ST PAUL'S

THE CATHEDRAL CHURCH OF LONDON

604–2004

St Paul's

The Cathedral Church of London

604–2004

edited by

DEREK KEENE

ARTHUR BURNS

ANDREW SAINT

YALE UNIVERSITY PRESS

NEW HAVEN & LONDON

Typeset by Best-set Typesetter, Hong Kong
Picture research by Julia Brown and Christine Faunch
Maps and plans by Tracy Wellman
Designed by Sally Salvesen
Printed by Conti Tipocolor, Italy

Library of Congress Cataloging-in-Publication Data

St. Paul's : the Cathedral Church of London, 604-2004 /
edited by Derek Keene, Arthur Burns, Andrew Saint.
p. cm.
Includes bibliographical references and index.
ISBN 0-300-09276-8 (alk. paper)
1. St. Paul's Cathedral (London, England)
I. Keene, Derek. II. Burns, Arthur (R. Arthur) III. Saint, Andrew.
BX5195.L7S427 2004
274.21′2—dc22
2004002259

ILLUSTRATIONS

endpapers: Edward VI's procession along Cheapside, 19 February 1547,
detail of Fig. 23 (The Society of Antiquaries, London)

half-title page: View towards the crossing, *c.*1725,
detail of Fig. 33 (St Paul's Cathedral)

frontispiece: View into the dome with Thornhill's *Scenes from the life of St Paul*, 1715–17,
and statues of the Doctors of the Church (1892–94) round the drum

CONTENTS

Part One   Historical Overview

Part Two   Up to the Reformation

FOREWORD

Other cathedrals are called by the name of the cities which they serve but St Paul's is properly unique. The story which is unfolded in this book explains how this particular cathedral has come to have significance, not only for the city and diocese of London, but for the whole nation and even for people beyond these shores.

I am the first bishop since the early seventeenth century to live literally under the shadow of St Paul's. This has given me a privileged view of the way in which the dean and chapter are seeking to develop the tradition of the cathedral to serve changing times.

The newly adopted cathedral statutes, latest in a very long line of such documents, defines the role of St Paul's in clause 1. 'The Cathedral Church of St Paul in London is the seat of the Bishop of London and a centre for worship and mission.' The question is how to interpret this role in the context of contemporary London, a world city in which virtually every tongue and every community under heaven is now represented.

One of the pictures of St Paul's which still resonates is that of the dome during the blitz, wreathed with smoke and destruction but still intact. It is one of the pre-eminent icons of Churchill's Britain. London had been bombed, thousands had been killed yet Londoners were united in their defiance of tyranny.

It is still one of the proudest pages in the history of St Paul's and the memory of the Paul's Watch who saved the cathedral many times from the engulfing flames deserves to be treasured for many generations to come. In a very different London, however, the cathedral must study afresh, as it has always done throughout its history, how it can serve the present generation.

The dome remains a potent symbol of unity. That is implicit in the architectural form chosen by Sir Christopher Wren and enhanced by the decision of a Victorian dean and chapter to erect eight statues just below Sir John Thornhill's paintings. The statues were described by Dean Gregory, who features largely in the following pages, as 'the four eastern and the four western most illustrious doctors of the church'. The Church of England has always understood itself to be 'a part of the one, holy, catholic and apostolic church' with a vocation to work for the union of the one body now fragmented as a result of human pride. The dome with its union of east and west cries out for the cathedral to have an ecumenical spirit, impatient with the divisions which have multiplied throughout the history of the christian church.

One of the best innovations sponsored by the present dean and chapter has been the introduction of ecumenical canonries. These have given a seat and voice in the affairs and worship of the cathedral to a distinguished international company of ecumenical friends. The Bishops of Mozambique and Berlin-Brandenburg are canons. So are the administrator of Westminster Roman Catholic Cathedral, the director of the Evangelical Alliance, the dean of the Swedish Church and a Russian Orthodox professor who teaches at King's College London. It is particularly significant that the minister of Wesley's Chapel is also a canon of St Paul's. Many of the wounds which separate Anglicans and Methodists to this day were inflicted in London. London and its cathedral have an international duty to ensure that the process of reconciliation is fostered here.

The future of St Paul's must be as a high place of worship that welcomes and embraces all christians and where all the christians of London can feel at home. But that does not exhaust the ecumenical vision of the dome.

Wren's St Paul's was built in the aftermath of a destructive civil war, fuelled by religious conflict which killed at least 100,000 people. By playing a destructive role in the broils of the seventeenth century, christians helped to endow the european enlightenment with a distinctly anti-religious spirit. That ought to make modern christians humble but the faith which animated the rebuilding of St Paul's was not irrational. The architecture and the worship for which it was designed, breathe a sober confidence in the capacities of reason when deployed in the service of faith.

I deduce from this that there is a ground upon which we can meet our contemporaries especially our critics as equals and learn from them as we face together some of the great challenges confronting the human race in our time. London, which has commerce with every part of the globe is a crossroads and a good place to take counsel about the way ahead for the human community with its great diversity of faiths and opinions.

I am occasionally cast down that while the christian community is preoccupied with parochial polemics, there seems to be little appreciation of the major dangers described, for example, in the Astronomer Royal's recent book, *Will the human race survive the twenty-first century?*

These are the themes which should be debated and faced under the dome and it was a delight to see a new constituency gathered there on several occasions to hear Nobel-prize-winning economists address so many of these global issues.

The notion that history has directly applicable lessons to teach is unconvincing. As St Paul's navigates into the unknown future, however, some knowledge of the past diverts the pressure of the passing moment and gives us room for manoeuvre. A lively sense of the many different ways in which human society has been understood and organised saves us from being oppressed by any sense of inevitability about where we are now. A historical memory gives us room to respond to changing circumstances and not merely to react.

I hope and expect that this survey of the fourteen-hundred-year-long story of St Paul's will deepen the understanding and enrich the imagination of all those who love the place and who believe that the greatest christian centuries are to come.

THE RT REVD & RT HON RICHARD CHARTRES DD FSA
Bishop of London

EDITORS' PREFACE

This is not the first history of St Paul's. William Dugdale's *History of St Paul's*, published in 1658, was the first formal history of an English cathedral. Both in its original and in its later editions it remains an influential and important resource, despite its many successors. These include Dean Milman's *Annals of S. Paul's Cathedral* (1868) and the *History of St Paul's* edited by Dean Matthews and W. M. Atkins (1957), both of continuing value for information and ideas. Among other studies covering major aspects of the cathedral's history, G. L. Prestige's *St Paul's in its Glory, 1831–1911* (1955) and Jane Lang's *Rebuilding St Paul's after the Great Fire of London* (1956) stand out for their distinction. Dugdale's enterprise was a reaction to the Interregnum and to the crisis occasioned by the abolition of the cathedral for the second time in its history. In happy contrast, our History celebrates one thousand four hundred years of the history of this ever-active, ever-changing, and almost wholly continuous London institution. Almost from the beginning, St Paul's attained a unique position among English cathedrals. The volume starts by reporting new thinking concerning Christianity and the cathedral in fourth-century London, from which there appears to have been no direct line of descent to St Paul's. It goes on to shed fresh light on every aspect of the cathedral's fortunes, spiritual life and architecture, through repeated phases of destruction by fire and ambitious reconstruction, of doctrinal and political challenge, and of dynamism and uncertainty. High points in the twelfth, thirteenth and fourteenth centuries were followed by the turbulence of Reformation, Civil War and the Great Fire, by a nineteenth-century heyday and, within living memory, by new uncertainties. Two world wars each had a profound impact, and while writing this book we have witnessed the second total rebuilding of the cathedral's environs within a generation.

With our contributors, we have tried to capture the quirky distinctiveness of the most prominent of England's cathedrals. Historically it has not been the wealthiest of them, nor at the top of the formal hierarchy, but one which owes its origin, its standing and much of its unique character to its close association with the largest and most dynamic city in the land. The history of St Paul's offers food for thought concerning central questions on the shaping of the nation and the state, on the church in society, and on the striking degrees of engagement and disengagement between Londoners and the great monument of cult and authority in their midst. As Britain's most coherent and conspicuous monumental building, the present cathedral left to us by Sir Christopher Wren also raises many issues about the purpose, destiny, flexibility and upkeep of such structures.

No previous history of St Paul's celebrated an anniversary. This one arose from the dean and chapter's desire to do so by sponsoring the endeavours of a collective of historians and others, some of them actively engaged in the current management of St Paul's and its fabric, to describe and understand a wide variety of themes in their history. This is the history of the dean and chapter and their church, but it is the authors' rather than an official view. As editors we have greatly appreciated this freedom to explore and write. The cheerful companionship of the cathedral chapter and staff has made an essential contribution to the history, and special thanks are due to the dean, John Moses, for his lively collaboration. Many others have helped the work towards completion. Deserving above all of our thanks is Christine Faunch who, as research assistant to the project, explored and made accessible through her lists a remarkable quantity of uncatalogued St Paul's materials in boxes at Guildhall Library. She also made a major contribution to the picture research, and sought out and organized a mass of historical information for authors. At St Paul's, the librarian, Jo Wisd0om, has been a highly valued source of advice, information and administrative support; successive cathedral registrars, Bob Acworth and John Milne, have ensured that bills were paid; Martin Stancliffe and Bob Crayford have provided much information on the fabric; and the chancellor, Canon John Halliburton, gave valuable support in the early stages. At Guildhall Library Stephen Freeth, in the manuscripts department, and John Fisher, in the department of prints and maps, have provided outstanding assistance and expert advice. English Heritage has provided much informal and support, including photography by Derek Kendall.

Julia Brown took on the picture research and ordering at a crucial stage and completed a complex task with meticulous professionalism. Tracy Wellman translated our ideas for maps and plans into elegant reality. Yale University Press, in the shape of John Nicoll at the start and Sally Salvesen at the design and production stage, has been a wise and supportive publisher. As general editor, I have received much advice and practical assistance from colleagues at the Institute of Historical Research, University of London, above all from Olwen Myhill. The support of the Leverhulme Trust has enabled me to devote much more time to the project than would otherwise have been possible.

Given that historians depend so much on their eyesight, not least in the final stages of such a project, it is appropriate to conclude by remembering St Erkenwald, the great refounder of the cathedral whose shrine there was associated with care for the eyes. We hope that he would have approved of a history published on the feast day of his predecessor Mellitus, first bishop of the present diocese.

DEREK KEENE
General Editor

NOTES ON CONTRIBUTORS

NIGEL ASTON   Lecturer in Early Modern European History, University of Leicester. Author of *Religion and Revolution in France, 1780–1804* (2000).

CAROLINE BARRON   Professor of London History, Royal Holloway, University of London. Her book *London in the Later Middle Ages: Government and People, 1200–1500* was published in 2003.

ROGER BOWDLER   Historian, English Heritage. He has published a number of articles on commemorative topics and the iconography of death.

ROBERT BOWLES   Consulting engineer and a partner with Alan Baxter & Associates; responsible for the practice's work on St Paul's and other major buildings in London.

SIMON BRADLEY   Editor of the Pevsner Architectural Guides (Yale University Press) and author of the volumes on *The City of London* (1997) and *Westminster* (2003).

PETER BURMAN   Director of Conservation and Property Services, National Trust for Scotland, and chairman of the St Paul's Fabric Advisory Committee; author of the guidebook, *St Paul's Cathedral* (1987)

ARTHUR BURNS   Senior Lecturer in Modern British History at King's College London, University of London. His publications include *The Diocesan Revival in the Church of England, 1800–1870* (1999) and an ebook edition of Dean Church's *The Oxford Movement: Twelve Years, 1833–1845* (2003).

DONALD BURROWS   Professor of Music, the Open University. His many publications include, as editor, *The Cambridge Companion to Handel* (1997),

JAMES CAMPBELL   A registered architect and an architectural historian specialising in the history of building construction. His book *Brick* was published in 2003.

CAROL CRAGOE   English Heritage; an architectural historian, she has published on Gothic architecture and on the development of English parish church chancels.

DAVID J. CRANKSHAW   Lecturer in the History of Early Modern Christianity, King's College London, University of London. He has published on the important provincial convocation of 1562, whose opening session was held at St Paul's.

VIRGINIA DAVIS   Senior Lecturer in late Medieval History, Queen Mary, University of London. Author of *Clergy in London in the late Middle Ages* (2000).

KERRY DOWNES   Emeritus Professor of the History of Art, University of Reading, and author of monographs on Wren, Hawkesmoor, Vanbrugh and Rubens, and of *Sir Christopher Wren: the Design of St Paul's Cathedral* (1988).

ROSAMUND FAITH   Economic historian, author of articles on the St Paul's estates and of *English Peasantry and the growth of Lordship* (1997).

DONALD GRAY   Canon Emeritus of Westminster Abbey, former Chaplain to the Queen. His *Earth and Altar: the Evolution of the Parish Communion in the Church of England to 1945* was published in 1986.

DIANA GREENWAY   Formerly Professor of Medieval History, Institute of Historical Research, University of London. Editor and translator of *Historia Anglorum, the History of the English People by Henry, Archdeacon of Huntingdon* (1996).

JEREMY GREGORY   Senior Lecturer in the History of Modern Christianity, University of Manchester. His *Restoration, Reformation and Reform, 1660–1828* was published in 2000.

GORDON HIGGOTT   Historic buildings inspector in the London division of English Heritage; co-author of *Inigo Jones: complete Architectural Drawings* (1986).

STEPHANIE HOVLAND   Graduate student, Royal Holloway, University of London; co-editor of a forthcoming edition of Dean Worsley's household accounts.

RALPH HYDE   Formerly Keeper of Prints and Maps, Guildhall Library, London. Author of numerous commentaries on maps and depictions of London and on panoramas of English towns.

W. M. JACOB   Archdeacon of Charing Cross, editor of *Theology* and author of *Lay People and Religion in the Early Eighteenth Century* (1996).

DAVID J. JOHNSON   Lately Clerk of the Records, House of Lords Record Office. Author of *Southwark and the City* (1969), he has for long been working on the estates of St Paul's.

DEREK KEENE   Leverhulme Professor of Comparative Metropolitan History and formerly director of the Centre for Metropolitan History, Institute of Historical Research, University of London. Author of numerous books and articles on London and other cities between the seventh and the nineteenth century.

HANNES KLEINEKE   Research officer at the History of Parliament and co-editor of a forthcoming edition of Dean Worsley's household accounts.

JEAN MORRIN   Teaches at King Alfred's College, Winchester. She completed her doctoral thesis in 1997 at the University of Durham on the estates of the Dean and Chapter of Durham.

ELIZABETH NEW   In 1999 completed her doctoral thesis at Royal Holloway, University of London, on 'The cult of the Holy Name'.

JOHN NEWMAN   Formerly Reader in the History of Architecture at the Courtauld Institute, University of London, he is author of several volumes in the 'Pevsner Architectural Guides' and contributed architectural chapters on the sixteenth and seventeenth centuries to *The History of the University of Oxford*.

NIGEL RAMSEY   Department of History, University College London, University of London. Co-editor of *A History of Ely Cathedral* (2003) and of the *History of Canterbury Cathedral* (1995), to which he contributed the chapter on the library and archives.

JAMES RAVEN   Professor of Modern History, University of Essex. Author of *London booksellers and American customers: transatlantic literary community and the Charleston Library Society, 1748-1811* (2001), he is investigating the book trades in the vicinity of St Paul's.

MARIE-HÉLÈNE ROUSSEAU   In 2003 completed her doctoral thesis at Royal Holloway, University of London, on chantries and chantry chaplains at St Paul's.

ANDREW SAINT   Professor of Architecture, University of Cambridge. His books include *The Image of the Architect* (1983) and *Towards a Social Architecture* (1986).

LUCY FREEMAN SANDLER   Professor of Art History, New York University. Her major publications include *Gothic Manuscripts, 1285–1385* (vol. 5 of *A Survey of Manuscripts Illuminated in the British Isles*, 1986)

ANN SAUNDERS   Editor of the annual journals of the Costume Society and the London Topographical Society. Her publications include *John Bacon, R. A., 1740–1799* (1961).

JOHN SCHOFIELD   Cathedral Archaeologist of St Paul's and a curator at the Museum of London. His publications on the archaeology of London include *Medieval London Houses* (1995)

TERESA SLADEN   An architectural historian specializing in architectural decoration, she contributed the chapter on mosaics to *The Albert Memorial* (2000).

MARK SMITH   Lecturer in Modern Church History, King's College London, University of London. Author of *Religion in Industrial Society: Oldham and Saddleworth, 1740–1865* (1994).

IAN SPINK   Professor Emeritus, Music Department, Royal Holloway, University of London, has published widely on English music, including *Restoration Church Music, 1660–1714* (1995).

MARTIN STANCLIFFE   Surveyor to the Fabric of St Paul's Cathedral and architect to Lichefield Cathedral, he teaches regularly at British schools of architecture and at ICCROM, Rome.

TIMOTHY STOREY   Member of St Paul's Cathedral choir, completing a PhD thesis at Durham University on music at St Paul's.

PAMELA TAYLOR   Historian and archivist, has published many articles on the estates and interests of the bishop of London and St Paul's during the early Middle Ages.

ALAN THACKER   Reader in Medieval History and Executive Editor of *The Victoria History of the Counties of England*, Institute of Historical Research, University of London. A specialist on Bede and on the cult of saints, he is co-editor of *Local Saints and Local Churches in the Early Medieval West* (2001).

J. J. WISDOM   Librarian, St Paul's Cathedral, and Assistant Librarian, Guildhall Library.

JOHN WOLFFE   Professor of Religious History, Open University, and author of *God and Greater Britain: Religion and National Life in Britain and Ireland, 1843–1945* (1994) and *Great Deaths: Religion and Nationhood in Victorian and Edwardian Britain* (2000).

TABLES

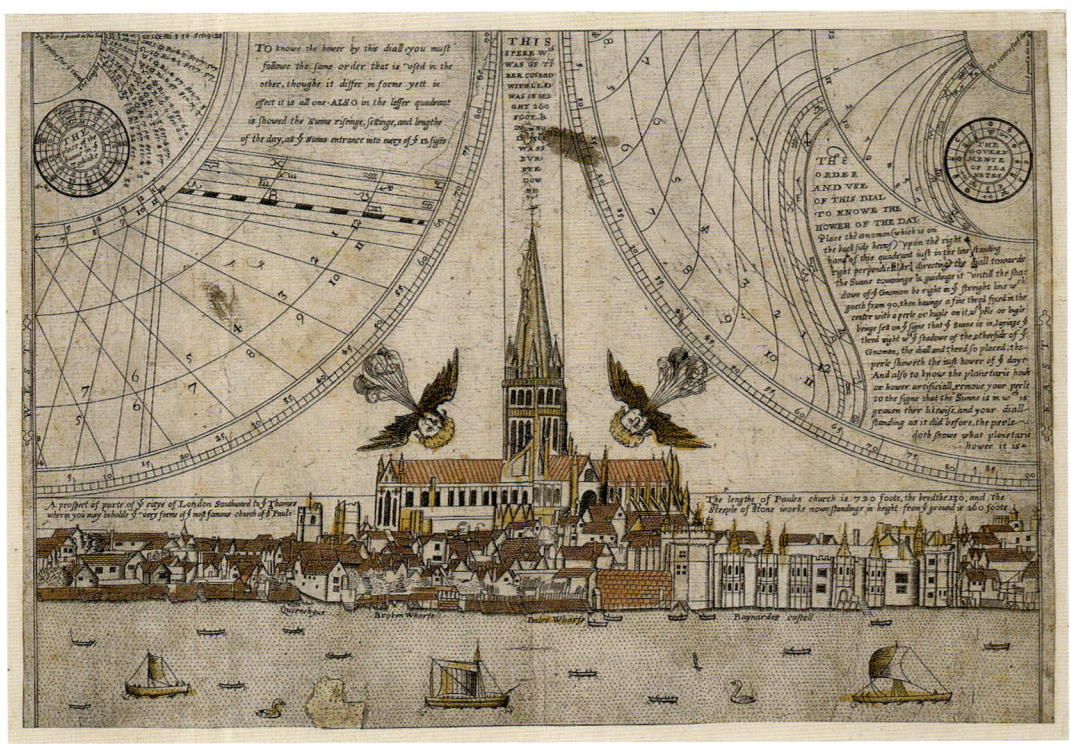

Prospect of ye Citye of London, executed after the spire of St Paul's burned in 1561, but showing it in its original form. (The Society of Antiquaries, London Plans IV, f.3★)

Part One

Historical Overview

I

ST PAUL'S AS ST PAUL'S

Derek Keene and Pamela Taylor

St Paul's, along with Canterbury Cathedral and Westminster Abbey, is one of the trio of great churches that stands for the historic presence of Christianity in England and for the links between church and state. That two of those churches are in the capital demonstrates the long-standing pre-eminence of London in the affairs of Britain; that the see of the Primate of all England is not reflects both political circumstances at the time of the foundation of St Paul's and the distinctively oblique relationship between London and the kingdom that has persisted ever since. While the abbey has been bound up with the Crown and its counsellors, St Paul's, though keeping up a continuing intimacy with monarchs, has been closer to other sources of power – to the people and business of London and to St Paul himself. Since at least as early as the twelfth century, St Paul's has dominated the landscape of its city in a manner unmatched by any other English cathedral. The monumental churches on the site have thereby served as unique symbols of the city and of national identity. The way in which St Paul's has risen again after destruction by three Great Fires of London (in 962, 1087 and 1666) and conspicuously survived other great fires (in 1135 and 1940) has added to its significance as an expression of the strength and endurance of London. Two of those occasions (1666 and 1940) were associated with warfare and serious external threats to the realm.

The distinctive identity of St Paul's is expressed in its name, for it is the only English cathedral commonly known by its dedication alone: always 'St Paul's', never 'London Cathedral'. Since the Norman Conquest it has been the 'church of St Paul, London', a style similar to that of other cathedrals, but unlike elsewhere the less formal title has always been 'the church of St Paul', 'St Paul's' or even 'Paul's', never 'the church of London'. The use throughout England of the name *Paulesbyrig* to denote the cathedral precinct suggests that this practice in naming the church originated well before the conquest.

What explains this unique nomenclature? Certainly, from early in its history there has been an especially strong sense of the presence of St Paul as the cathedral's protector, despite the lack of any corporeal relic of the saint. Moreover, the dedication – to St Paul alone rather than to Saints Peter and Paul – was rare for a major church in England. Other great cathedrals such as Canterbury and Winchester had multiple dedications from the beginning and acquired additional patrons as time went on, but in London St Paul has remained unchallenged, even by St Erkenwald. The cathedral and its surroundings came to be known by names – Paul's Walk, Paul's Cross, Paul's Churchyard – that were embedded in the national consciousness as places of assembly and for the circulation of news and ideas. Those names may resonate less today, but Wren's great church continues to perform a national role. The monumentality of St Paul's, its traditions and its associations with London enhance the impact of public events there, whether the restoration of King Henry III's rule in 1266, the duke of Wellington's funeral in 1852, or the Falklands Victory Service in 1982. In these long-established ways, we all know St Paul's.

1. Detail of Fig. 28, a fictitious view of the medieval cathedral ablaze in the Great Fire, 4 September 1666

2

BEFORE ST PAUL'S

John Schofield and Derek Keene

Present-day St Paul's, like its predecessors, occupies a prominent position just below the brow of the more westerly of the two low hills where the Romans established the city of London.[1] Those hills have shaped the city ever since. The natural subsoil is gravel overlaid in patches by brickearth, a light brown, wind-deposited soil. Surveyors and engineers from the time of Wren onwards have called the brickearth 'potter's clay', and it is likely that their observations concerned the redeposited earth floor surfaces of Roman buildings as well as the undisturbed soil. Ground levels in the city have been raised dramatically since early Roman times. In the vicinity of St Paul's, the pre-Roman ground surface seems generally to have been about 16 feet below the present pavement, and is likely to have been uneven in character.

As at York or Lincoln, the setting of the cathedral has enhanced its dominance over the city as a whole. From the site, one could look south over the river Thames and west over the Fleet valley, where the Fleet itself ran on the line of the modern Farringdon Street. In the mid nineteenth century there was a fall of about 42 feet from the pavement outside St Paul's to the high-water mark due south at Paul's Wharf. Before the Great Fire of 1666, there would have been a comparable, though less steep, fall from the cathedral to the bank of the Fleet. The level ground immediately to the north of the cathedral extended east about 330 yards to a point about half-way along the modern Cheapside before dipping slightly. From the junction with Poultry, the ground sloped more steeply into the valley of the Walbrook, which divided the eastern and western hills. At this point the Walbrook was at its narrowest. To the south, the valley and stream opened out towards the Thames, while to the north there was a wide boggy area, commemorated in the later name Moorfields, through which several convergent streams flowed. To the north of the site of St Paul's, a broad expanse of more or less level ground, bounded by marsh to the east and by the Fleet valley to the west, extended about 660 yards into the modern Smithfield ('smooth field'), where a broad ridge begins to rise gently towards Islington and Highbury.

St Paul's and all earlier features in the vicinity have thus occupied a relatively well-drained piece of ground, readily accessible from the river on the south side and from crossings of the Walbrook and Fleet to east and west. There was a good land route to the north and a fine view south across the river and the marshes beyond. Nevertheless, the site itself was often wet and muddy, apparently with streams running across it from north to south, immediately to the west of the present cathedral. One or more of those streams probably originated in the neighbourhood of Smithfield, although the city wall and ditch constructed around AD 200 would have interrupted their flow. The gravel acted as a substantial reservoir and where it was exposed on slopes there were springs, a notable feature of the city in Roman and later times.[2] Thus, even after the building of the city wall, streams flowed, at least intermittently, across the area and would have been much augmented after rain. Holes dug down to the gravel encountered a steady supply of water. Two parallel streams in broad hollows have been observed just north of the modern Newgate Street. One turned west towards the Fleet, while the other continued south. Both hollows were filled in and became marshy during the Roman period. Immediately north of the cathedral site, evidence for the second Roman stream was perhaps removed by a later ditch on the same alignment, more than 60 feet wide and over 15 feet deep. This later ditch appears to have continued south, where it has been observed between the

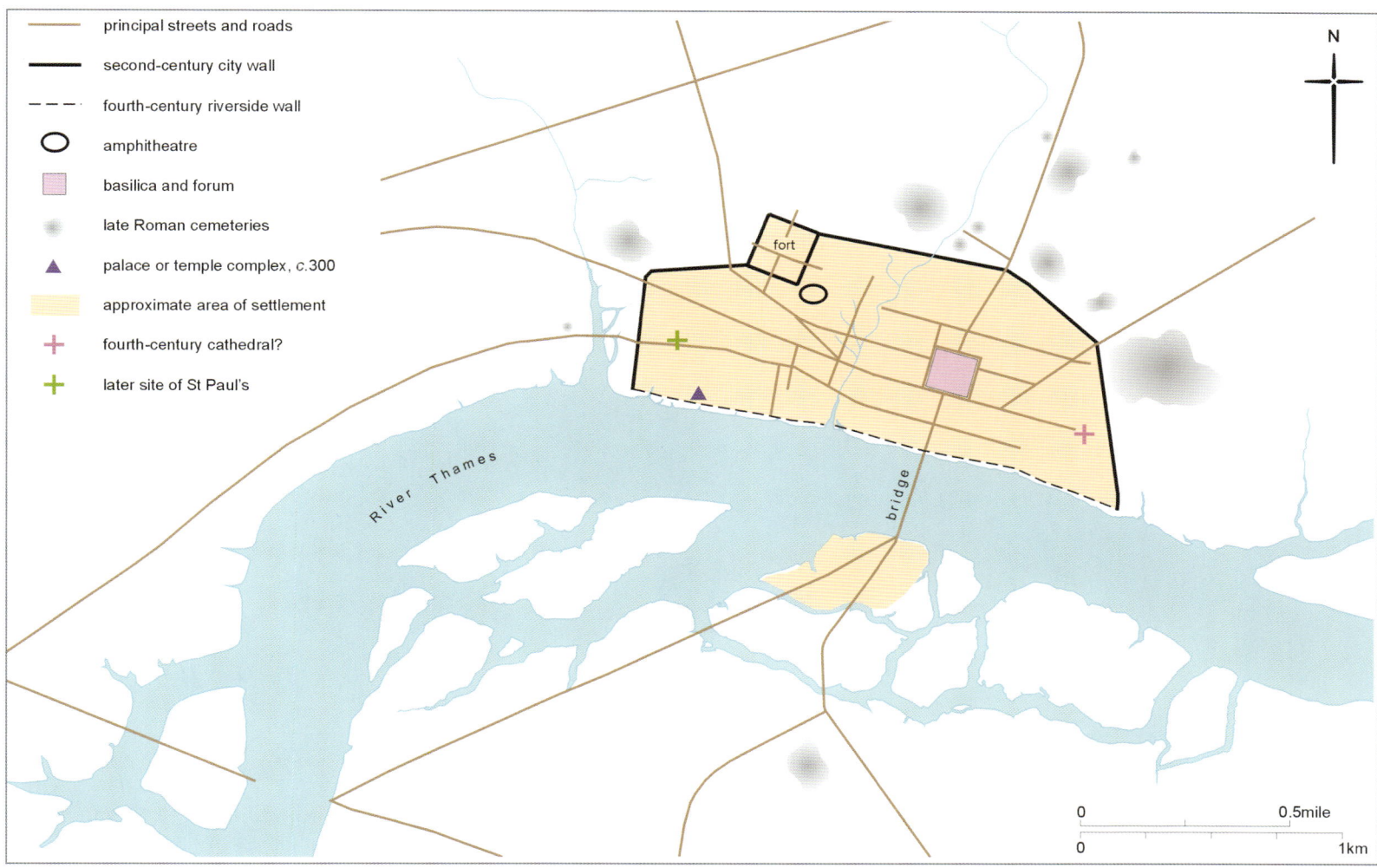

2. Late Roman London, showing the principal topographical features, the site of what may have been the fourth-century cathedral and the later site of St Paul's

modern Addle Hill and St Andrew's Hill, and was presumably a substantial boundary or defensive feature. The date of this ditch is uncertain, being attributed by some reports to the ninth century or earlier and by others to the later eleventh century. To the north of the cathedral, it was filled in during the late eleventh or early twelfth century (p. 18), while near Addle Hill it may have been filled in a little later.[3]

The prehistory of this area is simply stated. Although occasional prehistoric finds are made in the city, there is no clear evidence of habitation on the western of the two hills until the arrival of the Romans. There is little prehistoric material to report from modern observations in the St Paul's precinct or its immediate neighbourhood: Neolithic or Bronze Age flints and Bronze Age pottery found immediately south-east of the precinct do not amount to evidence for a settlement.[4] Yet the site of London had probably long been a distinctive place, and it is now argued that the Romans adopted the name for their settlement from one that for many centuries had denoted the river below a crossing on the site of the later London Bridge.[5]

The river crossing was key to the foundation of the Roman city, whose centre, marked by a forum and basilica, lay on the eastern hill. Nevertheless, a major Roman road on the line of the present Newgate Street seems to have been one of the original features of the settlement, and within twenty years of the foundation buildings were being laid out on the western hill. Though checked by destruction in Boudicca's rebellion (AD 60–1), London grew rapidly during the first and second centuries.[6] By about AD 70, a Roman street probably crossed the site of the

cathedral from west to east on a line between Ludgate (a later Roman gate) and the modern Watling Street, but the evidence for this street is slight. Traces of two secondary roads running south from Newgate Street to the north of the present cathedral have also been found and perhaps date from the first or second century.[7] At that time, the area later occupied by St Paul's was probably outside the formal boundary of the town, which seems to have followed a north–south line some 30 yards to the east of the present cathedral. This was a suburban location, initially characterized by digging for gravel and brickearth, pottery kilns and a cremation cemetery, traces of all of which have been found in the churchyard area.[8] From early in the second century there was extensive building in the neighbourhood, mostly of timber houses and workshops with brickearth foundations and floors. The more substantial buildings, including bath-houses and large residences, lay well to the south on the river frontage and to the east of Walbrook.

The city wall of about AD 200 enclosed the settlement for the first time. It incorporated the late first-century fort at its north-western corner, and extended thence to the Fleet valley and the Thames to protect an extensive built-up area. There were at least six gates in the wall, including, in the immediate vicinity of St Paul's, the predecessors of Aldersgate, Newgate and Ludgate. Cemeteries were set up outside the wall, while those within were closed down or forgotten. Industries were no longer practised in the area of the later cathedral, which became a predominantly residential district, with large masonry buildings. Some of those buildings may have been erected before the city wall, perhaps following a widespread fire of about AD 125. The 'late Roman' phase, from about 200 to about 400, may include several structures in this neighbourhood which cannot be precisely dated. The buildings with sumptuous mosaics summarily recorded in the nineteenth century along the north side of St Paul's Churchyard, probably belong to this period.[9] A hoard of 530 coins was deposited at the east end of the present Paternoster Row at the end of the third century.[10] This evidence, however, is insufficient to convey a sense of the overall pattern of activities during these centuries in the area later occupied by the cathedral precinct.

To the south, near the river, the picture is clearer. During the second and third centuries substantial quays were extended into the river, while nearby were monumental public buildings and temples, stone from which was incorporated in the defensive wall built along the river frontage during the third century. After the construction of that wall, but before about 300, a monumental building, perhaps serving as a palace or temple complex, was erected on a specially constructed terrace due south of the later cathedral.[11] The full extent of the structure and its influence on the later topography of the neighbourhood are not clear, but it overlooked the site of the later Paul's Wharf. By the early thirteenth century, a large stone house a short distance to the west belonged to the cathedral and was known as 'Diana's Chamber', a name which persisted into the late fifteenth century and was known to later antiquaries.[12] This name may allude to an episode in the mythical history of Britain, composed by Geoffrey on Monmouth in the 1130s. In this tale, the goddess Diana prophesied that Brutus, subsequently the founder of London, was to rule Britain.[13] Geoffrey's history, which refers to landmarks in the vicinity of St Paul's and was addressed to an élite with interests at court, would have been well known to canons of the cathedral. Later, Bishop Gilbert Foliot (d. 1187) reckoned that its prophecies and its account of the supposed earlier history of London justified the elevation of his see to metropolitan status. Remains of Roman monuments on the site by the river, still visible or newly revealed in the twelfth century, may have prompted the naming of Diana's Chamber. Moreover, a contemporary of Foliot's, in a jocular allusion to the mythical history, accused the bishop of intending to re-establish the ancient cult of Jupiter.[14] These appear to have been the ultimate origins of the sixteenth-century or earlier stories, for which there is no support in archaeological fact, that the cathedral itself occupied the site of a Temple of Diana or one of Jupiter.[15]

After 300, Roman London displayed few signs of prosperity, and buildings in many parts of the city were demolished. Pottery finds indicate some fourth-century activity in the St Paul's area and coins of several fourth-century emperors up to Valens (364–78) were found in 1841 in association with a substantial building beneath the north-eastern corner of the later churchyard. London remained an important administrative centre up to the late fourth century. Soon afterwards, the army was withdrawn and the economy collapsed. Despite signs of some continuing activity, London seems soon to have become more or less depopulated.[16]

Late Roman London was part of a Christian empire, but we know little of Christianity in the city at that time. Restitutus, bishop of London, attended the Council at Arles in 314, representing one of the four recently established metropolitan sees of Britain, and bishops of London may have been among those

groups of British bishops occasionally recorded during the fourth century.[17] There is also some evidence for Christian martyrs, including a bishop, in London before the conversion of Constantine in 312 (p.113). In the fourth century there were perhaps several Christian places of worship in the city in addition to the cathedral, which contemporary and later Continental practice suggests would have been within the walls. Not one of these sites has yet been identified for certain. A few Christian artefacts of the period have been found in and near London, but some of them may have been deposited at much later dates.[18] Can there have been any connection between the cathedral dedicated to St Paul, which we assume was established on the western hill in 604 and almost certainly occupied that site from the re-establishment of the see later in the seventh century, and any late Roman features in the vicinity? In other cities, especially in Gaul and Italy, there was sometimes an association between a late Roman site of public authority, or place of burial or cult, and a later major church. In the case of London, however, such evidence as there is suggests that there were no such links in the immediate vicinity of St Paul's. Moreover, any connection, however indirect, with the third-century palatial structures to the south remains purely conjectural. We may never be able to explore these questions further: the digging of foundations for Wren's cathedral, not to mention those of its predecessors and of other buildings in the vicinity, has been too destructive. Very recent excavation, however, revealed four burials, possibly of fourth-century date, in Paternoster Row to the north of the present cathedral.[19] A late Roman cemetery in that neighbourhood could be significant for the siting of the later cathedral, but the dating and interpretation of these burials remains uncertain. The earliest burials so far known to have been associated with St Paul's were those of King Sæbbi (d. c.694) and a group dating from the late eighth or ninth century recently discovered just north of the nave of the medieval cathedral.[20]

There is also the possibility that the church of the Roman bishop of London was in some other part of the city. A tradition recorded in the sixteenth century held that long before Augustine's mission the parish church of St Peter in Cornhill had been founded by King Lucius as the seat of the archbishop of London. The tradition owes something to Bede's story, later elaborated by Geoffrey of Monmouth, of a supposed Christian king of Britain during the second century, and presumably became attached to the church of St Peter because it was the seat of the bishop's jurisdiction in the eastern part of the city. There is no good evidence that St Peter's had a significantly more ancient origin than any other city parish church.[21] Moreover, by the early fifteenth century there was a similar tradition at St Paul's that traced the cathedral to the time of the supposed King Lucius (pp. 40, 121). A more serious candidate for the site of the Roman cathedral has recently been identified in the south-eastern part the city, which during the fourth century emerged as a focus of power and authority. In that area, just north of the modern Tower Hill, traces of a large building of basilican plan dating to shortly after 350 have been excavated. This building has some resemblance to the contemporary basilica of St Tecla, Milan, and so may have been an important church, but it is equally possible that the structure had a purely secular use.[22] The site of the church of Bishop Restitutus and his immediate successors remains to be conclusively identified.

3

FOUNDATION AND ENDOWMENT: ST PAUL'S AND THE ENGLISH KINGDOMS, 604–1087

Pamela Taylor

Despite London's earlier see, the foundation of St Paul's in 604 marked a fresh start. When St Germanus visited St Albans in 429 an ecclesiastical hierarchy was still in place, but the structure of town-based bishoprics vanished thereafter. By 597, when St Augustine's mission landed in England, although there were many more indigenous Christians around than Bede would have us believe, they belonged to a localized religion; 'all the British bishops' whom Augustine unsatisfactorily met in 603 were west of the areas of Anglo-Saxon settlement.[1]

Pope Gregory had instructed Augustine to re-establish the Roman structure, with metropolitans at London and York.[2] In retrospect, this would have been sensible as well as historically correct, but at the time the pope's vision was impracticable. Conversion was directed not at towns but at kingdoms, and via their rulers. Augustine landed in Kent partly because Ethelbert of Kent was then the most powerful king south of the Humber; London lay within the province of the East Saxons, whose ruler was Ethelbert's nephew and subject to him.[3] Only if Ethelbert had decided to absorb the East Saxon territory completely and move his own chief city to London would St Paul's have become the archbishopric. In the event, Augustine stayed at Canterbury, where his team was augmented by fresh arrivals in 601, two of whom were sent out in 604 to establish new sees.

We have an unusually good account of St Paul's foundation, written by Bede in the 730s, but based on reliable Kentish and Vatican sources transmitted by 'Nothelm, a priest of the church of London' – bishops apart, our first named member of the community.[4]

In the year of our lord 604 Augustine, archbishop of Britain, consecrated two bishops, namely Mellitus and Justus, Mellitus to preach to the province (*provincia*) of the East Saxons, which is divided from Kent by the river Thames and borders on the sea to the east. Its capital is the city of London, which is on the banks of that river and is an emporium for many nations who come to it by land and sea. At that time Sæberht, Ethelbert's nephew through his sister Ricula, ruled over the people (*gens*) although he was under Ethelbert's suzerainty.... When this province had accepted the word of truth through the preaching of Mellitus, King Ethelbert built the church of the holy apostle Paul in the city of London, in which Mellitus and his successors were to have their episcopal seat.... [Ethelbert also built the church for Justus at Rochester]; he also bestowed many gifts on the bishops of each of these churches and that of Canterbury; and he also added both lands and possessions for the maintenance of those who were with the bishops.[5]

This description conveys much solid information, but also leaves important points vague. We are told that St Paul's was newly built but neither precisely where nor why. It was definitely within the walls (*in civitate*) and, although we cannot be certain about it, probably already on the summit of the western hill. A charter of *c*.704–9 calls St Paul's *Paulesbyri*, denoting an enclosure, a term still in use in the 1050s.[6] By the 730s Bede's 'emporium for many nations' at London had developed along the Strand west of the walled city and was known as the *wic*. Much of the expansion was later seventh century, and the settlement's exact starting date is unclear, but royal initiative may well have been essential, and could perhaps have been Ethelbert's. Such economic activity as occurred within the walls seems also to have been concentrated on the western side, between St Paul's and the river (Fig. 3).[7] It is also possible that Ethelbert and/or Sæberht already had a palace

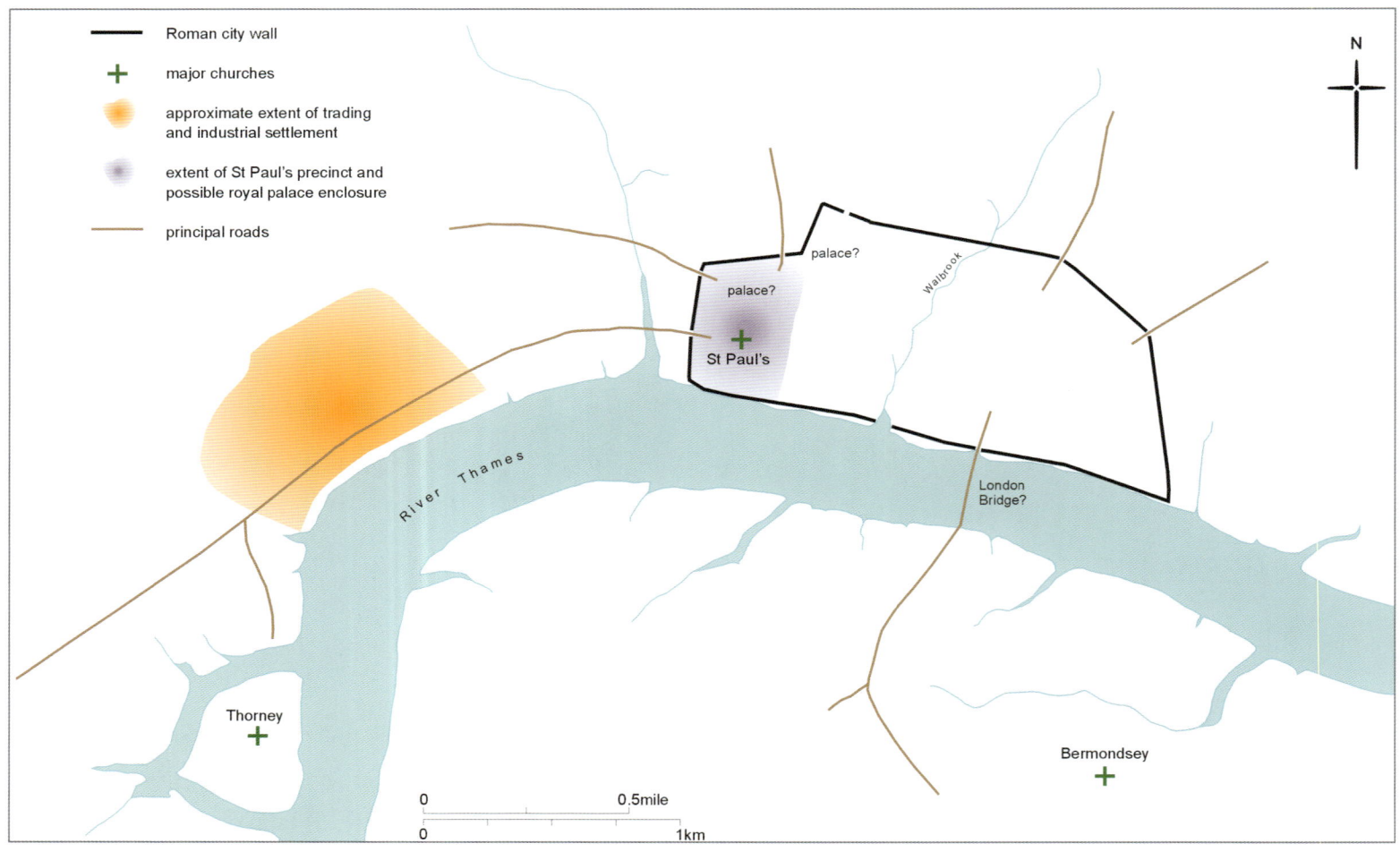

Legend (top map):

- Roman city wall
- + major churches
- approximate extent of trading and industrial settlement
- extent of St Paul's precinct and possible royal palace enclosure
- principal roads

N

palace?
palace?
Walbrook
St Paul's
London Bridge?

River Thames

Thorney
Bermondsey

0 ____ 0.5mile
0 ____ 1km

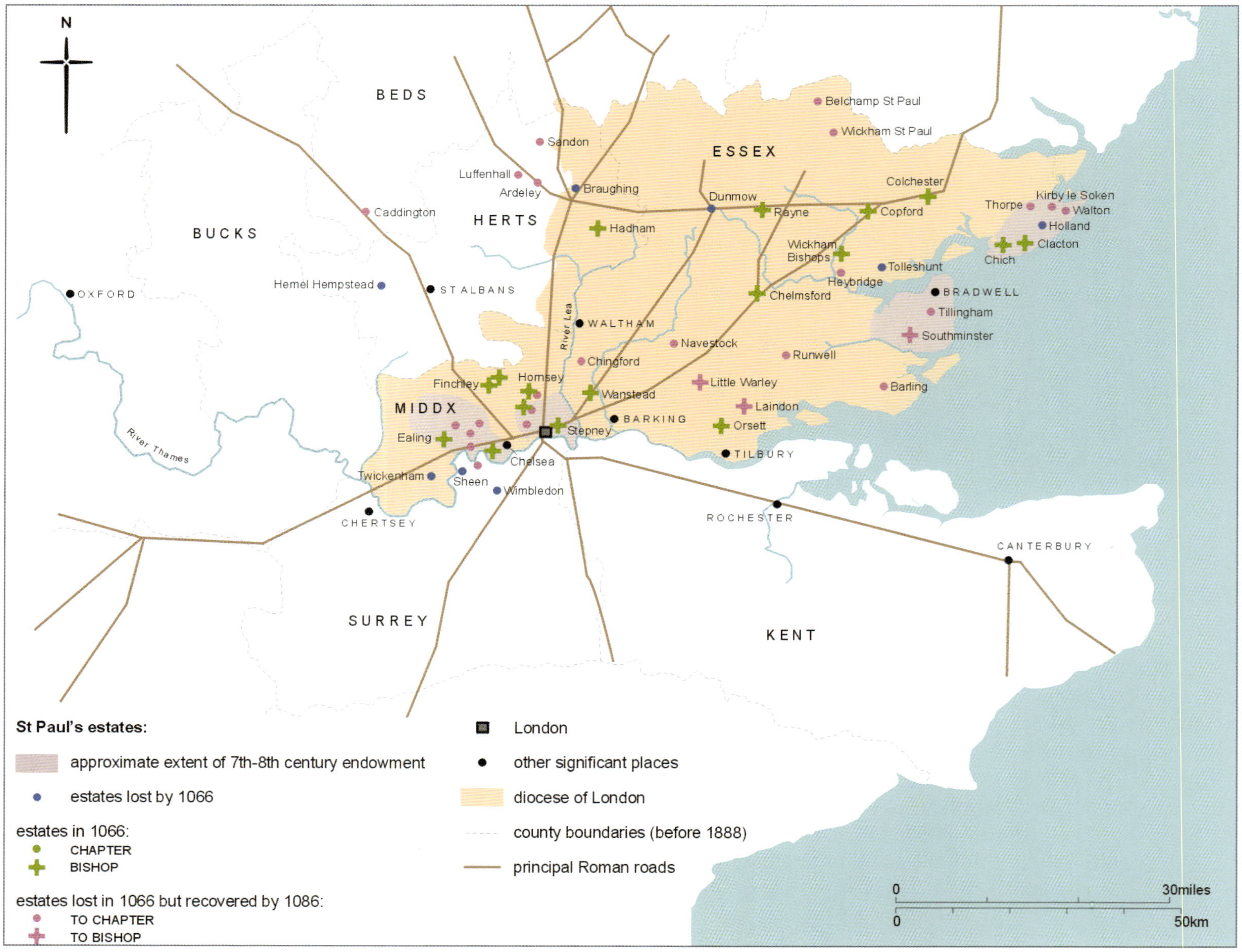

Lower map labels:

N

BEDS
Belchamp St Paul
Sandon
Wickham St Paul
Luffenhall
Ardeley
ESSEX
Braughing
Caddington
HERTS
Dunmow
Colchester
Thorpe
Kirby le Soken
Rayne
Walton
Hadham
Copford
Holland
Wickham Bishops
Chich
Clacton
Tolleshunt
Hemel Hempstead
ST ALBANS
Heybridge
BRADWELL
OXFORD
Chelmsford
Tillingham
River Lea
WALTHAM
Southminster
Navestock
Chingford
Runwell
Finchley
Hornsey
Little Warley
Barling
Ealing
Wanstead
Laindon
MIDDX
Stepney
BARKING
Orsett
River Thames
Chelsea
TILBURY
Twickenham
Sheen
Wimbledon
CHERTSEY
ROCHESTER
CANTERBURY
SURREY
KENT

St Paul's estates:

- approximate extent of 7th-8th century endowment
- estates lost by 1066

estates in 1066:
- CHAPTER
- + BISHOP

estates lost in 1066 but recovered by 1086:
- TO CHAPTER
- + TO BISHOP

- London
- other significant places
- diocese of London
- county boundaries (before 1888)
- principal Roman roads

0 ____ 30miles
0 ____ 50km

complex in the vicinity. The exact location of the palace abandoned when Edward the Confessor moved the court to Westminster in the mid eleventh century is unknown, but it seems to have been either immediately adjacent to St Paul's or slightly further north.[8]

The 'many gifts' that Ethelbert bestowed are unspecified, but presumably included precious items for liturgical and ceremonial use, honouring God in a way easily understood by a society with a deep-seated attachment to gold.[9] The king also gave land 'for the maintenance of those who were with the bishops'. The accumulation of the cathedral's medieval endowment (the sixteenth century brought radical alteration) is one of this chapter's central focuses. This is partly due to the shortage of surviving evidence for other activities, but it also reflects an important reality. In a world before stocks and shares, only land could provide the income to fund the clergy's work both centrally and throughout the diocese, so that both in 604 and subsequently the acquisition and retention of estates was an essential preoccupation. This also means that what we know of the scale and chronology of endowment provides some sort of guide to how the cathedral was being rated, as both a religious and a political investment, at different periods. There are, however, pitfalls, with the documentation so incomplete and unreliable that any interpretation can be contested.[10]

Two points seem basic. First, at London as elsewhere, there is a distinction between grants of very large areas of land, which were usually both early and royal, and smaller, more heterogeneous acquisitions.[11] Orders of magnitude are significant, even though the exact acreages conferred by assessments in hides, *cassati* or *manentes* are unknowable. Secondly, and a fact either misunderstood or ignored by the later canons, the separation of the endowments of the bishop and chapter was a later development, and until the tenth to eleventh centuries grants were made indifferently to both. Medieval St Paul's possessed four large blocks of endowment, discernible behind their later division (Fig. 4).

Bede is silent about the scale and location of Ethelbert's grants, but the medieval canons always claimed two foundation estates. For one, Tillingham in Essex, they also claimed the king's charter, but the charter is untrustworthy, and although documents were sometimes written to consolidate a genuine tradition, they could also be manufactured to create one.[12] The other, for which no charter was ever claimed, was the land accepted by William the Conqueror as 'the twenty-four hides which king Ethelbert gave to St Paul near the wall of London', and probably equating to the later block of prebendal lands in Moorfields, St Pancras and modern Camden.[13] This is a far more plausible candidate, but needs to be seen in conjunction with the bishop's manor of Stepney. The bishop cited no charter for this estate, but in Domesday Book (1086) it was assessed at over fifty hides, and included not only Stepney and Hackney immediately east of the 'twenty-four hides', but also Clerkenwell to their west.[14] Adjacent acquisitions further north had been added to Stepney, but were probably attached for administrative convenience to an earlier core.[15]

At least by 1200 the bishops also had the overlordship of a block of land within the city but at a distance from the cathedral, the contiguous sokes (estates with jurisdiction) of Cornhill and Bishopsgate, with Bishopsgate leading out into the manor of Stepney.[16] These could have been acquired in later exchanges, but can equally plausibly be considered part of the same foundation grant. The 'twenty-four hides' and Stepney encircled a large portion of London's walls, and Bishopsgate guarded the main north–south route through the city. This was therefore a strategically significant area, and arguably one more likely to have been assigned to the cathedral by Ethelbert than by any subsequent king.

Bede tells us that the East Saxon province and diocese were coterminous, but supplies only the eastern and southern boundaries, the sea and the Thames. Even this poses a difficulty, since in the late seventh century the diocese may also have extended south into Surrey (see below). The northern and western boundaries remain deeply problematic. From at latest the twelfth century up until the nineteenth, the diocese covered the counties of Essex and Middlesex and rather less than the eastern third of Hertfordshire (Fig. 4), but in the early period its area fluctuated, affected by the fortunes of the East Saxon kings. By the late sixth century their province extended west of the River Lea into what would become Middlesex, which included both London and, until the tenth century, much of Hertfordshire. Kentish suzerainty over the East Saxon kings collapsed soon after 604, and the second half of the century witnessed the expansion of the midland kingdom of Mercia. The name Middlesex, 'territory of the Middle Saxons', first recorded in 704, could represent either an earlier unit swallowed up by the East Saxons or, more probably, a new grouping devised within the expanding Mercian hegemony; certainly at the time Mercia was putting this western part of the East Saxon kingdom under more direct rule than the eastern.[17]

The county of Hertfordshire was not formed until the tenth century. The Tribal Hidage, probably a Mercian list of the 670s, names the East Saxons and also two identifiable groups within the later west Hertfordshire: the *Cilternsætan* ('Chiltern-dwellers') at the western edge and the *Hicce* around Hitchin at the northern; but the other known tribes of the area, from the *Brahingas* around Braughing westward to the *Wæclingas* around St Albans and, probably, Hemel, are not in the list and had therefore (like the equally absent Middle Saxons or their constituent tribes) already been absorbed into a larger unit.[18] This was probably initially the East Saxon kingdom and, from 604, the diocese. Archbishop Theodore (668–90) separated dioceses from their tribal origins and rationalized them, a process which included the creation of several new sees within Mercia. These included one at Leicester created before 679 for an artificial grouping, the Middle Angles; this later became part of the enormous diocese of Lincoln, whose southern, that is Middle Anglian, portion included west Hertfordshire.[19] Yet in 704 King Offa of the East Saxons gave his bishop land in Hemel Hempstead, firmly in the later west Hertfordshire.[20]

The question of when and why the diocese acquired its definitive shape recurs throughout this chapter. Beside the desirability of knowing the exact area which St Paul's served, the issue is also inextricably intertwined with the other dominant themes of the cathedral's history. Founded by an external king whose overlordship soon evaporated, London's see faced a uniquely complicated political future, passing at various times – and the eastern and western halves of the diocese often differentially – under

3 (*above left*).   London *c*.800. The existence of churches at Thorney (later Westminster) and Bermondsey is likely, but not certain

4 (*below left*).   The diocese of London and the estates of St Paul's between the seventh and the eleventh century. Some identifications shown are uncertain, while small, short-term or obscure acquisitions are not included

5. St Peter's, Bradwell on Sea, Essex, built in the mid seventh century for the Northumbrian missionary, St Cedd, at a time when St Paul's cathedral in London had been suppressed. The site, that of a Roman coastal fort, adjoined the large Tillingham estate which may have been part of St Paul's original endowment earlier in the seventh century. View of *c*.1920, shortly after restoration of the chapel

Mercian, West Saxon and Viking hegemony. For an archbishopric to have been at the disputed margins of so many rival claimants might have been an advantage, but for a bishopric, and particularly one so physically close to Canterbury, it was an enormous handicap. Much as rulers coveted London, its bishop was never central to their plans, and besides the heartland bishoprics of Mercia or Wessex, the archbishopric provided an alternative investment. Since the largest and most valuable estates were almost always early royal gifts, St Paul's and its bishops embarked on a future of high status but modest endowment.

Within little more than a decade, the question was whether there would be any future at all, for in 616 both Ethelbert and Sæberht died, and their heirs promptly reverted to paganism. Sæberht's three sons and co-heirs nevertheless arrived to watch Mellitus offering mass and demanded – not, one imagines, privately – 'Why do you not offer us the white bread which you used to give to our father...while you continue to give it to the people in church?' Rejecting the bishop's explanations of the prior need for baptism, they refused to enter the font (*fontem illum intrare*) and summarily drove him and his followers into exile.[21] Ethelbert's son soon reconverted, but was powerless when 'the people of London refused to receive Mellitus, preferring to serve idolatrous priests'.[22] Despite Mellitus's courage, and the interest of an episode which shows St Paul's with a font, perhaps a baptistery, and provides our earliest vignette of an actual service, it is obvious that the conversion had so far been at best superficial. In the new political circumstances (Sæberht's three sons died fighting the still pagan West Saxons, who were successfully ending Kent's hegemony) a further mission was impossible.[23] It would be interesting to know whether St Paul's was converted to a temple or became derelict.

The next mission occurred *c*.654 when, at the request of King Sigeberht of the East Saxons, Oswiu of Northumbria sent Cedd to evangelize. A peripatetic missionary of the Irish school, Cedd was not interested in re-establishing a centralized London-based see. Instead, he travelled throughout the province and built churches, where his priests lived by a rule, notably at Bradwell on Sea (the Roman fort of Othona) and Tilbury (Fig. 5).[24] In 665, in the hiatus after Cedd's death, one of the two East Saxon kings led his people into apostasy while the other remained faithful. Jaruman, bishop of the Mercians, undertook an emergency mission, and the description of his travels and the way in which the reconverted people 'abandoned or destroyed the temples and altars they had erected and opened the churches' suggests a territorial division of the kingdom; but Bede is silent over which part was which, or what, if anything, was happening at St Paul's.[25] The next bishop, Wine (from 666 to ?before 672), driven out of the West Saxon see, bought London from the king of Mercia, a simony which may have led to his ostracism by the new archbishop, Theodore (668–90).[26]

After this difficult start, St Erkenwald (675–93) is credited with setting the see on a secure and London-based footing, earning his veneration at St Paul's as its second founder.[27] He probably had the advantage of Kentish royal blood, and was certainly a major political as well as ecclesiastical figure, adept at acquiring endowments for the two foundations he had made before he became bishop: a monastery at Chertsey in Surrey and a nunnery at Barking, Essex, both on or close to the Thames.[28] As the political tides swirled, Chertsey's original endowment by Ecgberht of Kent was greatly expanded by Frithuwald, a Mercian sub-king in Surrey, while Barking's East Saxon endowment was enlarged by Mercian and West Saxon kings. Consulted by Ine of Wessex as 'my bishop' when drawing up his law-code, which may indicate that the diocese of London extended into Surrey, Erkenwald seems also to have been a major influence in developing the diplomatic of East and West Saxon charters.[29] Given all these aspects of his career, it is remarkable that no shred of evidence backs the St Paul's tradition that he 'bestowed great cost on the fabric thereof; augmenting its revenues very much with his own estate; and procuring divers ample privileges thereto'.[30]

The shakiness of the seventh-century English church, so amply reflected in London, was general and systemic, and Erkenwald worked particularly closely with Archbishop Theodore to reestablish it on a firmer basis. If Surrey, or part of it, was not initially within the see, the bishop's previous position as abbot of Chertsey and his special relationship with Theodore provide a possible explanation for its acquisition. Erkenwald was asked to attend Theodore's reconciliation with St Wilfrid, which took place in London, where the archbishop probably already had a house.[31] When Theodore instituted regular metropolitan provincial church councils, or synods, the London diocese seems to have been a favourite location, remaining so until the series petered out in the mid ninth century. Hertford, the first in 672 (assuming this was not Hartford in Huntingdonshire), was later in west Hertfordshire but probably then within the diocese, and Brentford (781), Chelsea (at least eleven between 785 and 816) and London itself (?795, 845) certainly so. But recent arguments that almost all were deliberately held here are flawed while so many places remain unidentified. *Clofesho* in particular, designated at Hertford as the only future meeting place, became in the event, with at least eleven meetings between 716 and 825, joint favourite with Chelsea, and may well have been within Middle Anglia; *Aclea*, with three meetings, may have been in Kent; *Astran* and *Adtuifyrdi* (one each) are unlocated, while Hatfield (679) may well have been in Yorkshire, as is Austerfield (702/3).[32]

Under Erkenwald's successor Wealdhere (693–705 × 716), London became for a while a more straightforwardly Mercian see. Wealdhere wrote the first surviving letter 'from one Englishman to another' to his archbishop in 704–5, concerning a forthcoming conference at Brentford to resolve differences between the king of the West Saxons and 'the rulers of our country'; and the Surrey section of the diocese may have been transferred as part of the settlement.[33] He also enhanced his see's endowment. The land at Hemel mentioned above was lost before *c*.1000, and a grant of thirty *cassati* at Twickenham, Middlesex, probably made to him personally, had gone before the 840s, possibly to his kin.[34] Two permanent acquisitions, though, were fifty *manentes* at Fulham transferred in 701 by Bishop Tyrhtil of Hereford (whose possession of them still needs explaining) and a further ten *manentes* in adjacent Ealing. These formed either all or part of the second of St Paul's four large-scale endowments, comprising both the episcopal manor of Fulham (which included Ealing, Acton and, probably as a later addition, distant Finchley) and the chapter estates in adjacent Willesden, Neasden, Harlesden and Twyford.[35]

A third large block of land was granted to Wealdhere's successor, Ingwald (705 × 716–745), by Suæbred, King of the East Saxons, seventy *cassati* in the 'regio known as Deningei'. This was the district between the rivers Crouch and Blackwater in Essex, although if the king was granting the entire *regio*, then some of it, including the eponymous township of Dengie, was later irretrievably lost.[36] There may have been an earlier connection. By 1086 the largest St Paul's estate in the area was the thirty-hide episcopal

manor of Southminster, whose name, 'the southern minster', was probably formed in contrast to the northern minster of Bradwell-on-Sea, St Cedd's mission centre. Bradwell, too, was in other hands by 1066, but the canons were holding nearby Tillingham (just over twenty hides), their alleged foundation estate. Did Cedd choose Bradwell because St Paul's already owned it, or did the canons forge a mistaken link with Ethelbert rather than with Cedd or Suæbred? There is no way of knowing.

There is also no way of telling when the cathedral obtained its fourth complete block of territory, which appears in Domesday Book as fifty-five hides divided between the bishop's manors of Clacton and Chich (later St Osyth), the canons' manor of the Naze (Kirby and Thorpe le Soken and Walton on the Naze) and Birch Hall (lost by the canons shortly before 1086). The area belonged to St Paul's by *c*.950, but given its size is likely to have been a far earlier acquisition.[37]

Difficult as it is to chronicle the acquisition of the estates, in turning to look at how they were utilized the silence is impenetrable. Cathedrals had pastoral responsibility for the whole diocese, but even the most ardently peripatetic teams could not hope to provide continuous care. The obvious next stage of providing local centres can be seen in Cedd's activities in the 650s, and also to some extent in Erkenwald's pre-episcopal foundations at Chertsey and Barking, although no nuns, and by no means all monks, could operate as priests. Such minsters (the same Latin word, *monasterium*, applied to communities of both monks and secular priests) covered their extensive parishes through teams of clergy, and the most extreme advocates of what has become known as the minster model postulate a precisely planned grid.[38] Minsters can often be identified, even after their downgrading to more local parish churches, by their location on royal estates, physical size, collegiate status and residual rights to such things as burial fees. But even if the search for such a rigidly homogeneous system were wise, London is particularly difficult territory in which to pursue it. The monarchy largely withdrew from estate ownership in Middlesex/Hertfordshire in the tenth century, leaving suggestive names such as Kingsbury but little other evidence – and any argument that churches on such estates 'must' have had minster status is entirely circular.[39]

One of the biggest gaps in the minster model has been the failure to consider the role of ecclesiastical estates in the creation both of minsters and of the parish churches which supplanted them, despite those estates accounting throughout for very high percentages of both acres and souls. Within the four blocks of St Paul's own endowment, minsters existed at Southminster and at Chich, whose name was changed to St Osyth in honour of the royal seventh-century saint celebrated there, but in neither case do we know whether the cathedral created or, perhaps more probably, inherited the minster.[40]

In neither of the Middlesex blocks is there any sign of a minster, except, perhaps, at St Pancras, where the dedication is almost certainly early but the church, within the 'twenty-four hides', is too close to St Paul's to fill an obvious need as a pastoral centre.[41] In 1593 John Norden recorded the belief that St Pancras was older than St Paul's, and local legend asserts that it originally served a nearby Roman settlement.[42] This is extremely unlikely. Not only are there no supporting archaeological finds in the vicinity or church fabric, but St Pancras, supposedly a Diocletian martyr, was probably a later invention.[43] Nevertheless, he was greatly venerated in Rome in the sixth and seventh centuries, and several early extra-mural churches dedicated to him in

6. Tombs of Sæbbi, king of the East Saxons (left, d. 694) and Ethelred, king of the English (right, d. 1016), the only kings known to have been buried at St Paul's, as they appeared in the medieval cathedral, etching by Hollar for Dugdale's *History*, 1658. The grey or black marble sarcophagi dated from the mid twelfth century

England may have imitated the Roman topography.[44] An altar stone with an incised cross was rediscovered under the church in 1847 and the cross-type has been claimed as seventh century, but it was in fact current until at least the fourteenth, while the earliest parts of the existing, small church do not predate the twelfth.[45]

The question of the relationship between St Paul's and its see's undoubted minsters remains an important, if insoluble, problem. To name only the most prominent, if St Albans, within west Hertfordshire, was originally within the diocese, then Mellitus inherited the cult centre with England's strongest claim to uninterrupted Christian observance; it was also one of the focuses of Offa of Mercia's attention, as, perhaps, was Westminster.[46] Waltham, well before the tenth-century installation of its Holy Cross, was clearly another major centre, as too was Erkenwald's foundation at Barking.[47] It is obvious from better documented sees and from Bede that many lesser minsters were little more than private family concerns, and that in the eighth century, as episcopal authority increased, many were brought under diocesan control or disbanded. This presumably happened at London, but apart from the possible interpretations of the Chich and Southminster endowments, and of a ninth-century lease in Braughing (see below), there is simply no evidence.

Evidence of the religious life at St Paul's is equally unavailable, but the cathedral's relationship with its city is brought briefly into focus by two grants from Ethelbald of Mercia to Bishop Ingwald of remission of tolls on a ship, presumably at London. Ethelbald made similar grants to two Kentish religious communities and to Worcester Cathedral, so Ingwald was not uniquely favoured, but he was at least benefiting from his cathedral's location.[48]

Whether eighth-century St Paul's continued to benefit from London's trade is unknown, but its status and endowments seem otherwise to have been faltering. Its bishop settled to a consistently low place in the episcopal hierarchy revealed in charter witness lists, and there are no signs of any grants to match the Middlesex estates such as Harrow, Hayes and Twickenham acquired by Canterbury at that time.[49]

The cathedral's failure to benefit from Offa of Mercia (757–96) is particularly noteworthy. Anxious to substitute direct for indirect rule in his sub-kingdoms, and unhappy with the resistance he encountered from Kent and its archbishop, Offa created a new archbishopric at Lichfield for the Mercians and Angles in 787, thus splitting the province and leaving London the only see north of the Thames still subject to Canterbury.[50] The foundation connections with Kent were thus perhaps acknowledged, and the Saxon sees kept together, but had Offa wanted to develop any other aspect of London's potential than the purely economic, he might have chosen to emphasize its northward links.[51] Genuinely pious as well as astute in his choice of 'national' saints for special devotion, the king promoted St Albans, and it is possible that St Albans's gain was St Paul's loss.[52] It is also conceivable that it was Offa who split the diocese of London, thus attaching St Albans to Middle Anglia.

The two possible indications that Offa was supportive of St Paul's are both dubious. The king took over the Kentish mint but also greatly expanded minting at London, and a London series coin inscribed with the name Eadberht and a monogram variously interpreted as M, for *monetarius*, moneyer, or EP, for *episcopus*, bishop, could reflect a coinage struck jointly with Eadberht, bishop between 772 × 782 and 787 × 789. By the 920s, though, only at Canterbury and Rochester did their bishops still have minting rights.[53] Whether or not Eadberht briefly had them, it is typical of St Paul's inability to benefit proportionately from London's economy that its bishop in general did not.

The second possible pointer is a brief notice in the Anglo-Saxon Chronicle that the bishops of Lindsey and London left the country in the year (796) that Offa died.[54] The obvious inference, not least from the subject order, is that they were too closely identified with him to feel confident with his successor, but the lack of evidence for any such identification, and the fact that Offa was co-ruling with Ecgfrith, his son and heir, makes this unlikely. The revision of the metropolitan structure proposed soon after Offa's death provides a more plausible context. Coenwulf, who succeeded Ecgfrith in December 796, had the advantages of no commitment to Lichfield and, since 792, a Mercian archbishop for Canterbury, but one reluctant to go there while Kent was still in revolt. In 798 Coenwulf therefore petitioned the pope to revive Gregory's original scheme, with London replacing both Canterbury and Lichfield as the southern archbishopric. Despite the historical and economic strength of the argument, the pope refused point blank, perhaps influenced by Kentish and West Saxon lobbyists unhappy at any enlargement of Mercian power.[55]

Only one charter is certainly recorded from ninth-century St Paul's: a lease by the bishop and 'congregation of brothers of the church of St Paul the Apostle' of land at Braughing to one Sigric for the substantial rent of four thousand silver coins, with reversion to the church of St Andrew. Everything about this transaction is obscure, including the charter's precise date (827 × 840), Sigric's identity, the nature of the interest of all the parties concerned and whether St Andrew's was Braughing's minster. It might represent a recycling of minster lands which had been transferred to diocesan control, but whether or not the reversion was really intended, the only recorded manor in Braughing in 1066 was in lay hands.[56]

In 825–6 Ecgberht of Wessex took control of Essex, along with Kent, Surrey and Sussex, but (except briefly in 829–31) Middlesex and London remained under Mercia, and the diocese was therefore once again split between kingdoms. Once again, too, kings, archbishop and bishops cooperated as necessary. Mercian and West Saxon coins were both struck at London, and the royal houses intermarried; archbishops of Canterbury, although technically owing allegiance to the West Saxon kings, occasionally attested Mercian charters in the 840s–860s, while bishops of London, judging from their very sparse attestations, seem already from the 860s to have been looking towards the West Saxon rather than the Mercian court.[57] This time, however, cooperation was also impelled by the Viking threat.

Assessing the Viking impact on the diocese is a nightmare, as, more seriously, it must have been for those who endured it. Viking armies attacked London in 842, 851 and 871, and the extra-mural trading settlement was contracting by *c.*850.[58] In 874 the Vikings deposed Burgred, king of Mercia, replacing him with their appointee, Coelwulf, and then in 877 divided Mercia between themselves and Coelwulf. It used to be thought that London was under direct Viking control from 877 until King Alfred of Wessex captured it in 886, but coin evidence provides a more subtle picture, with Viking power both less constant and less absolute. Coins in Alfred's name were being minted in London in the mid 870s – perhaps near St Paul's: finds include a trial-piece or weight from the churchyard – and they style him variously 'king of the English' and 'king of the Saxons and Mercians'.[59] Moreover, these were followed by coins for Ceolwulf, apparently issued after 877. Whatever the vicissitudes of London and Middlesex, Essex seems to have remained consistently under Wessex.[60]

7. Gravestone, early eleventh century, probably carved by a Scandinavian craftsman and commemorating a person of Scandinavian birth. Found on the south side of St Paul's churchyard in 1852. (Museum of London)

The only two extant copies of the undated treaty between Alfred and Guthrum, the Viking king of East Anglia, survive in a St Paul's manuscript, and the diocese was bisected by its terms.[61] The boundary between the respective territories was drawn along the Thames to the Lea and up the Lea to its source, before crossing to Bedford and thence northwards. The traditional interpretation is that the treaty was made shortly after Alfred's conquest of London in 886, and that Guthrum's was the eastern, Essex, side. A recent reinterpretation, however, has placed the date at 878 (thus, among other things, placing the city's reconquest earlier) and also reversed the sides. The jury is still, and perhaps permanently, divided and out, but the revised date has commanded wider acceptance than the topographical reinterpretation.[62] The treaty was in any case short-lived, and there were major campaigns across Essex in 892–6, and across the whole diocese as Edward the Elder pushed to victory in the 910s.

The lack of certainty about campaigns and control is unhelpful, but there are further reasons for doubt about the precise impact. The chroniclers, although guilty of ecclesiastical and pro-Wessex bias, give accounts of devastation which cannot be dismissed, and besides direct devastation, inaccessibility of resources must have been a recurrent factor. The Viking army which overwintered at Fulham in 879–80 apparently built the Thames-side embankment which later enclosed the bishop's palace and adjacent settlement.[63] On the other hand, place-name, coin-hoard and campaign evidence all indicate that only the northern edge of Essex was ever incorporated into the Viking East Anglian kingdom, and that despite the name of Dacorum (Danish) Hundred in west Hertfordshire, there was a similar absence of Scandinavian settlement in Middlesex/Hertfordshire.[64] Equally, coin and other evidence suggest a nuanced story. The Vikings were extreme players, but playing a pre-existing game in a world accustomed both to co-operation and to a whole spectrum of subjugation, from tribute payment through to extinction (as witness the East Saxon kings, last recorded in the 820s).[65] The complexities, and the possibility that London was treated separately from its hinterland, are suggested by the pattern of the London mintings.

On the specifically religious side, the degree of anti-Christian hostility from pagan overlords, as opposed to wealth-targeting raiding parties or the burden of raising tribute payments, is also debatable, particularly given that Guthrum converted to Christianity in 878, and that Alfred's desire for control may have added to the delays in filling episcopal vacancies.[66] The London episcopal list is incomplete between 867 and c.890 and the see may have been in abeyance.[67] It is possible that in the 880s an empty seat suited Alfred while he briefly considered moving the metropolitan see to London.[68] On the other hand, large-scale disruption is undeniable. Some minsters vanished permanently, and others were later refounded: if Hadstock was indeed St Botolph's foundation of *Icanho*, it was a notable casualty.[69] Barking was refounded, but its daughter house of Nazeing never reappeared.[70] Unlike lesser minsters, though, St Paul's was too important to be allowed to die. The episcopal line and, as far as we can tell, the previous endowment ultimately continued as before, even though between c.890 and the 910s the entire diocese and endowment cannot have been recovered. The formal legal position is unknown, but it seems that St Paul's carried on as best it could, and that its right to recover previously held estates when circumstances permitted was accepted.[71]

Bishop Heahstan (d. 897) was installed by the early 890s, in time to receive a copy of Alfred's translation of *Pastoral Care*, part of the king's general attempt to revive Christian practice.[72] Alfred also wished to revive the city of London's economy, but the extent of St Paul's involvement is, at best, unclear. In 889, before Heahstan was certainly appointed, the bishop of Worcester was granted a plot of land as a market-place, with its attendant tolls, in a document which stated that the king retained tolls on trade 'in the public street' or on the 'trading shore' (*ripa emptoralis*). Bishops of Worcester had a long-standing interest in London, having received remission of tolls on two ships there c.745 and a property near 'the West Gates' from King Burgred in 857 (perhaps in the suburban *wic*), but the incumbent was also one of Alfred's confidants.[73]

The see of London may again have been vacant, but its bishop seems definitely to have been absent from the meeting at Chelsea in 898 where King Alfred and Ealdorman Æthelred (the Mercian prince operating as a dependent ruler of Mercia), Plegmund, archbishop of Canterbury, and the bishop of Worcester planned London's *instauratio* (renewal or laying out); and as part of the process the archbishop and bishop received grants of adjacent river-frontage plots at *Ætheredes hyd*, later Queenhithe.[74] Plegmund was the Mercian whose elevation to Canterbury had probably replaced any idea of removing the archbishopric to London, and the personnel and outcome of the Chelsea meeting suggest that the city's redevelopment was part of a wider strategy for Mercia.[75] The bishop of Winchester, Alfred's heartland see, is as absent from the text as the bishop of London.

That St Paul's was in fact entirely excluded is perhaps unlikely. Alfred's laying out of new streets was small-scale, but seems to have covered the area from the Thames up to Cheapside, the latter abutting the cathedral precinct (and presumed palace site) and possibly *ab initio* a market street.[76] At the same time, Queenhithe probably became one of the main focuses of the 'trading shore', with a possibly associated cluster of -hithe (landing place) names extending westward towards Paul's Wharf, which, however, like the other -hithe names, is not recorded before the twelfth century.[77] St Paul's was definitely involved in other aspects of the tenth-century reconstruction. The rules of the London peace guild promulgated in the 930s are titled 'ordinance of the bishops and reeves of London', an ecclesiastical plural which presumably includes Canterbury, Worcester and any other see which had a London base. The bishops are unlikely to have been involved in the routine guild activities the ordinance describes, but it gives a rare direct glimpse of Bishop Theodred, taking a message from the king to the archbishop that the death penalty should not routinely be inflicted on men under fifteen.[78]

Such guilds were an interim stage before the full organization of shires and hundreds. King Edward's reconquest in the 910s was marked by the establishment of forts (*burhs*), including Hertford and Witham (911–2) and Maldon (916).[79] Like older *burhs*, including Colchester (reconquered in 917) and London, the new ones had an essential role in both defence and economic development, and Mercia was soon (although exactly when is unknown) divided into shires, each designed to support its eponymous *burh*. Hertfordshire must have been created primarily out of Middlesex, although with other land included on the north and west. Even the larger Middlesex could never have provided sufficient defensive resources for London, and it seems that all the shires within range, even as far away as Sussex, also owed additional duty there.[80]

The round numbers of hides in the hundreds (the subdivisions of the shire) of all the three counties of the diocese in

Domesday Book are sure evidence of a recently imposed structure.[81] The new hundreds remained almost without exception in royal hands, thus aborting the 'hundreds born private' which elsewhere allowed great landholders to control those in which their estates predominated.[82] Once again, royal concern with the area around London probably worked to St Paul's disadvantage.

The area of the London diocese had been recaptured by *c.*920, but further north both reconquest and the re-establishment of the ecclesiastical hierarchy were later, and Theodred, bishop of London (909 × 926–951 × 953), was also bishop of the East Anglian diocese centred at Hoxne. A brief flurry of evidence, which includes his will, shows Theodred, like Erkenwald before him, to have been a key figure in affairs of both Church and state. His name was probably German, as were those of four men, probably members of his ecclesiastical household, to whom he bequeathed chasubles. St Paul's was thus directly exposed to the period's important continental reform movement.[83]

Theodred's will includes bequests to the king, kinsfolk and churches in East Anglia, but only his grants to St Paul's are discussed here. To the cathedral went his two best chasubles, a chalice and cup, his best mass book, and his best relics (p. 115). Next came four estates specifically for the community, at Chich, Southery, Tillingham and Dunmow; at all except Dunmow, the slaves were to be freed. After land grants in Suffolk, none of them to St Paul's, he prescribed cash distributions, five marks to the archbishop, £10 to 'be distributed for my soul at my bishopric (*biscopriche*) in London and outside London', and a similar £10 at Hoxne. Next are the arrangements to be made on episcopal estates, one at Hoxne, then five at his main see: 'London' (*Lundenebyri*), *Wunemannedune*, Sheen, Fulham and Dengie (Southminster). All he had found on the first three London estates was to be left, but all he had added was to be divided, half for the cathedral (minster) and half for his soul, and all the slaves freed; at Fulham everything was to be left, unless anyone wanted to free any of the slaves; at Dengie what he had added was to be divided, but there is no mention of slaves.

The will thus gives a glimpse of the cathedral's chief but otherwise unrecorded activities, divine worship and estate management, while the concern to free slaves reveals both the importance of slave labour and increasing ecclesiastical sensitivity to the gap between preaching and practice. The later lists of stock handed down with each manor are foreshadowed in the distinction between inherited and acquired items. The will shows a bishop still deeply involved with his cathedral, but also some clear separation of the endowment: the first four estates are specifically bequeathed to the community, and the last five remain as episcopal demesne. It is therefore likely that Theodred provides a complete list of the episcopal estates, but neither the wording of the will nor what else we now know about the endowment indicates (as used to be thought) that this is true of the cathedral side.[84] The division was also still fluid: Chich appears in Domesday Book as an episcopal manor in 1066, but it was only part of the large block which also included Clacton and The Naze, separately entered and held by the bishop and canons respectively. Theodred seems to have been transferring the whole block, which was then redivided at some later date.[85]

Of the estates bequeathed to the chapter, Southery, outside the diocese, had been granted to Theodred by King Edmund, and was soon lost; Dunmow appears in the list of St Paul's estates made *c.*1000, but had gone by 1066. Chich and Tillingham were probably, as discussed above, long-established endowments.[86] On the episcopal side, London (taken to mean Stepney), Fulham and Dengie are old friends, but Sheen and *Wunemannedune* are both unfamiliar and significant.[87] Sheen is in riparian Surrey and by 1066 had been subsumed within the royal manor of Kingston.[88] *Wunemannedune* is almost certainly Wimbledon, nearby to the west, subsumed within the archbishop's manor of Mortlake by 1066.[89] Neither features in the *c.*1000 list, and they were perhaps transferred during the West Saxon succession crisis of 957, when the Thames became the boundary between Eadwig's Wessex and Edgar's Mercia, and all the bishops and ealdormen north of the Thames moved from Eadwig's court to Edgar's. Edgar also gained Wessex in 959, but the Thames thereafter remained the boundary between the Mercian and West Saxon parts of his kingdom.[90] The real puzzle is that Barnes, which is adjacent to Wimbledon, was a St Paul's estate *c.*1000, and held by the canons from the archbishop within Mortlake in 1066. When or why St Paul's had acquired estates in Surrey is unknown, but it is hard to see why Barnes should have been retained (or gained) when apparently related Wimbledon and Sheen were lost.

The importance of the bishop of London's role is dimly reflected in the later, weaker, sources. Under Theodred, the see rose to a regular second or third place in episcopal witness lists, and although his successors seldom maintained quite that ranking, they did not revert to the lowly pre-Viking position.[91] But a lack of holding power is also evident. Edgar appointed St Dunstan as bishop of Worcester in 957 and within the next couple of years as bishop of London, in illicit plurality. By 960 Dunstan was archbishop, and may have relinquished London immediately, although not certainly before 964.[92]

Dunstan's and Edgar's concern for religious revival extended beyond the restoration of the pre-Viking Church and, together with Saints Ethelwold and Oswald, they are particularly associated with monastic reform and with the peculiarly English movement to replace secular cathedral chapters with monastic ones. Dunstan was clearly a busy man, but the notable fact that St Paul's remained secular can hardly have been an oversight. Although re-examination of what used to be called the 'Tenth-Century Reformation' has destroyed belief in a standardized Benedictine world, either pre- or post-Viking, the movement was extremely powerful, and keenly felt within the diocese: some communities were reformed, including Westminster by Dunstan, who helped enlarge its endowment.[93] Two St Paul's clerics, Eadric and Thurcytel, left to become monks elsewhere (although for Thurcytel's attempted return after the general anti-monastic reaction, see below).[94]

Bishop Ælfstan (959 × 964–995 × 996) may have been a monk, as his two successors certainly were.[95] His role during his long episcopate was certainly vital, and he must have been a dynamic figure. When St Paul's burned down in 962, it may well have been under his aegis that it was rebuilt within the year (p. 128), and in old age he was one of those in charge of the fleet assembled at London in 992. Under bishops as distinguished as Theodred and Ælfstan, St Paul's may have been sufficiently reformed: among later statutes survives a 'Rule of St Paul', probably instituted there in the mid tenth century. It details appropriate behaviour in services and chapter, warns particularly against envy of others' revenues, slander and disobedience, and instructs 'do well what you have to do outside in the world, but let your zeal be within, impatient for the things that are eternal'.[96] Professor Whitelock considered but rejected the possibility that the rule was provided by Ælfstan's successor, Wulfstan (996–1002), London's greatest and most learned bishop, but a star whose trajectory soon made him also archbishop of York and bishop of Worcester.[97] The St Paul's liturgy, now silent to us, must have been highly regarded in the mid eleventh century, when Stow St Mary, in Lincolnshire, was endowed with the injunction that 'divine service (*theowdom*) be celebrated there as it is at St Paul's (*on Paulesbyrig*) in London'.[98]

Estate acquisition provides another indication of the cathedral's post-Viking status. It was Westminster Abbey, Dunstan's protégé, which acquired the five hides between the Fleet and the Tyburn (including the site of the now largely abandoned *wic*) as well as other lands which St Paul's must seriously have envied.[99] Nevertheless, despite lacking the cachet of monastic reformation, or any other grounds for competing with Canterbury, St Paul's managed to attract a respectable range of donations.[100]

Some or all of Islington (Middlesex) was still in lay ownership in 903 but belonged to the cathedral *c.*1005.[101] This may well also have been the period when the solid and heavily wooded block of land immediately to the north was acquired, comprising the later cathedral prebend of Brownswood and the episcopal estates of Hornsey, Finchley and Friern Barnet. Hornsey was attached to Stepney, but Finchley and Friern were added to distant Fulham (although most of Friern was given to the Hospitallers in the 1190s).[102] Wooded areas were frequently attached to distant centres to provide otherwise scarce resources, but this cannot have been the motivation here. Fulham, plentifully supplied with woodland on the clays of Hammersmith, Ealing and Acton, had no need of Finchley and Friern, and yet these were not attached instead to the less well-wooded Stepney.[103]

No part of this block can be identified in Domesday Book or any earlier St Paul's source, and some credence used therefore to be given to a fourteenth-century St Albans claim that all the abbey's land 'from Barnet to Londonstone', which would have included it, was confiscated by William the Conqueror. But a recently discovered boundary description for the grant of Barnet to St Albans *c.*1005 has now shown that Friern already belonged to a bishop, presumably the bishop of London.[104] The acquisition of these north Middlesex lands needs to be seen within various shadowy tenth-century contexts, among them the royal retreat from landownership in Middlesex of which Westminster Abbey was a conspicuous beneficiary, its corridor of estates through Hampstead and Hendon separating the west Middlesex St Paul's block, including Fulham, from Finchley and Hornsey.[105]

Another important dimension was the creation of Hertfordshire, probably to a large extent out of the former Middlesex. The county boundary between Middlesex and Hertfordshire ultimately followed the manorial one, contorting itself to place St Paul's Friern Barnet in Middlesex and St Albans's Barnet in Hertfordshire, but since such adjustments were sometimes made until the twelfth century, this does not help with precise dating. Nor does it shed any light on the division of the diocese. The whole of the new Middlesex, like Essex, was within the later medieval diocese, but only east Hertfordshire, up to the boundary provided in part by the Roman Ermine Street.[106] It seems improbable that the diocesan boundary between Middlesex and west Hertfordshire predates the separation of the two counties, but the sources are silent. The restructuring of the diocesan system north of the Thames in the mid to late tenth century, including the refoundation of the East Anglian diocese, provides a possible context, although with more manageable units the aim, it is hard to understand a transfer of west Hertfordshire from London to overlarge Dorchester.[107]

Further acquisitions between the 950s and 1066 – Orsett, Rayne, Copford, Glazenwood, Barling and Heybridge in Essex, and Hadham in Hertfordshire – cannot be described in detail here, but raise some general points.[108] First, despite the permanent gains, the reception of grants – which were often in the delayed forms of reversions or bequests – was always insecure. St Paul's kept a royal confirmation of a bequest of lands at Laver and Cockhampstead, but seems never to have obtained the estates; a grant of land at Weeley was in lay hands in 1066 and 1086, although St Paul's later had property there. The promised reversion of forty hides at Hadham resulted in only seven and a half. Moreover, then as at all periods, even estates that were received were readily lost. Holland, acquired by exchange in the later tenth century, had apparently gone by 1066. Thanks to an unusually honest account in the *Liber Eliensis*, the story leading up to this brief ownership also throws light into several other dark corners. Thurcytel, who had bought a place at St Paul's (*in presbiteratu emerat sibi locum*) but left to become a monk elsewhere, was expelled as abbot of Bedford in the 970s and sought readmission. The bishop (still at this stage involved in such matters) and community were unanimous in refusing, but friends' mediation and four and a half hides of land at Milton (Cambridgeshire) – rent during Thurcytel's lifetime and reversion thereafter – bought confraternity (*contubernium*). Milton duly reverted but the abbot of Ely made retention difficult, and the exchange for Holland – five hides next to other St Paul's estates in Essex – was agreed. The cash values were the same, but St Paul's benefited from an additional hundred sheep, fifty-five pigs, two men (presumably slaves) and five plough-oxen.[109]

In some grants the bishop was still seen as representing the whole community: Æthelric, for instance, bequeathed estates west of Rayne 'to St Paul's for the bishop (Ælfstan) for the provision of lights and for the communication of Christianity to God's people there'.[110] Other donations, though, were already specifically designated for either side: Ælflaed's will of *c.*1002 passed on her sister's reversionary grant of Hadham to the bishop (originally made *into Paulusbyrig æt Lundæne to bisceophame*) and added Heybridge for the community (*Dan hirede to brece into Paules mynstre*).[111] A degree of informal division of estates between bishop and cathedral was probably both early and widespread, but Domesday Book shows formal division (the later norm) further advanced at St Paul's than anywhere else. What caused this precocity is unclear, but since it is already visible in Bishop Theodred's will, its reflection in the grants is unsurprising.[112]

Knowledge of the St Paul's endowment was transformed by discovery of Richard James's seventeenth-century extracts from a roll, already missing when Dugdale was writing, which provided the only known copies of grants for Fulham, Ealing, Hemel, Islington, Dengie and Orsett, as well as information about Hadham, Braughing, Navestock, Laver, Cockhampstead and Shopland.[113] The discovery also left the eventual episcopal estates far better covered than the chapter's by reputable documents. Why this was so poses an interesting question. If the original grants of areas such as Fulham and Dengie in fact included later chapter estates, the canons may have faced the same dilemma. In any case, enthusiastically joining the twelfth-century circle of forgery which also included the abbeys of Chertsey and Westminster, they manufactured a confirmation from King Athelstan (925–39) legitimating at a stroke their possession of Drayton, Neasden and Willesden (Middlesex), Barnes (Surrey), The Naze, Heybridge, Runwell, Belchamp and Wickham St Paul's (Essex), and Sandon

LIST OF SHIPMEN

Entry in list	Modern place-name
Of Ticc IIII	Chich-St Osyth
Of Tillingaham II	Tillingham
Of Dunmæwan and of Tollesfuntan I	Dunmow and Tolleshunt
Of Naesingstoce and of Neosdune IIII	Navestock and Neasden
Of Hinawicun and of Tollandune II.	?Wickham St Paul's and Tollington
Of Gnutungadune and of Bræmbelege I.	?Hungerdown and Bromley
Of Tottanheale I.	Tottenham Court
Of Clopham II	Clapham ?*recte* Clapton
Of Baernun and of Ceswican I.	Barnes and Chiswick
Of Drægtune I	Drayton
Of Caddandune I	Caddington
Of Sandune I	Sandon
Of Ceaddingtune I	?Caddington
Of Fullanhamme V	Fulham
Of Forthtune IIII	?Fortune Gate
Of Stybbanhythe and of Gislandune II	Stepney and Islington
Of Orseathun I	Orsett
Of Ligeandune I	Laindon
Of Seopinglande and of tham westrum Orseathum I	Shopland and West Orsett
Of Bylcham I	Belchamp St Paul's
Of Coppanforda and Holande I.	Copford and Holland
Of Suthmynster V	Southminster
Of Claccingtune II	Clacton
Of Hæthlege and of Coddanham I	Hadley and Codham Hall in Warley

Note. For the source, nee n. 115. For more detailed discussion and a map, see Taylor (1992); also Kelly (2004), who prefers to keep Clopham as Clapham (Surrey), but accepts it would have had to have been a St Paul's estate.

with Rothe, Ardeley and Luffenhall (Hertfordshire), and copied and recopied it thereafter.[114] If there were any genuine documents for any of these estates (the only known one is a will for Heybridge), they were quietly lost, and although the forgery purports to be a confirmation – hence, presumably, the omission of the supposed foundation gifts of Tillingham and the 'twenty-four hides' – it was always cited as an original grant.

The first genuine list of the St Paul's estates is provided in a note made c.1000 of the distribution of obligations to provide [s]cipmen for manning a ship, and provides in passing the earliest references to most of the estates in the supposed Athelstan charter and to several of the later Middlesex prebends.

The list provides rare direct evidence of the national response to the renewed Viking attack from which the diocese had already suffered heavily: London was burned in 982, and although an army was repelled from the city in 994, Essex was repeatedly ravaged and its ealdorman and his followers killed at the Battle of Maldon in 991. With London crucial to sea as well as land

defence, Bishop Ælfstan was one of those in charge of the fleet assembled there in 992.[115] Interpretation of the list's wider significance, however, depends on knowing whether it includes only St Paul's estates, and whether it includes all of them. The arguments are very detailed, but the answers to both questions are yes, and its original editor's guess that St Paul's could somehow call on a few of its neighbours for help (or, put another way, that the bishop was acting in his civil role but for some reason only involving a very few outside estates, some of them outside the diocese) can be discarded.[116]

The list's pairings are mnemonic, by sound or proximity, so that Dunmow and Tolleshunt, to take the first example, owed one man apiece, making a total of fifty-eight men. This should almost certainly be sixty (scribal error is particularly easy with Roman minims), the normal complement of a ship. A royal edict of 1008 ordered the provision of a ship from every 300 hides throughout the land, organized through the shire and hundred (hundreds ideally contained a hundred hides), and some towns had separate quotas – Maldon's obligation to provide a ship is noted in 1086.[117] There is also evidence from the bishoprics of Sherborne and Worcester of private provision from 300-hide shipsokes, and although Domesday hidages cannot simply be projected backwards, the St Paul's list does seem to show a reasonable proportionality between the sizes of estates and their obligations, and to suggest a total endowment of around the 300-hide mark. The see of Worcester's triple hundred of Oswaldslow later became a highly privileged area of private jurisdiction, but this was not equivalent: at considerably poorer London the whole endowment was involved in a relatively short-term arrangement, and St Paul's never acquired any similar jurisdiction.

The obligation was imposed equally on episcopal and chapter estates, and it is possible that the list gives the chapter estates first, followed from Fulham onwards by the bishop's.[119] The obligation was also on all the lands, not simply the tenanted parts. This would change radically after 1066, when William I imposed knight-service obligations on bishops but not on their communities, and the bishop of London provided separate landed endowment for many of his contingent.[120]

Viking attacks more or less ended with King Cnut's accession in 1016. Bishop Ælfwig (1014–35) probably attended the London council which had instead chosen King Ethelred's son to succeed his father, a wrong call for which both city and cathedral paid heavily. Under such circumstances the flourishing cult of Archbishop Alphage (Ælfheah), murdered in 1012 by a Viking army based at Greenwich and buried at St Paul's, must have had a political dimension, and, strongly against the Londoners' wishes, the saint's remains were translated to Canterbury in 1023.[121] Adding obvious insult to injury, Cnut was a generous benefactor to Canterbury, Evesham, Winchester and elsewhere, and allegedly later transferred one of St Alphage's fingers to Westminster Abbey; St Paul's, meanwhile, lost not only the (lucrative) saint but also the extensive manor of Southminster (the latter's restoration by William I is a good example of successful institutional tenacity about endowment). Bishop Ælfwig's reluctant successor, Ælfweard (1035–44), who also continued as abbot of Evesham, was probably Cnut's kinsman, and a safer pair of hands. He was bequeathed an estate at Bentley in Essex but did not transfer it to his see, a failure perhaps typical of the man who, in the event, was London's last consecrated Anglo-Saxon bishop.[122]

That Edward the Confessor appointed two Norman favourites

to London, Robert of Jumièges (1044–51) and, after his translation to Canterbury, William (1051–75), is another tribute to the see's perceived importance. Recognition, however, had never equalled fondness. The unification of the kingdom under the erstwhile kings of the West Saxons had quickened London's emergence as the country's capital, and its economic and strategic pre-eminence were beyond question, but there had been no corresponding transfer of royal affection or symbolism: the kings remained attached to Winchester, where Old Minster was firmly the dynasty's church. When Edward the Confessor began the transfer, he deliberately chose Westminster, which thus received not only a grandly rebuilt church but also, in due course, the relocated royal court.[123] The London which became England's capital was always the London–Westminster conjunct. Robert's affections, too, may have lingered elsewhere: while bishop of London, he inscribed and gave an early eleventh-century English sacramentary to Jumièges, whose abbot he had formerly been.[124] His influence has also been suggested for similarities in the designs of the new mid century abbey churches at Jumièges and Westminster.[125]

Bishop William's commitment was more absolute, and in 1066 his Norman origins and mediatory skills may have helped soften William the Conqueror's wrath towards London and its cathedral. The bishop's name is curiously absent from the contemporary chronicles, but the later evidence of the annual civic thanksgiving processions to his tomb receives oblique contemporary support from Domesday Book (1086), which shows that while churches such as Ely which had withstood the Conqueror had proved easy meat for Norman predators, those such as Bury and St Paul's with trusted leaders had done well.[126] The king certainly remained wary of London, planting fortresses at either end of the city. The bishop held neither of these, but was granted a castle at (Bishop's) Stortford, strategically placed where Stane Street crosses the River Stort. King William also restored Southminster and, despite the enormous predatory pressures on estates close to London, allowed both bishop and chapter by and large to maintain and enhance their endowment. The canons lost part of Barnsbury (within Islington/Stepney) to Hugh de Berners, and some acres from several Essex manors to other forceful barons, but made more than compensatory, and probably equally illegitimate, gains in Essex (at Navestock, Barling, Chapel Lee and Norton Mandeville) and also gained or regained Caddington and Kensworth on the west Hertfordshire–Bedfordshire border.[127]

The bishop's acquisitions were greater, and by legitimate purchase, but mostly went towards endowing the knights with whom he now had to provide military service, an obligation no longer shared with the canons.[128] The histories of the episcopal and chapter endowments would in any case from now on be almost entirely separate, and this is one of the many ways, partly due to the conquest and partly coincidental, in which the years around 1086 provide a watershed. It was under bishop Maurice (1085–1107) that St Paul's assumed its later, better-known and better-documented form.

4

FROM CONQUEST
TO CAPITAL:
ST PAUL'S *c.*1100–1300

Derek Keene

In the same year before autumn, the holy minster of St Paul, the cathedral church of London, was burnt down, with many other churches and the largest and noblest part of all the city. Similarly also, at the same time nearly every chief town in all England was burnt down.[1]

The English chronicler's reaction to the fire of 1087 vividly reveals the cathedral as the focal point of London, the chief city of the kingdom. This second of the three great fires of London known to have occasioned rebuildings of St Paul's was perhaps the most significant of them as a turning-point in the history of the city's mother church. Fundamental changes were already taking place in its immediate surroundings and in its organization. Moreover, the great new church begun by Bishop Maurice after the fire was further to reshape and define London's landscape and identity. After Winchester cathedral, begun only eight years earlier, Maurice's church was perhaps the second largest structure to be erected in Christian Europe since the Emperor Constantine's basilicas in fourth-century Rome.[2] From its foundation, St Paul's would have served as one of the chief symbols of London and its bishop as the principal resident source of authority, governing in secular as well as spiritual affairs, but only in the two centuries following 1087 does it become possible to explore the relationship between city, state and cathedral, to visualize the church itself, and to identify the interests and relationships of many of the people associated with it. In this period the cathedral clergy were established in a constitution whose framework still endures. At the same time, the new church, from early in its history, served as a setting for public events without equal in the realm, just as its successor does today. In its scale the building reflected the ambitions of the bishops of London, but perhaps equally significant were those of the new Norman kings, aware of the political value of this great basilican public space in the largest and most powerful city of their territories.

In endowed wealth the mother church of London was of no more than middle rank among English cathedrals. Circumstances had denied it the metropolitan status which some thought was its due, a cause which in the twelfth century attracted a good deal of effort and was reinforced by interest in new fictional histories of Britain and London.[3] Indeed, there are signs of competition between St Paul's and other great churches: in size the new cathedral was a close rival to Winchester's, while the new focus on the cult of St Erkenwald was perhaps a response to developments at Westminster Abbey.[4] As dean of the province of Canterbury, the bishop of London had third rank in the hierarchy of the English church,[5] but both he and St Paul's owed their standing essentially to association with London, the richest city in the land and increasingly the seat of national power.[6] London has almost always been the largest and most prosperous British city, and along with Cologne was the leading urban phenomenon of Northern Europe during the eleventh and twelfth centuries, experiencing spectacular growth founded on its international trade and on its capacity to draw on the rapidly expanding resources of a hinterland that extended well beyond the diocese. Testimony to the city's wealth and population were its many parish churches, about 110 in all, of which most were probably founded by private householders or by neighbourhood communities by about 1100, when the city perhaps had well over 20,000 inhabitants. Over the following two centuries, London overtook rival English cities in its acquisition of an impressive portfolio of abbeys, priories, friaries and other religious institutions in

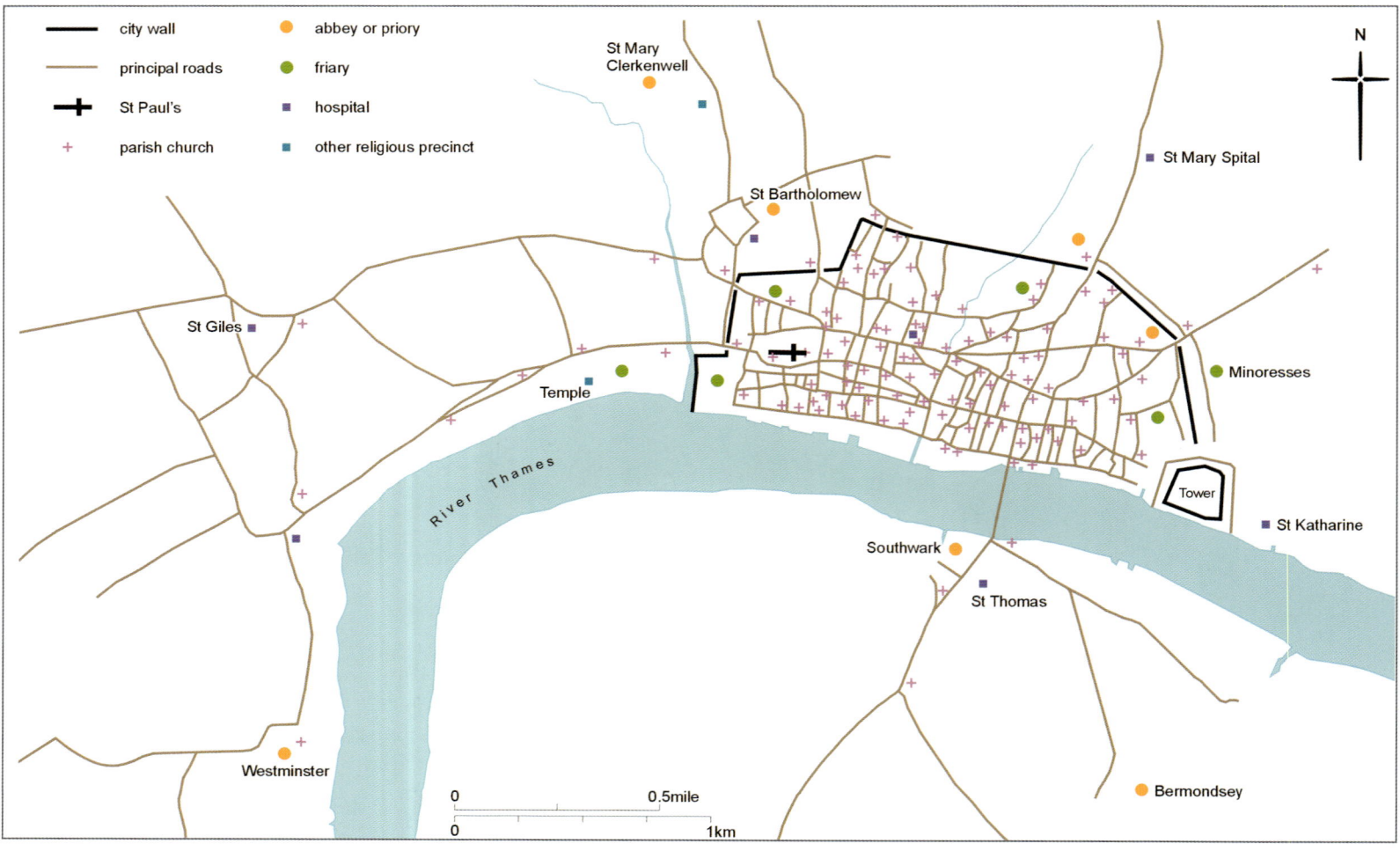

8.   The city of London *c.*1300, showing St Paul's, the religious houses of the city and the great number of parish churches

addition to its cathedral (Fig. 8). At the same time, its population may have quadrupled, reaching a peak about 1300 that was not to be achieved again until after 1550. In these two centuries, however, London came to be overshadowed by the seat of the French kings, Paris, and by a cluster of industrial and commercial cities in the Low Countries, while closer contacts with the Mediterranean world exposed it to the influence of much richer and more sophisticated urban societies. Nevertheless, London remained a bastion of the realm, a major source of public wealth and a spectacular showpiece. At the time of Duke William's invasion, Winchester was still in some respects the heart of the English kingdom, but control of London was essential to the conquest. Thereafter, London was the English city where monarchs spent most time and where the magnates of the realm set up houses close to the centres of business. Steadily, the institutions of government came to be settled on the edge of London, and during the last quarter of the thirteenth century London conclusively emerged in its modern role as the capital. The city itself had spread well beyond the Roman walls. On the south bank of the river there was another extensive suburb, but that was in another county and another diocese. Within the walls, and especially around the cathedral, where population densities were among the highest in the city, the intricate network of streets and lanes that had evolved was to remain largely unchanged until the nineteenth century (Fig. 9).

   The Norman Conquest had an immediate impact on the vicinity of St Paul's, where between Ludgate and the river a large fortification, later known as Baynard's Castle (of which

Montfichet's Tower was a part), was erected and passed into the control of one of the king's chief officers in London and later into the hands of the fitz Walter and the Montfichet families.[7] Before the thirteenth century, when it fell into decay, this fortification may have rivalled the Tower of London in strength. On its east side it seems to have incorporated a great ditch, possibly dug in the eleventh century, which extended well to the north of the site of the Norman cathedral (p. 3). This suggests that by the time of the 1087 fire the whole area immediately west of the cathedral had acquired a set of defensive works straddling Ludgate, Newgate and the city wall, later relics of which were Baynard's Castle, the Fleet Prison (where a substantial stone tower probably of late eleventh-century date has been discovered) and the street-name Old Bailey. By 1111 the bishop, in the course of building the new cathedral, had filled in the north part of the great ditch. In that year the king granted the bishop a part of that same ditch to the south belonging to Baynard's Castle, then in royal hands, to make the wall of his church and the street outside the wall.[8] This wall was that enclosing the south-west corner of the cathedral precinct, where it cut into the Baynard's Castle enclosure, while the street is now represented by Carter Lane (Fig. 20). This group of defensive works guarded the western approach to the city and, with St Paul's and the Tower of London, expressed the Norman regime's control of London.

   Before the Conquest, there had been a royal palace in the city. It was close to the cathedral, but perhaps not in Wood Street where later traditions placed it.[9] Most likely, as in some other European cities, it lay close to the cathedral, perhaps within the

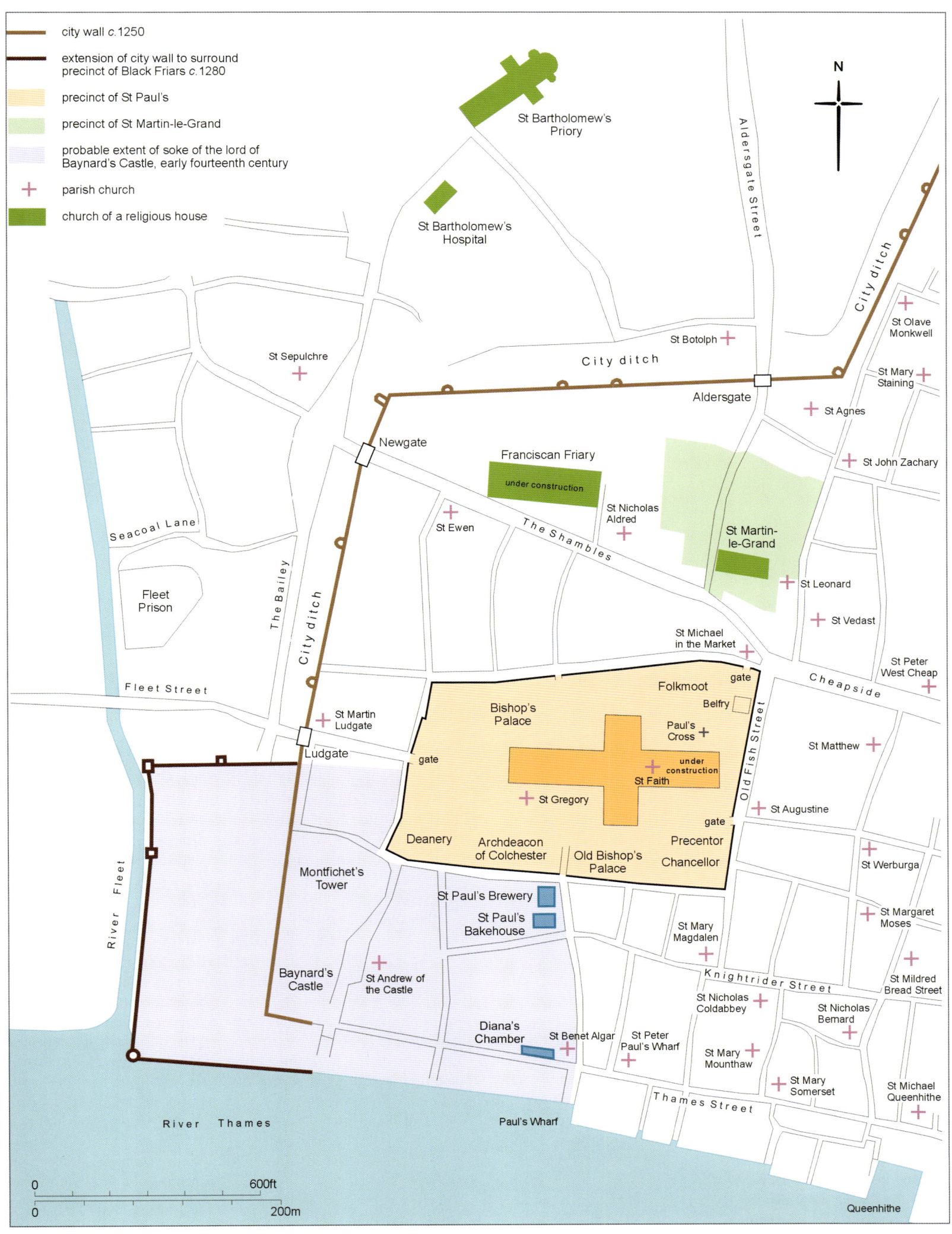

city wall *c.*1250

extension of city wall to surround
precinct of Black Friars *c.*1280

precinct of St Paul's

precinct of St Martin-le-Grand

probable extent of soke of the lord of
Baynard's Castle, early fourteenth century

✝ parish church

church of a religious house

N

St Bartholomew's
Priory

St Bartholomew's
Hospital

Aldersgate Street

City ditch

St Olave
Monkwell

St Sepulchre

City ditch

St Botolph

Aldersgate

St Mary
Staining

St Agnes

Newgate

Franciscan Friary

under construction

St Nicholas
Aldred

St Martin-
le-Grand

St John Zachary

Seacoal Lane

St Ewen

The Shambles

St Leonard

St Vedast

St Peter
West Cheap

Fleet
Prison

The Bailey

City ditch

St Michael
in the Market

Cheapside

St Matthew

Fleet Street

St Martin
Ludgate

Bishop's
Palace

Folkmoot

Belfry

Paul's
Cross

gate

St Augustine

Ludgate

gate

under
construction

St Faith

St Gregory

gate

Precentor

Chancellor

St Werburga

River Fleet

Montfichet's
Tower

Deanery

Archdeacon
of Colchester

Old Bishop's
Palace

Old Fish Street

St Margaret
Moses

St Paul's Brewery

St Paul's
Bakehouse

St Mary
Magdalen

Knightrider Street

St Mildred
Bread Street

Baynard's
Castle

St Andrew of
the Castle

St Nicholas
Coldabbey

St Nicholas
Bernard

Diana's
Chamber

St Benet Algar

St Peter
Paul's Wharf

St Mary
Mounthaw

St Mary
Somerset

St Michael
Queenhithe

Thames Street

River Thames

Paul's Wharf

Queenhithe

0   600ft

0   200m

9.   St Paul's and its immediate surroundings in the mid thirteenth century

precinct known as *Paulesbyrig*, and extended north and west from the cathedral to the city wall and Newgate, an area where important royal household officials had interests during the twelfth century.[10] Indeed, the royal church of St Martin-le-Grand, immediately north of St Paul's and founded by a leading figure in Edward the Confessor's government, was perhaps originally associated with the palace.[11] King Edward's building programme at Westminster may have included a residence intended to replace the palace in the city, but the move to a more spacious and less threatened site upstream could have been prompted by the construction of the new defensive work over part of its site, and may not have been fully accomplished until the building of Westminster Hall by William Rufus, under way in 1097.[12] The 'noblest part of all the city' destroyed by fire in 1087 may thus have included the environs of the palace itself. From that moment on, St Paul's occupied a new position in London's geography of authority and cult, as a site complemented by the abbey and royal residence at Westminster.

The new cathedral was begun in or soon after 1087. A major stage was marked by the translation of St Erkenwald's relics in 1148; it was perhaps largely completed by 1175, its tower finished in 1221, dedicated in 1240, and then its east end reconstructed and extended in the New Work finally completed in the 1320s. It dominated the city and its skyline in a way that its predecessor could hardly have done. The bulk of the church, occupying the brow of the hill overlooking the Thames, rose well above the city walls and all houses in the city, while its elegant and sumptuous spire,[13] perhaps the tallest in Europe, rose higher than any building in London before 1964. This striking erection featured prominently in representations of the city from *c.*1220 onwards (Figs. 10, 11, 16).

The surroundings of the cathedral were reordered by creating a new precinct, a process that involved the acquisition of private houses and the closure of streets, for which Bishop Richard de Belmeis I (d. 1127) was remembered.[14] The walls and gates of the precinct were probably complete by 1200 (p. 141). The new enclosure and cathedral incorporated the existing or nascent parish churches of St Gregory and St Faith, serving parishioners of a neighbourhood extending beyond the precinct walls. The former, first mentioned in 1009, adjoined the west end of the new cathedral nave on the south side, while the latter is first recorded in the twelfth century as occupying part of the crypt. An agreement of 1106 about the boundary between the churchyard and land belonging to St Martin-le-Grand reveals the process of defining the new precinct.[15] Elements of the earlier street pattern appear to have determined the position of gates in the precinct wall and perhaps also the small opposing doors in the north and south walls of the cathedral nave. Outside the south gate of the precinct, by the early twelfth century,[16] lay the canons' brewhouse and bakehouse (p. 307), to which some of the food renders from their manors would have been carried after being landed at the quays to the south (pp. 145–8).[17] At this time the extension of the city's quays into the river was one of the most remarkable expressions of its commercial vitality, from which the cathedral benefited. By 1127, for example, the bishop had assigned to St Paul's altar rent from his new quay at Paul's Wharf recently erected by his tenants.[18] The gate at the north-eastern corner of the precinct opened into Cheapside, the city's principal market street, which when originally laid out before 900 had probably been aligned on a larger royal and ecclesiastical enclosure. Shops at this end of Cheapside were occupied by goldsmiths, many of whom were also moneyers and exchangers of coin, hence the name 'Old

Change' for a part of the neighbourhood.[19] This indicates an association between moneyers and the principal site of royal authority that is also evident in other cities. Indeed, several London moneyers were related to canons of St Paul's, and one of them may also have been a canon.[20] A coin weight found in this part of the churchyard suggests that the association went back at least to the time of King Alfred.[21] By the thirteenth century, and probably from centuries earlier, this part of the precinct was used for meetings of the folkmoot, the open-air gathering of hundreds, if not thousands, of citizens that was the principal expression of their collective power. This may simply have been a convenient open space at the end of the city's principal street, but it is possible that the area had been formally set out as an assembly ground in association with the cathedral and the royal palace. The fortification of the western part of the city in the late eleventh century may in part have been intended to overawe the citizens at their main place of assembly. Adjoining the site of the folkmoot, in the corner of the precinct, was the detached belfry of St Paul's, a timber-framed construction erected in the 1220s but perhaps replacing a tower that occupied the site a century earlier,[22] whose great bell was rung to summon the folkmoot. The tower over the crossing of the cathedral was also described as a *campanile* and presumably contained the bells that marked the liturgical hours and those of the city markets.[23] South of the folkmoot was Paul's Cross, first recorded in 1241 (p. 31) and a focal point for public declarations. Streets near the precinct contained important food markets, stimulated in part by the needs and produce of the cathedral itself: corn in Cheapside, corn and meat in the street leading towards Newgate, and fish in streets towards the river.[24] Building the new cathedral also had an impact on its surroundings, promoting the industries of the Fleet valley. Before 1133, Henry the timber-merchant, probably warden of the Fleet Prison, had a wharf on the Fleet used by St Paul's ships bringing stone for the work.[25] The burning of lime gave its name to a lane nearby, and the enormous demands of the project and other building in London stimulated the shipping of coal from Newcastle, whence the adjoining Seacoal Lane.[26] The work-force was correspondingly large, and so St Paul's estates were exempted their customary contribution of labour to other public works in London.[27] Certain specialized crafts became a feature of the cathedral vicinity. The marbler among the local witnesses to the boundary agreement of 1106 probably worked or dealt in the black stone imported from Flanders; he had successors in the marblers who by 1300 were established around the churchyard and served a national market for monuments in finely carved and polished 'Purbeck marble'.[28]

The physical transformation of the neighbourhood was perhaps accompanied by a reordering of its secular administration. About 1130, the whole of the area around the cathedral, extending from the river to the city wall on the north side appears to have fallen into two of the city's wards, corresponding approximately to the later wards of Castle Baynard and Farringdon Within. The former was known as the Bishop's Ward and lay to the south of the cathedral, where the bishop's palace was situated. Further south, it included the church of St Benet Paul's Wharf, the more westerly of the bishop's two estate centres in the city. The other ward, to the north and west of the cathedral, was in the hands of a canon, Ralph son of Algod, member of an important London-based family. This ward later included land adjoining the city wall between Ludgate and Cripplegate and so may have some association with the western fortification and the royal palace.[29] The division of the area between the bishop and a canon may reflect the wider division of St Paul's city interests between the bishop and the canons and was possibly a special measure associated with the replanning of the whole district once known as *Paulesbyrig*. Later aldermen of these two wards were always laymen, so far as we know.

Following the construction of the cathedral and precinct, the major physical changes in the environs of St Paul's before the Reformation concerned the establishment of the two principal mendicant priories in London: that of the Franciscans, set up within Newgate from 1225 onwards, and that of the Dominicans, who from 1278–9 onwards occupied the site of Baynards Castle and Montfichet's Tower, adjoining the cathedral precinct. Neighbouring churches often opposed the insertion of friaries into city environments because of the potential loss of congregations and revenue. The bishop and chapter were certainly concerned about the Dominicans' church, which was planned to have the largest chancel of any Dominican church in England. St Paul's and the friars came to an agreement in 1278 whereby the new friary was to have only one entry from within the city walls and was not to encroach on the cathedral's property nearby. Strong support from the king and the archbishop (himself a Dominican) for the new church seems to have persuaded St Paul's to accept the project.[30] From then on, the north-west corner of the city was distinguished by its cluster of three great churches of architectural distinction, of which St Paul's remained by far the largest. There had been more distant, but significant, threats to the primacy of St Paul's in London from archbishops of Canterbury. Before 1089, Archbishop Lanfranc was responsible for establishing a base in Cheapside, where he commenced the substantial church of St Mary-le-Bow that soon became the focus of an extensive city district under the archbishop's own spiritual jurisdiction (Fig. 15). Between 1189 and 1199, partially executed plans for a powerful and well-endowed collegiate church under the archbishop's patronage at Lambeth may have seemed equally menacing.[31]

Before the Norman Conquest and into the twelfth century, the priests or canons serving St Paul's lived communally under the bishop, following an adapted rule of Carolingian origin which was also observed in other English secular cathedrals.[32] A part of the cathedral estate was assigned to the upkeep of the canons, who probably had the power to prevent the appointment of more members of their community than that income would support.[33] From Domesday Book it appears that by 1066 several canons held parts of the estate as individuals and that in 1086 there was a distinction between such lands and those held by the canons in common. From about 1090 onwards, perhaps under the influence of the Norman regime and taking advantage of the interval after the death of Archbishop Lanfranc, who had favoured monastic establishments at cathedrals, a group of English secular cathedrals adopted the prebendal system, common in Northern France, whereby each canon had his own endowment or prebend, often in addition to a claim (which could also be described as a prebend) on a common fund. There was some form of prebendal system at St Paul's by 1066, possibly reflecting the influence of the Norman bishops who had held the see under King Edward, but its development was slow and the permanent assignment of estates to individual prebends was probably not accomplished until well after 1150.[34] Nevertheless, later lists of the prebendaries trace their succession back to the time of Bishop Maurice, when a series of royal charters to the canons and the apologetic tone of Maurice's own confirmation to them of their rights and prebends – if some of these records are not later forgeries or 'improve-ments' of contemporary documents undertaken in order to justify the structures that eventually emerged – suggest that the decades after the great fire witnessed rearrangements in the endowment involving episcopal interference with the canons' interests.[35] Bishop Maurice himself, in pressing need of funds for building, may have appropriated a share of the income, as well as assigning it in new ways among the canons or restricting their tendency to appropriate cathedral lands to their individual prebends. There was an important liturgical side to these changes, for it was probably Bishop Maurice who divided the responsibility for the daily singing of the psalter in the choir by attributing responsibility for five psalms to each of thirty canons.[36] Thus, each canon's stall is identified by the opening words of a psalm.

As at other English secular cathedrals, the constitutional evolution of St Paul's followed a distinctive path. One notable and perhaps conservative feature, recalling earlier and persisting arrangements at some French and Italian cathedrals, was the prominence of the archdeacons among the dignitaries of the chapter.[37] Their main responsibilities as members of the bishop's household concerned the parishes of the diocese rather than the cathedral itself. At St Paul's, it seems likely that one or more archdeacons presided over the canons under the bishop until, or even after, the first appearance of the dean (between 1086 and 1103–4),[38] who eventually emerged as the ruler of the chapter and its common interests. The bishop's influence over his community of clergy at St Paul's and their estates remained strong for most of the twelfth century, not least under Gilbert Foliot.[39] However, the later decades of the century, especially under the rule of Ralph de Diceto – dean during Foliot's old age and afterwards, and then in later years remembered as a sort of founding father of the chapter – witnessed an important stage in the establishment of a more or less independent chapter based on an endowment clearly separated from that of the bishop. This change was gradual, probably with many steps no longer detectable today. Diceto's survey of the chapter estates and churches undertaken in 1180–1 was part of the process, as were the chapter's acquisition of its own seal by the same date and Diceto's statute of 1192 concerning residence, but it was not until the mid thirteenth century, in the statutes issued under Dean Henry of Cornhill, that the independent status and function of the chapter achieved formal recognition. These statutes specified that the chapter was to elect the dean and to induct new canons, but that appointments to other offices and to prebends lay with the bishop.[40] Within the cathedral, the prime responsibility of the dean and chapter was the maintenance of the offices in the choir. Thus they became responsible for the maintenance of the New Work begun in 1259,[41] while the bishop, exceptionally, maintained the fabric of the body of the church. The bishop presided in the choir at special feasts and his right to preside in chapter was recognized in the statutes. The chapter of St Paul's was less independent of its bishop than those of other cathedrals, but nevertheless acquired ordinary jurisdiction over the parish churches appropriated to its common fund, and prebendaries had similar rights over theirs. This exemption from archidiaconal control is recorded from the early twelfth century.[42]

Other offices, known as dignities, emerged gradually during the twelfth century within the community of canons that constituted the bishop's *familia* (household). In some cases the duties may have been performed on an *ad hoc* basis by individual canons, while in others responsibilities associated with one of the later dignities were undertaken by a canon with another title. Thus

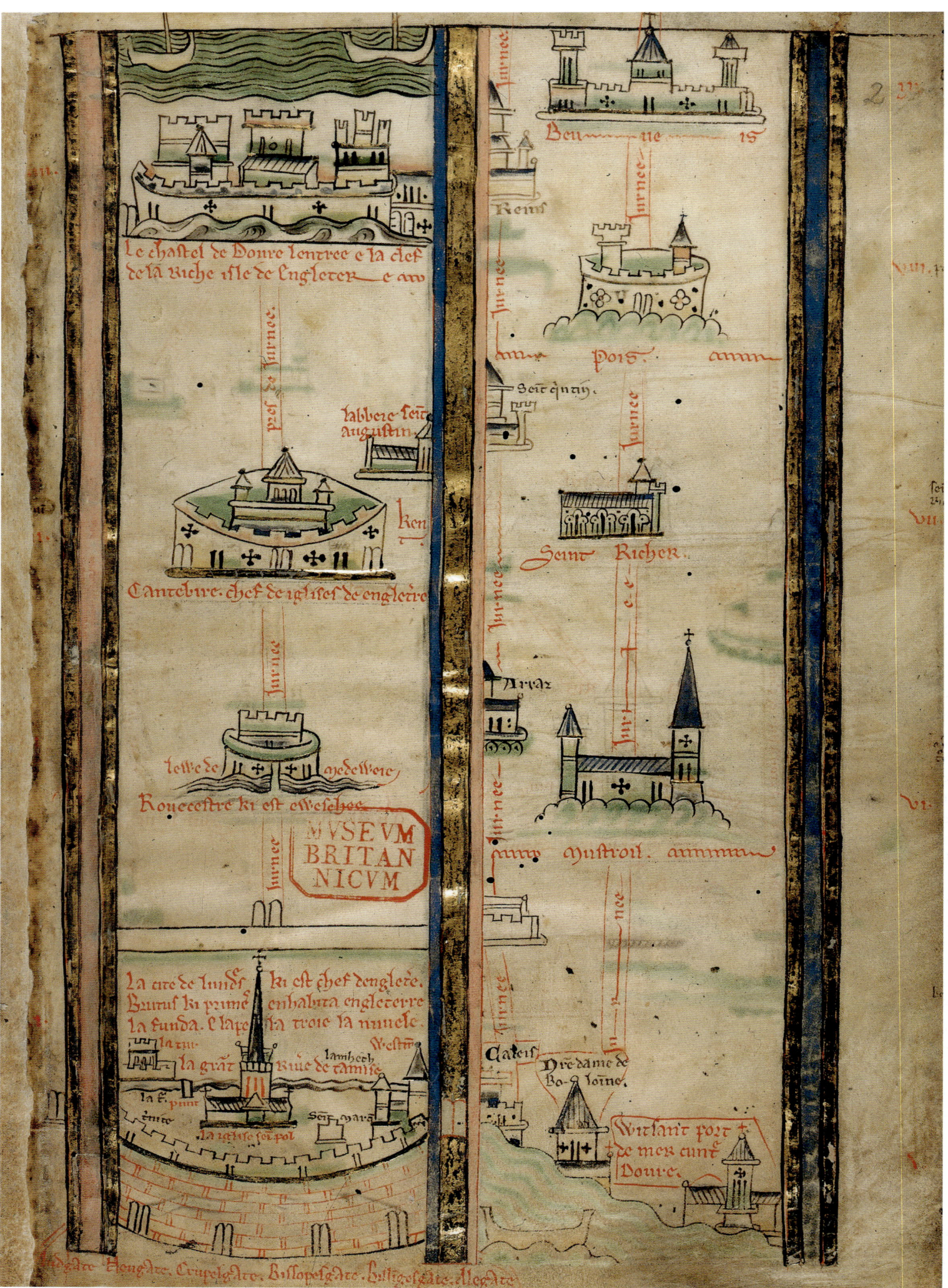

masters of St Paul's schools can be identified from before 1100, but not until about 1200 were they styled chancellor. Similarly, the treasurership was not formally endowed as a dignity until 1160–2, but the canon appointed had held the endowment by the gift of the previous bishop a decade earlier in an arrangement that perhaps expressed the bishop's attempt to assert control over his *familia* in the face of opposition from the archdeacon of London.[43] The community of St Paul's in the mid twelfth century was a hotbed of conflicting interests. There were cantors at St Paul's from at least 1104, but initially as members of the bishop's household and not as a regular officers, while the dignity of the precentor, who exercised a similar responsibility for the quality of song in the choir and supervised a singing master in the church of St Gregory, was not endowed until 1204. In other cathedrals, the precentor, who made a vital contribution to the chapter's central function of sustaining divine worship through the liturgy and its music, occupied a high position among the dignitaries, but not at St Paul's. This was because of the established position of the archdeacons, and especially the opposition of Peter of Blois, the learned and eloquent archdeacon of London notoriously conscious of his status and income, who appealed to Pope Innocent III on the matter.[44] From the early thirteenth century, there were eight dignitaries with separate endowments in addition to those of the thirty prebends. Their order of precedence was expressed by the position of their stalls in the choir: dean, four archdeacons (for the archdeaconries of London, Middlesex, Essex and Colchester), treasurer, precentor, and chancellor. A feature of the late twelfth and early thirteenth centuries was the establishment of houses within the precinct for use by the dignitaries and prebendaries (pp. 305–7),[45] another sign of their separation from the bishop's household. Ralph de Diceto in 1182–3 established the deanery with its chapel in the south-western corner of the precinct. By 1266 this chapel had been dedicated to Thomas Becket, the martyred archbishop of Canterbury, once Ralph's junior companion as a canon and by the 1180s being adopted by Londoners as their patron saint in addition to St Paul.[46] During the 1190s the prebendaries of Harleston and Caddington each conveyed to their successors stone houses they had built within the precinct.[47] In 1229–31 Henry of Cornhill, then chancellor, assigned to his successors in the dignity his houses on the south side of the cathedral.[48] From early in the twelfth century the master of the schools, predecessor to the chancellor, had had a house 'in the corner of the tower' (possibly, but not certainly, on the east side of the precinct near the belfry) and other canons had had houses adjoining,[49] but these may not have become prebendal endowments.

In addition to the dignitaries, there were other important offices held by canons or minor canons. From about 1181 there was a canon chamberlain who took financial responsibility for income other than the food rents.[50] At about that time, an income was assigned to an almoner. There was also a scheme for converting into a hospital for the poor those houses, appropriately situated close to Cheapside, given to the cathedral for that purpose

by Master Henry of Northampton, a learned canon and royal servant who had participated in the survey of the chapter's estate in 1180–1. The scheme came to nothing, but the almoner acquired important responsibilities, including the maintenance and education in grammar of eight boys suitable to serve in the church (whom he sent to the precentor's school for instruction in singing), the distribution of alms and the burial in the great cemetery of the poor and of beggars who died there or nearby.[51] In addition, there was a large staff of servants who undertook day-to-day duties in the cathedral, precinct, brewhouse and elsewhere: the responsibilities of the canons and minor canons who supervised them are detailed in the great collection of statutes compiled for Dean Baldock about 1300.[52]

The constitution of the chapter was the outcome of a complex evolution that achieved a delicate balance between established interests and acquired an arithmetical perfection. This doubtless contributed to the dean and chapter's conservative management of their secular affairs (pp. 145–6). Thus in 1282 they rejected a proposal from Queen Eleanor, wife of King Edward I, to endow a new prebend, being bound by their oath, they said, 'inviolably to observe the rights and liberty of their church'.[53]

Apart from the splendour of the architectural setting that it provided for the liturgy, and the splendour of its shrines and reliquaries (pp. 119–20), St Paul's was at the forefront of English church music during the thirteenth century. Along with those of other great churches, its canons and musicians, who were in touch with the latest developments overseas, played a part in the emergence of the new forms of polyphonic singing then being adopted in England. No surviving manuscripts of St Paul's polyphony from the period can be certainly identified, but the cathedral possessed what seems to be the earliest known book of the new music, now recognized as evolving independently from that of Notre-Dame in Paris. In 1255 this book was noted as having been donated by a cathedral treasurer in office during the late 1220s. The cathedral still owned the book in 1295, when it also possessed three other books of polyphony, one of them given by a prebendary who held office from before 1239 to about 1260 and another given by Ralph of St Gregory. Ralph presumably ran the precentor's singing school in the church from which he took his name.[54] Thus St Paul's seems to have been a focus for polyphonic innovation from before 1230, and it may be that the New Work was intended, at least in part, to provide an appropriate acoustic setting for the new music.

Many canons had duties outside London and so for much of the time were absent from St Paul's. They might be royal servants, holders of other ecclesiastical positions, representing St Paul's and other interests at the papal court or elsewhere overseas, or attending schools. One of the acknowledged purposes of cathedral endowments was to support such activities, but in the twelfth century and later the question arose of the degree to which absentees should be able to claim a share of the income. In the first half of the twelfth century, before the full development of the prebendal system, twenty or so canons seem normally to have been resident. From later in the century into the early fourteenth, the number of residents seems usually to have been fifteen or less, a smaller proportion than at some other cathedrals but presumably sufficient to maintain services. About 1150, it was accepted that non-resident canons could make no claim on the common fund.[55] Dean Ralph de Diceto's statute of 1192 drew a strict distinction between resident and non-resident canons, limiting the latter's claim on the common fund and defining the degree of

10.   Part of the itinerary from London to Apulia which prefaces Matthew Paris's 'History of the English' *c.* 1252. London and St Paul's are at bottom left; this part of the itinerary includes Rochester and Canterbury and continues as far as Beauvais (top right). Matthew's text alludes to the legendary history of London, while his sketch emphasises the centrality of the cathedral in the city's life and also shows the other major churches of St Martin-le-Grand and Holy Trinity Aldgate, with the Tower and Westminster Abbey in the background. (BL, Royal MS14 C.VII, fo. 2)

absence allowed to residentiaries. Later, a canon deciding to be resident was obliged to be present for three-quarters of his first year before being admitted as a stagiary (*stationarius*, 'resident', a term unique to St Paul's) whose residential requirements were less onerous. Both residentiaries and stagiaries had duties of hospitality – much elaborated in the fourteenth century – to the ministers of the church, to royal visitors, to royal officials and, in due course, to the mayor and aldermen of the city, who were entertained at the canons' houses.[56] Often such hospitality drew on the products of the brewhouse and bakery, as on the occasion in 1321 when the king attended the festivities at the summer feast of St Paul. He followed a procession round the cemetery, witnessed the boisterous presentation of a fat buck to the canons (*venatio*), heard mass in the cathedral and afterwards, at Westminster, was supplied with the famous hot wastels (fine bread or cakes) of St Paul's.[57]

The absence of canons meant that substitutes were necessary in order to maintain a full body of clergy in the choir. There seems to be a line of descent through the 'prebendary clerks of the choir' recorded in 1162, the 'deacons of the choir' (by 1191), and the 'poor clerks frequenting the choir' (1202–4), to the 'poor vicars of St Paul's' or 'poor clerks frequenting the choir and celebrating the daily office of the Virgin Mary' whose endowment was established by the bishop in the 1220s. They evolved into a formal body of thirty vicars choral, each answering to a canon, which by 1273 had a common hall in the precinct (Fig. 20).[58] Clearly, residentiaries and their vicars could be present in the choir at the same time. In contrast to other cathedrals, the vicars at St Paul's were deacons or subdeacons, and so the liturgical duties that elsewhere were undertaken by priest vicars were performed at St Paul's by minor canons, formally identifiable by the 1230s but probably of much

11.   Common seal of the 'barons' (citizens) of London. The seal matrix was made about 1220 and this side of the seal shows the city walls and what appears to be the spire of the cathedral rising up in front of the image of St Paul as protector of the city. (PRO, E329/428)

TABLE 1

Estimated annual values of property endowments at St Paul's, *c.*1290–1850

Category	Date							
	1291		1535		1650		1850	
	£[1]	%	£[2]	%	£[3]	%	£[4]	%
Common fund	?		725[5]	32	13,176	49	38,460	31
Dignitaries	144		464	20	6,035	22	24,879	20
Prebends	137		446	19	5,556	21	57,707	46
Minor Canons	?		248	11	1,486	6	4,000	3
Vicars Choral	?		?	?	468	2		
Chantry priests	?		410	18	–	–		
Almoner	?		?	?	181	1		
Total	?		2,293	100	26,902	101	125,046	100

Notes:

[1] Dignitaries' incomes: Astle, Ayscough and Caley (1802). Prebendal incomes: GL, MS 25504, fo. 90.

[2] Incomes after charges had been met: Caley and Hunter (1810–34), i, 360–9.

[3] Contemporary estimates of annual rack rent value based on reserved rent and fines; from Parliamentary Surveys and Close Roll (PRO, C54) entries of 1649 and later.

[4] See p. 337–8.

[5] Caley and Hunter (1810–34), i, 360–2. This figure is the sum remaining from the estates, including London property, pensions from churches and the revenues due to the chamberlain (which included some chantry income), minus rent charges, bread allowances to canons, pensions to vicars and payments to cathedral receivers, bailiffs, stewards and other officials and other payments. In 1547 the chantry endowments provided the dean and chapter with an additional £200 p.a. once rent charges and the expenses of the chantries, including payments to priests, had been met: see p. 481. A similar, but probably smaller, sum should be added to the £725 to represent the annual sum available to the common fund.

earlier origin and not always clearly distinguished from the predecessors of the vicars choral. By the later thirteenth century the minor canons constituted a group of twelve, answered to the dean and chapter and received prebends out of the common fund.[59] In this way the cathedral maintained a sufficient staff of priests to serve the number of altars, which as in other cathedrals increased during the twelfth century and afterwards.[60] About 1300, it was asserted that the minor canons and vicars of St Paul's went back to the foundation, an unlikely story even if we take the 'foundation' to date from Bishop Maurice's time.[61] The purpose of the statement was to bolster the standing of the vicars, who had had to cede precedence to the body of chantry priests that grew rapidly from the late twelfth century onwards. At St Paul's, the development of commemoration and celebration for the souls of the dead was stimulated by the formation in 1197 of a fraternity of beneficed clergy (*beneficii*, *beneficiati*) to support the celebration of the office for its dead members.[62] Soon after that date, chantries were being endowed with city property. According to lists from the mid thirteenth century, fifteen chantries had been established at nine altars in the cathedral and one in the chapel at the bishop's palace, while in addition sixty-three anniversaries of the dead were celebrated at altars in the cathedral. Most of those commemorated were bishops and members of the chapter, but also remembered were three kings (Ethelbert of Kent, Alfred and Henry II) and four women. Two of the women died about 1200 and seem to have been local residents: one was a maker of cloth of gold who perhaps supplied her products to St Paul's.[63] Other women were commemorated in the cathedral. About 1215 a chantry was established for William Marshal's daughter-in-law.[64] In 1279–80 Isabel Bukerel, who in widowhood had been notoriously dispossessed by the mayor, bequeathed an endowment for a chantry that came to be established at the famous Rood by the north door of St Paul's (pp. 40, 121) to benefit the souls of herself, her immediate

12. Thirteenth-century copper tonsure plate, cut down from a dish-base, and used to determine the extent of the shaven area on the heads of priests. See p.418 and n.80. (BM)

family and her husband's distinguished city ancestors.[65] A record of 1295 listed at least twenty-three chantries in the cathedral and precinct.[66]

The early endowment of St Paul's came to be split about equally between the bishop and the canons. Of all the endowed revenue pertaining to the cathedral in 1536, the common fund probably accounted for just under a third, dignitaries and the prebendaries just under a fifth, the chantries a little less, and the minor canons about a tenth; the incomes assigned to the vicars choral and the almoner are not recorded but probably represented less than 3 per cent (Table 1). In the mid and later thirteenth century, the proportion enjoyed by the dignitaries and prebendaries would have been somewhat greater. At that time, prebendal endowments at St Paul's were of small value by comparison with those at York, Salisbury and Lincoln.[67] Twenty-five of them were of no more than £6 a year and only two more than £10. That of Consumpta-per-Mare, from an estate eroded by the sea, was no more than 13s. 4d. The dean's dignity, by contrast, brought in £60 and the next largest, those of the treasurer and chancellor, about £26, sums comparable with prebends at York.[68] Moreover, dignitaries, who were obliged to be resident, sometimes held prebends in addition. Canons enjoyed other incomes from St Paul's, including pittances for attending anniversaries in the cathedral, but overall their incomes were never large. Residentiaries also received a shilling a week out of the common fund. Each canon, resident or not, got a weekly allowance of twenty-one loaves and thirty gallons of ale, which they presumably used for domestic consumption, for charitable purposes or sold. In the mid thirteenth century that allowance was estimated as being worth £4 6s. 8d. a year, an income exceeding that of sixteen of the prebends.[69] Those canons who were tenants of chapter estates had another opportunity for profit (p. 145). One attraction of a prebendal stall

at St Paul's, apart from the many advantages of residence in London, was that the source of the income was close at hand, an important requirement for effective property management in those days. Some prebendal income came from estates in Bedfordshire and Essex, but the bulk of it was supplied by land in Middlesex – especially those 'twenty-four hides next to the city wall', supposedly donated by King Ethelbert, which had been such a matter of concern to the canons around 1100 – and by rents in the city. In the seventeenth century, 93 per cent of the value of prebendal estates came from property in Middlesex and the city (Table 6; pp. 305–7). That proportion was probably smaller in the thirteenth century, but still large.

The background and careers of individuals within the religious community at St Paul's reflected the cathedral's situation within London, episcopal patronage, the crown's interest in rewarding its servants and supporters (especially as governmental institutions came to be settled in London), and in the thirteenth century papal provision.[70] Up to the 1130s, but to a rapidly diminishing extent thereafter, many of the canons of St Paul's, as elsewhere, were married. Consequently, sons not uncommonly succeeded fathers as canons. Moreover, bishops, deans and archdeacons promoted their sons and nephews, while bishops frequently reserved the office of archdeacon for kinsmen. The family of the powerful Bishop Richard de Belmeis I was prominent in the chapter over several generations.[71] Clerical marriage became one of the major concerns of church reformers and in 1129 a church council summoned by a papal legate was held in London, probably at St Paul's, where archdeacons and priests were ordered to put away their wives. This had little immediate effect, and the *focarie* of a group of secular canons who in 1137 were seized and imprisoned in a tower were probably, since Ralph de Diceto noted them in his chronicle, the ladies of the canons at St Paul's.[72] Yet even when clerical celibacy had become the norm, the bodily desires of the numerous clergy at St Paul's, like those of ecclesiastics generally, were a focus of attention, and by the late thirteenth century the precinct and adjoining lanes were identified as one of those districts in the city associated with loose women and fornication.[73] Marriage was one of the factors that contributed to the close links between some city families and the chapter in the twelfth century, but important families with roots in the city continued to contribute members of chapter, as did those of the gentry. Henry of Cornhill, canon and chancellor from 1217 and then dean from 1243 until his death in 1254, was from a city family that prospered in finance, as landowners, in royal service and in the church.[74] Thomas Eswy, canon from the mid 1250s and chancellor in the 1260s, was the son of a mayor of London.[75] Henry of Sandwich came from a knightly family in Kent and was brother of a knight in the royal household who in the 1280s and 90s ruled the city, at a critical moment of its history, as constable of the Tower. Henry was a canon before being elected as bishop in 1262, and may have been related to Stephen of Sandwich, canon by 1248 and subsequently archdeacon of Essex.[76] A significant proportion of bishops of London had an existing association with St Paul's, indicating that kings were careful about intruding outsiders and that progression from canon or dignitary to bishop at the cathedral was a recognized career for a royal servant.[77] Several canons were from aristocratic families, but did not always pursue a career at St Paul's. Henry III took advantage of an episcopal vacancy to appoint his half-brother to a prebend, among many other ecclesiastical positions.[78] Geoffrey Plantagenet, illegitimate son of King Henry II and eventually archbishop of York, held a prebend and

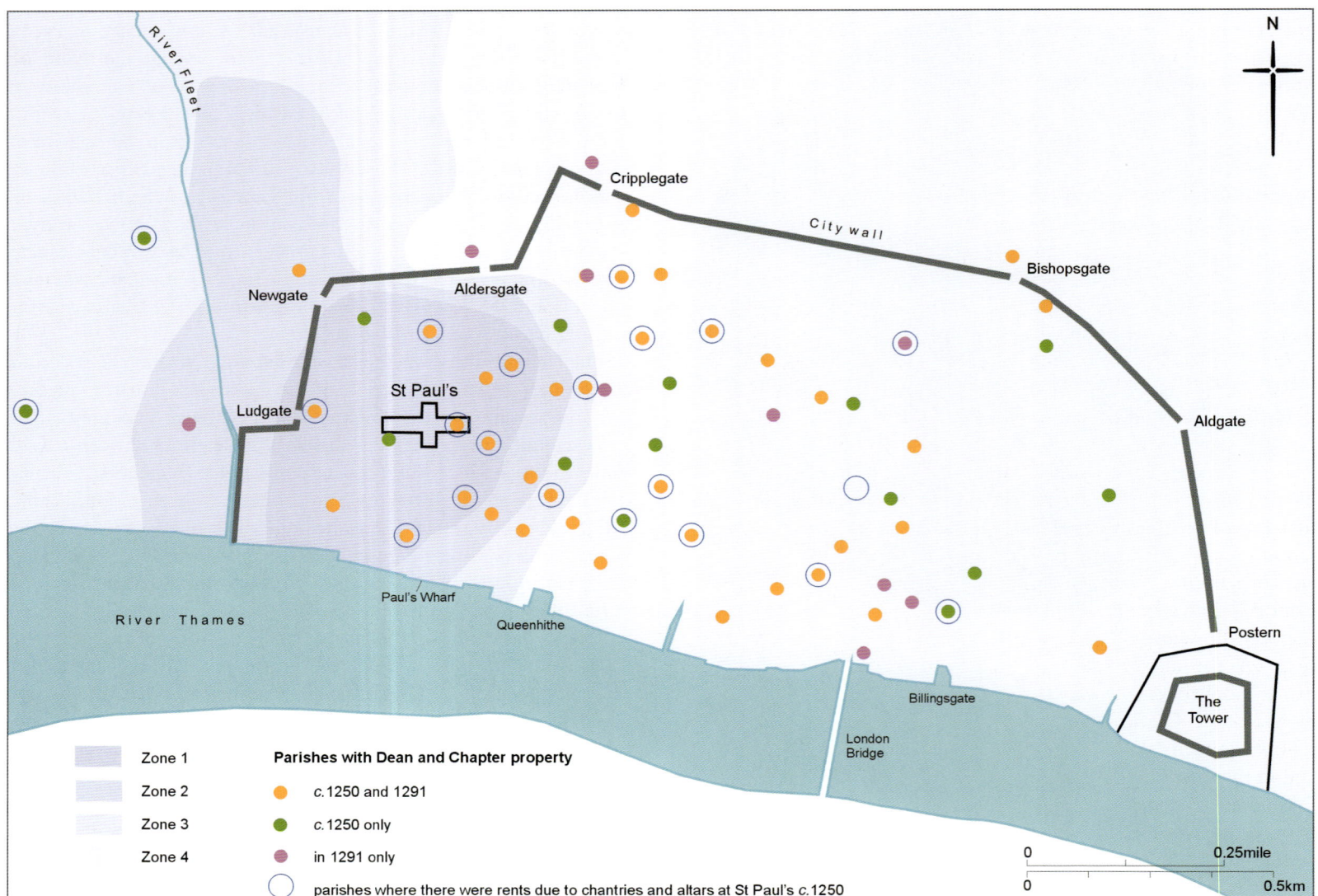

13.   City parishes where St Paul's owned property in the thirteenth century. See Table 3. The innermost zone of parishes comprises those of St Faith (whose church was in the crypt of the cathedral) and St Gregory (whose church adjoined the cathedral), with adjoining parishes. Zones 2 and 3 comprise successive rings of adjoining parishes, and Zone 4 the parishes beyond Zone 3. The boundaries of the zones correspond only approximately to the intricate pattern of parish boundaries

later the chancellorship. He can rarely have been present at St Paul's, but was perhaps responsible for establishing the commemoration of his father in the cathedral.[79]

London's strategic position had for long ensured that its bishops were prominent representatives of royal authority, while from the late eleventh century a number of them also held, or had held, important secular office as the king's chancellor or treasurer. Bishop Maurice was a former chancellor. Richard fitz Neal was treasurer while simultaneously archdeacon of Ely, dean of Lincoln and a canon of St Paul's, and continued in that royal office as bishop of London until his death in 1196, when he was succeeded as treasurer by his kinsman William of Ely, also a canon of St Paul's. John Chishull was both chancellor and acting treasurer while he was archdeacon of London, and again held those offices as dean of St Paul's, before his election as bishop in 1273. Canons held many lesser positions under the Crown. Hugh of Buckland (d. 1116–17), as sheriff or king's justice, administered a block of at least six counties adjoining London. Hugh's property at Ludgate suggests a close association with Roger, bishop of Salisbury, the head of King Henry I's government whose London base was at St Martin-le-Grand.[80] From later in the twelfth century, one of the largest identifiable groups of canons at St Paul's was those who

held posts in the royal government, for whom a house in London was especially convenient. They were promoted both by the king and by bishops who could thereby forward the careers of their juniors in government. Many such men also held more valuable prebends at York or elsewhere, but were more likely to reside at St Paul's than at a cathedral in the provinces. In the late twelfth and early thirteenth centuries, up to a third of the chapter were clerks in the royal household and acted as royal justices or diplomatic representatives. Later, they can be more clearly differentiated. Financial officials included Ranulph le Breton, who stood high under Henry III, from whom he received his prebend, but twice suffered political reverses and was once committed to the Tower. He died of apoplexy in 1246, while watching a game of dice.[81] Lawyers continued to be well represented on the chapter, reflecting the settling of the royal courts at Westminster and London's developing role as a centre for legal training.[82] The influential justice Martin of Pattishall died in 1229 as dean of St Paul's, having had a prebend there for more than twenty years, and was remembered in London as a man of wonderful prudence and of great learning in the laws.[83] Ralph of Hengham, prebendary of Caddington from 1280, was the best-known royal justice of the late thirteenth century, though perhaps not the author of the great common law treatise that bears his name. He was concerned to perpetuate his memory at the cathedral, and his tomb in the north aisle of the New Work survived into the seventeenth century (Fig. 67).[84]

A small but significant group among the thirteenth-century canons were foreigners, mostly Italians and non-resident, appointed by the pope. They often provoked opposition from Londoners. Two Roman clerks in the act of occupying a stall in the choir on behalf of an Italian whom the pope had provided to it were seized and killed by a mob in 1259. Master Cinzio the Roman, prebendary of Rugmere, was in 1231 arrested by those who opposed the Roman yoke, but nevertheless established himself in a house in the precinct and left a generous legacy to the cathedral.[85]

During the twelfth century, London, unlike Paris, Bologna or Oxford, did not develop a nascent university. Nor was St Paul's in the first rank among English cathedrals as a centre of learning. The practical skills of commerce and administration predominated. Nevertheless, by the 1170s London was well known for its schools and for the lively disputations, collegiality and extra-curricular activities of its scholars.[86] In this St Paul's played a part. Canon Durand, the first known master of its schools, was perhaps the well-known grammarian of that name.[87] Probably from his time on, the master regulated other schools in the city on the bishop's behalf, except those in parishes under the jurisdiction of St Martin-le-Grand or the archbishop of Canterbury.[88] These schools concentrated on grammar, rhetoric and other liberal arts, and in the later twelfth century several Londoners became famous as teachers of those subjects, both in England and overseas.[89] The names of two of Durand's contemporaries at St Paul's, the archdeacons Quintilian and his son Cyprian, indicate an interest in classical learning and especially rhetoric. Many of the canons of St Paul's were men of learning (p. 153) and, as at other cathedrals, a prebendal income and a share of the common fund (defined for that purpose in the residence statute of 1192)[90] was one way of financing a period studying law, theology or other subjects at Bologna, Paris and elsewhere. As a young canon of St Paul's, Becket had probably studied at Auxerre and Bologna. Young archdeacons were often at the schools. Ralph de Diceto as archdeacon had studied at Paris, while Gilbert Foliot, himself learned in civil law, as bishop of London had two archdeacons studying at Bologna.[91] Master David of London, born in the city and a canon of St Paul's by the time he was at the schools in Bologna, had previously studied at Clermont and Paris. His advocacy at the papal court on behalf of the king, Bishop Foliot and others was much admired.[92] St Paul's was also a focus for theological studies and may have established a theology school before the Lateran Council of 1179 laid down that all cathedrals should have one.[93] An earlier bishop, Gilbert the Universal (1128–34), had been a famous theologian, but also a lawyer (hence 'universal') and it was to his advocacy on behalf of the king that he owed his see: he seems not significantly to have intensified the atmosphere of learning at St Paul's.[94] Yet the cathedral was certainly a site of intellectual stimulation. As a young canon at the priory of Holy Trinity by Aldgate, Peter of Cornwall, a budding theologian, was taken by his prior to a synod at St Paul's where he heard a sermon on the scriptures by Bishop Foliot and was amazed at its number of distinctions, flowers of words and copious authorities. Later, two canons of St Paul's were among the dedicatees of Peter's *Pantheologus:* his teacher, Henry of Northampton, and the master of the schools, Ralph de Alta Ripa, the latter renowned as a cru-

sader as well as for learning.[95] Intellectuals and writers at St Paul's were often distinguished by their engagement with the affairs of the wider world (pp. 151–6).

In the thirteenth century, the tradition of legal learning continued at St Paul's, but the continuity of theological teaching and interest is less clear. A canon who died in 1213–14 left a house to be conferred on a residentiary, especially one who was a doctor in holy scripture or a teacher. There is no evidence of further provision until 1281 when the chapter appointed Richard Swinfield, archdeacon of London and a notable preacher and man of learning, to rule theology in its school, but lamented the absence of a teacher. Swinfield seems to have been succeeded as a teacher of theology at St Paul's by the archdeacon of Essex, Robert of Winchelsea, former chancellor of the University of Oxford and later archbishop of Canterbury, who recycled his Oxford theological lectures in London, presumably at St Paul's. Soon afterwards, Bishop Richard of Gravesend established a fund to support a divinity lecture under the supervision of the chancellor (p. 42).[96]

Canons of St Paul's shone in many fields, but often were simply passing through in the course of ecclesiastical, academic or bureaucratic careers. Thus the celebrated theologian Alexander of Hales appears to have acquired his prebend after the dispersion of the University of Paris in 1229, but later returned to Paris to teach and became a Franciscan.[97] One intellectually distinguished canon, however, based himself at St Paul's during his later years. This was Richard of Wendover (d. 1252–3), a physician who had studied at Paris and Salerno, wrote many treatises and attended the pope.[98]

St Paul's had an immense impact on its city, as a monument, as a focus of devotion and as a place of assembly. Not the least important of its roles was that of its cemetery as a place of burial for Londoners, both the poor and others who had no particular attachment to a city parish or who preferred St Paul's. Thomas Becket's parents were interred in the cemetery to the north of the nave, probably during the 1140s, and perhaps because their parish church of St Mary Colechurch in Cheapside was one of the minority that lacked a cemetery and it was not yet common for such churches themselves to be used for burial. Later, their tomb was marked by a chapel and became a focus of civic commemoration (p. 39). So many bones were cast up in the course of grave-digging that a charnel house was established in the north-eastern corner of the cemetery to accommodate them; in the 1270s a new chapel was established there and became a site of civic devotion within the precinct (p. 35). This same part of the cemetery, inside the great gate opening into Cheapside, was, as the meeting place of the folkmoot, one of the most important public spaces in the city. Another element in the close relationship between St Paul's and the governance of the city concerned the establishment of standard measures, essential in such a commercial place. The neighbourhood had long been associated with coinage standards and by about 1104 one of the canons, Algar, son and brother of a moneyer and perhaps also one himself, had a foot length inscribed on one of the pier bases of the new nave. This 'foot of Algar' or 'foot of St Paul's' was used for measurement in the city into the thirteenth century and for certain purposes later, although the king's standard, lodged at the Guildhall, eventually took over from it.[99] This is the earliest suggestion of the use of the nave for secular business, for which there is abundant later evidence. Thus, by the later fourteenth century, traders gathered every day in the church and its doorways, and it was the practice to assign places in the nave to twelve scriveners who wrote contracts and other documents for Londoners, while the routine presence of scriveners in the church is attested by 1314.[100] Moreover, it is tempting to speculate that around Algar's time there was some interaction between intellectual and governmental interests at St Paul's and the commercial life of the city, especially in the field of mathematics. At least two canons in the late eleventh century came from Lorraine, a region well known for commercial and mathematical skills. Albert of Lorraine held many canonries, including one at St Paul's, in which he was succeeded by his son Hugh. Robert of Lorraine, who seems to have come to England to serve in the administration of William the Conqueror and probably acquired his posi-

tion at St Paul's after he became bishop of Hereford in 1079, was later remembered for his knowledge of the abacus.[101] In the 1140s a treatise on the astrolabe was dated at London and astronomical tables were compiled for the meridian of the city, although neither text is known to have had a connection with the cathedral.[102] St Paul's also played a part in the city's military life. In time of war, it was stated in 1303 and 1321 but with reference to earlier practice, the mayor, sheriffs and aldermen assembled armed inside the cathedral and then in the space outside its great west door joined forces with the lord of Baynard's Castle, the hereditary leader of the citizen army, which marched behind the banner of St Paul.[103]

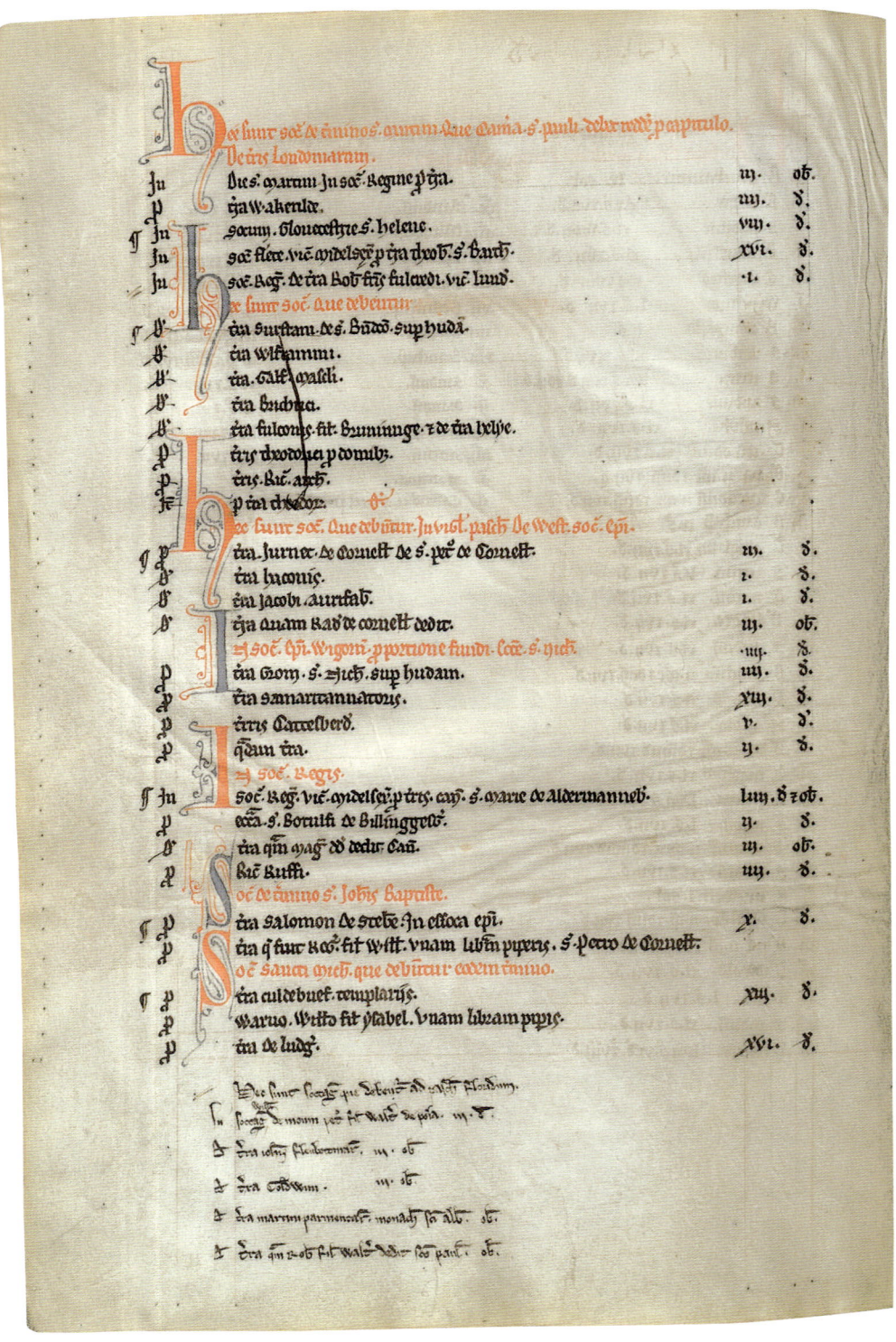

14.   Rental of the Dean and Chapter's properties in the city of London, mid thirteenth century. Land tenure in London was complex. This extract concerns the socage rents that St Paul's owed from some of its properties to ancient estates, including those of the king, the queen and the bishop of London. (GL, St Paul's collection, MS 25512, fo. 8v)

TABLE 2
St Paul's common fund: annual values, by counties from which it was due, 1086–1850

County	Date							
	1086		1535		c.1650		1850	
	£[1]	%	£[2]	%	£[3]	%	£[4]	%
Bedfordshire	11	7	69	5	588	4	1,642	4
Essex	113	67	512	40	2,748	21	8,352	22
Hertfordshire	24	14	119	9	1,564	12	2,749	7
Kent	–	–	–	–	131	1	1,249	3
Middlesex	6	4	147	11	2,772	21	6,789	18
Surrey	–	–	33	3	667	5	2,001	5
City of London	15[5]	9	413	32	4,706	36	15,678	41
Total	169	101	1,293	100	13,176	100	38,460	100

Notes:
[1] Domesday Book (including some lands later assigned to prebends).
[2] Caley and Hunter (1810–34), i, 360–1. The values include those of rents, farms, rectories and tithes, but not the rents due to the chamberlain (which came largely from London and included chantry revenues); no allowance is made for charges against these values. The total of values, including the chamberlain's rents, was £1,485 p.a., leaving £725 p.a. after allowing for charges.
[3] Rack-rent values, for which see Table 1; values include rectories, but not wood, for which only capital values are recorded.
[4] See pp. 337–8.
[5] Estimated on basis of the mid-thirteenth-century rental totals (see Table 3).

TABLE 3
St Paul's common fund: annual values for properties in city of London parishes, 1250–1850

Parish group (see Fig. 13)	Date									
	c.1250 (properties[1] only)		c.1250 (properties + pensions from churches)		1291 (properties only)		c.1650 (properties only)		1850 (properties only)	
	£[2]	%	£[3]	%	£[4]	%	£[5]	%	£[6]	%
1 (innermost)	13.6	48	18.9	37	41.4	63	2,907	62	8,211	52
2	1.5	5	2.6	5	3.7	6	113	2	1,030	7
3	2.7	10	5.3	10	1.1	2	542	12	1,986	13
4 (outermost)	10.6	37	24.9	48	19.5	30	1,141	24	4,451	28
Total	28.4	100	51.7	100	65.7	101	4,703	100	15,678	100

Notes:
[1] Principally houses, but including warehouses, gardens and other holdings.
[2] GL, MS 25512, fos. 1–7v.
[3] GL, MS 25512, fos. 1–7v.
[4] Astle, Ayscough and Caley (1802), 8–9.
[5] See Table 1, n. 3.
[6] See pp. 337–8.

As a landlord, St Paul's exercised a major influence in the city. A survey of the canons' city properties about 1130 shows that they were widespread, but the bulk of the estate by value probably lay in the vicinity of the cathedral, as it did in the thirteenth century (Fig. 3; Table 3).[104] The bishop was much less significant as a London landlord. St Paul's was one of a group of landowners in the city that had a jurisdiction over their tenants to some degree separate from that of the city courts. At the same time, the tenants and goods of the bishop and canons were free of certain city tolls. In 1253 the king allowed the city sheriffs an annual sum of £7 'for the liberty of St Paul', apparently in compensation for the loss of income to the city authorities that these privileges entailed. The allowance, however, had originated as two separate sums associated with the bishop's manors of Fulham and Stepney and with the canons' 'twenty-four hides' outside the city. The St Paul's sokes in the city (the areas where the cathedral had a jurisdictional privilege) were usually thought of as possessions of the bishop or of the bishop and canons jointly, although in the 1270s some citizens certainly believed that the canons had a soke of their own. This jurisdictional separatism faded away in the fourteenth century.[105] In 1536 almost a third of the dean and chapter's common fund (and so about 10 per cent of the endowed income of the cathedral as a whole) was contributed by city property and a further 12 per cent by land in Middlesex, proportions which were probably not much different in the thirteenth century. Around 1250, about half that city income was contributed by rents and houses in the parishes of St Gregory and St Faith and those adjoining them. By 1291, when the income from city properties appears to have more than doubled, that proportion had increased to 62 per cent, but was no greater in 1649 (Tables 1–3). The chapter's impact as a landlord was thus especially intense within a radius of 300 yards from the north transept door (Figs 13, 261). The estate was one of the most valuable in the city of London, but came to be overshadowed by those of other church landlords. By 1200, for exam-

ple, Canterbury Cathedral Priory had £50 p.a. from properties in the city of London, by comparison with the £30 due to St Paul's. Pensions from city churches, however, boosted St Paul's income to £58 but contributed no more than a further £3 to Canterbury.[106] Some of the new priories established in London from the eleventh century onwards also built up greater city rent rolls than the mother church. Thus, by 1290, the dean and chapter's annual income of £67 from city houses and rents was just exceeded by those of St Mary Overy, Southwark and St Bartholomew, Smithfield, and was about half that due to Holy Trinity Priory Aldgate.[107]

The canons especially valued their parish churches in the city. They are known to have had substantial interests in twenty-four of them in the twelfth century, more than a fifth of the total and far more than any other patron of churches in the city. In the thirteenth century they controlled twenty-one city parish churches and had lesser interests in a further five.[108] Some churches, including St Gregory's, may have belonged to the cathedral from long before 1100, but most of them were probably recent foundations that came into the possession of St Paul's during the twelfth century. Some may have been erected on land where the cathedral already had a claim, and so in due course came into the possession of the canons, but these may not have been a majority. Parish churches were pieces of real estate, and interests in them could be as complex as those in other types of city property. About 1119, for example, Deorman, nephew of the late Canon Algar, was in dispute with William, priest of the church of St Antonin, which Deorman claimed as his inheritance. In the presence of the bishop and the canons, the two parties agreed to divide their interest and Deorman promised that on his death his share should pass to the canons, who eventually acquired full control.[109] The canons themselves frequently used their churches as financial instruments through which to raise capital or rent, but the acquisition of so many city churches by the canons may also reflect an episcopal policy to ensure that as many as possible of the city's minute churches were in the hands of responsible patrons who would appoint priests effective in the cure of souls. The willingness of the churches' owners to entrust or sell them to the cathedral would also have been important. The canons' visitation of their city churches undertaken *c.*1181, and similar records from as early as 1138, indicate the care with which they managed them, and the impressive degree to which the churches were equipped with vestments, ornaments and books.[110] St Paul's churches lay principally in the vicinity of the cathedral and in another group near London Bridge, both areas of early and dense urban development. To the north of the cathedral there was a group of churches controlled by St Martin-le-Grand, while the Cheapside area included an enclave of parishes under the direct control of the archbishop of Canterbury, containing six of the thirteen city churches that the archbishop had entrusted to the monks of his cathedral priory (Fig. 15). These separate spiritual jurisdictions probably contributed to the formation of distinct religious cultures in their neighbourhoods, although the high residential mobility of London parishioners would tend to erode such differences.

As the mother church, St Paul's was the site and destination of great diocesan processions that filled the city streets at major feasts, especially during Whit Week. They emphasized the unity and importance of the city under its patron saint. By the mid thirteenth century, it was the practice on Whit Monday for all the rectors, vicars, parish chaplains and parishioners of the archdeaconry of London, a population comprising tens of thousands of residents of the city and Islington, to process to St Paul's. By 1302, a civic element had been grafted on to this procession, in the form of the mayor, sheriffs and aldermen, who according to a later record joined it at St Peter's in Cornhill. On the Tuesday and Wednesday there were similar processions for the people of the archdeaconries of Middlesex and Essex. These, too, acquired a civic component, and each of the three Whit Week processions had its own route through the streets and precinct. Other major ecclesiastical processions at St Paul's were probably limited to the cathedral and its immediate surroundings, including those on Palm Sunday and Ascension Day which the chaplains of the archdeaconry of London were obliged to attend.[111] The processions to St Paul's served as a foundation for an increasingly elaborated civic liturgy (p. 39) and, as we shall see, had a part in the even more splendid practices of royal entry.

The association between St Paul's and ideal of a well-governed city probably accounts for the special concern for order in the precinct under King Edward I, whose reign was marked by

15. Parish churches in the city of London owned by St Paul's and by other major ecclesiastical patrons during the twelfth and thirteenth centuries. St Mary-le-Bow was the headquarters of the archbishop of Canterbury's interest in the city

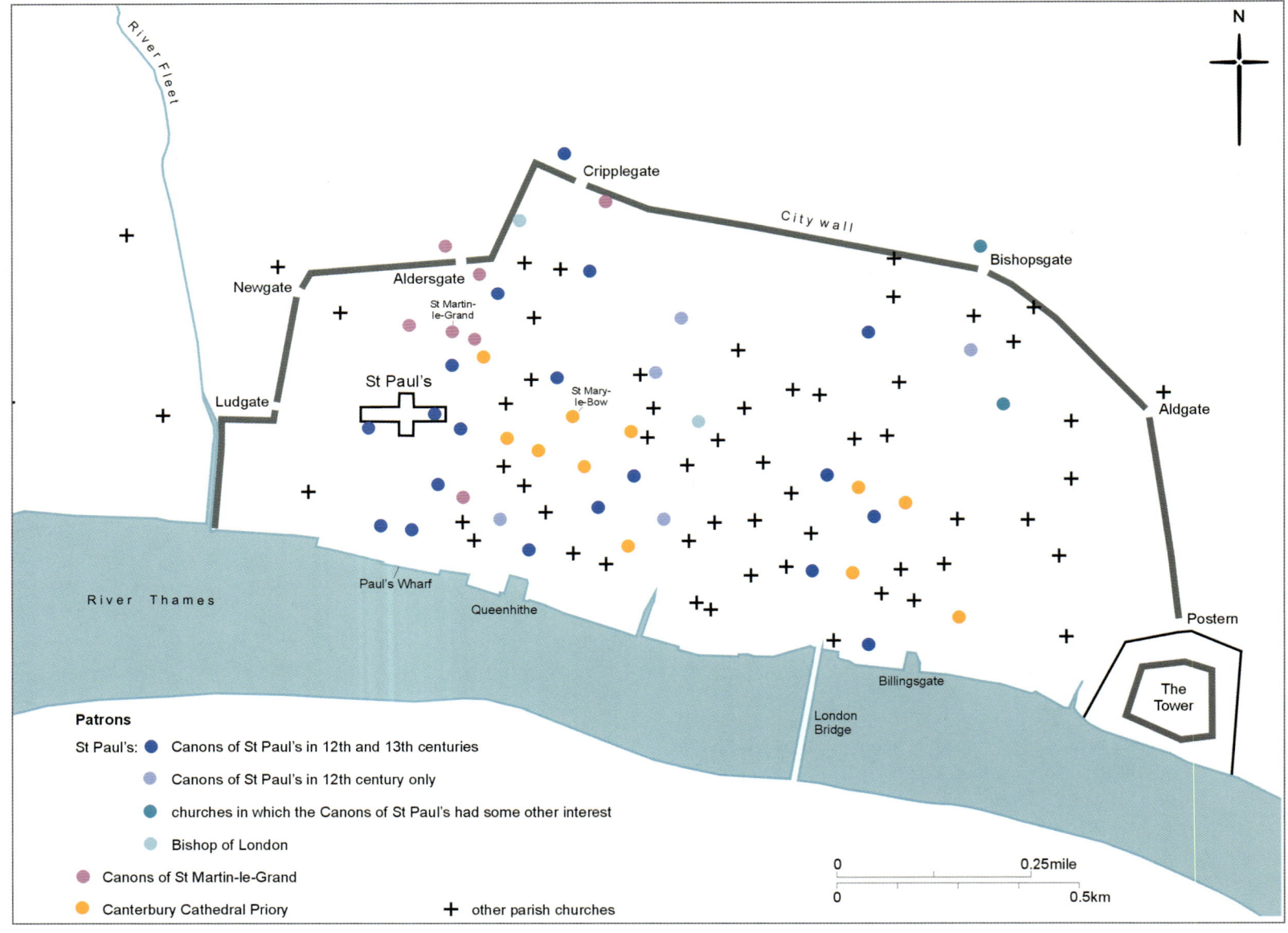

strong attempts to reform London. Early in his reign, city juries reported recent violence in the precinct: two clergymen murdered just outside the churchyard towards Cheapside, another murder nearby, a man attacked and killed as he entered the churchyard having left the members of the watch with whom he had been walking the city streets at night, and the cook slain by the other servants of a minor canon at his house in the precinct, plus accidental deaths.[112] In 1283 two prisoners escaped from the Tower and attempted to seek sanctuary at St Paul's: the sergeants who chased them decapitated one in the cathedral and the other in the little cemetery nearby.[113] Thus in 1285 the king granted the Dean and Chapter permission to enclose their precinct with a wall containing gates and posterns to be closed at night so as to prevent murders, fornications and other evils in the lanes thereabout and for the better security of the canons and ministers.[114] This was not the first enclosure of the precinct, but the integrity of the twelfth-century wall had been threatened by the recent building of houses against its outer face undertaken by the city authorities so as to increase their income.[115] On their side, the citizens were concerned about the obstruction of traditional ways into and through the precinct, a dispute that rumbled on for decades (pp. 34–5).

St Paul's and its precinct were as important as a theatre for the kingdom as they were for London itself. Major conflicts in both church and state were enacted and resolved there. In 1109 the new archbishop of York was consecrated at St Paul's and in the presence of bishops summoned by the king swore obedience to the archbishop of Canterbury.[116] Soon after 1136, a council of all England was held at St Paul's, at which a dispute over the control of the river Thames was settled.[117] In 1237 a great church council was held by the papal legate in the western part of the cathedral, where rising ranks of seats and a high throne for the legate were erected.[118] Other cathedrals accommodated such meetings, but the regularity of the practice at St Paul's during the thirteenth century was distinctive and reflected its situation in the capital.

St Paul's developed a role as the supreme setting for the formal reception of distinguished visitors to the kingdom. In 1184 the archbishop of Cologne and the count of Flanders came to England to offer prayers to St Thomas at Canterbury. The king met them and besought them to come to London to see the royal city, which on their arrival was bedecked (*coronata*) and resplendent, with joy and dancing in all the streets, and the guests were received with a solemn procession at St Paul's.[119] The dancing (*tripudium*) was probably performed by men from leading city families as a dignified expression of the loyalty and good order of the city.[120] Similar events, including the *tripudium*, appear in later accounts of royal processions through specially cleansed streets decorated with silk hangings to the cathedral. It was perhaps in this period, if not earlier, that the pattern of royal entries to London, so well known in the sixteenth century (Fig. 23), was established. The culmination of such occasions was marked by procession through the secular space of Cheapside into the sacred one at St Paul's by visitors who had set out from London Bridge after an approach to London by road or river from overseas.[121] There was such an event in 1194 when King Richard I returned to his kingdom from captivity overseas and was elaborately received in the city and with a procession of clergy and people at St Paul's.[122] Similar entries were those of the king's brother, Richard of Cornwall, returning to England from the Holy Land in 1242; of Richard's wife-to-be in 1243, followed a few days layer by their marriage at Westminster; and the receptions of the king

of Scotland and the sister of the king of Spain in 1255.[123] When in 1274, two years after his accession, King Edward arrived from abroad to take up a kingdom which for decades had been plagued by conflict, he was joyfully greeted in London by clergy and people, almost certainly in Cheapside and St Paul's. On the next day, he was crowned in Westminster Abbey.[124] The processions from St Paul's to Westminster achieved a peak of emotional significance in 1247 with the reception of a relic of Christ himself. Some of the Holy Blood was sent from Jerusalem to London, where it was kept safe for a while in the church of St Sepulchre outside Newgate. King Henry III ordered the clergy of London to assemble at St Paul's, whence, carrying his newly acquired relic, he led them on foot to Westminster, where the blood was to be housed.[125] St Paul's was also a site of ceremonial leave-taking. In 1241, at Paul's Cross, the king sought permission from the citizens of London, as representatives of his subjects, to cross to Gascony and there oppose the king of France. Four years later, he saluted the citizens in St Paul's before departing on an expedition to Wales.[126]

In the thirteenth century, St Paul's and Westminster Abbey developed complementary roles. Westminster was the site of coronations and came to be that of burial of the king and his family: the abbey church, adjacent to the royal residence and containing splendid relics and symbols of authority, encapsulated the sacral and bodily aspects of kingship.[127] St Paul's, equally splendid, was distinctive for its association with the material roots of power and for articulating the relationship between the monarch and his subjects, of whom the largest assembly was that of the citizens of London. That relationship between the two churches, not without its boundary disputes and tensions, endures today.

As London was the greatest material base of royal power, so it was the greatest potential source of opposition. In this, too, St Paul's had an important role. In 1191 a great assembly in the cathedral or churchyard, including Prince John, the archbishop of Rouen, bishops, earls, barons and the citizens of London, deposed William Longchamp, the unpopular justiciar of the absent King Richard, and also granted the citizens their commune, an event which should probably be counted as the formal origin of the city's mayoralty.[128] Five years later, the popular leader William fitz Osbert, opposing the leading citizens and their mayor, many times incited tumult and sedition in St Paul's.[129] These incidents were perhaps *ad hoc* protest meetings in the nave, but William was known for his learning in law and the tumults may have broken out in what were already customary business gatherings of lawyers and their clients. St Paul's was a major focus of opposition to King John during the crises of 1212–16. A majority of the canons sided with the barons against the king, making common cause with their fitz Walter and Montfichet neighbours at Baynard's Castle and with the citizens of London. Complaints against the king were made in 1213 at a great assembly of clergy and barons 'at St Paul', a phrase which suggests the almost tangible presence of the saint (cf. pp. 113–14). At a second council later that year, John resigned the crown and delivered the kingdom to the pope, while in 1214 at two great meetings in St Paul's the papal legate resolved the conflict between the papacy and the kingdom. During the civil war of 1216, when Prince Louis of France came to England to aid the barons, he was welcomed with a great procession at St Paul's, whose dignitaries entered his service. The chancellor had close links with the barons and, though excommunicate, was elected as dean.[130] Sermons at Paul's Cross urged Londoners to support the Prince.

Critical events in the crises of the next reign – involving divisions within the city, between the monarch and the city, and between the monarch and the baronial leaders of the kingdom – were also played out at St Paul's. During Whit Week 1253, the Londoners submitted to Henry III by swearing fealty to his son in St Paul's cemetery and paying the king £1,000 for their liberties.[131] During the fierce conflict over city taxation in 1258, the king's chancellor and leading adviser, John Mansel, who among his many ecclesiastical positions was chancellor at St Paul's, had the assessments read out at the folkmoot and then, in the hall of the bishop's palace, examined representatives from the city wards.[132] Several times during the years leading up to the civil war of 1264 the king was at St Paul's, lodging in the bishop's palace (once while his brother stayed nearby at St Martin-le-Grand) and holding a parliament in the chapter house. At one critical moment, the king's disaffected son attempted to take over the precinct, sending in officers who broke into the bishop's wine cellar and marked the canons' houses for requisitioning. After the battle of Lewes, when the king was in effect a captive, he was kept at St Paul's. With the tables turned after Evesham, the restoration of Henry's rule was enacted at St Paul's. Mayor and aldermen swore fealty to the king in the cathedral; the Exchequer was moved for a while from Westminster to St Paul's; a new constable of the Tower, who was to take charge of the city in place of the mayor, was sworn in before king and people at Paul's Cross; finally, in a symbolic emasculation of the opposition, the king at the cross ordered men from each city ward to demolish defences recently erected by the barons.[133] St Paul's was not to witness such events again, but during the crisis of 1297–8, when civil war threatened and there were many great meetings at the cathedral, King Edward I summoned a muster of the whole kingdom to meet *a seint Poul*.[134]

The sombre incidents of the mid thirteenth century, followed by the strong regime of King Edward I, seem to have initiated a change in the role or wider perception of St Paul's in national affairs. It remained one of the principal sites for national proclamations and the circulation of news, and continued as an important setting for the rehearsal of civic identity and memory, but by the fourteenth century it was becoming less significant as a site for highly charged public assemblies. Other more private political and social arenas gained in prominence: the Guildhall, parish churches and company halls in the city; and great national councils and parliaments at Westminster and elsewhere. Yet, as we shall see, the cathedral could still on occasion become embroiled in wider political conflict, as well as continuing to serve as a container for diocesan, national and civic cult and commemoration.

5

CATHEDRAL, CITY AND STATE, 1300–1540

Caroline M. Barron and Marie-Hélène Rousseau

Relations between the city of London and the great cathedral perched on its western hill were ambivalent. On the one hand 'between the cot on Cornhill and the cathedral at the other end of the city, there was little relation, however familiar a sight each might have been to the other'.[1] Yet 'the intimate link of church and city which revealed itself in the business dealings of the canons, in the chafferings in the nave... This link was a very solid one, and of vital concern to both partners; but there are few aspects of medieval St Paul's more elusive'.[2] Were the men of the cathedral precinct, the bishop, the dean, the canons, chantry priests and other cathedral clergy, miles apart from the men and women of medieval London, or was there 'an intimate link' between them?

By 1312 the major building work on the cathedral, the reconstruction of the east end and the lady chapel, was completed. This was followed by the building of a new chapter house and cloister, completed twenty years later (p. 139). After this most of the work on the cathedral took the form of repairs. The most characteristic additions of the fourteenth and fifteenth centuries were the building of the colleges in the precinct (Fig. 20): the group of lodgings for chantry priests which had begun to be erected by 1330, and perhaps as early as 1318, and were later known as the 'Priests' Houses' or St Peter's College;[3] the college for the minor canons in 1353; Holme's College for the priests of the chantry, founded by the mayor Adam Bury and enlarged in 1386 by his executor, the cathedral chancellor Roger Holme; and Lancaster College for the two priests who served the chantry established

16. St Paul's in the city landscape, early fourteenth century. The drawing serves as a device to denote text relating the story of the foundation of London. (BL, Cotton MS Nero D.ii, fo. 18)

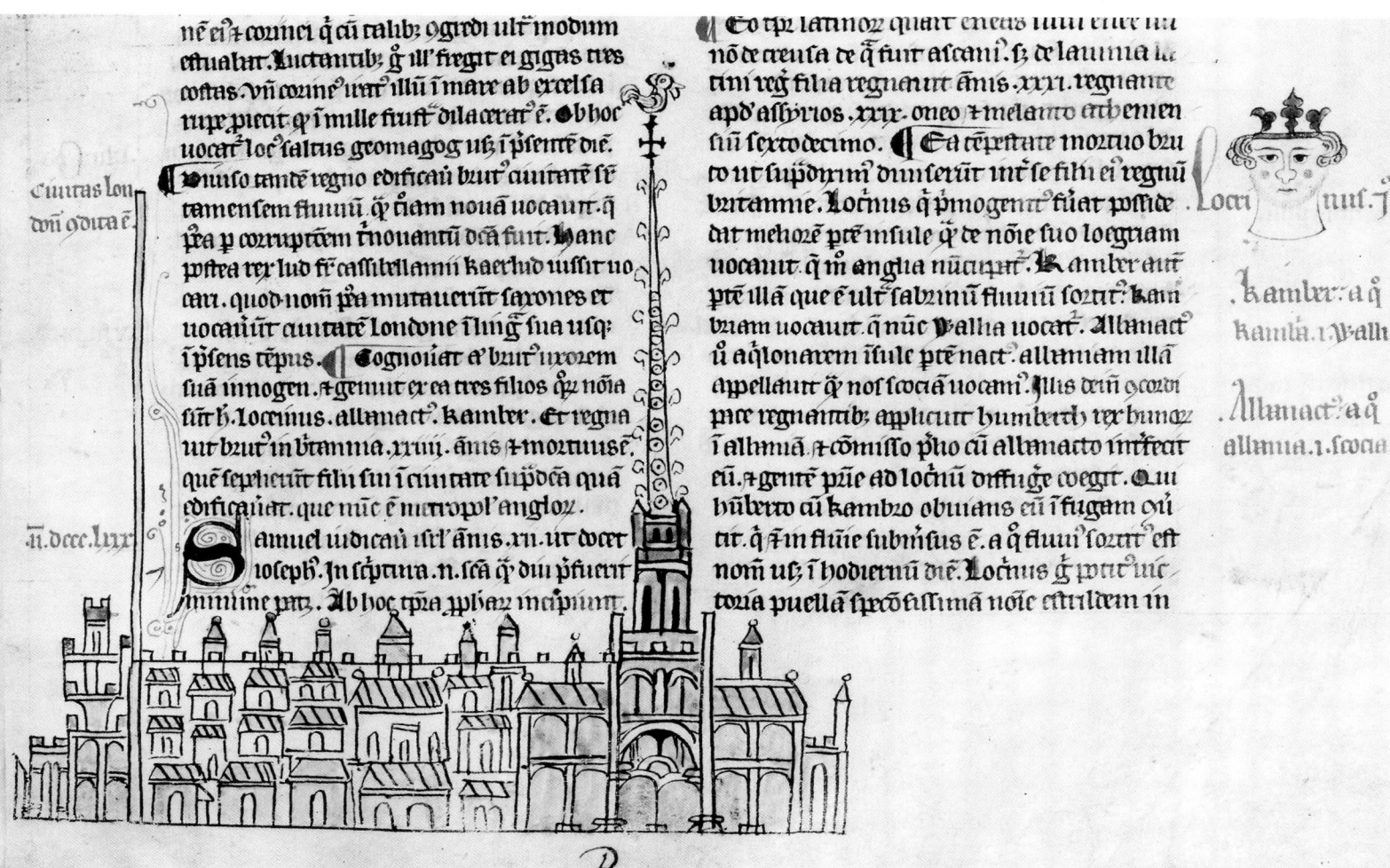

under the will of John, duke of Lancaster (d. 1399).[4] Another important group of new buildings, in the fifteenth century, was associated with the Pardon Churchyard (p. 35). The impressive scale of the cathedral is clearly demonstrated by its depiction in the mid sixteenth-century map-view of the city (Fig. 22).[5] This imposing complex of buildings cannot have failed to have both a visual and spiritual impact on the inhabitants of the city.

The cathedral and its precinct occupied a substantial area inside the city walls. Within this ecclesiastical complex lived a large number of clerical personnel, ranging from the dignitaries to the chantry priests (p. 38).[6] Half of the canons might be in residence at any one time, each in his own house: when Urban V instituted an enquiry in 1366 into pluralism among the English clergy, twenty-one of the thirty canons claimed that they were normally resident in London.[7] By the early sixteenth century, however, the number of residentiaries had fallen to four, plus the dean and sub-dean.[8] The minor canons were incorporated in 1394 and lived together in a college in the precinct according to rules revised by Bishop Braybroke in 1396.[9] About 1530 this college employed a butler, two cooks and other servants whom the minor canons remembered in their wills.[10] Thirty vicars choral lived together in a house at the west end of the precinct. More than thirty chantry priests occupied St Peter's College nearby, with smaller numbers in the other two colleges. By the reign of Edward VI more than fifty chantry priests were working in, and around, St Paul's.[11] In addition, there were the boys who attended the grammar school and the almoner's school (p. 23),[12] and the men of the households of the dignitaries and resident canons.[13] From the bequests in his will, it appears that the household of Dean William Say (d. 1468)

numbered some forty people,[14] while that of Dean Worsley (d. 1499) was a little smaller (p. 167). The bishops of London tended to be frequently seen in the city: Robert Braybroke (bishop from 1381 until his death in 1404) spent half his time in his London palace, and his household has been estimated at some eighty men.[15] In all, therefore, the precinct of St Paul's probably housed some 300 people (excluding the schoolboys), divided among separate households and colleges, but meeting together in the cathedral. This was a remarkable concentration of clerical personnel, equivalent to the number of communicants in a middle-sized city parish within the walls.

In one way the cathedral became more isolated from its urban surroundings in this period. By the later thirteenth century the dean and chapter felt that their precinct, once clearly closed off from the rest of the city, had become more permeable and subject to intrusion. In the 1280s they had secured royal support in making the enclosure more secure (p. 31), but their conflict with the city authorities over public access continued. In 1310 Edward II still found it necessary to instruct the mayor and sheriffs to ensure the safety of the canons and other people of St Paul's and their possessions, especially so as to enable them tranquilly to attend divine worship in the cathedral.[16] Meetings of the folkmoot in the north-eastern part of the precinct became less common, but in 1321 the mayor and citizens complained to the royal justices that the folkmoot could not meet 'because the dean and chapter had enclosed the place where it was wont to be held'.[17] At the same time, the city authorities also claimed other land near the cathedral as public space or highway.[18] The demise of the folkmoot, however, appears to have been associated less with the clo-

17.   Early fourteenth-century sketch of London added to a text of Geoffrey of Monmouth's 'History of the Kings of Britain'. The drawing, placed below Geoffrey's fanciful account of Billingsgate, shows St Paul's as the focal point of the city, its spire reduced to fit the available space. (BL, Royal MS 13 A.iii, fo. 28v)

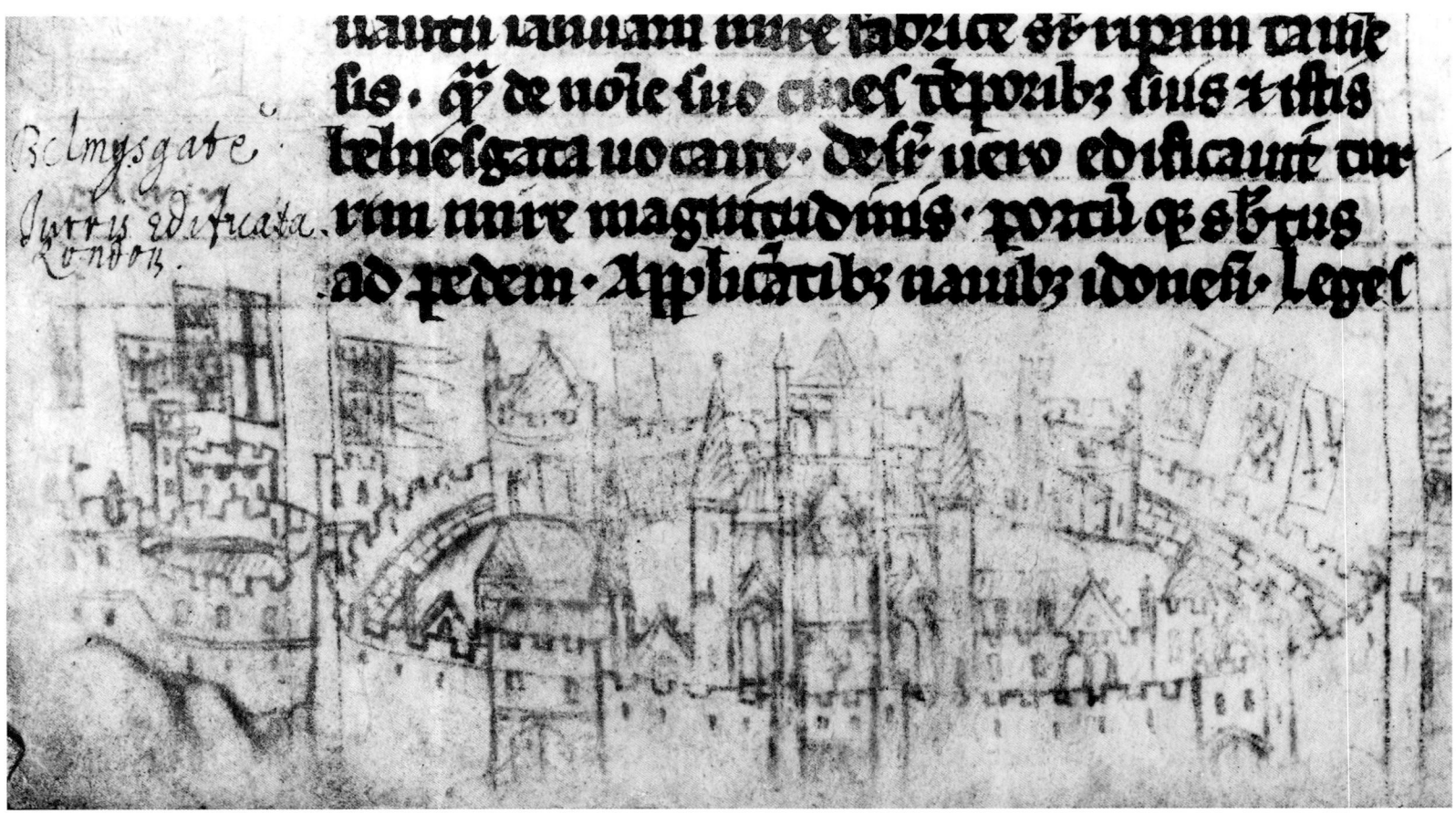

sure of the precinct than with the rebuilding of the London Guildhall. It was there, rather than in the open air of St Paul's churchyard, that the citizens held their political meetings from that time on.[19] The city's claim to land or rights of way within the precinct was still being made in the 1440s and 1450s, when the dean and chapter erected a set of bars and a cross to the west of the cathedral (where there had formerly been a gate), presumably to control access from Bowyer Row (now Ludgate Hill). Protests that they had been built on the common soil of the city were ineffective.[20]

This renewed physical separation of the cathedral precinct from the engulfing city may have been symptomatic of a more pervasive detachment. Of 2,500 wills proved in the London Husting Court between 1258 and 1358, the period in which the choir of St Paul's was completely rebuilt, only forty-nine record bequests either to the old or new work at the cathedral. In this same period nearly 134 record bequests to London Bridge, then undergoing major repairs. The picture changes somewhat in the period 1358–1544, when 114 testators out of 1,332 with wills proved in Husting remembered the cathedral church and only ninety-two made bequests to the Bridge.[21] But St Paul's was not among the churches that Londoners were accustomed to remember with small monetary bequests. At that level the friaries and parish churches attracted more attention. In Middlesex, by contrast, about fifteen per cent of testators in the fifteenth century made a small bequest to their cathedral.[22] The size and authority of the cathedral attracted interest from afar, but within the city it had to compete with an exceptional mass of devotional attractions, both large and small. Residents of London thus appear to have engaged with St Paul's selectively.

Burial in St Paul's churchyard seems to have become increasingly popular among Londoners. In the twelfth and the thirteenth centuries the canons had their own graveyard ground and lay people seem usually to have been interred in the great cemetery occupying the north-east part of the precinct, where there was a charnel house.[23] About 1277, a new chapel was constructed over the charnel house (*ultra ossamenta mortuorum*), a project in which the city authorities perhaps took an interest from the beginning. Thus in 1276 Henry de Edelmeton expressed a wish for burial 'in the little cemetery of St Paul's' but by the time of his death in 1279 had changed his mind and wished to be buried next to the new chapel, to which he switched his endowment of a chantry chaplain originally destined for his parish church.[24] In 1277 Roger Beyuin had left money for the fabric of the new chapel and an endowment for a chaplain, to be appointed by the mayor.[25] In 1282 the mayor and citizens agreed to provide ten marks towards the cost of 'the new chapel dedicated to the Virgin' and a further endowment for a chaplain there.[26] When Hugh de Sturmere was appointed as chaplain in 1302 he was required to open the chapel to pilgrims at specified times, including the days after Whitsun when the mayor and aldermen made ceremonial visits to the cathedral (p. 30).[27] In the fourteenth century the chapel fell into decay and in a sermon at Paul's Cross the archbishop of Canterbury offered a pardon to all who would help to repair it. Consequently, in 1379 a fraternity dedicated to Christ, the Virgin and All Souls was founded with the intent of encouraging support, principally by means of processions to the charnel chapel on the feast of All Souls and on the Sunday after Epiphany.[28] Few bequests to this fraternity are known,[29] but the mayor and citizens continued to take a strong interest in the chapel. In 1418, for example, John Bridgewater, the Beyuin

chantry chaplain, was given an annual civic livery in recognition of his 'great services'.[30] Bridgewater served until his death in 1427 and it may have been his long tenure of the post that inspired the city's common clerk, John Carpenter, acting as executor of Richard Whittington, to augment Beyuin's original endowment.[31] The chapel's civic connection was strengthened by Henry Barton (d. 1434–5). A wealthy former mayor and perhaps a member of the chapel fraternity, Barton was buried in fine tomb in the chapel. His obit there was to be celebrated on the feasts of All Saints and All Souls and attended by the clergy of the Guildhall chapel. Inducements were provided for the mayor, aldermen and principal officers of the city administration also to attend.[32]

Other parts of St Paul's precinct came to be more clearly defined as burial places. During the dispute of 1321 there was a reference to the new use for burial of the space to the east of the cathedral, perhaps available now that the New Work was complete.[33] Another burial ground was defined in the angle between the nave and the north transept. This area had been used for lay burial between the eighth and the tenth century and probably also in the eleventh and twelfth (p. 27).[34] It may have been the 'little cemetery' mentioned in 1276. Early in the thirteenth century the canon's cemetery seems to have lain to the north.[35] This part of the cemetery became known as the 'Pardon Churchyard', a name which suggests that its reordering was a response to the crisis occasioned by the Black Death of 1348–9. It was, or eventually became, an elite and enclosed burial place, perhaps modelled on the late thirteenth-century *Camposanto* close to the cathedral at Pisa. This burial place is first mentioned by name in the will of William Blith, saddler, drawn up in April 1349, in which he requested burial in the churchyard of St Paul's church called *Pardonchirchehawe* above the burial of his father, who had died in 1341.[36] Between 1358 and 1544 sixty Londoners with wills proved in Husting asked to be buried in one of the St Paul's churchyards. Often poorer Londoners, such as widows, requested burial there.[37] Burial in St Paul's cemetery may not always have been a voluntary choice. The cathedral authorities arranged for the interment there of the destitute who died nearby, and some parishes lacked cemeteries (p. 27). Moreover, burial in parish cemeteries sometimes came to be restricted. In 1459, for example, the alderman John Hatherle specified that the churchyard of his parish church of St Michael Queenhithe, overlooked by his house and a new vestry he had built for the parish, should cease to be used for burial 'except under pressing necessity, and that deceased parishioners and others were in the future to be buried in St Paul's churchyard'.[38] At the other end of the economic scale, members of wealthy families such as the Giffords and Bucklands chose to be buried in the new Pardon Churchyard.[39]

In the late sixteenth century John Stow noted that 'many persons, some of worship, and others of honour', had been buried in the Pardon Churchyard and that their monuments surpassed those in the cathedral. Stow also recorded its remarkable transformation in the early fifteenth century, noting that Thomas More, dean 1406–21, had built or contributed substantially to the costs of the cloister surrounding the churchyard; had rebuilt the 'faire chappell' in the its centre, where Gilbert Becket, father of St Thomas, had been buried; and was himself buried within the cloister. Stow described Gilbert Becket as the first builder of this chapel, but it seems unlikely that such a chapel would have been constructed at that date. Moreover, in 1429 Dean More was described as the founder of the chapel, dedicated to St Anne and St Thomas, and it was presumably there that his chantry was established.[40] But the burial of St Thomas's parents at this spot was probably one of the factors that made burial in the Pardon Churchyard attractive to the elite. More's colleague and successor as dean, Reginald Kentwood (d. 1441), was buried there, as presumably was Kentwood's successor Dean Lisieux (d. 1456), who expressed the wish to lie near More.[41] According to Stow, John Carpenter (probably about 1430) had paid for a series of painted boards to hang in the cloister, depicting the Dance of Death.[42] Stow noted their resemblance to the *Danse Macabre* that had been painted on the south wall of the Cemetery of the Innocents in Paris in 1424–5, when the city was in English hands. The Parisian *Danse* is the earliest known and probably most influential example of a genre that became widespread in Europe from the mid fifteenth century onwards. From a representation of it printed in 1484 we know that it showed figures of Death accompanying representatives of all levels of society in a grim dance.[43] Carpenter commissioned John Lydgate (who had been in Paris in 1426) to produce an English version of the poem which accompanied the Paris paintings, and this was inscribed on the panels at St Paul's. Lydgate's text refers to a mayor, artisans, merchants and burgesses who, along with the nobility and clergy, took part in the dance.[44] Direct evidence is lacking as to why John Carpenter chose to make this particular benefaction: his will of 1441 does not indicate any personal affection for the cathedral.[45] It is possible, however, that, as with the chantry in the charnel chapel, he commissioned the paintings in his capacity as an executor of Richard Whittington (d. 1423), thereby fulfilling intentions that Whittington himself had not fully worked out.[46] Use of the Parisian model at that particular time was perhaps a self-consciously up to date expression of English pride and strength. Moreover, the whole project, carried out under Dean More and Carpenter, possibly with Whittington's active support, seems to have included a strong civic element: the Pardon Churchyard was associated with the city's patron saint, and the Dance of Death portrayed the place that city society occupied within larger social and cosmological schemes. The paintings may even have depicted elements of the city's landscape, just as a generation later similar paintings executed in Lübeck and Tallinn did for those cities.[47] Certainly the 'dance of Pauls', as the London paintings came to be known, was one of the sights of the city, and Carpenter himself, in his great collection of city customs, accorded the tomb of Becket's parents a notable place in civic ceremonial.[48] There was a further association between the Pardon Churchyard and civic life, for the chaplains from More's chantry were to give the Easter sermons before the mayor and citizens at St Mary Spital outside Bishopsgate.[49]

Few of the cathedral clergy in this period appear to have been Londoners by birth. Between 1264 and 1535, the wills of only two deans, four canons and one minor canon were proved in Husting and concerned London tenements that they held in their own right. Only two of these testators, both born in London and having family links there, remembered the city or its inhabitants in their wills.[50] Martin Elys, a minor canon, in 1393 left money to his relatives, who were London waxchandlers, and made a bequest to the fabric of London Bridge, but it is clear that his loyalties were to St Paul's and his fellow minor canons.[51] The other civic benefactor was Dean John Colet, who described himself in his will drawn up in June 1514 as 'dean of St Paul's, citizen and mercer of London, freeman of the city, son and heir of Henry Colet, late knight and alderman'.[52] A few other clergy had strong London connections. Robert Aslyn, a minor canon and subdean

who died in 1539, willed that his fellow canons and his cousin, a London citizen and pewterer, be invited to his funeral dinner, while the craft of pewterers was to attend his funeral service.[53] Thomas Boleyn, canon 1447–51, was the brother of Geoffrey Boleyn, mercer, mayor 1457–8. Ralph Shaa, doctor of theology and canon 1477–84, was the brother of Edmund Shaa, mayor 1482–3.[54] It is noticeable that the men elected as dean of St Paul's in the fifteenth century had links with the diocese of York rather than with London (e.g. Booth, Say and Worsley).

Service with bishops and deans, however, offered a career path for Londoners. Thomas Horstone, son of a city draper, trained as a notary, became secretary to Bishop Braybroke – in whose service he was ordained a priest – and on Braybroke's death in 1404 acquired the prebend of Cantlers, which he held until his own death in 1410.[55] Braybroke's household accounts reveal the extent of his patronage of Londoners.[56] Several of his servants were London citizens, such as the notary Denis Lopham and the bishop's 'wardrober' and general factotum John Chertsey, a London draper who was 'the most experienced and wealthiest' of Braybroke's lay retainers.[57] Braybroke bought furs and cloth from several London merchants,[58] and when he was staying at his house at Much Hadham in Hertfordshire, his valets were sent to London to buy expensive textiles and accoutrements.[59] Dean William Worsley likewise used London tradesmen to supply his household (p. 168).[60] Bishop Braybroke's modern biographer believed that he took a lively, and indeed partisan, interest in political events in London in the 1380s, on occasion intervening to speak for the citizens when they were in trouble with the king.[61] But it is difficult to assess whether in this respect Braybroke was an isolated or simply a well-recorded case.

There were, inevitably, points of intersection between the city and the close. In the first place, the dean and chapter held a very considerable estate which not only included manors outside London, but also a large portfolio of urban property in the city (pp. 29–30, 305–7). In 1535 the dean and chapter's common fund (excluding the income received by the chamberlain) included over £400 annually from rents in the city and suburbs, over thirty per cent of the total (Table 2). Although at one time or another the dean and chapter probably held tenements in most city parishes, their main London estate was clustered around the cathedral itself, especially towards the river (Table 3; Fig. 13). The city's records of this period bear witness to the active role played in the city by the dean and chapter in their capacity as landlords. Whereas the bishop of London, whose urban estate was small, appears only rarely, the dean and chapter were constantly called to defend or repair their properties.[62] The cathedral and the city could co-operate as landlords: in 1430 the city leased its adjacent derelict wharf adjoining Paul's Wharf to the dean and chapter for ninety-nine years, so that the chapter might rebuild the two wharves together.[63]

By the later fourteenth century the dean and chapter held the advowsons of nineteen of the city's parish churches,[64] a smaller total than in 1300 and earlier (p. 29). In 1366 sixteen of these churches were held by chantry priests in the cathedral, and it

18. London *c.*1480, from a manuscript of the poems of Charles duke of Orleans prepared for Edward IV and Henry VII. Charles (d. 1465) spent many years in captivity in England and is shown here at the Tower of London. London Bridge is clearly depicted in the background, and behind that the great church with a spire is probably intended as St Paul's. (BL, Royal MS 16 F.ii, fo. 73)

seems likely that those priests served the cure themselves and were active in their London parishes, thus reinforcing links between the cathedral and the city (p. 161).[65] In 1547 only one of the St Paul's London churches (St Gregory by St Paul's) was served by a member of the St Paul's clergy – John Waklyn, minor canon and chantry priest – although fourteen of them were specifically stated to be served by a resident vicar. Thus, in what was probably an established tradition of the cathedral taking particular care of its parish churches (p. 29–30), the St Paul's churches seem more likely to have been served by a resident priest than city churches as whole, of which only half were clearly served by a resident vicar or rector.[66]

The cathedral was an important secular and civic space. The body of the church, especially the vicinity of the font, was the preferred location for the formal conduct of legal business. Lawyers and men hoping to act as jurors or witnesses gathered, deeds were written and sealed, and debts were repaid.[67] Churchyard and precinct were used for a variety of trading and other secular activities.[68] Around the feasts of St Bartholomew (24 August) and the Nativity of the Virgin (8 September), wrestling took place there, although attempts were made to forbid it,[69] and at the summer feast of St Paul there was a boisterous 'hunt' in the churchyard and cathedral (p. 24). As in the thirteenth century (p. 31), both church and churchyard were places where disorderly assault, both verbal and physical, might be expected.[70] In 1395, as the mayor was walking up Ludgate Hill towards St Paul's, a disaffected tailor followed him into the churchyard shouting abuse, pursued him into the church 'taking him by the sleeve and shouting and arguing with him', and then out again into Paternoster Row, where he violently threatened him.[71] The four virgers were to keep the cathedral free from such disturbances: by expelling women of ill fame, porters, beggars and minstrels who 'undevoutly' made a noise near the altars in the cathedral; and by guarding the precinct entrances with chains to prevent the entry of wheeled vehicles.[72] In 1385 Bishop Braybroke, adding to a mayoral prohibition of 1327, threatened with excommunication all those who bought and sold in the cathedral, or who played football, both within and without the church, or shot at crows and doves, thus endangering the glass in the windows and other ornaments.[73] Such efforts are unlikely to have kept profanity out of the cathedral or its precinct. There were few covered public spaces for trading or recreation in the city and the sheer size of St Paul's made it difficult to police. One purpose of the isolated, enclosed areas in the cathedral, such as the chantry chapels (pp. 164–6), may have been to shelter them from such activity and to create oases of liturgical calm and spiritual focus.

The number of chantries had continued to increase since the thirteenth century. About 1370 there were seventy-four chantry positions in the cathedral, but not all of them were filled, not least since the market value of their stipends had fallen. Bishop Braybroke in 1391 reformed the chantries, amalgamating endowments so as to reduce fifty-nine positions to twenty-seven. More chantries were founded subsequently, but there were further amalgamations and some chantry positions were held in plurality by minor canons. Thus, at the dissolution of the chantries in 1548, forty-seven chaplains together with twelve minor canons were maintaining between them a total of seventy chantries.[74]

Until the late thirteenth century, most of the chantries at St Paul's were established for the cathedral clergy, and of all those founded before the amalgamations of 1391, only twelve (including those at the charnel chapel) appear to have been for lay

Londoners (pp. 24–5). The community of citizens, acting through the mayor and chamberlain, took a special interest in the chantries and was patron of three of them: Beyuin's at the charnel house; that of the clerk, Henry de Guldeford (d. 1313); and that of the wealthy draper and mayor, Sir John Pulteney (d. 1349).[75] The interest of the Londoners in the chantries at St Paul's is evident in the complaint by the mayor in 1345 that the number of chaplains singing mass in the cathedral was not in proportion to the number of chantries endowed there by Londoners.[76] Moreover, many Londoners augmented or re-endowed chantries set up for cathedral clergy. Some, like Thomas de Bredestrete, who in 1310 left tenements to endow the chantry of a minor canon who had died ten years earlier, may have been acting as executors or trustees of the deceased.[77] Others, in return for undisclosed benefits, seem simply to have enlarged the income of well-established chantries, as did Geoffrey Meleman for the priests of Holme's College in 1499.[78] The pepperer John Grantham in 1330 obtained masses to be said for his soul by the priest of the chantry of Canon William de Haverhull (d. 1252) in return for increasing its income.[79] In the fifteenth century, the new Pardon Churchyard and chapel were a focus of such interest. Thus, Walter Caketon, embroiderer, in 1429 provided for an additional chantry priest in the chapel recently founded there by Dean More, perhaps in return for burial in the Pardon Churchyard, while in 1442 John Stile augmented the endowment of the chantry of Dean Thomas de Eure (d. 1400).[80] But as time went on, it is clear that Londoners who could afford to establish permanent endowed chantries chose to set them up in their parish churches rather than in the cathedral.[81]

Given the size of St Paul's and the number of its chapels, altars, images and lights, the evidence for vigorous support of them by lay fraternities is small. Only three fraternities based on St Paul's made returns to the enquiry of 1388: one dedicated to the Virgin's Assumption that met in the Lady chapel; one dedicated to St Katherine and All Saints that met in the chapel of St Katherine in the south transept and was probably associated with the haberdashers' craft; and one dedicated to All Souls that met in the chapel over the charnel house.[82] Wills provide little evidence of widespread support for these fraternities. Two further St Paul's fraternities are mentioned in fourteenth-century wills, but not in the returns to the enquiry of 1388: a guild of the Resurrection is recorded between 1372 and 1393;[83] and a guild of St Anne that met in the crypt had been established by 1372, when it was to have the key to the chapel door from outside,[84] but it is not mentioned after 1378.[85]

Londoners established hundreds of religious fraternities,[86] but associated them with their parish churches rather than the cathedral. Awareness of this deficiency at the cathedral may have prompted the establishment in its eastern crypt of a fraternity dedicated to the new and widely popular cult of the Name of Jesus during the episcopate of Thomas Kempe (1448–89) (pp. 162–3). Kempe, who established a chantry in the cathedral, may have been responsible for the idea but does not mention the cult in his will. Dean Lisieux (1441–56) certainly supported it, but his intended chantry at the Jesus altar was never established.[87]

Likewise, the craft guilds or companies of London focused their religious activities on parish or other churches rather than on the cathedral. This was but one aspect of the complex relationship between London's civic institutions and St Paul's. As in many European cities, London's cathedral had since the twelfth century or earlier played an important role in shaping civic space (p. 20). Moreover, the link between the cathedral and elements of city government strengthened from the later thirteenth century onwards, although not to the extent that occurred in many Italian cities. In the twelfth and thirteenth centuries, representations of crafts in the fabric of some cathedrals of northern France and Italy indicate that groups of craftsmen contributed funds for the building and decoration of cathedrals – although that interpretation has been challenged in one important case – but in general the devotional focus of crafts was in city churches other than the cathedral.[88] The case of London, for which comparable evidence is lacking, may well have been similar. From the fourteenth century some crafts certainly had chapels at St Paul's, but often in association with a base in a parish church or elsewhere, which in due course became the more important focus. Moreover, the growing perception of secular bodies, such as town governments or guilds, as suitable custodians of chantry endowments gave craft fraternities a new role at St Paul's. The fraternity at St Paul's dedicated to St Katherine was probably the original association of the haberdashers. In 1380 it was described as the fraternity of pouchmakers, a craft closely associated with the haberdashers, and both the wardens who drew up the guild return in 1388 were haberdashers. By the early fifteenth century, however, the haberdashers' fraternity dedicated to St Katherine had established a link with the parish church of St Mary Staining near the haberdashers' hall.[89] The company's link with the cathedral was revived in 1525 when the Haberdashers' Company was made responsible for the chantry of Canon Dr Dowman, set up at the cathedral altar of St Martha and St Mary Magdalen in the south transept.[90] The craft with the longest-lasting relationship with the cathedral was that of the tailors. At some point between 1361 and 1375, the bishop granted to the tailors the use of a chapel by the north door of St Paul's 'halowed in thonoure of St. John Baptiste'. In his will of 1382, the embroider Thomas Carleton asked to be buried in the chapel and made the tailors' fraternity responsible for maintaining his chantry there. This chapel quickly became a distinctive showcase for the tailors' fraternity, beyond their specific responsibility for the chantry which they fulfilled until 1548. But the tailors also had a chapel at their hall, probably dating from before the time they established themselves at St Paul's, and in the fifteenth century their parish church of St Martin Outwich, close to the hall, became the principal focus of their devotions.[91]

In the later fifteenth century, craft fraternities may have developed a renewed interest in St Paul's. The coopers' craft, dedicated to the Virgin, met in the Lady Chapel, and armourers in the chapel of St George. The yeomen fraternity of the dyers chose to meet in St Paul's, where they kept a common store of cash and plate, in order to distinguish themselves from the masters of their craft who met in the church of St James Garlickhithe.[92] The scriveners, who as writers of legal documents did much business in the cathedral, in 1450 decided to hold a mass of the Holy Ghost 'at Paules if hit may be hadde goodly' on the Sunday after midsummer, to be followed by the craft dinner.[93] The saddlers took responsibility for the chantry of Canon John Wythers (d. 1535), located in the 'long chapel at the north end' of St Paul's: in return, the two priests were to attend saddlers' funeral services.[94] Thus, despite an increase in the crafts' devotional focus on parish churches, the interdependence between them and the cathedral developed in several ways, indicating a measure of trust and co-operation.

St Paul's played an important part in civic ceremonies, especially those concerning the community of citizens and its protectors, of whom St Paul and the St Thomas of Canterbury were the chief. The cult of St Erkenwald played no part in these devotions. At least some of these practices had been established by about 1300, and possibly much earlier in the history of the mayoralty (p. 30), but the details are recorded only in a prominent section of the city's *Liber Albus*, compiled in 1419. An important day in the civic calendar was the feast of SS. Simon and Jude (28 October), when the mayor was elected. On the next day, accompanied by the aldermen, the sheriffs and the liverymen of the crafts, the new mayor rode to Westminster to take his oath at the Exchequer. Then, after dinner, he processed with the men of his livery company and the aldermen from the birthplace of St Thomas in Cheapside to St Paul's, where between the two small doors in the nave they prayed for the soul of Bishop William (1051–75), who they believed (perhaps incorrectly) had obtained from William the Conqueror important privileges for London (p. 15). They then moved into the churchyard where the bodies of St Thomas's parents lay, and near the tomb (presumably in the new chapel in the Pardon Churchyard) prayed for all faithful departed.[95] There were seven other days, all in winter, when the mayor, his household, the aldermen and the 'good men' of the crafts, ceremonially attended St Paul's, where the mayor occupied the stall next to the dean's: the feasts of All Saints (1 November), Christmas, St Stephen (26 December), St John the Evangelist (27 December), the Circumcision (1 January), Epiphany (6 January) and the Purification of the Virgin (2 February).[96]

The major civic ceremonial at the cathedral was linked to the long-established archdeaconry processions at Whitsun (p. 30). On the three days after Whitsunday the mayor, aldermen and city officers followed processions of parish clergy and parishioners to St Paul's. On the Monday, with the people of the city, they gathered at St Peter Cornhill, processed along Cheapside into the cemetery and then passed round the south side of the cathedral. On the Tuesday they assembled with the people of Middlesex at St Bartholomew's Priory, entered the city through Newgate, processed down Old Change and into the cemetery through St Augustine's Gate. On the Wednesday they assembled at the church marking St Thomas's birthplace in Cheapside and then with the people of Essex processed along Cheapside to the cemetery. On each day they entered St Paul's through the great west door and remained in the nave until the *Veni Creator* had been chanted by the vicars and organs. The mayor and aldermen then ascended to the altar, made offerings and returned home.[97] Pentecost was a moment of transition in the civic calendar when the mayor and aldermen decided on their summer liveries. Alderman John Sely in 1382 appeared for the Monday procession wearing a cloak that did not meet the specification for the year, and was obliged to entertain his fellow aldermen to dinner at his own cost on the following Thursday.[98] The civic processions were an important element in Londoners' personal associations with the cathedral. By 1429 Henry Barton, whose obit was later celebrated in the charnel chapel, gave a large silver thurible to St Paul's, with the injunction that it be used to cense the mayor, citizens and all people assembled in St Paul's on the three days in Whit Week.[99] More modestly, John Watson, a brewer who died in 1522, asked to be buried near Paul's Cross and requested that the wardens and liverymen of his craft, when they came with the mayor to St Paul's on Christmas Day, should 'turn towards his grave and there say a *Pater Noster* and *Ave Maria* for his soul'.[100] The Reformation swept away the censing of processions and the offering of masses for souls, and in 1548 the Whitsuntide processions were replaced with 'three solemn sermons'.[101]

Some bishops and deans aimed to foster a closer relationship between the city and St Paul's. Early in the fourteenth century a new cathedral statute imposed heavy obligations of hospitality upon resident canons in their first year in office, including two large banquets to which they were to invite not only the bishop, the stagiaries and the whole choir, but also the mayor and aldermen, the justices and the greater people of the court, 'so that the liberties and honour of the church might be maintained, and friendship continued between the church and city, and so that the royal court look more favourably at us'. Bishop Braybroke, as part of a major programme of retrenchment and reform (pp. 38, 21, 159–60), greatly reduced this burden of hospitality,[102] but he also took a close interest in the affairs of the city and it may have been with an eye to strengthening its ties with the cathedral that he attempted to revive the cult of St Erkenwald (p. 121).[103]

Erkenwald's shrine had been restored and enriched in the early fourteenth century (pp. 120, 138),[104] but seems subsequently to have attracted little interest from Londoners. Only four legacies to the shrine or the chaplains there are known from between 1368 and 1391; these included a girdle of *blew* left by Thomas Morice, a lawyer and common serjeant of the city, and a sapphire jewel left by a grocer, to help those with 'infirmities of the eyes'.[105] Such legacies suggest an already significant connection between lawyers and the cult, for the colour blue signified wisdom and students of law and other scholars were often portrayed as short-sighted. There was a fraternity associated with the shrine, but mentioned only in wills of 1378 and 1404.[106] Braybroke in 1386 re-established the two festivals of the saint. This promotion of the cult, together with the bishop's wider interest in the reform of St Paul's and in city affairs, may have been behind the composition of the alliterative poem on the life of St Erkenwald written about this time or later. This work abandoned the miracles recounted in the earlier Life (pp. 116–17) in favour of a story modelled on the famous legend of how St Gregory (d. 604) released from Hell the soul of the Emperor Trajan. The story concerned a just judge of London in pagan times who had been buried at St Paul's: his magnificent tomb was found during excavations below the 'new work'. The judge was enabled to come back to life for just long enough to allow St Erkenwald to say the words of baptism. The judge's uncorrupted body then instantly crumbled to dust. The poem recalls some of the mythical history of London (p. 4) and vividly evokes the physical setting of the cathedral as a focus for both civic and national life. The community of Londoners plays a major role, along with the mayor, under whose predecessor as 'duke' of London the judge had served. Underlying messages seem to concern the reform of the cathedral (associated with a building project) and the good governance in the city following a period of conflict, both appropriate for Braybroke's time. The poem appears to be aimed at the rulers of London and the lawyers who assisted them, and it has been suggested that the author was Ralph Strode, the city's common serjeant – and Chaucer's 'philosophical' friend – who died in 1387. But this attribution is far from certain and in some respects the poem seems distant from London, being written in the dialect of the north-west Midlands and surviving in only one manuscript, which is associated with Cheshire.[107] This new account of Erkenwald appears not to have found a wide readership and to have done little to generate interest in the saint among the civic élite. There are no recorded bequests from Londoners to the shrine of St Erkenwald after 1404, although the cathedral clergy further endowed the cult (p. 121). Lawyers, however, continued to take a special interest in the saint. In the fifteenth century at Lincoln's Inn they observed St Erkenwald's day as one of the four major feasts celebrated in the Inn, and new serjeants at law on their induction processed to St Paul's where they offered at the shrine of the saint and were then assigned to their pillars in the nave.[108]

By contrast, the rood at the north door of the cathedral was an object of widespread veneration (p. 121). According to beliefs recorded in the early fifteenth-century 'little chronicles' of St Paul's, the mythical King Lucius (p. 4) had found it in the river Thames in about 140.[109] A later version of the story identified it as the cross which Joseph of Arimathea had set up at Caerleon and which, having subsequently been thrown up by the sea, washed up the Thames to the later site of Paul's Wharf.[110] The 'little chronicles' were also written out on a hanging table (*tabula*) in the cathedral, and in addition the story was depicted 'in a wyndowe byhynde the sayd Rode'.[111] Doubtless the presence of this wonderful rood at the door of the north transept encouraged the tailors to adopt the nearby chapel of St John the Baptist and the clustering of chantry chapels nearby, including those of Isabel Bukerel, Adam de Bury and Roger Holme (pp. 24, 133). John Paston in 1465 urged his mother to take his sister Margery to 'the Rood of Northedor' to pray there 'that sche may have a good hosbond', while Henry Courtenay, earl of Devon, visited it three times between January and March 1519.[112] The tables (*tabulae*) hanging in the cathedral seem to have been an important medium for conveying historical messages to visitors, some of whom added their contents to their own collections. The texts of three of the tables were prefixed to a set of civic annals compiled for a Londoner in or soon after 1442,[113] while a later text of the St Paul's 'little chronicles', perhaps derived from the tables, contained additional London material, including a list of mayors to 1491.[114]

Another attempt to strengthen the bond between Londoners and their cathedral was made by John Colet (dean 1505–19; Fig. 19), the son of a wealthy London mercer. Dean Colet, like Bishop Braybroke, was an energetic reformer and attempted both to raise the standard of divine service in the cathedral and to improve its reputation in the city.[115] In his famous Convocation sermon, Colet called the wider church to reform.[116] His new rules governing the St Paul's clergy, drawn up in 1518, imposed especially strict rules on the fifty or so chantry chaplains, insisting that they should be of good character and personally examined by the dean before being admitted. Those who were *secutores chori* were to take part in the daily services of the cathedral and to live together in St Peter's College. They were not to wander around the city, nor to leave it without the express permission of the dean.[117] Earlier he had given his attention to the foundering fraternity of the Holy Name in the cathedral crypt, and the guild as he reformed it was both prestigious and wealthy (pp. 162–3). Colet strengthened the formal role of city institutions in the cathedral's affairs in 1512 with his reform of the long-established grammar school. The school, which had flourished in the twelfth century (p. 27), seems to have been less notable in the later fourteenth and fifteenth, when its pre-eminence was challenged by a number of unlicensed

19. John Colet, dean of St Paul's 1504–19, as portrayed on the cover of the Ordinances of St Paul's School by William Segar, 1585. The bust and cadaver are modelled on Colet's monument in the cathedral. Colet was the leading humanist connected with St Paul's and the founder of the school in its modern form. (Mercers' Company)

IO.COLET.DECA[...]S.PAVLI

ISTVC RECIDIT GLO=
RIA CARNIS

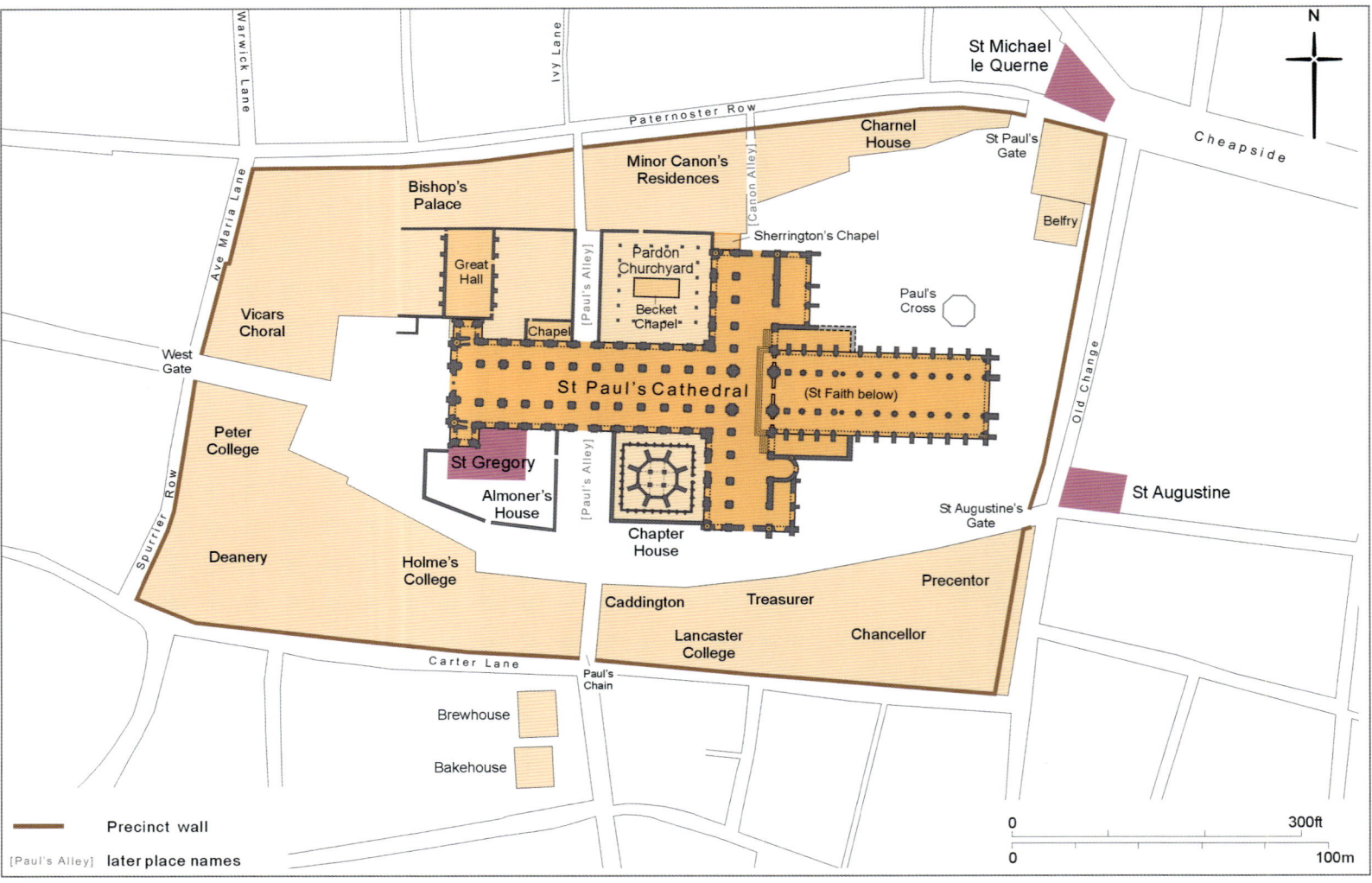

20. St Paul's precinct *c.*1500. For developments since the mid-thirteenth century compare Fig. 9

grammar-school masters.[118] Responding to the rising demand for education, and for education with humanist content, Colet reorganized the school, enlarged it to provide for 150 boys, provided some free places and inserted the study of Greek into the curriculum. He also encouraged the boys to take on the role of bishops at the customary St Nicholas feast and to preach sermons, presumably as a means of practising Latin rhetoric.[119] Using his inherited wealth, he provided the school with new premises on the east side of St Paul's churchyard and made over this property, not to the Dean and Chapter but to the Mercers' Company which was to run the school. Colet and the mercers were engaged in several joint enterprises at that time and, like other city companies, the mercers were extending their responsibilities as patrons of religious institutions.[120] Only a dean with the intellectual and financial clout of Colet, and a company with the standing of the mercers, could have removed the education of boys at St Paul's from the control of the cathedral.

Colet reshaped St Paul's as an educational hub in the city. Two centuries earlier, the cathedral had also been an important intellectual centre. Continuing a policy initiated in the late thirteenth century (p. 27), bishops in the first half of the fourteenth appointed Oxford theologians of distinction as chancellors of St Paul's with responsibility for promoting lectures in theology, the lectures themselves being normally given by deputies. The sequence culminated with Thomas Bradwardine, chancellor from 1337 to 1349. This was one of the periods in which London seems to have made a special contribution to philosophical and theological

learning. Apart from those associated with St Paul's, cutting-edge theologians deploying new intellectual tools were at work at the London friaries, especially those of the Franciscans and Dominicans close to the cathedral. This excitement doubtless promoted the business of text production in the vicinity of the cathedral (pp. 430–2). At the same time, to judge from the book legacies of its school masters (pp. 414–15), the almoner's school at the cathedral excelled in teaching the arts and other subjects subordinate to theology. After the Black Death, which killed Bradwardine, St Paul's reflected wider changes in intellectual interests. In the second half of the fourteenth century the chancellorship went to lawyers, anticipating the longer-term shift in the choice of university courses from theology to civil or canon law.[121] In theology, innovation lay with Wyclif and controversial Lollard ideas, rehearsed in London and elsewhere. On the side of orthodoxy, several fifteenth-century canons at St Paul's had close links with the universities and other networks that promoted learning. The new library over the east wing of the Pardon Churchyard cloister established by Walter Sherrington, prebendary from 1440 to 1449, was one expression of this concern and by 1500 St Paul's had an impressive collection of books and an exceptionally well-ordered archive (p. 417). Thomas Chaundeler (d. 1490), warden of New College, Oxford, for over twenty years and a pioneer of humanism, held a prebend for the last thirteen years of his life.[122] Lawrence Booth, who had been a prebendary of the cathedral since 1449 and was dean in 1456–7 before moving on to be bishop of Durham, was master of

Pembroke College, Cambridge, from 1450.[123] Ecclesiastical careerists such as these may have had little direct impact on London, but St Paul's was nevertheless an important site for theological teaching. William Ive, D.Th., gave theological lectures in its 'schools' in 1464,[124] attacking the erroneous teaching of the London Carmelites, and Bishop fitz James (1506–22) tried to enforce the statutory provision that the cathedral's chancellor should lecture in theology.[125]

In the thirteenth century St Paul's had been in the forefront of musical development with its adoption of polyphony (p. 23) and it seems that in 1298 the elaboration of its organ music provoked the dean to forbid the choir to stand around the organ in the choir screen (*pulpitum*) to sing the mass: they were to sing their solos nearer to the altar in the choir.[126] As the taste for polyphonic music developed, so more chantry founders specified that their commemorative services were to be sung rather than said. The London mayor John Pulteney (d.1349), in setting up his chantry in the chapel of St John the Baptist near the north door, left ten shillings annually to pay the boy choristers to sing an anthem of the Virgin before her statue in his chapel every evening after Compline.[127] Fifteen years later John Barnet, who had risen from a canonry at St Paul's to a bishopric, gave a generous gift of land in Essex to endow a daily anthem to be sung after matins in the choir before the image of the Virgin.[128] Richard Martin, bishop of St David's, who had been the archdeacon of London, at his death in 1482 asked to be buried by the rood of the north door and left money for the choristers each year to sing the Jesus antiphon *Sancte Deus, sancte fortis* before the rood.[129]

Dean Colet was also concerned to promote music, 'one of the greatest glories of the late pre-reformation English church, namely the extended, florid, virtuosic and technically highly-demanding polyphony of the day, written in five parts for boy's treble, alto, two tenor and bass voices'.[130] To this end Colet drafted new statutes in which the eight choirboys were to be taught singing and reading by the almoner to fit them for service in the choir (in fact the number of boys seems to have risen to ten by 1507) and in his reorganized Jesus guild (see p. 163) music was to play a prominent part: indeed it would seem that it was Colet's intention to use the resources of the lay members of the guild to fund cathedral music. Not only was the guild to pay the minor canons, eight chantry priests, the six vicars and ten choristers to sing 'solemly by note' at the feasts of the Transfiguration and the Holy Name, but a Jesus mass was to be sung every Friday in the crypt, and the master of the choristers was paid 26s. 8d. each year to see that three *Salves* were sung in the crypt every day after Compline. It was probably the Jesus guild that commissioned Robert Fayrfax, a gentleman of the Chapel Royal, to compose his mass of the Holy Name – *O Bone Jesu* – and he also wrote other music for the guild.[131]

Music in the cathedral was the concern of a minor canon who acted as sub-dean, and two other minor canons, known as 'cardinals', were responsible for discipline and order among the singers. The main singing tasks were carried out by the vicars choral: originally there were thirty of these men, but by the sixteenth century their numbers had been reduced to six. The numbers of choristers had, however, risen from eight to ten and the chantry priests were usually expected to take part in singing the services in the choir. As time went on chantry founders came increasingly to specify that their chaplains should assist the choir at certain services.[132] Only a few names of individual musicians at St Paul's are known to us. Richard Cotel (active 1397–1408), one of the

cardinals, wrote a short treatise on descant[133] and John Aleyn (d. 1437), the sub-dean, may have composed a motet praising the skill of English composers.[134] William Pasche, one of the sixteenth-century vicars, and William Whitbroke (d. 1565), the sub-dean, were both known as composers.[135] But the most famous of the cathedral musicians in this period was probably John Redford (d. 1547), one of the vicars and the 'master of the almonry', i.e. the choir master. Redford composed music (perhaps the famous anthem *Rejoice in the Lord Alway*), wrote plays, and also songs for the choristers to sing including one complaining about their master.[136] When he died Redford left bequests to each of the choristers and to his fellow vicars and requested burial in the Pardon Churchyard, which was to be demolished within two years.

As the cathedral of the capital city, St Paul's continued in its established role in the service of a larger constituency than the diocese of London. Councils of the ecclesiastical province of Canterbury almost always met at St Paul's rather than at the nominal seat of the southern metropolitan. For the meeting in 1309 the archbishop rode in procession from Lambeth to Southwark and, after crossing London Bridge, proceeded through the city to St Paul's where he celebrated mass, blessed the people and preached a sermon.[137] Just as the city itself was fertile ground for the generation of new ideas and events with a national impact, so the cathedral served as a site to signify their importance. John Wyclif was summoned to answer charges of heresy there in 1377 and the Lollards chose to nail their challenge to the contemporary church – the Twelve Conclusions – on the doors of the cathedral in 1395. Always a focus of royal interest, St Paul's came to have a special significance for the Lancastrian dynasty after John of Gaunt chose to be buried there in 1399. It was to St Paul's that Henry Bolingbroke came in September 1399 and, after the battle of Shrewsbury, he went first to St Paul's to offer thanks for victory before moving on by boat to Westminster. Richard II's body was displayed there so that all might see that he was dead: Henry V lay there in state and the bodies of those who died at the battle of Barnet in 1471 were brought there for public view.[138] Following his defeat of Lambert Simnel at the battle of Stoke, Henry VII was 'censed with the great senser of Powles by an angell comming oute of the roof'.[139] St Paul's was also used to stage public celebrations of diplomatic initiatives and alliances. These included the marriage ceremony of Prince Arthur and Katherine of Aragon that took place in the cathedral on the feast of the translation of St Erkenwald (14 November) 1501, following a magnificent series of pageants in the city. On this occasion, in the second bay from the west in the north aisle of the nave, there was erected a scaffolding 'mountain' on which the marriage took place, partly screened from public view. On the south side was a lesser structure where the mayor and aldermen stood. After the ceremony, and open to the public gaze, the wedding party led a splendid procession along a raised platform extending from the great west door to the choir, where mass was celebrated.[140] In 1518, for the proclamation of a general peace in Christendom that marked the recently concluded peace with France, a similar platform was erected, specifically so that the king and the foreign ambassadors might be seen. With the change of alliance signalled by the visit of the Emperor Charles V to London in 1522, both king and emperor attended a service at St Paul's.[141] Important as Westminster was as the burial place of the English kings, it was the abbey church of a monastic community, while St Paul's was a more public space serving both the city and the kingdom.

21. Bishop John Fisher of Rochester preaching a sermon at St Paul's following the death of Henry VII. A generic woodcut from Wynkyn de Worde's *A Tract to Commemorate the Funeral Sermon of Henry VII*, 1509

Since the early thirteenth century, if not earlier, one of the major focal points in that space had been Paul's Cross, in the great cemetery, where announcements were made, sermons preached and dramatic political events enacted in the presence of great crowds of Londoners (pp. 20, 31–2). The citizens' folkmoot no longer met there, but the tradition of assembly continued. Here in 1356–7, Richard fitz Ralph, the learned secular from Oxford who became archbishop of Armagh, delivered his vitriolic sermons against the friars.[142] Here also, twenty years later, the less forceful Thomas Appleby, bishop of Carlisle, was attempting to preach when a riot between goldsmiths and pepperers in Cheapside became so intense that the wounded stumbled into the churchyard and his preaching was disturbed.[143] In 1382 the cross was damaged by an earthquake and five years later Archbishop Courtenay offered forty days' indulgence to those who would help to repair it. The Lollard preacher William Taylor delivered an inflammatory sermon at Paul's Cross in 1406.[144] Bishop Kempe (1448–89) had the cross entirely rebuilt, added a roofed pulpit for preaching and adorned it with his own coat of arms.[145] The mayor and aldermen who gathered to hear the special civic sermons at the cross during Whitsun were protected from the weather by a cloth or awning, supplied, apparently as early as 1420 and still in 1461, by one of the city sergeants.[146] By the 1480s a covered gallery, described as 'the place where the doctors commonly stand in the upper storey' and serving also to accommodate powerful or distinguished visitors, appears to have been built along the north side of the choir wall, facing the cross, so that some listeners might be placed in a more advantageous, and drier, place in which to hear the preacher (Figs. 24, 93).[147] It was here that Canon Ralph Shaa, the brother of the London mayor, on 22 June 1483 preached his infamous sermon claiming not only that Edward IV's children were bastards but that Edward himself was not the son of duke Richard. The sermon was not well received and Shaa died a year later of remorse requesting burial 'afore the blessed figure of our lord Jhesu callid the rode of North door'.[148] It was evidently at Paul's Cross that in 1521 Bishop John Fisher preached for two hours against Martin Luther, before Cardinal Wolsey and other high-ranking clergy, foreign ambassadors and a great crown of Londoners: Lutheran books were burned there afterwards. During the upheavals of the Reformation, as earlier, St Paul's was an important site for the assertion of orthodoxy and ideas associated with those in power, but at the same time, because it was such a public place, it attracted anonymous expressions of contrary opinions. The bull condemning Luther that was posted on St Paul's door after Fisher's sermon was soon found to have had scrawled on it anti-papal views; the door was also used for posting heretical tracts.[149]

It is right to see an ambiguity in the relations between the city of London and St Paul's cathedral: an intimate link on the one hand and a distant relationship on the other. But, in spite of the efforts of Bishop Braybroke, Bishop Kempe and Dean Colet, and of some Londoners like the skinner Henry Barton, it seems that indifference may have triumphed over intimacy.[150] There was ambiguity also in the response of the cathedral clergy to the changes of the sixteenth century. Colet was succeeded as dean by the royal secretary Richard Pace, who was almost continuously absent for the seventeen years of his tenure, and Pace's successor, Richard Sampson, held the deanery in conjunction with the bishopric of Chichester until his conservative tendencies led him into conflict with Cromwell in 1540 and he ended up in the Tower. Whether the cathedral clergy, if firmly led, might have resisted change is uncertain but, as things were, they complied with royal commands. In 1534 seventy-eight of the St Paul's clergy (including eight canons, ten minor canons, thirty-one chantry priests and six vicars choral) formally accepted the king as the supreme head of the English church.[151] When the dean, four years later, was required to remove the famous rood at the north door and the statue of St Uncumber, he chose to do so at night for fear of protests,[152] and there was indeed an affray when the high altar was taken down in 1550.[153] On the other hand by February 1540 there were six English Bibles placed in the cathedral which stimulated impromptu sermons, and St Paul's was one of the first English cathedrals to introduce the new liturgy in 1552.[154] There were no recorded protests when the Pardon churchyard cloister, together with the panels of the *Danse Macabre*, were pulled down on the orders of Protector Somerset in April 1549 'so that nothing therof was left but the bare plot of ground'.[155] In the end, perhaps Londoners felt that St Paul's belonged more to the nation at large than it did to them, and so it was in the parish churches in the sixteenth century that the fiercest battles for the minds and souls of the Londoners took place.

6

COMMUNITY, CITY AND NATION, 1540–1714

David J. Crankshaw

Can any period have been more tumultuous in the history of St Paul's Cathedral than the early modern era? The institution faced religious reformation in the sixteenth century, temporary dissolution in the seventeenth, and two serious fires. It also underwent four building campaigns: in the 1560s–80s, attempting to repair the damage caused by the fire of 1561; in the 1630s, seeking to remedy the general state of dilapidation; in the early 1660s, aimed at reversing the degradation of the Civil War period; and after the Great Fire of 1666, creating the magnificent structure that we see today. St Paul's fulfilled many functions and encountered many problems in what has been called the 'Confessional Age', when much radical Protestant opinion was openly hostile to the continued existence of cathedrals. A central question concerns the extent to which St Paul's had become the 'mother church' of the realm – a focus for nationalism and a symbol of unity – by the time of the Hanoverian succession.

The cathedral's metropolitan context made it a special focus of attention. Moreover, London's transformation under the Tudors and Stuarts had an important bearing upon the city's capacity to fund the building campaigns.[1] The immediate motor of this

22. St Paul's as depicted in the 'copperplate map' of London of the 1550s, now in Dessau Museum. The last known view before the spire was struck by lightning and fell in 1561. (Museum of London)

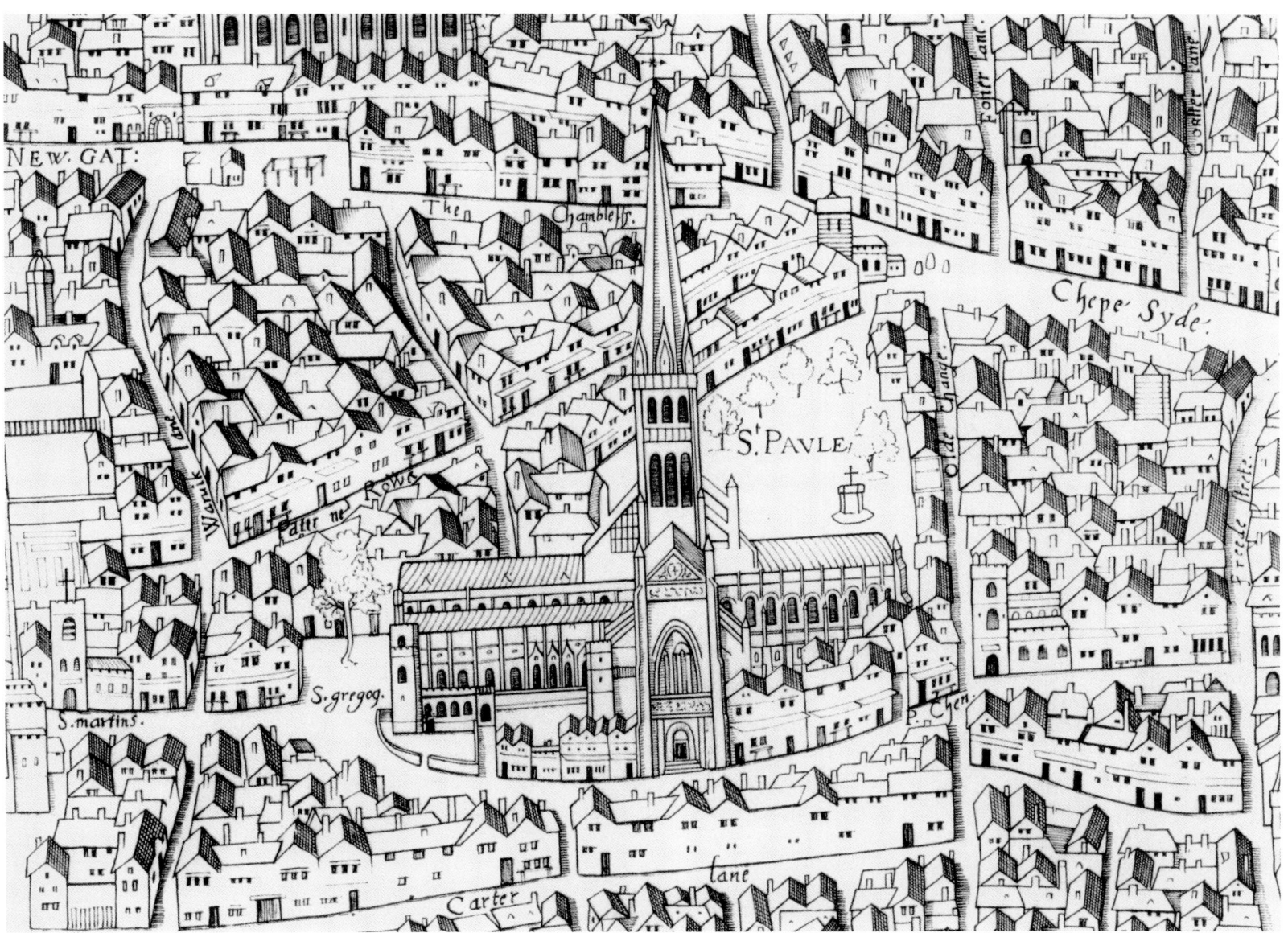

transformation was population growth, manifested in increasing density and geographical expansion. In 1500, with perhaps 50,000 inhabitants, London ranked tenth or lower among European cities, but by 1700, with more than half a million, it was the largest. London likewise increased its share of the nation's population. It had always overshadowed other English cities to a remarkable degree, but its predominance now became awesome: the second city, Norwich, contained about a quarter the population of London in 1500, but less than a seventeenth in 1600 and 1700. Metropolitan growth was fuelled by immigration, principally from elsewhere in England. Others hailed from overseas, drawn by economic opportunity or driven by political or religious persecution; they constituted a substantial alien presence, alarming to some.

The metropolis expanded on all sides, irregularly and seemingly uncontrollably, so that by 1700 less than a third of the population lived within the bounds of the ancient city. The varied and specialized suburbs of the capital became increasingly important to its commercial and social life, and by the late seventeenth century a sharp contrast between west and east had emerged, later being consolidated in the notion of a 'West End' and an 'East End'.

This growth was driven by trade, across the North Sea and then increasingly across the Atlantic. By 1700 London was on the verge of becoming the dominant European city of trade and finance. This brought immense wealth and made London of vital interest to the state. The metropolis contained the largest, most varied, and most specialized concentration of manufactures, and its products became progressively competitive abroad. London increasingly became a place of seasonal resort for the aristocracy, gentry and members of parliament. As a centre for litigation and legal education, it boomed. Moreover, by 1600 the capital boasted four of the country's nine major public schools, including St Paul's School, refounded in 1508–10. Public lectures and demonstrations added to the possibilities for mental stimulation, as did the coffee houses where many of them came to be held. London was also an ecclesiastical capital, for the southern province was administered from Lambeth Palace and the Court of Arches, sitting at the city church of St Mary-le-Bow, rather than from Canterbury. From the 1590s onwards, there was a sustained revival of church-building and beautification in both rich and poor parishes. In the Jacobean period at least sixty-three parish churches were affected. Although the ecclesiastical authorities, ceremonialists and evangelical Calvinists alike, offered encouragement, these projects answered local needs: to accommodate a growing population, to fit interiors for post-Reformation worship, to articulate parochial pride and identity, and to proclaim munificence.[2] Parish churches again became a focus of concern in the early eighteenth century.

By 1700 the reshaping of the metropolis into contrasting neighbourhoods was becoming clear: the crowded but sober commercial heart of the city, an emerging district of fashionable residence and consumption towards Westminster, a legal quarter, busy manufacturing districts in suburban and marginal areas, and distinctive zones of poverty.

In the middle of this maelstrom stood St Paul's. Did the cathedral bulk large in the lives of early modern Londoners, especially since so many of them were immigrants or lived outside the city? For many, sheer survival was their priority; the successful had other preoccupations. Parochial loyalties were strong. What can St Paul's have meant to London's provincial visitors, many of whom looked westwards, towards Westminster, rather than to the city?

One characteristic of early modern London, however, counted in the cathedral's favour, as the Henrician Reformation, for all its contradictions, ushered in the evangelizing Protestant revolution of the Edwardian era. This was Londoners' literacy, for the citizens (of both sexes) constituted the most literate (or least illiterate) community in England. Protestantism is a religion of the word, both written and spoken. Surrounded by booksellers, and boasting the great external pulpit of Paul's Cross, St Paul's would provide the setting for many of the climactic events of the Reformation.

REFORMATION AND COUNTER-REFORMATION

Despite a threat in 1532, St Paul's emerged from the initial legislative phase of the Henrician Reformation, completed by the 'Act for the Extinguishing of the Authority of the Bishop of Rome' (1536), with its secular status intact. Its spiritual jurisdiction, however, had been on a new footing since 1535, when, as the king's vice-gerent, Thomas Cromwell had inhibited all ordinary jurisdiction and had then granted specific licences, including one to St Paul's in October, for the resumption of spiritual jurisdiction 'at pleasure'. The cathedral now functioned entirely under the auspices of the Royal Supremacy. The St Paul's licence followed the local vice-gerential visitation, one result of which was the confiscation of the cathedral's relic of 'Our Ladies Milke'.[3] October also saw the culmination of the tussle for control of Paul's Cross, an evangelical victory made all the more necessary by recent conservative preaching on the doctrine of purgatory by Bishop Stokesley and a 'popish' prebendary. Another preacher at St Paul's, probably John Hilsey, had opposed these views. A regime that in 1534 had commandeered the pulpit, supplying bishops to preach up the Royal Supremacy on six consecutive Sundays, would hardly settle for half measures now, and so in October Cromwell licensed Hilsey, now bishop of Rochester, to appoint Paul's Cross preachers.[4]

Archbishop Cranmer prepared the way for further change with another Paul's Cross preaching campaign, undertaken early in 1536 by himself and six other bishops: purgatory was attacked, the pope denounced, and the Royal Supremacy affirmed. Hugh Latimer's sermon at the opening of Convocation at St Paul's in June was a quasi-official manifesto for reform that assaulted the main components of popular piety.[5] Convocation later agreed a book of Ten Articles, composed on the king's authority. An interim statement embodying a diluted version of Lutheran compromises, this is the first official doctrinal formulary of the Church of England. It famously reduces the seven sacraments to three and affirms a version of the core evangelical belief in justification by faith; but it also defends, in qualified terms, intercession for the dead, the cult of the saints and the use of images and ceremonies. There followed a decree which severely pruned the number of saints' days. In an attempt to enforce conformity to both the Ten Articles and the decree, Cromwell issued a set of Royal Injunctions in August 1536. Their most striking feature is the requirement that every parish priest provide a copy of the Bible in Latin and English by August 1537, a requirement largely ignored by the bishops for a year or more. The outbreak of the conservative Pilgrimage of Grace in late 1536 was one reason for caution. Once the crisis had blown over the evangelical offensive revived, beginning with the release in 1537 of the 'Bishops' Book', a Lutheran text amended to meet conservative objections, but still too radical for the king. Cromwell's second set of Royal Injunctions, promulgated in October 1538, was evangelical and in

23.   Edward VI's procession along Cheapside on 19 February 1547, the day before his coronation, with St Mary-le-Bow to the left and the cathedral to the right of centre. Copy by S. H. Grimm, 1785, of a contemporary wall-painting at Cowdray House, Sussex, destroyed by fire in 1793. (The Society of Antiquaries)

parts dismissive of tradition: images inspiring offerings or pilgrimages were to be taken down; the burning of candles before images was to be forbidden; and the veneration of images and relics was to be denounced in sermons.[6]

St Paul's witnessed the effects of this intensifying assault. The famous Rood of Grace from Boxley Abbey in Kent was displayed at Paul's Cross in February 1538 and smashed to pieces.[7] In August, Dean Sampson removed three of the cathedral's greatest pilgrimage attractions: the Rood of the North Door; the image of St Uncumber; and the image of Our Lady of Grace.[8] At another Cross sermon in November, the phial containing the Holy Blood of Hailes was held up for public contempt.

Other notable events took place at the cathedral in these years. Standing at the west door, the entire choir censed the king and queen as they rode past in December 1536. The following year elaborate services were held to mark Jane Seymour's pregnancy, the birth of the future Edward VI and then her death. Complying with the important poor law of 1536, the Lord Mayor instituted Sunday charitable collections at Paul's Cross from Lent 1538.[9]

The evangelical cause suffered a serious setback in November 1538 when a royal proclamation ordered Anabaptists and sacramentaries to quit the realm and affirmed several traditional doctrines. Henry had had enough of the reformers' programme, as was further signalled in early June 1539 when a three-line whip brought both archbishops and eight bishops to St Paul's for the lavish performance of a *Dirige* for the soul of Isabella, wife of the Emperor Charles V.[10] The ruthless Act of Six Articles, passed later that month, confirmed that the political tide had turned. It was the beginning of the end for Cromwell, who would be executed in July 1540.

The reversal of fortune became apparent at St Paul's in September 1539, when Bishop Stokesley was given a magnificent Catholic funeral prior to burial behind St Erkenwald's shrine. Although the shrine was demolished during 1540–1, along with the loft formerly supporting the Rood of the North Door, indicating that a species of reform was still afoot, gospellers (evangelicals)

soon complained that Edmund Bonner, Stokesley's infamous successor, had erected new images.[11] Bonner had caused bibles to be set up in the cathedral, he was alleged to have done so in order to entrap 'the busy Bible men of London'. A tailor given to reading Scripture aloud in St Paul's every holy day was arrested, apparently because the 'canons of Poolis toke displeasure' at his lectures, which rivalled their own 'mummynge masse and matyns'; his suspicious death in prison provoked much concern.[12] Obits continued to be said in the cathedral between 1541 and 1547.[13] Otherwise, the regular round of worship was punctuated now and then by great processions and special services held between 1544 and 1546 to mark victories over the Scots and French, and then peace with France.[14]

These were dangerous times for gospellers, not least after May 1543, when a statute sought to restrict access to vernacular Scripture. The new dispensation was buttressed that same month by a revised statement of doctrine, commonly called the 'King's Book', which was much more conservative than the 'Bishops' Book' of 1537. Paul's Cross was inevitably the venue of choice for the recantations of those who fell foul of these prescriptions. One famous victim was Dr Edward Crome, the evangelical rector of St Mary Aldermary. Another was Nicholas Shaxton, the evangelical bishop of Salisbury who had been among the preachers at the Cross early in 1536, had resigned his see in 1539, and at the Cross in 1546 was said tearfully to have exhorted his auditory to 'abolish' the English books that had occasioned his descent into error.[15] Conservatives even tried to bring down Cranmer in 1543. But the primate, surviving the 'Prebendaries Plot', prepared a new litany, which became the first officially sanctioned vernacular service: St Paul's first heard it sung in October 1545.[16] Conflicting signals demonstrate the void at the heart of royal policy for, unlike Luther, the king had found no coherent replacement for the doctrine of purgatory.[17] The regime seemed to be undermining traditional piety when it forced a priest to do penance at Paul's Cross for feigning a miracle, yet only months later underlined its opposition to evangelical advance by having heretical literature burnt at the Cross.[18]

Between 1541 and 1545 several of the cathedral's minor clergy seem to have shared the Supreme Head's muddle. Thomas Bringborn, for instance, left money for his fellow minor canons to sing masses for his soul, but also devised his best tippet to John Ponet, a man of firm evangelical views. Richard Hoper, one of the cardinals, endowed obits for twenty years, but also bequeathed his English Bible to his sister. Wills occasionally suggest members' intellectual tastes. The minor canon John Buckworthe possessed one of Erasmus' works and an unidentified French book of philosophy. Robert Skammenden, a chantry priest at Holme's College, owned books by Justinian, Richard of St Victor and St Bernard of Clairvaux, as well as works entitled 'Simple soule' and 'pystylle of priuate counselle'.[19]

These years witnessed swings in the fortunes of evangelicals and traditionalists surrounding the king, but many of his intimates were themselves gospellers and manipulated an increasingly debilitated sovereign. Thus, on Henry's death in January 1547, evangelical politicians were able to seize power in the name of the nine-year-old Edward VI, who had received a de luxe Protestant education. On the day before his coronation, the young king processed from the Tower to Westminster (Fig. 23) and at St Paul's saw a foreign high-wire artiste slide down a cable stretching from the cathedral's steeple to a ship's anchor lying next to the deanery.[20]

The regime's religious programme commenced with a new set of Royal Injunctions, followed up by a royal visitation. In London proceedings began in September 1547, when some images were removed from St Paul's and the Epistle and Gospel were read in English during the celebration of high mass. In November, the rood and its flanking imagery were demolished by night; the accidental fall of the great crucifix, killing at least one labourer and injuring others, provoked papist priests to claim, according to one chronicler, that the tragedy 'was the will of God for the pulling downe of the said idolls'. At the end of the month, a picture of Christ's resurrection and an image of Our Lady were destroyed after a Paul's Cross sermon.[21] December saw parliament pass the unpopular Chantries Act, which dissolved almost all colleges, chantries and fraternities. The cathedrals' main endowments were protected, but nothing could save the propitiatory foundations within their walls. A detailed chantry certificate gives us some idea of what was lost at St Paul's.[22] The fate of the redundant cantarists remains to be investigated, though some of them seem to have been pluralists, and one or two held domestic chaplaincies.[23]

A vernacular liturgical form was provided for the reception of communion in both kinds, a central tenet of Protestantism. On the orders of William May, dean since 1545, St Paul's adopted the new form in May 1548, when the customary Whitsuntide censing of the cathedral and the symbolic release of doves were discontinued. The choir now sang in English at matins, mass and evensong; no mass was held unless there were communicants.[24] Among the most vociferous of the gospellers who inveighed against the mass that summer was John Cardmaker, lecturer at St Paul's.[25] By the end of the year, the churchyard charnel house and chapel had been put to secular uses, cart-loads of bones being conveyed to Moorfields and Finsbury for unceremonious dispersal. This was apparently at the expense of Reyner Wolfe, the evangelical Dutch printer formerly based in Strasbourg, who acquired the chapel and rented adjoining properties as accommodation for booksellers.[26]

Meanwhile, Cranmer undertook more drastic liturgical revision, producing the first *Book of Common Prayer*, which contained pragmatic concessions to conservative sentiment. The new liturgy was due to come into force on 9 June 1549, but one local source records that St Paul's and some London parishes adopted the prayer book precociously at the beginning of Lent, when private masses were 'putt downe'.[27] Dean May then ordered the removal of the reserved sacrament from the cathedral's high altar. All of this was too much for Bishop Bonner, provoking the battle of wills that would climax with the bishop's deprivation and imprisonment in October 1549. As the regime attempted to combat the spread of Anabaptism, a stream of Anabaptists, including the notorious Joan of Kent, appeared before Cranmer and other commissioners in the cathedral's Lady Chapel. Those abjuring their errors bore penitential faggots at Paul's Cross. Then the cathedral clergy stopped wearing grey amices, instead donning either surplices with academic hoods (the prebendaries) or tippets (the minor canons). So far as St Paul's was concerned, the most dramatic event that summer was the archbishop's sudden arrival on 21 July to denounce insurgency: triggered by a wide variety of grievances, some religious, serious revolts had broken out in southern England. Vested in a cope and alb, though wearing neither a chasuble nor a mitre, Cranmer entered the choir after matins and delivered an exhortation against 'sumptuous apparell' and other vices. In the litany, performed according to the prayer book, the primate himself sang the collects, adding a prayer specially composed for the occasion, and then personally administered the sacrament to the dean and seven other communicants. Cranmer once again usurped Bonner's episcopal stall in August, when he came to give thanks for Lord Russell's relief of Exeter, using his sermon to execrate the western rebels for their popery.[28]

The pace of religious change quickened markedly following the coup of 1549, which led to the political ascendancy of John Dudley, later duke of Northumberland, and the translation of Nicholas Ridley to the see of London in 1550. A zealot, Ridley had an immediate impact at St Paul's, insisting that the altar lights be extinguished before he would penetrate the choir and requiring the replacement of fixed stone altars by portable wooden communion tables, thus anticipating the government's general order of November 1550. The high altar was demolished overnight in June, the new table being placed on the same spot, while a veil was hung beneath the steps leading to the upper sanctuary so that communicants would receive the sacrament unobserved. The secular affrays in St Paul's soon afterwards were probably no coincidence. Clerical conservatism was certainly alive and well in October, to the extent that the Privy Council ordered the cathedral communion service to be observed, for reports suggested that 'it was used as a verie masse'. Christmas brought the suppression of the '*Rectores chori*, wyth all their coppys at procession'. Shortly before Easter 1551, Ridley moved the communion table westward into the middle sanctuary, rotating it on to an east-west axis, so that the officiating minister now stood in the middle of its south side. He also walled up the grates on either side of the choir in order to prevent people from peering inside at communion time.[29]

In September 1552 Dean May ensured the discontinuation of organ playing, while in October, on Ridley's orders, the subsidiary altars were demolished, together with the stone reredos behind the former high altar; John of Gaunt's impressive monument would have been pulled down too had the Privy Council not intervened. The way was being paved for implementing the revised and unequivocally evangelical *Book of Common Prayer*, due to come into use on 1 November. The bishop himself officiated on the specified day, when his vestments and those of the dean

24.   A sermon being preached at Paul's Cross, apparently in the presence of James I, the queen and the prince of Wales who occupy the Sermon House, top right. Detail from the Gipkyn Diptych of *c.*1620 (see pp. 56–7, 174) (Society of Antiquaries)

and prebendaries were consistent with the stringent rubrics of the new liturgy: copes and chasubles had been discarded. Then more of the fabric of the upper choir was removed and the communion table was shifted further westward, to a site amid the choir stalls. In compliance with government orders, a lengthy list of Catholic church goods was compiled and in May 1553 all objects not reserved for continued use at St Paul's were conveyed away.[30] But the Edwardian regime was doomed, for the king was already ill with the infection that would kill him on 6 July.

The dean and chapter seem not to have been implicated in Edward's desperate attempt to secure England's Protestant future by diverting the Crown to Lady Jane Grey. There were murmurings of discontent at Paul's Cross, probably on 16 July, when Ridley reminded Londoners that both Mary and Elizabeth were debarred from the succession by their illegitimacy. That same

day a letter denouncing Lady Jane Grey and her Privy Council was found in the cathedral.[31] News that Mary had proclaimed herself queen had reached London as early as 10 July and on 19 July, as a huge crowd assembled in St Paul's churchyard, she was proclaimed queen in Cheapside. The Lord Mayor then led the excited throng into the cathedral, where the choir sang a solemn *Te Deum* and the organ boomed once again. Bells rang out across the city in jubilation, though whether at triumphant Tudor dynasticism or at the prospect of Catholic renaissance is obscure. Mary marched into London on 3 August. On his release from the Marshalsea, Bonner headed straight for St Paul's, where he ostentatiously knelt on the steps to pray.[32] The situation remained highly volatile and later that month one of Bonner's chaplains – having made the mistake of decrying his master's imprisonment, of praying for the dead, and of castigating gospellers as libertines – was attacked as he preached at the Cross. The following week the preacher was protected by 200 or more halberdiers.[33]

The formal undoing of reformation could not begin until parliament convened in October, but Catholic practice was voluntarily revived at St Paul's almost immediately with vespers and the Latin mass. Reconstruction of the upper sanctuary was begun, but with too much haste, for the works collapsed and had to be restarted.[34] Perhaps the dean and chapter were anxious to have everything finished in time for the queen's ceremonial procession through the precinct on 30 September, on the eve of her coronation: pageants were performed in the churchyard and a Dutch acrobat daringly disported himself at the steeple's summit. The unmarried cathedral clergy assisted at the coronation itself. Further elements of traditional worship were gradually re-introduced over the ensuing year: mass at the high altar; the reservation of the sacrament, suspended above the high altar under a rich canopy of cloth of gold; the Latin litany, the prebendaries processing in their grey amices; the Apostles' Mass; and the rood, now painted in the queen's colours. The feast of St Erkenwald's translation was apparently remembered in November 1554.[35] At least one Londoner in 1554 confidently expected the re-appearance of the cathedral's famously devout Jesus fraternity, though restoration did not occur until July 1556, when the Crown gave it an elaborate constitution. This may have been 'the foundation of a Counter-Reformation fraternity, rather than the restoration of a medieval one'.[36]

Held in the Long Chapel in October 1553, a disputation between Catholics and Protestants was one of several important national events that took place at St Paul's. Some participants in Wyatt's Rebellion were hanged in the churchyard in February 1554.[37] In March, the capital's married clergy were deprived of their benefices in the consistory court at St Paul's.[38] Two Protestant members of chapter – John Bradford and John Rogers – had already been dislodged on the pretext of sedition. Three others, including Dean May, experienced deprivation by June. Edmund Grindal, the unmarried precentor, resigned around the same time.[39] The new dean, John Feckenham, embarrassed the government in November by boldly telling his Paul's Cross auditory that the lay owners of former ecclesiastical property were morally obliged to return it. Much to Mary's delight, however, the dean, who was her confessor, appeared at court in March 1555 at the head of sixteen ex-monks seeking permission to return to the religious life. When the Westminster Abbey community was refounded in 1556, Feckenham became abbot and was succeeded at St Paul's by Henry Cole, Bonner's chancellor.[40]

The cathedral's Marian heyday fell during Feckenham's tenure, when royal visits were more frequent than at any other time in the century. Fresh from their Winchester nuptials of July 1554, the king and queen stopped to hear a *Te Deum* in the course of their state entry to London in August. This time the Dutch acrobat descended by rope from the top of the chapter house. Accompanied by a train of peers, Philip returned to the cathedral on 18 October to hear mass sung by compatriots drawn from his own choir. The most momentous event was the public commemoration, on 2 December, of England's reconciliation with Rome, which came shortly after Cardinal Pole's absolution of the realm in a ceremony at Whitehall. Parochial representatives from across the diocese were joined at St Paul's by the Lord Mayor and aldermen, by members of the livery companies and by the entire city clergy wearing copes. Dressed

in consistorial robes, Pole landed at Baynard's Castle and was brought to the cathedral by the Lord Mayor. The bishops of Winchester and London met him at the door and led him to the high altar. After the singing of a *Te Deum*, the cardinal retraced his steps to the door in order to receive the king, who arrived from Westminster with a guard of 400. Bonner then said mass, during which Gardiner gave the kiss of peace to both the king and the cardinal. After the service, Philip and Pole repaired to a balcony for Gardiner's Paul's Cross sermon. Addressing an attentive crowd reportedly more than 15,000 strong, the preacher declared that he had been empowered to grant absolution, thereby restoring the papal supremacy, as agreed by parliament. All knelt down in silence as he did so. It was pure theatre.[41] The feast of the Conversion of St Paul (25 January) provided another welcome opportunity for lavish display, beginning with a general procession from the cathedral to Leadenhall and back, Bonner carrying the sacrament under a canopy borne by four prebendaries. Attended by Pole and a large body of courtiers, the king rode over from Whitehall for the ensuing mass.[42]

Mary's government now approached its tipping point in popular estimation. Pole issued commissions for the trial of those who stood accused of heresy. As a result, almost 300 individuals suffered execution between February 1555 and November 1558; many others died in confinement. St Paul's supplied three Protestant martyrs, all condemned for denying the mass: John Rogers, John Cardmaker and John Bradford. Many of the 113 heretics condemned by Bonner were tried in the consistory court at St Paul's, where the bishop often conducted the proceedings in person.[43] For metropolitan gospellers, therefore, the cathedral must surely have acquired grim associations. As the last of London's residents died for Protestantism in June 1558, Mary's health was beginning its terminal decline and the wheel of fortune turned once again.

THE ELIZABETHAN CATHEDRAL

The in-coming regime ensured that a reliable Protestant delivered 'a godly sermon' at Paul's Cross on the first Sunday of Elizabeth's reign.[44] But the cathedral saw no change to Catholic ritual up to June 1559, by which juncture the legal foundations of the Protestant settlement had been laid, restoring a slightly amended version of the 1552 prayer book. This was a tense time, given the general acceptance of Mary's restoration of the old faith and the problems attending the return from exile of evangelical divines espousing a wide variety of views. Economic problems, pestilence, and the risk of invasion added to the sense of crisis. The evolution of government ecclesiastical policy was complex, and remains controversial.[45]

At Paul's Cross on 14 May, Edmund Grindal, returned from exile, announced the restoration of 'King Edward's Book'; but members of the chapter were conspicuous by their absence and St Paul's maintained 'popish' services for longer than many city parish churches. Bishop Bonner, who refused to resign in favour of Grindal, was deprived of the see on 30 May, to be followed shortly afterwards by Dean Cole and the treasurer. Progress was now brisk. Neither mass nor evensong was celebrated at St Paul's on 11 June 1559, when the reserved sacrament was removed from the building and William May again took possession of the deanery.[46] A royal visitation of the national church was then launched. At St Paul's in August the visitors – with May and Grindal (now bishop-elect) lending their support – directed that the high altar and rood be demolished, and that liturgical attire be restricted to the surplice. Later that month the Catholic goods stripped from London's parish churches were burned in the cathedral precincts and elsewhere. Prayer book services were revived at St Paul's at the end of September; in October the visitors deprived four of the archdeacons and at least two of the prebendaries.[47] Yet various Catholic objects remained in the cathedral until 1565, when Grindal decided they ought to be sold.[48] Moreover, about thirteen Marian appointees to prebends(i.e. up to Bonner's deprivation) survived the visitation, a number reduced by deprivation, resignation and death to five by the time of Grindal's translation to York in 1570.

Preferments to St Paul's made by the Crown after Bonner's deprivation and then by Grindal – totalling thirty-two to prebends and eight to dignities – favoured heavyweight reformers.[49] The early Elizabethan chapter could scarcely have been more militantly evangelical, and it is difficult to think of any other phase of the early modern period when it was so cosmopolitan, accommodating two Scots, a Frenchman and native divines able to draw upon experience in the varied Protestant milieux of Emden, Frankfurt-am-Main, Geneva and Strasbourg. Those who had been in Frankfurt included Dean Nowell (in office 1560–1602). Appointees included those who had lived in retirement under Mary (William May, Herbert Westphaling), one who had been imprisoned (John Veron), and one who had fled the country under Edward VI, returning to hold a benefice under Mary (John Bullingham). Eleven were protégés of Grindal.[50] Eleven were, or became, famous as preachers at Paul's Cross, in the cathedral, at funerals in the city, or at court.[51] Seven were later elected bishops.[52] Robert Crowley was one of the most interesting additions (1563) to the chapter. Returning from Frankfurt in 1559, he took Paul's Cross by storm, gathered a clutch of benefices and became unofficial leader of the radical core of those city ministers who were unwilling to compromise over the use of the surplice; by 24 September 1565 he was deprived of his prebend. John Wyllocke (prebendary 1570–85) was an ex-friar from Scotland who in 1540 had preached in London against confession; returning from Emden to Scotland in 1558 he became a moderator of the General Assembly, all the while continuing to hold the rectory of Loughborough; in 1576 it was reported that he never administered communion because he refused to wear a surplice. Yet in the same chapter, between 1559 and 1601, was Gabriel Goodman, characterized recently as 'a root of that anti-Calvinist stock which would run through Archbishops Richard Bancroft and Richard Neile to Laud, blossoming in the high Anglicanism of a future age'.[53]

On 4 June 1561 St Paul's faced a catastrophe that would blight it for decades to come: lightning struck the spire, starting a fire that destroyed the entire steeple and most of the roofs below, though the stone vaults of the latter were largely untouched. The bells crashed down beside the organ. Little else was damaged inside the cathedral, except for the communion table. The fire was successfully contained, but an Italian report put the cost of the damage at more than 100,000 ducats.[54] The event was widely reported,[55] but Elizabethan efforts to repair the damage were no more than fitful (pp. 171–3). Speculation about the cause of the disaster focused on human negligence and divine wrath,[56] not least on account of the ungodly practices to be found in different parts of the building (cf. pp. 52–3). Strenuous attempts were made to raise money for the repairs,[57] but there were

Dyversyties of opinions whether Paul's ought to be reedyfied considering howe yt was dystroyed by the finger of god because yt was abused, and many thought yt was pietas in deum pietas in patriam to haue buylded againe and the steple to be higher then ever yt was ...[58]

There was much reluctance to contribute funds, especially among the clergy.[59] Of the £5,968 raised by the end of September 1566, 54 per cent was supplied by London residents through a tax and a benevolence, 24 per cent by the clergy of the southern province, 11 per cent by Queen Elizabeth, 5 per cent by Bishop Grindal, 2 per cent by the dean and chapter, 2 per cent from the sale of timber, and 1 per cent from the Courts of Common Pleas and King's Bench.[60] By 29 October 1561 repairs had progressed sufficiently for the new Lord Mayor and his entourage to be able to pay their customary visit.[61]

For many in the chapter, rebuilding was to be matched by the completion of the English Reformation. Dean Nowell, recently commissioned to produce a Latin catechism for use in schools, was prominent in the 1563 convocation of the southern province, whose opening session was held at St Paul's; he was perhaps an agent of the bishops' programme. There was much sympathy in the lower house with radical proposals – including ones for the abolition of organs, copes and surplices – especially among clergy then or later associated with St Paul's. But the reformers' efforts did not prevail and the queen's veto of a disciplinary code demonstrated her unwillingness to modify the 1559 settlement.[62]

Although the 1563 convocation achieved immediate success in the approval of a statement of doctrine that would eventually become known as the Thirty-Nine Articles, its failure to establish a new code of discipline was a serious blow to reformers and set the scene for the Elizabethan phase of the controversy over vestments. In 1565 five members of chapter, including Nowell, were among twenty divines who petitioned for freedom of conscience in the matter – thus countering the queen's instructions to Archbishop Parker – but the bishops' over-riding Erastianism won the day.[63] This pyrrhic victory radicalized some nonconformists into espousing presbyterianism, and meant that the bishops increasingly lost the initiative in reform to a nascent puritan movement. Cathedrals suffered collateral damage. The sniping reached a crescendo in the Admonition Controversy, when London preachers dilated on the alleged iniquities of the 'loytering lubbers' staffing cathedral foundations; a later petition addressed to parliament urged their total destruction.[64] Underlying this attack was the perception that rich cathedrals, largely unscathed by the turmoil of the Henrician and Edwardian Reformations, were gorging on the income from appropriated rectories, a situation made worse by the fact that many of the prebendaries were pluralists and non-residents. Whereas pre-Reformation critics had complained that too few prebendaries resided at their cathedrals, leaving their duties to be performed by vicars, Elizabethan precisians attacked them for living idly in their precincts instead of preaching in their parishes.[65] At the heart of the debate was an awkward question: what was the point of Protestant cathedrals? Their former large contingents of intercessionary priests were now redundant; the pilgrimage business had been finished off; most saints' days had been abrogated; and vast processional spaces were no longer required. Nor did a bishop really need a cathedral: neither Grindal nor Bancroft appears to have set foot in Canterbury as archbishop. In identifying the benefits brought by cathedrals, Archbishop Whitgift of Canterbury scarcely mentioned their religious functions.[66]

Did conduct at St Paul's justify the hostility? Bishop Sandys' 1574 visitation suggests that prebendaries may not have neglected their parochial cures: doubtless some of the five absentee dignitaries, and some of at least eighteen missing prebendaries, were temporarily resident in country livings.[67] Moreover, critics can hardly have had St Paul's in mind when they complained about the paucity of preaching. Since the beginning of the reign, a host of distinguished men had mounted the Paul's Cross pulpit. Apart from bishops and prebendaries, they included the veteran Miles Coverdale, the bible translator; John Foxe, the martyrologist; John Knewstub, the leading puritan divine; Laurence Chaderton, the influential first master of Emmanuel College, Cambridge; and Stephen Gosson, author of a vicious attack on the London stage.[68] One of the more controversial Elizabethan Paul's Cross sermons was preached in February 1589 by Richard Bancroft, the future bishop of London and archbishop of Canterbury.[69] Notwithstanding the appearance of these stars, it was hard to attract preachers to the Cross. University preachers simply could not afford to come up to the capital 'at their own great cost', as one of the bishop's chaplains explained at the height of the crisis in 1591–2. The city corporation repeatedly rebuffed supplications for help. In the end, Bishop Aylmer bequeathed £300 in 1594, and another substantial donor was Bess of Hardwick, the countess of Shrewsbury. Further contributions generated a sum sufficient to provide each preacher with a fee and lodging.[70]

Preaching was not confined to Paul's Cross. The long-established cathedral divinity lectureship (p. 27) was held from 1570–1 to 1572–3 by the young and zealous Cambridge graduate Edward Dering, who tended to presbyterianism and had a serious interest in practical divinity. A fearless preacher, he famously upbraided Elizabeth in a court sermon of February 1570; but his recklessness led to suspension.[71] His successors were lesser men. There were also two cathedral readers: one in the Evangelists, the other in the Epistles. Early in the 1570s they included the former Marian captive and exile, Thomas Mountain.[72] The readerships were later usually filled by the minor canons. Stipends were also paid to 'preachers in the choir', of whom there were normally two a year in the early 1570s, rising to four a year towards the end of the decade; Dering was one for a while. Later preachers included Richard Porder, a recent graduate with puritan sympathies; minor canons; city ministers; and one Thomas White, who was probably the future founder of Sion College. The prevailing puritan ethos was reinforced by certain prebendal appointments during the 1570s and 1580s.[73]

How active were members of the chapter in the task of evangelization? Nowell was certainly a popular preacher, appearing at Paul's Cross on at least nine occasions, delivering a Spital sermon in 1563, and frequently being engaged to speak at funerals of the London well-to-do. His court preaching probably did most to enhance his reputation, for he inaugurated the prestigious Lent series of sermons on every Ash Wednesday between 1561 and 1592, although Elizabeth did not always listen to him with approval.[74] The dean was an influential figure beyond the pulpit: in the highest levels of government, in Crown ecclesiastical patronage, and in city circles.[75] He was also an effective Protestant propagandist and a staunch defender of conventions and standards.[76]

So far as one can tell, St Paul's prebendaries were not the 'loytering lubbers' of puritan polemic. Some of them – including John Mullins, John Pulleyn and Thomas Watts – petitioned the Lord Keeper in connection with the disposition of Crown livings and regularly examined candidates for ordination.[77] Certain prebendaries – including Arthur Bright, David Dee, George Dickins, Edward Layfield and Robert Temple – were probably much sought after as occasional preachers in the city's parishes, for prior to their capitular appointments they had occupied metropolitan lectureships, for which the market was highly competitive.[78]

The dean and chapter remained the largest single patron of London benefices. To its credit, the chapter stood aloof from the fashionable practice whereby patrons temporarily granted away the use of their advowsons. Despite periodic tension between chapter and bishop, the chapter seems not to have pursued an independent course in appointments. In general, posts were granted to chapter members – and as the bishop had mostly collated the prebendaries to their prebends, the bishop exerted a considerable indirect influence over capitular patronage. The poorer livings tended to be dispersed among the cathedral's minor canons. Nevertheless, some important nonconformists retained a toe-hold in the capital's ministry at the chapter's hands, including Thomas Spering, a troublesome cleric in the 1580s.[79]

That St Paul's occupied a central place in the realm can scarcely be disputed. It was on the gate of the episcopal palace, for instance, that John Felton posted the papal bull excommunicating the queen and sanctioning her deposition; and it was in the churchyard that he suffered execution in 1570. The government was particularly keen to keep Paul's Cross preachers 'on message' as the damaging Admonition Controversy gathered pace. Referring to Thomas Cartwright's *A Replye to an answere*, which poured from the presses in 1573, a correspondent reported that there was 'continuall preaching at Pawles against the boke, a thing reported to be injoyned etche man that occupieth that place'.[80] The greatest propaganda coup for mainstream English Protestantism came with the miraculous triumph over the Armada in 1588, which seems to have been given its first public recognition at Paul's Cross on 20 August, when Dean Nowell preached a sermon of thanksgiving. On Sunday 24 November, sporting her crown, the queen finally arrived, and stepped out of her chariot to find a chair of estate waiting for her, placed upon a carpet laid outside the west door. Here Bishop Aylmer gave her a book containing the cathedral statutes, which she promptly returned signifying her confirmation. After the litany had been sung in the choir, she entered an area known as the 'Duchie of Lancasters', just off the north choir aisle and near the tomb of John of Gaunt (Figs 67, 78). Here there was some kind of royal box, from which she heard the bishop of Salisbury preach outside. This was her only visit to Paul's Cross. The crowds were huge.[81]

The post-Armada cathedral comes alive in the records extant from Bishop Bancroft's visitation of 1598.[82] Apart from revealing strife among the minor canons and their wives, the bills of presentment tell us much about the building's immediate environment and the uses to which parts of the interior were put.[83] One virger was worried that, in entering the precincts to make arrests, city functionaries were infringing the jurisdiction of the dean and chapter. The cathedral's hallowed space was being polluted by smoke and smells emanating from the chimneys of sheds erected in the 'Crosse Church yard'. Respondents complained that surrounding shops opened for trade on the Sabbath, and in service time.

Schoolchildren played in the churchyard, breaking windows and disquieting members of the congregation. Some individuals inhabited properties giving access to the roof, and had damaged the leads. Too many Londoners possessed keys to the cathedral, enabling them to throw open its doors 'at vnlawfull times in the night'.

There was unease about profanation. Carpenters leased some of the vaults; trunkmakers occupied parts of the crypt and cloisters. The chapel beneath the far end of the south aisle was let to a glazier, whose cart wheels had damaged the steps at the south door. St John the Baptist's Chapel was redundant and lacked glazing. The 'muche vnglased' chapel of St Katharine intermittently served as a schoolroom. Building materials were kept in St George's Chapel and the partly-glazed Long Chapel. Residentiary canons vested themselves with surplices and hoods in the Duke of Lancaster's Chapel. Cushions and copes, 'and suche things as belonge for the sarvyce of ye churche', were held in the vestry itself, which was termed a 'severed place', perhaps signifying a secure area; this phraseology suggests that the copes were in regular use and were considered to be valuable.

St Paul's was an attraction for tourists. Notwithstanding the 1561 fire, they were encouraged to climb to the steeple for the view, whether or not divine service, or a sermon, might be in progress below. A Swiss visitor noted in 1599 that 'every Sunday many men and women stroll together on this roof'.[84] They made great whooping noises when they reached the top and dropped stones, which landed in the minor canons' garden, hit the leads, or fell inside the structure itself 'vppon those that walke there'.

Moreover, the cathedral was 'foule continually', producing a 'very evill savour greatly preiudiciall to mens health Especially in Winter'. Two minor canons reported that drunkards and 'other Idle & masterles people' were suffered 'to lye and sleepe vpon the formes, and aboute ye quire dores...where they doe verie often tymes leave all yt is within them verye lothsome to beholde'. The visitors' waste was swept up into a muckhill. The church was apparently cleaned every three or four weeks, but that did not extend to the regular removal of the dunghills, or even to the extrusion of the piles of 'parynges and duste' which persistently lay 'in Corners'.

St Paul's was a thoroughfare and meeting place. Even during services, nobody tried to prevent tradesmen from passing through the Lower Church with their burdens. It was also plagued by beggars. Poor folk, including many women with babes in arms, were to be found 'sittinge aboute ye pillers of ye Church and aboute the Quire Dores' after every service and sermon. Through the virgers' negligence, undesirables occasionally managed to penetrate to the choir at service time, obscuring the minor canons and drowning out their voices. Duchy of Lancaster officials had apparently attempted to control entry to the Upper Church by making a door in the north aisle, allowing a woman door-keeper to stand there and take money.

The huge nave – 'Paul's Walk' or 'Duke Humphrey's Walk'[85] – was notorious for the concourse of people and business, as noted in 1563:

> the south alley for usurye and Poperye, the north for Simony, and the Horse faire in the middest for all kind of bargains, metinges, brawlinges, murthers, conspiracies, and the font for ordinary paimentes of money.[86]

There were also the 'serving man's pillar', where domestic staff were hired, those 'masterless men that set up their bills in Paul's for services', and the *Si Quis* door, where clergymen advertised their availability for benefices and lectureships.[87] In the 1620s the nave was

> a heap of stones and Men with a strange confusion of languages ... It is the great Exchange of all Discourse and no business whatsoever but is here stirring ... It is the Market of yong lecturers, whom you may cheapen here at all rates and sizes .... All Inventions are emptied here, and not a few Pockettes .... It is the other expence of the daie after Playes Taverne, and a Bawdie house ... The visitants are all men without exception, but the principall Inhabitants ... are stale Knights, and Captaines out of service ... which after all turne merchants here, and traffick for Newes.[88]

There was little room for the sacred. Bell-ringers frequently failed to toll adequate announcement of services, forcing minor canons to 'come short' to the liturgy; and services either continued beyond the appointed hour or were 'vnreverently...knitt .... vp' before properly finished. Morning prayer was apparently held in the Jesus Chapel, underneath the sanctuary, while evening prayer seems to have been said in the choir; the choir men habitually lit an inadequate number of candles on dark evenings. What was termed the middle choir was too small, and the vicars choral pleaded with Bancroft for it to be enlarged so that standing children might be accommodated. This refers to the ten choristers, who used themselves 'very vnreverentlye in there seates talkinge and playinge, or els ... ronninge abowte the quiere to gentlemen and other poore men, for spurre moneye', which they claimed from any person entering the church wearing spurs. The minor canons and vicars choral were slack: unauthorized absence from portions of the service was universal and talking in the choir at inappropriate times was not unknown; they were unwilling to attend term-time divinity lectures.

The most important conclusion to be drawn from these records is that the ceremonialism that would flourish under the early Stuarts already existed before the advent of Dean Overall in 1602. The vicars choral appear to have championed the drive for greater reverence. Two of them opined that

> yt is a generall Fault amongst vs all and we do wysh yt myght be reffourmed of euery one of vs that at the Confession of our synis and asking mercy and pardon at godes handes For our offences at the begining of Servis that everie one should kneele and tvrne his Face towards the est and lykwyse at the Crede to stand vpp with his Face towarde the est and also to knele at the Rest of the prayers and not to Sitt one our tayles as Commonly we doe without any Reverence att all which is a verie Scandall to those that be present ...

Another vicar remarked that

> at the confessyon tyme we ought to kneelle on our knees towards the easte w[i]th our faces, which we for the moste parte do not, neyther at the Gloria Patri do not stand vp turninge our faces towards the easte, as in her majesties Chapell and other Cathedrall Churches they do with reverence ... in the vpper quier, wher the communion table dothe stande, ther is suche vnreverente people walking with their hattes on there heades commonlye all the service tyme ...[89]

This important statement corroborates other evidence that at St Paul's the eastward removal of the communion table to the sanctuary – a characteristic feature of seventeenth-century Laudianism – took place under Elizabeth, as early as the first decade of the reign. When the Marian high altar was demolished in 1559, it was replaced by a communion table located on the western side of the stone pulpitum dividing the choir from the nave. It was evidently there at the time of the fire (p. 51) and had been replaced on the same spot by 1562, but by October 1564 it had been shifted to the upper end of the choir.[90] This new site cannot have been far from that of the Marian high altar. If it was in the centre of the upper choir, as seems likely, then for the vicars choral in 1598 to call for those sitting in the lower choir to kneel towards the east, or with their faces turned towards the east, was to call for them to show reverence to the communion table or to the space once filled by the high altar. Apparently some already followed that practice. Many evangelical Calvinists would have regarded it as idolatrous.

To face east at specific points in the liturgy was not required by the 1559 prayer book. Yet, as an early manifestation of ceremonialism, the gesture was consistent with the predilections of some of the more recent recruits to the chapter, suggesting an incipient anti-puritan reaction, shading into anti-Calvinist reaction. The earliest of these appointees was the Spaniard Anthony Corro (1582), whose anti-Calvinist credentials seem certain.[91] Another was Lancelot Andrewes (1589), whose role in the emergence of English anti-Calvinism was crucial. Probably known to Dean Nowell since 1573, Andrewes owed his St Paul's prebend most immediately to Lettice Knollys, countess of Essex and Leicester, but ultimately to Sir Francis Walsingham.[92] Finally, Richard Bancroft became treasurer by royal grant in 1586: while his precise doctrinal alignment remains a matter of controversy, his anti-puritan bias is beyond question.[93] Viewed in the light of these appointments, the ceremonialist inclinations of the St Paul's vicars choral underline recent observations that the cathedrals survived the Reformation because they provided a 'source of patronage from the powerful to the deserving or from the powerful to themselves'; that they were also 'a useful siding into which one could shunt able but awkward clergy'; and that 'cathedrals acted as a liturgical fifth column within the Elizabethan church', demonstrating the ceremonial possibilities provided by Cranmer's prayer book of promoting 'the beauty of holiness in the face of Protestant denials that such beauty was a legitimate goal of Christian worship'.[94]

THE EARLY STUART CATHEDRAL AND THE FUND-RAISING CAMPAIGN OF THE 1630S

On 24 March 1603, the day of Queen Elizabeth's death, King James VI and I was prayed for publicly in the cathedral. A *quondam* chaplain-in-ordinary of the late queen, John Overall, was now dean, having succeeded Nowell in 1602.[95] Likened to the 'newe moone' on account of his gravity, learning and life, Overall was a strident anti-Calvinist, and the ceremonialism already stirring in the cathedral was now given full rein. In September 1602 a foreign observer noted that gentlemen came to the cathedral 'to hear the beautiful music ... The singers as well as the preachers wear white surplices, making use of many Popish ceremonies, all kneeling down on entering the church and otherwise keeping good order.'[96] Some were offended. The letter writer John Chamberlain complained of 'a new devised order to shut the upper doores in Powles in service time, wherby the old entercourse is cleane chaunged, and the trafficke of newes much decayed'.[97] Thomas Scott, a godly critic, had different objections: could 'these Controwlers of others proue that Christ or his Apostles did ever ordayne, or left unto vs, Crossings, Copes or Surplices?' He answered his own question:

whie are not these also Idolatrous and blasphemous fondnesse? Surely they are, yf they cannot prove them pure and religious wo[r]ship, for in God[es] service there is no mean betwe[en]e these two; all that is not pure worship, is [ydolatr]ie and Blasphemie ... have you not seene Doctor Overall, and his pide attendant[es], act their part[es], at the high Alter, in Powles?... Ho ye end that mens eyes should be fedd with nothing else (whie with nothing else in Rome, yf with some what else [perhaps edifying sermons] in Powles &c?) but with madd gazings, and foolish gaudes?[98]

Other visitors concentrated more on the cathedral's size and usefulness as a vantage-point. In around 1605 one poetaster recorded his reaction:

'Lord!' thought I, 'what a church is heere!'
And then I swore by all christen soules,
'Twas a myle long, or very neere.[99]

In 1606 King Christian IV of Denmark ascended the steeple:

and when he had suruayed the cittie, hee helde his foote still whilest Edward Soper, keeper of the Steeple, with his knife cutte the length, and breadth thereof, in the Lead: ... [T]he said Soper, within few dayes after, made the Kinges Charecter in gilded copper, and fixed it in the middest of the print of the Kings foote, which was no sooner done, but some rustie mindes of this yron age, thinking all gold that glistred, with violent instruments attempted to steale it ...[100]

The playwright Thomas Dekker advised gallants paying to climb the steeple to

draw your knife, and graue your name, (or for want of a name, the marke which you clap on your sheep) in great Caracters vpon the leades ... and so you shall be sure to haue your name lye in a coffin of lead when your selfe shall be wrapt in a winding-sheete: and indeed the top of Powles conteins more names then Stowes Cronicle.[101]

William Camden, the historian *alumnus* of St Paul's School, focused instead on the memorial inscriptions of the interior, publishing a selection of curious epitaphs in his *Remaines of a Greater Work Concerning Britain* of 1605.[102]

The most notable events of the early Jacobean period occurred outside the building. On 30 January 1606 four Gunpowder plotters were executed in the churchyard. In May Henry Garnet, the Jesuit Superior in England, suffered the same fate. The Jesuit John Gerard claimed that it had been suggested that a recanting Garnet would preach at Paul's Cross. Instead, Garnet resisted Overall's efforts to force him to admit treason and convert, and then professed his faith, all to such effect that the crowd ensured that the hanged man was dead before drawing and quartering commenced (without the customary accompanying applause).[103] Gerard's narrative is partially corroborated by a letter written to the king of Spain; another eye-witness, the Swiss pastor Johann Jacob Grasser, reported that Garnet had died 'an eloquent and daring man'.[104]

25. London from Southwark in about 1630, from a painting of the Dutch school. (Museum of London)

26. John Donne, dean of St Paul's 1621–31. This unusual portrait by an unknown hand, now in the Deanery, is inscribed 'Aetatis suae 49 1620', i.e. the year before Donne became dean. A copy or replica in the Victoria and Albert Museum has been ascribed to Cornelius Janssen. Donne had been ordained in the cathedral less than seven years before his installation as dean, an appointment which he owed to royal favour. A widower, he lived with his mother south-west of the cathedral in the deanery, according to Stow 'a fayre old house', which he improved and hung with a collection of religious art, including 'the picture called the Skeleton'. Half courtier and half ascetic, Donne devoted much effort to his sermons, many of which were published during his lifetime, adding to his fame. He preached in the cathedral at major festivals and on some other occasions, as well as several times at Paul's Cross. An efficient administrator of the cathedral's estates, he also sat often in ecclesiastical courts, but seems not to have greatly involved himself in the campaign for restoring the fabric. (St Paul's Cathedral)

In passing Gerard noted that a place in the stands to watch the execution cost 12*d*. Such stands regularly appeared in the churchyard at times of general festivity, such as the discovery of the Gunpowder Plot. Thereafter, the Lord Mayor and aldermen assembled at St Paul's to hear a sermon every 5 November, the Butchers' Company spending 3*s*. in 1606–7 'for the standing at Powles for the new holiday of thanksgiving'.[105] This transformation of the precincts into a public arena continued during the Interregnum: in 1653–4, for example, the Barber–Surgeons' Company hired a cloth 'to lay over the Rayle of our standing in Paull's Churchyard when the Lord Protector was enterteined by the Citie at Grocers hall'.[106]

Paul's Cross

Paul's Cross fascinated foreign tourists. A summer visitor in 1609 wondered whether the alfresco Sunday sermons continued in winter; they did, though heavy rain might force a retreat indoors. He also remarked upon the splendour of the mayoral processions to and from church.[107] At the head of the processions 'senators' in short chestnut gowns and silk caps preceded a sword-bearer, the Lord Mayor and more 'senators'. The presence of the sword *within*

the cathedral, however, was later controversial. Sensitive to perceived challenges to the rights and customs of the cathedral, the dean and chapter, perhaps egged on by Bishop Laud, also complained of arrests in the cathedral liberties by officers claiming mayoral authority.[108]

Alongside aldermen, Paul's Cross sermons also attracted lawyers. In 1627 new readers in the Inns of Court were ordered to repair to Paul's Cross wearing their caps 'in such decent and orderly manner as anciently hath been used'.[109] Dress codes also mattered to the livery companies: the Butchers' Company fined one Mr Greenby in 1616–17 'for cominge in his clothe jerkinge to Pawles'.[110]

The preachers the bishop of London selected for these audiences (Laud insisting on a preview of the text!) constituted a varied group. The incomplete chronological register of Paul's Cross sermons[111] reveals that some were bishops, others dignitaries such as Roger Parker, precentor of Lincoln, whose 1606 'Invective Oration' against the House of Commons led to his imprisonment in the dean's household.[112] There were university divines (mostly Oxfordians) and domestic chaplains to public figures, including the king. Few intramural incumbents feature among London-based preachers, who comprised mostly lecturers or readers from places such as the Inns of Court and St Katharine by the Tower. Preachers also came from across the Home Counties and East Anglia, including the puritan William Whateley, the 'roaring boy' of Banbury (1608), and Nathaniel Kitchener, preacher at Gravenhurst (1614), whose sermon was printed with a short commendatory poem written by a friend, beginning thus:

> In naught save in Christs Cross Paul Glory had,
> In naught more then in Pauls Crosse may we glad,
> Whereby men doe this Tripple honour raise,
> God glory, this Land Good, & Their selves praise.[113]

Others came from much further afield, such as Griffith Williams, parson of Llanllechid in north Wales (1621), whose sermon derived from lectures he had delivered at the cathedral when a lecturer there.[114]

The canons of St Paul's themselves took turns to preach (in the vernacular) on feast days.[115] We know that in 1608 George Downham, prebendary of Caddington Minor and advocate of *jure divino* episcopacy, preached in defence of kneeling at communion, the surplice and the use of the cross in baptism.[116] In 1619 the 'Mr Shingleton of Oxford' preaching against Lord Chancellor Francis Bacon was probably Isaac Singleton, prebendary of Broomesbury.[117] Noted for his 'powerfull kinde of preaching by his gesture & Rhetoriquall expression', John Donne (Fig. 26), Overall's Arminian successor-but-one, preached twice in 1622, on one occasion providing the official explanation for a largely still-born royal order forbidding preaching on affairs of state and permitting only deans or above to discuss 'the deepe poynts of predestination, election, [or] reprobation' before 'any popular auditorie'.[118]

No fewer than fifty-five of the 184 extant Paul's Cross sermons printed between 1570 and 1638 discuss predestination. Those from before 1630 (including twenty-seven preached under James) all took an orthodox Calvinist line, with Arminianism openly denounced for the first time by Roger Ley in 1619. By contrast there is no Jacobean evidence of anti-Calvinist preaching at Paul's Cross, and no Arminian Paul's Cross sermon was published before 1632. The last Calvinist Paul's Cross sermon, however, was printed in 1628.[119]

Sermons at Paul's Cross condemned much: simony and sacrilege (Roger Fenton, 1604), the 'dead sleep of security' (Thomas Cheaste, 1608), pride and stage plays (Robert Milles, 1611), swearing (Abraham Gibson, 1613), the vanity of ambition (Charles Richardson, 1617), Catholicism (Richard Stock, 1606, among many others). Mary Magdalen's love for her Lord (Thomas Walkington, 1620), and predictably 'good order' (Robert Harris, 1622), were eulogized.[120]

Many Jacobean sermons were Jeremiads, in which Old Testament prophecies of the troubles of Israel and Judah were applied to the contemporary situation, although predicated on a 'reformist' Calvinist eschatology rather than revolutionary millenarianism.[121] They were thus not the preserve of opponents of the status quo: one preacher inveighed against the presbyterian Thomas Cartwright and his disciples. Preachers delivered theatrical sermons with more emotional than intellectual force, preached against the backdrop of a culture suffused with providential tales of disaster, prodigy and accident; hence, for all their bullying, they may have been crowd-pleasers.[122]

The idea of a 'national covenant' – a special relationship first between God and Israel and then between God and England – has been suggested as central to the Jeremiad's 'Israelite paradigm'. Others, however, urge the importance of distinguishing between occasions on which Israel was cited as a Biblical *type* for the *invisible* church (the communion of saints only some of whom were English) and more frequent instances when Israel was loosely cited as an example of a *visible* church, when not Israel's *chosenness* but her *sinfulness* formed the basis of comparison with contemporary England. Many Jeremiads thus sought to convince hearers that repentance was necessary to avert God's imminent judgment, such as John Fosbroke's sermon of 1617 later published as *England's Warning by Israel and Judah*, which attributed the 1603 plague, the Gunpowder Plot and the death of Prince Henry in 1612 to God's displeasure at England's sins.[123]

Appropriately enough, public penance for offences ranging from slander to sedition was still performed at the foot of the Paul's Cross pulpit, from which the preacher would execrate the penitents. These included a drunken Mary Frith, *alias* the notorious pipe-smoking whore and fence Moll Cutpurse, who did penance in 1612 for wearing men's apparel; her confederates picked pockets during the sermon. In 1617 Sir Griffith Markham's wife, swathed in white sheets, appeared for having bigamously married her servant.[124]

Fabric and fund-raising

By the 1610s the cathedral fabric was in a bad way. In 1600 a falling piece of the south battlements was reported to have 'kild a carmans horse without doing more harme'.[125] A structural survey costing the necessary works, executed by royal request in 1608, had no significant results. The stone importer Henry Farley's complaints at the condition of 'the *Queene of Churches* in this *Land*' eight years later had more effect.[126] King James' visit to the cathedral on 26 March 1620 to view 'the Ruines' signalled renewed interest.[127] Bishop King of London stressed to the congregation that the church was

> your Sion ..., other are but Synagogues, this your Ierusalem the mother to them all, other but daughters brought vp at hir knees; ... to this doe your Tribes [the livery companies] ascend in their greatest solemnities; ... this [is] vnto you, as S Peters in the Vatican at Rome, S. Marks at Venice, and ... [the temple] of Diana at Ephesus ...[128]

Addressed to more than sixty individuals, a special commission for repair of the cathedral was issued in November 1620. The preliminary survey established that there would need to be a 'general Benevolence' (pp. 175–6). King James and both Bishops King and Montaigne made handsome contributions, but the effort petered out, Thomas Smethwick being permitted to reinvest his 1627 contribution in the East India Company 'vntill some fitter opportunity'.[129]

The year 1628 saw the appointment as bishop of London of William Laud, who found that he 'could not rest under the shade of those vast Ruines of ... his own Cathedral ... without continual thought, and some hopes withal of repairing those deformities in it'.[130] King Charles, who attended a sermon at Paul's Cross in May 1630, was persuaded to act. The fresh commission issued in April 1631[131] argued that St Paul's was of national significance, calling it

> the goodliest Monument, and most eminent Church of our whole Dominions, and a principall ornament of ... the Imperiall Seat and Chamber of ... Our Kingdome, whither ... there is continuall confluence both of Our owne Subiects, and of Ambassadours from forreine Princes, and other Strangers.[132]

It foresaw a lengthy and expensive task ahead, but hoped that Laud's promise of £100 a year would encourage others to contribute; moreover money left by the intestate departed would be diverted towards the project. Elsewhere Gordon Higgott describes the consequent restoration work (pp. 176–82). But the story of the fund-raising campaign itself may help to explain the cathedral's shocking fate during the Civil War.

On 16 May 1631 Laud told the Privy Council that St Paul's was 'a disgrace to o[u]r Country, and the Cittie, and a common imputat[i]on and scandall laid vpon o[u]r Religion, by o[u]r aduersaries, as voyde of charety and true deuoc[i]on'.[133] The next day the bishop of Norwich (perhaps in his capacity as king's almoner) handed over £400.[134] As the campaign gathered pace, a royal letter encouraged the Lord Mayor and aldermen to set an example to lesser citizens, eliciting in September a corporate offer of £200 a year for ten years.[135] Soon after, briefs were sanctioned for collections within the city and its liberties, while Laud approached at least some of the livery companies.[136] In 1632 followed commissions for collections elsewhere in the London diocese, in all counties and in certain towns.[137] That sent to Kingston-upon-Hull, for example, empowered the mayor and sheriffs to summon substantial inhabitants and landowners in the hope of eliciting contributions, while churchwardens were enjoined to target poorer people either in church or at home.[138] In October 1632, the Privy Council sent begging letters to 115 peers.[139]

It was recognized that notorious abuses, such as the nave being 'vsed like a Streete', might jeopardize the campaign. Early in 1632 the Privy Council invited the dean and chapter to suggest reforms.[140] A particular headache was children entering the cathedral on Sundays and festival days and playing as 'children vse to doe till darke night ... hence cometh principally that inordinate noyse, which many tymes suffereth not the preacher to be heard in the Quyre'. Luckily the culprits dwelt in the dean and chapter's peculiar, and so their parents might be dealt with by the cathedral authorities. The dean and chapter were encouraged personally to challenge anyone 'loitering' during services, especially 'foryners and straungers' (mostly 'men of ... qualitie'). 'Ancient wryteing' prohibiting the transit of burdens should be more visible, and carriers turned away. Recalcitrants should be prosecuted in the ecclesiastical courts, while 'Contemptuous pro-phanation' should bring in the Court of High Commission. Rules emerging from these discussions[141] were posted on the cathedral doors. The defence offered in a High Commission hearing of 3 May 1632 by a countryman caught 'pissing against a pillar' in St Paul's en route to his wedding – that he did not realize that he was in a church – has sometimes been cited as evidence of the cathedral's secularization, but the case itself more importantly reveals Laud's insistence on rigorous enforcement.[142] However, such reforms are unlikely to have influenced fund-raising much beyond the capital.

Some commissioners at least were diligent and brisk. In central Essex churchwardens were given just twelve days to organize collections for the 'magnificent structure' of the 'mother Church' of their diocese.[143] Elsewhere in Essex there were differing responses: Roydon parishioners blamed their paltry contribution of 11s. on the burden of local church repairs; yet in Fyfield the parson alone gave 10s. and promised to repeat the gift for six years. In Little Parndon the 'more able' gave £3 9s., while 'ye poorer sort, youth & servantes' offered 13s. 4d.[144] At Waltham Holy Cross money was collected in the church itself.[145]

Beyond the diocese we again see variations in both methods of assessment and responses. In southern Herefordshire the Laudian Viscount Scudamore could only get about halfway to his target of matching its subsidy assessment, while the northern county did much worse.[146] In Hampshire, collections based on assessments for purveyance, though uneven, lead some to conclude that 'the levy was not unpopular'.[147] In Kent the parishioners of Charing alone gave £6 13s. 8d., led by the moderate puritan Sir Robert Honeywood, who gave £2 despite recent differences with the king.[148] In the Welsh Marches, as many as 344 of 367 substantial persons expected to contribute in the Shropshire hundred of Oswestry did so.[149]

Laud was particularly concerned that the clergy were not being effectively canvassed, and this led to revised commissions being issued in 1634 and the new archbishop enjoining his bishops to galvanize their clergy.[150] Thus in a widely copied speech Corbet of Norwich offered his clergy 'one word in St: Paules bee-halfe, hee hath spoken maney a one in ours; hee hath raysed our inward Temples, let us help requit him in his outward', and received £150 in donations, some perhaps his own money distributed to poor clergy whose largesse might encourage others.[151]

Some contemporaries welcomed this campaign, either as a challenge to the worldliness of the age and church, or as a means of underpinning the cathedral's public role: in a sermon delivered in St Paul's the Lincolnshire preacher Gyles Fleming claimed that

> the generall and publike imployment which this Church is used for, pleadeth no lesse for the repairing and beautifying of it: Other Cathedrals, serving onely for the publike affaires of those Provinces that they are in. This for the use of the whole Church of England, in which respect we may stile it, Cathedram Cathedrarum, The mother of all our Cathedrals.[152]

Others cavilled. The puritan Dr John Burgess of Pembroke College, Oxford, reputedly cast down in the college hall the begging letter circulated by the university's chancellor and demanded that St Paul's be destroyed, since 'there was no authority for sacred buildings in [Biblical] precept, and … the divine majesty could be more rightly worshipped in woods and mountain caves (as in olden times)'. The university authorities insisted on a public recantation, but Burgess fled.[153]

The slow flow of money into the coffers also hinted at discontent – by January 1633 only one small contribution had resulted from the county commissions. Commissioners were instructed to certify the names of any ill-disposed persons to the Privy Council; in 1634, Bartholomew Garwell was forced to confess his 'great error in haueing vttered vnbeseeminge words' and apologize for his 'refractoriness and euill example' in refusing to contribute.[154] Determined individuals could provide a focus for resistance. In the Stour valley, Thomas Cotton (brother-in-law of the puritan John Bastwick, who dismissed Inigo Jones's west front as 'a seat for a priest's arse to sit in') and William Ball – whose contribution of 12d. at Colchester had set a local ceiling on giving to those who thought it bad 'man[n]ores to exceed theire better[es]' – were identified as a particular problem.[155]

Shortfalls in collections led to desperate expedients. In 1635 Bishop Juxon of London commuted public penance for adultery into a £10 fine payable towards the restoration; in 1636 the king decreed that all Court of High Commission fines should be diverted to the campaign for a decade or more.[156] Some litigants would later complain that contributions towards the repair had been required before they could secure absolution.[157]

Even London was backward, only one small sum from one ward having been received by April 1633. This slackness may have reflected suspicion of the king's motives and commitment: in a letter forwarded to the aldermen, Charles told Laud that

> wee are not ignorant what iealousies have beene cast amongst our loving people by some ill affected p[er]sons both to our selfe and that glorious worke, To the worke, as … Not fitt, being a slaunder vpon Gods service, and not to be compassed, being a scandall vpon the Nation. To our selfe, as if … the worke were but p[re]tended … to gett some great so[m]me of money together, and then to turne it to other vses.[158]

The corporation was not the only hindrance: Thomas Edwards, the puritan lecturer at St Botolph without Aldgate and author of *Gangraena*, regarded his lack of cooperation as a badge of honour, boasting later 'I... never gave a penny to the building of Paul's'.[159]

Yet many contemporaries judged the campaign extremely effective. Roger Ley, curate of St Leonard's Shoreditch, thought it a 'great success'; Dugdale wrote in 1658 that 'multitudes' had contributed 'most freely'. Heylyn, Laud's associate and later panegyrist, while noting 'many rubs, and mighty enemies', reported that money had come 'flowing in apace'.[160] Recent historians have been less impressed.[161] But a proper assessment requires the systematic investigation of chapter records, particularly the huge paper ledgers and audit volumes recording monies received. What does such an investigation suggest?[162]

Laud's own commitment is easily demonstrated: he gave £1,331 13s. 4d. between October 1631 and October 1640, one gift being intended for repair of the steeple; the archbishop later bequeathed £800 in case repairs resumed.[163] The general support offered at the outset by the remainder of the episcopate appears to have gradually fractured, though not straightforwardly along theological lines. Although twelve Arminians contributed in more than 70 per cent of the accounting years in which they could do so,[164] three leading anti-Calvinists suddenly abandoned the campaign and four gave nothing.[165] Six Calvinists contributed in most years in which they could; five terminated donations,[166] one of them, John Williams, perhaps doing so in response to the Laudian harassment which caused him to spend much of the 1630s 'either under investigation, on trial, or in prison'.[167] A determination to hold to a shrinking middle ground may at first have encouraged Calvinist contributions, but a threshold seems to have been reached on the eve of the First Bishops' War in 1638–9. What is more remarkable is that some Calvinists, principally Davenant, nonetheless continued to contribute.

The St Paul's chapter themselves gave £50 per annum between 1631 and 1640, and an extra £100 in 1639–40.[168] Just two other chapters (Lichfield and Exeter) made corporate contributions, but only five deans failed to contribute as individuals; the twenty-three contributing deans who remained unmitred during the period averaged an impressive £60 12s. 9d. Several other cathedral clergy made personal contributions, including a Calvinist prebendary of St Paul's, Samuel Fell.[169]

Among the parochial clergy it is striking that clerical donations did not necessarily decline in proportion to distance from the capital. The diocesan clergy of Lincoln, Norwich, Coventry and Lichfield, Carlisle and Durham all underperformed, whereas those of Canterbury and Winchester, but also Chester, exceeded themselves. There was a distinct lack of enthusiasm for the appeal in East Anglia and the Midlands. It is hard to establish whether such variations reflected the attitudes of the clergy themselves or those of their ecclesiastical superiors, although the clergy of Gloucester diocese, who gave nothing, perhaps shared a pervasive puritan sympathy with the marginally more responsive laity of the county. Individual clerical donors not surprisingly included royal and archiepiscopal chaplains. Among them were Christopher Wren's Arminian father, who made four donations,[170] and Dr Cornelius Burgess, who in 1632 contributed £5 to the cathedral in whose history he would shortly play a significant role.[171]

The universities made significant contributions despite being afflicted with fierce theological controversy: £594 came from Oxford and £542 from Cambridge. The most curious university contribution was the nigh £54 donated by Cambridge scholars' servants, indicating the appeal's remarkable social reach.[172] The king was the most generous layman, contributing some £12,421 16s. 2d., of which £9,491 16s. 2d. (over one third of this for the west end restoration) was unambiguously a royal benefaction. Government gave its (tardy) support, the Privy Council forwarding £610 6s. 1d.[173] Few peers dug into their pockets. Seventy-one peers (including some Catholics) contributed overall, individual contributions ranging from Baron Craven's £500 in 1633[174] to eighteen sums of less than £50. More than half of the nobility were thus disinclined to help a project closely associated with Laud and the king. Robert Greville, second Baron Brooke, allegedly wished that 'some of us shall live to see no one stone left upon another of that building'.[175]

The most fruitful lay county collection took place in Middlesex (£2,030); the least successful in Northumberland (£10). Eight English counties contributed higher proportions of the general lay collection than predictable on the basis of near-contemporaneous final Ship Money assessments. Berkshire, Hertfordshire, Kent, Middlesex, Surrey, and Sussex all lie close to London, but County Durham and Somerset do not. The underperformers were Cornwall, Yorkshire and Northumberland, whose coolness surely reflects remoteness; and a cluster of counties in south-central England: Gloucestershire, Bedfordshire, Buckinghamshire, Cambridgeshire, Huntingdonshire, Northamptonshire, Oxfordshire, Warwickshire, and Worcestershire.

Add these results to those for the general clerical collections, and it is apparent that those giving the highest proportion of their taxable wealth were the inhabitants of southern England, becoming less generous from east to west. More significantly, residents of central England were less generous than some living in the peripheries. Even if a contributory factor was administrative incompetence, this in itself perhaps tells us something about perceptions of the cathedral. The English cities deserve separate notice: despite its county's failure, Gloucester supplied a creditable £130. The highest sum came from Bristol (£266), while Oxford's £102 seems a foretoken of its later royalism. Fifteen English cities contributed. Seventeen smaller towns also organized collections; the most successful was Newcastle-upon-Tyne, where the mayor and burgesses between them produced £60 of the £112 raised.

What of London itself? The city's laity raised about £7,130, a considerable achievement. The best response came from the wealthy central wards and those immediately to the north and west but still within the walls. Taking particular note of the number of 'substantial' households as revealed in a 1638 tithe survey, nine wards underperformed and eight overperformed.[176] Apart from an area to the north-east of St Paul's, the overperformers broadly lay in the east of the intra-mural metropolis, whereas the underperformers, saving Bishopsgate, were generally located centrally. Thus the richer citizens were perhaps relatively least generous, although they may also have contributed as individuals or through livery companies, of which four gave £300 or more, while twenty-five gave under £50.

How much money was received altogether? From the accounts it can be deduced that £101,450 4s. 8d. passed into the Chamber of London between May 1631 and November 1644, the bulk of it in 1633–5 and 1636–8. A fresh round of letter-writing saw a significant increase in 1639–40, which then collapsed as the regime began to implode. To raise such a sum in a decade was no mean achievement: after the Restoration it would take nearly twenty years to accumulate a similar sum – and that was largely the product of the coal tax. Some have argued that only the contributions of a few individuals, such as Sir Paul Pindar, prevented utter failure.[177] Pindar's recorded contributions – the finance for the repair of the pulpitum and choir, plus £4,000 for part of the transepts – have been widely (and wildly) exaggerated.[178] Monies from other sources certainly exceeded those from the general collections. Yet the English and Welsh general lay collections together constituted nearly 20 per cent of all receipts. And if we include problematic entries, the general clerical collections and the contributions of London laymen, then we account for a third of the entire fund. In comparison the king provided some 12 per cent, the episcopate and male peerage both less than 10 per cent, and the London livery companies less than 4 per cent. Given other demands on their purse the amount donated by the provincial populace is impressive, especially since many donors can never even have seen the cathedral. And although inequalities of wealth ensured that the largesse of a well-heeled minority outweighed the meagre offerings of the multitude, it is significant that the fund-raising looked beyond the gentry to tap the limited resources of the common people, who were not coerced into payment. Hence, a substantial number of the king's subjects possessed a personal stake in the cathedral's future.

Those who failed to contribute were no doubt partly motivated by fear of an open-ended commitment, localism (some in Lincolnshire emphasized that their own cathedral might suffer 'a more neare approchinge mischife'),[179] and the burden of the Crown's own financial exactions.[180]

Such mundane explanations can suffice to explain the gradual decline in giving. The fascinating question of whether or not anti-Laudianism was an important contributory factor, however, remains as yet incapable of definitive answer. It should be emphasized that St Paul's itself did not experience drastic innovations during the Laudian ascendancy, having long been at the forefront of the new ceremonialism. There are none the less intriguing hints of its impact. A key element in the Laudian programme was the permanent relocation of communion tables (now termed altars) at the east end of chancels in a railed enclosure. In St Paul's the communion table/altar had been repositioned under Elizabeth. In 1633, however, the dean and chapter (particularly the royal chaplains Dean Winiffe and Archdeacon King) commanded the implementation of a similar rearrangement in St Gregory's, which abutted the cathedral fabric and lay within its peculiar jurisdiction. When five parishioners appealed against the alteration, Laud transferred the case to the Privy Council, where the king himself ruled in favour of the capitular authorities. The king subsequently reversed his ruling, and it was probably no coincidence that in 1637, by which time the incident was perhaps embarrassing, the Privy Council ordered the demolition of St Gregory's, ostensibly on the grounds that it compromised the structural integrity of the cathedral.[181] News of the 1633 St Gregory's *cause célèbre* certainly escaped from London, as indicated by the diary of John Rous, a Suffolk minister, who noted that there had been 'Much to doe about ceremonies, high altar and copes, &c at Paules'.[182] A hint of possible consequences for the restoration appeal survives in a poem written around 1635 by Dudley, 3rd Baron North, who opined that

Good works to nurse, made good men ope their purse:
St. *Gregories* curse, may make *Pauls* fare the worse.

Make not them glad who wish St. *Gregory* sad,
For being the Lad, who first turn'd Tables had ...[183]

By 1638, the restoration was so far in hand that another versifier had the cathedral, personified and proud as Punch, singing its own praises:

As famous as I ever have bin
I now shall receive my high renown
And all my honours returned me agen
I am old Paul of London town,
Now God preserve our Gracious King
Lord Mayor and the aldermen
which have been pleased in this noble thing
To give old Paul a new trimming agen.[184]

Such a mood of complacent and triumphant optimism, however, was to be short-lived.

WAR, FIRE AND RECONSTRUCTION

What was St Paul's like on the eve of the Civil War? The metropolitical visitation which Laud imposed on a reluctant chapter in 1636[185] found an establishment at nearly full strength claiming to do its duty. Prebendaries mostly officiated in person, but pluralists retired to the country in the summer or when disease struck, leaving the sub-dean to organize worship. A few absented themselves 'under pretence' of attendance at the Chapel Royal; Laud sought to identify those in fact present at neither. Some key personnel no longer inhabited their official residences, or indeed the close. Residentiaries rented accommodation; the minor canons occupied their college's properties, where the two cardinals rented rooms; and vicars choral lived 'in the towne'. Laud sought to restrain the practice of leasing property – the result was precincts teeming with lay 'inmates', fuelling complaints of the profanation of the churchyard; the cathedral vaults still served as warehouses.[186]

The provision of sermons remained lavish. A lecturer, Stephen Hall, preached thrice weekly in term time, while two others (but, under Donne, the dean and residentiaries themselves) preached alternately on Sunday afternoons. On holy days a dignitary, prebendary or deputy preached in the morning, a lecturer in the afternoon. For the great festivals the bishop (or his substitute) preached in the morning and the dean (or a residentiary) in the afternoon; prebendaries covered the lenten occasions. As for vestments, all usually wore surplices and hoods, but square caps had only been sported on 'extraordinary occasions'; Laud now insisted that caps always be worn to the choir.

With St Paul's effectively a Laudian flagship, protest mounted, evident in libels found about the precincts. One paper of August 1637 asserted that Laud leased the cathedral from the devil, another that 'the Government of the Church of England is a candle in the snuff, going out in a stench'.[187] On 15 October 1640 a mob in search of the bishops invaded the hated Court of High Commission temporarily sitting in the Convocation House;[188] a week later followed a 'great mutiny in Pawle's Church'. During a separatist trial supporters of one defendant stormed the court, causing the judges to flee for their lives, one escaping through a window. The insurgents reportedly tore down the benches, smashed the altar and destroyed books containing the Laudian canons of 1640.[189] As the case continued, on 1 November some sixty 'rude people' ransacked the nearby vicar-general's office assuming that it was connected with the Court of High Commission.[190] Clergy attending Convocation at St Paul's three days later found themselves guarded by horsemen and musketeers.[191]

The cathedral restoration generated more local resentments. In November 1640 the parishioners of St Gregory's complained to the House of Commons that, having recently repaired the church at a cost of some £1,500, the churchwardens had been forced to begin stripping and dismantling the building, causing intolerable inconvenience to a rapidly growing population. A parliamentary committee eventually ruled the demolition illegal, criticizing its promoter, Inigo Jones (Fig. 27), as a 'busie instrument'. Some demanded reconstruction, to which Jones should personally contribute £300; others suggested the allocation of part of the cathedral to the displaced parishioners – the MP Sir Simonds D'Ewes believed that this would better become St Paul's than 'the images that weere sett upp in it', advocating the punishment of those who had made 'an Idoll' of the cathedral. Unexpended funds collected for the repair of St Paul's ultimately financed repairs enabling sermons to be preached in St Gregory's once more by 1651.[192]

Laudian innovations polarized 1640s London.[193] Altars and rails were physically attacked from shortly after the opening of the Long Parliament in November 1640; by the end of 1642 most of London's were probably gone. In 1643 legislative encouragement led to an intensified campaign, which subsequently took on surplices, organs and fonts, all finding fewer defenders than had altars. Presentments against opponents of the prayer book had ceased in 1642, although popular support ensured that it was still used in certain London churches a year later. Meanwhile the Commons actively assisted the systematic ejection of 'undesirable' ministers: pluralists; ineffective or infrequent preachers; and those judged 'scandalous' on account of immorality, the teaching of Arminian or popish doctrine, or the introduction of Laudian ceremonial.

Ninety-nine London ministers were ejected in a campaign peaking in 1643; during the 1640s perhaps 80 per cent of London parishes (excluding Southwark) suffered clerical sequestration. The religious ferment had two further ingredients. The Catholic presence in the metropolis, and the exposure of alleged 'plots', fed fears of a popish coup. Secondly, religious radicals, exiled or forced underground during the 1630s, now resurfaced, organized and proselytized. In the early 1640s perhaps only 1,000 Londoners, generally of middling status, belonged to separatist congregations. As yet relatively untouched by the authorities, these unpopular elements, drawn from a wide area, were growing in prominence.

St Paul's was not immune to the surrounding ructions. A 'fanatiq [and] frantiq' illiterate Sevenoaks husbandman was committed to Bridewell in May 1640 for preaching 'absurdly' in the churchyard; the following January Lord Brooke's chaplain, troubled by the 'great tumult' in St Faith's in the cathedral crypt, refused to preach.[194] When zealots entered St Paul's during a September 1641 service to see if a Commons' resolution condemning rails and the positioning of communion tables against the east wall had been acted upon, they found the city marshal guarding a railed and altarwise table. The visitors promised to set to the task themselves if this was still the case a week thereafter: Dean Winnife ordered the requisite changes.[195] The troublemakers were also rumoured to have intended to deface various ornaments and overthrow the organ,[196] which remained the subject of disparaging separatist preaching. Humphrey Gosnold allegedly told his auditory that 'those...Organs, which are set up in *Pauls* Church, and other places, makes more noyse with their roaring, then all the Bulls of Basan did, when Ogg their King passed by them in tryumph'.[197] On 9 October 1642 the organ only narrowly escaped destruction in a 'riot … of some importance' (during which an officiating minister was allegedly struck) thanks to the 'furious resistance' of opponents of radical reformation.[198] Parliament instructed the Lord Mayor to close the cathedral,[199] the dean and chapter unsuccessfully petitioning the Lords on 1 November for its reopening.[200] Mayor Pennington suffered lampoons:

> 1643: *A Bill on St*. Paul's *Church Door.*
>
> This House is to be let,
> It is both wide, and fair;
> If you would know the price of it,
> Pray ask of Mr. Maior.
> *Isaack Pennington*[201]

The organ was finally demolished by order of a parliamentary committee in 1644.[202]

Such travails, however, were the least of the cathedral's problems. Deans and chapters came under attack both in the London Root and Branch Petition presented with 15,000 signatures to the Commons in December 1640 and in the lost puritan Ministers' Petition and Remonstrance of the following month. In March 1641 godly MPs were to the fore in a discussion on 'The Greatness of the Revenues of Deans and Chapters, the little Use of them, and the great Inconveniences that come by them'.[203] One of four cathedral representatives asked to put their case on 12 May was Dr John Hacket, shortly to become a prebendary of St Paul's (his claim that talk of the suppression of cathedrals had hit the bookselling trade was surely a direct reference to the cathedral); a leading witness for the remonstrants was Cornelius Burgess, shortly to play a very different role in the

27. Inigo Jones, from a miniature by Samuel Cooper. The involvement of Jones, as the King's architect, ensured that the project was identified in the city with the royalist cause. (Private collection)

cathedral's history. Burgess accepted that the application of capitular property to lay uses was sacrilege, but questioned whether cathedrals currently realized the lofty ideals of their defenders.[204] The remonstrants apparently wished cathedral posts to be annexed to city parishes, with their holders, better integrated into their urban milieu and more active as preachers, assisting the bishop in diocesan administration. Meanwhile not dissimilar proposals emerged from discussions in the Lords to which Hacket and Burgess again both contributed, and by the end of the year a failed bill had offered a combination of an enhanced role for cathedral clergy in diocesan administration and measures to limit the damage pluralism caused to parochial interests.[205] Others, whose views were expressed in an unsuccessful bill approved in the Commons in mid 1641, envisaged 'the utter abolishing … of all … deans and chapters, archdeacons, prebendaries, chanters … [and] canons'. The 'Episcopall partie' had again to see off plans for disendowment in the Grand Remonstrance of December 1641.[206] Crucially, however, in demands received in April 1641, the Scots made the bringing of the Church of England into conformity with the presbyterian Church of Scotland the price of their military assistance to parliament, tipping the scales towards not just Root and Branch reform, but reform on a presbyterian model. To the accompaniment of bonfires and bell-ringing throughout London ('ordered cunningly' by Pennington, noted Laud), bishops, deans and chapters were voted down in the House of Commons on 1 September 1642.[207] A resolution to sequestrate their incomes followed, while the bill abolishing the institutional structure of the established church was passed by both Houses on 26 January 1643.

Royal assent was never obtained, but this did not prevent parliament from seizing capitular assets. In May 1643, at least one person believed that the imminent demolition of Cheapside Cross by the London Common Council signalled that 'Paules is soone after to follow'.[208] What actually happened was bad enough. On 2 January 1643 the Commons resolved that the deanery should become a prison.[209] In May a Commons' committee ordered the burning of the cathedral's copes; the gold thus extracted to be sold for the benefit of the Irish poor.[210] In 1644 ornaments were confiscated: a 'Chest, or Silver Vessel' was to be sold to provide the necessaries for 'the Train of Artillery', while the proceeds from the sale of a mitre and crosier were be disposed of by the Commons.[211] In September authority was given for up to £3,000 of the restoration fund to be diverted (supposedly temporarily) to pay troops' wages; then £100 per annum was redirected from the capitular revenues to support parochial ministry.[212] It was probably with a view to eventual liquidation that the Committee for St Paul's in February 1645 called for the sorting, surveying and safe-keeping of tools and materials assembled for the repairs, the resulting inventories revealing that some 2,982 tons of Portland stone stood unused, as well as much timber, engine parts, and lead, iron and glass, distributed around the cathedral.[213]

The spoliation of cathedral property was matched by the harassment of the senior clergy in post in 1640–2. All but three of the eleven dignitaries had been preferred under Charles I, two being appointed after the beginning of the Long Parliament among a cluster of promotions possibly intended to increase the ecclesiastical regime's reputation: the popular preacher Josias Shute as archdeacon of Colchester and the Arminian Richard Steward as dean, succeeding Winniffe (both in 1642).[214] Of the prebendaries Zachary Goddell, the longest serving cathedral cleric of the seventeenth century at his death in 1660, had been appointed in 1590;[215] eleven had been appointed under James and twenty-two under Charles, mostly through episcopal collations.[216] Four appointments, however, had been made by royal grant. Three are easily explicable: William Bray (1632), chaplain to Laud, Thomas Wykes (1636), chaplain to Juxon, and Richard Steward (1642), clerk of the Closet; less so is the puritan Robert Thompson (1631). Of 381 St Paul's prebendal incumbencies occurring between 1540 and 1714, at least twenty-two resulted from such grants, eight under the routine arrangements obtaining during vacancies in the see. But even Henry VIII had only intervened thrice, making remarkable the fact that Charles I broke the convention of episcopal patronage no less than four times in the eleven years prior to March 1642, when the king recommended Hacket for a vacant residentiaryship seemingly already disposed of by the pledges of the prebendal electorate.[217]

The Laudian 'infection' produced by these appointments provoked puritan attacks. Richard Steward was never installed as dean, and ended up a leading figure among the exiles in Paris, eulogized by John Evelyn as 'a very great loss to the whole Church'.[218] Thomas Paske, archdeacon of London, lost his parochial livings and appeared before the House of Lords in 1642 claiming to be troubled by the unauthorized publication of a letter in which he had described the damage wrought by parliamentary troops at Canterbury Cathedral.[219] Laud's relative and ally Edward Layfield, archdeacon of Essex, was charged by the Commons in 1640 with introducing Laudian ceremonies and identified as 'notoriously disaffected to Religion'; he went on to suffer several sequestrations on various grounds of pastoral neglect, reputedly being imprisoned in most of the London jails and even on a ship.[220] After deprivation from his parochial benefices

Richard Clewet (or Cluet), archdeacon of Middlesex, became dependent on doles from a former parish. Even the Calvinist archdeacon of Colchester, Josias Shute, was imprisoned for failing to contribute to the parliamentary war effort.[221]

The prebendaries fared little better. William Haywood was deprived of St Giles in the Fields for introducing Laudian ceremonies and for other offences including preaching against parliament; he eventually retired to Wiltshire to keep a school.[222] Three prebendaries – Robert Cottesford, John Montford (Mountfort) and Richard Taylor – feature in John White's *First Century of Scandalous, Malignant Priests* (1643); Montford was another to endure imprisonment.[223] Charges of Laudian innovation were levelled against many other prebendaries,[224] among them Joseph Crowther who in 1651 became chaplain in France to the future James II.[225] Others ended up less comfortably: Thomas Soame, formerly a prolific pluralist and an outspoken royalist, died in 1649 with personal effects valued at only £20.[226] In fact only one dignitary and four prebendaries in post in 1642 escaped deprivation or sequestration.[227] Much less is known about the minor clergy, although Stephen Hall, the lecturer, suffered sequestration from his Cambridgeshire living and according to Walker was imprisoned for more than three years in Southwark Compter.[228] In 1644 and 1645 the Committee for Sequestrations ordered the Lord Mayor and aldermen to pay the inferior personnel their stipends, while several individuals were granted money in 1655 and 1657 by the Trustees for the Maintenance of Ministers.[229]

The vacuum left by the departure of senior clergy was filled in December 1643 by the parliamentary appointment of a public lecturer: Cornelius Burgess.[230] The cathedral was now at a low ebb, one commentator earlier that year lamenting that

> I see *Religion* in torne ragged weeds, and with slubber'd eyes sitting upon *Weeping-Crosse*, and wringing her hands, to see her chiefest Temple (*Pauls Church*) where God Almightie was us'd to be serv'd constantly thrice a day, and was the Rendezvouz, and ... Mother Church, standing open to receive all commers ..., to be now shut up, and made only a thorowfare for Porters; to see those scaffolds, the expence of so many thousand pounds, to lye a rotting; to see her chiefest *lights* like to be extinguished; to see her famous learned Divines dragg'd to prison, and utterly depriv'd of the benefit of the Common Law ...: Methinks, ... I see *Religion* packing up, and preparing to leave this Island ..., crying out, that this is a Countrey fitter for *Atheists* than *Christians* to live in; for God ... is here made the greatest *Malignant*, in regard his House is plunder'd more than any.[231]

Burgess's appointment itself, however, could seem to others the worst development yet. His fiery preaching provoked ridicule:

> Wee'l break the Windows which the Whore
> Of *Babylon* hath painted,
> And when the Popish Saints are down,
> Then *Burges* shall be Sainted;
> There's neither Crosse nor Crucifix
> shall stand for men to see,
> *Romes* trash and trumpery shall go down,
> *And hey then up go we.*[232]

Burgess was a phenomenon, 'a personality of national stature'. Despite appointment as a chaplain-in-ordinary soon after Charles I's accession, he had condemned Laudianism in apocalyptic terms in Fast Sermons delivered to MPs in 1640, calling on the

Commons 'to form a national covenant with God to carry the English Reformation to its fruition'. He would present 'the drift toward civil war as an extension of the cosmic war against antichrist', and regularly lead intimidating 'tumults out of the city ... to the Parliament doors, to see that the godly party ... might not be outvoted'. In 1642–3 he served as chaplain to the earl of Essex's regiment, and acted as an assessor for the Westminster Assembly at least until 1646.[233] He nevertheless preached frequently at St Paul's. Soon after his appointment as public lecturer he was granted by far the largest salary paid to any lecturer in the period 1560–1662: £400, with a convenient dwelling.[234]

This generosity no doubt reflected the authorities' need for a formidable and crowd-pulling preacher to compensate for the physical loss of Paul's Cross. Preaching had been transferred to the choir during the restoration work.[235] In 1635 labourers had 'pulld downe ... the Roomes where the Prebends of the Church, the Doctors of the Law; and the Parishioners of St Faiths did sett to heare Sermons at St Pauls crosse'; the pulpit itself was probably demolished in 1641.[236] It was nevertheless clearly intended that Paul's Cross would be restored. In 1643 the Commons acceded to a petition from the Court of Aldermen that the Lord Mayor and aldermen nominate and appoint men to preach every Sunday 'att the place to bee appointed in Paules Church yard', and 'vntill that place bee prepared and fitted for the purpose', at some other appropriate location.[237] The Court of Aldermen had earlier ordered the removal of 'Stones rubbish pales and Shedds' littering the churchyard while 'a...fitt place w[i]thin the said yard for a pulpitt to stand in' was identified.[238] A newsletter asserts that in February 1644 the itinerant Antinomian preacher John Simpson had preached 'at *Pauls* Crosse', but in reality he had merely utilized the site of the former pulpit, now a thoroughfare.[239] One must conclude that the pulpit was probably never restored. Burgess himself held forth in the eastern choir, walled off from the rest of the interior and entered via a window.[240]

Burgess was confirmed in the St Paul's lectureship in April 1645, when parliament also decreed that he should occupy the now dilapidated deanery. Some £535 (plus £80 in petty expenses) had been spent on the restoration by October 1645. Burgess himself paid part of this before presenting the corporation with the bill for the remainder, at which point the Court of Aldermen decided that the lecturer should be reimbursed £402 out of the cathedral's rents.[241]

Burgess's activities were overseen by a four-man 'Committee for Paules'.[242] Parliament too kept close watch: in 1646 the Lords commended to the Lord Mayor the dismantling of the remainder of the steeple.[243] Things could still go amiss: the library, plate, 'Rich pulpit Cloths' and utensils disappeared prior to the corporation's seizure of the property, perhaps taken by a former committee for sequestration, or simply embezzled by cathedral staff.[244]

A new wave of iconoclasm swept the city in 1643–4, the prayer book was abolished in 1645, and there were more sequestrations, increasingly on grounds of 'malignancy' – speaking or acting against parliament. The Westminster Assembly devised a presbyterian ecclesiastical polity. London's parishes were notionally assigned to twelve classes constituting a single province; eight were established. St Paul's joined fifteen parishes in the First Classis, covering an area which, judging by signatures to a 1646 presbyterian petition to the Common Council, was a 'focus of high presbyterian activity' – this perhaps explains the district's poor showing in Laud's 1630s fund-raising campaign.[245] The fact that a 1652 certifi-

cate outlining the state of the First Classis was penned at the cathedral suggests that it may have served as the classis' administrative headquarters; from May 1647 the provincial synod's earliest sessions convened in the former Convocation House.[246]

The new presbyterianism proved divisive. One challenge to the regime came from Independency, whose limited numbers were belied by its increasing boldness and overestimates of its strength; other Londoners increasingly turned against the sects. The fate of St Paul's, situated as it was amid a heavy concentration of radical activists should be seen in this context of growing diversity and militancy.[247] In 1647 the army emerged as a radical political force, marching on London when Westminster politics collapsed. Thus began a sequence of events that resulted in the cathedral's nave being used as a barracks and stable, essentially in an effort to bully the corporation into contributing funds for the army's subsistence. That troops were to be quartered in St Paul's was reported before the outbreak of the Second Civil War which climaxed in the Cromwellian victory at Preston in August 1648, celebrated at the cathedral in a service attended by the livery companies.[248] Two foot regiments, cavalry and artillery finally arrived on 8 December 1648, transforming the cathedral into a 'filthy *Stable* ... filled ... with Hay and Horses, ... so that of a *House of Prayer it is become a Den of Thieves*'. Troops obliged to sleep on the cold stone floors in the absence of the bedding that had been ordered nearly burnt it down by constructing pyres from scaffolding and 'other cumbustible matter' before the Lord Mayor promised to provide coal.[249] Yet preaching continued: Nathaniel Homes, Independent pastor and preacher to Colonel Scroope's regiment, delivered a sermon on 11 December, causing one writer to aver that the desecration had been exaggerated.[250]

Hostile contemporaries railed against the soldiers' supposed antics. In January 1649 a newspaper claimed that

> The Saints in *Pauls* were the last weeke teaching their Horses to ride up the *great Steps* that lead into the *Quire*, where (as they derided) they might perhaps learne to *Chaunt* an *Antheme*: but one of them fell, and broke both his *Leg* and the *Neck* of his *Rider*, which hath spoiled his *Cha[n]ting*, for he was buried on *Saturday* night last. A just *Iudgement* of God on such a prophane and *Sacrilegious* wretch ...[251]

Others complained that the cathedral had become

> a jakes for the worser beasts their masters, whose religion is Rebellion, whose piety is to blaspheme God [and] Revile ... the King ... it seems that this last week, one of their Mares foaling in the Church, the souldiers took upon them to Baptize the Colt, and taking one *Hawes* and *Cobitt*, made them stand for the Godfathers, and one *Rachell Barber* (one of their Ammunition bagages) for the godmother; whereupon one of them making his Cloak into the fashion of a Canonicall Gowne, took one of his fellowes Head-pieces, who was absent, pissed therein, and ... began to scoffe ...[252]

There was also more routine vandalism. In 1650 statues of the king and his father were contemptuously 'throwne downe';[253] a year later the churchyard's inhabitants secured a proclamation to prevent troops becoming a nuisance there, proscribing (among other activities) random searches of passers by and the noisy nocturnal games (such as nine-pins) that disturbed the rest of the 'weake and indisposed'.[254]

The abolition of deans and chapters finally received legislative sanction in 1649; two years later the wholesale demolition of cathedrals was being canvassed, including St Paul's. In this period of the cathedral's history lie the origins of the claim by a gullible nineteenth-century historian that 'Oliver Cromwell entered into a negotiation with a chief rabbi for authorising the immigration of Jews from Holland in consideration of receiving £200,000 and granting old St Paul's to become a synagogue'. In an eighteenth-century variant of the tale, Jews had promised £500,000 in return for the repeal of penal laws and the use of the Bodleian Library for 'their Traffick'; once more, St Paul's would become a synagogue. Both versions probably derive from Clement Walker's 1649 *History Of Independency*, where the asking price was £700,000. But although the rumour was widely current in the mid seventeenth century, reliable evidence there is none. The story is most significant in demonstrating the extent to which even the degraded cathedral symbolized England's Christian heritage.[255]

Such associations no doubt increased the anguish caused by the indignities heaped on the edifice. Roger Ley thought 'the most hateful sight I ever saw' was the use of one chapel 'albeit shut off by a door with iron and brass bolts, [as] a privy'.[256] Heylyn recorded that

> The Pavement of the Church [was] digged up, and sold to the wealthier Citizens, for beautifying their Country-Houses; The Floor converted into saw-pits in many places ... The Lead torn off in some places also; the Timber and Arches of the Roof being thereby exposed to Wind and Weather; Part of the Stone-work which supported the Tower or Steeple, fallen down, and threatning the like Ruine unto all the rest; The gallant Portico at the West-end ... obscured first by a new House looking towards Ludgate; and afterward turned into an Exchange for Haberdashers of small Wares, Hosiers, and such Petit Chapmen: And finally, the whole Body of it converted to a Stable ... for the better awing of that City ...[257]

During 1649 Burgess found the capital's religious climate increasingly uncongenial, and resolved to retire to Wells, where his turbulent career would enter a new phase. Nevertheless he not only retained his original lectureship, but acquired another, Dr White's, in 1654. Presumably now an absentee, he was finally removed from his lucrative positions in 1656. Samuel Annesley, former chaplain to the earl of Warwick, succeeded him in 1657, but at the much reduced salary of £120 per annum.[258]

The cathedral's institutional dissolution and consequent lack of internal records obscures its history during much of the Commonwealth and Protectorates. Huygens tells us that in 1651–2 the Lord Mayor and aldermen worshipped in a 'neatly restored' chapel at the building's eastern extremity, probably St Dunstan's, assembling behind a curtain before taking their reserved seats, indicated by tapestries.[259] The cathedral remained the city's premier meeting place and notice board: it was here that the eccentric millenarian and pantheist 'Thereau John' (Thomas Tany) hoped to dispute with representatives of the universities in 1652.[260]

The cathedral's empty vastness commended its use as a meeting place for separatist congregations. In 1653 the Council of State agreed that Captain Edmund Chillenden's congregation could meet 'without interruption' in the former St George's Chapel, now the Stone Chapel.[261] The presence of Chillenden, a 'Fifth Monarchist' with a long history of religious radicalism, inevitably generated trouble. On 16 October 1653 a mob of apprentices appeared outside the Stone Chapel, ostensibly to dislodge Chillenden and his fellow Baptists. Chillenden was

insulted; stones were thrown through the windows; there was retaliation. The troops who eventually dispersed the apprentices demanded of sheriffs sent by the city fathers worshipping in the choir that they be disciplined. When a sheriff queried on what authority Chillenden employed the chapel, he raised his pistol and responded 'By this authority!' A committee of the Council of State responded to this affair (which cost several lives and caused severe injuries) with a declaration forbidding the disturbance of peaceable assemblies, so long as they were neither popish nor idolatrous. The incident may also have encouraged Cromwell to contemplate the construction of a 'Citadell' 'to bridle the City of London', which John Aubrey suggested 'was to have been the Crosse building of St Paule's church'.[262]

In 1657, the Council of State approved the creation of another meeting place for a separatist congregation belonging to the very John Simpson – now a Baptist – who in 1644 had preached on the site of Paul's Cross. It was ultimately decided to locate the meeting on the site of the former Convocation House, now *sans* both floor and roof, although it seems that construction never commenced.[263]

Those with an eye to prognostications of 'regime change' were now beginning to look for events 'savouring of prodigy'. One such was the collapse of part of the cathedral roof in January 1654 – no prodigy in reality, since supporting scaffolding had lately been removed. Several persons were killed; one newsletter claims that about thirty children had been buried in the rubble. The Lord Mayor and aldermen petitioned Cromwell to re-use the fallen lead for pipes to improve the city's water supply.[264] England was now lurching dramatically from one governmental crisis to another as the republican regime tortuously negotiated its way through a bewildering variety of experiments, challenges and controversies. The regime became paranoid. Convinced that the exiled Charles II was poised to invade, Cromwell in December 1657 ordered the Corporation of London 'to prepare a convenient place in or neere Poules church for the quartering of 600 horse and foote for the safety of the Citty'. St Paul's once again became a stable.[265]

Cromwell's death and the failure of his son's brief protectorate deepened the crisis. London emerged as a locus of opposition to the army, with the Baptist sectaries the only reliable supporters of the Committee of Safety now in charge. The Common Council received petitions from householders and seamen calling for the expulsion of the soldiers quartered at St Paul's and elsewhere.[266] Since the city was daily expected 'to bee in eares with the souldjery', there was talk of putting 'hand granadoes in Pauls and other places to fire the Citty if they should stir'; according to a letter of 16 December 1659 several loads had indeed been sent into the cathedral.[267] On 2 February 1660 General Monck's men marched triumphantly into Whitehall. Authority now rested with the Rump Parliament restored on 26 December and a reconstituted Council of State. On 12 February Monck accompanied the Lord Mayor to a sermon at St Paul's; then on 28 February, a solemn day of thanksgiving for the re-admission of excluded members of the Long Parliament, he joined 'a great auditory of select persons' to hear Dr John Gauden preach 'an excellent sermon, tending to loyalty'.[268] Events were now moving rapidly towards a restoration of the monarchy. The reconstituted Long Parliament dissolved itself on 16 March 1660, having issued writs for what would be known as the Convention Parliament. The prospects for cathedrals were improving.

28.   St Paul's ablaze during the Great Fire of London, 1666, from a contemporary painting. (Museum of London)

Restoration and destruction

On 8 May 1660 Charles II was proclaimed king in London. Two days later, on a day of solemn thanksgiving, Richard Baxter, the nonconformist Kidderminster divine and apostle of reconciliation, preached at St Paul's before the Lord Mayor, aldermen and livery companies.[269] When Charles arrived in the capital on 29 May, he was presented with a sumptuous Bible while the whole company of London ministers, assembled on a special platform outside St Paul's, looked on.[270]

Preaching at the cathedral in the immediate aftermath of the proclamation, Dr Thomas Pierce, a victim of puritan persecution, was strikingly outspoken in calling for a 'petition for the restoration of Episcopacy, a divine institution'.[271] It proved impossible to attain a meaningful consensus in fashioning a religious settlement; at least 845 ministers were deprived over the next two years. Leading presbyterians may partly have been alienated by the surprisingly quick recovery of deans and chapters, and no doubt feared being outnumbered in an overwhelmingly traditional hierarchy.[272] If so, St Paul's probably played a determinative role, for the chapter was among the earliest to function again after the Restoration, granting a lease on 30 August 1660.[273]

Nationally, by May 1660 some two-thirds of cathedral chapter posts stood vacant by the deaths of deprived clergy. Patronage generally lay with the Crown, which was swamped by unsolicited requests for specific posts, many of which succeeded, despite the petitioners' lack of previous capitular experience and their service under the puritan regime: of eight men nominated to the Canterbury chapter, for instance, five had effectively 'collaborated'.

Indeed it has been suggested that such a pattern of preferment indicates that the king did not wish chapters to become 'the stronghold of the more extreme episcopalian clergy'.[274]

But St Paul's was different. Here capitular office was normally in the gift of the bishop – and Juxon, one of the few surviving pre-war bishops, made appointments almost immediately. Many former officeholders were restored, including the archdeacons of London, Essex, and Colchester and the chancellor. Three rank-and-file prebendaries briskly reclaimed their posts, and Juxon filled the remaining sixteen prebends between 14 and 27 August 1660. All but five of these new appointees[275] feature in the standard biographical register of mid seventeenth-century episcopalian sufferers.[276] Gilbert Sheldon, Juxon's successor in autumn 1660, followed a similar course, five out of his eight appointees displaying clear episcopalian credentials.[277] Thus, as a 'stronghold' of episcopalianism, the St Paul's chapter differed markedly from those reconstituted by the Crown.

Two staunch royalists first presided over the Restoration chapter. Matthew Nicholas, formerly dean of Bristol, had apparently been granted the deanery by Charles I, but only came to occupy it, aged and infirm, in July 1660. On his death in August 1661 Charles nominated John Barwick, before the Civil War the protégé and chaplain of Bishop Morton of Durham. He had been employed by the exiled court during the last year of the Interregnum to attempt to induce the surviving bishops to consecrate new prelates. Having turned down a bishopric himself, he was now a reforming (or restoring) dean of Durham and royal chaplain. In spite of poor health, he set out to continue reform upon his removal to London.[278] Barwick died in 1664 and was succeeded by the future nonjuring archbishop William Sancroft, who scarcely covered himself in glory by remaining secluded at Tunbridge Wells and then Durham throughout the Great Plague of 1665, in which several of the cathedral's dependents perished.[279]

The most significant challenge now facing the dean and chapter was to restore traditional worship in a city imbued with a pronounced presbyterian ethos. By late 1661 it was clear that the country as a whole would accept nothing less than the re-establishment of the Church of England, as enacted by what became known as the Clarendon Code (1661–5). Under its centrepiece, the Act of Uniformity (1662), over a third of London's ministers were ejected. Inevitably, the settlement's uncompromising nature provoked a backlash. In January 1661, St Paul's was occupied by a Fifth Monarchist insurrection, perhaps fifty strong, led by Thomas Venner, a London cooper who believed that Christ's reign on earth could be precipitated by an armed rebellion of saints. As trained bands and armed volunteers gathered to expel them, the Vennerites retreated, but by the time they were hunted down a few days later, the city had been panicked by exaggerated reports of the scale of the rising. The government responded by prohibiting all unauthorized meetings and all religious services not held in churches, or in private houses, attended only by residents. By the end of February, over 4,688 Quakers had been imprisoned nationally.[280] St Paul's featured in another protest when two female Quakers disrupted a service: one, clad in sackcloth with her face blackened, poured blood onto the altar before addressing the congregation. It must have been a startling sight, not least because, according to a 1662 Quaker pamphlet, the woman's hair also dripped blood.[281]

Amid these dramas, pre-war practice was gradually reintroduced in the cathedral. After so long an absence, the rituals of Dean Barwick's election, confirmation and installation were sufficiently novel for one observer to recount each in some detail; another ritual, the Lord Mayor's ceremonial visit to St Paul's during his procession, was restored shortly after.[282] In services, the prayer book had already been reintroduced in May 1661, when the organ was recommissioned.[283] Barwick set about restoring frequent communions. He also made tireless efforts to reform abuses such as those afflicting the college of minor canons, whose corporate revenues had decayed during the puritan revolution, partly through misappropriation; membership too had dwindled, while irregularities marred the few appointments made since the early 1640s. Bishop Sheldon also played his part: concerned to integrate the cathedral into London's religious life, he scheduled one of four new weekly public lectures to be held there.[284]

The cathedral environs also required attention. In October 1661 a royal proclamation ordered the removal of the market transferred during the Protectorate to the churchyard, now a dumping ground for refuse. Secular structures had encroached once again, unlicensed buildings pressing against the cathedral walls; in July 1662, the chapter authorized a clean-up.[285]

The main obstacle to complete rehabilitation was the lamentable condition of the fabric. As early as February 1659 the House of Commons was warned that 'If you go about to do any thing with it now, all the workmen in the world will tell you the foundation is rotten.'[286] Three years later *On the Fall of the Southside of S. Paul's Cathedrall* discussed either the collapse of January 1654 or a more recent catastrophe:

> Homer's vast Illiads found so small a Cell,
> They were recluse to th' Cloister of a Shell.
> Their Fate attends this Ruine; *Pauls* must be
> Unto it self both URN and ELEGIE.
> But must the Marble from thy Carkass rent,
> Thy Glory once, now turn thy Monument?
> Can there no Sheet, or Sere-cloath be allow'd,
> But thy own Lead to be thy Fun'rall Shrowd?[287]

This situation required improvisation, such as a makeshift choir based on Burgess's preaching area (p. 182). In October 1661, however, the king decreed that renovation would be partly funded from arrears of impropriations not pardoned by the Act of Oblivion, supplemented by the unexpended monies formerly set aside to augment ministers' maintenance; then, on 18 April 1663, he granted a commission for the collection of funds.[288]

Restoration began in earnest in August 1663, but the appeal failed to generate receipts until a year later.[289] In the capital fundraising was no doubt hampered by a dispute that arose when the Lord Mayor and aldermen, beneficent though tactless, sent in workmen to provide seating for them in the east end, instructing them 'to set up the Citty armes over the head of the seat made for the Lord Mayor'. This unprecedented act was interpreted by the dean and chapter (who had not been consulted) as a deliberate challenge to the cathedral's autonomy. In conciliatory gestures, the corporation successfully begged for retrospective consent while the chapter agreed to the collection of poor relief in the cathedral on the day of humiliation appointed for the death of King Charles. But Barwick and his colleagues were determined that the city authorities should not pay for the seats, lest a financial obligation preface political interference.[290] The contretemps may have had a lasting effect, for the corporation made no recorded contribution to the restoration prior to the Great Fire.

Some £6,031 was collected by June 1666, £2,450 from the dean and chapter themselves. Fourteen other donors were headed by the king (£1,627), with Bishop (later Archbishop) Sheldon providing £869; only two other bishops made donations, although Brian Duppa, the late bishop of Winchester, bequeathed £300. If any general collections were attempted, they failed: just £14 emerged from the single see of Coventry and Lichfield. The other contributors were all laymen, both eminent (Lord Chancellor Clarendon giving £50) and obscure (an esquire named Cole giving £10).[291] Despite the implication that a full restoration would not become feasible for some time, John Evelyn was apparently sanguine about plans to substitute 'a noble *Cupola*' for the tower when, as one of three project surveyors, he inspected the cathedral on 27 August 1666.[292]

A week later, the prospects looked very different. Old St Paul's was destroyed in the Great Fire of London, which broke out on 2 September 1666. Although the fire began in the eastern city, a severe drought, a strong easterly wind and the quantity of combustible materials lying in riverside warehouses ensured that the conflagration spread towards the cathedral. Stonebuilt churches, above all St Paul's, with its immensely thick walls and surrounding open spaces, appeared to offer some protection. Churchyard booksellers deposited their wares in the crypt alongside piles of cloth, while stopping up the least route 'through which the smallest spark might penetrate'. At about 8.00 p.m. on 4 September, however, some burning matter momentarily settled on the cathedral's roof, 'already scorched …

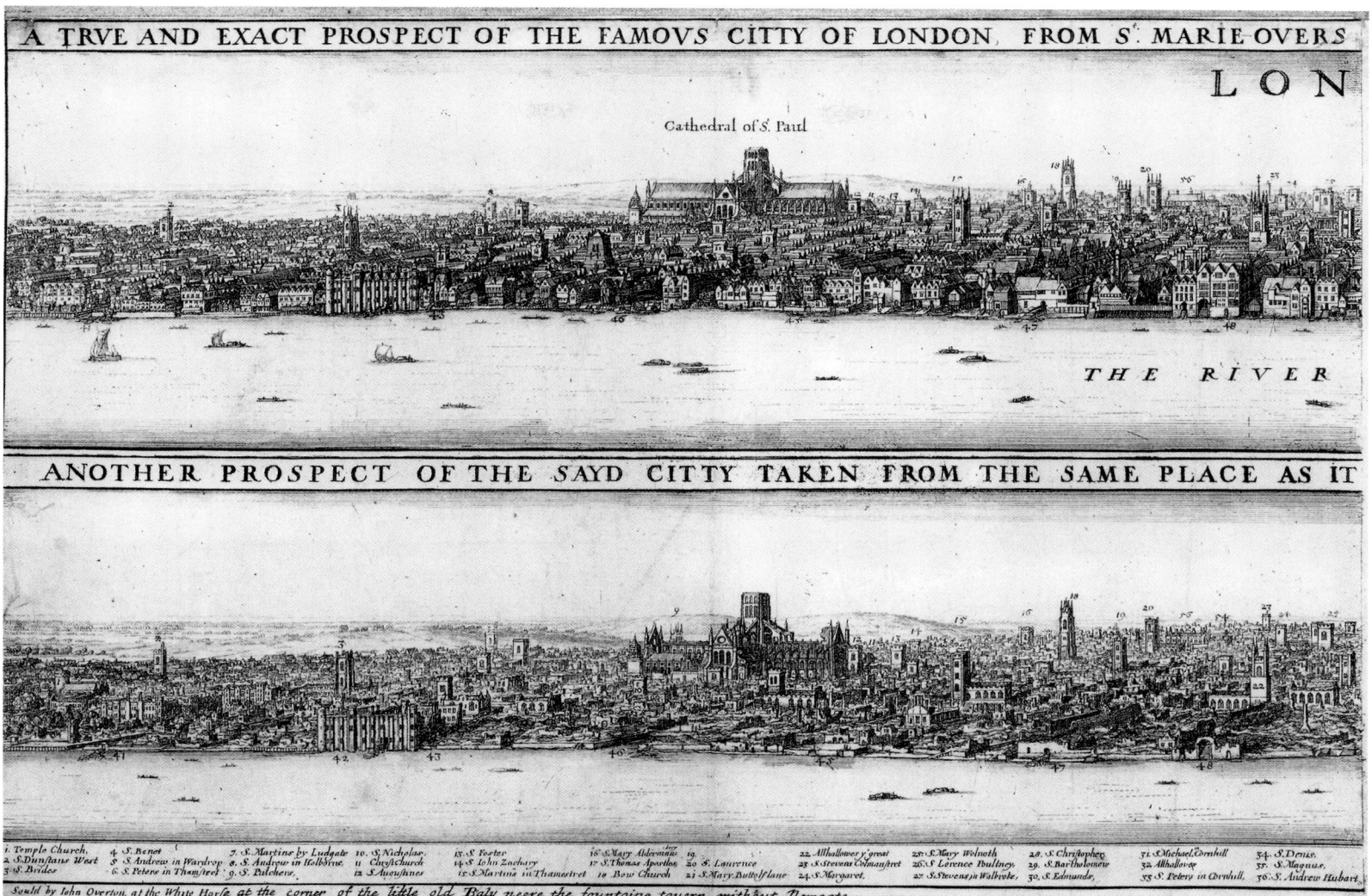

A TRVE AND EXACT PROSPECT OF THE FAMOVS CITTY OF LONDON, FROM S. MARIE OVERS

LON

Cathedral of S. Paul

THE RIVER

ANOTHER PROSPECT OF THE SAYD CITTY TAKEN FROM THE SAME PLACE AS IT

Sould by Iohn Overton, at the White Horse at the corner of the little old Baly neere the fountaine tauern without Newgate

29.   Etchings by Hollar showing twin views of the City of London with the cathedral in its context before and after the Great Fire of 1666. (GL)

by the violent heat of the air'. It ignited the fabric. Scaffolds erected to assist the restoration assisted the fire's rapid spread. The roof collapsed; stones flew like grenades. Heavy blocks smashed the floor and exposed St Faith's to the inferno: its contents burned for a whole week. On 6 September, the surrounding ground almost scorched the shoes of the schoolboy William Taswell, who nearly fainted from the overpowering heat and was amazed to see molten bell metal. Masonry still fell noisily from the ruinous walls; he observed the corpse of an old woman, 'whole as to skin, meagre as to flesh, yellow as to colour … Her clothes were burnt, and every limb reduced to a coal'. A day later John Evelyn described the 'beautifull Portico … rent in pieces'; 'all the ornaments, Columns, freezes, Capitels & proje[c]tures of massie Portland stone' dislodged; and the roof lead wholly melted. In fact the lead over the east-end altar was untouched. And Dean Barwick's physician brother, like others, found providential the survival not only of the rafters and lead over the place in which the dean had 'pour[ed] out his eucharistic vows', but also of a little oratory where he had regularly said private prayers. Another curious survival was the perfectly preserved body of Robert Braybrooke, bishop of London until his death in 1404, which emerged from the disintegration of his tomb to face the gawps of the crowd.[293]

How did Londoners react to the loss of St Paul's? Sir Philip Warwick was doubtless not alone in thinking the fire providential, cleansing the edifice from the 'contamination' of the Civil War.[294] Others may have found their world-view badly shaken, in that St Paul's had quite simply been a measure of things. Thus in 1635 Sir William Brereton had judged the eight 'great and stately pillars' of Durham Cathedral to be 'as great as Paul's'; in 1652 Salisbury Cathedral was thought 'the best constructed in all England' save for St Paul's; in 1646 in Switzerland Evelyn saw a horse plummet 'more than thrice the height of St Paules'. Now the yardstick was gone.[295]

Rebuilding

The remaining early-modern history of St Paul's is largely the story of the construction of Wren's masterpiece (pp. 186–219). But again the financing of the work has its own story to tell.

There were essentially four sources of funds. The king's commission of 1663 continued to elicit gifts. In June 1667 the dean and chapter forwarded £226 raised from the sale of material salvaged from demolished houses and then (if erratically) sustained annual payments of £50 until 1677. Dean Sancroft gave £450 in 1675; £100 came from his predecessor's executors. This time the episcopate was generous. Sheldon alone supplied £1,300 between 1668 and 1676, while many others either maintained subscriptions or made occasional gifts, typically of £50 a time; St Paul's also benefited from several episcopal legacies – thus £800 came from Juxon's estate in 1676–7. It became customary for each new archbishop and bishop to present £50 (later £100) to the fund in lieu of the gloves formerly given to guests attending consecration din-

30. The cathedral from the north-west, by Antonio Canaletto, 1754. (Paul Mellon Collection, Yale Center for British Art)

ners, this alone raising £400 in the decade from 1668. Layfolk were no less munificent: £600 received in 1678 was part of the bequest of Edith Chafein of Guildford.[296]

Secondly, a duty levied on coal provided the lion's share of the funds. Such a levy (of 1s. per chaldron) had been instituted in 1667 for the reconstruction of secular properties. In 1670 an additional duty of 2s. per chaldron was introduced, of which three-sixteenths was allocated to the cathedral. From 1677 the same proportional allocation was applied to the original levy. The 1685 Coal Dues Act not only extended the levy until 1700, but also assigned 60 per cent to St Paul's, reducing the share allocated to parish churches, now mostly rebuilt. Although an act of 1697 cut the levy to 1s. per chaldron and trimmed St Paul's share, it was once more extended, this time to 1716. However, a further duty of 2s. per chaldron, wholly appropriated to St Paul's, was introduced for the years 1708 to 1716 by a statute of 1702. Obscurity surrounds the process by which the coal duty

thereafter became a long-term feature of the cathedral's annual income.

It has been calculated that the levy contributed £3,415 to the cathedral between 1 May and 29 September 1670. In the subsequent six accounting years the annual yield averaged £4,053. For the decade after the 1677 changes to the rate income averaged £5,518 per annum. The total sum received across both tax periods was £88,490, from which the cathedral's contribution to the costs of collection must be deducted. Thereafter the levy awaits its historian. Income fluctuated due to changing demand, according to the severity of the winter; wartime disruption of the coal trade; and the effects of evasion and fraud. On the other side, London's growth served to increase the potential yield.[297] The variations from month to month inevitably meant that the pace of construction was less than smooth.

Work on the cathedral's east end began in June 1675.[298] By 1679 the coal duty account had been reduced to a balance of

31. William Sherlock, dean of St Paul's
1691–1707

32.   View of the chapter house on the north side of St Paul's Churchyard, *c.* 1720. Engraving by
John Harris. (GL)

£971 by disbursements of £34,271.[299] It was obvious that additional funding was essential. In 1678 the commissioners therefore
turned to a third expedient: public subscriptions. The king and
the duke of York promised £1,000 and £200 a year respectively;
prominent noblemen, including the earl of Danby, signed up for
annual sums of less than or equal to the £100 to which
Archbishop Sancroft and Bishop Henry Compton of London
committed themselves.[300] The dean and chapter renewed their
former annual subscription of £50; only two archdeacons and
two prebendaries also subscribed as individuals.[301] Although eight
more of their colleagues may have subscribed during the next few
years, the majority of non-contributors in the chapter around
1683 included long-serving members such as William Braborn
and Matthew Smallwood,[302] while the subscriptions themselves
were no more impressive than those promised by some metropolitan parochial clergy.[303] The call for subscriptions enjoyed some
success outside London: certainly, plenty of Cambridge heads of
houses and fellows proffered support, and the dean and chapter of
Norwich cathedral contracted to pay £50 over five years.[304]

The fourth fund-raising expedient was the issue in 1678 of a
brief printed as a broadsheet for mass circulation, followed by
another in 1682.[305] Some feared that the brief would 'not have
that desir'd effect amongst the inferior people'; this proved to be
the case in some places.[306] Recording the total amount forthcoming, and sometimes individual contributions, a series of
parochial certificates, some entered on the backs of the printed
briefs, survive for Wales, thirty English counties, and the cities of
Bristol and London.[307] At Asthall in Oxfordshire, 12*s.* was 'taken
out of ye Common Stock' 'by ye Consent of the Parish', indicating a communal decision to back the rebuilding.[308] In
Bedfordshire, by contrast, a Farndish churchwarden 'was twice
about ye Parish, and ye people would give nothing'; while
Sundon parishioners took the opportunity to dispose of a 'cropt'

sixpence and threepenny-bit.[309] In fact £65 of the contributions
collected nationally between December 1678 and July 1682 took
the form of 'Counterfeit mony'![310]

The Building Fund receipts muddy different types and sources
of contribution, but some preliminary judgments are still possible.[311] The diocese of London topped the list. The sums collected
in the sees of Peterborough and Oxford were strikingly high
given their small areas, while Lincoln, Coventry and Lichfield,
Canterbury and Chichester underperformed. This picture contrasts with the pattern of contribution in the 1630s, when the
Midlands had been conspicuously unresponsive and the south-
east strongly supportive. Was the change a consequence of the
Civil War, or of the impact of London's expansion upon provincial markets?

In the capital itself, we have records for seventy-six of the
ninety-seven intra-mural parishes and for thirteen of the seventeen
parishes and non-parochial precincts located in the liberties. The
absence of records may in fact indicate that nothing had been
gathered.[312] Many of the defaulting parishes clustered around St
Paul's. Save for the parishioners of St Gregory, St Martin Ludgate
and St Michael le Querne, the cathedral's neighbours seem to have
been reluctant to endorse the rebuilding through a general
parochial collection, perhaps on account of residual nonconformity in former presbyterian strongholds. Otherwise, the pattern of
contribution reflects the city's social topography, with the greatest
outlay in the wealthy west end. There was nevertheless ample support from several parishes lying at the eastern end of the intramural city – precisely the districts spared from destruction in 1666.

Of the £126,564 raised for either restoration or reconstruction
between the Restoration and March 1685, £68,945 – 54.5 per cent –
derived from the coal duty. Some 20.5 per cent came from clerical
gifts, legacies, and subscriptions, compared to 9.5 per cent from those
of the nobility and gentry; 11.5 per cent resulted from briefs. The

clergy thus appear to have contributed disproportionately to their numbers, and no doubt to their wealth, particularly as they were probably also represented among those responding to the briefs. The most generous interpretation would put the voluntary contribution of the laity at 21 per cent of the total. Hence, in purely voluntaristic terms, the emergence of Wren's St Paul's seemingly owed far more to clerical generosity than it did to lay munificence.[313]

In 1696–8 the cathedral faced a prolonged formal visitation by Bishop Compton (Fig. 348), the first since 1636. In the face of capitular hostility, Compton was thorough. Dean Sherlock's admission that the cathedral possessed no book of statutes led to the preparation of that establishing the cathedral's pattern of worship for the next century, subject to minor modifications by Bishop Gibson in 1724. Morning prayer was held daily at 6 a.m (7 in winter) in 'ye Chapell' and at 10 a.m. in the choir; evening prayer at 3 p.m. in the choir and 6 p.m. in 'ye Chapell', where a minor canon officiated. The first lesson was to be read by a vicar choral and the litany sung by two minor canons; the sub-dean would celebrate communion in the absence of the dean or residentiary. Communion was to be celebrated every Sunday and feast day. Latecomers, and those inappropriately vested, were to be fined, as were prebendaries who failed to preach according to the rota.[314]

Critics lamented the poor rate of progress in reconstructing St Paul's, not least in contrast to the surrounding parish churches:

> These Flames Impartial were, and mow'd down all;
> Nor could you e're have had a nobler fall;
> Sharing your Fate, when others did attend,
> Ambitious of their Mother-Churches End.
> The difference this: although y'ad all one death,
> On them alone the Fates bestow'd new breath:
> They only rose again, 'tis only they,
> Who seem to antidate the general day.
> ...
> One part begun, unfinish'd does admire,
> After so many years to be no higher:
> It looks upon those Heaps of Stones below,
> And fancies them to be remiss and slow.[315]

But Wren knew that what was gradually coming into being would enjoy more than a merely local significance. It was to be the Mother Church of the realm – an unparalleled setting for the affirmation of national unity and the celebration of national triumph. The architect was reported in August 1697 to have ordered the workmen to hasten the completion of the choir so that a *Te Deum* could be sung there upon the conclusion of peace.[316] The new cathedral's first Sunday service was held on 5 December 1697 before an 'innumerable multitude'; John Evelyn left before Sherlock's afternoon sermon because 'the presse of people was so great'.[317] That day also witnessed the building's inaugural marriage ceremony. Seventeen more took place in 1698; thereafter, they averaged twenty-four a year to 1715.[318]

And so began the regular round of worship. The preaching on offer often impressed;[319] some sermons certainly made a mark, most famously Dr Henry Sacheverell's inflammatory high-church attack on low churchmanship and occasional conformity delivered before the corporation on 5 November 1709 (pp. 343–4).[320]

Tourists inspecting the new building included Celia Fiennes, who thought it

> almost finish'd and very magnificent, the Quire with curious carved work in wood; the Arch Bishops seate and the Bishop of Londons and Lord Majors is very finely carv'd and adorned, the alter alsoe with velvet and gold; on the right-side is placed a large crimson velvet elbow chaire which is for the Dean; this is all finished (with a sweet organ) but the body of the church ... is not quite done.[321]

Some idea of the appearance of the high altar is provided by an engraving of 1698 showing a richly bound bible (or prayer book) flanked by two tall candlesticks.[322] But contemporaries were probably most impressed by Queen Anne's state visits (pp. 364–6). The queen's appearance at St Paul's on 23 August 1708 to celebrate Oudenarde prompted Anne Clavering to inform a northern kinsman that 'Our thanksgiving service at Pauls was an incomparable one. I hope you will give it a reading.'[323] What better evidence could there be for the rebuilt cathedral's centrality in the life of the nation?

7

HISTORY, 1714–1830

W. M. Jacob

After the upheavals of the seventeenth century, including the destruction and rebuilding of the cathedral under the later Stuarts, the eighteenth-century history of St Paul's can appear relatively uneventful; certainly, there is little 'eventfulness' in the surviving chapter records! The contents of this Hanoverian component of the historical overview may in consequence seem somewhat anomalous. The impression is only likely to be heightened since those matters that *did* disturb the apparent calm of capitular life are discussed in thematic chapters covering this period elsewhere in this volume: the decoration of the interior of the cathedral, the arrival of the monuments, events associated with the central place of the cathedral in the life both of nation and church during this period, the development of music and liturgy, or of the relationship between the chapter and its parishes.

Even if such matters are reincorporated into the picture, however, little of the evidence for developments in these areas is to be found in what one might anticipate to be a key source: the chapter minute-books. This is partly explained by the fact that some of these subjects fell wholly or partly outside the purview of the chapter: thus financing the maintenance of the fabric and the employment of the surveyor were a responsibility of the trustees of the fabric fund, and music and liturgy were the province of the minor canons (who included the organist). It is nevertheless striking that in this period the minute-books record little more than the granting and renewal of leases of chapter property, and the identities of those present at the meetings (which can at least tell us something about the intensity of the relationship between dean and residentiaries and their cathedral).

This chapter therefore first sets out the framework within which the institutional life of the cathedral was carried on, briefly describing the religious context of the period and of the cities of London and Westminster. It goes on to discuss the roles and relationships of the personnel of the cathedral during the period – the servants, the virgers, the musical establishment, the prebendaries, the dignitaries, the residentiaries, and the dean. In discussing prebendaries, dignitaries, residentiaries, and deans, attention has been paid to evidence about their backgrounds and education, the incomes of their offices, and the extent to which they were 'guilty' of the alleged plurality of officeholding which has subsequently served to bring the Hanoverian church so much into disrepute; all these issues, indeed, illuminate the role of the cathedral and its clergy within the wider context of the Georgian Church of England. Finally, the evidence for the business of the dean and chapter during the period is reviewed and assessed.

The cathedral foundation at St Paul's was an independent corporation, incorporating a number of other semi-autonomous corporations, but, unlike that of any other English cathedral, without responsibility for financing the maintenance of the cathedral fabric. The foundation had its own historic rules, officials, customs, traditions, lands and revenues, as did the bodies it embraced. It thus resembled many other corporations and institutions of Georgian England: the universities, the Inns of Court, the departments of state and institutions of government, and the royal court and household. Despite the attentions of reformers in the sixteenth and seventeenth centuries, these bodies and their officers proved resilient to radical reform, making modest adjustments as circumstances required. They were conservative, but not sclerotic institutions, whose workings could be arcane. A prime aim of this chapter is to explain the activities of the cathedral, and the attitudes and mental frameworks of its members.

The principal object of St Paul's cathedral was as a place of worship and prayer, and as the seat of the bishop of London. By offering a round of daily and Sunday worship, and providing sound preaching of the Christian faith according to the formularies of the Church of England, the cathedral provided an example of religious stability in the capital and the vast diocese of London, which embraced the cities of London and Westminster (and thus the financial and mercantile centre of the United Kingdom and its colonies, the seat of government and the royal court), as well as the rural counties of Middlesex, Essex, and part of Hertfordshire. It also provided a venue for state religious ceremonies (apart from coronations and royal funerals), and for great London church occasions, such as the festivals of the London Charity Schools and the Corporation of the Sons of the Clergy (pp. 348–51, 363–71).

Although not a metropolitan cathedral and seat of a primate, St Paul's was the mother church of the greatest European city. It was the most modern cathedral, and among the largest, in Europe. It had a national and international religious, political, architectural, and artistic significance. It was a popular tourist attraction. Engravings of it sold in large numbers, and it was one of the most significant landmarks and most familiar images of London (pp. 319–29). Its precincts were the centre of the London book trade, and leading booksellers and theological publishers were to be found in the churchyard (pp. 433–8).

God, and the things of God, were central in people's lives during this period.[1] In the wars that bridged the seventeenth and eighteenth, and then the eighteenth and nineteenth centuries, divine judgement and providence were seen at work in political and military events by all sections of society. God was regarded as having saved the nation from the Counter-Reformation tyranny of Louis XIV and James II, and from the heterodoxy and oppression of Revolutionary and Napoleonic France. Being right with God was a high priority for governments and citizens. The new modish cathedral in the centre of the city of London was an important symbol and means of ensuring the spiritual welfare of the nation, and of averting divine judgement, by ordering worship aright, and teaching sound doctrines and morals.

The cathedral was not alone in exercising this role. It was surrounded by more than forty parish churches in the city, most of which had recently been rebuilt, and themselves had dynamic religious lives. Visitors to the city in the early eighteenth century noted that churches were crowded: in 1714 James Paterson commented that 'there is scarce an Hour of the Day, but a Devout Person may have the Opportunity of serving God in Publick after the Manner of the Primitive Church'.[2] That year twenty-five city churches had daily morning prayer and twenty-six daily evening prayer; in 1746 twenty-three had daily morning prayer and daily evening prayer, while another twenty had morning prayer on Wednesdays, Fridays, and holy days. In addition to the cathedral, in Westminster the Abbey, St James's Piccadilly and St Paul's Covent Garden had two sittings of morning prayer daily.[3] Preaching and teaching were not neglected. In 1714 every city church had at least one endowed lecture on a Sunday, paid for from endowments or from voluntary contributions. There were thirty-two weekday lectures, twenty-eight of which were funded by members of religious societies of men.[4] In 1719 the Society of the Trustees of the London Charity Schools estimated that £10,000 a year was raised in London to fund education in accordance with the principles of the Church of England for the children of the poor, supporting about 3,000 boys and about 1,700 girls in some 120 schools in London parishes.[5] In the first half of

the eighteenth century, at least, the cathedral was thus at the heart of a city with a lively church life.

In St Paul's daily and Sunday worship only occupied the choir, a relatively small part of the building. The only other regularly used part of the building was the consistory court (at the south-west corner), where testamentary, defamation, and matrimonial cases were heard, as well as others of more obvious ecclesiastical concern. Litigants and defendants thus joined a wider public in coming into the cathedral in large numbers. Doctors' Commons, the society of church lawyers, had its meeting place nearby.[6]

THE PERSONNEL OF THE CATHEDRAL

The cathedral was a large and varied community. At the humblest level were a labourer, someone who looked after the silver, the constable, an organ blower, a clock-winder, and a library keeper. These posts were at various times held in various combinations of plurality. There was a dean's virger and three other virgers, two bell-ringers and a teacher to teach the choristers to read and write.[7] In the early nineteenth century, at least, there were also three 'Sunday attendants'. At a more elevated level the clerk of works was responsible to the trustees for the fabric. The chapter clerk and steward managed the dean and chapter's estates and funds.

The musical and liturgical establishment comprised six vicars choral and ten singing boys, reduced to eight in the middle of the eighteenth century. One vicar choral was almoner and master of the choristers; another was organist, employing a deputy to sing; until 1769 the statutes of the cathedral required a vicar choral to read the first lesson at the daily services.[8] There were twelve minor canons in holy orders. These included a junior and a senior cardinal and a sub-dean elected from among their number.

The cathedral had thirty prebendaries appointed by the bishop of London. They included the dignitaries of St Paul's – the precentor, chancellor and treasurer: a smaller group than in earlier times – who were separately appointed for life by the bishop; their posts were sinecures. Four of the prebends were held by the three residentiaries and the dean. The residentiaries were formally elected from among the prebendaries, but were appointed by the Crown, their appointment to a prebend often being effectively simultaneous with their acquisition of their residentaryship. The bishop of London was visitor. The bishop had his throne in the cathedral; and the five archdeacons of the diocese of London had stalls in the choir.

The virgers

The virgers 'minded' the cathedral, and formed the front-of-house staff, as well as conducting the dean and residentiaries to their places in the choir. They were nominated to their posts by the chapter, and were presented for admission to office by the treasurer to the canon-in-residence. The virgers were required to take oaths of allegiance and supremacy and canonical obedience, and to subscribe a pledge to appear at the chapter house annually on Audit Day to surrender their wands of office to the dean. The wands were returned for the succeeding year providing they had faithfully performed their duties.

The virgers were important not least for their prominent role in admitting and conducting around large numbers of visitors to the cathedral. In the early nineteenth century, at least, an entrance fee of 2d. was charged, and this was used to pay the virgers, who in the 1830s each received about £100 a year from this source.[9]

33.   Inside the nave of Wren's cathedral looking towards the crossing, *c.*1725. The body of the church west of the screen was confined to visitors and occasional uses. This generally accurate depiction of the interior shows a low railing erected in front of the choir screen to keep out dogs, and also indicates the painted treatment originally given to the stonework, though the painted coffering shown on the saucer domes seems never to have been executed. (St Paul's Cathedral)

Virgers were permitted to pay deputies to show visitors the crypt and the ball of the dome. Virgers also conducted people to their seats for services (it was claimed that they received bribes for good seats in the choir). From 1766 the dean's virger had an additional responsibility as deputy surveyor of the fabric, the dean and chapter requiring him to undertake a weekly inspection of the cathedral.

Despite the annual requirement for surrender of their wands, virgers were not easily dismissed. In 1778 Henry Argent was sacked for gross misconduct, but following a formal and public apology, and an undertaking not to reoffend, he was reinstated. On being dismissed again in 1781 for a long sequence of 'irregular, disorderly and disobedient behaviour', he took his case to the Court of King's Bench, which, in 1783, granted him a *mandamus* for his reinstatement, and compelled his successor to withdraw and hand over the profits he had received since his appointment.[10]

The musical and liturgical establishment

The vicars choral were usually pluralists, often also singing at Westminster Abbey and/or the Chapel Royal (pp. 394–5). They also participated in secular concerts to supplement their incomes. These multiple activities linked the cathedral's musical establishment to the vibrant musical and cultural life of eighteenth-century London, and related the musical life of the cathedral to contemporary music. Vicars choral were initially appointed only for a probationary year, with the proviso that unless a vicar choral should 'behave himself unworthy of the said office' the appointment would be made absolute. If nothing untoward occurred, they swore the requisite oaths and were admitted 'according to the statutes and laudable customs' of the cathedral as members of a body with its own property and endowments. This provided their income, augmented from the 'cupola fund', monies accrued from fees exacted from visitors to the whispering gallery, library, and the upper parts of the cathedral. Once a month this was

TABLE 4
Values of prebendal stalls, *c*.1720 and 1835

Net yearly values (yearly values for 1835 and probably also for *c*.1720)

c.1720	<£5	£5–10	£11–20	£21–30	£31–40	£41–50	£51–60	£61–70	£91–100	£101–150	£151–200	£200–300	£340–500	£1,200<
Number of stalls	6	1	1	1	3	3	1	1	1	1	2	4	4	1

1835	<£5	£5–10	£11–20	£21–30	£31–40	£41–50	£51–60	£61–70	£71–80	£81–90	£91–100	£101–110	£300	£600–1,000	£1,001 <
Number of stalls	2	4	8	1	0	0	0	1	0	0	0	1	1	3	3

Source: GL, MS CF 54/3; *Liber Ecclesiasticus*, 50–1. By comparison at Lincoln Cathedral in 1835 more than half the prebendal stalls had incomes of less than £20 a year; more than a quarter less than £10; and only four had incomes of more than £75 a year: Thompson (1994), 224–5.

TABLE 5
Status of fathers of prebendaries, 1714–1830

Period	Status of father:								
	Peer	Baronet	Knight	Gentleman	Professional	Clerical	Tradesman	Army	Plebeian
1714–1750	1	1	1	12	3	30	2	0	5
1751–1830	3	3	29	6	32	5	2	6	0

Note: this records all known fathers, save for two identified as 'farmers', two as 'government officers' and one as a 'dramatist'. Information on clerical backgrounds and preferment is derived from Foster (1887–92), and Venn (1922–54).

divided among the vicars and the minor canons in proportion to their recorded attendance at services. Like the virgers, vicars choral had effective security of tenure, even if their voices deteriorated with age.[11]

The twelve minor canons lived in St Paul's College, a group of small houses at the western extremity of St Paul's Churchyard. They were responsible for maintaining the daily round of services. They had been incorporated in 1394, with their own endowments (p. 34). The minor canons recruited their own members; when a vacancy occurred, they would nominate two candidates to the dean, who chose one.[12] The stipends yielded by the endowments of the College were small (p. 338), but were augmented by a share in the cupola fund: in the early nineteenth century it was alleged that minor canons were less frequent in their attendance at the cathedral during the winter months, when visitors – and hence the cupola fund – were at a low ebb.[13]

Minor canons might hold an additional office in the cathedral as sub-dean, succentor, sacrist, or librarian. They were also, in many instances, presented to parochial livings in the vicinity of the cathedral in the gift of the dean and chapter, the incomes from which further augmented their incomes.

As incumbents of city parishes and permanent residents in the metropolis, minor canons formed an important link between St Paul's and the city. But by far the most important contribution they made to the cathedral was in sustaining its worshipping life. The minor canons were responsible daily for saying morning prayer in the Morning Chapel at 7 a.m. in summer and 8 a.m. in winter; singing morning prayer in the choir at 9.45 a.m. and evensong at 3.15 p.m.; and celebrating holy communion after morning prayer on Sundays and holy days. In the absence of the canon residentiary on duty, a minor canon might preside and occupy his stall at a service. It was a minor canon who as succen-

tor chose the music for all the services. The minor canons sang with the vicars choral, forming two-thirds of the singers. During the eighteenth century, although ordained, they were usually professional musicians of considerable competence (p. 395). If the demands of the liturgy were thus heavy, there were limits to the commitment of the clerics involved: the senior minor canons, the cardinals, were exempted from saying early morning prayer, while in 1750 the other minor canons employed a clergyman to read these services at a stipend of £10 a year.

Minor canons (and the vicars choral) were under the supervision of the sub-dean, in turn supervised by the canon-in-residence. However, because residentiaries only served a month's duty at a time, there was a lack both of continuity and consistency in this supervision. Furthermore, the freehold nature of the minor canon's office meant that those who proved unsatisfactory could only be dismissed after due process of law.

In the early nineteenth century the musical establishment appears, from the evidence of Maria Hackett, a regular attender at the daily choral services, to have been unsatisfactory. Miss Hackett, through supporting a young relative as a chorister, discovered that following the sale of the Almonry, where the boys had been accommodated, no provision had been made for their accommodation, or general and musical education; she forcefully raised this omission with the bishop and the dean and chapter.[14]

The prebendaries

Those prebendaries not residentiaries had as their only duty preaching by turn at the morning service on festivals and saints days (or to appoint deputies to preach on their behalf). The St Paul's statutes enjoined them to appear in the cathedral as frequently as possible, although how often they actually attended the cathedral is unknown. Because there was no mechanism or forum for them to meet, they played little part in the life of the cathedral.

With the exception of the prebendaries of Lincoln, Hereford and Exeter, the prebendaries of St Paul's were the poorest in England, although some individual stalls were of considerable value (Table 4).

In addition to this income each prebendary received £3 10s. a year 'bread money', the commutation of the ancient allowance of bread from St Paul's bakery (p. 146). In fact five prebendaries – those of Ealdland, Ealdstreet, Twiford, Portpool and Consumpta-per-Mare – received nothing but 'bread money'. If a fine for the renewal of a lease fell due during a prebendary's tenure then he might benefit from a significant windfall: the prebendaries of Chamberlainwood and Wilsden, with rental incomes valued at £5 and £12 a year respectively, had during the three years ending in 1831 received fines for renewal of leases amounting to £1,500 and £5,250 respectively.[15] But none of the fifteen stalls valued at under £50 a year in the 1720s could be expected to make their occupants' fortunes. Where stalls were endowed with estates, prebendaries were responsible for managing them, and securing the income. Managing these estates could be difficult (pp. 336, 339). It might also be hard to ascertain the value of a stall. Bishop Blomfield thought he was generous in preferring William Hale to the prebend of Islington in 1829, believing it was worth £200 p.a., but Hale discovered after his installation that the income was only £100 a year.[16]

Many of the 215 clergy preferred to prebendal stalls between 1714 and 1830 retained them for long periods. Caddington Minor and Islington each had only four occupants over a period of 116 years; and only Mora had more than ten occupants during this time. What sort of men became prebendaries of St Paul's? The prebendaries were mostly sons of the 'middling sort'. The status of the fathers of 140 of the 215 prebendaries during the period can be identified (Table 5).

Although this sample represents only two-thirds of the total, it is unlikely that many aristocratic fathers were unrecorded. The considerable increase in the sons of 'gentlemen' after 1750 may reflect a growing tendency among professional men – lawyers, medical doctors and successful merchants – to designate themselves as 'gentlemen'. Indeed, a general examination of the backgrounds of London diocesan clergy has shown that most clerical sons of 'gentlemen' were from urban rather than rural backgrounds.[17] The fact that thirty of the fifty-five fathers identified in the earlier period were clergy echoes the finding that half the prebendaries of Lincoln in 1750 were sons of the cloth.[18] Of the clerical fathers only one can be identified as an incumbent in the city of London.

Of prebendaries whose schools can be identified, twenty-three were educated in London (nine at Westminster, five each at Merchant Taylors and Charterhouse, three at St Paul's and one at Haberdashers). Of the others, sixteen had attended Eton, and two each Harrow and Winchester. Forty-three prebendaries are thus known to have attended elite schools. The university education of 189 can be identified. Of these 103 were Cambridge graduates, and eighty-six from Oxford. Many had attended the largest and richest colleges: thirty-eight had studied at Christ Church Oxford, twenty at St John's College Cambridge, and fifteen at Trinity College Cambridge. A significant proportion had achieved high status in their universities. Nearly half had doctorates: ninety doctors of divinity, six doctors of civil law and six doctors of law. Another eleven were bachelors of divinity and four

were bachelors of law. Only sixty-four had not progressed beyond MAs, and a mere six held nothing more than a BA.

Prebendaries were appointed by the bishop of London, and an examination of the careers of 149 of them that can be traced during the period shows a significant correlation between appointment to a stall and holding office in the service of a bishop, being presented to an episcopal living, or being closely related to a bishop. Six were sons or sons-in-law of a bishop. No fewer than five of these had been preferred to their stalls by Edmund Gibson, bishop of London from 1723 to 1748 (three sons and two sons-in-law); moreover two of Gibson's grandsons also became prebendaries. One prebendary was a bishop's nephew. Forty-eight prebendaries had also been presented to an episcopal living, of whom fifteen had benefited from two such presentations, and six from three. One prebendary was subsequently preferred by the bishop to the chancellor's stall, another was already cathedral treasurer (both positions lucrative sinecures). Eight prebendaries had already served as domestic chaplains to a bishop; twelve went on to hold archdeaconries in the diocese.

A high proportion of prebendaries already held livings in the city (thirty-two) or the diocese (forty-four) when appointed to their stalls, which suggests that bishops of London may have followed the late seventeenth-century policy of Archbishop John Sharp of York in appointing worthy parochial incumbents in his diocese to prebendal stalls.[19] A further seven were subsequently presented to city parishes, and twenty-seven to livings in the diocese. If prebendaries saw themselves as having a close identity with the cathedral, this may have created a network of clergy seen as representing the cathedral's interests across the diocese. There was, however, no forum in which prebendaries could seek to represent the diocese to the cathedral.

The only formal corporate duty of the prebendaries was to elect residentiaries, the dean, and the bishop. There is no evidence of meetings of this greater chapter to elect residentiaries and deans, but they do appear to have convened to elect bishops. After the elections in the chapter house in 1809 and 1829 the prebendaries proceeded to the choir where a *Te Deum* was sung, and in 1829, Bishop Charles Blomfield was personally installed after the first lesson at morning prayer.[20] Otherwise the prebendaries' only formal attendance at the cathedral was as individuals coming to take their preaching turns, when they would probably only have encountered the canon-in-residence, or perhaps the dean.

Some prebendaries were part of wider networks. Ten during the period served as chaplains to the king or his consort. Forty-six were prebendaries of other cathedrals or collegiate churches; ten held two other prebendal stalls; twelve were residentiaries or dignitaries of other cathedrals, and four were deans elsewhere. This reflected the fact that prebendal stalls, not having cures of souls, were not subject to the legislation against pluralism. Whether this overlapping of personnel encouraged communication of good practice between capitular bodies cannot be ascertained. In addition nine prebendaries of St Paul's were archdeacons in other dioceses. Eighteen subsequently became bishops. Most prebendaries, however, died in office, and probably a prebendal stall at St Paul's was the most prestigious office achieved by the great majority.

The lack of interaction between the dean and chapter and the prebendaries may be illustrated by the fact that during this period only four prebendaries not residentiaries were presented to livings in their gift subsequent to their appointment as prebendaries. It is also striking that – no doubt because prebendal stalls were in the

34. Henry Godolphin, provost of Eton 1683–1735 and dean of St Paul's 1707–26, a portrait by George Perfect Harding. (Eton College)

gift of the bishop – it was most unusual, as in all cathedrals, for a minor canon to be promoted to a prebendal stall. There was only one instance of this happening at St Paul's during this period, that of Thomas Hilman.

The dignitaries

The dignitaries of St Paul's – the precentor, the chancellor, and the treasurer – were neither ex-officio prebendaries nor residentiaries. Most had, however, other connections with the cathedral. Four dignitaries during this period had been presented to prebendal stalls by the bishop prior to their preferment as dignitaries, and one (Hugh Chambres Jones, appointed treasurer in 1816), was later advanced to an archdeaconry held in plurality. They could thus derive a healthy income from the monies yielded by these other posts in combination with the dignitaries' remuneration: in the 1720s the precentor's office was valued at £534 5s. ½d., the chancellor's at £929 6s. 8d. and the treasurer's at £381 2s. 7d. (these estimates of annual value presumably took account of fines for renewal of leases, since in 1835 their annual rental incomes were returned as £58, £74 and £65). The possession of these sinecure offices did little to encourage a contribution to the life of the institution. The dignitaries had no duties apart from taking or finding a substitute for one of the preaching turns on a festival or saints day.

The residentiaries

The three residentiaries and the dean, who all also held prebends, together comprised the dean and chapter, the formal body corpo-

rate of the cathedral. They each kept three separate months of residence a year, during which they were required to attend the daily services, to read the lessons and preach at evensong on Sunday afternoons (before which they were required, by ancient custom, to entertain to dinner the minor canons and vicars choral who had attended the morning service), and were available to authorize decisions about estates (p. 337). Residentiaries did not remain at the cathedral outside their month of residence, and neither the deanery nor the residentiaryships were regarded as full-time commitments. The dean and chapter consequently had no meaningful corporate life. Houses were assigned to residentiaries who were under a duty to maintain them in good repair, but they did not necessarily live in them. Sydney Smith, at the end of our period, let his residence house in Amen court and lived in the West End.[21] The day-to-day running of the cathedral was left to subordinate members of the community. Even the residentiaries' apparently meagre roster of duties was not always fulfilled, and in the early nineteenth century the ever-vigilant Maria Hackett was critical of their attendance at services. In March 1813 she pointed out to John Hughes that 'The Dean's attendance for the last ten months has not amounted to so many days. I believe Dr Weston has not been in the Cathedral since July [and] Dr Wellesley above thirty days in the year.'[22]

Customarily residentaries were appointed by the Crown. The three residentiaries and the dean shared the annual balance in the common fund of the cathedral after the payment of stipends and allowances, while the dean also had separate estates. In 1762 the residentiaryships at St Paul's were valued at £800 a year; in 1831 the chapter divided a total of £9,049.[23] The duke of Newcastle with some justification described a canonry at St Paul's as 'the [best] Ecclesiastical preferment in the King's disposal next to bishoprics and the deanery of Durham'.[24]

Of the twenty-five residentiaries who held office between 1714 and 1827, thirteen held bishoprics during their clerical careers, of whom one, Richard Terrick, subsequently became bishop of London; five held deaneries, of whom three, Francis Hare, John Hume and Thomas Newton, became deans of St Paul's; and four also held dignities at other cathedrals. One residentiary, Gerald Wellesley, brother of the duke of Wellington, moved to a better-endowed post that was neither a deanery nor a bishopric – the rectory of Bishop Wearmouth in County Durham – having already been a canon of Durham for the last four years of his residentiaryship at St Paul's. Only nine residentiaries died in office without having received further preferment, suggesting that a residentiaryship at St Paul's was usually a step to further advancement in their careers. During the 1720s there were occasions when *all* the residentiaries were simultaneously deans of other cathedrals. In 1747, 1758, 1766, 1767, throughout the 1770s and in the 1780s, all the residentiaries attending chapter meetings were also bishops. Having such a concentration of deans and bishops from across the country had at least the potential for opportunities for consultation and sharing good practice.

With few exceptions residentiaries held some of the poorest prebendal stalls. Two exceptions were Robert Tyrwhit (residentiary 1733–42), who held Cantlers (1732–42), worth £495 16s. 8d. in the 1720s, and Christopher Wilson (1758–92), prebendary of Finsbury (1745–92) worth £1,218. It is perhaps not insignificant that Tyrwhit and Wilson were both sons-in-law of Bishop Gibson. Nevertheless, there are indications that on at least some occasions it was felt inappropriate that such lucrative combinations of office persist. When Samuel Baker became a residentiary in 1728, he resigned Brownswood to which he had been preferred a year earlier, worth £432, and took the income-less stall of Ealdland. But it was not just from their share of the common fund and the prebendal stalls they held that the residentiaries profited from their association with the cathedral. Seven were presented to choice livings in the gift of the dean and chapter. Thus John Jeffreys was rector of St Nicholas Cole Abbey, 1746–92; Christopher Wilson (bishop of Bristol from 1783), rector of Barnes (valued at £375 a year in 1835) from 1758 until his death in 1792, when he was succeeded by Jeffreys. The rectory of Therfield in Hertfordshire, valued at £937 a year with a residence house, was held by Philip Yonge from 1757 until 1761, and then by Samuel Weston from 1798 and then by Gerald Wellesley from 1822 until 1832.

The residentiaries of this era were mostly men of learning. All had doctorates, and only eight had no traceable publications. Most published sermons and pamphlets; a few, notably Francis Hare (residentiary 1707–26 before his promotion to the deanery), with four volumes of collected works to his credit, were notable apologists. Their scholarship extended beyond divinity. John Taylor (1757) was reckoned to have produced some good editions of the Greek orators; Richard Farmer (1788–97) was a friend of Dr Johnson and a Shakespearean scholar; John Green (1771–9) was reckoned a good scholar, with an 'elegant pen' in Latin and English; Thomas Jackson (1792–7) was a botanist; John Douglas (1776–87) was a Milton scholar who also edited Captain Cook's journals and Lord Clarendon's state papers, and at George III's request catalogued the libraries at Windsor and Kew.

The deans

Deans of St Paul's were men of distinction. The dean was nominated by the Crown, and, if not already a prebendary, the bishop conferred a prebendal stall on him. He was then admitted as a residentiary, and elected dean by the prebendaries. The dean kept monthly turns of residence with the other residentiaries. In addition to a fourth share in the profits of the cathedral, the deanery had its own estates, and the dean also benefited from the income of his prebend.

From 1727 when Francis Hare (1726–40) was appointed bishop of St Asaph, all deans of St Paul's during this period were simultaneously bishops: Joseph Butler (1740–50) of Bristol; Thomas Secker (1750–8; Fig. 36) and John Hume (1758–66) of Oxford; Frederick Cornwallis (1766–8) of Coventry and Lichfield; Thomas Newton (1768–82; Fig. 37) of Bristol; Thomas Thurlow (1782–7) and George Pretyman (1787–1820) of Lincoln; and William Van Mildert (1820–6), Charles Sumner (1826–7) and Edward Copleston (1827–49) of Llandaff. The dioceses of Bristol, Oxford, and Llandaff were the worst-endowed dioceses in England and Wales: the incomes from the endowments did not meet the annual expenses of office. In 1735, for example, Secker computed the revenues of Bristol to be worth £360 a year, and in 1762 it was valued at £450.[25] As the second city of the kingdom Bristol, required a good income for the bishop to maintain appropriate state and hospitality in his see city, and Bishop Gibson proposed that the deanery of St Paul's should be permanently annexed to that diocese.[26] Although Van Mildert reckoned the average income of Llandaff at £1,403 10s. 7d., in 1835 its net revenue was reckoned at £924.[27] In order to be viable such dioceses had to be held *in commendam* with another office. The expenses of becoming a bishop were considerable. Thurlow's legal fees alone for his consecration and appointment to Lincoln in 1779

amounted to £561 5s. 5d.[28] In addition there was the expense of furnishing and possibly repairing the episcopal residence(s), a carriage, and accommodation in London during parliamentary sessions, as well as travel expenses and hospitality. The deanery or a residentiaryship thus provided an ideal base for a hard-pressed bishop of a poorly endowed diocese, as well as an additional income. Episcopal deans usually resigned if they were lucky enough to be translated to a more lucrative see, as was the case with Butler and Van Mildert, both preferred to Durham, Secker and Cornwallis to Canterbury, Hume to Salisbury, and Pretyman (by then Pretyman-Tomline) and Sumner to Winchester. Nevertheless the deanery could be held *in commendam* with a see where it was hard to see the pluralism as necessary. The residentiary John Douglas appears to have been popular among the London clergy (he was elected a proctor in convocation in 1780 and in 1784), and was disappointed not to secure the deanery in 1787 when Pretyman was appointed. In his autobiography he noted ruefully that the new dean's diocese of Lincoln was worth £2,000 a year; complaining at the continued practice of holding the post *in commendam*, he commented that 'there should be more Residence and Hospitality at ye Deanery than a bishop can possibly comply with, unless he neglects his Episcopal function'.[29]

Such successful clerical careers reflected the fact that as Crown appointees, deans were usually well-connected with the court or the current ministry. Hare had been Sir Robert Walpole's tutor at King's College Cambridge, and was a member of Queen Caroline's circle; Butler had also been taken up by the queen, and was a close friend of Lord Chancellor Talbot. Secker was part of Talbot's circle, but was appointed on the nomination of Lord Chancellor Hardwicke and the duke of Newcastle, who had been tutored by Hume. Newton was a protégé of William Pulteney, earl of Bath, and of Lord Bute, and had been a member of the Leicester House group around George III's father, Frederick, prince of Wales. Thurlow was the brother of a lord chancellor; Pretyman had been William Pitt the younger's tutor and then his private secretary; Van Mildert was a member of the Hackney

35. The cathedral in its context shortly after completion, from the northwest. Anonymous English painting of *c*.1725. The size of the open space both inside and outside the railings is exaggerated. (Private collection)

36. Thomas Secker, dean of St Paul's 1750–8 and archbishop of Canterbury 1758–68, after Joshua Reynolds. (NPG)

Phalanx, with which Lord Liverpool had strong sympathies; Charles Sumner was much favoured by George IV; and Copleston, while 'liberal' in theology, was Tory in politics, and was preferred by George Canning.

Most deans were men of intellectual distinction. Hare, as has been noted, was an able apologist, a prolific author, and a Latin scholar. In 1736 he published an edition of the Hebrew psalms, but his theory of Hebrew versification was subsequently superseded by the work of Robert Lowth. Butler's *Analogy of Religion* remained a textbook for ordination candidates for more than a century, and shaped the thought of many nineteenth-century figures, including Gladstone. Secker's charges to his clergy as a bishop became useful handbooks for clergy and his *Lectures on the Catechism* were employed by generations of clerics as a basis for teaching children about the Christian faith. Newton's edition of Milton's *Paradise Lost* was in its eighth edition by 1773, and his *Dissertations on the Prophecies* were translated into both German and Dutch. Pretyman-Tomline energetically defended the Church of England against Calvinism and Roman Catholicism, while his *Elements of Christian Theology* was widely recommended to ordinands. Van Mildert published both Boyle and Bampton lectures; a leading high-church divine, while dean he produced a ten-volume edition of the works of Daniel Waterland, a notable Church Whig theolo-

gian. Copleston was a prominent 'Oriel noetic' and played a considerable part in the reforms of the college as provost and of Oxford University in general. At Llandaff he learned Welsh to be better able to minister in his diocese. In the nineteenth century those defending cathedrals against hostile reformers often cited their role as havens for learned clergy, providing an intellectual strike-force for the Church in its conflict with unbelief and heterodoxy. The eighteenth-century deans of St Paul's serve as a striking example of this aspect of the cathedral's function.

THE BUSINESS OF THE DEAN AND CHAPTER

The formal business conducted by the dean and chapter and recorded in the chapter act books was almost entirely concerned with granting leases of their estates. The only examples of other business recorded there were an agreement to remit the fees for the interment of Sir Christopher Wren in March 1723, and in April 1771 when they agreed to confirm the arrangements for the disposal of chapter patronage, a complex procedure allocating 'turns' to specified individual members of the chapter (pp. 372–3).

At St Paul's the dean and chapter had no responsibility for oversight of the funding of the maintenance of the cathedral fabric,

37. Thomas Newton, bishop of Bristol 1761–82 and dean of St Paul's 1768–82,
by Joshua Reynolds. (LPL)

which was often the main items of business, apart from the renewal of leases and patronage, on the agendas of other capitular bodies. This was in the hands of a fund under the trusteeship of the archbishop of Canterbury, the bishop of London and the Lord Mayor, established by act of parliament to administer the residue of the monies from the tax on coal imported into London which had financed building the cathedral. The trustees appointed a surveyor of the fabric, and were responsible for the general maintenance of the cathedral and examining and auditing the fabric accounts. This fund was augmented by monies from a benefaction in 1679 by Dr William Clarke, dean of Winchester, of the profits from the estate of Tillingham in Essex, which was held on a long lease from the dean and chapter (pp. 338–9). The independence of the trustees did not prevent the ever-efficient Thomas Secker looking into their activities and pointing out that the capital had been badly invested, that some of it had been lost, and that expenditure had been poorly administered. The intervention resulted in important changes in the adminstration of the fund in 1753 (p. 338). It was the bishop of London as trustee, not the dean and chapter, who opposed, but ultimately permitted, monuments in the cathedral.

The dean and chapter minutes of this period are frustratingly silent on proposals for decorating the interior of the cathedral, the ordering of its life, the employment of staff, the liturgy and music, and the exercise of their peculiar jurisdiction. Nor is there comment on what must have been major events in the life of the cathedral, such as the state services of the later eighteenth century, or even the theft of the cathedral plate in 1810. Most surprisingly there is no record of a formal response by the dean and chapter to Bishop Gibson's visitation in 1724.[30] This only serves to underline the importance of the business of leasing to the residentiaries.

Only seldom were all four members of the chapter present at any one chapter meeting.[31] Until 1722 they all attended a March meeting, which was usually audit day. Thereafter evidence for a formal audit day disappears. However, Sydney Smith noted that the dean and chapter dined together once a year when they distributed the dividends.[32] Chapter meetings appear to have been held when business needed to be conducted. There were usually between six and nine a year, but in 1733–4 there were three meetings, whereas in 1797–8 there were twelve meetings, and in 1765 and 1803 thirteen. Residentiaries who were also bishops, who might be expected to be in London for the parliamentary sessions, were not notably better attenders than others. The numbers turning up declined sharply after 1801. In 1801, 1803–6, 1810, 1812, 1816, 1818–19 and 1821, on average only one residentiary was present at each chapter meeting. This may be linked with the

38.   *The Minister endeavouring to eke out Dr. Pr.ty...n's Bishoprick*: a satire against pluralism by James Gillray, 1787. William Pitt, the prime minister, is depicted placing the dome of St Paul's over the crossing of Lincoln Cathedral. Pitt had simultaneously bestowed the deanery of St Paul's and the bishopric of Lincoln on his former tutor and private secretary, George Pretyman. (GL)

ending of the custom of bishops holding residentiaryships rather than the deanery *in commendam*. Majendie was the last residentiary appointed a bishop to retain his office when he was elevated to the see of Chester in 1800, retaining it until translated to the better-endowed diocese of Bangor in 1808. Except when prevented by ill health (as in the case of Newton), the deans were the most frequent attenders at chapter meetings. Apart from long spells during 1792, from May 1798 to May 1799, and from April 1802 until March 1803, Pretyman-Tomline seldom missed many meetings in succession.

Day-to-day business may have been handled by the dean if in residence, or perhaps the canon-in-residence. As bishops and thus members of the House of Lords, they usually spent the parliamentary session in London, and so were probably present in their cathedral more often than deans of other cathedrals. Indeed deans rather than other residentiaries left their mark on the cathedral. Henry Newman, the secretary of the Society for Promoting Christian Knowledge, thus blamed the new dean, Francis Hare, for in 1727 turning out the society (together with the SPG and the Corporation of the Sons of the Clergy) from the upstairs room of the chapter house as their regular monthly meeting place, and offering them, in exchange, the downstairs court room ('very inconvenient now and will be more so in the winter', grumbled Newman).[33]

Dean Secker apparently generally overhauled the business of the cathedral and reviewed the accounts. In 1754 he made an agreement with the vestry of St Faith's parish concerning their share of St Paul's churchyard. He put the archives in order, indexed the records and collated the old statute book correcting mistakes in its transcription and making his own extracts. Secker also agreed with the residentiaries that 'we would ordinarily preach our Afternoon Turns ourselves, or exchange them with others; which was pretty exactly observed'. Secker usually resided from September until April each year, spending December and the summer months in his Oxford diocese. When in London he attended church twice a day. His autobiography throws a little but rare light on the shadowy world of the eighteenth-century chapter, not least in its record of the process of his appointment. Becoming dean of St Paul's was an expensive business. Secker noted that the fees for his installation amounted to £204; the cost of his installation dinner £34 10s. Bishop Butler was tardy in vacating the deanery, and Secker only gradually moved in from his rectory at St James's Piccadilly, taking some books with him every day when he went to the cathedral. He spent £650 on improvements to the deanery, but only recovered £150 for dilapidations from Butler.[34]

Newton too resided at the deanery for the greater part of the year, spending the summer months in his diocese. When his health deteriorated his physicians advised him not to risk the chilly cathedral, and George III dispensed him from his duties. From 1779 his health was too poor even to permit attendance at chapter meetings. However, he was active in the abortive proposals for a decorative scheme for the interior of the cathedral, designed by Sir Joshua Reynolds and Benjamin West (pp. 241–2). At the deanery, he secured the demolition of shops in front of the house to create a carriage entrance, and secured leases and kept some property in hand to form a garden. He also enlarged the drawing room, and installed sash windows.[35]

Pretyman-Tomline remained an adviser of Pitt once at St Paul's, especially in economic matters. His closeness to Pitt ensured that St Paul's again became the arena in which great events of state were celebrated (pp. 367–7). It is striking that at St Paul's he did not use the limited patronage available to him as dean for the benefit of his family as he notoriously did as bishop of Lincoln.[36]

On Pretyman-Tomline's resignation after thirty-two years in office on his translation from Lincoln to Winchester in 1819, Lord Liverpool offered the deanery to Van Mildert, who had become bishop of Llandaff earlier in the year. He was also allowed to keep the rectory of St Mary-le-Bow, and his regius professorship at Oxford with its rectory of Ewelme *in commendam*. Liverpool made two conditions when offering the deanery to Van Mildert: he must reside at the deanery for six months each year, and do something about the allegedly scandalous state of the cathedral. Liverpool wrote to Van Mildert:

> It has long been felt that the Church of St Paul's has been greatly neglected and I understand that the Service is performed there in a much less creditable manner than in any other Cathedral in the Kingdom...I know I speak the sentiments both of the Archbp of Canterbury & of the Bp of London that this is an occasion on which a thorough Reform ought to take place as to all these particulars.[37]

This injunction to take up the cause of reform may have been inspired by the accusations of neglect levelled by Maria Hackett

39.   The transepts and crossing looking south, aquatint by A. C. Pugin and Thomas Rowlandson for
The Microcosm of London, published by Rudolph Ackermann, 1809. (GL)

(Fig. 333) against the Dean and Chapter. In 1817 she had pub-lished her *Registrum eleemosynariae D Pauli Londoninensis*, a tran-script of the medieval almoner's register, on which she had based her critique of the treatment of the choristers. Earlier, between January 1811 and August 1813 Hackett had written twenty-eight letters to the bishop, dean, various residentiaries and chancellor, suggesting simple and relatively inexpensive remedies to improve the education and care of the boys. The bishop had replied cour-teously, but the dean and residentiaries appear to have largely ignored her missives. She threatened to publish her correspon-dence with them, and in September 1813, after finally securing what she regarded as an unsatisfactory interview with a residen-tiary in May, petitioned the Court of Chancery on the choristers' behalf. In August 1814 the Master of the Rolls found that a char-ity had been established for the boys in the fourteenth century, but advised that a formal inquiry into the administration of the charity would be too expensive. She continued to accuse the dean and chapter of neglecting the boys, until in 1828 Dean Copleston arranged for a master to teach and maintain them (p. 404).[38]

Almost immediately after his appointment Van Mildert had to respond to the proposal that Queen Caroline, George IV's estranged wife, should attend morning service on Sunday 26 November 1820. On Liverpool's advice, he remained at Christ Church. Liverpool made Thomas Hughes, who was in residence, responsible for the arrangements, instructing him to conduct the service 'in the usual manner without alteration or addition, or without any deviation from the accustomed course'. In the event the queen attended morning prayer on Wednesday 29 November 'accompanied by the common council of the city of London and a guard of honour composed of 1,000 gentlemen on horseback' (Fig. 283).[39] Van Mildert's fears of riot or sacrilege proved unfounded.

Van Mildert was the first dean to be actively concerned for the fabric, launching an ambitious programme of repairs and improvements in the cathedral and deanery. At the latter the extensive repairs cost nearly £2,000, including a 'new water closet'. He did not actually move in until May 1823, having pre-viously shared a house with Joshua Watson, a leading member of

40. The former deanery in Dean's Court to the south of the cathedral, built in the 1670s for Dean Sancroft under Edward Woodroffe. A watercolour of 1881. The building ceased to be the deanery in 1977. The site is approximately that of the pre-Fire deanery. (GL)

the Hackney Phalanx, in Great George Street. He persuaded the chapter to agree to an 'experiment' of heating the choir, promising that it would involve them in no expense as Liverpool had offered government assistance. By 1823 Van Mildert felt that the success of the experiment was so modest as scarcely to justify it: the heating machine poured warm air into the dome, 'the cold air...consequently descending with such force as to be almost intolerable to those who officiated in the Choir'. At best, he thought running the machines constantly 'outside the hours of service' might raise the ambient temperature and reduce damp. Gas lighting was also introduced into the choir, experimentally, in May 1822.[40]

Occasional further insights into cathedral life are afforded by various sources. An analysis of the register of preachers identifies those preaching in place of residentiaries or prebendaries, if telling us nothing of the sermons themselves. In 1727 of thirty-one preachers listed, eight were current or former fellows of Oxbridge colleges, seven were incumbents or lecturers of city parishes, while five more were incumbents elsewhere in the diocese; three subsequently became prebendaries, and three bishops; three were published authors. In 1828, however, the pattern was different. Of twenty-four preachers listed, four were minor canons (two of whom preached four times each); only two were current or former fellows of colleges, five were city incumbents or lecturers while two held parishes elsewhere in the diocese; one had been Bampton Lecturer at Oxford in 1813 and one of the minor

canons, Richard Barham, was the author of the *Ingoldsby Legends*. One preacher who preached twice does not appear to have been a graduate, and one, who signed himself 'of Wadham College' Oxford, does not appear in published sources as such.[41] It is hard to avoid the impression that in 1828 the substitute preachers were men of less distinction than those a century before.

The register notes occasional innovations. From 1795 a preacher was recorded for the first time on Good Friday at both morning and evening services, and again on Christmas Day (when on this and subsequent occasions the preacher was the dean, who also usually preached on Easter Day). It also indicates that the cathedral was closed fairly regularly; every five years between 1728 and 1740, and then every three years until 1755, usually for four to six weeks during August and early September. In 1755 it was closed for fifteen weeks from June to September. It was closed for similar periods in 1760 and 1765, and in 1765 it was noted that the preachers were 'at Guildhall', as they were in 1766 when it was closed from 15 June until 16 November. Thereafter the closures were less regular. Very occasionally they affected major festivals: on Christmas Day 1805 it was noted 'No service on Account of Preparations for the Funeral of Lord Nelson'.

Other sources provide some evidence of efficient administrative organization within the cathedral. They demonstrate the careful planning undertaken for the thanksgiving service for the recovery of George III in 1789, necessary in order to seat members of both Houses of Parliament, the court, and members of the common council of the city in the choir. Tickets were issued for seats in the west gallery, the north portico and 'Scaffolds in the Churchyard' for spectators. The next time the king came to the cathedral, in 1797, there were similar preparations, and evidence also survives of catering arrangements. The Lord Mayor requested that in the vestry room 'no large Table will be required as no Second Breakfast is intended to be given, but a considerable number of chairs will be wanted'. It was suggested that they might be hired from the 'Cabinet makers in St Paul's Churchyard ...which the Chaplain will take care of'.[42]

There are occasional hints of the atmosphere prevailing within the cathedral community in surviving private correspondence and diaries. In the 1720s Dean Godolphin, his wife and the then residentiary Francis Hare regularly corresponded with James Lucas, the clerk of works. The letters suggest warm goodwill among the chapter. Hare wrote in November 1724:

I hope the Dean of Sarum [John Younger, residentiary at St Paul's 1698–1728, in residence at the time] continues well, I have often pitied him during the very cold days we have had. Pray my humble service to him and his Lady...I hope the Dean of St Paul's is well the last time I heard of him, was yt he had a cold, as you have opportunity inquire after him...

With commitments elsewhere which scattered them across the country, the residentiaries also visited one another outside the metropolis. In December Mrs Godolphin wrote that 'We are in great hopes of seeing the Dean of Worcester [Hare] today; our Chariot is to go to Slow [Slough] to meet him.' Francis Hare stayed at Eton where Godolphin was provost. When Dean Godolphin was at Eton, he was in regular touch with Lucas, whom he asked to buy shares for him. Mrs Godolphin wrote Lucas friendly and relaxed letters. He did much shopping for her: tea, fabrics, fish, and oranges, and more personal items such as 'stays' for herself and 'drawers' for the dean – on one occasion he was asked to buy a 'gout chair' for her sister, to be sent by the first ship to Pendarres. Other items were dispatched backwards and forwards from the deanery to Windsor by barge.[43]

John Douglas's autobiography is one of the best surviving sources for the concerns and experiences of a late eighteenth-century residentiary.[44] Douglas secured his residentiaryship in 1776 by exchanging it – with the prime minister Lord North's approval – for his canonry at Windsor which was thus acquired by the outgoing residentiary Shute Barrington. Douglas noted that he 'laid out a considerable sum in improving and repairing' his 'House in Amen Corner' before his family occupied it in May 1777. Douglas generally resided in February and October each year, spending the summer at Windsor, but in 1780 was in residence during the Gordon Riots. He secured troops to be stationed in St Paul's Churchyard, which he claimed 'saved our part of the town wch otherwise was in great Danger'. He 'entertained the whole Party, Officers and Privates (about 150 horse and foot) the first day, at my own Expense. Afterwards I settled it, that ye Dean and Chapter provide for the Officers and ye Wards for the privates.'

Crime was rife in Hanoverian London. In 1787, when Douglas was alone during his residence apart from 'the Porter, a female and her maid, at ye Porter's Lodge and my Coachman at ye Stables', he experienced it at first hand:

> A rascal of a footman who had unfortunately got into my family by the Imposition of a Sham Character availing himself of his Knowledge of the circumstances got into my House (we suppose by a false key) in ye Night between ye 4th and 5th March, broke open all ye Drawers and Presses in my Library and Dressing room and carried off all my valuable trinkets, snuff boxes, curious coins, medals, &c. He was apprehended … and fortunately some of the Articles (the trifling ones) were found upon him or at pawnbrokers, where he had got money upon them. He was gently used at the Old Bailey, acquitted of Burglary but found guilty of that sort of Stealing wch is punished by Transportation.[45]

When Douglas was, to his surprise, offered the bishopric of Carlisle in 1787, he was permitted to retain his residentiaryship *in commendam*. However, on the death of Bishop Harley, the dean of Windsor, in the following year, George III offered Douglas the deanery in exchange for his residentiaryship at St Paul's. Douglas thus returned to his former and favourite haunt (it incongruously provided the backdrop to his portrait as bishop of Carlisle), although he was allowed to remain temporarily at St Paul's 'in order to get me Dividend of some fines then in agitation'.[46]

CONCLUSION

The period 1714–1830 was an era of quietude in the history of St Paul's between the upheavals of the destruction and rebuilding of the cathedral, and the 'modernization' of the Victorian period. Most English eighteenth-century minds did not incline to radical reappraisal of institutions, whether of state or church. The medieval constitution of the cathedral was not questioned, but

modestly adapted. In 1714 the dean and chapter inherited a newly-built cathedral, the fabric of which was maintained by independent trustees. Music and liturgical matters were in the hands of the semi-autonomous corporations of the vicars choral and minor canons. The cathedral actually needed little hands-on attention from the dean and chapter. Their task was to be present, in turn, to preside over the cathedral's round of worship for and on behalf of the diocese, and to guard and defend the ancient heritage and endowments of the cathedral.

Occupation of the deanery, residentiaryships, or prebendal stalls did not place great responsibility or duties upon an individual. It conferred instead the dignity of a great institution of which they became a part. It provided freedom to undertake other, less well-provided for tasks in the Church. For most of the period the deanery in particular, and some residentiaryships, provided additional income, and a base in London during parliamentary sessions, for bishops of poorer dioceses. These positions also provided financial support and recognition and status for distinguished apologists for the Church and defenders of orthodoxy: Hare, Butler, Secker, Pretyman, and Copleston.

In these ways, providing a round of daily worship and weekly celebrations of the holy communion, and as a centre of godly learning, the cathedral throughout the long eighteenth century fulfilled Thomas Cranmer's expectations of a cathedral in the reformed Church of England.

The longevity of some residentiaries encouraged periodic criticisms that they were out of touch with current issues, and that they lacked political sympathy with current ministries and so failed to form effective links between church and state (p. 366). Quite simply, they outlived the ministries on whose advice they had been nominated by the Crown; their deaths or preferment being eagerly awaited by current ministers anxious to replace them with more sympathetic figures. Similarly, reformers of alleged abuses lived to be seen as reactionaries by succeeding generations. This was particularly true in the 1820s and 1830s as ancient institutions and arcane practices came under the microscope of reformers, supported by a radical press. However, a reading of Miss Hackett's researches and correspondence with the dean and residentiaries makes it hard to avoid the conclusion that the then dean and chapter displayed a woeful indifference to issues relating to the standards of worship and provision for the poorest members of their foundation, the choristers. However, despite the allegations of complainants and reformers, worshippers did not abandon the cathedral. In July 1824 *The Times* reported that the choir was crowded at Sunday evensong; with not a seat to be had except in the gallery, and that only by slipping 'half a crown' to a virger; Sydney Smith claimed in 1839 that he had 'very often' counted 150 people at evensong on weekdays.[47] But as public attitudes to the affairs of great public institutions began to change in the early to mid nineteenth century, and the term 'reform' became increasingly central in the lexicon of contemporary politics and debate, those hostile to the cathedral could find effective if often anachronistic Hanoverian ammunition at St Paul's.

8

FROM 1830 TO THE PRESENT

Arthur Burns

The modern history of English cathedrals has been characterized by four important trends: a diminution of their significance in national life; the increasing importance and changing nature of relations with both the worshipping laity and the wider public; a growing sense of financial crisis fuelled by the ever-burgeoning cost of maintaining the fabric; and administrative and financial reform. While all these trends are in evidence at St Paul's, its history also distinctively reflects the cathedral's location in one of the most extensive and rapidly expanding capital cities of the last two centuries. St Paul's has retained a national and civic 'presence' other cathedrals have lost, with important consequences for its internal history. Deans and canons have sometimes been selected with more concern for their national role than their suitability for chapter life. This is one explanation for the fact that the St Paul's community has sometimes been an unhappy one, its equanimity also disturbed by the scale of the challenges confronting a chapter at times almost borne down by its sense of responsibility for both fabric and Christian mission.

These themes permeate the modern history of the cathedral, but with varying intensity: thus in 1830 concern for the fabric was an optional matter of decoration, cleaning and improvement; by 1930 it was demonstrating the insatiable appetite for funds which has characterized it ever since, staking its claims to priority of attention with the compulsory closure of the cathedral as a 'dangerous structure'. For convenience's sake this overview is therefore subdivided to reflect broad shifts in the dynamics of the cathedral's history. In 1868 a period of modest internal reforms and more dramatic externally imposed changes was succeeded by forty years in which the reputation of the cathedral was transformed by the activities of a predominately Anglo-Catholic chapter. The retirement of Dean Gregory and the appointment of Dean Inge in 1911 was a similarly epochal moment, ushering in what in retrospect can seem a time of troubles only terminated by the outbreak of war in 1939. The changes in the public reputation of the cathedral resulting from the Second World War, combined with the wider social and political changes that ensued, have coloured much of the post-war history of the institution.

REFORMERS REFORMED: 1830–1868

The 1830s were a challenging decade for the Church of England. The Whig government installed in 1830 was unsympathetic. Political radicals were provoked by the episcopate's collective resistance to the 1832 Reform Act, and decried the church's role in 'Old Corruption', the nexus of patronage believed to corrupt the body politic. Cathedral offices, apparently combining few duties with extravagant rewards, and often in the Crown's gift, were singled out for attack. Friends of the church also sought reforms, aimed at rewarding the 'working' clergy in the parishes. In their schemes too, cathedrals stood to lose: with politicians ruling out state subsidy, where else might monies to improve the parochial system be found?

It was to cathedrals that the Ecclesiastical Commission given permanent form in 1836 turned to fund reform. In 1840 an Ecclesiastical Duties and Revenues Act authorized the plunder of cathedrals to bolster parishes and dioceses. At St Paul's, prebendal estates were designated for transfer to the commissioners, leaving the office of prebendary effectively an honorary one. The individual incomes of the residentiaries and dean were to be capped at £1,000 and £2,000 per annum respectively, and the surplus from the common fund placed at the commissioners' disposal. The dean economist and ascetic Edward Copleston. His income as bishop of Llandaff, some £900 p.a., paled beside the more than £5,000 he earned from St Paul's, and Copleston was an active presence throughout his twenty-two years as dean. It was Sydney Smith, however, who emerged as the dynamo of the chapter (Fig. 312).

No other contemporary cleric claimed so public a reputation as a reformer. Smith had helped to make the *Edinburgh Review* the leading organ of Whig reformism, frequented Holland House (to many clergy, effectively enemy HQ) and publicly supported the 1832 Reform Bill. He was appointed to St Paul's in 1831 by the Whig premier Earl Grey, who viewed the post as 'A snug thing, worth full £2,000 a year'. Perhaps Smith's residentiary colleagues when first appointed, the invalid Thomas Hughes and the 'languid' violinist Frederick Blomberg, so regarded their positions, but not the new canon.[2]

Smith's activism certainly made the canonries snugger: the common fund benefited as contracts were renegotiated and bills scrutinized. But Smith also secured improvements in the management of the fabric fund that did not impact on canonical incomes. He initiated the cleaning of the monuments that in 1819 he had judged 'a disgusting heap of trash'.[3] A library stove was installed to preserve newly repaired books from damp; conversely water was introduced as part of a system of precautions against fire which also included insuring the building (previously a curious oversight in the case of this particular cathedral!).

Hale's arrival brought Smith an ally and sometime rival in reforming energy. A trusted lieutenant of the bishop of London since 1829, Charles James Blomfield, Hale shared his patron's relentless activity. He soon assumed various responsibilities offloaded by the ageing Smith. The latter had bemoaned the hardship of winter preaching in St Paul's: 'sentences are frozen as they come out of my mouth, and are thawed during the course of the summer, making strange noises and unexpected assertions in various parts of the church'.[4] The only solution, he jested, was to 'warm the county of Middlesex'; Hale less ambitiously sealed the openings through which what heat there was escaped. In 1841 it was Hale who instigated a programme of cleaning the fabric.

Despite occasional friction, Smith and Hale collaborated in perhaps the most difficult area of internal reform, that involving the wider cathedral community. The choirboys were one focus of attention. In 1835 Smith produced recommendations intended to improve standards, effectively blaming the succentor, E. G. A. Beckwith, for a regime offering the unappealing combination of overambitious repertoire and superannuated choristers. The chapter effectively sidelined Beckwith in 1838, instructing the organist to consult other minor canons on repertoire; the succentorship remained effectively in abeyance until its 'restoration' (still held by Beckwith) nine years later.[5] The schooling and living conditions of the choristers were also kept before the attention of the chapter, not least by the indomitable Maria Hackett (Fig. 333). In 1836 an investigation rebutted criticisms, but five years later Hale suggested an increase in the establishment and the relocation of the school from the Adelphi Terrace home of the almoner, William Hawes. Smith opposed and frustrated the scheme; on his death in 1845, however, Hale removed the school to the chapter house, and the following year himself assumed the office of almoner, diverting its income to the support of choristers. It was not until 1853 that settled arrangements were complete under a new almoner whose residence at 1 Amen Court served as the school.

More truculent objects of reforming attention were found in the vicars choral, virgers and minor canons, as the chapter sought

41. William Hale Hale, archdeacon of London 1842–70, photographed in 1869. (SPCL)

of St Paul's would cease to be a residentiary, and an additional residential canonry (it was from this act that the position of the residentiaries as the 'canons' of St Paul's was formalized) in the bishop's gift would be created for the archdeacon of London. The parochial patronage of individual stalls and the dean would be vested in the bishop. The act also limited the number of minor canons in each cathedral to six.

These were far-reaching reforms. Their short-term impact at St Paul's was mitigated by the unusual status of the college of minor canons (ruled to preserve it from the axe) and the commissioners' respect for life-interests. The new arrangements for the deanery did not come into force until 1849, while the last of the prebendaries appointed under the old dispensation finally expired in 1875.[1] The most immediate consequence was the appointment in 1840 of William Hale Hale as archidiaconal residentiary, but until deaths among his colleagues released funds, Hale was deprived of an appropriate income from the common estate.

Many cathedral chapters resented such revolutions in their affairs at a time when they were already implementing their own reforms. St Paul's was no exception. Chapter minutes of the 1830s and 1840s demonstrate a desire for improvement and efficiency. Presiding over the work was the dean since 1827, the political increased control over their activities. The upheavals resulting from the work of the Ecclesiastical Commission encouraged an assault on often long-standing arrangements, and a chill in relations among the cathedral body was signalled in 1843 by the substitution of a monetary payment for the dinners traditionally provided by the residentiary to those participating in the Sunday morning service.[6]

The persistent sore of erratic attendance among the vicars choral was confronted in the mid 1840s.[7] In the early 1830s Smith had made the vicars liable to dismissal (new virgers were also required to agree to resign at the dean and chapter's request, reaffirming the position of the statutes muddied by the courts' intervention in the case of Henry Argent in 1783).[8] Then in 1843 Hale drafted regulations making appointment tenable at the pleasure of the chapter, enforcing retirement at fifty-five and prohibiting membership of any other choir. Their introduction provoked such anger that the chapter retreated; a second attempt at reform collapsed four years later. It was only when a new statute was confirmed in 1848 that stricter regulation was imposed, although, crucially, the vicars' freehold survived.[9]

Chapter encountered similar problems with the minor canons. Their role in Sunday morning service and the definition of 'attendance' were reviewed in the early 1840s (pp. 354–5).[10] Relations were further soured when in 1850 the chapter decreed that the Commission reforms required that in future the chapter should no longer be bound to appoint minor canons from among candidates furnished by the college.[11] A declaratory statement to this effect when the chapter next appointed one of the college's candidates inflamed the dispute. Senior minor canons complained to the bishop of London as visitor not only of this innovation, but also of systematic neglect of the interests of the college by residentiaries who kept the best chapter livings for themselves and their relations, and who permitted the incomes of the minor canons to stagnate while capitular revenue soared (p. 373). If the 1840 Act was to be followed when it came to appointment, why was its ruling that each cathedral should have only six minor canons ignored, when such a reduction would at least have increased each minor canon's share of their common fund?

Blomfield's judgement in 1854 largely favoured the chapter: the status of the college as a royal foundation incorporated under charter meant that it could not be reorganized without a specific order-in-council. Blomfield nevertheless insisted on a new statute governing the disposal of chapter patronage, and in 1855 an order-in-council ratified a scheme giving the minor canons precedence over all but the dean and residentiaries in the disposition of livings close to the cathedral. Meanwhile, a compromise on the appointment of minor canons saved the constitutional point for the chapter while restoring traditional practice.

Clearly, then, St Paul's was a site of active reform. Smith and Hale were particularly energetic, but the other residentiaries appointed in this period were also ornaments rather than liabilities to the cathedral. The evangelicals Thomas Dale (1843–70), Henry Montagu Villiers ('the most influential churchman in London' at St George's Bloomsbury, 1847–56), William Weldon Champneys (1851–68) and Henry Melvill ('the most popular pulpit orator in London' at St Margaret's Lothbury, 1856–71) were star parochial incumbents; so was the high churchman James Endell Tyler (1845–51).[12] The remarkably extended career of Charles Almeric Belli, precentor from 1819 to 1884, attracted criticism even within the cathedral: Smith branded him the 'Absenter', a reputation confirmed much later, in 1872, when the

dean's virger almost turned him away from a service unrecognized. The body of the prebendaries, however, contained few scandalous and many distinguished individuals who, like their eighteenth-century predecessors, gave substance to the claim that cathedrals sustained learned clergy: the Oxford professor of Greek Thomas Gaisford and the biblical scholar Thomas Hartwell Horne among them. Alongside were figures prominent in the lively London world of church voluntary organizations such as Henry Handley Norris and William Parker, secretary of the SPCK. Even the minor canons had their own celebrity in Richard Barham, author of the *Ingoldsby Legends*.

More generally, as the site of important national clerical festivals and now home to a national pantheon (Fig. 222), St Paul's was better placed than many provincial cathedrals to answer a utilitarian critique. In addition, it ranked only middle of the table in terms of its wealth as exposed in the Ecclesiastical Duties and Revenues report of 1835 (the gross income of the common fund of £11,140 being dwarfed by the £21,551 of Canterbury and £35,071 of Durham).[13]

Yet despite all this, and having in Smith so well-connected a canon, St Paul's figured particularly prominently as a target for criticism in debates over cathedral reform in the 1830 and 1840s. It was a misfortune that Bishop Blomfield of London was also the driving force of the Ecclesiastical Commission (as a fellow commissioner tartly observed, 'Till Blomfield comes, we all sit and mind our pens, and talk about the weather').[14] An instinctive utilitarian, Blomfield was reputed to have observed that 'the only use of Deans was to ask the Canons to dinner, & the only use of the Canons was to accept the invitation'.[15] This outlook informed his memorable verdict on the indefensibility of the St Paul's establishment during the debate on the 1840 cathedrals measure (p. 372).

Blomfield irritated many; none more than Sydney Smith. The latter conceded that 'the best reason for destroying the Cathedrals is the abominable trash and nonsense they have all published since the beginning of the dispute',[16] but took it upon himself to do better. A series of public letters highlighting the instance of St Paul's accused his diocesan of seeking to 'become the *Church of England here upon earth*'.[17] He scored palpable hits, such as his contrast between the episcopal commissioners' faith in the bishops as reformers and suspicion of chapters. But this was not vintage Smith. His wit failed to counteract an impression of self-interested opposition. Smith's reforming principles had been forged when the aim was to protect property from arbitrary interference rather than to redistribute it for the public good. The veteran reformer ruefully acknowledged his new persona as a reactionary: 'Whenever you meet a clergyman of my age', he lamented in 1835, 'you may be sure that he is a bad clergyman'.[18] Bitterness coloured his responses to even minor matters. As we have seen, when first appointed residentiary Hale could not share in the common fund; the chapter therefore resolved that his fellow canons should employ him as a deputy in respect of the consequent reduction in their own duties. Smith accompanied his cheque to Hale with a note so 'unexpected as it is undeserved' that Hale returned it. Insisting that Hale accept it, Smith was unapologetic: 'I consider myself fully entitled by law to a fourth of all emoluments which I enjoyed before your admission to the chapter and shall resist at Law any attempt to diminish them'.[19]

Many chapters protested to the Commission that its proposals involved the violation of ancient endowments, statutes and precedent. Here St Paul's was further compromised in reform debates by internal factors. Until Hale and William Sparrow Simpson

42. *St Paul's from the River Thames, looking east*, by David Roberts, 1863. One of a series of record paintings commissioned from Roberts by the railway and building contractor Charles Lucas. On the left, the City of London Gasworks; on the right, old Blackfriars Bridge, demolished while the painting was made. (Private collection)

(appointed a minor canon in 1861 and a year later librarian) organized its muniments, even the chapter sometimes failed to locate relevant documents.[20] More seriously, disputes within the cathedral saw statutes, benefactors' wishes and precedent invoked by *critics* of the chapter. Thus Maria Hackett accused the almoner of neglecting his statutory duties; minor canons argued that the nepotistic disposal of chapter patronage and the disposition of cathedral revenues ignored the donors' intentions.[21]

Another reason for St Paul's prominence in reform debates was its location: it loomed large in the vision of government, parliament and anticlerical Londoners, as illustrated by an extended debate on public access to the cathedral.

In the wake of parliamentary reform, emboldened radicals and reformers judged that the cultivation of 'respectability' among the unenfranchised would promote further expansion of the electorate. This was the background to a petition introduced in parliament in 1837 by the radical Joseph Hume, demanding free public admission to St Paul's as one of a number of institutions containing either paintings or marmoreal essays in civic virtue conducive to moral edification. The Whig home secretary Lord John Russell secured the backing of the queen before inviting the dean and chapter to improve on existing arrangements under which a fee of 2*d*. was charged to view the interior save at set times (9.45–11.00 a.m. and 2.45–4.00 p.m. on weekdays, and 10.00–12.00 a.m. and 3.00–5.00 p.m. on Sundays).

The chapter response was robust. Such matters were no business of government. Already a decision to remove (on Sundays only) barriers confining access to the transepts and crossing had

caused trouble; more might produce 'a Royal Exchange for wickedness'. The chapter's insistence that 'a church ought not to be regarded in the light of a gallery of art' was nevertheless weakened by the fact that save for occasional services the cathedral beyond the choir fulfilled little spiritual purpose (indeed, in 1853 a correspondent to the *Illustrated London News* could blithely recommend the removal of the floor of the crossing to allow visitors a better view of the last resting place of Nelson and Wellington!).[22] The chapter eventually undertook to extend the free access by an hour, and here matters rested until Hume secured a select committee on the question in 1841, which renewed the call for more public access. When Henry Hart Milman was appointed dean in 1849, his brief from Russell, now prime minister, specifically highlighted the matter.

The 1841 committee's minutes shed interesting light on the public frequenting the cathedral.[23] The minor canon R. C. Packman estimated that on the barrier-free Sundays between two and three thousand visitors entered the cathedral, primarily London artisanal families; weekday tourists came from out of town. All witnesses agreed that visitors could be a nuisance, but differed over the nature of the problem they posed. Smith and virger James Sykes blamed the London crowd: they smoked, snacked and solicited in the crossing; some defaced walls, monuments or servicebooks; others relieved themselves in pews and dark corners. In contrast, Packman was more concerned by 'gentlewomen with plumes of feathers, not of a bad character, but strings of person walking up and down, looking at each other, and lounging about'; a view supported by virger John Lingard, who

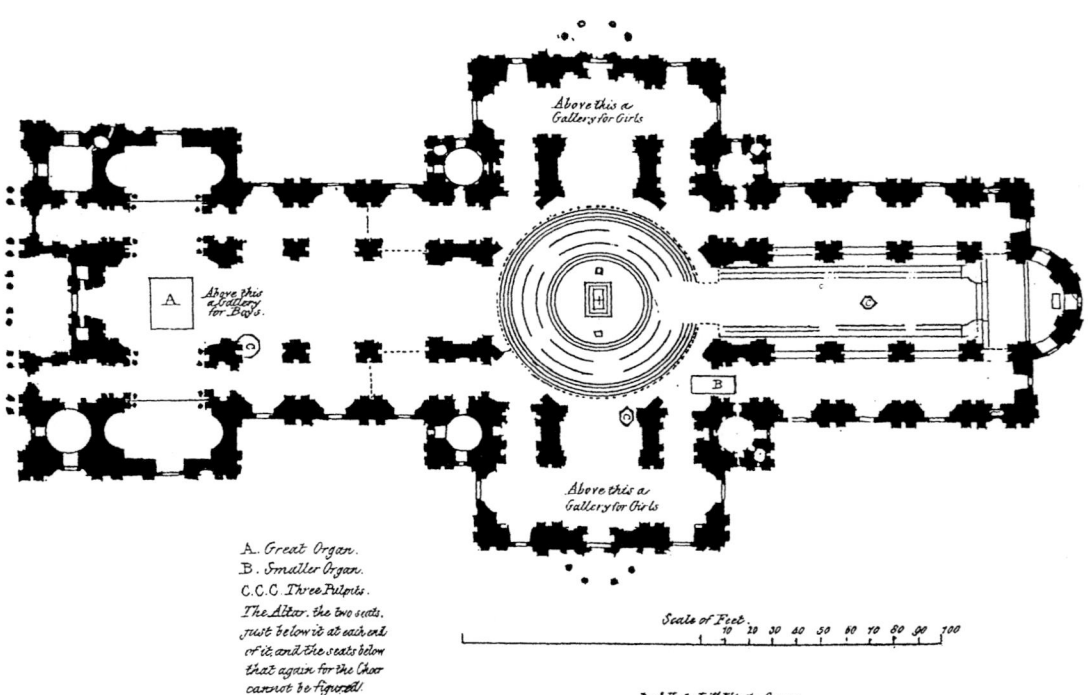

43. An anonymous *Plan for a More Extensive Application to Divine Service of the Hitherto Unoccupied Portions of ... St Paul's Cathedral*, 1839, featuring a dome altar and multiple pulpits.

thought that the poorer classes 'if they are spoken to...behave better than a great many who style themselves gentlemen'. Such contradictory responses reveal not only the different perspectives of Whig grandee and humble virger, but also the impact of the tensions within the cathedral community: Packman was the residentiaries' most vocal critic among the minor canons, and seized the chance to rehearse his view that remunerating virgers and minor canons by fees encouraged the 'evil' of regarding the cathedral endowments as 'the individual property of the dean and chapter'.

Financial implications certainly complicated the question of access. Tourism was vital to the everyday economy of the cathedral. In 1841, four junior virgers received a salary of £7 14s. 2¾d. But in a good year they might divide £500 from the 2d. fees (indicating an annual paying-visitor total of 60,000). Still more came from tours of the crypt and visits to the ball and cross (in the touristic *annus mirabilis* of 1862, with Wellington and his carriage and the knock-on effects of a Kensington exhibition to add to the attractions, this yielded £1,160); virgers also received one fifteenth of the 'cupola money' – in 1841, 1s. 6d. for a visit to the west gallery, model, library and bell. This generated some £30 (£120 in 1862) for each individual. The remainder of the cupola money (£2,640 in 1862) was allocated to the vicars choral and minor canons.

Dispensing with fees would require another source of remuneration to be agreed with the Ecclesiastical Commission. In 1845 Hale unsuccessfully argued that the monies transferable on the death of two residentiaries would be better reallocated to replace the fees supporting vicars choral, minor canons and virgers; in 1850, against the background of the impending Great Exhibition and an anticipated surge in visitor numbers the following year, the Commission released £400 for the virgers and £200 for additional vicars choral on condition that entrance fees were abolished and the vicars' estates managed more effectively. Thus the cathedral gained six assistant singers and the most unpopular element in the system of charging disappeared. In 1860, however, a request for a similar grant to subsidize the new evening services and to substi-

tute for cupola fees not only generated no new money but saw the previous subsidy declared *ultra vires*. Fees, however, were not reinstituted, and the chapter absorbed the additional costs from their share of the surplus in the common fund.

The cathedral under Dean Milman

Milman's installation in 1849 set the tone for future appointments to a deanery now free of its association with distant sees. Although an effective parochial clergyman, it was as a man of letters that Milman had achieved real distinction. Like Smith, he was a key contributor to a leading review, in his case the Tory *Quarterly*; but it was his *History of the Jews*, published in 1829 and described by Arthur Stanley as 'the first decisive inroad of German Theology into England',[24] that established a scholarly reputation confirmed by the monumental *History of Latin Christianity* completed at the deanery in 1855. Milman (Fig. 301) was Lord John Russell's appointment, and this with his liberal Anglican churchmanship retrospectively ensured that, in comparison with that of later high churchmen, his contribution to St Paul's was neglected. Milman had in fact a romantic affection for his cathedral, clearly expressed in his genial *Annals of S. Paul's*. This volume, together with Hale's contemporary editions, began a tradition of capitular ruminations on both the distant and modern history of the cathedral, reflecting a newly emotional attachment to the cathedral among its clergy.

The Milman era not only saw a continuation of institutional reform but also developments in worship and major alterations to the fabric, more commonly associated with his successors. The most famous state service of the nineteenth century, Wellington's funeral of 1852, was its outstanding event. There were many other occasions during the 1850s and 1860s, however, on which services marked significant moments in national life, such as thanksgivings for peace and other deliverances, and national acts of humiliation. These, while not unique to the cathedral, received national attention and with the funeral provided a basis for the later wider revival of the tradition of state services (pp. 356, 384). Such services utilized the whole body of the cathedral, and so related to another major development encouraged by Milman.

It is striking how little the debate over access in the 1830s and 1840s related to worship. A solitary anonymous pamphlet of 1839 bemoaned the 'cold and chilling air' generated beyond the choir by the absence of regular worship and icily marmoreal pantheon. Its author proposed the removal of the organ and screen, and a new altar on a raised circular dais under the dome surrounded by seats for the cathedral clergy (Fig. 43). The nave would accommodate male worshippers; the transepts women; the choir the 'quality' and regular communicants. The acoustic challenge of preaching to this congregation was solved by having lessons read from four separate reading desks and sermons preached from three separate pulpits simultaneously. The vast congregations anticipated would, the author hoped, derive from a programme of domestic visiting based at the cathedral and the provision of opportunities for quiet religious reading during the day.[25]

A little of this ambitious programme was realized on Advent Sunday 1858 with the institution of Sunday evening services under the dome. The 2,500 chairs provided were overwhelmed by the more than 10,000 who sought admission (Fig. 300). Bishop Tait preached, sharing Milman's enthusiasm for the experiment. The predominantly evangelical chapter may have been further motivated by the immediate occasion of the innovation, the cessation of similar events at the evangelical assembly-point of Exeter Hall on the Strand. The success of the service generated a series running from January to Easter each year, and led to the introduction of wandsmen on the cathedral floor in 1861, as well as almsboxes to help meet the additional expenditure involved.[26]

These developments informed the decorative projects launched under Milman, who had already encouraged F. C. Penrose, surveyor of the fabric from 1852 (Fig. 251), to initiate discussion on decoration. The commencement of the dome services was accompanied by the creation of a St Paul's Fund to support both this initiative and 'the embellishment of the interior of the cathedral'. By 1862 the fund had raised £12,000 and undertaken work costing £13,000; by 1868, following the institution of the 'National Guinea Subscription' in 1865, income and expenditure both totalled £25,000 (pp. 243–49). Of particular consequence for worship were the erection of a pulpit under the dome and the removal of the organ from the screen in order to permit the instrument's enlargement. The striking result (Fig. 124) prompted the decision that the organ should not be replaced and the new vista further improved by the removal of the screen, while a new, 'great' organ in the south transept was joined there by a platform for the large, mixed voluntary choir recruited to enhance the Sunday evening services.

All this activity increased St Paul's public profile. The preparations necessary for Wellington's funeral, the spectacle itself and the ingenious scaffold erected for the restoration of the dome frescoes in 1853 provided ideal subject-matter for the *Illustrated London News*, which regularly carried dramatic engravings of the latest developments (Figs 174, 288). This was fortunate, for in the adoption of the appeal to fund work on the fabric, public interest acquired new and enduring financial significance. It helped that the commitment of cathedral chapters to 'improvement' was by now receiving public recognition; the conception of cathedral office as a sinecure consequently became less prevalent. As Hale wrote to Mansel on his appointment, 'Formerly a Dean might lead a life of repose, whether at his deanery or away from it. This cannot be now.'[27]

POMP AND PASTORALIA: 1868–1911

Some prime ministers find the ecclesiastical patronage at their disposal an irritating burden; others fume at clerical longevity. The most 'ecclesiastical' of modern premiers, William Gladstone, had the privilege of overseeing a change of personnel at St Paul's that shaped a distinct epoch in the cathedral's history. Disraeli had provided the foundations in appointing Henry Longueville Mansel dean in 1868, and then Robert Gregory as canon to replace Champneys. In 1870 Gladstone elevated Dale to the deanery at Rochester, and appointed Henry Parry Liddon to a canonry; in 1871 the death of Melvill made room for Joseph Barber Lightfoot. Gladstone was still premier when Mansel died that July, and he raised Richard William Church to the deanery. Beyond the reach of the prime minister's hand, Archdeacon Hale died in 1870, to be replaced by Piers Calverley Claughton, the choice of a bishop of London, John Jackson, in office only since 1869. The sense of a new era in the life of the cathedral was reinforced in the same year by the resignation after sixty-two years' service of the chapter clerk, Christopher Hodgson, and the death of William Sellon, steward of manors since 1835.

Both Mansel and Church, though from a different school of churchmanship, were in the Milman mould of public intellectual. At Oxford, Mansel had delivered a widely influential and controversial series of Bampton lectures which, denying the capacity of metaphysics to make meaningful statements about the nature of God, in an attempt to disarm liberalizing theology had inadvertently cleared obstacles from the road to a coherent agnosticism. Church (Fig. 46) received the call while a parish priest. But he was neither obscure nor obscurantist. In Oxford, Church's proctorial 'Non placet' had saved his mentor John Henry Newman's *Tract XC* from formal condemnation by the university in 1845; unfinished at his death was his classic study *The Oxford Movement*.[28] Church continued the tradition of literary deans. He was a founder of the influential high-church newspaper the *Guardian*, and had written for the *Saturday Review*. 'Conservative by instinct', he had nevertheless a width of sympathy which made him both a political disciple of the pre-Home Rule Gladstone and, while theologically orthodox, less nervous of new developments than Mansel.

Church unfairly judged the deanery of Milman's day as 'a place of literary leisure'. No longer. He saw his own task as the 'very tough practical business' of setting 'St Paul's in order as the great English cathedral'. This would require the conclusion of a satisfactory financial settlement with the Ecclesiastical Commission and the continued restoration of the fabric; he would also have to 'fight and reduce to order' the vicars choral.[29]

Church hoped he would find willing allies in the residentiaries. Gregory, like Church, was an evangelical won over by the Tractarians, but came from a narrower, northern Wesleyan background and espoused a patriotic protectionist conservatism. He had proved an effective pastor in a deprived Lambeth parish, and was an able administrator who would serve as treasurer of the National Society while canon. Although Gregory was a Puseyite rather than a ritualist, he believed that 'so many things are mixed up with [the] cause that I value above all things' that he stood by ritualists when they came under attack. Worship was thus an obvious focus of his attention at St Paul's.

Gregory provided energy and purpose, Liddon the 'star turn' in the pulpit. Liddon was the closest disciple of Edward Pusey, and had built a significant reputation as a preacher in 1860s Oxford.

Shortly after his appointment to the canonry, he was elevated to a chair, but it was St Paul's that most effectively showcased his talents and his disdain for trends in Oxford led him to resign his professorship in 1882. Among the other residentiaries of the 1870s, Lightfoot, Hulsean professor of divinity at Cambridge, was a leading biblical critic, conservative but rigorous. He had accepted his canonry only on the condition that his residence need not interfere with the Cambridge terms, and he generally took a back seat. When in 1879 he accepted the see of Durham, it was yet another sympathetic professor, the Oxford medievalist William Stubbs, who took his place. Claughton's main contribution to the developments of the 1870s was not to obstruct the 'united force' Canon Scott Holland retrospectively attributed to the chapter as a whole.[30]

The first item on Church's agenda was a settlement with the Ecclesiastical Commissioners, towards which Mansel and Gregory had already made considerable progress. In 1868 legislation had encouraged plans to commute the cathedral property by permitting consideration of cathedrals' requirements for capital expenditure. Three years of hard negotiation by Gregory paid off when in 1872 the Commission agreed to provide an annual income of £18,000 in return for the transfer of most capitular property, and to allocate an additional £30,000 for capital expenditure. The estates of the vicars choral were simultaneously commuted for £900 per annum. Further negotiations led to the Saint Paul's Cathedral, London, Minor Canonries Act of 1875, that finally authorized the gradual reduction of their number to the six envisaged back in the 1830s.[31] Future minor canons lost their freehold and individual estates (but not the corporate estate), and would not be permitted to hold other benefices; in return, they were guaranteed a minimum income and pensions, while the commissioners agreed to erect six residences in what became Amen Court. A year later, the estates of both college and individual canons were commuted by order-in-council.

The chapter also revisited another long-standing financial issue, the cupola money. In 1871 the minor canons agreed to exchange their share for an annual grant from the chapter, while it was agreed that in future virgers should receive a fixed salary. Although it was not until 1874 that the vicars choral came to terms, the fund was now – like the income from the crypt – more directly under the control of the residentiaries. These developments, like plans for major expenditure, demanded more active financial management. Some concern that Gregory might effectively supplant the dean prevented his appointment to the office of cathedral treasurer in 1869 as part of a wider scheme of making the main cathedral offices tenable by residentiaries rather than prebendaries, but the plan was eventually implemented in the 1880s. A decade before, Gregory had been elected chapter treasurer with control of its finances, a post he retained long after he was elevated to the deanery.

The financial settlement facilitated a renewed commitment to enhancement of the fabric and precinct. Confident in the financial future, in 1872 the chapter contemplated spending the capital of the fabric fund on a one-off programme of initiatives; the trustees preferred to underwrite an initial burst of activity on condition that future calls on the fund should not exceed its income. Another token of confidence was the decision to build a choir school to support a more substantial choir; a sad consequence of the delays which postponed the opening until 1875 was that Maria Hackett, who died in 1874, did not live to see it (Fig. 336). While this construction went on to the east, outside the

cathedral to the west negotiations with the City led to easier pedestrian access as the forbidding railings were removed, and the churchyard was gradually transformed into a garden managed by the Corporation.

More contentious was the continuation of the programme of decoration and alteration. This had stalled in the late 1860s. A fresh appeal for £250,000, a tenth of which was donated in response to Gladstone's spirited speech at the public launch, was boosted by the thanksgiving service for the recovery of the prince of Wales in 1872, a second appeal being launched on the back of its success. The works contemplated were extensive and sometimes controversial (pp. 250–4). The chapter favoured ecclesiologically informed gothic where others preferred a more restrained classicism in keeping with Wren's architectural legacy. Delays and false starts followed, until the dean and chapter assumed full responsibility for future work and in the 1880s concentrated their energies on the choir and a scheme for a new high altar. By 1888 a reredos was in place, but the altar did not appear before Gregory succeeded Church in 1891. Church's incumbency nevertheless also saw a new peal of bells donated by the Corporation and city livery companies in 1878, and a reordering of the crypt, made possible by the removal of lumber associated with the construction of temporary structures for occasional services.

Meanwhile Gregory was more immediately successful in an attempt to address the shortcomings of the musical establishment. He had a widely publicized confrontation with the choir after a poor turn-out on All Saints' Day 1869, and with Hale's co-operation revived weekly Saturday chapter meetings to impose a new discipline on the singers (witness the attention devoted to fines in the reminiscences of the vicar choral William Frost).[32] With John Stainer's appointment as organist in 1872, a new and distinguished chapter in the history of the choir commenced (pp. 405–7). The voluntary choir was also reorganized (out went the women) and from 1873 became central to a new tradition of oratorio performances.

The chapter's commitment to these innovations stemmed from their concern to furnish a setting for an ambitious programme of services and devotion. Such innovations inevitably courted controversy during the 1870s and 1880s, when ritualism embittered church-party conflict. Moreover, Church himself, though a moderate with little interest in vestments, like Gregory felt compelled publicly to oppose the anti-ritualist Public Worship Regulation Act of 1874 and subsequently to protest against the imprisonments that followed. Liddon, too, got involved, joining Church to debate the act with Archbishop Tait. Evangelical enemies of ritual grew suspicious of goings-on in the cathedral.

Significant changes to the services began under Mansel. On Christmas Day 1868 decorations appeared on the altar, and a new St Paul's Day observance was established. Under Church, innovation and controversy increased. In 1871 the Purchas judgment outlawed celebration of communion in the eastward position. In a deliberate attempt to force the issue, Gregory and Liddon refused to comply. Their defiance paid off; no prosecution was brought and Church, too, celebrated in the eastward position. Choral communions were introduced at Whitsun 1872, and from Easter 1873 took place every Sunday and saint's day. Daily communions began in 1877; the three hours' devotion on Good Friday was introduced in 1878.

Angry 'Protestants' lived up to their name. A member of the Protestant Working Men's League stormed out of the first Good Friday devotions and attempted to organize a protest in the north porch; Easter 1883 saw an agitator rush the altar, his cries of 'Protestants to the rescue!' being stifled by Gregory's handkerchief stuffed into his mouth; two years later on Good Friday, Gregory's brawn again came in handy when it was the credence table that was targeted. The new reredos, with its representations of a nursing Virgin and the crucifixion, provoked the most controversy. The Church Association gathered over 9,000 signatures for a petition against the innovation and instituted proceedings under the Public Worship Regulation Act. Frederick Temple, the liberal bishop of London, vetoed the suit, but the issue smouldered on until the House of Lords upheld his decision in 1891. Together, these incidents cemented the cathedral's reputation as a bastion of Anglican high churchmanship.

As well as attending to the conduct of services, the chapter built on earlier efforts to make full use of the building and bring more to worship there. Marriages and baptisms were celebrated for the first time since the eighteenth century. Services were rescheduled better to suit the congregation (and on weekdays the needs of city workers). In answer to a request 'from some young city men', a daily compline was introduced and later a midday service.[33]

The increased emphasis on choral services acknowledged the attractive power of church music. But sermons also drew congregations. The roster of preachers from within and beyond the chapter was probably unequalled in quality at the time; above all, there was Liddon. Liddon's sermons became one of the attractions of the London summer, particularly after the sensational success of a series of Lenten lectures at St James's Piccadilly in 1872. 'Sermon-tasting' was popular among the increasingly mobile late nineteenth-century audience for religious instruction, and it flocked to the cathedral. Virger Green recorded on Sunday 15 May 1872 that 'Liddon preached from the dome pulpit, as there was not room in the Choir, and continued to do so'.[34] The afternoon nave services thus inaugurated are said to have attracted congregations of up to 6,000.[35] Sunday evenings, too, were popular. Henry Scott Holland described 'a guileless mass of clerks and sweethearts holding each others' hands and glad to use common hymn-books. The people of St. Paul's are not purse-proud city gents . . . ; they are all humble folk.'[36]

Occasional services were similarly well attended. The disruption caused to regular worship by preparations for the annual service of the charity children was one explanation for its abolition in 1877. But this loss was balanced by new occasions expressing the cathedral's role as mother church to the diocese (encouraged by the reinvigoration of diocesan life that had marked the mid century):[37] services for diocesan associations, a devotional day for the clergy of the London Mission of 1874, and services for clerical retreats (1878). There were more national church society festivals and episcopal consecrations; St Paul's also hosted services for the Lambeth Conference of 1878. Thus increasingly the cathedral reclaimed the position asserted in the chapter's submissions to the 1854 Cathedrals Commission of being 'a central cathedral for the whole Church of England'.[38]

This last assertion merged imperceptibly into a growing claim to a wider national and imperial function, memorably encapsulated in Canon Sidney Alexander's later description of St Paul's as 'the parish church of the British Empire'. The thanksgiving service for the recovery of the prince of Wales in 1872 proved the first spectacular in a relationship with the Crown that flowered with the service on the steps for Queen Victoria's Diamond Jubilee in 1897 (Fig. 320). Royal occasions were complemented by memorial services for distinguished Britons and visits by foreign dignitaries. A growing stock of imperial heroes underlined the new emphasis; well into the twentieth century, General Gordon's mock tomb was garlanded by visitors, while Lord Roberts's unmarked grave became 'a great place of pilgrimage to the British soldier'.[39] The cathedral benefited from aligning itself with public sentiments that could stimulate the charitable generosity on which future care of the fabric would depend. There was none the less genuine enthusiasm within the chapter for such developments. They chimed with both Church's liberalism and Gregory's Unionism, and in William Sinclair, archdeacon-canon from 1889 and author of some rather undigested *Memorials of St Paul's* in 1909, they found a champion. At the Imperial Federation Banquet of 1891 he announced a desire to see 'the banners of the knights of St Michael and St George waving above the remains of the heroes of the French War', testifying that 'the victories of peace are no less glorious than the triumphs of war'. Long discussions led to an appeal in 1903 to create a chapel for the Order of St Michael and St George, a scheme praised by the *Daily Telegraph* as bringing the cathedral 'ever closer [to] the empire of which it is the religious centre'. The chapel opened in 1906, its restricted dimensions ensuring that ceremonial would involve the whole cathedral. Bishop Henry Montgomery, prelate of the order, proved both a creative liturgist and its faithful servant until his death in 1932, praying for each individual member at the altar rail (Fig. 194).[40]

St Paul's thus became an increasingly ubiquitous symbol of church, city, nation and empire. This made the cathedral vulnerable to symbolic assault by those who wished to alter existing arrangements in any one of these. Its national role coloured the reredos controversy: a 'retired rector' warned that 'a shattered navy would not be so terrible, would not be so ruinous, would not be so full of menace to the Empire, as the growth of this Down-Grade Babylonianism' at St Paul's.[41] In 1887, a service was stormed by socialists who hissed Canon Gifford's sermon while Gregory and other clergy provided impromptu alfresco worship for the marchers left outside; in 1905, unemployed workers staged another invasion after climbing Ludgate Hill to the accompaniment of the 'Marseillaise'; in 1913, suffragettes planted a bomb under the bishop's throne.

Yet if it was becoming the parish church of the empire, St Paul's could not straightforwardly be dismissed as the parish church of the establishment, not least as a result of the changing theological complexion of the chapter.

St Paul's remained a high-church stronghold at the end of the century, evangelical representation being confined to Archdeacons Gifford and Sinclair. But high churchmanship was changing. Henry Scott Holland, appointed canon when aged only thirty-seven by Gladstone on Stubbs's elevation to Chester in 1884, had been influenced by the idealist T. H. Green at Oxford, where he belonged to the 'holy party' from which in 1889 emerged *Lux Mundi*, a bold effort to foster a Catholic theology appropriate to modern society and thought. From the cathedral pulpit, Liddon spearheaded the orthodox attack on the volume's editor, Charles Gore; Gregory two years later would sign a declaration repudiating what he saw as the underlying heresy of the book, which some believed to have killed Liddon. Holland penned its opening essay.

It was not only theology that marked Holland out. Green's influence also encouraged a realization of thought in action; Holland wrote of his appointment to Green's widow that it 'will, I trust, take me nearer to work that he would hold dear, among working-men of that great city'.[42] Holland could not embrace

44. Amen Court, residence of the canons of St Paul's, looking east in 1912. To the right, the backs of the original houses built under Edward Woodroffe, 1671–3; in the distance, additional houses designed by Ewan Christian, 1878–80. (SPCL)

45. Interior of No. 3 Amen Court, *c.*1900. (SPCL)

the ILP or the Labour Party, but he was an advanced Liberal, and it was from Amen Court in 1889 that Holland helped establish both the Christian Social Union and, seven years later, his journal *Commonwealth*. The CSU has been dismissed as 'central, respectable and vague', but the political incoherence of its social-service activism was compensated for by its influence: no fewer than sixteen of fifty-three bishops appointed between its foundation and 1913 came from its ranks.[43] In Henry Scott Holland, as later in John Collins, St Paul's gave a platform to an Anglican promoting a distinctively Christian politics which would significantly influence the future direction of official church policy.

Despite their differences, the chapter of this period worked well together. Holland shared his colleagues' love of the cathedral, as did another high-church (but Tory) appointment, Liddon's replacement in 1890, William Newbolt, who later wrote of the 'glamour about St. Paul's at this time'.[44] Both Holland and Newbolt (a former curate of Butler of Wantage) threw themselves into a developing ministry directed at the city that had commenced in the 1870s. First target were young clerks and warehousemen lodging in commercial premises in the vicinity of the cathedral. In 1871 Gregory had inaugurated a 'semi-secular' lecture series that for some years attracted exclusively male audiences of a thousand or more; then followed more select (and awkward) 'soirées' at the chapter house. In 1876 William Russell and H. C. Shuttleworth were appointed as minor canons explicitly to assist with such work, and they established confirmation classes and a communicant guild. Shuttleworth lectured in warehouses on both secular and sacred topics (in 1883 a short-lived club and reading

46.   Two late nineteenth-century deans: *above*,
Richard William Church; *right*, his successor,
Robert Gregory, being conducted along the south
chancel aisle by Virger Robert Green, *c*.1900. (SPCL)

room were established) and began to attract women (especially
nurses from Bart's) to his ministrations. From 1871 working men,
whose presence in the cathedral as tourists had caused alarm in
the 1830s, were conducted on guided tours on Saturday afternoons by the canon residentiary.[45] The chapter also supported
pastoral work in livings in its patronage: in 1871 there was a substantial endowment of large parishes carved out of St Pancras, and
in 1896 the chapter resolved to have annual collections, the proceeds of which they would match to secure augmentations from
Queen Anne's Bounty. When the last of the *ancien régime* prebendaries expired in 1875, at Gregory's suggestion his accumulated
profits and a gift from Lightfoot re-endowed a stall to maintain
the diocesan inspector of religious knowledge in schools.[46]
Meanwhile Church demanded increased attention to the spiritual
needs of the ever-expanding cathedral staff. This enjoyed only a
limited success; but improvements to their material conditions,
including a new provident fund, summer holidays for the choirboys and residences for virger and bell-ringer, were no doubt
informed by the same spirit.

Newbolt took pastoral work in a new direction, beginning
with the creation in 1893 of what became the St Paul's Lecture
Society. This was a private organization that met in the cathedral
once the nights closed in to hear talks on 'Catholic faith and practice'. By 1914 it had over four hundred members and conducted
weekend retreats in the Trophy Room. In 1898 Newbolt gathered
a handful of warehousemen for spiritual instruction in his residence, and three years later persuaded them to constitute themselves the Amen Court Guild. The creation of cells preserved its
essentially domestic aspect as this 'delightful little bit of
pastoral work' grew until it, too, had well over four hundred
adherents by 1921.[47]

Robert Gregory as dean

Such developments were underpinned by the sympathetic support of Robert Gregory. When Church died in 1890, Gregory's
obvious claims on the office had outweighed the absence of

comparable intellectual distinction. There was a tradition to be
preserved and work undone; Gregory, for all his seventy-two
years, was central to both. The new appointee would not retire
until 1911.

As dean, Gregory gave fresh impetus to the decorative programme (pp. 254–6). The new high altar was finally installed in
1891, and the Jesus Chapel ('dull and gloomy', judged Newbolt)[48]
behind it dedicated; between 1892 and 1894, statues filled the
niches in the drum of the dome. The next grand project was the
Richmond mosaics, completed in the choir in 1896. Between
1898 and 1901, the success of the decoration encouraged city livery companies to finance further mosaics in the quarter domes
under the Whispering Gallery; the choir aisles were similarly
enhanced by 1907. Stained glass, most lost in the Blitz, completed
the 'Byzantine splendours' of the decorative scheme.[49] More pro-
saic improvements included a new clock in the south-west tower
in 1893; electric lighting, paid for by the American financier
Pierpont Morgan in 1902; and a new hot-water heating system.

Gregory generally presided over continuity rather than change,
as in the pastoral and liturgical developments already considered.
Chapter appointments remained predominantly high-church:
Gregory's canonry was filled by George Forrest Browne, a
Cambridge professor of archaeology, succeeded on his elevation
to the bishopric of Bristol in 1897 by Arthur Winnington-
Ingram. The latter's appointment as bishop of London in 1901
brought in another high-flyer, the future primate Cosmo Gordon
Lang (curiously addressed as 'Charles Gore' by Gregory during his
installation). When Lang departed in 1909, an Anglo-Catholic
whose long future career would be confined to the cathedral,
Sidney Alexander, took his place. The nature of the chapter
none the less changed. The burgeoning activity of the cathedral
required more commitment than scholar-canons retaining their
Oxbridge chairs could supply: Browne resigned his within the
year. Three years later, however, he was appointed suffragan bishop
of Stepney and, like Winnington-Ingram and Lang, held this position in plurality with the canonry, thus linking the cathedral more
closely with diocesan life.

47.   An appropriately 'gloomy' portrait of W. R. Inge, dean of St Paul's 1911–34. (SPCL)

In terms of devotion to the cathedral, however, Gregory had no equal. He resigned the treasurership in 1904, but regularly attended chapter meetings until illness intervened in 1907. Now in his eighties, his thoughts turned to the succession. There seemed but one candidate. 'Remember, Holland, when I am gone, that the secret of a place like this lies in punctuality', he informed the heir apparent.[50] Ironically, however, the end to academic pluralism which Gregory applauded would frustrate the plan. In 1910 Asquith offered Holland a Regius chair, and he was gone. ('The parting from here is *horrible*. I resisted and refused, but it was made inevitable.')[51] Perhaps this prompted Gregory's decision to retire rather than die in office. In February 1911 he resigned; by July he was failing; in August he was dead. By then in post – though not in the deanery itself, which Gregory retained in retirement – was a dean of a very different kind.

GLOOM AND DOOM: 1911–1940

The appointment of William Ralph Inge to the deanery of St Paul's can be interpreted either as a radical break from St Paul's tradition, or its resumption. In contrast to the earlier established public figures, Gregory had won his reputation while at St Paul's. Inge was different: 'Asquith, I am told, wishes me to revive the tradition of the Deanery as the most literary post in the Church – the tradition of Colet, Donne, Tillotson, Milman, Mansel and

Church,' he recorded in his diary.[52] Inge's career had been predominantly academic, culminating in four years as Lady Margaret Professor of Divinity at Cambridge from 1907. His lectures on *Christian Mysticism*, speaking engagements on both sides of the Atlantic and publications such as *Studies of English Mystics* (which revived interest in Julian of Norwich) enhanced his reputation, as did the two-volume *The Philosophy of Plotinus* written at the deanery.

It was not Inge's academic writings, however, but rather religious reflection and the *Lay Thoughts of a Dean* (1926), generally taking the form of *Outspoken Essays* (1919–22) or *Assessments and Anticipations* (1929), which secured him wider fame. Inge spoke from the pulpit, after dinner, on the platform, in the lecture hall, and on the radio; further ruminations appeared in a range of newspapers before resurfacing in book form. The logorrhoea stemmed partly from the financial prudence of both the dean and his 'fanatically economical' wife:[53] the journalism paid handsomely. But Inge also coveted a 'very wide pulpit for the advocacy of various things I care about', and he believed that articles in the *Evening Standard* – 'a vulgar little paper' – made him 'one of the best known men in England'.[54]

The impact of Inge's writing came not merely from its profusion but also its content. 'Dean Inge . . . says things that no other public man would dare say, at times provoking his fellow countrymen almost to fury,' observed one commentator in 1931.[55] Inge's robust socio-political outlook blended Conservatism, a tendency to depression and eugenics, but rejected any notion of a specifically Christian politics. This put him outside the prevailing current of ecclesiastical social thinking. Inge was an active member of the Eugenics Society: his essays overflowed with the 'vital statistics' of birth and death rates and social engineering. He called for the sterilization of the unfit, and in 1921 rowed with Archbishop Davidson following an article deploring the education '*at our expense*' of working-class children who would 'take the bread out of the mouths' of more promising breeding stock.[56] Such views prompted suggestions that 'Dr Inge's Heaven would in practice be reserved for men and women capable of taking a double-first'.[57]

Another judgement was that 'Dr Inge looks out of his deanery windows and sees the world as a steep slope reaching down into the sea.'[58] Inge's secular pessimism was famously exposed when shortly after his appointment he addressed the London Women's Diocesan Association on a subject he acknowledged to be 'a red rag for me', 'The Co-operation of the Church with the Spirit of the Age'. Inge deplored such co-operation. Democracy was 'a superstition and a fetish'; so was progress. Almost overnight, St Paul's acquired its 'gloomy dean'. The soubriquet stuck. Inge pasted into his scrapbook a cutting from the *Church Family Newspaper* announcing 'Baby daughter of the "gloomy dean" of St Paul's christened in the cathedral'.[59]

Inge thus fulfilled Asquith's hopes for a public figure. He did so despite increasing deafness and crippling shyness. When the newly appointed minor canon John Collins had his first interview with Inge, a few inconsequential opening remarks subsided into twenty minutes of mutual silence. Mrs Inge subsequently confided to a disquieted Collins that he had been 'a *great* success with the dean'.[60] Collins would come to respect Inge and, no stranger to controversy himself, to value his provocations. Inge's relations with other members of the cathedral community were more difficult.

Asquith had not in fact asked only for a literary dean; he also wanted worship maintained 'at the standard of sober beauty' established under Gregory.[61] Inge was less suited to this aspect of his brief. St Paul's was a flagship for Anglo-Catholicism by 1911; and Inge represented a radical departure from this tradition, having early abandoned his family's high churchmanship. By the time he arrived at St Paul's, he had emerged as a leading modernist, and from 1924 served as chairman of what under his tenure became the Modern Churchman's Union.

Inge was not the only new arrival. Holland's successor was J. G. Simpson, a son of the manse with 'the Kirk in his bones';[62] but the appointment of E. E. Holmes in 1912 to replace Sinclair not only brought together the chapter that would remain unaltered until 1928, but ensured that the prevailing tone would continue to be set by the Anglo-Catholicism common to Newbolt, Alexander and Holmes. When Inge consulted the outgoing archdeacon on his plans, the now embittered Sinclair told him bluntly that 'As long as Alexander and Newbolt are both here you are not going to be allowed to do anything'; he was also reminded that he would not even possess a casting vote in chapter meetings: 'No one who is not an Anglo-Catholic has a chance of being appointed to a Chapter living' (there was indeed a resolution not to appoint clergy who celebrated communion at the north end, and Inge's liberal candidates were blocked).[63]

Inge's lack of sympathy with the matters closest to the hearts of his capitular colleagues is apparent from his thoughts at the end of his first full Sunday of cathedral worship: the 'services seemed to me a criminal waste of time . . . However, I believe I can, without giving offence, pursue my theological studies in my stall.' He was wrong: 'I find it won't do to read books – the congregation would not notice, but the choir . . . would. The noise gets on my nerves and interferes with consecutive thought – I am conscious of growing irritation and dislike of the Cathedral.'[64] Inge took grim pride in his suffering: in 1924 he noted that his cathedral attendances outnumbered Newbolt's. The best he could find to say of his relations with his colleagues at the end of his first year was that they were 'tolerably pleasant'. Looking back in 1949, Inge ruefully compared the position of the dean to that of a 'mouse watched by four cats'.[65]

Of two novel and daunting challenges that Inge's chapter encountered, the First World War found them better prepared. The tradition of state services readily accommodated this new national crisis. Kitchener was commemorated and Roberts interred in the cathedral; and if the unknown soldier was laid to rest in Westminster Abbey, it was not impossible that he had been recruited by the stirring rhetoric of Winnington-Ingram from the cathedral steps (Fig. 322), or prayed for in one of the well-attended services of intercession that punctuated the war years. What Alexander later recalled as the 'heart-searching succession of memorial services'[66] – for fallen nurses, guardsmen, cavalry, artillery, navy, railwaymen – imparted a newly democratic note to the cathedral's response to war. Both militaristic and memorial services cemented the place of the cathedral in the ritual life of the metropolis, as testified to by the spontaneous popular demand for a service on Armistice Day, crowds filling the precinct when one was duly arranged (pp. 387–8).

The war inevitably disturbed the internal life of the cathedral. A vicar choral was given leave of absence as a territorial in May 1914, the first of a number of such departures which depleted the choir: from June 1916, two services a week featured boys' voices alone. In 1915, Sunday evening services were suspended on account of the blackout. On 30 September 1917, 'friendly fire' damaged the south-east cornice; the following March, an unexploded British shell penetrated the south transept; most

CROSSING THE NAVE.

48. Firewatchers cross the cathedral in front of Penrose's pulpit of 1860. Drawing by J. Begg from *Saint Paul's Watch Founded June 1915, Terminated Nov. 1918*. (SPCL)

alarmingly, matins on 7 July 1917 was punctuated by the sound of direct (enemy) hits on the neighbouring Central Telegraph Office. The cathedral had prepared for raids. In June 1915, Alexander and the surveyor Mervyn Macartney (Fig. 254) established the St Paul's Watch, a company of over 250 volunteer architects, professionals and cathedral staff to respond to nocturnal fires. In fact, it was not wartime infalgration but inflation that most damaged the cathedral. In January 1918 a concerned chapter noted the impact of rising wages and considered fund-raising expedients, including collections at Sunday afternoon services for the explicit purpose of keeping them going. Expenditure on the library was curtailed. The cathedral having survived on a reduced complement of minor canons during the war, in 1920 the sixth minor canonry was indefinitely suspended and the incomes of those remaining augmented.[67]

These financial worries added to concerns relating to the second, more fundamental challenge of the early twentieth century: the condition of the fabric. Alexander, now treasurer, here found a cause close to his heart. By 1911, for more than a decade the surveyors had monitored the effects of settlement and the possible impact of public works in the vicinity, but a report in 1907 concluded that there was no immediate cause for concern. A quite different verdict came from the engineer Francis Fox in 1913. This was to Alexander 'the birthday of the whole movement' for the restoration of the fabric, whereas Inge was 'sceptical about the danger, which was exploited, I feared, from interested motives'.[68] Only a further report in 1914 persuaded chapter to act (pp. 299–300). An appeal for £70,000 was launched, principally to fund the strengthening of the piers supporting the dome. The works, carried out by men too old for call-up, were inevitably disrupted by the war. By 1922 the money was gone, but the job unfinished; Alexander published an appeal in *The Times*, this time for £100,000. Work progressed; but on Christmas Eve 1924 the chapter suffered a humiliating 'act of insolent rudeness' (Inge) when the city surveyor served them with a 'Dangerous Structure' notice 'as if they were owners of a small shop in Aldersgate Street' (Alexander).[69] This concentrated minds both in and beyond the cathedral. It was swiftly decided to seal off the choir, dome and transepts to enable repairs to be expedited. All that was needed now was the money. Alexander again wrote to *The Times*, now seeking £140,000. The screen went up, and it was not until 25 June 1930 that the cathedral was formally reopened at a special thanksgiving service. Much remained to be done by Godfrey Allen, who succeeded Macartney as surveyor, but the crisis was over. Five years later, the passage of the City of London (St Paul's Cathedral Preservation) Act, which protected the building from environmental disturbances, offered a more certain future for the restored structure.

The fundraising necessitated by the repairs had been a remarkable achievement. Historic links with the City paid dividends: the first appeal had received £15,000 from the Corporation and livery companies; the Stock Exchange and merchant houses also contributed. A shortfall of £10,000 in 1920 had within days elicited a gift of £100 each from one hundred firms. *The Times* had been crucial in publicizing the later appeals: printing a daily list of new subscribers, in 1925 it had collected over £200,000 within a month (Inge believed this explained the hostile press the cathedral received in other prints). The fundraising was also widely and rightly recognized as Alexander's achievement, not least by Alexander himself.

A chapter at odds
The fabric had been restored; relations in the chapter deteriorated. This was not all down to Inge. Canon Simpson, uncomfortable with the chapter's apparent wartime endorsement of prayers for the dead, boycotted its meetings from 1915. By 1920 chapter was 'instructing' a reluctant dean to ask if Simpson intended a *de facto* resignation.[70] But it was not until his appointment to the deanery of Peterborough in 1928 that Simpson departed. In his place Baldwin installed W. H. Elliott, who 'had felt for years that the pulpit of St Paul's was meant for me'. Within a year 'the back-biting and bad spirit in Amen Court' had shattered the illusion and his nerves. Inge judged him a whinger; twenty years later, Elliott riposted that, if anything, he had downplayed the 'hostility' of Amen Court, and that Inge was culpable for having given up and taken refuge in his scholarship rather than 'knocking down the grinning idols of a disgraceful apathy'.[71] In 1930, the same year Elliot resigned and was replaced by the high churchman Oliver Chase Quick, Archdeacon Holmes was succeeded by the evangelical E. N. Sharpe and the death of Newbolt brought in another conservative high-church theologian, Kenneth Mozley. Alexander now had no rival in experience or commitment to the cathedral. This made all the more unfortunate the increasingly open hostility between Alexander and Inge, whose 'blistering acidity' John Collins judged had 'shrivelled' the senior canon.

Alexander surely had Inge in mind when in 1930 he contrasted Dean Church's character with 'the egoism and inhumanity which are the scholar's besetting sins'; at a St Paul's Day dinner from which Alexander had absented himself to avoid an encounter, Inge announced that 'We are sorry not to have the Senior Canon with us, but Saturday night is his bath night'. In 1934 Inge would write to Dick Sheppard that the 'poisonous reptile' Alexander 'is insane, poisoned at last by his own venom'.[72]

By then, Inge had had enough. As his retirement approached, there was much discussion of the merits of rival candidates for the succession and the qualities desirable. It was argued that the dean of St Paul's was 'the church's mouthpiece to many who read and think and form public opinion but seldom "go" to church'; in contrast, the prime minister's office advised 'that a man with strong human qualities is needed to thaw the present chill, and that administrative and organising capacity are perhaps more important at this time than either great preaching power or great scholarship'. Some in the City, and other London residents, advocated Alexander as Gregory *redux*. The Assyriologist and Egyptologist Sir Wallis Budge informed Archbishop Lang that 'Whatever I am and have I owe to St Paul's, its peace, its restfulness... Alexander has watched the cathedral day and night for 25 years or more... As he has fulfilled his duties as a canon the Dean and Chapter have got all his life and service *for nothing*.' The archbishop, however, had ruled out Alexander 'for obvious reasons', nor would Ramsay MacDonald countenance him. Also in the ring were Tubby Clayton, Eric Milner White and Dick Sheppard (vetoed by Lang on grounds of 'health and irresponsibility'). Inge (stressing that 'nobody here wants the senior canon') first recommended Vernon Storr, but then the dean of Exeter, Walter Matthews (Fig. 53). Inge reported that 'his tiresome wife, of whom he lives in terror, says she hates London. I am going to see Mrs M alone one day this week, and if she is recalcitrant I shall give her a straight talk about the duties of a great man's wife. I am not afraid of her at all.'[73] The much maligned 'Mrs M' had good reason for fearing the move, but her objections, and objections to her, were overcome. John Collins left the cathedral shortly after the announcement and visited Alexander to say goodbye. The senior canon indicated his desk: 'That drawer contains all my plans for St Paul's: nobody will ever see them now.'[74]

Dean Matthews and Dick Sheppard
Matthews was a true Londoner: born in Camberwell, a parish priest in Crouch End and then dean and professor at King's College London. Inge described Matthews as an 'Orthodox Modernist';[75] certainly he was an ecumenically minded 'thinking' theologian. On his appointment to St Paul's in 1934, Matthews was president-elect of the Modern Churchman's Union; like Inge, he would lecture abroad and ruffle Anglo-Catholic feathers. Matthews was nevertheless a very different, more sympathetic personality, sensitive in both senses of the word. Hopes that this might produce an improved atmosphere in chapter were dashed when the disappointed Alexander unavailingly protested that Matthews's London degrees disqualified him from office.

Matthews's appointment nearly coincided with the introduction of new statutes under the Cathedrals Measure of 1931 that, as enacted in 1936, drew a line under some of the recurring issues of the previous century. Canonical duties were detailed; after extended negotiation, the minor canons kept the notion of a college, but effectively lost the last vestiges of 'quasi-independence' and were subjected to increased regulation, as were the vicars choral. Bishop and chapter both emerged with strengthened authority. The authority of the dean, however, was not augmented.

Lacking new constitutional powers, Matthews needed reinforcements. Matthews wanted and got Dick Sheppard to fill a canonry vacated by Quick. Instructed by both archbishop and premier to revitalize St Paul's, Matthews had in mind Sheppard's remarkable pastorate at St Martin-in-the-Fields, where he had famously opened the church round the clock to meet the needs of the destitute and servicemen. Sheppard (Fig. 49) was also a pioneer of religious broadcasting: from 1924, monthly services were relayed from St Martin's, making it a national institution. Enviably well connected, Sheppard was nevertheless a brave appointment. He was dismissive of many of the central concerns of the other canons, plagued by ill health, and famously impetuous and impatient ('the stuff of which Fuhrers and dictators are made', judged Matthews).[76]

There was friction. Alexander and Mozley told Sheppard that he spent too little time in the cathedral. As the international situation worsened, Sheppard achieved celebrity through the Peace Pledge Union, which emerged from his letter to the press in 1934 asking all renouncing war to send him postcards stating the fact; in 1937 (when despite its misgivings, chapter sanctioned a PPU mass in the crypt) he toured the USA on its behalf, and was elected rector of Glasgow University ahead of Churchill. Sheppard's frequent indispositions only exacerbated the problem.

The absences also reflected Sheppard's discomfort in his new post. Alexander thought Sheppard failed to understand that a cathedral was not a parish church; Sheppard that Alexander forgot what a church was for. Early on, Sheppard protested against the use of the Athanasian Creed by refusing to turn east during the 1934 Christmas Day service. On more than one occasion he drafted manifestos for reforms: among them, reordering Sunday morning worship to make it less intimidating; new short lunchtime services for city workers; opening the cathedral until 7 p.m. with a constant clerical presence; illuminating the cross and a night-time light over the door to signal a new openness to the laity. Sheppard called Matthews to arms, in February 1935 proposing a joint ultimatum – 'the Mussolini touch was essential' – to the chapter backed by a threat of highly publicized resignations.[77] Matthews himself was prepared to resign over the reordering of Sunday mornings, and consequently won the day; but generally the alliance proved only fitfully effective, as in fashioning the monthly broadcast Empire Services, and in bringing in cribs and Christmas trees (a gift secured by Sheppard from the king, which could not be refused). Some victories proved own-goals. A watchnight service initiated on the steps saw Sheppard howled down by the crowd, and was the kind of thing Alexander had in mind when preaching from the cathedral pulpit against 'stunts and innovations' in its worship.[78]

For Sheppard, these minor victories counted little. From early 1935, resignation was in the air, and Matthews's efforts to lighten the mood struck a faintly hysterical note: Sheppard's presumably rhetorical threat to hurl himself from the Whispering Gallery during the Athanasian Creed elicited in January 1935 the following message:

Dear Dick,
I love you!
Don't jump off yet,
    Yours aff. Walter.[79]

49.   Canons to the left of them, I: between the wars, H. R. L. (Dick) Sheppard, canon 1934–7, a walking advertisement for his Peace Pledge Union in a 'wet and foggy' Strand, February 1936. (SPCL)

Four months later, Sheppard was on the brink again, drafting a letter to *The Times* explaining his impending departure, citing 'certain omissions in the religious, social and administrative witness of the Cathedral which I am too experienced, and, let me add, impatient to tolerate'. In 1936 it was Mrs M's turn to plead, now having to defend the dean from criticism of his leadership.[80] Immediately following a 'sticky' chapter in September 1937, Sheppard dictated an indictment of the cathedral far more damning than that of 1935:

I do not consider that St Paul's Cathedral is in any kind of way fulfilling its functions. As a converting power it is negligible.... It is impossible to describe the inhumanity of the place... As to the Cathedral's attitude towards social problems and the values that really matter in this war-saturated world I dare not express myself. Until I came to St Paul's I would not have believed that such aloofness from reality on the part of almost everyone concerned could exist in a corporate body... Whether or not I make this memorandum public depends on whether or not I

50.   St Paul's Watch: members of the Second World War contingent atop a roof opposite the north-west corner of the cathedral, *c.*1942. (SPCL)

Top Row.   G. PHYPERS.   V. COATES.   R. JOHNSON.   F. HARRIS.   S. EMPSON.   W. OAKMAN.   E. WALDRON.   J. MUTCH.   J. ROBERTS.   A. SANDERS.   G. DOWNES.   W. SMELLIE.
J. RUNDLE.   L. PARRISH.   J. CAIE.   W. SMITH.   E. MOTT.   F. BLANDFORD.

Second Row.   H. WALDEN.   G. SARGEANT.   J. WALKER.   A. JEFFERY.   N. ROLLIN.   G. BUCKLE.   F. HANCOCK.   L. ALMOND.   J. LANHAM.   J. PARROTT.   J. GUNSTONE.   F. ROWLEY.
D. STEALEY.   J. O'RIORDAN.   J. COCKS.   W. G. JENKINS.   F. LEAVER.   C. ATKIN.   H. WINTER.   J. COFFIELD.   A. BUCKHURST.   S. GIBB.   J. WILSON.   C. FRISBY.   C. ROGERS.
M. JENKINS.   T. WILSON.   E. GOSLING.   W. WILLIAMS.   S. HAWKINS.

Third Row.   F. ADAMS.   T. CALNAN.   R. HUGGINS.   W. PINNER.   D. COOPER.   C. ADD.   G. RIPLEY.   S. HOOKER.   S. HUME.   R. S. KERR.   A. PHIPPS.   H. WILLIAMS.
H. LESTER.   R. LILLYCROP.   M. CLARKE.   F. FOSTER.   R. SCHILLING.   F. POCOCK.

Bottom Row.   J. WRIGHT.   S. EVANS.   S. TAYLOR.   D. JENKINS.   H. MAYDWELL.   N. HERBERT.

think the exposure of what I would frankly call the scandal of St. Paul's might not be of assistance to the Church at large … on the whole I believe its work is not merely negative but actually harmful to organized Christianity to-day.[81]

A month later, Sheppard was gone, but not through resignation. Physically broken, his marriage failing, Sheppard's heart stopped in Amen Court as he worked into the night of 31 October 1937. The funeral was a national event, broadcast by the BBC. But it was a miserable end, and a huge blow to Matthews. Even Mozley, for all his differences, wrote a touching tribute, although the word 'stunts' surfaced here, too.[82]

So an unhappy era began to draw to a close. The role of personalities in creating the febrile atmosphere of these years, however, should not obscure the seriousness of the issues. Not just Sheppard, but Matthews and earlier Elliott had despaired of the religious life of the cathedral of the 1920s and early 1930s. Sheppard encapsulated the critique in condemning his colleagues for 'attempting to maintain the traditions of Dean Church and Dr. Liddon, and obstinately refusing to realize that, except for a handful of people of a very conservative type, those traditions are of as little service to the people as they are to the Kingdom of God'.[83] It must have hurt Alexander to hear 'those traditions' dismissed as pastorally lazy, for Sheppard failed to acknowledge that they, too, had been forged as bold pastoral initiatives, and made the cathedral for Alexander 'the church of the London citizen … the home of the poor'.[84] Moreover, the national function of the cathedral was ignored, while Sheppard did not allow for the practical difficulties presented by the restoration of the fabric. But those who called for a more 'parochial' approach were right that the rapidly changing environment of the city, with its declining resident population, demanded new initiatives. Sheppard and Matthews were both articulating views that they had heard expressed in the streets around the cathedral.

It might not be too much to say that the cathedral was now becoming unpopular: surrounded by a largely indifferent popula-tion, and with a shrinking band of friends in high places. That all was not well was obvious to all; and the wider world who mourned Sheppard would have all the gory details brought to their attention when Ellis Roberts published a remarkably indis-creet and raw biography. Roberts attacked the chapter's 'purely formal interpretation of their duties' in the 'old mausoleum', and printed both sensitive correspondence and Sheppard's indict-ments. Matthews (the 'little Dean') was portrayed as not up to the job.[85] But how St Paul's could have weathered this gathering storm of outspoken criticism had other events not intervened remains a hypothetical question. Roberts's volume was published in 1942; by then such debates belonged to another age.

FRIENDLY BOMBS?

St Paul's had a good war. Indeed, a crisis that threatened the very physical survival of its fabric proved the salvation of the institu-tion, endowing it with a renewed sense of purpose and an enhanced national standing.

Before hostilities commenced, the threat of war had already stimulated action. After Munich, Sheppard's successor, F. A. Cockin, arranged weekday intercessions that attracted crowds of city workers and spawned the St Paul's Guild of Prayer, whose members undertook to pray daily either within or in sympathy with the cathedral. The chapter generally found a healthy distrac-tion from their internal divisions. Godfrey Allen, the surveyor, was placed in charge of arrangements. The choir school was evacuated to Truro in August 1939, and remained there until the end of the war in Europe; once war was declared, there was a further exodus, this time of Gibbons carvings, Tijou metalwork, the Wren model and rare books. Less portable treasures were repositioned or walled up. A strong room and air-raid shelter were created in the crypt; emergency rations were stockpiled.

If high-explosive bombs were one concern, perhaps more wor-rying was a more familiar enemy: fire, this time in the form of the incendiary. Alexander and Allen responded by recreating a St Paul's

Watch. The first firewatchers were recruited from the staff (including choir and minor canons), but on the outbreak of war Allen persuaded the secretary of the RIBA to issue an appeal for help that yielded forty volunteers, soon after joined by another twenty or so, allowing a team of around twelve on any one night. A crypt HQ controlled a command post at the top of the main stairs that relayed reports from roof-top look-outs. The endless drills – dealing with bombs and casualties, hoisting heavy equipment, devising routes through the roof spaces in blackout conditions – generated considerable camaraderie, enhanced once raids led to the provision of sleeping facilities in the crypt. The mess room established by Matthews and Sheppard for cathedral workmen now served the watch, more as common room than caff, one member dubbing it 'the best club in London'.[86] Alongside the architects (including A.R.G. Butler, Sidney Caulfield, Horace Farquharson, Donald McMorran, J.M. Richards and C.M. Oldrid Scott) the watch recruited artists, exiled politicians and intellectuals. John Betjeman was probably its most famous member; but it could, for example, have staffed an outstanding history faculty (H. J. Habbakuk, W. E. Hancock, W. N. Medlicott, Sir Bernard Pares, Richard Titmuss and Francis Wormald). Not surprisingly, lectures were arranged.

Matthews recalled his time with the watch as an unforgettable experience of companionship and commitment. All was not always so congenial: as recruitment became difficult in 1942, GPO 'conscripts' were assimilated, and the logbook records an effectual mutiny when 'all post office men refused to do Patrol', leading to what was described as a 'good clear out'.[87] But for all the tensions, by the end of the war the socially diverse and multinational watch knew they had been part of a remarkable collective enterprise. There can be no doubt of the individual heroism required of those who stood on or within the roof under what Matthews called the 'wild beauty' of the Blitz skies.

During the day, the chapter resolved to attempt to sustain business as usual. Matthews worried that the aged Alexander and ailing Mozley would have been better served by retreat from the front line once the inhabitants of the precinct felt it necessary to retire to the crypt for shelter at night. In Alexander's case, at least, he need not have fretted, for the senior canon was complaining to others that 'people are now threatening me with all kinds of mysterious reactions, collapses and catastrophes if I continue to "carry on": the fact is that they are seeking excuses for their own perpetual and prolonged absences!'[88] Save for brief periods when the

51. The north transept floor after a direct hit early in the morning of 16/17 April 1941. (GL)

52.   Ludgate Hill after an air-raid in May 1941, looking east, with St Martin Ludgate and St Paul's in the background

police insisted on suspension, daily services were sustained, even while sirens wailed. National days of prayer attracted good congregations. Already before the war, the ecumenical service celebrating the silver jubilee of George V and Queen Mary (Fig. 323), broadcast by the BBC in 1935, had heralded a new era of successful national services; now Matthews, a former royal chaplain, worked closely with Crown and government to sustain a regular programme of state occasions. As the war progressed, these were increasingly occasions of hope or celebration of deliverance (in 1943 thanksgivings for the Battle of Britain and for the more recent victory in North Africa, in 1944 for the liberation first of Paris, then of Athens), punctuated by others of a more sombre nature, such as a memorable memorial service for President Roosevelt in April 1945. Matthews personally contributed further to the war effort by undertaking official missions to neutral countries and making regular broadcasts on the BBC.

The cathedral did not escape unscathed. On 10 October 1940 a 500-pound bomb penetrated the choir, shattering the high altar. On 17 April 1941 a direct hit on the north transept destroyed the vault over the central bay of the crypt, bulging the walls of the transept and blowing out much of the glass that remained; a land mine that fell near the site of St Paul's Cross fortunately failed to explode (as, earlier, had a high-explosive bomb which landed near the south-west tower) (Figs 51, 258). Remarkably, there were no human casualties, but the fabric required immediate attention, and Allen and the works staff patched and mended under the most difficult circumstances. This was the last major damage the cathedral sustained, however. By August 1943 it proved possible to restore the broken choir arch that posed a serious threat to the soundness of the vaulting.

If April 1941 saw the most serious structural damage, it was the night of 29 December 1940 that defined St Paul's as a symbol of London's fortitude. Twenty-eight incendiaries fell on the cathedral and the precincts, the watch combating the resultant fires in the roof timbers without the assistance of the failed mains water

supply. The city was aflame; but for once the cathedral's familiar nemesis spared the building. Textile workers were evacuated into the crypt as fire consumed the surrounding businesses; film cameramen on the roof of the cathedral captured remarkable images of the statues on the parapets starkly defined against a wall of fire.[89] At the height of the raid, Churchill telephoned the Guildhall to insist that the cathedral must be saved, and the symbolic importance with which the building was thus invested was confirmed by the publication of Herbert Mason's iconic photograph of the dome and towers amid fire and smoke (p. 461; Fig. 388). The chapter house was not so fortunate, and was burnt out, along with two houses in Amen Court. These buildings, however, only shared the fate of the majority of neighbouring structures in the course of the Blitz; to the north and east St Paul's now rose dramatically from a jagged landscape of urban destruction.

On both VE and VJ days, St Paul's was one of the sites to which crowds flocked. No fewer than 35,000 attended the services that on VE day, as in 1918, were hastily arranged to meet public demand. It was as if the pre-war difficulties had never existed. But whereas in the era of Church and Gregory it was the religious life of the cathedral which sustained its reputation, this was not so now. Members of the watch, as one observer noted in 1944, 'were not necessarily churchmen; certainly it was unlikely that they were regular worshippers...but they were men to whom St Paul's mattered a great deal' (enough, indeed, to pay for the keystone of the restored chancel arch); as the dean put it in his address at the disbandment of the watch, 'You felt that something beautiful was threatened.'[90] It was the symbolic value of the building and the almost providential aspect of its survival that mattered most. Much of this sentiment was newly kindled in the furnace of war. Matthews heard of a woman at Mansion House underground station on VE day who, though not religious, felt that 'it's meant something that it was there and people praying in it. It's kept us going.'[91] Some of those who emerged from the crypt after the big raid took with them a sense of identification with the cathedral

53. The dean and chapter in session, 30 December 1950. From left to right, G. L. Prestige, canon 1950–5, W. R. Matthews, dean 1934–67, and Marcus Knight, canon 1944–60

that would draw them back to great occasions at St Paul's for decades to come.[92] From within the Christian tradition, some, like Lord Simonds, the former lord chancellor, could believe it 'a daily miracle that it should survive; that it did survive was a daily hope and inspiration and a symbol that the Christian way of life should not perish'.[93] Thus, as the celebration of victory gave way to the challenge of post-war austerity, St Paul's perhaps had more friends than it had possessed for half a century. It would need them.

POLITICS AND PRESERVATION

When the war ended, Dean Matthews was already sixty-five, but would remain in post until the mid 1960s, his authority bolstered by his war record. His career began to echo that of Inge: journalism for the *Daily Telegraph*, theological scholarship, even an honorary fellowship from the Eugenics Society. But the atmosphere in his cathedral was improving rather than deteriorating. By 1950 the chapter was very different from that of 1939. Mozley and Cockin had resigned in 1941 and 1944 respectively to be replaced by one liberal theologian, Marcus Knight (a former pupil of Matthews; Fig. 53), and one Anglo-Catholic, Vigo Auguste Demant, a former director of research for the Christian Social Council; in 1947 Oswin Gibbs Smith took the place of Archdeacon Sharpe. Demant's departure in 1949 brought in the patristic scholar G. L. Prestige (Fig. 53). But the most significant change resulted from the death in 1948 of Sidney Alexander. His last years had been difficult. His colleagues, tiring of his autocracy, had secured Matthews's co-operation in dislodging him from the treasurership and installing the dean himself. In a sad echo of Sheppard's end, Alexander died alone and largely unloved in his dilapidated residence, the drawing-room of which served as his coal cellar. In a final gesture of support for the cathedral that had been his life, the residue of Alexander's estate was left to members of the cathedral staff.

The choice of replacement was a bold one – perhaps only possible in the context of a Labour government containing Sir Stafford Cripps. Like the cathedral he now returned to, John Collins (Fig. 54) had enjoyed a good war. His imaginative and brave ministry at RAF Yatesbury had attracted wide notice. When demobilized, Collins returned to his former position as dean of Oriel College, Oxford, as 'an insider of the Anglican church and an insider of the Establishment: but a rebel against the pretensions of both'.[94] Blossoming friendships with Cripps, Victor Gollancz and Richard Acland combined with his wartime experiences in compelling him to issue a call to 'Christian Action' in response to the challenge of post-war reconstruction, from which resulted the organization of that name. Cripps saw in Collins a new model clerical leader and urged on him the canonry to which he was installed in January 1949.

There is a temptation to portray Collins as a second Dick Sheppard. Certainly he could be a provoking colleague: it did not augur well that at his first chapter dinner he announced that 'as a sow returns to its vomit, so I have returned to St Paul's'; like Sheppard, too, he argued that 'unless we can bring the cold stones of St Paul's to life we might as well hand the place over to secular authority as a national monument to a dead past'.[95] He preached that living artists and modern music should be introduced to prevent the cathedral becoming a museum: after the press had publicized the sermon, the organist threatened resignation and Collins received a round-robin from the canons suggesting that it was *he* who should go, which he melodramatically ripped up during the next meeting of chapter.[96] The tensions surrounding his appointment, however, partly reflected Matthews's initial resentment that he had not been consulted (and the active opposition of both Bishop Wand of London and Archbishop Fisher).[97] Ultimately, Collins's vision of how to invigorate the cathedral was much more in sympathy with its traditions than was Sheppard's. He had understood and valued Alexander, and was liturgically conservative. Matthews warmed to Collins, particularly after Collins organized

54. Canons to the left of them, II: during the cold war, John Collins, canon 1948–81, on the road from Aldermaston at the head of the Campaign for Nuclear Disarmament march, 30 March 1959. Left to right: Jacquetta Hawkes, Collins, Ben Levy. In the second row stepping out, Michael Foot

and led a choir tour of the USA and Canada in 1953. Some of the 'excitements' of Collins's contribution to cathedral life indeed resulted from excess of zeal, as in his early abortive and embarrassing initiative as newly appointed chancellor to make the library a centre of scholarship (p. 427). He could wax rhapsodic on the cathedral: 'In my more imaginative moments, I have seen St Paul's, set in the heart of the City of London, as an inspiring symbol of the power and love of God over a civilization that is largely dominated by Mammon... As a centre of Christian action, it seemed to me then [1949], as it seems to me now [1966], that St Paul's offers exciting possibilities.'[98] In at least one sense, St Paul's did become a centre of Christian Action, for the headquarters of the movement was now located in Collins's residence in Amen Court.

Retrospectively, it can be suggested that Collins's appointment was also fortunate in view of the cathedral's oft-repeated claim to be 'the parish church of the Empire'. Like the empire itself, this still had creative potential in 1945. Since the end of the First World War, the Order of the British Empire had sought a suitable location for a chapel: St Paul's had been first considered in 1917 and remained a candidate throughout the inter-war years. Doubts about St Paul's focused on the proposed location for the chapel: in 1947 Sir Robert Knox commented that 'Personally, I do not much like the idea of inviting GBEs to put their stall plates in a Crypt. Most of them are getting on in years, and it seems... to resemble an invitation to them to make some preparations for removal elsewhere.' The chapter, too, had concerns, both architectural and about the significant non-Christian constituency among the order's 85,000 members. Debate was still ongoing when the death of Canon Prestige in 1955 shifted the balance of opinion, and in 1957 an appeal was launched to raise the necessary funds. This proved extraordinarily successful, suggesting that the argument employed by those who had long advocated the choice of the cathedral – that the site should 'mean something to Overseas members who may never have an opportunity in the future of visiting it' – had no little force. The first service in the new chapel was celebrated in May 1960 (Fig. 205).[99] Just three months before, in Cape Town, Harold Macmillan had announced that the 'wind of change' was blowing through the continent of Africa.

The Order of the British Empire would undergo its own brand of decolonization. But the imperial associations of St Paul's were in need of recasting if they were not now to become a liability. By 1979 even a former high commissioner of Australia would sneer at the Order of St Michael and St George's service as 'a brassy celebration of the British Empire... The pompous vulgarity of the whole thing disgusted me... the poor imperial relics, my contemporaries, tripping, or more like stumping up and down the aisle in a series of ridiculous processions.'[100] Back in 1950, however, Collins was moved by a reading of Alan Paton's *Cry the Beloved Country* to extend Christian Action in to the field of race relations, and to deliver anti-apartheid sermons in the cathedral. He preached against George VI's convalescence in South Africa and denounced the South African premier, Dr Malan, as a 'wretched man hag-ridden with fear', provoking Archbishop Fisher to shake the turbulent priest by the lapels of his jacket. In 1954 Collins toured South Africa, making no secret of his sympathy with the ANC, and on his return publicly disowned official church policy. It was all too much for some. One morning, his tearful daily help informed Diana Collins (whose own activism alongside her husband gave the significant female presence in the close a new prominence) that the League of Empire Loyalists had daubed the slogan 'HANG CANON COLLINS – BANDA'S REBEL HEADQUARTERS' in indelible paint on 2 Amen Court. Nothing daunted, Collins went on to make his residence the headquarters of the British Defence and Aid Fund to support the defendants in treason trials in South Africa, which after the Sharpeville massacre channelled funds from foreign governments to the opposition.

Both Christian Action and Collins alienated many in their activism. It was not just on race that Collins spoke out: Christian Action was prominent in campaigning against capital punishment, and the decision to create the Campaign for Nuclear Disarmament was taken in Amen Court. Collins served as its first chairman, and in 1962 was arrested during a protest in Trafalgar Square. Collins brought these issues into the cathedral through his sermons, which at times verged on the party political: indeed, in 1964 he did preach in favour of Labour electoral success.

Nor was it only Collins who took preaching in new directions.

He did much to open up the pulpit both to non-Anglican clergy and to the laity. Collins persuaded chapter to invite non-conformists to preach, but when on four successive Sunday evenings free churchmen occupied the pulpit, the high-church *Church Times* ceased to publish the names of the preachers during Collins's residences. (Some years before, in 1941, its editor, the future Canon Prestige, had denounced Matthews as 'an ecclesiastical Quisling' for organizing a centenary celebration of General Booth's conversion.)[101] Laymen were no less controversial; it was perhaps unfortunate that the appearance in January 1950 of the first such preacher, Stafford Cripps, coincided with the calling of a general election. Dean and chapter certainly had grounds for irritation with some of the consequences of Collins's lead: in 1951 General Sir Giffard Le Quesne Martel announced an anti-Communist pilgrimage to the cathedral to call for a purge of undesirable elements, which attracted the attendance of palace officials; two years later, the *Record* newspaper claimed that Collins was using the cathedral to advance Communism.

No doubt to many of those offended the goings-on in the cathedral represented a betrayal of St Paul's tradition. But they might equally be regarded as a recovery of certain aspects of it. The hostile Protestant invasions of the late Victorian cathedral need to be remembered alongside its Anglo-Catholic achievements. Indeed, its Victorian vibrancy reflected not only its national symbolism, but its provision of a forum in which important contemporary national issues (including above all the identity of the national church) were contested, not least by a chapter whose own position on these was not in fact that prevalent in the establishment, but rather had something almost counter-cultural about it. The war years had seen St Paul's reclaim its national standing. Now its critical role was recovered in Collins's activities, and the preaching of those whom he invited to the cathedral pulpit (in later years including Martin Luther King and then his widow, Coretta), providing a running commentary on national and international concerns informed as much as the building's establishment ritual by a sense of the cathedral's importance not just in Britain, but in a wider English-speaking world.

After the war, this latter dimension of the cathedral's identity was deliberately expanded to embrace not only the shrinking Empire and burgeoning Commonwealth, but also the USA. Wartime services, perhaps especially that commemorating President Roosevelt in 1945, provided a starting-point, as did the crypt memorial to W. M. L. Fiske, the first American pilot killed in the Battle of Britain. The choir tour led by Collins in 1953, a minor fundraising success, was also significant. But most important was the creation of an American Memorial Chapel (Fig. 197), given by British citizens to commemorate the sacrifice made by Americans based in Britain during the Second World War. Originating with Lord Trenchard, the scheme was embraced by Matthews partly as a means of restoring the apse area damaged during hostilities. In 1951 General Eisenhower handed over a handwritten role of honour containing more than 28,000 American names that became the central feature of a restrained but American-themed setting designed by Stephen Dykes Bower and Godfrey Allen. Appropriately, the chapel backed on to the new high altar, itself dedicated as a memorial to the Commonwealth war dead.

Restoration

Much of the immediate post-war history of the cathedral was inevitably dominated by the theme of restoration of the war-damaged fabric (pp. 261–3, 301–2). For the chapter, this raised two recurrent questions: what to do, and how to fund it? The first was difficult enough. The damage done to the reredos forced a choice between restoration and replacement and, perhaps inevitably in a period when Victorian architecture had comparatively few champions, it was the latter course that was adopted. Stephen Dykes Bower was primarily responsible for the high altar and baldacchino that dominate the restored east end, formally reopened in May 1958. Four years later, the other part of the cathedral severely damaged by bombing, the north transept, was finally rededicated. The war was only indirectly responsible for one of the most troublesome aspects of the rebuilding. City planners, not bombs, threatened to obliterate the choir-school building in Carter Lane. Negotiations conducted by Gibbs-Smith led to Godfrey Allen being asked to submit plans for a new building on the site of St Augustine, Watling Street. The opening of the new school (Fig. 340), on 4 May 1967, was virtually the last act of Matthews's incumbency and due cause for celebration, but it was not Allen's building that then came into use. The rejection of his design had in 1956 provoked the embittered resignation of the individual widely credited with the safe custody of the fabric during the war.

These works were expensive in contemplation and even more so in execution. They were accompanied by many smaller projects necessary to modernize or repair the fabric and decoration. Even before the war, the cathedral finances were parlous: Matthews described the cathedral when he arrived as 'living on the margin of solvency', the value of the Ecclesiastical Commissioners' payments having been seriously eroded by inflation and rising costs while simultaneously, as the chapter were painfully aware, the value of the property for which it was compensated had risen significantly.[102] The chapter house, gutted in the Blitz, had before this suffered the perhaps greater indignity of being leased to Lloyd's Bank as Alexander struggled to raise revenue. It was decided to restore and reclaim the building after the war, adding a further expensive project to an already lengthy list. Meanwhile, recurrent costs spiralled. Matthews compared various items of expenditure in 1954 with their equivalents twenty years before: maintenance of the fabric had risen from £4,000 per annum to £14,000; maintenance of the choir school from £4,700 to £8,100; payments to the vicars choral from £2,900 to £7,000.

Faced by both the particular demands of post-war reconstruction and the longer-term challenge of meeting rising costs, the chapter needed to maximize income. In 1944 Alexander and Matthews had taken an important step in reforming the cathedral's financial management. The thirty-three-year-old David Floyd Ewin (Fig. 295), a member of the watch, was appointed receiver and registrar, the post for the first time being separated from that of chapter clerk. Ewin would remain in post until 1978, providing remarkable continuity in the financial affairs of the cathedral. After the war, external advice was sought on the chapter's investment portfolio, helping to ensure this produced significant income.[103]

Part of the cost of reconstruction was met by the state through the War Damage Commission. Alexander estimated that the chapter itself might need to find £100,000, but was confident that this could be raised from firms and individuals in the City without a formal appeal. Both Alexander and Matthews were old hands at public speaking and public eating (although the latter was conscious that Inge, for all his puritanism, had allowed the pleasures of the table to feature too prominently in his *Diary of a Dean*). By

now, the cathedral could draw on a fund of goodwill built up over a century in the Square Mile, sometimes reinforced by Masonic links. Alexander's estimate was soon exceeded by money collected. But his estimate was woefully short of the actual sum required. A more formal appeal was in the end unavoidable, and from a committee of City men chaired by Sir Christopher Chancellor emerged a target of £400,000 and an aspiration towards an additional annual income of £20,000, to be raised by what became the St Paul's Campaign. The funds collected were administered by the St Paul's Cathedral Trust, a body uniting dean and chapter with appropriate laymen. Thus it was now institutionally recognized that the future maintenance of the building could no longer be the sole responsibility of the cathedral establishment.

Both cathedral congregations and visitors rallied to the cause. Collections at services, fees for admission to the dome and crypt and collection boxes all yielded significantly more by the mid 1950s than they had in the 1930s. This partly reflected increased visitor numbers and interest in the icon of wartime defiance. But it was clear to Matthews that such a mood needed a more efficient conduit if it was to yield maximum benefit to the cathedral.

One consequence of the travails of the inter-war cathedral may have been the failure of St Paul's to generate a friends organization. Canterbury had one from 1927; York from 1928; Norwich from 1929; Hereford from 1932.[104] Matthews found in the wartime watch an echo of the Exeter Friends (established in 1929) that he had valued in his previous post, and looked to set up a similar body. It proved surprisingly difficult. Matthews later complained that Canon Demant and others, fearful that the Friends might compromise the chapter's authority, and perturbed by the energy Margaret Babbington had displayed as steward of the Canterbury Friends, had prevented the cathedral from tapping

into the goodwill apparent at the end of hostilities. An initial meeting was consequently not held until April 1952, when eighty-four prospective members, many watch veterans, assembled to constitute the Friends under the joint presidency of the Lord Mayor and bishop of London. The Queen Mother accepted an invitation to serve as patron. Matthews, whose devotion to her dated from her days as duchess of York, correctly anticipated that she would not regard the role as honorific, but rather take a keen interest in both organization and cathedral. Throughout the remainder of her long life, the Queen Mother regularly attended the Friends' festival services and receptions. The fiftieth anniversary tribute to the Friends of 2002 reflected the patron's contribution to the organization's success, both through the number of contributors identifying an encounter with the Queen Mother as the highlight of their involvement, and in the fact that she featured in more illustrations than either cathedral or chapter. This focus on the Queen Mother should not be dismissed merely as a symptom of establishment royalism. Not only did her sustained commitment to the organization earn affection, but she represented a vital and increasingly poignant link with the mythologies of the Blitz central to the construction of the modern public identity of the cathedral. This nexus was never better expressed than in 1999, when she unveiled in the precinct a memorial to the citizens of London killed in the Blitz (Fig. 247).[105]

Matthews always felt that the Friends were not quite as much a success as they might have been. At the end of the first year, membership was in the 600s; five years on, in 1957, it stood at 1,721. Matthews suggested that had the Friends been launched at the end of the war the figure might have been 10,000. Ambitions of an altogether grander kind were voiced by Canon Freddy Hood (Fig. 55) at the Festival Service of 1963: 'We dare to envisage twenty thousand or more men, women, boys and girls, each com-

DOME

The Magazine of The Friends of St. Paul's Cathedral
Number 6 Winter 1968-9

mitted to God within the life of his own church, yet, so to speak, part of our worldwide congregation with St Paul's as a dynamic centre': equally extravagant was the first edition of the Friends' magazine, *Dome*. By 1964 both the ambitions and *Dome* had been trimmed, but continuing disappointment at the organization's performance reflected unrealistic assessments both of the prospects of, and the effort required to realize even modest growth in, an organization whose identity was rooted in the particular historical moment. Moreover, unlike provincial cathedrals attracting higher numbers, St Paul's had to compete with other metropolitan landmarks, not least the Abbey. As it was, subscriptions, donations and sales helped sustain the activities of the choir (an individual choristership being sponsored in 1957), routine maintenance and the purchase of furnishings, most notably the new pulpit erected in 1964, commissioned by the Friends from Lord Mottistone (Fig. 198). By 2002, the grand total of donations to the dean and chapter stood at £676,000, worth far more in real terms.[106]

In 1967 Matthews could look back with satisfaction on his time at St Paul's. The chapter had had its differences, but nothing to match the pre-war tensions. The repair of holes in the dome left by ack-ack shrapnel – more 'friendly fire' – had brought the work of restoration virtually to a close. An anonymous donation of £10,000 allowed the cleaning of the west front between 1961 and 1963; the former Lord Mayor Sir James Harman organized an appeal for £150,000 to finance the subsequent removal of grime up to four inches thick from the remainder of the building. The chapter house had been reclaimed, and a new choir school constructed. The tradition of state services had been triumphantly sustained, culminating in 1965 in the memorable funeral obsequies for Sir Winston Churchill (p. 389; Fig. 324), one of the first great television occasions in the cathedral (perhaps between 850 and 900 million people world-wide watched or listened). The

comparative absence of innovation in other aspects of the cathedral's activities reflected the conservatism of chapter throughout Matthews's tenure, and further Anglo-Catholic appointments. Prestige had been succeeded by the former bishop of London and church historian William Wand (at whose episcopal enthronement in the cathedral in 1945 an ultra-Protestant demonstration had recalled earlier disturbances). Freddy Hood, a keen promoter of the Friends (founding the North American branch in 1964) and a popular priest in the city, had been principal of the Anglo-Catholic Pusey House.[107] The only canon retaining much taste for experiment in outreach and services (if not liturgy) was the archdeacon of London, Martin Sullivan, the most recent appointment of 1963, who in a long parochial career both in Britain and his native New Zealand had embraced a variety of pastoral challenges. His junior position, however, provided little opportunity to influence cathedral policy. This was all about to change.

AFTER MATTHEWS

It was widely assumed that the Labour prime minister Harold Wilson would choose John Collins to succeed Matthews. A popular alternative tip was Edward Carpenter, the similarly left-leaning canon of Westminster, a distinguished church historian and theological liberal. The quixotic Wilson instead sprang a characteristic surprise by appointing Sullivan. Sullivan suffered a series of bemused and disparaging press profiles, in which 'safe' and 'middle of the road' were among the kinder judgements. Both Carpenter and Collins felt the blow heavily. The new dean was sensitive to the feelings of the more senior clerics over whom he now presided, but it was perhaps a relief that Hood retired in 1970 and Wand in 1975. Fortunately, Collins swallowed his pride and did not become Alexander to Sullivan's Matthews.

Sullivan's incumbency was not without its achievements, being notable not least for the quality of the musical life of the cathedral. As ever, the needs of the fabric loomed large. Another national appeal, for £3 million, was launched under the leadership of Derick Heathcoat-Amory and Sir Peter Studd, who made it the theme of his mayoralty; it was also promoted in the USA, where the banker Hoyt Ammidon raised $500,000 within four months. When it closed in 1973, the appeal, though in certain respects controversial (p. 302), had met its financial target.

Sullivan acknowledged that he did not belong in the well-established tradition of scholar-deans, and instead prioritized pastoralia, in particular reaching out to the young. A new crib echoed Sheppard's pre-war initiatives. In 1969, monthly Sunday 'worship in the round' was introduced in the crypt, while the normal evening service (briefly rechristened the 'people's service') was shortened.

The crypt was a key venue for a 'festival of youth' featuring speaker meetings on moral and religious issues that Sullivan launched in 1968. Perhaps in reply to an imagined rebuke from Alexander's ghost, Sullivan invoked a term already well established in the St Paul's lexicon to argue that the festival was 'not a stunt or gimmick'.[108] Evocative vignettes of 1960s 'outreach' nevertheless enlivened the pages of *Dome* at this time: Mary Hopkin performing under the dome, folk dancing, a 'festival of jazz praise', a fashion show. The exterior suffered various indignities, including the architectural equivalent of the then fashionable lava lamp, the *son et lumière*. Sullivan himself was grimly determined to unbend, but found Hopkin too loud and guiltily wished the youngsters attending 'dry-cleaned' and shorn of their

57. 'The Dean and Chapter with the Cathedral team', 2002. Lucy Winkett, the first woman priest appointed to the chapter (then a minor canon), is fourth from the right in the second row

flowing locks.[109] An apotheosis of sorts occurred when the dean arrived at the cathedral while paratroopers were conducting harness jumps from a platform on the west front to encounter a press pack expectantly anticipating a decanal descent (Fig. 56). Sullivan gamely complied; shortly after, he had publicly to endure Cardinal Heenan's observation that whereas Christ had resisted the temptation to leap from the pinnacle of the temple, the dean had been found wanting.

Heenan featured in another difficult moment for Sullivan when in 1969 Archbishop Ramsey persuaded chapter to allow a Roman Catholic to preach in the cathedral for the first time since the Reformation. Mindful of the precedents for vigorous Protestant reaction to Anglo-, let alone Roman, Catholicism, chapter agreed to position plain-clothes policemen throughout the expectant congregation, while a uniformed snatch squad lurked in the Lord Mayor's vestry. Cries of 'traitor' when Ramsey rose to speak prefaced more serious scuffles when Heenan entered the pulpit. Sullivan took a dim view not only of the fra-

cas, but also of Heenan's sermon (he was not instinctively ecumenical, as was later apparent in the Silver Jubilee service). The strongest public reaction to a cathedral service, however, was reserved for chapter's decision in August 1971 to allow the use of Galt McDermot's setting of the communion service for a celebration in the cathedral. McDermot's other compositions included the musical *Hair*, the (fully dressed) cast of which would attend the service. The correspondence columns of the national press heaved with outraged letters.

The excitements and embarrassments early in Sullivan's incumbency perhaps made the comparative calm in the years before he announced his resignation following the Silver Jubilee service of 1977 welcome, not least to the dean. His retirement was followed three years later by that of John Collins.

The cathedral under Alan Webster

That Collins's departure did not mark the end of political controversy associated with St Paul's was largely due to the fact that to succeed Sullivan James Callaghan selected Alan Webster. A theological liberal, he brought with him a modernizing agenda informed by his experiences as dean of Norwich and as a parochial clergyman who had cut his teeth in Leslie Hunter's Sheffield. Theology and politics closely intertwined in both his insistence on a Christian engagement with contemporary issues and his concern that the internal polity of the church (not least in cathedrals) be more inclusive. Such views ensured that his tenure would have its difficult moments.

As in Collins's day, Amen Court (which, following a decision under Sullivan to lease the old deanery in future, now housed the dean as well) became a centre for 'guerilla action' in both church and state. Another continuity with Collins's years was the contribution of women: indeed, a cause close to Diana Collins's heart, the ordination of women, was promoted by Margaret Webster, the first full-time secretary of the Movement for Women's Ordination, fully supported by the dean. The then bishop of London, Graham Leonard, was a prominent opponent of the movement, and 'unofficial' protests – such as that which led to the forceful ejection from the cathedral of silent but banner-waving protestors during the July 1980 ordination service – could cause embarrassment. Amen Court itself generated controversy in 1982, when Elizabeth Canham, an Englishwoman ordained in the USA, celebrated communion in the basement of the deanery. News got out; there was a critical leader in *The Times*, while Leonard issued a lengthy statement condemning the service.[110]

The most famous 'difficulty' of Webster's incumbency came with the service of thanksgiving and remembrance after the Falklands War of 26 July 1982, discussed in detail elsewhere (p. 390). Along with the Royal Wedding service of the previous year, it demonstrated Webster's commitment to a revival of the ecumenical tradition in state services (he once called the cathedral an 'ecumenical laboratory') as well as his determination to make the church's voice heard on major issues. It was rumoured that Mrs Thatcher's disapproval of the refusal to celebrate victory was reflected shortly afterwards in her choice of the former lawyer Graham Routledge, a theological and political conservative (indeed a former parliamentary candidate), as canon. Routledge would certainly lead opposition to Webster, but he made his own positive contribution to cathedral life, not least as a keen supporter of the Friends.[111]

The Falklands service was only the most obvious manifestation of active 'political' engagement. The controversial report of the Archbishop's Commission on Urban Priority Areas – *Faith in the City* (1985) – was welcomed by a dean conscious of the contrast between the City and surrounding poverty as a polarity recalling Blomfield's comparison of cathedral and city 150 years before. Webster sought to involve the City itself in a Christian response to deprivation. A group of committed laity (including the industrialist Sir Richard O'Brien, chair not only of the archbishop's inquiry but also formerly of the Manpower Services Commission) had already been meeting in the deanery and conducting fact-finding missions; it now summoned City workers to two-hour discussions in the chapter house. Although an exchange of letters with the premier revealed only the gulf between thinking in Downing Street and in the deanery, the group continued its work; in 1987 it promoted a meeting at the Bank of England between leading businessmen and the archbishop of Canterbury, who subsequently penned a conscience-pricking letter to the directors of some two hundred City firms.

The prominence of City representatives in these decanal projects indicates that the attempt to provide a challenging Christian witness in the Thatcherite economy did not straightforwardly distance the cathedral from its City neighbours. Relations with the City were probably less cosy than at other times, but dean and chapter appreciated that the economic challenges facing the cathedral made lay professionals vital not just as a source of financial support, but also of advice. Webster consulted more widely beyond the cathedral on finance than his predecessors – indeed, he felt that the affairs of the cathedral needed to be made more open in order to rally support. In 1978 he broke with precedent in showing the then Lord Mayor Kenneth Cork, both a committed Christian and an expert in bankruptcy, the cathedral accounts.[112] A more formal approach was the creation of a 'Court of Advisers' including O'Brien, Robin Leigh Pemberton, the governor of the Bank of England, and Sir James Swaffield, director-general of the GLC, as well as public figures with a particular interest in the cathedral such as Charles Groves and Roy Strong. Important for the future was the involvement of Elspeth Howe, who in 1992 would be appointed to chair the Archbishops' Commission on Cathedrals. In 2000 Peter Chapman, a former chorister and accountant who had served on the court, would be appointed the first lay canon of St Paul's after a revision of its statutes under legislation derived from Howe's Commission's report.

The cathedral Friends were another crucial lay resource, and here, too, Webster sought to make more of lay commitment. The secretary was given a target of 5,000 members and general reinvigoration, a process that involved the introduction of a bookstall and recruiting desk on the cathedral floor. Recruitment received a significant boost with the Royal Wedding of 1981 (Fig. 325; p. 390). Memberships from overseas experienced a sudden surge, and although many of the hundred or so joining each month in 1981 quickly dropped away, the organization emerged strengthened, with a membership of over 4,000 by the mid 1980s.

The increased emphasis on the Friends reflected their significance in managing one of the most important developments in the recent history of the cathedral, the growth of mass tourism. What from 1964 became known as the 'Working' Friends had long provided volunteer guides; from 1976 they joined the virgers in leading so-called 'super-tours' embracing Amen Court and the chapter house, while from 1979 Maurice Sills and John Eames voluntarily assumed the heavy responsibility of conducting schools visits (over three hundred a year). The planned expansion of the Friends aimed in part to provide additional manpower to supplement the hundred or so Friends already acting as guides.[113]

More generally, the chapter considered how best to cater for, manage and exploit the growing tide of visitors; in 1978 Webster noted that a single week in July had seen 105,000 visitors, and the year as a whole perhaps 2.5 million. The crypt emerged as central to plans to create space and a focus for visitor activities. In winter 1979–80 *Dome* carried Robert Potter's elaboration of a long-term scheme to create bookshops, better catering facilities and attractions for which an admission fee would be charged in the form of a 'treasury' and a display of the Great Model.[114] The refectory and treasury opened in 1981, followed in 1983 by an audio-visual presentation and a religious bookstall.

The promotion of tourism and its accompanying commercialization caused dismay in some quarters, but the chapter had little choice. Already the old deanery was being leased and investment income maximized. In 1980–1 the first of a regular series of audits of the cathedral's financial situation in *Dome* explained that although the cathedral trust fund could still support maintenance, the works department faced cutbacks, and that despite donations for the crypt development and organ (from the Garfield Weston Trust) and the new treasury (£40,000 from the Goldsmiths' Company and £20,000 from the bishop of London), the general fund of the cathedral had been overspent for two years running. Income was expected to fall £100,000 short of expenditure for the coming year. It had therefore been decided to introduce admission charges for the east end.[115]

The royal wedding of 1981, however, temporarily provided relief. Never before had the full potential of St Paul's as the setting for a television spectacular been so effectively realized; Sir Alastair Burnet observed that among Wren's lost drawings must be one for the positioning of cameras.[116] The public flocked to the scene: visitor numbers matched previous records, the shop doubled its sales and donations were significantly up. 'Out of the red for 1981' proclaimed a headline in *Dome*; indeed, despite warnings of difficult times ahead, £15,000 was donated to home and overseas charities as a thank-offering. The new admission charges were dropped. Two years on, nevertheless, the long-term trend was worrying, with expenditure having exceeded income in four of the previous five years and another deficit on the cards. The choir was only one aspect of the cathedral feeling the pinch, with six of eighteen vicars choral sacrificed as an economy measure. In 1984 the choir school itself became a focus of concern, with an appeal launched by the Lord Mayor, Sir Allan Traill, specifically to secure its future. Without tourism, now accounting for virtually half the cathedral's annual income, the situation would have been far worse.[117]

For all its economic travails, the chapter did its best to ensure that pastoral matters were not overlooked. There were new attempts to make spiritual contact with visitors and to improve the pastoral relationship with cathedral worshippers. The two groups were not mutually exclusive: it was tourists who ensured that Sunday services in the depopulated city still attracted some eight hundred to the morning service, and perhaps five hundred to communion. Webster later told the *New York Times* that 'Europeans, including the English, are weak on church-going...it takes Americans to fill St Paul's' (not perhaps as novel a state of affairs as one might assume, for in 1854 the cathedral had been described as 'the great resort of foreigners, especially of Americans').[118] The strongest attendances were for the extravagant (and expensive) orchestral 'July masses' inaugurated by the organist, Christopher Dearnley (the musical life of the cathedral, for all its publicized difficulties, generally continued at a high level: pp. 410–12).

During the 1970s the minor canons (particularly Michael Moxon and Samuel Cutt) had played a key role in the pastoral ministry of the cathedral, and Canon Evan Pilkington, who had arrived in 1976 with a strong parochial record, had formed a 'pastoral committee'. With Pilkington's encouragement, by the early 1980s a member of the clergy was on duty on the floor of the cathedral each day, also providing hourly 'welcome-prayer spots' from the pulpit. There was a new midday Eucharist aimed at visitors, first on Wednesdays and then daily. Webster also hoped that the introduction of contemporary religious art might provide a new focus for devotions.

The dean led the way when it came to the congregations, although his hopes that the services themselves might be modernized and held more often under the dome were largely unfulfilled. (He was particularly impressed by the services held in the cathedral by the Taizé community in 1986–7, when seats were removed to allow some 7,000 worshippers to sit or kneel on the floor of the nave, dome and parts of the transepts.) Webster nevertheless broke down the distance between clergy and worshipping laity in other ways, mingling with those assembling before the service, and inaugurating a 'congregational consultation', with all subjects open to discussion, as well as a series of congregational retreats.

The recent past

Webster retired in 1988. It is impossible as yet to address subsequent events from a serious historical perspective. Under Webster, however, the cathedral became recognizably the same institution it remained at the end of the twentieth century. It is not inappropriate, therefore, briefly to consider how some of the important themes already apparent from the account of his tenure have developed over the past fifteen years.

Webster's successor, Eric Evans, had previously spent twenty-five years in the diocese of Gloucester, the last thirteen as archdeacon of Cheltenham. He proved a popular appointment, and his tenure was marked by fewer tensions both within and beyond the cathedral than his predecessor's. Evans was, however, dogged by serious ill health that limited his capacity to provide dynamic leadership. He bore his incapacity with fortitude: Robin Bawtree, appointed secretary of the Friends in 1995, on first meeting Evans was given a guided tour of the deanery with the dean trailing his oxygen machine behind him.[119] Evans announced his impending retirement in March 1996, but in August died in post. His successor, and dean at the time of writing, was John Moses, formerly provost of Chelmsford. Among other changes in chapter, perhaps the two most historically significant have been the arrival of the first lay canon in 2000, and in 2003 the announcement that John Halliburton would be succeeded by the first woman cleric (Claire Foster, the second lay canon, had preceded her as the first woman) appointed to chapter, Lucy Winkett, whose arrival as a minor canon in 1997 had been a source of some controversy within the cathedral community.

The cathedral's constitution has also undergone important recent changes, as in the 1830s partly driven by legislation. The Care of Cathedrals Measure (1990) required each cathedral to establish a fabric advisory committee to oversee works, subject to the regulatory authority of the Cathedrals Fabric Commission for England, thus significantly eroding the autonomy of the chapter in a key aspect of its activities. (Such renewed interest on the part of the state in cathedral affairs encouraged the chapter to break with a tradition of sturdy independence by beginning to consult more regularly with sister institutions in the defence of cathedral interests, a development anticipated when Webster became the first dean of St Paul's to attend the Deans and Provosts Conference.[120]) The Cathedrals Measure (1999) led to revision of the constitution and statutes. As enacted in April 2000, these affirm the growing importance attached to lay involvement in cathedral governance. Chapter itself is expanded by the addition of three persons (of whom two at least must be lay canons) appointed by bishop and dean, chosen with regard to the expertise they bring to the chapter. The constitution also provides for a council to further and support the work of the cathedral,

58.   The nave in 2002

consisting of a lay chairman, chapter representatives, three lay members representing the cathedral community, and eight further lay members appointed by the bishop to represent local, diocesan, ecumenical or national interests. Together with the new lay canons, this has superseded the former Court of Advisers. The former Greater Chapter is replaced by a new College of Canons, while a company of honorary canons that can include not only laity but also non-Anglicans has been added to the list of cathedral offices. A sign of the times is the formal incorporation of a finance committee into the constitutional structure.

For the chapter, finance predictably remained an abiding preoccupation. A financial controller was appointed in 1991. Tighter budgetary control, such as ensuring that special services were properly costed, helped to ensure that 1992 saw the first budgetary surplus for five years. By the end of the decade, the cathedral also had a development office and director of fundraising. Chapter minutes reflect an increasing dependence on grants and sponsorship for specific events and developments, bringing with it the particular difficulties associated with this revenue stream in a public religious institution. In 1993–4 there was welcome news when Paul Newell made the cathedral his designated charity as Lord Mayor; the St Paul's Cathedral Trust was established in the USA to handle the transatlantic dimension of an appeal which in all raised over £4.5 million, some of which went to finance immediate projects, but £2.2 million of which was deposited in the Endowment Trust for St Paul's established in 1971.

The more businesslike approach to fundraising inevitably extended to the management of tourism. In 1992 it was estimated that tourism-related employment at the cathedral already amounted to sixty-three paid employees assisted by two hundred volunteers. The crypt was gradually transformed into what by 1997, in a phrase redolent of the era, Dean Moses dubbed 'the People's Boulevard', complete with café, restaurant, toilets and conference room (Fig. 202). Most controversially, in May 1991 the chapter bit the bullet and reintroduced charges for access to the main floor; the only other cathedral to make such a charge at the time was Ely. Although the total number of visitors in 1992 (1,400,000) was significantly lower than at York Minster or Canterbury (2,250,000 each), St Paul's income from admission charges was five times greater than that of its nearest rival, York, which only charged for particular attractions. In the same year, the net income produced by charges, donations and purchases by visitors at St Paul's was £2,052,000, again dwarfing that of its only serious competitor, York (£807,000).[121]

In 1992 tourism and trading accounted for 31.7 per cent of St Paul's annual income; by 1998 this had risen to 67 per cent. As the cathedral's *Annual Report*, itself evidence of both the professionalism of its financial operations and of its adaptation to the *fin-de-siècle* culture of audit (also apparent in the shooting of a fly-on-the-wall television documentary), noted in 2000, 'In finance terms, the Cathedral is a very different organization to the one that existed before admission charges were introduced.'[122]

Welcome though the revenue from tourism was, the chapter was understandably concerned that so much of its income should derive from a source so vulnerable to events beyond the cathedral's control, as in the aftermath of the destruction of the World Trade Center. Major projects, moreover, would continue to depend on other fundraising, and thus it was that in 2000 the St Paul's Foundation was created as a limited company charity to fund a £40 million programme of interior and exterior restoration and cleaning, which has attracted significant individual donations of £10,800,000 from the banker Robin Fleming and £5,000,000 from Sir Paul Getty.

Under Dean Moses, the cathedral has in fact embarked on an ambitious and integrated strategy for the future, which embraces not only such work on the fabric, but also worship, ministry and mission. By 2004 there had been important developments in the worship of the cathedral, such as the restoration of sung matins and an informal evening service on Sundays, but perhaps most importantly the belated realization of one of Webster's wishes with the construction of a Dome Sanctuary, its dais providing a focus for worship at the heart of the cathedral. Together with the placement of a dramatic new pyx in St Dunstan's Chapel, reserved for private prayer, and discussions concerning a new font, this reflects a newly determined effort to explore the potential of the interior to express sacramental order and Christian life.

The cathedral's ministry has also developed in new directions. A small lay community of young graduates sharing in the life and work of the cathedral was established in 2001; there has also been a conscious effort to establish more effective links with the diocese, through such initiatives as events for newly ordained deacons and parochial incumbents. Other developments hark back to much earlier attempts to extend effective ministry to the City. A series of major public lectures on ethical and moral issues has been established, while in 2001 Ed Newell was appointed to a canonry with the brief of developing a St Paul's Institute as a forum for education and debate concerning ethical questions related to the financial and business worlds, and to the life of a capital city.

And thus, as it approaches its 1,400th anniversary, St Paul's remains very much a going concern (in every sense). It retains its key role as a centre for national religious expression and yet also a place of personal devotions. At the same time, much has inevitably changed. For example, the casual visiting public, clearly perceived as a threat to the successful preservation of the building in the 1830s, by 2000 had become an indispensable resource in securing the finance necessary for the task. On the other hand, despite being overshadowed by new prestige developments in the metropolis with their own iconic status – Canary Wharf, the 'erotic gherkin' – St Paul's has successfully maintained its place as a signifier for London, even in youth-oriented contexts: thus in 1998 the cyber-heroine Lara Croft – 'Tomb Raider' – battled over and through a virtual St Paul's; and advertisers continue regularly to exploit the dome's recognition factor. It is nevertheless the case that much of its status continues to derive from the particular circumstances of St Paul's symbolic importance in the 1940s. As the Second World War recedes beyond collective memory, the cathedral will once more need to reinvent itself in the popular imagination of an increasingly multicultural nation and metropolis. This will be a significant challenge. In confronting it, the cathedral's future guardians can draw both warning and inspiration from its history over the past 170 years.

Part Two

Up to the Reformation

9

THE CULT OF SAINTS
AND THE LITURGY

Alan Thacker

The cult of the saints was probably established in London well before the foundation of St Paul's. Recently it has been convincingly argued that the early Christian community in the city venerated one Augulus, a Roman bishop of *Augusta* (as *Londinium* was known in the later fourth century), who suffered martyrdom with eight companions, presumably sometime before the conversion of Constantine in 312.[1] The location of any such grave and cult is of course uncertain; most probably they would have been associated with an extra-mural burial ground. Unlike that of Alban, however, the cult does not seem to have survived the disruption of Romano-British Christianity in south-eastern England and almost certainly it had disappeared before the seventh century.

THE PATRONAL CULT AND EARLY SECONDARY RELICS

The foundation of the Anglo-Saxon episcopal complex in London was accompanied by the introduction of relics providing a new focus for the cult of the saints. The Italian missionaries from whom the clergy were drawn seem to have had little contact with Romano-British Christianity and either encountered very few native cults or were reluctant to adopt them. They knew nothing of, or ignored or suppressed, veneration for Augulus. Instead, they introduced relics of their own, brought from Italy or acquired *en route* in Gaul, in particular those of the great apostles and martyrs of Rome.[2] In London, St Paul became the patron of the new episcopal see: we know that the association goes back to earliest times since Bede expressly notes that King Ethelbert (Æthelberht) of Kent established a church there dedicated to the apostle for the first bishop, Mellitus (604–c.617).[3] In promoting this cult, Mellitus, like the other Roman missionaries, had to rely on what are now known as secondary relics – that is, relics created from items such as strips of cloth which had been placed in contact with the primary corporeal remains or the tomb which enclosed them. He could not bring with him any of the primary remains themselves, for in the early seventh century the Roman church in particular guarded its holy dead with especial zeal, permitting no fragmentation of the body nor even interference with the tomb. Presumably, therefore, the dedication indicates that the London's new cathedral held a piece or pieces of cloth sanctified by having rested on the apostle's tomb in the great Roman basilica of San Paolo fuori le mura on the Via ostiense. Such a relic may have been enclosed in the principal altar or displayed in a separate reliquary.[4]

As the cathedral's patron, Paul was the embodiment of the church – in a memorable phrase, its 'undying landlord'.[5] This relationship seems to have been felt with especial intensity by the London chapter who, alone among English cathedral establishments, designated their church simply by its titular saint. The cathedral clergy's attitude is especially apparent in their early rule, which goes back to the tenth or early eleventh century. 'Paul is the superior of you all by his calling in teaching and preaching; . . . Paul provides for you in temporal things; . . . you are nourished by Paul's food and drink – when you go out from Paul's chapter, never cease for the rest of the day to obey his saving exhortation . . . He is God's minister, an avenger to execute wrath on him who doeth evil.'[6] The feast days of the saint, his

59. Detail of the 'Prospect of ye City of London' showing the cathedral from the south. Executed after the spire burned in 1561, but showing it in its original form. (The Society of Antiquaries, London Plans IV, f.3★)

conversion (25 January) and his commemoration with St Peter on 29 June and alone on the following day, would always have been events of particular solemnity in the liturgical life of the cathedral (p. 117).

By the late eleventh century, the Anglo-Saxon cathedral of St Paul's was associated with a group of churches (pp. 127–30; Fig. 9), some of whose dedications are suggestive of an early date, an indication perhaps that from the earliest times the episcopal complex had possessed other significant secondary relics besides those of the apostle. In particular, *Paulesbyrig*, the early enclosure, included a church dedicated to Gregory the Great, the pope responsible for the English mission, in existence by 1009 and after 1087 adjoining the south-western side of the nave of the rebuilt cathedral. Further west on Ludgate Hill, there was a third church dedicated to the Gallic saint, Martin of Tours.[7] The fact that Pancras, a martyr favoured in early seventh-century Rome, was later recorded as titular of a large ancient parish a mile or two outside the walls suggests that he, too, may have been an object of veneration to the early community.[8] Churches or altars were dedicated to these saints elsewhere in seventh-century England (in particular at Canterbury) and in contemporary Gaul and Rome. We may suppose, therefore, that although we cannot identify them precisely, the secondary relics which Augustine and Mellitus brought with them contained items derived from these saints.[9] The gifts sent by Pope Vitalian to King Oswiu of Northumbria later in the seventh century provide an analogy. These included relics of the apostles Peter and Paul and of several Roman martyrs, including Pancras and Gregory.[10] All this would suggest that in the seventh century the cathedral included a distinctive group of Roman and Gallic saints' feasts in its annual observance.

PRE-CONQUEST TOMB CULTS AT ST PAUL'S

By the early eighth century St Paul's had also acquired a local saint of its own, drawn, as in the cathedral churches of Gaul, from the ranks of its first bishops. The founding bishop, Mellitus, would have been an obvious candidate to be so honoured, had he not been buried at Canterbury, the see to which, after his expulsion from London, he had been transferred in 619.[11] It was, therefore, Erkenwald (Earconwald), Mellitus's third successor as bishop of the East Saxons (675–93) and the man often regarded as the cathedral's second founder, who was singled out to achieve the status of local saint. In thus augmenting the secondary relics of Roman apostles and martyrs introduced by the Gregorian mission with the most highly esteemed relic of all, an entombed body, St Paul's was placing itself at the forefront of the development of an English cult.[12] Only a few other contemporary English episcopal churches, such as Lindisfarne and Lichfield, had so honoured one of their bishops; there is no evidence for tomb cults of this kind in Canterbury. The reasons for this modishness can be discerned in the career and family connections of Erkenwald himself.

Appointed bishop of London with responsibility for the East Saxons by Theodore, archbishop of Canterbury, shortly after the synod of Hertford, perhaps in 675, Erkenwald continued to hold the see until his death in 693.[13] Notably well connected, he received grants from the West Saxon king Cædwalla (686–8), assisted Cædwalla's successor Ine (688–726) in the formulation of his law-code[14] and shortly before Theodore's death in 690 played an important part in that archbishop's reconciliation with the Northumbrian bishop Wilfrid.[15] Erkenwald's name suggests that

he may have been of royal Kentish blood and a relative of a princely Frankish family, that of another Earconwald (Erchinoald), mayor of the palace and patron of Balthild, English queen of the Neustrian Franks in the mid seventh century. The bishop was brother to Ethelburga (Æthelburh), foundress of Barking (whose own name also points to Kentish regality), and himself founded Chertsey. With such connections, he was probably in touch with the most advanced ecclesiastical circles, those responsible for introducing Frankish ideas about local cult into England. Members of the Kentish and East Anglian royal families, bearing the significant names of Earcongota and Æthelburh and probably his relatives, were the object of translations in the Frankish royal monastery of Faremoutier-en-Brie in the late seventh century. As such, they were very likely the first English saints to be so authenticated. These developments, focused as they were on Erkenwald's relatives, may have had an impact on the development of cult in London in the 690s.[16]

The English historian Bede (d. 734) was in touch with the nuns of Barking and obtained information about Erkenwald from them. He expressly tells us that his account was derived from a lost Barking *libellus*, a source clearly concerned to promote Erkenwald as the object of a cult.[17] From it, Bede learned that the horse-drawn litter used by the bishop when he was ill was preserved by his disciples (*discipuli*) and continued to effect many cures; splinters from it had become miracle-working secondary relics.[18] That the Barking miracle stories are focused on a secondary relic, the litter, rather than the tomb, is not especially surprising – the tomb, after all, was not in their monastery but in London. Probably the prominence accorded to the litter means that it was preserved at Barking itself.

While no early *libellus* survives to illustrate the cult-making activities of Erkenwald's other monastery, at Chertsey, that community also had an early interest in its founder. In a letter written before 745, Abbot Sigebald of Chertsey promised Archbishop Boniface, if he outlived him, that he would commemorate him at mass with 'our father Earconwald'.[19] Chertsey's continuing devotion to the saint is indicated by the production of a late list of English saints' resting places, claiming that he was buried there. This flies in the face of all other such lists which firmly locate Erkenwald's tomb in London.[20]

Clearly Erkenwald was venerated in both his monasteries from an early date. It would seem likely, therefore, that, as the resting-place lists suggest, he was also venerated then in his see church, where, despite the late claims of Chertsey, he was clearly buried. Our only account of the pre-Conquest enshrinement comes from a mid twelfth-century source, the London canon Arcoid. The picture that he presents is not wholly consistent, but he is clear that Erkenwald's burial was located at the pre-Conquest cathedral church.[21] In the arrangements destroyed by the fire of 1087, as he describes them, the saint's remains lay within a wooden chest (*theca lignea*), covered by an ancient silk and linen pall (*palliolum*). The whole was raised upon a stone-built substructure located to the east of the high altar (*altare dominicum*). All this derives from very early exemplars, ultimately depending upon a Merovingian model, established for Martin of Tours, and represented in late seventh-century England by the shrines of Cuthbert at Lindisfarne, Benedict Biscop at Wearmouth and Chad at Lichfield.[22] Such dispositions point to early origins; even if in this case, they probably represented a conservative recreation of the original arrangement, realized within a year of St Paul's destruction by fire in 962.[23]

Elsewhere, in apparent contradiction of this account, Arcoid says that the tomb (*sepulcrum*) of the saint lay 'outside the minster' (*extra monasterium*).[24] The difficulty may be resolved by assuming that by *sepulcrum* Arcoid was designating a monument marking the original burial place of the saint, where he lay before being translated inside the church. In late tenth-century Winchester, for example, Swithun's physical remains lay in a splendid reliquary within the cathedral, while the site of the saint's original burial place outside the earlier church was commemorated by a cenotaph in the western atrium.[25] It is not at all unlikely that Erkenwald similarly had more than one cult site in London's pre-Conquest episcopal complex.

Erkenwald's main feast-day, the day of his death or deposition, is recorded on 30 April (once on 29 April) in thirteen tenth- and eleventh-century calendars. He is also invoked in many late Anglo-Saxon litanies.[26] All this is evidence that by then he was well established as a saint. At most, however, the calendar entries and the litany invocations are evidence of a widespread liturgical commemoration; they tell us little of the observance of the cult at St Paul's itself in the Reform period. Most significant perhaps is a second entry, on 7 July, in an early eleventh-century calendar from Wessex, which evidently records a secondary feast, perhaps a commemoration of the translation implied in the physical arrangements described by Arcoid.[27] Otherwise, all that is known about the cult before the late eleventh century derives from a few miracle stories.[28] One early relic, perhaps dating back to pre-Conquest times, was the 'very ancient psalter of St Erkenwald' (*psalterium sancti Erkenwaldi vetusissimum*) mentioned in the inventory of 1255.[29]

Associated with the cult of Erkenwald in the earliest source was that of Sæbbi, king of the East Saxons (664–94) and responsible through Bishop Jaruman for his people's conversion. His reign coincided with Erkenwald's episcopate and indeed he and the bishop may have been related.[30] Shortly before his death, he abdicated, received the religious habit from Erkenwald's successor Waldhere and became a monk in London. His burial by Bishop Waldhere at St Paul's, in the presence of his sons and successors, was marked by a wonder: the sarcophagus intended for his interment miraculously expanded to accommodate the royal body. Like those relating to Erkenwald, the stories about Sæbbi are recorded in the *Historia Ecclesiastica* and again derive from the lost *libellus* of the nuns of Barking. They suggest an early attempt to establish a royal cult in St Paul's.[31] Sæbbi, however, is not mentioned in the resting-place lists and his later feast day (29 August) does not occur in the early calendars.[32] It would seem, therefore, that his cult never really got off the ground. That is not surprising, since on the whole English cathedrals (as opposed to monasteries) did not favour royal dynastic cults.[33] It may therefore be that there was always more enthusiasm for this holy king at his family monastery of Barking than at St Paul's.

After its brief emergence into the historical limelight in Bede's *History*, St Paul's vanishes again from view, and indeed we can say little more about its functions as a cult centre until after the Conquest. We do know, however, that in the tenth century Theodred, bishop of London from *c.*926 to the early 950s, left the church his 'best relics', perhaps acquired together with some vestments on a visit to Pavia.[34] Theodred, one of the richest and most eminent of all the pre-Conquest holders of the see, also bequeathed to the community at St Paul's four estates in Essex and Norfolk (pp. 12–13), including that of Chich with its cult of St Osyth, later important in the cathedral. We know nothing of

the nature of his relics, but almost certainly they may be identified with those attributed to Bishop 'Theodore' and inventoried at the beginning of an Anglo-Saxon Old Testament still owned by the cathedral in 1245.[35] Theodred himself, according to William of Malmesbury known popularly as 'the Good', was treated as a saint of London in a list of English saints' resting places transcribed at Peterborough in the twelfth century. Nevertheless, although he was undoubtedly buried at St Paul's in a tomb of particular prominence (p. 127), there is no evidence of a cult at the cathedral.[36]

Theodred, whose diocesan responsibilities extended to Suffolk, was a devotee of the cult of the East Anglian martyr-king Edmund, to the guardians of which he left estates in his will.[37] These tenuous links between Edmund and St Paul's were much intensified during the Danish wars of the early eleventh century. In 1009 the king's body was brought for safety to the church of St Gregory, *infra atrium Sancti Pauli*, where it remained for three years, working numerous miracles. In 1012, when the guardians wished to return the body to Suffolk, the impact of the cult had been such that Bishop Ælfhun (1002 × 1004–1015 × 1018) sought in vain to retain the relics and remove them to the cathedral.[38] Edmund's feast was long to remain of significance in the cathedral liturgy (p. 117).

Just as it was losing Edmund, St Paul's acquired its own martyr cult. The story of the translation of the relics of Alphage (Ælfheah), archbishop of Canterbury, killed by the Danes at Greenwich on 19 April 1012, is a remarkable one. Alphage's initial resting place after his murder was in St Paul's, where he immediately became the object of veneration and his remains worked many wonders. In 1023 this London cult was suppressed when Cnut forcibly removed the saint's remains to Canterbury, apparently in the teeth of opposition from the citizens. Osbern, a monk of Christ Church, Canterbury, produced a vivid record of these events in the late eleventh century.[39] According to him, the martyr's body was enshrined at St Paul's, in a monument attached to one of the walls of the cathedral comprising the tomb itself, covered by a stone slab, and a superstructure of masonry, adorned with a candelabrum. In a swift and secret operation, masterminded by the king and by Æthelnoth, archbishop of Canterbury, this structure was demolished and the miraculously undecayed body, covered by a cloth snatched from the high altar, was taken to the river to be shipped across to Southwark. From thence it was carried under armed guard to Canterbury. Osbern's reliability has been questioned on the grounds that another late eleventh-century account of the episode does not mention its violent and clandestine nature.[40] Nevertheless, the removal of the remains, which were then perhaps its major object of veneration, was a severe loss to St Paul's and is unlikely to have been accomplished without opposition, especially if the cult was a focus of hostility to Danish rule.[41] St Paul's, however, appears to have retained one or two relics. The martyr's blood-stained cowl remained there until given to Ramsey Abbey in 1044, and a chasuble, 'said to be St Alphage's', was still in the treasury in 1245. Adorned with gold thread and gems, it seems to have been of a grandeur and elaboration appropriate for high-grade Anglo-Saxon workmanship.[42]

The last Old English bishop of London, Ælfweard (1035–44), was a keen collector of relics.[43] Most of those we know about were given to the abbey of Evesham, which he held in plurality with his see, and to Ramsey Abbey, whither he withdrew after being stricken with leprosy. Despite the lack of record, however, he probably also encouraged relic cults at St Paul's. He

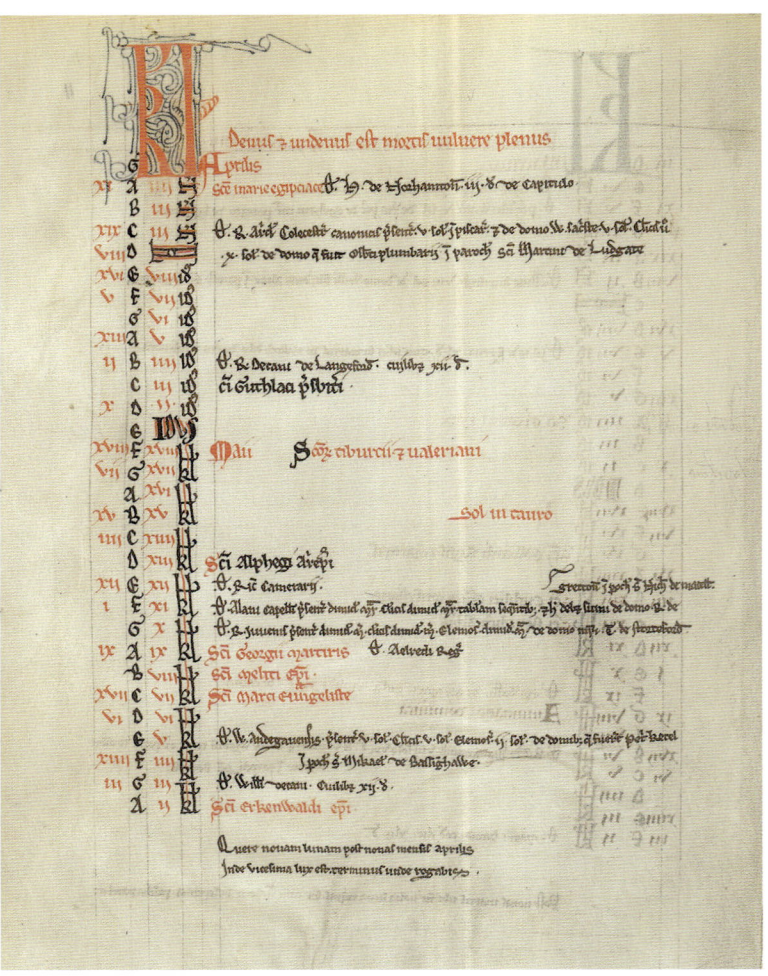

60.   Excerpt from a thirteenth-century calendar of St Paul's, showing feasts of St Mellitus and St Erkenwald picked out in red (GL, St Paul's collection, MS 25512, fo. 11v)

perspective.[47] That life, which introduces Mellitus as the teacher of Erkenwald, a detail unknown to Bede, was clearly centred on the corporeal remains. Its main episode is a lengthy account of the removal by the canons of St Paul's of the saint's body from Barking, where he had died, in the face of opposition from the nuns themselves and the brethren of Chertsey. The story vindicates the Londoners, to assist whose passage the swollen waters of a river in spate miraculously divided, thereby enabling them successfully to bring the body back to their city.[48]

Before Maurice died in 1107, Erkenwald's marvellously preserved remains had been translated to the new crypt, where they were installed in a place of honour on the right side of the parochial altar, presumably transferred thither from a church demolished to make way for the Norman cathedral.[49] In the twelfth century Erkenwald's feast day seems to have been a major event, its observance commanded throughout the diocese and culminating in elaborate ceremonies in London. The tomb itself had become a focus of miracles and votive offerings by the 1130s. Prayers were said and processional masses held there on the saint's feast days and on the anniversary of particularly celebrated miracles.[50] By 1139 a new wooden shrine, plated in silver and gold, was under construction.[51] In 1140, however, whatever plans there were for a fresh translation had hurriedly to be anticipated after an attempt to steal the body from the crypt. The saint's remains, by then enclosed in a lead sarcophagus, were taken to the chancel of the upper church, evidently sufficiently complete to accommodate them and regarded as a safer place, more easily watched over. The lead coffin was enclosed in a stone structure specially built to house it and miraculously adjusted to do so when found to be defective. The translation, effected on 16 February 1140, was accompanied by miracles.[52] In 1148 these provisional arrangements were superseded by a fresh translation. The saint was then relocated to a place of honour behind the high altar of the Norman presbytery, where he remained until the building of the New Work in the early fourteenth century.[53]

The revival of Erkenwald's cult was accompanied by a revival of interest in other early saints with whom Erkenwald himself had been, or could be, associated. A particular beneficiary was the founding bishop, Mellitus, who had himself been the object of a promotion (together with the other early archbishops) in the celebrated translation of 1091 at St Augustine's, Canterbury. He was now regarded as Erkenwald's teacher, and by the thirteenth century he shared with the latter the primary cultic site, attached to the high altar.[54] From the late eleventh century, if not earlier, there was also a church dedicated to St Augustine himself just to the east of the cathedral, where, after the completion of the new enclosure in the twelfth century (p. ••), it stood just outside the precinct gate.[55]

By the mid twelfth century there are signs of an attempt to promote Sæbbi, credited with responsibility for Erkenwald's appointment to the see, and termed *sanctus* and most gentle of kings (*mitissimus regum*) by Arcoid.[56] He was given a new tomb, together with the Old English king Ethelred II (978–1016), perhaps at the time of the 1148 translation.[57] Significantly, he is recorded as a saint in a resting-place list compiled or transcribed at Peterborough about that time, although the cult does not seem to have developed thereafter.[58] By then, too, there is interest at St Paul's in Erkenwald's sister Ethelburga and the other saints of Barking. As early as the 1080s, Goscelin had dedicated his lives of Ethelburga and her tenth-century successor Wulfhilda to Bishop Maurice,[59] and in the 1140s Arcoid included in his account of Erkenwald's miracles a wonder performed at Barking

presumably intended, for example, that his cathedral should benefit from his removal of relics from the shrine of St Osyth at Chich (an act of hubris credited with bringing upon him the affliction that forced his retirement). He is likely also to have fostered the cult of St Alphage at St Paul's before taking the martyr's cowl to its new home in Ramsey.[44]

THE REORGANIZATION AND REVITALIZATION OF THE CULTS AFTER THE FIRE OF 1087

Although according to Arcoid, writing in the mid twelfth century, Erkenwald's feast day was widely observed even before the fire of 1087, paradoxically, the burning of the old minster gave fresh impetus to the cult. Belief that the saint's shrine miraculously survived the fire unscathed added to his prestige.[45] Moreover, the ambitious new work of replacement simultaneously required enhanced offerings to help with funding and provided new opportunities for enshrinements along the lines being developed contemporaneously at Canterbury, Winchester, Ely and elsewhere.[46] Like other senior ecclesiastics of the time, Bishop Maurice (1085–1107) was clearly interested not only in the native saints of his cathedral church but also in those from nearby, such as Erkenwald's sister Ethelburga and her successors at Barking, and St Osyth at Chich.

Naturally, Erkenwald became the principal focus of the revitalized cathedral cults. Between 1087 and the 1120s, perhaps around 1100, he was the subject of a life, clearly written from a London

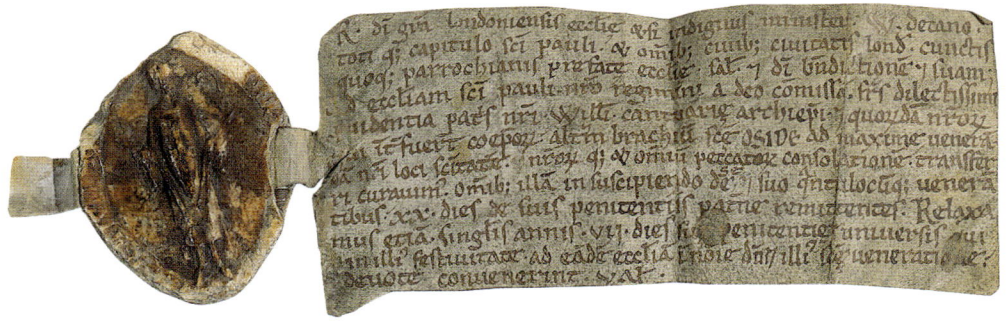

61. Bishop Richard of London grants an indulgence to all who venerate the newly acquired arm of St Osyth: a charter of the 1120s. (GL, St Paul's collection, MS 25122/1140)

jointly by the bishop and his sister.[60] By Arcoid's time, too, there is evidence of the beginnings of interest in Cedd, the seventh-century bishop responsible for the conversion of the East Saxons after the collapse of the Roman mission.[61] These interests were to evolve further in the thirteenth century, by which time King Ethelbert of Kent had also joined the company of the church's local saints (p. 118).

One of the most developed of these promotions of local Old English figures was that of St Osyth (Osgyth), allegedly a late seventh-century royal abbess. Saints of that name appear to have rested at Chich (Essex) and at Aylesbury (Bucks).[62] The East Saxon cult, the only one firmly attested in the resting-place lists, was fostered at Chich (St Osyth's) with a translation in 1076 and confirmed by Bishop Maurice, who translated the remains a second time, to 'a higher place, behind the high altar'. The cult was further promoted by Bishop Richard of Belmeis (1108–27).[63] Belmeis had originally sought to take over Osyth's land at Chich, but in 1119, after a partial recovery from a stroke, attributed to the intervention of the saint, he repented and founded a new and enriched community of canons regular to act as guardians of the shrine. In the 1120s he brought a relic (an arm) to London and granted an indulgence to all who venerated it (Fig. 61). This translation to St Paul's took place in the presence of William of Corbeil, archbishop of Canterbury (1123–36) and previously prior of St Osyth's, who acquired the other arm for his own cathedral church.[64] Here again there is evidence of a link between St Paul's and the metropolitan church in the promotion of cults.

The Norman clergy of St Paul's did not restrict their investment in saints simply to those who were mentioned in the Bible, martyred in Rome, or endowed with local associations. Their growing interest in figures venerated generally throughout the West is illustrated by the introduction of another cult, that of St Faith, the virgin martyr of Conques. Brought to England shortly after 1100,[65] it was evidently established almost immediately at St Paul's, if (as Arcoid implies) the parochial altar in the crypt was dedicated to the saint by the time that St Erkenwald was translated thither, before the death of Bishop Maurice in 1107.[66] Interestingly, the cult of St Faith was also observed in Canterbury by the mid twelfth century.[67]

THE EMERGING PATTERN IN THE LATE TWELFTH AND EARLIER THIRTEENTH CENTURY

The developing pattern of cult at St Paul's emerges clearly from its calendars, which record the feast days given especial prominence at the cathedral, above and beyond the universally highly graded dominical, Marian and apostolic feasts. The calendars were an important expression of the cathedral clergy's corporate identity, indicators of the local figures from their own past whom they wished to honour and of others from the wider world with whom they wished to identify. The annual liturgical round therein laid out, together with the special prayers or collects, rituals and music by which it was expressed, constituted the church's distinctive use, famed from the twelfth century for its splendour and above all its elaborate processions.[68] The liturgical year was determined by a number of factors, including in particular the identity of the titular saint, St Paul, honoured at the high altar, and of the local bishop, St Erkenwald, honoured primarily at his tomb. Conscious of a glorious past stretching back to the introduction of Christianity among the English, the London clergy added to their calendars a number of saints associated with that era. They also included other saints with strong connections with London and Canterbury, as well as those honoured in churches nearby and in the diocese or at newly established altars in their own cathedral (pp. 118–19).

The earliest surviving calendar from St Paul's, copied into a twelfth-century English psalter later at Sens and now in Paris,[69] dates apparently from the 1150s or 1160s.[70] It offers evidence of a distinctive annual cycle, the principal saints' feasts being highlighted in blue, green and red, with others, less honoured, in black. In particular, it gave especial emphasis to two celebrations of St Paul himself: his conversion (25 January) and commemoration (30 June), both being entered in blue and in capitals, distinctions otherwise accorded only to certain Marian feasts and the deposition of Pope Gregory the Great (12 March).[71] Other major highly ranked days included those of St Erkenwald, his deposition (30 April) and translation (14 November), both entered in red, and of two archbishops of Canterbury, SS Mellitus (24 April) and Dunstan (19 May), the former in red, the latter in blue. Other Canterbury saints in the calendar included the archbishops Augustine (26 May) and Alphage (19 April), and the Kentish abbess Mildred (13 July), all entered at the lowest grade, in black.

Among the early martyrs customarily honoured in the liturgy, the calendar gave prominence to the English protomartyr Alban (22 June) and SS Vincent (22 January) and Lawrence (10 August), of both of whom the cathedral may already by then have had relics (pp. 118–19). Also singled out, in blue or red, were the virgin martyrs Katharine (25 November) and, probably, Margaret (20 July), both of whom later had altars in the cathedral, and St Faith (6 October), already in the crypt and entered in black.[72] A number of East Anglian saints were highly graded, including the martyr kings Ethelbert (Æthelberht, 20 May) and Edmund (20 November),[73] and Abbot Botolph (Botulf) of Iken (17 June), by then titular of a parish church near St Paul's and of others in the city.[74] Other local saints, such as SS Etheldreda (Æthelthryth) of Ely (23 June) and Osyth of Chich (7 October), were entered with less honour, in black. One or two widely venerated saints, later known to have had altars in the cathedral or churches in the precinct or nearby, were graded highly with entries in blue, including SS Mary Magdalen (22 July), Leonard (6 November), Martin (11 November) and Nicholas (6 December).[75]

This calendar seems to have been associated with a wider ordering of the liturgical Use of St Paul undertaken in the mid twelfth century, probably by the learned canon, Master Alberic (see pp. 153, 413). Certainly, in the mid thirteenth century, another period of liturgical definition (see below), Dean Cornhill (d. 1254) gave an ordinal to the cathedral which included a calendar and was said to be *secundum Albericum*.[76]

The deanship of Ralph de Diceto (1180/1–1200) appears to have been important for the reordering of the cathedral's liturgical life, as for so many of its other activities (p. 21). In particular, he seems to have been responsible for the establishment of new altars, providing new focuses of cult to put alongside holy tombs such as Erkenwald's and portable reliquaries like that of Osyth's arm. He was, for example, almost certainly responsible for the early introduction of the cult of the martyred archbishop, Thomas Becket, who had been a canon at the cathedral. Diceto's deanery chapel, which he established in 1182–3, is later recorded as dedicated to Becket (p. 21), and shortly after its construction Bishop Richard III (1189–98), set up altars to the archishop and to the French martyr, St Denis, in a gallery at the west end of the cathedral (*super testudines in occidente ecclesie*).[77] The same bishop also established an altar to the Merovingian queen Radegund, served by a perpetual chaplain.[78] Soon to become important locations for chantries (p. 119), by *c*.1200 these altars belonged to a group of active cult sites before which lamps burned perpetually, maintained by the gifts of the cathedral clergy and the faithful. By then or a little later, there were altars to the Virgin, St Erkenwald and St James,[79] and, in the crypt, to the Northumbrian king Oswald, for the upkeep of which a payment of 2*s.* was made annually on the saint's feast day (5 August).[80] By then, too, the rood, which was to remain one of the greatest cult objects in the cathedral until the Reformation, had been installed in the cathedral. In this early period it stood before an altar dedicated to St John the Evangelist, served by a perpetual chaplain and already perhaps near the south door of the cathedral nave.[81]

Diceto also formed a relic collection which he bequeathed to the cathedral and which provides important clues to the developing pattern of cult at St Paul's as revealed in the calendars and inventories of the earlier thirteenth century. His collection included relics of Christ, Mary Magdalen, the Roman martyr-popes Stephen and Alexander, the Roman martyrs Lawrence, Hippolytus, Mark and Marcellian, the Gallic bishops Martin of Tours and Maximinus of Trier, the Northumbrian king Oswald, the Frankish abbot Remaclus, the English abbess Walburga, the otherwise unidentified martyrs Eugenius and Victor, and an unnamed companion of St Maurice.[82] An eclectic assemblage, it anticipates the grading of feasts and the dedication of several thirteenth-century altars, including perhaps that of St Oswald, already noted.

An early thirteenth-century calendar shows that the pattern established by the later twelfth century remained fairly stable. In addition to recording the cathedral's principal feasts in red and other significant saints' days in black, it included commemorations or obits of local clergy and of other figures revered for their associations with London and its see (Fig. 60).[83] Unsurprisingly, the principal feasts remained those of SS Paul and Erkenwald, although, oddly enough, Erkenwald's secondary feast, his translation, was omitted from the original text and had to be entered shortly afterwards. As before,

feasts highlighting the Roman mission included Mellitus, Gregory the Great and Augustine of Canterbury, the last by then upgraded. By then, too, the cathedral was developing a strong interest in the mission's English patron, King Ethelbert of Kent, whom it regarded as its founder and whose day of death (24 February) was added to the calendar shortly after it was written, along with the obits of Alfred and Henry II. The links with Canterbury in the crucial areas of liturgy and cult were also indicated by the continuing inclusion of the feast days of Archbishops Dunstan and Alphage and Abbess Mildred, all at a lesser grade, entered in black.

Other feasts continued to reflect the cathedral's links with cult sites in its Essex diocese and in East Anglia. St Osyth, in accordance with her ambiguous origins, is entered in black under two feast days, 3 June and 7 October. The East Anglian martyr-kings Ethelbert and Edmund and Abbot Botolph were all still accorded the highest grade, and Abbess Etheldreda of Ely was again entered in black.

Thomas Becket, who by the early thirteenth century had been adopted by the citizens as second patron of their commune after St Paul, was a predictable new addition. His main feast, the day of his martyrdom (30 December), was entered in red and the feast commemorating his translation in 1220 (7 July) in black (although by the 1230s it was treated as a solemnity and had become the main London feast).[84] Other highly graded feasts, mostly reflecting the presence of significant relics or altars, included SS Mary of Egypt (2 April), Petronilla (31 May), Margaret, Mary Magdalen and Katharine, the last two of which were upgraded to rank with the feast of St Michael (29 September) about this time.[85] Significant black-graded entries include Oswald, archishop of York (28 February) and a group of martyr-kings, the West Saxon Edward (18 March), the Mercian Kenelm (17 July) and the Northumbrian Oswald (5 August). Perhaps the most notable omission is the feast of Erkenwald's sister, St Ethelburga of Barking (11 October), from both this and the earlier Paris calendar.

In the 1230s Bishop Roger Niger (1228–1241) issued orders, in conjunction with Peter Newport, archdeacon of London, requiring the solemn celebration throughout the city of specified feasts which with one or two exceptions reflect the Use of St Paul as represented in the calendars just discussed. That these feasts are described as customarily doubted by chaplains newly arrived in the city and that they included the commemoration of St Paul and the deposition and translation of St Erkenwald suggests perhaps that the cathedral had some way to go in establishing the observance of its main cults in London as a whole.[86] A related group of feasts was the subject of further regulation by Bishop Fulk Bassett (1241–59). Bassett alleged that there was scandalous diversity in the solemnity with which certain feasts were treated in the diocese and sought to standardize the degree to which works of piety and servile labour could be performed on those days.[87] The feasts of St Paul, the deposition of St Erkenwald (but not the translation), the translation of St Thomas Becket and the feasts of St Edmund king and martyr and St Katharine were declared solemnities to be observed by all. Those of SS Dunstan, Ethelbert king and martyr and Oswald were restricted to the city, while those of SS Alban, Osyth and Ethelburga were to be treated as solemnities only in their own deaneries.[88] The need for this regulation again perhaps suggests that the cathedral's use and the special cults which it reflected had had only a limited influence in London.

A more developed picture of impact of the use in the cathedral itself emerges from contemporary and mid thirteenth-century records of its altars and the honour paid to them. By then, the cult of the Virgin had risen to especial eminence. At her principal altar, probably in the nave,[89] mass was celebrated daily by a priest and six clerks from the choir; there were bequests to fund tapers to adorn it and lights to burn before it.[90] The nave also contained an important altar to the apostles, at which there was a weekly solemn mass. They and the altars of SS Michael, Radegund and John the Evangelist, all served by perpetual chaplains, were especially favoured for chantries, and chantries were also established at the altars of SS John the Baptist, James the Less, Stephen and Lawrence, Chad (the brother of Cedd), and Thomas and Denis. Reference was made to the feast days of SS Oswald, Chad and Katharine, to the service of St Radegund and the office of St Anne.[91] Other records show that commemorations were also made by 1247 at altars dedicated to St Nicholas and St Ethelbert, king and martyr, and by the 1260s to the recently canonized Edmund, archbishop of Canterbury, and the English king, Edward the Confessor.[92] By 1257 the much revered rood had been set up near the great door in the north transept, with the altar of St James beneath it.[93]

The continuing devotion to St Paul is reflected in the special acts of charity commanded by Henry III on the feasts of the apostle's conversion and commemoration in 1244, when the bishopric was in royal hands after the death of Roger Niger. The provision for the conversion was especially lavish: 15,000 paupers were to be fed in the churchyard (*in atrio*) and 1,500 wax tapers lit in the church.[94] The feelings of the contemporary clergy for their patron are perhaps evidenced in their ownership of a treatise in praise of St Paul, a sermon on his life and death, and a handsome glossed copy of the Epistles.[95] In the mid thirteenth century the cathedral also acquired a new unofficial cult. Bishop Roger Niger, clearly an attractive personality warmly admired by the chronicler Matthew Paris, was believed to have worked miracles from his tomb almost immediately after his death in 1244. Although not canonized, Matthew tells us, he was regarded locally as a saint.[96] There is evidence that in the 1250s and 1260s some English bishops took the same view and granted indulgences to their flock to visit the tomb.[97]

Two important thirteenth-century inventories help us to envisage the physical expression of cult within the cathedral.[98] By then, St Paul's abounded in relics, enclosed within altars, portable shrines and liturgical objects. In particular, they formed a dominating presence on or around the high altar in a variety of shrines (*feretra*) and other precious containers made of silver and ivory and filled with eclectic collections derived from all kinds of saints. The high altar was particularly associated with the shrines of the two early bishops – Erkenwald and Mellitus. The exact arrangement is unclear, but it seems likely that by then the two reliquaries lay side by side on the altar itself or on some abutting structure. In 1245 Erkenwald's *feretrum* was of wood, covered externally with silver plates adorned with images and precious stones, and surmounted by two silver angels.[99] The shrine of Mellitus was also of wood, surmounted by a single angel of gilded copper and covered in the front with figured silver plates.[100] The nature of the relics that it housed is, however, uncertain. Clearly, the cult was of considerable importance in the thirteenth-century cathedral, which also possessed two silver-plated arm reliquaries of the saint, one of them adorned by Bishop Eustace (1221–8) and expressly said to contain bone donated by the monks of St

Augustine's.[101] We may suppose that St Augustine's was the source of the other relics of Mellitus, all presumably distributed after the translation of 1091.[102]

The community also had relics of the two Ethelberts – the confessor-king of Kent and the martyr-king of East Anglia. A portable shrine covered with 130 precious stones and other ornaments and inventoried in both 1245 and 1295 was said to contain relics of a King Ethelbert, otherwise unidentified but possibly the martyr, since he was titular saint of an altar in the cathedral at this time.[103] By 1295 the cathedral had two other reliquaries, one containing a jawbone of Ethelbert of Kent, the other a head-shrine of Ethelbert of East Anglia. By then, if not earlier, therefore, St Paul's interest in the Kentish king had developed into a full-blown cult. In 1245 the cathedral also possessed arm reliquaries of St Osyth and St Oswald, the former presumably acquired in the 1120s, the latter perhaps when the altar was established around 1200. The community also claimed to possess the staff (*baculus*) and other relics of Thomas Becket and a pillow (*auricularium*) of St Edith, probably the saint of Wilton.[104]

By 1245 the cathedral's collection of dominical relics included a fragment of the Cross, enclosed in a cross-shaped silver-gilt reliquary. The most important of the items derived from universally venerated saints appear to have been two ribs of the Roman martyr, Lawrence, enshrined in a portable *feretrum*, apparently of relatively recent construction, covered in plates of gilded silver and adorned with a crystal and other precious stones. Another probably contemporaneous relic list mentions a head of St Gameliel and relics of St Augustine (of Hippo) and St Agnes.[105]

A number of twelfth- and thirteenth-century bishops gave reliquaries (*feretra*) to the cathedral. That of Bishop Richard III (Richard fitz Neal, 1189–98) was particularly esteemed. Known as the *feretrum* of the Virgin, because hairs from the saint had been placed within it, it also enclosed a small gold casket containing a tooth of St Vincent. Another episcopal *feretrum*, said to be especially beautiful – of solid silver gilt – and to contain many relics, was the gift of a Bishop William, perhaps Richard III's successor, William of Sainte-Mère-Eglise (1198–1221). There were also relics in a black chest (*cofrum nigrum*), believed in 1245 to have been the gift of Bishop Gilbert (perhaps Gilbert the Universal, 1127–34).[106] All these reliquaries were probably kept in the treasury.

THE COMPLETION OF THE NEW WORK AND THE LATER HISTORY OF THE CATHEDRAL'S CULTS

A further major reordering of medieval cult in St Paul's took place with the construction of the New Work, begun in 1259 and not completed until the 1320s. Inventories of the 1290s and the earlier fourteenth century enable us to identify the principal cult sites – the most important chapels and altars – in the cathedral as a whole during this period. They mention the Carnary (charnel) chapel, dedicated to the Virgin and established in St Paul's churchyard in the 1270s (p. 35), the chapel of St John the Evangelist 'in the south part of the church', the parochial chapel of St Faith in the crypt and the chapel of St Radegund, also probably in the crypt.[107] By then, besides these, the most important locations for chantries comprised altars dedicated to the Virgin, in the nave and in the south transept opposite the chapter house door; to the Apostles, in the nave; and to SS Michael and Silvester, both probably in the New Work.[108] Other altars at which chantries were established in the late thirteenth or fourteenth century included

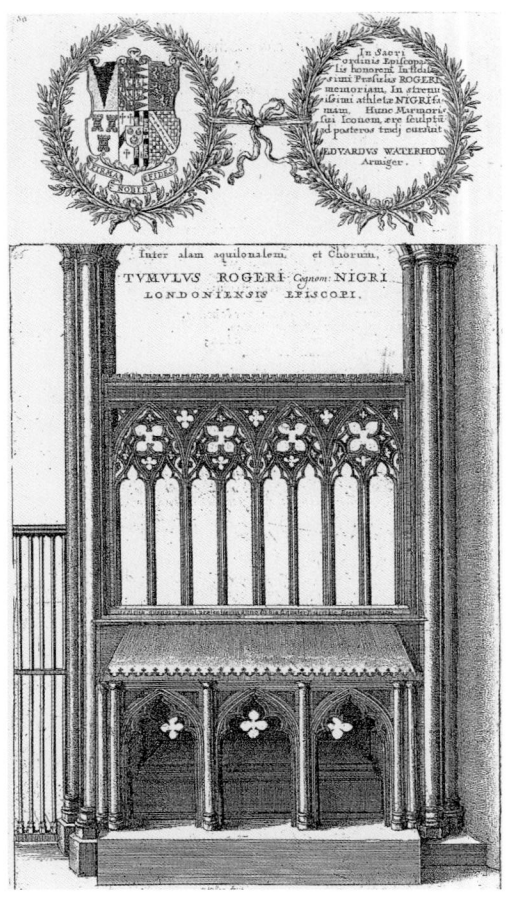

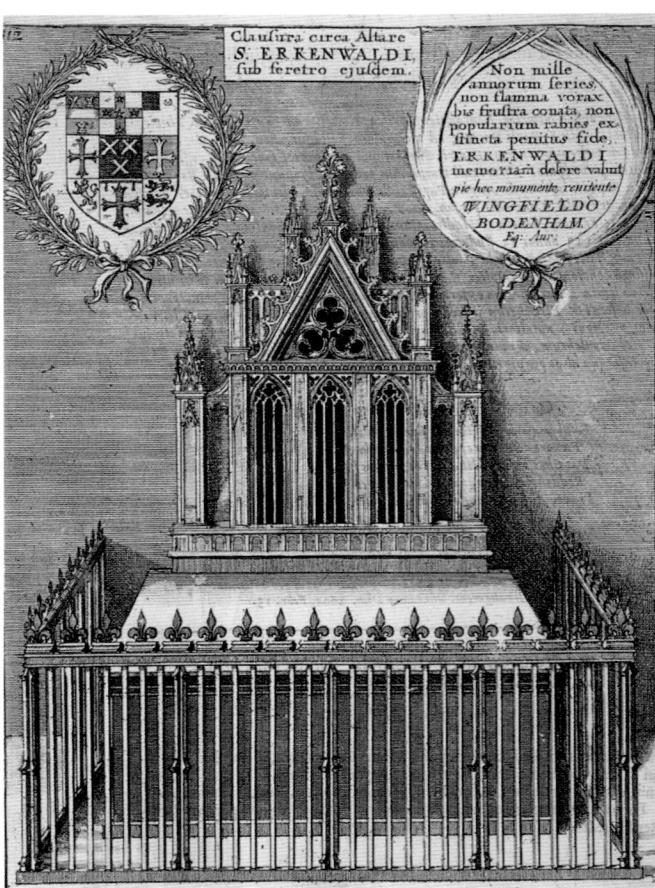

62 (*far left*). The tomb of the saintly Bishop Roger Niger (d. 1241), drawn by Hollar for Dugdale's *History*, 1658. This new shrine was erected in 1326. (GL)

63 (*left*). The enclosure around the altar and tomb of St Erkenwald below his shrine and behind the high altar, drawn by Hollar for Dugdale's *History*, 1658. The shrine was completed in 1326 and some or all of its structure removed in 1552. The railings may be the remains of the 'grate' erected there in 1401. (GL)

those of St Chad and his brother St Cedd, SS Hippolytus, Stephen, Katharine, Andrew, Margaret (before the rood at the north door), and Thomas (in the south transept near the chapter house door). There was also a new altar near the door leading to Ivy Lane in the north side of the nave.[109]

In the New Work – increasingly the location of the main cult sites – the crypt altar of St Faith and the chapels of St Radegund and of St John the Baptist (the latter in a separate structure at the south-west angle) were probably established at a relatively early date.[110] The ritual furnishings of the upper church and choir were, however, only put in place after the paving of the four easternmost bays in 1313.[111] The centrepiece of the new arrangements was the new shrine of St Erkenwald set up to the east of the stone screen behind the high altar, at this period part of the Lady Chapel (Fig. 67).[112] Bishop Gilbert Segrave laid the first stone on the day of his enthronement on 24 March 1314,[113] and soon afterwards, in May 1314, consecrated the principal eastern altars, those of the Virgin, Thomas Becket and Dunstan (situated respectively at the east end of the central, north and south aisles).[114] At the west end of the Lady Chapel, St Erkenwald's own altar had been set up by about 1320, enriched by a munificent bequest of Bishop Ralph Baldock (1304–13), whose executors established a perpetual chantry there, served by two priests; Baldock himself appears to have had an interest in improving the cathedral liturgy.[115] In 1326 the saint was finally translated to his new home, an elaborate house shrine with a gable and fashionable decorated tracery (p. 138, Fig. 63).[116]

The final stage in the completion of the New Work was the reordering of the choir. This had been going on at least since 1309, when a new altarpiece was commissioned, but reached its high point in the 1320s.[117] About 1325, a major new monument, the elaborate oratory and chantry chapel dedicated to the Virgin,

St Laurence and All Saints, was built in the south choir aisle by Canon Roger de Waltham and apparently linked with the chapel of St John the Baptist in the crypt below (pp. 164–6). In 1326, a week after the translation of St Erkenwald, the body of Roger Niger, described as a saint, was moved to a new shrine in the north arcade (Figs. 62, 67).[118] The first mass at the high altar was celebrated in 1327, and the new ritual arrangements were finally brought to completion in 1339, when Bishop Richard Bintworth consecrated that altar to St Paul, and its collaterals to north and south to St Ethelbert, king, confessor and founder, and St Mellitus.[119]

While all this was going on, the cathedral's continuing role as a focus for the expression of the feelings of London's citizens about contemporary political events was demonstrated in 1322, when it was the setting for a short-lived cult of Edward II's cousin, Thomas of Lancaster. An image of the earl, set up in St Paul's shortly after his execution at Pontefract, was venerated by crowds of worshippers and even worked miracles – events which provoked the king to write to Bishop Stephen Gravesend condemning the cult and ordering its suppression.[120] Despite the king's efforts, however, it was of sufficient importance for an office honouring Thomas as soldier saint and martyr to be composed.[121]

Apart from the fleeting veneration of Thomas of Lancaster, the cult of the saints did not change substantially in the cathedral in the fourteenth century.[122] A resurgence in devotion to Erkenwald, stimulated by the translation, resulted in some notable bequests in the ensuing two decades,[123] and an important office for his feast, later enjoined on the diocese as a whole, was certainly in use around this time.[124] In 1339, presumably in association with the consecration of the high altar, the shrine was further beautified, the chapter employing three goldsmiths to work on it for an entire year.[125] Thereafter, however, interest seems to have slackened off (p. 40), and when in 1360 John, the captive king of France, visited the cathedral, his gift of twelve nobles to the shrine was eclipsed by that of twenty-six nobles to the rood at the north door.[126] In 1386 Bishop Robert Braybroke (1381–1404) found it necessary to issue injunctions, reiterated in 1393, enforcing the solemn observance of both of the saint's feasts throughout the diocese: they were to be kept as 'first class feasts' in the cathedral, when the parochial clergy of the diocese were expected to come to the cathedral in their copes and walk in procession with the canons and ministers of the choir.[127] That action clearly inaugurated another revival of interest in the cult. Almost certainly it stimulated the production of a new Middle English life of the saint, a work clearly aimed at a London audience but apparently of limited distribution (p. 40). It also seems to have elicited further gifts, and in the autumn of 1401 the shrine itself was repaired and greatly enriched. The new work included a gilded image of the saint himself, the provision of a further eight statues and the surrounding of the whole by a splendid iron grate. In 1407 Dean Thomas de Eure further endowed the cult, leaving £100 to be invested to provide revenue for the maintenance of the fabric of the shrine, the lights which burned before it, the festival masses on the two feast days, and the chaplain who served the saint's confraternity.[128] In 1436 the saint's casket (*capsa*) was adorned with Bishop Robert fitz Hugh's pontifical ring, a gift of the Venetian doge.[129]

Devotion to the Virgin was expressed with ever more elaboration. By the mid fourteenth century an especial focus was a much venerated image, attached to the second column of the south nave arcade. Regular offerings from the faithful were collected in a box fixed nearby, and in 1365 John Barnet, then bishop of Bath and Wells, gave a water mill, other property, and rents worth 43s. a year to maintain a daily office before it.[130] In the New Work, besides the Lady Chapel itself, there was yet another cult site, Roger de Waltham's oratory. A gift of twelve nobles by the French king in 1360 to an image of the Virgin 'beside the choir' (*encoste le cuer*) was clearly to one of the images amongst the sculpture adorning that chapel.[131]

Another continuing focus of cult was the north transept. Here, in 1349, Sir John Pultney, a former lord mayor, founded a chantry chapel dedicated to St John the Baptist and served by three priests.[132] Here, too, was the cathedral's second major object of veneration, the rood at the north door, devotion to which seems to have grown in the later Middle Ages (p. 40). Its offerings were considerable, in the 1340s amounting to nearly £650 in two years.[133] Housed upon a wooden platform, flanked by the altars of St James and St Margaret and approached from below by two flights of steps,[134] by the early fifteenth century the rood was reputed to be that which Joseph of Arimathea set up at Caerleon, and to have been set up in the cathedral in earliest times by King Lucius (p. 40). By then, too, the cult of Becket as patron of the citizens was being boosted by civic veneration for his parents, buried in the Pardon Churchyard north of the cathedral nave (p. 39).

The late medieval cathedral's enduring and conservative devotion to its local cults was evident from its attachment to its ancient Use, the special liturgical prayers and rites still offered and observed in the choir services on feast days. In 1376 Dean Appleby strongly resisted an attempt to replace that Use with the increasingly influential Use of Sarum at the dean and chapter's church of St Giles Cripplegate, an action which prompted the parishioners, most unusually, to petition the pope directly to sanction the new custom.[135] In 1414, when Bishop Richard Clifford finally imposed Sarum on the cathedral certain feasts were exempted. Besides those commemorating St Erkenwald himself, they included several of long-standing local interest to St Paul's, namely SS Ethelbert of Kent, Oswald of Worcester, Chad, Mellitus, Ethelbert of East Anglia, Lawrence, Hippolytus, Radegund, Osyth and Ethelburga. For them, the long-established readings and collects of the traditional local use still pertained.[136] In the mid sixteenth century the petty canon Thomas Batmanson was still sufficiently interested in that use to add these collects to a late fifteenth-century service book.[137]

While its Use mattered greatly to the cathedral, there is little to suggest that it had much appeal elsewhere. A service book following the Use held by the church at Writtle (Essex) in the mid fourteenth century was then over fifty years old and may simply have been discarded by the cathedral.[138] In London itself the opposition to the Use at St Giles's is reflected in what appears to have been a general reluctance on the part of the laity to participate in the cathedral's liturgy and cult. Despite the relaunches of the early fourteenth and early fifteenth centuries, interest in St Erkenwald was limited and for the mayor and citizens the principal event in the cathedral's year was the Whitsun processsions (p. 39). There were few fraternities or guilds, although there are signs of an emergent interest in the later fourteenth century. A guild of St Katharine was established to maintain a light in the saint's chapel in 1352, a guild and chapel of St Anne were set up in the crypt in 1371, and a guild of All Souls founded to restore and maintain the dilapidated charnel chapel in 1379. By 1389 there was a guild of the Annunciation attached to one of the chapels of the Virgin, perhaps Waltham's oratory,[139] and there is also some evidence of a guild attached to the shrine of St Erkenwald about this time (p. 40).[140] Thereafter, however, enthusiasm for such organizations seem to have declined at St Paul's until the later fifteenth century, when they came to play a more significant role in liturgy and cult at the cathedral. In the mid 1440s the east end of the New Work's north aisle housed a chapel of St George, replacing the earlier altar of St Thomas Becket, and in 1453 the city's armourers established there a newly incorporated eponymous guild.[141] By 1450 the cult of the Holy Name had been established in the east end of the great crypt; served by the wealthy Jesus Guild, it was a vehicle for opulent ceremonial (pp. 162–3). Later still, at the very end of the Middle Ages, the invented transexual saint Uncumber seems to have acquired a cult of some significance at St Paul's; in July 1538 her image, 'standing in her old place and state, with her gay gown and silver shoes on', was still the object of veneration.[142] Indeed, it was viewed as of sufficient importance shortly afterwards to be one of the first cult statues to be removed by the royal commissioners (p. 47).

The many and various cults at St Paul's, a dominating element in its religious and liturgical life since its foundation, were brought to an end in the mid sixteenth century. In 1538 Henry's commissioners visited the cathedral and took down the rood at the north door and the image of St Uncumber.[143] St Erkenwald's shrine, still intact in June 1539 when the cathedral celebrated an obit for the consort of the Emperor Charles V, is last mentioned in September of the same year.[144] Presumably, as elsewhere, around this time the saint's physical remains in their gilded and jewelled casket were removed; spoils from an image of St Erkenwald, almost certainly that from the shrine in St Paul's, had been delivered to the king by June 1540.[145] Destruction on a much greater scale took place immediately after Henry's death in January 1547.

In September, the royal visitors arrived at the cathedral to begin the elimination of its remaining images. Together with the great rood, they were all finally removed on 17 November, in a night of violence during which two workmen were killed and 'divers others sore hurt.'[146] The destruction of the charnel chapel followed in 1548 and in 1549 the sacrament house and the Becket chapel in the north cloister were also taken down.[147] Later in the same year, the morning mass of the apostles and all masses of the Virgin were abolished and Communion was prohibited except at the high altar.[148] The high altar itself was pulled down (again clandestinely and at night) to be replaced by a Communion table in 1550.[149] The purging of the cathedral of Catholic cult was brought to completion in 1552 when at Bishop Ridley's command the chapels and altars, the priests' sedilia on the south side of the presbytery and the stonework behind the high altar (including, presumably, the substructure of the shrine of St Erkenwald) were all 'plucked down'. On All Saints' Day in that year, the bishop celebrated according to the rite of the new Protestant prayer book for the first time.[150] Despite the brief restoration of Catholic worship under Mary (1553–8), the apparatus of medieval cult never recovered from the assaults it endured under Edward VI. In 1559, after the accession of Elizabeth I and the appointment of a new Protestant bishop, Edmund Grindal, the restored altars and images were removed for a final time.[151]

IO

THE ARCHAEOLOGY
OF ST PAUL'S

John Schofield

The idea that wonders and potentially decipherable mysteries from the past are to be revealed by delving into the lower depths and fabric of St Paul's was well established by 1400 and was vividly expressed in the new miracle story of St Erkenwald composed about that time. The story focuses on the discovery of an ancient tomb beneath the crypt and relates an unsuccessful attempt to understand its meaning by research in the cathedral library. In that period, too, there seems to have been a new interest in material features of the cathedral which supposedly demonstrated its ancient origin (p. 40), and somewhat later another story related the discovery of cattle skulls in the course of digging a foundation to the conjectured origin of the cathedral as a temple of Jupiter.[1] Unfortunately for the modern archaeologist, the digging and delving associated with the successive reconstructions of the cathedral and of other buildings round about have been so constant and so thorough that very few remains of those earlier structures survive, either in the ground or in the archaeological record.[2] This essay surveys archaeological discoveries at the cathedral since the seventeenth century and assesses what may yet remain to be revealed.

ARCHAEOLOGICAL EXPLORATION OF THE FORMER CATHE-DRALS AND THEIR SURROUNDINGS

During the construction of the present cathedral between 1668 and 1714, Wren and others noted Roman and later constructions and objects which were exposed or dug up: their notes form our best impression of the earliest Roman period on the cathedral site (pp. 2–4). There were pottery kilns in two places, cremation burials, coins and the usual array (for London) of pottery from elsewhere in the empire. None of the finds can now be traced, but some of the makers' stamps on pots were transcribed at the time: they are of potters working in Gaul between the first and the third century.

Wren was intimately acquainted with the pre-Fire cathedral and with the ruins that remained standing afterwards. What he saw of those parts of it which had long been demolished and of the churches that preceded Bishop Maurice's great construction begun in 1087 has to be gleaned from throwaway lines in *Parentalia*. He noted 'that though several times the fabrick had been ruined, yet that the foundations might remain, as originally they were laid, and upon observing, that they consisted of nothing but Kentish-rubble stone, artfully worked, and consolidated with a exceeding hard mortar, in the Roman manner, much excelling what he found in the superstructure'.[3] It is not stated where this was in relation to the present cathedral.

Fortunately, antiquaries were already combing the site. Payne Fisher, in his 1684 account of the tombs in the pre-Fire cathedral and their inscriptions, relates how several of the more substantial ones, though damaged, could be seen in the ruins for years after the Fire. Some of the tombs of medieval bishops had been broken open, allegedly by the Fire itself; they included the marble coffin of Bishop Braybroke (d. 1404), whose well-preserved skeleton was exposed and marvelled at, until it was reburied by Dean Sancroft. Fisher himself handled a chalice found in another tomb, conjectured to be that of a bishop.[4]

In August 1675 John Conyers watched the excavations at the east end of St Paul's. He noticed that the burials were in two general layers, a total of 17 feet thick; saw construction levels possibly from the church of 1087; and noted 'shreddes of the pretty green serpentine hard stone or Egiptian marble and the porphery or

64. The north end of one of the two buttresses of the fourteenth-century chapter house exposed by Penrose in 1879. View (probably drawn by H. W. Brewer) looking south-west, showing the ornate mouldings of one of originally eight supports for the chapter house above. The remains of the buttress survive in the ground south of the present nave. (SPCL)

Redd and whit[e] such like a Jasper and other Collourd stones as was used in the mosaick worke of St Edwards the Confessours monument at Westminster'.[5] Perhaps he had found one of the masons' yards or tomb-makers' workshops which had been close to the medieval cathedral (p. 20). Conyers also observed a Roman kiln under the north end of the new transept in 1677.

In terms of archaeological investigation, nothing is then reported until the work of the antiquary Charles Roach Smith and others in the 1830s and later, who recorded high-quality late-Roman buildings on sites immediately north of the cathedral. These decades produced two important post-Roman objects: a coin weight of a late ninth-century moneyer, also from a site on the north side (p. 20), and an eleventh-century tombstone in Scandinavian style, from a site towards the south-east corner of the churchyard (Fig. 7).[6]

The pre-Fire cathedral was reconstructed in a series of drawings by E. B. (Benjamin) Ferrey, who submitted them to the Royal Institute of British Architects in 1868 and was awarded the silver medal of the Institute and five guineas. They were at a scale of eight feet to the inch, and the ground plan is six feet three inches long. The elevations and sections were correspondingly enormous and now hang in the north triforium aisle of the present cathedral. Ferrey's reconstructed plan, elevations and sections were published in Longman's *History of St Paul's Cathedral* (1873). Unfortunately they contain much speculation and, although admired, are not used by scholars today. Moreover, they were immediately overtaken by new discoveries in the ground.

F. C. Penrose, appointed as Surveyor to the Fabric in 1852 (p. 296), began a new phase of dedicated investigation, scrupulously recorded, into selected features of the pre-Fire cathedral and its precinct. In the 1870s he found the east end of the New Work, conserving it in four small, below-ground chambers east of the present cathedral. At the same time he also found the site of the adjacent Paul's Cross as rebuilt in the fifteenth century (its site now marked on the ground); found and conserved the remains of the fourteenth-century chapter house (Fig. 64); and in smaller holes located the walls of the north transept, what may be St Gregory's church, and the junction between the west end and the portico designed by Inigo Jones. Penrose's observation of the west end is problematic, since the accounts for building the post-Fire cathedral suggest that the workmen dug out much of the west end of its predecessor, further than was really needed. From these remains Penrose began to work out the outline of the medieval building and its appendages.[7] He adjusted the plan engraved by Wenceslas Hollar for Dugdale's *History* of 1658 to fit his surveyed findings, and produced a plan of the pre-Fire cathedral in relation to that of its successor. Penrose's reconstructed plan is only now being tested and adjusted, 130 years later, by current work in and around St Paul's.

Surveyors of the Fabric in the first half of the twentieth century were more concerned with the upkeep and stability of the cathedral, though the records of their test pits, still kept at St Paul's, include tantalizing glimpses of earlier structures. Penrose's collection of moulded stones from the medieval fabric was housed in the triforium, uncatalogued and only occasionally visited by scholars (Fig. 65).[8]

Despite the unparalleled opportunities presented by reconstruction after the Second World War, and the beginning of modern urban archaeological excavations at Winchester in 1961, attitudes in the city of London were not friendly to archaeology. During the 1960s, the two archaeologists working independently there, W. F. Grimes and Peter Marsden, made small observations of Roman and later buildings in the area around St Paul's and Marsden excavated on the site of the church of St Augustine adjoining the precinct.[9] In 1969, the present cathedral works department was constructed underground on the north side of the nave. This did not compromise Wren's building, but the evidence for the previous 1,700 years of activity on the site, much of it to do with the cathedral, was hastily dug out by a dragline. This had been an important area for burial and in the fourteenth and fifteenth centuries had acquired a uniquely significant group of structures expressing the culture of the cathedral and its association with the city (pp. 35–6, 415–16). In these salvage conditions Robert Crayford, a concerned member of the architect's team, recorded Roman and medieval pits, the foundations of the Pardon Cloister and Becket Chapel, at least one other medieval building north of the cathedral, several graves from which coffin lids or fragments of stone coffins were recovered, the drain constructed by Wren on the north side of the cathedral, traces of the post-Fire buildings removed in 1710 to increase the space in the churchyard, the foundations of the wall which held the iron railings of the enclosure at that time, and the foundations of the chapter house.

The next phase of archaeological exploration of the cathedral and its churchyard began in the early 1990s, when urban archaeology had become established practice and cathedrals became obliged to look after their physical heritage. Between 1994 and 2001, a programme of building work, mainly in the crypt

65. Fragments of stonework from the cathedral of eleventh- to seventeenth-century date,
a major resource for understanding the medieval building, displayed in the library aisle.
In the foreground, a bust of Somers Clarke, surveyor to the fabric, 1897–1906

(p. 110), required archaeological excavation in advance. This revealed fragments of Roman buildings, Saxon burials north of the medieval nave, and fragments of medieval foundations which were largely unintelligible due to their digging out after 1668. Piercing of the crypt walls in two places provided spectacular new evidence about the pre-Fire cathedral. As could be inferred from the building accounts for Wren's structure, the crypt walls contained moulded stones from its predecessor. These included, from the north wall of the nave crypt, many stones from Norman piers, probably from the nave of the medieval building; and, from the south-west tower, stones from Jones's portico and from his recasing of the nave and transepts between 1633 and 1642.

The most recent phase of exploration took place between 1999 and 2001, during the preparation of this book. Despite the almost total destruction of a vast extent of historic deposits to the north of the cathedral by the Paternoster Square development during the 1960s, some pockets of strata survived and were excavated in modern conditions during the recent reconstruction of the neighbourhood. Immediately north of the cathedral, fragments were found of foundations from the bishop's palace, and more of the great western ditch which was filled in probably shortly before 1111 (p. 18). A notable find was a single sherd of pottery dating to 650–850, in a medieval context, in the north-west corner of the medieval precinct.[10]

THE SURVIVAL OF EARLY STRUCTURES

How much of the early cathedrals and of Bishop Maurice's great successor to them might survive beneath the ground? We can only give approximate answers.

Wren's building programme of 1675–88 destroyed most earlier deposits – certainly those relating to the medieval cathedral – within the footprint of the present cathedral, but there are still large areas of the churchyard where such deposits may survive, especially along its south side and under the north-east churchyard, including the site of the folkmoot (p. 20). These strata may still contain information about the location of the first cathedral on the site and its relationship to the pre-existing topography (p. 127).

At its greatest extent, about 1300, the medieval cathedral extended beyond the outline of Wren's structure to both east and west, where its remains have been observed, and it is just possible that parts of the terminal walls of the two transepts also survive.

The south half of the medieval chapter house and its cloister are now visible south of the present building. Though much, perhaps the majority, of the area of the medieval precinct and its buildings has been destroyed, it seems that the area south of the present cathedral, including the present coach park, is a large island of substantially intact archaeological strata. This may be the most important surviving resource which in the future will enable us to enlarge our present fragmentary understanding of the surroundings of the early cathedrals and of the religious and secular activities pursued there.

THE PRESENT STRUCTURE AS AN
ARCHAEOLOGICAL RESOURCE

As recent discoveries have demonstrated, the walls of the crypt contain many hundreds of reused carved stones from the earlier cathedral, but usually with their crucial mouldings facing into the rubble core. Only two of these stones, carved originally in the twelfth century, show their mouldings out into the crypt, though elsewhere the walls are clearly composed of irregular, sometimes rounded pieces (for instance, in the passage down from the north-west door and in the west wall of the conference centre). The cathedral walls above ground, behind their faces of Portland ashlars, probably also contain pre-Fire rubble. The carved stones found so far are from Romanesque and later piers, arches, windows, screens and tombs. Because many were inside the building in 1666, and were then quickly reused, some still have traces of original paint, from which colour schemes inside the cathedral can be reconstructed. The pieces of fluting and capitals from Jones's portico still carry the soot of the Great Fire. The geology of the medieval stones is also revealing. Many

of the twelfth-century stones recently recovered are from Taynton, Oxfordshire, where before 1066 the abbey of St Denis, near Paris, acquired an estate including a quarry.[11] Taynton Stone seems to have been much used in south-east England as a substitute for the finer Caen stone from Normandy, which was also used at St Paul's.

Deposits from the period after about 1500 lie immediately beneath the present-day ground surface, and are subject to damage from the slightest intrusion, such as the construction of drains or the planting of trees. The site of Inigo Jones's portico, fragments of which were found within the crypt walls, itself lies in the area west of the present cathedral: the condition of any surviving remains is unknown. Most strata relevant to the later history of the precinct are likely to have been destroyed, but recent observations point to the survival of construction debris from the 1670s and of temporary works on the cathedral building site.

Wren's cathedral is an exceptional store of information on building techniques and craftsmanship for its period (pp. 207–19). When maintenance works are undertaken, recording takes place of moulded stones, timber and iron work, and the use of stone and brick. The roof over the nave, untouched by war damage, must be one of the largest seventeenth-century roofs in Britain. Wren's great iron chain in the entablature of the dome peristyle was recently inspected during repairs. Not only was it found to be sound, but the examination cast important new light on engineering aspects of the construction (p. 217).

Although the construction of the present cathedral and other buildings nearby has been immensely destructive of archaeological deposits relevant to St Paul's, significant survivals remain. Those survivals, and the cathedral fabric itself, still have much to tell us of the history of St Paul's and of the city itself over 2,000 years.

II

FABRIC, TOMBS
AND PRECINCT 1087–1540

Carol Davidson Cragoe

The devastation caused by the 1087 fire gave Bishop Maurice (1085–1107) the opportunity to build a church that would be 'the honour and glory of London'.[1] Work on what would become one of the largest buildings in Europe, let alone in England, was sufficiently advanced in 1102 for Archbishop Anselm to hold a great council there; but it was not completed at Maurice's death in 1107, and his successors struggled with 'the expense of a burdensome work'.[2] A fire that ravaged London in the 1130s damaged the cathedral and probably necessitated some rebuilding; the vaults and west end were not finished until the late twelfth century, and the central tower and spire were still under construction in the early thirteenth. No sooner was the building finished than first the choir and then the chapter house were rebuilt in a programme completed by the mid fourteenth century. The spire was damaged by fire in the later Middle Ages and completely destroyed in a fire of 1561. Although most of the walls of St Paul's remained upstanding after the Great Fire of 1666, it was too badly damaged to be salvaged and was entirely rebuilt. This essay focuses principally on the architecture of the cathedral in use between 1087 and 1666 and attempts to recreate something of its appearance up to the Reformation. It also briefly examines the Anglo-Saxon cathedral that burned in 1087, some of the medieval tombs and the buildings of the precinct surrounding the cathedral.

THE ANGLO-SAXON CATHEDRAL AND ITS SURROUNDINGS

The present-day cathedral is at least the fourth on the site. Its predecessor, burned in the Great Fire, replaced the building destroyed by fire in 1087, which in turn replaced one burned in 962. It is likely that the cathedral has been in much the same location since the re-establishment of the see in 604, or at least since the time of St Erkenwald (bishop 675–93), but there is no clear indication of continuity with any earlier religious or burial activity on the site (p. 4). Wren apparently saw earlier foundations during the construction of his cathedral, and he noted that 'several times the fabrick had been ruined, yet that the foundations might remain, as originally they were laid.'[3] He gave no further details as to the shape or exact position of these foundations, but it is possible that the position of the Anglo-Saxon cathedral influenced the layout of the later building. The north and south nave doors of the post-1087 cathedral were approximately in line with Ivy Lane to the north and the lane to Paul's Wharf on the south (Fig. 9) and so may represent the remains of an earlier street to the west of its predecessor.[4] The site of the existing church of St Gregory (p. 115) may also have conditioned the positioning of the new nave.

As the Anglo-Saxon cathedral was rebuilt within a year of the fire of 962, it is possible that it was constructed of wood; however, contemporary cathedrals for which we have good archaeological evidence, such as those at Winchester and Canterbury, were built of stone, so it is more likely that it was a stone building that required only minor repairs.[5] By the time it burned again in 1087, it had 'an elegant ceiling [supported] by means of wooden beams strung across between the tops of the two walls'; there was a crypt with windows, through which the tomb of bishop Theodred could be seen by passers-by, and the ancient shrine of St Erkenwald stood behind the High Altar.[6]

The group of parish churches around the Romanesque cathedral (Fig. 9), including those of St Gregory, St Faith, St Martin at Ludgate, St Augustine outside the precinct east gate and St Michael outside the north-east gate, suggest that its predecessor

66 (*left*). Drawing, possibly fourteenth-century, of St Paul's from the north-east, also showing the detached bell tower at the corner of the precinct. Scratched on an inside wall of the tower at Ashwell Church, Hertfordshire

67 (*below*). Plan of the cathedral from Dugdale (1658) showing the location of monuments and other features. It is not possible to show all the key numbers on the plan. The principal monuments have been identified as follows, translating from the text:

9 chapel of Thomas Kempe, bishop of London
10 tomb of Sir John Beauchamp
14 tomb of John Donne, dean of St Paul's
15 monument of John Colet, dean of St Paul's
17 monument of Sir William Cockayne
18 monument of Sir Nicholas Bacon
26 monument of Sir Christopher Hatton
29 tomb of Henry Lacy, earl of Lincoln
30 tomb of Robert Braybroke, bishop of London
31 tomb of St Erkenwald
34 tomb of Ralph de Hengham
36 monument of John of Gaunt, duke of Lancaster
40 tomb of Ralph Niger, bishop of London
43 tomb of King Sæbbi, king of the Saxons
44 tomb of King Ethelred, king of the Saxons
51 Ralph de Baldock, dean of St Paul's and bishop of London

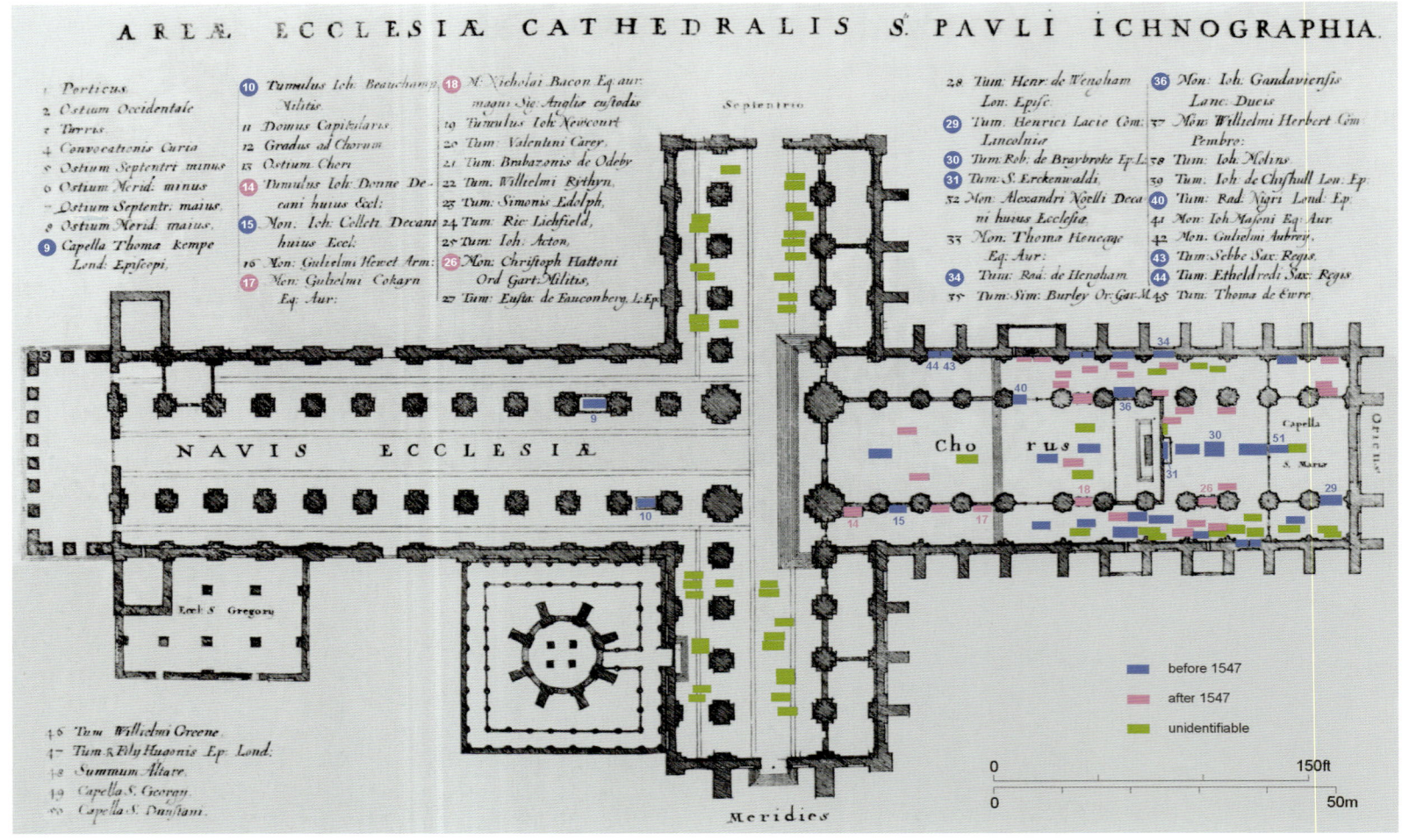

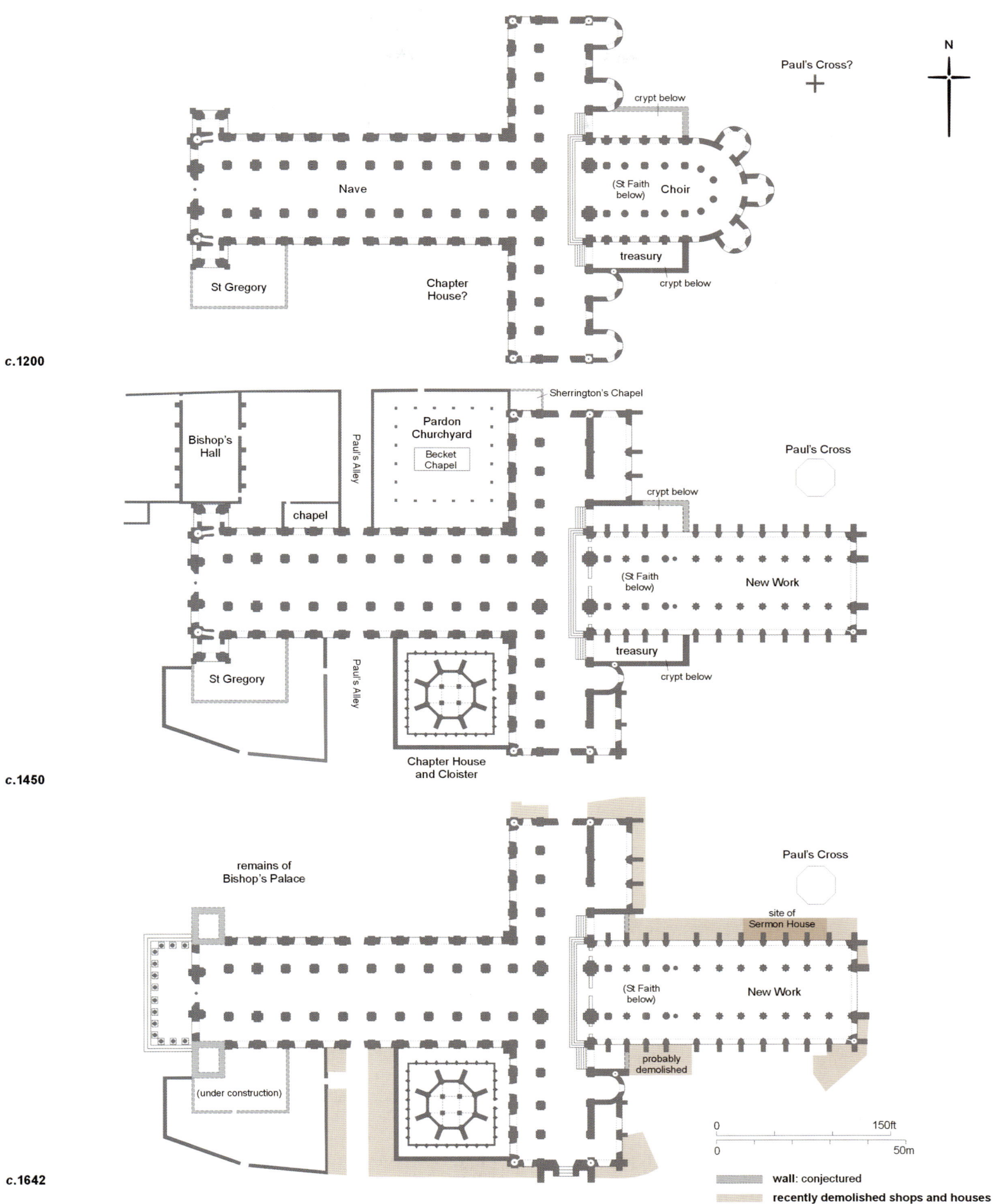

68.   Reconstructed plan of the cathedral *c.* 1200, *c.* 1450 and 1642

69.   Ruins of the crossing, south transept and nave during demolition *c.* 1672, seen from the north-east, drawing by Thomas Wyck. Remains of the Romanesque crypt and treasury are visible in the centre, above and left of the central male figure, while parts of the Gothic crypt to the east are seen in the lower left corner. (GL)

was surrounded by a family of chapels similar to those known to have existed around many major churches in western Europe in the centuries before 1100 (p. 114). St Gregory's was within the cemetery (*atrium*) of St Paul in 1009, when the body of St Edmund was temporarily deposited there (p. 15). This church was presumably also destroyed in the fire of 1087 and was rebuilt adjacent to the cathedral's nave. The earliest evidence for St Faith's is twelfth-century, when it was in the crypt under the cathedral choir (pp. 116, 131), but it may have replaced an earlier chapel.[7]

REPRESENTATION AND REALITY

It is now very difficult to recreate the ambience of the cathedral and its surroundings, as most of the things which provided its real character, such as images, tombs, chapels and other liturgical objects, were removed after the Reformation. The coloured glass was a particular loss: an inventory of *c.*1645 included, in addition to nearly 8,000 loose quarries or panels of window glass, 600 feet of 'old glass', and 'the broken glass. . . which may make ten barrells'.[8] Today, the only visible remains of the pre-1666 cathedrals

are a few fragments of walling and a collection of stones discovered during excavations around the modern precinct, but many drawings and engravings of the building were made between the thirteenth and seventeenth centuries and contemporaries occasionally commented on the its fabric and ornaments. While much of this evidence is vague, inconclusive, or simply not as detailed as we might wish, comparisons with other cathedral and monastic churches built in England during the Middle Ages can extend our understanding.

The earliest representations of St Paul's are from the thirteenth century, and include the chapter's second seal[9] and sketches in Matthew Paris's mid thirteenth-century itineraries (Fig. 10). These, and other later medieval views such as a drawing scratched into the tower wall at Ashwell church in Hertfordshire (Fig. 66), are too schematic to provide conclusive evidence about architectural details, but they do demonstrate that from the moment of its construction the cathedral's towering spire was a powerful symbol of the city of London (Figs 16, 17). Sixteenth- and seventeenth-century images (Figs 22–3, 91, 93, 94–5, 102) provide more details, but individual views do not always agree. A suite of drawings, including a partial plan produced by Wren for a proposed restoration in 1666 (Figs 104–6) and several post-Fire sketches of the ruins after the Great Fire offer other clues about the cathedral's appearance, as do scattered documentary references to the building.

By far the most useful, but also the most problematic, representations of the cathedral are the engravings created by Wenceslaus Hollar for Sir William Dugdale's *History of St Paul's*, published in 1658. Dugdale's text, the first monographic account of a major English church, also provides information about the structure and its history. Hollar's engravings lend the cathedral a magnificently bleak grandeur, stripped as it was of most of its tombs, altars, images and other liturgical objects, but by the time he saw the building it was in very poor repair (pp. 182–3), so he was instructed by Dugdale to draw the building as it had been and not as it was.[10] For this reason, many of his views need to be treated with caution, especially where they show liturgical fittings, such as the choir stalls, which are known to have been destroyed; images of tombs similarly improve on the badly damaged reality, and his plan (Fig. 67) is partially inaccurate and not to scale. However, where architectural fragments survive, they often match details shown by Hollar, suggesting that he generally tried to reproduce what he saw, albeit sometimes in a simplified or idealized form.

Taken together, the evidence suggests that the medieval cathedral had an aisled nave and choir, both twelve bays long, with a crypt under the entire choir (Fig. 68). The five-bay transepts had aisles on their western sides and enclosed chapels on the east. The original east end of Bishop Maurice's eleventh-century cathedral was apsidal, but it was replaced in the thirteenth century with a much longer, flat-ended choir known as the 'New Work'. This had a large rose window which clearly caught the imagination of contemporaries, as Chaucer poked gentle fun at the foppish clerk Absalon, who had a pattern like *Poules wyndow* cut into the tops of his shoes.[11] A stone tower and the famous wooden spire topped the central crossing, and there were small towers at the west end of the nave outside of the line of the aisles. The cathedral was hemmed in on all sides by the buildings of its precinct, including cloisters in the angle between nave and transepts on both sides, and the parish church of St Gregory against the south-west end of the nave. The following discussion progresses from east to west – the way the cathedral was built – before returning to later alterations in chronological order.

THE ROMANESQUE CRYPT

Church construction in the Middle Ages usually began at the east end, to bring the principal liturgical spaces into use as quickly as possible. At St Paul's, the Romanesque east end, begun soon after the fire of 1087, was altered during the New Work choir extension, but Wren discovered its foundations during the building's demolition and noted that it had an apse 'after the usual Mode of the Primitive Churches'.[12] He gave no more details, and it is unclear whether this meant an apse with an ambulatory and radiating chapels, like those used at the contemporary churches at Norwich, Ely and Bury St Edmunds, or a series of graduated apses 'in echelon' at the ends of the aisles and main choir vessel like those of the first Romanesque choir at Canterbury.[13]

The crypt under the choir was built first. A small portion of it is visible in a drawing made after the Great Fire by Thomas Wyck (Fig. 69) and Dugdale remarked on the similarity in style between

it and the Romanesque nave and transepts.[14] Its piers would have been placed under those of the choir above, and its vaults were painted.[15] Like the Gothic crypt to the east (Fig. 74), there may have been an additional row of piers down the centre. Used by the parish of St Faith's until 1551, this part of the crypt was subsequently let as warehouse space.[16] St Erkenwald's shrine was adjacent to the parochial altar until his translation into the upper church in the 1140s, but this probably indicates only that the crypt was used for several purposes and not that the parish grew up around the shrine.[17]

The entrances to the crypt were via steps and doors in the second bay of the transepts. That in the north transept was probably the principal entrance to St Faith's, as its parish later covered an area to the north and east of the cathedral. The steps led into projecting crypt bays set in the angle between the transepts and choir, an arrangement similar to that used at the contemporary church of Bury St Edmund's.[18] On the south side further arches led eastwards from this bay and also south from the main crypt into a crypt-level space underneath the treasury next to the south choir aisle (see p. 134).[19] The evidence for an outer crypt on the north side is more circumstantial, but access to the crypt was the same on both sides, suggesting a similar internal arrangement. Externally, the entire length of the north choir aisle was, by the late fifteenth century (p. 44), built up to the aisle window-sills with galleries for hearing sermons at the adjacent Paul's Cross and later with bookshops (Fig. 24), but these may have incorporated an older stone structure alongside the western choir bays, with timber buildings to the east.[20]

It is not clear that there was any form of outer crypt around the original Romanesque east end. On the south side the outer crypt aisle was connected at the east to the chapel of St John the Baptist between the buttresses of the westernmost bay of the Gothic crypt, but it is unclear whether this replicated an early arrangement or was a later change. Outer ring-crypts were unusual in the late eleventh century, but such an arrangement would find parallels at the much earlier Old St Peter's in Rome, at Canterbury's Anglo-Saxon cathedral, and in particular at Archbishop Thomas of Bayeux's post-Conquest rebuilding of York Minster, begun at much the same time as St Paul's.[21] It would also explain William of Malmesbury's remark about the great breadth of 'the crypts'.[22]

THE ROMANESQUE CHOIR

The late thirteenth-century New Work choir extension greatly altered the eleventh-century choir, but some older masonry, including the four western pairs of arcade piers (Fig. 68) and part of the aisle walls, seemingly survived, recased in Gothic guise, until the Great Fire. It is unclear if this was the extent of the Romanesque choir without its apse. Four straight bays between the crossing and the apse was a common arrangement for late eleventh-century great churches, and the apparent retention of the Romanesque crypt only under these bays suggests that this may have been the case at St Paul's.[23] However, it is also possible that the choir was longer and that there were originally five straight bays before the apse.

Arcades with alternating pier designs were popular in the late eleventh- and twelfth-century Romanesque period: the variety visually lightened the massiveness of the construction. A common arrangement of this type juxtaposed smooth, cylindrical piers with more complex 'compound' piers made up of a group of round or rectilinear shafts. Hollar's views (Figs 71, 73) suggest that

CHORI ECCLESIÆ CATHEDRALIS S. PAVLI PROSPECTVS INTERIOR.

71.   The choir looking east, etching by Hollar from Dugdale (1658). The choir stalls (provided by Sir Paul Pindar in 1634) are shown as incorporating covered upper seating, but as they had been destroyed in 1645 the accuracy of Hollar's depiction is questionable

We know little of the liturgical arrangements of the Romanesque choir. The usual position for choir stalls in this period was in the central crossing area, so the choir screen would have been in the western crossing arch or even in the eastern part of the nave. The high altar probably stood on the chord of the apse; St Erkenwald's shrine joined it in 1148 (p. 116). Other work on the choir at about this time, either in conjunction with the translation or following damage during the 1130s fire, included the creation of new tombs (Figs 6, 67) for the Anglo-Saxon kings Sæbbi (d. 694) and Ethelred (d. 1016).[28] Set into niches in the north choir aisle wall, their sarcophagi, which were similar but not identical, were made of a dark grey or black marble.[29] They had unusual, almost classical fluting on the lids, and blind arcading similar to some on part of St Erkenwald's shrine (Fig. 63). A plain black marble chest with a gabled lid, located in a niche in the south choir wall opposite the Saxon kings, and another with a carved cross-shaft on the lid located in a niche in the north wall probably belonged to twelfth- or early thirteenth-century bishops.[30]

THE TRANSEPTS

The transepts, on either side of the central crossing space where the choir met the nave, housed a number of altars and other important liturgical sites, including the *Crux borealis*, a miraculous rood by the north transept door which was a major focus of devotion (pp. 40, 121). There was also an elaborate wall painting of Jesus flanked by donor images of Margaret Beauchamp, countess of Shrewsbury (d. 1468), in heraldic robes, and her children over the nearby entrance to the crypt.[31] Recent research has demonstrated that the transepts, five bays long and with aisles on their west sides, originally had chapels along the east, with projecting apsidal chapels in the third and fifth bays (Fig. 68). In the later Middle Ages, the eastern chapels were converted into aisles, although some of the later plans show those aisles as if they were original (Figs 67, 89).[32] Such transepts would have been similar to those at Bury St Edmunds – which had both apsidal chapels and aisles on their east sides – but with the circulation space rationalized by placing the aisles on the west side of the transept to allow the use of both the aisles and the eastern side of the main transept vessel as additional chapel space. The ghosts of these chapels appear in the clusters of monuments on the plan (Fig. 67).

Of the original apsidal chapels, only that in the third bay of the south transept retained anything of its original late eleventh- or early twelfth-century form in the seventeenth century, by which time it was used as the Morning Prayer chapel; it had a tower, or perhaps just an upper storey, above it.[33] The interior of the transept west aisles had Romanesque blind arcading with broad, round-headed arches, round-arched vaults[34] and galleries connected to those over the nave aisles on both north and south (Fig. 69). The external elevation of the transepts may have been similar to that of the Romanesque nave bays (Fig. 77) with pilaster buttresses and round *oculus* windows in the gallery, but the south transept clerestory was rebuilt, perhaps added when the central tower was built early in the thirteenth century.

A new chapel, possibly incorporating part of an apsidal chapel in the fifth bay, was built against the end bays of the south transept in the late twelfth or early thirteenth century. This may have been the original Lady Chapel, said to have been opposite the chapter house door in the west wall of the south transept.[35] The cathedral possessed relics of the Virgin by the late twelfth century

choir piers at St Paul's originally had such an alternating arrangement. Counting out from the crossing, the second and fourth sets of piers had cylindrical cores with large, flat pilaster shafts on their inner faces, while the first and third sets were more angular, suggesting compound piers cased in later shafts.[24] Thus, the piers alternated, beginning at the crossing: compound, round, compound and round. A further set of compound piers would have provided a balanced composition before the round piers typically used around an apse; this would have given a five-bay choir similar to that at Bury St Edmunds.[25]

Whatever the length of the choir or the shape of the piers, Arcoid's comment in his life of St Erkenwald of *c*.1140 that the Anglo-Saxon cathedral was destroyed by fire because it had a wooden roof, unlike the stone vaults built in his day, may indicate that the Romanesque choir was vaulted.[26] The choir at Durham was vaulted at about this time and vaults were apparently intended from the outset in the St Paul's nave (pp. 134–5). Such an arrangement would have made St Paul's one of the first, if not the first, fully vaulted cathedral in England. It is interesting to note in this context that the church at Copford (Essex), built *c*.1120–30 on the bishop's manor, was the only fully vaulted Romanesque parish church in the country.[27]

72. Interior of the nave looking east, etching by Hollar from Dugdale (1658)

(p. 119), and there were a number of gifts to an altar of the Blessed Virgin in the 1230s and 1240s.[36] Although there was also an altar of the Virgin in the nave, the six clerks and a priest of the choir who were recorded in the 1220s as celebrating a daily mass of the Virgin probably had a larger, purpose-built chapel.[37] There was also an altar or chapel dedicated to St John the Evangelist somewhere near the south transept door, but its precise location is unclear.[38] The south transept was subject to structural problems throughout its history. The tall lancet windows in its clerestory (Fig. 77) may have been installed in the thirteenth century, perhaps at the time the tower was being completed. The transept was repaired again in the late fourteenth century, when Henry Yevele installed a large multi-light window and a new south door, visible in sixteenth- and early seventeenth-century views, after an earthquake in 1382.[39]

By the mid sixteenth century, the eastern aisle or former complex of chapels in the north transept was known as the 'Long Chapel' (p. 39). From the fourteenth century onwards, it had apparently contained several different altars or chapels and almost certainly represents an enlargement and rebuilding of a pair of Romanesque apsidal chapels like those on the south transept.[40] The popularity of this area for burials and chapels was largely due to the presence here of the miraculous *Crux Borealis* (p. 40). A chapel, probably the Long Chapel, behind the rood at the north door was under construction in 1355, and was presumably the chapel where, in 1385, Adam de Bury wished to be buried before an altar to St Mary Magdalen then about to be erected. De Bury's chantry there was subsequently enlarged by his executor, Roger Holme, and some or all of this space became known as 'Holme(s) Chapel', which in the fifteenth century was said to be beneath the rood. Described by John Stow as a 'fair chapel of the Holy Ghost', it contained an altar of St James and St Lawrence.[41]

The complex of chapels near the north door also included a chapel dedicated to St John the Baptist, which from the later fourteenth century was maintained by the tailors' craft (p. 39). A rental of 1570 seems to place the chapel of St John (presumably the tailors' former chapel) to the north of the Long Chapel, although this may simply indicate that it was in the north-east bay of that chapel.[42] The fine chantry chapel of Sir John Pulteney, built under the provisions of his will of 1348, was similarly in the north part of St Paul's, but its relationship to Holme Chapel and the tailors' chapel is unclear.[43] In the fifteenth century, Walter Sherrington's executors built a chapel against the external north face of the transept next to the Pardon Cloister (Figs 20, 68); after the Reformation, this was converted into a house.[44] By the

explained by the presence of a structure between it and the choir. The presence of outer structures on both sides of the choir aisles would help to explain why Jones's work on the choir only encompassed the eight eastern bays and not the four western bays.[48]

73. Eastern bays of the choir, built from 1259 onwards, looking east towards the Lady Chapel beneath the rose window, etching by Hollar from Dugdale (1658)

THE NAVE

Bishop Richard I de Belmeis (1108–27) 'marvellously advanced the work on the walls of the new church', begun by Bishop Maurice, and 'completed a great deal of the work which had been begun', suggesting that some or all of the nave dates from his episcopate.[49] None the less, the fire in the 1130s must have delayed progress, and may have required some rebuilding. Worked stones discovered during modern excavations, including a chevron jambstone and pieces of palmette ornament, point towards a mid twelfth-century date for parts of the building, but it is not known exactly where these were located in the medieval cathedral.[50]

The nave (Figs 72, 95) was twelve bays long, with a gallery, clerestory and rib vaults over both the aisles and central vessel. In addition, there were crypts of some form under part of the nave: a parliamentary survey of 1649 mentioned 'all that vault under part of the south aisle of the [nave] of Paul's church'; there is a further reference to 'vaults' under the north side of the nave, but these may have been later medieval burial vaults.[51] Unlike the alternating piers in the choir arcade, the nave had uniformly compound piers. Each bay was separated by a triplet of tall shafts supporting the springing of the vaults, making it seem very lofty, an impression reinforced by the stilting of both the main arcades and the gallery arches, as if they were being forced inwards and upwards by the piers. There were tall, narrow blind arcades on the aisle walls below the windows, and the aisle vaults were supported on triple wall responds matching those on the main piers (Fig. 72). The aisle windows were large, with round heads and later tracery which survived Inigo Jones's seventeenth-century restoration in the eastern bays on the south side (p. 180), behind the chapter house, perhaps because of difficulties in reaching this area (Fig. 77).

The clerestory in these south-eastern bays retained its pre-Jones arrangement of gabled or triangular-headed windows linked by a string course, although it is not clear whether the western part of the clerestory (Fig. 77) had similar windows.[52] This shape was common in Anglo-Saxon architecture, but it is unlikely that this part of the cathedral survived the fire of 1087; therefore, these windows have been variously dated to the late eleventh century, c.1200, and after 1561.[53] The last can be discounted as there is no evidence that the clerestory was rebuilt after the fire of that date (pp. 172–3), but either of the others is a possibility. However, the motif, which was repeated (Fig. 95) for the east windows of the Gothic crypt and on the detailing of the buttresses, was sufficiently unusual in English architecture after the Norman Conquest to suggest that its use in the clerestory at St Paul's was a specific quotation from something Anglo-Saxon within the cathedral, perhaps the shrine of St Erkenwald, which was miraculously preserved in the fire of 1087.[54]

Today, church and cathedral naves are principally places for people to sit or stand while services take place elsewhere in the building, but in the Middle Ages the nave also had many liturgical sites of its own. At St Paul's, for instance, the Romanesque choir screen towards the east end of the nave had altars associated with it. There were also altars in the gallery at the west end of the

post-Reformation period, the transept had a porch containing a few memorials removed from the churchyard.[45]

THE TREASURY

The second bay of the south transept extended eastwards above the outer crypt aisle and alongside the choir to form a treasury or sacristy (Fig. 68), where the cathedral's extensive collection of liturgical vestments and other precious objects was stored.[46] This structure appears, without a label, on several plans (e.g. Fig. 89), but its identity is confirmed by references to Roger of Waltham's chantry in the fourth bay of the south choir aisle 'opposite the sextry'.[47] Access was apparently from the first bay of the choir via a bridge across the entrance to the crypt (Fig. 76). The treasury was probably contemporary with the choir and transepts, as its length was approximately equal to that of the surviving portion of the Romanesque choir, and its interior had generously proportioned blind arcading similar to that on the interior of the west wall of the south transept (Fig. 69).

There may have been a similar structure on the north side of the choir: one drawing (Fig. 76) shows a matching bridge over the crypt entrance on this side, and the evidence for a stone building along the north side of the crypt was discussed above. Furthermore, the Long Chapel on the north transept apparently stopped short of the choir aisle wall (Fig. 104), an arrangement best nave, and in the aisles (pp. 118–21). An image of the Virgin on the second pier of the south arcade, with an associated altar, was an important cult site by the mid to late thirteenth century and attracted a number of chantries and burials.[55] Another, more secular cult site in the nave was the area around the tomb of Bishop William (d. 1075), who was commemorated annually by the mayor and aldermen (p. 39). His tomb had presumably been removed from the remains of the Anglo-Saxon cathedral after the fire of 1087. After it was defaced at the Reformation, a wall plaque in his honour was put up by Sir Edward Barkham.[56]

THE VAULTS AND WEST FAÇADE

Work on the cathedral was still ongoing in 1175, when Bishop Gilbert Foliot appealed for funds so that 'you may see the too-long protracted work completed in your day'.[57] One of the projects undertaken at this time was the completion of the rib vault over the nave (Fig. 72). Some form of vaulting had always been intended, as the triple respond shafts (one each for the main transverse and two crossing ribs or groins) on each pier ran unbroken by string courses or other banding from the floor to the base of the clerestory. After the vaults were completed, the main roofs were finished, possibly by Godwin the carpenter and his brothers Ranulph and Richard, whose services were obtained by the dean and chapter *c*.1174–81.[58] There were many donations to the fabric fund in the late twelfth and early thirteenth century, including one by Bishop Richard III in the mid 1190s for window glazing and repair.[59]

The structural work on the nave, including the vaults and west façade, must have been completed by the time of the consecration *c*.1189–98 of altars dedicated to SS Denis and Thomas Becket in the west gallery.[60] The west façade had a triple portal 'curiously wrought of stone', with 'a massie pillar of brasse' in the middle of the central doorway.[61] The sixteenth-century *Prospect of ye Citye of London* (Fig. 59) shows three tall lancets, small openings in the west gable and stair turrets at the nave corners matching those on the transepts and choir. The *oculi* over the doors of Jones's façade (Fig. 100) were almost certainly reworked Romanesque openings lighting the gallery. This latter was an unusual feature for the later twelfth century, but westworks or western galleries had been built earlier in the century at a number of major churches, including Winchester, Ely and Bury, so its presence probably indicates that the lower part of the façade and the west end of the nave were earlier than the upper parts.

The original design of the west end may have been intended to include a tower or towers, although this was seemingly never fully executed. Wren remarked on 'the great Piller adjoyning to the N.W. tower' [presumably that by the bishop's palace] and noted that 'there had been a considerable Addition, and a new Front to the West, but in what Age is not ascertained.'[62] Similarly, in a letter of 1668 Dean Sancroft remarked that 'The second Pillar [from the west end] is bigger than the rest'.[63] Furthermore, several early views (Figs 22, 59) show what may have been a small stair turret or a buttress for an unfinished tower two or three bays from the west end.[64] Whether this was to have been the usual pair of towers over the west ends of the aisles or a more unusual single, axial tower over the west end of the nave like those at Ely and Bury is not clear, but the latter seems more likely given the other similarities between Bury and St Paul's.

In the event, this early design was abandoned except for the internal west gallery, and two low flanking towers were built adjacent to the west ends of the aisles, probably as part of a late twelfth-century screen façade which was also never fully completed. Stow described these towers as being 'of auncient building …made for bell towers'.[65] The northern tower was part of the accommodation of the bishop's palace, and the southern tower, later known as the Lollards' tower, was the bell-tower for St Gregory's parish church; they served as prisons from time to time. Both towers were accessible from the cathedral at ground (Fig. 89) and gallery levels.[66] Screen façades with flanking towers were a feature of major English churches such as Wells and Salisbury in the thirteenth century, and some of the earliest examples, including St Botolph's, Colchester (*c*.1160–70), Earl's Colne Priory (late twelfth century) and St Alban's (*c*.1195 but never completed),[67] were near London and roughly contemporary with St Paul's.

It is possible that the west front and vaults were the work of an architecturally inclined chaplain of Ralph de Diceto, the late twelfth-century dean. Called William 'the Englishman', this man built a church at Acre in Palestine *c*.1192. He may be, although the connection is far from certain, the same William the Englishman who had completed the choir at Canterbury cathedral between 1177 and 1184.[68] While this attribution is speculative, St Paul's was largely completed during Diceto's time, and the possible connection is strengthened by the dedication of one of the St Paul's west gallery altars to St Thomas of Canterbury, who had been Diceto's fellow canon at St Paul's (p. 23).

THE TOWER

The cathedral's cruciform, or cross-shaped, plan suggests that it was intended to have a central crossing and tower of some type from the outset. Hollar's view shows the crossing piers (Fig. 72) as similar to those in the nave, with multiple half-shafts around an angular core, implying that they were built in the late eleventh or early twelfth century, but the accuracy of this view is questionable. In particular, he does not show the arches 'of later years' that had been inserted into the crossing to strengthen it.[69] The crossing area always had serious structural problems, apparently because of a lack of sufficient buttressing, and it is possible that the tower and spire built in the thirteenth century replaced an earlier tower.

An annalist noted under 1221 that the tower of St Paul's was finished, and it appeared, complete with its spire, on the common seal of the city of London (Fig. 11) of about that date.[70] Between 1223 and 1226, timber was provided for new choir stalls; these would have been located under the crossing, where the choir remained until the fourteenth century.[71] By the mid thirteenth century, the spire was the iconic image of London (Fig. 10). The stone tower rose 260 feet above the floor of the crossing; the lead-covered timber spire that topped it was said to be 274 feet high, although the total height was not more than 500 feet, probably because the parapet and pinnacles of the tower rose well above the base of the spire.[72]

The tower was never stable, and 'on the outside of the tower, the buttresses… [were] erected one upon the back of another to secure three corners of the inclining sides (for the fourth wants a buttress)'.[73] Its lower lantern stage, just above the main rooflines, had three hugely tall windows on each face that lit the crossing below and may have been an inspiration for the lantern begun, but never completed, at Westminster Abbey later in the thirteenth century. The upper stage, separated from the lower by a band of blind arcading, had similar, but shorter, lancets. Its decoration,

ECCLESIA PAROCHIALIS St FIDIS
PROSPECTVS INTERIOR.

FIDEM HAC EXHIBET, ILLA DEVM.

74.   The thirteenth-century Gothic crypt looking east, etching by Hollar from Dugdale (1658)

apparently including shafts with crocket or foliate capitals (Fig. 84), was typical of its period. Some illustrations suggest that the openings had tracery, but this may have been a later insertion. In comparison, the spire was a plain affair which gloried in its height, not its decoration. Topped by a ball and cross with a weathercock, it was almost entirely unadorned except for a small opening with a little gable in the centre of each face between the tower pinnacles. The cross had to be re-erected twice in the early fourteenth century, and the spire itself may also have been partially rebuilt at the same time.[74] It was struck by lightning in 1444, but the fire was put out.[75] Repaired again in 1553, it was entirely destroyed by a fire in 1561 and never subsequently replaced (pp. 172–3).

THE FIRST GOTHIC CHOIR

The completion of the tower did not mark the end of building work at St Paul's, and the cathedral's dedication in 1241 took place while construction was ongoing, a not uncommon occurrence. From 1228 onwards, numerous indulgences were offered in return for contributions to the fabric, including a papal indulgence of 1252 for the completion of building work.[76] The principal project undertaken at this time was the remodelling of the eleventh-century choir in a more up-to-date Gothic style (Figs 68, 71).[77] The structural bones of the old choir were left standing, but the piers were recased in new shafts, probably detached and possibly made of Purbeck marble, with foliate capitals. The remodelled gallery had paired lights separated by clusters of shafts, each with its own individual capital. There were plate tracery trefoils in the spandrels with a hoodmould over each pair of openings. The slender vault shafts, also possibly of Purbeck, had annulet rings at the base of the gallery and supported bundles of seven ribs springing from a single small capital, similar to those in the vaults of the nave at Lincoln and the choir at Ely, both also dating to the second quarter of the thirteenth century.

The east end of the cathedral was subsequently greatly extended during the New Work, and it is not clear what, if anything, had previously happened to the east end. The fifth bay east of the crossing was considerably wider than the others and may have been intended for eastern transepts like those at Lincoln, which would suggest that there was an intermediate east end for which

we now have no evidence. On the other hand, the original Romanesque apse may simply have been left until the later thirteenth century. At both crypt and choir level, Hollar's views show an intermediate pier (Figs 73, 74) placed off-centre in the fifth bay at approximately the point where a pier would have been had the Gothic pier spacing been carried further west, suggesting that the wide bay was little more than a setting-out error.

THE NEW WORK

The cathedral's Lady Chapel, known as the 'New Work', was begun early in 1259 and removed all traces of the former apse, so that the choir stretched for twelve bays ending in a flat wall of glass with an enormous rose window (Fig. 75).[78] It included an extension to the crypt (Fig. 74) which from the mid fifteenth century housed the Jesus Chapel (pp. 162–3) until that was suppressed after the Reformation; in 1551 the parish church of St Faith was moved into the space, it being deemed 'a place more sufficient for largenesse and lightsomnesse' than the older part of the crypt.[79] The presence of the parish church in the western part of the crypt meant that the Jesus Chapel had its own external entrance (visible in Fig. 102) on the north side, where a bonfire was made on the vigil of the feast of the Holy Name of Jesus.[80] This entrance may already have existed in 1372, before the cult of Jesus was established there (p. 121). The eastern bays of the upper part of the New Work, including the vaults and rose window, must have been complete by 1295, when the altar of the 'Blessed Virgin in the New Work' was included in a list of the cathedral's chantries.[81] Bishop Fulk Basset (d. 1259) was commemorated at this altar and Dean Peter de Newport (d. 1260) at the altar of St Thomas to the north, since the New Work was begun during their tenure.[82]

As the choir had so recently been updated, its enlargement was probably a direct response to the rebuilding of Westminster Abbey (from 1245 onwards) in a French style at the expense of King Henry III. There was a strong rivalry between the abbey and St Paul's, as each church had a close relationship with the Crown and both could claim to be national seats of authority. This rivalry also reflected tensions between the jurisdictions – both spiritual and secular – based in the city and those operating outside it (pp. 17, 31). Perhaps because of this, the design of the New Work presented a direct architectural challenge to the abbey through its use of

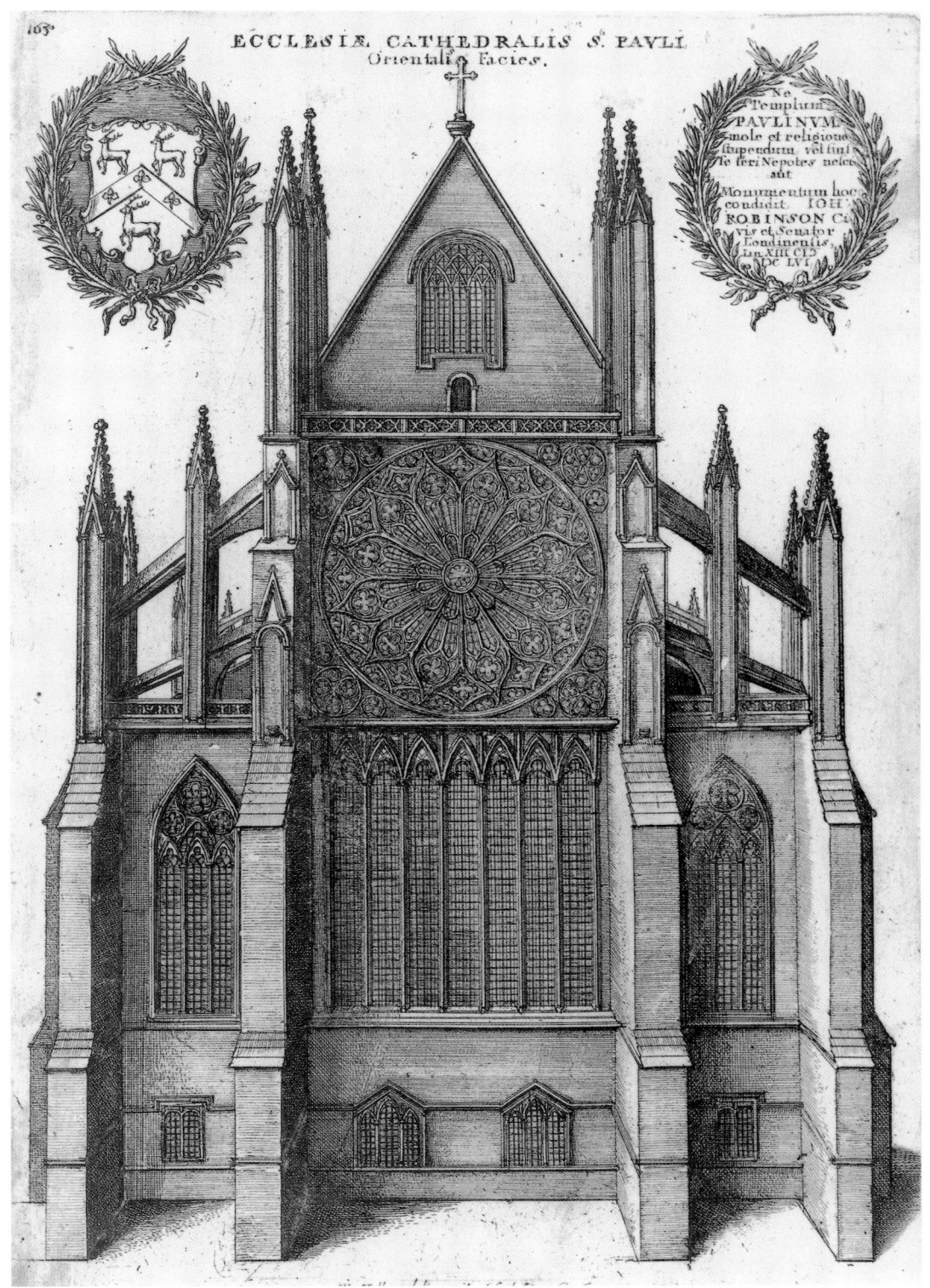

75.   The cathedral's east end, etching by Hollar from Dugdale (1658)

deliberately English motifs, such as the cliff-like flat east end, in contrast to the most important elements of Westminster's design, such as the eastern 'chevet', an apse ringed by chapels, which had been drawn from French models. Adding architectural insult to injury, where the cathedral's designers used French motifs, as in the patterns of the window tracery, these were stylistically considerably more advanced than those used at the abbey only a few years before.[83]

The detailing of the New Work was derived partly from that of the reworked western part of the choir, but with an added level of architectural complexity reflecting the influence of important mid thirteenth-century English buildings such as Lincoln. For

instance, the new piers had more complex, sixteen-shafted piers with turned capitals and elaborate arcade arches with many small mouldings. The gallery had newly fashionable bar-tracery trefoils, and the openings were enclosed in up-to-date continuous mouldings without capitals.[84] It was architecturally very influential, and by the early 1280s had spawned a number of imitators such as St Etheldreda's chapel in the Bishop of Ely's Holborn palace (begun 1284).[85]

Some aspects of both the New Work and the remodelled Romanesque choir, such as the vault (Figs 71, 73) and wall arcading (Fig. 102), were seemingly very similar, but it is not entirely clear how, or indeed where, the two sections were joined together.

137

The steps towards the west end of the choir probably marked the join, but different views place them (variously) in the third bay (Fig. 71), the fourth bay, the third and fifth bays (Fig. 104), the fourth and fifth bays, or nowhere at all (Fig. 89). Wren's elevation hints that the detailing was continuous through these middle bays and thus that the join was further east, but comparison with other views suggests that his illustration shows the building after remodelling to be carried out as part of the construction of his proposed rotunda. In particular, he omitted the intermediate pier in the fifth bay and put multiple shafts and a high base on the fourth pier.

The name of the designer of the New Work was not recorded, but its most innovative feature, the ogees – reverse S-curves – at the ends of the individual lights within the rose window (Fig. 75) suggest that it was at least partly designed by the important late-thirteenth-century mason and architect Michael of Canterbury. Ogees became ubiquitous in later medieval architecture, but their first use in England, aside from the St Paul's rose window, was on the Eleanor crosses (begun 1291) and at St Stephen's chapel in the palace of Westminster (1292–7), both also designed by Michael.[86] Other architects whose names have been put forward in connection with the project include Richard Crundale, Simon of Pabenham, and Robert of Beverley, all of whom were working on important commissions in and around London in the third quarter of the thirteenth century.[87]

Despite the completion of the east end in the late thirteenth century, work on the choir was still ongoing in the early fourteenth century: in 1300 all offerings were assigned to the completion of the New Work, and *c.*1310 a new clutch of indulgences was issued in return for contributions to the fabric fund.[88] Although there appears to have been some actual construction in these years, such as the addition of a new chapel between the buttresses on the south side of the choir attributed by Stow to 1316,[89] most of the work was decorative and finishing. The centre of the choir was paved *c.*1312 by Adam le Marbrer, who had long had workshops in the precinct, and the choir windows were glazed about the same time.[90] A new suite of liturgical fittings was also

created, including an elaborate painted retable for the high altar. Ordered in 1309 from the London craftsman Richard Pickerell, it had a wooden frame and cover with folding leaves, all adorned with precious stones, enamel work and metal statues.[91]

The other major project in this period was the creation between 1313 and 1326 of a new shrine for St Erkenwald, the centrepiece of the cathedral and its liturgy (pp. 119–20). It was replaced after the Reformation by a commemorative plaque,[92] but Hollar's illustration of the surviving fragments (Fig. 63) may show one end of an elaborate stone superstructure originally placed above the main shrine base, similar to that reconstructed on St Werburgh's shrine in Chester cathedral. The bottom had a row of round-headed blind arcading, with fluting at the corners, perhaps a remnant of something created for the 1148 translation; the upper section was arranged like the end wall of a church, with three 'windows' and a buttressed and pinnacled gable above. There were tiny bases for statues on the buttresses.[93] New railings were made *c.*1400 as part of further elaboration of the shrine. They are unlikely to have survived into the seventeenth century, but Hollar's view was apparently 'a true representation from the very original draught, made for a direction to the smith that wrought [them]'.[94]

The canons moved into their new choir and used the high altar for the first time in 1327.[95] The new choir screen (Fig. 76) was probably completed by that date, as the great rood over the old screen had been taken down two years previously to be repainted, an event notable for the lucky escape of the almoner, despite the destruction of many liturgical ornaments on the altar at which he was celebrating, when the rood was dropped by careless workmen.[96] The liturgical arrangements of the Gothic choir were much altered between the Reformation and the mid seventeenth century, but Hollar's view and plan (Figs 67, 73) give some sense of their earlier arrangement. The choir screen was placed across the eastern crossing arch. It had a deeply recessed central doorway with a vaulted interior, flanked by four ogee-gabled statue niches and matching doorways in the walls blocking the ends of the choir aisles. A loft was removed in 1643.[97] It has

77. The fourteenth-century cloister and chapter house in the angle between the nave and south transept, etching by Hollar from Dugdale (1658)

been suggested that the screen was designed by William Ramsay, who was working on the chapter house in the 1330s,[98] but while it has stylistic parallels to Ramsay's earlier work, it is quite unlike the chapter house itself.

Beyond the screen in the choir proper, the stalls occupied the western choir bays below the steps leading up to a platform for the matitudinal or morning altar. The high altar was raised on a further small platform; a large reredos, largely or entirely destroyed by the seventeenth century, presumably separated it from the shrine in the Lady Chapel to the east. In 1551 the iron grates in choir arcades near the high altar were bricked up to protect the privacy of communicants.[99] In the Middle Ages, all the choir arcades were probably closed by barriers such as the iron grills closing the two-light stone tracery screens shown by Hollar in the wide fifth bays (Figs 71, 73). These stone screens may have been the inspiration for the early fourteenth-century stone chancel screens in London diocese parish churches such as Great Bardfield and Stebbing (Essex).

THE NEW CHAPTER HOUSE

In 1332 the royal mason William Ramsay was exempted from jury service while he was 'especially and assiduously [giving] his whole attention to the business of [St Paul's]',[100] notably to the creation of a cloister, with a new chapter house at its centre, in the south-west angle of the nave and transept (Fig. 77). One of the first examples of the 'Perpendicular' style which was to dominate English architecture for the next two centuries,[101] it replaced an older chapter house, in existence by *c.*1240, which had stood on much the same site as its replacement.[102] In a grant for the project, the dean and chapter stated that they wished their cathedral to 'resemble others', suggesting that Ramsay's brief was to create a building akin to the fully glazed polygonal chapter houses recently built at Lincoln, Salisbury, Wells and Westminster.[103]

Both the octagonal chapter house and the square cloister were two-storeyed to improve the light and air circulation in this cramped space and to ensure that they could be seen above the high surrounding walls. The chapter room itself, with its huge windows, was on the first floor above an open undercroft. The lower part of the room on the outside had panels of blind tracery with corbels for statues; the mullions continued up into upper windows, creating a panelled effect over the whole building. The prominent buttresses at each angle were like 'a crown surrounding the casket within'.[104] At least one further set of tall pinnacles soaring above the roofline must have been intended, along with finials on the gables and a more complex parapet, but there is no evidence that these were ever built, as they were not shown on any of the early views.[105]

The cloister was about 100 feet square externally, a size dictated by the length of the transept arm.[106] Excavated fragments suggest that both the upper and lower storeys had three-light openings,[107] which were linked, as on the chapter house, by continuous mullions through a band of blind panelling. Similar blind panels of *c.*1351 at St Stephen's chapel, Westminster had figures painted on them,[108] and there might have been a similar scheme at St Paul's. Access to the lower part of the cloister and chapter house undercroft was through a door at the east end of the south aisle; the upper chapter room was reached by means of a set of large steps in the middle bay of the west aisle of the south transept. These led up to the upper walk of the cloister, and presumably from there to the chapter house across some form of bridge.[109]

TOMBS AND CHANTRIES

Most of those commemorated by impressive monuments in the cathedral (Fig. 67) and its precinct were clerics, prominent citizens of London or their relatives, as during the Middle Ages burial there was seemingly never particularly fashionable with the aristocracy. Notable exceptions included Henry de Lacy, earl of Lincoln (d. 1310), a major benefactor of the New Work; John of Gaunt, duke of Lancaster (d. 1399); and Margaret Beauchamp, countess of Shrewsbury, who was associated with the Jesus Guild (d. 1468; p. 163). Late sixteenth- and seventeenth-century

78. Tomb of John of Gaunt, duke of Lancaster, and his first duchess, Blanche, erected *c.*1374–8, from the Hatton/Dugdale *Book of Monuments*. (BL Add. MS 71474, f.183r)

antiquaries such as Dugdale, Stow, Weever and Fisher were able to record only about one hundred or so of what must have been thousands of medieval burials within the cathedral and its precinct, and of these, only about two dozen were drawn before the Great Fire.[110] In part, this was because the charnel house chapel and the Pardon Cloister (pp. 35–6), among the principal places for élite memorials at St Paul's during the later Middle Ages, were cleared away after the Reformation, with more than 1,000 cartloads of bones being taken to Finsbury Fields for reburial. Moreover, Protector Somerset took away 'much goodly stonework' from tombs and chapels in the cathedral for the construction of Somerset House on the Strand, tombs were cleared from St Faith's and many of the remaining tombs were damaged during the Civil War.[111] Brasses were particularly vulnerable. Dugdale remarked on the large numbers of monuments 'torn away and for a small matter sold to Copper-Smiths and Tinkers' such as Allen Gamon and Roger Sylvester, who bought 'seven score pounds of olde and broken latyyn [brass]' from St Faith's.[112]

What remained suggests that the cathedral's rich and varied collection of tombs were largely made by the tomb-makers, masons and brass workers who served a national market from

workshops clustered around the cathedral, both in the churchyard and on Paternoster Row.[113] Because of this, many of the monuments were among the earliest of their type. Bishop Eustace Fauconberg (d. 1228) had one of the earliest full-length sculpted stone effigies of a bishop, while the lost brass commemorating Bishop Henry de Sandwich (d. 1273; p. 25) was almost certainly the earliest English episcopal brass.[114] The canon and jurist Ralph de Hengham (d. 1311; pp. 26–7) had an early 'Camoys'-type brass: his figure was surmounted by a canopy supported on corbels, while the background was powdered with heraldic stars and sheep.[115] Henry de Lacy's tomb was said by Stow to have been 'fowly defaced',[116] but it was probably originally of the canopy type seen on important royal tombs at Westminster Abbey; as the niches on its base did not have ogees, it may have been made in the early 1290s, before the completion of the New Work.[117]

Initially a 'tomb-free zone' was created around the high altar and St Erkenwald's shrine to emphasize their sanctity.[118] For instance, clerical tombs such as those of Eustace de Fauconberg, Ralph de Hengham and Bishop Henry de Wengham (d. 1262) were placed within the wall arcading of the new choir, while Canon Roger of Waltham's chantry (d. 1341) was in the south choir aisle (pp. 164–6). Other tombs made around the time of the completion of the New Work, such as that of Henry de Lacy, made around the time of the completion of the New Work, were placed in the Lady Chapel.[119] Only the sainted Bishop Roger Niger's tomb (Fig. 62; p. 120) was included within the screen

79. Tomb of Sir John de Beauchamp (d. 1388) in the south nave arcade, etching by Hollar from Dugdale (1658)

enclosing the presbytery, an early example of this arrangement.[120] Although the upper part of his tomb was made for his translation in 1326,[121] the actual tomb chest was probably the thirteenth-century original.

None the less, tombs soon encroached on the area around the high altar. One such was that of Sir Simon Burley (d. 1388), built into the north choir aisle wall, and Hollar's plan (Fig. 67) indicates that the eastern choir bays had many other late medieval monuments, especially brasses, in and around the choir, although most were too defaced for their dedications to be recorded. The most elaborate survival was the tomb (Fig. 78) created by Henry Yevele and Thomas Wreke *c.*1374–8 for John of Gaunt and his first duchess Blanche (d. 1376), the parents of the future King Henry IV.[122] Placed within the north choir arcade, just to the west of the high altar, it was a virtuoso creation made of freestone and alabaster from the Lancaster estates at Tutbury, with an elaborate canopy similar to the reredos that Yevele made for Durham Cathedral at much the same time.[123]

John of Gaunt also founded a chantry, later known as Lancaster College, in the chapel between the buttresses of the fifth bay of the choir on the north side; it was apparently linked to the crypt below by a staircase with windows.[124] Among its contents was an elaborate cross which had an enormous round foot in the shape of a castle with sixteen large and small turrets around the exterior walls, and thirteen turrets around the inside walls. The matching candlesticks had images of the Crucifix, the Virgin Mary, St John, the Four Evangelists and Saints Peter and Paul; their bases had castles with pinnacles, windows and 'curious towers'.[125] The presence nearby of the cult-site of Blanche's great-uncle, the pseudo-saint Thomas, earl of Lancaster (d. 1322) probably influenced Gaunt's decision to have his tomb and chantry in the cathedral (p. 120).

The nave and transepts were also important places of burial. Among the notable lay burials in the nave was Sir John de Beauchamp (d. 1368), whose tomb (Fig. 79) adjacent to the miraculous image of the Virgin was probably an early work of the well-known architect Henry Yevele.[126] Important clerical burials included Bishop Michael of Northburgh (d. 1361), whose brass was placed 'without the great west door', and Bishop Thomas Kempe (d. 1489), whose chantry-chapel was in the third bay of the north nave arcade. Kempe's chapel continued to be a place for episcopal burials in the post-Reformation period.[127] The tomb of Bishop Richard fitz James (d. 1521) was near the north-west crossing pier; but burning timber falling from the spire in 1561 destroyed its grey marble effigy and two-storeyed timber chapel.[128]

THE PRECINCT

The precinct surrounding the cathedral was reorganized from early in the twelfth century onwards (Fig. 20). Bishop Richard de Belmeis I bought nearby houses and lanes for that purpose and the precinct walls and gates appear to have been complete by the late twelfth or early thirteenth century (p. 20). The cemetery wall at the north-east corner was mentioned in 1106, and the south wall towards the western corner of the precinct some five years later, suggesting that the enclosure had much the same dimensions by then as in the later Middle Ages.[129] Both the eastern wall and the great gate leading to Cheapside were mentioned *c.*1200, and other features in the north-east corner of the precinct, such as the great cross and the bell-tower, were in existence by the early thir-

teenth century.[130] Other gates recorded at this time included the postern in the north wall (by 1226), the gate by the church of St Augustine (by 1246) and the gate towards Ludgate (by 1277).[131]

Within the enclosure lay the bishop's palace and the houses of other cathedral dignitaries; St Gregory's church with its church-yard and rectory; the Pardon Cloister and Becket chapel; the chapter house and its cloister; many of the canons', vicars' and chantry priests' residences; the great churchyard with its cross, bell-tower and charnel house; the almonry and deanery; and a host of lesser buildings including craftsmen's shops and workshops.[132] There were also a number of other buildings connected with the cathedral, including some of the canons' houses and the brew-house and bakehouse, outside the precinct.

The southern part of the precinct along Carter Lane was occupied by substantial residences for cathedral dignitaries, including the precentor, chancellor and treasurer, established from the late twelfth century onwards (pp. 21–3, 305–7). The 'Old Paleys' was also here and was converted into Lancaster College for the chaplains of John of Gaunt's chantry in 1403.[133] It was probably the original bishop's palace since in the early twelfth century the focus of his property holding was to the south of the cathedral (p. 20). On the other side of Paul's Chain, the alley leading up to the south nave door, stood the deanery (pp. 23, 305), several canons' houses, Holme's College and, next to the gate leading towards Ludgate, the chantry priests' houses or St Peter's College (p. 33), part of which in 1554 became Stationer's Hall.[134] The close and hall for the vicars choral lay to the north of the gate.

East of the vicars' lodgings, adjoining the cathedral's north aisle, was the bishop's palace, which had been moved to this location by the 1230s.[135] This may have been its intended site since the time of Bishop Maurice, but it could not be built here until after the cathedral itself was finished. A large building, surrounded by a garden, it incorporated the cathedral's north-west tower, which, like the Lollards' tower, served as one of the bishop's prisons. It had a chapel, probably two-storeyed, adjacent to the north nave door, and there was also a door from the palace directly into the consistory court in the north aisle.[136]

The Pardon Churchyard, subsequently the Pardon Cloister, was in the angle of the nave and north transept. This was a long-established site for élite burial and in the early fifteenth century was provided with an impressive new cloister containing a chapel which apparently housed the tomb of the parents of St Thomas of Canterbury, certainly contained the chantry of Dean More (d. 1421) and additionally was an important site for civic devotion (p. 35–6, 39). A few years later, Walter Sherrington's executors built a library over the east walk of the cloister, associated with his chantry chapel at the north door of the cathedral (pp. 415–16). With the exception of its east walk, the cloister and everything in it were demolished in 1549 on the orders of Protector Somerset, who used the stone for his new house; Sherrington's chapel was replaced by a 'faire house' in the reign of Edward VI.[137]

North of the Pardon Churchyard were canons' residences (where they had once had a cemetery: p. 35) and the hall of the minor canons. The north-east part of the precinct was given over to the churchyard, with the charnel house on the north side.[138] In the 1270s a chapel dedicated to the Virgin was built over the charnel house and became another focus of civic devotion (p. 35).

To the south-east of the charnel house, near the side of the choir, were Paul's Cross and the site of the folkmoot. The cross (Fig. 24), which was used for proclamations and preaching, was made 'of timber, mounted on steps of stone and covered with lead'. Remains discovered during excavations in 1878 showed it to have been 37 feet across, and located about 12 feet from the north choir wall. First mentioned in 1216, it was rebuilt by Bishop Kempe, whose heraldry decorated the lead work of its roof (pp. 31, 44).

The great bell-tower, which stood beyond the cross on the eastern edge of the precinct near Cheapside, may first have been mentioned in the 1220s, when Richard de Greenford agreed to find the timber for its construction,[139] but there could be an early twelfth century reference to its predecessor (p. 23). Large detached bell-towers were once very common, with examples known of at Salisbury, Canterbury and Ely, among others, but they have almost all now been demolished except for a few examples near East Anglian parish churches.[140] Built of stone, with a timber spire, the Ashwell drawing (Fig. 66) suggests that it was a miniature version of the crossing tower and spire, which itself contained bells (p. 20).[141] It had four bells, used to call people to assembly at the folkmoot and for services in the Jesus chapel in the crypt, which Stow remarked were 'the greatest that I ever heard of'. From the mid fifteenth century, those who occupied the Jesus chapel appear to have been responsible for maintaining the bell-tower. The spire and bells were removed in or before 1547, but the name 'Jesus Steeple' and the stone base appear to have survived until the fire.[142]

The precinct also encompassed St Gregory's parish church, which stood against the south-west end of the cathedral's south aisle. It was presumably built at the same time as the nave, with which it shared a wall, but it was entirely rebuilt by Inigo Jones in the seventeenth century and little is known of its previous form. Its general shape suggests that it had a nave and chancel with a single aisle alongside both, and several views show a crenellated parapet, suggesting that its roof was rebuilt in the later Middle Ages. By 1353 it had its own rectory house, located between the church and the cathedral's south nave door.[143]

CONCLUSION

When thinking about St Paul's in the Middle Ages, it is all too easy to be swayed by the prejudices of sixteenth- and seventeenth-century eyewitnesses such as Wenceslaus Hollar, John Stow, William Dugdale and Sir Christopher Wren, whose views and accounts form the basis of our understanding of its form and character. But far from being impartial observers, these men were using the building to score political, religious and personal points of their own: Wren, for instance, wanted a contract for major building works, while Dugdale – a Royalist and supporter of the High Church faction – wanted it restored as a symbol of the monarchy's greatness. By attempting to display the cathedral in its medieval glory, Hollar – at Dugdale's request – expressed an implicit criticism of its decline since the Reformation. Yet while the Reformation was undoubtedly catastrophic for St Paul's and other great churches, the later Middle Ages seem not to have been marked by great concern for the fabric of the cathedral. There was much new building at London churches during the fifteenth and early sixteenth centuries, but not at St Paul's.

Aside from repairs to the spire in the mid fifteenth century and the installation of new tombs, the last major alterations to the cathedral complex were in the early 1400s, and these were centred not on the cathedral itself but on its precinct. Thus it is likely that much responsibility for the decay into which the building fell after the upheavals of the 1530s and 1540s lies with the previous century or more of benign neglect. Perhaps, had Henry VIII not fallen for Anne Boleyn and for the material, and other, attractions of church reform, this genteel decline would have been reversed in the mid sixteenth century. There is certainly evidence for reform and liturgical revival at St Paul's in this period. After a lull in chantry foundations, there was a renewed burst of enthusiasm for them towards 1500, and a similar revival of interest in the cathedral among craft guilds.[144]

Whether this revival would have extended to the cathedral's fabric is less clear. Tombs such as that of John Colet (Fig. 19) with its strongly classicizing frame and sixteenth-century brasses which also used classical details[145] show that the new Renaissance motifs then being used in Italy and France were becoming very fashionable at St Paul's in the 1520s and 1530s. Would this enthusiasm for the Renaissance have spread to church architecture had the Reformation not put an abrupt end to virtually all ecclesiastical building projects? Certainly the adoption of new styles for English domestic architecture in the later sixteenth century suggests that had church construction continued in this period as well, it, too, would have been revived and encouraged by new fashions. But here we enter the realms of fabrication rather than fabric-history: at a distance of more than 450 years, we can only say that the medieval cathedral of St Paul's was an extraordinary and impressive creation of the eleventh, twelfth and thirteenth centuries, but by the mid sixteenth century it was quietly mouldering away.

12

ESTATES AND INCOME,
1066–1540

Rosamond Faith

For the members of a small new religious community in unfriendly and unfamiliar surroundings, securing a regular supply of food for their table and clothes on their backs was an important early preoccupation. A stable community had different needs from a bishop whose business might well take him out and about and who could expect hospitality on his travels, and King Ethelbert provided land 'for the maintenance of those who were with the bishop' when the new see for the East Saxons was established in London (p. 5). This need for separate provision for the community seems to have been recognized by Bishop Theodred, who, in his will (d. after 955), granted some of his personal land to the community as *beodland*, 'table land' (p. 12). These properties were also known as *solanda*, possibly *sceolanda* or 'shoe lands', intended to provide an income to pay for their shoes. After the Conquest, the community's principal 'table land' was identified with twenty-four hides 'next to the wall of London which king Ethelbert gave to St Pauls' and was granted exemption from geld and the (by then archaic) traditional obligations of 'works and expeditions' by William I and his sons. Such exemption was traditional for minster 'inlands' or lands directly exploited for the support of a monastic community, and Domesday Book notes that in Edward's time some land at Fulham and Willesden was explicitly known as being 'for the canons' food'. As well as the 'twenty-four hides near London', there were small *solandae* at Drayton and Chiswick in Middlesex and at Tillingham in Essex.[1]

Some important features of St Paul's estate-management policy may stem from the fact that the cathedral escaped the tenth-century drive to replace clerks in many minsters with monks and remained a college of secular clerks. Members of the community obtained more individual rights to property than monks would have done. The 'twenty-four hides' were, or became, a collection of smallish holdings dispersed among those of other landlords. Some of them were used to support individual canons: Ralph, Durand, Gyrth and Walter are named among their Domesday tenants. Such holdings were antecessors of the later prebends, lands permanently assigned for the support of the occupants of individual canonical stalls in the cathedral (p. 21). Two canons held land in Stepney in 1086 as tenants of the bishop.[2] Perhaps from the time of Dean Wulman and Bishop Maurice (1085–1107) the purpose of the prebendal system was primarily liturgical: the recitation, over the year, of the entire psalter by the thirty major canons of the cathedral. In due course, nine prebends were created from the 'twenty-four hides' to provide each with a small cash income. There were also prebends further afield: one, called Consumpta-per-Mare ('consumed by the sea'), had been much reduced by erosion from Essex's vulnerable coast. The prebends provided only part of the canons' income: each major canon was also entitled to a weekly allowance of bread and beer, and twelve pence. In addition, there were the other members of the community, and their servants, to be fed. These demands were met from the resources of what came to be known as the 'country manors'. By 1066 St Paul's had ten manors in Essex, four in Hertfordshire one in both Hertfordshire and Bedfordshire and one in Middlesex. Some further property was acquired after the conquest. By 1086 Caddington (Beds.) and Kensworth (Herts., later Beds.) had both been given by 'Young Leofwine', Lee Chapel and Norton in Essex had been acquired by gift, and the canons had 'taken over' and 'annexed' land at Barling and Navestock, both in Essex. Barnes (Surrey) was given by two brothers for entry into some kind of cathedral fraternity by 1108 and Sutton (Middx) was acquired by 1181. By 1180–1, lands in Stepney and Acton, which would formerly have belonged to St

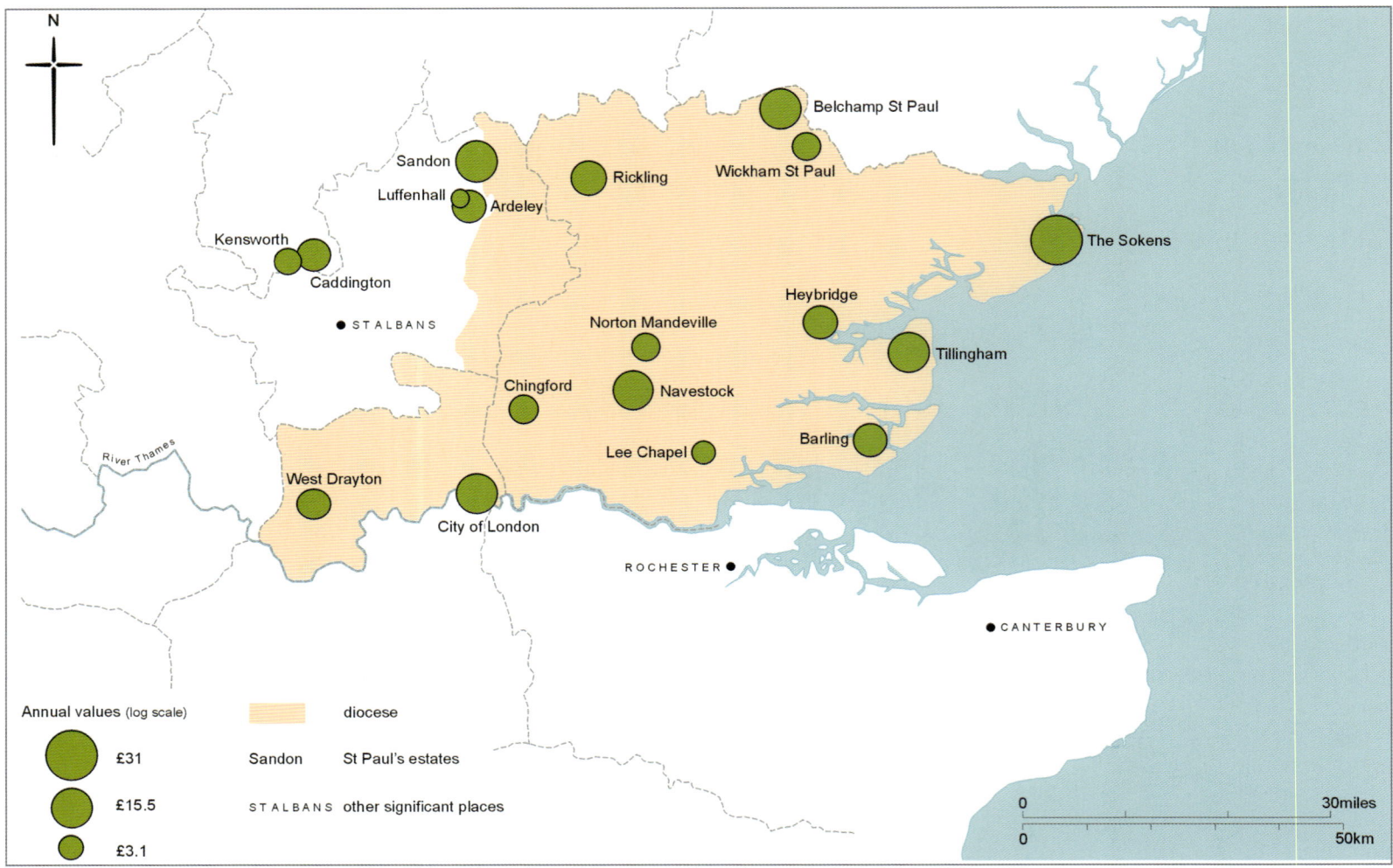

80. St Paul's estates and their annual values in 1086. For total annual values by county, see Table 2 (p. 29). The value for the city of London is an estimate

Paul's, and the church at Lambourn (Berks.) were acquired to provide a separate estate for the dean.[3]

Although this was not a big estate by the standards of the old established religious houses, it lay within an area which was highly populated and was to become among the more prosperous areas of medieval England. By far the largest property was 'the Soke of St Paul's', the area known now as The Sokens in eastern Essex. This consisted of The Naze, once a large promontory, and the vills of its hinterland: Walton, Thorpe and Kirby. It was the relic of an ancient soke, a jurisdictional area whose inhabitants owed attendance at its court and other obligations. It retained many aspects of its distinct identity, including the peculiar jurisdiction that passed into lay hands after the dean and chapter lost the estate in 1544.[4] The valuable grazing of the Essex coastal marshes was one of the major resources of The Sokens and of three of the canons' other Essex manors which profited from it, Barling, Tillingham and Heybridge. Five others lay on the heavy London clays: Belchamp St Paul and Wickham St Paul in the north-east of the county, Navestock and Chingford in the heavily forested south-west, and Runwell on the edges of the Thames marshland. The Hertfordshire and Bedfordshire manors lay in the area of more workable boulder clay soils which became incorporated in the Middle Ages – perhaps already by the Conquest – into large-scale open-field systems. These manors had by far the most impressive agricultural assets: six plough teams were at work on the home farm at Sandon in 1086, while it was judged that there could be

ten at Caddington – as many or more than the demesne of the whole of the four vills of The Sokens combined. The total yearly value of these properties in 1086 was about one hundred and fifty pounds: not very much by the standards of the contemporary church. Westminster Abbey, admittedly a larger community with eighty monks, had property worth over six hundred pounds.[5] However, in contrast to the monks of Westminster, and in contrast also to their own bishop, the canons managed to keep most of their estate 'in hand' rather than granting it out to military subtenants. Instead, it was managed in order to meet several demands: to provide regular supplies for the community and its servants, to bring them in a cash income and to provide a comfortable living for favoured individuals. The chapter's estate policy was essentially and literally conservative: to hold on to what they had and to secure their position locally by buying out the rights of other landlords. It was evidently considered a priority to ensure that the manors which produced supplies for the chapter were properly kept up. Whenever we are able to glimpse management strategies at work, we sense a preoccupation with maintaining and improving the capital value of the property, especially its buildings, rather than maximizing revenues. It is thanks to this preoccupation that, while central accounts have largely failed to survive which would have informed us about the income the canons received from their property, the care with which they inspected and recorded their capital assets in the form of manorial surveys and estate-wide enquiries has given us much valuable information.

Well into the fourteenth century, the property was primarily managed to produce regular deliveries in kind, known as 'farms'. This was by then an extremely old-fashioned system, essentially that by which the itinerant kings and perhaps also the greater landlords of Anglo-Saxon England had been supported by *feorm*, supplies of food and drink delivered from their estates. By the time of the Conquest, it was common to find a division on many great estates between, on the one hand, manors kept 'in demesne' – kept in hand and managed by a bailiff to produce supplies for consumption and/or sale – and, on the other hand, manors leased out in return for a set return in cash, kind or both: a relic of the *feorm* system. But some major Benedictine houses at this time still secured their supplies by fastening on individual manors the obligation to provide the community with food for a set period: Ramsey, St Albans, Ely and Bury employed this system. The St Paul's system combines elements from both. The manors were virtually all leased, generally to individual canons, a practice forbidden by statute but seemingly winked at. As part of his rent to the chapter, the lessee or 'farmer' of each manor owed a regular payment in kind, the 'farm' (*firma*), which went to the direct support of the residentiaries. He also owed a substantial yearly sum in cash, and in the twelfth century a new lessee had sometimes to pay a substantial entry-fine on taking up the lease. The manors were generally let for life, or for the life of the tenant and his designated heir, and it was not uncommon to hold the lease of more than one manor at a time. It was the obligation of the lessee to supply the farm due from his manor and see that it was delivered to London and to pay the rent in cash also due from it. He was responsible for paying whatever was due to the sheriff and hundred bailiff in tax and other public obligations. He was held responsible for returning the property with the same amount of live and dead stock as it had when he received it and as it is recorded in many cases in the lease itself. The leases and their accompanying very detailed inventories are among the earliest surviving estate records from post-Conquest England. Canon Hale's edition of a selection, with many other estate records of St Paul's, was a pioneering work in medieval social and economic history. His painstaking work on the leases and accounts unravelled the complexities of the farm system and I follow him here.[6]

The lease of one of the canons' manors was a valuable acquisition and considerable profits could be made by a lessee. Great landlords in the twelfth century were at risk from depredations by unscrupulous lessees. It probably stood the chapter in good stead at the time that most of their known lessees at this period were canons of the cathedral. Others were members of a cathedral fraternity, or had important positions in other churches than St Paul's. Members of the chapter were subject to its supervision and discipline and the worse depredations of unscrupulous lay tenants were avoided. They were often rich men. A lessee was 'usually a man of substance, and often a man of standing' and, in Stubbs's view, 'rich as the church was, no canon was allowed to become a residentiary who could not afford to spend seven or eight hundred marks the first year'. By the fourteenth century he had a round of expensive obligatory entertainments to pay for (p. 24). Did the canon lessees live on their properties? This is very difficult to determine. After a dispute arose over the matter, Dean Ralph drew up rules about non-residence at the cathedral, but these seem to have been concerned more with calculating what an absent residentiary should be allowed to receive than with forbidding absence altogether. Considering their elevated social position, and the official responsibilities which demanded the presence of many of them in London, at Westminster or at court, it is likely that many would have been absentees and put in subtenants, as the dean certainly did in the fifteenth century. But in the thirteenth century, while they may not have been permanently resident on their manors, they undoubtedly visited them and kept an eye on their management. In 1259 the canon lessee visited Sandon for nine weeks and at harvest time, each visit giving rise to a good deal of preparation and expenditure.[7] The survival of so many fine houses on the chapter's manors from this period is testimony to the amount of investment made in them. Like manors owned by the laity, the dean and chapter's country properties each had its court (*curia*), a complex of residential buildings and, ranged near them, the buildings of the home farm. The accommodation for the lessee or his representative was a main house, generally referred to as the hall (*aula*), with a separate chamber (*camera*). Later on, as at Barnes (Surrey) in the fifteenth century, the living accommodation is likely to have grown piecemeal, with an upper floor inserted and the services attached to one end of the hall. By the sixteenth century, the houses were substantial, many having been rebuilt. There was a range of associated domestic buildings: latrine, chapel, kitchen, bakehouse and brewhouse. From the twelfth century on, there may well have been a deer park and fishponds, those statements of upper-class lifestyle and diet.

The chapter's farm buildings may well have surpassed their domestic houses in magnificence.[8] Twelfth-century leases record their dimensions and present a unique and important insight into the size and layout of the working manors, as well as to the contents of the work buildings. In a number of cases, it is possible to compare the details of the leases with the sites of the manors today. The barns tend to stand out as the largest and most impressive monuments on these manors. Where standing remains survive, the earliest fragments are thirteenth century in date and compare favourably with other big barns of the period, such as the twelfth-century Cistercian barn at Coggeshall Essex and the thirteenth-century Templar barns at Cressing Temple, Essex. The court at Sandon, Hertfordshire is described in a lease of 1155 which lists two large barns and two smaller barns, along with a hall, chamber, cowhouse, bathhouse, malthouse, pigsty and fowlhouse. A further lease of 1239, and a building inventory compiled between 1239 and 1259, describes the overall layout and size of the buildings. The manor was divided into three units: a domestic area and two work yards. One of the work yards was devoted to the barns, the other to livestock. Some other buildings lay outside. What is striking, both in the sources and on the ground today, is the dominance of the barnyard. It occupied a large rectangular area in the eastern part of the complex, with the stockyard between it and the domestic area. The medieval hall undoubtedly lies beneath the present house, which occupies the top of a low broad hill: the surviving barns are visible for miles across the rolling open chalk lowlands. In contrast, the area of the stockyard (which is now a lawn) would have been sandwiched between the house and the barns, and although its own cowhouse and dairy are described as significant buildings in their own right, it is the barns that would have drawn the eye. The largest barn defined the east side of the yard and measured 80 feet long and 34 feet wide. It had an entrance porch that was 12 feet wide between the posts and 19 feet long, and the entire structure was made from good oak and ash timber. Such details are given for the other structures as well, while the third barn, which faced the gate, measured 17 feet high to the tie-beams.

At Belchamp St Paul, the lease of 1174 × 80 goes further by describing the crops that were to be stored within its barns. The oat barn, for instance, had oats filling its west side, oats and barley in the east aisle as high as the tie beams, and barley in the south aisle. The rest of the barn was empty. Such detail provides a wonderfully rich insight into how these structures were used, and presents the St Paul's material as unique in its detail for the study of agrarian practice in this period. These were very substantial and outstandingly large and well-built structures which would have made an impact on the surrounding landscape. Some, at least in part, are still standing today, testimony to the care devoted to their upkeep over the centuries. Keeping these large numbers of buildings in repair was a problem and after the plagues of the fourteenth century builders' wages were rising: the more work that could be done from materials on the manor, and by unpaid labour, the better. Some repairs to farm buildings were the responsibility of the manorial tenants: at two of the manors of The Sokens, they had to repair the great barns of the home farm. Some canon lessees undertook new building on their own account: it was reported in 1335 that Mr William de Melford had built a 'handsome and suitable' new hall at Heybridge. But in general the cost of repairs seems to have fallen on the chapter, and they took care by means of periodic visits to see that only necessary work was done, that costs were kept down and that the work was done economically. Local men were sworn in to giving their opinions on all these aspects and their expert knowledge must have been invaluable. At Runwell in 1335, for instance, they stated that shingles were needed for the roofs of the hall and the chapel, at present thatched, and some of the old shingles could be reused. The building at the end of the hall should be moved next to the hall, where it would be big enough to serve as bakehouse, brewhouse and kitchen, and should be tiled for fear of fire (always a risk with thatch). The barn should be shortened by six bays, and with the timber thus gained the granary could be repaired. A new upper millstone should be installed and the present upper millstone should replace the faulty lower one, and so on. Generally, manors were run as separate units by their lessees, but in the case of buildings we can see some traces of policies adopted with the larger needs of the estate in mind. The coastal manors always had the threat of flooding to contend with, which burdened them with extra costs. Oaks felled at Hadleigh were taken to Barling to repair the sea wall there after the sea had broken in and flooded a large area.[9]

The whole leasing system was geared to providing for the needs of the chapter and its ancillary population. A week's farm was intended to provide their supply for a single week of bread and ale, but it is doubtful whether the supplies ever actually came in the form of such perishable items. One manor was still required in the thirteenth century to provide malt, but on the rest this obligation had been commuted into payments of 'maltsilver'. At the end of the thirteenth century, the 'farm of a week' consisted of grain alone: sixteen quarters each of wheat and oats and three quarters of barley. Some twelfth-century leases include the provision that if the lessee planted a vineyard, the chapter was to have a share of the wine. The farm included cash sums to pay the wages of the workers at the bakehouse and brewery and alms. When the grain arrived, it was ground at the chapter's mill and was brewed and baked at St Paul's own bakehouse and brewhouse to provide loaves and beer for the community under the supervision of the warden of the bakehouse (*custos bracini*). The thirty major canons were entitled to three loaves a day and thirty gallons (*bollae*) of

beer a week; the minor canons, the servants and some of the officials of the cathedral proportionately less: 'good beer [i.e. from the first brewing] . . . for the Residentiaries, and common beer for the rest'. The beer was brewed from oats as well as barley: in this as in so many other ways, St Paul's was old-fashioned.[10]

Receiving weekly supplies of the grain essential to the production of two such essential commodities as bread and beer in a rapidly expanding metropolis put the canons in an enviable position. The brewery and bakehouse ran at a profit, presumably from the sale of grain, ale or bread which were surplus to requirements. In the 1240s, when canon Geoffrey's allowance was assigned to the support of a chantry, it was valued at the enormous sum of 125 marks (£83, perhaps reckoned as sixty years' purchase, as an allowance was reckoned at six marks a year). Additional income came from the money rents which all the manors owed in addition to their farms, the London rents, which were already substantial by the twelfth century, oblations and perhaps the sale of tithes from the churches on the country manors. A papal letter of 1181 × 85 indicates that there was conflict over entitlements to this income. Absent canons 'by ancient institution' of the church were entitled to the weekly rations and twelve pence allowance plus their *solanda* 'and can claim nothing when absent from other revenues'. The absentee canons had evidently wanted to establish individual claims to a share – what came to be called the 'dividend' in later medieval colleges – of the chapter's common revenues.[11]

At some stage, perhaps more than once, the delivery of food farms was regularized into a regular cycle. One such reorganization may have been under the first dean, Wulman (1086 × 1107), whose bishop, Maurice, was certainly responsible for some rearrangement of the prebendal system (p. 21). By the late twelfth century, an elaborate cycle of farms was attributed to Wulman's time: fifteen of the eighteen country manors owed produce assessed in terms of so many weeks' and days' (and in some cases, fractions of days') farm, amounting to precisely fifty-two weeks, six and five-sixths of a day's farm. Evidently the aim was to provide supplies sufficient for every week of the year.[12] Such a rigid system would have had to bend or it would break, and leases of the mid twelfth century show various accommodations being made by which the farm was commuted, or partly commuted, into cash payments, or payments were reduced for the first years of the lease. On his accession as dean in 1180–1, Ralph de Diceto, having surveyed the manors and their obligations, rationalized the system yet again. He reduced the overall weeks' supplies to forty-five, taking some manors out of the cycle altogether and ending the payments of single day's and fractions of days' farm.[13] In a period when many major landlords were profiting from rising prices and sending the grain from their manors to market, the continuing importance of these elaborate deliveries in kind in the domestic economy of the chapter is striking evidence of St Paul's institutional conservatism.

As did university colleges, ecclesiastical bodies had the advantage being administered by a supply of leisured and literate men. They collected and preserved their archives, kept full records and were prepared to go to law and call on the excommunicatory powers of the bishop to secure their rights. While the properties of a monastic house were under the care and control of the chamberlain, who might be able to create a 'house style' of management and record-keeping which he passed on to his subordinates and successors, the chamberlain at St Paul's seems to have been less involved with estate management, and individual deans had a fairly free hand, subject to the chapter's approval, in managing the estate. Ralph de Diceto, dean from 1180 to about 1199 or 1200, was a notable example. An early example of the analytically mind- ed historian, he was also a vigorous administrator with much the same outlook as his contemporary Abbot Samson at Bury St Edmunds. He set about systematically perambulating the estate, recording the cathedral's properties and investigating losses: the results were recorded in a major survey of which only fragments survive. This was in line with contemporary best practice: the twelfth century was the great age of medieval estate surveys. All proprietors of great estates depended on the knowledge of local people for their information, to safeguard them against fraud and damage from their own lessees and officials, and Ralph's injunc- tions to make enquiries through sworn local juries show how important this source of information was:

> In order that the truth may more easily appear: as to the capac- ity of the manors, the number of tenants now more, now fewer, we have decreed that there be chosen those who, bound by having taken a religious oath that to what is asked they will nei- ther suppress the truth nor knowingly assert what is false but according to their conscience will state in common for how many hides each manor defended itself towards the king in the time of King Henry in the time of Dean William [i.e. *c*.1111–35], what monetary rewards are paid each year to the sheriff or to the hundred bailiff and what and by what means is paid to the college of canons, how many hides are there in demesne, how many assized, how many are free and how many geldable, how many acres are there in demesne arable, how many in meadow, how many in woods, either sown or unsown, how much stock can be put either on marshland or on other pasture. Which tenants enjoy liberty, which are burdened by works, which are rent payers or which are cottagers. What of improvement should accrue to each manor and which manor suffers loss either in the deterioration of buildings or in destruction of woodlands. Who has moved or overstepped boundaries. Because the first intention of the wicked is indeed always to cause loss, the careful reader about the inquiry into the manors will note anything that is missing lest he impute it to the negligence of the enquirers or to the error or fraud of the jurors.[14]

Another collection of surveys has survived more successfully. Named after its illustrious model, like several other similar large- scale projects on other estates, the 'Domesday of St Pauls' was drawn up on the orders of Dean Robert de Watford in 1222 and consists of very detailed surveys of the demesne lands followed by a custumal listing the manorial tenants' rents and obligations.[15] Further surveys were made in the 1290s and copied into registers with the relevant Domesday entries and leases, but by and large the unstable conditions of the later Middle Ages, and perhaps administrative fashion as well, made this kind of magisterial record-making increasingly obsolete, and no comparable survey of the estate seems to have been made until Colet's visitation of 1505 (see below).

Another keen administrator, and one who seems to have been something of an innovator, was Canon Fulk Lovel, archdeacon of Colchester from 1263 × 67 to 1285. We can see him at work as les- see of the canons' manor at The Sokens in Essex. Among the manor's assets were its extensive saltmarshes, extremely valuable sheep grazing used by the flocks of both the manor and the manorial tenants. The marshes were periodically flooded by the

sea and the local people had learned to live with the fact, moving their sheep off when necessary. Lovel sought a more interven- tionist solution. He ordered the marsh pasture at Walton to be enclosed by a sea wall and a droveway to be constructed for driv- ing the sheep on to it. Local conditions defeated him: the wall was wrecked by the sea and a meeting of the chapter agreed with local opinion that it was not worth repairing only to be destroyed by the next storm, although the droveway should be kept up. At Sutton (Chiswick, Middlesex), where Fulk also leased the manor, he had the fields measured in extreme detail, down to the last half- acre.[16] This greater precision was coming to be part of what was considered good estate practice. St Paul's even had its own stan- dard measure, 'Paul's foot' (p. 27).

The lessee put the day-to-day management of the manor in the hands of a bailiff, whose clerk drew up the yearly account and who sometimes had a reeve working under him. The bailiffs effec- tively ran the manors, with occasional visits of the lessee to super- vise the harvest or of the steward to hold the manorial court, whose profits went to the chapter. It was probably the bailiff who made the important day-to-day decisions about deploying the work-force, planting and harvesting. The lessee was in the position of a temporary lord of the manor and in some respects represent- ed the legal lord, the chapter. On many manors he was obliged to maintain the gallows and tumbril – signs of the right to hold a court leet, or delegated royal jurisdiction. Occasionally an incom- ing lessee would be formally obliged to 'deal rightly' with the ten- ants and the permission of the dean and chapter was notionally required for the permanent alienation of demesne land, but in fact he had a pretty free hand in creating small tenancies.

For its lease to be a profitable undertaking, a manor needed to produce an income in cash and kind well above what was sent up to St Paul's every year. Many factors were involved. As assets, the lessees took on the manor's resources in the arable land, farm stock and equipment of the home farm as well as the labour and rent due in varying amounts from different classes of tenants. Outgoings were the 'farm' in grain and cash, the costs of admin- istration, the necessary investment in repairs to buildings and equipment, and the tithe due to the parish church from the demesne or home farm. Also due were the public payments the manor owed to the shire and hundred, and tax. With very few manorial accounts to guide us, it is difficult to judge how far lessees were successful in making a profit, let alone whether the chapter would have done better to take all their manors 'in hand' and run them themselves rather than leasing them. We can, how- ever, get an idea of what the possibilities were for profit and loss to the lessee. First of all, he had to provide the farm. By and large, the manors with the largest amount of arable land sent the most supplies: Sandon, Belchamp, Tillingham and Ardeley. The excep- tion was The Sokens, an entire district or soke, with a large home farm and a cash rent of £50 by the late twelfth century, by far their most valuable property. It owed no farm and possibly was excluded from the supply system because it included the remains of the prebend called Consumpta-per-Mare.

The grain for the 'farm' came from the demesne arable. Here the major cost was labour, of people and livestock. There were two sources of labour: the permanent workers on the home farm and the tenants. Wage labour, if it was employed, does not figure in our documents. The plough team was the major capital and labour cost and the heavy clays of most of the manors meant that large teams were needed. While eight-ox teams were the most common, eight oxen and two horses were needed for Belchamp's

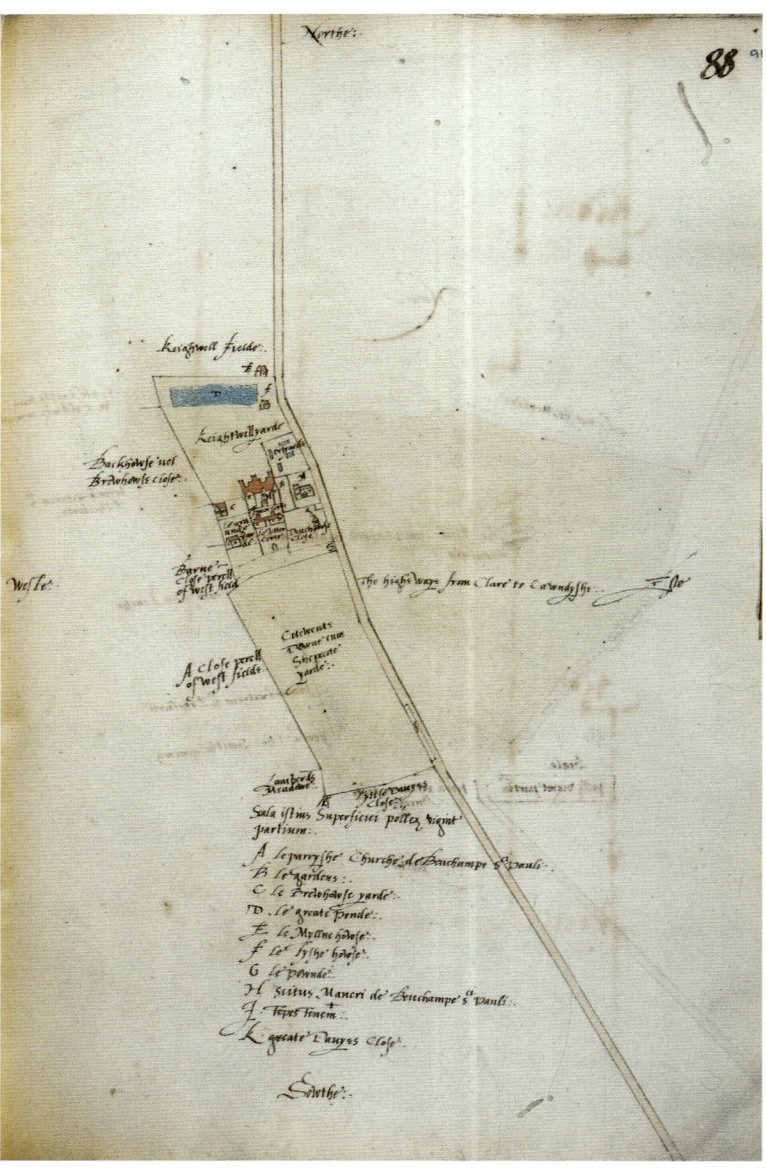

81. Map of the manor of Belchamp St Paul, Essex, belonging to St Paul's, drawn by Israel Amyce, 1657. (GL, St Paul's collection, MS 25517/1)

four demesne teams and Thorpe's one, while at Navestock and possibly also at Heybridge two huge teams of twenty head were required. On most of the manors, one or two horses were kept for harrowing: the use of horses was an innovation in which Essex was a leading county. Although the plough teams at work on the demesnes were large, not many teams were kept, and their numbers did not increase in step with the expansion in demesne arables which took place from the late twelfth century. There were probably two main reasons for this. It was difficult to provide keep – pasture in summer and meadow for hay or other supplies of winter feed – for the numbers of cattle necessary to provide these numbers of male stock (cows were seldom used). Of more significance for the overall management of the manors, however, was the fact that the canons as lords of their manors, and their lessees as their deputies, had rights over their tenants' labour, equipment and livestock. As the 1222 surveys put it: 'The wainage [cultivation] of the demesne can be done by' *x* ploughs in demesne 'with the customs of the vill' or 'with the customs of the work-tenants (*operariorum*)'. Their tenants' ploughs accounted for between 20 and 58 per cent of the ploughing on most of the canons' manors.[17]

Although St Paul's had its own wharf in the city (p. 20), and one might have thought that supplies from the north-east Essex

manors would have been brought to London at least in part by water via the Stour and the coast, in the twelfth century only Barling and Heybridge seem to have sent their farm, or part of it, by boat. In the thirteenth century Navestock sent its farm by boat, via Dagenham, the lessee providing the skipper. The rest went by road, most probably by packhorse. Transporting the corn owed as part of the farm was an obligation on the manorial tenants, who were expected to use their own horses rather than the livestock and carts of the home farm. The Tillingham corn was thrashed and taken to London by nineteen tenants accompanied by a farm worker, with their food provided. Sandon tenants carried twenty-five loads a week between Michaelmas and Pentecost. It was evidently considered a sensible deployment of the available labour supply to use tenant labour and livestock for this purpose and on some manors it was reckoned as equivalent to a certain number of days' week-work. In spite of the elaborate arrangements for transporting the farm by means of tenant labour, however, there were discrepancies between the amount of labour needed and the amount notionally available: at Sandon there was a shortfall, at Ardeley a surplus.

The boats and packhorses bringing up the canons' grain must have been a familiar sight in medieval London, and its daily baking, malting and brewing into the canons' bread and ale two equally familiar smells. That they lived so well on the produce of their manors may have caused resentment among their fellow-citizens who had to work for a living. An episode recorded in the mid twelfth-century miracles of St Erkenwald was designed to show the importance of the proper observance of saints' days – and this saint's day in particular. A working man who refused to stop work and join the crowd in the cathedral for the services celebrating Erkenwald's feast (30 April) is reported as saying to a priest who reproved him:

> You clerics have so much time on your hands that you neglect your own business and meddle in what doesn't concern you …you're free to keep every day as a holiday, and you get to grow soft with idleness and to eat other folks' food. You can sing without care both day and night, for no necessity compels you to work. Your life should be thought of more as a game or stage play than as a real occupation. If someone would feed me every day for free, and clothe me, damn me if I wouldn't strain myself for him, no matter if he wanted me to sing high or low.[18]

Ploughing the demesne and transporting the farm are only two of the contributions made by manorial tenants to the running of the manors. Their overall contribution was much greater. The lessees could call on some very long-established obligations which had been imposed on the people living on St Paul's lands before the Conquest. As regular farm workers, they had the bordars and slaves recorded on the manors in 1086, the bordars with their own smallholdings and often with one or two draught stock of their own. These would have been responsible for the ploughing that was done by the demesne teams, and for the care of the demesne livestock. There were seldom more than about a dozen of these permanent farm-hands, although at Sandon, the major grain-producing manor, there were twenty-three. 'Boons', or set numbers of days or specific tasks, were another long-established form of labour, which all tenants on the manors owed. Boons earned traditional entitlements of food and drink for the tenants who performed them and their families, who were sometimes expected to turn up too. For some tasks, food and drink was to be provided; for some, not. At Sutton in Chiswick, different, and sometimes overlapping, groups of tenants had to weed the farm-yard, scythe the hay and collect it from the meadow and spread it on dry ground (Sutton's meadows were very near the Thames), toss and cock it as it dried, send men to load the hay carts and stack hay (thirteen in all, who would be given wheaten bread and ale), bind the cut corn, supply carts for carrying the corn, load the sheaves on to the carts, gather nuts in the grove. Harvest time on a big manor was a large-scale affair at which many officials were present as well as the harvesters, and all had to be fed. At Sandon, harvest costs in 1325 included stipends paid to the reeve, the claviger who had charge of the keys to the barns, the rider who supervised the harvest on horseback and took messages to and fro, the reap-reeve who oversaw the harvesters, the *meyator* in charge of the stacking, the tithe collector and the 'warden' (*custos*), a brewer and baker, gleaners and nightwatchmen. Bread, meat, doves, beer, geese, saltfish, herrings, eggs, milk, butter, cheese, barley malt and flour and pottage were provided for the harvesters' meals. Gloves were given to the farm labourers and to ten ploughmen.[19] A third source of labour was week work, a certain number of days owed each week on unspecified tasks, owed on all the manors by various classes of tenants and universally considered the most servile form of obligation: most of the ploughing, ditching, muck carting and spreading was done by week-work.

One of the management decisions that had to be made was how best to deploy this diverse customary labour supply. Different economic circumstances dictated different policies. The canons' estate comes into view in our records in a period of expanding agricultural production, fuelled by and responding to a rising population and, from the late twelfth century, monetary inflation. Landlords could do well in these conditions, particularly those like the lessees whose major outgoing – the 'farm' – was a fixed quantity. The chapter as a whole received fixed supplies of a commodity, grain, whose price was rising. Whether the chapter or the lessees were its instigators, there was a general policy of expansion on many of the manors in the twelfth century and some enlightened improvement policies were adopted. The arable of the home farms was enlarged, mostly by taking in land from the forest, and was improved by marling (spreading lime as a top-dressing), draining and double ploughing. In the expanding economy of the twelfth century, landlords were in the market for the labour of both livestock and people. The canons bought Alwin the Lame of Cromer (Herts) and all his children for 60 shillings in the Hertford county court in 1191, probably something of a bargain as he brought with him a mare and cart and twenty-eight sheep.[20] A cheaper solution was to exploit the pressing demand for land from a growing peasant population by increasing the number of tenancies held for labour rent. By creating new permanent tenancies on land which had formerly been part of the home farm – a process known as 'assizing' land – a landlord could increase both his supply of labour and the amount of regular 'assized rent' coming in. Although the canons wished to be informed about such arrangements, they were not unduly bothered by the consequent loss of land from the home farm. The lessee of Kensworth was given a free hand to let as much land as he saw fit, and the 'Domesday' surveys of 1222 were concerned only that the land was let 'well and to the profit of the canons'. There was, however, an enquiry in 1240 into unauthorized lettings at Belchamp, when the manor was in the hands of Hugh of St Edmunds as *custos* or guardian. The policy of 'assizing' land was aimed at getting the best return from assets: the calculation was that more could be had from the rent and labour of a good ten-

ant than from keeping so much land in the demesne or home farm or using it to provide smallholdings for the farm workers. This did not mean that rent income was more important to the canons and their lessees than cultivating their demesnes. On the contrary, the policy of assizing unwanted demesne land was to increase productivity and during the two centuries after the Conquest the picture is of investment and improvement.[21]

The owners of large estates had to make a fundamental decision about how they managed them: whether to lease their properties out in return for a fixed rent, or keep them 'in hand', run by a bailiff and sending their produce and cash profits directly to the estate owner. Many landlords in the thirteenth century whose properties had previously been leased took this latter course, hoping to profit directly from rising prices, and perhaps also to avoid the risk of their tenants' establishing a claim to ownership of their leased properties. The canons' estate comes into view in our records in a period of expanding agricultural production, fuelled by, and responding to, a rising population and from the late twelfth century a time of inflation. That they continued their policy of leasing in these conditions cannot have been for commercial reasons: the institutional culture of St Paul's must have played a part. The lessees at this period were either canons or men who had a strong connection with the cathedral. Statutes restricted the amount they could expect from the cathedral's resources (see pp. 23–4). Such men had come to expect perks: a prebendal house in London, and an attractive house and profitable manor in the country. There would have been little enthusiasm for upsetting these arrangements in favour of direct management, whatever economic rationalism may have dictated.

From the early fourteenth century onwards, conditions were very different. A prolonged agrarian crisis from 1317 to 1322, in which cattle disease and crop failures combined, struck the rural economy very hard. Plague, at its most dramatic in the Black Death of 1348–9 when the population was reduced by between a third and a half, returned in the 1360s and was to recur sporadically through the following century. Workers were now in short supply and found themselves in a good bargaining position. It took legislation to keep down their wages and to prevent them seeking work where it paid best. The restrictions of serfdom, particularly the compulsory labour of week work and boon works, always resented, now seemed intolerable. In 1381 endemic peasant discontent broke out into open protest and violence. The Peasants' Revolt of that year was directed against many national targets but also at the local lords of manors, particularly ecclesiastical ones. The canons' Essex tenants must have been aware of the marches from that county to the capital, and the dramatic Smithfield meeting at which the peasants' leader Wat Tyler was murdered by mayor Walworth took place a stone's throw from the cathedral. There seem to be no recorded instances of attacks on the lands of the dean and chapter. St Paul's may simply have been regarded as a good landlord and escaped unscathed. However, the bishop's tenants *were* implicated in the uprising and his boatman John Pecche of Fulham was one of Wat Tyler's men. And it may well be significant that almost no manor court rolls from the chapter manors survive: these were a favourite target of the peasant rebels and were burned on the bishop's manors of Fulham and Chelmsford.[22]

Underlying changes in the rural economy were at work. During the fifteenth century and well into the sixteenth, agricultural prices were depressed and relatively stable. There was no longer any great advantage in receiving rents in corn, which could be bought cheaply locally. It was becoming harder to cultivate the demesne (the home farm) for profit and many landlords were now commuting their manorial tenants' customary obligations for cash. Here, too, the chapter was conservative: the harvest was still being brought in by the tenants at Kensworth early in the sixteenth century and a good deal of the ploughing was still done by them, too.[23] Many major landlords reacted to the overall changed economic conditions by leasing out their home farms in whole or in part to their manorial tenants, as did Westminster Abbey. But St Paul's was trapped in a rather inflexible position as regards its estates. The system of long leases of entire manors to individual canons was well entrenched and the lease of a substantial chapter property had long been one of the perks that a canon could reasonably expect. It was still possible to use the properties to confer favour within the community: in 1502 Master John Forster, a prebendary, had Sandon for his lifetime rent-free in lieu of an annuity granted him by the dean and chapter. But now it was not only canons who benefited from the fine houses and well-established home farms of the estate. Members of the gentry and London merchants were now among the lessees of the chapter manors and might expect to pass their lease on to their sons. In common with other institutional landlords, the chapter was beginning to experience some of the disadvantages of the leasing system which had served them for so long. Some leases were unfeasibly long, effectively for life. Arrears were rife: a common problem for fifteenth-century landlords. Repairs were expensive, and their costs often borne by the landlord. The elaborate and unwieldy system of corn deliveries was breaking down. By the early sixteenth century the bakehouse and brewery were dependent on buying in most of their corn locally. Now Barnes, Drayton and Sutton – relatively close to London – sent wheat only four times a year and the laden packhorses were no longer to be seen each week bringing the corn up from the more distant country estates.[24] From the Conquest until the fifteenth century, the canons' impressive barns, the sight of their supplies making their slow way to London, the diversion of the labour of so many country people to plough their lands and harvest their crops and of income to pay their rents, the employment of local men as reeves, haywards and harvest supervisors, the great meals at which the harvest workers were fed, the tithes paid to their churches, the constant presence of their bailiffs and reeves and the occasional presence of their stewards holding the courts to which all the tenants of their manors were summoned must cumulatively have made the presence of St Paul as landlord vividly felt in the neighbourhoods of the country manors. From the fifteenth century on, the chapter was a more nebulous and distant reality. Work on its home farms had been largely commuted for cash rents. The manors were no longer feeding it directly, their lessees were now less likely to have been canons than members of the country gentry, whose well-built houses were appropriate to their status.

After a period during which the administration of the chapter's properties seems to have been in the doldrums, the advent of Dean Colet in 1504 must have brought a welcome breath of reform. He at once undertook a visitation of the whole estate. Unfortunately, this cannot be traced in the archive, but an inspection of Kensworth in 1509 survives which records the manorial lands in the laborious detail that the splendid surveying techniques of later in the century were to make redundant.[25] As was becoming increasingly common, lay administrators now played an important part in running the estate finances. From the time of Bishop Warham (1502–3), a receiver general was in charge of all the estate income, drawing up an overall account. No doubt the stewardship of Essex, held by the earl, and the stewardship of all the courts in Hertfordshire and Middlesex were sinecures and the administrative work would have been done by their lay subordinates, no longer by canon lessees and their reeves and bailiffs. This fact has deprived us of much information about the estate. The principal source of information available at the end of our period comes from the valuation of church property made in 1535–6 known as the *Valor Ecclesiasticus*, Henry VIII's survey of the assets of religious houses compiled as a preliminary to their dissolution. It is a bald summary of what they might have expected to receive each year in tithe and rent, both of entire manors and tenants' holdings, court profits and sales of wood. It says nothing about sales of produce or what had come to be an occasional but increasingly important source of landlord income, and one that went some way to compensate them for the depredations of sixteenth-century inflation on rents that had become fixed and customary. This source was entry-fines: sums paid on taking up a lease. Nevertheless, the *Valor* shows that the properties that had been the most valuable in the early endowment still held their relative value by the mid sixteenth century. These were the manors of the grain-producing chalk uplands, Caddington, Kensworth and Sandon. 'St Paul's Soke' in Essex was still valuable on account of its sheer size and the rents paid by its growing population. Growing timber was now valued as a separate asset and a significantly appreciating one in a period of extensive building. The *Valor* indicates that the estate expected surprisingly little from this source, and considering how much of the land lay in well-wooded Essex, we might suspect that it does not tell us the whole story. The real change in the canons' 'portfolio', however, was in the newly important part played by properties classed as in 'the city and the suburbs': £413 out of a total of net yearly value of £727 for the common fund. This overall sum fell far behind Westminster Abbey's £3,470, but it would in the future stand the canons in good stead that such a large proportion of their income now came from the city or nearby, not valuable properties at the time of Domesday Book but assets which the rapid spread of urbanization would in the long run prove to be the most profitable.[26]

13

HISTORICAL WRITING
AT ST PAUL'S

Diana E. Greenway

Was there a distinctively Pauline tradition in the histories that were produced by members of the medieval chapter of St Paul's? A Pauline voice? Certainly the annals and chronicles compiled at St Paul's were far removed in content, if not in style, from their counterparts from the English monasteries. A major purpose of monastic historical writing was the education of young monks in the heritage and customs of the house, with the result that the focus tended to be local. At the English secular cathedrals, however, since the canons were not bound to be resident, the horizon was broader. At St Paul's, above all, where members of the chapter were well placed to observe political events and gather news, and many canons were themselves involved in royal and ecclesiastical administration, historical writing reflected a close interest in great national and international issues, especially matters concerning the relationship of church and state.

The most elementary type of historical writing in the Middle Ages was the keeping of annals, in which notes of principal events were entered year by year, with little to suggest cause and effect. This basic genre was developed into more complex narratives, or 'chronicles', also arranged chronologically, but less disjointed and offering at least some idea of development, causation and motivation. Both annals and chronicles were produced by members of the medieval chapter of St Paul's. They might cover any length of time, from a few years in the author's life to the history of the world since the Creation. Universal histories consisted largely of compilations of extracts from earlier works, woven into largely derivative texts, while histories of shorter chronological scope could contain contemporary eyewitness reporting of events.

Annals and chronicles are recognizably 'historical' in that they attempt to record actual happenings with accuracy. But St Paul's also produced books in other genres, which, although treated as historical in the Middle Ages, fail to satisfy a modern definition. One was hagiography, the writing of saints' lives and miracles which served as aids to devotion. In the first half of the twelfth century, the revival of the cult of St Erkenwald, whose shrine was at St Paul's, led to the writing of both the *Life* and the *Miracles* of the saint.[1] Another pseudo-historical genre, which had a moral purpose, is represented at St Paul's by the work of the early fourteenth-century canon, Master Roger of Waltham. His *Compendium Morale* is a highly derivative collection of 'historical' examples illustrating the virtues and duties of princes (p. 164). A third type of pseudo-history written at St Paul's was legendary history, which was intended primarily to entertain. The *Petit Bruit*, written around 1300 by the prebendary of Wilsden (Willesden), Master Ralph de Bohun, is a short history of the kings of England from Brutus to Edward I in Old French,[2] in the genre of the fanciful *Brut* histories that ultimately derived from Geoffrey of Monmouth's legendary *History of the Kings of Britain*. The *Petit Bruit* has some original elements, in that it rearranges the *Brut* chronology and introduces new fictitious characters.

In the field of serious history, Ralph de Diceto was one of the most notable of medieval historians. Probably a native of Diss, in Norfolk, he had a long career at St Paul's, as archdeacon of Middlesex from 1152 to 1180 and dean from 1180 to his death in 1199 or 1200. His two principal works were a universal history from the Creation down to 1148, called the *Abbreviationes Chronicorum* ('Brief Chronicles'), and a more detailed history of his own time, 1147–99, entitled the *Ymagines Historiarum* ('The Reminders of History'), which is one of our most valuable sources for the reigns of Henry II and Richard I.[3]

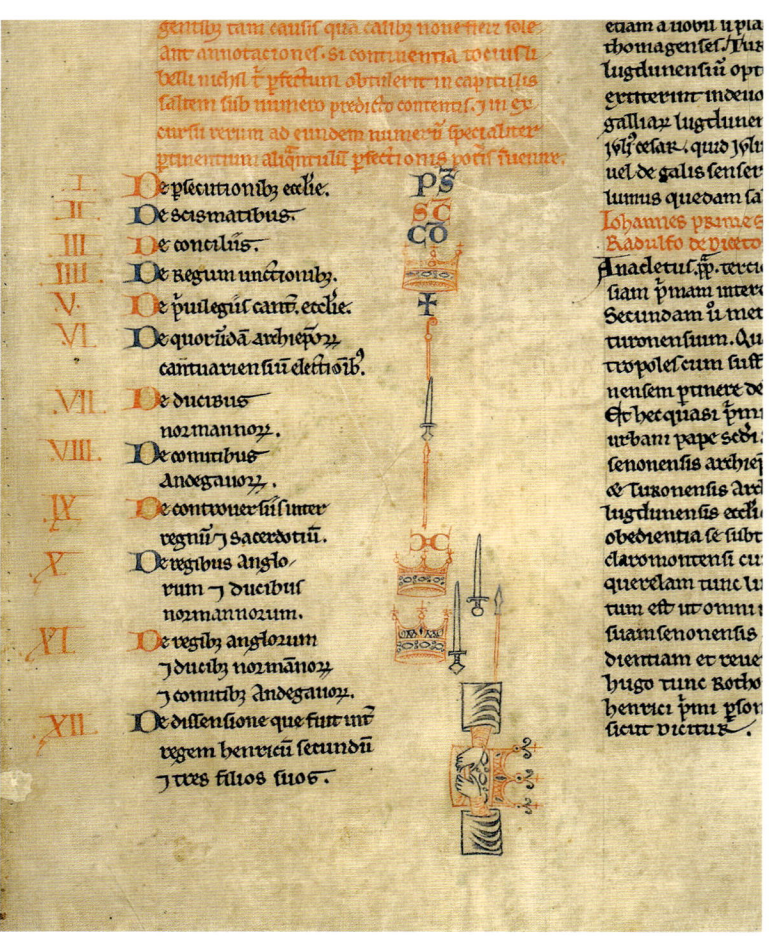

82. Ralph de Diceto's system of symbols designed to help readers find topics in his chronicles written at St Paul's, late twelfth century. Compare Gransden (1974), Plate VII. (BL, Cotton MS Claudius E.iii, fo. 3v)

Ralph was a man of considerable erudition, a graduate of the university of Paris, who read widely in history, theology and ecclesiastical law. He had a well-ordered mind. His chief purpose in writing his two historical works was to make his own learning accessible to a group of men who were too busy to read at length – the administrators in church and state with whom he was familiar as dean of St Paul's. Ralph had learned much about the organization of knowledge from the writings of the Parisian teacher Hugh of Saint-Victor, and used a combination of headings, marginal symbols, tables, lists and summaries to render his works truly 'reader-friendly'.[4] The system of symbols, set in the margins of his works, was designed to help his readers find material on particular topics, such as the anointing of kings and conflicts between Church and state (Figs 82–3). He also provided summaries of various kinds, which could be used for quick reference, including a short history of Normandy and a summary of the conflict between Henry II and Thomas Becket. A similar method may be observed in the official record of the survey he made as dean of St Paul's manors and churches, the manuscript of which is very similar in layout and script to the manuscripts of Ralph's historical works.[5]

His first work, 'Brief Chronicles', consists of a patchwork of passages culled from earlier chronicles. His second book, a history of his own time, he entitled 'The Reminders of History', a term which the early Christian writer Cassiodorus applied to those 'very brief reminders of the times', the chronicles of Eusebius, which had been translated from Greek into Latin by Jerome.[6] Ralph's appropriation of the phrase for the title of his book was

ambitious, in that he thereby associated himself with the greatest writers of the early church, but it was also humble, acknowledging the frailty and incompleteness of the historical record, which is a mere 'reflection' of events. He endeavoured to make his work as authentic as possible by incorporating lengthy quotations from contemporary letters, about 120 in number. These documents underpin and supplement the material he gained from first-hand observation and friendships. In particular, he was familiar with such prominent figures as Bishops Gilbert Foliot and Richard fitz Neal of London, Richard of Winchester, Arnulf of Lisieux, and William Longchamp of Ely, Hubert Walter, archbishop of Canterbury, and Walter of Coutances, archbishop of Rouen.

Ralph's reporting of events reflects his somewhat conservative ideal of the harmonious working together of the English church and the Angevin kingship. His esteem for Henry II determined that the starting-point of the 'Reminders' would be the beginning of Henry's adulthood, the ceremony of his knighting. A deep interest in the king's Angevin background lay behind his inclusion of material drawn from Angevin sources and of so many details about Aquitaine that his nineteenth-century editor, Bishop Stubbs, suggested that Ralph himself might have had Aquitanian origins. As the monarchy depended for its effectiveness on the administrative services and counsel provided by members of the

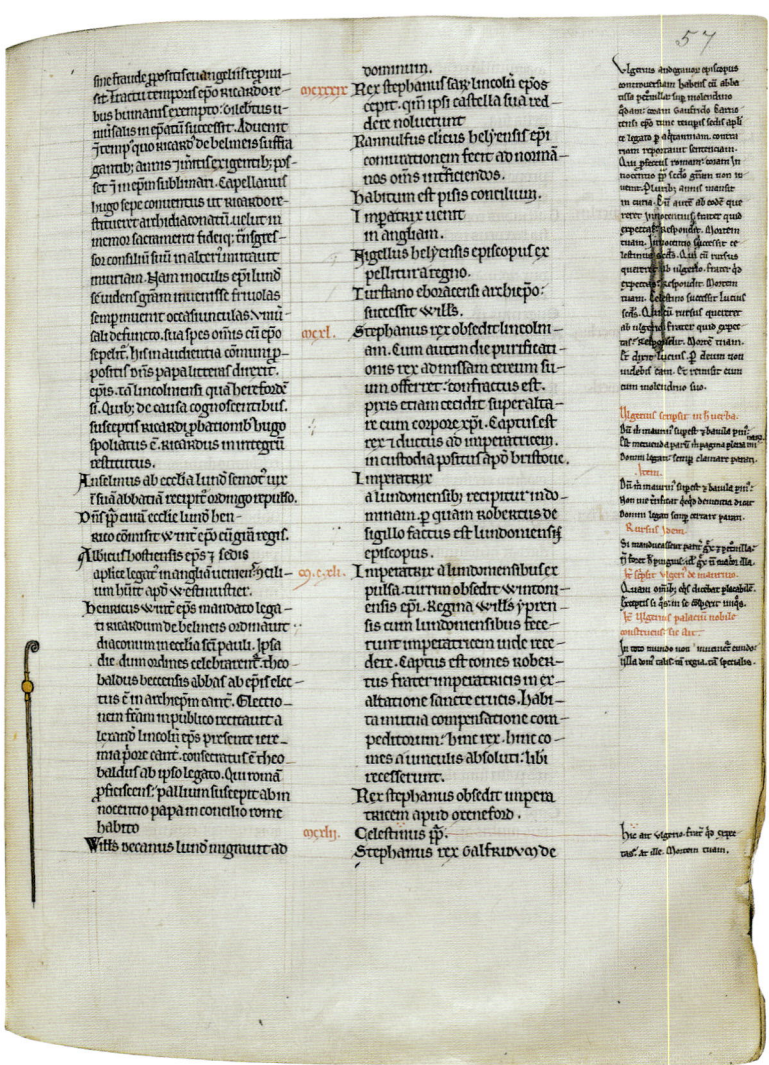

83. Ralph de Diceto's use of blank space for additions to his chronicle and of the crozier symbol to indicate matter concerning the archbishop, late twelfth century. (LPL, MS 8, fo. 57r)

clergy, a harmonious relationship with church leaders was essential to good government. This seemed assured when the king had his chancellor, Thomas Becket, promoted to the archbishopric of Canterbury. Ralph clearly shared the king's dismay when Becket insisted on resigning the chancellorship, and the alliance of church and state began to crumble. The Becket controversy brought him personal distress: at Northampton in 1164, when the king brought charges against Becket, Ralph was seen by another witness to weep bitterly. But his narrative of these events is cool and detached, giving no hint of his feelings and putting the emphasis firmly on the quoted documents of the case – letters from the king, the archbishop, the pope and other chief players in the action.

The process of composition of Ralph's two chronicles was lengthy, probably stretching over twenty years or more. In the two earliest manuscripts there are numerous signs of revision, and additions are written in the margins.[7] Ralph explains that when he began the 'Brief Chronicles' some earlier histories were not to hand, and so extracts from them took the form of marginal insertions.[8] The 'Brief Chronicles' is a monumental compilation, incorporating quotations and extracts from scores of texts, attesting to a large network of scholars who supplied Ralph with source-books to supplement the cathedral library's resources. Ralph had the help of several scribes, whose hands can be seen in the main texts of the 'Brief Chronicles' and the 'Reminders' and copying additions into blank spaces and into the margins of the two earliest manuscripts (Fig. 83), and at two places even inserting extra scraps of parchment.

In a sense, therefore, Ralph's histories were produced collaboratively at St Paul's. In the second half of the twelfth century the cathedral clergy were renowned for scholarship: 'I do not know their equals for learning,' wrote a contemporary.[9] There was a school, run by distinguished teachers, and there were several university graduates in the chapter. This was the milieu in which the canon Master Alberic of London perhaps wrote a recension of the *Mythographus tertius Vaticanus* (a handbook of classical mythology).[10] Such men doubtless had some influence on Ralph's researches, and it is even possible that some had a hand in the writing of the 'Brief Chronicles' and the 'Reminders'. We cannot know what degree of control Ralph exercised over his team of helpers, though we may guess that it may have relaxed a little towards the end of his life. The authentic 'Reminders' end at the coronation of King John on 27 May 1199, and the short continuation to March 1202 was perhaps compiled by one or more of Ralph's team.[11]

It is disappointing that after Ralph, although there was considerable annalistic activity in thirteenth-century London, only a little of it can be shown to have originated at St Paul's. A set of annals covering the period 1064–1274, in an early fourteenth-century manuscript at Corpus Christi College, Cambridge, was given the erroneous title *Annales Sancti Pauli* by Felix Liebermann, who printed small extracts in 1888.[12] The entries between the years 1064 and 1217 are laconic and sometimes inaccurate, and are probably drawn from an unidentified set of monastic annals. Certainly there is a London interest in some of the annals after *c.*1218, and also in the royal charters of rights copied on the final leaves of the manuscript, but there is no Pauline emphasis. Crucially, the particular annal on which Liebermann based his identification – a note relating to the dean of St Paul's and the constitutional position of the precentor, under the year 1257 – appears also in the *Annales Londinienses*, a composite set of London annals running from 1194 to 1330.[13] These two sets of

annals share a core of material between 1218 and 1274, containing adaptations of the St Albans *Flores Historiarum* and additions, some of London origin: this common core derives from a lost compilation, of which the Corpus copy has the superior text. Both also contain independent elements, which in the Corpus annals have a concern with appointments to the English episcopate, and suggest ecclesiastical, but not Pauline, authorship, while those in the *Annales Londinienses* have a secular, civic focus, suggesting lay authorship. It is remarkable that both omit some notable events at St Paul's which are however recorded in the semi-official city chronicle, the *Chronicon Maiorum et Vicecomitum Londiniarum* ('Chronicle of the Mayors and Sheriffs of London'), covering the years 1189 to 1274. These three compilations are survivors that attest to the existence of a range of annalistic writing in London in the thirteenth century, much of it now lost.

The *Flores Historiarum* ('The Flowers of History'), which was used in the common core of the *Annales Londinienses* and the Corpus annals, was an abridgement of earlier histories taken down to the year 1249, by Matthew Paris, a monk of St Albans. It achieved considerable popularity in the second half of the thirteenth and first half of the fourteenth centuries and itself became the subject of abbreviation and continuation by many writers. Texts circulated which incorporated material added after 1249. In some copies the pre-1249 text was abbreviated, in others it was filled out with additions, and in some others there was both abbreviation and addition. Several of these continuations of the *Flores* were compiled in London – at Westminster Abbey, in the city, and at St Paul's.

A *Flores* continued down to 1308 was abridged at Westminster Abbey, where it was also given some Westminster additions. Shortly after 1308 this text came to St Paul's, perhaps on the initiative of Bishop Ralph of Baldock (1304–13).[14] At St Paul's extra material was interpolated in the earlier section, chiefly for the thirteenth century,[15] and further annals were added at the end, covering the period from January 1309 to April 1341.[16] These annals are not separately titled in the only surviving manuscript, now at Lambeth Palace Library, but are undubitably Pauline and were given the title *Annales Paulini* ('Pauline annals') by their editor, William Stubbs.[17]

The interpolations written at St Paul's in the thirteenth-century section of the *Flores* must have been drawn from some contemporary notes or annals that have not otherwise survived. They are of some historical interest, recording such events as the dedication of St Paul's in 1240,[18] which is integrated in the text, and the visitation by archbishop Boniface in 1248,[19] which is a marginal addition. The existence of both kinds of interpolation – integrated and marginal – indicates that the text was worked on at St Paul's over a period of time: the Lambeth manuscript was a new copy, made at St Paul's and incorporating some added Pauline material, and this in turn received further Pauline additions.

The material added after January 1309, the *Annales Paulini*, falls into three distinct sections.

The first section, covering the period from 1309 to early 1332, is concerned almost exclusively with London and St Paul's.[20] One area of interest is the king's government: meetings of parliament, changes in chancery and exchequer, trials and executions. Events in the city form an even larger area, ranging from notes on extreme weather and occurrences such as a stag found in Shoe Lane and tournaments at Stepney and Cheapside, to accounts of law sessions at Guildhall and St Paul's, of riots and the murder of

84. Drawing of St Paul's from the west, fourteenth century, in the margin of the 'Pauline annals' beside the account of the renewal of the cross on the steeple and the dimensions of the church in 1314. (LPL, MS 1106, fo. 96v)

the bishop of Exeter, and all kinds of issues concerning the liberties of the city, its mayor and citizens. Ecclesiastical affairs are given the greatest prominence. Church councils and convocations meeting in London are recorded, and many London churches and religious institutions are mentioned in the course of the narrative, but the central place in the annals, year after year, is occupied by the cathedral of St Paul's. The annalist describes the visits of archbishops and cardinals, of the king, bishops and earls, and meetings of the clergy; the reading out of ordinances, papal letters and excommunications; murder affray, plunder and violence in church and churchyard; notable ceremonies. Building work in the cathedral is reported, including an account, under the year 1314, of the erection of the new cross on the spire, which is accompanied by a sketch (Fig. 84).

That the annals were composed within the cathedral community is quite clear. The deaths and elections of the bishops are of great significance, and their careers, as of several of the canons, are followed with interest and in some detail. The stories of an accident in the nave, in which the almoner had a lucky escape when part of the rood fell down on the altar in 1325, and of how the canons ordered hot cakes to be prepared for the king's visit in 1321, demonstrate an intimate association with the cathedral, as does the reporting of news coming from estates of St Paul's, such as the whale stranded at Walton on the Naze in 1326 and the queen's stay there in the same year.

The second section of the *Annales*, covering the years 1332–7, is of a different character, sharing a good deal of material with the chronicle of Adam Murimuth, and in these years the compilation takes a different turn, reflecting Adam's wider interests – English relations with the papacy, the French and the Scots. Analysis of the shared text shows that the compiler of the *Annales* borrowed from Adam Murimuth, and not vice versa. The version of Murimuth's chronicle that was used was the first edition, ending in 1337.

Although Murimuth subsequently continued his chronicle to 1341, and later still to 1347, the third and final section of the *Annales*, covering 1338–41, has no Murimuth material. The focus is once again on London and St Paul's. In fact, every event in this short section, with one exception (Edward III's visit to Antwerp and the birth there of prince Lionel), has a direct link with the cathedral: the bishops, the altars, the steeple, processions and ceremonies.

As we have seen, the second section of the *Annales Paulini* used another Pauline chronicle, that composed by the Master Adam Murimuth. This was yet another continuation of the *Flores*, which Murimuth entitled *Continuatio Chronicarum* ('Continuation of Chronicles').[21] Although he was not a canon until 1325, when he was already aged fifty, Murimuth had connections with the diocese and the cathedral from at least 1308.[22] In that year he appears as an advocate in the court of Arches, and by 1312 he was rector of Hayes in Middlesex. He represented the dean-elect, John de Sandale, at the papal court in 1314, and became official of the bishop in 1319 and vicar-general in 1321.

Murimuth's first patron, however, was the bishop of Exeter, Walter de Stapledon, who granted him a yearly salary in 1308. Murimuth already possessed the degree of Doctor of Civil Law, doubtless from Oxford. As a lawyer, he specialized in taking cases to the papal court at Avignon, and represented several different English clients in the years between 1311 and 1319, including the university of Oxford, the archbishop of Canterbury and the king. As the king's envoy, he was also engaged in diplomatic missions, especially in France, in the 1320s and 1330s.

The rewards and support for this career in public service were a string of ecclesiastical benefices: canonries in the cathedrals of Hereford, Wells and Exeter, and rectories in Gloucestershire and Kent. But he was rebuked in 1334 by Bishop Grandisson of Exeter for his absence from Exeter, where he was precentor, and in 1337 he exchanged the precentorship for the rectory of Wraysbury (Bucks). As official of the court of Canterbury from 1335 to 1339 and the archbishop's vicar-general in 1339, Murimuth seems to been more often in London after his final mission to France in 1337. St Paul's became more central in his life: he had transferred from the prebend of Ealdstreet to that of Nesden in 1328, and in 1338 he took on the lease of the chapter manor of Barnes.[23]

Murimuth set out to continue the *Flores Historiarum*. Exeter was the only English cathedral where he could find a copy, and this went down only to 1302. He therefore used a copy from Westminster Abbey, which ended in 1305. This was probably the text continued at St Paul's in the *Annales Paulini*. Murimuth claims to have kept notes on the chief events of his own time which he used in writing his account.

What Murimuth chose to write, however, is brief and uninformative, especially in his first edition, which went down to 1337. He was evidently writing some time after the events recorded, for there are several references to matters 'which will appear below': at some of these points, the interval was as much as three or four years. After 1338 the annals become fuller, though it is clear, as pointed out by his editor, E. Maunde Thompson, that Murimuth knew a good deal more than he intended to say.[24] His main theme was English relations with the continent, and chiefly with the popes and the kings of France. Murimuth belonged to an increasingly vehement body of opinion that opposed papal intervention in England and the English Church. He disliked the visits of foreign cardinals and papal taxation. He objected to papal provisions to English benefices, especially of foreigners, though he also criticized English bishops appointed by the pope. This opposition was part of Murimuth's fiercely English patriotism. At this time, when relations with France were breaking down, on the eve of the Hundred Years' War, the papal curia was located at Avignon and subject to the influence of the French king. Although Murimuth was critical of the oppressive measures Edward III adopted to finance the war, he was a strong supporter of the English invasion of France. From 1339 down to the end of the final version of his chronicle in 1346, he packs his narrative with relevant documents, twenty in all, quoted verbatim, consisting chiefly of the king's correspondence with the French king, including his claim to the French crown, and with the pope, supplemented by diplomatic dispatches and an account of the proceedings that led to the Statute of Provisors, banning papal provisions, in 1343. Doubtless at St Paul's Murimuth was in a good position to gather information, but it was through the contacts he had made in his earlier diplomatic career, rather than his canonry, that he was able to gain access to some of these texts.

One more piece of historical writing may have belonged to this burst of activity at St Paul's in the early years of the fourteenth century. The anonymous so-called *Vita Edwardi Secundi* ('The Life of Edward II')[25] was possibly written by a canon of St Paul's. It has no contemporary title, and was given its misleading title by its first editor, Thomas Hearne (1729), who believed it to have been written by a monk of Malmesbury.[26] In fact, it is not a biography of Edward II but a chronicle covering the years 1307–25, probably intended as yet another continuation of the *Flores*, and it is clear that it was not composed by a monk. It is

possible to build up a profile of the anonymous author who compiled the work in several stages between 1310 and 1326. He was familiar with the principles and practice of the civil (Roman) law, had connections and sympathies with the marcher lords and an exceptional interest in Scottish affairs. Judging from the fullness of his record for the years 1315–23, his career was then at its peak. The text ends abruptly in 1325 and appears to have been completed before September 1326. In looking for a match for this profile, Denholm-Young suggested a canon of Hereford and St Paul's, Master John Walwayne.[27] He was a doctor of civil law, the agent of the earl of Hereford in England and also in Scotland, he retired as escheator on 10 January 1324 and was dead by 18 July 1326. This remains an attractive, though unproven and unprovable, conjecture.[28]

No other substantial histories were to be written at St Paul's until the early sixteenth century. The only compilation that bears the cathedral's name is the 'Little Chronicles of St Paul's'.[29] This general chronicle from the Creation, written in the early fifteenth century, includes fifteen meagre jottings concerning St Paul's for a period of over 1100 years, beginning in 140, when an image of the crucifix was found at the north door (or when the image of the crucifix later at the north door was found), and ending in 1369, when Blanche of Lancaster was buried in the church. No trace survives of any more serious historical enterprise having been carried on at St Paul's in the fourteenth and fifteenth centuries, a period when London saw a flowering of vernacular chronicles written by laymen.

But in June 1513 a major historian was collated to the prebend of Oxgate. This was Polydore Vergil.[30] An Italian from Urbino, he had come to England in 1502, at the age of about thirty, as the deputy of his relative Adriano de Castello, the papal tax-collector. Before gaining his prebend of Oxgate in St Paul's,[31] he had already been appointed to prebends in Lincoln and Hereford, and since 1508 he had also been archdeacon of Wells.

Vergil's career as a writer had begun before he came to this country. In 1499 the first edition of his first historical work, *De Inventoribus Rerum*, had been published in Venice, in three volumes, and he was to add five more books to this immensely learned and popular work in the second edition printed in Basle in 1521. The theme was 'the first begetters of things', 'who first invented or began all things or arts; who first established particular provinces or towns; by whom the names come of provinces, towns, peoples...who first held certain offices...who first did anything splendid or unusual'. This was a highly original way of writing universal history from Adam down to his own time. Vergil consulted a prodigious number of sources – writings from Greek and Latin antiquity, the patristic and early Christian period and the Middle Ages, as well as the works of his contemporaries – and made use of his own observations. Among the illustrations drawn from his own experience, he mentions the garlands worn by the clergy of St Paul's on the patronal festival.

The second of Vergil's historical works was an edition of the sixth-century British text by Gildas, *De Calamitate, Excidio et Conquestu Britanniae* ('The Disaster, Ruin and Conquest of Britain'), which was published in 1525, probably in Antwerp. This was a landmark in British historiography, the first in a long and continuing tradition of critical editions of insular Latin historical texts.[32] Indeed, since the most important of the Gildas manuscripts (Cotton MS Vitellius A. vi) was seriously damaged in the fire in the Cotton Library in 1731, Vergil's text has provided a vital witness for later editors.[33] Vergil's interest in Gildas, the first

British historian, arose from his work on the *Anglica Historia* ('English History'), in which he was to challenge the generally accepted legend of King Arthur. Vergil realized that Arthur and his exploits were not found in Gildas's sixth-century account of the Saxon invasions, but originated much later, in the work of the twelfth-century writer, Geoffrey of Monmouth.

Vergil's long-term historical project was the *Anglica Historia*, begun in 1506 or 1507, at the request of King Henry VII. By 1513 he had written a narrative from the earliest history of Britain down to the battle of Flodden in September 1513. Over the course of the next twenty-one years, he made extensive revisions and additions to the text. The first edition, taking the history down to the death of Henry VII in 1509, was printed in 1534 at Basle. Vergil's account of the reign of Henry VIII, which he had been writing at least since 1513 and which he continued right down to the birth of Prince Edward in 1538, was not to be printed during the king's lifetime. When a second edition was published at Basle in 1546, it ended like the first in 1509. It was not until after the deaths of both Henry VIII and Edward VI, and in the year of his own death, 1555, that the final section of Vergil's text, covering 1509–38, was printed in the third edition, also at Basle.

Vergil's *Anglica Historia* used a wide range of earlier sources, supplemented by his own observation of antiquities still visible in his day and by his collection of oral traditions and the memories of his older contemporaries. For the events of his own time, he used his own experience and the information that came to him through friends and acquaintances. As his biographer points out, 'Vergil was a Londoner, even if only by adoption'.[34] As the occupant of a comfortable house in St Paul's Churchyard (p. 307) and a member of Doctors' Commons in Paternoster Row, he was excellently placed to enjoy the companionship of the leading intellectuals of the time, many of them fellow canons of St Paul's. In his edition of Gildas he had benefited from the learned collaboration of Master Robert Ridley, Doctor of Theology, a canon from 1524 to his death in 1536[35] and chaplain of Bishop Cuthbert Tunstall. Tunstall had encouraged the work by providing both a manuscript of Gildas and Ridley's services as co-editor, and was the dedicatee of the edition. Vergil's participation in the cathedral community was of considerable intellectual value to him: of the fourteen English humanists listed by him as his friends in 1521, eight were members of the chapter. Of Dean John Colet, who died in 1519, Vergil speaks with admiration in a passage on the foundation of St Paul's School which he added between 1513 and 1534. He knew the first three High Masters, William Lily, John Rightwise and Richard Jones. The first of these honoured him in

an epigram. When Vergil left England in 1553, to return to die in his native Urbino, his deep learning and his capacity for friendship would have been sadly missed at St Paul's.

Vergil's narrative gives a reasonable, detached view of English history. He sought to present the truth, so far as he could establish it, in classical style. He rejected the romantic notions of the Trojan origins of Britain which, since Geoffrey of Monmouth, had been woven and embroidered into the fabric of insular history, preferring to stay close to the evidence of Caesar, Tacitus and Gildas. For much of the medieval section he was dependent on Bede and on the *Polychronicon* continued to 1461, texts of which were available in print.

The *Anglica Historia* had to fulfil the expectation of its royal patron. Polydore Vergil was an elegant propagandist for the new dynasty, presenting the period from the deposition of Richard II down to the accession of Henry VII as a prelude to the establishment of the house of Tudor: he emphasizes the horrors of the conflict between the rival dynasties of Lancaster and York. His portrayal of Richard III as deformed, crafty and cruel became the accepted view of the king, largely through Grafton's translation, printed in 1543.[36] The marriage of Henry Tudor to Elizabeth of York, which Vergil attributed to divine intervention, created the 'true and established royal line'. He welcomed the accession of Henry VIII with high praise for his many qualities, including 'humanity, benevolence and self-control'. But as the reign proceeded, he grew disenchanted, fearful and critical. In 1514 he experienced at first hand the capricious injustice of the king and Wolsey, when he was thrown into prison on a trumped-up charge. It is scarcely surprising that on his release in the next year he did not present his *Anglica Historia* to the king as he had planned. He carried on writing his account of the reign, though with less enthusiasm, down to 1538, but delayed publication until both the king and his son Edward VI were safely dead.

No other English cathedral was so well represented among the historical writers of the Middle Ages, with two major historians of European stature – Ralph de Diceto and Polydore Vergil – and several lesser figures. Although there were breaks between periods of activity, there was a distinct tradition at St Paul's that favoured the production of narratives concentrating on political events, the problems confronting royal and ecclesiastical government, and international relations. The Pauline voice was the confident voice of those accustomed to leadership, a voice that spoke the language of the well-informed and professionally detached public servants who were the colleagues and neighbours of the canons of St Paul's.

14

THE LESSER CLERGY IN THE LATER MIDDLE AGES

Virginia Davis

The senior clergy of St Paul's Cathedral were the canons headed by the dean. However, the men who held these positions were not only senior members of the English church hierarchy, they were also usually important figures in royal or ecclesiastical administration, men with relatively little time to devote themselves exclusively to their cathedral duties. Distinguished twelfth-century absentees included Thomas Becket before his promotion to the archbishopric of Canterbury. In addition, the development of the prebendal system in the eleventh and twelfth centuries, which left individual canons responsible for the administration of specified cathedral lands, made absenteeism relatively easy.[1] Attempts were made, at St Paul's as at other secular cathedrals throughout England, to encourage residence by canons through the use of payments from the common resources of the cathedral made only to those in residence. In the twelfth century, this was confirmed to the resident canons of St Paul's by Pope Alexander III (1159–81).[2] However, despite such strategies to encourage residence by the canons, absenteeism by the major canons was increasingly common and over the centuries a system developed to ensure that the worship in the cathedral did not suffer as a result of the frequent absenteeism of the canons.

The bulk of the daily liturgical life of St Paul's, as in any major secular cathedral, was underpinned by the work of the lesser clergy, a varied body of men who together supported the religious offices of the cathedral. There were three main groups of lesser clergy by the later Middle Ages; the twelve minor canons who deputized for the major canons in singing the daily services, a duty carried out in other English cathedrals by men described as vicars choral; the chantry priests who were responsible for daily services at the many endowed chantry altars in the cathedral; and up to thirty vicars choral who contributed to singing of the daily offices in the cathedral. In addition, within the precincts of St Paul's Cathedral were occasional hermits such as the East Anglian Thomas Blaksale who settled himself as a hermit in the cathedral grounds in the late 1360s. Blaksale was subsequently ordained as a priest in the spring of 1371 on condition that he abandoned the hermit's habit he habitually wore.[3] A snapshot of the lesser clergy at late-medieval St Paul's is provided by the body of men who in 1534, on the eve of the Reformation, accepted the royal supremacy of Henry VIII: it included nine or ten minor canons, thirty-one chantry priests, six vicars choral and twenty-three others.[4]

Lesser clergy may have been important to the functioning of London's cathedral church from the eleventh century, but they are not documented before the later twelfth and the constitutional structures are unclear before the thirteenth. A late-thirteenth-century claim that the original foundation of the church had included minor canons and vicars was an idle boast, and it is possible that a clear distinction between the two was not made until the thirteenth century. By the early fourteenth century, the two groups lived separately in lodgings near the cathedral assigned to them by the dean and chapter.[5] The twelfth century also marked the appearance of chantry priests. These men were technically superior in status to the vicars choral, but their precise duties depended on the terms of the foundation of the individual chantries. The chantries – foundations dedicated to the saying of masses for the soul of the founder and his or her relatives – were founded by bishops, canons, great men of London and noblemen. There was an explosion of chantry foundation in churches and cathedrals all over England from the mid fourteenth century, but at St Paul's chantries began to proliferate much earlier (pp. 24, 38).

85.   Initial letter from the charter of incorporation of the minor canons
of St Paul's, 1394. (GL, St Paul's collection, MS 29410)

In the thirteenth century, the individual vicars choral were appointed by the individual canons and were subject to their jurisdiction, their role from the outset being to support the liturgical round of worship within the cathedral. This practice allowed the canons to absent themselves from the cathedral for much if not all of the year. A set of regulations of 1290 emphasized that that the vicars choral should consist of equal numbers of men who had been ordained as sub-deacons or deacons and that they must be able to sing in the choir.[6] The distinctions between these three groups, however, is an artificial one, for it becomes clear – especially after 1350 when the survival of records improves – that there was considerable overlap between the three groups of lesser clergy, in particular with many minor canons also doubling as chantry priests.

The key role of the minor canons was expressed in the papal confirmation of their incorporation as a collegiate institution. Their duty was to serve God day and night. They had been long established, but in 1353 they followed the example of the chantry

chaplains who earlier in the century had built themselves a communal residence. Such a residence must have helped to avoid some of the problems of otherwise finding lodgings in the vicinity of the cathedral. Those problems are encapsulated in the petition of one of the minor canons, Nicholas Husband, who in 1315 obtained permission to build a new residence within the precinct on complaining that his existing house was too far from the cathedral and portraying dangers from robbers and others who roamed the area by night, including a crowd of loose women.[7] While Husband's claims are likely to have been exaggerated in order to support his petition, none the less he portrays a vivid picture of the position of the cathedral in the centre of London life.

In 1356, in a charter from Dean Richard of Kilvington, it was stated that the minor canons excelled all other chaplains in name and honour and they were able to officiate in the place of major canons at the great altar and the choir, a statement of corporate pride which was confirmed by Bishop Sudbury of London and by Pope Urban VI in 1373.[8] The position of the canons as a legal entity was finally clarified during the late fourteenth century episcopate of Ralph Braybrooke. Braybrooke took his duties *vis-à-vis* the community of clergy at St Paul's very seriously, a commitment which caused some hostility from traditionalists as he struggled to clarify hitherto obscure customs and traditions. In 1394 he instituted a formal college of minor canons at St Paul's, twelve canons in total, headed by a warden. The twelve minor canons wore surplices with 'almuces of calaber [capes lined with fur] and black cloaks' and had a common establishment with a hall for communal eating, situated just north and west of the cathedral north transept.[9] Braybrooke was in fact regularizing a situation already partially in existence. In the mid fourteenth century one of the minor canons, Robert of Kingston, had bequeathed his house to provide a common dining hall for the minor canons[10] and late fourteenth-century wills confirm that many of the minor canons already ate in a common hall. Will evidence from the same period also shows that some dwelt in separate houses, both within the churchyard and beyond its walls. The minor canons continued to build upon this and in 1395–6 they defined their rules and customs and obtained a charter of incorporation from Richard II (Fig. 85).[11]

Braybrooke's reforms, made in the turbulent conditions of the later fourteenth century, were important because they gave the college of minor canons a legal identity as a community with a common seal and a common chest in which they could safeguard their documents and records. Although the minor canons remained subject to the dean and chapter, this move by Bishop Braybrooke marked an important step in ensuring their self-identity. As a corporation, they could communally own property. Lands and rents dedicated to their upkeep were listed in the 1404 papal confirmation of Braybrooke's actions.[12] A grant of Pope John XXIII in the early fifteenth century clarified the minor canons' position as far as holding benefices was concerned.[13] Each was allowed to hold for life, in addition to his canonry and minor prebend, a chantry in the cathedral and a parish church or other benefice involving cure of souls which required personal residence. This stipulation – that minor canons could hold chantries – must have both further blurred the distinction between the three groups of lesser clergy and increased the tension or rivalry between the vicars choral and the chantry priests.

The papacy was supportive of the needs to provide for liturgical service in the cathedral despite the competing claims of the city's numerous parish churches. A papal grant of 1418 granted automatic permission for the minor canons to draw upon the fruits of their benefices held elsewhere as if resident and allowed them to farm out the benefices if they were outside the diocese of London.[14] Thus many minor canons would have had a fairly substantial income. While these men were described as 'minor canons', in fact they would have seen themselves – and would have been seen by others – as winners in the race for promotion in an age when far more men were being ordained to the priesthood than there were benefices to support them. Across England as a whole, the supply of clergy far exceeded the availability of benefices; for the late thirteenth century, it has been estimated that there were four or five men being ordained per parish.[15]

There was no shortage of clergy in late medieval England, although some of those ordained had limited education and few prospects of attaining high office within the church, or even a parochial benefice. It has been suggested that in the last quarter of the fourteenth century the majority of the clergy being ordained were unbeneficed.[16] The clerical poll taxes of 1379–81 demon-

strate this clearly, showing that many London churches had at least five or six chaplains attached to them, men who would assist in the liturgical round of the worship in the parish.[17] In the parish church of St Mildred Bread Street, 300 yards from the cathedral, in 1379 there were seven chaplains in addition to the rector. The surviving records from William Coleyn, the man responsible for collecting the 1381 tax from the clergy of St Paul's and the extensive territory of its peculiar jurisdiction, point to both the scale and diversity of lesser clergy connected with the cathedral. Each of the beneficed clergy on his list owed 6s. 8d., and the others lesser sums.[18] The image which emerges from the clerical poll tax of this period is that of a city and hinterland in which a great variety of clergy were active in many different roles.

The activities of the late medieval minor canons are relatively well documented in the surviving codes of statutes. They were expected to have been ordained as priests and they annually elected a warden from amongst their number. In addition, they were proactive in choosing new members whenever a vacancy occurred, assembling and choosing two potential replacements to be nominated to the dean and chapter, who would choose between them. The sub-dean was the most important of the canons, a position recognized by Bishop William Warham's grant of a privilege to him that he might wear grey fur, as the great canons did. The sub-dean was chosen from amongst the minor canons by the dean. The second and third minor canons, who had the title, unusual outside Rome, of 'cardinals', were responsible for discipline amongst the minor canons; they were expected to monitor attendance and punctuality at the services. They ate communally, listening to a reading from the Bible at dinner-time. They were expected to be within the precincts of the cathedral by 9 o'clock in summer and by 8 o'clock in winter, the statues expressing concern that thus they would be refreshed to perform their key role of serving God. The statutes were also concerned to regulate the activities of the canons, and various breaches of the statutes – from frequenting taverns to brawling with fellow canons or refusing to serve in an office within the college – were punished by fines. The statutes present a picture of what was expected of men living such a communal religious collegiate life.[19]

Some of the minor canons were rectors of churches close to the cathedral, the closest being the parish church of St Faith, which was within the cathedral fabric. Nicholas Overton, one of the most senior of the minor canons (junior cardinal 1413–29; senior cardinal 1429–37, minor canon 1437–45) was also rector of St Mildred Bread Street,[20] whose proximity to the cathedral may have meant his parishioners saw something of him. Others held benefices in more distant parts of the country. John Seton, a minor canon from *c.*1437–42, was also the rector of Crewkerne in Somerset. His contemporary Walter Adam was a minor canon from May 1435 until his death in 1445, by which time he was sub-dean of the minor canons, and was also rector of the Northamptonshire church of Middleton Cheney for part of this period.[21]

Those who were minor canons were very rarely *en route* to the position of canon. The two groups can better be seen as on parallel roads, with those holding cathedral prebends doing so primarily as rewards for royal or ecclesiastical service elsewhere and those holding minor canonries being men who were committed to the liturgical service of the church. How did one become a minor canon? Many of them had come up through the route of vicar choral. The vicars choral were expected to be of the clerical rank of sub-deacon or deacon and the records of London ordination lists bear this out.[22] An analysis of lists of men who are described at the moment of their ordination as either vicar choral or minor canon of St Paul's makes it is clear that this rule was adhered to, with no one being ordained as a priest who is described as vicar choral. A substantial number of those initially described in the ordination lists as vicars choral had become minor canons by the time they were ordained as priests. Richard Hokyngton, who was described as a vicar choral at ordinations in 1386 and again in 1391, is listed as a minor canon by 1394, when he was ordained priest. Hokyngton then spent his career as a minor canon until his death in 1429, by which stage he had attained the rank of senior cardinal or second minor canon.[23] Likewise, John Goode was initially described in 1420 and 1421 as a vicar choral and subsequently from 1423 as a minor canon, a position he retained for the remainder of his career, holding it alongside benefices as indicated above.[24] So, one route to a position as minor canon was by becoming a vicar choral though the patronage of the major canons. An alternative route was through the practice of the exchange of benefices between clerics, a popular late-medieval practice, the mechanisms of which are not fully understood.[25] Thus Robert Gervays was a minor canon from 1384 to 1393, when he exchanged his position with one John Horewode, rector of Rotherfield Greys in Oxfordshire, becoming the rector of Rotherfield Greys while Horewode joined the ranks of the minor canons. Horewode retained that position until 1405 when he exchanged again, moving away from St Paul's.[26]

Individual experiences and backgrounds show how men joined this group of minor clergy. Martin Elys was a minor canon who died the year before Bishop Braybrooke's reforms took effect. His background was that of a family of wax chandlers in London, but in this he may have been unusual because it is difficult to trace connections between many minor canons and established London families. Elys's will clearly demonstrates his commitment to the cathedral as the central focus of his life.[27] He wished to be buried in the churchyard dedicated to the canons and he left bequests to the canons, the minor canons, chaplains of the cathedral and other clergy. Income from rents and houses was gifted to the dean and chapter. His fellow minor canons were left his library, which was extensive for the period, and his silver, brass and pewter utensils, while he left his chalice and portfiroy with music to the church of St Faith, of which he had been rector for nearly thirty years. Fellow minor canons to whom he was evidently close received sums of money and household goods. Despite his London background, Elys had connections beyond the city and left the Hertfordshire abbey of St Albans a precious image of silver gilt representing the Resurrection. His distinctive spirituality seems to be expressed in his bequests to the highly devout Carthusian order. Humble, or cautious, to the end, he requested the seal of the Court of Canterbury be fixed to his last testament in place of his own 'little known' seal. The picture which emerges from Elys's will is one of a man with a strong commitment, primarily to St Paul's but also to other elements of the church in England. He was also well educated, to the extent that he owned Latin books and may have attended Oxford or Cambridge, although there is no other evidence that he did so.

Chantry priests were a distinctive group of clergy in many late-medieval English churches, great or small. Their services were needed and desired by many testators, especially in the two centuries following the Black Death. Those testators who could afford to made provisions in their wills to establish a permanent chantry where a priest would say daily masses for their souls in perpetuity. St Paul's Cathedral, as the mother church of the diocese of London and a focus for worship within the city itself, had a very large number of chantries.[28] Some had been established by the men and women of the city and the diocese, but the majority were founded by cathedral clergy rather than Londoners, a reflection of the fact that many Londoners had a closer spiritual relationship with their own city parish church than the huge cathedral situated in their midst. One result of the clerical domination of the foundations in St Paul's was that the majority of the chantries were in the gift of the dean and chapter, who chose the chantry priests. A fourteenth-century list of chantries lists seventy-three chantries with their values and the names of the contemporary chaplains; by the time of the dissolution of the chantries in 1548, there were thirty-four chantries with a gross annual value of nearly £650, served by forty-seven chaplains.

Not everyone who wanted to found a chantry in the cathedral or in parish churches was able to do so; some with lesser assets at their disposal founded obits, anniversary masses for souls. Some men who set out to found chantries left endowments which were not adequate to realize their intentions, especially with the collapse in land values after the mid fourteenth-century pestilences. In the late fourteenth century the reforming bishop of London, Robert Braybrooke, expressed his concern that the chantries in the cathedral were too poor to sustain the clergy who served them. Bishop Braybrooke feared that these clergy might either bring the church into disrepute by their impoverished existence or neglect the chantries while they sought to enhance their income elsewhere. He felt that some of the chantries must be united if their resources were adequately to support their priests. With royal permission, in 1391 Bishop Braybrooke amalgamated the chantries in twos and threes to provide an income which was often substantially above the recommended stipend of seven marks (£4 13s. 4d.) p. a. stipulated by the archbishop some years previously. Braybrooke combined fifty-nine chantries into twenty-seven groups.[29] This meant that the men serving the chantries were often well rewarded and might have been expected to have been committed to their posts. Braybrooke reinforced this by forbidding those holding benefices from also holding a chantry, although he exempted the minor canons from this prohibition. Nearly fifteen years earlier, in 1378, Archbishop Sudbury had denounced the poor moral standing of chantry priests throughout his province of Canterbury and their greed and gluttony. Sudbury proposed to deal with this by reducing the chaplains' stipends to seven marks a year or to board and three marks.[30] This attack on the lifestyle and income of the chantry priests is hard to reconcile either with the evidence of the income available to chantry priests or with Bishop Braybrooke's concern about the poverty of St Paul's priests. Archbishop Sudbury's concern may partly have arisen not as a result of dealing with the chantry priests of St Paul's, with whom he would have been familiar from his period as bishop of London (1362–75), but rather from a wider concern about absenteeism from parochial benefices which became widespread after the Black Death. This problem was highlighted by Geoffrey Chaucer who, in the prologue to his Canterbury Tales, criticized rural priests who abandoned their parishes. The good parson:

> . . . sette nat his benefice to hyre
> And leet his sheep encombred in the myre
> And ran to Londoun, unto Seinte Poules
> To seken him a chaunterie for soules,
> Or with a bretherhed to been witholde.[31]

Concern for the effective regulation of the body of chantry priests at St Paul's Cathedral continued to be expressed by successive deans of London, not least because this group formed a substantial proportion of the lesser clergy attached to the cathedral. The wealth of the cathedral made it a focus for criticism of the clergy, not least as the late-medieval reformers attempted to renew the English church from within. Early in the sixteenth century, Dean John Colet tackled the perceived problems of the body of chantry priests and the other cathedral clergy who he felt were failing to live up to their calling. In a famous convocation sermon preached in 1512, Colet complained that priests were more attracted by ideas of greed and gain rather than religious devotion; he identified the wealth of the cathedral as a major part of the problem. Colet had found that many priests attached to the cathedral were more concerned with hunting, sports, plays and other leisure activities rather than devotion and, in an attempt to tackle the abuses, in particular of the lesser clergy, he drew up new statutes to regulate each group of the cathedral clergy.[32] As part of his reforming programme, Colet also produced a corpus of extracts from the collected statutes to provide an easily accessible code of statutes so that chantry chaplains could not plead ignorance of what was expected of them.

The dean and chapter of St Paul's possessed the advowsons – that is, the right to present the incumbent – of a wide range of parish churches within the city and diocese of London and beyond the diocesan boundaries. Within the city itself, after 1300, they were able to present the priests to nineteen parish churches.[33] Outside the city, they held the right to present to valuable parochial benefices such as, for example, St Martin's in West Drayton in Middlesex. Twenty-four parishes within the diocese can be identified as being under the patronage of the cathedral chapter in the fifteenth century.[34] They also were patrons of other parish churches situated elsewhere in England. This reservoir of patronage offered the chapter of the cathedral a resource with which to reward those connected with the cathedral, formally and informally, as the close examination of a number of benefices demonstrates.

No parochial benefice was closer to St Paul's Cathedral than the church of St Faith in the western part of the crypt under the choir. It served as a parish church for stationers and others dwelling in the north churchyard and in an adjoining area outside the precinct. Given its situation, it is hardly surprising to find that some, at least, of its rectors were drawn from men closely connected with the cathedral; in the fourteenth century, these included the minor canon Martin Elys whose career has been detailed above. By the fifteenth century, the parish church appears to have become a resource for men who were also prebendaries of the cathedral such as Richard Hayman and John Forster, canon from 1481 until his death, who also held the St Paul's benefice of St Peter le Poor from 1484.[35]

The dean and chapter did not have complete control over the holders of the benefices in their gift. A late-medieval culture in which incumbents of benefices exchanged their benefices between themselves, with fairly nominal reference to the patrons concerned, meant that benefices might change hands rapidly after the initial presentation had been made. This was the case in the church of St Gregory, adjoining the south side of the cathedral. From 1398 to 1423, this parish church had a long period of stability under its parish priest, John Tykhill.[36] Tykhill had been a priest serving the chantry of Isabel Bukerel in St Paul's, but he resigned the chantry on being presented to the parish church, presumably because to hold both positions would not have met with Bishop Braybrooke's approval. Tykhill had had long experience of the London churches since in 1381 he was one of the chaplains at St Mildred's Bread Street, which was also in the gift of St Paul's. On Tykhill's death, chapter presented Hugh Bramburgh to St Gregory's and within two years Bramburgh had exchanged it for the Leicestershire benefice of Thurcaston.[37] His successor, Richard Ulverston, held it for only a few months before a further exchange brought to the parish a high-flying doctor of theology, Thomas Chace, who was to hold it from 1426 to 1437. The appointment of this highly educated priest, however, was to be of little benefit to the parishioners of St Gregory's, since Chace was already chancellor of the cathedral, ex-chancellor of the University of Oxford and held many benefices throughout the country as well as being chaplain to Humphrey, duke of Gloucester. He was elected, but not confirmed, as bishop of Meath in 1434, and went on to be Chancellor of Ireland. In 1437 Chace exchanged St Gregory's for the Essex parish of High Ongar.[38] The dean and chapter's churches elsewhere in the diocese of London were equally subject to the ebb and flow of individual ecclesiastical careers with 'chop-church' exchanges rather than the active choice of chapter determining who the actual rectors were. Thus, the parish church of Stoke Newington was held in 1414 by William Battysford, who exchanged it the following year with John Wrastlyngworth.[39] Wrastlyngworth within a year exchanged it again with Walter Stoning, who moved on to Wallingford in Berkshire, again within a year. The chapter as patrons would have formally accepted the changes, but appear to have had little to do with the selection or the incumbent.

When the dean and chapter did have a vacancy and an opportunity to present, what lay behind their choice of men to present? Most lucrative benefices tended to be used to reward men already senior in the church or with influential connections with the Crown or aristocracy. Analysis of the ways in which the dean and chapter used their reserves of patronage indicates no particular patterns of preference, such as, for example, the promotion of Londoners. At any time, the body of powerful and well-connected senior churchmen would have had many petitioners for benefices from amongst their entourages and connections and might have been seeking to reward men or to strengthen links with the king, with major aristocratic figures and with influential London figures. The decisions which lay behind each individual presentation to a benefice must have been influenced on every occasion by a range of considerations. The needs of the parishioners in many, perhaps the majority, of cases would not have been a major factor, although care is likely to have been taken to ensure that the parishioners were adequately served and that the resources existed to ensure that a vicar would be paid. In their patronage of the lesser clergy, the dean and chapter thus followed principles similar to those by which they themselves had obtained their positions.

15

FRATERNITIES: A CASE STUDY OF THE JESUS GUILD

Elizabeth New

In 1459 the Jesus Guild met in the crypt of St Paul's and was formally established there 'until a better [place] be provided';[1] in fact, the fraternity remained within the cathedral until its final dissolution a century later. The location of the guild was not as rare as might be supposed, for a number of fraternities met within St Paul's, and laymen established guilds in several other English cathedrals.[2] What was unusual about the fraternity of the Holy Name was the way in which it was integrated into the liturgical life of St Paul's. The exceptional survival of the early sixteenth-century records of the fraternity of the Holy Name allows a rare insight into the activities of a voluntary association, largely composed of the laity, which chose to meet and worship within the cathedral in the century before the Reformation.[3]

The idea of the 'Holy Name' – that is, reverence to and acknowledgement of the inherent power in the name Jesus – formed part of Christian tradition from the earliest times,[4] while the use of the 'sacred monogram' (usually IHS or IHC from the Greek $IH\Sigma OY\Sigma$, Jesus, and XPC from *XPICTOC*, Christ) to represent the Holy Name were used throughout the Christian world.[5] There was a long tradition of devotion to the Holy Name in the western church, but it was not until the late thirteenth century that a cult began to evolve.[6] The fourteenth century saw a rapid development of the devotion across western Europe, and it soon gained widespread popularity in England.[7] The earliest known text of the mass of Jesus in England is found in a missal of *c.*1383,[8] and during the first half of the fifteenth century it became popular throughout the country.[9] Masses were at first instigated mainly by individuals or family groups, but from the mid-fifteenth century many were supported by religious guilds, the Fraternity of the Holy Name in St Paul's being one of the earliest.

In 1450 Dean Thomas Lisieux requested burial within 'the chapel of Our Lord and Saviour Jesus in the great crypt'.[10] Unfortunately, it is not clear whether this chapel was established before, or in conjunction with, the fraternity. Otherwise, our earliest evidence for the existence of the Jesus Guild is from the 1455 will of Thomas Batail, a London mercer.[11] Dean John Colet supervised a reorganization of the fraternity in 1507, in response to mismanagement which had left the guild in financial difficulty and led to a neglect of religious services. Colet may also have seen the fraternity as a way to improve the liturgical and musical standards in St Paul's, and to encourage the laity to use the cathedral.[12] Under Colet, new ordinances were drawn up, with an emphasis upon correct liturgical observance and organizational responsibility, and the guild thrived until its dissolution in 1547. The fraternity was revived under Queen Mary in 1556 and reorganized once again, with a greater role for priests and strong links with the parish of St Faith, elements which had been absent from the pre-1547 foundation.[13] The guild was finally dissolved three years later, following the accession of Elizabeth I.

The early sixteenth-century records of the fraternity reveal a wealthy guild with complex patterns of income and expenditure. The annual income varied, but increased from £144 6s. 8d. in 1514–15 to £408 1s. 7½d. in 1534–5. Bequests were received on an irregular basis and the guild had a small amount of land and property which it leased out, but the main source of income was the 'farm of devotions', payments made by individuals or groups for the right to collect the offerings made to the guild within particular dioceses in return for prayers and remembrance at its services. These farmers operated throughout the land, from Durham to Canterbury, Chichester and Exeter, and even (unsuccessfully) in Ireland. The money generated in this way usually accounted for over half the total income.

The religious observances of the fraternity were set out in the ordinances, and the accounts show that these were carefully followed. The most important day in the liturgical calendar of the guild was the feast of the Holy Name (7 August), although the Transfiguration (6 August) was also celebrated. The subdean, the other eleven minor canons, eight chantry priests, six vicars choral and ten choristers of St Paul's were to be present at the services on these feasts.[14] All the clerics, with the exception of the subdean, stayed after high mass on the feast of the Holy Name to sing *Placebo* and *Dirige*, and returned on the following day to celebrate a requiem mass for the departed brothers and sisters of the fraternity. In addition, a vicar and the choristers sang antiphons before images of Jesus, the Blessed Virgin and St Sebastian every evening and a mass of Jesus was celebrated by one of the cathedral cardinals (the second and third of the minor canons, responsible for discipline in the choir) each Friday.[15]

The chapel of Jesus occupied the eastern part of the crypt below the New Work, the western part of which was used as the parish church of St Faith (p. 136).[16] The appearance of the chapel can be gleaned from the accounts. Its walls, pillars and vault were plastered and limewashed and decorated with the sacred monogram, while a great Jesus light (probably a candelabrum) and numerous candles and torches, in addition to several windows, would have made the undercroft a bright place. The chapel housed four altars (dedicated to Jesus, the Blessed Virgin, St Anne and St Sebastian), a number of statues and several tombs, including that of Margaret, Countess of Shrewsbury (d.1468).[17]

The Jesus Guild maintained a considerable collection of vestments and the chapel was equipped with most types of liturgical plate, ranging from cruets to a holy water stock. In 1529 the fraternity bought four new chalices costing £12 3s.; it is no surprise that in the same year a lockable 'hamper' was also purchased.[18] In addition to the vestments and plate, the number and variety of books owned by the fraternity highlight a concern for a high standard of worship. The Jesus chapel housed a pair of organs,[19] which not only emphasizes the wealth of the fraternity but also the importance placed upon music in the liturgy of the Holy Name.[20] The Jesus Guild employed the choristers of St Paul's to sing in the chapel, and on occasion paid the choristers of the Chapel Royal to attend important services. The fraternity also possessed different settings of the Jesus mass, one written by the renowned composer Robert Fayrfax.[21]

The accounts and testamentary evidence contain the names of almost 250 individuals involved with the guild.[22] The great majority were Londoners, but there was a wide spread of other members from the Midlands, southern England and the southwest. There was a notable group from the borders of Wales, perhaps drawn in through connections with the Countess of Shrewsbury and her relative Lord Sudeley, both of whom were associated with the fraternity. This aristocratic element, however, was small by comparison with the numbers from London companies who dominated the membership. The guild had no formal links with any particular craft except, perhaps, the Waxchandlers' Company, which held its annual elections, mass and obits in the Jesus chapel on the feasts of the Transfiguration and Name of Jesus. The company also supplied wax for the chapel and assisted with the maintenance of the fittings, in return receiving liveries with the sacred monogram.[23] The Mercers' Company, however, provided by far the largest number of members of the fraternity, and other members came from a wide variety of occupations, ranging from haberdashers, merchant tailors and goldsmiths to innkeepers, tallow chandlers and shearmen. Clergy were also involved with the guild. The dean of St Paul's was *ex officio* rector of the fraternity, but several deans demonstrated an exceptional interest in the guild: Roger Radcliff (d.1471), for example, asked to be buried in the *le crowdes* (the undercroft) of St Paul's. Four other priests requested burial in the chapel, including an archdeacon of Middlesex, a dean of the Court of Arches, and a subdean of St Paul's.[24]

The fraternity was well represented in the highest levels of London civic society and included five London knights, four mayors and fifteen aldermen among its members.[25] Some of these individuals were very wealthy: John Aleyn, a London mercer and active member of the guild, was in 1541 assessed for tax upon goods worth £3,000.[26] The London members resided in many different parts of the city. Thus the forty-four brothers and sisters whose parishes of residence can be identified lived in thirty-one different parishes. This was in contrast to most London guilds, which drew their membership largely from within their own parish or craft communities.[27] Indeed, the parish of St Faith, whose parishioners worshiped within the cathedral crypt, does not appear to have provided any members of the fraternity before its refoundation in 1556.

In common with other English religious guilds, the fraternity of the Holy Name was open to both men and women of good character who wished to enjoy the spiritual and temporal benefits offered, although it differed from most guilds in several ways.[28] Perhaps of greatest significance was the lack of material and postmortem support for members of the Jesus Guild, something which was in marked contrast to the majority of fraternities.[29] The Jesus Guild offered a variety of religious celebrations, prayers and an indulgence, but no tangible benefits such as funerary provision or help in times of need, support which was offered by most of London's parish guilds.[30] Instead, it offered a popular dedication and services performed in some splendour by numerous cathedral clergy in fine vestments, to the accompaniment of organ music. Few fraternities could provide such an impressive liturgy, reformed by one of Europe's leading theologians (Colet) and based around an immensely popular devotional feast, and certainly no London parish guild could afford this. The fraternity of the Holy Name in St Paul's cathedral provided a form of spiritual commonality and liturgical refinement which could be found nowhere else in London.

16

THE CHANTRY CHAPEL OF ROGER OF WALTHAM

Lucy Freeman Sandler

Medieval chantries were endowments by pious individuals that were intended to provide the funds for priests to celebrate masses and recite the Divine Office on behalf of the living and the dead in perpetuity, in the hope of shortening their time in Purgatory. The great era of chantry foundation was the thirteenth and fourteenth centuries.[1] By the end of this period at St Paul's Cathedral fifty-seven chantries had been founded, primarily for bishops of London, cathedral officers and canons and their relatives.[2] Ordinarily, the chantry priests performed their liturgical ceremonies at one of the many existing altars of the church. Only a few chantries were housed in purpose-built structures.[3] Among these was the chantry founded by the fourteenth-century canon of St Paul's, Roger of Waltham. The sixteenth-century antiquary John Leland wrote that Roger's chantry chapel, his 'oratory', was famous there, and that its sculptures and paintings were described in a book (now lost) he had seen in the cathedral.[4]

In fact, the chantry chapel of Roger of Waltham was among the earliest such structures at St Paul's, and the only one of which a contemporary description exists. The description is preserved in the texts of several agreements between Roger and the dean and chapter of St Paul's, originally kept in the cathedral treasury in a box containing all the documentation relating to Roger's endowment.[5] Duplicate copies of the charters and ordinances were once kept at the abbey of Holy Cross at Waltham, Essex, where Roger had probably been born.[6]

Roger of Waltham became a canon of St Paul's around 1306.[7] He held the prebend of Caddington Minor until his death in 1341.[8] Canons of St Paul's were often employed in the royal administration and Roger of Waltham was no exception; he is recorded as serving Edward II in several capacities between 1322 and 1325.[9] Apart from his official positions, Roger is known as the author of a political treatise for the instruction of rulers, the *Compendium morale*.[10] This work survives in more than fifteen copies.[11] According to Leland, it was widely circulated and one copy was still at St Paul's in the sixteenth century.[12] Added to the main text in some copies of the *Compendium morale* are a number of devotional texts, reflecting the pious side of Roger's interests.[13] The same pieces are found in another compilation, the most personal revelation of Roger's piety, a unique manuscript produced between 1325 and 1335.[14] The volume contains numerous devotional texts in prose and verse, in addition to moral exempla and other extracts from Seneca's writings, and a summary of the scientific and philosophical works attributed to Aristotle. Written throughout in an expert court hand (the kind of script used for royal documents), the first part is richly illustrated with initials and large miniatures that include representations of Roger at prayer before the sacred objects of his devotion, and the two further parts are joined by a full-page 'philosophical Trinity' showing Plato, Seneca and Aristotle.[15] The volume is clearly stamped as Roger of Waltham's own, personal book not only by its repeated images of Roger himself, in the robes of a cathedral canon, but by his own words, written on scrolls held in his hands, with texts begging the sacred figures to whom he is shown praying to intercede on his behalf (Fig. 86).

Roger of Waltham's personal miscellany dates from the same decade as his chantry chapel, whose first beginnings were in 1325 when Roger was licensed to alienate in mortmain to the dean and chapter properties in the city of London with a total value of £8 6s. 8d. a year.[16] The dean and chapter were to use the funds to establish a perpetual chantry for his soul and the souls of his relatives and his first patron, Antony Bek, bishop of Durham

(d. 1311).[17] The endowment of the chantry was increased in 1326 by Roger's grant of a messuage worth £3 6s. 8d. a year.[18]

Roger's endowments of 1325 and 1326 provided for a first and then a second priest to recite the daily office and the office of the dead, and other prayers, and to celebrate masses with collects for Roger, both before and after his death. The funds were also to be used for housing the priests, for sets of ecclesiastical vestments, altar furnishings and liturgical books, for payments to minor canons and vicars choral for participation in solemn processions and masses on the feasts of the Invention and the Exaltation of the Cross, and the birth of St John the Baptist, and for the distribution of alms to 100 poor people at ten feasts a year.[19]

Roger's chantry occupied two sites in succession within the cathedral. The first, like that of most other chantries founded at St Paul's in the thirteenth and early fourteenth centuries, was a pre-existing altar in the chapel of St John the Evangelist in the south transept, already a popular altar for chantries.[20] By July 1329, however, Roger's chantry had been moved to 'the altar of St. Lawrence newly constructed by him [Roger] at the back of the eastern end of the choir on the south side'.[21] Such a construction was apparently envisaged in the ordinance for the chantry of March 1329, which noted Roger's 'former' establishment of a chantry at the altar of St John and then detailed new provisions for ceremonial processions on feast days, including that of St Lawrence, as if in anticipation of the building of a new altar in honour of the martyr-saint.[22] In October of the same year, the form of the chantry was described as 'an altar, or rather chapel',[23] suggesting an enclosing structure, and a document of 1332 described this structure as an oratory (*oratorium*).[24]

This new structure was built in honour of God, the Virgin Mary, St Lawrence and All Saints and its altar was dedicated to St Lawrence.[25] St Paul's had not previously had an altar solely dedicated to St Lawrence, but the cathedral did possess a valuable portable reliquary shrine of the saint (p. 119).[26] When the altar in Roger's chantry chapel was dedicated to St Lawrence, this shrine may have been given a fixed home.

On the beam of the chapel, either inside the structure or over the entrance door, there were seven candles, each weighing two pounds, to be lit every Sunday at high mass, at every mass celebrated for Roger in the chapel, and whenever feast-day processions approached the structure. These candles were to be replaced on major feasts of the Virgin from the oblations of the faithful collected in locked boxes both within and outside the chapel.[27]

The interior of the chapel was ornamented with statues of the Deity and angels, St John the Baptist and St Lawrence, and the eastern end of the exterior with a statue of St Mary Magdalen. The eastern wall behind the altar was painted with the Joys of the Virgin — the Annunciation, Nativity or Adoration of the Magi, the Resurrection and Ascension of Christ, and the Assumption of the Virgin. In vault of the chapel were paintings of the celestial hierarchy — evidently the deity, angels and saints.[28]

The document of 1332 also describes a 'glorious tabernacle' built on the south aisle wall of the choir opposite the chapel. This tabernacle contained a sculptured tableau of the Nativity, including statues of the seated Virgin, the Christ Child in a cradle between reclining figures of the ox and the ass, and St Joseph seated at the foot of the Virgin. Surmounting the arch over this group was a statue of the standing Virgin with the Christ Child in her arms. In addition, on a transverse beam between the 'head' (the altar end) of the oratory and the Nativity group, were crowned statues of the Saviour and the Virgin seated in a

86. Roger of Waltham praying before the Coronation of the Virgin, as if before the tabernacle opposite his chantry chapel in the cathedral; from a compilation of texts expressing his personal piety, c.1330. (Glasgow University, MS Hunter 231, p. 83)

tabernacle — a Coronation or Triumph of the Virgin — and standing statues of the virgin martyrs Katherine and Margaret. According to one interpretation of the document of 1332, the area between the oratory structure and the wall tabernacle, evidently below the transverse beam with its Coronation of the Virgin, was to be the site of Roger's burial. On the other hand, this part of the document could be interpreted as primarily an agreement to prohibit burial in that space, on account of the fragility of the vault (perhaps of the crypt below), except to stagiaries and those with the special permission of chapter, the reference to Roger's intended burial place (which may have been above floor level in the chapel) simply denoting the general locality (*in precinctu illius loci*). Unlike the wall tabernacle, whose figures and enclosing arch probably projected in relief, the grouping on the transverse beam most likely consisted of free-standing figures carved in the round, placed under a four-sided canopy. To span the aisle, the beam would have had to have been supported from below, perhaps by a screen-like arched opening, and to lighten the load, it seems probable that the carved figures were executed in wood rather than stone.

The agreements between Roger of Waltham and the dean and chapter supply a uniquely detailed contemporary description of an elaborate work of art in which sculpture and painting were integrated in an architectural setting. Had Roger's chantry chapel survived, it would undoubtedly have been a work of surpassing magnificence. The only work that still stands to which Roger's chantry can possibly be compared is the Percy tomb-chapel of *c*.1340 in Beverley Minster.[29]

Detailed as the fourteenth-century descriptions may be, they leave open questions of the precise site of the oratory, its form and the arrangement of its constituent elements. In the seventeenth century, John Weever observed that the tomb of Sir William Cockayne, built in 1626 and still partly preserved in the crypt of the Wren cathedral, had been erected on the site of 'an altar built to the honour of God, the blessed virgin, St. Lawrence, and all saints, by one Roger Waltham'.[30] He transcribed the altar inscription, probably from a memorial tablet,[31] and although his transcription is faulty and incomplete, the original phrasing echoes that of the surviving documents for Roger's oratory, mentioning the existence of painted vaults and statues, the seven candles and the provisions for alms. Cockayne's tomb (no. 17 in Hollar's plan of St Paul's) was sited against the back of the choir stalls in the fourth bay, just before the steps that rose towards the high altar in the presbytery (Fig. 67).[32]

The position of the Cockayne tomb fixes the site of Roger of Waltham's chantry chapel. It was on the outside of the choir enclosure. The solid backs of the choir stalls would have formed one side of a projecting structure that had an interior and exterior adorned with statues, like later 'closet' chantries.[33] The vaulted interior (*volta*) again presaged later chantry structures. The materials used, according to the document of 1332, were both stone and wood,[34] recalling the wide use of stone for the lower parts of tombs, rood screens and chantry chapel walls, and wood not only for their finely carved figural and decorative components but also for their upper structural parts, such as vaults of tomb canopies.

The consecration of the high altar in the newly rebuilt choir of St Paul's took place in 1327.[35] This great ceremonial event may have provided the impetus for Roger of Waltham to transfer his chantry to a purpose-built altar and enclosure in the south aisle of the new choir. This structure had been begun by July 1329 and finally, by August 1332, as a complete oratory, had been further elaborated into a richly sculptured complex spanning the south aisle of the choir and projecting from the aisle wall itself.[36]

Completion of Roger's chantry chapel probably coincided with the erection of the pulpitum surmounted by a Crucifixion group at the entrance to the new choir,[37] a structure whose details, to the extent they are recorded in Hollar's engraving (Fig. 76), seem to bridge the Decorated and the Perpendicular styles. Roger's chantry chapel could well have had similar design features. But his foundation was not to last for ever. In 1391 the income supporting Roger's two chantry priests was consolidated by Bishop Braybrooke with that yielded by the thirteenth-century chantry foundation of Bishop Fulk Basset and his brother Philip Basset, chief justiciar.[38] From then on, one priest performed the duties and received the income formerly shared by three. Along with the rest of the chantries at St Paul's, Roger of Waltham's was suppressed in 1547[39] and its physical substance destroyed in 1552.[40]

17

THE HOUSEHOLD AND DAILY LIFE OF THE DEAN IN THE FIFTEENTH CENTURY

Hannes Kleineke and Stephanie Hovland

By the later Middle Ages, the deanery of St. Paul's was one of the most important non-episcopal benefices in England, and its incumbent could expect to lead a lifestyle to rival that of some of the wealthiest of laymen. Records illustrative of the domestic establishments and daily life of the greater clergy of late medieval England are scarce, but in the instance of St Paul's the fortunate survival of an almost complete run of the accounts of the receiver general of William Worsley (dean 1478–99) dating from 1479 to 1497 provides a rare insight into the life of the dean and his household.

Within the city, the base of this household was a mansion in the cathedral precinct (p. 23). Some deans also maintained a separate establishment further afield, but within easy reach of London. When William Worsley was not in residence at the cathedral or occupied elsewhere in England, he often stayed in a house at Hackney, perhaps the building later known as 'Brooke House'.[1]

In the fifteenth century, the members of the dean's household usually numbered between twenty-five and thirty.[2] Many of the servants were drawn from London families, but they invariably also included kinsmen of the deans themselves. Among the household servants of William Say (dean 1457–68) was his nephew William, and William Worsley in later life employed his kinsmen Edmund Worsley and Philip Booth as joint receivers.[3] There was some continuity between the establishments of successive deans: a certain James Ratherford served both Roger Radclyffe (dean 1468–71) and Worsley, and a younger kinsman and namesake of Dean Radclyffe officiated as Worsley's receiver for much of his career at St. Paul's.[4]

The organization of the dean's household appears to have followed common contemporary patterns. At the head of Dean Worsley's establishment, Roger Radclyffe combined the office of steward of the household with his duties as receiver general. There is less definite evidence of the departmental organization of the household below this official, but the subdivision of items of expenditure in Worsley's accounts suggests that there was a separate kitchen, which took charge of the establishment's supply with foodstuffs, a buttery, responsible for wine and ale, and a stable, headed by the keeper of the horses. Responsibility for Worsley's extensive annual purchases of clothing and napery appears to have been divided between a chamberlain, who controlled the acquisition and distribution of clothing and livery for both the dean and members of the household, and a naperer responsible for other clothware.[5]

Despite their extensive pastoral duties at the cathedral, fifteenth-century deans also maintained private religious establishments. Both Thomas Lisieux (dean 1441–56) and Roger Radclyffe included their chaplains among their executors, while the will of William Say named at least three clerics among his household servants, and William Worsley paid wages to up to five chaplains at a time.[6] Some of these chaplains were recruited from among the minor clergy of the cathedral: Worsley's personal chaplains included Thomas Bromley, chaplain of the de Bruera chantry, and William Roke, a minor canon at the cathedral and chaplain of the Foliot chantry.[7] Others acquired their positions by virtue of their connections with particular institutions: Dean Worsley, who had studied at Cambridge, seems to have had a predilection for graduates of that university. At least two of his chaplains, John Slade and Thomas Watson, may have joined his household shortly after completing their studies, and two others, Thomas Smith and Thomas Turner, were probably also Cambridge men. Another chaplain, Thomas Cartwright, accompanied Worsley to London from his previous place of residency at Southwell Minster.[8]

Central to the daily activities of the household was its provision with foodstuffs and other supplies. As well as providing for the household servants, the dean was required to offer hospitality to the lesser clergy of the cathedral on a regular basis.[9] Furthermore, his public role meant that he often had to play host to important visitors, including members of the royal family. Such an event involved substantial additional expenditure. In 1481, when Dean Worsley entertained King Edward IV's stepson, Thomas Grey, marquess of Dorset, a variety of cloth items had to be acquired specially, and damaged silver plate was repaired.[10]

Even in the later fifteenth century some bread and ale were supplied by the cathedral's bakehouse and brewery as part of the dean's allowance from the common fund, but other supplies had to be purchased. Routinely, the bulk of the provisions consumed by the dean's establishment were bought from London merchants, although fuel was acquired further afield in the Home Counties and fish could on occasion be brought from markets nearer to the coast.[11] The London brewers John Essenwolde, Richard Prowell and William Whitney, as well as the unnamed owner of *le Herteshorne* (probably the brewhouse of that name near the Tower of London) and the Hackney brewer Richard Dene sold ale to Dean Worsley, while Alexander Berebrewer, master of *le Hermitage* (also near the Tower) provided him with beer. A London vintner supplied a range of wines, including claret, Malmsey and Rhenish wines.

The range of dishes consumed in the deanery was extensive. While on fast days an array of fish was served, on other days quantities of pork, beef and mutton were eaten, all enriched with a variety of spices. Far from being austere occasions, the feasts held in the presence of important guests were livened up by the performances of mimes and minstrels, formally attached to the king's court and the establishments of great lords, but specially hired for these occasions.[12] By the end of the fifteenth century, the splendid hospitality on offer at the dean's table was widely renowned, but within a few years the tradition was discontinued by the more austere John Colet (dean 1505–19).[13]

On occasion, the need to respond to events on the national stage left its mark on the life of the dean's household. The household servants were expected to be present at important occasions at the cathedral, such as the funeral of King Edward IV, for which the members of Worsley's household were provided with a special black livery.[14] At other times, duties in connection with benefices held by the dean further afield or special royal missions necessitated travel away from London. Worsley regularly visited a canonry he held at Southwell Minster and in 1481 accompanied King Edward IV on his expedition towards Scotland.[15] On such occasions, a smaller, riding household would accompany the dean, while the majority of the establishment remained behind in London.

When appearing in public, the dean's attire proclaimed his status for all to see. Richly furred gowns in a variety of colours were newly acquired for Worsley every year and could be combined with, for example, a silken girdle and modishly pointed shoes bought in 1481–2.[16] Even for the potentially strenuous journey to Scotland alongside the king, Dean Worsley ensured that the briganders (a type of body armour) worn by him and his attendant household chaplain were covered in velvet and decorated with gilded keys.[17]

The funds necessary to support the dean's activities were drawn partly from the spiritual revenues of his benefices and partly from his estates. In addition to the portion of the cathedral estates traditionally assigned to the deanery, the dean, like other stagiaries, usually took further lands to farm from the chapter. The sums at

87. Dean William Worsley (d. 1499) depicted on his brass inlay memorial at St Paul's, as drawn by Hollar for Dugdale (1658)

the dean's disposal were substantial: at the end of the fifteenth century, William Worsley's disposable annual income regularly exceeded £300 and often came to as much as £400, sums which placed the dean's household among the 200 wealthiest in late-medieval England.[18] Nevertheless, the administration of a landed estate comparable in size to that of a minor baron made further demands on the dean's time. In addition to the visitations of the chapter's churches that he was required to conduct, he might on occasion also ride around and inspect his manors and personally examine the accounts of his estate officials.[19]

Towards the end of his life, Dean William Worsley became remarkable for reasons entirely disconnected from his duties at St Paul's. For reasons now obscure, in 1495 he allowed himself to be drawn into a conspiracy seeking to depose King Henry VII and to replace him with Perkin Warbeck, the Flemish pretender who was posing as King Edward IV's younger son, Richard, duke of York. When the conspiracy was discovered, Worsley was arrested and placed in the Tower of London, where he remained for a period of sixteen weeks.[20] Uniquely, the dean's household now had to provide for its master's comfort in his unusual circumstances. A number of the household servants accompanied the dean into captivity, and various kinds of meat and fish, as well as wine and sweetmeats, were regularly sent to the Tower for Worsley's table, while the more important servants who remained outside sought to negotiate terms for the dean's release with the king.[21]

Although they eventually succeeded in this, Worsley's stay in the Tower had apparently affected his health. In the months following his release, ointment had to be provided for the dean's back, and within three years he was dead, albeit perhaps not of a broken heart on account of his disgrace, as one sixteenth-century chronicler believed.[22]

Part Three

From the Reformation to the Present

17

THE FABRIC TO 1670

Gordon Higgott

The history of the fabric of St Paul's from the end of Henry VIII's reign until the decision to build a new cathedral on new foundations in 1673 is marked by two disastrous fires, in 1561 and 1666, and two periods of iconoclasm, under Edward VI and during the Civil War and Commonwealth. The restoration of the cathedral by Inigo Jones under Charles I from 1633 to 1642 was aimed chiefly at the repair of the external stonework, which had decayed over a long period through the corrosive effect of coal smoke in the wet London atmosphere. Jones's crowning achievement was the west front and portico, built in Charles's name, but unfinished at the outbreak of Civil War in 1642 (Fig. 99). It survived only twenty-four years until gutted by the Great Fire, but its memory endured in several of Wren's designs for the new cathedral and in the detailing of the Corinthian order at the lower stage of the new building.

THE AFTERMATH OF THE REFORMATION

Save for the plundering of St Erkenwald's shrine in 1540, the fabric of the cathedral suffered little under Henry VIII, but the accession of Edward VI in 1547 heralded a wave of iconoclasm. On 17 November that year, the great rood was pulled down, and ten months later the king's commissioners began their visitation of St Paul's, when all images were removed.[1] Two months after Bishop Ridley supplanted Bonner in April 1550, he had the high altar destroyed and a wooden table set up in its place. At Easter 1551 this was moved down from the raised platform 'into the midst of the upper choir' and set, like a table, in an east–west direction. Communicants knelt around it, their privacy secured by closing up 'the iron grates of the choir on the north and south sides with brick and plaster'.[2] Just before the publication of a new prayer book on 1 November 1552, Ridley ordered the remaining altars and parclose screens in the cathedral to be destroyed, the chapels dismantled and the reredos and sedilia defaced or torn down. The Communion table was now moved 'in the lower quire where the priests sing'.[3]

The greatest act of destruction at St Paul's during Edward VI's reign was perpetrated by the Lord Protector, the Duke of Somerset, in April 1549. He demolished the Becket Chapel in the Pardon Churchyard, and 'the whole cloister, the Dance of Death, the Tombs and Monuments; so that nothing thereof was left but the bare plot of ground' (it was later converted into a garden for the petty canons).[4] Somerset used the stone for his new town house on the Strand. Only the library above the cloister on the east side was spared; its ground-floor arcade is shown against the west aisle of the north transept on a schematic plan of the pre-Fire cathedral (Fig. 89).[5]

THE FIRE OF 1561 AND ITS CONSEQUENCES

The disaster from which the cathedral was never to recover fully before the Great Fire occurred after lightning struck the spire during the afternoon of 4 June 1561. Fire burned downwards to the battlements of the steeple 'so furiously, that within the space of four hours the same steeple, with all the roofs of the church, were consumed, to the great sorrow and perpetual remembrance of the beholders'.[6] A tract published six days later describes how

88. The dome of Wren's cathedral from the south-east

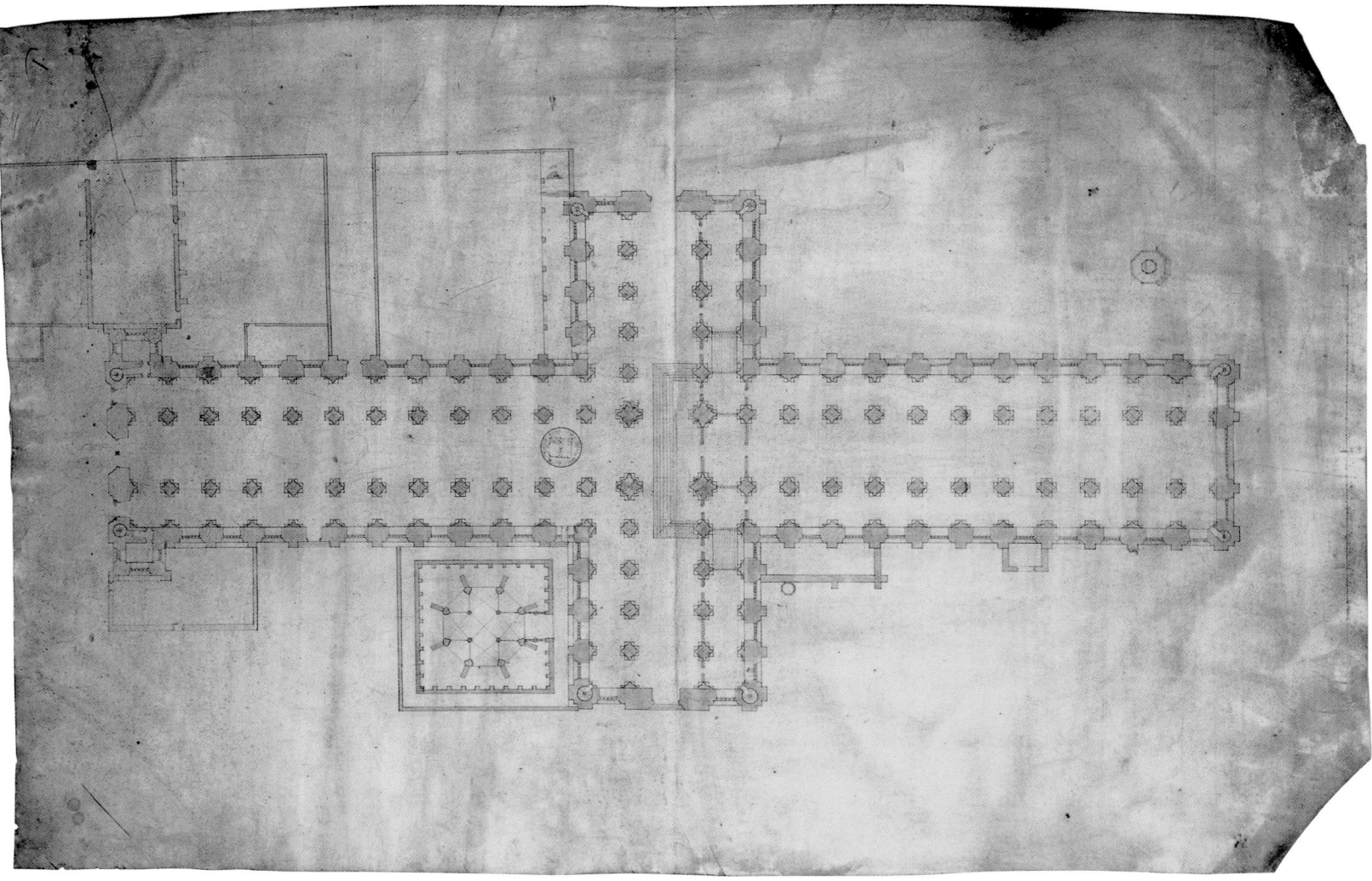

89. Ground plan *c*.1550–1630. Anonymous drawing, pen and ink on vellum. It does not show the bays of the nave and choir correctly, but is broadly consistent with the ground plan after the destruction of the Becket chapel in the Pardon Churchyard in 1549 and before Inigo Jones's restoration works, 1633–42. (AS, Wren Collection II.1)

the roofs of the nave, choir and transepts were destroyed completely, but that the vaults still stood 'unperished'.[7] When Christopher Wren surveyed the cathedral soon after the Great Fire in 1666, he concluded that falling timbers in the earlier fire had cracked these high vaults, causing a 'spreading out of the walls above ten inches in some places from their true perpendicular'; Inigo Jones had tried to correct the fault, but his recasing work had 'gon away from its perpendicular alsoe, by this second fall of the roof in this last fire', so that the building was now almost beyond repair.[8]

The initial response to the fire was one of enormous collective effort in which the Lord Keeper, Sir Nicholas Bacon, played an important role on behalf of the queen at meetings with the lord mayor, the archbishop and the bishop.[9] On 24 June the queen instructed the mayor and the Archbishop of Canterbury to impose levies on the citizens of London and the clergy of the southern province, while she herself promised a thousand marks in gold (£666 13s. 4d.) and a thousand loads of timber from the royal forests. This last commitment brought the involvement of her surveyor, John Revell, a former Master of the Carpenters' Company, who was to play a central part in the re-roofing campaign until December 1563.[10] The Carpenters' Company gained immediate approval to build temporary roofs of boarded rafters before the winter and replace them afterwards with permanent roofs. Stow wrote that 'within one Moneth next following the burning thereof, the church was covered with boord & lead, in

the manner of false roofs against the weather'.[11] This exaggerates the speed of the re-roofing work but describes what was achieved by the time of a thanksgiving service on All Saints' Day, 1 November 1561.[12] In a crude sketch by the Venetian Alessandro Magno in 1562, the tower is covered in scaffolding (a structure he mistook for a newly built timber-framed tower) but the roofs are shown intact.[13]

During a lull in carpenters' work in the first half of 1562, preparations were made for replacing the temporary roofs with permanent structures. These were pre-assembled under Revell's direction at the queen's manor at Welbeck (Notts), and also at Guisborough (Yorks), before being disassembled and shipped to London. Revell had 'the oversight of the frames and workmen', implying a role in the design of the new roofs.[14] The timbers started to arrive at St Paul's for assembly in mid 1562. The number of carpenters sharply increased from three in July to more than forty in September and October. A second phase of permanent roofing followed in March and April 1563, after which few carpenters are listed in the accounts.[15] The main problem was lack of money for new lead.[16] A plague in this year would have taken its toll on the work-force and may have killed Revell, who died after a short illness in December 1563. As a result, the second stage of the re-roofing campaign was never completed. There is no evidence in the accounts for permanent roofing of the two transepts, or anything more than a temporary structure on the crossing tower. One reason for the falling away of interest may have been that the temporary roofs over the transepts were judged good enough for the longer term. They were repaired rather than renewed in the 1630s, but their underlying fragility appears to have been exposed in 1654, when the removal of scaffolding around the tower brought down part of the south transept vault and the entire roof.

Stow writes of the steeple that 'divers models were devised and made, but little else was done, through whose default, God knoweth'.[17] John Revell's shared interest with the queen in the replacement of the spire of St Paul's is demonstrated by his New Year's gift to her in January 1562 of 'a marchpane [ceremonial sweetmeat] with a model of Powle's Church and steeple in paste'.[18] It is likely that he drew (or at least procured) the remarkable colour-washed design for a new spire for St Paul's that bears the date 1562 beneath an aedicule containing a statue of St Paul (Fig. 90).[19] The design is for a timber structure, clad almost entirely in lead. Classical balustrading and obelisks on the parapet appear as Italianate versions of the destroyed fourteenth-century battlements and pinnacles, visible in van Wyngaerde's view of *c*.1540 (Fig. 91). It is by far the most magnificent surviving architectural drawing from sixteenth-century England and is clearly the work of an accomplished draughtsman familiar with Renaissance detail. Moreover, it suggests that the 520-foot dimension given by Stow for the height of the medieval spire was exaggerated.[20] Assuming an overall width of fifty feet at the bottom of the parapet (the width of the tower in a survey of 1609), the height of the replacement spire would have been about 215 feet to the top of the cross, making a total of about 420 feet for the entire tower and spire from pavement level – roughly the height of the spire of Salisbury Cathedral.[21]

The account ends in December 1564, and an audit of September 1566 reveals that £6,702 was spent, against an original estimate of £17,738 for permanent roofs and a spire. The queen only paid out £266 of her promised largess, probably because the greater part of her gift of oaks had gone unclaimed.[22] However, she regarded the cathedral as the shared responsibility of the City and the bishop of London, rather than her own. In 1576 she was 'very urgent about the rebuilding of the Spire', and threatened to summon the 'Mayor and six of his best brethren before her' to explain themselves.[23] The mayor told the Privy Council in 1580 that the City could do no more, and the bishop of London protested that it was beyond the revenues of his whole see to put the matter right.[24] A mayoral committee reported in 1582 that the walls were 'laid open and greatly spoiled with rain, the gutters cut off and other defaults permitted'.[25] In that year the queen appointed Sir Christopher Hatton to inquire into why the 'principal ornament' of the chief city of the kingdom was still in decay. Two years later, he advised that £9,000 would be needed to complete the steeple in stone, as well as £2,490 for repairs to the nave, chancel and floors of the cathedral.[26] Nothing further was done until James I's reign, by which time 'the corroding quality of the coal smoke, especially in moist weather'[27] had hastened the decay of the stonework. Added to this was the long-standing abuse of the nave and transepts of St Paul's ('Paul's Walkes') for secular business of all kinds.

JAMES I'S INITIATIVES IN 1608 AND 1620

On 24 July 1608 King James I wrote to the mayor and bishop of London, urging them 'to remove the scandal that hath long lien upon our city of London especially, but in a manner upon the whole realm, for the neglect of the repairing of the steeple of

90. Design for the spire in pen, wash and gouache, drawn or procured by John Revell, Elizabeth I's Surveyor of Works, 1562. (Society of Antiquaries)

91. Part of Anthonis van den Wyngaerde's panoramic *View of London*, mid 1540s. The most reliable illustration of the spire of St Paul's before its destruction in 1561. (Ashmolean Museum, Oxford)

mitted. It shows the west elevation of the existing tower, which had no buttress on its north-west corner. The design mimics the ogee-shaped crown of the nearby steeple of St Mary-le-Bow (Fig. 94) in a curious, almost self-conscious blend of Renaissance and medieval motifs. The clustered obelisks derive from an engraving of Antonio da Sangallo's design for St Peter's, the lunettes on the octagonal crown are from Michelangelo's dome of St Peter's, and the classical loggia is an adaptation of the loggias at Palladio's Basilica in Vicenza. But the design was hardly a practical response to the decays of the steeple.

A crisis in James's finances in 1610 and Salisbury's death in April 1612 probably put paid to the king's involvement in the short term. But petitioning by Henry Farley, a stone importer, and the author of a polemical tract, *The Complaint of St Pauls to all Christian Soules* (1616), appears to have goaded the king into action.[31] James decided to visit the cathedral in person and on Sunday, 26 March 1620 he knelt at the great west door at the head of a long procession. After a sermon at Paul's Cross by Bishop King – the event shown in the diptych commissioned by Farley from the painter John Gipkyn (Figs 93–94)[32] – he declared that he would fast on bread and water to see the restoration work done. He ordered another investigation into the decays of the cathedral in April and on 16 November issued a royal commission under the great seal of England. This was directed to the lord mayor and aldermen, the Archbishop of Canterbury, the whole Privy Council, some of the bishops and many individuals, including Inigo Jones, Surveyor of the King's Works. At least six of the commissioners (including three privy councillors) were to meet and consider what repairs were needed and how funds could be raised. They were then to appoint surveyors and officers to carry out the work, but this last stage was not reached during James's reign.

The commissioners found that while the bishop had charge of the 'whole body of the Church', and the dean and chapter of the choir, neither had funds for regular repairs, let alone wholesale restoration.[33] They therefore advised that 'a general Benevolence throughout the whole kingdom should be attempted', with the nobility and gentry taking the lead. The king headed a national subscription with a promise of £2,000, Prince Charles gave £500,[34] and Bishop King committed £100 per annum out of his revenue, but though a large quantity Portland stone was paid for by Bishop Mountain when he succeeded on Bishop King's death in 1621, no repair work was begun.[35]

The purchase of stone probably arose from a survey begun in April 1620, which set out costs for replacing stonework around the whole cathedral and rebuilding the tower, 80 feet high and 50 feet square, using 20,000 feet of Ketton and 10,000 feet of Portland stone.[36] The total was in excess of £20,000. This is a stonemason's estimate rather than a full schedule of repairs. It represents a bid for work and does not anticipate any new features, either on the tower or at the west front. As such, it was hardly likely to inspire benefactions or impress the commissioners, some of whom suspected that 'under the pretence of this needful repair' the king aimed at the ruin of the bishop and other members of the church.[37] The problem was lack of leadership. The king's authority over parliament and the country fell to a new ebb during 1621; his health was failing, and his finances were in ruins. Without visible royal support, interest in the restoration campaign quickly waned. Nothing seems to have been achieved after 1620, nor is there evidence of Inigo Jones supplying designs for refacing the cathedral. Soon after King

St Paul's Church'.[28] James promised to contribute liberally towards the repairs himself and, observing that the 'whole body' of the cathedral (the nave and transepts) was 'not only in decay, but in danger of ruin in some parts', ordered a costed survey and statement of available funds. The estimate of 24 October 1608 put the repairs at £22,537 2s. 3d., of which more than half was needed for the steeple.[29] The estimate did not envisage any new structure but recommended that the top thirty-three feet (belfry stage) of the tower be taken down and rebuilt – a sign that the 1561 fire had caused lasting damage to the stonework of the steeple. The other major element of the bill was for replacing the stonework of the nave, aisles and west front, suggesting that the Romanesque parts of the church were those 'most in danger of ruin'.

A design by Inigo Jones for a new termination on the steeple of St Paul's is datable to this period (Fig. 92).[30] Jones had travelled in Italy sometime between 1597 and 1603, and within five years had become the court's leading designer of stage scenery and costumes. In 1608 his main private patron was the Lord Treasurer Robert Cecil, the Earl of Salisbury. Cecil probably commissioned this design at about the time the survey was sub-

Charles's accession in 1625, the royal favourite, the Duke of Buckingham, 'borrowed' some of the Portland stone for his watergate at York House.[38]

THE RESTORATION CAMPAIGN OF 1631–42

It was in the context of King Charles I's personal rule, which began in 1629, and within the orbit of his Privy Council, that the restoration of St Paul's Cathedral was planned and carried out from 1631.[39] For the next eleven years the fabric of the cathedral was effectively in the hands of the king, his councillors and his officers, rather than the dean and chapter, the bishop or the lord mayor (although responsibilities overlapped). The centralized system of control and accountability explains both the success of the restoration programme between 1631 and 1642 and the abuse that the cathedral suffered once the king was forced to relinquish his authority.

The architect of the restoration, in the broadest sense, was William Laud, the high churchman whom Charles appointed bishop of London in 1628 and elevated to the archbishopric of Canterbury in 1633.[40] Laud helped devise and implement the king's policies of reforms in the Church of England, which aimed at restoring uniformity of worship, good order and the 'beauty of holiness' to church services and buildings. He established a mechanism by which funds for the repair of the cathedral could be obtained in a commission of 5 January 1631 'for inquiring into the execution of the laws for relief of the poor and supervising of the administration of gifts for pious uses'.[41] This was followed on 10 April 1631 by the king's royal commission for the repair of the cathedral. It renewed the terms of King James's commission and gave Laud the authority to set up a register of subscriptions and issue letters patent for receiving public contributions.[42]

The City of London was to manage the money and in May 1631 an account was opened in the Chamber of London.[43] By October 1633 nearly £18,000 had been raised and work on refitting the choir and repairing the choir screen was already complete, although without any expenditure from the account. This was the gift of Sir Paul Pindar, an ambassador in Constantinople under James I who in 1639 was also to pay for the embellishment of the south transept front (Fig. 95).[44] Pindar funded the repair of the chancel screen, or pulpitum, 'adorning the outside thereof with many faire polished pillers of black Marble, and with curious carved Statues of Kings and Bishops, the First Founders and Benefactors of the whole Fabricke', and decorating its inner side 'with divers Angels and other ornaments'. The choir stalls were refurbished and a 'faire rayle of Wainscot, and a great number of Cherubins' were added, 'all which work he hath caused to be sumptuously gilded and painted with rich colour in Oyle'. The choir and the 'upper part of the Presbytery' were hung with tapestries. The altar table is not mentioned, but it was probably in the presbytery, or upper choir. Significant in view of the probable date of 1631–2 is the wainscot rail. Although we cannot be sure of its exact position, it was almost certainly an altar rail, inserted in accordance with the liturgical reforms implemented by Laud on the king's instructions with increasing vigour during the 1630s.[45]

The commissioners first met in December 1631 to agree procedures for acquiring and demolishing houses and cellars that encroached on the cathedral – work that went on throughout 1632.[46] In January 1633 the king ordered that work should begin

92. Design by Inigo Jones for a new termination or crown on the mediaeval tower, *c.*1608. The tower rises behind and above the existing west elevation, whose north-west corner is correctly shown without a buttress. (Worcester College, Oxford)

on the south side at the east end of the choir, and he appointed a committee of six from the commission of 'pious uses', including Laud, to have charge of the repairs and authorize the accounts. This committee made Inigo Jones surveyor on 4 February, a task he agreed to undertake without charge, nominating Edward Carter as his 'substitute', or executant architect. Carter thus became the highest paid official, earning five shillings a day 'for his continuall attendance in receiving directions for the going forward of the worke'.[47] John Webb, then about twenty-one, was made clerk engrosser, to write fair copies of the accounts, but he also served as Jones's draughtsman. In December 1639 he received a large payment of £120 for seven years' work, 'Copying severall designes and Mouldings and makinge the Traccery of them according to Mr Surveyors direccons for the workmen to followe for all the tyme'.[48]

The survey of 1620 had indicated that the south side of the choir was most in need of repair. This part could claim precedence over others, since it included the 'vestry' and 'Dean's Chappell' in several separately roofed bays beneath the aisle windows, the latter apparently in the wider bay, eighth from the east.[49] The accounts opened in April with payments for work on the three most easterly bays of the choir on the south side.[50] Over

93. St Paul's 'unrestored', from the diptych by John Gipkyn commissioned by Henry Farley, probably in 1620, when James I visited the cathedral and heard Bishop King preach on the restoration of St Paul's. The king is seated with Queen Anne and Prince Charles in the upper floor of the Sermon House; below are the Lord Mayor and Aldermen. The text, 'View O King how my wall creepers have made mee work for chimney sweepers', refers to the houses, with chimneys, built on the east side of the north transept. (The Society of Antiquaries)

the next four years, Edmund Kinsman and his team of seventy masons, carvers and labourers worked from east to west on this side at least as far as the eighth bay.[51] They renewed the stonework of the walls, buttresses, pinnacles and parapets (mostly in Portland stone) and replaced much of the tracery of the aisle windows in Ketton stone. From about April 1634, Kinsman was joined by Thomas Stanley's team at the east end and by the teams of Richard Chilton and subsequently John Moore on the north side of the choir.[52]

The repairs to the medieval tracery and ornament involved the construction of a 'Tracery house for the drawing out the windowes pinacles &c at the South end being called the ladies chappell'. This was a timber platform, apparently in the southernmost bay on the east side of the south transept. Sixteen quires of paper were used 'to paper the Chapell windowes' to create an even light for the drawing of full-sized timber templates.[53] These were cut out from 'slit deales' or planks, planed and glued together by the joiners. Templates for the Gothic tracery would have been prepared by the

masons themselves, but those for new classical details, like the 'modell of a cornice and ffreeze for the upper of the church', paid for in January 1636, would have been drawn by Webb.[54]

From 1635 a small team under William Hilliard spent up to four years painting the internal walls and tracery of eastern arm, the vestry and Dean's Chapel on the south side of the choir, and the Morning Prayer Chapel on the east side of north transept.[55] In January 1636 the painters were employed 'in grinding of colors and laying in stone color in oyle the inside of the great window at the East end'.[56] Payments for 'best blue verditer', indigo, vermilion, 'lambeblack' [lamp black] and 'dry verdegrease' [verdigris, or green] suggest polychromatic effects in areas like the Dean's Chapel, where the painters were still 'grinding colours' in July 1639.[57] The intention was to distinguish the choir and the eastern chapels from the main body of the church and give particular emphasis to the spaces used by the clergy in daily worship. Such embellishment was commended by the author 'R.T.', who explained in his Laudian tract *De Templis* (1638) 'That when we

94. St Paul's 'restored', from the Gipkyn diptych. This imaginary restoration adds a crown to the tower not unlike Inigo Jones's proposal of 1608 and reglazes the windows. (The Society of Antiquaries)

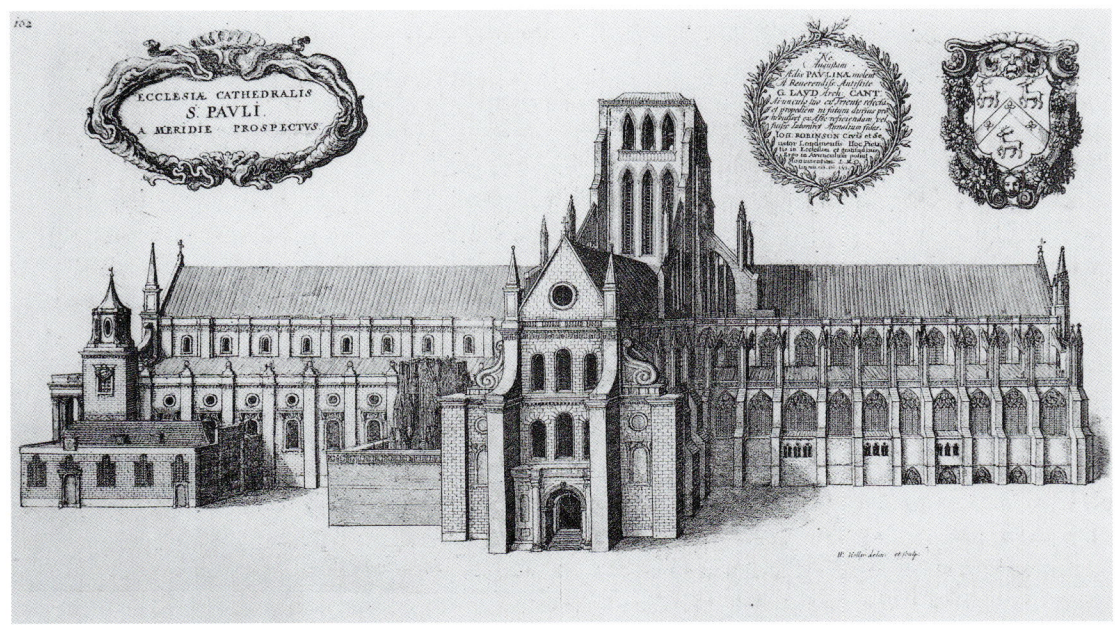

95. View from south in *c.*1656 (partly reconstructed). The south transept front was restored with money from Sir Paul Pindar. The church of St Gregory is shown on the left. Etching by Hollar for Dugdale (1658)

96. Preliminary design by Inigo Jones for the west front, c. 1631–3. (British Architectural Library/RIBA)

97. The west front and portico as designed by Inigo Jones, c. 1634. Engraving by Henry Hulsbergh after a drawing by Henry Flitcoft, in William Kent's *Designs of Inigo Jones* (1727), vol. II. For scale, see Fig. 101.

enter into this place, more holy & divine thoughts may possesse our minds, occasioned by the differing structure, and more glorious ornaments'.[58]

CLASSICIZING THE 'BODY' OF THE CATHEDRAL

On St George's Day, 23 April 1634, King Charles informed Archbishop Laud of his intention 'to undertake the whole repair of the west end of that church without having any to share in the honour of that particular with us'.[59] The king had been slow to contribute to the repair fund himself,[60] but now wished to dispose of 'all false and scandalous rumours' that 'the work were but pretended by us to get some great sum of money together, and then turn it to other uses'. His commitment to the west front would 'rise to a far greater sum' than his promised £500 for ten years, and he instructed Laud 'to call upon our surveyor to use all care and industry for the setting forward of the work'. A separate account for the west end was opened in November 1634 and work began clearing the ground, while Edward Carter visited the island of Portland to negotiate the quarrying and transport of 'the great stones' that would be used for the Corinthian west portico – the main object of the king's benefaction.[61]

The king's decision to embellish the west front at St Paul's rather than restore the spire reflected a trend in continental church architecture since the late sixteenth century towards lavish architectural and sculptural display on entrance fronts. This was exemplified in Paris in the vast, three-tiered façade of the Jesuit church of Saint-Louis (now Saint-Paul-Saint-Louis) on the rue Saint-Antoine, which was patronized by Charles's brother-in-law Louis XIII.[62] A preliminary design by Inigo Jones for the west front is in this idiom, and is datable from its draughting technique to the early 1630s (Fig. 96).[63] With its superimposed orders and rich sculptural ornament, including angels bearing palm leaves

and an 'IHS' monogram in a sunburst (a favourite Jesuit motif), it is closer to the Roman baroque than any church design in England before Wren's Great Model of 1673–4. The design may be contemporary with Pindar's embellishment of the choir with similar ornaments in c.1631–2 and was probably rejected as too overtly Catholic for the façade of the cathedral.

The king's benefaction of 1634 was probably made on the basis of Jones's revised design for the west front, in which a giant Corinthian portico, ten columns wide and surmounted by statues of kings, replaced the Italianate scheme of applied orders (Fig. 97). The portico allowed Charles to proclaim his regal munificence through an inscription on the frieze.[64] The statuary may have been intended to celebrate the association of the monarchy with St Paul's, although only two figures were executed – those of Charles himself and King James (Fig. 100).[65] Jones retained the giant scrolls, circular windows and flanking turrets of his earlier scheme, but treated the entire façade with a type of channelled rusticated walling frequently illustrated by Palladio in Book IV of the *Quattro Libri* (on Roman temple architecture).[66] Jones applied the same walling to the nave and transepts, and set Roman block cornices (also from Palladio) in place of Romanesque corbelled courses at eaves levels, pineapple finials over the aisle pilaster buttresses, and obelisks in place of turrets and finials above the main bastions of the three gable ends. At main parapet level he placed a large block cornice above a frieze of lions' heads and foliate 'drops'. This frieze later puzzled Sir Roger Pratt, who thought it 'seems somewhat to allude to the Dorick order, where the Bobbins are set for the Triglifes, and the Lyons heads for the Metopes'.[67] Summerson described it as 'quasi-Tuscan' and went on to characterize Jones's recladding work as 'a deliberate quest for the primitive', like his contemporary work at Covent Garden.[68] But while Jones undoubtedly sought simplicity of treatment, not least for reasons of cost, many

98 (*above*). St Paul's from south-west *c.* 1640–54, showing the tower scaffolded. Drawing by Martin van Overbeek. To the right of the cathedral, the cupola-capped tower of St Mary-le-Bow. (Museum of London)

99 (*below*). Drawing of *c.* 1672 by Thomas Wyck of the west front and portico. The inscription and balustrade survived the Great Fire intact. In the background the gable end of the south transept is visible. (BodL, Gough Maps, f.2v)

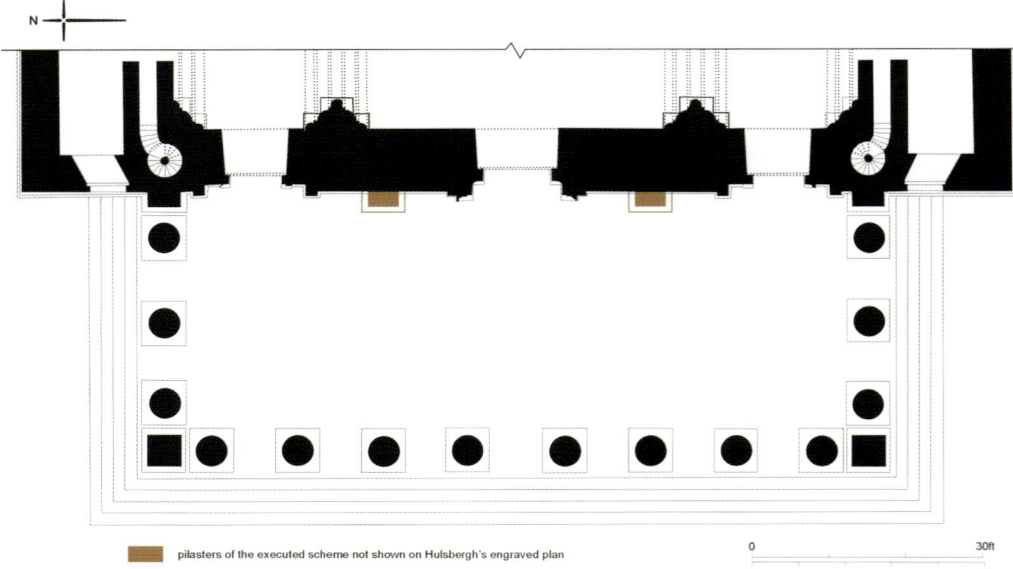

100 (*left*). View from the west in 1656 (partly reconstructed) showing the west portico, built 1635–42, but left incomplete on the outbreak of Civil War. The statues of King Charles and King James were destroyed in 1649. To the right of the portico, the church of St Gregory, partly pulled down by Jones and subsequently repaired. Etching by Hollar for Dugdale (1658)

101 (*below left*). Reconstructed ground plan of Inigo Jones's west front and portico, built 1635–42, based on archaeological and documentary evidence, and an engraved plan by Hulsbergh in William Kent's *Designs of Inigo Jones* (1727)

pilasters of the executed scheme not shown on Hulsbergh's engraved plan

of his cladding details were borrowed from illustrations of the temples and public buildings of imperial Rome, where they appeared in the context of Corinthian or Composite orders.[69]

Jones's cladding increased the depth of the walls by at least one foot. In 1668 Wren and Dean Sancroft discovered that this 'flagging' had not been properly keyed into the existing walls.[70] It may have been fixed only with mortar, secured in place where necessary by a temporary system of timber clamps attached to beams on the inside walls.[71] Above the main cornice, Jones rebuilt the gable ends, the parapets and the uppermost parts of the western towers, and repaired the roofs. In July 1640 preparations began 'for the takeinge downe of the Steeple'.[72] That November, 'A gent', who 'hath desired to have his name concealed', gave £600 'for & towards the repaire of the decaies & ruines of the steeple of the Pauls Cathedral church'.[73] From this wording,

straightforward replacement appears to have been intended. But though the entire tower was scaffolded (Fig. 98), no demolition had begun when work ceased in September 1642.

In the interests of uniformity, Jones removed almost all traces of the medieval and particularly the Gothic fabric from the exterior of the nave and transepts, even though he had faithfully restored the Gothic stonework of the choir. Wyck's view of the inside of the ruined south transept shows the main Gothic window arch overlaid with three round-headed openings – a change that would have reduced light to the crossing area (Fig. 99). At the west end, Jones ordered the partial demolition of the church of St Gregory next to the south-west tower (for which he was arraigned by the House of Lords in December 1641), and in April 1638 the destruction of the chapel of the bishop of London's house adjoining the north-west tower (Fig. 100).[74]

102. View of the choir from the north dated 1656. The staircase and doorway at the east end of the north choir aisle gave access to the 'Preaching place', set up in the choir in 1649. Etching by Hollar for Dugdale (1658)

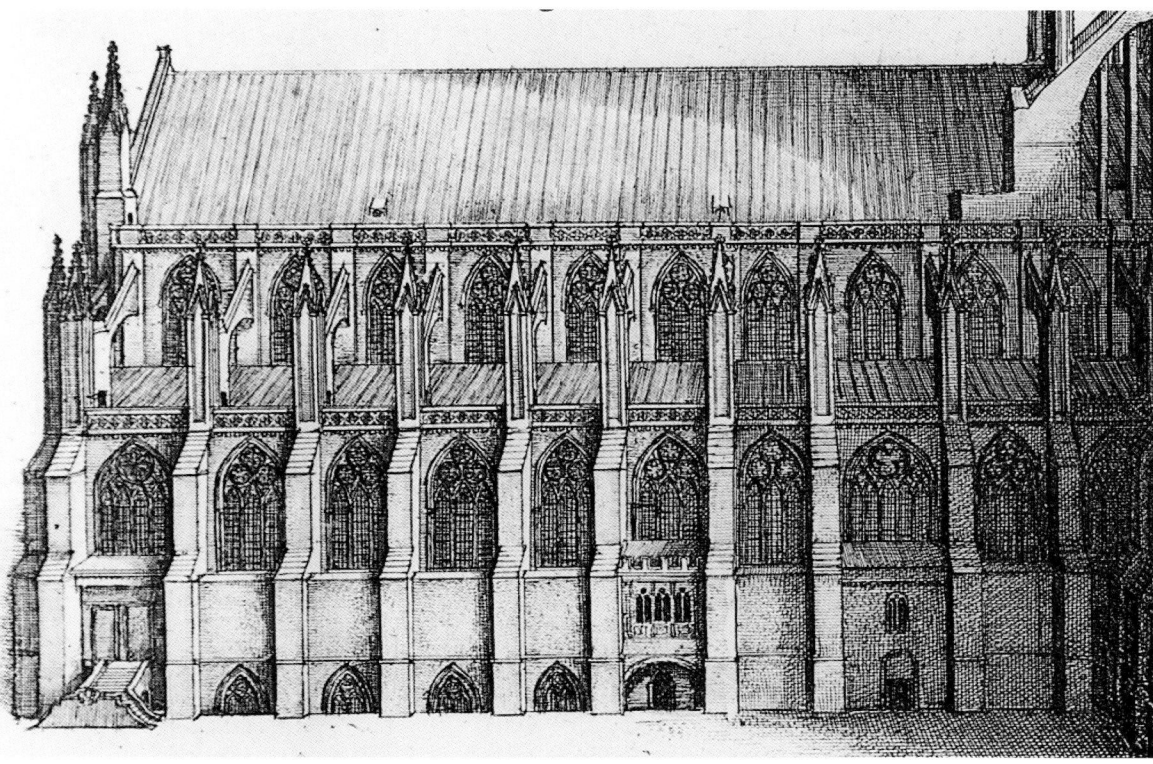

The portico itself was one of Jones's greatest achievements and marked the culmination of his personal quest for an authentic revival of ancient Roman architecture, based on his knowledge of the original monuments and his study of Renaissance treatises. John Webb wrote in 1665:

[Jones] reduced the Body of [the cathedral], from the Steeple to the *West* End, into that Order and Uniformity we now behold; and by adding that magnificent Portico there, hath contracted the Envy of all *Christendom* upon our Nation, for a Piece of Architecture, not to be paralleled in the last Ages of the World.[75]

Jones was probably influenced by Roman temples he had seen in Italy in 1613–14, especially those of Antoninus and Faustina in the Roman Forum and Castor and Pollux in Naples, which had been converted to churches in such a way as to leave their porticoes projecting forwards of modernized façades.[76]

Jones took the idea of a colonnade lined with statues from Palladio's reconstruction of the Temple of Venus and Rome,[77] but turned this into a three-sided portico ten columns wide and four columns deep (Figs 100, 101). The corner columns were square and paired with round columns on each side, giving strength to the angles. This arrangement was without precedent in antiquity and was to influence the way Wren grouped his columns on the west front of St Paul's.

Thomas Wyck's rough sketch of the ruined portico gives an impression of the prominence of the pedestals and balustrading in the overall scheme (Fig. 99). Jones designed this balustrading with the aid of a full-sized timber model, which he erected *in situ*, and then had altered and painted between July 1638 and November 1639.[78] He positioned the pedestals and balusters in accordance with his interpretation of an obscure passage in Vitruvius about optical correction.[79] The columns themselves were four feet in diameter (not five feet, as the scale on the 1727 engraving implies) and followed Palladio's rules both for the height of the columns

(38 feet high, or nine diameters) and for the height of the entablature (a fifth of the column height). This made a total of about 45 feet for the full height of the order to the top of the cornice.[80] The cornice derived from the temple of Antoninus and Faustina and was borrowed by Wren for the main order of the new cathedral. The portico remained standing until it was demolished in 1687–8 to make way for Wren's west front.[81]

Twenty years earlier, Wren had praised the 'excellent beauty and strength' of Jones's portico, which though burned by the Great Fire, 'time alone and weather could have noe more overthrown than the natural rocks; soe great and good were the materialls, and soe skilfully were they laid after a trew Roman manner'.[82] He was referring to Jones's use of Roman constructional techniques, involving the largest possible blocks of stone finely jointed together. John Webb emphasized this aspect of Jones's achievement when he wrote that it took two years to find a stone in the Portland quarries 'for the great Architrave, incumbent on the middle Intercolumn of the *Portico*', which even then was 'in Length not fully twelve Foot' (that is, short of an optimum twelve-foot width, which would have made the central intercolumniation eight feet, or two diameters wide).[83]

The portico was intended to be separately embellished, so as to be distinct from the west front as a whole; and though Dugdale wrote that it was intended as an 'ambulatory' for those who had previously done business in the nave, there is no evidence of it being used in this way.[84] Its rear wall appears to have been clad in fair-faced ashlar, not the rustication shown in the 1727 engraving (Fig. 97).[85] The three western doors had surrounds of white Carrara marble, and black Belgian marble was intended for the steps but was not installed.[86] Payments to Thomas de Critz in October 1639 for 'paynting in stone colour in distemper in the way of Releive three great figures of the Apostles tenn foot 8 inches high', and in January 1641 'for drawing of severall figures of Kings for the Ornament of the west end', suggest figurative

103. Part of a view of St Paul's and the City of London from near Arundel House, anonymous drawing of *c*.1654–66. This view post-dates the removal of scaffolding that precipitated the collapse in January 1654 of the south transept vault and roof. (BM)

decoration on the walls and panelled ceiling.[87] However, the ceiling was probably not finished – or at least not painted – before work ceased. A 'great modell for part of ye seeling of the portico' was made and carved between May and November 1641, but the accounts for the final year say nothing specific about its construction or finishing.[88] Roger Pratt described the ceiling in 1660 as having square panels, formed into octagons, 'joined to each other by a kind of square Guiloche' – perhaps a Greek key ornament – and decorated with 'large vases [roses?] either of fir or wainscot'.[89]

By late 1641 the prospects for completing the restoration works must have looked gloomy. Contributions to the restoration fund fell off dramatically in the year up to September 1641, when only £1,569 was paid in.[90] Between 1634 and mid 1637, the king had contributed over £8,000 towards the west front from his own funds, but his personal payments fell sharply thereafter, and he relied on monies from ecclesiastical fines in the Court of the High Commission, a move that undoubtedly created resentment against the restoration campaign.[91] The fines were imposed from 30 May 1637 and amounted to at least £1,670 by September 1640.[92] Even so, the total of £10,661 10s. 8d. given in the king's name from 1634 to 1640 (including the fines) was nothing like the amount actually spent on the design and construction of the west front and portico. The audited accounts state that £9,439 was spent on the 'West End' between November 1634 and October 1641, compared with £71,060 on the 'East End...North & South Sides'.[93] But from about 1637 many works for the west end – including payments for carpenters' and joiners' works and the carriage of stone – were paid for in the other accounts.[94] This discreet system of creative accounting must have had Laud's blessing, and appears to have been managed so that the audited expenditure at the west end roughly matched what had been given for that purpose in the king's name.

By October 1642, £101,325 had been paid into the Chamber of London since 1631 and all but £305 had been spent.[95] The

workmen must have known their wages would not be paid, and work appears to have stopped soon after Parliament announced its intention to abolish bishops, deans and chapters in September 1642. In the final months, Jones appears to have concentrated all his efforts on completing the stonework of his portico and west end. In July and August 1642, masons were setting 'Pyramides stones' weighing eleven tons either side of the gable end and carvers were busy on the cornice of the gable end, the flutes of the columns, the lettering of the frieze, and the 'Enrichments of the Rayle and base below and above the balesters on the front of the Portico'.[96] The portico was probably still scaffolded when the site was abandoned. There is no record of King Charles ever visiting the cathedral to see the restoration works in hand.

CIVIL WAR AND INTERREGNUM, 1642–60

After the abolition of the cathedral's establishment in January 1643, the mayor and aldermen of London assumed responsibility for the building and its precinct. Paul's Cross had probably already been demolished; they now ordered the destruction of the organ loft (above the pulpitum) and in March 1644 the seizure of 'all money, goods, and materialls, bought, or given and brought into any place for the repairing or furnishing of this Church'.[97] Jones's deputy, Edward Carter – a presbyterian – was now consulted on works at St Paul's. In February 1645 the Corporation's 'Committee of Paules' met and, 'upon conference with Mr Carter', drew up an inventory of the materials.[98] Two months earlier, the last £200 of the repair fund had been paid out towards the 'building upp and repairing of half of the parish Church of St. Gregory', and in August 1645 the House of Lords ordered that the parish be given some of the left-over materials.[99] The fully glazed church that Hollar shows adjoining the south-west tower was probably largely reconstructed from salvaged Portland stone at this time (Figs 77, 95). With its simplified Venetian windows and motifs borrowed from the St Paul's restoration, it may well have been to the designs of Carter himself.[100]

Carter was probably responsible for what Dugdale described in 1658 as 'a Preaching place' for the St Paul's 'lecturer' Cornelius Burges in the eastern part of the choir arm in 1649. It was separated from the rest of the eastern arm by 'a new partition Wall, made of brick' within the choir proper, and appears to have been entered by a new staircase and doorway at the east end of the north choir aisle shown in Hollar's view of the north side of the cathedral in 1656 (Fig. 102). The partition wall and north-east entrance were needed because from December 1648 Fairfax's army used the nave and transepts for stabling their horses, 'making plentiful fires with the seats'.[101] In 1650 the Council of State directed that the statues of King James and King Charles should be taken down and broken.[102] Three years later, the scaffolding around the tower and inside the crossing area was removed and assigned to Colonel Jephson's regiment in lieu of pay, precipitating a collapse of the south transept vault on 27 January 1654.[103] A commissioners' minute of 1664 states that 'one Capt John Wheat still liveinge about the towne, took away the Scaffoldinge of the steeple & threwe downe the roofe of the south Isle, and carried away the materialles in the night tyme'.[104] In his history of St Paul's, published in 1658, William Dugdale laments: 'the whole roof of the South Cross [south transept] is already tumbled down; and the rest in severall places of the Church, often falling'; and he explains that since the cathedral may now 'be utterly destroyed, and become a wofull spectacle of ruine', his purpose is to give 'some representation, as well to the present age, as future times, of what it hath been'.[105] This is why Hollar's engravings in Dugdale's *History* give no hint of the semi-derelict state of the cathedral in the later 1650s: he 'restored' the cathedral to an imagined state of perfection before the Civil War. Thus, in the choir he shows conjectural fittings and an altar table, set behind a rail, that would either have been destroyed or concealed behind the partition wall (Fig. 73).

The actual state of the cathedral in the late 1650s and early 1660s can be judged from a topographical view that shows the south transept open to the skies (Fig. 103). We know from a survey by William Webb, in November 1657 that the roof and floor of the chapter house had collapsed and the northern half of the cloister garth had been demolished (Hollar shows the entire cloister intact) (Fig. 77).[106] By then many houses had been built around the walls of the nave, and two-storey shops constructed inside Jones's west portico, 'its stately pillars...shamefully hewed and defaced'.[107]

FROM THE RESTORATION TO THE GREAT FIRE, 1660–66

After the Restoration in May 1660, the priorities at St Paul's for King Charles II and his new bishop of London, Gilbert Sheldon, were the re-establishment of the choir as a physical entity in the eastern arm of the cathedral and the repair of the fabric. Shortly after he took office in October 1661, Dean John Barwick created a makeshift choir by enlarging Burges's 'preaching place' by 'the length of one arch into the old quire' and constructing a new partition wall. This wall – probably no further west than the line of steps between the eighth and ninth bay from the east end – was a temporary measure, 'until the repairs of the remaining part of the old fabric should be fully perfected'.[108] At the same time, the king was consulting the young professor of astronomy at Oxford University, Dr Christopher Wren, about 'the rebuilding of St Paul's'.[109] This vague reference, in an undated letter to Wren from his friend Thomas Sprat, suggests that Charles II sought advice on the structural condition of the crossing tower and south transept as a result of the collapse in 1654.

Charles II formally announced his intentions for the repair of St Paul's in the commission he issued on 18 April 1663.[110] His decision-making procedure gave wider discretion to the bishop of London and dean of St Paul's, one of whom had to be present at every meeting of at least six commissioners (in practice, both attended every meeting from 1664 to 1668). This group – no longer subordinate to the Privy Council – was empowered to decide the nature and sequence of the work year on year, the extent of demolition (within the context of 'repairs'), the methods of financing and the appointment of subcommittees to manage the work.[111] Money was to be raised by national subscription, but the 'Register' of contributions was entrusted not to the City of London, through the Chamber, as in 1631, but to the bishop of London, with Sir John Cutler as receiver (shortly afterwards made treasurer at St Paul's).[112] For the first time since before the fire of 1561, major repairs at St Paul's Cathedral ceased to be a direct function of the king's Office of Works. Moreover, the commissioners had the power to appoint 'other persons of known ability and integrity'. In the climate of scientific enquiry and dilettantism that prevailed in the 1660s, they used this discretion to seek alternative advice beyond what was initially available to them from surveyors and craftsmen in the king's Office of Works.

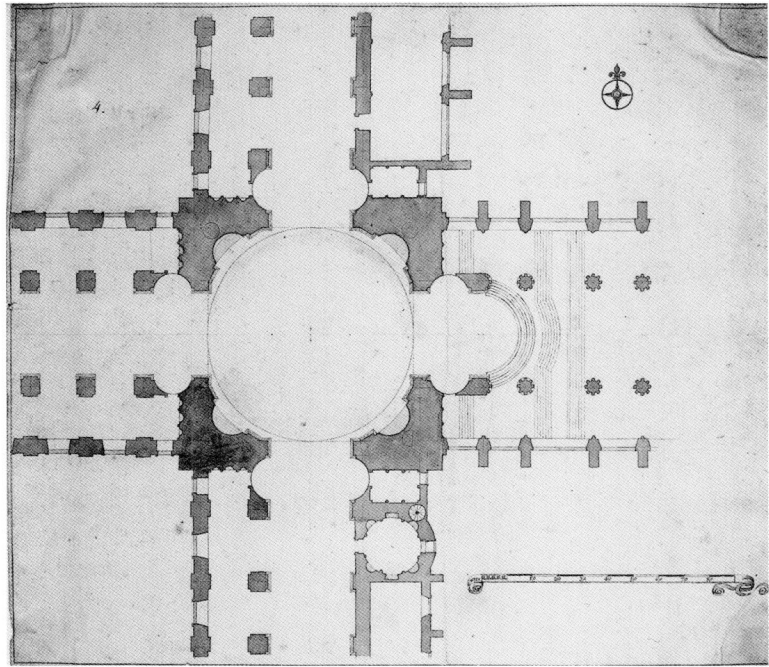

104.   Plan by Wren, before the Great Fire, of a proposed new domed crossing to replace the ruined medieval crossing and tower, and to include a new choir vestibule, May–August 1666. (AS, Wren Collection, II.4)

The crucial problem was what to do with the tower and crossing area. Following a commissioners' meeting on 27 July 1664, the Surveyor-General Sir John Denham, his 'Surveyor Assistant' John Webb and the king's master mason Edward Marshall recommended the complete demolition of the tower and crossing piers down to the pavement, the removal of the adjoining high vaults and aisle roofs, and the reduction of the piers at the angles of the crossing 'into such new Order as [Denham and Webb] shall think fitt; so that they endeavour to make the grand Nave of the [cross] somewhat wider'.[113] They foresaw the rebuilding of the south transept vaults and east arcade, the latter having been 'beaten down' by the collapse. The steeple would have to be scaffolded first of all, and at least 3,000 tons of Portland and Beer stone would be needed each year for its reconstruction. Webb's guiding hand is apparent from a note he made in November 1663 listing all the timber that would be needed 'from Norwey for the scaffolding of St Pauls steeple'.[114] This timber was delivered in June 1664, before the commissioners had instructed Denham and Webb to prepare their report.

The commissioners may have been alarmed at Webb's strategy, and the speed with which he was moving at a time when contributions to the repair fund were only about £3,000, for in January 1665 they consulted Roger Pratt, an experienced and well-travelled gentleman-architect who was then working for one of the commissioners, the lord treasurer, the Earl of Clarendon. They also asked the paymaster Hugh May for advice on the repair of 'vaultes and pillars'.[115] Pratt counselled against the demolition or scaffolding of the tower, suggesting instead a survey after the roofs and crossing vaults had been repaired and the south transept vaults rebuilt in rendered brick.[116] His advice on the reuse of existing stone was adopted in May 1665, when the commissioners ordered some vaults to be 'made good with Chalk, Stone or brick & overlayed with a strong finishing mortar' rather than built new, and the 'Consistory Court' in the north transept to be 'taken downe & the stones employed to the best advantage of the Church'.[117]

105. Elevation and section by Wren, before the Great Fire, of proposed new dome and crossing area, looking east, May–August 1666. The dome is inspired by Bramante's unexecuted scheme for St Peter's, Rome. (AS, Wren Collection, II.6)

John Webb's efforts were henceforth directed solely towards repairs of the portico, the western part of the nave and the ruinous north nave aisle. In the fifteen months up to the Great Fire in September 1666, Webb repaired the roof and wainscot ceiling of the portico, and the columns, marble doors and frieze, whose inscription had been 'stopped up' with plaster.[118] The problem of the crossing area, meanwhile, was being contemplated by Christopher Wren during his nine-month visit to France.[119]

Wren's eloquent report to the commissioners on 1 May 1666,

submitted about six weeks after his return, must have been written with knowledge of Webb and Pratt's contrasting advice on the extent of demolition and rebuilding needed at the crossing.[120] He dismisses the idea of piecemeal repair (advanced by Pratt) and proposes a dome to replace the tower, and classical recasing of the nave and transepts, with the vaults rebuilt in rendered brick for lightness and economy. With compelling logic, he explains that he would not propose anything 'of meer Beauty to be added but where there is necessity of rebuilding & when it will be neer the

106.   West to east section, by Wren, before the Great Fire, of proposed new dome and crossing area, May–August 1666. The double-shell masonry and timber construction derives from contemporary Parisian examples, notably Lemercier's Sorbonne Chapel. (AS, Wren Collection, II.7)

same thing to perform it well as ill'. The cramped and defective crossing area would be widened by one bay on all four corners by removing the piers at the 'inner Corners and the Cross' to create a 'spacious Dome' in the middle. The cathedral, 'which is much to narrow for its height', would then seem to

swell in the middle to a large Basis rising into a Rotundo bearing a Cupolo, & then ending in the Lantern: & this with incomparable more Grace in the remote Aspect than it is possible for the lean Shaft of a Steeple to afford.

The same amount of lead would be used for the dome as for a spire, and 'the same quantity of Ashler makes the Corners outward that would make them inwards'. The 'infirm and tottering' tower would be reduced to form a construction platform for the dome, built around and above it before the tower was demolished, thus saving a 'world of Scaffolding poles'.

Wren's drawings, finished in August 1666, show a dome inspired by Bramante's unexecuted scheme for St Peter's published by Serlio, and by the tall, double-shell Parisian domes he

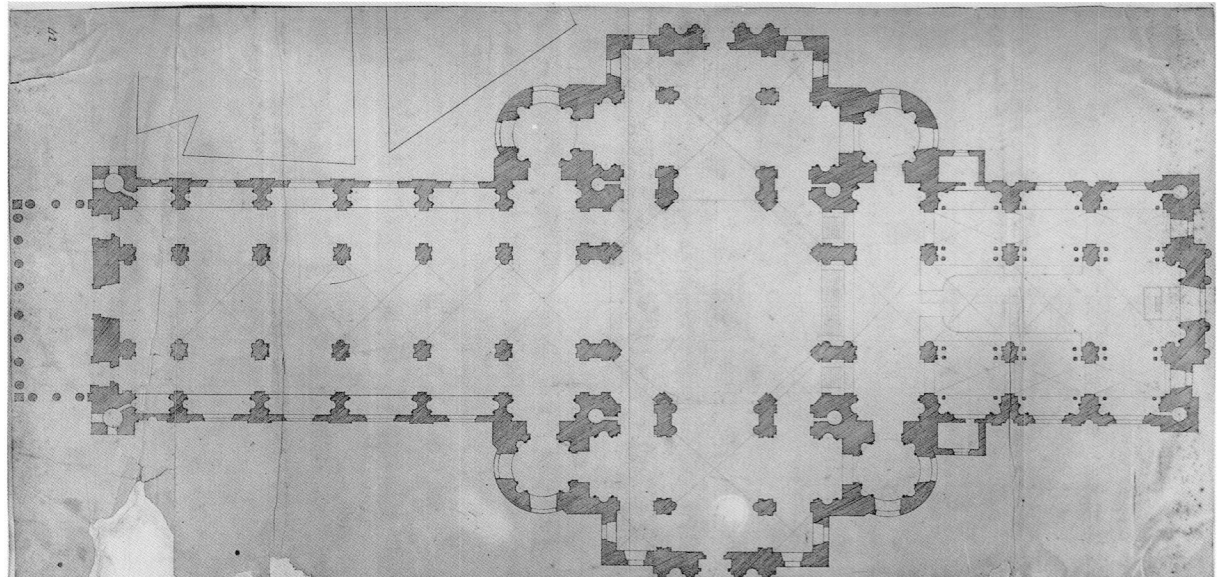

107. Ground plan for a new cathedral on the existing alignment. Modelled partly on Palladio's reconstruction of the Basilica of Maxentius, or Temple of Peace, in Rome, it incorporates a reconstruction of Inigo Jones's west portico. Drawing by Christopher Wren, datable to 1668. (AS, Wren Collection, II.42)

had seen in Paris at the chapel of the Sorbonne (1635–42), the Val-de-Grâce (1643–67) and the Jesuit church of Saint-Louis (1627–41), engravings of which were also the source for his proposed internal recladding (Figs 105, 106).[121] His plan of the crossing area shows the western part of the choir transformed into a vestibule, with a stepped ascent to a new choir area further east. New vestries, the Morning Prayer Chapel, the chapter house and the Consistory Court would have been accommodated in adapted, classicized spaces on the eastern sides of the transepts.

Wren appears to have developed this proposal after consultations with Roger Pratt in the summer of 1666. Pratt reported to the commissioners that he had 'conferred with Dr Wren & Mr May' about his proposal, for which a measured survey and 'Draught' had not yet been prepared.[122] He was concerned that 'In the Steeple' Wren was proposing an alteration 'somewhat else upon new foundations', and thus would have exceeded the terms of the 1663 Commission. These terms were clarified retrospectively in 1673, when the Commission for Rebuilding St Paul's emphasized that the previous commission was concerned with 'upholding and repairing' the cathedral, and did not authorize the commissioners 'to begin and complete a new fabrick upon new foundations'.[123]

Matters came to a head at a site meeting on 27 August, where Wren, Pratt, May, Dean Sancroft, Bishop Henchman and others were joined by John Evelyn, who had recently been appointed as 'one of the three Surveyors of the repaires of Paules' (the others being Webb and either Pratt or Denham).[124] Evelyn describes how agreement was reached on the principle of demolishing the tower and rebuilding it on 'a new foundation':

> and we had a mind to build it with a noble Cupola, a forme of church-building, not as yet known in England, but of wonderfull grace: for this purpose we offered to bring in a draught and estimate, which (after much contest) was at last assented to, and that we should nominate a Committee of able workmen to examine the present foundation.[125]

A week later, on 2 September, the Great Fire started in Pudding Lane on the eastern side of the city. By Tuesday 4 September it had reached St Paul's, and burned so fiercely that night that William Taswell, a schoolboy at Westminster, later claimed that he had been able to read his pocket edition of Terence by the light of

it.[126] Evelyn thought that the 'Scaffalds contributed exceedingly' to the spread of flames. The high vaults of the choir that had survived the blaze in 1561 now collapsed, breaking into the crypt of St Faith's, where the flames, fuelled by thousands of stored books, put the magnificent eastern arm of the cathedral beyond hope of repair (Fig. 69).

At the west end, Evelyn lamented that he had found

> that beautifull portico (for structure comparable to any in Europe, as not long before repaired by the late King) now rent in pieces, flakes of vast stone split asunder, and nothing remaining intire but the inscription in the architrave shewing by whom it was built, which had not one letter of it defac'd.

The Portland stone ornaments of the portico and west front, calcined in the heat, 'flew off, even to the very roof'.[127] But along the flanking walls of the nave Jones's recasing fared better, leaving this part of the cathedral the most capable of repair, or at least of temporary use.

WREN'S FIRST DESIGNS FOR THE NEW CATHEDRAL, 1668–70

Henceforth, only Wren's advice was sought. His report to the commissioners in February 1667 set the parameters for their response to the crisis over the next two or three years.[128] He recommended building a temporary choir and auditory in the western seven bays of the nave, after which they should consider 'a more durable and noble Fabrick to be made in the place of the Tower and eastern parts of the Church'. Work on this temporary structure began in March 1668 under the direction of Edward Woodroofe (or Woodroffe),[129] but the collapse of a pier in the nave in April caused Jones's recasing to lean out perilously from the original nave walls. Dean Sancroft now judged that there was no alternative to complete demolition and summoned Wren urgently.[130] Wren reiterated that there was 'noe medling with the old worke' and restated the agreed aim of 'a greater and fairer work intended upon the ruines of the East end'.[131] But though he was reluctant to offer a design without knowing what funds would be available, Sancroft summoned him from Oxford on 2 July 1668 to 'prepare something to be proposed to his Majesty (the Design of such a Quire, at least, as may be a congruous Part of a greater and more magnificent Work

108.   Wren's First Model, 1669–70. Oak and pear wood by William Clere. The photograph shows the ten-bay choir and auditory and the internal staircase structure behind the missing east-end loggia. At the opposite end was a separately hinged dome portion with porticoes on three sides. (St Paul's Cathedral)

to follow)'. The commissioners wanted him 'to frame a Design, handsome and noble, and suitable to all the Ends of it, and to the Reputation of the City, and the Nation', on the assumption that 'Money will be had to accomplish it'.[132] The king must have agreed this strategy, for on 25 July he issued a warrant for the demolition of the eastern arm and tower,

> in such manner as shall be judged sufficient to make Room for a New Choir of a faire and decent fabrick neare or upon the old foundations: And also that care be taken to preserve the Cornishes, Ashlers, and such other parts of the former Works towards the west, as shall be deemed usefull for the new fabrick, lest they be spoiled by the fall of more of the walls, which seem to threaten immediate ruine.[133]

The 'handsome and noble' design, of which the choir was to be part, appears to be represented among the surviving Wren drawings by a ground plan for a new cathedral on the existing alignment which includes a plan of the choir stalls (Fig. 107). This design relates by its scale (sixteen feet to the inch) and architectural character to the pre-Fire designs of 1666. It has a version of Jones's portico at the west end, and its plain wall treatment suggests scope for the reuse of cornices and ashlar from the 'former Works' of Inigo Jones.

On 30 July 1669 Wren was appointed Surveyor to the Fabric of St Paul's and became head of an office, with Woodroofe as his draughtsman-assistant and John Tillison as Clerk of Works.[134] He began work on his first complete design for the new cathedral, now known as the First Model (Fig. 108). The model was constructed between October 1669 and March 1670 by Wren's principal joiner, William Clere, and was Wren's response to the cathedral's straitened financial circumstances before Parliament agreed a tax on coal to fund the rebuilding of St Paul's and the

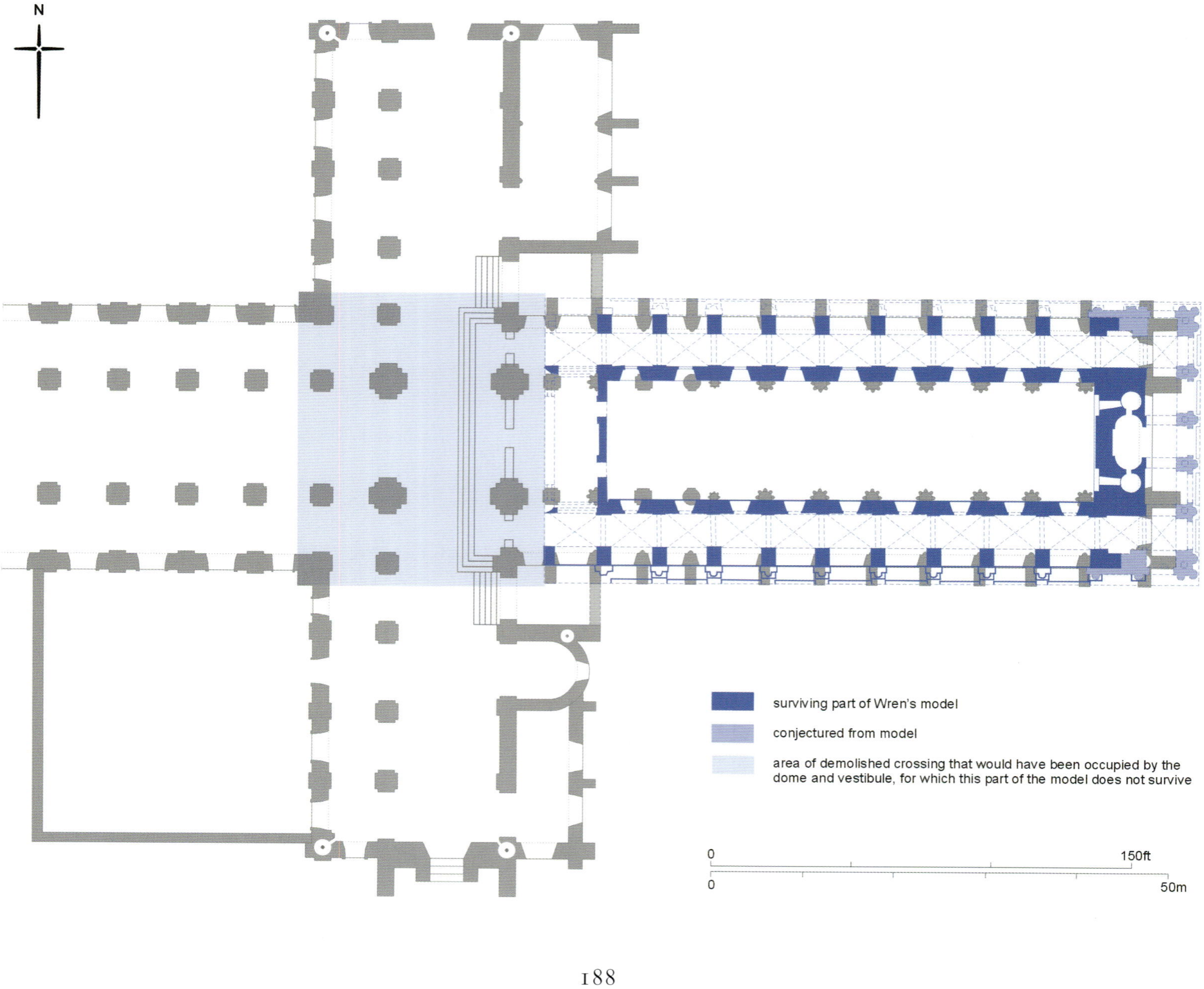

surviving part of Wren's model

conjectured from model

area of demolished crossing that would have been occupied by the dome and vestibule, for which this part of the model does not survive

N

0   150ft

0   50m

109 (*above*). Wren's First Model, 1669–70. Eighteenth-century copy of a lost original Wren office drawing showing the section looking east, and typical bays from the internal and external elevations. (Private collection)

110 (*left*). The plan of Wren's First Model overlaid on that of the eastern arm of the pre-Fire cathedral at main floor level. The missing dome portion of the design would have fitted the crossing area

City churches on 1 May 1670.[135] It marks a clear stylistic break with Jones's classical work on the pre-Fire cathedral, but respects the terms of the warrant of July 1668, which required the new building to be 'neare or upon the old foundations'. The surviving portion of the model is for a ten-bay choir and auditory on two levels, with the gallery level providing additional seating. Doors on two levels at the east end would have provided separate access for the clergy. The two original floor levels are shown in cross-section on an eighteenth-century copy of a lost original design, on which parts of the arcaded internal and external elevations are also shown (Fig. 109). The choir floor would have been raised half a storey above a sunken basement, supported by a central line of piers, as in the medieval crypt. This part of the structure would have fitted the area of the former eastern arm in both plan and section, while a missing vestibule and dome portion at the west end (known from a description in *Parentalia* and a critique by Roger Pratt in 1673) would have occupied the former crossing area (Fig. 110).[136] In Wren's compact scheme, the aisles became external loggias at ground level, providing shelter for those who had previously done business in the nave of the old cathedral – an arrangement probably suggested to him by Palladio's basilica at Vicenza, whose external elevations were the inspiration for his two-storey arcades.

Roger Pratt observed in 1673 that Wren's model was 'one long continued body only', unlike any other church he had seen, ancient or modern. This opinion reflected the doubts of the commissioners in 1670. Some had considered it too far removed from 'the old Gothick form of cathedral churches', while others thought it 'not stately enough, and contended that for the Honour of the Nation, and the City of *London*, it ought not to be exceeded in Magnificence, by any Church in *Europe*'.[137] The arrival of a secure annual revenue of more than £4,000 from coal tax allowed the latter opinion to prevail, and led to the decision to construct a new cathedral on new foundations that was formalized in the Commission for Rebuilding on 12 November 1673.

111. Wren's Great Model for St Paul's Cathedral. Charles II approved a design in December 1672 – possibly the Greek Cross design shown in Figs 143 and 144 – and ordered that a model of it be built 'soe large that a Man might stand within it, the better to consider all the proportions of the same as well within as without' (GL MS CF 54/5). The model is 20 feet 11 inches long (6.36 metres), 13 feet 1 inch wide (3.97 metres), and 13 feet high (3.95 metres), and scaled at 2 feet to an inch (1 : 24). It was built in oak and pear wood by the joiner William Cleere (or Clare) and his team between October 1673 and late summer the following year, when it was being painted in 'stone and lead colour, within and without' and 'gilded with copper' (WS, XVI, 204–7). Eighteen statues adorned the parapets, and the dome and vaults were plastered and painted in *trompe l'oeil*. The king's Commission for Rebuilding St Paul's, issued in November 1673, specified this model as his approved design; but some time late in 1674 or early in 1675 the St Paul's clergy rejected the Great Model as 'not enough of a Cathedral-fashion', one objection being the circular form of the choir. Wren's inspiration for the dome came from early designs for St Peter's in Rome by Bramante and Antonio da Sangallo and from the contemporary church architecture of François Mansart, whose sketch-plan for the Bourbon Chapel at Saint-Denis of 1665 may have informed the plan for a central dome surrounded by an ambulatory of eight alternately circular and oval spaces. The projecting portico, with columns 50 feet (15.25 metres) high, looked back to Roman temple architecture and to Inigo Jones's west portico of the old cathedral, much admired by Wren. (St Paul's Cathedral)

19

WREN AND THE NEW CATHEDRAL

Kerry Downes

Wren, who had been interested in architecture at least since the late 1650s, completed his self-education in France in 1665–6; it was there that he dreamed of a great cupola crowning an interior suffused with light and dominating the surrounding city. On his return to England in late March 1666, the prospect of realizing that dream was faint. While a royal commission deliberated on repairing old St Paul's (see pp. 183–6), the national economy could not give it priority. After the Great Fire, the question was whether London would have any cathedral; the old one soon proved irretrievable, but rebuilding would take many years and much money.

The design whose building commenced around midsummer 1675 was at least his seventh, and it was not much earlier that he awoke to the hugeness and implications of his undertaking – organizing men, materials, money; problems of geometry and statics, even surveying a site full of standing ruins; then in his forty-third year, he might still be saddled with the task at three-score and ten. The massiveness of the piers and bastions around the dome area at crypt level shows how well he prepared for what would eventually rise above them.

THE REQUIREMENTS FOR AN ARCHITECT

Wren became the architect of St Paul's by royal warrant in November 1673 when the Great Model was the approved design.[1] He was uniquely qualified for the job. He had a good constitution, surviving actively into his ninety-first year – all the more important because after the rejection of the Great Model there was no model: what the commission's minutes call 'the Design' consisted of a set of drawings in his own keeping and another locked up in the office. A model's virtues were not only 'the Incouragement and Satisfaction of Benefactors that comprehend not Designs and Draughts on paper' but also 'the inferior Artificers['] clearer intelligence of their Business', especially if in the absence of the architect or for some other reason 'the work should happen to be interrupted or retarded'.[2] After the making and rejection of two models, Wren had 'resolved to make no more Models, or publickly expose his Drawings, which (as he had found by Experience) did but lose Time, and subjected his Business many Times, to incompetent Judges'.[3] The new building's appearance, beyond an outline plan, was known to very few, and two printmakers anxious to show the new building in advance were reduced to fantasy: Godfrey Richards (1676) adapted a Great Model elevation to the Warrant plan (Fig. 114), and the elevation in Ogilby and Morgan's 1682 London map is an optimistic (and acknowledged) invention (Fig. 268). Models of a different kind – expendable, accurate but simple, for a structure or a detail – were used to guide the builders.[4]

There could have been other contenders. John Webb was fifty-five at the time of the Fire. Sir Roger Pratt had virtually abandoned architecture for husbandry when he belatedly inspected and described Wren's First Model. Hugh May had the king's ear and was involved before the fire, but, as a brilliant house designer, he perhaps would not have wanted the job. Wren, too, had the king's ear. Charles II had engaged him over St Paul's in 1661 as an expert, not as a commissioner (see p. 183), and in the same year had tried to tempt him to Tangier with the promise of the Surveyorship of Works in due time. In 1669 Sir John Denham died and Wren did succeed him as Surveyor.

Wren had learned the management skills for resources, money, materials, time and the work-force. Applying his experi-

112.   Sir Christopher Wren, portrait by Johann Closterman, *c.* 1695. The cathedral is shown with the transepts as built but with the west towers and dome not yet finalized. (Private collection)

ence with the Sheldonian Theatre to the far larger scale of the cathedral, he ensured that one trade smoothly followed another in every part of the construction, maintaining the work-force over long periods.

He understood as well as anyone the Vitruvian tripos of 'Commodity, Firmness and Delight'.[5] Wren designated these terms, formulated by the ancient Roman architect and theorist Vitruvius and never improved upon, the 'principles' of architecture, in which all three must be considered in a proper mutual relationship. He was not a theoretician: his writing is fragmentary and occasional. His interests in the natural and mathematical sciences involved the co-ordination of brain and hands: optical and mechanical devices, dissection, microscopic and telescopic draw-

ing, plane and solid geometry, and finally the field that became his life and his passion – architecture.

He was familiar with Anglican liturgy, customs and ceremonial. His uncle Matthew was a Laudian bishop, his father Dean of Windsor and registrar of the Order of the Garter. However, his upbringing was not sheltered: during the Civil War and in the Oxford of the 1650s he encountered other aspects of Protestant religion, for better and for worse.

He was exceptionally capable of understanding and visualizing three-dimensional forms, in space and in mass and relative to one another, developing his innate talent through his geometrical work, applying it first to geometrical problems of the solar system. Later, it was indispensable in understanding all those parts of

113 (*right*). View from the north-east, by Sutton Nicholls, 1695. The north transept is still hidden by scaffolding and wattle screens, leaving the public with little idea of the appearance of Wren's building. From a unique proof impression before letters. (GL, St Paul's collection)

114 (*below right*). 'The new Model of the Cathedral of St. Paules as its now to be Built'. Plate added to the third edition of Godfrey Richards's translation of Palladio's First Book of Architecture, 1676. The dome and quadrant curves of the Great Model are adapted to the straight lines and Latin-cross plan of the actual building

the cathedral that lie between the exterior and interior aspects – parts known to maintenance staff where they are hollowed into passages and staircases, and to no one where they are solid.

He also learned to understand scale – human scale, the scale of the whole and the parts of a building and the relation of architectural to human scale. Not all designers of buildings manage this; Wren took time to develop it, but it is manifest in his cathedral.

THE CHARACTER

Most of all, Wren had *genius*. It would be simplistic to say that he was appointed to St Paul's by default, but there is no evidence of competition. From his teens, contemporaries considered him brilliant: 'a youth of absolutely marvellous talent';[6] a 'miracle of a youth';[7] 'a miracle of a man, nay, even something divine'.[8] Since he published little and seldom completed projects or provided details of his reasoning, it is not immediately obvious why they were so impressed. However, if we accept that they were not deceived, we may be able to look afresh at the qualities of his great church, a building that over three centuries has been more often faulted than praised.

The most effusive early tribute is that of Thomas Sprat,[9] who presented him as the paragon of the Royal Society philosopher (scientist), in the mould formed by Francis Bacon: working by induction, deriving general principles from experiments or accumulated data. In a famous essay, Sir John Summerson[10] portrayed Wren as a creative heart overruled by a rationalistic head, and this interpretation appealed strongly to the generation that rediscovered the more exciting baroque of Hawksmoor and Vanbrugh. Recently it has become fashionable to fault Summerson and his generation, even to discredit his brand of art history as too obviously of its time.[11] To do this in respect of Wren misses the point, for Summerson himself found Wren too fascinating to abandon. His later image, presented briefly in a short monograph,[12] is closer to the truth: the mathematician who found architecture the most exciting, actual and even passionate demonstration of geometrical truths, the only ones, except those of revealed religion, 'that can sink into the Mind of Man void of all Uncertainty'.[13] In what read like incomplete lecturing notes, Wren discussed two 'causes' of beauty: geometry and association with 'things not in themselves [i.e. geometrically] beautiful';[14] the architect should rely on reason epitomized in the logic of numbers and distrust fancy [imagination] which 'blinds the judgement'. But if Summerson could not abandon Wren, so Wren could not abandon fancy. Like Nicolas Poussin, a painter of his father's generation, Wren protested too much; neither would he have been such a great artist if he had not, albeit circumspectly, kept an essential place in his art for intuition.

Sprat misrepresented Wren. In his inaugural astronomy lecture at Gresham College, Wren named the preceding thinkers whose influence and achievement he most valued: Copernicus, Kepler, Galileo and Descartes, Harvey (the circulation of blood) and Gilbert (the earth as a magnet), whom, rather than Bacon or even Descartes, he calls the 'Father of the new Philosophy'.[15] A good enough reason, and perhaps the real one, for his omitting Bacon was that Bacon set little store by mathematics. Moreover, Wren's forte was geometry, the most *deductive*, visually the most demonstrative, and thus most intuitive of the mathematical sciences.

One may *become* an architect; Wren was slow to recognize that he was *born* an architect. The most significant difference this recognition made was in his attention span. Architecture takes a long time. The mathematician who sent to Paris a geometrical proof when the rules specified a numerical one, who showed how to solve it but did not bother to do so, became the architect who spent hours scrupulously redrawing details for the sake of a few inches' difference, who, having finished his drawings 'with a great deale of paines', would 'not repent the great satisfaction and pleasure I have taken in the contrivance' even if nothing were to come of them.[16]

Wren, who learned to draw well as a child, later advocated its universal teaching as second to writing and the basis of 'all Mechanick Arts'.[17] But, like Inigo Jones before him, he had no architectural training. Since the early Renaissance, it was acceptable to practise architecture as a gentleman – the path established by Leone Battista Alberti and followed by Pratt – or as an artist or craftsman – such as Brunelleschi, Raphael, Michelangelo and Jones. The first path was open to Wren; so was a third. It was widely accepted that, with the implicit authority of Vitruvius, architecture was a branch of mathematics embodying both the statics of structures and the creation of order and beauty. When he began in the autumn of 1661 to advise on the old cathedral, his talent was unproven, but he had made 'new designs tending to strength, convenience and beauty in building' in his postgraduate days at Oxford – thus probably before 1657.[18] He had read Vitruvius and probably also Serlio, Alberti in Latin and Palladio. His father understood building, and in the mid 1650s young Wren would have brought a habituated and analytical eye to the many important recent buildings in Oxford (including his own college, Wadham) as well as in London. Of all these, few besides Jones's works were strictly classical; Jacobean and Caroline architecture was based on considerable but indirect knowledge of ancient Rome and modern Italy by way of France, the Netherlands and Germany. In this context, Wren's first buildings, Pembroke College Chapel in Cambridge (1663–5) and the Sheldonian Theatre in Oxford (1664–9), were recognized by contemporaries as advanced. He went to Paris with a decade's private study behind him. To old St Paul's he brought a decade's experience in statics, longer in geometry. And by the time the Great Model was being drafted he had been in part-time practice also for a decade.

Wren learned by looking, by watching, and by questions and dialogue. His visit to Paris, the length of an academic year, taught him what he could not learn at home. The debate as to whether he went as a scientist or an architect is fruitless because he made no distinction. However, the two figures he expressly wished – and undoubtedly managed – to meet there were the senior French architect François Mansart and the sculptor-architect Gianlorenzo Bernini, who on a royal invitation had recently arrived in Paris. Moreover, in a letter – our major source for the visit – Wren wrote, 'the Louvre for a while was my daily Object, where no less than a thousand Hands are constantly employ'd in the Works… which altogether make a School of Architecture, the best probably, at this Day in Europe'.[19] And on his return he wrote (in the context of dome-building) of seeing several large structures 'in rising, conducted by the best Artists, French and Italian, and having daily conference with them'.[20]

THE BRIEF

There were no prototypes for a post-Renaissance Protestant cathedral. After eight years of experiment and discussion, a brief was agreed between architect, clergy and monarch; had it been written out in detail in 1674, it would have comprised the following:

- A traditional Latin-cross plan, with nave, chancel and transepts; this was only established as a prime requirement after the Great Model showed the alternative to be unacceptable.
- New foundations, avoiding the old as far as possible. Wren pressed for this as early as April 1668.[21]
- Provision for daily liturgy, the preaching of sermons and ceremonial assembly. Only the last of these anticipated an attendance of more than five hundred; for over a century, the chancel served both for worship and as an 'auditory'.
- A large and impressive building, appropriate to a symbol of the capital city, the Church of England, the monarchy and indeed the whole country; Wren had written of the old cathedral as 'a pile as much for ornament as use'.[22]
- Wren himself was committed from the start to a lofty cupola riding over the city as a landmark without, and providing a spacious and exciting climax within.
- Bell-towers.
- A modern building, comparing favourably with recent architecture elsewhere in western Europe. Christopher Wren junior says that the chapter and other clergy 'thought the [Great] Model not enough of a Cathedral-fashion' and Wren 'turn'd his Thoughts to a Cathedral-form (as they call'd it) but so rectified, as to reconcile, as near as possible, the Gothick to a better Manner of Architecture'.[23] The arbitrary equivalence of 'style', 'manner' and 'form' does not mean that his father considered an alternative Gothic design with pointed arches; Wren dismissed such a choice in his report of May 1666, urging Sancroft to 'goe to the charges of trew latine'.[24] Reconciliation in this context can only mean a Gothic (i.e. Latin-cross) plan and, in our terminology, a classical style.
- As an enterprise funded principally by a new tax on London's coal supply, the avoidance of conspicuous extravagance was not to prejudice the requirements of excellent workmanship or appropriate materials, detailing and ornament, but no overall budget was set.
- To restore as soon as possible the traditions of divine service, the building, whose construction speed depended on the rate of income, ought to be completable in stages. Wren was anxious that it *should* be completed, but the twenty-two years taken to finish even the choir were due as much to political and finan-

115.   West-east section of Wren's Warrant Design, belatedly approved on
14 May 1675. (AS, Wren Collection, II.14)

cial causes as to his efforts to advance work in other parts. It was also recognized at the start that all four legs of the dome must, for stability, rise simultaneously.[25]

A possible further provision, a portico giving sheltered exterior space for secular transactions as Inigo Jones's had done, was dropped before construction began; the new coffee-houses were more comfortable.

In all this Wren was the prime mover, for he alone understood the implications of every part of it. The Warrant Design (Fig. 115) meets this brief, very neatly and simply. It has been seen as a reversion to much earlier ideas,[26] partly because it does not appeal to modern taste and partly because of its Jonesian western portico and fenestration. Certainly ideas reappear from a Latin-cross plan (Fig. 107) datable to 1668,[27] and almost certainly made after a fall of masonry on 25 April 1668 put paid to ideas of a temporary church in the ruined nave.[28] Wren had only acquiesced in this project because of the clergy's enthusiasm;[29] he was not surprised at the accident, and begged Sancroft '(as I have alwaies enclined since the fire) to set your thoughts upon a new fabrick upon new foundations, artificiall durable and beautifull, but less massive, and to use the old but as you would use a quarry'. He came to London with 'old designes', and again in July to help the commission 'to frame a Design, handsome and noble, and suitable to all the Ends of it, and to the Reputation of the City, and the Nation';

it was now assumed 'that Money will be had to accomplish it',[30] and on 25 July an order was issued by the Secretary of State for demolishing the eastern arm and tower 'to make room for a new Choir, of a faire and decent fabrick neare or upon the old foundations'.[31] However, the status of this early Latin-cross plan is uncertain: it assumed the same orientation as the old cathedral, which Wren never favoured, and his work at St Paul's was not official for another year.[32] There are no related drawings and, for all its high degree of finish, it may be no more than what today is known as a 'sketch-plan'. But it does contain several features that, after the model-making episodes of 1669–73, reappear in the Warrant Design: a Latin cross with short transepts, a large dome spanning the aisles, carried on eight piers and abutted by big corner bastions, a Jonesian west portico and a basically classical vocabulary with broad bays and cross-vaulting throughout.

In reality, the Warrant Design is a fresh response to a new situation, after the huge scale and painted vividness of the Great Model finally made up the clergy's minds about what they did not want and, by default, what they did want. Moreover, Wren took the Warrant more seriously than some modern commentators do. He provided a Latin title to the drawings, and the dramatic angels, over-life-size, that swoop down with garlands in the spandrels under the dome are not the work of a half-hearted architect.[33] The design is broad, bold, unconventional (particularly in and over the crossing) and simple in vocabulary; Wren, who

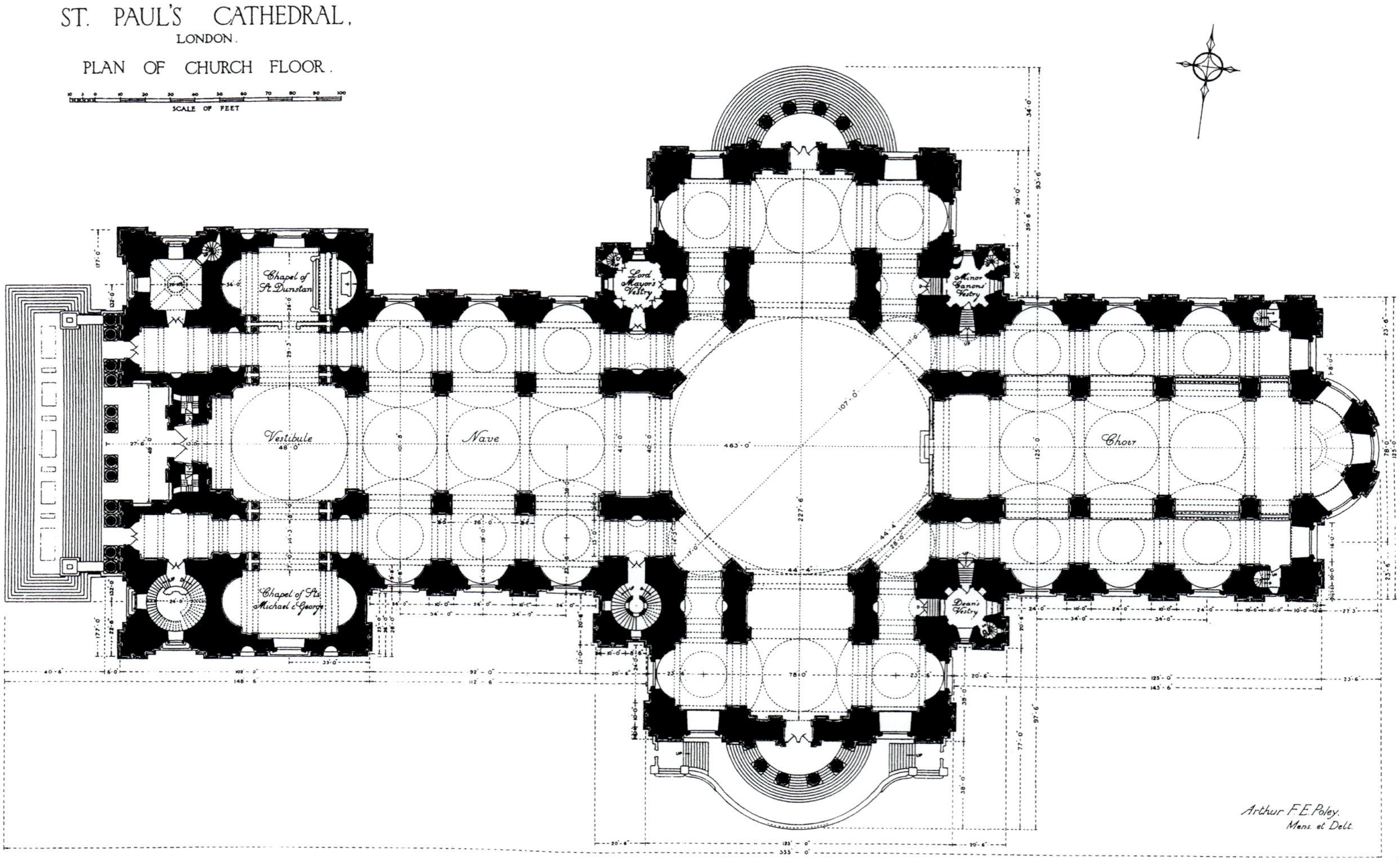
ST. PAUL'S CATHEDRAL,
LONDON.
PLAN OF CHURCH FLOOR.
SCALE OF FEET
Chapel of St Dunstan
Lord Mayor's Vestry
Minor Canons' Vestry
Vestibule
Nave
Choir
Chapel of St Michael & George
Dean's Vestry
Arthur F.E. Poley.
Mens. et Delt.

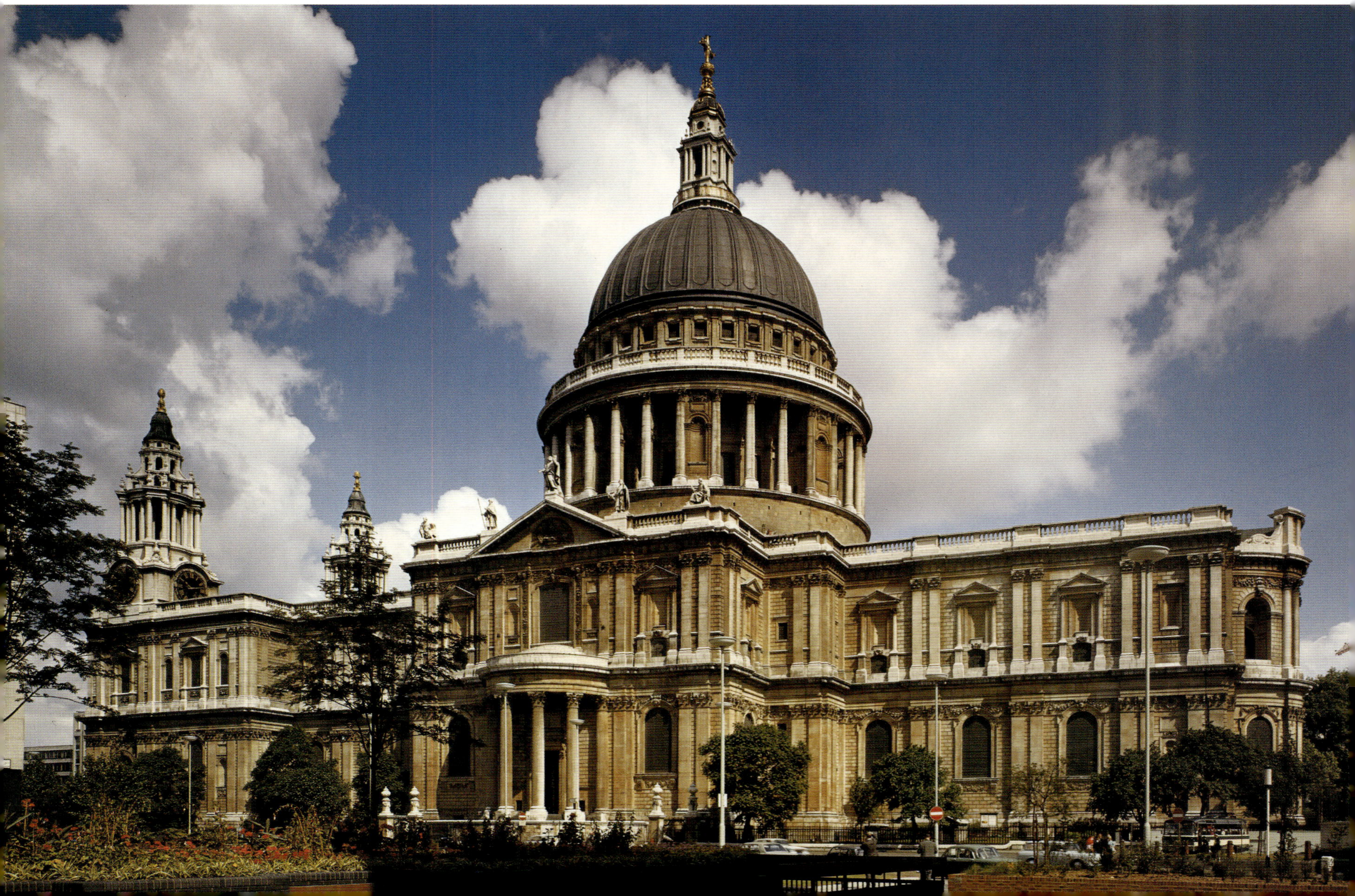

was capable of great speed, could have devised and drawn it out in a couple of weeks. It is the key to reconstructing the brief set out here.

A first stone was placed without ceremony on 21 June 1675, and the east end was set out again around that time.[34] The theory that – for no good reason – he aligned his building on sunrise for Easter Day 1675 is based on an inaccurate diagram.[35] Wren's reasons for the reorientation were the rebuilt street pattern, the available space, the line of Ludgate Hill and, most important, the desire to avoid old foundations.[36]

Wren followed the brief to the end, but the vagueness of architectural thinking at the time allowed him considerable latitude which, with the particular sanction of Charles II, he exploited. In doing so, he transformed a set of fulfilled requirements into a unique monument, but also, like many works of genius, an equivocal one which cannot be understood in terms of any previous work, or according to prior assumptions about the nature of a cathedral.[37]

THE EXTERIOR

Thus one of the earliest – albeit satirical – commentators on the building, Joseph Addison, interpreted its exterior as a palace rather than a temple (see p. 451).[38] This impression persists, not only through the deep-rooted English equation of Gothic style with religious function, but because it is iconographically accurate. Most Renaissance long churches, like earlier ones, are basilican, with one-storey aisles flanking two-storey middle naves. Whether or not they have additional entrances through the transepts, their long sides often display a great deal of buttressing and roofing (e.g. the Gesù in Rome or the Redentore in Venice) and are visually subordinate to the west[39] front. St Paul's, on the other hand, has a continuous two-storey exterior without any obvious engineering. The Latin-cross plan is concealed (Fig. 117). The north and south sides are almost symmetrical about the transept porticoes, the extra length at the west being occupied by bell-towers and by chapels with the library and trophy room above (Figs. 116, 350). The single-bay transepts appear as central salients in the 'palace front', the negative corners between the four cross arms being hidden by the huge positive corners of the central square mass that provides both abutment and visual support for the massive dome.

To a London viewer, there are obvious parallels with Jones's Banqueting House, with a similar use of two applied orders and a similar rustication pattern. Because the long side view occupies a larger visual segment, it is dominant, to the city and the world, from near and far. Moreover, the near view was limited from the start. In London, as in some other densely packed city centres, the cathedral was inextricable from the urban scene, and with the streets of post-Fire London already crowding around the churchyard when building began in 1675, a large open space with a single show façade was not a practical possibility. This did not deter eighteenth-century printmakers from showing the cathedral in a wide open space (Fig. 118). Instead, St Paul's offered a *front* in every direction except east. In the far view, on the other hand,

118 (*above*). *The North-west Prospect of the Cathedral Church of St Paul's London*, view by D. Stopendaal, Amsterdam, *c.* 1725. One of several popular early views showing St Paul's extracted from its surroundings. A previous engraving has been copied and reversed in printing, so that the building appears as if from the south-west but with the north portico steps. The reversal was possibly deliberate, for use in a viewer with a mirror. (BM, Crace Collection)

119 (*right*). View from the north-west, by Robert Trevitt, published in 1703. (GL)

until the twentieth century the whole upper half stood clear above other buildings (Figs 120, 356). This huge two-storey mass provides visual support for a very large dome, so large that its diameter spans across the aisles, so tall that in clear weather only intervening building development and the earth's curvature limit its distant perception, 'at Sea Eastward, and at Windsor Westward'.[40]

Wren understood tempo, rhythm and movement in architecture. At St Paul's the tempo is slow, the rhythm flexible and the

116 (*above left*). Survey plan of the main floor of the cathedral, measured by Arthur Poley and published in *St Paul's Cathedral, London, Measured, Drawn and Described* (1927)

117 (*left*). The cathedral from the south, *c.*1965

120.   The City of London from the terrace of Richmond House, Whitehall, by Antonio Canaletto, *c*. 1747. (Trustees of the Goodwood Collection)

121 (*opposite*).   The west front, *c*. 1965

movement small. Superimposed orders of coupled pilasters divide the nave and choir elevations into grids of near-square parts; horizontal and vertical emphases are balanced, and the large bays are too few in number to establish a rhythm along the elevations. Then the pilasters enclose some corners (e.g. the corner bastions supporting the dome) but allow others to stand proud as sheer masonry (e.g. the transept ends); the east and west ends of the façades are treated differently from the rest, and from each other. The effects are interesting and lively, but only skin-deep, a sheen on the massive solid geometry of the whole. Wren wrote that 'Fronts ought to be...rather projecting forward in the Middle, than hollow'.[41]

This is true of the long sides as wholes, but in the transept ends the plane of the wall surface, and the pilasters and entabla-

tures that articulate it, do not advance consistently towards the centre as happens in typical baroque buildings; anthropomorphically, these fronts *are*, but they *do* nothing. And yet the inhibition has a positive element: when construction reached the upper walls, Wren enriched the design with chains of carved vegetation down the middle pilasters and with a false frieze at capital level. This, and the shifting wall plane, tend to confuse the analytical eye and favour the holistic perception of the complete transept end as a unit. But the entire long fronts can also be read this way; their division into few large units, more easily perceived intuitively than construed analytically, is a hallmark of baroque architecture. The false frieze, inserted throughout the lower order, was a favourite device of Wren's; it had the authority of the Banqueting House and ultimately of

122.   Aedicule on south transept

123.   The nave looking east, engraving by E. T. Dolby, *c.* 1852. (GL)

Palladio's illustrations of his Palazzo Thiene (though not the actual building).[42]

Our reading of the exterior is permanently compromised by the balustrade at the top of the walls that blurs the hard geometrical edge Wren intended. This was ordered by the new building commission in 1717 in imitation of Jones's Banqueting House; 'ladies', wrote Wren, 'think nothing well without an edging'.[43] The balustrade over the peristyle of the dome, however, *is* part of his design, easing and softening the transition from the close-packed columns of the peristyle to the almost hemispherical[44] cupola above. Thus vertical emphases dissolve upwards into equilibrium. Michelangelo's dome of St Peter's (as altered in execution by Giacomo della Porta) seems to soar; Wren's dome floats. The dome only assumed its final form about 1704, on the eve of construction. By then, thanks to the extension of the coal tax, the city skyline had been embellished with several tall and inventive steeples (e.g. besides the earlier St Mary-le-Bow, St Dunstan in the East, St Bride, Christ Church) and others were projected (St Vedast, St Magnus, St Stephen Walbrook). So the dome stands out, apparently geometrically simple, among the varied and elaborate shapes of the church steeples, in whose company the bell towers in their final form take their place (Fig. 120).

The dome, like the church it crowns, looks entirely different outside and inside. The casual observer may not be aware of this, or may retain but never account for a confused impression. All the moral force of nineteenth-century criticism descended on Wren's 'dishonesty'. There was even some bantering talk of a proposal to

remove the outer leaded timber dome and leave exposed the brick cone that, unseen, carries the lantern and counterpoises the inner dome (Figs 136, 138).[45] But the strongest and most persistent criticism is of the screen walls that form the upper half of the exterior elevation (see p. 213 and Fig. 380). Wren's aesthetic – typically baroque – admitted no problem: 'In things that are not seen at once, and have no Respect one to another, great Variety is commendable'.[46] Wren was not a paper architect, and one of the marvels of St Paul's is the way in which the visual exterior and interior each 'have Respect' to their common structure. The substantial separation of inner and outer domes, of spacious interior and crowning landmark, already characterized his pre-Fire proposal of August 1666 (Figs. 105, 106), and was a device he learned in Paris. The almost complete disparity in the church body came later, possibly by 1668 but very probably in detail by 1675 when building started.

Very few external features betray what is inside. Apart from the obvious ones, the main west, north and south doors and the windows over them, the most significant is in the west front (Fig. 121), where the partial replacement of pilasters by full columns, twelve below and eight above, expresses and coincides with the basilican cross-section with side aisles below and clerestory above. The windows set deep in the peristyle can be seen from outside; however, the square recesses just under the leaded dome are blind, lined with Irish black marble,[47] for there is nothing significant behind them to light.[48] The upper windows of the apse also go through, although the glazing is visibly several feet below the outer apertures; this device appears in engravings of Antonio da

124. The crossing and choir, after the removal of the organ and screen and before the installation of the reredos. One of the earliest known photographs of the interior, by James Valentine, c. 1880. (Yale University Arts Library)

Sangallo's design for St Peter's, which had a comparable difference between internal and external levels.

In one other feature the interior disposition is consistently expressed outside: the small segmental-headed triforium windows immediately over the first outside cornice (Figs. 120, 122). This (in every sense) transparent honesty counted for little with the critics, for it is implicated in the larger deception of the screen walls. The screens' external effect has been described; in order to understand how and why Wren came to invent them, it is necessary to consider the interior, demonstrably of Latin-cross form and flooded with light, the quality he so much admired in Gothic Salisbury where, in his report of 1668, he praised the medieval architect who 'knew better that nothing could adde beauty to light'.[49] An early visitor found the new St Paul's 'extraordinarily light',[50] and indeed it was, for the whole had been painted – probably primarily to conceal the many patches and variations in the ashlar facing[51] – and dust and soot had not yet begun to dull its luminosity.

THE INTERIOR

No one on entering the building can fail to notice the crossing, framed by the nearest of its four great main arches and limited by the farthest (Figs. 58, 123); the twenty-four tall windows in the peristyle make it the lightest part of the building and provide about three times the window area of the Warrant dome. However, from the west door the crossing cannot be perceived spatially, and its full expanse in all dimensions is only apparent from much closer, almost under the great arch at the east end of the nave. Only there can the great height of the inner dome be seen, or, more significantly, the width of the crossing which incorporates that of the side aisles (Fig. 124). This dramatic use of space and light goes back to the pre-Fire proposal to replace the crossing and tower by a 'Spacious Dome or rotunda with a Cupolo or Hemispherical Roof', likewise spanning the aisles (Fig. 104). Cupolas that do this are exceptional – Florence Cathedral[52] is the obvious example – and there was none of this sort in Paris when,

in 1665, Wren had met domes for the first and only time. But there is a plausible prototype nearer home, although from an earlier age.

Wren's uncle Matthew, bishop of Ely from 1638 to his death in 1667, returned to his see in 1660. In 1663 he engaged his nephew to design the new chapel of Pembroke, his old Cambridge college. This, if nothing else, would have provided an occasion to see one of the marvels of English Gothic construction, the octagon of Ely Cathedral, built in 1322–42 (it may be noted) after the failure of the main piers and the collapse of the tower and crossing. Spatially, the timber and glass octagon is the nearest thing to a dome in English medieval architecture; it spans sixty-five feet on the cardinal axes and is lit by a central lantern and four large windows in the diagonal faces between the main roofs; in Wren's time, these all contained clear glass. The choir stalls were then under the octagon and the vista from the west was virtually closed below triforium level by a stone pulpitum carrying a small organ.

Already, too, in the pre-Fire design Wren envisaged a dome with an internal diameter four-fifths of the eventual building (85 feet against 107 feet), a drum and peristyle (cylindrical rather than slightly conical), an inner dome of brick slightly taller than a hemisphere,[53] a higher outer dome of timber covered with lead, and a tall lantern and finial. Moreover, the heights at each stage – drum, inner and outer shells, and finial – are within a few feet of the final ones (Figs 105, 106).[54] Thus was the original dream embodied in the final reality.

The French source usually cited for the double-shell dome of masonry and timber is Lemercier's church of the Sorbonne; however, it was anticipated by Mansart's church of the Visitation, in the newly fashionable rue Saint-Antoine, a convent church which was open to visitors. This has a stone lower shell and a timber upper one; moreover, in the Visitation the lantern windows introduce light into the church, whereas the Sorbonne dome is almost blind since the lantern is only lit indirectly by lucarne windows high in the outer dome. The Visitation is circular, whereas the other churches have the typical Counter-Reformation short Latin-cross plan. Further along the same street, another Latin-

125 (*above left*).   The nave looking west

126 (*left*).   View of the crossing looking north-east, published by Robert Sayer *c.* 1750. (GL)

127 (*above*).   Timber screen and iron railings installed *c.* 1708 in front of the Chapel of St Michael and St George (formerly Consistory Court chapel) in south aisle, view in 1956

cross building, the Jesuit church (now Saint-Paul-Saint-Louis) by Martellange and Derand, has a well-lit lantern and dome.

As Wren was not one of those who 'comprehend not Designes & Draughts on paper' for whom models are a necessity, he would also have absorbed from his 'daily conference' – and from drawings – other buildings incomplete or merely projected: the chapel of Le Vau's Collège des Quatre Nations (perceptibly oval), Guarini's never completed Theatine church (Sainte-Anne-la-Royale) and Mansart's projected funerary chapel attached to Saint-Denis, which was under consideration in 1665–6 and the basis of Hardouin-Mansart's later dome of the Invalides.

But visitors do not generally make straight for the centre even of a church simpler than St Paul's. The first impression, of the distant bright crossing, is formed in the context of the broader, peripheral view, of huge size but not inhuman scale: huge because

inside the building we see it at close quarters occupying our whole vision, and human because the architecture begins at a human level. Outside, there is indeed a high basement: the pilaster shafts commence twelve or thirteen feet from the ground (Fig. 117). But out of doors we naturally distance ourselves for a more comfortable view, and in the context of street, people and traffic the scale evokes wonder rather than fear. Inside, where everything is close, the height to the shafts, only about four feet, is below the eye-level of an average child of eleven (Figs. 33, 123).

This seldom receives comment, and when the interior is full of furniture it may not be consciously noticed. But it is very different indeed from Wren's previous conception. In the pre-Fire crossing, the corresponding point was about eight feet (Fig. 106). The First Model's outside loggias, which might also have been

202

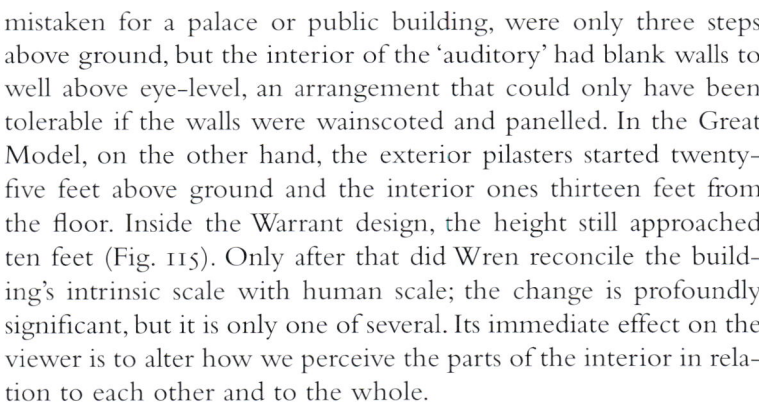

128.   South nave aisle looking east in 1980 The monument on the right is to Bishop Middleton, 1832

129.   Looking into the north choir aisle and choir from the crossing in 1991

mistaken for a palace or public building, were only three steps above ground, but the interior of the 'auditory' had blank walls to well above eye-level, an arrangement that could only have been tolerable if the walls were wainscoted and panelled. In the Great Model, on the other hand, the exterior pilasters started twenty-five feet above ground and the interior ones thirteen feet from the floor. Inside the Warrant design, the height still approached ten feet (Fig. 115). Only after that did Wren reconcile the building's intrinsic scale with human scale; the change is profoundly significant, but it is only one of several. Its immediate effect on the viewer is to alter how we perceive the parts of the interior in relation to each other and to the whole.

To say that Wren changed a five-bay nave into a three-bay one with a vestibule is true; to expand on this statement may therefore seem needless, and that may be why writers seldom do so. But the change is only part of a comprehensive process, and how he made it and how it alters our perception of the interior are important matters, all the more so because, like the Warrant Design itself, they are so seldom discussed. The first point to make is that Wren preserved the letter, and the floor area, of the Latin cross, but the spirit is that of an interior space centralized around the crossing (Fig. 126). Anyone familiar with Renaissance and later churches would expect on entering St Paul's to see a long nave of identical bays; instead, the space is divided into few large spatial units more or less corresponding to the large units of mass outside. Even from

the side aisle doors, the western part of the interior is higher, broader and more open, with a large saucer-dome ('the west dome' in building accounts) and with large arches opening to the north and south chapels that project outside east of the towers (Figs. 116, 117).

The distinctness of this space from the nave proper is also made by the very large pier masses that support the four corners of the 'west dome' and define the space beneath it. From the west end, these piers seem similar to those at the east end of the nave under the crossing arch; as we see those distant piers sharply foreshortened, it is not obvious how much bigger they are. So the large piers, near and far, frame and define the intervening three bays which, being all the same, form a group – a larger unit – to the eye. If we choose the side aisle, we see it sharply foreshortened, the west and crossing ends narrower than the main three bays (Fig. 128). Walking down the church, we discover that the choir, apart from its furnishings and the later mosaic decoration, comprises an identical group or larger unit, defined at the far east end by the half-bay that terminates in the apse.

Here, some historical imagination is needed. Firstly, Wren had considered the 'excessive length' of the old cathedral no more than picturesque.[55] Until the 1860s, his functional chancel was divided from the unfurnished crossing and nave by a wooden screen and organ case (Figs. 123, 155). Secondly, later polychrome decoration in the spandrels below the Whispering Gallery

130.   Proposed south elevation of the first complete design on the final
plan (the 'Definitive Design'), with a dome inspired by Michelangelo's for
St Peter's, Rome. The drawing differs from the building in many details,
from the basement upwards. (AS, Wren Collection, II.29)

interferes with the illusion he devised for the transition from
unequal up to apparently equal arches meeting in sharp points on
the main cornice; he had used a similar device in St Stephen
Walbrook.

In both nave and choir the arrangement of piers and arches is
confirmed by the vaulting, for each bay in the group of three is
covered by a vault with oddly shaped pendentives adjusting the
rectangular plan to a saucer-dome, an innovative substitution for
the cross-vaults of the Warrant (Fig. 115). Except for the west end,
the groups of three saucer-domes are framed by very broad
coffered arches – the west and east crossing arches and that over
the eastern half-bay terminating the choir. Each transept is only a
single bay, with a saucer-dome between the crossing arch and the
end wall.

It is of course quite possible to read the interior in other ways,
but the reading presented here not only follows the diversity and
distribution of architectural elements but also relates closely to
that rarity in Wren's practice, an acknowledged precedent: the
ancient basilica of Maxentius in Rome, a large cross-vaulted hall
three bays long, flanked and supported on either side by three
barrel-vaulted side rooms. Wren wrote a perceptive and original
analysis of this ruined building in his fourth *Tract*,[56] based not
only on Serlio and Palladio but also on other, untraced, sources;[57]

however, his interest was more than antiquarian, for in one respect
St Paul's is very close to his source. The columns that originally
supported the Basilica's main vaults had each a section of entablature, but it was not continued along the wall between them. Wren
commends the omission as, in his view, taking account of the
requirements of light inside the building, and in his final paragraph he cites other ancient examples with similar justification.
His adoption of the same feature at St Paul's, with pilasters instead
of columns and with only the cornice continued, was comparably
pragmatic, and is another element in the transformation from the
Warrant. It also reinforces our reading of the three bays as a unit
distinct from other parts of the design. For the identification we
have the authority of his son, who cites the basilica in answer to
contemporary criticism of his father's unorthodoxy: 'In this the
Surveyor always insisted that he had the Ancients on his Side'.[58]
Although less directly than in the basilica, Wren's motive is again
light and the sensation of light.

By this point, the visitor will have reached the crossing (Fig.
129) and will not only have taken in its expanse, its height, its illumination and Thornhill's grisaille dome painting, but also, looking
all around, will have observed the continuity of the smaller order
of pilasters – Composite instead of the Corinthian of the large
order – that encircles the whole interior supporting the arcades

and the aisle vaults and figuring prominently in the view through the secondary arches at the corners of the crossing, 'so the Aisle of the whole length of the church is of itself a long and graceful Portico, without being interrupted by the legs of the Dome'.[59] This is particularly striking at the level of the capitals, whose volutes and leaves become part of a rich and continuous false frieze. In many places there is also, just below the aisle windows, a moulded band, an interlace with flowers.

Thornhill's painting emphasizes the height of the inner dome, a dimension Wren had carefully calculated not to appear extreme; even so, the beholder has no idea either of its relation to the exterior or of the hidden cone which carries the lantern and secures the stability of the whole (Fig. 138). What is inescapable is the bulk of supporting masonry – eight great piers linked by arches at two levels to the four corner bastions that also appear outside between the cross arms. It is only here, and in the deeply coffered crossing arches, that the building's massiveness appears.

THE TRANSFORMATION

There is substantial evidence for the conclusion that, up to the roof-line and apart from decorative details, the cathedral was completed according to Wren's 'Definitive' design of 1675; surviving drawings tell us something – but not everything – of how he reached that design. Rather more is known of the evolution of the dome from the 'former design' shown in a well-known south elevation (as it had become by 1700 and was described in a related sectional engraving)[60] to the final structure, because shortly after 1700, with the body of the church virtually complete, Wren exchanged secrecy for publicity and allowed several prints to be engraved and published.[61] The 'former design' shows a drum with sixteen windows between buttress-piers and an outer cupola with ribs and the same profile as St Peter's, its unmistakable prototype (Fig. 130).[62] It is far more massive than the Warrant dome, and Wren prepared appropriately for such a structure. Around the turn of the century, he finalized the thirty-two-column peristyle shown in the 1702 prints; the hidden cone, the outer cupola and the lantern were only finalized later, and differently.

Drawings document the particulars of the complete design up to the roof-line,[63] but we would have very little idea of how Wren developed this extremely complex building had not the architect (and his son and subsequent owners) preserved the little Warrant drawings, already obsolete when authorized on 14 May 1675.[64] As the basis of the brief, these drawings set out the design from which, according to his son, Wren was allowed by Charles II 'the Liberty . . . to make some Variations, rather ornamental, than essential, as from Time to Time he should see proper'.[65] Wren used his liberty to transform the building, but so cleverly that in no respect could he be convicted of abandoning his brief. We know something about one stage in the transformation from a small group of unfinished drawings that Sir John Summerson called the 'Penultimate design';[66] these concentrate around the crossing, and show Wren – not surprisingly – working systematically upwards from the ground and outwards from the centre. At this stage, he had reworked all the plan dimensions and *most* of the vertical ones up to the main internal entablature; however, ambiguities and uncertainties in subsequent drawings – including the church floor height from ground – support the argument that the whole, including the screen walls, was settled while the Warrant drawings awaited a decision from Whitehall.[67]

131. Impost capitals in the choir. The garland retains the convention of hanging from two pins

132. Impost capitals in the nave. These were carved later than the choir; the flowers are more realistic, the carving is more daring and the arrangement much freer

Wren's approach to design embraced alternative modes, plain or enriched, simple or complex, and this is not a matter of date or development. The Warrant design is sparsely ornamented, rather plain and simple (Fig. 115). The plan appears to embody a 10-foot module, if we take the effective widths of nave as 40 feet, aisles as 20 feet, and arcades and aisle walls as 10 feet. In the final design, surfaces are more varied, detailing richer, the components and their combinations more complex. In the design as a whole, any neat proportional scheme disappears with the nave 41 feet, aisles 19 feet, arcades thinner and aisle walls thicker. This is enough to establish that the building could not prudently have been started on Warrant foundations.[68]

These changes are among the first; linked to them were the redesign of the west end and the effective reduction of the nave, the application of coupled pilasters to the whole exterior and the reversion from equal to unequal arches under the dome. Equal arches are unique to the Warrant; Ely, and Wren's plans from 1668 through to the Great Model, have unequal ones. Wren seems to have wanted more space, illumination and structural lightness in the main naves, lower and narrower side aisles, and a more diffused statical system. In the Penultimate drawings, he experimented with big windows above the diagonal arches, whose light would supplement the sixteen oval windows in a truly hemispherical dome,[69] but this was a blind alley. Other crucial interior changes were dropping the plinth under the pilasters by more than half and lowering the cornice of the large order by some seven feet; the first humanizes the interior scale, the second – requiring the omission of most of the entablature – gives the main spaces virtually a two-storey elevation and thus a considerably loftier appearance. (A constant is the aisle windows, which is why they now break up into the exterior false frieze.)

This lightness (in all senses) is enhanced by the change from cross-vaults throughout to saucer-domes on pendentives derived from a hemisphere. In his second *Tract*, Wren recommended this construction as needing less abutment.[70] The 'Greek' (Byzantine) examples he cites, including the Hagia Sophia, cover square areas; rectangles present problems since the semicircular arches on the short sides will be smaller and lower than on the long sides. That is what happens in the aisles; in the main vaults Wren ingeniously adapted the system, making the clerestory lunettes tall half-ovals[71] and thus as high as the semicircular cross-arches. Decorated spandrels link them to the saucer-domes and fill in the pendentives.

The spandrels, curved in three dimensions, are but one of the devices Wren invented in the final design for decorative texture, enriching both interior and exterior but without detriment to the building's monumental character. Few seem borrowed rather than invented, the most notably derived feature being the aedicules in the screen walls (Fig. 122), inspired by (rather than copied from) Serlio's reconstruction of a windowless feature in the Pantheon.[72] Wren's aedicules work visually in the elevation as if they were windows and incorporate the real triforium windows, but of course there is nothing behind them to be lit. Comparable elision and combination occur in the lower storey, where the window heads form part of the false frieze – baroque ambiguities Wren seems to have invented (Fig. 117). The 'spherical arches' (as the accounts call them) around the insides of these windows seem to be the source for the outside niche windows in the base of the west towers (Fig. 121); the perspective windows of the Palazzo Barberini in Rome are not their source, for their panels create no illusion.

As carvers and moulders became more skilled and their sense of form more painterly, decorative panels became freer and more undercut; for example, in the imposts of the chancel and (later) nave and transept arcades (Figs 131, 132). Wren considered the classical orders good servants and bad masters.[73] Besides curtailing the nave entablatures, he pared down those of the arcade imposts and flattened their cornices so that they do not oversail the main pilasters. He invented a reduced Corinthian for the peristyle capitals, effective for details 170 feet above ground (Frontispiece).

In a basilican church, side aisles have a ritual and a statical function. The first was not required at St Paul's, 'our Religion not using Processions'.[74] The second is to support the main naves. Structurally, the changes from the Warrant make for less mass and less thrust in the body of the church, even though in the Penultimate drawings Wren introduced flying buttresses inside the aisle roofs. The emphasis on the aisle walls – fourteen feet thick in

133. Putti over the Dean's door, south side of nave. (SPCL)

the main piers – must therefore have another reason. The beautiful low dome and the bright crossing windows of the Penultimate were indeed a blind alley, closed by raising the corner bastions and the screen walls, as they are now and always will be known. Modern structural theory suggests that these play no significant part in the stability of the building;[75] however, Somers Clarke, looking down from the peristyle, concluded 'in a flash' that they did,[76] and Wren clearly thought so too. His discussion of structural problems at Westminster Abbey in 1713 touched on walls as abutments,[77] and why else did he make the screen walls so thick? Concealment was not their primary function, although, once they were envisaged, the buttresses could be higher and bigger without having to become orthogonal walls like those flanking Palladio's Redentore in Venice. In any case, Wren considered the similar walls above the Basilica of Maxentius to be the origin of Gothic flying buttresses;[78] moreover, the soldiers' church of the Invalides in Paris, begun a year after St Paul's, has a fine set of highly visible flying buttresses.

Besides the cross-bracing which Wren believed the screens to provide for the whole crossing, they gave visual support to whatever over-sized dome he could imagine, and dominating two-storey elevations to the exterior which complement the two-storey design within. Architecture involves not merely the recital of the Vitruvian tripos but the reconciliation of its elements as in a Venn diagram. All the changes are interlinked; it is quite a different matter from redesigning the dome and west towers a quarter of a century later.

Ever since it was published in *Parentalia*,[79] it has been a commonplace that St Paul's was built to one man's design during his life-span whereas St Peter's in Rome required 145 years and twelve architects. This is much more than a guidebook cliché, for Wren's building is not only large – even for a cathedral – and complex; it is also a unique response to unique problems.

20

THE CONSTRUCTION OF
THE NEW CATHEDRAL

James W. P. Campbell and Robert Bowles

The rebuilding of St Paul's after the Great Fire was one of the largest building projects of seventeenth century. It is also one of the best documented. This essay is concerned with how the cathedral was built, in terms of the process of construction and of the structure that resulted. While many drawings survive, crucial ones appear to be missing, making interpretation of the development of the design and Wren's intentions difficult. The building works present the opposite problem: there is almost too much material. Over one hundred books of accounts and related documents survive for the rebuilding of the cathedral.[1] Even the summaries and extracts from these compiled by the Wren Society in the 1930s fill four large volumes. In addition to this material, the building itself provides its own clues in the form of archaeological evidence. Such a wealth of information means that as well as being the most significant work of architecture erected in seventeenth-century England, St Paul's is also the most important and complete source for understanding the processes of building construction in the period.

THE CONSTRUCTION PROCESS

At the time of the Great Fire, the old cathedral was undergoing repair works (pp. 183–6). These were brought to an absolute halt by the events of September 1666. When those responsible for overseeing the works returned to the site after the fire, they found the cathedral was in a much worse state than they might have hoped. Inigo Jones's portico was burnt beyond rescue and the destruction was even worse at the east end, where the vaults had fallen into the crypt. In the rest of the church, the timber roof had been destroyed, but some of the stone vaults of the side aisles and around the tower in the nave and choir remained intact. The lead that had covered the roof had melted and was intermixed with the rubble on the floor of the church. Winter was approaching and further damage was being caused by rain, wind and frost.[2]

Through necessity, the tidying-up operation began almost immediately. Presumably responsibility fell formally to the cathedral office of works under the direction of the cathedral surveyor, Sir John Denham,[3] but in view of Denham's state of mental health in 1666[4] we can assume that the work was delegated to those on site with perhaps some intervention from others in the Office of the King's Works in Whitehall.

Accounts suggest that the office of works at St Paul's in these early years consisted of only a few individuals. John Tillison was clerk of works, having replaced Thomas Gammon in 1664.[5] He was subsequently joined by Edward Woodroofe (also spelt Woodroffe) who helped oversee Wren's first attempts to patch up the cathedral and acted as assistant surveyor from January 1668,[6] although he was not officially appointed to that post until June 1674.[7]

CLEANING UP

As the initial intention was to save as much of the cathedral as possible, the priority in the late 1660s was to make the building safe. First, the rubble had to be removed and the floor cleared. In 1663, the king had formed a commission to study the possibilities for repairing and rebuilding the church.[8] Various experts had been consulted before Wren entered the field with a report on the state of the cathedral in May 1666, followed by a grand design for the crossing (see pp. 184–6).[9] After the events of September 1666, Wren, Roger Pratt and Hugh May were asked again to consider what was

N

0   150ft
0   50m

134.   Plan showing the position of the present cathedral in relation to its predecessor

to be done,[10] but only Wren (who had the advantage of knowing both Archbishop Sheldon and Dean Sancroft personally) appears to have been seriously involved. In a report of February 1667 he lists the damage, rejects the possibility of repair but suggests building a temporary roof over the nave.[11] He seems to have gone on to produce an innovative design for this roof involving the use of small timber planks rather than long beams to economize on timber (presumably based on the designs contained in Philibert de l'Orme's *Nouvelles Inventions Pour Bien Bastir*, published in 1561),[12] but after analysing its cost and finding it more expensive, he abandoned it in favour of a more conventional design.[13]

In the meantime, the difficult task of reclaiming the lead from the old roof had already started. In 1667 a plumbery had been set up in Convocation House Yard which was surrounded by high walls.[14] Lead was valuable and here it could be stored safely and melted down for reuse. As the weather improved, labourers began to move the tons of dust, burned timbers and fallen stones that lay in heaps in the body of the church to yards outside it.

In January 1668, the commissioners issued an order for the erection of a temporary choir in the nave and the walling-in of the site.[15] The contract for the new roof was signed with Thomas Gammon, carpenter, in March.[16] The timber walling was erected, and helped to keep the public out of what was undoubtedly a dangerous site, but the temporary roof could not be completed. In April, Dean Sancroft wrote to Wren in Oxford, reporting that the work about the west end 'is fallen about our ears' and summoning him immediately to London to advise on what was to be done about the remainder of the cathedral which was also in imminent danger of collapse.[17] From this point on, Wren became acting surveyor. He ordered the demolition of the remainder of the choir and the crossing tower with Denham and Sancroft in August 1668[18] and his position was formally confirmed in July 1669, shortly after he became Surveyor of the King's Works following Denham's death.[19] At this date, there was still no money for the rebuilding of the cathedral.

DEMOLITION

The first task facing the new surveyor in 1668 was to demolish those parts most likely to fall and consolidate what remained, but as plans for a new cathedral were formulated, the idea of consolidation gradually gave way to removal.

It is easy to dismiss demolition as a minor process, but in the case of such a tall building it was involved and dangerous. Large amounts of stone and rubbish had to be removed and disposed of. In two months in 1669 alone, no fewer that 1,250 carts of rubbish were transported down Ludgate Hill.[20] A veritable army of labourers and carters was employed to carry out this work. The riskier operation of climbing up the outside of the cathedral and battering pieces until they fell down was subcontracted to John Simpson and Henry Russell, who employed labourers to do the work.[21] There is no evidence of any scaffolding being used and as a result there were a number of deaths and serious injuries.[22]

The great piers that supported the cathedral closer to the ground could not be dismantled by hand, forcing Wren to use a combination of explosives and battering rams to destroy them. Rightly or wrongly, *Parentalia* claims originality for the blasting aspect of this operation.[23] Gunpowder was commonly used in siege warfare by engineers to undermine walls, but it is not clear if it had been used in peacetime demolitions before. In January–March 1672 a gunner was paid to come from the Tower of London to advise on the operations.[24] As it turned out, its use proved too dangerous and the work had to be completed using iron-tipped battering rams.[25]

OFFICE OF WORKS

Managing such a large operation demanded careful administration. Before the fire, the office of works had been based in rooms at the sign of the Saracen's Head in St Paul's Churchyard which were furnished with ten chairs, a table and a carpet.[26] These offices may have burned down, for immediately after the Great Fire work began on a new set of offices in Convocation House Yard.

The convocation house, the original octagonal chapter house of the cathedral, had long since fallen into disrepair.[27] In the 1660s only its empty shell remained in the centre of the yard, both the floor and the roof of the building itself having fallen in. The magnificent two-storey cloister surrounding it seems to have collapsed completely, leaving only a high wall. This yard now became the centre of operations, chiefly because it was easy to secure. Here all records, drawings, models and expensive building materials were stored safely under lock and key and from 1670 it was guarded by two mastiff dogs, kept by John Tillison for the purpose.[28]

The new office was built between October 1666 and March 1667, probably on the south side of the yard.[29] It was two storeys high, the lower rooms being used as stores, and the upper for drawings and administration. A small building was constructed beside the entrance gate and it was here that workmen were ticked off in the register on their way into the cathedral. The first-floor office was hung with green baize[30] and the wooden floors and skirting were painted black.[31] In its centre was a long table surrounded by seven chairs.[32] There were also cupboards for storing drawings and accounts, and tables around the side for working at and laying out drawings. It was probably also used for the meetings of the commissioners and for the weekly meetings with the various master craftsmen.[33]

Wren's regular attendance on site only appears to have started in early 1672. In December of the previous year he had had two additional rooms added to the office,[34] one for himself and one for the storage of models. Wren's personal office was panelled and had its own drawing table and cupboards,[35] curtains and a fireplace with a map of London over the mantelpiece.[36] It was from here that he surveyed the works until eventually the office itself had to be dismantled to make way for the nave of the new cathedral and moved to another more temporary structure nearby.

In 1673 the convocation house itself was reroofed and converted to become a room for the Great Model, which was made there and stayed there until it, too, had to move because of the building works and was placed inside the cathedral.[37]

A useful list of office staff is provided in the Wren Society volumes.[38] Initially the offices seem to have housed only Tillison and Woodroofe. Tillison was clerk and paymaster, while Woodroofe, who was also surveyor for Westminster Abbey, is likely to have been part-time, acting as assistant surveyor at St Paul's and covering for Wren in his absence. In 1669 John Oliver[39] may also have worked here, designing the deanery. Woodroofe died in 1675 and was replaced by Oliver, who remained in the office until his death in 1701, when he in turn was replaced by Thomas Bateman. In 1685 Tillison also died[40] and was replaced by two people, Lawrence Spencer as clerk and Thomas Russell, who became Clerk of the Cheque (replaced by Richard Maples in 1703). They were joined by John Scarborrow in 1688 (replaced by William Dickinson in 1696) who helped John Oliver by acting as 'measurer'. There was only one dedicated draughtsman employed by the office and that was Nicholas Hawksmoor, who first appears in the accounts in 1690–1. Occasionally reference is made to servants belonging to these staff not otherwise mentioned in the accounts, but the part they played and their number are unclear.[41] So possibly the office contained more staff than this short account suggests.

135. Comparative sections through the choirs of old and new St Paul's drawn by Godfrey Allen, 1924, showing Wren's classical design juxtaposed with the slenderer Gothic cathedral. (*The Builder*, 18 Jan. 1924)

The office had to manage the flow of money and materials in and out, make sure that the craftsmen were attending and monitor the progress of works. It was a difficult task that left little time for drawing, but then the construction of St Paul's probably relied less on drawings than might be supposed.

THE USE OF DRAWINGS AND MODELS

A large number of drawings survive for St Paul's. Some are in the collection of All Souls College, Oxford, most of which are catalogued in the Wren Society's volumes, where many are reproduced.[42] In the fuller catalogue of those that remain in the cathedral's ownership (now on loan to the Guildhall Library), Kerry Downes has noted that few of the drawings actually show the cathedral as built.[43] As he suggests, there are two possible explanations for this: either the working drawings (those actually used on site) became too dirty to retain and were thus disposed of; or such drawings never existed.

Contracting at St Paul's was carried out by parcelling out the works to teams of craftsmen, each working on a section and being paid either by the day or according to the amount they built. All they needed were instructions on a day-to-day basis for the piece they were working on and a steady supply of materials. In most cases, an oral command would do and many issues could have been (and no doubt were) solved on the scaffold. The accounts are full of entries for profiles in the form of timber templates, drawn on wood by Wren, the draughtsmen or the clerk of works and cut out and strengthened by joiners. These were provided for cutting stonework. Setting out of the various pieces was done at full size on tracing floors, of which there were a number (presumably one for each team) around the site. As each block was cut, it could thus be compared to the template and then to its neighbours laid out on the tracing floor, before being lifted into position for final fitting. None of this required a single paper drawing.

For particularly complex parts of the building, models were prepared. A large number of models are listed in accounts for various purposes and they vary in size and complexity, from simple models of parts of the cornices to whole sections of the dome made on a large scale in stone.

The drawings which were produced were probably mostly intended for the design team rather than the craftsmen, to enable the office to test out ideas at an early stage or later to make sure that the parts would fit together and to enable them to draw sections accurately on the tracing floors.[44]

SITE ORGANIZATION

Although the surveyor and his staff were in charge of the work, the job of finding the labour and directing the building work could only be carried out by skilled master craftsmen in the various trades. Carpenters, joiners, bricklayers, labourers, painters, plasterers, plumbers and watchmen were in most cases paid by the day. Other craftsmen (including, most importantly, the stone masons) were paid at an agreed rate by measuring the work that had been carried out.

The medieval arrangement whereby the masons were in charge of the works did not operate at St Paul's. Instead, the cathedral was built by a number of teams of masons working simultaneously and in competition. In the early years, two teams operated, one led by Joshua Marshall[45] and the other by Thomas Strong.[46] On Marshall's death in 1678,[47] his contract was split and taken over by Edward Pierce and Jaspar Latham, while another contract went to Thomas Wise, making four teams in total. Two more, one led by John Thompson and the other by Samuel Fulkes, were added in 1688. Strong's contract passed after his death in 1681 to his younger brother Edward Strong, who saw the work to completion. Of the others, Nathaniel Rawlins took over Latham's contract in 1693, while Christopher Kempster[48] and Ephrian Beauchamp took over Pierce's in the same year. William Kempster, Christopher's brother, took over Thompson's contract in 1700.[49]

The master carpenter was one of the most important craftsman on site. That job was given to John Longland and his partner Israel Knowles. Longland became one of the longest-serving craftsmen at St Paul's, working for over thirty-one years on the project before his death in 1706. His business partner Knowles died in 1692. For a couple of years, he worked with Thomas Woodstock until he, too, died, at which point Longland formed a partnership with his former apprentice, Richard Jennings.[50] On Longland's death in 1706, it was Jennings who took over the contract and supervised the completion of the dome.[51]

The carpenters working under Longland had to provide all the scaffolding and the formwork on which the stone was erected. Lifting stone to the upper floors was one of the most difficult parts of the works. A series of wooden ramps or 'bridges' were erected at lower levels, allowing stone to be pulled up, while a whole series of A-frames and pulleys allowed more straightforward lifting operations. Rubbish and mortar were moved in wheelbarrows and long ladders were used to reach the upper levels. All of these were made and maintained by the carpenters.

They also made the site huts and lodges for the masons to work in, which frequently had to be moved, and they built the elaborate temporary roof structures that kept the rain and snow off the works as the cathedral gradually grew. When walls were high enough, large 'engines' were built to lift the stones aloft. Lastly, all this was kept from view by screens which the carpenters built to hide the cathedral from prying eyes.

To carry out all this work effectively, the master carpenter needed to co-ordinate with the other master craftsmen on a regular basis, and this was done through formal weekly site meetings, held every Saturday, presumably in the office of works.[52] It was said that Wren attended St Paul's every Saturday, no doubt participating in these meetings. In this way, he could communicate the design, as it developed in his mind or on paper, directly to the workmen.

THE DESIGN

Wren's first designs for St Paul's pre-date the Fire and relate to the repair of the building. After the Fire, there was still much talk of repair rather than rebuilding, so it was only later that designs started to emerge for the whole cathedral. No one doubts that the First Model Design preceded the Great Model which was itself replaced by the so-called Warrant Design and that it was this last scheme that won royal approval and finally meant that building work could proceed. However, interpretation of the next stage in the design process is fraught with controversy and uncertainty.

We do know that the cathedral Wren began in 1675 was not being built to the Warrant Design because the two designs had different dimensions, proportions and layouts at the crossing. The question then remains: was the cathedral built to any of the surviving plans, and if so, which?

One suggestion is that it was being built to a set of plans which are collectively termed the 'Definitive Design' and appear to have been drawn by a single hand, supposedly in the 1670s. This is the theory put forward, on evidence of various kinds, by John Summerson in 1961 and subsequently supported by Kerry Downes.[53] Another, earlier theory has a growing number of contemporary adherents. According to this version, the Definitive Design drawings are not in Wren's hand but another later one, possibly that of Nicholas Hawksmoor, who could not have started work on the cathedral before the mid 1680s.[54] If that is so, when construction began in 1675 there was no intention to have screen walls or flying buttresses, and no fixed idea about the form of the dome.

It is only by examining the fabric that we can see whether, in what ways and at what stages it was possible for Wren to change his mind during construction. While such an approach cannot prove or disprove the existence of a Definitive design in 1675, it can at least say whether the alternative is a workable hypothesis. With all this in mind, we can now discuss how the cathedral Wren constructed was put together and the structural implications of the decisions he made.

136 (*right*). The dome in isometric projection, showing hidden aspects of the construction. This celebrated large-scale drawing was measured and made by R. B. Brook-Greaves and Godfrey Allen, 1923–8, and published in a limited edition by the Architectural Press. (SPCL)

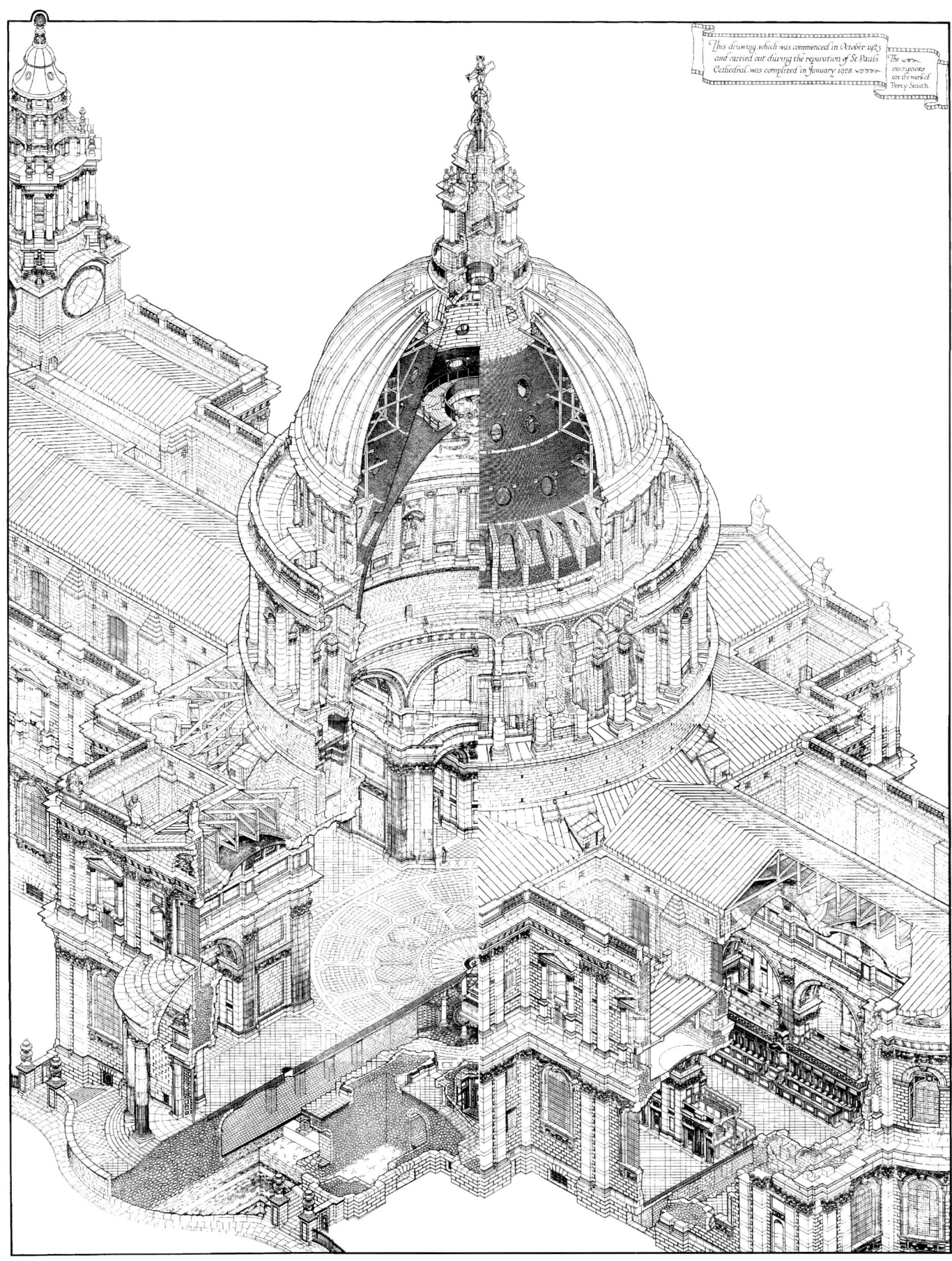

This drawing, which was commenced in October 1923 and carried out during the reparation of St. Paul's Cathedral, was completed in January 1928. The inscriptions are the work of Percy Smith.

To WILLIAM DUNN. *F.R.I.B.A.*

who first suggested the idea of shewing the construction of St. Paul's Cathedral by Isometric Projection
~ this drawing is inscribed by MERVYN EDMUND MACARTNEY. *F.S.A.* Surveyor to the Fabric ~

Measured and drawn by R.B.BROOK-GREAVES in collaboration with W. GODFREY ALLEN

Valuable assistance has been rendered by Matthew Dawson F.R.I.B.A. & E.J.Bolwell

Published by the Architectural Press   Photo & Collotype. Donald Macbeth

THE STRUCTURE OF THE CATHEDRAL

In comparison with the amount that has been written and published about the architectural aspects of Wren's cathedral, little has been published about the building as a structure; much of what does exist was prepared in the wake of a crisis or to promote or resist some proposed change. Wren himself left no published account of how he approached what we now call the engineering of the building, nor any extended discussion of his approach to structure in general. An interpretation of his views has to be deduced from what others recorded him saying about particular issues, from examining the fabric and the building accounts, from his brief tracts on architecture and from reading the reports he wrote to explain his opinions when he was consulted about buildings such as Salisbury Cathedral, Westminster Abbey and Old St Paul's.[55] These last contain some generalized statements, but need to be taken with caution, since each was written for a particular context.

Nor is there anything approaching an engineering textbook written by any of Wren's contemporaries. Structural engineering only emerged as a fully separate discipline about a century ago, by which time the requirement was for buildings and structures of a very different form from St Paul's. So the analytical and mathematical modelling tools that have been developed by later engineers are often inappropriate or misleading when applied to massive load-bearing masonry structures. Few engineering textbooks attempt the analysis of existing structures of this type.[56] This does not mean that such analysis can tell us nothing about the way structures behave, merely that it cannot tell us as much as we may hope.

The challenge that Wren faced was to produce a building of monumental and classical appearance whilst working with construction techniques and a plan-form which both derived from the great Gothic cathedrals. The proportions of the piers, walls, arches and vaults throughout his design were quite different from those of its Gothic predecessors, and generated different structural problems. The dome presented the greatest challenge of all, since Gothic buildings do not have them. Classical buildings with large domes existed in continental Europe, but all were of different proportions from what was required at St Paul's, or had been the subject of concern as to their structural stability, making them dubious precedents.

Wren's designs solved all these problems using forms that were often bold and inventive but rarely so removed from what had gone before as to experience the problems which often beset the first generation of radically innovative structures. He had time on his side. Work progressed slowly, allowing numerous trials and tests to be carried out and the design to be continually refined and adapted as the need arose. To an extent, it was a process of trial and error. For instance, Sir Dudley North gave a vivid account of how crypt arches destined to carry the main floor of the cathedral had twice collapsed during construction until Wren realized that they did so because the abutments were temporarily out of balance, and adjusted working methods accordingly.[57] No doubt many other such instances during the decades when the cathedral was rising have gone unrecorded. The idea that the cathedral was in some sense 'designed' or worked out and then built unaltered to that design is misleading. Like most building (even today), the evidence suggests that much of the design was developed as work progressed.

FOUNDATIONS

Settlement due to the consolidation of the ground below the foundations was a problem for St Paul's from the beginning of construction, despite all the care that the Surveyor took to reduce its effects. The first stones of the new cathedral were laid on 21 June 1675 at the south-east corner of the building.[58] *Parentalia*, the Wren family memoir which gives the earliest extended history of building the cathedral, alleges that Wren 'began to lay the foundations in the West-end and...proceeded successfully through the *Dome* to the East End',[59] but this is one of many questionable statements in the book. Wren's son, Christopher, who almost certainly wrote this account, was born in 1675 and for this early period must have relied much on stories told to him later by his father and others. The building accounts are clear: the foundations were started at the east end and worked westwards. It could not have been otherwise, because much of the west end of the old cathedral, including its foundations, were not demolished until the middle of the 1680s. Only at the east end was the site clear and excavated, ready for work to begin.

Parentalia goes on to recount how Wren found that the ground in the north-east 'Angle' of the cathedral was unreliable and how he had to build a special foundation there.[60] Mervyn Macartney, who carried out surveys and published details of the foundations in 1914, ordered test pits to be dug in the north-east corner of the cathedral to look at this extraordinary foundation, but nothing of the sort was found.[61] The story may be apocryphal, but it is possible that such an ingenious foundation does exist, buried elsewhere, deeper within the fabric.

The plans of the old and new cathedrals were very different. Wren rotated the axis of his design (Fig. 134) and the setting-out of the piers and walls bore no relation to what had been there before. As *Parentalia* explains,

> To have built on the old Foundations must have confined the *Surveyor* too much to the old Plan and Form; the ruinous Walls in no Part were to be trusted again, nor would old and new Work firmly unite, or stand together without Cracks.[62]

In some cases, the positions of the new foundations inevitably coincided with the old, but the new piers are much larger than the medieval ones, generating correspondingly larger foundations. No attempt was made to combine the two. Instead, all the old work was removed and the stone recovered was reused.

Wren had already investigated the ground by digging pits before determining how the cathedral was to be founded.[63] There he had discovered that beneath the soil the natural ground comprised 'potter's clay' (nowadays normally called brickearth) over sands and gravel over clay. Water lay on the top of the clay, in the bottom of the sand and gravel. A decision was made to form the foundations in the potter's clay, at a depth of between 4 feet and 7 feet 6 inches below the floor of the crypt.

From a modern standpoint, Wren's decision to found the building in the potter's clay was perhaps the worst of the technical decisions made during the construction of the cathedral. Potter's clay is a wind-blown mixture of sand, clay and silt which varies in its proportions and properties and consolidates unpredictably when loaded. Where it has never been loaded or saturated, it can appear firm on the surface but undergo gross settlements when loads are applied. It is also prone to swelling and shrinking due to changes in moisture content.

Had Wren chosen to excavate slightly deeper and found his building in the sand and gravel which lies below the brickearth, this would have provided a much firmer formation and led to less settlement. No doubt Wren shared the belief (first outlined in the Bible and still commonly held today) that founding in sand or gravel is unwise. It is true that sand when excavated is loose and appears to have no strength, and excavations in sand below the water table tend to collapse as water flows in. But these situations do not represent how the material behaves when confined naturally in the ground, where it actually provides a stable base for foundations.

The result of Wren's decision to found his massive piers for the dome (larger in size than those for the crossing of Old St Paul's) in potter's clay was that they began to settle immediately on construction, but by different amounts in relation to the rest of the building. Most of this differential movement is now known to have taken place before the construction of the dome itself. But the movement continued in unpredictable ways well after its completion. This settlement was still a cause for concern in the twentieth century, when major works were undertaken in 1925–30 to repair the damage done (see pp. 299–300). Modern monitoring has shown that it has now effectively ceased.

WALLS

The walls and piers of St Paul's are generally constructed with a rubble core faced with new Portland stone ashlar. This method of building, though traditional and indeed standard in massive masonry construction, was one that Wren himself had criticized in his pre-Fire survey of the piers of Old St Paul's in 1666:

> They are only cased without, and that with small Stones, not one greater than a Man's burden; but within is nothing but a Core of small Rubbish-stone, and much Mortar, which easily crushes and yields to the Weight.[64]

Nevertheless, Wren had little choice but to employ a similar form of construction for his new cathedral, as the alternatives (a wall-core of solid squared and dressed ashlar construction, or of solid brick faced with ashlar) would have been prohibitively slow and expensive. However, he took care that the stones for the casing were massive, accurately shaped with thin joints, and of varying depths so that they were well keyed into the core.

While the outer face of the walls is of Portland stone, much of the infill material is rubble from the old cathedral. Other types of stone were used, including Burford, Reigate, Headington, Kentish Rag, Beer, Ketton, Caen, Guildford and Tadcaster stones.[65] Maintaining an adequate supply of stone was a continual problem throughout the works.[66]

Mortar for the walls was carefully chosen. In this period, the basic ingredients for mortar were lime, sand and water (the same materials mixed, with animal hair, were used to make plaster). The mortar was 'non-hydraulic', i.e. it did not harden under water and was comparatively weak. Lime mortars need a long time to absorb carbon dioxide from the air and thus gain their full strength. Wren experimented with adding a number of pozzolanic materials to produce stronger, quicker setting mortars and plasters to suit his purposes in those areas where strength was particularly important.[67]

Perhaps the most important feature of the walls was not the way they were made but the variation in their thickness. In a Gothic cathedral, the walls are typically constructed to be as slender as possible and need to be stabilized by regular buttresses. Wren had rejected this arrangement, which would not have produced regular 'classical' elevations. Instead, both the Great Model and the Warrant design had indicated thick walls, with huge niches on the internal faces between the piers at church-floor level. Accordingly, in the cathedral as built, the external walls between the church floor and the triforium level are two and a half times as thick, over a similar height, as the equivalent walls in the old cathedral (Fig. 135). This meant that no external buttressing was required. Crucially, this feature also allowed the thinner upper screen walls above triforium level to be added on top after the completion of the ground-floor walls, which were more than thick enough to withstand the extra loads involved, both from these screen walls and from the flying buttresses they hide, supporting the nave vaults and roof.

FLYING BUTTRESSES AND SCREEN WALLS

If we presume that the Definitive design belongs to the 1680s, then the question remains of how late the screen walls (Fig. 360) could have been added and why. Their presence is bound up with the decision to include a triforium gallery, not shown in the Warrant design, and with the position and form of the buttresses which Wren had always needed to support the main nave vaults and roof. In an intermediate design, flying buttresses were to take their path through the roof of this new triforium gallery.[68] Finally, they were lifted above its roof space, thereby increasing the usable floor area of the gallery. To conceal these conspicuous and unclassical features, Wren used the screen walls to raise the parapets of the aisles in nave and choir to main-roof level, thereby giving the cathedral its continuous cornice all round. Exactly when these changes were made remains a mystery.

The introduction of screen walls brought other advantages, including a reduction in the amount of carved masonry which would have to be procured and constructed before the choir could be roofed and made permanently watertight. The clerestory walls could be quite plain on the outside, as they would be hidden from view. The choir could then be vaulted and roofed, and fitting-out could start, while the masons continued working on bringing the outer decorative screen walls up to their full height wholly outside the building. So it is likely that the screen walls were adopted by Wren because they combined a number of advantages (structural, aesthetic and economic) while also enabling him to introduce a triforium gallery with its extra space in a manner acceptable to the commissioners.

One controversial recent study of St Paul's has suggested that the screen walls are not structurally necessary and that the flying buttresses could have been omitted.[69] But even if 'static equilibrium' is possible without them, there are other factors to be considered, such as movements due to changes of temperature and moisture content, and the desire to avoid cracking in the plastered vaults – far more likely in the absence of buttresses.

VAULTS

The first set of main masonry vaults to be constructed in the cathedral were built between October 1675 and November 1676,[70] those for the crossing in 1677–8,[71] while those for the nave were started in 1678 between the piers supporting the dome and not finished until 1689.[72] The vaults of the crypt were

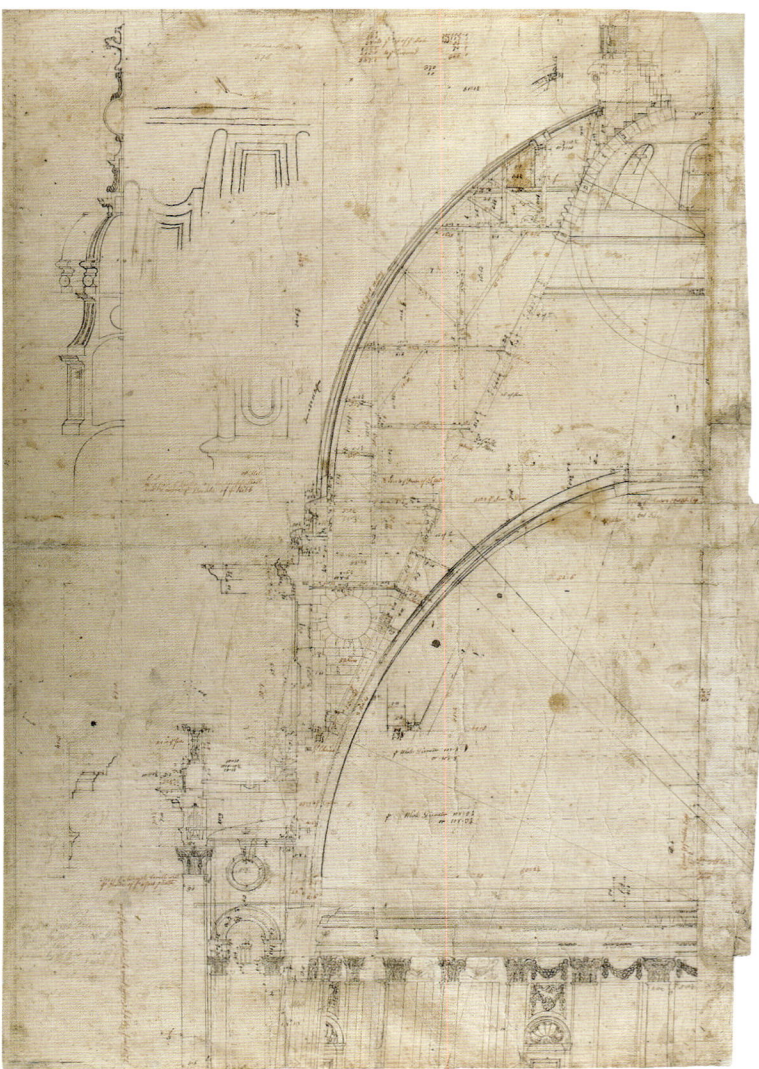

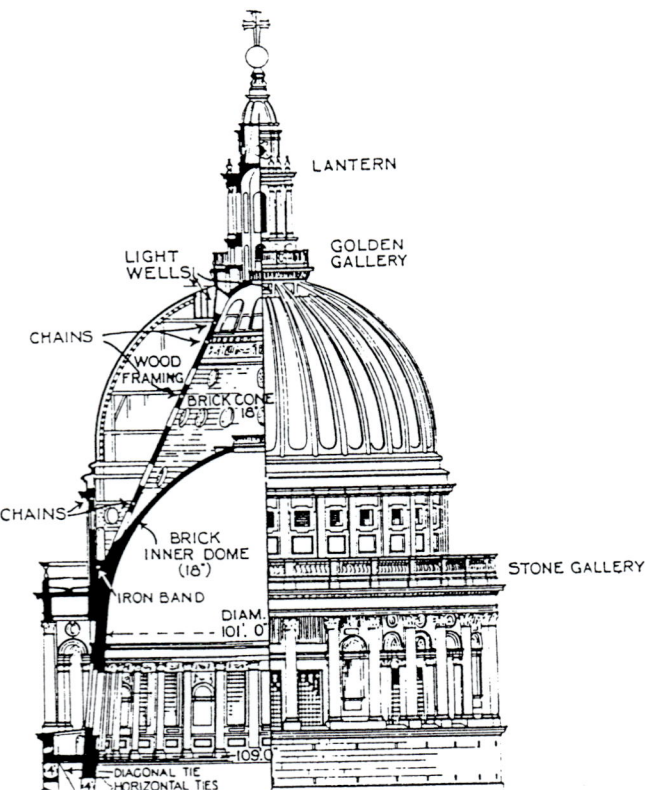

138. Section and elevation of the dome of the cathedral from Banister Fletcher's *History of Architecture on the Comparative Method*, showing the position of the various iron chains. The great chain is labelled 'iron band' and the recently discovered chain (F in Fig. 139) runs through the gallery masonry, to the lower left of the great chain in the section.

137. Survey drawing of section through the dome as built, possibly made by John Gwynn in the 1750s and revised during Robert Mylne's surveyorship, *c.* 1789. (SPL GL) This drawing shows the profile of the inner dome to be made up from segments of circles with different diameters and centres

TIMBER ROOFS

constructed from brick rather than stone. All the vaults were built on elaborate sets of timber formwork supported from the floor. On completion of each vault, its formwork was dismantled and presumably reused where possible.

The high vaults of the cathedral over the aisles and nave appear from below as a series of inverted saucers, with carved stone perimeters, supported by four pendentives. The masonry is two bricks thick at the crown, and the geometry is less complex than it appears at first, since the saucers and pendentives are all parts of the same spherical surface. When viewed from above, the saucers are seen breaking through a flat brick floor, which is pierced by numerous small holes, invisible from the ground, through which ropes could be passed to draw up scaffolds for painting the undersides. The flat floor also conceals low barrel-vaulted tunnels which help to further reduce the weight of the structure while maintaining lateral support.[73] The regular bay system is complicated at the west end by the widening of the nave and the insertion of a much larger saucer-dome in the space between the library and trophy room. Although in terms of structure this is identical to the other vaults, it has important consequences for the configuration of the timber roof above.

Following medieval precedent, Wren's interior vaults do not keep out the rain. Instead, above the vault is a large space covered by a completely independent timber structure spanning between the nave walls. Wren chose a tried and tested structural form for the roof, but one that was rare in England at the time: the king-post truss.[74] The critical member of such trusses is the tie-beam. While it was possible to make a tie-beam from two pieces of timber joined together with a tension splice, a method that Wren employed elsewhere, it was preferable and safer to use a single timber. Oak was the wood of choice. Twenty-foot oak timbers were fairly easy to procure in the seventeenth century, and thirty-foot ones were achievable, but every foot beyond that was increasingly difficult to find. In order to achieve a minimum cross-section of the order of one foot square, the tree from which a timber was produced would have had to be much taller, with a straight trunk. Wren's chosen span at St Paul's was no less than forty-two feet. The search for trees tall enough to produce timbers of adequate length and cross section was accordingly long and difficult.[75]

The king-post roof provided a long span at a low pitch and was thus ideal for hiding behind a parapet. In classical buildings in the English climate, parapet gutters too often leak, and the most common cause of failure of these roofs is the rotting of the ends of the timbers at this point. It was a problem Wren himself commented upon.[76] At St Paul's, he placed the gutters over side passages above the walls, lower than the ends of his trusses. The gutters could thus easily be repaired and replaced and any leakage would not damage the main structural timbers. Wren's provisions for managing roof leaks included the floors of these passages, which were not paved

139.   Isometric cutaway drawing showing the complexity of the ironwork and masonry jointing in the peristyle. The chain marked F is shown along with the iron hangers which supported the blocks during construction, discovered during restoration of the peristyle in 1997. The nuts were tightened or loosened to adjust the line and level of the architrave stones before the cornice and frieze stones were added. (Alan Baxter Associates)

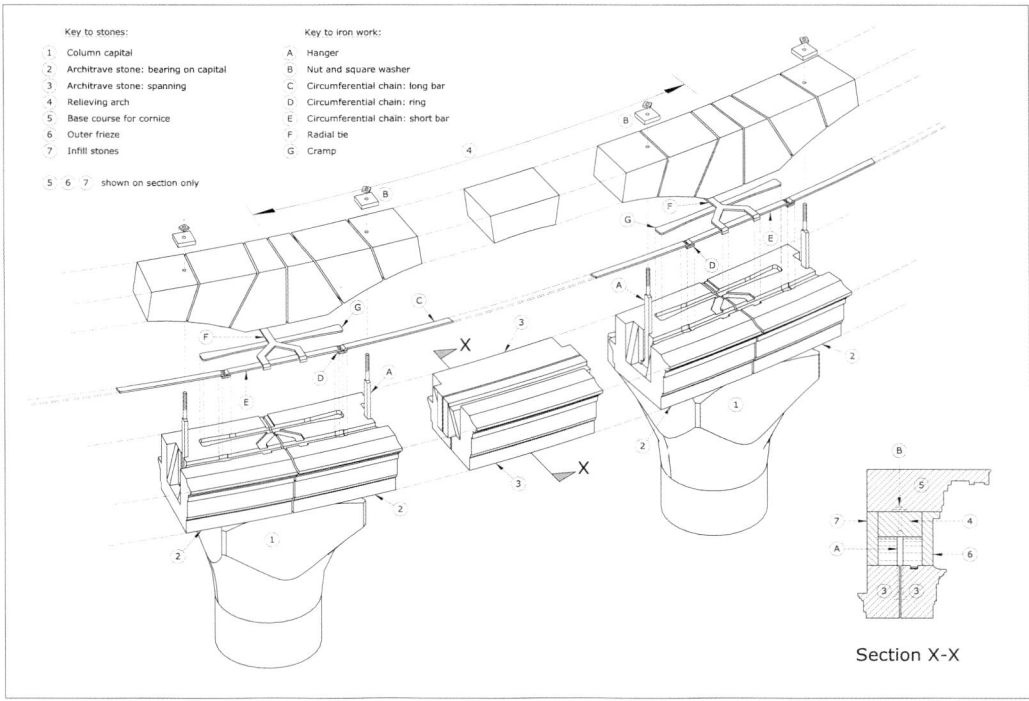

Key to stones:
1   Column capital
2   Architrave stone: bearing on capital
3   Architrave stone: spanning
4   Relieving arch
5   Base course for cornice
6   Outer frieze
7   Infill stones

5   6   7   shown on section only

Key to iron work:
A   Hanger
B   Nut and square washer
C   Circumferential chain: long bar
D   Circumferential chain: ring
E   Circumferential chain: short bar
F   Radial tie
G   Cramp

Section X-X

with brick as in the roof spaces generally, but with stone flags, laid to fall to small holes in the clerestory walls, through which water could run off.

For the most part, the roof is uniform throughout, the same structure being used for the nave, choir and transepts with only the most minor variations. However, at the west end the enlarged saucer-dome over the vestibule creates a problem. Here, the dome rises to a point where it would clash with a tie-beam set at the normal level. Unless the roof is raised at this point, which would create an odd profile on the outside of the cathedral, the geometry of the truss must be adjusted. Wren's solution was to insert two trusses with raised tie-beams. Such trusses can be designed to carry similar loads to those whose tie-beams are not raised, but the deflection under load is greater. To reduce this effect and the consequent dip in the roof ridge line, the trusses have braces beneath the tie beam. Similar structures are used over the great portico at the west end. The stiffness of these trusses was, however, less than ideal, and indeed by 1902 those in the portico were reported to be resting on the vaults.[77]

THE DOME

As he was finishing the Great Model, Wren was setting out on the ground the first dome, presumably to the same design. Once work was under way, in 1676 we find him setting out the curve of the new dome on the floor of the cathedral so that the piers and vaults below could be properly constructed.[78] Yet the dome was not to be finally completed until 1710. During that long period, scholars agree, it went through many versions and revisions. Just as there is uncertainty over which design Wren started to built in 1675, so there is equal confusion over the various stages of design of the dome and when decisions were made.

In 1693 we find a flurry of design work on the dome, particularly in the form of models. Either Wren was making a number of different versions of the same design, testing various features of each or, less probably, he was trying out a number of completely different design approaches in search of a workable solution. Until this point, there was no need for Wren to complete the design of the dome. His son says that after the Great

Model he had forsworn models of the whole design for public presentation.[79] There must have been much speculation over the form of the cathedral's crowning feature and it can only have been to his own advantage to be allowed to keep his cards close to his chest.

The dome provided both structural and aesthetic challenges. Aesthetically, a dome which looked right from within would generate too modest a profile externally, but a dome designed to look right on the skyline would look like a chimney from immediately below. Structurally, the challenge was to produce a structure that would not crack and would be as light as possible.

The substructure that Wren built to carry his dome comprises eight piers and four bastions, which seem to terminate at triforium level and support great arches, but in reality extend almost up to the whispering gallery. They support a drum, which in turn bears a hidden cone of masonry surmounted by a stone lantern. Outside these is the external timber dome that dominates the city's skyline. In other words, there are three separate domical elements (Figs 136, 138). These basic structural elements are clad and disguised in a variety of ways. The real elegance of Wren's solution is that it allowed the structural and aesthetic aspects of the design to be developed independently of each other.

The inner drum is a *frustum* (a cone with the end sliced off) rather than a cylinder, making the ideal structural shape for transferring its weight to the piers. The taper is imperceptible when viewed looking upwards from the church floor, and hidden from the outside by the outer drum and peristyle colonnade which are cylindrical. They serve to hide the taper, while their weight helps to take the line of thrust from the inner dome and the brick cone in between vertically on to the piers. The inner drum carries a simple dome of uniform thickness which is almost a hemisphere. However, the top section is slightly flatter, being part of a sphere of larger diameter than the lower section. This dome supports nothing other than its own weight. It is built entirely of brickwork, and contains no iron other than the chain around its base. It is a most remarkable structure, because it has no cracks of any sort, even though the construction outside and below it has distorted and cracked.

The key structural element is the hidden brick cone in

140. *The Night Watch in the Dome*, by Henry Rushbury, 1918. (Imperial War Museum)

141. Timber framework between the brick inner cone and the outer dome

between the inner and outer domes. It starts at the level of the stone gallery and supports the crowning stone lantern, which weighs some 700 tons. This lantern in its turn provides pre-compression to the cone, improving its stability. The cone is hidden from the outside by the lead-covered timber of the outer dome, and from the inside by the brick inner dome. Numerous iron chains and ties are built into its brick walls. Some resist compressive forces which can be calculated, while others provide tensile capacity in the masonry which helps to resist the effects of settlement and thermal movements.

The outer dome is a simple arrangement of radial timber frames, boarded and clad in lead. It rises from a cylindrical wall on the inside of the stone gallery. Immediately inside the base of this wall is a paved passageway laid to falls for the containment of roof leaks.

The question has often been raised as to the connection between the ingenious dome of St Paul's and the structural 'science' of the period. In particular, there has been debate about the role played in the design by Robert Hooke and by the theories of structural statics that he was developing.[80] Wren and Hooke had been discussing the ideal shapes for arches and domes in the Royal Society in 1670–1.[81] Wren had come up with one solution and Hooke with another. The two were close friends and in 1675 Hooke reported that he showed his conclusions to Wren and 'he altered his designs by it'.[82] This, however, was many years before Wren finalized his design for the dome.

Unlike modern engineers, Wren and Hooke in their deliberations of the 1670s were not trying to calculate the forces in a structure and devise a form of construction capable of carrying them. They were endeavouring to determine what shape to make

a structure, so that the forces on the different parts of it could flow through it to the supports without generating tension, since masonry is very weak in tension.

The ideal shape for an arch or dome is the 'line of thrust' generated by the loads which it carries, including its own weight. Since masonry is extremely strong in direct compression, if a well-built masonry arch or dome can be set out to follow the line of thrust, it can be very thin.

Hooke had presumably realized that it should be possible to determine the line of thrust by making and loading models (the traditional way of designing domes on the continent). However, models in compression have to be stiff, and when collapse occurs the evidence of where it originated is destroyed. If a model withstands collapse, it still provides no guidance as to how to modify the shape to get closer to the perfect answer.

The breakthrough which Hooke described in 1671 was the discovery that the ideal shape for a compression structure is the same as for a tension structure carrying equal but opposite loads. Such a model can be represented by a string or chain hung between two points, with loads in the form of weights hung from it. A tension model of this kind does not have to be stiff, nor is it subject to buckling. The string immediately adopts the ideal shape, the inversion of which provides the shape needed in compression.

Hooke applied this principle in two dimensions for an arch, by suspending weights from a lightweight chain and observing the shape that it adopted. The principle could then be extended to three-dimensional structures such as domes, if a suitable modelling medium could be found. String or chain nets appear at first sight to be suitable, but they soon become slack in one direction or another under load, and invalidate the model. Nevertheless, where the loading of a dome is symmetrical all round, as in the dome at St Paul's, a cross-section may be proposed which, when rotated, generates a conoid that has no tension in it. Hooke called the ideal section for a dome carrying no loads other than its self-weight a 'cubico-parabolic conoid'.[83]

It is interesting to consider the extent to which Hooke's theories may have been applied to each of the three structures making up the dome of St Paul's. The structure of the outer dome is a simple timber frame comprising vertical and horizontal timbers with some bracing, built off the cone. The profile of this must have been determined entirely by the aesthetics of the external silhouette. The lengths of the timbers could have been changed without making significant differences to the loads on the cone and, more importantly, to the stresses within it. These are dominated by the cone's own weight and that of the lantern.

The cone and the inner dome both exemplify the application of Hooke's theory. But they are more than just examples. They are, within the limitations of masonry construction, the two 'limits'(in the mathematical sense) of his generalized theory.

The cone and lantern are probably about as close an equivalent as one could get in masonry to the inversion of a single heavy weight at the centre of a weightless conoid. The cross-section is two straight lines, which, when rotated, generate a cone (Fig. 141). The weight of the lantern is large in comparison to that of the cone, so the effect is close. The inclusion of bands of ironwork compensates for the lack of perfection in the model.

The inner dome, on the other hand, is a shell which carries no loads other than its own weight. It is protected from the elements and from wind loads by the cone. Its construction is therefore precisely that which should generate no cracks if it is built to the ideal shape – the cubico-parabolic conoid.

The shape of the inner dome is often assumed to be a hemisphere, or at least part of a sphere, but that is not the case. A survey drawing dating from the late eighteenth century (Fig. 137)[84] shows that its cross-section is made up from parts of three different spheres. The resulting shape is very close to the theoretically perfect curve for a dome of constant thickness whose only loads are its own weight.[85] We do not know if Wren (with or without Hooke) originally set the dome out to the precise theoretical curve, but for practical purposes of setting out masonry it makes sense to approximate it to a series of parts of spheres, each one of which could be simply set out by a mason with a line fixed at a centre.

There remains a mystery about the overall significance that Wren and Hooke attached to the dome structures at St Paul's. Did they just think that they had been fortunate to have been able to apply two examples of the weights-and-chain theory in one place – or did they intend it to serve as silent proof of the general condition for the equilibrium of masonry conoids?

IRON

As has already been noted, iron played an important part in the structure of the dome, but it was also used extensively elsewhere. Wren used wrought iron exclusively. In comparison with other building materials, wrought iron was expensive and required a great deal of skill to achieve anything that was not very simple, so its use was always deliberate and carefully thought out. Every iron component had to be individually made, even if it was to a standard pattern. The design of iron components had to take account of the fact that iron was produced in individual ingots. To join

one ingot to another, or to join the two ends of a single ingot to form a ring, meant forge-welding. This difficult process involved raising the temperature of the iron well above that needed merely to manipulate it, almost to the point at which it would melt, and hammering it together until an acceptable bond was achieved. A joint might look satisfactory but be fatally flawed. The structural ironwork in St Paul's therefore avoids forge-welding wherever possible.

Wrought iron corrodes when in contact with oxygen and water. Exposed iron can be protected by painting it regularly, provided that it is accessible, but iron let into masonry cannot be regularly repainted. It is susceptible to corrosion even when it is not exposed to the elements, since in some conditions water can condense from the atmosphere within the structure itself. The problem of corrosion, which can cause serious spalling problems in masonry, was well known to Wren and his contemporaries. They addressed it by embedding the ironwork deep inside masonry, well away from exposed surfaces, and encapsulating it in lead, poured in after the iron was positioned. The lead had the additional advantage of providing a slightly resilient layer between the iron and the stone, reducing the risk of cracking due to hard spots.

Wren used wrought iron in the cathedral in several different ways. The most obvious are the numerous visible elements: window stays, hinges and railings, as well as the splendid gates and screens by the celebrated Huguenot smith, Jean Tijou. In addition, there were hidden chains incorporated within the dome and the entablatures to help them resist tension loads, and a variety of cramps and ties. Much of the more complex structural ironwork in the upper stages of the cathedral was supplied in 1704–7 by the smith Thomas Robinson.[86]

One of the most ingenious uses of iron was recently uncovered in repair works to the peristyle (Fig. 139). Here, the wide span of the flat masonry entablature immediately above the column capitals gives rise to the need for ironwork. There are three distinct sets of iron components, each fulfilling a different structural function. A complete chain runs all the way round the circumference, with radial ties at each column position. This serves to counteract the effects of creep due to temperature changes and helps the structure to cope with differential movement in the masonry. Then there are cramps connecting the two stones which bear on each capital. Finally, iron hangers support the joints between the capital stones and the suspended stones. These have threaded ends with nuts and hang from a secret relieving arch hidden behind the frieze stones. There is an item in the original accounts for 'nicking up' these hangers.[87] The relieving arches and hangers appear to be structurally superfluous now, but were probably part of the temporary works during construction, left in on completion. They reflect the limits of the equipment then available for lifting and propping heavy stones.

THE DEAN'S (OR GEOMETRICAL) STAIR AND WESTERN TOWERS

The two western towers were among the last parts of the cathedral to be constructed. We know that Wren and Hooke were always looking for experimental possibilities in their buildings; they had even designed the Monument as a zenith telescope.[88] No doubt they also used St Paul's for similar purposes. A hole in the main floor under the dome, later filled in, made the full height of the cathedral from the top of the lantern to the bottom of the crypt originally accessible. This would have maximized the length

142.   Looking up the Dean's (or geometric) stair in the south-west tower, 1986. The shaft was built first and the steps were subsequently slotted into holes then cut to receive them, and wedged in place with iron 'shims'.

of a suspended pendulum, a favourite experiment of the members of the Royal Society.[89]

There is also evidence that Wren had visions of using the south-west tower of St Paul's to house a giant telescope.[90] Such a telescope required a hollow space down the centre of the tower. This helps to explain one of the cathedral's most splendid but puzzling features: the great staircase in the south-west tower, which allows access to the triforium and library.

Commonly known as the Dean's Stair, sometimes as the 'geometrical stair', this structure (Fig. 142) rises in a spectacular stone spiral from church-floor level to the triforium, a height of some fifty feet. The eighty-eight Portland-stone treads are arranged around the perimeter of a cylindrical space some twenty-four feet in diameter. Unusually, the steps were not built into the masonry as the walls were raised. Instead, the stone ashlar walls enclosing the space were completed first and the treads were let into the masonry later. Each tread is accurately shaped to bear on the edge of the one below, and to fit as tightly as possible into the surrounding masonry. To achieve absolute tightness, metal wedges were driven into the ashlar above each tread. The iron handrail plays no structural role, and there is no hidden iron in the treads, except for some repairs. The only original ironwork apart from the wedges is hidden in the cantilevered landing stones at the top, where metal tongues in the vertical joints allow loads to be shared between adjacent stones.

The first staircase of this type in England is found in Inigo Jones's Queen's House, Greenwich, fitted out in the early 1630s. They were still rare when this one was completed in 1705, but were to become common in grand Georgian houses, where the ground and principal floors might be linked in this way. What distinguishes the geometrical stair at St Paul's is the height to which it rises in one unbroken sweep.

The precise manner by which loads from such stairs reach the ground has been much debated. Though individual treads or short runs of treads are often cracked, cases of complete collapse are rare. This demonstrates a measure of redundancy in a nevertheless daring and delicate system. Such stairs are vulnerable to impact damage to individual treads, and the contact between one tread and the next can be broken by slight movements in the surrounding walls. The geometrical stair at St Paul's has been damaged by impact to individual treads and by stress concentrations due to the iron wedges. But the cracks in the walls appear to have done little to compromise the robustness of the stair itself.

THE CATHEDRAL COMPLETED

The last stone of the cathedral's structure was laid on 26 October 1708 by two sons named after their fathers.[91] Christopher Wren junior had been born in the year the foundation stone was laid;[92] Edward Strong was son of the mason who had taken over from his brother as one of the master masons of the works in 1681.[93] The elder Wren presumably watched from below. It was a couple of days after his seventy-sixth birthday.

In many ways, it marked the end of an era. Inside and around the cathedral itself there was much left to do, but the political climate was turning against the architect who had served successfully under so many different governments for so long. Some inkling that the tide was changing had occurred in 1707 when a lobby from the copper merchants attempted unsuccessfully to force a ruling through Parliament that the dome should be covered in copper rather than lead, which was Wren's preferred material. A new dean and a residentiary appointed in 1707 proved even more troublesome. Arguments soon ensued about the finishing of the dome and about the building of the railing around the churchyard. Wren's adversaries proved more than a match for the old surveyor. He found his craftsmen accused of embezzling funds, while he was accused of having lost control. The evidence for such a claim was questionable, but it had an effect. John James was appointed as master carpenter to replace the carpenter whose honesty had been called into question and although Wren was reappointed surveyor in 1712, the dean remained openly hostile. After the accession of George I, he ceased to attend committee meetings. John James had been appointed his assistant and it was he who oversaw the finishing of the cathedral.[94]

Of all the members of the original office of works who had been involved in the rebuilding of St Paul's at the beginning, in 1675, only Wren lived to see the building completed. There were decisions taken in the finishing of the cathedral in the later years which he definitely disagreed with, and parts of the work which show the signs of other hands, but the responsibility for the overall design of St Paul's Cathedral was undeniably his. It was his life's work. Like any structure of such a size and complexity, it is not without its flaws, but it remains a unique and remarkable monument to the achievements of one of history's most extraordinary individuals and of those that worked under his direction.

21

FITTINGS AND LITURGY IN POST-FIRE ST PAUL'S

John Newman

'But that which contributes not a little to the Beauty of this choir, are the Galleries, the Bishops Throne, Lord Mayors seat, with the Stalls, all which being contiguous, compose 1 vast body of curious carved Work of the finest Wainscot, constituting 3 sides of a quadrangle.'[1] In these words Edward Hatton, writing a decade after the opening of the choir in 1697, draws attention to the unique character of Wren's liturgical furniture for the new cathedral. The fittings in medieval cathedral choirs provided a throne for the bishop and stalls for the dean and chapter and the other clergy and singing-men, in an enclosure from which lay worshippers were excluded. Wren, by contrast, integrated the choir stalls with galleries for the congregation at two levels above and behind them. This was in order to provide together in the eastern arm the two essential components of Protestant cathedral worship, a choir and what contemporaries called an 'auditory'. The stalls and galleries extended the length of the north and south sides of Hatton's 'quadrangle', while towards the east it lay open where the altar stood in the eastern apse of the building. At the west end the stalls and the upper gallery returned to flank the great organ in a magnificent case, supported on four pairs of marble columns. The mid nineteenth-century reordering, which opened up a vista through the length of the whole cathedral by removing the western stalls and columns and splitting and resiting the organ and its case, has destroyed the original effect of the interior of the cathedral: an enclosed eastern arm set aside for worship, with the rest as a vast promenading area. There was one other small space reserved for services, the Morning Prayer Chapel opening from the north-west corner of the nave.

In order to understand how Wren's cathedral came to be furnished in this novel fashion, it is necessary to consider the pre-Fire arrangements in the medieval choir, and to establish what acts of worship were intended to be performed there.

In all post-Reformation English cathedrals the clergy continued to occupy the stalls in the choir, but in some the practice developed of hearing sermons in the nave, in particular where the mayor and corporation attended services. For example, at Wells a nave pulpit of stone was set up as early as the 1540s, and a plan of the nave of Chichester Cathedral in 1635 shows seating around a 'sermon place'.[2] Plans published by Browne Willis in 1727–30 show pulpits outside the choir enclosure at Ely, Hereford, Oxford and Bristol.[3] At St Paul's, however, the nave had become dominated by secular activities long before the Reformation, and the condition of 'Paul's walk' and the uses to which it was put remained a scandal throughout the sixteenth and early seventeenth centuries.[4] It was at Paul's Cross, outside to the north-east of the cathedral, that sermons were delivered on occasions of national thanksgiving or by celebrated visiting preachers.

Sermons at Paul's Cross were discontinued *c.*1633 and preaching thereafter took place in the choir instead.[5] Shortly before then, Sir Paul Pindar, a rich City merchant and former ambassador in Constantinople, paid, among other things, for the repair of 'all the decays and defects of the Wainscot worke of the Quier'[6] (see p. 175 and Fig. 71).

When, after the Restoration, services in the cathedral got back to their pre-war routine, the members of the establishment resumed their daily round of worship. But it is clear that provision also had to be made for preaching services attended by city dignitaries. Thus a member of the chapter, writing to the dean during the aftermath of the Plague, in December 1665, refers to the re-establishment of services in the following terms:

143 (*right*). Plan of Wren's 'Greek cross' design, *c.* 1671–2. (AS, Wren Collection, II.21)

144 (*below right*). Section of Wren's 'Greek cross' design, *c.* 1671–2. (AS, Wren Collection, II.23)

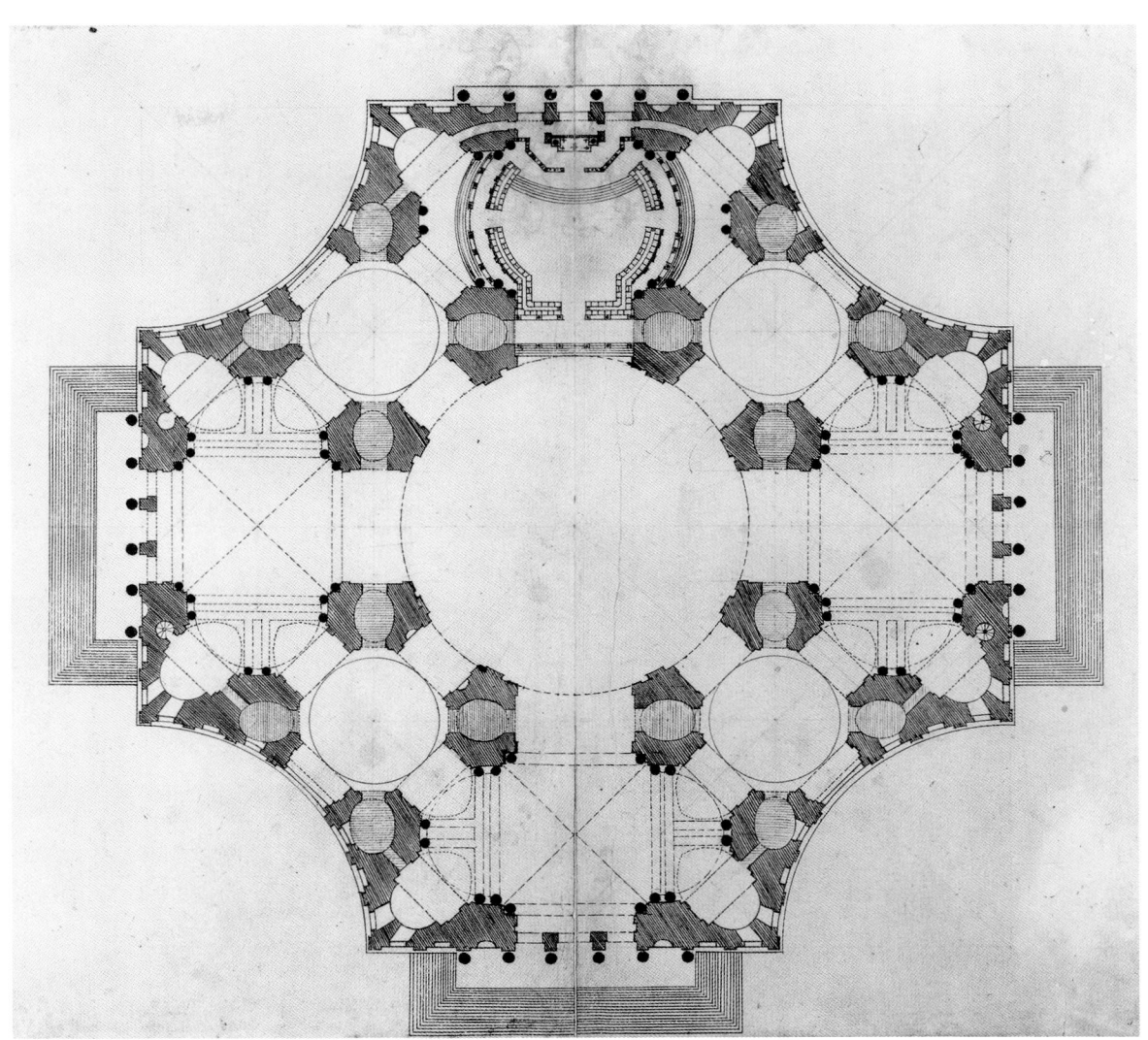

145.   St Dunstan's Chapel, originally the Morning Prayer Chapel, looking west in 2002. The chapel was fitted out for daily services in 1698

if the choir begin at Christmas the solemn services, we are obliged to preach our customary sermons before my Lord Mayor upon Christmas night, Twelfth night and Candlemas night as also upon the Holy days in Christmas week.

The size and nature of the congregation at such times is indicated by a contemporary letter, which refers not only to the lord mayor, but to aldermen and the city livery companies.[7]

In spite of all this, one must not assume that, after the developments of the 1630s, the physical linkage of choir and auditory was considered automatic at St Paul's. Wren, in discussing his ideas for the further restoration of the medieval cathedral in May 1666, listed the various functions which had to be accommodated in the building as 'a Quire, Consistory, Chapter House, Library, Court of Arches & preaching Auditory'.[8] In his mind at least, 'choir' and 'auditory' seem to have been quite distinct from one another. After the Great Fire, he proposed fitting up the ruined cathedral for worship by concentrating choir and auditory in the Romanesque nave, as being the least damaged part of the building, siting the choir in two bays towards the east and the auditory in three or four bays further west. Once again, he envisaged two different spaces for two distinct functions.[9]

During the seven years from 1668, when the decision was taken to pull down the ruins of the old cathedral and build anew, until the commencement of construction in 1675, Wren made at least five strongly contrasting designs, all of which must have required him to consider how worship would be conducted in the new setting. Yet, tantalizingly, only three of his many surviving drawings for these projects give any indication of his thinking on this issue; otherwise, they represent his ideas exclusively for the structure of the building and not for its furniture. The first of these three drawings is the highly finished plan for a Latin-cross cathedral dated by Gordon Higgott to *c.*1668[10] (see p. 187 and Fig. 107). This shows the eastern arm firmly separated from the rest of the building by a flight of ten steps, then a broad preliminary bay followed by a three-bay choir. Within the two western bays of the choir, the outlines of north and south stalls are indicated, returning at the west to form a deep screen, probably to support an organ loft, with a wide central entrance. In the east bay, the altar is set well forward of the east wall, railed in on three sides and with a reredos of some sort behind. As far as one can tell, this is a conventional scheme, providing seating for a choir only and not an auditory.

Much more specific indications of choir seating are given in the plan and section of the so-called 'Greek-Cross' design, which became the basis of the design of the Great Model[11] (Figs 143, 144). The clergy objected to the Great Model design because 'the Quire was design'd Circular'.[12] The Greek-Cross plan shows what they were objecting to, a choir confined within the easternmost space, with seating arranged two deep in stalls which are shown bowing strongly outwards on a circular plan, a highly unconventional arrangement quite unlike the straight, parallel ranges of normal stalls. To the west, the stalls return straight, to flank a central entrance. In all, about ninety-six seats are indicated, enough for the entire cathedral establishment with a small surplus. In order to accommodate a congregation of any size, further seating would have been required. But none is indicated, nor is a pulpit shown, either within the choir or elsewhere in the building. The section drawing would seem to rule out the possibility that upper-level galleries were intended, for the choir enclosure and the colonnade surrounding it are indicated as being no more than about seven feet high. So these designs, too, are for a 'choir' but not an 'auditory'.

One other of Wren's early designs, however, deserves consideration. This is the First Model. Predating the Greek-Cross design and Great Model, it belongs to the period before the increase in the coal tax in 1670 laid the 'silver foundations' for a monumental building.[13] The First Model (Figs. 108–10) represented a cathedral which would consist of nothing more than the bare essentials for worship, a domed vestibule and a rectangular body ten bays long. The single surviving drawing related to this project makes clear, better than the mutilated remains of the model itself, how the body would be fitted up for worship, even though no fittings are indicated (Fig. 109). One can assume that at the level of the main floor parallel ranges would be set against the side walls facing one another, while galleries would have run above and behind their full length. Such an arrangement has much in common with the scheme Wren ultimately devised. It has long been recognized that in his First Model design Wren adumbrated the interior of what he came to consider his most successful parish church, St James's, Piccadilly. But perhaps it should also be seen as his preliminary insight into the way the cathedral clergy and choristers and a large congregation could all be seated together. All in all, the evidence of Wren's preliminary designs, such as it is, remains inconclusive. The drawings of the Warrant design, on the basis of which construction began in 1675, contain no indication of any fittings whatever.

The monumental cruciform cathedral which was constructed from 1675 left open the possibility of separating choir and auditory by fitting up the nave for sermons. But we can be fairly sure that this was never contemplated. Wren's close association with William Sancroft, dean of St Paul's throughout the period of design, and from 1677 archbishop of Canterbury, makes it likely that Sancroft's ideas on matters of worship would have prevailed. So it is worth noting the archiepiscopal enquiries which Sancroft made in 1683 into the forms of services held in cathedrals within his province. The nature of the replies which these elicited[14] makes it clear that Sancroft was intent on encouraging two

reforms in particular: one was the celebration of Holy Communion weekly, the other was the removal of all nave sermons into the choir. If he wanted the choir to double as the 'auditory' in other cathedrals, one can surely assume that he would have insisted on it in the cathedral with whose rebuilding he had been so closely involved and in which he continued to take a keen interest.

St Paul's Cathedral, however, had more than a diocesan role. As the cathedral of the capital city of England, it was, as has already been noted, the setting both for services attended by the lord mayor and Corporation of London and for services of national thanksgiving: as Henry Compton, bishop of London, put it in 1678 in his appeal for funds, 'Our Kings have used upon extraordinary occasions to resort to it there to pay their solemn acknowledgements to Almighty God for publick blessings and deliverances granted to this Nation.'[15]

The first reference to Wren's designs for the choir fittings comes in the autumn of 1693,[16] shortly before construction of the high vault of the choir was put in hand.[17] He brought to a meeting of the commissioners on 2 October 'The Designe by him prepared for the Inside of the Choire... for their Approbation thereof, or further Direction therein'. No decision was taken on that occasion, and it was not until the following May that Wren exhibited his designs again. This time, they found favour and the commissioners urged him to proceed as fast as he could, 'being very desireous to hasten ye same, so as ye Choire may be fitted for Divine Service as soon as possible may be'.[18] For all this note of urgency, it would be another three and a half years before the choir was ready for its first service.

Towards the end of this period, in 1696, Bishop Compton embarked on a visitation in which, among other things, he sought to re-establish the daily and weekly services of the cathedral on a footing of decency and order. Compton's ensuing injunctions regulated the chapter's private devotions and public worship.[19]

Each residentiary canon in his own stall each day was to say the portion of the Psalms appointed for that prebend, the first words of which were to be inscribed over his stall, as they had been in the old cathedral since at least the early fourteenth century.[20] The minor canons should together say morning and evening prayer daily in the Morning Prayer Chapel, at 6 a.m. and 6 p.m. in summer and at 7 a.m. and 6 p.m. in winter. Public prayers should be sung in the choir each weekday at 9 a.m. and 3 p.m., and on Sundays at 9 a.m. Residentiaries and minor canons should normally attend, and so should the vicars choral and choristers. The Venite and Psalms should be sung antiphonally. Hymns and anthems, as authorized by the dean, should be chosen to relate to the Psalm or the lesson for the day, 'so that all the faithful who are present at the prayers may join in the singing, at least in their hearts, if not with their mouths'. Sermons should be delivered in the choir on the main feast days, by the dignitaries and residentiaries (or their substitutes) according to a set rota. Holy Communion should be administered every Sunday and on other feast days, 'if a suitable number of the faithful are present who can communicate along with the Minister'. On these occasions, the choir should sing the Sanctus and the Gloria.

These statutes, then, envisaged two spaces for worship, the choir and the Morning Prayer Chapel (Fig. 145). Since the Middle Ages, the chapel had been a space separate from the choir, and the thirty minor canons were to meet for prayers there twice daily. Earlier in the seventeenth century, they had gathered in the Jesus Chapel in the crypt.[21] Wren sited his Morning Prayer

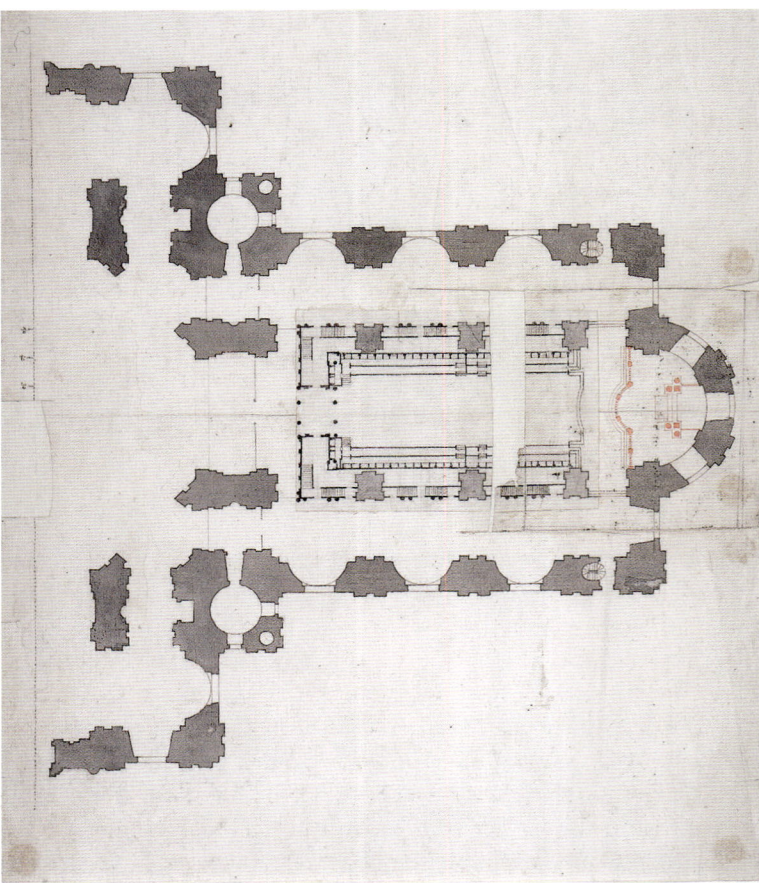

146.   Plan of eastern arm of the cathedral, Wren office drawing of
c. 1693/4. The seating is shown largely as executed, but without a bishop's
throne at the east end of the south stalls. The stalls and piers are overlaid
on an earlier plan which indicates a different arrangement of the west
return stalls, and access to the galleries by means of spiral stairs projecting
into the aisles. (AS, Wren Collection, II.30)

On these occasions, the congregation would have required considerably more seating than was provided in the choir stalls.

There is no evidence that Wren produced a three-dimensional model of the whole scheme, though the joiners did make a number of part-models, two of which survive.[26] Thirty-one drawings also remain. In order to understand Wren's scheme in its entirety, it is necessary to look at a drawing of the eastern arm produced by his office in *c.* 1693–4, a detail of which was subsequently published by Hulsbergh in 1726, and which may be presumed to show Wren's own final intentions for the choir[27] (Fig. 146). These make it clear that in two important respects Wren's original concept was compromised in execution. First, he conceived a layout that was absolutely symmetrical across the east–west axis, with the bishop's throne sited centrally in the south stalls, facing the lord mayor's seat in the centre of the north stalls; so the present elaborate bishop's throne beyond the east end of the south stalls was clearly an afterthought, a very early one. More damagingly, Wren's intention to have a free-standing, columned reredos behind the communion table in the sanctuary, large enough to form a visual focus for the entire choir space, was completely thwarted.

These and other points can now be considered in more detail, by a discussion of the three components in turn: first the western screen and organ, then the stalls and galleries, and finally the sanctuary.

The present state of the choir and its furnishings differs considerably more from Wren's original arrangements than is generally realized. The nineteenth-century reordering not only opened up the east–west vista, but also moved the stalls and galleries bodily one bay westwards and raised the entire floor level of the choir.

Although the choir of the new cathedral was first used on 2 December 1697, when the thanksgiving service for the Peace of Ryswick was held there, at that time the organ was only partially playable and other minor works were still incomplete. More seriously, the choir arm was separated from the still-unfinished dome and nave by a temporary timber screen. Only with its removal and the erection of Jean Tijou's wrought-iron gates across the west end of the choir aisles in 1705 could the setting for public worship in the cathedral be said to be entire.[28]

The western screen bore aloft the magnificent central organ case. The screen was of the Corinthian order, with a deep entrance defined front and back by groups of four columns of white veined marble on foliate pedestals.[29] The west-facing columns carried a timber entablature and pediment, creating the effect of an entrance portico. Within this portico, the paving was marked by a band of patterned marble, which contrasted with the white marble floors of vestibule and choir and served as a threshold since there was no flight of steps to separate the two spaces. On the timber screen to left and right of the entrance, the Corinthian order continued as pilasters, with paired columns at the outer angles.[30] All the carved enrichment, including the swags of fruit and flowers between the pilaster capitals and the scrolling foliage in the friezes, was the responsibility of Grinling Gibbons.[31]

The organ case which stood above the entrance portico was to be 22 feet high, 18 feet wide and 6 feet deep, following a decision taken by the commission as early as 10 May 1694 after consulting the master of the choristers, Dr John Blow, and the organ maker, Bernard Smith.[32]

The siting of the organ seems at first to have been a matter of debate. Plenty of precedents are known for placing an organ centrally on the pulpitum or choir screen in English cathedrals dating

Chapel at ground level, but equally isolated from the choir, off the north-west corner of the nave. It required nothing more than a reading desk, set beneath the north window, and seating for the minor canons. The desk and most of the original pews still survive.[22] The importance of the Morning Prayer Chapel is indicated by the fact that it was fitted up for use by the early months of 1698, years before work on the nave was completed.[23]

The choir, on the other hand, required four items of liturgical furniture, Communion table, organ, pulpit and litany desk, together with seats for the full cathedral establishment of dignitaries, residentiaries, minor canons, vicars choral and choristers, about seventy in all, and also for those members of the public who might want to attend services on weekdays or Sundays. The 116 seats in the two rows of north and south stalls, together with the western return stalls which Wren's design provided, could therefore be thought adequate for the entire congregation envisaged in Bishop Compton's statutes.

However, the statutes do not mention the services regularly attended by the lord mayor, aldermen and other city dignitaries. As we have seen, such civic services could be quite frequent.[24] More significant still had been the great services of thanksgiving or penitence at which the cathedral establishment had demonstrated its loyalty to king or Parliament as prudence dictated during the turbulent decades of the mid century. The lord mayor might order the printing of the sermon delivered at such services.[25]

147 (*right*). Section through choir looking west, showing screen and organ case, *c*.1693–4. (GL, St Paul's collection)

148 (*below right*). Elevation and profile of the choir stalls, Wren office drawing of *c*.1693–4. (GL, St Paul's collection)

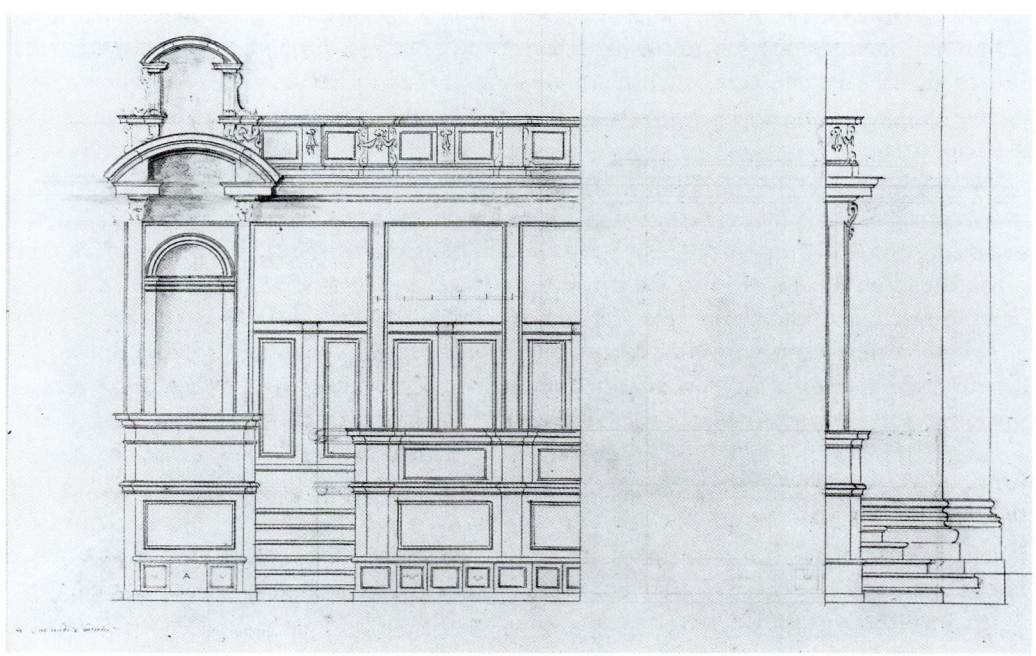

149.   Organ case on the north side of the choir in 2002

150.   Seating in the upper gallery above the south side of the choir in 2002

back at least to the mid sixteenth century. From the Restoration onwards, however, much larger organs began to be built, so that when positioned axially they interrupted the vista through the length of the building. This can still be seen in respect of the earliest surviving example of such an instrument, John Luxmoore's in Exeter Cathedral, dated 1665. In pre-Fire St Paul's Cathedral, however, as Hollar's engraving shows (see Fig. 265), the organ had been placed not on the pulpitum but under an arcade arch above the north choir stalls.[33] So it is perhaps under-standable that the possibility of siting the new organ in a similar position was considered by Wren. A pair of elevational drawings for the organ case,[34] one sited under an arcade arch, the other apparently free-standing, show that the design was being devel-oped before the position of the organ had been fixed. Furthermore, it is the design for the arcade site which employs the disposition eventually executed, with rectangular side towers framed by Corinthian pilasters. An organ of the dimen-sions specified on 10 May 1694 could just have fitted under the arcade. However, Wren must surely have been opposed to the non-axial placement of the organ. The arrangement adopted (Fig. 147), placing the organ in its boldly monumental case axially over the entrance screens, reinforced the separateness and enclosed nature of the choir and auditory within the eastern arm of the cathedral.

The choir seating is one of those neat and satisfying inventions of which Wren the mechanical philosopher was master (Figs 148, 156). As already explained, it is devised to provide both a 'choir' and an 'auditory'. The choir was represented by the stalls, primarily intended to seat those who made up the cathedral establishment and had the duty to say or sing divine service in the cathedral daily. In the mid 1690s this body numbered fifty-five, thirty prebends or residentiaries, among whom were the dean, the four archdeacons, the treasurer and the precentor, together with the chancellor, the reader in theology, twelve minor canons, six vicars choral, three virgers and two bell-ringers.[35] To these must be added about ten singing boys. The upper or principal stalls provided sixty seats, twenty-eight on the north side, twenty-eight on the south, with two return stalls at the west end on each side.[36] However, as with medieval choir stalls, there was also a second set of stalls and desks at a lower level extending in front of the north and south stalls, providing a further fifty-six seats. Furthermore, the dean, archdeacons and principal officers of the chapter all had their official stalls, as well as the stalls allocated to them as prebends; so the sixty upper stalls could not quite accommodate the full establishment. The build-ing accounts distinguish between the prebends' and singing-men's seats. However, the north and south stalls are interrupted where they pass in front of the central pier on each side by a

151 (*above*). Middle gallery above the south side of the choir, facing east in 2002

152.   Detail of cherubim by Grinling Gibbons over choir stalls in 2002

153 (*below*). The choir stalls in 2002

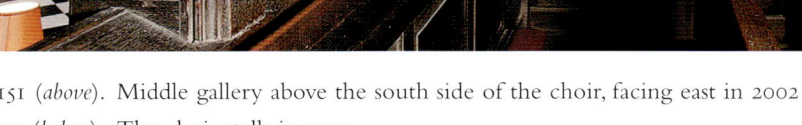

154.   Engraving by Robert Trevitt showing the south side of the choir, during the thanksgiving service attended by Queen Anne and both Houses of Parliament on 31 December 1706, published in 1710. (GL)

broader, shell-headed stall under a lofty canopy. These were to be the bishop's (south) and lord mayor's (north) thrones. Almost, but not quite, all of the prebendal stalls lie west of these thrones, and it is understandable that the dean and chapter should have been troubled at the prospect of the bishop sitting among them. So, as already mentioned, while construction of the stalls was under way it was decided to erect a second bishop's throne in the traditional position beyond the east end of the south stalls. References in the building accounts to the bishop's and lord mayor's 'seats' as well as to the bishop's 'throne' make clear the timing of this change of mind.[37]

The upper or prebendal stalls have panelled backs framed by mullions, every other one of which is taken up to support a richly decorated overhanging horizontal canopy. However, the canopy is set at a level high enough to allow for an intermediate row of rectangular apertures like boxes in a theatre, each the width of two stalls. These open into the lower or 'middle' galleries, while behind the canopy above is a further level of seating, the upper galleries.

What made it possible for Wren to provide these two tiers of gallery seating was the plan of the choir piers. These are rectangular, set twenty-six feet apart from one another and each no less than nine feet deep. This enabled the galleries to be constructed in blocks between the piers, two full blocks and a half block on each side, unlike the stalls, which run continuously in front of the inner faces of the piers. The great depth of the piers provides space not

only for the galleries themselves, but also for stairs at the back, giving access from the aisles. The middle galleries, with handsome coffered ceilings, are subdivided into six per block and provided with seats in front and a rear pew hard up against the back wall and probably intended for servants. (The present front pews are not original.) The upper galleries, being deeper, have space for three rows of pews and are without subdivisions within the blocks. The two eighteenth-century engravings of thanksgiving services (1706 and 1789)[38] (Figs 154, 310) agree in showing two people in each middle-gallery opening, i.e. twelve per block, so there were front seats for fifty-two people in all at that level. In the upper galleries the seating arrangements were more spacious and substantial, facilitated by the canopy overhang. But the engravings make clear that at that height people had to jostle to gain a view of what was going on below. One may reasonably calculate that about one hundred per side could be seated in the upper galleries. This would give a grand total of seating in the galleries (including servants) of just over three hundred.

At the rear, the galleries and the straight flights of stairs leading to them are hidden from the choir aisles by handsome timber screens (Fig. 334). In each bay, two pairs of three-quarter columns frame three doorways and support an entablature and balustrade.[39]

The seating in the galleries, conveniently approached from the choir aisles, was intended to be occupied by persons of quality. But Wren also made provision for humbler seating in the body of the choir. A fixed bench ran in front of the choristers' stalls, as is which particularly captured the imagination of contemporaries. John Evelyn noted 'The pulling out the formes, like drawers, from under the stalls is ingenious',[42] and the Revd George Hickes commended the use of something similar for the churches to be built under the Act of 1711.[43] Unfortunately the benches do not survive, lost in the raising of the choir floor in the mid Victorian alterations, nor does there seem to be any visual record of them in use.

The focus of attention for the 'auditory', whether seated in stalls or galleries or on the drawing seats, was the preacher. A tall but apparently plain and unimpressive hexagonal pulpit surmounted by a small tester was made, at the modest cost of £107, by the joiners Roger Davis and Hugh Webb in the early months of 1698 and Grinling Gibbons provided a little enrichment for it.[44] It appears in eighteenth-century engravings of the choir always in the north-east corner of the choir floor, though it was probably made to be movable.[45] The mobility of the pulpit may explain its otherwise puzzling slightness.

Architecturally, and to a lesser extent liturgically, the focal point of the choir was the *mise-en-scène* in the centre of the eastern apse. However, it was here that Wren suffered his greatest disappointment. His concept of a marble altar-piece with lofty twisted columns is recorded on the engraved plan of 1726[46] and in the words of *Parentalia*, where it is described as 'consisting of four Pillars wreathed, of the richest Greek Marbles, supporting a Canopy hemispherical, with proper Decorations of Architecture and Sculpture'.[47] Although it is asserted in *Parentalia* that it was because of the difficulty of obtaining suitable decorative marbles[48] that the altar-piece remained unexecuted, it is also likely that such a reminiscence of the baldacchino in St Peter's, Rome would have raised the anti-papist hackles of the clergy.

The model which survives in the cathedral is for something less ambitious, a reredos to be set against the east wall of the sanctuary rather than a free-standing baldacchino (Fig. 157).[49] This, too, has twisted columns, which are paired and flank a tall, round-headed opening, presumably intended to be filled with an altar-piece painting.

These projects were quickly set aside, for already in March 1697 preparations were put in hand to create a monumental setting by the simplest possible means – gilding and painting the architectural members of the apse itself. According to *Parentalia*, this was 'intended only to serve the present Occasion'; but no attempt seems to have been made to replace it during the eighteenth century. During the second half of 1697, payments were

155. Engraving by Robert Trevitt showing the choir looking west, 1703 (The Society of Antiquaries)

shown in early engravings by Trevitt and Lens; but provision was also made for seating across the floor of the choir. This consisted of forty-eight retractable benches, twenty-four on each side, which when not in use ran back on wheels between the joists under the stalls (Fig. 156). The design for the panelling which concealed them when not in use is recorded in Wren's elevation for the stalls.[40] The building accounts itemize the various components of these 'drawing seats', their joinery, their steel handles and spindles and their *lignum vitae* wheels.[41] They were a feature

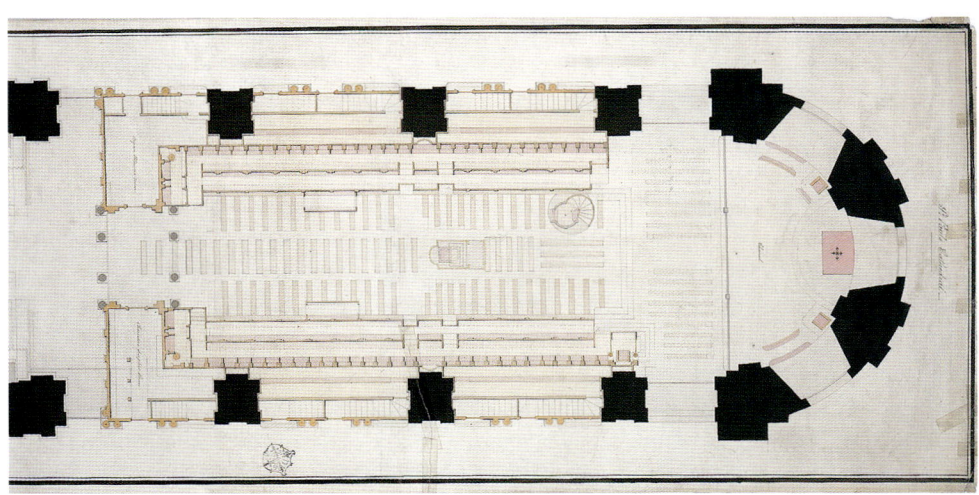

156. Survey plan by F. C. Penrose of the choir in its former position, showing seating arrangements in December 1848, including the original retractable benches. (SPCFA)

157. Wooden model, probably made in 1696, for an unexecuted reredos. (St Paul's Cathedral)

made to John Moore for double-leaf gold and to William Thompson for gilding mouldings, foliage in the frieze, palms and laurels and a 'glory', and also for painting the apse to look like veined marble and the four pilasters with gold-veined ultramarine.[50] Edward Hatton (1708) describes this 'Altar-Piece' and notes that between the pilasters the wall was covered with panels of crimson velvet.[51]

The engraving of 1726 and the compiler of *Parentalia* ignore the realities of Protestant England in referring respectively to '*summum altare*' and 'high altar', since there was but a single 'altar' in the entire cathedral. Liturgically, too, what was placed in the centre of the apse was not an altar but a Communion table. The heated controversies of the 1620s and 1630s between the advocates of a fixed altar, led by William Laud, and those who argued for a movable table, had cooled well before the end of the century. The post-Restoration convention envisaged a wooden movable table railed within an eastern enclosure, an arrangement thereafter found in parish church and cathedral alike. At St Paul's Cathedral, Bishop Compton's statutes of 1696 refer to the 'holy table' and the sacrament to be celebrated at it as the '*sacramentum Coenae Dominicae*' (the Lord's Supper).[52] However, there are numerous non-technical references, for example in the building accounts, to the 'altar' as well as to the 'communion table'. Broadly speaking, the wooden table is referred to as the 'communion table' (payments to John Smallwell the joiner and Grinling Gibbons the carver), but its setting, the apse itself, its decorated marble paving and the steps and rail which formed its western boundary was generically the 'altar'.[53] Even at pavement level, however, Wren's original proposals were simplified: where he had envisaged a flight of three steps up to the apse, bowed out boldly in the centre, and an elaborate balustraded rail (for which Hawksmoor made a sketch design),[54] a single straight step was laid across the chord of the apse, with two steps further west,

forming a platform-like area between the east end of the stalls and the 'altar'. Geometrical patterns in coloured marbles decorated the pavements at both levels.[55] However, the most eye-catching feature of the east end was the wrought ironwork supplied by Jean Tijou: the gates which enclosed the 'platform' to north and south, for which Tijou received no less than £708, and the Communion rail, which cost £260 in 1707 and thus was one of the last fittings to be installed.[56]

In considering the choir furnishings as a whole, two further features need discussion, one practical, the other symbolic. The first is the matter of lighting. Natural illumination, from the large clerestory windows and from the two tiers of windows in the apse, will have been adequate during daytime; but for times when daylight was insufficient, artificial lighting had to be provided. In practice, however, such lighting seems to have been extremely limited. The main payment for light fittings is £40 in January–March 1698 to Mary Sherlock, widow of the ironmonger Edward Sherlock, for two brass 'branches' to hang in the choir and two brass 'lanthorns' to hang in the side aisles. Trevitt's engraved view of the choir looking west shows the 'branches' to be small, four-branch candelabra, which must have been quite ineffective in giving general illumination to the choir.[57] However, it seems that the choir stalls were fitted for candles, as the joiner Charles Hopson was paid for fixing 'Brass Sockets for Candles' in the choir,[58] though no early view indicates candles or their holders. A list of items still to be supplied as late as February 1711 includes 'brass candlesticks for the Choir', so it was clearly possible to conduct services without them.[59]

So to the sculptural decoration of organ, stalls and galleries. What significance was this lavish display intended to hold for those attending services in the choir? All the carved decoration is in timber and was provided by Grinling Gibbons. He presumably was working to instructions from Wren, even if he made his own preparatory drawings. The only drawings in Gibbons's hand are the two for the organ case already discussed, showing abundant swags of fruit and flowers rather different from what was executed. The few surviving designs from Wren's office for the stalls and their canopies indicate inconspicuous vases and swags of drapery. This is quite unlike the scheme carried out in 1696–7, which is inhabited by a host of celestial figures, winged and robed angels, winged putti (the 'boys' of the building accounts) and winged infant heads or cherubim (Fig. 152).

Angels and cherubs had been used in England since early in the seventeenth century to decorate religious buildings and in particular monuments. According to Dugdale, Sir Paul Pindar in refitting the choir of the old cathedral 'beautified' the east face of the pulpitum 'with figures of Angels', and erected wainscot 'with excellent carving; *viz.* of Cherubims and other Imagery, richly gilded'.[60] The fabric of Wren's cathedral, too, is carved with numerous cherubim, over doors, under windows and on the keystones of the arcade arches (Fig. 133). But the angels and cherubim on Wren's choir fittings are unprecedentedly concentrated and conspicuous. The angels, many blowing or holding trumpets, adorn the organ case, two angel terms flanking the chair organ, four more, two east and two west, beside the central pipes of the main organ, and eight nearly life-sized, full-length figures standing on the angles of the towers. On the organ case, pairs of boys support drapery, or hold up wreaths or the royal arms. But boys are also concentrated on the canopies over the principal stalls. The bishop's throne, by contrast, has a more elaborate and towering canopy, set on enriched columns and adorned by rich scrolls

158. *La Communion des Anglicans à Saint Paul*, engraving by Jakob van der Schley, 1736. This shows the seating arrangements at an ordinary Sunday service and the manner of taking communion. The thoroughgoing segregation of the sexes is striking. (GL)

La COMMUNION des ANGLICANS à SAINT PAUL.

and cherubim. But the main array of cherubim, their mouths open in song, is on and under the overhanging cornice of the north and south stalls. These give the most convincing impression of a heavenly host.

Perhaps this impression was intended. This is certainly suggested by a sermon preached by the dean, William Sherlock, in November 1699, two years after the opening of the choir for worship.[61] The occasion was the Anniversary Meeting of the Lovers of Music (the St Cecilia festival), and the dean used it to reflect on and justify the use of music in religious services and in particular the practice of antiphonal singing as practised in cathedrals. Sherlock disputes the then fashionable recourse to the primitive Church as a model for modern practice, but points instead to the Bible. For him, the exhortations in the New Testament 'to Sing to God, To admonish one another in Psalms, and Hymns, and Spiritual Songs', although they may not be 'an Apostolical Institution of a Quire nor do prescribe the particular Forms of Cathedral Worship', yet provide justification for them. More particularly, he notes that the vision of the prophet Isaiah (chapter 6, verses 1–3) is considered a paradigm of cathedral worship: there 'the seraphims are represented crying one to another, Holy, holy, holy, is the Lord of Hosts, Heaven and Earth are full of his Glory. This is acknowledged to be a great Example of Antiphonal Singing, in which One Answers another.'[62] By this line of thinking, there is a particular appropriateness in the concentration of Gibbons's songful cherubim on the cornice overhanging the stalls from which the canons and singing-men chanted antiphonally. But it should be noted that the stalls in the pre-Fire cathedral, as repaired by Sir Paul Pindar, were 'beautified . . . with a faire rayle of Wainscot and a great number of Cherubims artificially carved.'[63]

The new choir was inaugurated with a thanksgiving service for the Peace of Ryswick, on 2 December 1697, in the presence of the lord mayor and aldermen and representatives of the city companies. Henry Compton, bishop of London, preached on the text

'I was glad when they said unto me, Let us go into the House of the Lord'.[64] It would have been interesting to know what allusion, if any, he made to the new building and its fittings on this occasion; but unfortunately the king declined to attend the service, with the result that it was decided not to put the sermon into print.[65] Only John Blow's newly composed anthem on the same text survives.

It was during the first half of Queen Anne's reign that the cathedral saw a series of state services, which utilized the new *mise-en-scène* to overflowing. The seating arrangements for these occasions were regularly reported in the *London Gazette*.[66] In all cases, whether or not the queen was present, a chair of state was placed on a dais at the west end of the choir and the stalls and galleries were occupied not only by civic dignitaries and their wives but also by members of both houses of parliament, peeresses and other ladies of rank. But the character and meaning of the gathering depended on whether or not Parliament was in session.

In November 1702 and December 1706, when Parliament was in session, the House of Lords (forty-nine peers and thirteen bishops on the first occasion, fifty-six peers and nine bishops on the second) sat on broad, upholstered benches in the body of the choir, as if they were in the House of Lords.[67] Members of the House of Commons, of whom there must have been up to two hundred present, were placed in the stalls and the upper galleries, the Speaker taking the canopied stall on the south side normally reserved for the bishop. The lord mayor, aldermen and sheriffs were squeezed into the east half of the middle gallery on the south side, with their wives in the gallery opposite; peeresses occupied the west half of the south gallery at this level, facing foreign dignitaries and their wives. The clergy were displaced to the east end of the choir, the dean and chapter seated within the altar rail and other 'eminent divines' outside it.

The appearance of the choir on these most ceremonial of occasions is vividly conveyed in Robert Trevitt's engraving of

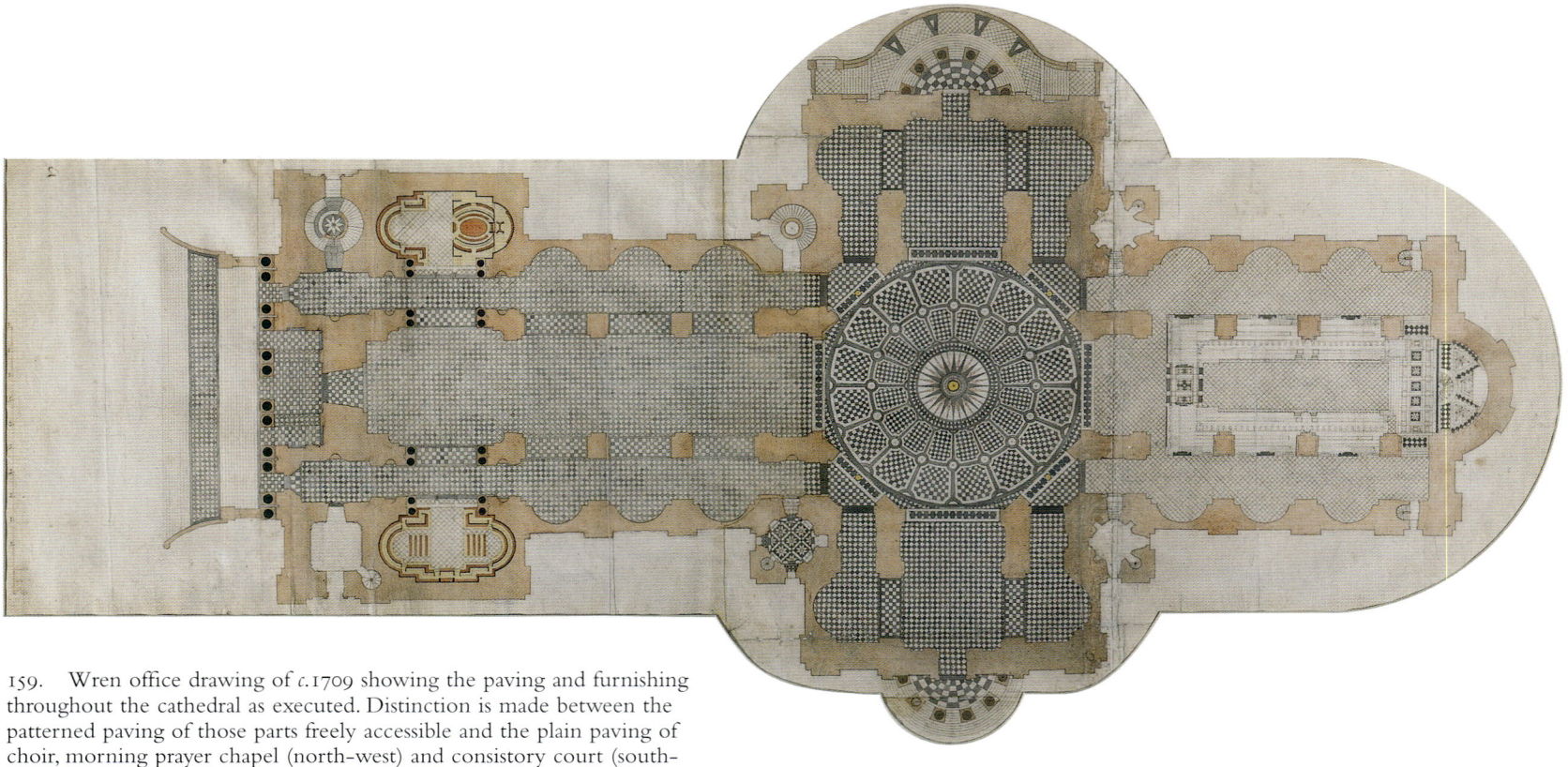

159.   Wren office drawing of *c.*1709 showing the paving and furnishing throughout the cathedral as executed. Distinction is made between the patterned paving of those parts freely accessible and the plain paving of choir, morning prayer chapel (north-west) and consistory court (south-west). (GL, St Paul's collection)

the service on 31 December 1706 (Fig. 154). Besides those already mentioned, Trevitt also indicates, for instance, the heralds flanking the queen's throne, the ladies of the bedchamber in the lower south-west stalls, and the musicians in the upper galleries flanking the organ.

At the other thanksgiving services, when Parliament was not sitting, a different, somewhat less crowded, seating pattern was adopted. Information is fullest for the service in 1704, but it is clear that seating was similar at them all. Peers and privy councillors occupied only the prebendaries' stalls on the north side, and on the south side the corresponding stalls were filled by the ladies of the bedchamber, with the maids of honour in the lower stalls. Peeresses and other high-ranking ladies flanked the queen in the middle galleries, while further east at that level there sat, on the north, foreign dignitaries and their ladies with the lady mayoress and aldermen's and sheriffs' wives, and on the south, the lord mayor himself, aldermen and sheriffs. In the upper galleries various musicians were gathered on either side of the organ, but further east those members of the House of Commons who were in town were placed on the north side, further ladies and 'other persons of distinction' on the south.

There were many other services regularly throughout the year where the clergy retained their stalls and civic dignitaries and, one may assume, their wives, sat in the galleries. The lord mayor regularly ordered the sermons which were preached on such occasions to be printed.[68] From these we discover that, during the first fifteen years of the new choir being in use, anniversary services were held on a fast day for the Fire of London, and in commemoration of the Martyrdom of Charles I, and for such groups as the Sons of the Clergy, the Lovers of Music and gentlemen educated at St Paul's School and at Eton College. These and others like them must have been the services for which Wren's great auditory was most effectively used, with

the clergy and choristers in their rightful places in the stalls and civic dignitaries and the rest of the congregation in the galleries above.

For Sunday-by-Sunday worship, Wren's stalls and galleries came to be used in a different way. The only visual record of an ordinary service in the early eighteenth century is Jakob van der Schley's engraving of 1736, 'La Communion des Anglicans à Saint Paul'[69] (Fig. 158). Clergy who were in residence but not officiating occupied the lower west stalls, leaving the rest of the stalls for laymen. Women sat in the middle galleries, and seem to have taken Communion only after the men present had done so. This segregation of the sexes was made complete by the two different means of access, to the stalls from the choir itself, but to the galleries only from the aisles.[70] Nor was this a novelty in 1736: reference can be found already at the end of 1704 to 'the 3 Galleries where the Women sit,'[71] and John Macky, writing in 1714, greatly approved. He saw the galleries as

> a Conveniency that keeps the Ladies free from the Crouds, which the greatest Quality are necessitated to submit to abroad; besides, it makes the Appearance in the *Choir* on a Solemn Day the more noble; that Circle of Ladies giving a Lustre to a *Holy-Day*.[72]

In conclusion, it should be re-emphasized that Wren, acting on the instructions of the dean and chapter and probably in deference to the advice of Archbishop Sancroft, prepared only two places within the cathedral for worship, the choir and the Morning Prayer Chapel. The crossing, transepts and nave were intended as monumental unfurnished spaces where clergy and laity would promenade or process. Nothing brings out the contrast more vividly than the enormous plan[73] made to record the floors of the cathedral when newly laid (Fig. 159). Where worship was conducted, the marble paving was white; elsewhere, there were patterns in black, white and veined marbles.

22

EMBELLISHMENT AND DECORATION, 1696–1900

Teresa Sladen

Although Sir Christopher Wren had no hand in choosing either the painted or the mosaic decoration now to be seen in St Paul's, the mythic stature of the man, coupled with the shabby way in which he was treated during the final stages of the project, has led most subsequent decorators to ask the same question. Had the commissioners not overruled their architect and taken the matter of painting the dome into their own hands, how would Wren have wished to see his building completed? Even the most cursory glance at the decorative history of the cathedral suffices to show how many different answers were found to this question, all coloured by the aesthetic of their time. But because so many of these schemes were carried out in Wren's name, an essay on this subject must start by trying to unravel what he himself might have done.

The evidence of Wren's approach to decoration is both limited and contradictory. First of all, there is the statement made by his son in *Parentalia* that Wren had wanted the dome of St Paul's clad in mosaic.[1] At first sight, this seems surprising, but mosaic was, after all, a classical form of decoration and, in the contemporary debate over the virtues of the Ancients as opposed to the Moderns, Wren was firmly on the side of the Ancients. Writing from Paris in 1665, he said: 'Building certainly ought to have the Attribute of eternal, and therefore the only Thing uncapable of new Fashions.'[2] At this time, he much preferred the 'masculine Furniture of Palais Mazarine' which housed the Cardinal's 'great and noble Collection of antique Statues and Bustos' and included examples of 'true Mosaicks' brought from Italy, to the more 'feminine' style of contemporary French decoration.[3] Furthermore, he knew that Michelangelo's dome in St Peter's had been treated in this way and, while in Paris, would have seen the chapel of the Sorbonne where the dome was painted to simulate mosaic of the type used in the great church at Rome.[4]

But several things make it hard to argue that Wren was ever deeply committed to the use of mosaic at St Paul's. By the time he visited Paris, the compartmentalized form of mosaic decoration employed on the dome of St Peter's in 1591–3 (Fig. 160) and painted on that of the Sorbonne in 1641–4 was already out of fashion in both Italy and France.[5] Furthermore, the cost of mosaic would have been likely to exceed any sum sanctioned by the commissioners.[6] Nor do any of the surviving drawings made during the development of Wren's scheme for St Paul's show this type of decoration.[7]

The alternative to mosaic was some form of painted decoration and, bearing in mind his love of the arts of the Ancient World, it is not surprising that in 1673–4 he had the dome of the Great Model painted with coffering similar to that of the Pantheon in Rome. This was a building he would have known well from printed sources and there seems no reason to doubt that this type of coffering, undivided by ribs, is what he would have favoured at this date.

But times change and anyone sensitive to developments in their own field will be affected. When Cardinal Mazarin died in 1661 and Louis XIV took the government of France into his own hands, he and his finance minister, Jean-Baptiste Colbert, set out to strengthen and control the institutions underpinning the art and architecture of the nation. Soon, the intense interest focused on all the arts, coupled with the major building campaigns undertaken by Louis XIV, led to France, rather than Italy, coming to be the prime centre of art and architecture in Europe.

160 (*above*). The dome of St Peter's, Rome, showing the mosaic decoration introduced by Cavaliere d'Arpino, *c.* 1590

161 (*right*). Section of the church of Les Invalides, Paris, showing concealed windows which lit the surface of the upper dome. Engraving attributed to Pierre Le Pautre, made during construction, 1687. The decoration is not shown in its final form. (Bibliothèque nationale, Paris)

During the first half of the seventeenth century, a number of domed churches had been built in Paris, all of which Wren would have seen in 1665.[8] But what he could not have seen was the domed church of Les Invalides built to the designs of Jules Hardouin Mansart between 1677 and 1691 and decorated by 1706.[9] This far outshone its predecessors; not only was it structurally innovative, but it combined painting and decoration in a fresh and dazzling way. In order to throw light into the sky painted on the upper dome, the architect provided a ring of windows concealed by the rim of the lower cut-off dome. Beneath this, the cove of the lower dome was divided into a series of tall rectangular panels suited to the compositional form of paintings. The development of the design and proposed decoration of Les Invalides was documented and spread abroad by the constant flow of engravings from the print-making industry in Paris (Fig. 161). It soon became the most famous church of its day.

Wren was evidently well aware of the progress of the church of Les Invalides while it was under construction.[10] A sectional drawing related to the so-called Definitive design of St Paul's, and now believed by recent scholarship to have been produced in the late 1680s or early 1690s, has concealed windows in the dome similar to those of Les Invalides (Fig. 162).[11] Furthermore, the surface of the upper dome in this drawing is covered with squiggles, indicating some form of baroque illusionistic painting. This shows that by the time Wren was working on this design, he was not only

aware of the structural form of the dome of Les Invalides but also understood the reason for the concealed lighting.

Another design for the dome, dateable soon after this one and inscribed with the words 'Sr. Chr: Wren's owne hand', is of even greater significance (Fig. 164).[12] It shows a section of the dome, but in this case the inner dome is taller and the surface is subdivided by ribs which frame rectangular panels. This scheme of decoration seems to be based on one that appears in two engravings of the interior of Les Invalides issued in the 1680s, before the final form of its decoration had been decided.[13]

It would be difficult to argue that these designs, made before the final form of the dome of St Paul's was settled, represent Wren's final wishes. What they do suggest, however, is that his ideas on the subject of decoration were not fixed at some early point in his career, and that he was not isolated from, or unaffected by, developments taking place in France. Even so, had he thought the decoration of his dome an integral part of the design, he surely would have provided drawings to show what he had in mind. The absence of these suggests that, although he would have had views on the type of decoration appropriate, he did not think it enormously important.

Further evidence regarding Wren's wishes for the decoration of St Paul's is provided by the scheme carried out in the choir. This was the only part of the building to be entirely decorated before Wren fell out with the commissioners. Even so, as John Newman

162 (*above*). Section of the dome of St Paul's, related to the Definitive Design, *c.*1690, showing concealed windows and some form of decoration on the surface of the upper dome. (GL, St Paul's collection)

163 (*above right*). The east end with the communion table at the end of the seventeenth century, from a lost engraving reproduced in J. D. Chambers, *Divine Worship in England* (1877). (SPCL)

164 (*right*). Half-section of the dome inscribed 'Sr. Chr: Wren's owne Hand', showing the inner dome decorated with rectangular panels similar to those in Le Pautre's engraving of the church of Les Invalides of 1687. (BM)

165. Decorative scheme proposed for the saloon at Blenheim by James Thornhill, *c.* 1714. (Ashmolean Museum, Oxford)

166. Early 'architectural' scheme of decoration for the dome with square coffering, by James Thornhill, *c.* 1708. (Courtauld Gallery, London)

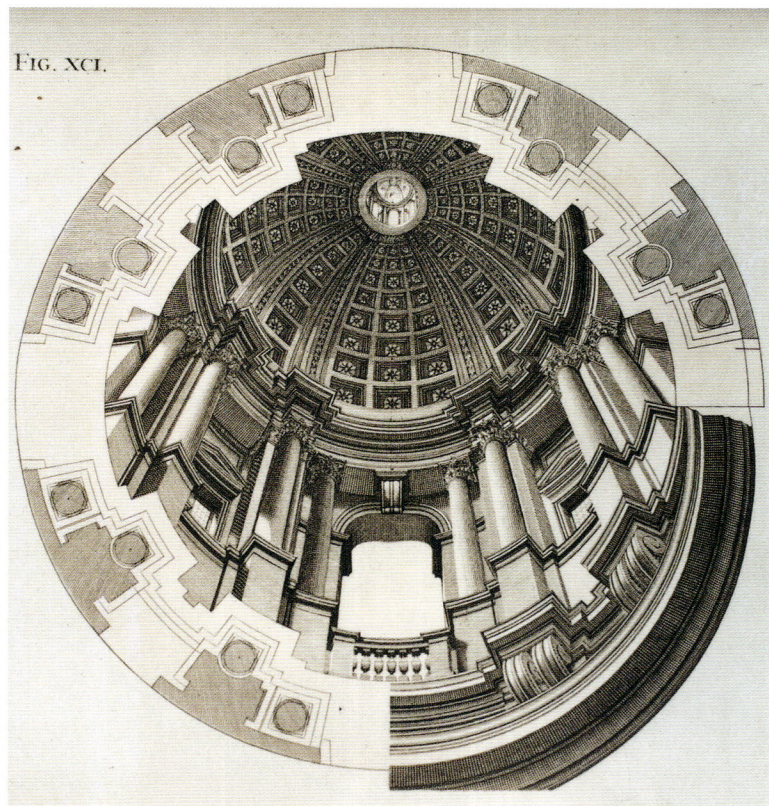

167. Diagram showing the cupola painted on the flat ceiling of Sant'Ignazio, Rome, printed in the English translation of Andrea Pozzo's book on perspective (Pozzo, 1707)

points out (see pp. 229–30), Wren's plan for a grand marble altar placed beneath a baldacchino was set aside, and the relative simplicity of the decorative scheme (Fig. 163) may have had more to do with the commissioners' desire for a certain Protestant decorum than with Wren's personal taste.

The overall effect of the choir, though more magnificent, must have been similar to that of the city churches, with their chaste white walls, dark woodwork and gilded mouldings. In September 1696 the plasterer Henry Doogood was paid for 'Whitening and Collouring' the vaults, aisles and both sides of the choir.[14] A year later, the painter William Thompson was employed to decorate 'ye Circular Part of the Choire' in a more elaborate manner. Here, the walls were painted to resemble white marble, a foliate frieze was painted beneath the modillion cornice, the mouldings were lavishly gilded, and the four fluted pilasters were 'hightened with Ultramarine and Vain(ed) with gold'.[15] The most striking elements of the choir would have been the apse glittering with gold, Gibbons's bravura display of carved woodwork and Tijou's remarkable iron gates.

Another ten years were to pass before the vaults of the nave, transepts and dome in the crossing were ready to receive plaster. This took place between 1706 and 1708.[16] During the two following years, Wren had all the stonework in the cathedral up to the level of the great cornice covered with a grey or stone-coloured oil paint.[17] And finally, towards the end of 1710, the plasterers were paid for whitewashing 'the Vaultings of the whole Church' while the painter redecorated the choir apse and refurbished the ornamental work there.[18]

168. Alternative early 'architectural' scheme of decoration for the dome, by James Thornhill, *c*.1708.
(Courtauld Gallery, London)

In 1708, with the cathedral near completion, it was time to decide on the decoration of the dome. In April that year, the commissioners asked Wren to procure suitable designs.[19] It is not known whether he did so but, under these circumstances, it would have been natural for him to turn to the painter who was making such a success of the decoration of another of his buildings, the Naval Hospital at Greenwich.[20]

This was James Thornhill, who at just thirty was beginning to make a name for himself. His style owed a good deal to that of the Bolognese painter, Antonio Verrio, for whom he had worked at Hampton Court, and also to that of his French contemporary Louis Laguerre.[21] Where he excelled, however, was in his outstanding ability as a scenographic painter and it was probably his more disciplined approach to the depiction of painted architecture that made him popular with the office of works.[22] People were, at this period, deeply interested in the 'science' of three-

dimensional drawing and in 1707 John James, one of the architects working under Wren, published the first English translation of Fra Pozzo's *Rules and Examples of Perspective for Painters and Architects* (Fig. 165).[3] Wren, Hawksmoor and Vanbrugh all put their names to the 'Approbation' at the beginning of this book. The series of 'architectural' schemes Thornhill devised for the decoration of St Paul's show how much he learned from Pozzo's diagrams (Figs 166, 167).[24]

These 'architectural' sketches must predate the meeting of 25 February 1709, because this was when the commissioners stipulated that the dome should be painted with figures and after that there would have no incentive for Thornhill to produce schemes of this kind.[25] So if, as seems likely, they were made at Wren's request, these drawings are of great significance as the best indication we have of the type of scheme he might have approved, had he retained control of the decoration of the dome. One

document which may be thought to support this thesis is the estimate he made in 1711 listing the works needed to finish the cathedral. Here he says that painting the dome with figurative scenes would cost £3,500, but adds in brackets 'But if the same be painted with ornaments of architecture in Basso Relievo, and the mouldings heightened with gold, it may be done for two thousand pounds, and *several are more inclined this latter way than the other*' (my italics).[26]

Thornhill's early sketches for the decoration of the dome show just how inventive he was as a designer of painted architecture. In the most restrained scheme, the area between the ribs is filled with square coffering similar to that shown in the illustration in Pozzo's book; in another, the same area is occupied by a coffered niche containing a cartouche supported by angels; while in the other three Thornhill has painted arches between the ribs, creating the illusion of a view out to the sky beyond. It is not unreasonable to suppose that if any of these schemes had been carried out they would have been painted largely in white with the mouldings picked out in gold, as shown in the sketch Thornhill made for the decoration of the saloon at Blenheim *c.*1714 (Fig. 165).[27] These colours would have matched those in the choir where the vaults and saucer domes were painted white and the mouldings in the apse enriched with gilding.

But just when the time had come to decorate the dome, the commissioners began to obstruct their architect's plans. At the meeting held on 25 February 1709, ignoring any proposals he may have put before them, they suddenly raised the question of figurative decoration.[28] Wren was then asked to list all the works still to be done in the cathedral and provide estimates of their cost in time for the next meeting. This took place just one week later and there is no evidence to suggest he met their demand. None the less, on that day the commissioners decided

> That the inside of the Dome be painted with figures, but confined to the Scripturall History taken from the Acts of the Apostles, and that such Painters as are willing to undertake the same, do bring their Designs & Proposals (bothe as to sume and time) to the Commissioners to the Chapter House…on Tuesday 5th Day of April next.[29]

Thornhill was the only English painter to respond to this appeal. The other contestants were two Frenchmen, Pierre Berchet and Louis Cheron, and two Italians, Giovanni Battista Catenaro and Giovanni Antonio Pellegrini. The Venetian Pellegrini, who seems to have come to this country chiefly in the hope of gaining this commission, was the only foreign painter of any stature.[30] In February 1710, all the other competitors having apparently been eliminated, Thornhill and Pellegrini were asked to paint their designs on two small models prepared for that purpose.[31]

The stipulation that the dome should be decorated with 'panels of histories taken out of the Acts of the Apostles' presented both painters with a difficult task since there were no obvious prec-

edents.[32] On the one hand, it required the division of the dome into a series of compartments, each containing a different Act, and on the other, as these were historical events, it ruled out the type of celestial scene usually chosen for ceilings and vaults. As neither model has survived, it is not possible to do more than speculate on what the artists may have proposed at this stage.

If Pellegrini's sketch of a dome painted with a cloudy sky heaving with angels represents the scheme he produced for St Paul's, he must have decided to ignore the commissioners' instructions.[33] Schooled in the manner of Correggio, he may have felt he could not do justice to the project in any other way. Thornhill, on the other hand, probably followed the brief and divided the dome into eight compartments, each containing a scene from the life of St Paul.

The earliest surviving figurative paintings made by Thornhill for the dome are the ones Robert Mylne, then Surveyor of the Fabric, purchased for the cathedral in 1776 (Fig. 169) He described them as 'the first designs' of Sir James Thornhill.[34] Thomas Newton, who was dean at the time, said they were 'higher finished than usual in order to be carried and shown to Queen Anne'.[35] It seems likely they were made to gain the support of the queen when the artist realized the commissioners were not going to choose his scheme.

These paintings show what difficulty Thornhill was having in developing a scheme of the type required by the commissioners. Struggling to find a satisfactory method of dividing the dome into eight panels, he painted coffered ribs, similar to those used in the lower part of the dome of Les Invalides, between the eight figurative scenes (Fig. 170). Since he did not visit Paris until 1717, he must have learned of this scheme from a contemporary print of the interior of Mansart's dome such as the one drawn by Delamonce in 1711.

At Les Invalides, the apostles painted by Jean Jouvenet are portrayed as flying figures seen through rectangular openings in the near-vertical wall of the lower cut-off dome. But when Thornhill adopted the same type of framing device for the upper, overarching surface of the dome of St Paul's, the effect was very different. The panels no longer looked like windows and their awkward triangular shape was unsuited to pictorial composition. Furthermore, because he had to depict historical events, the people in his paintings needed to stand on the ground. As a result, the lower halves of the panels are crowded with figures which 'weigh down' the compositions and eliminate the sense of uplift so important in the decoration of a dome.

The minutes of the commissioners' meetings between February 1710 (when Pellegrini and Thornhill were asked to paint the models) and May 1711 (the last meeting of this commission for which there are minutes) make no further mention of the decoration of the dome. But it was probably either at this time or in the final months before the commission was dissolved in October 1711 that Louis Laguerre may have entered the field with a new scheme for St Paul's.[36] For, according to notes made at a later date by the antiquary George Vertue, it was Laguerre who was

> first chosen unanimously by the Commissioners of St Pauls to paint the Cupola of that Church in proper Colours he having made many approved sketches and designs for that purpose an actual agreement being made he began to draw and dispose the work in the Cupola, an order (a month afterwards) came from the Commissioners to forbid his proceeding any further (by some political contrivance) prevented his doing of that great work.[37]

169 (*above, far left*). St Paul before Agrippa. One of the presentation set of eight oil paintings made by James Thornhill for Queen Anne, *c.* 1711. (Yale Center for British Art, New Haven)

170 (*above left*). Detail of a section of the church of Les Invalides, Paris, showing the form of the panels painted by Jean Jouvenet on the inner dome, drawn by Delamonce, 1711

171 (*left*). Part of Thornhill's decoration of the dome of St Paul's, as executed

Part of this statement is difficult to reconcile with the known facts. Although it is possible that Laguerre made sketches for the decoration of St Paul's, if he was 'unanimously chosen' by the commissioners, the minutes do not record the fact. By this time, the building of the cathedral had entered a very troubled period; the commissioners had fallen out with Wren and were embroiled in a number of disputes that had brought work to a virtual stand-still. Wren was fighting back; first, he sent a private petition to the queen, complaining of the way in which the commissioners' behaviour was preventing him from completing the cathedral, and then followed this up with an appeal to Parliament. These actions were to lead to the dissolution of the commission in October 1711.[38] Under these circumstances, even if the commissioners had been disposed to appoint Laguerre to decorate the dome, they may have been too preoccupied with other matters to give the necessary order.

The other puzzling statement made by Vertue is that Laguerre started to lay out his scheme on the surface of the dome. It is hard to see how he could have done so, as the 'tredways' necessary for such an operation were not in place at the time.[39] But when Vertue later wrote of Thornhill's having given an entertainment in the dome he said the artist 'had drew [*sic*] the principal grand lines [of his scheme] before' and then added, as an afterthought, 'Or Mr Laguerre had begun it'.[40] This suggests that Vertue was not altogether sure of his facts.

The final decision concerning the decoration of the dome was not made until 1715. By that time, Queen Anne had been replaced by the first Hanoverian monarch, the Whigs had swept back into power and the proportion of low church bishops on the commission had been increased. These men would have been anxious that the decoration of St Paul's should look neither foreign nor Roman Catholic. Even if Archbishop Tenison never actually said 'I am no judge of painting, but on two articles I think I must insist: first that the painter be a Protestant; and secondly that he be an English man', these words probably expressed the majority view.[41] This would have given Thornhill an advantage over Laguerre and, just three days after it came into being, the new commission asked him to undertake the decoration of the dome.

At the crucial meeting, held on 28 June 1715, the commissioners chose 'the middlemost of the 3 Designes which now hang in the Chapter House' and stipulated that the decoration should be carried out in monochrome rather than in full colour.[42] The following year, when Dudley Ryder visited Thornhill at work in the dome, he observed that there were indeed 'three models' pinned on the wall, 'one of which is chosen'.[43] He added that all the models were 'divided into eight columns or pieces of architecture, in each of which some one story of St Paul is described'.

It is difficult to distinguish between the words 'model' and 'design' in this context, but it seems likely that what the commissioners chose, in the first instance, was the architectural frame which was to surround the figurative compositions. This took the form of a continuous arcade with a scene from the life of St Paul placed in each opening. The form of the painted architecture certainly emphasized the earthbound nature of the figures and the scenographic approach looked back to the type of decoration made popular by Verrio in the 1670s. The commissioners may have preferred this scheme because it owed less to France than any of the other 'models'.

In fact, Thornhill's design seems to have been based on one he saw when he visited the Low Countries in 1711. The sketch in his notebook of the interior of St Martin, Tournai shows that here a ring of piers with tunnel-vaulted spaces in between was painted on the surface of the dome.[44] By reducing the architecture of this scheme to a relatively thin arcade, Thornhill was able to create a framing device for a series of figurative scenes.

In the second half of 1715, the carpenters erected 'tredways' round the dome and the labourers cleaned and swept the scaffolding so that the painter could start work.[45] By May the following year, Thornhill had marked out the main lines of the composition on the dome.[46] Four months later, he had painted the architectural elements of the scheme, though these were not yet gilded, but had not started the figurative painting.[47] The entire work was finished during the next twelve months and the scaffolding taken down in the latter part of 1717.[48] The following year, Thornhill painted the lantern.[49] And then, in 1720, the commissioners asked him to provide 'models' for painting the drum and the quarter spheres and spandrels beneath.[50] Owing to a shortage of funds, however, the painting of the quarter spheres and spandrels was postponed and Thornhill only painted the peristyle and wall of the whispering gallery.[51] The final payment for this work was made in September 1721.[52]

Opinions on Thornhill's paintings in St Paul's have differed from one period to another but, on balance, they have not been favourable. Even Dudley Ryder, no great expert on painting, was not unduly impressed. When he said 'we shall now at last be able to vie with Paris for history painting which we have been so deficient in before', he was flattering Thornhill, for he added in the privacy of his diary, 'The models have a pretty good spirit in them, but there does not seem to me to be the air of grandeur and majesty in describing the postures and faces which appears in the most masterly pictures'.[53]

Sentiments of this kind and a general feeling that Thornhill's scheme did not do justice to Wren's building have been echoed by critics ever since. In 1938 the Wren Society claimed there was 'a well founded tradition' that Wren disliked Thornhill's paintings in the dome and had favoured the scheme proposed by Pellegrini.[54] There does not appear to be any evidence for that. What is clear, however, is that it was the commissioners and not Wren who, at every stage, decided what form the decoration was to take. It was they who ruled that the dome should receive figurative decoration; they who wanted a series of scenes from the lives of the apostles; and they who insisted the whole should be painted in grisaille. They did not perceive that the height of the dome, combined with the way it was lit, made it unsuitable for figurative decoration.[55] It is probable that both Wren and Thornhill were aware of this fact but could do no more than bow to the commissioners' wishes.[56]

When the paintwork beneath the dome was finally complete, the interior of the cathedral must have presented a harmonious, if relatively plain, appearance. The lower parts of the nave, transepts and choir were unified by the greyish white paint Wren had applied up to cornice level. Above this, the vaults, spandrels and saucer domes throughout the building were whitewashed and the mouldings picked out in a slightly darker colour.[57] The only parts of the interior to receive more elaborate treatment were the apse in the choir and the dome and peristyle in the crossing.

In the choir, the pilasters round the apse were painted blue and 'veined with gold', the mouldings over the altar lavishly gilded, and the metal gates and altar rail burnished to look like gold.[58] Under the crossing, Wren's grey paint was carried on up into the peristyle, but here the fluted pilasters, swags and insignia of the painted architecture were enlivened with plenty of gilding. The

172.   Detail of a section of the choir drawn by Alexander Gough in 1848, showing C.R. Cockerell's colour scheme. (GL, St Paul's collection)

moulded cornice above the peristyle was also gilded, as were the architectural elements of the paintings in the dome. The figures in the dome would have stood out because they were painted in the light shades used to portray simulated sculpture.[59] And to crown it all, the mass of rosettes in the cap of the dome and lantern above glittered with gold. The interior of the cathedral may not have matched the grandeur of the exterior, but, when the paintings were finished, the plaster was still white and the gilding fresh, it must have been a fine sight.

FROM 1722 TO 1848

The clergy may have been satisfied with the interior of the new cathedral but the connoisseurs of the art world were not. For if the standard of English art was taken as a measure of the health of the nation, its inferiority to that of France was a serious matter.[60] As a result, the need for some form of academy of the kind found on the continent was under constant discussion. Thornhill himself had planned the establishment of a national school of painting to be state-funded and housed in a building on the present site of the National Gallery.[61] But this came to nothing, and in 1749 a journalist and propagandist, John Gwynn, took up the campaign. In a series of publications, he called for the founding of a public academy, the improvement of London and Westminster and, as a key element of both causes, the 'completion' of St Paul's Cathedral by means of an elaborate programme of painted decoration.[62]

In *London and Westminster Improved*, Gwynn observed that the cathedral 'suffers greatly for want of decorations in both painting and sculpture' and argued that Wren had always intended the walls to be covered with paintings.[63] Referring to the 'desolate appearance of the naked pannels', he likened the building to 'a carver's

shop in which there is usually great choice of frames, but not one picture'.[64] In 1755–6, in conjunction with Samuel Wale, he published a *Transverse Section of St Paul's Cathedral decorated according to the Original Intention of Sir Christopher Wren* to show how he thought the interior should look (Fig. 275). Of course, none of the extra decoration shown in this drawing was ever carried out, but it is interesting to note, only thirty-five years after the building was finished, this first example of a respectful desire to 'complete' Wren's great work. The plea for more decoration was to be made over and over again during the next hundred and fifty years.

In 1768, two events came together which could have resulted in the cathedral acquiring the type of decorative scheme advocated by Gwynn; these were the founding of the Royal Academy, under the presidency of Sir Joshua Reynolds, and the appointment of Dr Thomas Newton as dean of St Paul's. In 1773 Reynolds approached Newton, stressing how important the patronage of the Church was for the future development of painting in England, 'individuals being for the most part fonder of their own portraits and those of their families than of any historical pieces'.[65] He suggested that six of the best qualified Royal Academicians, including himself, Benjamin West, Angelica Kauffmann, Giovanni Cipriani, James Barry and Nathaniel Dance, should provide paintings for the decoration of St Paul's entirely free of charge.[66]

Newton, an enthusiastic supporter of the arts, hurried off to gain the support of the king. But although George III was delighted with the proposal, Richard Terrick, the bishop of London, was not. He refused permission on the grounds that the paintings would be seen 'as an artful introduction of popery'.[67] After this, hoping not to lose the opportunity altogether, the dean suggested that Sir Joshua Reynolds and Benjamin West should

173. Interior of the dome, drawing made by John Coney in 1817 showing the architectural decoration of the peristyle before it was repainted by C. R. Cockerell in 1821. (Victoria & Albert Museum)

paint pictures to fill the panels above the two doors near the Communion table. The subjects of these were to be, in the case of Reynolds, Jesus lying in the manger, and in that of West, the giving of the tablets to Moses.[68] But the bishop vetoed this as well. George III was so disappointed that he planned to build a Chapel of Revealed Religion in Windsor Castle instead, but, owing to illness and intrigues at court, this, too, came to nothing.[69]

In fact, the century between 1721 and 1821 saw little decoration added to the interior of St Paul's. In 1752 Henry Flitcroft, then Surveyor to the Fabric, reported that the cathedral had neither been whitewashed nor painted since the building was finished, adding that the lower parts of the history paintings in the dome were beginning to decay.[70] The problem was that the income of the cathedral, derived from the residue of the money raised after the Great Fire, was barely sufficient to cover the upkeep of the building, let alone its refurbishment. When Thomas Secker was made dean in 1750 and examined the accounts, he saw that the capital was dwindling and insisted on stringent economy.[71] The result was that although works of routine maintenance, such as painting the ironwork, were undertaken, no major schemes of redecoration were carried out in the next seventy years.[72]

Throughout this entire period, only two of the painters' bills were for more than £100. The first of these was submitted in

1767. At this time, major repairs were made in the area of the crossing and there was scaffolding reaching up into the peristyle. After the masons had finished their work, the painters 'Scrap'd clean'd & twice paint'd [the windows] in ye Colonnade', painted the piers which had been rebuilt and reduced 'Several New Pieces of Stone . . . to the Colr of Old'.[73] The rest of the bill was for painting various items of ironwork, including the railing of the Whispering Gallery.

In 1789 a General Thanksgiving was held to celebrate the recovery of George III (see pp. 367–9). On occasions like this, when the cathedral was fitted up for a major service attended by the Royal Family, Court and both Houses of Parliament, hasty attempts were made to improve the appearance of the interior. In this case, labourers were employed in 'Cleaning, dusting and rubbing Choir, Organ, Bishop's Couch and Body of Cathedral'; the colour of the railing of the Whispering Gallery was changed from grey to 'fine Yellow'; and all the marble in the choir, including the columns under the organ were cleaned and polished.[74] The Surveyor to the Fabric, Robert Mylne, was given a gratuity 'For his great Trouble and Expences Repairing and Cleansing the Fabrick for the General Thanksgiving'.[75]

The 1789 thanksgiving took place at the end of a decade during which Mylne had undertaken major repairs to the cathedral (see p. 294).[76] In 1791 the painter was paid the relatively large sum of £1,81 14s. 6d.[77] We do not know exactly what was done, but it seems likely that this was when the pilasters in the choir were painted to resemble Siena marble.[78] Some seven years later, in 1798, as well as doing a little work in the peristyle, the painter touched up the rosettes in the cap of the dome.[79]

Robert Mylne died in 1811 and the post of Surveyor of the Fabric then passed to S. P. Cockerell. There is no record of work undertaken during the eight years he remained in office but in 1819, when he was succeeded by his son, C. R. Cockerell, the situation changed. By this time, the decoration of the cathedral was in a poor state.[80] Spurred on perhaps by the enthusiasm of the young new surveyor, in July 1821 the dean and chapter agreed that 'the Interior of St Pauls required cleaning and beautifying' and authorized Cockerell to carry out the work.[81] This took place the following year and was the first comprehensive redecoration of the cathedral since its completion one hundred years before. The total cost was £1,834, the painter being paid £1,414 for his work while the remaining £420 was spent on 'Gilding for the Interior of the Choir'.[82]

When Cockerell redecorated the choir, he returned the pilasters in the apse to Wren's original colour.[83] This was the first example of the more archaeological approach to the decoration of the cathedral which those who adhered to the classical style attempted to pursue throughout the nineteenth century. Cockerell wrote in his diary: 'We must after all appeal to principles – if in painting them blue we are wrong, Sir Christopher Wren is wrong'.[84] A section drawn by Alexander Gough in 1848 shows the choir as painted by Cockerell (Fig. 172).[85] There is no evidence to suggest that the redecoration he carried out throughout the rest of the building was any less conservative.

The possibility of restoring Thornhill's paintings in the dome was also discussed at this time, but the dean and chapter thought the scaffolding required would be too expensive.[86] E. T. Parris, a young artist who was later to paint a panoramic view of London round the circular wall of the Regent's Park Colosseum (see p. 329), claimed that on hearing this he 'immediately . . . contrived an apparatus for the purpose of getting at the paintings'.[87] It was not until 1829, however, that Cockerell, hoping the paintings might be restored, showed the model of the apparatus to the dean and chapter.[88] Parris's estimate 'for restoring the whole of the painting and gilding above the Whispering Gallery was £1000, and no charge for scaffolding!' But this was still thought to be beyond the means of the cathedral.[89]

The effect of redecoration does not last long if a building cannot be kept clean, and within twenty years the walls, vaults and monuments in the cathedral were once more covered with grime. This was the situation when in 1840 Archdeacon Hale, an energetic man with a particular interest in the architecture of the cathedral, was appointed to one of the canonries of St Paul's. Canon Sydney Smith, then treasurer, made Hale responsible for the maintenance of the building, though he made it clear that any major works should be handled by the surveyor, C. R. Cockerell, in conjunction with the chapter.[90]

Being a practical man, Archdeacon Hale decided to address the problem of the pervasive London dirt that blew in through the many unglazed openings on the stairs and in the crypt. In 1841 the changes included 'Doors put at top of the stone staircases . . . The Gold about the Altar washed and cleaned. Additional seats, and many other details of painting etc.'[91] Then the following year,

> The church was shut during the months of August, September, and part of October. The whole of the choir, except the vaultings, was dusted, and the great part of the walls was cleaned by a single coat of paint.[92]

In addition to this, the north and south transepts were dusted, all the monuments cleaned and 'Many loads of dirt were removed from the vaulting over the Aisles'. Two years later, the cathedral was closed again while the nave and 'circle under the Whispering Gallery' were cleaned and dusted.[93] At the end of the process, presumably to make it easier to clean, a coat of varnish was applied to the paintwork.[94]

When Henry Hart Milman was made dean of St Paul's in 1849, he claimed that nothing important in the way of 'completion and decoration' had been carried out in the cathedral since Wren's death.[95] That was fair comment, since in the early years of Victoria's reign the interior must have looked, by and large, much as it had in 1723. After all, Cockerell had returned the choir to something approaching its original appearance, and no further decoration had been introduced.

But there was change of a negative kind. Thornhill's paintings in the dome were so damaged and blackened with dirt that they were hard to see (Fig. 173). Although the scheme of fictive architecture in the peristyle was probably partially repainted in 1822, it may have lost some of its detail in the process. And, finally, if the practice of adding varnish to the paintwork was extended to the vaults, it would have been at this time that they became, or began to become, darker in colour. Wren's whitewashed saucer domes and vaults were an important feature of the original interior, so this was a change for the worse.

FROM 1849 TO 1900

Throughout the eighteenth and first half of the nineteenth century, all the regular services in the cathedral were held either in the choir or in the Morning Chapel, neither of which could accommodate large congregations. When Milman was appointed dean in 1849, he was instructed by the bishop of London to carry

174.   Scffolding in the dome during E. T. Parris's restoration of the paintings, from the *Illustrated London News*, December 1853. Thornhill's decoration in the peristyle is shown before it was painted over by Penrose in 1859

out measures which would enable St Paul's to play a greater part in the worshipping lives of ordinary members of the Church of England.[96] With this in mind, he decided to reorganize the cathedral so that evening services could be held in the vast space under the dome. But this was not all. Cultivated and urbane, Milman wanted to transform the interior of St Paul's in order to draw people into the building. As he put it,

> I would see the Dome, instead of brooding like a dead weight over the area below, expanding and elevating the soul towards heaven. I would see the sullen white of the roof, the arches, the cornices, the capitals, and the walls, broken and relieved by gilding . . .[97]

Three years later, when Cockerell's protégé Francis Cranmer Penrose became Surveyor to the Fabric, Milman encouraged him to work out a scheme for the decoration of St Paul's and then place the matter in the public arena. Accordingly, Penrose wrote a paper on the subject and read it at a meeting of the Royal Institute of British Architects.[98] This event was followed two months later by a general discussion.[99]

On the first occasion, Penrose, like the scholar he was, started by laying out what he took to be Wren's views on the decoration of the cathedral. He suggested that the original architect would have favoured a 'thoroughly architectural design', and went on to say that 'there is still a good deal of architectural device in [Thornhill's decoration of] the present cupola, and we cannot much blame that'.[100] He therefore saw 'the restoration of the cupola in chiaro scuro, with a very large amount of gilding . . . as the starting point for the other decorations' and thought that

175.   Decorative scheme proposed for the peristyle and drum beneath the dome, by F. C. Penrose, 1856–7. (GL, St Paul's collection)

'surface painting in colours would be out of place' in the area beneath the dome.[101]

He took a different view of introducing colour to the choir. Here he thought the three sections of the apsidal vault 'were evidently intended by Wren for some coloured decorations' and recommended architectural decoration – that is, painted coffering – in the saucer domes of the choir, with monochrome figures in the spandrels. As the pilasters of the apse had already been painted in imitation of lapis lazuli, he thought it might be right to add a little colour to the panels beneath the windows, but that was all.[102]

But this restrained approach, taking its cue from the decoration already in the building, did not find favour with the other speakers; what they wanted was much more colour, especially in the area of the dome. What was the point, asked J. W. Papworth, of seeking the opinion of others if the decision to retain Thornhill's painting had already been taken? The building would simply remain as 'gloomy and miserable as at present'.[103] Parris diplomatically replied that though stone, with plenty of gold, should predominate, the panels nearer the ground might be painted with colours.[104] Archdeacon Hale objected to the 'heathenism of the statues' and wanted the cathedral painted from end to end as a 'great pictorial bible'.[105] And finally George Gilbert Scott spoke

in favour of stained glass, though he emphasized that it must be pot metal glass and not the enamelled variety. He went on to say that, if the money could be found, then mosaic would be the proper material to use for the decoration of the dome. This was endorsed by Penrose.

But despite the views expressed at this meeting, and before the idea of lining the dome with glittering mosaics had taken firm hold, the dean and chapter decided to restore Thornhill's cycle of paintings. So in 1853, some thirty years after it was first proposed, Parris erected his scaffold and started work (Fig. 174).[106] He found the bottom twenty-five feet of the plaster all round the dome so perished that it had to be cut back to the brickwork.[107] The repainting and restoration of Thornhill's paintings took three years to complete.

While Parris was at work, Penrose turned his mind to designing a scheme of decoration for the peristyle, drum and spandrels of the main piers beneath the dome. This can be seen in a drawing he made *c.*1856–7 (Fig. 175).[108] He planned to repaint Thornhill's scheme of fictive architecture in the peristyle, adding a blue background and touches of red, place a gold mosaic text round the wall of the Whispering Gallery, and insert gold mosaic panels with blue borders in the spandrels of the main piers.[109]

In 1857 St Paul's was caught up in the controversy surrounding the competition to select a sculptor to design the monument for the duke of Wellington. After the first ill-judged decision had been quashed, it was Penrose who advised the First Commissioner of Works, Lord John Manners, that Alfred Stevens's entry was not only superior to the others but also the one best suited to the style of the building.[110] Stevens's work exemplified an important trend in art at this time, the cult of Michelangelo and the continued pursuit of the classical ideal. Unlike the Gothic Revival, which was seen as particularly British, this movement had its roots in Europe. It was this, coupled with the association of the classical style with Roman Catholic architecture, which led to the constant wrangling over the decoration of the cathedral in the second half of the nineteenth century.

Dean Milman never wavered from the view that St Paul's should be decorated in the classical style, and the committee set up for this purpose was of like mind. Besides himself, four canons and a number of wealthy businessmen, three architects initially sat on the committee, C. R. Cockerell, Sir Charles Barry and Sir William Tite, all of whom were best known as designers of classical buildings.[111] It was this body, revealingly called the Committee for the Completion of St Paul's, which was the driving force behind the changes proposed for the interior of the cathedral during the next ten years.

The committee began by concentrating on the reorganization of the space under the dome. Thornhill's paintings having been restored, the windows in the peristyle were reglazed, gilding was added to the cornice, lantern and railings, and large numbers of chairs were purchased to accommodate the expected crowds of worshippers.[112] To prepare for the new work in the peristyle, Thornhill's swags and fluted pilasters were painted over – never to be seen again.[113] Then, in 1859, it was decided to enlarge the organ. At this time, Penrose tells us, there was no intention of moving Wren's organ from its original position. But after it had been taken down from the screen,

> so great an improvement was noticed in the appearance of the church and so great a disinclination arose again to block the central vista with an object which would have been considerably

increased in solidity and there being indisputable evidence that Sir Christopher Wren had wished the organ to be placed under one of the arches on the north side of the Choir that the organ builder was told to rebuild it in that position.[114]

No doubt Penrose believed his own argument regarding Wren's intentions, but a more important element in the equation was probably the desire of the clergy to make the high altar visible from the nave. Be that as it may, the change led to a string of consequences. Opening up the vista immediately shifted attention from the area of the dome to that of the choir and apse. Wren's plan had comprised two spaces; the nave with its climax under the dome, and the choir with its high altar in the apse. But when the two were linked, the high altar in the choir suddenly looked small and insignificant. So now the committee turned its attention to the decoration of the apse and choir.

The best guide to the plans for the choir at this stage is provided by Penrose's coloured drawing entitled *Sir Christopher Wren's Altar Piece, a Study, for the Completion of the Apse of St Paul's* (Fig. 176). This shows the organ in its new position on the north side of the choir and the walls and vaults decorated much as Penrose had suggested at the RIBA meeting in 1852. Although Penrose planned to fill the panels in the apse with mosaics similar to those proposed for the spandrels in the crossing, the only parts of this decorative scheme actually carried out were the gilding of the apsidal barrel vault and the coffering painted in the eastern saucer dome.[115]

By this time, word of the plan to add figurative decoration to St Paul's had got out and two ambitious young painters, Frederic Leighton and G. F. Watts, both trained abroad and inspired by the works of Michelangelo, were keen to display their skill in the field of mural decoration. In 1860 Mrs Sartoris, the former opera singer Adelaide Kemble, wrote to Dean Milman on Leighton's behalf, saying how keen he was to be involved with the decoration of St Paul's.[116] The following year, Watts, in correspondence with the dean, offered to help in any way he could. Milman responded warmly, promising to bear him in mind when mosaic ornament or fresco painting was to be introduced.[117]

When the committee decided to proceed with the decoration of the choir, Watts and Leighton, together with Alfred Stevens and a Frenchman, Baron Henri de Triqueti, were asked to submit drawings to show how it might be done. The artists were to follow Penrose's iconography and design a scheme with an image of Christ the Intercessor in the centre of the apsidal vault and figures of Moses and Elias in the panels to either side. Stevens did not respond to the invitation, but Watts, Leighton and Triqueti all sent their proposals. The remarkable drawing made by Watts is still in the keeping of the Watts Gallery (Fig. 177).

The following year, growing anxious about the situation, Leighton wrote to his friend F. G. Stephens, the art critic of *The Athenaeum*, 'I have heard nothing more of St Paul's but feel more and more convinced it was a job from the beginning'.[118] Stephens then obligingly wrote an article praising the drawings of Leighton and Watts and dismissing the feeble design submitted by Triqueti for its failure to attain the 'grandeur of treatment' needed in figures so high above the ground.[119] But despite this, the Frenchman's scheme was the one chosen.

The committee's decision may have been governed by the fact that Triqueti's reputation was largely based on his use of incised and inlaid marble to provide a 'permanent' and washable form of pictorial decoration. When Milman wrote to the bishop of

176.   *Sir Christopher Wren's Altar Piece, a Study for the Completion of the Apse of St Paul's*, by F. C. Penrose, *c.* 1860. (SPCL)

London saying he wanted more colour in the cathedral, he added that this should be provided by 'foreign or native marbles, the most permanent and safe mode of embellishing a building exposed to the atmosphere of London'.[120] It therefore seems likely that anxiety about the ability of fresco to withstand damp and the need to keep the decoration clean was the deciding factor in this case.

Meanwhile, the dome had not been forgotten. In August 1862, Penrose asked Alfred Stevens to design a mosaic depicting the prophet Isaiah for one of the spandrels of the piers under the dome.[121] And some time afterwards, perhaps as compensation for not having been chosen to decorate the chancel, Watts was also asked to design a mosaic of St Matthew the evangelist for one of the spandrels. Stevens's mosaic was unveiled in 1864, and that of Watts two years later (Fig. 178).[122] The finished products did not do justice to the original designs and neither received much acclaim.

In 1855 Alfred Stevens designed a decorative scheme for the dome of the Reading Room at the British Museum.[123] The proposal came to nothing, but when in the 1860s the replacement of Thornhill's paintings was under discussion, he seized the opportunity to develop another grand scheme for the decoration of a dome. His design for the Reading Room employed the 'rib and medallion' pattern used at St Peter's in Rome and this was also the basis of his scheme for St Paul's (Fig. 179–80). But in this case, by

177 (*above*).   G. F. Watts's design for the panels of the vault over the altar, 1863. (Watts Gallery, Compton)

178 (*below*).   Spandrel mosaics in the dome, 2002. Right, St Matthew by G. F. Watts, unveiled in 1866, with later alterations; left, Daniel, by Hugh Stannus after a sketch by Alfred Stevens, installed *c*. 1890. The mosaics were made by Salviati in Venice

179.   Model of the dome, worked on by Alfred Stevens between 1862 and his death in 1875. A photograph taken before deterioration. (SPCL)

180 (*top*).   Detail of Stevens' model as it appears today. (SPCFA)

181 (*above*).   Dado panel ('By the Waters of Babylon') from the apse model painted with Henri de Triqueti's frieze of incised stonework. (SPCFA)

combining caryatids, roundels and enthroned figures to form the architecture of the design, he achieved a far more dynamic effect. There was also to have been a rich mosaic frieze round the wall of the Whispering Gallery and sculpture in the niches of the peristyle and under the arches of the quarter domes. Both in its overall conception and in the quality of its draughtmanship, this scheme far outshone anything proposed for the cathedral either before or since.

In 1866, Penrose's model of the apse of the choir, which had been repainted with Triqueti's scheme of decoration, was exhibited at the Royal Academy.[124] The dominant colours had now been changed from Penrose's blue and gold to Triqueti's green and red. A frieze of monochrome figures against a dark red background, to be carried out in stone, was painted round the dado; the pilasters were painted to resemble verde antico rather than lapis lazuli; the splays of the windows were green; the foliate frieze was green and gold on a red ground; and the rectangular panels

above the doorways to the aisles along with the three sections of the half-dome were filled with mosaics on a gold ground.

While the scheme for the apse was being reworked, the 'Completion' committee was also debating what kind of stained glass would be right for the cathedral. Charles Winston, an expert on the properties of ancient stained glass and a friend of Archdeacon Hale, was asked to join the committee. Winston suggested that he and Penrose should visit Glasgow Cathedral to examine the series of windows there recently designed by a number of well-known German artists.[125] The reason for looking to Germany was twofold. Firstly, craftsmen in England had, up to this time, concentrated on the design of Gothic Revival glass and this was thought unsuitable for a classical building. And secondly, those practising the art of stained glass in England were generally considered artisans rather than artists and the subcommittee wanted 'to see the art of staining glass fall into hands much higher

N° VII

in the scale of art than any that had yet exercised it'.[126] Only in Germany as yet were painters of international repute making designs for stained-glass windows.

The artist chosen to design the pictorial elements of the stained glass in the apse and at the west end of the cathedral was Julius Schnorr von Carolsfeld, one of the most gifted of the Nazarenes. He and Penrose co-operated over the design of the windows, Schnorr drawing the figures and Penrose the architecture. These windows broke new ground, establishing principles for the design of stained glass in classical buildings which were to be used for the next fifty years.

The most successful of Schnorr's designs was that of the great west window installed in 1866 (Fig. 182).[127] Describing the window in 1894, T. F. Bumpus, a good judge of stained glass, wrote in *Church Review*,

> I beg to direct the reader's attention to the remarkably fine effect produced at the west end of the cathedral by its large painted window – one of the Munich School it is true; but a vastly superior specimen... Viewed at sunset this portion of the cathedral, with the two great isolated columns of the first nave arcade in the foreground, is the most solemn and impressive I know.[128]

Sadly, this window was destroyed in the Second World War.

The stained glass Schnorr designed for the apse was less satisfactory. Here the deep splays of the windows, painted a 'black green colour' in conformity with Triqueti's design, had already restricted the light and the addition of coloured glass made the situation worse (Fig. 183).[129] Perhaps this was when the Committee for the Completion of St Paul's began to have doubts about the suitability of Triqueti's decorative scheme for the apse. In any case, neither the mosaics for the vault nor the frieze of incised stonework he designed for the dado was ever installed.

With the death of Dean Milman in 1868, the first phase of the Victorian drive to 'complete' the interior of the cathedral came to an end. During the next three years, all the members of the chapter changed and those who replaced them had a very different attitude to the role of church decoration. The next dean was Henry Mansel, but he died within three years and was succeeded by the unworldly Richard Church. Two other important appointments made at this time were those of Canon Gregory and Canon Liddon.

As young men, Church, Gregory and Liddon had all been involved in the Oxford Movement. Such had been the success of this movement and its architectural counterpart, the Ecclesiological Society, in affirming the Church of England's links with its pre-Reformation and Gothic past that by 1870 most people, certainly the vast majority of the clergy, had come to regard Gothic as the only truly Christian style. By contrast, classical art and architecture were widely thought to be secular, even pagan, in feeling.

Although he was not to be dean for another twenty years, it was Canon Gregory who now became the driving force behind the decoration of the cathedral. An astute and rather overbearing man (see Fig. 46), by taking control of the cathedral finances he placed himself in a powerful position within the chapter. Although contemptuous of the decorative work carried out under the auspices of Milman and Penrose, he realized he needed

183.   Photograph of the apse model exhibited by F. C. Penrose in the Chapter House in 1872, showing Triqueti's dado panels, the Schnorr/Penrose windows, W. F. Woodington's mosaic designs for the apsidal vault and Penrose's decoration of the presbytery vault. (GL)

to increase his knowledge of classical architecture if he was to have a decisive influence in this area. So, soon after his appointment he went to Italy 'to see how other churches of a similar style ... were decorated'.[130]

Gregory claims that on his return he merely suggested that the Completion Committee should be revived. But that is not what happened; an entirely new committee structure was created, comprising a General Committee, an Executive Committee, a Fine Art Committee and a Finance Committee.[131] The first meeting of the Executive Committee, which included the dean, Canon Gregory, Canon Liddon and several other eminent clergymen, together with all the members of the Fine Art and Finance

182 *(left)*.   Design for the great west window by Julius Schnorr von Carolsfeld, 1862. (Victoria & Albert Museum)

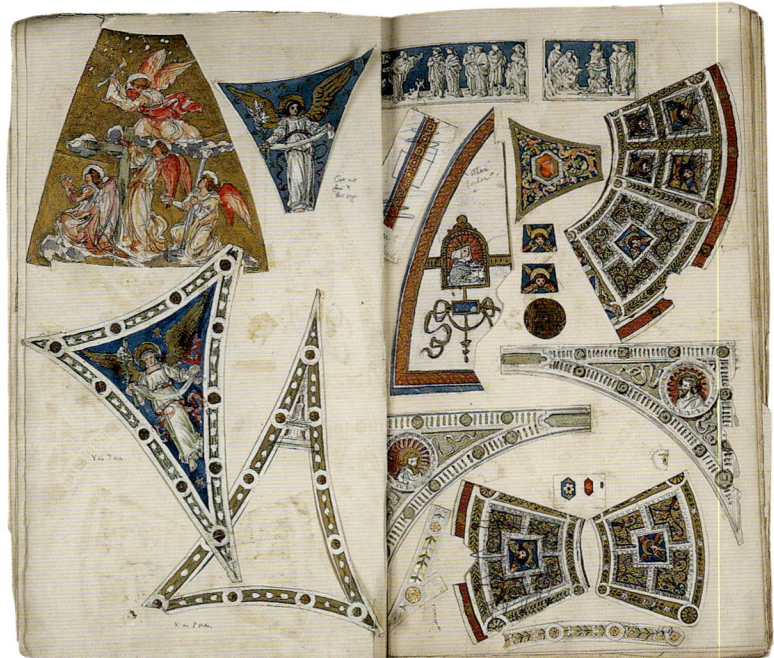

184, 185.   Sketchs for the decoration of the east end by William Burges, *c.* 1873. *Above*, one of the saucer domes. *Right*, spandrel panels, frieze and elements of the apse. (SPL)

186.   Burges's model of the east end showing the stained glass, mosaic and painted decoration he proposed in 1873–4

Committees, took place in May 1870.[132] This was followed in July by a public meeting held at the Mansion House to launch a national appeal to raise funds for the 'Completion of St Paul's'.[133]

The new Executive Committee was determined to dispel the tide of adverse criticism with which the decoration recently carried out in the cathedral had been met. As a first step, it was agreed to ask William Burges, an architect whose reputation was based on his designs for Gothic buildings, to devise an iconographical scheme for the decoration of St Paul's. A. J. B. Beresford-Hope, the former chairman of the Ecclesiological Society, and member of both the Executive and Fine Art Committees, rushed off to discuss the matter with his protégé.[134] At this point, Burges would have realized that, should his scheme be accepted, he would probably be asked to carry out the work. Even so, with Penrose still in post, he was in a delicate position.

Astonishingly, however, just a few weeks after Burges had agreed to make the report, he published an article pouring scorn on the previous approach to the decoration of St Paul's. Pretending to believe Penrose would continue to oversee the decoration of the cathedral, Burges mockingly pointed out that he shared 'with Mr Cockerell the distinction of being [one of the] *ultimi Romanorum*'.[135] He continued that, as the architect in charge, Penrose should be given a free hand and not be subject to the whims of a committee. He then went on to attack the use of fashionable painters and sculptors to carry out 'sacred subjects' at St Paul's, not failing, of course, to mention foreigners.

It is difficult to imagine that Burges would have written in this way unless he thought most committee members would agree with him. He had the support of Beresford-Hope and must have known that Dean Church, Canon Gregory, Canon Liddon and many others would be sympathetic to an ecclesiological approach to the decoration. But he should have known better; some members were deeply worried by the idea of employing an architect with little feeling for the architecture of Wren, and even those who admired his work must have been alarmed by the tone of this article.

In fact, when Burges was asked to carry out the decoration of the cathedral, a majority of the members of the Fine Art Committee were violently opposed to his appointment.[136] But this group of men, though they sat on the Executive Committee, did not hold enough votes to overturn the decision. The whole thing led to a huge and very public row and caused so much friction between the members of the two committees that, from this time onwards, they were quite unable to work together.

Much of the correspondence printed in the press attacked the cathedral on the grounds that Penrose was being unfairly treated. To dispel this impression and avoid yet another public relations disaster, the dean and chapter put Penrose's models and drawings on display in the chapter house.[137] These included his model of the apse, which retained the figurative panels designed by Triqueti beneath the windows but now had decoration by a different painter, W. F. Woodington, in the vault (Fig. 183); the large, as yet unfinished model of the crossing, which Penrose, like Stevens, had been making at his own expense; and several coloured perspective drawings of the choir.

Attempts were now made to persuade Burges to work in tandem with Penrose, but this he flatly refused to do. In due course, Burges was asked to carry out the decoration of the cathedral while Penrose retained his post of Surveyor to the Fabric and was given the right to comment each time Burges revealed a new part of his scheme.[138] In March 1873, having been instructed to adopt the style of 'the best Italian Architects and Artists of the 16th century', Burges went off to spend a month in Italy with his assistant Henry Lonsdale.[139]

Burges's drawings for the decoration of St Paul's are imbued with the gaiety and prettiness typical of mosaics designed by Renaissance painters such as Raphael and Pinturicchio (Figs 184–6). But, as contemporary critics were quick to point out, when Burges's decorative schemes were carried out by his rather pedestrian group of assistants, the finished products did not live up to their early promise. This was the issue on which the whole argument over the employment of the artists for the decoration of buildings turned. Burges wanted total control and sacrificed art in the process; the opposed group wanted art of the finest quality and were, for this reason, prepared to concede a measure of freedom to the artists concerned.

By the summer of 1874, the conflict between the architect and his opponents on the Fine Art Committee had become so serious that Burges softened his position; he approached Frederic Leighton and asked him to design the mosaics for the apse.[140] Then, as a sop to those members of the committee who had wanted perspectives rather than models, he instructed Axel Haig to make coloured drawings of the scheme. But it was too little too late. By this time, the public, stirred to anger by all the correspondence in the press, was thoroughly roused, and the dean and chapter decided to suspend the programme of decoration.[141] Burges's appointment was formally revoked in 1877.[142]

Meanwhile, work had been going on which had greatly altered the appearance of the interior. In May 1872 the chapter had asked the Decoration Fund to provide for 'cleaning the roof and walls'.[143] During the following nine years, Wren's grey paint was removed from the area of wall beneath the great cornice in the nave, aisles, transepts, choir and choir aisles. At the same time, the vaults, which may already have been treated in this way, probably received a further coat of varnish or shellac. This would have reversed the tonal relationship of wall and vault; the walls becoming lighter and the vaults darker.

In 1877 a new Decoration Subcommittee was appointed for the 'Completion of St Paul's' to be chaired by the Reverend Lord Alwyne Compton rather than the dean. The purpose of this body

187. Lithograph of the cartoon for the mosaic decoration of the dome designed by Frederic Leighton and Edward J. Poynter, published 1884. (GL)

was 'with the funds in hand (exceeding £40,000) to carry into effect, as far as possible . . . the decoration of the dome with mosaic in a similar style to St Peters at Rome'.[144] Responsibility for the decoration of the choir, on the other hand, remained in the hands of the dean and chapter.[145]

The first act of the new subcommittee was to buy Alfred Stevens's model of the dome, the artist having died two years before.[146] Because of its sketchy nature, the design needed to be worked out in much greater detail before it could be transferred to the dome. The two men eventually chosen for this task were Frederic Leighton, by this time the most revered classical painter in England, and Edward Poynter, then head of the South Kensington School of Art. Both regarded Stevens as a genius and, referring to his design for St Paul's, Leighton declared 'I think that no English artist, dead or alive, could have furnished so striking a decorative scheme'.[147] None the less, he went on to say, 'an artist competent to design work of the order here imperatively called for, would find it impossible to follow, slavishly, in the wake of another man, albeit his superior'.[148]

During the next twelve months there was much discussion of both the iconography and composition of the scheme. Leighton thought the circles, lanterns and ribs should remain totally unaltered, and that this aspect of the work should be entrusted to 'a capable and talented pupil of Stevens', but the designs in the circles and the prophets and sybils should be done '*de novo*'.[149] He agreed to paint the groups in the large circles himself, while Poynter took on those in the smaller medallions together with all the other figurative elements of the design (Fig. 187). The 'mechanical part of the work' was entrusted to Hugh Stannus, one of Stevens's former assistants.

188.   The chapel at Temple Newsam, Yorkshire, with the classical reredos designed by G. F. Bodley, *c.* 1877

But this was not all. Edmund Oldfield, an expert on iconography, thought Stevens's Old Testament subjects out of place in the dome and recommended scenes from the Book of Revelation instead.[150] Others considered the naked caryatids at the base of the ribs unsuitable for the decoration of a church and, as a result, these were replaced by groups of saints on earth, each accompanied by an angel.[151] In fact, by the time the matter was settled, few aspects of Stevens's scheme remained unchanged.

As well as drawing the architectural parts of Leighton and Poynter's cartoon, Stannus designed a scheme of his own. This, too, adopted the rib-and-medallion format, but, despite his knowledge of Stevens's work, Stannus was not a sufficiently skilled designer to carry off a project of this magnitude. In fact, the Leighton/Poynter proposal, the 'ribs' of which combined both figures and architecture, was closer to Stevens's original conception. Leighton's 'And the Sea gave up its Dead', designed for the central roundel, is an extraordinarily powerful image, and photographs of fragments of the model painted with the rest of the scheme show what a spirited effort Poynter also made to match the quality of Stevens's draughtsmanship.

Unfortunately, when the cartoons were unveiled in September 1884, neither was deemed a success. The fact that the gold ground of the Leighton/Poynter scheme, which was to be carried out in mosaic, was merely painted on canvas, would not have helped. But even so, the great height of the dome, combined with the inadequate lighting, would have made it impossible for people standing in the crossing to see the scenes in the roundels clearly. This brings us back to the form of the dome itself; it was not designed for, or suited to, the display of figurative decoration.

In the late 1880s and early 1890s, the six remaining mosaic designs, three by Watts and three by Stevens, were installed in the spandrels of the crossing.[152] Between 1892 and 1894 the niches in the drum were gilded and the eight statues of the Doctors of the Church, four designed by C. E. Kempe and four by Woodington, were put in place.[153] But the failure of the great scheme of mosaic decoration in the dome had put an end, once and for all, to the dreams of the classicists, while the Decoration Subcommittee was by this time a spent force.

Meanwhile, the dean and chapter had been considering what to do in the choir. In 1883 a new subcommittee, consisting of Dean Church, Canon Gregory and the canon in residence, was set up to advise on the introduction of a new high altar. At the

first meeting, it was decided that 'Mr Burges having died... Without any hesitation Mr Bodley was chosen'.[154]

George Frederick Bodley was the leading exponent of the later Gothic Revival which, turning away from continental sources, took English church architecture of the early fourteenth century as its model. But though much favoured in Anglo-Catholic circles for his gothic buildings, the choice of his firm for the work at St Paul's seems to have been based on the success of the classical reredos he designed for the chapel at Temple Newsam, a country house near Leeds (Fig. 188).[155] The Reverend Frederick Sutton, who collaborated with Bodley in the design of organs and took a very active interest in the decoration of St Paul's, was keen that the cathedral should be 'Bodleyfied'.[156] To this end he asked Mrs Meynell Ingram, the owner of Temple Newsam, to invite Dean Church to see her newly converted chapel, where Bodley's reredos had been designed to complement the early Georgian fittings. In September 1877 she wrote to her brother, 'I hope to have the house full for the shooting and have asked among others the Dean of St Paul's (not that he shoots however I suppose) as Mr Sutton is wild for him to see the reredos here in hopes (I imagine) that St Pauls may follow at a respectful distance in our wake!'[157] All this suggests that it was Dean Church, rather than Canon Gregory, who was behind the employment of Bodley's firm to carry out the work in the choir.

Now that the screen at the west end of the choir had been removed, the intention was to provide a high altar of sufficient size and grandeur to form the main focus of the interior. It was to be placed in the easternmost bay of the choir with the space in the apse behind it forming a separate chapel. In 1884 Bodley's partner, Thomas Garner, provided a design. This consisted of a central pedimented reredos which, though much more elaborate, had a good deal in common with the one devised by Bodley for Temple Newsam, and an altar in front. Initially Garner planned to adapt Tijou's iron screens to connect the reredos to the walls of the choir. Then it was suggested that a semi-circular marble screen 'to range with the architecture of the church' would be preferable and he added quadrant wings to either side.[158] The design of the wings was based on those of a reredos thought to have been made by Inigo Jones in the seventeenth century.[159] The reredos was completed in 1888, the new altar being added three years later in 1891 (Fig. 189).

Garner also designed a scheme of painted decoration for the apse and bay of the choir containing the reredos. His drawing of the decoration for the apse shows a thoroughly 'architectural' scheme, the colours of which, grey and white combined with a good deal of gilding, look back to those used by Wren (Fig. 190).[160] But though the dean and chapter appear to have been satisfied with the reredos, there were differences over the scheme of painted decoration. Mr Harding, the cathedral clerk of works, recounts that in 1887 Garner tried some 'experiments in painting the wall surfaces of the choir. Unfortunately this painting was carried out to a rather large extent before it was stopped'.[161] Then in 1889 'cartoons of angels' were tried out in the panels above the choir cornice but these were not implemented.[162]

By this date, Dean Church was seriously ill and all momentum behind the work in the choir seems to have been lost. But when he died in December 1890 and was succeeded by

189 (*right*).   The reredos, 1888, and high altar, 1891, by Thomas Garner. The bronze standards left and right of the altar steps were cast in 1891 by Barkentin and Krall after Renaissance originals in St Bavo, Ghent

190. Decorative scheme for the apse designed by Thomas Garner, *c.* 1887. (GL, St Paul's collection)

192. Clerestory window designed by William Blake Richmond, *c.* 1893. (SPCL)

the forceful Robert Gregory the situation changed once more. As a keen advocate of Burges's pictorial approach to the decoration of the cathedral, Gregory is unlikely to have been impressed by the more subtle 'architectural' scheme proposed by Bodley and Garner. It is not surprising, therefore, especially now that the scheme for the dome had been abandoned, that there was a return to the idea of figurative mosaics. In his *Autobiography* Gregory wrote,

> It fortunately happened that, within a few days after my being appointed Dean, a friend of Mr. (now Sir) W. B. Richmond, suggested to me that he should be employed to give designs for mosaic work, with which the roof and spandrels in the choir and other parts of the Cathedral might be decorated.

After this things moved swiftly. Richmond's first cartoon was put in place for inspection in July 1891 and an agreement sealed with the artist in the same month.[163]

The earlier mosaics in the cathedral had been prefabricated in Italy. Because they have an entirely flat surface, they do not sparkle in the way that mosaics composed of tesserae set at slight angles to each other will do. Richmond decided to use the second type of mosaic. In 1892 Mr Harding, the clerk of works, tells us that

The first two mosaics by Richmond came in for the spandrels over the North East Choir Arch. These panels had been worked at his studio on slate slabs, in sections the slates were nearly one inch in thickness, so that when the putty and mosaic were on, the thickness was very near two inches. This of course entailed cutting away a good deal of the stonework, and also, owing to the weight, required well fixing.[164]

The thickness and weight of the panels were not the only problems, however. Although the mosaics had apparently looked right in the studio, when they were put in place their style was found not to be bold enough. Black outlines had to be added to the figures and the tones of the drapery deepened.[165] After this, the mosaicists worked on scaffolding in the cathedral, setting the tesserae in cement applied directly to the wall.

The next mosaic carried out was the one in the saucer dome immediately over the reredos. While this was being installed,

192 (*right*). Mosaics by Richmond in one of the saucer domes of the choir

Bodley and Garner were fitting up the chapel behind the high altar, to be called the Jesus Chapel (Fig. 302). Wren's pilasters in the apse were replaced in grey marble and the lower three windows there filled with stained glass designed by Kempe.[166] These windows, which replaced the German ones, were largely made of clear glass with delicately drawn classical detail picked out in yellow stain.[167] The mosaics in the three panels of the apsidal vault and the stained glass in the upper part of the apse and the clerestory, all of which could be seen from the choir, were designed by Richmond.[168]

In order that the mosaics should not stand out as isolated blocks of colour surrounded by plain stonework, painted decoration was added to the wall, and

> all the plane surfaces, whether in gold or in colour, have been broken up with small patterns scarcely distinguishable from below, to remove any sense of monotony. Similar treatment has been applied to the stone ribs of the roof in the apse and the choir bay; to the great ring of sculpture round the saucer dome in the choir bay; to the canopy of clerestory windows and generally to the parts which do not lend themselves to mosaic treatment.[169]

For the next four years, Richmond continued to work in this manner throughout the choir without, apparently, any adverse criticism. It was when the mosaics began to overflow into the space under the dome that a clamour of furious protest began. In March 1899 *The Globe* described them as a 'vicious glittering disfigurement of Wren's work', as if 'a little perky French milliner [was] attempting to brighten up a work by Michael Angelo'.[170] In April, George Aitchison led a deputation from the RIBA to meet the dean and express their reservations.[171] The following month, students of the Royal Academy, Slade, Westminster, Birkbeck and other metropolitan art schools assembled to protest against the 'Desecration of St Paul's'.[172] The two things they and many others found most objectionable were the 'petroleum stencilled frieze' (painted round the arches of the quarter domes in the crossing) and the 'audacious demolishing of the stonework of the structure itself to provide a bed for these detestable mosaics'.[173]

All this was too much for the dean and chapter. In December, Harding was ordered to 'remove all the stencil work from the North East and South East Quarter Domes, also a good deal of the red paint colour to be taken out of the Choir Cornices'.[174] In 1900 the decision was taken to remove the 'mosaic treatment over the pilasters in the Apse' and, though this was not done, it shows the committee's state of mind.[175] Their confidence was gone, and in 1901 the dean and chapter turned down Richmond's scheme to add further mosaics to the wall of the Whispering Gallery.[176]

Once again, those who believed the quality of Wren's acknowledged masterpiece was in danger of being destroyed had raised their voices against those who felt the importance of the building lay in the message it conveyed rather than the style of its architecture. This was at the heart of the battle which raged throughout the Victorian period. All those who promoted classical schemes of decoration, no matter how unsuitable they may have been, echoed the desire expressed by John Gwynn in 1755 to decorate St Paul's 'agreeably to the original intention of Sir Christopher Wren'. But for those who favoured an 'ecclesiological' approach to the decoration, the language of Wren's building was a serious problem; not because the baroque style was out of fashion but because it was not considered conducive to Christian worship.

The story of the decoration of St Paul's, no matter how fascinating, is not a happy one. While Wren was grappling with the problems posed by the construction of so vast a dome, it is unlikely that he gave much thought to how the inside was to be painted. There is little evidence to suggest that he ever expected the dome to receive anything more than a relatively modest scheme of 'architectural' decoration. It was the ambition of others which led to the series of proposals for ever more elaborate plans to transform the interior of the cathedral. But none of the works which were carried out, from Thornhill's cycle of paintings in the dome to Richmond's mosaics in the choir, can be deemed a total success. There were two fundamental reasons for this. The first was that Wren conceived his great dome purely in architectural terms; it was not designed for the reception of an elaborate scheme of figurative decoration. And the second was that removing the organ and screen to make the choir the main focus of the building posed a problem that no amount of further embellishment could ever solve.

193 (*right*). General view of the choir in 2002 showing mosaics by Richmond, and baldacchino by Stephen Dykes Bower and Godfrey Allen, 1954–8

23

DECORATION, FURNISHINGS AND ART SINCE 1900

Peter Burman

Entering the cathedral in 1900, the visitor would have been struck by an appearance very different from that presented a century later. Perhaps the overwhelming difference would have been a much darker tonality than obtains today. Nevertheless, a process of lightening and freshening had then already begun, the rich-hued mid Victorian stained glass having been in large part replaced by lighter glass. Work was close to completion on the mosaic decoration of the choir and its aisles, too, adding a note of glittering magnificence to the interior of the eastern arm.

Among the principal liturgical furnishings of the cathedral, Francis Penrose's congregational pulpit, commanding the dome and the nave, occupied the south side of the entrance to the choir. Beyond it, the vista opened up by the removal of the choir screen and organ in 1861 had not long been logically completed by a high altar and grand Parian marble reredos, designed by Thomas Garner of the firm of Bodley and Garner and dedicated on St Paul's Day, 1888. The reredos remained controversial. A guidebook of 1906 by George Clinch remarks that

> the opposition on religious grounds which some folks have felt to the subjects represented in the sculptures, renders it difficult for one to give an entirely unbiased critical opinion, and, moreover, there is even now as we write just a trace of newness and freshness about the reredos which the gentle hand of time will eventually tone down.[1]

The visitor of 1900 would also have been able to note fairly recent embellishments to the Morning Chapel off the north aisle at the west end. The equivalent chapel off the opposite aisle was in transition; it was then called the South or Consistory Chapel, having recently reverted to its original use as the Consistory Court of the diocese, after a period when the incomplete Wellington monument was placed there. For the time being, it doubled as a baptistery, so here, too, was temporarily located Francis Bird's font, banished from its original position nearby in the second bay from the west of the south nave arcade. The crypt below was dominated by the presence of memorials, including the focal sarcophagi of Nelson and Wellington; and by the sumptuous if incongruous presence of Wellington's funeral carriage.

During the twentieth century, many of these spaces were to change radically. The font was shifted again, first to the south and then the north transept; Penrose's marble pulpit was replaced in the 1960s by a baroque revival equivalent in timber; while the high altar and reredos, after significant but far from irreparable wartime damage, gave way in the 1950s to the present baldacchino. At the west end, the Morning Chapel became St Dunstan's Chapel in 1905 and the Consistory Chapel turned into the Chapel of St Michael and St George in 1906. A small space at the foot of the north-west tower was converted into the Chapel of All Souls, a memorial to Lord Kitchener. In the crypt, the eastern chapel of St Faith-under-St Paul's became in the 1960s the Chapel of the Order of the British Empire (or OBE Chapel).

Along with this went a succession of attempts to impose order on the number and quality of the memorials in the crypt. Here, many of the recent changes have responded to the huge growth in the number of visitors and the need to provide facilities following large services in the cathedral. The western area or nave of the crypt was gradually developed, particularly during the 1990s, as in effect a visitors' centre. But commemoration has not been forgotten. The Chamber of the Great Commanders of the Second World War was created around Wellington's sarcophagus in the 1970s, while the OBE Chapel has undergone further development from the 1990s.

What is most striking in the story of the many twentieth-century changes to the cathedral's interior is the continuity of an arts-and-crafts tradition – that is to say, the consistency and patience with which successive Surveyors to the Fabric have sought out and collaborated with the best British craftsmen of their day, and endeavoured to ensure that the results harmonized with the cathedral's dominant and unique aesthetic.

The period around the turn of the nineteenth to the twentieth centuries was a time of architectural and artistic achievement in many European countries, not least in England, where the Arts and Crafts Movement was at its height. The Surveyor to the Fabric at this exciting moment, between 1897 and 1906, was Somers Clarke. A Gothic revivalist by training, Clarke had for years been in partnership with J. T. Micklethwaite (who sometimes assisted him at St Paul's and was Surveyor to the Fabric of Westminster Abbey at just this time). But he had broad interests, including an active involvement in Egyptian archaeology, and indeed he retired to Egypt on relinquishing the surveyorship. As a member of the Art Workers' Guild, Clarke was keen to promote collaboration between architecture and the other arts within the cathedral. He was an individualist with pungent opinions, whose forthright attitude to his ecclesiastical clients may be gauged from the advice he gave his successor on the subject of remuneration, 'Beware of the amiable imbecilities of parsons!'[2]

Somers Clarke's main achievement within St Paul's during his short tenure of office was the Chapel of St Michael and St George, though it was not long to remain as he left it. This substantial double-apsed side-space, shielded from the south aisle by an imposing screen (Fig. 127), had never hitherto enjoyed regular religious use. It was fitted up for the consistory court of the diocese of London in 1708, with a low horseshoe of legal seating at its eastern end.[3] Seldom used, it had been earmarked back in 1858, quite inappropriately, as the location for Alfred Stevens's Wellington monument, after whose eventual completion in 1878 sporadic attempts were made to hold court hearings against its awkward and colossal backdrop.[4] But in 1894, just before Clarke's appointment, the Wellington monument was moved to the spot C. R. Cockerell had first intended for it, the second bay of the north nave arcade. The consistory court could now return, and for the next few years the chapel served also as a baptistery and housed the cathedral's font.

These arrangements were destined to be short-lived. Since 1891, the archdeacon-canon, William Sinclair, had been promoting the idea of a space or chapel within the cathedral as the spiritual home for the chivalric Order of St Michael and St George. This order had been founded in 1818, its members being honoured for services in overseas territories and foreign affairs. The liberation of the so-called 'Wellington Chapel' seemed to offer the perfect answer, and in 1895 Dean Gregory agreed it in principle. For a time, the relocation of the font, so recently put there, proved a stumbling block between the chapter and the order and delayed the project, which was eventually set in train at the end of the Boer War in 1901–2.[5] The timing signifies renewed recognition of St Paul's as the cathedral of empire at the start of a new century.

The initial transformation of the chapel was carried out at the expense of the order in 1904–6 by Somers Clarke (with some help from Micklethwaite). It was a difficult assignment on a limited budget:

194.   Chapel of St Michael and St George looking east, showing reredos, prelate's throne and stalls designed by Mervyn Macartney from 1909 onwards

> Whilst the elaborate stall work of St George's, Windsor or at Henry VII Chapel for the Order of the Bath could not be rivalled, there must be a standard of decent splendour which is demanded by the fact that the Order is in St Paul's Cathedral, below which you cannot go.

Clarke told his clients in 1902.[6] The new work had not only to cohere with the entrance screen fixed in Wren's day but also to take in discarded carvings from Gibbons's choir stalls. Clarke's reaction was to make a clear differentiation:

> the stalls, the canopies, and the lower ranges of seats ... are designed to be in harmony with the chapel but not imitate the work of the Choir Stalls. The carving of Grinling Gibbons is unique of its kind. It would seem a foolish thing to produce a poor imitation of that which is so individual and so beautiful ... The wood work would be of teak. This is a fitter and better wood for the purpose than the wainscot oak we now get, a material which does not even come from a British possession.[7]

Accordingly, in the arrangement inaugurated by Edward VII in June 1906, the chapel housed thirty-three teak seats, mostly canopied, round three sides including part of the apses, with plainer stalls and seats in front of them incorporating some old decorative ironwork from the choir. The western apse at the back was filled with a row of three richer canopied stalls for the sovereign flanked by the grand master and the chancellor of the order; here probably were incorporated the limewood carvings from the old choir. The new carving throughout was by

195. Design for stalls and organ case in the western apse of the Chapel of St Michael and St George, by Mervyn Macartney, 1926. Not as executed. (SPCL)

J. E. Knox of Kennington. 'The work is flat in character and very refined in design', reported *The Builder*.[8] Over each stall hung a brocade banner embroidered in silk with heraldry on the advice of W. H. St John Hope. Clarke's scheme was completed by four large plaster panels of arms in the vault (savaged by the College of Arms for 'heraldic inaccuracies') and by a memorial window from Powells in light glass with emblems of the order and the figure of the donor, Sir Walter Wilkin, in a corner. An original suite of altar ornaments consisting of a cross, candlesticks and flower vases (now displayed in the Treasury) was due to the art-metalworker William Bainbridge Reynolds.[9]

At this stage, a reredos was contemplated, but it was not to be carried out by Somers Clarke, for in 1906 (the year of his partner Micklethwaite's death) he retired from the surveyorship at the age of sixty-five and handed over to his friend and fellow Art Worker, Mervyn Macartney. It fell to Macartney to complete the original conception of the St Michael and St George Chapel for the order, along with his other responsibilities to the dean and chapter. The transition was smooth, since Macartney continued to consult Clarke as the scheme developed (Fig. 194). Nevertheless, his instinct was to cleave more closely to the style of the original cathedral fittings. The chapel's reredos, dedicated in 1909, shows this clearly and would look well in a city church. Incorporating old wreathed pillars discarded from the choir, and taking its proportions from the adjoining screen, it is of oak, not teak, and is surmounted by two flanking figures carved by Abraham Broadbent and a central figure of St Michael added in 1916. The central panel was filled in 1918 with a painting of St Michael overcoming Satan, by J. Eadie Reid after a Raphael in the Louvre.

This is now in store, having been replaced by the present figure of a youthful St Michael carved in 1970 by Edwin Russell (Fig. 303). A handsome altar rail in gilt bronze was also installed in 1909 by Bainbridge Reynolds, who also at about this time initiated the fine series of floor memorials in aluminium to members of the order.[10]

Further embellishment of the St Michael and St George Chapel, combined with a complete revision of the seating arrangements, took place in stages between the world wars. First signs of dissatisfaction surfaced with a resolution of the chapel committee in 1913 requesting Macartney 'to advise the Officers how best to make the chapel more worthy of its associations'. Later, it was said of Somers Clarke's seating, 'He was given a certain sum and with it he did his best. But the authorities have never really been satisfied with the result.'[11] Changes were urged on in particular by the order's ambitious prelate, Bishop Henry Montgomery, who planned all sorts of enrichment and even hoped at one stage that the order might quit the chapel and colonize the whole north choir aisle. Macartney produced a general scheme in 1914, but in the event, changes were made piecemeal. They began with a new prelate's seat or throne for Montgomery to the left of the sanctuary in 1923. Then, after Clarke's death in 1926, features installed by him started to be removed or transformed. In 1928–9 the sovereign's throne and its environs in the western apse were entirely remade, with new carving by Henry Poole and, after his death, E. R. Broadbent, but once again incorporating the old limewood features. Surviving watercolours suggest that Montgomery and Macartney had hoped for an organ case above at this end, the whole composition being encrusted with exuberant carving (Fig. 195). In another rendering, the canopy to the throne is simpler but sumptuously draped. Finally, between about 1930 and 1937, most if not all of Clarke's teak chairs and stalls were replaced with stalls of oak.[12]

In 1905 the Morning Prayer Chapel opposite the Chapel of St Michael and St George on the north side was renamed the Chapel of St Dunstan, after the great reforming figure who had been one of London's early bishops. As its older name implies, the chapel had always been used for morning prayer, but by this time the cathedral was offering a variety of services in different spaces. It was now being used principally for services of Holy Communion where relatively few people would be present, and had already been enriched with mosaics – by Salviati in the western apse (1874) and by Powells in the eastern apse (1884). It was not greatly changed in 1905, but different ways of furnishing and arranging the chapel have been tried at different times since then.

The present arrangement, made under Martin Stancliffe, reflects the need for a place of reflection and prayer close to the main north-west entrance of the cathedral, where the visitor may enter without payment. The original Wren communion table from the choir, a magnificent late seventeenth-century table made by William Samwell, which had for some decades been placed against the east wall of the south choir aisle, has been brought here; and its proportions fit the chapel well. The Sacrament is now reserved in the chapel, providing a focus for devotion and stillness, and a finely chased hanging pyx by the silversmith Rod Kelly was completed to accommodate this need in 2000.

Also during Somers Clarke's surveyorship, electricity was introduced to the cathedral at the expense of the financier Pierpont Morgan (1899 onwards). Great care was taken over the electrical fittings. They were designed by Clarke in a sometimes uneasy collaboration with the Arts and Crafts architect and metal worker W. A. S. Benson – the first English designer to realize the artistic opportunity offered by the introduction of electric light.[13] At the west end of the nave stand two magnificent bronze candelabra, modelled by the sculptor Henry Pegram in 1898 (Fig. 58) They appear to have been originally destined for the sanctuary, but on Canon Newbolt's advice Clarke placed them instead in their present position. Pegram was clearly an artist in whom Somers Clarke felt confidence. The crypt contains two fine memorials by him, to Sir George Martin and William Huggins, and in the north transept is his memorial tablet to Sir John Stainer of 1903. The railings which continue over the main entablature of the nave installed in Wren's time in the eastern arm of the building are also by Somers Clarke. These were his personal gift to St Paul's.

Mervyn Macartney's period as surveyor (1906–31) was dominated by the major structural works which were found to be necessary soon after he took office and closed only with his retirement (pp. 299–300). His major artistic contributions to St Paul's were therefore confined to the completion of the St Michael and St George Chapel and to the creation in 1922–5 of another chapel which, while less conspicuous, was nevertheless critical to the embellishment and spirit of the cathedral in the inter-war years. That is the Chapel of All Souls, also known as the Kitchener Memorial Chapel. It houses one of the finest ensembles of sculpture in the cathedral.

The chapel occupies the space at the foot of the north-west tower and is entered from the vestibule. It is an intense space, exceptional in St Paul's for being wholly devoid of woodwork. The backdrop is Wren's: a square room with canted corners which support the broad ribs of the vault. The ribs are ornamented with coffering and rise to an octagonally framed centrepiece carved with oak leaves and acorns. In the furnishings and sculpture four major figures were involved: Macartney as Surveyor to the Fabric, William Reid Dick as sculptor, and Detmar Blow and George Frampton as consultants respectively for the architecture and for the sculpture. The carving is all Reid Dick's and in Portland stone, except for the effigy of Kitchener (see Fig. 245).

At the base of the eastern wall is a stone altar, the front panel decorated with a frieze of putti in low relief. Behind and above, a reredos culminates in a *pietà*, a work of plasticity and tenderness in which the Virgin supports the body of the dead Christ and kisses his right arm, the two bodies arranged in powerful *contrapposto*. Inserted into the centre of the west wall a tall inscription panel records the creation of the chapel as a memorial not only to Lord Kitchener (d. 1916, when the ship in which he was sailing, *HMS Hampshire*, was sunk off the coast of Orkney) but to all those who fell in the war of 1914–18. Flanking the tablet are the military saints, Michael and George, while centrally placed before them at strikingly low level is the pristine white marble effigy of Kitchener, by Reid Dick. The high-quality lettering and the metalwork, including entrance gates, grilles to the recess with the roll of honour and standard candlesticks, are all by Bainbridge Reynolds, as are the silver and crystal altar cross and candlesticks.

Macartney was succeeded in 1931 by his own former personal assistant, W. Godfrey Allen. As assistant surveyor, Allen had already been to the fore in the works of strengthening the dome. Despite the heroic part he played in saving St Paul's during the Second World War (pp. 301–2) and his efforts in repairing the war damage immediately afterwards, he was to be marginalized in respect of the post-war arrangements for the interior.

The first step towards what was to become the liturgically and artistically charged project of replacing Garner's high altar occurred in 1946, when the dean and chapter solicited schemes from several prominent church architects, namely Stephen Dykes Bower, Edward Maufe, John Seely (Lord Mottistone) and Oliver Hill, for an American War Memorial Chapel behind the high altar, to commemorate those American allies who had died in the Second World War. It appears that Godfrey Allen provided them all with a standard set of drawings, so that they had the measurements and context which they needed. It was at first the intention to retain the Bodley and Garner reredos, though not necessarily the high altar, which had suffered more severely from war damage. In the event, the reredos was to be dismantled completely and broken up, so that only two of its most significant carvings were retained in the cathedral: the Crucifixion and the Virgin and Child. These were placed to form a focus for the east ends of the the north and south choir aisles, but are no longer in position at the time of writing.

The strategy of replacing the reredos with a baldacchino emanated from Stephen Dykes Bower, whose winning design went boldly beyond the terms of the original commitment to an American War Memorial Chapel. A civilized, fastidious and scholarly architect, Dykes Bower was steeped in the Gothic tradition and was to be Surveyor to the Fabric of Westminster Abbey from 1951. Yet at St Paul's he was clear that architects in that tradition whom he admired had gone astray. In a meticulous and powerfully argued report of August 1946, Dykes Bower lavished praise upon the refinement and quality of Bodley and Garner's reredos: 'One generation may well pause before removing so masterly an effort of its predecessor'.[14] But, he maintained, it was an unsuitable termination for the climax of St Paul's, for which Wren's original intentions had been plainly laid out in *Parentalia*: an altar surmounted by a baldacchino 'of four Pillars wreathed, of the richest Greek marbles supporting a Canopy hemispherical, with proper Decorations of Architecture and Sculpture'. Wren, so *Parentalia* professed, had been refused the chance to build this 'after a good Roman manner' (see pp. 229–30), and put aside his design for the high altar 'in expectation of a fitter opportunity'.[15] The aftermath of war now at last provided that opportunity.

Dykes Bower was well aware that Wren had originally provided an enclosed choir with an organ over a great screen to the east of the dome (see pp. 223–9). The evidence for the scale, position and exact design for such an altar and canopy in relation to that original arrangement was fragmentary, though he reviewed it in full. His concept of the new baldacchino was therefore for the cathedral as it had come down to the mid twentieth century, with all the changes of the previous century, and especially the removal of the screen, the placing of the organ cases in two halves north and south, and changes to the floor levels. Soon after the opening out of the choir in the 1860s, Penrose had indeed experimented with designs for raising just such a baldacchino over the high altar (Fig. 176), only to be denied the opportunity in his turn, as Dykes Bower also knew.[16] This, therefore, was the third attempt to endow St Paul's with a baldacchino.

All these schemes, Wren's included, derived ultimately from the great baldacchino raised by Bernini over the papal altar in St Peter's, Rome, with its scale, splendour and memorable spiral or 'Solomonic' columns. That in its turn had been based on the former canopy with twisted, vine-wreathed marble columns over the shrine of the apostle in the Constantinian basilica that preceded the present St Peter's. The true origin of these columns probably

196 (*left*). A craftsman puts finishing touches to the baldacchino, 1958. (SPCL)

197 (*below left*). The American Memorial Chapel (by Stephen Dykes Bower and Godfrey Allen, 1954–8), looking towards the reredos with a column of the baldacchino in the foreground

lay in honorific thrones of the Roman east, yet according to a tradition dating back to the late Middle Ages, they had been brought from the holy of holies in Solomon's Temple in Jerusalem.[17] So, consciously or not, the elevation of such a baldacchino over the high altar evoked and renewed the cathedral's links with early Christianity and its roots in Judaism.

The proposal Dykes Bower put forward in 1946 was for a baldacchino close enough to the plans of Wren and Penrose before him, carried on marble columns, but for a long and distinctive double-altar of marble below it which would serve both the body of the church and the American Memorial Chapel in the apse behind. This would be small in scale but rich in detail, and would form a kind of ambulatory or pilgrims' route round the back of the high altar: a place to which visitors could have ready access (unlike the high altar sanctuary), and where they could pause, examine the roll of honour, ponder, pray, and pass on. The conviction of the concept quickly caught on, but it was destined to undergo some evolution. The idea of a shared altar, entailing westward-facing celebration in the chapel, vanished, while the marble columns of Wren's vision disappeared in favour of oak, no doubt for reasons of expense in the climate of post-war austerity. The contemporary literature generally refers the authorship of this revised design to 'Stephen Dykes Bower and W. Godfrey Allen', but there is no evidence that Allen enjoyed any major creative responsibility. That it was completed to acclaim in 1958 is to the credit of both architects; there is no reason to suppose that their relationship was anything other than good.

As completed, the high altar itself is an exceptionally long one, its length dictated by the scale of the cathedral around it. It is of a pure white marble and has front panels carved with the emblems of the Eucharist. On the altar stands a lofty cross and a pair of candlesticks, classical–baroque in style, made of gilt metal, designed by Dykes Bower and given by the Goldsmiths' Company. The baldacchino (Fig. 193) soars above, supported (as in Penrose's designs) at each corner by a triplet of columns: two are fluted, one square and one round, while the third column in the most prominent position adopts the Solomonic shape of Bernini's Roman canopy. There, the columns are single and cast of bronze, plundered from the roof of the Pantheon, but the St Paul's columns (Fig. 197), like the whole of the baldacchino apart from the marble bases, are of oak, richly gilded in many of its parts. Crowning the massive entablature are pediments of heroic proportions, triangular to the north and south, broken and segmental to the west and east. From the broken pediments hang tassels of painted and gilded wood, taking up the theme of winged cherubs' heads which occurs so often in the ornament of Wren's cathedral (Fig. 196).

Above and within the framework established by the pedimented sides rises an elliptical dome, supported on a tall attic stage pierced with oval openings which are themselves richly ornamented. Four gilded urns, with flames issuing forth, stand round the attic stage. On the gilded cupola of the dome stands a figure of the risen Christ, his hand extended in benediction; while left and right stand angels in postures of adoration. Only one English precedent can be found for the figure of the risen Christ above a canopied baldacchino, and that is on the ciborium in the church of Holy Redeemer, Clerkenwell, of some seventy years before and only about a mile away.

Placed near the high altar, on either side, are two superb bronze candlesticks with rich Renaissance ornament. These are casts taken in 1891 from a pair in the cathedral of St Bavo, Ghent; the originals, ascribed to Benedetto da Rovezzano, may have been made to accompany Cardinal Wolsey's sarcophagus, now in the crypt of St Paul's as the sarcophagus of Admiral Nelson.

The achievement of the baldacchino and high altar cannot be too highly stressed. Their completion provided the opened-up cathedral with the focus that it had been lacking for almost a century, and with strong historical justification. To judge from old photographs, the Bodley and Garner reredos had never made a decisive impact in the long view from the west. The Dykes Bower baldacchino certainly does. Much energy had been expended over many years by clergy, architects and artists in devising a fitting climax to St Paul's. Yet none possessed the certainty of scale and touch of the scheme finally realized – at about the last moment that such a scheme, based wholly and unapologetically on scholarship and historical styles, could have seized so prominent a place within the cathedral without great public controversy.

The American Memorial Chapel in the western apse behind the high altar and baldacchino was dedicated in 1958 (Fig. 197). Here, the floor of black and white marble, the altar with its sunburst throw-over frontal, the reredos, cross and candlesticks, the curved stalls, communion rail, and casket for the roll of honour were all designed by Dykes Bower, working with Godfrey Allen. Of particularly good quality are the eight carved limewood drops on the pilasters of the reredos and stalls, all carved by George Haslop. They depict American birds, fruit and flowers and prove that the highest craft skills were not lacking in the second half of the twentieth century when opportunity offered. The various embellishments to St Paul's since the Second World War have frequently furnished such opportunity.

Allied to the high altar, baldacchino and American Memorial Chapel project, but a little later in date, was the commission to fill the six windows in the apse with stained glass by Brian Thomas, *c.*1960 (the blitz having blown out almost all the glass in the cathedral). Dykes Bower and Allen had anticipated a scheme that would 'conform in style with Sir William Richmond's glass which was destined to harmonise with the mosaic decoration of the choir'.[18] In the event, a different aesthetic prevailed. The commission for the three lower windows came about as a result of Thomas's membership of the Art Workers' Guild, of which Godfrey Allen was master at that time; the smaller windows, based on the 'I AM' texts of St John's Gospel, a theme suggested to Thomas 'by the intelligent curate of my local church',[19] followed once these had been installed. The predominant tones are blues and golds, chosen no doubt to complement the mosaic-work and the baldacchino, but in the event denser and stronger than Richmond's glass. The iconography is less important than the general effect from a distance.

After Godfrey Allen's resignation in 1956, the dean and chapter appointed as his successor John Seely (Lord Mottistone), who in turn was followed on his death in 1963 by his partner Paul Paget. Seely and Paget were active in the post-war reconstruction of the city of London, working on several city churches and other historic buildings as well as St Paul's. Lord Mottistone's two main achievements in the cathedral were his designs for a new pulpit and for the OBE Chapel in the crypt. The pulpit, designed in 1960 but not installed until 1964, is a vigorous essay in the style of Wren, informed by study of those which survive in the city churches, but with a swagger of its own (Fig. 198). Like the original furnishings in the choir, it is of oak beautifully set off with limewood carvings. The canopy carries an openwork cupola with

198. The new pulpit by Lord Mottistone (of Seely and Paget), 1963–4, shortly after completion. (SPCL)

199. *The Light of the World*, by William Holman Hunt. A copy by the artist of the original painting at Keble College Chapel, Oxford. (St Paul's Cathedral)

an elegantly designed urn as its finial, while round the cupola winged cherubs and urns hold up heavy swags of flowers. The two putti bear aloft the collar and badge of the Order of St Michael and St George. The panel below the canopy supports, as is traditional, a crucifixion, sculpted by Edwin Russell.

The next surveyor, the well-known conservation architect Sir Bernard Feilden, was mainly taken up anew with the structural stability of the cathedral (pp. 302–3). But during Feilden's time (1969–77) the Chamber of the Great Commanders was created in the crypt (p. 292). Further work of his period involved the repositioning of the font in the north transept, and the furnishing of part of the same transept's eastern aisle as the Middlesex Regimental Chapel, with an altar supported on oval columns of engraved glass designed by Feilden and the sculptor John Skelton. This has now been replaced by an altar behind which is the cathedral's copy of Holman Hunt's painting, *The Light of the World*, originally donated by the social reformer Charles Booth in 1907. The boxed frame around it, designed by Martin Stancliffe,

provides the celebrated painting with a secure setting and the chapel with a devotional focus (Fig. 199). Set in the wall of the sanctuary is an aumbry carved with the pelican in its piety, by Tony Webb, chief carver in the cathedral works team for many years at the close of the twentieth century (Fig. 200).

The surveyorships of Robert Potter (1978–84) and Sir William Whitfield (1985–90) were largely also marked by quiet progress with the repair and conservation of the cathedral fabric, but under Martin Stancliffe, the surveyor since 1990, a good deal of internal work has taken place. The most conspicuous scheme has been the creation of the sanctuary under the dome, the subject of much debate and design work during the last years of the twentieth century. The use of the dome area has preoccupied the cathedral authorities for over a hundred and fifty years. Temporary liturgical furnishings having been tried from time to time, during the 1990s a series of experiments took place. The conclusion was that the eastern segment of the dome area was suitable not only for choirs and orchestras on great musical occasions but also for a perma-

200. Aumbry door by Tony Webb installed in the Middlesex Chapel, north transept, 1978. (SPCL)

201. Henry Moore, in wheelchair, contemplates his *Mother and Child* in the north choir aisle, 1984. This sculpture is one of a growing number of independent works of art which have been introduced into St Paul's, as into other British cathedrals, since the 1960s. (SPCL)

202. The crypt looking east in 2002

nent liturgical focus allowing fuller congregational participation in the celebration of the Eucharist, on the lines of practice in many great cathedrals abroad, such as Cologne and Milan. The form of the altar platform responds to the spatial qualities of this central point in the cathedral, while the use of different woods in inlaid patterns picks up the design vocabulary of Wren's cathedral within a more contemporary idiom. The furnishings, which have yet to be completed with a bishop's throne and canopy, have been also designed by Stancliffe.

At the time of writing, work is in progress on a carefully researched cleaning of the whole interior of the cathedral (Fig. 203). The final result should be that Wren's interior will glow with greater luminosity. The mosaics and painted decoration of the late

nineteenth century will also have been cleaned and conserved. As a result, there will be a stronger sense of the layers of history and indeed fashion which give the cathedral its sense of belonging not only to the world of Wren but to all the generations since.

The crypt is the area of the cathedral which has seen most dramatic changes since 1945. It was constructed beneath the whole area of the cathedral, and its plan reflects the broad divisions of the main floor of the building. It was intended as a burial place, and the solemn entrances from the north and south transepts are a reminder of that. In time, the crypt has come to fill many functions, particularly during the past century. Until the 1980s, its nave had something of a museum aspect, with Wellington's funeral carriage, the Great Model and Penrose's discarded pulpit all

203.   Looking west across the arm of the newly cleaned north transept in 2002. In the background the font, designed by John James and made by Francis Bird, 1726–7

presented to the visitor as relicts of different layers of the past history of the cathedral. Gottfried Semper's riotously ornamental funeral carriage (Fig. 318) was dispatched to the present duke of Wellington's seat at Stratfield Saye, Hampshire – a loss to the London public of the most conspicuous and visible object designed by a great German architect during his short time of residence in Britain. But the Great Model, properly repaired, lit and interpreted, is now displayed in the Trophy Room above the Chapel of St Dunstan; and Penrose's pulpit has been taken up to the same level over the north nave aisle, where other objects from the nineteenth and twentieth centuries are preserved.

The west end of the crypt now has the air of a visitor centre. The visitor descends stone stairs at the north-west corner of the building, to be first greeted by a restaurant. Turning into the crypt, there is a café on the right and beyond it the doors of a meeting room, now joined to the 'beehive', a circular space beneath the famous Geometric Stair. East of these comes an extensive shop, opposite which on the north side are lavatories, staff rooms and various facilities for the works department. On the south side, one of the most attractive recent adaptations has been the creation of a new Song School and Music Library, though these are not seen by the visitor, as they are part of the working life of the cathedral. All these changes were carried out during the 1990s under the design and supervision of Martin Stancliffe. Wall surfaces, floor surfaces, lighting, new furniture, screens (and particularly those of the shop, which catch the chunky character of Wren's woodwork) have all been carefully considered throughout, so that the secular character of the west end of the crypt does not impact negatively on the mausoleum-like character of the central and eastern parts.

The hinge between the two is to the west of Nelson's sarcophagus, under the dome. In 2004 the caesura between them is likely to be marked by the installation of gates commemorating Sir Winston Churchill, designed by the Somerset artist-blacksmith James Horrobin. Further east lies the Chamber of the Great Commanders. Its main focus is the austere, red porphyry sarcophagus of the duke of Wellington, designed by Francis Penrose in 1858. Also by Penrose are the standard candleholders in all four corners and the magnificent mosaic floor. Under Bernard Feilden's surveyorship, the walls were equipped with a series of memorial tablets to field marshals who were leaders of the military forces of the British Commonwealth during the Second World War. The tablets are set out and lettered in such a way as to complement and provide a context for the Wellington sarcophagus. The dedication plaques and three of the tablets are by John Skelton, while others are signed by other well-known letterers of the late twentieth century, Jack Trowbridge, Paul Wehrle, Helen Bicknell and John Poole.

204 (*right*). St Faith's Chapel in the crypt in 1956, shortly before its transformation into the OBE Chapel. In foreground, mosaic floor by F. C. Penrose and memorial to Bishop Mandell Creighton. To the left, the blackened remains of the Woolley monument (1614). (SPCL)

205 (*below right*). The OBE Chapel by Lord Mottistone (of Seely and Paget), 1959–60: in the foreground, screen with glass panels by Brian Thomas. View of 2002

The north transept of the crypt currently contains the cathedral treasury, created under Robert Potter's surveyorship in 1981 to display precious objects and embroidery. The entrance gates were designed and made by a young artist-blacksmith from Gloucestershire, Alan Evans, as the result of an invited competition. The treasury brings together fine metalwork, vestments and other treasures not only from St Paul's but also from churches in the diocese of London. Among the objects belonging to St Paul's are plate and altar furnishings made by Bainbridge Reynolds for use in the Chapel of St Michael and St George (including an enamelled morse designed by Princess Marie Louise, a granddaughter of Queen Victoria); the Communion Service of the OBE Chapel, part of the ensemble of furnishings and works of art designed by Lord Mottistone; the cope worn by Bishop Mandell

Creighton at Queen Victoria's Diamond Jubilee Service in 1897, (Fig. 304) and the Jubilee cope, stole and mitre designed by Beryl Dean and made for Bishop Gerald Ellison to wear during the present Queen's Silver Jubilee Service in June 1977. At the time of writing, this space was being replanned to fulfil a function in the interpretation of the cathedral.

The east end of the crypt forms an area about half that of the choir above. It was anciently known as St Faith-under-St Paul's, and here baptisms and funerals associated with that 'cathedral parish' (St Gregory's having been united ultimately with St Martin, Ludgate) took place. In May 1960 the area was rededicated as the Chapel of the Most Excellent Order of the British Empire (Figs 204, 205). As with the American Memorial Chapel and the Chapel of St Michael and St George, the furnishings form a remarkably complete ensemble of their period. They were designed by Lord Mottistone in collaboration with the artist Brian Thomas. The altar has a throw-over frontal of deep red velvet with the badge of the order in gold and silver thread and the motto 'For God and Empire'. Baroque-style chairs, a charming font in silvered wood, vibrant carpet and vinyl floor tiles add to the quaintness of the ensemble. The most ambitious feature, artistically speaking, is the screen surrounding the sanctuary of the chapel. This is of black-painted wrought iron, in a baroque style, incorporating sixteen panels of painted grisaille glass by Brian Thomas. On the left side of the entrance are shown George V and Queen Mary, and on the right side Elizabeth II and the Duke of Edinburgh; the panels behind the altar show Queen Elizabeth the Queen Mother and George VI. Other panels depict animals, activities, landscapes, buildings and people emblematic of the diverse parts of the formerly far-flung British Empire. The cross and candlesticks on the altar are also of wrought iron, and of a commendable delicacy. Lord Mottistone also designed special Communion silver for the chapel, dedicated in October 1963.

The OBE Chapel consists in effect of a chancel, occupied on special occasions by the clergy and members of the Royal Family, and of a nave for the congregation. Members of the order and their families have the right to baptismal, wedding and funeral offices here, and memorial services are often held. All this requires adequate seating, a sense of enclosure and gravity, and adequate musical presentation. To meet these needs, Martin Stancliffe added a screen across the west end of the chapel (1993–4), comfortable new chairs with leather seats and backs and fresh lighting. To mark the hundredth birthday of Queen Elizabeth the Queen Mother in 2000, the dean and chapter commissioned from the sculptor Martin Jennings a bronze portrait bust, marking her service as patron of the Friends of St Paul's for over fifty years. At the time of writing, a new floor is shortly to be laid, replacing the vinyl tiles; fragments of Penrose's mosaic floor beneath will be taken up for display elsewhere, but the ledger stone over the grave of Bishop Mandell Creighton (d. 1901) will be revealed.

Summing up the effort lavished on the embellishment St Paul's over the past century is an impossibility. The last words may perhaps be left to Stephen Dykes Bower, who concluded his report of 1946 advocating the present baldacchino with the following admonitory yet uplifting words:

> The larger the building, the more difficult it is to achieve a sacramental, devotional atmosphere. Churches of the largest size must needs exert their influence by other means – by their numinous quality, their majesty and sublimity. It is as a temple of the spirit, the seat of Godhead that St. Paul's with perennial magnetism, speaks to every responsive mind.[20]

24

THE POST-REFORMATION MONUMENTS

Roger Bowdler and Ann Saunders[1]

206. Tomb of Sir John Woolley, 1614. Etching by Wenceslaus Hollar from Dugdale's *History*, 1658. Note the 'correct' Corinthian columns and the cadaver beneath the seated figures. (GL)

THE POST–MEDIEVAL MONUMENTS[2]

Thanks to their collections of memorials, Anglican churches are temples of remembrance as well as places of worship. The visitor to St Paul's on the eve of the Great Fire would have found an exceptional collection of monuments, surpassed only by Westminster Abbey's. Some were on the grandest scale, and all but two were to perish in 1666. Guides to the tombs appeared, sure testaments to their standing. Henry Holland's *Monumenta Sepulchralia Sancti Pauli* of 1614 gathered the epitaphs together; it was updated in 1633 as *Ecclesia Sancti Pauli Illustrata*. Another guide to them appeared in 1684, long after most had been lost.[3] Dugdale's history of 1658 contained an unprecedented sequence of etchings by Hollar depicting the monuments. Thirty-three monuments, concentrated in the east end, were marked on the accompanying *ichnographia*, and there were others besides. The disappearance of so many outstanding tombs in the Great Fire was the greatest loss ever suffered by English sepulchral art: at least they live again in Hollar's engravings (Figs 6, 62, 63, 79, 206).

The startling Woolley monument of 1614, now reduced to lumps of blackened effigy, would once have been among the finest funerary monuments of its day (Figs 204, 206). The gargantuan, soaring tomb of Sir Christopher Hatton (d. 1591), the prominent Lord Chancellor and courtier, was overwhelming even by the ambitious standards of the Elizabethan age, and can be seen

207. Tomb of Sir Christopher Hatton, d. 1591. Drawing by William Sedgwick from Dugdale's 'Book of Monuments', 1641. (BL)

208. Monument to John Donne, d. 1631, in the south choir aisle. Made in the workshop of Nicholas Stone, based on a portrait of the dying dean in his shroud

as the *ne plus ultra* of English monuments (Fig. 207): not surprisingly, it prompted adverse comment as soon as it was erected.[4] Posthumous fame is not always reflected in a memorial: the most renowned Elizabethan to be interred in St Paul's was Sir Philip Sidney (d. 1586), who had to wait until the 1980s for a memorial. Sir Anthony Van Dyck (d. 1641) had to wait until 1928 for his monument to be replaced after the Great Fire.

Only one effigy survived 1666 intact.[5] Happily, this was the remarkable figure of John Donne (d. 1631), dean of St Paul's, produced in the workshop of Nicholas Stone (Fig. 208).[6] The most famous of all English resurrection monuments, it shows Donne's shrouded body released from its urn: the reconstituted body is whole but not yet living, awaiting the moment of Christian triumph over death. It originally stood at the west end of the south choir aisle, facing southwards, and was replaced in its present position (with a brand new surround) in 1873.[7] Before then, it had languished in the crypt (Fig. 209) with the rest of the calcined monumental lumber.[8] Dean Donne bore his final illness with stoic fortitude: 'all this mellows one for heaven, and so ferments me for this world, as I shall need no concoction in the grave, but hasten to the resurrection', he wrote shortly before his death.[9] Izaak Walton's hagiography included an

account of how the dying dean posed for his deathly portrait, clad in his shroud and perched upon an urn, while a nameless artist took his likeness. This final portrait formed the frontispiece to his posthumously published sermon, *Deaths Duell* (1632), and was no doubt copied by Stone's carver, Humphrey Moyer, too. Walton called it 'as lively a representation...as marble can express: a statue indeed so like Dr Donne, that – as his friend Sir Henry Wotton hath expressed himself – "it seems to breathe faintly, and posterity shall look upon it as a kind of artificial miracle".'[10] Resurrection monuments were coming into vogue in England at this time: they normally consisted of tableaux of figures starting up from their coffins at the sounding of the last trump, but Donne's was different, emphasizing bodily reconstruction. It attracted considerable notice. Sir Ralph Verney, a Royalist *émigré* in France in 1651, instructed his agent to 'see Dr Dunns & other Tombes at Pauls or Westminster' before discussing the design of the memorial to Verney's wife and parents.[11] The Donne tomb looks firmly to the world to come. Most subsequent memorials in St Paul's would emphasize worldly achievements and human qualities: not until the mid nineteenth century would the specifically Christian monument make a return.

209 (*top*). Watercolour of effigies in the crypt, by G. F. Sargent *c.* 1847, including that of John Donne, before the monument was reinstated upstairs. (GL)

211 (*above*). One of the *memento mori* cartouches over the entrances to the crypt from the transepts. Parishioners of old St Faith's church retained burial rights inside the rebuilt cathedral. (SPCL)

210 (*top*). 'Bus queue' of repositioned monuments in the south aisle of the crypt in 2002. In the foreground, Admiral Malcolm by E. H. Baily, 1842, and calcined effigies from the Heneage monument, *c.* 1594

212 (*above*). Relief of swaddled babies, a detail from the tomb of the bookseller John Martin, d. 1680, and his wife. Attributed to Edward Pierce, this was the earliest substantial monument to enter the rebuilt cathedral. (SPCL)

Monuments might have been kept out of the body of the cathedral for most of the eighteenth century, but they found their way into the crypt from an early date. The bony cartouches over the entrances to the crypt announce the subterranean realm of the dead (Fig. 211). The parishes of St Faith and St Gregory retained the right to inter their dead here, and the increasingly questioned custom of intra-mural burial was suffered to continue because of this. The finest (and earliest) Stuart monument in the new crypt was that of John Martin (d. 1680), a City printer, shown kneeling in the *orans* position with his wife, either side of a neat pile of books; below them is a melancholy predella panel showing two swaddled and short-lived babies (Fig. 212). One Thomas Cooke (d. 1692) was buried beneath a ledger slab outside the area of St Faith's, the earliest memorial in the crypt space of the cathedral proper.

The earliest wall monuments in the new cathedral were erected in memory of Wren's immediate family. Wren is on record as

wishing to do away with the age-old custom of burial in vaults inside churches,[12] but evidently underwent a change of heart when it came to his own family. Wren's first wife, his daughter and his sister all have finely executed cartouches to their memory in the cathedral. The most interesting is the rectangular relief, baroque in conception, of the '*desideratissimae virginis*', Jane Wren (d. 1702). A skilled musician, she is depicted as St Cecilia playing on a cloud-borne organ, while an angel strums a lyre and cherubim hover in attendance. It was executed by the Rome-trained, Catholic sculptor Francis Bird, who was carrying out much work elsewhere at St Paul's under Wren's direction. The standard work on English sculpture might dismiss it as 'childish' and 'grotesquely immature',[13] but it still tells us much about the influences which worked on the imaginations of Wren and his contemporaries.

Wren's own grave was covered with a heavy ledger slab (Fig. 213). Above it is a marble tablet, incised with the famous Latin

213. The tomb of Sir Christopher Wren, d. 1723, engraving of *c.* 1818. Wren's understated memorial was the outstanding feature in the crypt until the arrival of Lord Nelson in 1806. (SPCL)

epitaph: *si monumentum requiris, circumspice*. The humility of the memorial slab contrasted with the inscription's supreme assurance, which summoned the freshly built heaps of architecture to pay homage to their creator. The presence of Wren's tomb ensured that the crypt would henceforth become a place of pilgrimage. A commentator of 1825 remarked 'admired as this inscription has been, yet one can say from experience, that the direction to "look around," when the reader is in the midst of a dark gloomy vault, has a very contrary effect to that intended'.[14] The neoclassical cult of commemoration prompted later architects to lend greater sepulchral support to Wren's fame. Robert Mylne, in 1807, caused the inscription to be repeated on a tablet erected on the organ gallery in the choir; around this time also, James Elmes proposed a substantial monument for the centre of the crossing beneath the dome.[15] It came to nothing.

The post-Fire rebuilding had a dramatic and unprecedented impact upon new monuments within the cathedral. It was customary for cathedral authorities elsewhere to welcome the fees from erecting monuments: exceptionally, St Paul's managed to keep memorials at bay for most of the eighteenth century. In a complete departure from Anglican custom, they were banished from the main body of the church. Wren's richly articulated interior left few areas of smooth masonry where monuments might lodge. The vast interior remained unadorned and unsullied. It cannot be overemphasized how unusual this state of affairs was, and how marked were the contrasts with London's other great church, the ever-more-densely thronged Westminster Abbey.

Applications for above-ground monuments were bound to come, however. In the early 1760s, the debate was opened.

When Bishop Newton was only one of the residentiaries, a statuary of some note came to him in his summer month of residence, desiring leave to set up a monument in St Pauls for one who had formerly been a Lord Mayor...he went to consult with Archbishop Secker...[who] much approved of the design of monuments, saying what advantages foreign churches have over our's, and that St Pauls was too naked and bare for want of monuments, which would be a proper ornament, and give a venerable air to the church...Bishop Osbaldeston, he was violent against it; Sir Christopher Wren had designed no such

things; there had been no monuments in all the time before he was Bishop, and in his time there should be none...churches, he said, were better without monuments than with them.[16]

The death of the Earl of Chatham in 1778 raised the issue again. Horace Walpole wrote to his antiquarian friend William Cole that 'the City wants to bury Lord Chatham in St Paul's, which as a person said to me this morning, would literally be robbing Peter to pay Paul. I wish it could be so, that there might be some decoration in that nudity, *en attendant* the re-establishment of various altars.' Cole's reply hoped that 'his bones may lie at St Paul's. Such a beginning would put it in fashion and ornament the walls that want covering.'[17]

Chatham's monument ended up in the Guildhall, which was to become a second City pantheon to national worthies. St Paul's continued to hold out against the insertion of monuments, but the 'nudity' of its interior could not resist the swelling neoclassical tide, which brought in its wake a veritable lust for commemoration. The resulting memorials form an outstandingly coherent group of heroic tributes, unrivalled in Britain or abroad. So unusual are these monuments that they demand special and more detailed attention.

THE MEN OF PEACE

It was to John Bacon the elder that the honour fell of carving the first three exemplary figures to be admitted to the body of the cathedral. The first of all was a memorial to the philanthropist John Howard (d. 1790; Fig. 214), who had devoted his life to the improvement of prison conditions and died far away in the Ukraine, still intent on his investigations. An attempt to raise a statue to him had been made during his lifetime, but Howard had vehemently rejected the honour. Once dead, however, he could not decline it; money was subscribed, a committee formed,[18] and the Revd John Pridden suggested that 'upon a proper application' St Paul's might be willing to accept the tribute, notwithstanding that Howard had been a nonconformist. Everyone was behind the scheme. Alderman Boydell, creator of the Shakespeare Gallery in Pall Mall and chairman of the committee, wrote to the dean, requesting permission. In March 1791, the dean and chapter gave their consent, a group of Royal Academicians met at the cathedral

215 (*above*). Monument to Samuel Johnson, writer and lexicographer, by John Bacon senior, 1791–6. (SPCL)

214 (*left*). Monument to John Howard, prison-reformer and philanthropist, by John Bacon senior, 1791–5. The first memorial erected in the body of the cathedral. (SPCL)

to select the most advantageous position for the sculpture – before the main south-east pier supporting the dome – and Bacon was chosen to execute it. The committee resolved

> That the Monument consist of a Figure (7 feet 8 inches high) of Mr. Howard relieving a Prisoner to be placed upon a Pedestal (7 feet high) with proper Emblems and Inscriptions – so that the Expence do not exceed Eighteen-Hundred Guineas & that the Work be executed with all convenient dispatch this being the first Monument which the Dean and Chapter of St. Paul's have ever permitted to be placed in that Cathedral.

In June, Bacon produced a model which was approved by the committee; it may well have resembled that which he had already carved for Thomas Guy in the chapel of the hospital, showing the benevolent alderman raising up a sick man to lead him to safety and care.[19] Bacon was duly advanced £500, but early in the following year trouble began. The clergy, the committee, the academicians and the sculptor arranged to meet again at St Paul's; Bacon arrived last, to find that his original design had been discarded and a single figure substituted. Dr Pridden reported to Samuel Whitbread:

The objection of Mr. Bacon that he could not well delineate the character of Mr. Howard without a secondary figure appeared to them of no weight... It was justly observed by one of the Committee (Mr. West) that public characters require no embellishments, that an exact representation of Mr. Howard with no other inscription than

John Howard

the

Visitor of Prisons

would convey a full idea to succeeding generations of the work of our philanthropist.

Bacon reluctantly assented, the price was reduced by 500 guineas, and the work began; the sculptor was never reconciled to the alteration.

The motivation behind the change of plan may have been concerned with the raising of a memorial to the lexicographer Dr Samuel Johnson (Fig. 215), who had died in 1784. Johnson and Sir Joshua Reynolds had been close friends, and the artist was determined that the writer should receive proper recognition.[20] He was buried in Poets' Corner in Westminster Abbey, where Bacon

216.   Relief panel from monument to William Jones, jurist and orientalist, by John Bacon senior, 1799. Emblems of Indian culture studied by Jones are depicted between mourning classical figures

217.   Monument to Richard Rundle Burges, killed at Camperdown while commanding the *Argent*, by Thomas Banks, 1805. (SPCL) The heroic nude stands shameless in the Christian temple

had also been selected to erect a figure for a modest £600. But once Howard's monument was admitted to St Paul's, nothing less would content Sir Joshua – Johnson must be in the cathedral, too. In July 1791, Reynolds attempted to filch Howard's place for his friend, but Samuel Whitbread firmly repulsed him; the north-east pier was selected for the doctor.

Bacon was now working on two more than life-sized figures and trying to placate two eager and impatient committees. The Howardian Committee requested an assurance that theirs would be unveiled first; Bacon promised that it would be. Both bodies were demanding; Bacon wrote to his wife that he was being harassed on two sides.

By the autumn of 1795, both works were nearing completion. Bacon informed the Howardian Committee that Mr Sewell wanted to draw the figure for the *European Magazine*; did they want it in the *Gentleman's Magazine* as well? Meticulous discussions went on about the punctuation of the inscription; 'a blunder will be more easily excused in my pen than in my chisel', wrote Bacon, rather grimly.

Howard's monument was unveiled on 23 February 1796, Johnson's early in March. It is worth looking carefully at the pair, since they set the pattern for everything that came later. Howard stands attired in a Greek tunic. Spurning fetters, he steps forward confidently, a huge key in his right hand and, gathered in his arm, a sheaf of papers and scrolls relating to hospitals and prisons. The focus of his life's work is revealed on the pedestal relief where Howard, again in classical garb, stoops to raise up a prisoner while a helper carries a tray of food and water on his head and, in the very lowest of relief, a gaoler unlocks the door to free those who have been unjustly confined. Johnson is swathed in a toga, his chest and shoulders bare. His head rests on his left fist while his right hand reaches across to open a scroll with a Greek inscription. The attitude seems clumsy, but we may guess that Reynolds suggested adopting the pose of Heraclitus in Raphael's 'The School of Athens'.[21] Bacon himself had never left England, but Reynolds had spent much time in Italy and would have been jealous for every detail of his friend's memorial. The pedestal is filled with a long Latin epitaph composed by Samuel Parr, Johnson's lifelong verbal sparring partner. The figures unveiled to the contemplation of the public, Bacon published an open letter, describing what he had attempted to achieve, in the *Gentleman's Magazine*.[22] The choice of a single figure for Howard still rankled but he felt he had succeeded in capturing something of Johnson's essence.

It was not long before he received a third commission. Sir William Jones, Chief Justice of the High Court at Calcutta, died in 1794; and two years later the governors of the East India Company decided to set up two statues in his memory, one in St Paul's and another in 'a proper place' in Bengal.[23] Bacon was selected to provide that in St Paul's. Jones's father had died when the child was three; his mother had nourished the boy's precocious genius and he had entered Harrow School at the age of seven, where he astonished everyone by his linguistic abilities. He continued these interests at Oxford and then turned to the law for a living. Appointed to Calcutta, he showed his sympathy for the language, poetry, laws and culture of India and he founded the Asiatic Society to express that respect. The climate killed him within ten years, but in that time he achieved a codification of the Indian legal system. His widow's memorial to him, by Thomas Banks, in the chapel of University College, Oxford, shows him surrounded by native friends, with the inscription 'A Nation deserves to be judged by its own laws'.

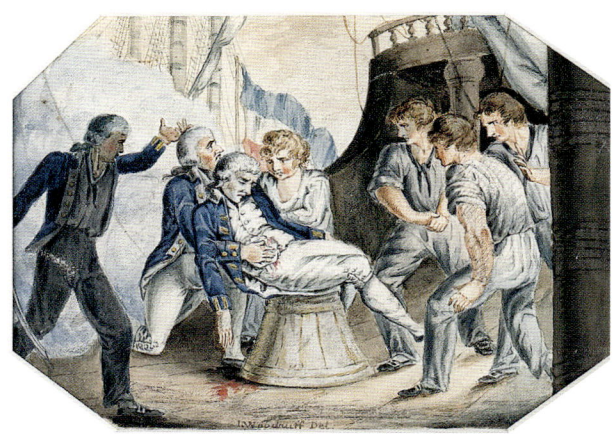

218 (*above*). The death of Captain Faulknor on board the *Blanche*, 1795, contemporary watercolour. (Private collection)

219 (*left*). Proposed design for monument to Captain Robert Faulknor, drawing by Richard Smirke for J. C. F. Rossi, after 1800. (GL)

220 (*right*). Monument to Captain Robert Faulknor, as executed by J. C. F. Rossi, 1803. (SPCL)

Bacon shows his subject bare-shouldered, clad in a toga. He holds a scroll, the constitution of the Asiatic Society, and rests his elbow on his *Translation of the Institutes of Menu*. The book rests on a pillar decorated with reliefs of books for Jones's learning, scales for his work as a judge, callipers for his mathematical interests, an astrolabe, and a lyre for his poems. But as with Howard's memorial, the real delight of the monument is the exquisite bas-relief on the pedestal where symbolic figures bring truth and enlightenment to an Indian scene; a small goddess sits serenely enthroned, embracing an image of Brahma and holding a tablet with a complex scene (Fig. 216).[24]

If there were going to be monuments in St Paul's, then these three bravura figures made a splendid beginning. They have an endearing quality. One early nineteenth-century visitor is recorded as having done reverence to Howard and Johnson, believing them to be representations of St Peter and St Paul.[25] Later critics are, however, particularly scornful of Johnson; 'a tired gladiator, meditating on a wasted life' is one comment. But the most perspicacious judgement comes from the sculptor himself in a letter to his son:

> Mr. Rigaud has been at St. Paul's and likes our work very much. Even Howard, he says, is not as grand as Johnson but the notion is extremely good and he could not help thinking that one figure seemed to be going about what the other was projecting – this was pleasing to me and I know it will be to you.

The fourth position under the dome was taken by a milder memorial, a statue of Sir Joshua Reynolds. In contrast to Bacon's three neoclassical figures, Reynolds wears his Royal Academician's robes over everyday dress, holds a copy of his own *Discourses* and leans against a pillar whereon is carved a portrait of Michelangelo,

whose name was the last word that he uttered in his final discourse to the Academy. The sculptor was John Flaxman. Compared with the drama of Bacon's figures, Sir Joshua seems strangely calm and domestic; the Latin inscription was composed by the antiquary, Richard Payne Knight. The Academy refused to contribute to the cost; Lady Thomond, Reynolds's niece and heiress, fretted at the slowness of the work; it was unveiled in 1813, twenty-one years after the painter's death.[26]

THE HEROES MOVE IN

Before Howard or Reynolds was in position, the whole approach to statuary in St Paul's had changed. On 1 February 1793, Revolutionary France declared war on Great Britain and Holland. A war had begun that was to last, with scant intermission, for twenty-two years. That conflict would be fought not only across the European land mass, but also across the oceans. During those wars, the government voted and paid for thirty-three marble memorials to the nation's heroes. All but two came to St Paul's.

These were not the first national monuments to naval or military heroes; Westminster Abbey already held memorials to Captain James Cornewall, killed in 1744 in a victorious action against the French (the first ever to be voted by Parliament) and to General Wolfe (a particularly distinguished work by Joseph Wilton). What is amazing is the sheer scale of the commitment.

The first three memorials were to Captain Robert Faulknor (Figs 218–20), to Major-General Thomas Dundas and to Captain Richard Rundle Burges (Fig. 217);[27] the sculptors commissioned were John Charles Felix Rossi, the younger John Bacon and Thomas Banks, the selection being made by the academicians.

221 (*left*). Detail of a painting of Charles Towneley and friends at his house in Westminster, surrounded by his collections, by Zoffany, 1781–3. (Towneley Hall Art Gallery and Museum, Burnley)

222 (*below*). Monuments existing and proposed in the cathedral, from Dugdale (1818)

MONUMENTS ERECTED BY 1818: 1, Doctor Johnson; 2, John Howard; 3, Sir Joshua Reynolds; 4, Sir William Jones; 5, Captain Westcott, Generals Craufurd and Mackinnon; 6, General Dundas, Generals Mackenzie and Langwerth; 7, Captain R. Faulknor, Captain R. W. Miller; 8, Captain R. R. Burges, Captain G. N. Hardinge; 9, Sir I. Brock; 10, Sir R. Abercromby; 11, Sir John Moore; 12, Lord Collingwood; 13, Earl Howe; 14, Viscount Nelson, Captain J. Cooke; 15, Marquis Cornwallis, Captain Duff; 16, General Le Marchant; 17, Captains Mosse and Riou; 18, Lord Rodney; 19, Sir William Myers; 20, General Hoghton; 21, point beneath the dome, below which is Lord Nelson's Sarcophagus.

MONUMENTS EXECUTED BUT NOT YET ERECTED: a, General Sir Thomas Picton; b, General Sir William Ponsonby; b, General Hay; b, Generals Gore and Skerritt; c, Sir Samuel Hood; d, Colonel Cadogan; e, General Ross; f, General Bowes.

OTHER FEATURES IDENTIFIED: A, Minor Canons' Vestry; B, Dean's Vestry; C, Lord Mayor's Vestry; D, Font; E, Morning Prayer Chapel.

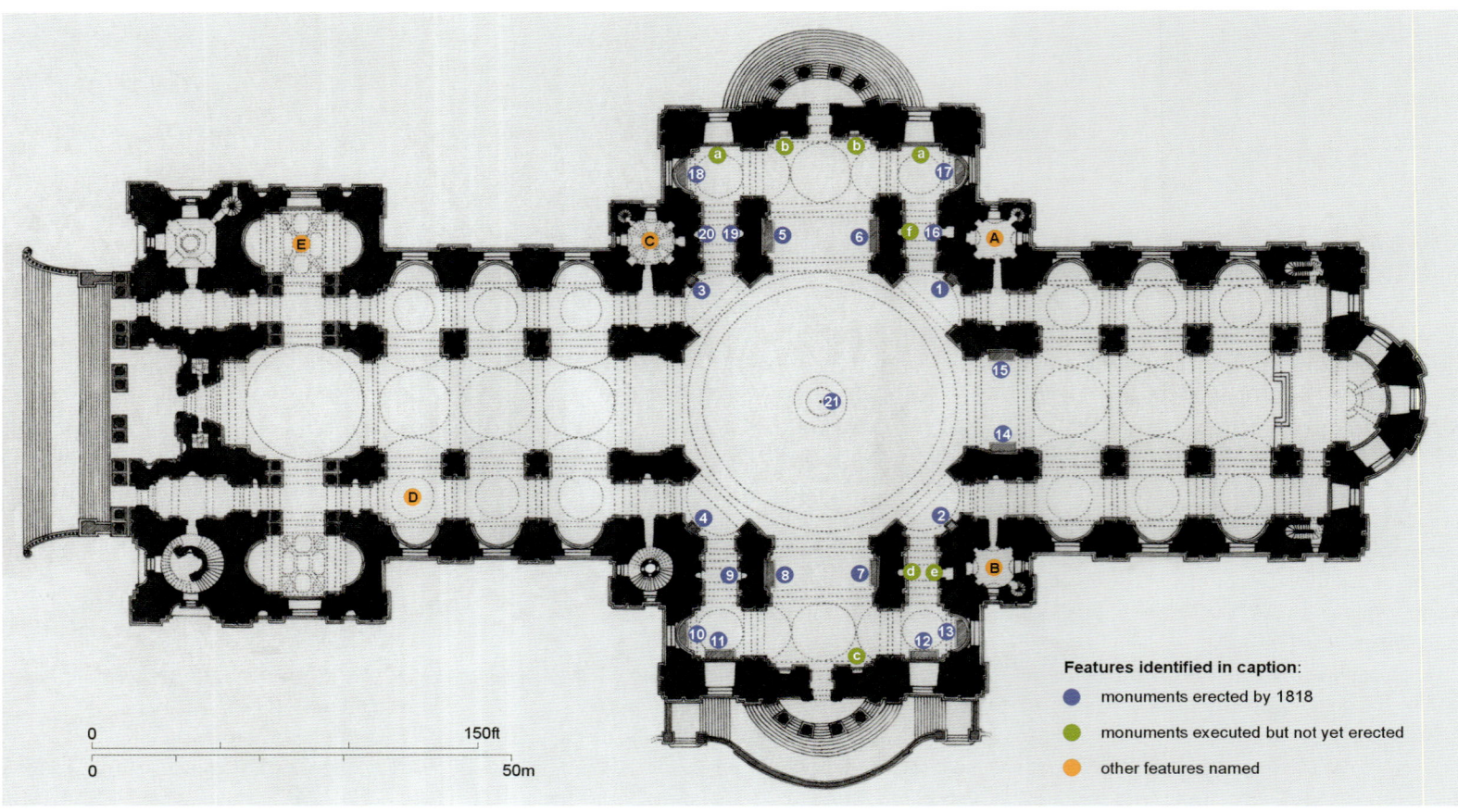

Features identified in caption:

● monuments erected by 1818
● monuments executed but not yet erected
● other features named

Faulknor was an immensely popular hero. In an engagement with the French off the West Indies on 5 January 1795, the bowsprit of *La Pique* came athwart Faulknor's vessel, the *Blanche*; he seized it, lashing it to the capstan, thereby converting the entire side of his ship into one battery, but in the course of the action he was killed. His intrepidity caught the imagination of the nation; a one-act opera celebrating his courage was given several performances that summer at Covent Garden.[28]

Dundas's end was less heroic. A brave soldier and a capable governor of Guadeloupe, which had been captured from the French, he died of fever in June 1794. When the French retook the island, his body was exhumed and exposed to wild animals; Parliament answered the insult with a marble memorial. In contrast, Burges, captain of the *Ardent* under the command of Lord Howe, had

died in October 1797, successfully breaking the enemy line off Camperdown on the Dutch coast.

Reaction to these memorials, when they were finally installed, was mixed. Banks had been lucky to get the commission, worth £5,250, for Burges; his initial enthusiasm for the French Revolution had led to his arrest for seditious speeches – this while the elder Bacon was patriotically drilling his workmen in the yard behind his premises – but by the time the work was offered to him, his feelings had clearly changed. Burges is represented by a portrait head on an idealized heroic body, naked save for a chlamys flung negligently over one shoulder. He stands on a substantial pedestal on which, across a cannon and a most realistic coil of rope, Victory hands him a sword. The pedestal is carved with sea gods and marine tributes.

Though George Lewis Smyth declared 'the statue of Burgess [*sic*] cannot fail to command praise; the attitude is fine and the air brave', other critics considered that it 'brought the blush of shame to the cheek of modesty'.[29] Rossi's group for Faulknor was even less successful. The hero, scantily clothed, falls backwards into the arms of Neptune; the sea god turns to catch him while Victory places – one is tempted to say pops – a wreath on his head. Rossi's original design shows a sculpture almost twice as tall, with Britannia and a lion surmounting the main group.

Bacon's group for Dundas is the most graceful of the three; Britannia, attended by a companionable lion and by Sensibility, a young plant in her hands, crowns a bust of the hero, the pedestal of which is decorated with Britannia defending Liberty against Anarchy and Hypocrisy.[30]

The government felt uneasy at the results of their expenditure; perhaps the academicians were not the most reliable arbiters, and a committee might keep matters under proper control. Accordingly, under instructions from the prime minister, Addington, such a committee was formed in 1802, with Charles Long, MP, later Baron Farnborough, as chairman.[31]

If the actions of the heroes, reported in dispatches and published in newspapers, are one strand of this story, and their representations by the sculptors the other visible thread in it, then the deliberations of this committee are the link between the two. First known as the Committee for the Erection of Monuments, but soon to be spoken of – half respectfully and half mockingly – as the Committee of Taste, it had great influence over the art world of the day. A knowledge of the composition of the committee is essential to the understanding of why a cohort of large white marble neoclassical figures people the aisles and transepts of St Paul's.

Charles Long, the chairman, was artistic adviser to both George III and George IV. He was assisted by Sir George Beaumont, whose paintings became the nucleus of the National Gallery; by Reginald Pole Carew, the Home Secretary; by the connoisseur William Locke; by Henry Bankes, MP and a trustee of the British Museum; by Sir William Hamilton's friend, Charles Townley, whose collection of Greek and Roman antiquities was purchased by the British Museum (Fig. 221); and by the acerbic and arrogant Richard Payne Knight, who nevertheless freely bequeathed his collections to the same museum. Later, others would be added – Thomas Hope; Granville Leveson-Gower, marquess of Stafford; George Legge, third earl of Dartmouth; John Joshua Proby, Lord Carysfort, a fine classical scholar; George Howard, Lord Carlisle, Trustee of the British Museum; George O'Brien Wyndham, Lord Egremont, Turner's patron; Robert Banks Jenkinson, Lord Hawkesbury, later prime minister as Lord Liverpool; and (according to the artist and diarist Joseph Farington) Sir Uvedale Price, author of a celebrated *Essay on the Picturesque*.

All these men had received a classical education, the majority had made the Grand Tour, and most had their own collections of antique sculpture, often housed in specially and expensively designed galleries. To them, nudity was the proper garb for a hero, and white Carrara marble the obvious material. Zoffany's portrait of Charles Townley, seated in his study, surrounded by his collection, says it all.[32] All were deeply interested in classical art and familiar with the latest archeological discoveries. But they were not artists and had no practical experience of stone carving.

The post of secretary to the committee went to Robert Gillman, already secretary to the British Institution formed to encourage art in Britain. No minutes have been traced, nor is there any mention of the monuments in the chapter records; either matters were settled by word of mouth or the cathedral clergy accepted that, if the government had voted the funds, then it was their patriotic duty to accept the monuments. Perhaps they were proud to house a national Valhalla; a floor-plan of the cathedral in the 1818 edition of Dugdale (Fig. 222), shows the position of each one already executed and lists those that are still to come. Sydney Smith, speaking a generation later,[33] had no taste for the monuments, but the mood was very different in the harshest of the wartime years.

To the committee fell the commissioning of the next four monuments, tributes to Admiral Lord Howe, to Captains Mosse and Riou, to Captain Westcott and to General Sir Ralph Abercromby. Models were displayed in the Treasury, one each from Banks, Flaxman, Rossi and Westmacott.[34] Farington records:

> As there appeared by this mode to be no competition, it was resolved that each sculptor shd. be called upon to produce models for the other three monuments besides that which He had delivered, – or drawings of designs if He preferred it.
>
> It was also resolved to go to St. Paul's & consider the Places where such models shd. be placed. I told Sir George [Beaumont] that there was a standing Committee of Members of the Royal Academy appointed for that purpose.

The academicians were eager to join in the selection of artists and the positioning of sculpture. Farington recorded that he had talked to his fellow academician, Thomas Lawrence, who

> conversed on Tuesday last at Woodlands with Mr. Lock and Willm. Lock respecting the *Committee of taste*. When the Committee met (Mr. Long in the Chair) Wm. Lock gave his opinion of the propriety of consulting or referring questions upon the merits of designs laid before the Committee to the Members of the Royal Academy or to such Artists as might be thought best qualified to give judgement. This was warmly *opposed* by Mr. Knight who was the chief if not the only speaker.—Mr. Long seemed to sit, as Chairman, only to see how the ayes & noes counted.—Knight carried it. Mr. Banks gave proof of his taste by observing on the advantage which Sculptors wd. derive, or rather that their view should by the Committee be pointed to the Great Altar at St. Peter's in Rome, a design of Bernini in which *twisted Columns* & many flourishing fancies appear.
>
> Lawrence observed to them that Mr. Knight's taste was just that which shd. not be adopted. It was founded on Sensual feeling.—The simplicity of Raphael, His Purity, &c afforded no gratification to Knight,—His pleasure was derived from the luxurious displays of Rubens.—Wm. Lock said he had noticed this at the Marquiss [*sic*] of Stafford's where Knight was profuse in his admiration of a sensual picture by Rubens but did not notice pictures by Titian to which Rubens would have bowed.[35]

Flaxman began work on Howe's memorial. The aged admiral, described by Horace Walpole as 'undaunted as a rock and as silent' and known as Black Dick by the Navy, had died in 1799. Flaxman portrayed him in uniform holding a telescope; attended by a somewhat somnolent lion, the admiral leans against the prow of his ship, the *Queen*. Britannia sits enthroned on the deck while History, supported by Victory, records Howe's relief of Gibraltar and his success off Ushant. The memorial was not achieved without difficulty. Flaxman designed it, but the cutting was done by

223.   Detail from monument to Sir Ralph Abercromby, by Sir Richard
Westmacott, 1803–9

his assistants. Howe's figure was made disproportionately large and months of work were spend chipping away to reduce the size and then in repolishing the marble. Afterwards, Flaxman always made a full-size model before work began on the stone.[36]

Westcott's monument went to Banks. Having risen from cabin boy to command of the *Majestic*, this hero was killed at the Battle of the Nile in 1798. Westcott's memorial represents him as semi-naked, a tunic slipping off one shoulder. He slumps into the arms of a winged Victory who staggers, struggling to crown him with a laurel wreath. It is not the happiest composition, but the relief on the pedestal deserves examination. On the front, a river god,

the Nile, is surrounded by small genii, while to the left is wrought the explosion of the French flagship, *L'Orient*, at the height of the battle, with stylized plumes of smoke billowing into the air.

High on the wall of the south transept is a more modest tribute to another hero of the ensuing campaign, Captain Ralph Willett Miller, RN, who fell at the siege of Acre. It is a tablet by John Flaxman, showing Britannia with her lion and Victory hanging a plaque on a palm tree; it is an early example of sanserif lettering. No official memorial was voted to Miller; his brother officers were so incensed that they commissioned the sculptor themselves.[37]

Two more of Nelson's captains, James Mosse and Edward Riou, lost their lives in his next major engagement, off Copenhagen. This commission went to Rossi, but his original design was altered and amended by the committee. The finished result is dignified; a pair of large winged figures sit in front of a noble sarcophagus, holding portraits of the captains with a long inscription describing their feats, but an anonymous critic declared the sculpture 'despicable, both in conception and performance'.[38]

So far the Navy had had the honours, but the Egyptian campaign, following the landing at Aboukir Bay, gave a hero to the Army. General Sir Ralph Abercromby died of wounds received at the Battle of Alexandria. The commission for his memorial, at £6,500, went to (Sir) Richard Westmacott, and is one of the most individual and spirited in the entire pantheon (Fig. 223). The general, having received the fatal sword thrust, falls from his horse into the arms of a kilted highlander; the horse rears up, about to crush beneath its hooves a naked figure representing the enemy. Flaxman and Rossi had said that Westmacott had not yet achieved a nude figure and that he was determined to show what he could do,[39] but the hero is represented in uniform, not as a classical demi-god.

The next round of commissions came after Trafalgar, fought on 21 October 1805. In addition to Nelson's, memorials were voted for Captain George Duff, commanding the *Mars*, and Captain John Cooke of the *Bellerophon*. The younger John Bacon provided Duff's tablet (£1,575) with a magnificently muscled sailor sinking to his knees in grief; Duff, who had run away to sea at the age of nine, was truly beloved by his crews, so that his was one of the few ships that remained loyal during the Nore Mutiny. Cooke's was given to Westmacott and is a companion piece to Duff's; Britannia crouches, overwhelmed with sorrow at the loss of so noble a man; two putti flank her, one with her trident and the other naughtily trying on her helmet.

The honour of carving Nelson's memorial – a profitable one at £6,500 – went to Flaxman, though he was not allowed to follow his own ideas unhindered (Fig. 224). Farington reported:

> Mr. Knight mentioned the liberality of Westmacott who had permitted that Flaxman should adopt part of a design he had made for a monument to Nelson.[40]

Flaxman took it calmly; he told Rossi he would indeed 'adopt the sentiment of Westmacott for Lord Nelson's monument but ...the composition of the figures [would] be his own'. He eschewed both the neoclassicism of Banks and the realism of Westmacott's Abercromby. His Nelson stands calmly beside a coil of rope and an anchor stock; he is in uniform with all his decorations, a magnificent fur pelisse which the Grand Vizier of Turkey had presented to him concealing the lack of his right arm;[41] the loss of the other eye is indicated. Nelson's chief victories are listed around the pedestal on which are carved river gods with the Nile reclining on a sphinx; a British lion growls menacingly at the base while Britannia instructs two midshipmen – one, very young, clutching a sextant – to follow the example set by the hero.

When Nelson fell, fatally wounded, at Trafalgar, the command of the fleet passed to his friend, Cuthbert Collingwood. Having won the victory, the admiral remained at sea, despite failing health, for the next five years, and died at last on his ship, the *Ville de Paris*, in March 1810. His body was brought back to England, given a state funeral and buried close to Nelson's sarcophagus. Westmacott was commissioned to carve his monument (Fig. 225); the price set was £4,200. The admiral lies on the deck of a man-

224.   Monument to Lord Nelson, by John Flaxman, 1808–18. (SPCL)

of-war, still clasping a sword, his body draped in colours taken from the enemy. Fame kneels over him and Neptune, surrounded by mawkish little river gods, gazes at the hero. Four tiny roundels, carved along the line of the ship, show the Genius of Man learning to sail the oceans and to forge the instruments of war.

Collingwood's was the last monument, bar one, to a naval hero. The very last, executed by Charles Manning, is to Captain George Hardinge of the *San Fiorenzo*, who in March 1808, off the coast of Ceylon, engaged *La Piedmontaise*, a vessel more than twice the size of his own. The battle lasted for three days. The French ship was at last captured but Hardinge lost his life. The tablet (£1,575) shows

225.   Detail of monument to Lord Collingwood, by Sir Richard Westmacott, 1811–17. (SPCL)

226.   Detail of monument to Sir John Moore, the hero of Corunna, by John Bacon junior, 1815. (SPCL)

a sarcophagus across which Fame lies, prostrate with grief, while a seated Indian mournfully clasps the British colours.

By this time, a new factor had entered the game. The marbles brought from the Parthenon by Lord Elgin reached England in January 1804. Since Elgin was then a prisoner of war in France, they remained in fifty huge packing cases for three years until their owner was freed; half the collection was unpacked and put on display in June 1807. The artists and sculptors were awestruck, overwhelmed by what they saw. Benjamin Haydon brought Henry Fuseli to see them and recorded in his diary:

> . . . he strode about the collection in his fierce way, saying 'the Greeks was Gods! – they was Gods!'[42]

The members of the Committee of Taste were less impressed. Several of them were members of the Society of Dilettanti; their preference was for the smooth elegance of the Apollo Belvedere; vigorous roughness, the naturalism, the spontaneity of the Parthenon marbles were alien to them. Even before the sculptures were unpacked, the most vocal of the committee, Richard Payne Knight, taunted Lord Elgin, publicly declaring – without having seen them – that they were of little value. He sneered:

> You have lost your labour, my Lord Elgin; your marbles are overrated; they are not Greek: they are Roman of the time of Hadrian.[43]

It took the resolute support of the artists, a visit from Canova and the deliberations of a select committee to win for the marbles a proper appreciation of their true worth and a home in the British Museum.[44] The enlarged committee continued its task of selecting and advising the sculptors. By now, marble supplies in England were running low,[45] and the artists, worn down by the seemingly interminable war and by the stress of participating in frequent competitions, were criticizing each other and complain-

ing of the committee's interferences and alterations.[46] There were others, too, who were impatient of the great sums spent on sculpture. Haydon thundered to his diary about

> Masses of marble scarcely shaped into intelligible boots, spurs, epaulets, sashes, hats, & belts huddled on to cover ignorance and hide defects. Why is this infatuated attachment to an art? Surely divide your favours and affections. If you shower thousands into the lap of Sculpture and fatten her to idleness with one hand, scatter hundreds into the lap of Painting also that her preternatural efforts without friends, without patronage, may be fostered & saved from being wholly without effect. No, year after year and day after day monuments & money are voted in ceaseless round without discrimination, without thought.[47]

The war went on. British military activity, now concentrated on the Iberian peninsula, for the time being ended in evacuation from Corunna following the death of Sir John Moore on 16 January 1809. A memorial to the hero was urgently demanded; Parliament voted for it nine days later and the sculptors were ready to compete. A Committee of Subscribers for an additional monument was set up in Glasgow; to it, James Moore, Sir John's brother, reported from London:

> At the British Institution there are I believe ten models for the monument of Sir John Moore. I pretend to little taste, but I preferred that by Rossi, where the General is represented, dying on the lap of Hispania.[48]

The energetic gentleman then sought out Joseph Nollekens (who had never joined in any of the competitions and now refused the Glasgow commission) and visited Westminster Abbey and St Paul's. Nevertheless, the committee's vote for Moore's monument in the cathedral went to the younger John Bacon. Farington reported:

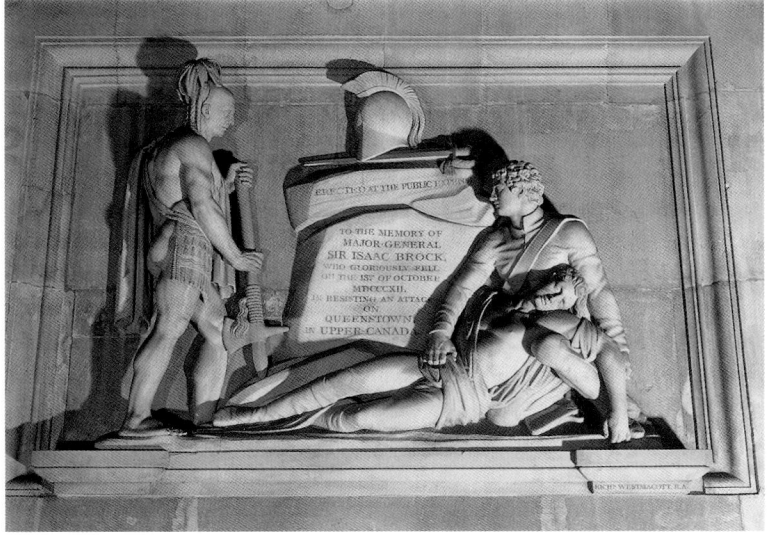

229.   Horse's head from monument to General Sir William Ponsonby, killed at Waterloo, designed by William Theed senior, sculpted after his death by E. H. Baily, 1820. (SPCL)

227 *(top)*.   Monument to General Daniel Hoghton, killed in the Peninsular campaign, by Francis Chantrey, 1812–16

228 *(above)*.   Monument to General Sir Isaac Brock, killed in Canada, by Sir Richard Westmacott, *c.* 1815 Homage is paid by an American Indian

At the decission [*sic*] for the monument of Sir John Moore – Sir George Beaumont, Mr. Thos. Hope & Lord Carysfort were for Rossi – while Charles Long, Bankes & P. Knight with another or two were for Bacon.

Rossi declared he would never compete again. On the finished work, Valour and Victory lower the general into his tomb with a rope of laurel while the spirit of Spain mournfully raises a flag above the dead man (Fig. 226).

Wellington's long, harsh Peninsular campaign began in the summer of 1809. Victory at Talavera (July 1809) cost the lives of Major-General E. Mackenzie and Brigadier-General J. R. Langworth; hideous casualties at Albuera (May 1811) included Lieutenant-General Daniel Hoghton (Fig. 227) and Lieutenant-Colonel Sir William Myers. Ciudad Rodrigo (January 1812) took Major-General Robert Crauford and Major-General Henry Mackinnon; Vittoria (June 1812) Colonel Henry Cadogan; Salamanca (July 1812) Major-General John Gaspard Le Marchant and Major-General Bernard Ford Bowes; and a reckless sortie at Bayonne (April 1814) – across the frontier on to French soil at last – killed General Andrew Hay.

Meanwhile, in June 1812, goaded by maritime disputes and hoping to add loyal Canada to the United States, America declared war on Britain. Sir Isaac Brock lost his life in defence of Canada (Fig. 228), Generals Gibbs and Pakenham succeeded in burning the White House and most of the rest of Washington with it, but were killed attacking New Orleans, while General Robert Ross died in a successful attack on Baltimore. Further afield, Major-General Robert Gillespie was killed in the defence of Nepal on the Indian frontier, while back in Europe, Generals Gore and Skerrett fell at Bergen-op-Zoom in the Netherlands. In April 1814 Napoleon abdicated and was sent to Elba, only to escape and, returning to France, raise a last army to fight at Waterloo. The Allies' victory there cost the lives of General Picton and Major-General Sir William Ponsonby, whose horse stumbled (Fig. 229), leaving its rider to be speared by a French lancer.

Parliament voted memorials to all of these men, and eventually added five more: Admiral Viscount Duncan, who had commanded the Fleet off Camperdown in 1797; General Lord Heathfield, who had defended Gibraltar with exemplary stubbornness in an earlier war; Admiral Lord Rodney, who had defeated the French off Dominica; Admiral John Jervis, Earl St Vincent, who had taken his title from his defeat of the Spanish in 1797; and Marquis Cornwallis, Governor-General of India and conqueror of Tippoo. Duncan's monument was assigned to Westmacott, and St Vincent's to Edward Hodges Baily; Rossi, over the years, was commissioned to execute the other three. The results are so variable that it is hard to credit that they are all by the same man – Heathfield has a particularly uninspired bas-relief, and Rodney, flanked by History and Fame, seems spiritless, but Cornwallis's memorial is another matter. It caught the eye of James Moore:

> There is a monument by Mr. Rossi about to be erected in St. Paul's. I have seen it, though it is still unfinished, and there is a small model of it in the exhibition. It is in memory of the Marquis Cornwallis. A statue of the marquis in the robes of the Garter is placed on a lofty Pedestal; below there are three allegorical figures. One is a beautiful female Hindoo, looking up at the marquis; I believe he had one of the daughters of Niobe in his head, when he designed it. The robes of the Garter give a cumbrous appearance to the principal figure, but on the whole, it has a magnificent effect.

The beautiful Indian lady represents the River Ganges with a semi-naked turbanned figure beside her for the River Begareth, while the Britannia, sitting with her trident on the opposite side of the group, has an unusually oriental air. This monument, with that to Nelson, was placed dominantly at the entrance to the choir.

Francis Chantrey's three plaques, to Bowes, Cadogan and Hoghton, all commemorate young men who died within months of each other in the Peninsular campaign. The sculptor must have looked closely at the Parthenon marbles. Each panel gives a low-relief scene of the action, with the hero's death standing out in higher relief – Hoghton cheers on his men who advance uphill with fixed bayonets at Albuera (Fig. 227); Bowes falls as his troops breach the walls of Salamanca; the dying Cadogan is supported as his men press on to conquest at Vittoria. Sir Isaac Brock's tablet by Westmacott is conventional enough save for one of the mourners – a magnificently accoutred North American Indian, Tecumseh. The same sculptor fashioned the companionable figures of Generals Pakenham and Gibbs, the latter resting his hand on his friend's shoulder.

Finally there is Sir William Ponsonby's memorial, designed by William Theed and carved by Edward Hodges Baily. The dying soldier lies, naked, supported by the horse that failed him; he reaches up, to take a wreath from Victory; the horse's head (Fig. 229) is a direct quotation from that in the pediment of the Parthenon. Smyth did not approve of it, calling it a 'vulgar combination of Nature and Art', but the Victory and the horse's head are eloquently carved.[49]

It takes years to carve a large marble memorial. The final examples were not installed until the 1830s, but the plan of the cathedral published in Ellis's 1818 edition of Dugdale's *History of St Paul's* shows that the nave now housed a pantheon to the heroes of the long wars with France (Fig. 222). Collective commemorations were in the air; as early as April 1800, John Opie had written to the editor of the *True Briton* to propose the erection of a huge circular building dedicated to that purpose; the Royal Academy minutes devote ten pages to the scheme.[50] Now London's cathedral possessed such a tribute. The model was the Panthéon in Paris, once the church of Ste Geneviève, rededicated in 1791 by the French Assembly to the memory of exemplary citizens.

Because of the entrance fee to St Paul's, those whose efforts had won so many victories were expected to pay for the privilege of looking at the memorials. The government reacted by insisting during the winter of 1837 on the cathedral permitting several hours of free access each day, excepting Sundays. The chapter agreed, unwillingly, Sydney Smith remarking tartly that 'the public [had] thought fit to erect St Paul's into a receptacle for public monuments', but he had to give way, and old sailors and old

soldiers could now view the marble tributes freely and remember their own part in the struggle. In 1841, the Select Committee on National Monuments published a table of what the monuments had cost the country; in all, it amounted to an astonishing £110,575.[51]

With the enlargement of the organ and opening up of the choir in 1859, Nelson and Cornwallis were moved from their original positions across the entrance to the eastern arm. Subsequent generations made other adjustments; some heroes were moved down to the crypt, many were lowered from their pedestals and are now regarded from the wrong angle. By the beginning of Victoria's reign, the metropolitan cathedral had been transformed into a Valhalla commemorating those of the previous generation who had fought out the long wars against France and Napoleon – wars as bitter, as widespread and as full of courage on both sides as any other conflict.

LATER MEMORIALS

The arrival of the 'Peninsular School' memorials permanently changed the mood of the cathedral. The martial tableaux injected a tributary character to modern-day valour within the sacred walls, resulting in an upsurge of popular interest in St Paul's. Not even the 2d. entrance fee (finally abolished in 1851)[52] put off the growing numbers of visitors, keen to witness this dramatic spectacle and re-enactment of heroic deaths, and to stand beside the remains of Lord Nelson. Maria Hackett's oft-revised *A Popular Account of St Paul's Cathedral* of 1813 consisted largely of epitaphs and descriptions of tombs, remarking that 'the arrival of Monuments and Statues in honour of the illustrious dead, have added materially to the interest excited in the mind of the visitor'.[53] Even foreigners concurred: 'the starkness of the walls, following the Reformation of Henry VIII, made the church seem gloomy and repellant to the eye; this has been overcome by setting up statues and tombs of various great men'.[54] Never again could the cathedral be accused of barren emptiness.

Artists continued to be honoured. After Reynolds was laid to rest in 1792, his part of the crypt saw a steady stream of artistic burials, becoming something of a Royal Academicians' pantheon, with ledger slabs to John Opie (d. 1807), Benjamin West (d. 1820), Henry Fuseli (d. 1825) and George Dance (d. 1825). Sir Thomas Lawrence joined them in 1830, but his grave is not marked. Interestingly, the only Royal Academician ever to be expelled has the most imposing of the early artists' memorials in the crypt. James Barry died in 1806, but in 1819 his bust was modelled and moulded in Coade stone, and then placed in the crypt.[55] The first sculptural memorial to enter the crypt for over a century, it anticipated the wave of later memorials that was so richly to embellish the subterranean space.

The process of commemorating heroes went on well after Waterloo. Major General Robert Gillespie was killed during the Gurkha War in 1814, but his mural monument by Chantrey, in the established tradition, was only erected in 1826. The naval hero Captain Sir William Hoste was accorded a prominent statue by Thomas Campbell in the south transept, unveiled in 1833. Its form pointed to the direction monuments in St Paul's were now taking. Allegory was banished: the standing figure was fast becoming the thing – sober, economical of space and with firm classical precedents. The figure by William Behnes in the south transept of Major General Sir John Thomas Jones (d. 1843) even has an epitaph which opens 'This statue . . . erected by his

230. Monument to Bishop Reginald Heber, by Francis Chantrey, 1835. Formerly in the chancel, it was later banished to the crypt. Other versions of this memorial to the colonial evangelist are in Calcutta and Madras. (SPCL)

231. Angel from the Melbourne monument, by Carlo Marochetti, after 1853. The first avowedly Christian monument erected in the cathedral since the seventeenth century. (SPCL)

surviving brother officers of the Royal Engineers'.[56] Twenty years later, such a figure would be erected not in a church, but on the street or parade ground. These monuments were national tributes, not grave-markers, and turned to traditions of public commemoration for inspiration. Later on, from the mid century onwards, memorials in St Paul's would return to older tomb-types: under the influence of the Gothic Revival, the recumbent effigy would find its way into the cathedral.

After Waterloo, it was not the military alone which erected monuments inside St Paul's. The professions, and in particular medicine, began to appear as their social standing rose. Statues to the surgeons William Babington (d. 1833) by William Behnes and to Sir Astley Paston Cooper (d. 1842) by E. H. Baily were erected in the south transept, alongside the Abercromby and Moore memorials. Clerical monuments, too, began to appear. At first, these commemorated Anglican worthies busy overseas. Chantrey's magnificent figure of Bishop Reginald Heber (d. 1826) first occupied the east end of the south choir aisle in 1835. It has subsequently been dismantled and banished to the crypt; a tomb of the highest quality (Fig. 230), it deserves better. Heber died at Trichinopoly, and there are two earlier versions of Chantrey's tomb in India, in Calcutta and Madras.[57] The detached relief of Heber blessing native converts returned to the theme of Sir

William Jones's memorial forty years before: the comforts of Christianity that attended imperial expansion. John Lough's memorial in the nave to Bishop Middleton (d. 1822), the first Anglican bishop in India, erected in 1832, expressed the same sentiment but in a coarser manner, with the over-scaled bishop looming over suppliant, 'doll-sized' children.[58]

The first statesmen to find their posthumous way to St Paul's rather than to Westminster Abbey were the Melbournes: the prime minister William Lamb, second viscount Melbourne (d. 1848) and his diplomat brother Frederick, third viscount (d. 1853). Designed and modelled by the Piedmontese sculptor Carlo Marochetti, it consisted of a pair of sentinel angels (Fig. 231), each as langorous as any Rossetti damsel, guarding a pair of heavy black doors and leaning on their trumps. Across the lintel is written 'Through the gates of death we pass to our joyful resurrection'. Not only was this the first monument to statesmen: it was the first modern memorial in St Paul's to employ Christian imagery directly. Perhaps for this reason, Dean Milman wrote of it with great warmth: 'I never consented to any proposal to erect a monument in St Paul's with less hesitation or with such perfect conscientiousness as that to the admission of Viscount Melbourne into our Valhalla.'[59] The *City Press* pronounced in 1870 that 'the statuary is not despicable if judged as a whole, and since

233 (*above*). *Pilgrims to St Paul's*, engraving of a lost painting by J. E. Millais, 1868, depicting veterans paying their respects to Nelson's sarcophagus in the sombre gloom of the crypt

232 (*left*). Monument to J. M. W. Turner, d. 1851, by Patrick Macdowell. The painter is depicted in the act of observing the celestial firmament. (SPCL)

MAROCHETTI'S angels have guarded Viscount MELBOURNE'S tomb, many a one has had a feast of beauty there that has kindled all the emotions that belong to acts of worship'.[60] These angels were to make a reappearance on one of the sculptor's most prestigious commissions: the Scutari memorial at Istanbul of 1856–7.[61]

After Reynolds, the second artist to gain a memorial upstairs was J. M. W. Turner (d. 1851). The Irish sculptor Patrick Macdowell carved an animated figure for the south transept, depicting the rapt artist confronting the spectacle of the heavens as he gazes out of the east-facing window (Fig. 232). No other memorial had achieved such a satisfying relationship with the fabric of the cathedral itself. The first architect to be remembered upstairs (other than Wren) was C. R. Cockerell (d. 1863), Surveyor to the Fabric as well as the cleverest neoclassicist of his generation. His memorial consisted of a profile portrait, suspended from an Ionic column of his beloved Bassae order, and surrounded by slightly too much Romano-Christian embellishment for its own good. Its designer is unknown; F. C. Penrose, his successor as surveyor, may well have had a hand in it.

If the great commemorative development of the eighteenth century had been the admission of memorials within the body of the church, that of the nineteenth was the introduction of monuments within the crypt. Nelson's arrival beneath Wolsey's abandoned sarcophagus in the crypt in 1806 ushered in a new era. His tomb became an object of pilgrimage, best depicted in Millais' now-lost painting *Pilgrims to St Paul's* (Fig. 233) which showed two veteran Greenwich pensioners paying homage to the great admiral.[62] A letter of November 1852 to the *Illustrated London News* expressed dismay at the state of the crypt:

> On frequent occasions, when visiting the tomb of Nelson, I have been pained by the forlorn, dismal, and dirty aspect of the whole scene...[which] has exhibited a striking contrast to the well-kept, clean, and tasteful appearance of the Panthéon at Paris...I trust that...[it] may be made more what a national mausoleum should be, and more worthy of the sepulture of England's noblest sons.[63]

No longer could the cathedral muddle along: it now had to shoulder the responsibilities of a 'national mausoleum'. The arrival of Wellington's remains in 1852 made action imperative.

The saga of the monument to the Iron Duke took decades to play out. His remains had arrived amid splendour (see p. 384; Figs

284

234 (*right*). Granite sarcophagus of the Duke of Wellington, as completed to F. C. Penrose's design, 1858

235 (*below right*). The Duke of Wellington's coffin suspended on chains above Nelson's sarcophagus. After the state funeral in 1852, Wellington's remains found a precarious temporary home while more fitting quarters were prepared. (SPCL)

316–18), only to be left hanging literally in mid air (Fig. 235). But the matter of a fitting receptacle could not wait. Penrose designed a temporary sarcophagus of granite and marble, while work on the 'Wellington Chamber' in the crypt got under way. The earlier tomb shared the same severe characteristics as its permanent successor. The former was described in 1854 as 'very good. The massive forms of the memorial harmonising well with the deep gloom and solid properties of the crypt, which is a place well worthy of a visit. The extent seems wondrous; in parts the darkness is seemingly deepened by the gas-lights, which dimly illuminate up the tombs of the warriors.'[64] This gas-lighting was an innovation;[65] the present-day electric lighting that has replaced it has eliminated the atmosphere of respectful awe that formerly characterized a visit to this most solemn part of the church.

Wellington's permanent sarcophagus (Fig. 234) was of pink Cornish porphyry, which reputedly took two years to scoop out by hand. It rested on a base of grey Cornish granite, with sentinel lions at each corner. His body was finally translated on 15 April 1858: at last, 'the dust of England's greatest general reposes at length in a not unworthy mausoleum'.[66] Dean Milman was highly complimentary: it was 'in perfect character with the great man . . . in its grave splendour, and . . . time-defying solidity, emblematic of him who, unlike most great men, the more he is revealed to posterity, shows more substantial, unboastful, unquestionable greatness'.[67] Penrose designed the surrounding chamber to extend this mood of martial power: the granite skirting answered the monument's base, while the heraldic mosaic floor (worked by female felons at Woking) now joined with that around the Nelson tomb to form a ceremonial heart to the crypt. Four granite gas-lit candelabra stood as sentinels. Soon after, in 1859, the body of Wellington's fellow-commander, Sir Thomas Picton, came to join him in the crypt, having been claimed from a closed-down burial ground in Bayswater Road.[68] Picton's monument already stood in the north transept, so this was a rare case of a memorial preceding its associated burial.

In the meantime, Britain's army had once again become involved in a European war. Three of the ensuing monuments to casualties of the Crimean War were by Marochetti, the most successful sculptor of the 1850s. That to Major General Sir Arthur Wellesley Torrens, 'mortally wounded at the battle of Inkermann', was a spirited tableau in the established 'Peninsular School' style, full of martial detail, showing a triumphant charge of the Guards with Torrens at their head. The second memorial, to the Cavalry Division, was a closely studied relief of diverse uniforms, like a cigarette card rendered in marble.[69] It showed that a change had affected military memorials. No longer was it only the most senior casualties who warranted remembrance: entire regiments, including lesser ranks, now gained monuments. Not only stirring deeds, but participation in campaigns, were commemorated. More unusual still was the third of Marochetti's monuments, to the officers of the Coldstream Guards killed at Inkermann.[70] The

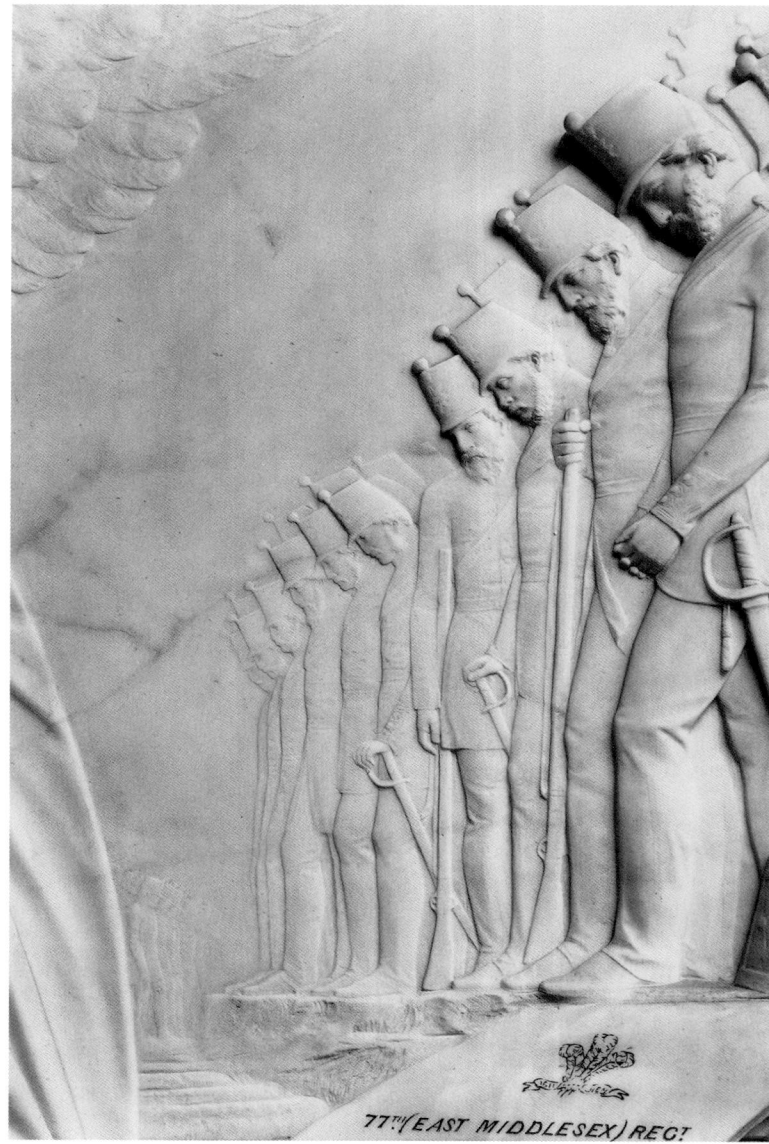

236. Detail of Crimean War memorial to the 77th (East Middlesex) Regiment, by Matthew Noble, after 1856. (SPCL)

237. Wall monument to Edwin Landseer, by Thomas Woolner, 1882. Landseer's best-known painting, *The Old Shepherd's Chief Mourner*, is depicted in relief. (SPCL)

relief shows a monument on the field of battle, with the names of the fallen just legible; these names are repeated in larger letters below. It was an effective way of showing the sheer distance that separated the battlefield from Britain. This theme of the pathos of distant death was taken up by Matthew Noble's relief to the '15 officers and 542 Non Commissioned Officers Drummers and Privates sustained by the 77th Regiment during the Crimean Campaign 1854 1856' (Fig. 236). It showed long lines of soldiers standing before a long mass grave, in which coffins await their final covering of earth. Few, if any, would ever see these men's actual graves, and such cenotaph-memorials thus played an important role in providing a focus for grief. The Crimean War was the first conflict to generate public war memorials as we know them today.

The democratization of remembrance was underscored by the creation of a regimental chapel in the north transept in the mid 1870s, dedicated to the 77th 'East Middlesex' Regiment.[71] This marked the arrival of a local, London-based flavour to monuments in St Paul's, which had hitherto been a national pantheon. The Cardwell Reforms of 1872 ushered in permanently located regimental depots: these fostered a spirit of local pride, and cathedrals across the country, including St Paul's, began to acquire

regimental shrines. Another monument to show the increased respect accorded to deceased lower ranks was the pair of brasses in the north nave aisle, erected in 1876 in memory of the 300-odd men drowned on board the ironclad HMS *Captain* in 1870: all are named, irrespective of commissioned rank. This would have been unthinkable half a century earlier.

Developments were afoot down in the crypt. Much of it had previously been out of bounds. The ending of the annual charity children's service in 1877[72] meant that the huge heaps of timber used for temporary stands no longer had to be stored, freeing up much space: this resulted in the opening up of the east end, through the formation of St Faith's chapel. In 1878 the west end of the crypt was cleared also, having hitherto 'always been used as a complete lumber place'.[73] The way was now clear for the arrival

238. Wellington monument, by Alfred Stevens, 1857–78, with crowning equestrian figure by John Tweed. Though first intended for its present position in the north nave arcade, the monument was initially assembled in the former Consistory Court chapel on the south side of the nave. It was removed to its rightful position in 1894, after which Tweed in 1912 added the equestrian figure on the basis of Stevens's model

239. Detail of the Wellington monument. Bronze sarcophagus and recumbent effigy by Alfred Stevens. (SPCL)

240. 'Oriental homage to a great British warrior', by A. Forestier: Indian troops in 1902 before the tomb of General Charles Gordon, by Joseph Boehm, 1885. (GL)

241. Brass memorial to Special Correspondents who died in the Sudan, by Herbert Johnson, 1887. (SPCL)

of scores of monuments down below. 'Painters' Corner', the area around Wren's grave, was spruced up in the early 1870s,[74] prompted by the burial of Sir Edwin Landseer, the royal favourite and animal artist supreme, laid to rest here in 1873. The very lions in Trafalgar Square had wreaths placed in their mouths as their modeller's cortège passed by.[75] He received a fine memorial by Thomas Woolner in 1882 which combined a leonine profile portrait with a relief after his masterpiece, *The Old Shepherd's Chief Mourner* (Fig. 237). After Landseer, crypt monuments arrived thick and fast.[76] These included some of the finest ledger slabs ever designed: J. E. Boehm (d. 1890) has a Gothic Revival brass, with depictions of the sculptor at work; Sir John Everett Millais (d. 1896) lies beneath a Renaissance-inspired slab designed by R. Norman Shaw, befitting his stature as a painter-prince, while Sir Arthur Sullivan (d. 1900) rests beneath a sumptuous Grecian ledger of beaten bronze.

Upstairs, monumental matters were progressing less smoothly. The greatest headache for the cathedral authorities was the protracted affair of the Wellington monument. This was the last of the national, publicly funded monuments to enter St Paul's. So complex is the story, it has a monograph devoted to it;[77] only a précis can be given here. Expectations surrounding the nation's memorial to the Iron Duke were of the highest order. Some 250,000 persons, or five per cent of the population, watched the funeral procession. Fifty-thousand people later filed past Gottfried Semper's funeral carriage when it was on show in Marlborough House, before it came to St Paul's, where it remained on view in

242.   Monument to the poet and editor W. E. Henley, by Auguste Rodin, 1907.
Henley had been an early champion of Rodin's: in return, the sculptor recast his
bronze portrait bust of 1886 for the memorial and designed the surround. (SPCL)

the crypt (Fig. 318) until its removal to the ducal seat of Stratfield Saye, Hants in 1981.[78] In 1857 a public competition for the design of a Wellington monument was held, organized by the office of works; the first verdict was set aside, and the fourth-placed Alfred Stevens eventually secured the commission with a towering Renaissance variation of the triumphal arch. Stevens then spent the years 1858 to 1870 making preliminary models and greatly exceeding both budgets and deadlines. He died in 1875, broken by the project.

The monument was eventually crammed into the former Consistory Court Chapel in the south-west of the cathedral in 1878; this was not Stevens's intended location, and the monument lacked its crowning equestrian statue. Lord Leighton took up the matter and led a campaign to have it completed and repositioned in the nave. It found its present position (Fig. 238) in 1894; in 1912 the equestrian statue, modelled by John Tweed after Stevens's designs, was eventually placed on top. By then, some sixty years had passed since the death of the duke, whose unmistakable profile reclines at peace within the troubled elements of the vast monument (Fig. 239). By way of comparison, it took twenty years

for Napoleon's translated remains to reach their final resting place in Les Invalides, as designed by Visconti, in 1861.[79] Wellington was, at best, indifferent to commemoration[80] and it is fair to say that his colossal sarcophagus is more in keeping with his character than Stevens's intense and allegorically laden pile. Nevertheless, the monument has a real claim to being 'the finest work of sculpture produced in this country during the 19th century'.[81]

Most monuments were erected with less ado. Gordon of Khartoum's monument, by Sir Joseph Edgar Boehm, was erected in its prominent place on the north side of the nave in 1885 (Fig. 240).[82] The recumbent bronze effigy, of quattrocento inspiration, depicted the Christian warrior at peace, the sumptuous cushion which supports his head contrasting with the coarse army-issue blanket beneath. Its calm is in stark contrast to his gory end, with which all onlookers would have been familiar. The subsidiary relief below is labelled 'in the school at Khartoum', and shows the gentler side of Gordon, instructing Sudanese youths (rather in the manner of the relief on the monument to Sir Henry Lawrence (d. 1857) in the south aisle, which depicts him giving succour to young innocents besieged within Lucknow during the Indian

243 (*far eft*). Monument in cast aluminium to the artist and children's book illustrator Randolph Caldecott, by Alfred Gilbert, completed in 1900. (SPCL)

244 (*left*). Statue to Bishop Mandell Creighton, by Hamo Thornycroft, 1905. This finest of episcopal monuments in the cathedral expresses Creighton's high churchmanship through Renaissance allusions. (SPCL)

245 (*right*). Recumbent effigy of Earl Kitchener and guardian figure of St Michael from the Chapel of All Souls, by William Reid Dick, within architectural setting by Mervyn Macartney, 1922–5. (SPCL)

Mutiny). Gordon was a martyr for the cause of Empire: his death unleashed an outpouring of public grief,[83] which was reflected in the memorial's prominent position: before the arrival of the Leighton and Wellington monuments, it would have stood in even more splendid isolation. It captured the mood of romantic imperialism of its day. 'Admirers of this Christian hero constantly bring fresh flowers, which the attendants remove when withered', remarked a guidebook of 1900.[84]

The same mood of colonial exertion is sensed in a number of late-Victorian monuments in the crypt. Foremost among them is the high-relief brass, erected in 1887, to other casualties of the Sudan Campaign: the seven special (or war) correspondents, headed by St Leger Algernon Hubert. Designed by Herbert Johnson, it showed a valiant reporter taking notes at the front line (Fig. 241); below, Clio and Britannia flank a poignant relief of a row of fresh graves, beside a parched camel skeleton. Journalism and publishing were trades close to St Paul's, both literally and historically: this monument effectively marked the arrival of memorials to men of commerce, albeit in an imperialistic and martial guise.

Men of empire form by far the largest group of persons commemorated within St Paul's. Which groups are under-represented? Ethnic minorities only appear in supporting roles. Surprisingly, perhaps, lord mayors and City dignitaries are thin on the ground, too. Women, in allegorical form, are plentiful: they are far scarcer as recipients of monuments. Of the eight monuments in the crypt to women, five are associated with the Wren family, or are of late Stuart date. The remaining three all commemorate philanthropists: Maria Hackett (d. 1874, erected in 1877), the 'choirboys' champion';[85] Maria Fussell (d. 1881, erected in 1902),

the notable donor of £111,000 with which thirty-two new parishes were created in the diocese of London; and Florence Nightingale (d. 1910), whose relief by A. G. Walker, showing the Lady of the Lamp, provides a welcome depiction of nurturing and compassion amid the legion tributes to high achievers, be they military, clerical or political. Other badly represented groups are writers, radicals, scientists, financiers and industrialists, doctors and lawyers. Only in more recent times have efforts been made to be more inclusive, and to fill gaps. Thus John Wyclif, 'Morning star of the Reformation', received his memorial 501 years after his death in 1384.

Those groups that were better represented were often clustered together, after the manner of 'Painters' Corner'. Nelson's coffin was flanked by Collingwood and Northesk, his subordinates at Trafalgar; in due course, twentieth-century naval commanders would congregate here, too. Colonial administrators gathered to the south-west of Nelson, while antipodean politicians clustered to his north-west. Reporters are grouped to the south of the painters, while clerics concentrate on the south side of the Chapel of the Order of the British Empire. Cathedral organists lie together on the north side, close to a group of recent tablets to deceased deans. Thus do zones of remembrance emerge out of the dense throng of monuments.

As the crypt filled up, memorials had to vie for attention. Some opted for size: none surpasses the vast Renaissance Revival concoction commemorating the colonial administrator Sir Bartle Frere (d. 1884), which took its cue from the Mason monument of 1566 in Old St Paul's.[86] Others opted for artistic excellence. Within this category comes Thomas Brock's memorial to Frederic, Lord Leighton (d. 1896), installed in the nave in 1902,

where the painter cuts a lonely figure among the warriors. Not only was this the last major tomb to be placed in the nave, it was also 'perhaps the most poignant of the New Sculpture's funerary monuments'.[87] Marble busts had proliferated, but the bronze bust by Auguste Rodin to the poet, editor and critic W. E. Henley (d. 1903), unveiled in 1907 within a frame also designed by Rodin, continues to stand out (Fig. 242).[88] So, too, does Alfred Gilbert's memorial to the illustrator Randolph Caldecott (d. 1886). Begun in 1887, but only unveiled in 1900, it comprised a painted aluminium figure of a child[89] clasping a portrait medallion (Fig. 243). It is one of the tenderest memorials in the cathedral, as befits 'an artist whose sweet and dainty grace, has not been in its kind, surpassed'. Gilbert himself received a memorial here, depicting Eros, after his death in 1934. Another great artist, John Singer Sargent (d. 1925), is remembered by a cast of his own sculpture of the Crucifixion, given by his sisters and erected by the Royal Academy. Its setting is cramped, and its lighting unflattering: but in terms of religious impact its effect is profound.

The close of the nineteenth century witnessed the flourishing of monuments to bishops. Senior churchmen had received prominent memorials in increasing numbers from the mid century onwards, and it became almost an acknowledged right for deans to receive monuments, from Dean Milman (d. 1868) onwards. Hamo Thornycroft's remarkable standing bronze figure in the south choir aisle to Bishop Mandell Creighton (d. 1901) depicted him as a Renaissance ascetic, smothered in Romish gorgeousness (Fig. 244): the sheer act of wearing a cope was a provocation at this time, so this was a bold conception indeed.[90] Creighton had succeeded Frederick Temple (d. 1902) on the latter's translation to Canterbury. He, too, gained a memorial at St Paul's: an intense

bronze relief by F. W. Pomeroy, installed in 1906, repeats the Creighton formula of showing a deeply cerebral head, offset against magnificent vestments. These elements provided fine opportunities for sculptors. The Temple relief was a variant of the same sculptor's kneeling effigy to Temple at Canterbury.

One of the most curious monuments in all St Paul's is Princess Louise's 1904 Boer War memorial to colonial troops in the south transept. This consists of an elaborate tablet beneath the figure of Christ being lifted from the cross by an angel with dramatically outstretched wings. Princess Louise, Victoria's youngest daughter, was a sculptor of no little ability: this is surely her masterpiece, as well as an example of virtuoso bronze casting, which used its slender site cleverly.

By this time, architects as well as the dean and chapter were growing increasingly uneasy about the sheer quantity of memorials inside St Paul's. Somers Clarke, Surveyor to the Fabric, led the charge. 'It is generally admitted', he wrote in *c*.1902, 'that S. Paul's Cathedral contains as deplorable a collection of monuments as can be found in any great church in Christendom. Whilst their historical interest is great, especially to all English speaking people as works of art they are for the most part contemptible.'[91] Such haughty contempt struck home. Late in 1913, *The Builder* discovered that the dean and chapter were trying to impose a ban on future monuments inside the main body of the cathedral: the journal begged to differ, observing that 'in the case of a building so intimately connected with the history of the country as is St Paul's a continuous series of monuments is a great factor in giving it historic interest and value'.[92] The debate continues to this day.

The last great monument to arrive inside the cathedral was that of Field Marshal Earl Kitchener, who drowned off the Orkneys on board HMS *Hampshire* in June 1916. The only British field marshal ever to die on active service, his death struck a sombre note.[93] A memorial fund raised £250,000: utilitarian imperatives set up scholarships and a medical school at Khartoum, but £30,000 was spent on what became the Chapel of All Souls, in the north-west corner of the interior. Kitchener's recumbent effigy (Fig. 245) made the reputation of its sculptor, William Reid Dick. One of the last of such figures, it depicted a Christian warrior, immaculately booted and spurred, basking in a shaft of uplifting light. The chapel, designed by Mervyn Macartney, became a memorial to all casualties of the Great War, and forms a counterpart to the Tomb of the Unknown Warrior in Westminster Abbey. There lies a body with no name: here rests a great name but no body, for Kitchener's remains were never recovered.[94] Seldom has an effigy captured the stillness of death so tellingly.

St Paul's is a world-war Valhalla, as well as a Napoleonic and imperial one. The memorials to other senior commanders are inevitably humbler than Kitchener's personal chapel, and the reticence and austerity of these modern military memorials are immediately sensed. Proportions, lettering and subtleties of effect came to take on the roles formerly played by size, symbolism, sculptural display and lavish materials. Partly this was a practical matter: space was at a premium, and *grandes machines* like the Bartle Frere ensemble could simply no longer be housed. Partly, also, it was a deliberate choice: living memory, not lapidary memorials, would ensure remembrance. Admirals of the Fleet Earls Jellicoe and Beatty (d. 1935 and 1936) lie alongside each other to the south-east of Nelson. Rivals in life, in death they vie for attention yet: the former's is larger and higher, the latter's more opulent and in front. Beatty's was designed by Lutyens, and the

246.   Wall tablet to Ivor Novello, by John Skelton, unveiled in 1971. (SPCL)

247.   Richard Kindersley lettering the memorial to London victims of the Blitz, unveiled outside the north transept in 1999. The inscription is a quotation from Winston Churchill

following description of this apparently plain affair reveals the infinite subtleties that today tend to go unnoticed:

> Once more, a supreme effect of dignity is achieved by the minimum of means. The proportion of the triangular shape is, of course, faultless. But one is most impressed by the thinness of its edge, almost like that of bronze; by the very flat angle in section of its outer frame; by the slight camber given to the whole surface; by the grand simplicity of the inscription; and, perhaps above all, by the bold raising of the carved coronet, finely executed through months of work in this hard and intractable material.[95]

Another military memorial that repays examination, but for historical reasons, is the neo-Georgian tablet by Sir Albert Richardson to Pilot Officer Billy Fiske (d. 1940). The first American pilot to die in the Allied cause in the Second World War, Fiske was a well-connected financier-playboy. Within a fortnight of his death in action, outline approval had been granted for the erection of a monument in St Paul's. This was unveiled by the Secretary of State for Air, Sir Archibald Sinclair, on 4 July 1941, less than a year later.[96] The plain, dignified tablet was accompanied by a small framed panel beneath, displaying Fiske's frayed pilot's wings. Still poignant, the understated memorial is remarkable on several accounts. It is the only monument in a national church to an individual pilot, and far and away the most prominent memorial to an individual Battle of Britain pilot; its prompt unveiling indicates the political seriousness with which the occasion was regarded. As such, it can be interpreted as a dress-rehearsal for the post-war American Chapel, an alliance-cementing tribute to transatlantic bravery and sacrifice. The modesty of the memorial is greatly outweighed by its historical implications, especially given the place of the Blitz in the modern perception of St Paul's. Recently, in 1999, an outdoor monument was erected outside the north transept to the 32,000 victims of the London Blitz, underscoring this association (Fig. 247).[97] It is

just one example from the growing number of retrospective memorials to past campaigns erected in recent times. The present desire to thwart oblivion by remembering the deserving and the overlooked has led to the erection of modern memorials to the Gallipoli campaign, the tragic 1915–16 siege of Kut-el-Amara, to Polish RAF airmen, the Murmansk convoys and the Korean War.

The recent history of memorials in St Paul's has been dominated by the erection of modest tablets of native English stone, embellished with fine lettering in the tradition of Eric Gill. Such are the tablets of 1979 which surround the Wellington sarcophagus and commemorate field marshals of the Second World War. Here, the names themselves – Slim, Montgomery, Alexander *et al.* – form the principal elements of the design. Three of these tablets were the work of Gill's nephew, John Skelton.[98] Another of Skelton's works in the crypt, different in look and recipient (Fig. 246), is the tablet to Ivor Novello (d. 1951). The outstanding actor and songwriter, now best remembered for his wartime songs 'Keep the Home Fires Burning' and 'We'll Gather Lilacs', might seem an unlikely candidate for admission into the Valhalla that is the crypt of St Paul's. The composer's epitaph is among the most lyrical of recent inscriptions: 'Blaze of lights and music calling, Music weeping, rising, falling, Like a rare and precious diamond, His brilliance still lives on'.[99]

St Paul's was conceived as a church, yet the presence of scores of outstanding monuments makes it something else besides. It has become a pantheon, and a crowded one at that: visitors become pilgrims amid its myriad tributes to the good, the great, the imperial and the brave. The 1985 Falklands Memorial in the crypt, by Richard Kindersley, is among the most recent arrivals but it reveals an important truth about the monuments of St Paul's. Under the name of Col. 'H' Jones VC, repeated underscoring by fingers has produced an unintended patina of honour. In St Paul's, people not only come to worship and to admire; they come to remember as well.

25

CONSERVATION OF THE FABRIC

Martin Stancliffe

All buildings change as they grow old, and St Paul's is no exception. Whatever the completeness of Wren's conception (and that changed markedly as the construction progressed), and whatever its state of completion at the time when he stood back from it (and it was clearly far from complete), there came a time when the original construction of the cathedral could be said to be over. Since that time, St Paul's has received remarkable continuity of care at the hands of a sequence of individual Surveyors to the Fabric, men who have been entrusted with the care of the fabric of the building from Wren's death to the present day. Their interests have intertwined with the needs of the varied life and use of the cathedral, the demands of its own ageing processes and the changing pressures of the world around it.

In the three hundred or so years of its life (a relatively short period for the life-expectation of a building constructed to such high standards), a number of issues have been a continuing source of concern: the structural stability of the building and its settlement; its adaptability to the changing demands of its use; the perceived need to 'complete' what Wren was felt to have left incomplete; and its stature as a symbolic building within London and the nation. Running in parallel with these greater issues are others, less important in themselves but recurrent over the generations: concern about the risk of fire; the need to keep the fabric weather-tight; its lighting, heating and security; its cleanliness; and, increasingly, its erosion by atmospheric pollution and by wear and tear resulting from its use. All of these introduce changes to the building, some more marked than others. This essay follows these changes as they intersect with the continuity of care required of successive Surveyors to the Fabric and with their own interests and expertise, as they have responded to the evolving needs of the building.

On Wednesday 20 September 1710, Wren attended the commission for the rebuilding of the cathedral, effectively for the last time. He had reported regularly to this body for some thirty-five years, hardly missing a single meeting. From that day on, apart from two courtesy appearances before the committee in 1715, his involvement came to an end, and the cathedral could be pronounced complete, allowing Wren to claim his final fee. From 1711, the day-to-day control of the work passed to John James, first as master carpenter and then as assistant surveyor.[1]

Although the initial construction work might be largely complete, the need for vigilant care to the cathedral had already made itself known. As early as 1689, structural movement had caused spalling in the stonework of the central piers, necessitating raking out and repointing of joints to avoid further damage. The problem of the unequal loading of the stonework as a result of the enormous imposed weight of the dome also continued to manifest itself. In order to rectify this, a great deal of stonework had already been replaced between 1690 and 1710. Looking back in 1715, the mason Edward Strong described the problem, recording that he had 'repaired all the blemishes and fractures in the several legs and arches of the dome, occasioned by the great weight of the said dome pressing upon the foundation; the earth under the same being of an unequal temper'.[2]

Wren, as an experienced architect, was well aware of the need for maintenance. Indeed, he discussed with the commissioners the necessity of providing a fund for this purpose; and as the completion of the building works approached they made representation that:

> to prevent the Church from coming again into the like ruinous
> Condition it was in before the Fire; and that so magnificent

248. *A suppliant before a divine*, by Nathaniel Dance-Holland. This is believed to represent Robert Mylne, surveyor to the fabric, begging Archbishop Secker for funds for repairing the cathedral shortly after his appointment in 1766. (Tate Gallery)

Flitcroft and told him that, in the light of the falling value of the fund, the trustees were minded to combine the roles of surveyor and clerk of the works, as 'clerk of the fabric' at a reduced salary. This produced an expostulation in the form of a 'Humble Memorial' from Flitcroft, in which he expressed

> his Duty humbly to Represent to your Lordships whether the Care of this Great and Noble Fabrick, which has hitherto been under the Inspection of an Able and Experienced Surveyor, ought not still to Continue so, in order to Represent to the Dean from time to time the State of the Building and to Direct the Works that are Necessary to be done, for the Security and Preservation thereof, and to Examine and Certifie the Value of the Works, when done.[5]

The trustees appear to have been persuaded by this argument, and in response reviewed the way in which the fabric fund was being used. Finding that it was being used to pay for a wide miscellany of everyday expenses, they determined that the fund would no longer accept responsibility for anything except the proper maintenance of the fabric. As trustees, they also determined to appoint 'one skilful architect to take care of the building who shall be called the Surveyor of the Fabric'. He was 'in person' to 'carefully survey the whole of it once every half year',[6] thus securing the continuity of care which extends to this day.

Information on work carried out to the fabric during the middle years of the eighteenth century is scanty, as befits the general condition of a building constructed to the highest standards and only recently completed. However, spasmodic reports indicate continuing trouble resulting from the settlement of the dome. The choice of Robert Mylne in 1766 to follow Stiff Leadbetter (who had succeeded Flitcroft as surveyor in 1756) may indicate an understanding on the part of the Trustees of what might be required (Fig. 248). Unlike James, Leadbetter and Flitcroft, all carpenters by trade, Mylne was from a family of masons; and this background perhaps better equipped him to analyse the structural condition of the cathedral. Mylne was an active and effective surveyor with a good grasp of structural issues: indeed, he was by outlook as much an engineer as an architect (his winning competition designs for Blackfriars Bridge had first brought him into prominence, and he was a leading member of the Society of Civil Engineers).[7]

Even before Mylne's appointment, some work was being done in the south transept; but in 1781 Mylne presented a report which drew attention to a 'business...of a serious nature...which for some years past has been observed by me with some degree of anxiety'. This report analyses the settlement of the dome and its effect on the surrounding structure, and proposes the insertion of 'Chain-bars to tye the Piers of the cupola and the South front wall together in a most effectual manner'.[8] This work necessitated the closure of the cathedral for nearly two years, and was reported complete in November 1782.

Mylne's long surveyorship spanned some forty-five years and ended only with his death. During this time, he replaced a good deal of external Burford stone with Portland; installed a complete lightning protection system (with advice from Benjamin Franklin among others); superintended the sprucing up and fitting out of the cathedral both for the major service for George III's recovery (see pp. 366–8) and for Nelson's funeral (p. 382) (recommending the use of the Rovezzano sarcophagus for his tomb and designing the pedestal to it); and he designed a new choir pulpit (the remains of which are still preserved in the triforium). Mylne

a Building may be preserv'd in truly good Repair; the Commissioners have all along hop'd that when the Building should be finish'd if the Mony given would allow it, a certain Sum should be laid aside for the Repairs of it: It being evident that the want of a sufficient Fund was the cause of the great Decay of the old Church; and in the Opinion of Sir Christopher, a much greater Expense would be necessary to keep the new Church in due Repairs, than did the old one.[3]

A fund was duly established, under the trusteeship of the archbishop of Canterbury, the bishop of London and the lord mayor of London.

On the death of Wren in 1723, James was appointed surveyor – a natural step, as there was still work to be done before the cathedral could be considered finished, for it was not until 1726, with the installation of Francis Bird's font, that the cathedral could really be pronounced complete. At the same time, even then there was the necessity for repair works, and James doubtless continued to be involved in this routine work. The desirability of having someone at hand who intimately understood the needs of the fabric meant that his services were retained during his lifetime.

James died in 1746 at the age of seventy-two, and Henry Flitcroft was appointed 'by a verbal order of the dean'[4] to succeed him. Like James, Flitcroft had started life as a carpenter, and the practical experience which this gave him doubtless recommended him to the cathedral authorities. However, when Thomas Secker was appointed dean in 1750, he found that he needed to review the whole issue of the funding of repairs. Secker sent for

249.   *A tribute to the memory of Sir Christopher Wren*, by C. R. Cockerell, surveyor to the fabric 1819–52, exhibited at the Royal Academy, 1838, and afterwards engraved for publication. All the buildings then attributed to Wren are gathered together by Cockerell before a dominant St Paul's. (Private collection)

appears to have had strong professional principles, and followed them, however unpopular this made him. Indeed, his determination to ensure that the cathedral obtained value for money nearly cost him his job when he attempted to ensure that a contract was given to the lowest bidder in the face of opposition from the dean and chapter who wanted to employ a contractor of their own choice who demanded a higher rate.[9] This accords with a contemporary description of him as 'a rare jintleman, but as hot as pepper and as proud as Lucifer'.[10] He also felt, like other surveyors since, a strong affinity with Wren, designing the monument to him in the crypt (until then, there had been no memorial to Wren in the cathedral other than his inscribed ledger slab) and requesting that he should be buried near him.

Mylne died in 1811, and with the appointment of Samuel Pepys Cockerell to succeed him, the care of the cathedral fabric moved on to a new phase. Cockerell was not only an experienced architect, but also uncle by marriage to William Howley, bishop of London (1813–28) and archbishop of Canterbury (1828–48). As he was already surveyor to both the Canterbury and London dioceses (whose respective prelates were both trustees of the St Paul's fabric fund), Cockerell's appointment was perhaps a natural one.[11]

During this time, the general maintenance of the cathedral continued: by 1815 the north-west tower was repaired, the lead roof to the nave substantially recast and relaid, and the peristyle and other windows were re-leaded. The post must have seemed worthwhile for S. P. Cockerell, as his son Charles Robert urged him to retain the surveyorship while relinquishing most other extraneous business.[12] Doubtless he hoped that he might follow his father; and this ambition bore fruit in 1819 when Charles was indeed appointed surveyor in his father's stead. His appointment brought a rather different kind of person to the surveyorship. Charles was then only thirty-one, and had returned a mere two years previously from his Grand Tour, during which time he had expressed to his father a reluctance to follow him as an architect ('you know that I am nothing but an artist and shall never be anything else'[13]). He was still only at the outset of his architectural career, and with limited practical experience. However, the warm support of his father, his family connections and a glowing recommendation from Robert Smirke were enough to secure him the surveyorship.[14] In this it is possible that an appreciation of his artistic skills may have been an additional recommendation. In particular, the growing introduction of monuments called for a discerning eye – a new facet of the surveyorship.[15] The younger

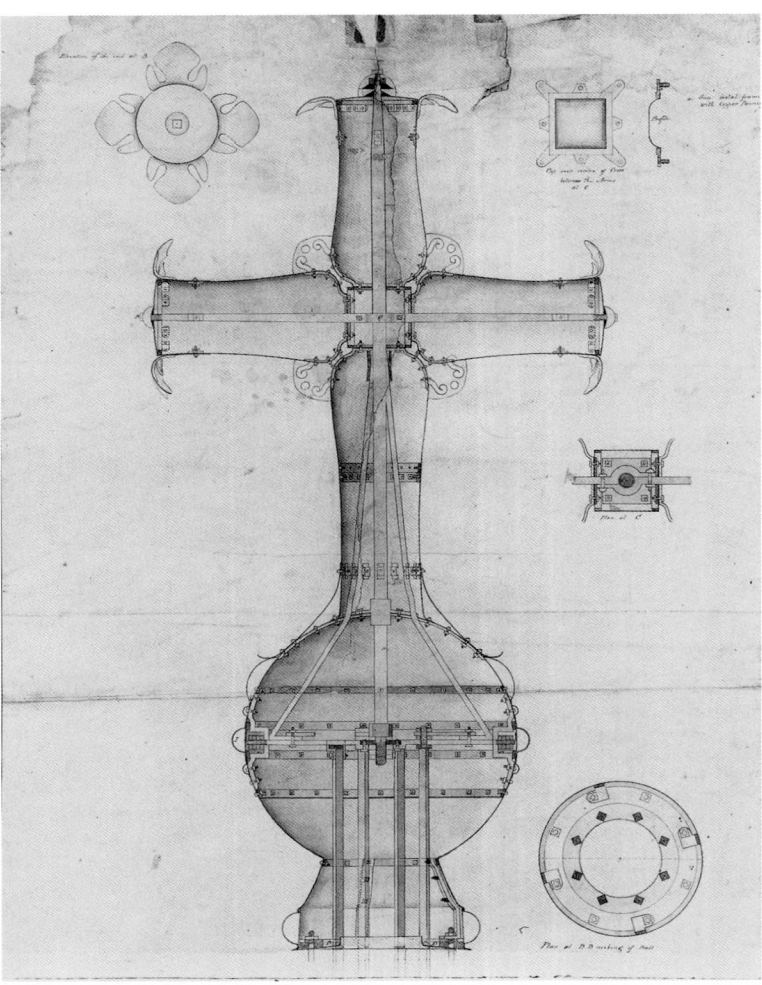

250. Drawing by C. R. Cockerell for restoring the ball and cross surmounting the cupola over the dome, *c.* 1821–2. (GL, St Paul's collection)

Cockerell became an enthusiast for Wren at a time when praise from others was often lukewarm. He gave pride of place to the cathedral in his fine painting *A tribute to the memory of Sir Christopher Wren* (1838; Fig. 249), and in his lectures as professor of architecture at the Royal Academy paid homage to the recognition of Wren's genius and example as expressed in St Paul's.[16]

The new surveyor threw himself into the practical work of the cathedral. The building, now more than one hundred years old, was beginning to need rather more attention. In his report of 5 April 1821, Cockerell expressed concern at a range of issues. He referred to the differential settlement of the dome (still clearly a matter of concern), to the problem of stone spalling as rusting iron cramps expanded, to the surface erosion of the Portland stone, and to the decay of exposed ironwork. The iron framework to the ball and cross surmounting the dome was in need of replacement, and Cockerell's fine drawing reveals the care he took to ensure the work was carried out properly (Fig. 250). The work was executed in 1821–2, along with other tasks which included redecoration of the interior, the introduction of heating stoves and, for the first time, gas-lighting in the choir. At the same time, he addressed the matter of funding for these works, and set out in a letter to the Archbishop of Canterbury the history of the fabric fund from 1737,[17] a document which shows the increasing complexity of the role of the surveyor.

Until this time, it seems that the surveyor, responsible as he was to the trustees rather than to the dean and chapter, had a fairly free hand around the building. The appointment of Sydney Smith

as a canon of St Paul's in 1831 must have come as something of a shock. Despite Smith's age (he was sixty at the time of his appointment), this forbidding character still had a great deal of energy. He immediately seems to have thrown himself into the detail of the maintenance of the cathedral, and on to a collision course with its surveyor. He was not initially an easy person to get on with: as Cockerell recorded, 'his early communications ... were extremely unpleasant; but when satisfied by his methods of investigation, and by a "little collision", as he termed it, that all was honest and right, nothing could be more candid or kind than his subsequent treatment'. His attention to detail was minute; and he seems even to have accompanied Cockerell on his twice-yearly inspections: 'nothing daunted him; and once, when I suggested a fear that his portly person might stick fast in a narrow opening of the western towers, which we were surveying, he reassured me by declaring that "if there were six inches of space, there would be room enough for him"'.[18]

The cathedral owed much to Sydney Smith at this time. Many were the issues which he sought to address: in particular, the fear of fire. The threat of fire has confronted every surveyor from Wren to the present day. The loss of Old St Paul's by fire was, of course, the reason why Wren's new cathedral was needed in the first place. Wren himself had made provision for fire engines, and the 1753 review of the fabric fund had included a decision 'that the old Fire Engine be repaired or a new one bought at the Expence of this Fund'.[19] Smith went further: 'he advised the introduction of the mains of the New River into the lower parts of the fabric, and cisterns and movable engines in the roof; and quite justifiable was his joke, "that he would reproduce the Deluge in our cathedral"'.[20] This might well have been prescient, as Archdeacon Hale a few years later was driven to having carts filled with glowing coals dragged through the church in winter to counter the bitter cold.

Like an undertone, the concern for the settlement of the fabric continued. In 1831 a proposal was put forward to drive a sewer close to the south side of the cathedral. Cockerell brought in Smirke and his own brother-in-law, the engineer Sir John Rennie, who agreed that the proposal represented a potential threat to the stability of the fabric, and managed to get the route diverted. In 1842 he again brought in Smirke, this time to provide a second opinion in surveying the structural cracking in the north-east pier of the dome; and his reports around 1850 continue to record cracking and flushing of stone. But in his last report of March 1852 he records: 'it is gratifying to be able to state that no new symptoms of settlement can be traced, nor further crushes in the supports of the cupola, or any other parts of the fabric'.[21]

Here at mid century there is a decisive change. Dean Milman, appointed in 1849, found within two years that a new surveyor was needed to replace Cockerell, whose health had failed and who had already retired from other architectural practice. In any case, after thirty-three years the energetic new dean doubtless wanted a fresh architect. Milman had clear ideas about what he wanted, and in Francis Cranmer Penrose he found a fellow enthusiast. Penrose at the age of thirty-four was at a similar stage to Cockerell when he had been appointed: he had not long returned from an extended European tour, during which, like Cockerell, he had become fascinated by the details of Athenian architecture. Also like Cockerell, Penrose had a great admiration for Wren, and indeed dedicated the heart of his professional career to 'completing' Wren's creation. In this he was to be severely disappointed; but the first twenty years of his surveyorship were intensely busy as he worked with Milman to try to solve the huge problem presented by the dirty, indeed squalid, interior and to fit the cathedral as a whole for increasingly more substantial usage.

Penrose was to be surveyor for forty-five years, equalling Mylne and almost rivalling Wren's own length of involvement with the building (Fig. 251). The issue of structural settlement was pushed into second place by the need to address what was widely felt to be the deeply unsatisfactory nature of the interior. Nevertheless, within his first year Penrose was filling cracks in the dome with cement as a 'tell tale' against which to record further cracking, and in 1859 he was reporting further signs of movement in the southern supports to the dome. In 1878 – in connection with plans for decorations – he took precise measurements of the dome, and found a 'very measurable amount of subsidence and disturbance'.[22] However, he concluded that most of this settlement had occurred during construction, and does not seem to have felt that substantial structural work was necessary, at least until the Central London Railway Bill was introduced in 1890.

The story of the major decorative schemes, which lasted for much of the rest of the century, is told on pp. 243–56. Against this backdrop of events, which included the appointment of William Burges as 'Architect' in a manner clearly extremely hurtful to him, Penrose continued to bring forward an extraordinary range of other work, aimed at enabling the whole cathedral to be used to its full capacity. Things were done on a major scale. When the original pulpitum organ was taken down for repair and the dean and chapter could see the potential for the use of the whole cathedral, undivided by Wren's screen, Penrose arranged for the choir stalls to be completely reconfigured, bringing them forward a whole bay, removing the screen, and raising the level of the choir by three steps. He used the salvaged remains of the screen to make porches for the north and south transepts in order to keep out the cold, and laid out the dome area for liturgical use, designing a new pulpit and placing an organ (at least on a temporary basis) in the south transept. When the discussions with Burges were at their height, he used the opportunity created by the lavish preparations for the thanksgiving service for the Prince of Wales's recovery in 1872 entirely to remove (with caustic paste, wet sand and an enormous amount of elbow grease) the remains of Wren's paintwork from all the interior stonework. He also brought the crypt into use, installing the massive tomb for the Duke of Wellington and designing the mosaic floors around it (see pp. 284–5).

Penrose brought a robust approach to problems of all sorts. He introduced gates at the half-level of the west steps which rose up by means of a hydraulic mechanism; he introduced mirrors into the peristyle to reflect more light into the interior of the dome; he renewed the lightning conductor system; he replaced the timber access stairs in the dome with iron to reduce fire risk and had the timber treated with fire retardant; he installed stoves in the crypt and inserted bronze grilles throughout the cathedral floor to allow the warm air up into the church above; he installed a gas retort (which exploded), a gas driven hydraulic system for pumping the organ (which never worked properly), and a hydraulic lift in the north transept for lifting furniture and equipment from the crypt (which was also removed when it did not work well); and year in, year out he organized the replacement of roofing lead, repairs to the marble floors and all the other tasks required for the continuing care of the building.

Throughout, Penrose did not forget his archaeological interests. He became intrigued by the remains of Old St Paul's which came

251 (*top*).   F. C. Penrose, surveyor to the fabric 1852–97, portrait in old age by J. S. Sargent, 1898. (Royal Institute of British Architects)

252 (*above*).   Team of workmen engaged on the 'dome experimental designs' under Penrose, Poynter, Leighton and Stannus, 1884. Standing to the right, E. J. Harding, clerk of works, from whose scrapbook the photograph comes. Back row, left to right: Waters, Raffield, Sladen, Brown. Front row, Collard, Huntingfield, Gurney (?), Simpson. (GL, MS 25809/1–2)

253. One of the transverse arches and bull's eye windows behind the peristyle of the dome, showing cracks. Photograph of 29 April 1902 taken as part of the first full photographic survey of the fabric, carried out on the initiative of Somers Clarke. The scale and annotated plan of the peristyle are for reference purposes. (SPCFA)

for so long, and to refocus them on the underlying problems of the structure. As there was not enough factual information to form an adequate defence in the face of threats from such projects as the Central London Railway (eventually built in 1896–1900), he instituted a series of measurements, taking levels, plumbing the dome and making photographic records (Fig. 253). His important report of 1902 presented a comprehensive analysis of the structural needs of the cathedral. Realizing that the resulting work would involve considerable expenditure, he brought in W. D. Caroe, architect to the Ecclesiastical Commissioners, to explore possible funding from that source, the original fabric fund having by this time dwindled effectively to nothing. Caroe authorized a schedule of works, which Somers Clarke put in hand. These addressed pressing structural needs, continuing the work begun by Penrose to restrain the west pediment, and attending to the stability of the south and north transepts. He dealt with the problems presented by the rusting of Wren's iron chain around the entablature of the peristyle, and also tackled the heating of the cathedral.

Somers Clarke, however, was not in robust health, spending each winter in Egypt, where he had archeological interests. Despite his affection for the building,[24] he resigned in 1906, recommending his friend Mervyn Macartney to succeed him. The dean and chapter seem to have welcomed the continuity which

254. Mervyn Macartney, surveyor to the fabric 1906–31, from a group-portrait in the Art Workers' Guild by J. P. Cooke, 1909–10. (Art Workers' Guild)

to light from time to time, collecting the fragments of moulded stone which were dug out from the core work of the walls whenever a new flue was installed or a new opening was formed; he carefully excavated and recorded the remains of the medieval chapter house; and he drafted a plan of the medieval cathedral and its relation to Wren's building, demonstrating that they were laid out on different alignments.

This vigorous activity for the first time introduced a significant amount of change. But the structural issues remained unsolved; and when a proposal was put forward in 1890 to run the Central London Railway tunnel close to the cathedral, Penrose consulted Francis Fox, a notable engineer whose career embraced both underground railways and historic buildings, and had the proposal modified. He also initiated major repairs to restrain the pediment at the west end of the nave. Nevertheless it must have been some time since he had scrambled around the upper parts of the cathedral.

Penrose retired in 1897, at the age of eighty. He was succeeded by Somers Clarke, the partner to J. T. Micklethwaite, at that time surveyor of Westminster Abbey. For a time, both of London's greatest churches were looked after from the same office.[23] Clarke inherited a situation which required a substantial change of approach. He needed to draw the dean and chapter's attention away from the decorative schemes which had preoccupied them this amicable handover of responsibility achieved, and Macartney was duly appointed (Fig. 254).

Almost immediately, Macartney found himself plunged into structural problems. Within weeks of his appointment, the dean and chapter, in response to yet another proposal to run a sewer close to the cathedral, set up a commission to help him examine and report on the building's structural stability. This commission was made up entirely of architects. They reported in 1907 that in spite of the settlement there was no immediate necessity for any extensive remedial measures, with the important proviso that the existing conditions of the subsoil and the existing water levels were maintained. They recommended careful monitoring of this and of all building operations in the vicinity of the cathedral; but they specifically advised against works of underpinning, on the basis that 'such operations would only be attended by fresh dangers'.[25] However, they did consider that 'there is a large amount of structural work required in repairing the fabric which should be proceeded with without delay'.[26] Macartney put these findings and his own research into a wider context in an important paper read to the RIBA in November 1907.[27] In the succeeding discussion Francis Fox, fresh from his triumph in stabilizing Winchester Cathedral through the combination of forced grouting under pressure for the superstructure and underpinning the foundations with the help of a diver, reminded the meeting of his earlier engineering consultations at St Paul's and voiced his concerns about the underground conditions in its vicinity, hinting that he considered the subsoil to be unstable.

During the next few years, Macartney continued with a programme of work; but it was not long before there were further threats. The dean and chapter consulted Fox, who, after much investigation (and a flurry of correspondence in *The Times*), produced a report in which his reference to subsoil conditions beneath the cathedral containing 'quicksand' raised a great deal of concern. Fox advised setting up another commission, and an expert body was duly appointed. This commission, the first to comprise both architects and engineers, studied the building carefully, but concluded with a fierce difference of views. This was not what the dean and chapter wanted, and so they asked Macartney and Caroe to reconvene and come up with a reconciled view. Their report, presented in 1914, set out a series of works for which a public appeal was to be launched, principally the repair and strengthening of the piers in the crypt and the eight piers of the dome.[28]

1914, the first year of the Great War, was 'largely spent in examination, and not in remedial work'.[29] Experimentation with pressure grouting along the lines advocated by Fox was carried out; but this did not impress Macartney who, in agreement with Caroe, began work on the strengthening of the first pier. Despite further disagreement, the work of cutting out and replacing the facing stonework of the pier continued, with limited grouting only. In his annual report to the dean and chapter, Macartney reported 'the lines on which I have hitherto gone viz restoring the building as nearly as I can to its original structural condition is a sound one'.[30]

Work was, however, extremely difficult. By 1918 the effects of war had slowed progress and increased costs considerably. Things went even more slowly in the next few years, perhaps because of the increased cost, but also reflecting the serious condition of the next pier to be dealt with. There is a sense of underlying concern, and it is perhaps no surprise to read in Macartney's report of

November 1921 that Sir Francis Fox (as he now was) had been involved in 'renewed activities'.[31] Another commission was suggested, again including both engineers and architects, with Godfrey Allen, Macartney's assistant, as secretary.

This commission initially reported in June 1922, but temporized until scaffolding had been erected. On its later findings, Macartney commented:

> After meeting for a period of nearly 18 months we are not yet in accord as to the method to be adopted in strengthening the piers that support the Dome. We are unanimous in our opinion that they want strengthening but not as to the means. I have purposely kept rather in the background as these gentlemen more or less differed from my views as to the treatment of this problem. It is a source of some gratification to me that I find that the solution of our troubles is not so easy as they thought.[32]

During the next year the situation did not improve: in particular, the issue of how to grout remained. A company engaged to carry out further experiments found the pressure had to be doubled in order to achieve any results, to Macartney's concern. He continues: 'So far there has been no open rupture between the Commission and myself but I felt constrained to protest against [the company] being employed above Church Floor level'.[33] A year later, he can only report 'I am unable to report much progress with respect to [the work of the commission]'.[34]

But while the commission was deliberating, concern was mounting in the world outside, fired particularly by the fall of a section of moulded stone from the vault of the nave. Two articles appeared in *The Builder*;[35] Sir Francis Fox published his autobiography, with a chapter devoted to St Paul's in which he again raised his view that the cathedral should be underpinned;[36] and two further books were in preparation, both to be published in 1925, critical of the approach to the problem.[37] In December 1924 the frustration and concern at the lack of progress felt by those outside the circle of the commission came to a head; and on Christmas Eve 1924 the dean and chapter were served with a 'Dangerous Structure Notice' by the Dangerous Structures Surveyor of the City of London.

This dramatic intervention galvanized the commission into activity. It immediately produced a second interim report, quickly followed by a final report;[38] and, following negotiations with the City authorities, the measures put forward in this were accepted, and the Dangerous Structure Notice was suspended pending the execution of the work. This was to be begun promptly. In its report to the Corporation, the subcommittee appointed to look into this matter also significantly drew attention to 'the great danger to the Cathedral from excavation for building operations in the immediate neighbourhood which may be carried down below the level of the Cathedral foundation', and recommended that 'the Government should be asked to take the necessary measures in this respect to safeguard such a National monument'.[39]

Macartney, towards the end of 1925, could record that the past year 'has been one of the most momentous in the History of the Cathedral';[40] and was able to report good progress with the works. They were of a major nature: a temporary wall was erected to divide the dome area from the nave; steelwork supports were erected to the piers and arches; and the work began with all speed. This involved not only grouting and repairing all the piers to the dome, but also the insertion of a large number of tie-bars in

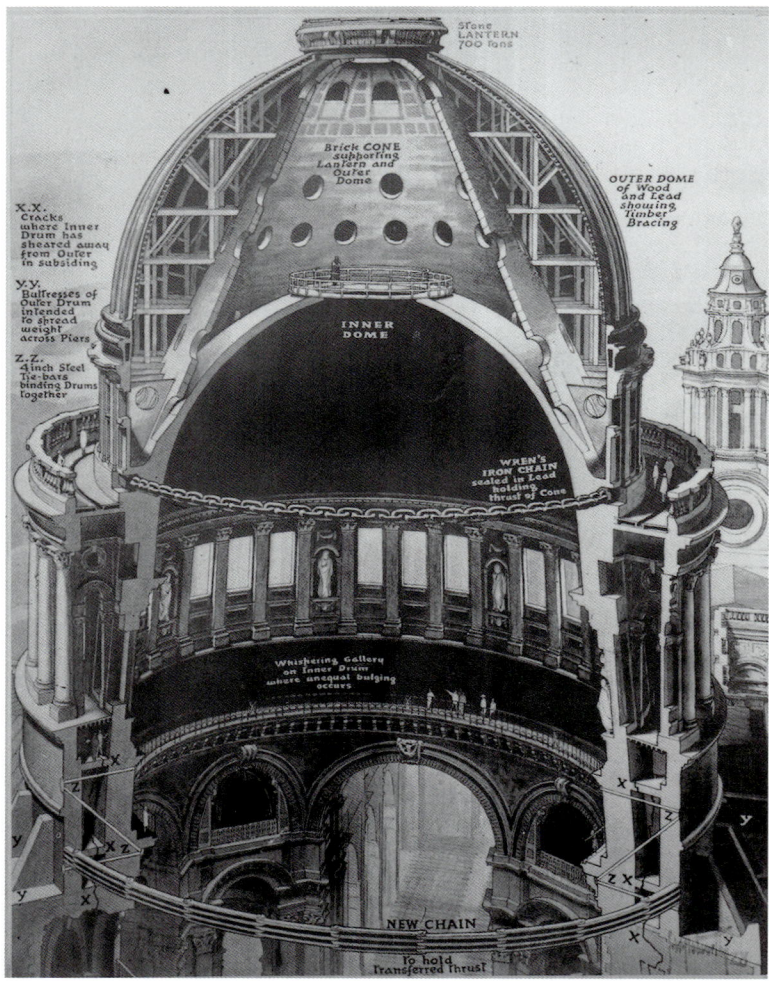

255.   Cut-away of the dome during the great restoration, showing old and new means of reinforcement. From *The Sphere*, 11 August 1928. The depiction of the old and new chains is schematic rather than accurate

256.   Unloading temporary steelwork for the great restoration outside the south transept, *c.* 1927. (SPCL)

the base of the dome, together with two new 'chains' of stainless steel, binding the base of the dome (Fig. 255). The extent of the works certainly put the dome and its supporting structure into a thoroughly sound state; but Macartney may (perhaps with some justification) have felt that they went further than was strictly necessary. In particular, he may have felt that damage caused by the extensive grouting might have been avoided; but he appears to have lacked the confidence to resist it.[41]

Throughout this whole period, much other work was carried on: the design of the Chapel for the Order of St Michael and St George, begun by Somers Clarke, was continued under Macartney (pp. 259–60); the Kitchener Chapel gradually developed (p. 261); and much was done to try and reduce the erosion to the roof-level statues. In addition, the opportunity presented by the thorough investigation of the construction of the cathedral (Fig. 253), and by the access which the major works provided, resulted in a thorough programme of recording, leading to the publication by Arthur Poley of a comprehensive set of measured drawings of the cathedral,[42] and the making of the celebrated and remarkable cut-away isometric drawing, first dreamed up by William Dunn and prepared by R. B. Brook-Greaves, the original of which still hangs in the cathedral (Fig. 136).[43]

The major work, which dominated this period, drew to completion in 1930 when a great thanksgiving service was held on 25 June. In that same year, Macartney presented his 'twenty fifth and final report' to the dean and chapter, a useful record of an extremely eventful twenty-five years.[44] By now Macartney was

clearly exhausted, and at the age of seventy-five felt that he had done his duty by the cathedral. His efforts were rewarded with a knighthood. He retired in 1931, soon after the completion of the work, but lived for less than two further years; as Godfrey Allen recorded: 'the long tenure of his office told on him more than is generally known'.[45]

There was still a great deal to be done in the aftermath of this major project, and what could be more natural than for Allen, who had acted as Macartney's assistant throughout and done much of the day-to-day work, to be appointed to succeed him as surveyor? First, it was essential to ensure that the foundations of the cathedral were protected from any risk arising from building operations in the immediate vicinity. Despite Sir Francis Fox, the foundations had not been considered by the commission to require strengthening; but the need to protect its footings remained paramount. As Macartney recorded in his last report: 'The Cathedral is now as safe as human ingenuity can make it but this condition can only be maintained if the sub-soil and the water it contains remain unaltered.'[46] With the help of the City, proposals were put in hand to draft legislation to achieve this, and these in due course led to the City of London (St Paul's Cathedral Preservation) Act, 1935, which still acts to ensure that the foundations of the cathedral are not threatened by development within a defined area around the cathedral.

One outcome of the major works was the setting up of a series of annual levels and measurements to demonstrate that movement to the structure was at a standstill. These measurements, taken with a great deal of accuracy, were continued on a regular basis for the next sixty years. As a more immediate consequence, the interior of the cathedral needed cleaning. The Thornhill paintings in the dome were conserved by Professor Tristram, and an attempt was made to clean the stone surfaces which had been stripped of their original paintwork in 1872. Here Allen had little success, and the improvement in the appearance of the stonework appears to have been modest.[47]

The height of the new generation of buildings being erected in the City during the 1930s began to cause similar concern to the depth of excavations into the subsoil (Fig. 257). In his report of 1932, Allen drew attention to the fact that 'quite recently the view from Blackfriars Bridge has been spoilt by the hideous new Telephone Exchange building in Queen Victoria Street'. He continued: 'The question of the height of buildings near St Paul's is a difficult one and I intend to investigate it thoroughly'.[48] The result of this initiative was the proposal for a code of practice to control the height of development within an area around the cathedral. Godfrey Allen expended much energy on determining a specific basis for this code, and it was greatly to his credit that it was accepted by the City and incorporated into its town planning scheme in 1938. The 'St Paul's Heights Code', as it is known, is still upheld today.

In 1938, experiments to clean the exterior stonework of the cathedral were under way when an ominous section appeared in the surveyor's annual report under the heading 'Air Raid Precautions'.[49] A report from the London Fire Brigade led to a thorough review of the fire-fighting capacity of the cathedral, together with proposals for a 'fire party' of sixty-eight men who would be trained to cover the building in the event of attack from the air. With war looming once again, the idea of the 'St Paul's Watch' (first formed during the First World War – see pp. 95, 99–100) was revived and Dean Matthews turned to Godfrey Allen to organize and lead it. As Matthews later recorded: 'It is difficult to state, without seeming to exaggerate, the debt we owe to Mr Allen. If any one man can be said to have saved St Paul's from ruin, it is he.'[50]

War brought a whole new phase of work to the cathedral. During the Blitz, the cathedral was hit by two 500-pound high-explosive bombs, and by seventy or more incendiary bombs (Fig. 258). In addition, a one-ton bomb fell immediately adjacent to the west steps, but fortunately failed to explode (earning Captain Davies the war's first George Cross for its removal). The two bombs which did explode did a great deal of damage: one within the roof space over the high altar, the other in the north transept where it exploded in mid air within the cathedral and caused extensive damage. Emergency repairs were put in hand immediately by the depleted works department, but the full repair was to occupy Allen for much of the rest of his surveyorship, together with the remodelling of the high altar and the formation of the American Chapel, in which Allen was joined by Stephen Dykes Bower. From these years date also a number of works, from the renewal of the heating system to discussion of the reordering of the Chapel of St Faith to form a chapel for the Order of the British Empire.

In his 1944 report Allen also drew attention to the potential presented by the devastation: 'If the Cathedral survives the war it will have greatly added to its importance historically and most people will expect it to be given a fairer place in the City of the future than it enjoyed in the past.'[51] These forward-looking words predicted a perhaps brighter future than was realized by the

257. Looking west from Cannon Street, montage prepared under the direction of Godfrey Allen showing the effect building to the limits allowed by the London Building Act of 1930 would have on this view of the cathedral. From 'St Paul's Heights. A survey of views showing the potential results of extensive reconstruction of buildings near the cathedral to the height authorised by the London Building Act 1930'. (SPCFA)

258. War damage in crypt, following the high-explosive bomb of 17 April 1941 which destroyed the north transept vault and caused the partial collapse of crypt vaulting beneath. (SPCFA)

259.   Post-war repairs to one of the saucer domes
in the north transept, 1959–60.. (SPCFA)

construction of Sir William Holford's Paternoster development to the north of the cathedral (see pp. 444–8). They were accompanied by a passionate plea for traffic to be moved further from the cathedral, a plea which should still be heeded today.

Godfrey Allen's surveyorship came to an unexpected end in 1956. The sorry tale is told with disarming frankness by Dean Matthews: Allen had been asked to submit a plan for the new choir school; but the dean and chapter brought in external advisers and other architects without consulting him, and Allen resigned, believing that they had not behaved properly towards him. Matthews wrote: 'It has been a lasting grief to me that the man who did so much for St Paul's and loved it so well should feel alienated from it'.[52] It was clearly also a lasting sadness for Allen, who for many years thereafter could not bring himself to revisit the cathedral which he had served for forty-five years. The story illustrates the power of the building to command the deep affection and respect of those who believe themselves called to serve it, and the consequent difficulty of accepting perhaps unintentional slights to their professional judgement and integrity.

Lord Mottistone, of the Seely and Paget partnership, was appointed to succeed Allen. By this time, the war repairs were nearing final completion, and Mottistone's principal contribution to the cathedral was the design of the Chapel of the Order of the British Empire (Fig. 205), a new dome pulpit to replace that originally provided by Penrose (Fig. 198) and a new lighting system.

With that internal work largely complete, attention again began to be given to the exterior of the cathedral, and in particular to its soot-blackened state. Experiments were carried out, and between 1961 and 1963 the west front was cleaned. The reception was mixed, some being hostile to the revelation of the cleaned stonework; but under Paul Paget (Mottistone's partner, who had been appointed surveyor following his death in 1963) the cleaning was extended to the whole exterior of the cathedral. The development of Holford's Paternoster scheme also created the opportunity to develop facilities for the works department, by excavating under the churchyard and creating workshops beneath the pavement, thus linking the chapter house with the cathedral.

Paul Paget retired in 1969, handing over the work of the surveyor's department in model order to his successor Bernard Feilden. Feilden had previously been involved in addressing major structural problems at York Minster, of the order of those which had faced St Paul's at the beginning of the century. He recognized that at St Paul's these had been successfully addressed by the 'great restoration' – in the area of the dome, at any rate; but he also recognized that the building had never been subjected to a fully comprehensive study as a guide to the care and repair of the cathedral far into the future. He set about a thorough inspection of every aspect of the building and presented the resulting report in 1971.

The heart of his study was the concept of 'planned preservation', looking forward to a thirty-year programme of work, based on 'the belief that each generation should face up to and solve its own problems, coupled with the view that a "stitch in time saves nine" and the duty to keep Wren's masterpiece aesthetically and structurally intact'.[53]

An appeal was launched on the basis of his plan of work. But to Feilden's concern this was not presented in terms of responsible future planning and wise harbouring of resources but instead on the basis that St Paul's was again somehow in danger: the posters prepared for the appeal showed the west front collapsing. Generous donations came in; the works department was increased in size; and work began on the west front in 1972. However, rapidly escalating construction costs during the 1973–5 period of sharp rises in oil prices hit the cathedral hard, and concern in the press that the appeal was misdirected also led to severe problems. In response, the dean and chapter determined that the appeal funds should be used for the running costs as well as the maintenance of all the chapter's properties, and not just for the cathedral. They directed that the numbers of craftsmen working on the cathedral should be halved.

260. Statue of St Peter on western pediment, showing erosion to the stonework, *c.*1973. (SPCFA)

This was a bitter blow; but although Feilden considered resignation at this time, he recalled that his title of 'Surveyor to the Fabric' placed on him a duty of care to the building, and that his resignation would not serve the fabric well at this critical time. Nevertheless, he argued strongly for the work which he considered to be necessary, and brought in Robert Potter and Alban Caroe to review the project. They fully vindicated Feilden's approach, and the chapter accepted the situation;[54] but the programme to the west front was curtailed, and the intended work to the south transept was cancelled. It was clearly a relief to Feilden when in 1977 he was appointed director of ICCROM in Rome and could, though sadly, leave St Paul's behind him.

Anxious to ensure continuity, the dean and chapter appointed Robert Potter in his place. He began preparations for the projected work to the south transept; but without funding, and with no commitment from the dean and chapter to continue this long-term programme, there was little prospect of taking work forward. Neither Potter, who retired in 1984, nor William Whitfield who succeeded him, had much opportunity; but Whitfield understood well enough what work was required, and, after a brief period as surveyor, recommended the appointment of a younger man who could make the necessary commitment to getting things going again; and Martin Stancliffe, writer of this chapter, was appointed in 1990.

He carried out a comprehensive review of the entire fabric to follow up Sir Bernard Feilden's survey twenty years earlier; and the resulting report has set the agenda for the next quarter-century and beyond. Its findings were that the fabric is in a remarkably sound state; but that despite this, care of the stonework needs to continue in order to ensure that it is kept weatherproof and clean (Fig. 260). The structural concerns which led to the major works of the 'great restoration' are well understood and are kept under review; as a result, the stonework damage to the south transept – never addressed as part of the 'great restoration' – could properly be undertaken without further damage occurring. It was clear that erosion of the stone is a continuing process and requires the recording of details of existing states. The review also showed that fire awareness and protection should always be a high priority; that the interior of the cathedral was both dirty and untidy; and that the liturgical layout and lighting of the cathedral could be improved to increase its dignity and expressiveness. Furthermore, it revealed that the crypt was underused, given the pressure on the cathedral to provide a wider range of services to its visitors and staff; and that the value of recording, archiving, conserving and curating the remarkable collections relating to the fabric should once again be recognized, and their permanent safety secured.

Much work has been done over the past decade to deal with these and a range of other issues, many of them reflecting the concerns of earlier generations. In particular, cleaning of the internal stonework has restored to the interior a unity and lightness in which Wren's architectural and decorative modelling can again be appreciated (Fig. 203).

Establishing and maintaining high standards of workmanship; careful programming to ensure that the life of the cathedral can continue as far as possible undisturbed; close control to ensure that scarce resources are responsibly deployed: these have always been the care of the surveyor. The evidence of both the fabric and of the surviving records indicates how faithfully their duty has been discharged by successive surveyors. What is new are the methods which are now felt necessary to control the work. The passing by Parliament in 1991 of the Care of Cathedrals Measure introduced for the first time the necessity for work to the fabric of the cathedral to be subject to approval by a body external to the cathedral authorities; it also required the establishment of a Fabric Advisory Committee. This body has greatly widened the scope of advice both to the dean and chapter and to the Surveyor to the Fabric, and has proved itself to be helpful in the continuing care of the fabric. The obligation to make formal applications through a process which involves public advertisement and consultation with a variety of bodies, including English Heritage, amenity societies and the City planning authorities, has also ensured that any work to the fabric has a broad basis of support. In parallel with this, the requirements for detailed understanding of the fabric, and for transparent accountability, have increased the numbers of people involved: archeologists, conservators, engineers, quantity surveyors and experts in many fields – even project managers.

The consequent need for the surveyor to have a comprehensive but at the same time detailed understanding of the fabric is all the more essential in the face of so much specialist involvement. All work to the fabric introduces change, and it is vital therefore that the work is coherently – indeed creatively – put together, and that the reasons for it and the implications of it are fully understood. Even to stay still requires conscious decision; and a living cathedral, among the most visited and most loved in the country, must continue to develop. Continuity is, after all, at the heart of the Surveyor to the Fabric's role.

26

ESTATES AND INCOME,
1540–1714

David Johnson

The upheavals of the sixteenth and seventeenth centuries caused changes to the patrimony and – briefly – dispossessed St Paul's of all its lands. In the city, the Great Fire was another blow. These were the most dramatic episodes in the history of the dean and chapter as landlords and they are well documented. From the records of the Commonwealth sales, beginning in 1649, it is possible to compile a virtually complete inventory of the estates owned by the dignitaries, prebendaries, minor canons and vicars choral, together with a contemporary estimate of the annual value of each estate (Tables 1–3, 6), while the lease books, accounts and related records, which survive in increasing completeness for this period, reveal the relations between the church and its individual tenants.

THE PATRIMONY

The Reformation affected St Paul's landholding indirectly; the dissolution of the monasteries flooded the land market and provided Henry VIII – and especially his courtiers – with bargains which, if they did not wish to keep them for themselves, they could trade with acquiescent landlords, such as cathedral clergy, in exchange for some of the latter's choice estates.[1]

The first effect on St Paul's can be attributed to Wolsey. He had acquired from Lesnes Abbey the rectory of Aveley in Essex in order to settle it on his new foundation, Cardinal's College in Oxford. On his attainder, Aveley was forfeited to the king, who granted it in 1536 to the dean and chapter of St Paul's in recompense for a pension of ten marks a year payable out of the same abbey.[2] The purpose of the next exchange, in 1540, is clearer. To enable Henry VIII to assemble the lands necessary to create Marylebone Park as a hunting ground conveniently close to Whitehall, Thomas Bennett was obliged to surrender his prebend of Rugmere – some 145 acres, mainly pasture and meadow – and to accept in return the parsonage of Throwley in Kent, which hitherto had belonged to Syon Abbey, and William Horsey had to surrender 55 acres of his prebend of Tottenham Court.[3] Four years later, a more wide-ranging series of exchanges was imposed. The king acquired several of the chapter's Essex estates, including the large area of The Naze or The Sokens, made up of the rectory manors of Thorpe, Kirby (though not the prebend of Sneating) and Walton, the manor of Beldams in Great Hallingbury and the rectory of Brikelsey (Brightlingsea); and also the manors of Chingford – where Henry made yet another hunting ground – and Foliat Hall in Ongar; and the rectory of Navestock. He also acquired Acton manor in Middlesex. In exchange, the cathedral received a selection of estates which had previously belonged to monasteries: in Essex, the manor of Hawksbury and other lands in Fobbing, Biggins manor and neighbouring lands in Chadwell, Horndon on the Hill rectory, and Rantisward marsh in South Benfleet; in Middlesex, the rectories of Tottenham, Kingsbury and Edmonton (which had briefly belonged to Lord Chancellor Audley but had previously belonged to Walden Abbey) and the manor of Whetstone, where the woods were carefully preserved prior to sale to the church; and in Hertfordshire, several estates in Walden Abbatis, subsequently renamed St Paul's Walden, Therfield rectory manor (which had been part of the jointure of Queen Katharine Howard, executed in 1542, and previously had belonged to Ramsey Abbey) and Hemel Hempstead rectory.[4]

Many of the estates which St Paul's surrendered soon passed to courtiers: for example, Chingford and Foliat Hall to Sir Richard Rich, who as chancellor of the Court of Augmentations had

TABLE 6
St Paul's prebends: location of their endowments and their estimated annual values,[1] 1650 and 1850

County	1650		1850	
	£[2]	%	£[3]	%
Bedfordshire	106	2	773	1
Essex	153	3	1,037	2
Kent	115	2	599	1
Middlesex:				
Middlesex, outer[4]	791	14	6,653	12
Middlesex, inner 1[5]	1,050	19	13,138	23
inner 2[6]	1,277	23	31,031	54
inner, sub total	2,327	42	44,169	77
Middlesex, total	3,118	56	50,822	88
City of London	2,048	37	4,419	8
Sussex			57	<0.5
Total	5,540	100	57,707	100

Notes:
[1] Includes rectories, but not woodland, for which only capital values are recorded.
[2] Rack rent values: see Table 1, n. 3.
[3] Rack rent values in CERC, S1, S2.
[4] Chiswick and Willesden.
[5] Harringay, Hornsey, Islington, Shoreditch, Stoke Newington.
[6] St Pancras.

negotiated the 1544 exchange; Acton to Lord Russell, Lord Privy Seal; and The Soken lands to Sir Thomas Darcy, Vice-Chamberlain of the Household, as an endowment to fit him for a barony.[5] Like Rich, Sir William Paget was also chancellor of the Court of Augmentations when he negotiated on behalf of the Crown the exchange of Drayton manor and rectory – the chapter's most valuable Middlesex property – for Charing rectory and the annexed Egerton chapel in Kent. He was then allowed to purchase Drayton for himself 'after the common rate' as a reward for his services. Next year, in 1547, the dean and chapter were persuaded to exchange the manor of Runwell for the sometime monastic estates of Mucking manor and High Easter rectory, all in Essex, and Runwell was immediately granted to Sir Anthony Browne, Master of the Horse.[6]

Thus Henry VIII did not compel the church to accept rectories (spiritualities) originally-owned by monasteries in exchange for manors and other lands (temporalities), unlike the policy later pursued by Elizabeth I. In spite of all the changes of the 1540s, about half the rectories owned by St Paul's in 1650 were part of its ancient patrimony.

The Acts of Parliament to dissolve chantries of 1545 and 1547 also brought changes, since quitrents and the like were payable to various beneficiaries, including members of the cathedral clergy, from this source.[7] The dean and chapter lost responsibility for overseeing over fifty, often fractious chaplains and also for administering their endowments. In 1548 it was reckoned that there were over forty-seven chantries in the cathedral and during that year most of their lands were sold, including Holme's, Lancaster and Peter Colleges, Sherrington's Chapel outside the north door, and even the Charnel Chapel in the north-east churchyard. Less than £13 p.a. had been payable out of chantries to the chapter and other cathedral servants but from other sources they had received £144 for performing obits.[8] Following the suppression of obits together with chantries, these sums became payable to the Crown but in some cases the dean and chapter held, and continued to

hold, the lands which generated the rents; Bowes and Paulhouse in Edmonton and Essex lands worth £14.10s. 0d. p.a. were among them.[9] This confusing situation was finally resolved in 1572 when rent charges on the lands exchanged in 1544–7, together with numerous quitrents payable from chantries, obits, etc., amounting to £110 p.a., were released to the dean and chapter in return for the surrender of quitrents of an equivalent value payable to them by the Crown.[10]

Thereafter, for the rest of the sixteenth century and throughout the seventeenth, the patrimony remained virtually unchanged, apart from a few minor losses. In the city itself, in the mid seventeenth century the dean, canons and petty canons owned well over 400 properties. As well as numerous houses, shops and sheds within the churchyard wall, such 'tenements' were concentrated in large blocks immediately to the north and south of the cathedral. Elsewhere, single houses or small clusters were scattered over the city. The country estates were almost entirely in the Home Counties, particularly beside the Thames estuary in Essex, in north-eastern Hertfordshire and in the eastern half of Middlesex, where some, such as Finsbury, were already inner suburbs of Tudor London. Just over the boundaries of these counties lay Barnes in Surrey, Caddington and Kensworth in (modern) Bedfordshire, and Charing and Throwley in Kent. Only Lambourn in Berkshire was more than fifty miles from the cathedral.

Within the cathedral precinct, bounded by Paternoster Row, Old Change, Carter Lane and Ave Maria Lane, and marked by a medieval wall (much of which was still standing in 1670),[11] the cathedral clergy owned a large proportion of the buildings. In the south-west corner, in the middle of a block of properties all owned by the dean, lay the deanery. This 'great messuage' of almost fifty rooms consisted of linked buildings of two storeys with garrets over, ranged round several courts and yards and a seventy-foot-square garden. Immediately to the east, 'a canonical house or mansion' with some adjoining small tenements belonged to the prebendary of Harleston, while the plots to the north, sometime Peter College and Holme's College, were sold in the 1540s as chantry lands. Continuing clockwise, in the north-west corner was the vicars choral's mansion. By the early seventeenth century, this had been divided into thirteen small tenements, eight along Bowyer Row and the rest encircling a small courtyard. Only the largest building of this group seems to have been used by the vicars; the other tenements were all leased out, one to a residentiary. Adjacent to the 'vicaridge house', facing the west front of the cathedral, a further two tenements and a mansion were owned by the prebendary of Pancratius, who also served as penitentiary. The remaining space of this corner was taken up by the (disused) bishop of London's Palace and, to the east of Paul's Alley, the Petty Canons' College and a few of their other properties. The college comprised separate dwellings and larger blocks divided into suites of chambers around a central courtyard, with a hall to the south. A large garden between the cathedral and the hall covered the area known as Pardon Churchyard, where a cloister had stood until its destruction in 1549. The garden was bisected by a diagonal path leading between the great and little north doors and during the Commonwealth period the northern half was built over.[12]

The north-east corner of the churchyard was largely open, to provide an auditorium for the preachers at Paul's Cross. Of the property that fringed the area, little belonged to the cathedral; north of the wall along Paternoster Row, the houses belonged to

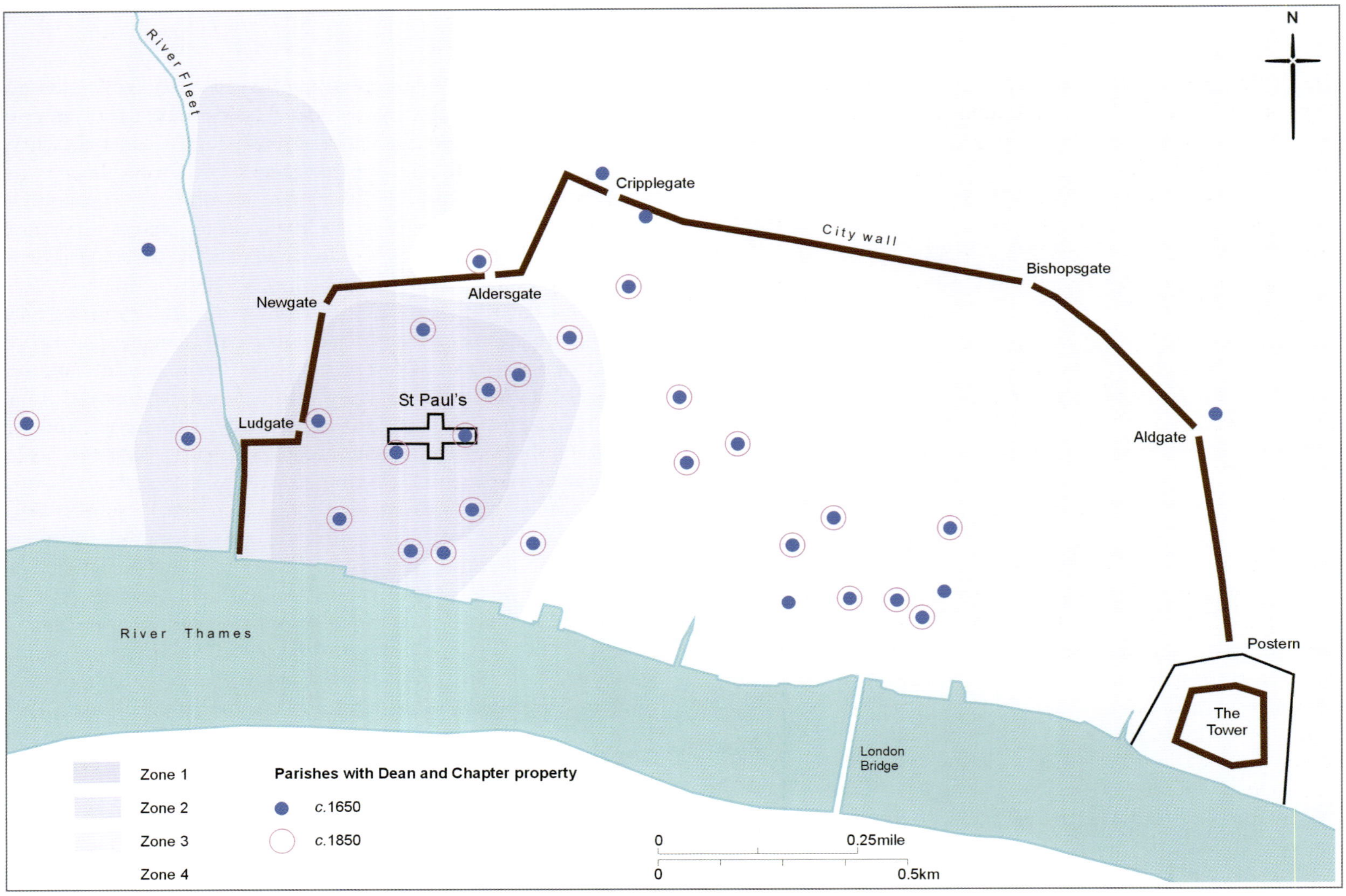

Top map labels:

N

River Fleet

Cripplegate

City wall

Bishopsgate

Newgate

Aldersgate

Ludgate

St Paul's

Aldgate

River Thames

Postern

The Tower

London Bridge

Zone 1
Zone 2
Zone 3
Zone 4

Parishes with Dean and Chapter property
● c.1650
○ c.1850

0   0.25mile
0   0.5km

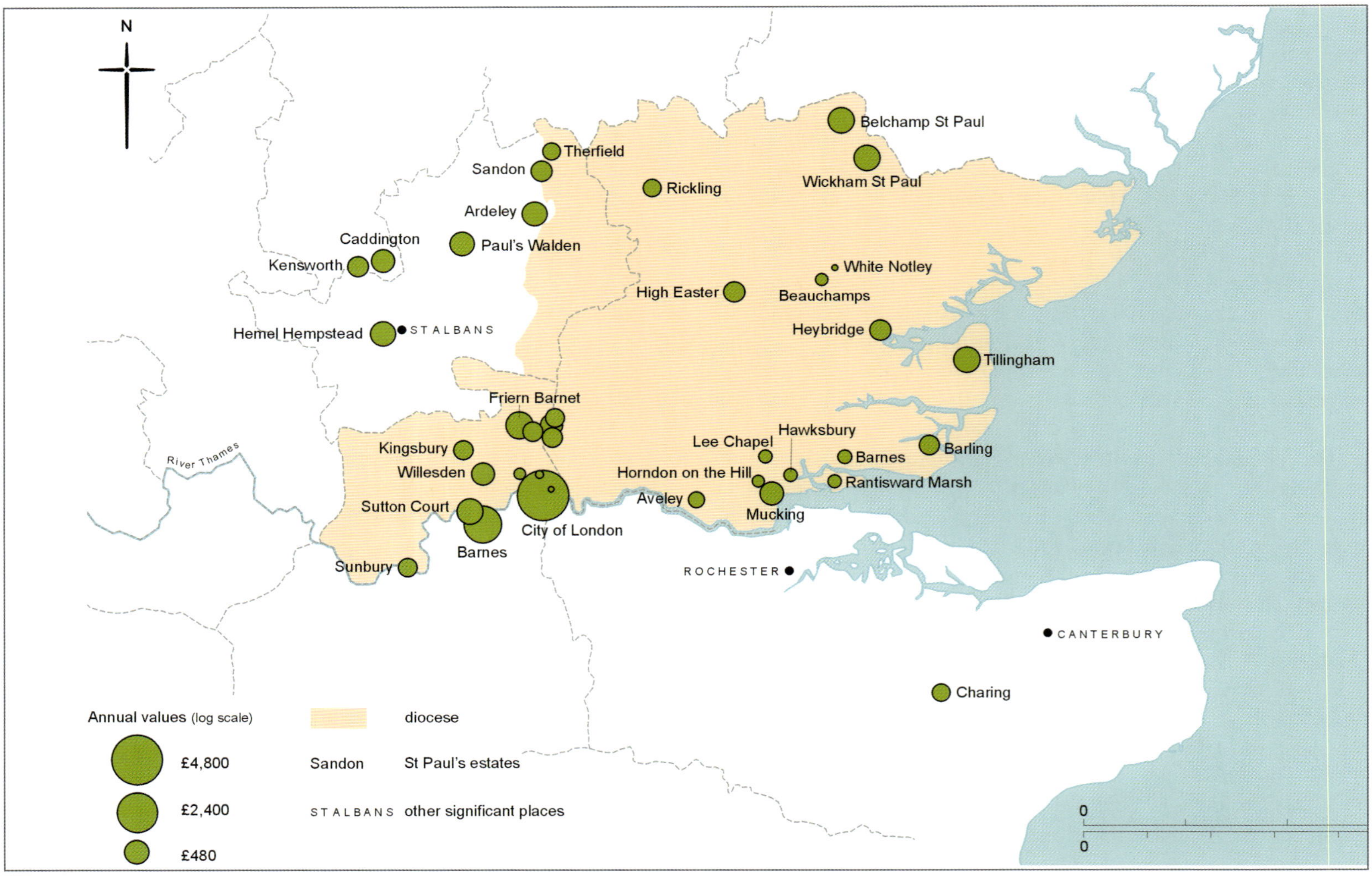

Bottom map labels:

N

Belchamp St Paul

Therfield

Sandon

Rickling

Wickham St Paul

Ardeley

Caddington

Paul's Walden

Kensworth

White Notley

High Easter

Beauchamps

Hemel Hempstead   ST ALBANS

Heybridge

Tillingham

Friern Barnet

Kingsbury

Lee Chapel

Hawksbury

Willesden

Barnes

Barling

Horndon on the Hill

Rantisward Marsh

Sutton Court

Aveley

Mucking

Barnes

City of London

Sunbury

ROCHESTER ●

● CANTERBURY

Charing

Annual values (log scale)

£4,800

£2,400

£480

diocese

Sandon   St Paul's estates

ST ALBANS   other significant places

306

the Bridge House Estate, and south of the wall to the bishop of London. Next to Paul's Gate, leading into Cheapside, the Jesus Steeple and two houses adjacent were alienated in 1546[13] so that the only property along the eastern border in which the chapter retained an interest was the school. However, the property south of St Augustine's Gate extending to Paul's Chain belonged almost entirely to St Paul's. The eastern end had long been the site of the precentor's mansion. By the fifteenth century it had been divided into tenements and by the seventeenth there were thirteen surrounding the Three Tuns Tavern. The precentor also had three rooms over St Augustine's Gate itself. Immediately to the west lay the chancellor's property. In 1649–50 it was sold as seven tenements, though a gatehouse, a coalhouse and a stable provide traces of the mansion which had once stood there. Next lay the property still known in the seventeenth century as the treasurer's mansion, consisting of several buildings grouped around two yards entered via Carter Lane and a further three houses fronting St Paul's Churchyard. To the west the land, originally the site of the old palace of the bishop of London, contained various tenements, including, at the north end, Lancaster College, a residence for chantry priests. Polydore Vergil was one of its neighbours when this was sold in 1548 (pp. 155–6).[14] The last block before Paul's Chain contained nine dwellings around a central yard, Raven Court, which were – as they had been since the twelfth century – the property of the prebendary of Caddington Major.

Like many medieval cathedrals, St Paul's was encrusted with shanty buildings between the buttresses and against the walls. Stow complained in 1598 that the south side in particular, including the chapter house, 'is now defaced by meanes of Licences graunted to Cutlers, Budget makers and other, first to build low sheddes, but now high Houses'.[15] Those in the angle between the north transept and the choir are well known from an early seventeenth-century painting which shows the king and the lord mayor and aldermen in the Sermon House by Paul's Cross.[16] Similar tiny shops, only four feet six inches deep but with a room over and a cellar beneath, were built against the wall of the Petty Canons' Garden. Most of these excrescences were cleared away in the 1630s during the Laudian refurbishment of the exterior,[17] but some had returned by 1649, when the churchyard was surveyed and divided into plots for sale.

Just beyond the churchyard, St Paul's owned several large blocks of tenements. These included 'the twenty-six tenements about the bakehouse' and opposite, on the eastern side of Paul's Chain, the Paul Head Inn and the Paul Head Tavern, 'new built' in 1610 but on the ancient site of the cathedral brewhouse. Another named group were the eight 'St Erkenwald tenements' which fronted on to Knightrider Street and backed on to the large complex of buildings leased to Trinity College, Cambridge, and sublet by them to the civil lawyers of Doctors' Commons. North of the cathedral were more public buildings: the Exchequer Office, leased to the chancellor, Lord Wriothesley, lay behind a group of small tenements on the west side of Warwick Lane and just north

of the College of Physicians, whose great messuage abutted on Amen Corner; on the eastern side of Warwick Lane, another Exchequer Office lay close to the Prerogative Office; and further east still, in Wood Street, the mayor and citizens leased the compter there.

The estates outside London varied enormously in value, acreage and type. In 1649 the Parliamentary surveyors estimated that the full improved annual value – that is, the rack rent – of five of the capitular estates exceeded £500 a year. The most valuable was Barnes manor in Surrey. The eighty-odd rooms of Barn Elms House were surrounded by buildings, barns, stables, gardens, orchards and fishponds covering nineteen acres and there were a further 444 acres of demesne land. The next most valuable capitular properties were the manor of Friern Barnet or Whetstone in Middlesex, estimated to be worth £624 a year, and three manors with rectories all worth over £500: Belchamp St Paul, Sutton Court and Tillingham. Belchamp St Paul was a typical manor (cf. pp. 145–6). The manor house, Paul's Hall, was large, with hall, parlour, kitchen and other domestic offices on the ground floor, a dining-room, gallery and ten 'lodging chambers' amongst other rooms above stairs, and further rooms, including 'a still house', round an inner courtyard closed by a gatehouse; an outer courtyard enclosed within a substantial wall contained more outhouses. All around were over 570 acres of demesne, mainly arable but with 82 acres of pasture or meadow and seventeen of coppice wood. Only about a tenth of the land seems to have been unenclosed, lying in common fields. At Belchamp St Paul, the dean and chapter also owned the rectory – that is, the right to take the great tithes and to use or lease the parsonage house and any land attaching to it – while the vicar had the small tithes, a vicarage house and glebe land. Here, the great tithes were worth £110 a year, while the vicar had a house, 33 acres and a pension of £20 a year payable by the lessee of the rectory, worth in all £44 p.a.[18]

All the prebendal estates were described as manors, with the exception of Holbourn and Mora, where there were only city tenements; Rugmere, where land had been exchanged for Throwley rectory; and Pancratius, which had both city tenements and Chigwell rectory.[19] Some prebendal estates had long since disappeared: Consumpta-per-Mare and Ealdland in Essex and Portpool in Holborn; Twiford was known to hold land in Willesden parish in 1523 but by 1620 it had been lost.[20] Ealdstreet was only saved by the determined efforts of the prebendary, Henry Halsteed, in the later seventeenth century.[21] Of those prebends which were recorded in the Parliamentary surveys, the most valuable by far was Finsbury, at £1,257 p.a. In form, Finsbury was like other manors, with courts, freeholders paying quitrents and pastures or meadows like Moorfields or Bunhill Field, but its demesnes were distinguished by the numerous – probably more that 150 – small tenements built over them in the sixteenth century and later. Next in value, at a little over £500 p.a. each, were Cantlers and Totenhall, both in St Pancras parish. In spite of being only one mile from St Paul's, Cantlowes manor house in 1650 was still surrounded by 213 acres of pasture and Tottenham Court was still surrounded by 240 aces of pasture, a coppice and several farmhouses.

261 (*above left*).   The Dean and Chapter as a property owner in the city of London, *c.* 1650 and *c.* 1850. See Table 3. For the parish zones, see Fig. 13

262 (*left*).   Annual values of Dean and Chapter estates *c.* 1650. For county totals and sources, see Table 2. The values exclude woodland, for which contemporary sources give only the capital value. The diocesan boundary is that of the historic diocese of London, excluding the archdeaconry of St Albans (a scatter of districts in Hertfordshire and Buckinghamshire) which formed part of the diocese between 1551 and 1845

THE COMMONWEALTH SALES

By the beginning of 1643, St Paul's had ceased to function as a cathedral. The bill to abolish bishops, deans and chapters, passed on 26 January 1643, appointed feoffees to take charge of their

263. Boyton Hall Farmhouse, Finchingfield, Essex, a sixteenth- and seventeenth-century moated manor house once part of the endowment of the minor canons of St Paul's

lands; but in practice the mayor and aldermen probably acted, since they were already responsible for maintaining order in St Paul's and choosing the Sunday preachers, and on 12 March they were appointed to sequestrate the houses and revenues of the cathedral and to pay the newly-appointed lecturer, Cornelius Burges, £400 p.a. from the receipts.[22] The city's Court of Aldermen thereupon set up a 'sub-committee for Paul's', and this group, several times augmented 'in regard of the great occasions vrginge more attendance then is vsually afforded there', met frequently at Campden House. Having received the money collected for the repair of the cathedral before the Civil War, they had also to consider such questions as whether to repair the 'steeple' (i.e. tower), what to do with the scaffolds still standing and, in 1649, how to provide soldiers billeted there with coal to prevent them burning the timber. Their main task, however, was to supervise the management of the estates. John Reading, chairman of the group, served as the steward but the sub-committee continued to pay the surveyor of the new work. They complained that they had no power to renew leases and that many of the necessary evidences were missing, with the result that they were unable to collect enough rents to meet the charges upon them.[23] Some substantiation of this claim is provided by the accounts for the last quarter of 1645, when less than £580 were received, well below a quarter of the annual rents of all the various ecclesiastics at St Paul's.[24] Four years later, new arrangements were made.

From the time of the earliest 'root and branch' debates in the Long Parliament, deans and chapters had been tarred with the same brush as bishops and it is therefore surprising that their lands were not put up for sale with those of the bishops in 1646. But in 1649 further delay was impossible. With the king executed, the House of Lords abolished and the army occupying London, there was no way of resisting demands that dean and chapter lands be used as security for the arrears of the soldiers' pay and on 30 April the necessary ordinance was passed.[25] The estates of deans and chapters were vested in fifteen trustees under Sir John Wollaston, who were to supervise their sale. Tenants were given first option to purchase, but if they failed to exercise this right, anyone might

apply. There were strict rules about how and when payment must be made. Settlement could be in cash, public faith bills for loans already made to the government, or receipts for money doubled (i.e. anyone paying a sum equivalent to the amount he was already owed by the state, with interest, could claim dean and chapter lands to the value of the doubled sum).[26]

The experience gained in the sale of episcopal lands was particularly relevant to the surveys on which the sales were based. The surveyors were not expected to produce measured plans but to estimate the value of each property by viewing the land, hearing evidence in courts of survey, examining records and – only on occasion – actually measuring fields, though city tenements were always recorded to the nearest inch. Basic surveying skills were easily learned from popular textbooks and most country gentlemen were able to understand court rolls and leases so that it was relatively easy to find competent surveyors to join the few identifiable professionals who produced the surveys of St Paul's lands. Each survey was checked by Colonel William Webb, the Surveyor General, and the scrupulous attention which he paid to detail is perhaps the strongest guarantee of their reliability.[27]

Using their expertise, the surveyors estimated the rack rental or full annual value of each property and by multiplying this by different factors depending on whether the property was in possession or reversion – that is, whether or not there was a sitting tenant – the contractors then set a sale price. It is interesting that St Paul's lands were some of the first to be sold and that the rates used to calculate the purchase prices were nearly always above the legal minimum, sometimes substantially so. Whatever doubts purchasers may have had about the wisdom of buying church lands, the St Paul's sales tend to support Edmund Ludlow's comment that 'such was the good opinion that the people had conceived of the Parliament, that most of those lands were sold at the clear income of fifteen, sixteen and seventeen years'.[28]

The sales of St Paul's lands produced a total of just over £152,000.[29] The most expensive was the dean's estate in Shadwell, which included nearly 700 houses built in the 1630s and 1640s.[30] At £9,540 5s., this was far more that the next nearest, Barnes manor in Surrey, at £5,945. At the other end of the scale, the quitrents of the manor of Barnes in Hadleigh, Essex, were, sold for only £7.[31] However, the sale price was of limited significance if the land was in reversion. The most extreme proof of this was provided by Finsbury prebend; although it had an annual value of £1,257 3*s.* 4*d.*, its sale price was only £1,085 because the mayor and aldermen – who were also the purchasers – had been granted reversionary leases which gave the city control until 1784.[32] The fact that tenants had the right of pre-emption contributed to the large number of small sales. There were sixty-one sales below £100 and a further fifty-four sales between £100 and £200, amounting to almost a quarter of all the purchases, so that the sales of St Paul's lands demonstrate that there was no attempt to restrict the sales to expensive lots which only the wealthy could afford.[33]

Of course, many of the purchasers of cathedral lands *were* wealthy Londoners and this fact has sometimes been interpreted as evidence of capitalist speculators seizing the opportunity to make easy money. St Paul's purchasers include a few examples of this category. Some 'persuaded' the sitting tenants to surrender their leases, or increased the rent when the lease fell in, or later resold their purchases at a profit, or, in the country, took in waste, cut down timber or enfranchised copyholds for a fee. But two facts reduce the force of this interpretation: many Londoners were either agents or tenant purchasers.

From the documents known as 'particulars' and from subsequent conveyances or litigation, it is clear that approximately half of all sales were made to agents acting on behalf of 'real purchasers'. A few of these agents were relatives or friends of the purchasers, but mostly they were professionals, generally London merchants and lawyers, often active in the land market and sometimes specializing in dean and chapter lands.[34] What is equally noteworthy is the large number of real purchasers who had some tenant right in the land they acquired. The surveys, particulars and other subsequent documentation indicate that 60 per cent or more of all purchasers were lessees, assignees or sub-tenants of the properties they purchased. When the lease was near expiry, the tenant had a good reason to purchase the freehold. Some families who had lived on the same estate for generations bought to preserve their inheritance, but the majority bought because their position as tenants gave them an advantage in purchasing what was likely to prove a useful investment.

THE DEAN AND CHAPTER AS LANDLORDS

When the dean and other residentiaries met in their irregular chapter meetings, it was almost invariably to consider the grant of leases of property. They negotiated leases of the capitular estates, registered leases made by the bishop and joined with the minor canons and vicars choral in leasing their property. They also registered leases made by individual prebendaries, but the latter acted independently and information about them as landlords is scattered and incomplete apart from the 'snapshot' provided by the Parliamentary sales.

The members of the chapter were experienced landlords. As prebendaries, often of other cathedrals as well as of St Paul's, they (usually) had estates of their own to manage and those who became residentiaries generally served for many years and took turns to act as receiver general. Moreover, they had a personal interest in acting commercially since the entry fines on capitular leases were distributed to them as dividends.[35] They were aided by a small, long-serving staff. The registrar and clerk of the chapter had custody of the muniments and engrossed the leases, for which he was paid 'seal money'; he was frequently asked to ascertain facts and to arbitrate in disputes. John Houghton (1663–86), like his successor, Thomas Gilbert, also served as attorney and solicitor, representing the chapter in courts of law. He was aided by the clerk of the chamber, who held this post with that of auditor, with responsibility for examining the accounts of the collector of rents in London and the bailiffs of the country estates. For more complicated legal advice, the chapter turned to the steward, a professional lawyer, who also presided at the manorial courts retained in their possession.[36]

Law and convention both constrained the chapter's landlord policy. In spite of official attempts to discourage them, 'long and unreasonable leases', often of ninety-nine years and sometimes in reversion, were usual for much of the sixteenth century and many of them were still in being in the mid seventeenth. But in 1571 the maximum term of twenty-one years or three lives was applied to the lands, houses and impropriations of deans and chapters and, in the following year, the maximum term for clerical *urban* property was set at forty years.[37] Thereafter, at St Paul's all leases conformed to the statutes. The chapter granted relatively few leases for three lives, but sole proprietors, such as the dean or a prebendary, were sometimes inclined to grant leases for lives even after 1634, when Charles I – at Archbishop Laud's prompting – instructed church landlords against this, notwithstanding the statutes.[38]

Rents charged by the church were traditionally below market rates and during the sixteenth century they became virtually fixed. Long leases contributed to this process. The registers of leases, which begin in 1536,[39] show that many rents set then were still being charged in the later seventeenth century. The difference between the beneficial rent paid by the lessee to the church and the full commercial rack rent was aggravated by prolonged inflation. To make up for this difference – the 'improvement' – churchmen, like many institutional landlords, charged a premium or entry fine every time they granted or renewed a lease. Evidence on how fines were calculated and how much was raised from them is scattered and particularly sparse before 1660, but in each case the chapter had first to assess the value of the improvement. They might send one of their officers to view the property or, after 1660, consult the Parliamentary survey, but more usually they relied on the evidence of subleases or assignments. The majority of lessees, both urban and rural, sublet and charged their subtenants a rack rent. This rent was sometimes disputed, but lessees also sought to minimize their income by claiming deductions or 'reprises' for exceptional expenditure, like expensive rebuilding, heavy taxes or personal misfortune – and the chapter was often sympathetic. Once established, the improvement was multiplied by a number of years' purchase to produce a figure for the fine, which the chapter and potential lessee (or his agent) would then haggle over. In the Tudor period this was a rough and ready process, the fines being round figures having only an approximate relationship to the improvement, but later, particularly after 1660 when the chapter minutes begin, increasingly careful calculations can be traced. Towards the end of the seventeenth century, the chapter was clearly applying published tables[40] which showed how to calculate the fine according to various rates of interest.[41]

Most tenants renewed their leases before the term had expired. Up to the Civil War, renewals might be requested at virtually any stage; afterwards, it became common to renew leases after seven years had elapsed and the chapter encouraged this by penalizing lessees who were late in applying with higher entry fines. The chapter thus ensured an unbroken series of tenancies with minimum effort: they were spared the trouble of finding new, untried tenants;[42] new leases could repeat old virtually verbatim, at the accustomed rent and for long at 'the ancient accustomed fine'; and all responsibility for maintaining properties (and in the country of compiling terriers and rentals in order to preserve the church's patrimony) fell on the tenants. Even when lessees disposed of their leaseholds, their assignees or executors were obliged to sign bonds to keep the covenants of the lease. The opportunity to renew leases encouraged tenants to improve their holdings. This was particularly true of those families which held the same St Paul's properties for generations. For example, under the Tudors and Stuarts, the Freshwaters at Heybridge Hall and the Glasscocks at High Easter rose from yeoman to esquire status; at Ardley manor, the Chauncys 'held the same by several leases for lives above the space of two hundred years last past'; and in Willesden the Roberts family had held some St Paul's land for centuries and Sir William was given special permission to purchase the freehold in 1651 though a contractor for the sale of dean and chapter lands.[43]

But it was not mere sentiment that made tenants keen to renew their leases. Even though they had to pay substantial fines, they were still able to profit, particularly from subleasing. In the city, the chapter frequently granted in one lease several adjoining tenements – houses of varying sizes, possibly with a garden, a yard or, by the river a wharf – which the lessee then sublet separately to poorer Londoners, who would certainly not have been able to afford the combined rent or the overall fine.[44] In the country, too, there were opportunities to profit, not only from farming close to the London market but also from felling timber, exploiting manorial rights and subletting parcels of demesne. The tenant's right to renew a lease was a valuable privilege which could be assigned – for a price.[45]

The importance of tenant's rights became most obvious at the Restoration. There was at first considerable doubt as to whether the lands of bishops and deans and chapters would be returned to the Church. By late 1660, however, when St Paul's had a new dean and the chapter had been reconstituted, it had become clear that no impediment would be placed on them and the appointment of a royal commission on 7 October to arbitrate in unresolved disputes confirmed this. Its members assumed that deans and chapters would normally respect the right of old tenants to renew their leases and would compensate purchasers who had not recovered their costs from the fines.[46] At St Paul's, many new leases were granted on these principles without great dissension, probably because so many of those in possession in 1660 had been tenants or were descendants, relatives or assignees of tenants.

Although the Parliamentary surveys clearly demonstrated the gulf between reserved and rack rents, the chapter increased scarcely a quarter of their reserved rents at the time of the Restoration. The main change was in leases of impropriate rectories where, in response to a royal order of August 1660 to ensure that vicars had incomes of at least £80p.a.,[47] many lessees had to pay a surcharge of £20 or more on their rents. Other covenants were largely unchanged. Nevertheless, this was a busy time for the chapter because problems were numerous.[48] The widespread use of discounted public faith bills by purchasers made it difficult to assess the actual money they had expended and the compensation

they deserved; many of them claimed that they had made costly improvements; some purchasers had taken the opportunity to incorporate church land into their own, neighbouring estates and had then further conveyed the land in marriage settlements and family trusts or had mortgaged it. Purchasers at second and third hand were particularly vulnerable since they had often paid commercial prices in hard cash and, like all reversioners, had had to defer enjoyment of their purchases. On the other hand, old tenants who were not purchasers still clung to their right to renew, and in 1660 many of their leases still had a few years to run. Each leasehold provided its own problems.

Scarcely had the dean and chapter disposed of their estates after the Restoration when they had to confront two further crises: the Great Plague halted the work of the chapter and added to arrears of rent; the Great Fire devastated most of St Paul's city properties. Rents continued to be paid for the surviving houses but almost all the other city tenants defaulted.[49] All the church's leases had covenants obliging the tenants to maintain and, if necessary, rebuild their leaseholds, but in face of so general a calamity they needed a further incentive. An extension to the lease was the obvious solution but the chapter was not authorized to extend any term beyond forty years. However, the Fire Court, which had been set up by Parliament to arbitrate between landlords and tenants, was empowered to do so and generally it decreed that leases should be made up to sixty or sixty-one years. Many St Paul's cases were brought before it, often to ratify an agreement already made.[50]

Although the Fire Court ordered some reductions in rent, St Paul's tenants were expected to pay their (modest) reserved rents continuously. Thus, the judges supported the chapter's refusal to reduce the rent of John Amherst even though his wife's former husband, Richard Higgenson, had spent £4,000 in redeveloping the Prerogative Office site in the 1650s. On the other hand, some tenants had to be compensated when municipal improvements, like the proposed quay alongside the Thames or street widening as at Ludgate Hill, truncated their holdings. The only houses that the chapter sought to rebuild were for residentiaries; they tried to gain possession of a site in Knightrider Street but the Fire Court decreed that the right of rebuilding belonged to the assignee of the lease and the chapter had to turn their attention to the site vacated by the Physicians' College at Amen Corner.[51]

RECEIPTS AND PAYMENTS

The size of the arrears caused by the Fire may have prompted the new dean, William Sancroft, to revise the accounting system which had been in operation since at least the mid sixteenth century. By consulting leases and earlier accounts, he established the arrears owing on each property. The regular covenants permitting the chapter to penalize and if necessary distrain defaulting tenants seem never to have been enforced. Sancroft collected some arrears and extinguished others, like those on Therfield mill 'long since decayed and fallen down', or the debts of the bailiff 'died – non solvent'. Then he set out a complete rental, including, under the appropriate parish, many small items of income such as quitrents – many deriving from chantries – which had often proved elusive. He was also careful to include the rent capons which his predecessors had neglected, presumably because payment in kind had dwindled and tenants were willing to forget their obligation to pay the monetary equivalent.[52] London rents had previously been collected under the headings *de antiquo jure* and *de nova fabrica*, but

264.	Dean Sancroft's scheme, in his own hand, for reducing the many sums due to minor canons, virgers and others to annual or quarterly payments. (SPCL)

these had long ceased to have any real meaning and Sancroft listed together all receipts from the city.

Payments were also simplified. Previously, the receiver general had made some payments to cathedral clergy, while the chamberlain had distributed 'bread money' – £3 10s. p.a. to each prebendary, less to the minor canons and vicars. But as this money had been drawn from the receiver general's account since at least the 1540s, it was an economy to combine the two offices. Sancroft was meticulous in setting out the numerous small payments due to the staff. In particular, he identified the sources of each *vaga portio*, a stipend, varying from £2 to £6, allocated to each of the minor canon's stalls. These payments were then 'digested into ye method of one pay-book, wherein every one may see presently what his dues are'. Many salaries, like the £20 due to the receiver general or the £6 13s. 4d. due to the steward, had not changed in one hundred years. The lion's share was taken by the dean and the residentiaries, who each received £110 as 'wages'.[53]

Changes in the totals of income and expenditure over the whole period are more difficult to explain. It is not always clear what is included in these sums – and the sums themselves are not always accurate – but the 'charge' of the receiver general, that is, the accumulated arrears plus the receipts for each year, rose from £1,192 in 1549 to £1,368 in 1594, £1,569 in 1641, £2,020 in

1664 and £3,554 in 1667. The last figure is inflated by Sancroft's discoveries but more particularly by high arrears. Over the next decade, the figure fell to £3,085 in 1675 and £2,584 in 1678, by which time London had been rebuilt. The rental component of this sum in the later seventeenth century was about £2,100, falling slightly in the early eighteenth century.[54] Fluctuations are to be explained more by variations in the amount of arrears than by any increases in rents, which remained largely static. Indeed, following the Fire, most city rents were frozen until after 1706. Nor did fines affect rental totals because they were recorded separately, if at all, and divided equally amongst the residentiaries.[55]

Apart from paying the staff, clerical and lay, the receiver general also met any necessary expenses. These included taxes, the cost of regular supplies like bread and wine, candles and parchment, and minor repairs to the fabric and furniture. Once these had been satisfied, any surplus on the year was divided equally amongst the residentiaries; this bonus was often over £200 each in the later seventeenth century and usually over £150 in the early eighteenth. This was, of course, in addition to the rents and fines they received from their prebends and dignitaries' estates and their wages as residentiaries. In recompense, from 1670 onwards the dean and chapter subscribed £50 each year towards the rebuilding of St Paul's; it was a small gesture compared to the full annual value of their estates.[56]

27

MUSIC, 1540–1640

Ian Spink

When Archbishop Laud made his visitation of St Paul's in 1636, the usual questions were asked about the size and composition of the choir. The dean and chapter replied:

> there are twelve petticannons, whereof two are cardinalls, six vicars chorall, an epistoler and aunciently a gospeller, an almoner who is yᵉ mʳ of the ten choristers... For the petticannons, they are a corporacion subordinate to the deane and chapter, having certaine rentes belonging to them besides some stipends from the deane & chapter. The vicars have likewise certaine rents besides stipendes from the deane & chapter. The almoner or mʳ of the choristers hath likewise certaine rents belonging to his place besides a pencon from the deane and chapter for instructing and mayntayning the boyes.'[1]

Thus, the choir consisted of twelve minor canons, six lay vicars and ten choristers. The title 'cardinal', unique to St Paul's in England, denotes the second and third minor canons – respectively senior and junior – who had responsibility for discipline and attendance, and catechizing the boys. In overall charge was the subdean, or first minor canon. The others had no particular titles, though they might serve as subchanter (succentor), sacrist, gospeller or epistoler.[2] Note that despite the presence of an organ since before the Reformation, there is no mention of an organist. Normally, one of the vicars choral was paid extra for taking on this task, and so the position became established without becoming statutory. The almoner might be a minor canon or a vicar choral, and was responsible for boarding the choristers and looking after their musical training, as well as religious and general education.

There is no roll of admissions to the minor canons and vicars before 1660. For this early period, members of the choir must be discovered from other sources, such as leases, visitations, etc. Once they had satisfactorily served a probationary year, they had tenure for life. Unfortunately, regular lists of choirboys do not seem to have been kept at any time, though we know the names of many by chance. As for what was sung, the music in the cathedral library goes no further back than the 1670s, though, of course, much of the general cathedral repertoire from the Reformation onwards survives independently.[3] With one of the largest cathedral choirs in England, and situated in the largest city, it might be expected that St Paul's, both 'old' and 'new', would have been one of the foremost exponents of this glorious tradition. At times this was certainly the case, but equally there seem to have been times when it was less so.

DEFINITIONS

It may be useful to define a few musical terms that will be frequently used in this and subsequent chapters – in particular, the two principal forms of English church music, service and anthem. The former denotes a musical setting of the morning and evening canticles, and the sung parts of the Holy Communion, unified by key. It may not include all items from the three offices, but one or two are normally complete. The anthem, on the other hand, is a setting of an independent text, usually scriptural (the psalms especially) but sometimes rhymed or from the prayer book and appropriate for general or particular use. In the early years of the Reformation, services and anthems tended to be in a simple chordal style that made the words clear, although polyphonic interest might not be completely excluded. Such music was described as 'full' when sung by the whole choir together, 'verse' when solo sections (necessitating an organ accompaniment) alternated with the chorus. All this was more or less in conformity with injunctions issued in 1559 advocating 'a modest and distinct song…as plainly understood as if it were read without singing'.

> [N]evertheless, for the comforting of such as delight in music, it may be permitted that in the beginning or in the end of common prayers…there may be sung an hymn [i.e., anthem]…in the best sort of melody and music that may be conveniently devised, having respect that the sentence of the hymn may be understood and perceived'.[4]

REFORMATION AND REACTION (1540–60)

According to one source, 'in Maye [1548] Poules quire…song all the service in English, both mattens, masse, and even-songe' for the first time.[5] Presumably vernacular settings such as those in the 'Wanley' partbooks of about this date were used, though they are not known to be directly connected with St Paul's.[6] English adaptations of motets by Sheppard and masses such as Taverner's 'Meane Mass' found there may well have been sung, and, significantly, there is a Magnificat by William Whytbroke, subdean from 1534, among the contents.[7]

'The playnge of organs at the devyne servys' ceased in September 1552.[8] But the new, more Protestant, prayer book of that year had little more than a year to run before the Catholic Mary came to the throne, and caused its repeal. A Latin *Te Deum* 'with the organs goinge' was sung to mark her accession on 19 July 1553,[9] and no doubt there was splendid music when she and her husband, Philip of Spain, visited the cathedral on 19 August the following year – similarly at the mass on 2 December when the Papal Legate, Cardinal Pole, received the Church of England back into communion with Rome.[10]

During this period of reaction, there was a return to the elaborate church music of Henry VIII's reign, and the liturgical use of the organ was resumed. An organ mass, *In die Sanctae Trinitatis* by Philip ap Rhys 'of Poles', dates from this time,[11] and the works of the old organist, John Redford, were revived.[12] Little is known of the instrument on which this music was played, except that it was said to have been like one in Durham Cathedral, 'the pipes beinge all of most fine wood, and workmanshipp verye faire'.[13] It would not have been large by modern standards – probably only a single manual with a handful of stops. It is traditionally attributed to William Beton.[14] As for the choir music, one source that to some extent reflects the St Paul's repertoire in the mid century may be the so-called 'Gyffard' partbooks.[15] Their contents include the 'Western Wind' masses of Taverner, Tye and Sheppard, and other masses (and Magnificats) by them. The connection with St Paul's is not exclusive, but the presence of a mass, 'On the Square' by Whytbroke, and settings of *Christus resurgens* by Redford and *Nesciens mater* by Thomas Wright (a vicar choral who died in 1558) supports the link, as do two further masses 'on the square' by William Mundy, one of which shares its material with Whytbroke's. Other pieces by Mundy include a Magnificat and the motet *Exsurge Christe*, a prayer for the removal of schism, which may perhaps have been sung at the mass reconciling the Church of England to Rome.

Mundy was certainly a vicar choral at St Paul's between 1559 and 1563, but in the latter year he joined the Chapel Royal 'from Poules'.[16] Whether his big five- and six-part votive antiphons and psalm-motets were written for St Paul's cannot be said, however. Certainly a work like the six-part assumption-motet *Vox patris coelestis*, lasting more than a quarter of an hour, must have sounded absolutely marvellous there, especially the passages with divided high voices.[17] It is not surprising that he was head-hunted for the Chapel Royal.

'THE CHILDREN OF PAUL'S'

This seems the best place to break into the musical history of St Paul's and deal with 'The Children of Paul's' – one of the leading companies of child actors in Elizabethan times.[18] These were, in fact, the cathedral choristers, and both the Chapel Royal and St George's Chapel, Windsor ran similar companies, though 'Paul's' appear to have been the queen's favourite.[19] Their tradition of play-acting went back to the Middle Ages, but from John Redford's time until the end of the century they played an important role in the history of English drama. Their earliest surviving play is Redford's *Wit and Science*, the manuscript of which also contains some of his organ music and dates from about 1545.[20] They performed before Princess Elizabeth at Hatfield House in 1552, and again at Nonsuch in 1559 after she became queen. Over the next thirty years, they appeared at least three dozen times at court.[21] When not performing at court, their theatre was probably in the cloister precinct, perhaps the undercroft of the chapter house at first, and later in a house erected in the north-west corner of the cloister.[22]

Redford was one of the vicars in 1534 and became almoner soon after in succession to Thomas Hickman, who died that year.[23] As such, he had power to 'take up' boys from any collegiate church and train them as choristers (likewise the masters of the Chapel Royal and St George's). Thomas Tusser, for example, tells how he was pressed into service from Wallingford:

> Thence for my voyce, I must (no choice)
> Away of forse, like posting horse,
> For sundrie men, had plagards then,
>   such childe to take:
>
> But marke the chance, my self to vance,
> By friendships lot, to Paules I got,
> So found I grace, a certaine space,   *John Redford*
>   still to remain: *an excellent*
> With Redford there, and like no where,   *Musician*
> For cunning such, and virtue much   *[organist of*
> By whom some part of Musicke art   *St. Paul's. M.*
>   so did I gaine.*[24]

Redford was succeeded by Sebastian Westcote,[25] who in turn was granted a warrant 'to repare unto sundry parts of this our realme for the takying upp of serten apte chyldren that may by his good educacon be framyd in syngyng'.[26] His indenture, with a few changes here and there, provided the basis of subsequent almoners' contracts, up to and including Randolph Jewett's in 1666.[27] The almonry house was to the south of the churchyard and there the choristers were boarded, two to a bed as we may assume from the 'fyve bedsteed[es], fyve mattress[es], fyve paire of blankett[es], fyve bolsters of floxe, fyve coverled[es] such as are accustomablie used for the Tenne Choresters' mentioned in his will.[28] At his death, he bequeathed his successors 'my cheste of vyalins and viall[es] to exercise and learne the children and Choristers there'.

Not surprisingly, choirboy plays made considerable use of music.[29] Unfortunately, none of the songs that survive with music from this early period can definitely be assigned to the Children of Paul's, but we know from other sources that they took the form of 'consort-songs', with treble solo supported by four-part instrumental accompaniment. (This was where Westcote's violins and viols came in.) William Mundy's 'Fie, fie, my fate'[30] is one such which has all the appearances of being from a play on the subject of the Prodigal Son, popular with the Children of Paul's at this time.[31] It is possible that such songs were a model for the emerging verse anthem.

At this time, there were two other musicians connected in some way with St Paul's, though they do not seem to have held official posts there. One is John Heywood, musician and playwright, a member of Redford and Westcote's circle who was involved with both the Children of the Chapel Royal and the Children of Paul's.[32] The other is Thomas Mulliner, sometimes said, erroneously, to have been Master of the St Paul's choristers, who has left an important collection of keyboard pieces, the so-called 'Mulliner Book'.[33] He seems to have had contact with John Redford, thirty-five of whose pieces are contained in the book, and was certainly aquainted with John Heywood. Little is known of him except that he was *modulator organorum* at Corpus Christi College, Oxford, in 1564.

Heywood and Westcote were both Catholics. The former had actually been condemned to death in 1544 for denying the king's supremacy in matters of religion, though he later recanted and was pardoned. Despite enjoying favour equally under Edward VI and Mary, he went into exile in 1564 and died abroad. Westcote's faith, too, brought him into conflict several times with authority. Repeated refusal to take Communion in the 1560s led to his deprivation as vicar choral, though he continued as almoner. It is not surprising that, living so close to his choristers, he passed on his religious sympathies to some of them, including Thomas Morley and Peter Philips, both of whom went on to compose a considerable amount of Latin church music – the latter especially, as organist to the Archduke Albert in Brussels.[34] As for Morley, he may or may not have thought better about being a Catholic later in life; his Latin settings are mostly early works or written for domestic performance.

The fortunes of the Children of Paul's seem to have declined after Westcote's death in 1582.[35] Thomas Giles's indenture as almoner, dated 22 May 1584, is the first in English and sets out his duties as follows:

> the said Thomas shall...teach or cause to be taught the said Children as well in the principles and groundes of Christian religion, conteyned in the littel Cathechisme...and in writinge, as also in the arte and knowledge of musicke, that they may be able, thereby to serve as Quiristers in the said Churche, and shall see them to be brought up in all vertue, civility and honest manners. Item the said Thomas doth covenant that he shall of his owne proper cost and Charges, provide as well convenient and cleane choyce of surpless as also all other manner of apparell...holsome and sufficient diet, holesome and cleane beddinge, w[it]h all things nedefull for them and in their sickenes shall see them well looked unto and cherished and procure the advise and helpe of Phisitians or Surjians if neede so requier of his owne cost and charges. Item when the children shall be skillfull in musicke...suffer them to resorte to paules schole tow howers in the forenone and one houre in the afternoon [in

summer]...and one hower in the forenone, and one hower in the afternone [in winter]...that they may learne the principles of gramer, and after as they shall be forwardes learne the said catechisms in Laten w[hi]ch before they lerned in Englishe and other good bookes taught in the said Schole.[36]

Giles was probably a competent enough choir trainer but less interested in the acting side. From 1589 or so, under his successor Edward Pearce, the Children of Paul's took on a new lease of life, with John Marston as their principal dramatist.[37] Their repertoire included several moralistic and satirical plays by Marston, Thomas Middleton and others, some songs from which were published by Thomas Ravenscroft between 1609 and 1614. Ravenscroft is listed as one of Pearce's choirboys in 1598. In *A Briefe Discourse* he described his master as 'a man of singular eminency in *his Profession*...in the *Educating* of *Children* for the ordering of the *Voyce*'.[38] and included Pearce's setting of 'Love for such a cherry lip', from Middleton's *Blurt Master Constable*, acted by the Children of Paul's in 1601. The popularity of the children's companies was declining with the public, however, and little is heard of the Children of Paul's after 1608.

ESTABLISHMENT AND GROWTH OF THE ANGLICAN TRADITION

At the beginning of Elizabeth's reign, the 1559 Act of Uniformity re-established Edward VI's Second Prayer Book and English as the language of the liturgy.[39] At St Paul's, the changes probably took place in June that year. A suitable basic repertoire would have been provided by John Day's *Certaine Notes* (?1560), which contained among other things the Whytbroke Magnificat already mentioned. It also included such well-known anthems as Sheppard's 'I give you a new commandment' and Tallis's 'Hear the voice and prayer'. A possible St Paul's connection may be evident in one manuscript which, despite a link that dates only from the 1630s, may reflect a situation of sixty or so years before.[40] Among its contents are services by Mundy (five in all), Robert Parsons, Sheppard and anthems by Tallis and Tye. Te Deums by 'Ramsey' and 'Woodson' are probably by John Ramsey and Thomas Woodson, both listed as vicars in 1574.[41]

Queen Elizabeth paid the first visit of her reign to the cathedral on mid Lent Sunday (24 March) 1560, where at 'Evening song... a good anthem was sung'.[42] As a leading composer and current member of the choir, William Mundy may have written one specially for the occasion – perhaps even his best-known anthem, 'O Lord, the maker of all things', which closely exemplifies the reformers' musical ideals.[43]

> O Lord, the maker of all things, we pray thee now in this evening, us to defend through thy mercy from all deceit of our enemies...

Whether or not Mundy remained at St Paul's after his appointment to the Chapel Royal in 1563, his music would surely have been sung there. 'O Lord, the maker of all things' notwithstanding, much of his work seems to disregard Reformation principles, however. His First Service, for example, is surprisingly complex and at times breaks into six and seven parts, while the anthem 'O Lord, I bow the knees' is quite densely polyphonic. Perhaps these were written for the Chapel Royal. As already suggested, he was also important in the development of the verse anthem, 'Ah, helpless wretch' being among the earliest examples of the form.[44]

The next important composer associated with St Paul's is Thomas Morley, described as 'organist of Paules church' in 1591.[45] Though born in Norwich, Morley is listed among the St Paul's choristers at the 1574 visitation,[46] and it seems likely that he had been brought there from Norwich by Westcote under his right to 'take up' boys from provincial cathedrals. Significantly, that same year Morley was granted the reversion of the post of organist and Master of the Choristers at Norwich Cathedral, and took this up in 1583. He remained there until 1587, when presumably he returned to St Paul's. How long he remained is not known, but one Thomas Harrold was organist by 1598.[47]

It would be quite understandable if Morley had relinquished his place at the cathedral due to pressure of work. His productivity as composer, arranger, author, editor and publisher during the remainder of his life was phenomenal. There is no knowing whether this, or his Catholicism, was the reason he wrote so little Anglican church music.[48] Nevertheless, there are two fine settings of 'Out of the deep' among his anthems, the earliest a verse setting from about 1580, the other an adaptation of his six-part *De profundis*, possibly made after his death. His First Service is a large-scale work mixing full and verse writing, and contains all the items of the liturgy. The second, a full setting of the Magnificat and Nunc Dimittis in triple-time, is obviously modelled on Byrd's 'Three Minnoms' service. A third, the so-called 'Short Service' about which some doubts as to authorship have been expressed, did not circulate widely. The Burial Service, the earliest to survive by any composer, is simple and deeply moving. Whether it can have been performed at the funeral of Sir Philip Sidney on 10 February 1587 may depend on exactly when Morley left Norwich for St Paul's.

Despite Morley's recent presence, one forms the impression that at the end of the century the cathedral music may have been in the doldrums. Bancroft's visitation of 1598 reveals no distinguished musicians in the choir, nor any personnel shared with the Chapel Royal.[49] Among the vicars we find the name of Nicholas Yonge, editor of the landmark publication *Musica Transalpina* (1588), but not otherwise noteworthy. Edward Pearce, Master of the Choristers, may have been too interested in putting on plays to coach the boys properly (*pace* Ravenscroft), though it was reported that the 'ten Quoristers…are now well instructed and fitt for their places'. Their surplices, however, 'are most Comenlie uncleane, and their apparrell not in suche sorte as decencie becometh'. As for their behaviour, one of the minor canons reported that 'the Children of the queere, either they use them selves very unreverently in their seats talkinge & playinge or else they be running aboute the quiere to gentlemen, and other poore men for spurr money'. Spur money was a fine traditionally exacted by choir boys – not only at St Paul's – from anyone entering the church wearing spurs.

The choirmen, 'both petticannons and vicars doe Come to divine service fornone and afternone ordely in their gownes and surplic[e]s excepte Mr Harrold [the organist] for he doth often offend therein wch by meanes of his shorte Cominge Goeth upp to the organ wth his Cloke'. As to leaving before the end of service, 'the wholl quier offendeth for many tymes and verie oft they goe forth wthout askinge leave…[M]orover it is a generall faulte amongst us all, and we doe wishe it might be reformed of everie one of us that at the Confession of o[u]r synnes…everie one should kneele and turne his face towards the east…alsoe to kneele at the rest of the prayers, and not to sett, on our tailes as Comenlie we doe wthout any Reverence at all.'

265.   Detail of Hollar's partly reconstructed view of the choir looking east, 1656. Since the organ and stalls were destroyed in 1644–5, the accuracy of their depiction is questionable. Dugdale (1658)

Thomas Harrold in his turn alleged that 'there is a disorder among the quier men, in that they use not to light their Candles at service tyme in the darke evenings, for whereas they have everie one a Candle they seldome lighte above 3 or 4 on a side when there should be 9, to the great disgrace of the Churche and their owne hinderaunce' – a possible implication being that while every man ought to have a candle, the boys did not, since they sang from memory. More relevant to his own position, '[t]he orgayns are so misused in the Blowing…that the Bellowes be broken, and the winde is not sufficiente to geve sownde to the insterment…The Organe lofte is greatly abused by ye bell ringers letting up of many people for monye, to the decaye of ye instrument, ye pipes beinge many of them under feet, and ye hazardinge of ye people underneath.' Despite all this, a German traveller, Paul Hentzner, commented in the same year: 'it has a remarkable [*egregium*] organ which, together with other instruments, makes excellent music at evensong'.[50] The 'other instruments' were probably cornetts and sackbuts from the city waits.

In the absence of specific indications as to the choir's repertoire at the turn of the century, it may be assumed that John Barnard's *First Book of Selected Church Musick* (1641) provides the foundation.[51] A minor canon from about 1623, Barnard published this collection with a view to generally raising standards throughout the country, and it would seem natural that he drew on what was sung at St Paul's. Applying a post-1600 cut-off to focus on the Elizabethan repertoire, we are left with a basic selection of services and anthems by Tallis, Byrd, Mundy, Morley and a few others.[52] Taking this putative repertoire forward to the Civil War (but remembering that it contained only works by dead composers), we may note the addition of Ward and Gibbons, and anthems by Weelkes and Adrian Batten – the latter a vicar from about 1628. The outbreak of the rebellion in 1642 put paid to plans for a second volume by those 'now living', doubtless to be drawn, like the first, from the so-called 'Barnard' manuscript part-books.[53] These not only reflect St Paul's, but constitute a vast private anthology embracing a much wider provenance. A closely related source known as the 'Batten' organ book does not, strictly speaking, belong to the set, but may well have been compiled by either Batten or the organist John Tomkins.[54]

In so far as there was a distinct repertoire of works by St Paul's composers, it must have included music by both Batten and Tomkins.[55] Batten was particularly prolific, with eight services, more than sixty anthems, a litany and several sets of preces. Taken as a whole, his music is sound but unimaginative. Tomkins, organist from 1619 (also of the Chapel Royal) and half-brother to Thomas Tomkins, is known to have written a service and eight anthems. The organ on which he played was probably the one said in 1609 to be thirty feet high, with nine stops on the great and six on the chair.[56] If so, it would have been the largest known in the country. According to one report, this instrument may have been rebuilt in 1631 or 1632, but, even so, is unlikely to have resembled the one depicted by Hollar – who was working ten or more years after it had been destroyed (Fig. 265).[57] In any case, judging by the number of transposed accompaniments in the Batten organ book (eighty out of a total of 256, mostly up a fifth) it would have been a 'ten foot organ' with bottom C of the keyboard sounding a pipe 10 foot long (nominally the F below). It thus needed accompaniments to be written a fifth higher, or transposed at sight.[58]

Other local composers whose works would have been performed were John Gibbs, almoner from 1613, William Cranford, a vicar choral from 1624, and William West, 'Pauli canonicis minor' who died in 1643.[59] Each is known to have written a service, but only Cranford wrote more than a couple of anthems. His setting of 'O Lord make thy servant' travelled widely and enjoyed a long lease of life. It was probably written to mark Charles I's coronation in 1625. Barnard himself composed a set of preces and responses for '27 March' and '5 November', respectively commemorating Charles I's accession and the discovery of the Gunpowder Plot. Surprisingly, perhaps, there is little sign that Martin Peerson, Gibbs's successor as almoner, contributed significantly to the music of the choir.[60] An excellent composer, he published two modernistic collections of vocal chamber music in 1620 and 1630, the latter mainly sacred, but somewhat remarkably, nothing is found in the Barnard/Batten sources. Nevertheless, eighteen or so substantial anthems survive elsewhere in manuscript – among them 'Blow up the trumpet' and 'I will magnify thee, O Lord' at Durham Cathedral – some of which must surely have been sung in St Paul's before the Civil War.

Comparing Archbishop Laud's visitation of 1636 with Bishop Bancroft's of 1598, one senses a healthier state of affairs consistent with other improvements that were taking place in the cathedral. Almost the only cause for concern was the fact that some of the choir 'under pr[e]tence of their attendance at the King's Chappell do too often absent themselves from yᶦˢ church', to which Laud characteristically replied '[a] waye would be thought on to find wher[e] they are absent fro[m] both; and the[n] to punish'.[61] History, however, had its own solution, for in January 1643 Parliament abolished all 'bishops...deans and chapters...vicars choral and choristers, old vicars and new vicars of any cathedral... out of the Church of England'.[62]

ALMONERS (MASTERS OF THE CHORISTERS) AND ORGANISTS 1540–1642

Almoners	*Organists*[63]
John Redford (?1534–47)	John Redford (?–1547)
Sebastian Westcote (1554–82)	Philip ap Rhys (1559)
Thomas Giles (1584–1600)	Henry Mudd (1573)
Edward Pearce (1599–1612)	Thomas Morley (1591)
John Gibbs (1613–24)	Thomas Harrold (1598)
Martin Peerson (1626–42)	John Tomkins (1619–38)
	Adrian Batten / Martin Peerson[64]
	Albertus Bryne (1638–42)

28

IMAGES OF ST PAUL'S

Ralph Hyde

Early in the morning on Saturday 14 June 1710, Zacharias Conrad von Uffenbach, student, book collector, connoisseur and, at this particular moment, London tourist, took a trip to St Paul's.[1] On arriving there, before doing anything else, he climbed to the dome to view the prospect of London. 'Right at the top of the tower,' he wrote in his diary, 'we found countless names written in chalk or scratched on stone, so we had ours done also by our man.' Descending to the floor of the new cathedral, he was overwhelmed by its magnificence. 'It is easier to make it out from the drawings and engravings that we bought than to describe it in words,' he exclaimed.

What prints did von Uffenbach buy? We do not know, but we do know what was on the market. For prints of the medieval building he may have looked at Daniel King's *Cathedrall and Conventuall Churches of England and Wales Orthographically Delineated* (1656), which included amateurish line engravings by King of the exterior. A work that he would have been more tempted to buy would have been William Dugdale's *History of St Paul's Cathedral* (1658), which was illustrated by many fine etchings of the interior as well as the exterior of the old building. These etchings were the work of Wenceslaus Hollar (Fig. 266), the Bohemian artist and printmaker brought to England in December 1636 by a peregrinating earl of Arundel. Hollar's etchings of St Paul's included a curiosity – a view of the building as

266.   South side of the mediaeval cathedral with the spire restored, etching by Wenceslaus Hollar from Dugdale (1658). The spire is based on the Elizabethan drawing illustrated in Fig. 90, p. 173

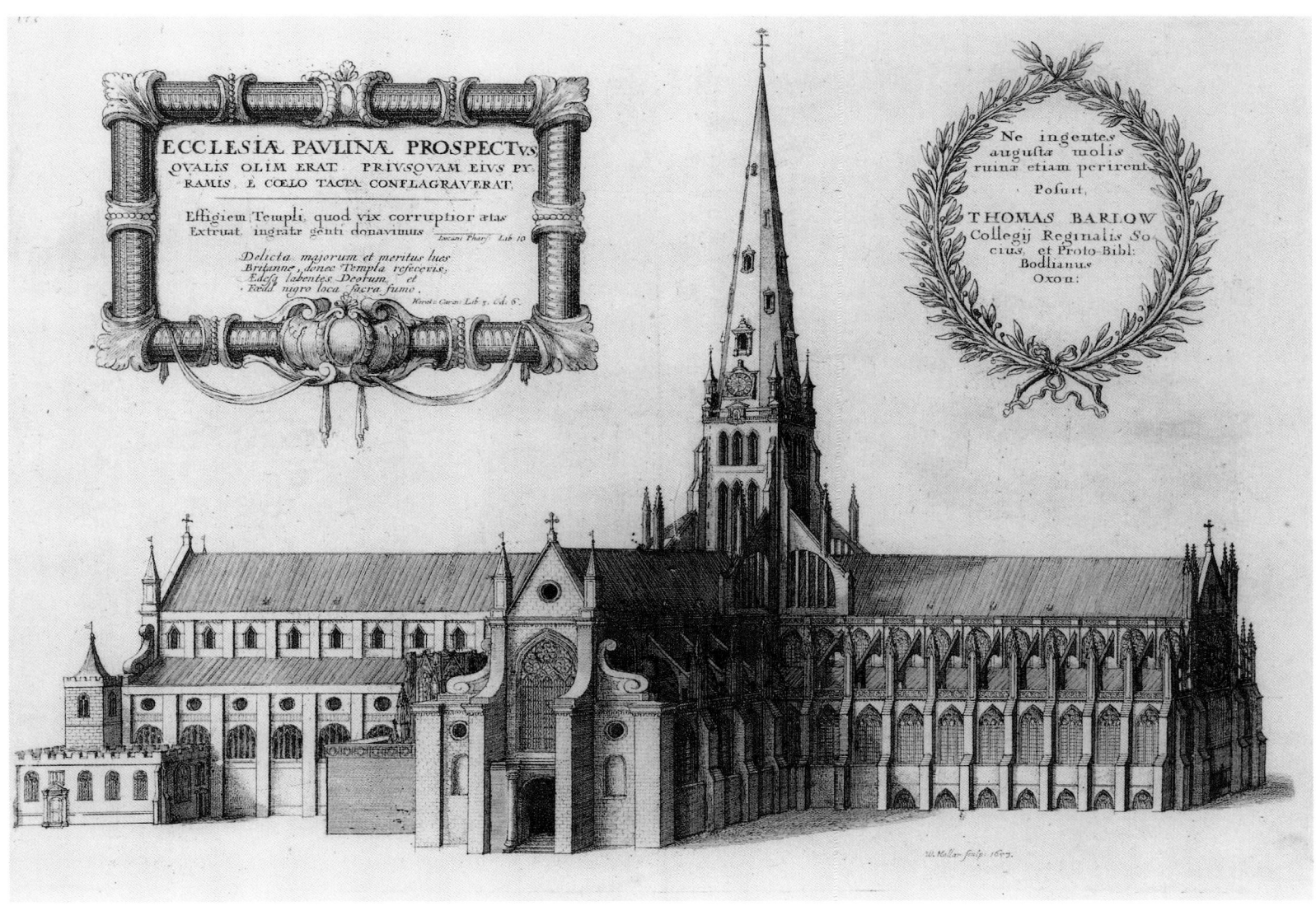

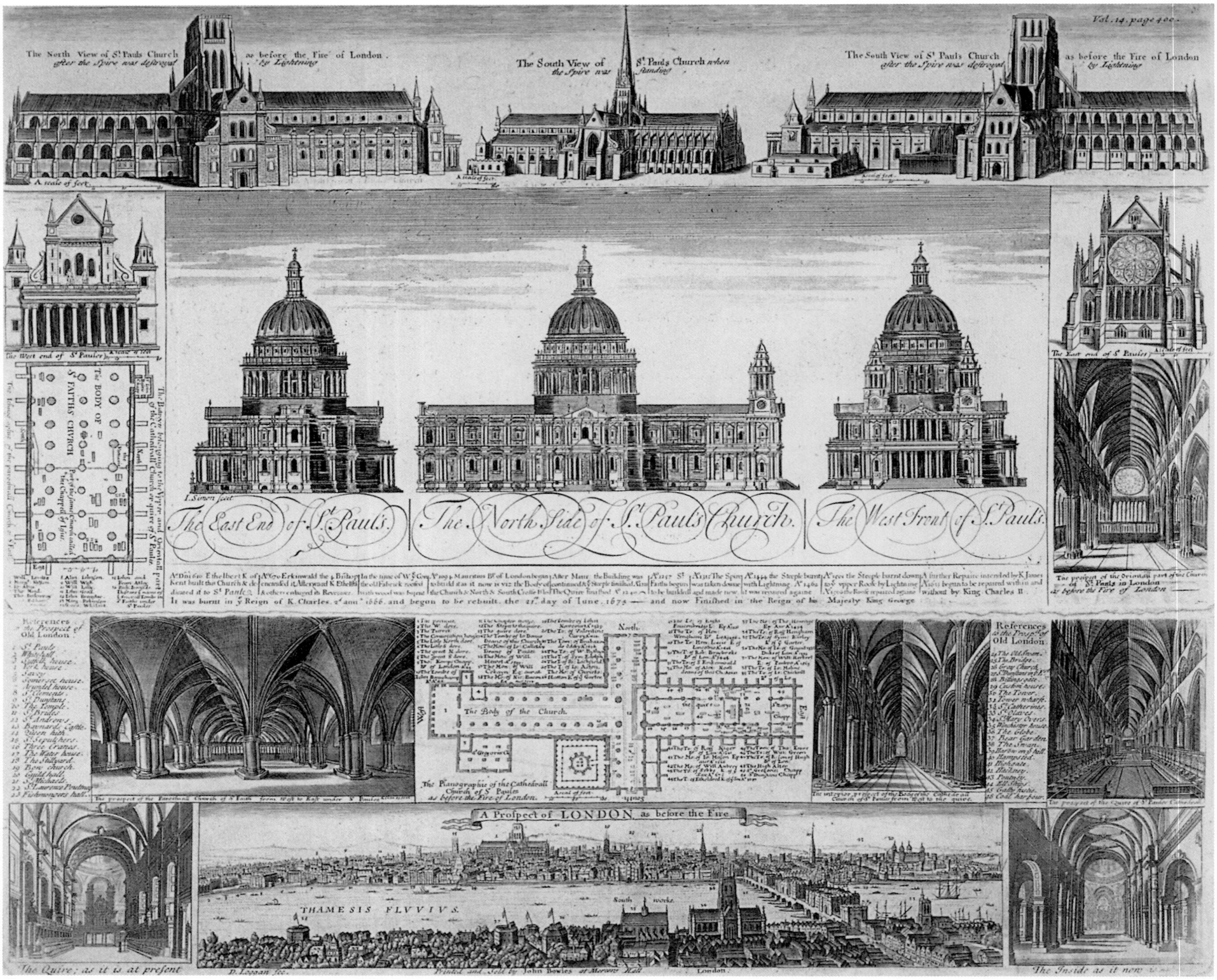

267.   Composite engraving of the old and new cathedrals by David Loggan and others, 1658 onwards, in the state published by John Bowles, *c.*1724. (GL)

268.   South side of the new cathedral, view as presented in William Morgan's wall–map of 1682, *London &c. Actually Survey'd*, based on guesses and imagination. (GL)

seen from the south, complete with Inigo Jones's additions, but also sporting the medieval spire.[2] For the spire detail, it looks as if he had access to the drawing of 1562 that is in the collection of the Society of Antiquaries (see p. 173).[3] Hollar also produced a second etching of the nave, dedicated to Philip Howard, a man related to his original benefactor. This did not appear in Dugdale's *History* and seems to have been issued in the first place as an independent print.[4] The second state of it carries the imprint of John Overton, and features in the 1672 edition of King's *Cathedrall and Conventuall Churches*.

There was another independent print featuring old St Paul's that von Uffenbach almost certainly would have been shown and perhaps would have purchased. Drawn by Daniel King, engraved by David Loggan and published by John Overton, its design was complex (Fig. 267). Basically it consisted of verses about the cathedral in Latin and English with small views of the medieval St Paul's arranged around them, all copied from Hollar's etchings for Dugdale's *History*. Across the bottom of the print appears a profile view of London from Southwark, related to the view in James Howell's *Londinopolis* (1657). The King–Loggan engraving appeared in 1658 and proved highly popular. It remained in print

269. Long section from Wren's 'Definitive Design', proof before letters, engraved *c.* 1698. (GL)

for eighty years or so, changing hands and being regularly adjusted and updated. By 1713 the poem had been replaced by three views of the exterior of Wren's St Paul's, and the text at bottom left and bottom right by views of Wren's interior. It was now in the hands of Thomas Bowles, who sold it at his premises in St Paul's Churchyard. To make it sound recent, Thomas Bowles asserted that it had been 'Finished in the Reign of her Majesty Queen Ann...' The copper plate was then acquired by John Bowles. He issued at least three states of it, from his shop over against the Stocks Market, where the Mansion House would eventually be built; and then from his shop set into the front of Mercers' Hall in Cheapside. One asserts that it was 'now Finished in the Reign of King George 1724'; the copy in the British Museum's Crowle Pennant carries a contemporary inscription claiming that it was finished in the reign of George II.[5]

Having found engravings of the medieval St Paul's, von Uffenbach would have wanted prints that showed the building under construction. Here he would have had a problem. A print took time to prepare, and any print issued showing the extent of progress on a specific date would have been old hat by the time it reached the print shops. Only one such print was issued, Sutton Nicholls's 'St Paul's Cathedral from the N. E.', published in 1695. This shows the building from the apse (strangely distorted) to the north transept (Fig. 113). The transept is still clad in scaffolding, and the masons' lodges where the stones would be prepared are much in evidence. There is no sign yet of the nave, however, though by this date it was under construction. Nicholls's address was The Gilded Ball at the east end of St Paul's Churchyard near Cheapside. The noisy building site was something he had daily to endure.

What the public really wanted, however, were prints that would show how the cathedral would look when finally completed. Here, Christopher Wren was unhelpful, and printmakers had no choice but to use their imagination. Godfrey Richards in Palladio's *First Book of Architecture* (1676) imagined it as the Great Model design with a Latin-cross plan rather than a Greek-cross plan (Fig. 114). In 1682 William Morgan published his huge wall-map, 'London &c. Actually Survey'd', heavily decorated with the names of peers and bishops and views of London's principal landmarks (Fig. 268).[6] Morgan apologized for his inaccurate representation of St Paul's with the explanation: 'For so much as is built is taken from the work itself: the rest is added according to the best information we could get, hoping it may not be very unlike when finished.' In the absence of anything official, other printmakers cribbed from Morgan. Morgan's fantasy thus features in Morden and Lea's *Book of the Prospects of the Remarkable Places in and about the City of London (c.*1687–1692),[7] in a collection of small London views issued in *c.*1690 by Johannes de Ram,[8] and in Vincenzo Coronelli's *Viaggi* (1697).[9]

In 1698 Sir Christopher Wren, aware of public curiosity and anticipating a demand for authentic prints, was minded to produce his own and set to work on them. He applied to William III for a licence – i.e. for copyright protection. The reference to them in State Papers Domestic[10] is intriguing:

> Licence to Sir Christopher Wren, knt., surveyor general; reciting that he hath not only with expense of much time and charge but also with great truth and exactness, according to the rules of art, delineated, described, and accurately engraven on copper several designs of the cathedral church of St Paul's, London, as it is rebuilt and to be finished... and granting to him the exclusive right of printing and publishing the delineations and descriptions for fifteen years.

One of the engravings referred to in the licence must surely have been Wren's 'Section of the Cathedral Church of S. Paul Lond: Wherein the Dome is Represented According to a Former Design...' (i.e. the Definitive Design) (Fig. 269). There is a proof of this print in the St Paul's Deposit at Guildhall Library which carries ink instructions to the engraver, in a hand that may be Hawksmoor's.[11] In the early years of the eighteenth century, three more approved engravings based on Wren's drawings appeared, each carrying the words, 'Ex Autographo Architecti': a plan at

270 (*left*). West front, engraved by Simon Gribelin, 1702. This was from the set of engravings officially approved by Wren for publication. The west towers and dome are not as executed. (GL)

271 (*above*). The choir and transepts looking east, as imagined by William Emmett and published by Thomas Bowles, 1703. The choir, opened in 1697, is depicted accurately, but the transepts and dome are largely fanciful. (GL)

272 (*below left*). Looking north across the nave towards the Morning Chapel, engraving by Robert Trevitt, published in 1703. (Pepys Library)

floor level with outlines of the crypt and peristyle; a north elevation; and a dramatic two-sheet west elevation, 1702. The engraver of the west elevation was the Huguenot printmaker and metal engraver, Simon Gribelin (Fig. 270).[12] For his trouble, Gribelin was paid £60.[13] The print displays the west towers, though not as executed, and the dome is not as executed either, being punctured with lucarne windows. There are no apertures in the drum.[14]

The appearance of Wren's authorized prints, and the existence of his fifteen-year licence, was not enough to stop the publication of unofficial views. In January 1702/3 Thomas Bowles advertised 'The South Prospect of ye Cathedral of St Paul's London'; 'St Paul's The East Prospect'; 'The Front or West End of the Cathedral Church of St Paul's in London'; and a plan of the building.[15] All were by William Emmett. Bowles claimed they had been 'Examined and Revised by some of the best Architectors, and approved by other Ingenius Persons'. In fact, 'The South Prospect' was a reversed copy of the authorized North Prospect, with a wall round the transept; and the 'Front or West End' was largely copied from Gribelin's authorized view, with rustication and the apertures round the drum added. Provided the prints 'met due encouragement', more were promised, showing the interior 'both in straight Lines and Prospective.' Sales must have been satisfactory for Emmett subsequently published himself from his house in New Street 'A Section of the Inside of St Pauls From East to West it being the Metropolitan Church of this Most Eminent City of London' and 'The Cathedral Church of St Paul's in London: A Section of the Cross Isle from North to South with a Prospect of the Choire & Dome.' The 'Section of the Cross Isle' is a striking and slightly disturbing fish-eye view (Fig. 271). The building is shown correctly up to the base of the dome, but the rest is fanciful. This print appeared in two forms, the complete image and a smaller

273 (*above*). South elevation of the Great Model, engraving by Henry Hulsbergh, *c*.1726. (GL)

274 (*right*). East end, drawn by T. Schwertfäger and engraved by Regimus Parr, published in 1747. (GL)

version, for which the copper plate was trimmed. Some copies of the second version carry the imprint 'Printed and sold by Joseph Smith in Exeter Exchange in the Strand', and it is in this state that it sometimes appears in the *Nouveau Théâtre de la Grand Britannia/Britannia Illustrata* (1724, etc.).

To be taken far more seriously are the prints of Robert Trevitt, for Trevitt had been officially engaged by the St Paul's Commissioners and the copper plates he had engraved remained their property.[16] Trevitt produced five prints of the cathedral that are essentially architectural, and one that is essentially ceremonial. The ceremonial view (Fig. 154) is entitled 'A Prospect of the Cathedral Church of St Paul, on the General Thanksgiving the 31st Decemr. 1706: Her Majesty and both Houses of Parliament Present'. According to an inscription on the Society of Antiquaries' copy,[17] the figures were drawn and engraved by 'Lu Duguerniese', presumably Louis Du Guernier II, who was born in Paris and died in London. The service, thanking the Almighty for 'the great and wonderful successes wherewith he has blessed the arms of Her Majesty and Her Majesty's allies in the last Campaign', is shown in progress in the completed choir.[18]

Trevitt was paid for the work he did for this engraving in 1710, which is presumably when it was published.[19] His more purely architectural views consist of a two-sheet *Ecclesiae Cathedralis Divi Pauli a Porticu Occidentale [...] Aspectus Interior...*; *A View of the Isle at the Entrance of the North Portico of the Cathedral Church of St Paul*; *A View of the Morning Chapel in the Cathedral Church of St Paul* (Fig. 272); *Chori Ecclesiae Cathedralis Divi Pauli: Aspect Interior a Parte Orientali ad Occidentalem*; and *Scenographia Templi Paulini a Parte Occidentali ad Borealem*. The first, published 'by the Permission of Sir Christopher Wren', was advertised in February 1702/3,[20] and the next three, also published with Wren's blessing, in August 1703.[21] They could be bought at Trevitt's house at the

sign of the King's Arms in Coleman Street. Since the west towers and dome on the final print are represented as built, it must have been published a few years later. One state of the Morning Chapel plate is interesting in showing reclining figures in the spandrels (a clue to Wren's intentions?)[22] The staffage is curious. The people appear to be clad in classical costume. The group on the left ignore at their peril a ferocious dog that charges at them from the right.

Following Sir Christopher's death in 1723, his son and heir, Christopher Wren junior, began preparing for publication a commemorative volume with the intended title, *A Specimen of the Works in Architecture of Sir Christopher Wren*. By 1729 he had assembled fifteen large copper plates (Tab 1–Tab 15). Nine were of St Paul's Cathedral – a somewhat miscellaneous collection. Most seem to have been engraved quite recently (two are actually dated 1726), but at least one of them (Tab 10) is one of the Wren authorized plates, the *Section of the Cathedral Church of S. Paul* mentioned earlier, that showed the dome 'According to a Former Design'. Four of them (Tab 5–Tab 8) represent the Great Model design, the plan being engraved by Benjamin Cole, the perspective by Jacob Schynvoet, and the south elevation and the east–west section by Henry Hulsbergh (Fig. 273). The plan of St Paul's as built (Tab 9) is by Hulsbergh, too. There is also a section of the south transept (Tab 11) by Gribelin, and the two smaller west and east and prospects (Tab 12–Tab 13) for which Sir Christopher Wren had received payment back in April 1703.[23]

The *Specimen* was never published. On the death of Christopher Wren junior in 1747, the plates were inherited by his younger son, Stephen. Stephen sold them to the booksellers Samuel Harding, Daniel Browne and William Bathoe, and 'Tab' plates can thus be found with the Harding, Brown and Bathoe imprint.

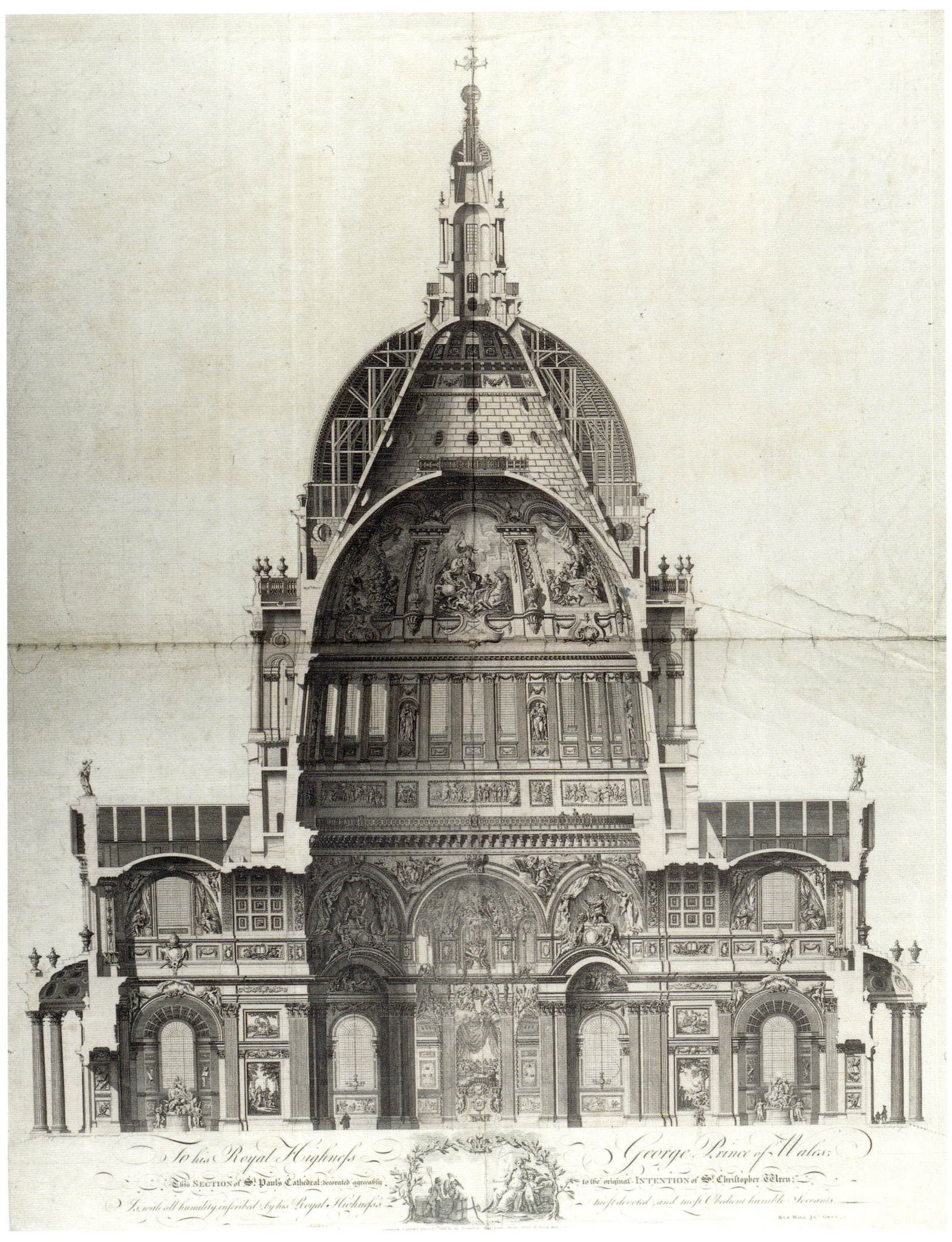

To his Royal Highness George Prince of Wales; This SECTION of St Paul's Cathedral decorated agreeably to the original INTENTION of St Christopher Wren; Is with all humility inscribed by his Royal Highness most devoted and most Obedient humble Servants.

As one would expect, several shops in St Paul's Churchyard stocked prints of the cathedral. Sutton Nicholls, as we have seen, published and sold the only print that showed the building under construction, and Christopher Browne at the Globe & Compass published and sold a 'South Prospect of the St Paul's Cathedral, London.' The most important print shop by far, however, was the Great Picture Shop of Thomas Bowles. This was situated next door to the chapter house in St Paul's Churchyard, and for well over a century catered for clergy, tourists and country chapmen.[24]

Thomas Bowles's imprint featured on a number of large architectural views of the cathedral. In addition to some of the Emmett's plates, there was 'The West Prospect of the Cathedral Church of St Paul's London', which he published with his relation John Bowles at the sign of the Black Horse in Cornhill; 'The North Prospect of the Cathedral Church of St Pauls'; 'The South East Prospect of ye Inside of ye Cathedral of St Paul's', engraved by H. Terasson; 'The East Prospect of the Cathedral Church of St Paul's', engraved by Thomas Platt; 'The Foundation or Ground-Plat of St Paul's Church'; and 'The Statue of Her Majesty, &c. Erected at the West End of St Pauls Anno. 1713'. In the second half of the eighteenth century these prints were still being printed off by Thomas's successor, Carington Bowles, at 69 St Paul's Churchyard, as the shop had become. Carington assigned plate numbers to the large St Paul's engravings and sold them for three shillings each.

The Bowleses' principal rivals were the Overtons and their successors. John Overton operated from the White Horse without Newgate, and was succeeded by Henry Overton; and Philip Overton operated from the White Horse in Fleet Street, later the Golden Buck, and was succeeded by Mary Overton and then Robert Sayer, Sayer & Bennett, Robert Sayer again, and then Laurie & Whittle.[25] Their large architectural plates included several that were after drawings by Bernard Lens: 'The Inside and Choir of ye Cathedral Church of St Paul's London', engraved by Jan Kip; 'The South East Prospect of the Cathedral Church of St Paul's London', engraved by John Harris; and 'The Western Prospect of St Paul's Church with the Queen's Statue, Erected on Thanksgiving Day for ye General Peace in ye Year 1713', engraved by Hulsbergh. Charming, crude and rarer is Henry Overton's 'Statue of Our Sovereign Lady Queen Anne, being of ye finest Marble, erected in Honour of Her Majesty at the West end of St Paul's Cathedral, London'.[26]

Architectural prints drawn in the manner of those by Bowles and Overton, showing the north, west, south and east elevations continued to be issued as the century progressed. There was a crude and derivative set by John King. 'T. Schwert fäger' (Theodor Schwerfeger?) introduced an element of unnatural perspective into his elevations (Fig. 274). They were engraved by Regimus Parr, published in 1747,[27] reissued in due course by Robert Sayer, and then reissued again in 1794 by Sayer's successors, Laurie & Whittle. Peter Schenk in Amsterdam issued an east prospect, a south prospect and a west prospect, all copied from William Emmett's views. By 1720 Schenk's plates had been acquired by Joseph Smith in the Exeter Change, Strand, London, who in each case supplied neat-lines, inserted an English title at the top, replaced the Dutch title below with a French title, and

corrected the lantern detail over the dome. In the case of the south prospect and the west prospect, he updated the west towers. The dome, however, he left alone, allowing it to continue with its lucarne windows. In Italy, Ferdinando Fambrini issued two views of the cathedral, one showing the east front and the other the west front. In the latter the neighbouring buildings in St Paul's Churchyard are unashamedly Italian. The artist unconvincingly accredited with both is none other than Canaletto.

Before leaving engravings that are essentially architectural, two items demand particular attention, a large two-sheet section of St Paul's and a companion two-sheet plan. Both were the work of the journalist and architect John Gwynn and the artist Samuel Wale, as part of Gwynn's campaign for the 'completion' of St Paul's by means of internal decoration (see p. 240).[28] To draft his section and plan, Gwynn set about taking the measurements of the building. In the dome he missed his footing and fell, his downward plunge being halted by a projecting piece of lead. There he hung until he was rescued.[29] Gwynn and Wale's 'Tranverse Section of St Paul's Cathedral, Decorated According to the Original Intention of Sir Christopher Wren' was engraved for them by Edward Rooker, engraver and actor, who, a contemporary noted, engraved fine plates of St Paul's in the morning and played Harlequin on the stage in the evening (Fig. 275).[30] The print, dedicated to the prince of wales, was published by Gwynn and Wale, at the Golden Ball in Little Court, Castle Street, near Leicester Square, on 27 May 1755, price twelve shillings.[31] 'The first specimen of architectural engraving', Horace Walpole declared it to be. The Gwynn and Wale plan, dedicated to the dean and chapter and engraved for them by James Green, was published on 21 June 1758, price five shillings. Section and plan were reissued by Alexander Poole Moore in 1801.[32]

In a different category altogether from the engravings mentioned so far are eight fine prints engraved after James Thornhill's scenes from the life of St Paul which decorated the dome. These were engraved by rather superior engravers, Bernard Baron, C. Simmoneau, N. D. Beauvais, Claude du Bosc and Gerard van der Gucht. In October 1719 Thornhill invited subscriptions, which could be taken out at the London print shops of Edward Cooper, Michael Hennekin and Thomas Bowles, and also at several bookshops in London and the provinces. Subscribers were obliged to pay half a guinea in advance, and another half-guinea on delivery. No more would be printed than subscribed for. On 2 May 1720 Thornhill presented a set of proofs to King George I, and on 9 May he delivered the prints to subscribers.[33] Most of the copies were printed in black, but copies have been seen printed in red and in brown.

We have looked at architectural prints and a set of fine prints. A third category becomes progressively more significant as the eighteenth century advances – topographical prints aimed primarily at the 'stranger market' – in other words, at country bumpkins and foreign visitors. Maps designed to meet their particular needs had begun to make their appearance in the mid 1720s with Thomas Bowles's 'Pocket Map of the Cities of London, Westminster and Southwark.' It was Thomas Bowles, together with John Bowles and J. Smith, who in the 1720s also published the first real London guidebook, the *New Guide to London: or, Directions to Strangers* (second edition 1726). Maps and guidebooks for strangers became plentiful in the 1750s.[34] And so did topographical prints.

The guidebooks directed strangers to what was almost a standard list of London landmarks, specifying, where necessary, the 'curiosities that strangers must pay for seeing.' Printmakers such as

275. Section of dome and transepts showing proposed scheme of paintings to enhance Thornhill's paintings in the dome, published by Samuel Wale and John Gwynn, 1755. (GL, St Paul's collection)

276. A zograscope, with a *vue d'optique* engraving of St Paul's positioned for correct viewing. (GL)

277. View from the south-east, engraving by Paul Fourdrinier, 1743. (GL)

Bowles, Overton and Sayer listed perspective views of precisely the same landmarks. Each measured approximately ten by sixteen inches. Sayer & Bennett in their 1775 catalogue list forty-six perspective views, including three of St Paul's, 'Price 1s. each; beautifully colored 2s. They make Genteel furniture when Framed and Glazed: likewise they are admirably adapted for the Diagonal Mirror or Optical Pillar Machine.'

The 'Diagonal Mirror or Optical Pillar Machine', otherwise known as the zograscope, was a simple contraption consisting of a convex lens mounted on a short pole, screwed into a circular base (Fig. 276). Behind the lens was a mirror sloping at forty-five degrees. To obtain and enjoy the required effect, you laid your print flat on the table, immediately behind the circular base. You then looked through the lens at the reflection of the print in the diagonal mirror. Since it was the reflection that you were looking at, the image itself needed to be reversed. Those prints specifically

created for this purpose – known as *vues d'optique* – consisted usually of images with plenty of perspective. Their titles appeared in the centre of the top margin in reversed capitals.[35]

Many of these *vues d'optique* were published by firms in Paris and Augsburg, who plagiarized, reversed, crudely coloured and retitled prints that were available in London. N. J. B. Poilly and Daumont in Paris, for instance, issued a *vue d'optique* of Robert Sayer and Henry Overton's jointly published 'North West View of St Pauls Cathedral London' engraved by T. M. Müller. Daumont and Basset both issued reversed copies of an engraving of the choir which had appeared in John Strype's *Survey of the Cities of London and Westminster...* (1754).

New large topographical views of St Paul's also appeared in the 1740s and 1750s. Like the smaller ones, they frequently passed through a sequence of states over a period of sixty years or more. Thus 'A Curious Perspective View of the Inside of St Paul's Cathedral, Shewing Part of the Dome, the Piers, and Arches which Support it, and the Entrance to the Choir and the Isles' was published first in mid century by Robert Sayer, then in 1794 by Laurie & Whittle, and then jointly in the early nineteenth century by Robert Wilkinson and Bowles & Carver.

A serious problem faced by topographical artists attempting to record the exterior of the cathedral was that it was so hemmed in by other buildings. Thomas Girtin encountered the problem when producing two images of St Paul's for *Public Edifices of the British Metropolis*: 'In executing these designs', the text informs us,

> the Artist has availed himself of a licence allowable in the Fine Arts; as, in order to present a more complete view of this magnificent edifice than any spot in the confined area which actually surrounds it would permit, he has, in his representations, enlarged the space that surrounds the building very considerably...[36]

This convention had been followed almost from the start. Joseph Smith's two-sheet 'Prospect of the Cathedral Church of St Paul's, London', published in 1720, solved the problem by not showing neighbouring buildings at all. Paul Fourdrinier of Craigs Court, Charing Cross, shows buildings in his large south-east view of 1743 (Fig. 277), but his churchyard is gargantuan and Ludgate Hill appears on the horizon. Smith's image was copied by an artist who produced a pair of large oil paintings of Westminster Abbey and St Paul's. The churchyard in the view of St Paul's is brought to life by staffage which includes clergy and visitors, a stagecoach pulled by five horses, and two figures who attract a crowd by fighting with quarter-staffs. On this occasion, buildings intended to represent those to the south of the cathedral have been added.[37] This painting shows the cathedral from the north-west. So too does Canaletto's oil painting now at the Yale Center for British Art (Fig. 30).[38]

Canaletto's *Thames looking towards the City* features a state barge that replicates very nearly the *bucintoro* in his painting of Venice on Ascension Day (Fig. 278). It also features a non-existent ten-storey warehouse on the river front. The view of St Paul's itself is accurate enough, but the height of the Queen Anne statue has been exaggerated, no doubt for effect.

As we have seen, Queen Anne's thanksgiving service of December 1706 gave rise to the earliest ceremonial image of St Paul's. George III's thanksgiving in 1789 for his (temporary) recovery from madness provoked several more (Figs 279, 310). Edward Dayes, court painter to George III and art tutor to the duke of York, painted the royal procession making its way to St

278.   Detail from *The Thames on Lord Mayor's Day, Looking towards the City*, by Antonio Canaletto, *c.* 1747. (Lobkowicz Collection, Nelahozeves Castle, Czech Republic)

Paul's, at the king's command. It would seem to have been the queen who commissioned him to paint the scene inside the cathedral. The royal party is seen processing from the west door towards the choir, the route being lined by Yeomen of the Guard and a double row of grenadiers. Beneath the dome, wooden staging had been built to a great height to accommodate the children from London's charity schools. By way of welcome, they lustily sang the 100th Psalm. Dayes's image captures that emotional moment. In it, the dukes of Cumberland, Gloucester and York, the prince of Wales, the king, the queen, and several princesses can be identified. A wedge of Christ's Hospital boys can be spotted on the right. The print was published by Benjamin Beale Evans of the Poultry in May 1793. A note on it states that it was engraved by James Neagle 'from a drawing in the collection of Her Majesty'. Queen Charlotte's collection was sold in a public auction in 1819, so it could be that the Dayes watercolour of the thanksgiving in the Guildhall Library collection is that item.

The actual service in the choir was recorded in an aquatint published by Robert Pollard on 24 June 1790. The print is fairly common, but to be understood it needs to be studied with a sheet entitled 'Explanatory References to the Print of the Choir of St Paul's on the Day of Solemn Thanksgiving…', which is rare. There is a copy of this key in the King's Topographical Collection.[39] It consists of a key block, the references and an account of the procession. An engraved plan depicting the choir on this occasion is also rare. This item was drawn by Robert Mylne, Surveyor to the Fabric, engraved by Thomas Medland and printed for John Stockdale.[40]

Towards the end of the eighteenth century, the convention for showing the cathedral standing in acres of vacant space was largely abandoned.[41] It is now represented more faithfully, looming over buildings or peeping round the corner at the end of a narrow, crowded street. The new style was introduced in 1792 by William Marlow. In Marlow's case, the crowded street is Ludgate Hill with the church of St Martin Ludgate on the left. The composition of Thomas Girtin's view of St Paul's from St Martin's-le-Grand is very similar in spirit (Fig. 281). It is thought to have been painted in *c.*1795. Girtin had grown up near St Martin's-le-Grand and was therefore very familiar with the noisy, bustling street with its dilapidated shop fronts. He died in 1802, and the print after the

325

279 (*above left*).   Interior during the thanks-giving service for the recovery of George III, 23 April 1789, by Edward Dayes, published in 1793. (GL)

280 (*above right*).   The dome and north side of the choir from Cheapside, engraving by Thomas Malton, 1797, from *A Picturesque Tour through the Cities of London and Westminster*. (GL)

281 (*left*).   The dome from St Martin-le-Grand, watercolour by Thomas Girtin. *c*. 1795. (Metropolitan Museum of Art, New York)

282. Lord Nelson's funeral under the dome, 13 January 1806, aquatint by F. C. Lewis after A. C. Pugin. (GL)

watercolour was published by his brother John thirteen years later. The dedication to the earl of Essex tells us that what we are looking at will become the site of the new General Post Office.

Another artist who adopted the new style was Thomas Malton, an architectural perspectivist who was responsible for *A Picturesque Tour through the Cities of London and Westminster* (1792–1801). This volume does indeed consist of a descriptive and iconographic tour through the capital. The iconographic element consists of a hundred fine aquatints. Ten of them are of St Paul's, so this one London landmark receives disproportionate attention (Fig. 280). The cathedral is viewed at first from Blackfriars Bridge (plate 48, the plate that concludes volume 1) and then from Ludgate Hill (plate 49, the first plate in volume 2). Next we have views of the west front and the south front (plates 50–51), and then three views of the interior, showing the nave looking from the west entrance towards the choir (plate 52), the nave looking from beneath the dome towards the west entrance (plate 53) and a view of the transept from the north entrance (plate 55). Then we have a view of the cathedral from the west end of Cheapside (plate 56). The hundred aquatints were supposed to conclude with a view of the opera house (which opera house is not clear). There was a hitch and Malton substituted yet another St Paul's view – this time showing it from the north-west corner of the churchyard.

In his text Malton, like so many commentators (see p. 452), extols the exterior of St Paul's and damns the interior. 'There is nothing to awaken curiosity or the charm the fancy, no splendours of decoration, no elaborate display of art in sculpture or painting, nothing but barren vacuity, through which at intervals a few wandering visitants glide like spectres escaped from the tombs.' He reminds his readers of the Royal Academicians' offer to decorate the panels, and its rejection. But Malton rejoices at the introduction of sculpture in the shape of the monuments to Samuel Johnson and John Howard, then recently installed (see

pp. 272–5). To give an idea of the effect, he sketchily introduces one of them into his view from under the dome (plate 53).

The St Paul's plate in Rudolph Ackermann's *Microcosm of London* (1808–1809), engraved by J. Bluck after Thomas Rowlandson and A. C. Pugin, like Malton's plate 55, consists of the view across the space beneath the dome from the north to the south transept. William Coombe's text once again contrasts the 'chilling nakedness' of the interior with the splendour of the exterior.

The most significant state occasion at St Paul's at the beginning of the nineteenth century was the funeral of Nelson (Fig. 282). The funeral car had been designed by the Strand printmaker Rudolph Ackermann, who was also an experienced and accomplished carriagemaker. London printmakers competed to be the first to bring out Nelson funeral prints. Ackermann, with his inside knowledge, was able to issue the first of his before anyone else. His aquatint of the coffin carries the date 7 January 1806 – two days before the event. On 13 January a rival, S. W. Fores, rushed out a view of the funeral car with a cheeky caption: 'The Public may be assured of the Correctness of this print, as Mr Elliot[t] of Bond Street [the upholsterer of the car] very kindly gave the Publisher every Assistance to complete it from the Car itself.' It was printed in aquatint to imitate black velvet, and sold for two shillings plain, two shillings and sixpence correctly coloured, and five shillings 'silvered at the top like the car'.[42] Besides views of the coffin and the funeral car, Ackermann announced the publication of 'Nelson's Emblematic Monument', offering those who subscribed a free copy of a print showing 'the correct representation of the banners, banderoles, trophies, &c. which were placed round the coffin in St Paul's'. The text on it would include a pedigree of 'the much-lamented Hero'.[43]

Two series of prints commemorating Nelson's funeral were published. In April, Cundee announced the publication of the first of these – four coloured aquatints – proudly boasting that they had been taken from actual observation during the water and

283 (*top*). *Queen Caroline's Procession to St Paul's, November 29, 1820. To return thanks for her Triumph over the Bill of Pains and Penalties*, popular woodcut published by T. Batchelar. (GL)

284 (*above*). *Going to St Paul's*, view by George Cruikshank from *The Comic Almanack*, 1845, showing parish officers leading children from local schools to the cathedral. (GL)

285. Bird's-eye view within the Colosseum, Regent's Park, showing panorama of London painted on canvas lining the walls, with west towers of St Paul's in foreground, by Thomas Hornor and E. T. Parris. Aquatint published by Rudolph Ackermann, 1829. (GL)

land processions and from inside the cathedral during the funeral service.[44] The draughtsman was the architectural artist, A. C. Pugin. The second series was published by Edward Orme, engraver and printseller to the king and royal family. The dates on his individual prints range from 12 January to May 1806. They would appear with other relevant Nelson prints in *Orme's Graphic History of the Life, Exploits, and Death of Horatio Nelson*.[45]

Making sense of the prints of the actual funeral service is difficult. The space under the dome was illuminated by a temporary, octagonal lantern bearing about 200 lamps. This is represented in the prints more or less consistently. The arrangement of mourners and banners within the enclosure installed under the dome, however, differs from print to print. Two items that can be profitably used with the prints are William Suttaby's *Inside of St Paul's Cathedral as Fitted up for the Funeral of Lord Nelson*, and a manuscript cross-section of the platform staging.[46]

The funeral of Nelson was an occasion that united the nation in grief, and was celebrated by a torrent of prints. Queen Caroline's attempted thanksgiving at St Paul's on 29 November 1820, intended to celebrate her triumph over the Bill of Pains and Penalties and 'to return thanks for her escape from a conspiracy', divided the nation, and was celebrated in just one or two pro-Caroline popular prints. One of them was published by Alderman Thomas Kelly of Paternoster Row. It depicts the moment when

she arrived at St Paul's. In another popular print, published by T. Batchelar, a banner reads 'Britons Behold your Queen' (Fig. 283).

The most popular regular function at the cathedral – popular with the public at any rate, less so with the clergy – was the united annual service of the London charity schools, instituted as a regular event in 1782 (see p. 350). Normally it took place in June. It occupied the nave and the entire space beneath the dome, the children being accommodated on staging, built tier over tier to a considerable height. The staging took one month to erect, blocked out the choir and transepts, and effectively put the cathedral out of action for other functions. The service itself was very moving, reducing hard men to tears. Several prints of the service were published in the nineteenth century. Richard Phillips of 77 St Paul's Churchyard published a line engraving by James Fittler after Edward Pugh in 1804, and Joseph Mead a steel engraving by W. H. Page after Frederick Mackenzie. An etching entitled 'Going to St Paul's' by George Cruikshank showed a procession of children setting off from their school, parish officers leading the way (Fig. 284). Later, the *Illustrated London News* would produce wood engravings of the event. The most attractive engraving by far, however, was an aquatint issued by Robert Havell junior – 'The Anniversary Meeting of the Charity Children in the Cathedral Church of St Paul' – published in *c*.1830 in aid of the Female Charity School in St Pancras.

286.   St Paul's and old Blackfriars Bridge from the south-west, by David Roberts, exhibited at the Royal Academy, 1862. This historicizing picture shows not only the old bridge before demolition but also the Lord Mayor's procession on the river, a ceremony discontinued in 1856. (The Worshipful Company of Goldsmiths)

Alterations at the cathedral were sure to trigger the publication of prints. In 1820 the Surveyor of the Fabric, C. R. Cockerell, was obliged to replace the corroded ball and cross atop the dome. Thomas Hornor, a Yorkshire land-surveyor, who earlier in the year had been making drawings from the Bull's Eye Chamber, was given permission to erect an observatory above Cockerell's scaffolding. With the aid of a graphic telescope, Hornor made about 300 sketches.[47]

Originally it had been Hornor's intention to produce a printed panorama made up of four long sheets. Subscribers were canvased by means of a prospectus which passed through several printings between 1822 and 1823.[48] It was illustrated with a view of Hornor's observatory and also a folded cross-section of the cathedral, copied from Wale and Gwynn's, demonstrating Hornor's

route to his observatory, up 616 stairs and four ladders. Extensions to the cross-section on left and right can also be unfolded to reveal St Paul's Churchyard. In the event, the prints were never published. Instead, the drawings became the basis of a 360-degree show panorama, painted by E. T. Parris and assistants within a specially designed rotunda called the Colosseum, built on the east side of Regent's Park (Fig. 285).

An anonymous aquatinted anamorphic view of London, *A View of London and the Surrounding Country Taken from the Top of Saint Paul's Cathedral*, was concocted from keys to this panorama in *c*.1845.[49] A vignetted north-east view of the cathedral appears in its centre.

Thomas Hornor was not the only panoramist to be interested in St Paul's. David Roberts, who year by year painted panoramas

287. Trigonometrical survey of London from the top of the dome, 1848. (GL)

for the Theatre Royal, Drury Lane and then at the Theatre Royal, Covent Garden, used the cathedral as a dramatic background for several easel paintings. Three of his oil paintings showing the Cathedral concern Lord Mayor's Day. That at Goldsmiths' Hall is of St Paul's and Blackfriars Bridge, and shows the Lord Mayor's Procession on the river (Fig. 286). To add drama to the scene, the size of the cathedral is greatly exaggerated. Guildhall Art Gallery has *St Paul's Cathedral with a Civic Procession*, an oil on panel, which depicts the Lord Mayor's Show at the top of Ludgate Hill making the turning into St Paul's Churchyard. The Walker Art Gallery, Liverpool has a companion to the Guildhall painting which shows the Lord Mayor's Procession at the foot of Ludgate Hill turning into New Bridge Street.

Thomas Allom, architect, architectural perspectivist and panoramist, had a vision of a more beautiful London. He produced two watercolours, now at the Victoria and Albert Museum, which reveal his dream for transforming the Thames by means of a spectacular embankment and quay.[50] St Paul's dominates the scene in both, and it is clear that Allom intends his scheme to complement the cathedral. In 1846 Allom published a pair of bird's-eye views which together provide a 360-degree (though overlapping) view of London, one being a view looking eastwards from the spire of St Bride's, the other a view looking west from

the upper gallery of the dome of St Paul's.[51] The views were engraved on steel, the St Paul's plate by John Henry Le Keux, and were published by Ernest Gambart, Junin & Co. of Berners Street. Lithographic versions of them were published in Paris, being drawn and lithographed by H. Walter, printed by Lemercier and published by Wild.

French lithographic printmakers supplied a wider, international market than their British counterparts. Jules Arnout in Paris designed and lithographed a number of St Paul's views. These tinted lithographs, occasionally coloured, were published jointly by Bulla Frères et Jouy in Paris; F. Ebner in Berlin; Ernest Gambart & Co. in London; and Emile Seitz in New York. The series includes a view of the Ambulatory 'Cathédrale de St Paul, bas coté'; two views of the nave from slightly different viewpoints ('St Paul's Inside View' and 'Cathédrale de St Paul, La Nef'); and a north-east view of the exterior from the corner of Cheapside ('Dôme de la Cathédrale de St Paul'). Arnout also issued an animated view of the cathedral from Fleet Street, confusingly entitling it 'Rue de la Flotte de Ludgate Hill.'

The funeral of the duke of Wellington on 18 November 1852 (see pp. 381–4) has been described as 'the most colossal religious spectacle ever staged in St Paul's at this or any other period of its existence'.[52] When the duke died on 14 September the printmakers, now into chromo- rather than tinted-lithography, went into top gear. Ackermann & Co., successors to Rudolph Ackermann, commanded the top end of the market. With Day & Son, lithographers to the queen, they published on 30 April 1853 a series of large, spectacular chromo-lithographs.[53] The one of the actual service in this series needs to be read with a 'Plan Shewing the General Arrangement and Sub-Division of the Seating on the Occasion of the Funeral of Field Marshal the Late Duke of Wellington', lithographed by Standidge & Co., at hand. The artist had been accommodated on the benches on the south side of the nave reserved for the press. For the funeral, the cathedral's windows were covered with heavy black cloth, obscuring all daylight. Lines of artificial lights trace out the main features of the architecture, and a corona of gas-jets run underneath the Whispering Gallery to illuminate the dome area.

The duke of Wellington's funeral was the last occasion to be celebrated by London printmakers in such a grand manner. In 1857, in the face of competition from France and the phenomenal success of the Art Unions, Ackermann & Co. dissolved their partnership. From this date, makers of quality prints scarcely ever concerned themselves with reportage. The reason for this must surely have been the arrival on the scene of illustrated newspapers. In 1842 the *Illustrated London News* (*ILN*) had been launched, a weekly newspaper, modestly priced and heavily illustrated with wood engravings, which rapidly acquired a large circulation. Soon there were rivals – the *Illustrated Times* and the *Pictorial Times*, for example – and from 1869 there was the *ILN*'s most serious rival, *The Graphic*. State occasions were celebrated by these illustrated newspapers with special commemorative issues, and within days of the event. The illustrations would not be coloured aquatints or chromo-lithographs, but nevertheless they could be very striking. This was definitely so with the *ILN*'s large fold-out wood engraving, 'The Funeral of the late Duke of Wellington in St Paul's Cathedral', by J. L. Williams, which showed the service in progress beneath the dome.

The *ILN* and its rivals also provided a vehicle for news illustrations of the cathedral that almost certainly would not have been recorded otherwise. In June 1848, for example, sappers and miners

constructed a crow's nest, somewhat in the manner of Thomas Hornor's observatory, though more sturdy, above the ball and cross. From there they took bearings in connection with the tri-angulation of the metropolitan area for the first Ordnance Survey of London. Wood engravings showing the crow's nest and the soldiers taking their observations appeared in the *ILN* (Fig. 287).[54] *Punch* carried a caricature.[55]

Another news event that resulted in noteworthy wood engravings was the restoration of Thornhill's paintings. Their lamentable condition had become apparent when the dome was illuminated with gas-jets for Wellington's funeral. The task of restoration was assigned to E. T. Parris (see pp. 242–4; Figs 174, 288). On 24 December 1853 the *ILN* carried a cross-section of the dome showing Parris's system of scaffolding, and explained how it worked. It also carried a dramatic general view of the dome showing the operation in progress. In 1856, when the work was nearing completion, the journal sent its artist aloft to record what was happening at close quarters. The resulting wood engraving[56] showed the ambidextrous Parris perilously standing on his platform, applying paint with a brush in his left hand whilst holding three house-painter's brushes in his right, a pot of paint at his feet. His curious clothing, we are told, had been designed 'to protect him from the gusts of wind which play around the huge vaulted space'.

Another St Paul's news story was the installation of the Great Paul bell. The new sixteen-ton bell was cast in November 1881 at the foundry of Messrs Taylor & Sons at Loughborough (Fig. 289). Several views of its progress appeared in the illustrated papers – the great bell being tested for tone at the foundry, the bell being hauled by road to London by road steam engines, the bell at Highgate, the arrival at St Paul's, the removal of masonry from a door to get the bell into the building, and the hoisting of the bell through the void in the Dean's Stair up to the top of the north-west tower.

The longest-running saga in the illustrated weeklies and the architectural press, however, was the decoration (or 'completion') of St Paul's (see pp. 244–56). From 1860 they carried illustrations of scheme after scheme. The *Graphic* celebrated the completion of

288. E. T. Parris on a cradle restoring Thornhill's frescoes in the dome, *Illustrated London News*, 9 August 1856. (SPCL)

289. The new great bell for St Paul's leaves Messrs Taylor's works, Loughborough, for London, *The Graphic*, 20 May 1882. (SPCL)

290. Preparations for the thanksgiving service for the recovery of the Prince of Wales, *Zig Zag*, 24 February 1872. (GL)

W. B. Richmond's mosaics in the choir on 4 April 1896 with a full-page wood engraving by the romantic Catholic convert, H. w. Brewer. One senses the artist's hearty approval.[57]

There was one state occasion that received saturation coverage in the illustrated weeklies, the Thanksgiving for the Recovery of the prince of Wales on 22 February 1872. Every element in the thanksgiving programme was recorded in wood engravings in the *ILN*, the *Graphic*, *Zig Zag*, *Day & Night*, the *Queen* and the *Penny Illustrated Paper*, and not just the pomp. Many of the illustrations are pure reportage, setting out to satisfy the public's curiosity on a host of minor matters. How were the stands in the cathedral erected? *Zig Zag* showed a veritable army of carpenters at work (Fig. 290). Everyone could see the exterior of the queen's pavilion, but what did it look like *inside*? *The Graphic* showed them. The Navy was responsible for the illumination of the cathedral on thanksgiving night, but how was it done? The *ILN* showed a group of bearded sailors on the Golden Gallery filling the lanterns that were to surround the dome, alternatively red, white and green.

In 1887 Queen Victoria celebrated the Golden Jubilee of her reign with a service at Westminster Abbey. The Diamond Jubilee

on 22 June 1897, however, was celebrated with a service held on the steps of St Paul's. The scene was captured by Andrew Gow in a large oil painting (Fig. 320), which was presented to the Corporation of London two years later. Subsequently the Corporation had a photogravure reproduction of it made by William Doig & Co. The *Daily Mail* published 'what is, we believe, the largest news illustration ever printed by any daily paper in this country', which showed the Diamond Jubilee procession as seen from the ball of St Paul's.

The 1880s saw the foundation by Seymour Haden of the Society of Painter Etchers, which led to the 'British Etching Revival'. The prints produced were issued in limited editions and with variant states, and the scarcity of the states artificially affected their value. St Paul's was the subject of several of them. Eighteenth-century printmakers had coped with the problem of the cathedral's cramped site by grossly enlarging St Paul's Churchyard; and mid nineteenth century artists had been largely content to show St Paul's from the south looming over the townscape, or from the west peeping round the corner at the top of Ludgate Hill. The solution adopted by Mortimer Menpes, Ian Strang and A. R. Blundell was to show the cathedral from the roof-tops. Mortimer Menpes's etching seems to have been taken from the roof of a building in Ludgate Circus. An advertisement on the roof of a building on the north side of Ludgate Hill announces Treloar's carpets. From 1903 William Monk regularly issued a 'Calendarium Londinense', otherwise known as the 'London Almanack' or 'Monk's Calendar', with an original etching as its headpiece.[58] In 1906 the subject was St Paul's from Fleet Street.

291. *The Preservation of St Paul's*: scaffolding for the great restoration in the dome, by Ian Strang, 1927. (GL)

292.   Looking from Newgate Street to St Paul's after the raid of 29
December 1940, crayon and watercolour by Richard Mathews. (GL)

The *Preservation of St Paul's*, as the operation of the 1920s to strengthen the dome (see pp. 299–300) was popularly called, was recorded in 1927 in an evocative etching by Ian Strang depicting the scaffolding beneath the dome (Fig. 291). On the completion of the work, the dean and chapter organized a thanksgiving service. It took place at midday on 25 June 1930 and was attended by King George V. The invitation card consisted of an original etching of the cathedral by Henry Rushbury, each copy signed by the artist.

These operations had made detailed measurement of the cathedral both necessary and possible. Arthur F. E. Poley had begun taking measurements during repairs to the west end in 1908. He was now able to make a complete record, and the thirty-two plates resulting from his labours appeared in 1927 as *St Paul's Cathedral, London, Measured, Drawn and Described* (Fig. 116).[59] R. B. Brook-Greaves, in collaboration with Godfrey Allen, measured and drew the cathedral in isometric projection, his gigantic drawing being completed in 1928 (Fig. 136).[60] The Architectural Press published a reduced, yet still large, reproduction of it in a limited edition of fifty copies. On the completion of the 'Preservation', Cecil Brown drew a colossal and formidably detailed section of the building,

dedicating it to the king, and also two very large plans, one at the triforium level, the other above the roof of the triforium, which he dedicated to the dean and chapter.[61]

It was as well that these repairs had been made. On 29 December 1940 the Luftwaffe launched a massive firebomb raid on the heart of London. The St Paul's Fire Watch quickly doused incendiary bombs landing on, or even penetrating, the building, and it was in large measure due to them that the cathedral survived.[62] Richard George Mathews, etcher, illustrator and graphic journalist, arrived on the scene the next day. A Canadian resident in London, he worked for the *Montreal Star* and was used to working promptly and to deadlines. Over the next few months, Mathews produced an extensive series of pencil, crayon and watercolour drawings of the bomb damage in the City. It includes a view of the cathedral from the ruins of Paternoster Row, which he made on 30 December 1941 (Fig. 292), and views looking towards the cathedral from Watling Street, Warwick Street and Newgate Street. Dennis Flanders, another graphic journalist, served as a member of the St Paul's Fire Watch.[63] On 30 or 31 December he make a drawing of the cathedral from Cannon Street, and a few months later another from Watling Street.[64]

Muirhead Bone made a drawing on the spot, 'The City and St Paul's after the Raid on the Metropolis'; and Henry Rushbury produced drypoints showing the cathedral from Paternoster Row in 1941 and from Cannon Street in 1942. The headpiece for the 'Monk's Calendar' for 1942 showed the cathedral surrounded by buildings destroyed by enemy action. Etched by Leonard Squirrel, it was after a drawing made on the spot by Frank Emanuel.

The perspectivist, Cyril Farey, who also served on the Fire Watch, made a number of watercolour drawings of the cathedral during the war years, including one of the interior showing the damage to the north transept.[65] Cecil Brown, meanwhile, produced a watercolour bird's-eye view of the cathedral, showing gaping holes in the roofs of the north transept and the choir, and the area immediately around the building. It would serve as a study for his very much larger *Tribute to London*, which covers the whole of the central part of the City and displays the situation when the clear-up was under way.[66] Yet it was not a print, drawing or painting but a photograph, Herbert Mason's 'The Miracle of St Paul's', taken during the height of the great air-raid of 29 December, that remains the most evocative and celebrated image of St Paul's during World War II (see p. 461; Fig. 368). It was to be as vital a contribution to the iconography of the cathedral as any of its famous predecessors by David Roberts, Edward Dayes or even Canaletto.

29
ESTATES AND INCOME,
1714–2004

Jean Morrin

From the beginning of Christianity in England, landed estates were the traditional means of support for the church. The financing of 'old-foundation' cathedrals such as St Paul's had evolved over a very long time. Cathedral chapters of the 'new foundation', endowed at the Reformation, had statutes specifying sources of income and expenditure, including the repair of the cathedral fabric.[1] There were no such rules for old-foundation cathedrals: here, clergy drew income from a variety of sources. In the years following 1840, government intervention removed or drastically restructured the cathedrals' estates; in 1871 those belonging to St Paul's (with the sole exception of Tillingham, Essex, reputedly part of the original seventh-century endowment which St Paul's retains to this day) were exchanged for an annual cash endowment.[2] This chapter examines the estates and income up to this enforced change, before discussing the transformation of funding in the mid nineteenth century and the impact of the new financial system.

THE CORPORATE ESTATES BEFORE REFORM

In the eighteenth century, the chapter of St Paul's comprised the dean and three residentiaries, selected from a body of thirty prebendaries. Each residentiary received a small fixed stipend (his 'bread money' as prebendary), the profits of his prebend and an equal share (dividend) of the balance of the corporate estate revenues (the common fund) remaining once the running expenses of the cathedral had been met. The non-resident prebendaries received nothing from the common fund.

The St Paul's estate that supported the common fund comprised land, buildings, tithes, woods and manors in the city of London and the Home Counties (Essex, Kent, Middlesex, Surrey, Hertfordshire and Bedfordshire; Fig. 293). Chapter, minor canons and vicars choral each had communal and individual estates in these areas. The cathedral dignitaries and prebendaries were also endowed with individual estates. The chapter estate was very stable in the eighteenth century. The only major property sale occurred when part of Doctors Commons, in the parish of St Benet Paul's Wharf, was sold to the College of Doctors in 1783 for £3,000.[3] The rental roll of the cathedral comprised fixed, not variable, rents amounting to £1,600 per annum in the late eighteenth century. The cathedral also benefited from the income from a fabric fund, entirely separate from the common fund.

From the beginning of the nineteenth century, the escalating financial demands of the state impacted on the cathedral's estates. The government invited landowners to buy out the land tax on their estates to help finance the French wars. To raise the necessary capital, between 1798 and 1811 St Paul's sold land which provided 16 per cent of its annual rental income to its tenants. Remaining tenants were charged a proportion of the redeemed land tax in addition to rent. All leasehold land in Sunbury, Friern Barnet, Paul's Walden, Ardeley and Wickham St Paul was sold. Similarly, the leasehold land in the dean's manor of Sutton Court was sold to the duke of Devonshire to redeem the land tax on the dean's separate estate. Further property was sold in Kentish Town, Edmonton, Hemel Hempstead, Belchamp St Paul and in the city of London in the parishes of St Andrew Hubbard, St Faith, St Gregory, St Michael le Querne and St Vedast. The fixed rent roll of the cathedral consequently fell to £1,347, and by 1850 further small sales had reduced it to £1,317.[4] Wood was also sold, and the profit invested in government stocks.

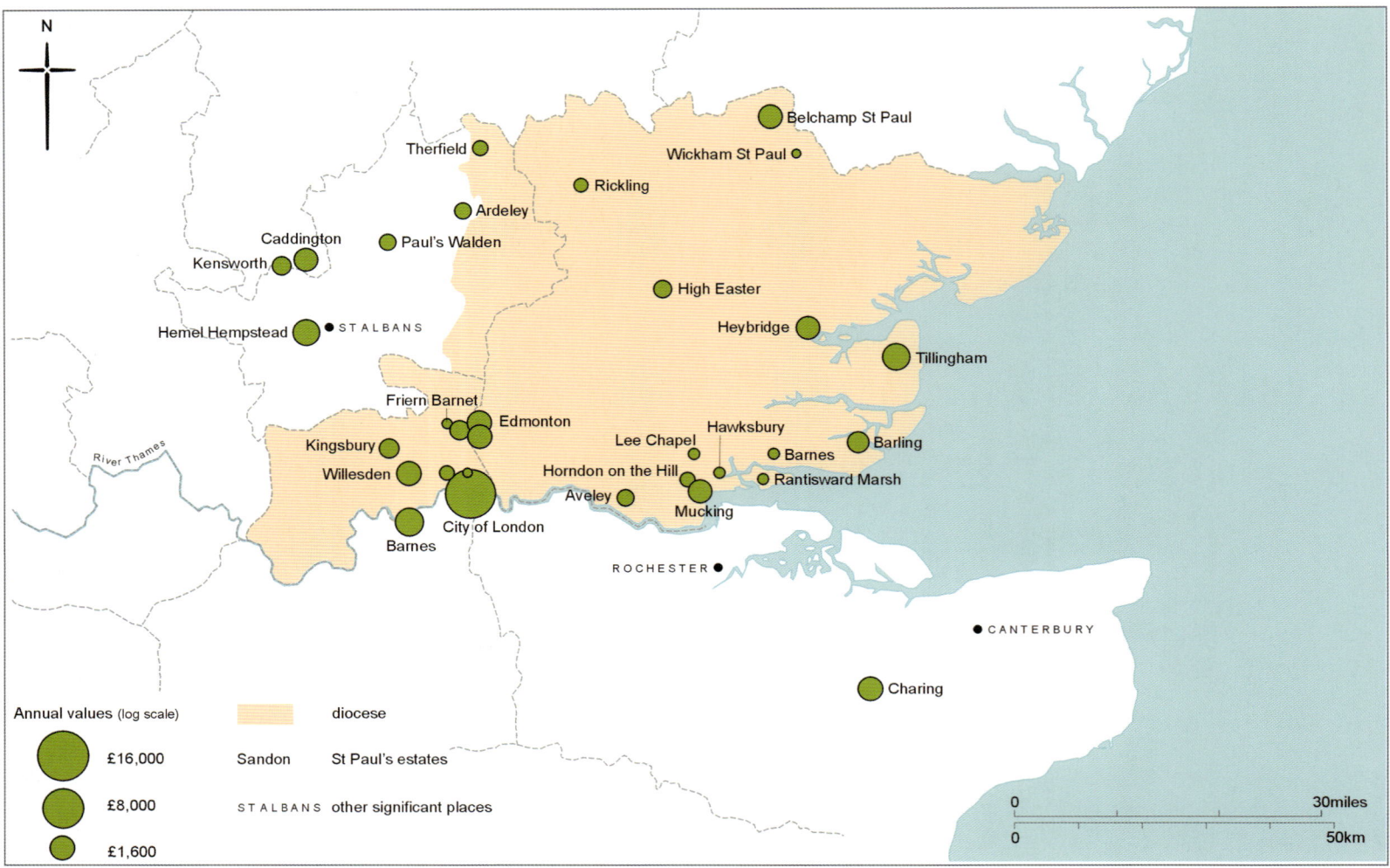

293.   Annual values of dean and chapter estates *c.* 1850. For county totals and sources, see Table 2, p. 29. The historic diocese of London is shown (see Fig. 262)

The chapter continued to collect rent and fines on its remaining estates. In the city of London, the chapter possessed houses, warehouses and other buildings on forty-year leases renewable every fourteen years. Over 80 per cent of St Paul's country leases were for twenty-one years, renewable every seven years on payment of a fine. Such leases provided a steady and largely predictable income, but failed to realize the full potential value of property.[5] During the nineteenth century, renewal fines on St Paul's country estates increased from 1.25 times to double the annual value of the estate. Property values also increased rapidly from the late eighteenth century, so, in contrast to the stability of the century after 1660, fines from the country leasehold estates increased dramatically between 1740 and 1840: fourfold at Belchamp, fivefold at Mucking and a massive eightfold at Tillingham (from £380 in 1738 to £3,232 in 1843). However, the tenants still paid less than economic rents.[6] Chapter officials valued some properties, but too often relied on tenants for information about often lucrative subleases. It was better when independent local sources could be consulted: when the lease of Charing and Egerton tithes was renewed in 1800, the vicar supplied details of crop yields (requesting that the lessees should not be informed of his role).[7]

Two archaic forms of tenure survived on the St Paul's estates: leases for lives, and copyhold tenure. On the country estates, fifteen leases (thirteen for Hemel Hempstead and Bovingdon tithes, the others for land attached to High Easter rectory and 140 acres of Rantisward marsh on Canvey Island) were for three lives – a

form of tenure condemned by the Crown in the 1630s. Income from such leases through fines was erratic, occurring only on the death of one of the people whose lives were specified. When this happened, huge fines for adding a new life benefited the chapter. One life dropped from the lease of High Easter rectory in 1855; the lease had last been granted in 1806 and the remaining lives belonged to individuals aged eighty-two and seventy-seven. To add a new life, the chapter charged £7,129, most of which they drew as dividend, almost doubling their average annual dividend: such windfalls explain their reluctance to run out leases for lives, despite the fact that their predecessors had been deprived of fine income for fifty years, and the annual rent was only £37.[8]

Leases for lives were not the only archaic survival on the St Paul's estate. Copyhold tenure, where tenants held their land by copy of the manor court roll, continued on its manors.[9] Chapter charged variable fines on entry to copyhold (except at Kensworth, where fixed annual sums covered rent and fines). Elsewhere during the nineteenth century, copyholders were slowly buying the freehold interest in their land, and some ecclesiastical landowners (for example, Durham chapter) had converted copyhold to leasehold in the sixteenth century after legal battles with tenants. In 1850, however, St Paul's chapter still received £1,600 a year from manorial rents and fines.[10] Copyhold survived on many secular estates in the home counties, and the pattern was reproduced on the St Paul's holdings here: its Essex manors of Barling, Tillingham, Heybridge, Wickham St Paul and Mucking; in Hertfordshire at Therfield, Ardeley, Paul's Walden,

Kensworth; at Caddington in Bedfordshire; at Barnes in Surrey; and at Friern Barnet, Tottenham and Edmonton in Middlesex.[11]

The canon in residence at St Paul's was always available to take major estate decisions. More routine administration was transacted by lay professionals – lawyers, surveyors and land agents – of whom the most important were the chapter clerk and the steward. Woods were managed by a land agent. Christopher Hodgson, who also served the archbishop of Canterbury and the bishop of London, acted as chapter clerk for sixty-three years from 1806 to 1869, negotiating the renewal of leases, representing the chapter at parliamentary committees, and managing the mid nineteenth-century changes on the estate.[12] The manorial courts and copyholders were managed by the chapter steward, the lawyer William Sellon.[13] Hodgson and Sellon instructed tenants to repair buildings and preserve trees; they increased fines if a tenant was late renewing a lease and reduced them if costly repairs were needed (for example, at the General Court Baron of Barnes manor in 1831 a Dr Patin, tenant of a large pond on the waste for which he paid £2 annually, was allowed ten years rent-free for 'his great expense in cleaning the pond and making new sluices').[14]

The chapter was an active landlord: any serious disputes or issues affecting the structure of the estate were referred to them for resolution.[15] In 1828 a Mr Pedley wanted to exchange his leasehold farm in Caddington for part of his own freehold farm, and proposed to obtain the act of parliament necessary for the exchange. Chapter determined that Pedley must provide adequate buildings on the land to be exchanged and bear the costs. After 1831 chapter occasionally granted building leases requiring an act of parliament, beginning with 6.5 acres in Eden Grove, Islington, where the tenant surrendered his twenty-one-year lease in return for a ninety-nine-year building lease. The economic rent payable was reduced to recognize the tenant's interest in the land, assessed at two-thirds. A general act permitting chapters to grant building leases passed in 1842 gave more security for large investments. During the 1840s, a series of building leases were granted in Barnes as the area was ripe for development.[16]

The pattern of tenure on the country estates became increasingly fragmented as the intensity of land use increased during the nineteenth century and portions were let to new lessees for development. The country properties nearest to London were the most likely to be developed: the Hammersmith Bridge Company acquired parts of Barn Elms manor. In 1828 Kentish Town parsonage was divided into seven leases and Willesden into fifteen. Bowes manor, Edmonton and Tottenham were divided. There was also development further afield: the Bedfordshire manor of Caddington was divided in 1828, and Hemel Hempstead rectory, a lease for lives, was divided into ten separate leases in 1810. There was much less scope for development in the crowded city properties around St Paul's.[17]

Who were the tenants of St Paul's? Most were male. In 1850 there were a few female leaseholders in houses in the city and outer suburbs of London. Most tenants of country estates were aristocracy or gentry: Lord Truro was charged over £4,000 to enfranchise his leasehold property in Charing and Egerton in 1855. In the smaller properties of the city and outer London, there were many craftsmen renting individual properties, although wealthier tenants still leased groups of property. Fines precluded impecunious tenants. Manorial land could none the less attract copyholders of very varied social status: the 150 copyholders of the manor of Cantlers in Kentish Town included the earl of Dartmouth, but also plumbers and builders.[18]

294. Extract from a map of Tillingham, Essex, in 1739, showing estate buildings. Tillingham was reputed to have been granted to the cathedral at its foundation and is still in the possession of the dean and chapter. (Essex Record Office, D/Dge P8)

By 1850 St Paul's Cathedral was not realizing the potential rental value of its common fund estates. In 1850 the total income actually collected by chapter from rents, fines and other common-fund estate sources was £13,811, but almost three times that sum could have been achieved from a system of economic or rack rents: the potential value of these was estimated by chapter officials at £38,460, demonstrating just how far short the income fell of its full potential.[19] In the city of London the parish with the greatest potential annual rental value was St Faith (£3,399 p.a.), while the parishes of St Benet Paul's Wharf, St Gregory by St Paul's, St Martin Ludgate, St Michael Wood Street, and St Martin Ironmonger Lane each contained property worth over £1,000 p.a. The total estimated rental value of city property in 1850 amounted to nearly £16,000.[20] The country estates, including manorial dues, were estimated to have potential economic rents of nearly £23,000 in 1850: Essex estates had a potential rental value of over £8,000; those in Middlesex of nearly £7,000; the Hertfordshire estates of nearly £3,000; Surrey £2,000; Bedfordshire over £1,500; and Kent over £1,000 (Table 2 and Fig. 293). The single most valuable country estate was Tillingham in Essex (Fig. 294), with an estimated rental value of over £2,000, but the Middlesex estates of Edmonton, Tottenham and Willesden were increasing in value as the metropolis of London expanded.[21] The chapter also had £15,710 invested from sales of woods, land tax and land sold for economic development such as railways and bridges. This gave a dividend of approximately £592 in 1850.[22]

THE ESTATES OF THE DIGNITARIES, PREBENDARIES, MINOR CANONS AND VICARS CHORAL (Table 1)

The dean, chancellor, treasurer and precentor had separate estates. In 1850 together these had a potential rental value of £25,000, but again this was not realized. The dean's estate had a net annual potential rental value of £21,015. Of this Shadwell, sold for the highest price in the Interregnum land sales, had a potential annual rental value of £15,837, but the property had been let on a ninety-nine-year lease with a perpetual right of renewal, and Dean Copleston (died 1849) drew only £2,000 a year from it.[23] The dean's land in the cathedral precincts had a potential net annual rental value of £3,312, in Whitechapel of £345; at Sandon (Herts) of £1,184 and at Biggins manor (Essex) of £338. The dean also received his stipend, the profits of his separate estate and his equal share (as a residentiary) of the surplus on the common fund. The treasurer, chancellor and precentor were not members of chapter, but held sinecure estates. The chancellor's estate had a potential annual rental value in 1847 of £2,213 and comprised land in the precincts and Hammersmith with the rectories of Boreham (Essex) and Ealing (Middlesex). The treasurer's lands, in Hertfordshire, had a net annual rental value of £1,651 in the 1860s.[24] But once more, as with the chapter and their corporate estates, the dignitaries realized nothing approaching these annual values. In 1835 the officers' incomes (from all sources) were reported as follows: precentor £58, chancellor £74 and treasurer £65 (p. 86).

As an old-foundation cathedral, St Paul's had non-resident prebendaries, twenty-six of whom enjoyed their manorial endowments as sinecures (the other four being the dean and residentiaries). Chapter did not value prebendal lands as they were outside their responsibility. The chapter surveyor could only tell a parliamentary committee that 'the prebends are different persons; they hold I believe, a great deal of property unconnected with the dean and chapter at all'.[25] Prebendal land was leased for three lives or twenty-one years. The prebends varied greatly in value. Nesden consisted of a quarter of an acre of land worth a few shillings per annum but charged with repairing a bridge, which sometimes cost the unfortunate prebendary £50 or £60. Finsbury with existing leases had a potential net annual rental value of £7,000 in 1859, and was expected to be worth ten times as much when the leases fell in.[26] Prebendal income, however, was once more much less than the value of the subleases of the estates. The net annual rental value of all the prebendal estates with their current leases was estimated in the mid nineteenth century at £58,000. Change of use from agriculture to industry and the running out of leases could have increased that value tenfold.[27] The difficulty of combining ministry with land management is illustrated by decisions made by the prebendary of Cantlers in 1813. Thomas Randolph kept one-third interest in his estate, but alienated two-thirds to his tenant, the marquis of Campden, in return for estate management. When valuing the prebend Cluttons recorded that the alienation to the marquis was 'not a good decision'. The prebendary was drawing about £2,000 annually from his third, but Cluttons estimated in 1850 that once the building leases expired the prebend should produce an income of £80,000 a year, only one third of which would revert to the church because of the Act of 1813.[28]

The minor canons of St Paul's had individual endowments, mostly located in St Benet, Paul's Wharf. Individual estates yielded £40–70 a year, except those of the sub-dean, worth £150 p.a. All received occasional renewal fines.[29] The corporate estates of the college of minor canons included $8/_{21}$ of the tithes of Halstead rectory and property in St Paul's churchyard, yielding £12 annually for each minor canon. The minor canons also had a share in the 'cupola fund' derived from payments made by visitors to the upper part of the cathedral. Although the minor canons with the vicars choral administered the fund, the virgers also received a share (they alone profited from showing the crypt and ball). Its net average annual income in the 1850s was £946.[30]

Each of the thirty medieval prebendaries had a vicar choral to represent him in the choir, but by the nineteenth century only six vicars choral remained, now laymen. Each received an income of about £40 per annum from a corporate endowment in Essex leased from the chapter, including the tenths of the rectories of Steeple Bumpstead, White Notley and a share of Halstead rectory ($^{13}/_{21}$ parts), the vicarage of Finchingfield and a house in Ludgate worth about £75 a year. Vicars choral also received a stipend, an allowance instead of Sunday dinners (from 1843) and a share in the cupola fund which together amounted to over £100 annually.[31]

The separate estates of dignitaries, prebendaries, minor canons and vicars choral interwove with the corporate estate of the chapter to produce a complex mesh of cathedral landownership, especially in the city of London and in Kentish Town. The prebends of Harleston, Chamberlainwood, Broomesbury, Wilsden, Mapesbury, Nesden and Oxgate all lay in the parish of Willesden.[32] Much land was held in Essex. As we have seen, the rectory of Halstead had many demands made on it: a pension of £1 12s. paid to the chapter; a yearly rent of £1 12s. to the chamberlain, £2 for singing books for the choir, and a payment to the minor canons. In 1838 the Halstead lease was renewed for a fine of £1,900 to which each vicar choral and minor canon had to contribute. The prebends of Ealdland, Weldland, Reculversland and Sneating lay near the chapter estate at Tillingham.[33] Close proximity could create tensions. In 1837 the minor canons owned property in St Paul's churchyard leased to Evan Edwards. Without the chapter's consent, Edwards inserted windows on the first and second floors that overlooked the chapter house yard and was fined one shilling a year for continued use of the windows. He had to frost the glass to prevent 'persons seeing through the same and over looking the chapter yard' and only the top of the sash was to open 'for the admission of air'. Chapter retained the right to build on their chapter yard.[34]

THE FABRIC FUND

The fund established by parliament after the Great Fire of 1666 continued to provide for fabric maintenance. From 1753 the use of the fund was clearly defined and the trustees (the archbishop of Canterbury, the Lord Mayor and bishop of London) were responsible for the upkeep of the fabric including repair of the organ, clock and bells (prior to 1753 it had been employed among other things to pay for coal, candles and wages for watchmen). Minor expenses were charged to the chapter's common fund. From 1753 the trustees appointed an architect as Surveyor to the Fabric and the chapter a deputy.[35]

From 1837 the fund was supplemented by income from Dean Clarke's Charity drawn from the Tillingham estate. William

Clarke (dean not of St Paul's but of Winchester), a St Paul's lessee at Tillingham, on 22 April 1679 bequeathed his lease of lands and tithes to trustees charged with raising the septennial fine, with the aim of augmenting ten small vicarages and paying any surplus for repairing St Paul's cathedral. The trustees failed to pay the surplus to St Paul's. In 1837, however, Sydney Smith obtained a decree from the High Court of Chancery declaring that:

> the overplus of the clear annual rents and profits of the said charity estates was properly applicable to the repairing and keeping in repair of the said Cathedral church of St Paul and the same should be from time to time paid over to the Lord Archbishop of Canterbury, the Lord Bishop of London and the Lord Mayor of London.[36]

By the mid nineteenth century the combined annual income from the two fabric funds was about £1,500, made up of £700 from the dividends on the parliamentary fund of £23,000 Old South Sea annuities, and about £800 from the yearly rents and tithes of Tillingham. The chapter were empowered to spend only the income, not the capital, from the fund. When they overspent, for example on repairing the chapter house in 1833, the trustees protested. Although the fabric fund and communal fund were separate, the chapter contributed on an *ad hoc* basis when major work on the fabric was required: an arrangement contrasting with that at other old-foundation cathedrals, where chapters had more formal financial arrangements: for example, Salisbury, where one-eighth of the dividend was assigned to fabric maintenance. In 1821 the surveyor, Charles Cockerell, reported deterioration in the fabric and estimated the cost of repairs at £2,950. The chapter borrowed £3,000 to fund the repairs to be repaid out of their dividends over the next five years, and sold timber worth £584 to pay for 'cleaning and beautifying' the interior of the cathedral. Chapter also agreed to warm the choir in winter at a cost of £132 annually.[37]

THE AGE OF REFORM

These complex financial arrangements had both strengths and weaknesses. Owning land maintained the presence of the church in the city of London and Home Counties, but its management was a distraction from the business of running the cathedral as a place of worship. For the chapter, there was always the temptation to reduce expenditure to increase dividends. Tenants gained great advantage from the beneficial leases. They had security of tenure, and near-certainty of renewal: leases were frequently the subject of mortgages and trusts beyond the term of the lease. Large estates were leased to substantial tenants who sublet the land, often at great profit, but this at least relieved the clergy of responsibility for much estate administration. Tenants were responsible for repairs and insurance. This leasing system suited clergy who were not farmers, but some of the land was neglected despite repairing clauses in leases. In Caddington in 1865, the farm buildings were 'in bad order' and much land was unlet by the tenant.[38]

Contemporaries were particularly critical of the management of the estates of dignitaries and prebendaries. These members of the cathedral body (other than the residentiaries) seemed to do very little in return for their lands, and moreover failed to realize their financial value. They did not develop land for building in prime development areas such as Kentish Town and Islington. Buildings (as was the case at Shadwell) were frequently in a poor state of repair.[39]

In the 1830s politicians seeking reform, like the reformist bishop of London, Charles Blomfield, believed that the potential revenue of church estates was not being realized. As we have seen, the evidence supports this view. The cathedral estate had a potential estimated net annual rental value of £39,000 in 1850, but less than £14,000 was realized, since fines equivalent to economic rents were drawn on only one or two out of every seven leases each year at a time when land values had massively overtaken old fixed rents. Of the net annual value of £80,000 attributed to the estates of dignitaries and prebendaries, only one-tenth was realized, while the potential value if existing leases were run out was ten times greater for some of the individual estates.

The administration of the estates feeding the common fund could also have been improved. Responses to enquiries were hindered by the absence of a complete version of the cathedral statutes. In 1872 leases and other estate documents were discovered uncatalogued in the attic of the chapter house. No one individual in the chapter was responsible for income and expenditure. Manors were not operated very efficiently: chapter had few manorial maps to establish what land a tenant claimed. When Tillingham manor was surveyed in 1837 in response to Ecclesiastical Commission enquiries, it was discovered that all the copyholders had died: new tenants were admitted in 1838–9, presumably as a result of the survey.[40]

The basis of cathedral finance was transformed by state-inspired reform beginning in the 1830s in the wake of the constitutional revolution of 1828–32. The bishops' role in opposing parliamentary reform in 1831 encouraged radicals to view clergy as 'enemies of liberty and the civil rights of Englishmen'. Cathedral endowments joined clerical pluralities and non-residence in the firing line. In June 1832 the prime minister, Lord Grey, appointed an Ecclesiastical Revenues Commission to enquire into ecclesiastical finances.[41] Four years later, a permanent Ecclesiastical Commission was established to supervise church reform. Given the prevalence of attacks on the 'rich endowments of cathedrals', and the absence of alternative sources of funds to finance reform within the church which would not impinge on the financial interests of the lay political classes, it was inevitable that cathedral endowments would feature prominently in its deliberations.[42] Even some of those well disposed to deans and chapters believed that they were not effective estate managers and that managing estates was a distraction from their spiritual role. The commissioners' reports duly proposed that much cathedral property should be redeployed to support spiritual provision in the parishes of industrializing England and its administration transferred to the commission.[43]

The most prominent member of the commission, Bishop Blomfield of London, in particular wanted to make better use of the church's resources and to establish a central professional bureaucracy that would manage estates much more efficiently than cathedral chapters. Blomfield looked at the 'slums around St Paul's crying out for ministers and saw the endowments of the cathedral wasted in pastoral idleness'.[44] Sydney Smith responded on behalf of St Paul's chapter, arguing that the system could work as it was: the chapter employed professional agents to ensure effective management (p. 86). Smith accepted that the retention of prebends by non-residentiaries was unjustifiable, but suggested that each stall could be annexed to a populous parish, or cathedral endowments taxed to raise money for poor livings. Smith lamented what he saw as the state's over-reaction to the clamour for reform, regretting that 'all is change, fusion and confusion'. In an open letter to Blomfield published in *The Times*, Smith accused Blomfield 'of having shaken the laws of property and prepared the ruin of the church by lowering the character of its members'. He opposed sending the profits of St Paul's to distant Northumberland, a sentiment echoed in many other cathedrals.[45] Smith's protests were to no avail. The Ecclesiastical Duties and Revenues Act of 1840 attacked cathedrals as 'the most overt symbols of the church's power'.[46] As in other cathedrals, under its provisions land that had been donated to St Paul's would be effectively confiscated and in future managed by a central body to benefit distant parishes with no thought to the original donors' intentions. All the individual endowments of dignities and prebends were duly transferred to the commissioners as life-interests expired. Non-resident prebendaries were abolished to be replaced by (truly) honorary positions. Future appointments as deans and canons were no longer to be directors of cathedral businesses, but in some sense salaried employees of the church, deans receiving £2,000 and canons residentiary £1,000 per year rather than the previous annual average at St Paul's of £2,500 each for the residentiaries. St Paul's was allotted an additional residentiary in the person of the archdeacon of London, but fewer minor canons were to be employed. The college of minor canons protested to the commissioners, stating that they had existed since 1396 as a corporation holding lands, and they had done nothing to merit the loss.[47]

By 1859 at St Paul's the separate estates of the dean and twenty-seven of the prebends had been transferred to the Ecclesiastical Commissioners, although the last prebendary under the old dispensation (Randolph of Cantlers) would survive to 1875.[48] For forty years in the mid nineteenth century St Paul's was thus effectively in transition between old and new systems. The task of responding to parliamentary inquiries and the commissioners fell mainly to Smith and, after his death in 1845, to Archdeacon Hale and Dean Milman. Despite the uncertainty and negotiations, the cathedral and estates still had to be managed. The chapter sought in vain to use the profits of the prebends for repairs at St Paul's rather than transferring them to the commissioners for the benefit of the church as a whole.[49] The chapter also argued that the dependence on the public's contributions to the cupola, crypt and ball funds to finance the cathedral staff vital to maintaining such an 'expensive cathedral for the gratification of public curiosity' should be replaced by adequate stipends.[50] Such measures would maintain the dignity of the metropolitan cathedral: 'this is demanded by the great and increasing concourse of worship not only of the higher classes, and those of more refined education, but of the middle and even of the lowest orders'.[51]

Reform took on a new dimension with an 1851 act that permitted the enfranchisement of cathedrals' corporate estates to tenants or other buyers who paid the chapter the difference between the value of the lease and the value of the land. The profits of sales went to the Ecclesiastical Commissioners for redistribution to benefit the wider church. If a chapter and Church-Estates Commissioners wished to retain land, usually for its potential development value, the tenant was paid the surrender value of the lease and the land was transferred to the management of the Ecclesiastical Commissioners.[52] Attention had to be paid 'to the just and reasonable claims of the present holders of lands under lease or otherwise arising from the long continued practice of renewal'. The price to be paid for the sale or enfranchisement was to be the value of the land less the value of the lease, and if the chapter declined to enfranchise, they had to pay for the surrender

of the lease at such valuation. All claims by lessees that they had a long-standing vested interest were ignored. In 1851 Roundell Palmer warned that lessees should not be advantaged by historically uneconomic rents as no one could 'acquire a vested interest in the mismanagement of public property'.[53] The Church Estates Commissioners approved all transactions and adjudicated disputes, for example over land which had a dormant value for mining or building or on which extraordinary improvements had been made.[54]

More generally, however, St Paul's suffered badly from the confiscation of separate estates and the reduction in corporate income. James Tate died in 1843, Sydney Smith in 1845, Frederick Blomberg in 1847 and Dean Copleston in 1849, so the life-interests protecting the *status quo* expired quite rapidly, bringing in new arrangements for the operation of the common fund. After the deaths of the residentiaries, one third of the profits of the common fund were paid to the Ecclesiastical Commissioners, leaving the new residentiaries (who would also lose the income formerly received from the prebends held in plurality with the residentiaryship) with less revenue from the fund. St Paul's, despite its status as the metropolitan cathedral, only drew an average of £12,500 per year in income from its estate between 1846 and 1852, little above the average income of £10,570 among the twenty-six cathedrals and two collegiate churches. The income from all the prebendal estates at St Paul's is not recorded, but whereas the potential net annual rental value of the estate supplying the common fund was £38,460 in 1850, the prebendal lands had an estimated potential rental value of nearly £58,000 annually and the individual estates of the dean, chancellor and treasurer of almost £25,000 a year (Table 1).[55]

As a result of enfranchisement, the rent roll of the corporate estate was reduced by nearly one fifth, from £1,317 in 1850 to £1,067 in 1871, with a proportional reduction in fine income. Properties were sold to tenants in Charing, Willesden, Tottenham Bowes, Kensworth, Caddington, Therfield, Paul's House, Beauchamp and Heybridge, West Leigh and Mucking; and in the city of London in the parishes of St Andrew Holborn, St Andrew Baynards Castle, St Benet Paul's Wharf, St Benet Sherehog, St Dionis Backchurch, St Mary Aldermanbury, St Martin Orgar and St Michael le Querne. The sale documents reflected the old and the new in estate management, with property descriptions dating from the 1666 Great Fire linked to professional architectural plans of the premises as in the sale of a forty-year lease in St Paul's Bakehouse of

> all those two messuages or tenements [which] at the time of the dreadful fire was in the tenure or occupation of Thomas Turner, Doctor in Divinity then or late Dean of Canterbury, situate, lying and being on the south side of a court commonly called or known by the name of Paul's Bakehouse near Paul's Chain in the Parish of Saint Gregory in London.[56]

In the case of some other property, the tenant's interest was bought out. The Ecclesiastical Commissioners wanted a viable estate after commutation, so land was retained in areas suitable for housing and commercial development.[57]

Beneficial leases were replaced by rack rents. Much land was ripe for development, but this process meant a huge loss of fine income in the short term. The financial cost of running out leases led to chapter's decision to exchange their estate for a cash endowment from the commissioners. Following the trend set by Carlisle and York in 1852, the treasurer of St Paul's commuted his individual estate for a cash sum in 1858.[58] From 1863 Archdeacon Hale and Hodgson the chapter clerk worked on schedules of cathedral resources and expenses to determine the appropriate commutation sum, well before an act of 1868 made enfranchisement or transfer of land to the Ecclesiastical Commissioners compulsory. It fell to Dean Mansel and Canon Gregory to conduct the negotiations between 1868 and 1871 that finally secured an adequate initial sum for the running costs of the cathedral. However, no provision was made for review in the event of rising costs.[59]

The estates of St Paul's were finally transferred to the Ecclesiastical Commissioners on 29 September 1871, save for

> the cathedral church, the precincts thereof, the chapter house, the surveyor's office, the deanery house, the canonical houses (Amen Corner), and the redeemed land tax charged on the same houses excepting also any right of ecclesiastical, educational, or other like patronage, any property held by the said Dean and Chapter for the benefit of the minor canons of the said church, or of any one of such minor canons, or for the benefit of the pittanciary and vicars choral of the said church … but including the almonry estate.

The chapter kept the proceeds of the cupola fund, the crypt fund and the ball fund. So a great tradition came almost to an end. In return, chapter was endowed with an annual commutation sum of £18,000 to pay all salaries and expenses, including £2,000 for the dean and £1,000 for each of the canons. Tradition did not *quite* die, as St Paul's was re-endowed with the Tillingham estate that partly supported the fabric fund. The pressing need for repairs to the cathedral was recognized in a one-off capital payment of £30,000. St Paul's had the option of being re-endowed with an estate yielding £18,000, but the chapter opted for a permanent annual payment. Thus they had an initial advantage over cathedrals such as Canterbury, Durham and York, which opted for re-endowment, as this avoided a downturn in rental income during the agricultural depression of the 1880s from which the new system of rack rents offered no protection. The depression caused some cathedrals to hand back their new endowments in return for annual payments. However, in the long-term the annual payment had its own disadvantages, as twentieth-century chapters found that commutation payments were not increased in line with inflation.[60] The property of the pittanciary and vicars choral was similarly commuted in return for an annual sum of £900. The minor canons' estate was transferred to the Ecclesiastical Commissioners in 1875 in exchange for an annual income of £2,000, although the annual value of their estate (the tithes of St Gregory by St Paul and property in Islington) had been estimated at nearly £4,000 just six years before.[61]

FROM REFORM TO THE PRESENT

Improvements in the internal administration of the cathedral finances responding to the new challenges accompanied the externally imposed reforms. The chapter recognized the need for one residentiary to manage the new financial system, especially as the long-serving chapter clerk Christopher Hodgson retired and the receiver William Sellon died in 1869. Canon Gregory was appointed treasurer, with responsibility for all income and expenditure, and served until 1904.[62] The chapter charged William Sparrow Simpson, the cathedral librarian, to produce a definitive volume of the statutes of the cathedral. In 1876 the chapter even managed to persuade the commissioners to dedicate

the endowment of the last remaining prebend of Cantlers to the endowment of a diocesan schools inspector and a small financial payment to prebendaries fulfilling their preaching obligations.[63]

By 1871 the cathedral was in need of major repairs; the surveyor noted that 'the stonework is not in the condition which it ought to be, but the fabrick fund is insufficient to arrest its slow but gradual deterioration'.[64] The chapter deployed capital and income from the fabric fund on repairs, but the trustees objected when the fund was reduced to £5,000.

Chapter also decided to separate the parts of Dean Clarke's charity from Tillingham, devoted to its different purposes. A sum of £10,000, mainly from the fund but partly from communal chapter funds, was transferred to the Charity Commissioners to provide for the augmentations of poor livings. The Tillingham trustees were then discharged from duty and handed the Tillingham lease back to the chapter. The proceeds of the Tillingham estate now belonged fully to the chapter, who also became responsible for the entire fabric fund and the fabric surveyor, Penrose.[65]

Still more money was needed to meet the needs of repairing and modernizing St Paul's as a 'religious and national' monument: an appeal fund was launched to raise £100,000. The progress of the fund and gratitude to subscribers was recorded in *The Times* in 1870.[66] Restoration and improvement of the fabric has depended ever since on appeals and trust funds established to support specific projects at St Paul's. After the First World War, serious structural problems were discovered, necessitating further fundraising: the Ecclesiastical Commissioners, the City of London and the general public all contributed. Economies were also made in the running costs.[67]

Proceeds from the Tillingham estate, let in six leases for economic rents, continued to support some of the costs of the cathedral. Chapter purchased 170 acres of reclaimed enclosed land from Mr George Battens in 1876 for £1,300, to consolidate the estate, and three copyhold cottages were purchased in 1880.[68] Its long and colourful history continued during the Second World War, when a gun emplacement was sited at Tillingham, and farmland was flooded in the 1953 floods, much time elapsing before the ground recovered. Today, the Tillingham estate of 1,568 acres remains the property of St Paul's and the dean and chapter pay an annual visit (Fig. 295). The estate, protected by a sea-defence wall, has developed into three farms: Tillingham Hall, Weatherwick and Marsh Farm (which includes a decoy pond for wildfowling and marsh land). Tillingham Hall has been divided into flats and there are fifteen residential leases, together with grazing leases. Tillingham is not, however, the only investment property of the cathedral, since in the 1970s the Old Deanery was rented out and the dean moved into Amen Court. Together, these properties are valuable contributors to the cathedral's income and assets: the combined value of Tillingham and the Old Deanery increased by £490,000 in 2001 to £4.3m (helping to offset the £1m losses on St Paul's financial investments in the same period) and they yielded a net profit of £200,000.[69]

After the Second World War, the repair of war damage was a major drain on finances. Restoration was financed by the War Damage Commission and contributions from the City of London. Another important source of income appeared when in 1952 the Friends of St Paul's developed out of the St Paul's Watch to 'help finance desirable improvements in the Cathedral [and] to foster interest in its history, architecture and its work', which the Friends have done ever since.[70]

295. Chapter visit to the Tillingham estate, 1957. Left in front, Dean Matthews; far right in Land Rover, David Floyd Ewin, the cathedral's registrar and receiver. (SPCL)

The maintenance and improvement of the fabric of St Paul's now depends on trust funds such as the St Paul's Cathedral Trust, which was recently merged into the City of London Endowment Trust for St Paul's; and the Garfield Weston Trust. Capital grants are also received from English Heritage (as part of a general policy of supporting the maintenance of the fabric of historic cathedrals) and from the Friends. In 2001 nearly £2m was received from these trusts in capital grants for specific repair and building projects. A director of fund-raising was appointed in 1998 to head the development office. A trust fund has also been established in America.

The running costs of the twentieth-century cathedral should have been financed by the annual commutation sum received from the Ecclesiastical Commissioners. By 2001, however, the £18,000 paid annually from 1871 would need to have been increased to about £830,860 per annum to have equivalent purchasing power. Neither the Ecclesiastical Commissioners nor their successors, the Church Commissioners, have increased the commutation payment in line with inflation.[71] Small increases had raised the sum to a mere £22,000 a year by 1960. From 1 October 1966, the annual payment was replaced by a capital grant of £310,000 invested in the Church of England property pool and a very small annual sum (£3,500 in 1966). In the 1990s the share in the property pool was replaced by a capital endowment invested by the St Paul's chapter and on which dividends are received. This is inevitably vulnerable to wider economic trends: financial investments lost over a million pounds in value in 2001.[72] The Church Commissioners also pay an annual contribution to the salaries of the dean and two residentiaries, worth £83,731 in 2001.[73] It was in light of the utter inadequacy of these financial provisions to meet the running costs of the cathedral that from 1991 the chapter was forced to charge for admission to the cathedral. The cost of maintaining St Paul's today as both a place of worship and a national heritage site is very high. In the 130 years since the new system of financing began, total annual income has risen to £7.5m, of which net income in 2001 was £1m, reduced to £500,000 by net losses on investments of £500,000.[74] Tourism is thus an essential source of revenue. The mid nineteenth-century enterprises that brought in £1,000 annually from the cupola, crypt and ball funds have developed dramatically. Tourist income from the shop, café, restaurant, conference facilities and admissions, amounting in 2001 to £4.9m, now provides for virtually all the running costs of the cathedral, including clergy salaries and all the facilities provided for worshippers and tourists.[75]

The present dependence on the fickle profits of tourism represents a sea-change from the old system of financing the running costs of St Paul's from the proceeds of landed estates over which the chapter exercised control. One can only speculate on the result had the nineteenth-century reforms not occurred, or if chapter had opted for a re-endowment in property rather than a commutation sum in 1871. It might not be unduly fanciful to suggest that perhaps the finances of the metropolitan cathedral would now have a more secure, and more dignified, basis.

30

PREACHING ANGLICANISM
AT ST PAUL'S, 1688–1800

Jeremy Gregory

On Saturday 5 November 1709, the cleric William Bissett, a Whig supporter and a low churchman, was among the congregation in the rebuilt St Paul's awaiting the sermon at the annual thanksgiving service for the discovery of the Gunpowder Plot in 1605. This was conventionally an occasion to celebrate the nation's deliverance from popery and arbitrary government, and to wax lyrical about the benefits of the Revolution of 1688, which, providentially it seemed to some, had also begun on 5 November, when the future William III landed at Torbay. In fact, the sermon – delivered by Henry Sacheverell, a thirty-six-year-old fellow of Magdalen College, Oxford, with something of a reputation for being a high-church zealot – has claims to be regarded as the most notorious ever preached in the cathedral (old or new). Bissett, who was sitting next to Sacheverell, later remembered that the preacher 'came into the pulpit like a Sybil to the mouth of her cave, or a Pythoness upon the Tripod', and recalled being surprised by 'the fiery red that over-spread his face... and the goggling wildness of his eyes'.[1] Instead of containing the usual platitudes, *The Perils of False Brethren, both in Church and State* (on the text 2 Cor. xi:26; Fig. 296), preached during one of the most intense periods of party strife in the century, was a swingeing attack on the incumbent Whig regime. The resulting uproar made it the hottest political topic of the year, and proved to be a vote-winner for the Tories in the general election in September 1710.

In Sacheverell's opinion, the Whig government had placed the Church of England in danger by siding with its nonconformist rivals. Indicative of the importance contemporaries placed on preaching in St Paul's as a way of influencing the rest of the country was the fact that he saw his sermon as an opportunity

to open the Eyes of the Deluded People, in this our Great Metropolis; being conscious of what prodigious importance it is to the welfare of the Whole Nation to have its Rich and Powerful Citizens set right in their Notions of Government, both in Church and State.

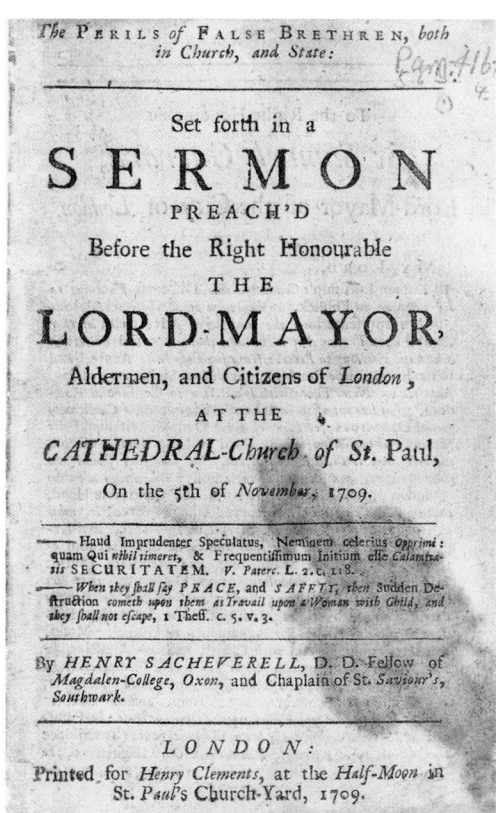

296. Title page of Henry Sacheverell's St Paul's sermon of 5 November 1709, *The Perils of False Brethren, both in Church and State*. (SPCL)

Sacheverell pointed to what he saw as a parallel between the Church of Corinth in Paul's time and the present-day Church of England, 'wherein her Holy Communion has been Rent and divided by Factitious and Schismatic Impostors, and her priests and professors (like St Paul) castigated, misrepresented and ridiculed'. But what was worse was that this was done not just by the church's enemies 'but by our pretended Friends and False brethren'. The true Church of England, he asserted, was against the toleration of dissenters. 'Let us therefore', he concluded, after an hour and a half of invective, 'as we are unhappy sharers of St Paul's misfortunes, follow his example and conduct in a parallel case. He tells us in his Epistle to the Galatians that he was obstructed in his preaching the Gospel', but persevered. Sacheverell urged his superiors to 'thunder out their ecclesiastical anathemas' against Whigs and nonconformists.[2]

Little might have come of the event, however, if Sacheverell, much against the advice of his friends, had not decided to have the sermon printed. He later claimed that Sir Samuel Garrard, Bt, the newly elected Tory mayor of London, who had given Sacheverell the original invitation to preach, had encouraged him to publish, although this was disputed.[3] It was the published sermon (printed by Henry Clements) which took Sacheverell's rant – in fact a reheated version of a sermon previously preached in St Mary's, Oxford in 1705, highly derivative of other high-church writings – beyond the cathedral walls and generated a public outcry, allowing it to be caught up in the wider high-church/low-church and Tory/Whig divisions (and ensuring that Bissett's printed response reached twelve editions by 1715). In the pamphlet war following the sermon, one critic, in *The Perils of Being Zealously Affected but not Well*, quoted St Paul's words against Sacheverell: 'the high-flying faction may call themselves Churchmen all they please; but St Paul would not allow 'em that Name, for he declares, that if any Man seem to be contentious, the Church of God hath no such custom'.[4] Another opponent dubbed Sacheverell an 'ecclesiastical incendiary' for raising such a false alarm, noting that 'anyone that reads and heeds St Paul's writings and Temper will soon perceive that nothing can be more opposite to the meek and gentle, to the charitable and forgiving, to the healing and most affective spirit of that Divine writer' than Sacheverell's invective; he accused Sacheverell himself of being 'the false Brethren'.[5] A third critic thought the sermon more suited to a 'Billingsgate Auditory than a Cathedral Harmony'; a fourth concluded that 'since the foundation of the City of London and the Conversion of this Island to Christianity, there has not been in any Age, within any Cathedral, such a sermon, so insolent, uncharitable, untrue'.[6] So great was the uproar that Sacheverell was impeached on the grounds of preaching sedition. He was, however, let off with such a lenient sentence by Tory judges (being forbidden to preach for three years) that it was widely supposed that they implicitly shared his fears for the church, and during his trial dissenting meeting-houses in London were burned by high-church mobs (on the night of 1–2 March 1710).

As the Sacheverell case shows, the Church of England was divided by major issues in the late seventeenth and early eighteenth centuries and these were often aired in the rebuilt St Paul's. In the years after the Revolution of 1688, clergy had to face the political question of how to treat the monarchy in the light of what seemed to some as the deposition of James II and an affront to the institution of divine kingship. Secondly, in the wake of the Toleration Act of 1689, which had granted limited freedom of worship to Protestant nonconformists, clergy had to decide how to deal with those who dissented from the national church. 'Were they', as G. V. Bennett once asked, 'ready to accept the place in English society of a basically voluntary body working within the legal conditions of the establishment or were they going to agitate for a return to the past when Church and State had conjoined in a single authoritarian regime?'[7] Thirdly, clergy (and London clergy in particular, many of whom worked in parishes in the gift of St Paul's) had to contend with the urgent problem of how they should combat what was perceived to be the growing vice and immorality of the age, leading Jeremiahs such as William Fleetwood, bishop of St Asaph, even during his thanksgiving sermon of 1708 for the victory at Oudenarde, to worry about the 'Abominations that almost over-run the Kingdom' and to warn his congregation in the cathedral of the fate of Sodom and Gomorrah.[8] How far should the church work alongside the laity and even dissenters in trying to create a holy nation, or should it instead pursue its own agenda? To a large extent, these issues were the ones that polarized high- and low-church clergy in the decades following 1688–9, and to participants the debates were a struggle over Anglican identity.[9] Institutionally, therefore, the most pressing concern for the Church of England during the first thirty years covered by this chapter was to find ways of healing these divisions and to present a united front.

The significance of the new St Paul's to the history of the Church of England in the eighteenth century was only in part that it became a prominent site where controversial ecclesiastical topics, such as those aired by Sacheverell, might find a sounding. More crucially in the long run, it quickly took on the role of being the natural meeting place for the church as an organization, functioning as the semi-official venue for some of the most important church-sponsored meetings of the period. The very size of St Paul's, and its location in the capital, made it a more convenient and suitable space for clergy gatherings than its potential rivals of, say, Westminster Abbey, Canterbury Cathedral or York Minster. After 1717, with the demise of Convocation (which did not meet again until 1852), it was the most regular rendezvous for leading members of the clergy from all corners of the nation. The nature of the sacred space, and the fact that clergy most frequently met in the cathedral within the context of a service, or a celebration of a church-led enterprise, ensured that debates and discussions were to a large extent constrained and contained, and this tended to focus activity on matters and concerns on which the great majority of clergy could agree. The cathedral thus became a place where divisions within the church could be healed. Even in the period between 1688 and 1720, when clergy were most clearly divided into opposing camps, there were a number of issues raised in the cathedral, particularly regarding pastoral work and the need to improve the lot of clerical dependants, where it is impossible to find a clear party divide, and in this context clergy gatherings in St Paul's were seen as instrumental in bringing rifts within the profession to an end. Roger Altham, in his sermon before the Corporation of the Sons of the Clergy delivered in the cathedral in 1706, observed that 'the design of this meeting is to cultivate that mutual good will among us, that may make us meet in the house of God as Friends'; Philip Bisse exhorted the same group in 1709 to 'endeavour to repair the Breaches, to heal the Divisions, that, to our real Reproach, are now first in this Age unhappily crept in even among the House of Levi'; his younger brother Thomas congratulated his cathedral congregation in 1716 that

297.   The two Houses of Parliament process along the Strand to St Paul's for the annual charity service, watched by children from the London charity schools. Engraving by George Vertue, 1715. (GL)

a pleasant thing it is, the more pleasant because rare, to behold brethren to dwell together in peace and unity. But to behold them to testify their unity by assembling in the House of God, is moreover a blessed thing.[10]

Although there were some contentious views expressed in the cathedral, in general meetings in St Paul's were far less concerned to articulate divisions than to find a common ground and a common purpose (in part, perhaps, because the managers of the church were increasingly more careful in their choice of preachers).

Those attending the services and festivals in St Paul's were not, of course, all members of the clergy. The majority attending most of the great occasions in the cathedral were laity, notably leading representatives of the London élite, such as the Lords Mayor and members of the corporation, as well as members of the nobility, who not only listened to what clergy had to say, but perhaps more significantly were exhorted to support and contribute to church-sponsored projects. The shift from the exclusively clerical enclaves of Convocation in Westminster Abbey in the seventeenth century (themselves divided into meetings of the 'upper' and 'lower' clergy', which sometimes resulted in bitter disputes within the clerical body)[11] to the celebrations in St Paul's in the eighteenth century, where clergy of all ranks and laity met together, is both an example of the ways in which the church achieved a corporate identity in the years after 1688–9 and a telling instance of Norman Sykes's insistence that what distinguished the Church of England in the eighteenth century was lay involvement.[12]

The rebuilt St Paul's itself reveals something of the preoccupations of the late Stuart and Hanoverian church, and gives some insight into the ideology of the Anglican Church during the long eighteenth century. The mere fact of the building of the post-fire St Paul's indicates much about the Church of England's aspirations – as does the frequent comparison with St Peter's in Rome, and the accompanying extensive discussion of what a

Protestant cathedral should look like and, indeed, was for.[13] To some, the building itself signalled the ways in which the Church of England had deviated from its Reformation principles;[14] to others, it marked the triumph of Anglicanism over popery and dissent.[15] Commentators managed to use both the anticipated greater scale of St Paul's and the realization that St Peter's was actually bigger as signs of the Church of England's superiority – in the latter case, the colossal size of St Peter's could be seen as a comment on the vulgarity and even despotic ambitions of Rome.[16] Not least the way that the rebuilding was paid for – by a tax on coal brought into London and by public subscription[17] – was viewed as helping to link the church to the wider world, indicating that the cathedral was a part of, rather than apart from, society, a point continually reiterated by preachers in St Paul's defining the Church of England's identity against popery and nonconformity.

The interior decoration of the cathedral also reflected its Protestant and Anglican emphasis: unadorned stonework and plain window glass reflected prevailing Anglican taste. Wren's intended Italian mosaics for the dome were vetoed as too popish,[18] and instead it was embellished between 1715 and 1719 by Sir James Thornhill's rather sombre frescos depicting key moments of St Paul's life (his conversion; punishing Elymas; preaching at Athens; curing the poor lame man; Paul's conversion of the gaoler; preaching at Ephesus; his trial before Agrippa; and the shipwreck; Fig. 171). These, in depicting St Paul as a man of action and engagement with the world, could be seen as an exemplar and as a model for how Anglicans were to behave in society, implicitly contrasting this with Catholic and nonconformist models which, it was alleged, pitted the individual against society.[19]

But the most important ways in which the new cathedral articulated and defined an Anglican identity was through the services performed there from 1697 onwards, well before the internal decoration was complete. Nineteenth-century reformers bemoaned what they considered the lax standards of worship in St Paul's during the eighteenth century, but it is clear that eighteenth-century Londoners and visitors who attended worship in the cathedral found it more than satisfactory.[20] Along with other cathedrals in the country, it could be argued that the most obvious contribution to the maintenance of Anglicanism of St Paul's was the very fact of the public nature of the worship and the regular round of daily and Sunday services maintained during the century. John Wesley himself, usually seen as a stern critic of the established church, sometimes worshipped there; for example, on 24 May 1738 he recorded that he went in the afternoon to a service at St Paul's where the anthem was 'Out of the deep have I called unto thee, O Lord' (to Henry Purcell's setting), and it was later on that evening that his heart was 'strangely warmed'.[21] After his conversion, he did on occasion speak harshly of the congregation at St Paul's, 'a considerable part' of which, he noted, were 'asleep, or talking, or looking about, not minding a word the preacher says';[22] nevertheless he himself continued for some time to attend the cathedral, and to take communion there.[23]

Within the service, the clearest mechanism by which St Paul's contributed to a definition of Anglican identity in the eighteenth century was through the preaching of sermons, and these demonstrate much about the self-presentation and self-perception of the Church of England. It is worth stressing at the outset how far Wren's designs for the new cathedral emphasized the centrality of the sermon in worship, and as such can be seen as articulating a Protestant, and indeed a specifically Anglican, world-view. Changes in the mid-nineteenth century have obscured to the modern visitor the ways in which the eighteenth-century cathedral interior

298. The first pulpit, a detail from the Trevitt engraving of 1706 (see Fig. 154). (GL)

resembled Wren's other London churches and had a similar function as a preaching box or 'auditory', where the focal point was the preacher in the canopied pulpit and the emphasis on hearing the word (Fig. 298).[24] The contrast was both with Catholic churches, where the sermon had a less central function (famously Wren wrote in 1711 that 'it is enough that they [Roman Catholics] hear the Murmur of the Mass, and see the Elevation of the Host'),[25] and with the often extemporized nonconformist sermon which was not (at least at the start of the period) so often printed, nor, it was alleged, so orderly or tightly argued. It was remarked as if some surprise that Samuel Salter, preacher at the Charterhouse, delivered his 1755 sermon to the Sons of the Clergy in St Paul's without notes.[26] It is also striking, as Sacheverell's sermon shows, how far it was one of the conceits of eighteenth-century preachers in St Paul's to take Pauline texts and to use examples drawn from St Paul's life to press home contemporary issues. Eighteenth-century clergy found what they saw as St Paul's emphasis on practicalities and this-worldly actions, as well as his stress on unity and concord, useful paradigms with which to address current concerns. A number of sermons preached in the cathedral, such as George Bell's *St Paul's Behaviour in the Cause of the Gospel* (1713), used the life of the apostle as an exemplar for what they considered to be true Anglican behaviour.[27]

Sermons delivered in the cathedral had a potential impact on many more than were present to hear them. If preachers were rarely able to lecture to the large numbers that in the sixteenth and early seventeenth centuries had gathered round Paul's Cross (pp. 50, 54, 56–7),[28] through the power of print, their message could nevertheless reach a far wider public. Many St Paul's sermons were published, particularly those preached at the most notable services of the year (often by the staunchly clerical Rivingtons, located at 62 St Paul's Churchyard, Innys and Manby, or Wyatts). Sacheverell's 1709 sermon, admittedly hardly typical and with a greater reach than other sermons preached during the eighteenth century, was heard by only a few hundred people in the cathedral, but was soon printed in an estimated 50,000 copies and was read by at least 250,000 people, an audience equivalent to the then electorate.[29]

There were, of course, sermons delivered weekly in St Paul's, and although some were published, most have been lost to the historian. Those that have more readily survived were the set-pieces preached at the major fasts and festivals of the Church of England: sermons delivered on 30 January for the martyrdom of Charles I in 1649; on 29 May for the restoration of Charles II; and on what one preacher called the 'double deliverance' of 5 November – for the discovery of the Gunpowder Plot in 1605 and the invasion of William of Orange in 1688.[30] Sermons were also preached at the annual fast days peculiar to St Paul's: the patronal festival of 25 January and on 3 September, in remembrance of the Great Fire of London in 1666 which had destroyed the medieval cathedral. The 5 November and Great Fire services, with their attendant sermons often delivered by clergy connected to the cathedral, were performed until 1859, and were usually frequented by leading representatives of the state (notably the Lord Mayor and members of the city of London corporation). Further sermons were delivered to the annual meetings of the gentlemen educated at St Paul's School, which gave preachers the opportunity to dwell on the beneficial relationship between the Church of England and education, often contrasted with the supposed superstition of Catholic, and ignorance of nonconformist, rivals.[31]

The very nature of the fasts and festivals observed in St Paul's encouraged sermons that memorialized past events, drawing out the lessons that could be learned from them and often indicating parallels between past and present. These sermons tell us a great deal about the Anglican mind-set in the late seventeenth and eighteenth centuries: it was extraordinarily historical, seeing the major events of the past as 'a soap-opera written by God'[32] (one 'to be continued...'). The incidents commemorated were seen as key times when God had saved the English/British nation and/or the Church of England, and preachers often rehearsed the crucial dates from the Reformation to the present that marked the special relationship between God, the British nation, and the Anglican Church. They invariably highlighted the importance of 1605 (the discovery of the Gunpowder Plot), 1660 (the Restoration), 1688 (the 'Glorious Revolution') and 1715 and 1745 (defeats of Jacobite risings) as examples of divine providence and divine intervention in the nation's history, which could be cited as evidence that England was indeed God's 'elect nation'. In his 5 November sermon of 1712, delivered at a time of fears over the Protestant succession, Thomas Sherlock reminded the St Paul's congregation why such events should be commemorated, observing that the Church of Rome 'this day out-did even themselves... But God prevented their malice and turned the mischief upon their own Heads. In memory of which Blessings this Day was deservedly distinguished in the English Calendar.'[33] But these dates were also warnings that the special relationship might be lost and the lessons from the past forgotten. Francis Browne noted in his 30 January sermon in 1713 that 'This day bears witness what it once produc'd, and I hope will ever be distinguished in our British Kalendar, not only as a memorial of what has been, but like the Marines sea-mark, to advise of future Danger'.[34]

Given that such sermons necessitated an overview of English history and a commentary on key events, they sometimes took the preacher into controversial areas. There were – as the Sacheverell case vividly demonstrates – occasions when preachers used sermons delivered in the cathedral explicitly to attack their enemies within the church. Only in 1733, however, when David Scurlock, deputizing for an indisposed prebendary at the height of the Excise Crisis, preached *A Caution against Speaking Evil of our Governors* (using St Paul's letter to Titus to defend Walpole's government and to condemn processions and petitions to parliament by those outside the electorate), was there anything remotely approaching the outcry occasioned by Sacheverell, and this was overtly political rather than church-based.[35] The great majority of preachers employed the review of past crises to preach peace, harmony and moderation (albeit on the terms set by the preacher). In September 1711, when party conflict was still rife within the church, John Strype, the ecclesiastical historian and curate of Leyton, preached before the Lord Mayor. The point of his sermon, *The Thankful Samaritan*, was stated to be to dispel the spirit of disunity within the church. This, he argued, was not the true spirit of the Church of England, whose liturgy asked for prayer for unity, peace, concord and forgiveness. Strype noted the 'great law of love' that St Paul had recommended at Ephesus, and he concluded:

> And were I to speak (if it could possibly be) to the whole kingdom of Great Britain at once, I would use the same words [Ephesians IV: 31–2]; 'Let all Bitterness, and Wrath, and Clamour, and Evil Speaking, be put way from you, with all

Malice. And be ye kind one to another, tender-hearted; Forgiving one another, as God for Christ's sake hath he forgiven you'.[36]

This stress on charity, moderation, unity and peace – *pace* Sacheverell – was central to the emerging rhetoric of the Church of England. In preaching the spirit of concord, however, preachers were sometimes challenged by the occasion. The 30 January sermon was particularly difficult to get right: on the one hand, there was the danger of venerating Charles I so much that the preacher could be accused of favouring arbitrary government, but, conversely, excessive criticism of Charles could be interpreted as an attack on monarchy. On 30 January 1737 Richard Venn, rector of St Antholin, London, in a sermon published along with others in 1740 after his death, 'for the benefit of the widow', affirmed that the execution of the king had indeed been a great scandal and went further than most in declaring that Charles had 'as a man, a Christian, and a Prince... exceeded all kings'. Venn admitted that the king could be accused of some political mismanagement, but 'nothing which could justify a Civil War'.[37] As William Crowe, rector of St Mary Magdalen and St Gregory, situated near the cathedral, noted in his 30 January 1724 sermon, it was difficult to find anything to say about the topic which would not 'inflame people'.[38] His solution was to avoid rehearsing the details of the day and instead to use his sermon, *The Duty of Promoting the Public Peace*, to urge patriotism, peace, unity and a charitable and benevolent public spirit (best represented by the Church of England). For Crowe, the lesson of 1649 was that people should not divide over small things, and he reminded both dissenters and churchmen seeking to widen the breach between the church and nonconformity of what he considered to be the 'generous and truly Christian declaration of St Paul': 'that the kingdom of God is not meat and drink (i.e. not light and indifferent matters) but righteousness and peace', which for Crowe stood against the 'abominations of popery or the extravagancies of fanaticism'. And in what was an attack on Jacobites, he praised George I for being a 'bulwark of the Reformation'.[39]

The most common way in which those delivering sermons in St Paul's attempted to find a consensus on which all could agree was to play down divisions within the church and to concentrate instead on extolling its superiority over its rivals. Playing the 'no popery' card was the most obvious device – as Thomas Sherlock, chaplain to Queen Anne and future bishop of London, announced in his 5 November 1712 sermon: 'There is nothing an Englishman has more to fear than the prevailing power of Popery',[40] although some speakers, again most notably Sacheverell, preferred to harp on the iniquities of Protestant nonconformity. Anti-Catholic rhetoric was unsurprisingly to the fore in John Dane's sermon of 23 October 1710, commemorating the 1641 massacre of Protestants in Ireland and preached in the cathedral 'before the Protestant Gentlemen of Ireland' on the subject of *The Reformation protected by the Providence of God; or the Deliverance of the Protestant Church of Great Britain and Ireland from the evil design of Papists*. Dane selected a Pauline text, 2 Cor. 1:10, which, he thought, 'suited with the occasion of our meeting': 'be thankful to God who delivereth us from so great a death'. Dane argued that although many had died in 1641, many thousands had escaped, which he took as evidence of divine intervention. But he reminded his congregation that, however much it was put down, popery had always fought back: 'For popery', he warned, 'like the Hydra, tho' never so many of its heads are cut off, others will yet still rise', as was witnessed in the years before 1688. Not only was it imperative that Protestants should unite against their common enemy, but, he claimed, more importantly, the only means to secure God's providence was for individuals to live a good life.[41] In similar vein, Benjamin Ibbot, rector of St Vedast's, Foster Lane, preaching at the 1711 day of humiliation for the Fire of 1666, informed his congregation: 'It was no doubt, a very frightful and shocking spectacle to view this Great city in flames...but the end of the world will be worse.' He advised his hearers that they should examine their hearts and remove what is offensive to God ('thus may every private person contribute towards a general Reformation, by reforming themselves').[42] For Ibbot and other preachers, the message was that although civil magistrates could do something by their authority and example, the best remedy was internal reformation. In 1770, from the distance of over a hundred years, East Apthorp, vicar of Croydon, in his 3 September sermon was more impressed by the blessings the Fire had given to the country. He recognized that the cause of both the Plague and Fire had been God's displeasure with the nation (citing the crimes of court and people before the Civil War, the war itself, the overthrow of monarchy and the corrupt nature of the Restoration government), but he also noted that no one had been killed in the fire – indicating God's benign providence – and he concluded that in fact the Fire had had the 'happiest effects' in checking atheism and reviving religion (especially among the aristocracy); moreover, it had led to the rebuilding of London. That project had been the work of a century, and Apthorp saw the reign of George III as the great fulfilment of an enterprise which embraced Wren's and Hawksmoor's churches; he celebrated 'our stately temples', which he believed 'becoming to the pure sublimity of our Holy Religion, undebased by the childish ornaments of Romish superstition'.[43]

Alongside the fast-day sermons, clergy in St Paul's were able to define the position of the Church of England during sermons delivered at what can be regarded as the corporate festivals of the Church of England, notably the annual festival of the Corporation of the Sons of Clergy and, from 1782, the anniversary meetings of the children educated in the charity schools 'in and about the cities of London and Westminster' established under the auspices of the Society for Promoting Christian Knowledge (SPCK).[44] These charity events, begun in 1655 – before receiving royal backing at the Restoration – and 1704 respectively, had been held in St Michael, Cornhill, St Mary-le-Bow, and other large London churches, such as Christ Church, St Sepulchre and St Andrew Holborn, before returning or moving to St Paul's. In the nineteenth century these Anglican festivals would be joined in St Paul's by the annual meeting of the missionary Society for the Propagation of the Gospel (established in 1701). The association of cathedral and societies was reinforced by the fact that until 1730 monthly business meetings of all three societies were held in the chapter house.[45]

In his Sons of the Clergy sermon of 1722, Pawlet St John, rector of Yelden in Bedfordshire, praised the support the Corporation had received from Charles II and Queen Anne ('whom', he said, 'were I capable of forgetting, or should I forbear to mention, the stones of this very Temple would call out'). He described the annual festival in Old Testament terms: 'Hither accordingly, one Day in every year, under the favour of his Authority, do all our Tribes come up to testify unto Israel, the Royal Bounty of our Founder.'[46] Both the Corporation of the Sons of the Clergy and the SPCK were seen as central to the Anglican project. The

Corporation of the Sons of the Clergy was a fundraising device to support the widows and children of deceased clergy, originally established to provide for those whose husbands had suffered in the Civil War. Sermons preached at the annual meeting put forward a defence of the Anglican clerical profession and stressed the benefits the clergy brought to the laity in attempts to get the latter to support the charity. By concentrating on the need to improve the lot of clergy, the Corporation could appeal to all shades of the clerical spectrum. The SPCK, with its aims of spreading religious instruction and education, principally through the foundation of charity schools and the distribution of religious tracts, was held to highlight the contrast between Anglicanism and Roman Catholicism (in which scriptural knowledge was believed to be deliberately withheld from the laity). Although the fundraising services were not held in St Paul's until the late eighteenth century, the London charity-school children (nearly 8,000 of them by 1793[47]) figured prominently in several of the major eighteenth-century state services held in the cathedral, beginning with the 1713 thanksgiving service for the Peace of Utrecht which included charity-school children singing from stands erected in the Strand. They also performed at the great service of thanksgiving for the recovery of George III from illness in 1789, this time under the dome, as in the charity-school festivals. Sir Gilbert Elliott described the scene (Fig. 299):

> Under the dome were piled up to a great height all round, 6,000 children from the different charity schools in the City, in their different habits and colours. This was by far the most interesting part of the show. You may see this any year for they are brought to St Paul's and placed in the same order every year, and I think it will be worth your while if you ever come within sight of St Paul's again. After the house of Commons and of Peers etc. were seated...and when the King approached the centre, all the 6,000 children set up their little voices and sang part of the Hundreth Psalm. This was the moment I found most affecting and without knowing exactly why I found my eyes running over and the bone in my throat, which was the case with many other people.[48]

The annual meetings of the Sons of the Clergy were regarded as a showpiece for the church. The opportunity was taken to define Anglicanism in contradistinction to popery and nonconformity. The preachers were usually distinguished (bishops, deans or influential clergy) and stressed the distinctive features of Anglicanism and the benefits the Church of England brought to English/British society. In urging their congregations to give liberally to the charity, it is not surprising that several preachers, such as Philip Barton in his 1735 sermon, took as a text St Paul's statement in 1 Cor. XII:13 exalting charity above faith and hope (although it is not clear what the apostle would have made of this being adopted as a slogan for Anglican charities).[49] The meetings themselves, moreover – attended by both clergy and laity – were taken to be representative of the ways in which the Anglican clergy were integrated into society. Christopher Wren, himself the son of a clergyman, was vice-president of the society in 1722, and from 1769 the meeting included a dinner for the archbishops, bishops, nobility, Lord Mayor and aldermen, as if to cement the alliance between church and state.

Despite the controversy caused by his 1709 sermon, Sacheverell was invited back to the cathedral nine months after the end of his suspension from preaching to preach before the Sons of the Clergy in December 1713, although this time he was hissed by the crowds gathered at the Royal Exchange.[50] Again he took St Paul as his text (on this occasion 1 Tim. VIII), to support the argument, as befitted the occasion, that the apostle took the marriage of clergy for granted, 'for (as he excellently argues) if a man know not how to rule his own House, how shall he take care of the Church of God'. Sacheverell maintained that St Paul directed clergy in the primitive church in the choice of wives to ensure that they should reflect well on the clergy (they should, he said, be 'grave, not slanderers...sober, faithful, in all things'), and he concluded that in no age since Paul's Epistle had been written had there been so many widows who so entirely fulfilled the 'excellent and moving Character required of them', to recommend them 'to our Kindness and favour'. Sacheverell also used the fact that Jesus on the cross committed his mother to the love and maintenance of his disciples as a further reason for supporting the charity, and he urged his congregation 'to contribute towards a Design, upon which the Credit of our Reformation does in some measure stand'.[51]

Sacheverell appears nearly to have learned the lesson of his controversial preaching, or at least on this occasion the very nature of the event ensured that the sermon would mostly reiterate themes on which all could agree. Along with numerous other commentators, he was keen to stress the ways that clergy sons had benefited and given lustre to all other professions

> as appears from this compounded Body drawn out of Church and State, City and Country, the Court and the Camp, the nobility and the Gentry, the magistracy and the Law, the Universities and Faculties, the Shops and Exchange, who all repair to this Holy Temple...to celebrate our Lineage.[52]

But Sacheverell could not resist using the opportunity to continue his high-church attack on low-church views. He concluded that, despite the evidence of excellence in the clerical profession, some things disgraced the profession, such as the 'false notions of charity and moderation' which were, he claimed, leading some members of the profession to side with 'sectaries', to speak evil of church dignitaries and to charge the 'best Church and government in the world' with popery.[53]

As might be expected, a recurring theme of the Sons of the Clergy sermons was that in the Anglican Church, in contrast to the Roman Catholic, there was no essential division between the clergy and the laity. This point was frequently raised to stifle anxiety that by giving to the widows and children of the clergy money was being transferred from the lay to the clerical estate. In 1734 George Lavington, prebendary of St Paul's and rector of St Michael Bassishaw, perhaps responding to fears that the church was gaining from deathbed bequests, was quick to point out that in recommending the charity he did not want to make the clergy rich and powerful. He reminded his congregation that clergy widows and their children were members of the laity, and in any case clergy contributed no small share to the charity, thus themselves transferring money to the laity.[54] In 1738 Edmund Marten in *The Usefulness of Assembling Ourselves to Promote Good Works* reassured his congregation that in requesting help for widows he had 'no desire that they may adorn themselves with plaited hair or gold or pearls'.[55] But this line had always to be tempered by the need to assert that the clergy *did* require maintenance and were worthy of support. In 1757, in the middle of the Seven Years War, Gloster Ridley, chaplain to the East India Company at Poplar and incumbent of Romford, Essex, preached of the need 'at this time especially, when our

enemies threaten our very protestantism', to support the clergy. He pointed out that the laity had done extremely well at the Reformation, at precisely the time when the clergy suffered from a diminution of their wealth: 'your wealth and their calamities', he told the lay members of his congregation, 'are twins of the same birth'. Echoing a number of other preachers, Ridley noted how the Reformation had saved the laity from papal dominion and from 'the papal militia of monks and friars'. He also attacked clerical celibacy in the Catholic Church which, he claimed, had 'opened a door to such impurities as shocked human nature; injuries that troubled private families; and the cruel slaughter of infants, whose numbers made the sword of Herod appear comparatively innocent'. Ridley emphasized the crucial role that the English clergy had played in the Reformation (understood as largely a clerical event directed by God) that, in anticipation of the protestant work ethic, had benefited the state by getting rid of numerous holy days and 'idle drones'. He also noted that having a married clergy had helped increase the population (good for national strength) and produced sons who had shone in all manner of professions and thus benefited the national community.[56]

Similar themes occurred in Arnold King's sermon of 1751. After arguing that 'we are Protestant Christians: religion and liberty go together', he asserted that in giving to the clergy's families the congregation was really giving to all society: 'for there is hardly a Family of any Consequence in the kingdom that has not, at one Time or other, been related to the clergy'.[57] In 1758 James Ibbetson reminded his audience that 'the marriage of the clergy has broken down the middle wall of partition between the interests of the clergy and laity, and that these children are the binds and cements of that union, which, we hope, will ever hold them together'.[58] Most Church of England clergy of the period could happily have endorsed this flattering portrayal of Anglican clerical marriage and its effects on society: even high churchmen shared in the distaste for celibacy (including Francis Atterbury, bishop of Rochester and leading high churchman, in his sermon on the same occasion in 1709),[59] which explains the frisson provoked in nineteenth-century Anglicanism when John Henry Newman advocated celibacy as the ideal for the religious professional. The sermons celebrated the end of celibacy and the cementing of Protestantism with the heterosexual clerical family, and this made the poverty of the clergy's dependants a real concern. Samuel Salter in 1721 warned lest the English clergy, in themselves the pride and glory of the Reformation ('as is universally said and allowed'), should 'in their nearest and dearest relations, become a scorn and a disgrace'.[60] Preachers painted affecting pictures of distressed widows; in 1790 Durand Rhudde maintained that what was worse for these unfortunates was that most clergy wives had been well educated and well brought up.[61]

Anti-popery and pathos did not exhaust the preachers' repertoire of arguments to encourage support for the Corporation. In 1709 Philip Bisse congratulated it on the fact that all money raised went to the objects of the charity: 'a method in every part directly opposite to that which universally obtained among the Foundations of Monastic Houses'. Thomas Ashton in 1753 linked the need for such a Corporation to the benefits of the present age, arguing that it was a 'wise defect of providence, which in the discreet profusion of its gifts, has contrived to put a kind of stop to its own bounty, to give us an opportunity of exercising ours'. He ventured that in contributing to the fund supporters would add yourselves to the nation of priests; have the merit without the hardship, of being preachers of righteousness; and having assisted the prophet in the execution of his office, shall, hereafter, by the divine justice, be made partakers of his reward.

In 1760 William Dodwell promised that 'the fatherless and the Widow…shall be our comfortable witness at that awful Season and shall testify to our Honour and Reward that we were under God, the happy Author of their preservation'; in 1722 Pawlet St John argued that sons of the cloth in particular should contribute: 'Then are ye Bastards, and not sons, if ye decline this opportunity of shewing piety at home'.[62]

We have seen that preachers stressed the crucial role of the Reformation in changing the fortunes of the clergy, but in some cases this resulted in much less positive evaluations of the event than we have so far observed. Thomas Mangey, vicar of Ealing, asserted in 1734 that the Reformation had made the parish clergy like 'mechanics'; in 1737, William Berriman's sermon argued that the Reformation had taken money away from clergy at precisely the time when their expenses were increased because they could have families.[63] In 1709, Philip Bisse complained that only in England was such a charity necessary because in both Catholic and reformed Continental churches clergy had a decent provision. His younger brother Thomas, at the height of the tensions between high and low church in 1716, went so far as to argue that the poverty of the present-day clergy could be laid at the door of the Reformation, while in 1758 James Ibbetson lamented the failure then to establish better provision for poor clergy, adding 'our enemies we know rejoice in this: they represent this distress as a mark of the divine displeasure on our Reformation'.[64] This line of argument was problematic not only in suggesting that the Reformation had not been an unmitigated blessing, but in the implication that medieval clergy had been better off than their Protestant successors. John Lewis, for example, a Whig low churchmen, responded to Thomas Bisse's sermon in print, defending the Reformation and arguing that Bisse had both a rosy view of the medieval clergy and an exaggerated sense of the contemporary poverty of the church. In claiming that 'it's certain that our Arch-bishops, Bishops and Parish Priests have generally a larger income than even the Popish bishops and clergy', however, Lewis was not likely to do much to stimulate charitable support for the cause.[65]

The Sons of the Clergy festivals in fact did relatively well as fundraising events, testifying to the effectiveness of the preachers' arguments. Until the 1720s, about £500 was collected each year; from the 1730s, approximately £1,000 a year was raised (equivalent to some £40,000 in 2004[66]). Apart from rents from estates and private donations, this represented the Corporation's main source of income and was crucial in supporting about 700 clergy widows and their children.[67] In order to increase the attraction of the charity event, and to maximize the collection, musical concerts, increasingly dominated by the music of Handel, were introduced from 1718. Until 1727, the meeting was in December, but it was then moved first to February, then to April, and by the mid-1750s to May, again to boost income through increased attendances.[68]

The charity schools established with the support of the SPCK have claims to be one of the most significant achievements of the church in the eighteenth century, and by the 1790s there were nearly 8,000 children educated in or near London, with a total of

nearly 45,000 educated in this way through Great Britain and Ireland. Nevertheless, the schools were criticized, especially from the 1770s, by those who feared that poor children were being overeducated. The annual meetings of the charity-school children held in St Paul's from 1782 (in either May or June to ensure as large a congregation as possible) provided an opportunity to defend the schools. At the first meeting in 1782, Beilby Porteus preached that Christ's special message had been to the poor. Porteus's sermon was a forthright defence of the work of the SPCK: 'it breathes the true spirit of Christianity, and follows, at a humble distance, the example of its divine Author, by diffusing the light of the Gospel more earnestly to the poor'. Porteus argued that without the schools many thousands of children would have had no education whatsoever, so the schools were essential to the public good. He also enumerated the ways that the SPCK provided for the poor once they had left school, giving them useful reading material that could turn them into staunch supporters of the church and 'preserve them from the artifices of popery and the delusions of enthusiasm'. During his sermon, Porteus pointed to the nearly 5,000 charity-school children who had been installed in a temporary amphitheatre under the dome: 'the effect of so large a number of children in that form, and uniting with one voice in the responses and in the psalm singing, was wonderfully pleasing and affecting'.[69] The size of the collection raised at this and subsequent meetings demonstrated the wisdom of having the children participating in the service, and in 1789 (whether inspired by sentimentality or satire is debatable) William Blake recorded the now annual St Paul's event in his poem 'Holy Thursday':

Twas on a Holy Thursday their innocent faces clean,
The children walking two and two in red and blue and green,
Grey-headed beadles walked before with wands as white as snow,
Till into the high dome of Paul's they like Thames waters flow.

O what a multitude they seem'd, those flowers of London town
Seated in companies they sit with radiance all their own.
The hum of multitudes was there, but multitudes of lambs,
Thousands of little boys and girls raising their innocent hands.

Now like a mighty wind they raise to heaven the voice of song
Or like harmonious thunderings the seats of heaven among.
Beneath them sit the aged men wise guardians of the poor.
Then cherish pity; lest you drive an angel from your door.

The meeting remained a popular event until the 1870s.[70]

During the 1790s, the tone of the sermons delivered in St Paul's became more urgent. Preachers used the pulpit to defend the church at a time when, during a period of economic distress and renewed dissent, and then Britain's involvement in the war with revolutionary France, the church seemed to be more under threat than it had been for over seventy years. In 1790, Charles Edward de Coetlogon, associated with the evangelical revival, assistant chaplain at the Lock Chapel and chaplain to the Lord Mayor for that year, preached a remarkable series of sermons in the cathedral. In his Good Friday sermon *The Surprize of Death*, de Coetlogon, in evangelical fashion, urged more public observance of the day: that 'the anniversary recollection of an event so remarkable and so interesting should be treated with indifference is among the numerous and most deplorable operations of human nature'. His sermon for 24 January (the patronal festival), *The Essential Deity of the Messiah*, addressed the threat to the church from unitarianism and rational religion; while his sermons for 30 January (*Religion and Loyalty the Grand Support of the British Empire*), 25 April (*Harmony of Divine and Human Legislation*), 29 May (*National Gratitude for Providential Goodness*) and 5 November all emphasized the importance of giving loyalty and support to the church in a period of impending crisis.[71]

In 1793 – the year that Britain joined the war against revolutionary France – Samuel Horsley, the bishop of St David's, in a charity-school sermon had to respond to heightened fears that the schools might foster insubordination in the lower orders:

> Our Lord's example, of preaching to the Poor, will with every serious believer, outweigh the objection, which hath been raised against these charitable institutions, by a mean and dastardly policy, imbibed in foreign climes, nor less unchristian, than it is inconsistent with the genuine feelings of the home-bred Briton; a policy which pretends to forsee, that by the advantages of a religious education, the Poor may be raised above the laborious duties of his station, and his use in civil life be lost… Fear not therefore to indulge the feelings of benevolence and charity, which this day's spectacle awakens in your bosoms.[72]

In seeking to present itself as a charitable and benevolent institution, the Church of England in the 1790s – led by cathedral chapters such as that of St Paul's – also wanted to show charity to exiled French Catholic clergy, seeing the atheism of the revolutionaries as now the more dangerous enemy.[73] Even before this date, some preachers had expressed a positive view of medieval Catholic clergy. Beilby Porteus as rector of Lambeth in his 1776 sermon to the Sons of the Clergy praised the medieval church's support for the poor and the monasteries' preservation of antiquities and encouragement of music, which, as he remarked, played such a crucial role in the clerical festival.[74] Arguing for the need to support contemporary Catholics, however, represented a shift in clerical rhetoric. In his 1795 Sons of the Clergy sermon, Charles Peter Layard responded to press attacks on the Church of England by claiming that there had never been a period when the clergy so worthily displayed their charitable nature as in their current concern for *émigré* priests. Because the church was helping others, its own poor should not be forgotten.[75]

Others, however, responded to the time of crisis by re-emphasizing the gulf separating Anglican and Catholic. In 1796, a year of intense socio-economic and military stress, Thomas Rennell (prebendary of Winchester, rector of St Magnus the

Martyr and one of the high-church Hackney Phalanx) preached to the same society, taking as his text 2 Cor. VIII:23–4. Rennell stressed the Church of England's role as the leading bulwark against popery, the result of a 'manly' Reformation, and this was the main claim which, he argued, the clergy had on the congregation's bounty. Rennell declared that Catholics' 'first, their darling object' was the subversion of the Church of England, and he blamed the French Revolution itself on Catholicism. The Church of England's essential opposition to popery could be seen in the doctrines of those sixteenth-century heroes of the Reformation, Cranmer, Latimer, Ridley and Hooper, which were still the teaching of the church. Church of England clergy had also maintained Christian orthodoxy against the fashionable spread of Arianism. St Paul's emphasis on the reciprocal love between ministers and congregations was applied to the contemporary situation. At a time of anticlericalism, growing controversy about tithes and Methodist and dissenting growth, Rennell noted that mutual support between ministers of the gospel and early Christians was a 'prominent feature of the Apostolic age'. 'The spirit of social religion', he affirmed

> seems to have never been so well understood, nor its practice so generally diffused… the primitive Christians well knew both how to command and how to obey. The absolute necessity of religious order and subordination, as arising out of the very nature and essence of Church communion they abundantly felt and acknowledged.[76]

It was this model of mutual cooperation between clergy and people that he hoped might be resurrected in the present age.

As we have seen, sermons preached in St Paul's during the eighteenth century aimed at demonstrating the Church of England's superiority to its rivals of popery and nonconformity. They presented an image of the church as a benevolent and charitable institution which benefited the whole of society. Clergy were effectively using the cathedral as a propaganda machine for the Church of England, hoping to confirm their congregations in the view that the established church had played and would continue to play a crucial role in the life of the nation, and attempting to persuade their listeners to give money to Anglican enterprises. In so doing, preachers generally minimized differences of opinion within the church, and to a large extent this emphasis was crucial to the healing of the party rivalry within the church which had so troubled it in the late seventeenth and early eighteenth centuries.

31

LITURGY, 1714–2004

Donald Gray

Although we have no hesitation in acknowledging that all the great buildings of Christendom were erected *ad majorem Dei gloriam*, it is easy to forget that they demonstrate that fact definitively when performing their primary function as 'houses for worship'. Too many church guidebooks choose to illustrate their individual glories with pictures of an empty building, bereft of the people of God about their duties. For Christians, however, 'worship is the pivotal activity that focuses and enriches life, giving meaning and purpose to existence'. 'The gathering together of God's people in loving, adoring worship is the most expressive manifestation on earth – a veritable "epiphany" – of the Church; it betokens and reveals the Church.' So writes A. G. Martimort in *L'Église en prière*.[1] Or, as the Second Vatican Council put it:

> All should hold in great esteem the liturgical life of the diocese centred around the bishop, especially in his Cathedral church; they must be convinced that the pre-eminent manifestation of the Church is present in the full, active participation of all God's holy people in these liturgical celebrations.[2]

Evidence of the content and performance of worship in St Paul's during the early eighteenth century needs to be assessed both with more regard to its context and with more care than has sometimes been the case in the past, just as is more generally the case with the pastoral and liturgical life of the Hanoverian Church of England. There remains a lingering tendency to disparage the spiritual life of the church in this period in a critique that has changed little since first advanced by the Tractarians of the mid nineteenth century. As long ago as 1914, J. Wickham Legg warned against accepting uncritically the self-serving Anglo-Catholic verdict on the eighteenth century as a time of 'general decay in religion' characterized by slovenly worship and erastian and avaricious clergy.[3] Earlier still, F. C. Eeles criticized those who insisted that regard for the externals of worship, 'let alone the use of what is commonly called ceremonial', was an innovation upon post-Reformation usage: Eeles claimed that a slovenly neglect characteristic of the early nineteenth century had been anachronistically projected on to earlier periods, when it was in fact in marked contrast to the practice of the better-appointed churches in the seventeenth and early eighteenth centuries.[4] Certainly there were more places than commonly supposed where the Prayer Book, Anglican canons and visitation articles were adhered to and with more than a legalistic determination, as demonstrated in the three volumes of *Hierurgia Anglicana* as well as in Wickham Legg's splendidly titled *English Church Life from the Restoration to the Tractarian Movement, Considered in Some of its Neglected or Forgotten Features*.[5] Recent research has if anything extended this rehabilitation to the later eighteenth century and beyond. F. C. Mather and Peter Nockles have demonstrated the continuing sacramental and spiritual dimension of pre-Tractarian high churchmanship, thus further problematizing any suggestion that a century and a half of decay followed a Caroline 'golden age'.[6] It is bearing in mind such warnings that we approach consideration of the liturgy and worship of St Paul's after the death of Queen Anne.

Evidence at the beginning of the period as to the daily and weekly pattern of worship in the cathedral is provided by James Paterson's *Pietas Londinensis* of 1714, an assessment of the 'Ecclesiastical State of London' describing all the churches and chapels-of-ease in and about the cities of London and Westminster and their times of 'public prayers, Sacraments and Sermons, both ordinary and extraordinary'. Paterson recorded the

'Manner and order of Divine Service' within St Paul's – which he considered

> perhaps the most ample and celebrated Piece of Architecture in the whole World…the Monument of London's Glory, the Confusion of Roman Cruelty, and the Trophy of our reformed religion, which triumphs over that as much as the new Temple exceeds the old.

Morning prayer was held every day in the Morning Chapel, in the summer at 6 a.m., in the winter at 7 a.m.; 'But in the Choir again at ten'. Evening prayers were 'Constantly at three a clock', and the Sacrament of the Lord's Supper was administered every Sunday of the year at noon.[7]

The doubling of morning prayer provided for both a proven need and also a continuing fashion at the opening of the eighteenth century. In the popular writings of Queen Anne's reign, constant allusion may be found to early six o'clock matins, the origins of which lay in the 1547 Royal Injunctions for Cathedrals.[8] The *Guardian* for 26 May 1713 contains an account of 'one who going to the six o'clock service found many poor souls who had really come to pray' in the cathedral, but also 'pretty young ladies in mops, popping in here and there about the church, clattering the pew doors behind them, and squatting into whispers behind their fans'. The situation was saved when 'a great deal of good company came in'. Nevertheless, the *Guardian* correspondent believed that it was 'worthwhile that the church keeps up such early Mattins throughout the cities of London and Westminster'. Paterson noted other examples of such services (for example, at St Anne, Limehouse, St James's, Piccadilly and Westminster Abbey). He also records that in 1714 the provision of daily worship in the parish churches of the city and of Westminster displayed a number of patterns of which the most common was 'Morning Prayers [*sic*] and no more' on the Litany Days (Wednesdays and Fridays). There was nevertheless a significant minority of churches which had both prayer book offices (for example St Andrew Holborn, St Andrew Undercroft, St Bartholomew the Great, St Bride Fleet Street and St Botolph Aldersgate).[9]

Ten years later, at Bishop Gibson's 1724 visitation, the chapter returned that, in addition to the daily morning and evening prayer, 'Morning Prayer is said also by the Petty Canons at 6 a.m. from Annunciation to Michaelmas and from then to Annunciation at 7 a.m.'.[10] Holy communion was celebrated every Sunday and every holy day 'when there are sufficient numbers' (Fig. 158). The answer to another query returned that the vicars choral and inferior officers (those not in holy orders) received the sacrament every month, or at least four times in the year.[11]

The later service of morning prayer, and that of evening prayer in the afternoon, both took place in the choir behind the substantial screen surmounted by the organ. This enclosed area, holding at most a few hundred worshippers, was the place where most divine services were conducted. Both services were sung by the choir together with the minor canons, members of the chapter being in attendance (although the regularity and frequency of such attendance was subject to constant criticism).[12]

No contemporary descriptions of worship in the cathedral in the early eighteenth century are known to survive. We do know that the choir had been fully recruited after the fire, and although Dean Godolphin (1707–26; Fig. 34) did not share the high churchmanship of his predecessor William Sherlock (Fig. 31) and others in the chapter, visitation returns show him to have conscientiously

maintained the daily round of worship. Gibson's visitation of 1724 provides a snapshot of contemporary practice and concerns. The bishop declared that the times of choral services 'had been found to be inconvenient', and directed that they should be changed to 9.45 a.m. and 3.15 p.m. 'both on the Lord's Day and on all other days'. He also tightened up a number of regulations, doubling the fines for absence at statutory services from 2*d*. to 4*d*. and decreeing that preachers wishing to provide substitutes must give at least three weeks' notice. Gibson further enjoined 'that neither the Dean nor the President of the Chapter admit any excuse for preaching in person, but such only as shall be canonical and reasonable'.

Gibson identified another matter as continuing to be detrimental to the decent conduct of divine worship: every day, including Sundays, great numbers of people could still be seen walking and talking in the nave. This was a tenacious survival of 'Paul's Walk', an intrusion that reduced the nave to little more than a thoroughfare and market.[13] Writing in the 1860s, in his *Annals of S. Paul's*, Dean Milman blamed the phenomenon on the absence of 'sacred objects, roods, images and shrines' and the abandonment of 'services which were daily, hourly', so that 'it cannot be wondered that the world took more entire possession of the vacated nave and aisles'.[14] In his day, Gibson demanded that these perambulations and conversations must cease; the dean and chapter should use all their authority to bring this disgraceful state of affairs to an end. He condemned as a further abuse one of the virgers' unofficial sources of income: 'Persons piously and religiously disposed may not be discouraged from attending Divine Service in the Quire by the Virgers refusing to open seats until money be given them.'[15]

During Anne's reign there had been frequent royal visits to St Paul's for thanksgiving services in honour of military and naval victories. George I went to the cathedral for a thanksgiving service on his accession – but never again (p. 366). The form of that service, on 20 January 1715, followed the style of those held in his predecessor's time, in which the singing of the *Te Deum* was the liturgical centrepiece. The settings were great choral affairs with orchestra, but what made them notable was the inclusion of gunfire, as the guns at the Tower of London, on the river and in St James's Park fired salutes first as the king took to his coach at St James's Palace, then at the singing of the *Te Deum* and finally on his return to the Palace.[16] This use of the *Te Deum* as a focus of liturgical thanksgiving echoed the practice of the medieval church and was consonant with the customs of orthodoxy. George II having failed to attend worship in St Paul's at any point in his reign, his grandson George III repaired the sixty-four-year gap when he decided to give thanks to Almighty God 'for the signal interposition of his good providence in removing from His Majesty the late illness with which he has been afflicted'. The order of service employed on 23 April 1789 included the litany read and chanted by the minor canons; a solemn rendering of the *Te Deum* in which the cathedral choir was joined by a chorus and 6,000 charity children (Fig. 299); and anthems specially written for the occasion. The service concluded with the communion service read by the dean and residentiary canons.[17] The next celebratory service was held in 1797 in thanksgiving for a series of naval victories. A striking piece of ceremonial was introduced into this service. After the first lesson, the flag officers and captains proceeded to the altar and delivered up a number of flags (French, Spanish and Dutch) captured from the defeated enemy fleets (p. 369).

299. Stands in the crossing packed with charity children for the thanksgiving service for George III, 23 April 1789. Coloured engraving by T. Prattent for *The Lady's Magazine*. (GL, St Paul's collection)

At these 'ovational pomps'[18] the music was of a high standard, under the direction of such distinguished musicians as Maurice Greene and John Jones. We can be reasonably sure that the daily performance of the *opus dei* was also accomplished with some expertise, even if it was not always conducted in as orderly and devotional a fashion as some would wish, or later generations would come to expect.

More detailed accounts of worship in the cathedral begin to emerge at the beginning of the nineteenth century, particularly when services were reckoned to be under threat for lack of human resources. Richard Harris Barham, author of *The Ingoldsby* Legends, was appointed a minor canon in 1821. In a letter of 7 June 1836, as the cathedral faced the prospect of far-reaching reform at the hands of the Ecclesiastical Commission, he wrote:

I do not believe that it is at all in contemplation to do away with the services or anthems at St Paul's; though if the number of minor canons is to be reduced to six, the chanting the prayers must necessarily be abandoned. The Dean is fighting hard to retain eight; but even that number – allowing for absence from ill health and other sufficient causes – would be too small to carry on the duty as at present conducted.

Barham noted that early prayers had 'quite fallen into abeyance'. The reader attended each morning, but had told Barham that he had no congregation. Canon Sydney Smith had expressed a wish to do away with the early morning service altogether; but this proposal was opposed and subsequently dropped.[19]

Barham's son describes his father's churchmanship as one that was 'high and dry but would tolerate no leaven of popery'. A further indication of the climate of churchmanship at St Paul's in the early nineteenth century and its implications for worship is revealed in Barham's comment on the appointment of Thomas Dale as a residentiary in 1845: 'I was half afraid of some sour and lank-haired Puseyite, with whom I might have had to carry on a perpetual warfare'.[20]

There is mixed evidenced as to the popularity of the services provided in this period. *The Times* (9 July 1824) reported such large congregations at evensong that the only way to obtain a seat was by slipping half-a-crown into the palm of the virger (some customs died hard). This contrasts with Easter Day 1800, when Dean Pretyman complained that 'no more than six persons were found at the table of the Lord'.[21] This is less surprising in the light of attitudes, recorded by John Jebb in 1843, towards the midday communion service, at that time the only Sunday eucharist. Jebb complained of a slovenliness 'long sanctioned' by the chapter:

But surely the Chapter of St Paul's must at length perceive how sacrilegious a mockery they have long sanctioned: suffering a pretence to be made of weekly communion, the Table being arranged for the feast, so as thereby to invite communicants, the Clergy being in numerous attendance; and then when the time arrives for its celebration, the Clergy are dispersed, the Altar is forsaken, and the expectant worshippers dismissed by the notice of a Virger, without even a diaconal benediction.

Jebb, who had set himself the task of investigating 'the will and spirit of the Church of England as to that peculiar mode of performing her ritual which is commonly known by the name of Cathedral or Choral Service', maintained that he had personally been subjected to a repulse of this kind 'some years ago: and such was the deep pain inflicted in consequence' that he had never since ventured to attend Sunday morning service at St Paul's. The custom, he believed, reflected 'discredit on that wealthy Chapter . . . in one of the most conspicuous churches in Christendom'.[22]

Jebb was not alone in his outrage. A young Frederick Temple, the future archbishop of Canterbury, attended morning service and remained in his place for holy communion. A virger accosted him: 'I hope, sir, you are not intending to remain for the sacrament as that will give the Minor Canon the trouble of celebrating, which otherwise he will not do'. Canon Gregory's account of this disgraceful incident concludes: 'Upon this Mr Temple left the Cathedral.'[23] A further report appeared in correspondence columns of *The Times* in October 1842. An anonymous clergyman recounted how the cathedral clergy, headed by the dean, left their places after the sermon and proceeded to the vestry while the waiting congregation 'went sorrowing away'. An editorial note testified that 'we have sufficient authority for the statement of our correspondent'.[24] The letter drew an immediate and explosive response from Dean Copleston, who denounced the anonymity of the correspondent and the temerity of *The Times*, demanding names and dates. He succeeded only in provoking further letters from other correspondents witnessing to similar incidents.

Correspondents also took exception to Copleston's attempted justification of cancellations of communion. He argued that the prayer book rubrics allowed celebration only if there were four (or three at least) 'desirous of taking the sacrament'.[25] Critics rushed to point out the further rubric obliging clergy in cathedrals and collegiate churches to communicate at least each Sunday 'except they have reasonable cause to the contrary'. When the dean eventually saw fit to respond in December 1842 (having in the interim been 'at a distance and engaged in important duties' in Llandaff), he outraged his critics by not engaging with the implication of the rubric regarding cathedral clergy and renewing his demand for the real name of the pseudonymous 'Presbyter'. *The Times* maintained the honourable press tradition of protecting its sources.[26] Copleston none the less was concerned by the issue. In 1840 he had asked Archdeacon Hale to investigate, and later told Hale that he had now given orders that if two communicants offered themselves the virger should 'report the fact in the vestry to the canon in residence or his deputy' and a service be held, as, with two of the cathedral clergy present, the rubrical number of four was achieved.[27]

Other criticisms of the liturgy at St Paul's came to light in the course of the dispute. Exception was taken to the omitting of lessons at morning prayer, and the consumption of the consecrated remains after communion by 'officers of the church' (virgers?) who had not communicated within the service.[28]

Jebb's *Enquiry into the Liturgical System of the Cathedral and Collegiate Foundations*, published in 1843, certainly had little good to say about the performance of divine worship at St Paul's: 'It is melancholy to contrast the neglect of St Paul's in its present state with the fullness of its ancient service.' St Paul's had 'a degenerate choir'; there was no voluntary, no anthem on Sundays in the morning or communion service, no anthem when the Litany was sung; the *Sanctus* was sung as an introit to the communion service.[29] Jebb did concede some recent improvements at St Paul's: the resumption of the singing of the Nicene Creed at the communion, and the abandonment of the custom of the officiant leaving the altar immediately after monotoning the opening phrase of the creed. The only remaining example of this particular 'gross impropriety', Jebb noted, was at Westminster Abbey.[30]

Further indications of the liturgical standards prevailing in St Paul's in the early nineteenth century are found in the diaries and correspondence of Archdeacon Hale, canon from 1840 (Fig. 41). William Russell, who edited the Hale documents (the originals are now lost), spoke of them as 'giving a glimpse of what a cathedral establishment was before and at the great revival'.[31] Hale tried to improve standards. In this he had the support of Sydney Smith, who 'appeared to be very strict upon the forms and ceremonies of the Church', though he had no time for the liturgical fashions of the Puseyites who 'make religion an affair of trifles, of postures, and of garments'. He told a correspondent of a sermon he had preached in St Paul's:

'I wish you have witnessed the other day at St Paul's my incredible boldness in attacking the Puseyites. I told them that they made the Christian religion a religion of postures and ceremonies, of circumflexions and genuflexions, of garments and vestures, of ostentation and parade; that they took up tithe of mint and cumin, and neglected the weightier matters of the law – justice, mercy, and the duties of life, and so forth.'[32]

Perhaps unsurprisingly, there were consequently no early manifestations of Tractarian influence on worship in St Paul's.

One of the great occasions of the year was the Festival of the Corporation of the Sons of the Clergy. Each year, for days beforehand, daily services were suspended in order that galleries might be erected. Hale found that one of these galleries intruded within the rails of the sanctuary and this he objected to: 'It is a practice which offends many persons as a positive desecration of the Church; and on the Sunday before the Festival almost prevents the Altar service from being decently performed.'[33]

Other innovations reflected long-standing concerns, notably the troublesome communion issue, which became an almost neurotic concern for both Hale and Copleston. Writing to the dean in August 1843, Hale observed that:

I made one change with respect to the Communion Service, which I hope your Lordship will not disapprove, that of remaining in the new seats within the altar rails while the sermon is preached. The preacher with a tolerable voice is easily heard there. I had no difficulty in persuading the Minor Canons to remain with me, and if the practice be continued there is an end at once of the possibility of the charge that we are unwilling to administer the Communion.[34]

Hale was also pleased with further innovations in 1846. Bishop Blomfield had conveyed his dissatisfaction with the repetitions involved in the setting of the Nicene Creed used during an ordination service; Hale suggested to John Goss that he might compose a new setting of the creed in a recitative form. The archdeacon expressed his admiration of the result, finding the enunciation very devotional.[35] Later the same year, Archdeacon Hale declared: 'How I enjoy Cathedral worship. I regard the possession of it as a merciful hearing of my prayers, for I am where in heart I desired to be.'[36]

From this 'heart-felt' declaration, and a comment in 1847 that the whole of the service was now performed in a manner 'more fitted to God's honour', there might appear every justification for William Russell's claim that before the publication of the Hale documents 'too little honour had been accorded to the memory of one who initiated so many of the reforms and improvements' which were only effectively carried out at St Paul's after his death in 1870.[37] But it is not altogether easy to reconcile this assessment and Hale's own definition of a cathedral as being 'like the Temple at Jerusalem, they are the Temples in each Diocese, where the daily service of prayer and praise is continually offered, with such attendance, dignity and ceremony as is due to divine service'[38] with the other, less flattering mid nineteenth-century accounts of worship at St Paul's.

A turning-point in these matters was the arrival in 1849 of Dean Milman from Westminster Abbey (Fig. 301). Milman was the first 'full-time' dean, his ten predecessors having combined the office with one of the less lucrative bishoprics. Even so, he was saddled with a chapter whose interests lay mainly in the parishes which they held in plurality with their cathedral appointments. Though distinguished in many fields, and doubtless devout and dedicated in regard to their cures, these clergymen were not tempted to take over-much interest in the cathedral's worship and liturgical affairs, as demonstrated in their attitude towards the principle of weekly capitular collegiate worship in 1842.[39] Towards the end of Copleston's tenure of office, Hale had prepared a memorandum for submission to the Ecclesiastical Commissioners applying for grants which would have placed the emoluments of the minor canons, vicars choral and virgers on a secure and dependable footing. This scheme would have doubled the number of choirmen, and consequently the reliability and standards of music at the twice-daily office would have been guaranteed. The proposals had not proved successful at the time, so during his first year of office Milman renewed the application, stating that:

301 (*above*). Henry Hart Milman, author and dean of St Paul's 1849–68. (NPG)

300 (*left*). First evening service under the dome, 28 November 1858. The pulpit by F. C. Penrose had just been installed. (SPCL)

the Dean and Chapter are strongly of the opinion that there is a prior and undoubted claim on all the revenues of the church for the celebration of divine service in a manner befitting the metropolitan cathedral, and for the decent maintenance of the servants of the church.[40]

This time, although the dean and chapter were not given all they asked for, significant financial improvements were made.

An important feature of cathedral worship under Milman was a sudden return to the use of St Paul's for services of national significance. There was a day of thanksgiving for the cessation of the cholera epidemic in November 1849; a service of thanksgiving for the plentiful harvest of October 1854; a day of humiliation for the Crimean War in March 1855; a day of thanksgiving for peace in May 1856; a further day of humiliation after the 'Indian Mutiny' in October 1857; and a service of thanksgiving after its ending in May 1859. In March 1866 there was another day of humiliation on the outbreak of the cattle plague.[41]

More generally, Milman was of a mind to improve standards of liturgy and worship in the cathedral. He had nothing in common with the ritualism of later high churchmen, yet his refined artistic sympathies inclined him to admire clergy who in their church services 'introduced some slight element of poetry into lives sunk under the weight of monotonous labour and the hard-fought struggle for their existence'. Milman believed there was a 'reaction from the plethora of preaching', and admired 'the orderly and beautiful' in worship.[42]

We have already noted Milman's concern regarding the abuses caused by the perpetuation of 'Paul's Walk'. As a resident dean, he was in a good position to monitor such matters. One of his first duties was to superintend the arrangements for the duke of Wellington's funeral on 18 November 1852. Although the service was basically the burial service of the Book of Common Prayer, well-chosen music, some specially composed for the occasion by John Goss, together with decorous ceremony in a cathedral

draped throughout in black cloth with a large proportion of natural light excluded, combined to produce one of the most memorable spectacles of the century (p. 384).[43]

The holding of a thanksgiving service for a plentiful harvest in St Paul's on Sunday 1 October 1854 was a remarkable and innovative action on the part of the dean and chapter. The idea that it would be right and proper to offer thanksgiving annually to the Almighty, whether the harvest was plentiful or not, does not appear to have taken root until the middle of the nineteenth century. It is true that before that time a special thanksgiving prayer to be used after the general thanksgiving was occasionally issued by authority, but in each case this followed an abundant harvest: the first such seems to have been produced in 1796, and in 1847 a complete form of thanksgiving (sentences, psalm, collects and lections) had been issued 'by her Majesty's special command'.[44]

Equally remarkable was the decision to commence a series of Sunday evening popular services in 1858 (Fig. 300). In 1852 Lord Shaftesbury had commenced Sunday evening meetings in Exeter Hall in the Strand, built in 1829–31 as a non-sectarian hall for religious meetings. Shaftesbury's meetings were considered by the incumbent of the parish in which the hall was situated as an intrusion, and he put his veto upon them. Critics prepared to pour scorn on a church 'which, while itself neglecting the opportunities of attracting large masses of the people offered by the noble spaces at its command, yet did not hesitate to warn off trespassers upon its province'.[45] A public debate ensued and as a result Bishop Tait of London decided to secure the opening of Westminster Abbey and St Paul's to popular evening services. The dean and chapter of St Paul's, while expressing their 'earnest, unanimous, and sincere desire to co-operate to the utmost of their power in the promotion of religious worship and the preaching of the Word of God in the metropolis, especially as regards those classes for which such services are more particularly designed', raised a number of practical difficulties, not least the financial considerations. They pointed out 'the scantiness of the funds which could be applied for such a purpose'. None the less, they complied with Tait's wishes, and the first service was held on Advent Sunday 1858, of which Virger Green recorded 'Dr Tait preached. Cathedral crowded, a great number of people outside unable to get in.' This event was also significant in that the service was held under the dome.[46]

However, this was not the first attempt to open up the cathedral for popular worship. From the first, the idea was in Milman's mind and he needed little persuasion from Tait. A mere two months after his installation, Milman had perceived the possibility of using the cathedral's empty spaces for popular services, and had convinced the chapter that it was feasible. In the year of the Great Exhibition (1851), a series of evening services were held in the nave.[47] Then, in 1860, in consequence of a plan for the enlargement of the organ, the screen between the choir and the dome was temporarily removed. The magnificent effect of the uninterrupted view of the cathedral from end to end made such an impression on Milman (and no doubt others) that it was decided the screen should not be re-erected. 'Since then', Milman's son and biographer wrote, 'the whole vast area of the building has remained, as he desired, available for public worship.'[48] These architectural improvements, together with the policy of holding services and musical occasions that were more accessible to the general public, were 'the first dawn of the new era that was approaching in the history of the cathedral'.[49]

During a conversation in 1868 with Robert Gregory, the minor canon J. H. Howard compared the state of affairs at St Paul's with the mythological Augean stables.[50] Nothing daunted, the newly appointed Canon Gregory enthusiastically set about the task of bringing Puseyite principles of dignity and order to the cathedral. Having suffered the indignity of a capitular installation (presided over by Hale) of which Gregory said 'A more miserable and disgracefully slovenly service I never saw', he perhaps commenced his work with a somewhat jaundiced view, which also served to strengthen his determination to revive 'the customs of reverent devotion and the care of all those who were engaged in the holy service' in the cathedral.[51]

Mansel, Milman's successor, was granted little time in which to make an impression on the cathedral. Yet in his mere three years of office he maintained the impetus for change established by his predecessor. On Christmas Day 1868 there were decorations on the altar for the first time, although the dean and chapter proceeded cautiously, deciding that an Epiphany star rather than a cross, in a time of much Protestant suspicion of signs and symbols, would be diplomatic.[52] Holy Week 1870 was marked by Mansel and the chapter giving instructions that there would be choral services but without organ accompaniment; a subtle move to recognize that solemn season.[53] The high-church care for detail was also apparent when the chapter told the succentor that they wished him 'to set Anthems as far as possible in harmony with the teaching of the seasons of the church as ordered in the Book of Common Prayer'.[54] It was in Mansel's time that the proper observance of St Paul's Day (25 January) was revived, as recorded, somewhat laconically, in the chapter minutes: 'Resolved, also that there be a celebration of the Holy Communion in the choir at 8 a.m. on the Feast of the Conversion of St Paul, in place of the ordinary Morning Service at that hour.' In the afternoon the dean preached in the presence of the bishop and seventeen of the prebendaries, who afterwards joined the chapter for dinner. Virger Green confidently asserted that this was to be an annual feast.[55]

Even these modest changes would have been viewed with disapproval by keen eyes carefully monitoring liturgical activity in England's churches and cathedrals in search of the least sign of advanced Puseyite activity influencing either the conduct of services and sacraments, or the furnishing and paraphernalia of worship. Mansel was an old-fashioned high churchman, as was Gregory, never a ritualist, but influenced from an early age by the *Tracts for the Times* ('In them I found what I wanted. With little or no external teaching but what was derived from the Oxford Tracts, I became a Churchman.')[56] When Canon Dale was appointed dean of Rochester in 1870, Gladstone nominated Henry Parry Liddon to succeed him as a canon, and when Canon Melvill died in May 1871 his place was filled by J. B. Lightfoot. Then, on the sudden death of Dean Mansel in July 1871, after much advocacy by Gladstone, Richard Church (Fig. 46) was appointed dean.[57]

The providential combination of Church, Gregory and Liddon had a profound influence upon the standards and style of St Paul's worship. They were of a mind, and that mind was Tractarian. Lightfoot's academic interests were elsewhere; while Archdeacon Claughton, the remaining member of the chapter, did not trouble himself over much with these matters. Thus 'the dean found himself in the rare position of heading a chapter which was prepared to act with practical unanimity'.[58]

Church, who had been very much part of the Oxford scene in the early days of the Tractarian movement, personified in his liturgical concepts the 'reserve' of that initial phase. Of all he did, his daughter said: 'He had the delicate sense of appropriateness, the abhorrence of all that was flaunting and slipshod, the love of the neatness and finish, that gave charm and taught reserve to the scholars of his day.' In a letter he wrote from the deanery in 1874, he mused:

> It seems to me that this is a time when ritual is taking shape which may be permanent, and that there is a chance, which never was before, of settling the outline and principle of an intelligent, appropriate, expressive, outward form or shape of worship, *with the lines* of the Prayer Book, fairly interpreted. Of course I mean according to the ideas of worship which belong to the movement.[59]

Church and his high-church colleagues were in temperament far removed from the frills and fancies of the later Anglo-Catholic ritualists; yet it is equally apparent they had high ideals for the conduct of worship. Of Liddon at the altar it was said that 'There was something about his manner of performing this, as he realised it, the greatest act of his life, which was all his own, although he was as far as possible from intruding his own feelings or personality.'[60]

The matter of enforceable liturgical parameters at St Paul's came to a head in 1871, in the wake of the Purchas Judgement by the Privy Council. This ruling, *inter alia*, declared the eastward position of the celebrant at holy communion illegal. Immediately the Church Association gave notice that they would give the bishops no peace until the decision was enforced. The next day, Gregory and Liddon informed the bishop of London (John Jackson) that they were unable to recognize in the judgement sufficient grounds to depart from their existing practice. An exchange of letters took place. Summoned to the episcopal presence, Gregory and Liddon told the bishop that they hoped he would take proceedings against them before doing so against any of the parochial clergy. Two months later, Jackson announced his intention to act in accordance with the judgement, and Liddon and Gregory responded with an open letter repeating their refusal to comply. The bishop's rather lame response was to say he would prosecute the canons if 'duly called upon, by the authorities of the cathedral to take cognizance of the offence'. There was never chance of that happening, so Gregory and Liddon continued to celebrate at the altars of St Paul's in the eastward position.[61]

Henry Scott Holland, canon 1884–1911, believed that there should be two principles informing the worship of St Paul's: in the first place, 'the whole cathedral must be used from end to end for public worship'; and secondly, 'the whole cathedral must be endowed with the living warmth which should belong to a house of prayer and praise'. Holland continued the high-church tradition at St Paul's along with W. C. E. Newbolt, who succeeded Liddon and joined the chapter in the last year of Church's incumbency. Therefore it is no surprise to read that Holland stated that 'above all, the central Eucharistic Act of the Church's Communion with God must occupy the house which was built to enshrine it'. The hole-in-the-corner nature of the cathedral eucharistic arrangements which then obtained had to be changed, Holland believed:

> It must be brought out of the corner in which it has hitherto lurked – the privilege of a secluded few who have it all to themselves at the obscure end of a Sunday morning service. It must show itself as the culminating moment of public worship, to which the varied gifts of music and art, by which men heighten their devotion, contribute their finest and fullest ministrations.[62]

Newbolt concurred in all of this, saying that at St Paul's

> the Church must offer to God its liturgy, a name given of old by the Athenians to certain public works, offered by the few on behalf of the many, and taken over by the Church to describe the sacred Altar service, the Church's public work.[63]

From 1871 onwards, this 'public work' was performed in the Morning Chapel (renamed St Dunstan's Chapel in 1905), newly furnished with an altar, on all holy days; then from 1 January 1877 there was a daily celebration. Also, in October 1871, it was decided that the holy communion service in the choir on a Sunday morning would be 'chorally rendered' and the blessing with which,

after matins, the people had been dismissed would be omitted.[64]

Gradually Holland's first principle regarding the use of the cathedral 'from end to end' came to pass. Services were now regularly held under the dome as well as in the choir. In addition to the Morning Chapel, other chapels were brought into use. St Faith's Chapel was formed in the crypt and early morning prayer transferred there in 1877; the Jesus Chapel was furnished in the eastern apse in 1894 (Fig. 302), and the Chapel of St Michael and St George was inaugurated in 1906.[65] With regard to Holland's second principle, the cathedral as a house of prayer, there were various attempts to increase the opportunities for public as well as private prayers. In 1870 a group of 'about 100 persons engaged in business in the neighbourhood' successfully petitioned the chapter, requesting that some portion of the cathedral be set apart for the purpose of prayer.[66] Then, in Advent 1873, following a request for a short daily evening service 'on the model of compline', such a devotion commenced. A similar, midday service based on sext, drawn up by Liddon, started in 1877.[67] From 1877 until 28 June 1901, the service bills record that the normal daily pattern of worship was thus:

(7.15: Holy Communion on Saints' Days in the North-West Chapel)
8.00: Morning Prayer in Crypt Chapel
10.00: Choral Morning Prayer in Choir
1.15: Short service in North-West Chapel ('Sext')
4.00: Choral Evening Prayer in Choir
8.00: Short Evening Prayers in Crypt Chapel ('Compline')

The last service of the day moved to 7 p.m. in 1898.

Early matins and compline having been dropped in 1901, the resulting simplified daily pattern was:

(7.15: Holy Communion on Saints' Days)
8.00: Holy Communion in North-West Chapel
10.00: Choral Morning Prayer
1.15: Short Service in North-West Chapel
4.00: Choral Evening Prayer[68]

Comparison can be made with Westminster Abbey services at roughly the same date. 'Snapshots' in 1873 and 1901 reveal nothing more than choral matins at 10 a.m. and choral evensong at 3 p.m.,

302. The Jesus Chapel behind the high altar, as fitted out for small services by Bodley and Garner in the 1890s (see p. 256). In the background, the tomb of Canon H. P. Liddon

303 (*above*).   Bishop Simon Barrington-Ward, prelate of the Order of St Michael and St George, in front of the altar in the Order's chapel, wearing the cope and mitre presented by Earl Beauchamp in 1911

304 (*above right*).   'Prussian cope', given to the cathedral by Offley Wakeman, 1896. Made from silk woven for the intended coronation robe of Princess Victoria, wife of Frederick III of Germany, but never made because of the Emperor's premature death. The cope was first worn by Bishop Creighton for the Diamond Jubilee Service in 1897, the first event for which copes were adopted at St Paul's. (St Paul's Cathedral)

305 (*right*).   Clergy at Queen Victoria's Diamond Jubilee service, 1897, wearing high-church attire including skull caps of cardinal-red velvet. Detail of a print published by J. P. Mendoza. (GL)

although Dean Bradley introduced (or perhaps more accurately, reintroduced) a shortened form of morning prayer in 1898. A daily eucharist at 8 a.m. commenced in Advent 1901, seemingly at the expense of early matins.[69]

A daily eucharist, compline, sext: all these demonstrated the 'Catholic' leanings of the dean and chapter at St Paul's, as did the arrival of the cope as a vesture of the clergy (Figs 303, 304). Its first appearance, surprisingly, occurred during the time of Liddon and Gregory's dispute with Jackson. On Trinity Sunday 1871, Jackson became the first post-Reformation bishop to wear a cope in St Paul's; the cope having won the approval of the Privy Council even if the eastward position did not.[70] The dean and chapter first emerged so robed for the service following Queen Victoria's diamond jubilee in 1897 (Fig. 305), a flattering imitation of their colleagues at Westminster ten years earlier.[71] The *Guardian* reported that in addition to the copes the dean and chapter wore 'scull caps of cardinal-red velvet'.[72] The chapter resolved to use these vestments on all major festivals. They further agreed that on those important days assistants should wear coloured stoles and, further, such stoles would be worn on all occasions on which holy communion was celebrated. At this juncture the chapter seemed not the least unwilling to let their liturgical preferences be known. They commissioned the design and production of a processional cross and ordered the altar candles be always lit at evensong.[73] Only Archdeacon Sinclair was unhappy with these resolutions, asking that his dissent be recorded in the chapter minute book and omitting all mention of these decisions in his *Annals.* Although there was little ornate ceremonial in the Sunday morning sung eucharist ('but what there is is carefully and well thought out' said Newbolt), any innovations naturally provoked reactions from Protestant objectors.[74] On Easter eve 1883, during evensong, a man leaped on to the high altar, throwing down the cross, crying out 'Protestants to the rescue'. During the service on Good Friday 1885 in the Morning Chapel, the paten and chalice were knocked over by another protestor, using his umbrella.[75]

St Paul's moved into the twentieth century with Gregory (now dean), Holland, and Newbolt still at the helm, so no change in liturgical style or churchmanship was likely. Contemporaneously the Church of England found itself in the midst of another of its attempts to bring order and discipline to its worship, with a royal commission on ecclesiastical discipline reporting its findings in 1906. St Paul's was not the subject of any investigations reported to the commission, but the diocesan bishop and canon Arthur Winnington-Ingram was extensively questioned by the commissioners on account of the prevalence of liturgical lawlessness in the London diocese. He was asked about the use of the cope in his cathedral. In reply he said, 'It is not used every Sunday by the celebrant. The celebrant does not always use the cope, only on days when all the canons wear copes; then the celebrant does.' However, the bishop said he always wore the cope in the cathedral at ordinations and at the bigger services, 'and also if I am there on Easter Day or on any eve of the great festivals'.[76]

There is evidence that the St Paul's chapter, although maintaining their high-church principles, none the less wished to proceed cautiously in these matters. One of the contentious issues often mentioned in reports to the Discipline Commission was the use of the mixed chalice (i.e. the adding of a small amount of water to the wine in the chalice). The commissioners' report criticized 'ceremonial' mixing (that is, during the communion service), but considered that the pouring of wine into a chalice already containing water much less objectionable.[77] At the chapter meeting on 20 February 1891 this latter practice was recommended by H. S. Holland and adopted by the chapter.

On Gregory's retirement in 1911, a priest of very different religious preoccupations began a long occupation of the deanery. W. R. Inge had little or no concern for the niceties of liturgical worship and scant respect for scholars of Christian worship: asked if he was interested in liturgiology, he replied that he was not, nor was he interested in philately and postage stamps. Tone deaf, and in later life hard of hearing, his diary abounded with 'petulant and almost profane language against dreary and interminable musical services which I had to attend'. 'Are we sure that the Deity enjoys being serenaded?' he asked.[78]

Notwithstanding his declared lack of interest, Inge kept a tight rein on liturgical matters. When the minor canons drew up a long series of resolutions about the services, he described it as 'a trou-

blesome matter'. The liturgical and ceremonial changes they proposed included the use of copes at the high altar each Sunday; in the communion service the saying of the Summary of the Law in the place of the Ten Commandments, the use of *Benedictus Qui Venit* and *Agnus Dei*; and the omission of the penitential opening at weekday matins.[79] All (save the *Agnus Dei*) were included within the provision of the *Revised Prayer Book* of 1927–8 and were covered by the bishops' policy statement that, as regards variations from the prayer book, they would be guided in the future by the 1928 proposals.[80] The minor canons' resolutions were reported to the chapter on 4 January 1930 and the dean asked 'to make acknowledgement of the letter', which he did purely formally. He believed the cumulative effect of the proposals would be 'to change the type of service which has always been maintained at St Paul's into one of a definitely "Catholic" type'. Inge thought that 'the cathedral services should be on the lines of what may be called Prayer Book churchmanship so that all churchmen should feel themselves at home in the Metropolitan Cathedral. It would be a great pity if this were changed.'[81] There were no changes.

The general atmosphere at the time (one of the canons said that St Paul's was 'dead almost beyond recall') was bound to influence the worship.[82] Not even the mercurial Dick Sheppard was able to make much impression in his admittedly brief time as a canon. Sheppard wanted to abandon the singing of the daily offices and use the choir for 'beautiful and dignified services of not more than 35 minutes duration at say, 12 and 6 o'clock'. He was reminded that he was at St Paul's, not St Martins-in-the-Fields. Sheppard did manage to introduce Christmas trees and the Crib despite being told that such things were 'all very well for provincial cathedrals, but would never do here'.[83]

When Dean Matthews succeeded Inge, he reported that 'The tradition of St Paul's which I inherited was strictly in accord with the Prayer Book.' Sunday morning service consisted of morning prayer and holy communion, all sung, with a sermon as part of the communion. Matthews's attempt to introduce a break between morning prayer and the communion, with the sermon at the end of morning prayer, was fiercely resisted by other chapter members. Matthews declared himself shocked that the chapter's intransigence meant the continuance of a pattern of worship which could result in 'the blessed sacrament [being] received carelessly and unheedingly as a quaint part of the tourist attraction' by strangers unfamiliar with Anglican liturgy who suddenly found themselves in the midst of a eucharist.[84] Matthews was also unhappy with a full choral matins each weekday morning at 10 o'clock: 'To a busy man, and we were busy, the idea seemed clear that the Kingdom of God might be better served if morning prayers were said.' He did succeed in getting the custom slightly changed by having matins said on Wednesdays and Fridays and the choir singing on those days at 1 p.m. 'when a congregation was able to attend by cutting short the lunch hour'.[85]

It was not until just half-way through Matthews's record-breaking occupancy of the office of dean that the chapter took any cognizance of the liturgical changes taking place around them. The liturgical movement had already begun to influence all the churches of western christendom. In England it was represented by the Parish Communion movement, which had a conse-

306. Service under the dome showing forward altar and platform, July 1999

quential effect on parochial practice and produced an enhanced awareness of the importance of eucharistic worship.[86] A small sign of a growing appreciation of these liturgical developments emerged in 1955, when Matthews, perhaps to curb some enthusiasms, drew up a statement agreed by chapter and circulated to all the cathedral clergy:

The Dean and Chapter are concerned to secure a reasonable degree of uniformity and therefore they request that the general limits to be observed by the cathedral clergy should be those provided by the 1662 Prayer Book with such alternatives and deviations as are permitted in the Revised Prayer Book of 1928. However, from the Comfortable Words onwards to the Prayer of Thanksgiving the 1662 book should be followed, except the Proper Prefaces and Benedictus as provided by the 1928 order may be used.

The dean then spelled out the consequences of this directive: the collect for the sovereign became optional; the Creed and the *Gloria* might be omitted on weekdays; either the 1662 or the 1928 intercession might be used. In conclusion, he asked for the clergy's 'good will and co-operation when they celebrate the Holy Mysteries'; an indication that there were those who would have gone further in a high-church direction.[87] But these modest changes were no more than the prevailing custom in the majority of 'middle of the road' parishes. Certain ceremonial details regarding the priest standing or kneeling during parts of the service were amended in May 1956; subsequently appropriate settings of the *Agnus Dei* and the use of the *Kyrie* were allowed at the sung eucharist. Later, office hymns on the eve of red-letter saints' days were introduced. About that time there was also a six-month experiment with 'a temporary altar at the east end of the dome area' – but it did not last long (November 1955–May 1956). Nor did an experimental weekday sung eucharist in the Jesus chapel. One change was agreed by chapter: immediately on its authorization, they adopted the *New Lectionary*.[88]

The authorization in November 1966 of *Alternative Services, First Series*, containing many of the 1928 proposals, had the result of 'legitimizing' the provisions of the 1955 decanal statement, but there was no move at that stage to incorporate the much more radical proposals of the Series Two services into Sunday worship at St Paul's. Members of the chapter who were eager and anxious to champion avant-garde causes in other areas adopted a conservative attitude towards liturgical changes. For instance, although John Collins wished the cathedral to be a 'centre of Christian action', he also wanted its worship to be 'the best and most beautiful in the Anglican tradition of liturgical worship' – which, for him, meant no changes.[89]

This continued to be the case until the end of Dean Sullivan's time. In 1978 the chapter and the college of minor canons had long and often acrimonious discussions on the future pattern of Sunday worship. The eventual result was the introduction of a monthly celebration on a platform at the chancel steps, facing westward and using Series 3; from 1980, Rite A of the *Alternative Service Book*. On all other Sundays, and on saints' and greater holy days, the modified prayer book form continued to be used at the high altar, except in July. During that month, full orchestral masses were celebrated with an altar under the dome. This pattern remained unchanged until 1997, after which every Sunday eucharist (except for the July orchestral masses) was celebrated at a 'nave altar' using Rite A. In 2000, after a number of experiments, the area at the foot of the chancel steps was completely redesigned to give maximum dignity to the Sunday service in this style and at that place (Fig. 306). *Common Worship* was introduced on its authorization at Advent 2000. At the weekday celebrations of the eucharist, the cathedral clergy had, since 1978, been permitted to make their own choice from any of the forms authorized in the Church of England.[90]

From the late seventies there were also changes in the conduct of special services. The 1977 Queen's Silver Jubilee service was a completely Church of England occasion, but by the Queen Mother's eightieth birthday service in 1980 it was realized that there were sensitive ecumenical considerations involved in these national occasions. At this service the cardinal archbishop of Westminster and the moderator of the Church of Scotland had not merely 'walk-on parts', but took prayers within the service.[91]

Sunday and weekday evensong remained in the prayer book form. At the end of the twentieth century, this fully choral service continued to be well attended, and had acquired its own enthusiastic following. This is due, not least, to the regular weekly broadcast of evensong by the BBC and the increasing availability of first-rate recordings of the service. St Paul's has each year made significant contributions to these broadcasts and added regularly to the discography of evensong.

The memorial service has proved to be one of the significant growth areas in the liturgy of the last quarter of the twentieth century. St Paul's has had to undertake its share of these services for 'the great and the good'. There has also developed another type of memorial service; that which follows a tragedy or disaster.[92] The call for the church to provide liturgical expression of widespread shock and horror and be able to respond quickly to such requests was well illustrated by the service held in St Paul's on 14 September 2001, just three days after the destruction of the World Trade Center in New York. It was a splendid example of St Paul's enduring ability, in the twenty-first century, to fulfil its role to bring before God 'all our thoughts, our pain, our prayers'.[93]

32

ST PAUL'S AND THE PUBLIC CULTURE OF EIGHTEENTH-CENTURY BRITAIN

Nigel Aston

Ten years after St Paul's was first used in 1697, the new state of Great Britain was inaugurated in the cathedral on 1 May 1707 when the first, specially commissioned collect acclaimed 'all the signal providences by which the Union of this island [is] brought to a happy conclusion: so that as we were before under one head, so are we now become one people'. The preacher on the occasion, William Talbot, bishop of Oxford, spoke of creating 'a hearty Union' from which prosperity and joy would follow,[1] but such worthy aspirations would not flow merely from an act of parliament or from Queen Anne's wearing the combined Order of the Garter and Order of the Thistle to symbolize the union. If a distinctively British public culture could not be created overnight, the role of a great building like St Paul's was potentially vital to fostering that 'unity among the brethren, commanded by God', which also figured in Bishop Talbot's sermon, inspired as it was by the 133rd Psalm.

The Church of England had acquired a metropolitan cathedral that in scale and significance rivalled St Peter's in Rome, without much thought being paid to the spatial possibilities it offered. What, beyond the customary routines and rhythms of Anglican worship, would the Church of England and the monarchy *do* with this magnificent edifice? The answer would only be worked out gradually in the century between British victories at Blenheim and Trafalgar, as St Paul's became the setting of choice for the celebration and commemoration of national events, occasions on which the monarchy, parliament, the mayor and citizens of London, and ordinary subjects were brought harmoniously together in thanksgiving. These services may have been based on the Anglican liturgy and exclusively conducted by dignitaries of the established church, but there was a sense in which they transcended the cathedral's basic confessional identity, implicitly reflecting the Protestant diversity of eighteenth-century Britain and conferring some sort of recognition on the contribution of non-Anglicans to the life of the state. Indeed an anonymous poem of the 1690s conveyed this hope that dissenters might not feel unwelcome in the cathedral:

> But yet to thee I open still my gate,
> Hadst thou but Grace to enter in thereat.
> Beneath my roof I have preserv'd a Room
> For thee and all thy sons that thither come;
> Where a safe shelter thou mayst always find
> From wasting Rains, and the tempestuous Wind.[2]

That process was assisted by the participation in the worship of the cathedral on major occasions of the mayor and corporation of the city of London. Central to the character of the eighteenth-century state were the limited civil and religious rights extended to Protestant dissenters under the 1689 Toleration Act and the prominence of some of them in the livery companies and counting houses of the city. Thus the great mayoral pew in the choir could be filled by a non-Anglican, one of those 'occasional conformists' whose activities so agitated Tory politicians during Anne's reign. The attendance of nonconformists in the state services both reflected their legitimate role in the life of the Hanoverian polity and encouraged their less socially exalted brethren to regard St Paul's as a place in which they, too, could feel comfortable. While many high churchmen undoubtedly resented the prominence of dissenters and moneyed men on state occasions, more moderate Anglicans might take comfort from seeing the representatives of a corporation whose reputation for Whiggery and disloyalty had been notorious during much of the

307. *The Statue of Her Majesty etc Erected at the West End of St Paul's, Ann[o]* 1713, an early engraving sold by Thomas Bowles. Due to erosion in the London climate, the original monument to Queen Anne by Francis Bird was replaced with a copy in 1886. (GL)

time the cathedral was being rebuilt at least appearing to toe the line. It may well be that Queen Anne's more positive evolving attitude towards Protestant dissenters and her sense of them as her loyal subjects was assisted by their participation in the thanksgiving services.[3]

St Paul's was a 'contested space' well into the eighteenth century. In Anne's time it was the Tories, both clerical and lay, who made claim to ownership based on the building's association with the Stuart monarchy, a claim which never went unchallenged. City of London interests also saw St Paul's as 'theirs'. In the four-way relationship between Crown, government, city and church, the Corporation's importance in a St Paul's context reflected its importance as a political force within British politics. The Lord Mayor had a permanent stall and a vestry next to the north transept; the sovereign had no such provision, a tangible indication that St Paul's, throughout the eighteenth century, was tied to the political nation in the first instance through the city of London rather than the monarchy. In a state that depended so heavily for its financial support on city funding via institutions such as the Bank of England and the New East India Company, the presence of its representatives was symbolically appropriate and hinted at the 'virtual representation' of the nation beyond the city boundaries.

The city had the place of honour in the first of the state services to be held in the new building. In 1697 peace had returned to Europe when the War of the Augsburg League was concluded by the Treaty of Ryswick, which finally extracted from Louis XIV of France legal recognition of William III's title to the English throne and, by implication, of the Glorious Revolution. Though the cathedral bells had yet to arrive and scaffolding was still in place, the opportunity to revive the Elizabethan practice of celebrating national victories at St Paul's and hymning the contemporary achievements of a Dutch sovereign could not be passed over. The king was duly invited to St Paul's. Exactly who issued the invitation is hard to establish: Archbishop Thomas Tenison of Canterbury was William's closest spiritual adviser in his last years; Bishop Henry Compton of London (Fig. 348), disappointed of the primacy in both 1691 and 1695, was no doubt keen to have the king present in 'his' cathedral. But as with all the state services, planning arrangements were primarily the responsibility of the dean and chapter. On 2 December 1697, a select number of the political élite were admitted to the nave to hear Compton give thanks for the new cathedral and the king's victories, taking as his text 'I was glad when they said unto me, Let us go into the House of the Lord'. Embarrassingly, the hero of the hour had not gone into this new House of the Lord. William III, who was suffering from a cold, instead heard a sermon at his palace of Whitehall. With a huge crowd expected, security risks were high; it was only a year after a Jacobite assassination attempt on the king (the Fenwick Plot) had been foiled. So St Paul's made do with the Lord Mayor, aldermen and several companies of city livery men. William's decision to give thanks in Whitehall might have been disappointing for those who had wanted a royal occasion in St Paul's, but it was not in itself unusual. There had been a thanksgiving at the end of each campaigning season throughout the Nine Years War (1688–97). On those occasions, it had been customary to have many different services rather than one national one, with the Commons at St Margaret's, Westminster, the Lords at Westminster Abbey and the royal court at Whitehall. 2 December 1697 thus turned out to be the city of London's day, not the sovereign's, and the practice of having one major thanksgiving service had to wait a little longer to emerge.[4]

William's status as the champion of international Protestantism was never in doubt; in contrast, in many high-church quarters his commitment to the Church of England – and therefore to St Paul's – was; somewhat unfairly, given the efforts he made to distance himself from his Dutch Reformed background after 1689. Such was emphatically not the case with his sister-in-law and successor in 1702, Queen Anne. Her reign coincided with a run of British victories in the War of the Spanish Succession (1702–13). These demanded commemoration in the cathedral, which found itself to be suddenly commensurate with the new state's international power in a manner that could not have been foreseen when work started in the 1670s. The importance of the new St Paul's in public architectural terms was reinforced by the absence of royal building schemes at the turn of the eighteenth century, despite the terrible (and modest) state of royal palaces in and around the capital and the recent loss of Whitehall in the fire of 1698. If Greenwich, Kensington or the Wren refashioning of Hampton Court could not compete with the palace of Versailles, St Paul's had a dominant physical presence that compared very favourably with the Invalides chapel and the recently completed chapel at Versailles.[5]

The obvious point that St Paul's was a palace for divine worship rather than a hubristic setting for acclamation of *le roi soleil* was not lost on contemporaries. One poet conveyed the point thus:

Let me not therefore add,
Nor the expression seem too bold, if I
This more than Royal House, the Palace call
Of the Supreme Celestial majesty.[6]

Not that Queen Anne had either the physical presence or the temperament to incline her to imitate Louis's magnificence. But she had a strong sense of her regal dignity, dynastic pride in abundance, and a determination to lead her country against Bourbon aggrandizement. As Dean William Sherlock put it during the Blenheim service, 'Can any thing be more glorious to your Majesty's Reign, than to break the power of France, and to humble a proud insulting Monarch?'[7]

Anne's personal interest in St Paul's and all it symbolized derived from her status as supreme governor of the Church of England, a responsibility she discharged with unflagging dutifulness. The construction of the cathedral had been a constant backcloth to her life and, encouraged by Compton, her favourite prelate and former preceptor, she was determined to use St Paul's for a state occasion at the earliest opportunity. Even before her accession, she had paid the cathedral a private visit prior to the Ryswick service and, as monarch, she returned seven times on official duties. First, on 12 November 1702 she came to offer thanks for the successes of John, earl of Marlborough in Flanders and for the destruction of the Spanish fleet at Vigo Bay by the second duke of Ormonde and Sir George Rooke. Further visits marked the spate of Marlborough's victories in the War of the Spanish Succession. On 2 August 1704 there was a celebration of Blenheim; on 23 April 1705 of the forcing of the French lines at Tirlemont in the Spanish Netherlands; on 7 June 1706 of Marlborough's great victory at Ramillies and the earl of Peterborough's successes in Catalonia; on 31 December 1706 the occasion was further 'wonderful successes'; there was a service for the Union on 1 May 1707; on 23 August 1708, as the nation tired of conflict and high taxation, the queen still led it in rejoicing for the battle of Oudenarde. The queen's immobility had always made it difficult to build a service around an elaborate royal procession from the west entrance through to the choir, and eventually prohibited her attendance altogether. She never again returned to the cathedral, not even for the final opening in 1712. Her absence at the service commemorating the bloody battle of Malplaquet was a tangible sign of her own war-weariness, and she was simply too unwell from gout to attend the thanksgiving for the Peace of Utrecht on 7 July 1713. The poet laureate, Colley Cibber, recorded her absence with memorable bathos:

See! Britain's Peers and senate move in state,
For whose appearance gazing millions wait . . .
tis true, we see our Peers and Senate come,
In state advancing to the sacred dome;
That glorious sight affords no small relief;
But still the QUEEN is absent . . . That's the Grief.[8]

On these festival days, the court appropriated the choir, in which captured French flags and other trophies of war were laid up. The cathedral in effect acted as the chapel royal for the occasion, with the lord chamberlain therefore responsible for the seating arrangements. Members of the royal household, peers, privy councillors, other great officers of state and both houses of parliament (when sitting), including the speaker and the serjeant-at-arms, all attended; the Lord Mayor, aldermen and sheriffs, foreign envoys and their wives were also there.[9] The order of seating was

not to everyone's taste, and it entailed sitting packed together, with several hours of waiting before the queen arrived to be escorted to her place in procession by the yeomen of the guard.

The social inclusiveness of the state services in Anne's time should not be exaggerated. The political nation could assemble *inside* the cathedral in harmonious order; humbler subjects observed the monarch's progress from *outside*. With the nave still awaiting completion, there was nowhere to put these people, and the thought of including a selection of ordinary Londoners would not have been entertained even if space had been available. There were no precedents for it, and the public-order risks were immense. The people's participation was desired only as appreciative spectators, with the streets leading up to Ludgate Hill from St James's affording space for spectators to assemble, await the sovereign and cheer or jeer at the politicians who went to the cathedral in their coaches. The services offered Londoners the chance to have a day off work for socializing (a welcome extra holiday in their Protestant calendar) and walk-on parts in constitutional life, irrespective of whether they were Anglicans or dissenters. On the day of the Blenheim service (and it was typical of the others), the Strand, Fleet Street and Ludgate Hill were railed off and hung with blue cloth. The militia was drawn up behind the barriers; people filled the streets, sat on the roofs and peered out of their windows to secure a vantage-point. It was a precarious exercise in crowd involvement, always risky in an early modern state. As the Dutch envoy reported, 'the crowds of people which followed Her Majesty's carriage [were] so great that it could scarcely move'.[10] In Anne's time, however, these were demonstrations of affection, and the queen and her ministers correctly calculated that there was no threat to her or to them. These were unforgettable moments for all participants and provided a comforting if transient sense of national accord. Bishop William Nicholson of Carlisle wrote on 31 December 1706 of attending the queen 'in Her glorious Procession to St Paul's; the Weather good, and the Shew unspeakably fine. . . . Decorum of both Houses, & c. very extraordinary.'[11]

The eighteenth-century state services at St Paul's were both the focal point and the mirror of comparable acts of worship and thanksgiving observed at every parish church in England and Wales (the Scottish Kirk also held services on these days). George Hooper, bishop of Bath and Wells, in his sermon marking the signing of the Peace of Utrecht in 1713, pointedly talked of

the general joy which the people have everywhere conspired to express . . . [This] should not only be gratefully and devoutly testified by them to the Divine Majesty in all their Religious Congregations throughout their several Cities and Places of Habitation, a-part; but be unitedly presented up to him by this great Assembly, the States of the whole Kingdom; and our Joint Thanks offered in the most Authentick manner, and as enacted before Him.

It was the presence of the sovereign and other members of the political élite that principally differentiated St Paul's from all other settings for these services and made it a national focus for celebration. Hooper could not resist setting up an explicit analogy with Old Testament examples:

So are the Tribes of our Israel, the Princes and Elders of the People, by the Direction of their Sovereign who sits on the Throne of Judgment, Victorious as David, and Peaceful as Solomon, come up now to the Great House of God in our Metropolis.[12]

The contrast with the situation in France, where the monarchy was leading the country in public acts of contrition, was marked and instructive. After an exceptionally hard winter and with the kingdom threatened by allied invasion, there was a procession of the relics of Saint Généviève, the patroness of the city, in Paris in May 1709 attended by most of the clergy of the capital, the cardinal archbishop and the sovereign courts, all processing to Notre Dame.[13]

The language of the St Paul's thanksgiving sermons was replete with providential references (particularly Old Testament ones) as preacher after preacher emphasized that victory could not be presumed and was dependent on Britons' responsiveness to divine commandments. Since all national favours flowed purely from God,[14] prayer was no less important than armies in achieving success, as George Stanhope, dean of Canterbury, insisted:

> Fleets and Armies are proper instruments of Defence: But Fervent Applications to the Lord of Hosts and God of Battles give a Turn to the whole Affair. Thus Religious and good Governours work unseen and at a distance; while their Piety and their Prayers qualifie their Forces for victory, and the chapel and the closet crown the Sea and the Field with Efficacy and Success.[15]

Moral reform and patriotism went together.[16] Magnanimity should be shown by all 'true sons of the Church', as Dean Richard Willis emphasized, thereby risking the anger of high-flying Tory clergymen, for 'To deal mildly and gently with those who dissent from us, is really the best and most likely method to bring them over to the truth.'[17]

Despite appeals to confessional harmony and an insistence that national unity was a precondition of God continuing to confer his blessing on British arms, Anne's twelve-year reign was notoriously one in which party strife reached its height: the contest between Whig and Tory was an ineradicable part of public life, deplore it though many Britons did, including the queen herself. Anne's Toryism was offset by a liking for non-party administration which maximized her prerogative rights and by the Whiggish preferences of her life-long friend and mistress of the robes, Sarah, duchess of Marlborough, wife of the queen's great captain-general in Flanders. By 1708, however, the queen was tiring of her 'Mrs Morley's' tutelage, as the grip of the Whig Junto on power reduced her own scope for manœuvre. When the royal coach arrived at St Paul's on 23 August 1708 for the Oudenarde service, its occupants were struggling to regain their composure following a quarrel provoked by the sovereign's refusal to wear the jewels the duchess had laid out. Even inside the cathedral, the row continued, and some worshippers overheard the duchess tell the sovereign to shut up when she tried to defend herself against the duchess's accusation that Marlborough's credit was waning.[18] The service actually intensified party warfare because of the 'Screw-Plot': the Whigs were accused of having connived with plotters to remove screws and bolts from part of the choir roof so it would fall on the queen and the cabinet.[19]

The duke of Marlborough's chaplain-general to the army in Flanders, Francis Hare, newly appointed canon residentiary (1707), was blamed by the Tories for suppressing evidence of the conspiracy. His nomination reflected the growing prominence of Whigs in taking plum posts in the cathedral. Sherlock's successor as dean was Henry Godolphin (1708–26; Fig. 34), brother of Marlborough's right-hand man in government, Lord Godolphin. They were a powerful duo, dominant in cathedral affairs after

Bishop Compton retired from the commission for rebuilding in 1707. Hare and Godolphin could not rely on their Whig credentials to carry all before them; their proximity to the grasping, reputedly treacherous Marlboroughs did not recommend them to George I's advisers after 1714, and their presence discouraged the new Hanoverian régime from using St Paul's for royal or national occasions. There were other disincentives. St Paul's was suspect because it had been unable to disengage itself from those Tory and high-church sympathies that, however much to the taste of Queen Anne and her last ministry, smacked of Jacobite treason after 1714. Many members of the incoming administration could not forget the humiliation heaped on their heads in 1709–10 when Dr Henry Sacheverell had used the pulpit of St Paul's to deliver his notoriously incendiary sermon about 'false brethren in Church and state' (pp. 343–4). Unseemly wrangling between the architect and the chapter also provided justification for sustained royal disdain under the incoming dynasty.

The thanksgiving service for the accession of George I held on 20 January 1715 – celebrating the bringing of 'his Majesty to a peaceable and quiet Possession of the Throne, and thereby disappointing the Designs of the Pretender and all his Adherents' – was the first and last to be graced by the presence of the new sovereign. The preacher invited Britons to rejoice at having as their rulers 'a Family at the Head of the Protestant Interest in Europe', but few of George's subjects felt any fervour for him:[20] the contested background to his accession and his lack of personal charm turned what was officially intended to be a focus for national celebration into a distinctively Whig festivity. In Anne's reign, Bishop Jonathan Trelawny had referred to the great thanksgiving services as 'in effect, the Act of the whole Kingdom':[21] affection for the monarch indeed cut across party lines. That was not the case after August 1714, when the claim of the first two Hanoverian kings appeared inadmissible to a sizeable minority of Britons and dubious to most. This, too, had an impact on the decline of St Paul's as a royal venue of choice: between 1714 and 1760, if there was a metropolitical church of preference for both George I and George II, it was Westminster Abbey, the place of their coronation and a royal peculiar. Visits to St Paul's by members of the royal family, where they occurred at all, tended to be unofficial, as in 1724 when Princesses Anne and Caroline visited the cathedral to hear their music master, Handel, play the renovated organ. All that was left of the royal connection with St Paul's in these decades was the statue of Queen Anne by Francis Bird (Fig. 307), expressing the western prospect from the new cathedral and symbolizing the earlier close link with the monarchy which had lapsed.[22]

Of course, it would be wrong to suggest that St Paul's languished. These were the decades in which it affirmed its Anglican identity and became a setting for a variety of choral and corporate services, many attended by the Lord Mayor and City Corporation. Even without the king or members of the royal family present, there were occasions in the life of the kingdom that demanded commemoration, but not according to the precedents set in Anne's time. Thus the excitement generated by George II personally leading the British and Hanoverian infantry into action at Dettingen on 27 June 1743 led to special prayers while the sovereign was absent on the continent. Three years later, the dynasty was rejoicing in its own survival and trusting that so too were its people. In late April 1746, St Paul's held a service of national thanksgiving for the defeat of the Young Pretender at Culloden, part of a wider range of tributes to the victorious duke of Cumberland encouraged by the government that tried to generate rather than reflect a national mood.[23] The national and international impact of the service was nevertheless blunted by the king's refusal to attend in person. It was the same story in April 1749 at the celebrations for the Peace of Aix-la-Chapelle ending the War of the Austrian Succession (1740–8) signed the previous year: the entire royal family went not to St Paul's, but to the Chapel Royal.[24] In one sense, such arrangements merely reverted to earlier precedents, but it also signalled that St Paul's was far too modern and newfangled for an *arriviste* dynasty looking to stress its continuity with Britain's more distant past. George II's advisers may also have feared staging a public celebration which could rebound against the monarchy, given the concessions made to France and Austria at the Peace, concessions some critics alleged were dictated by Hanoverian rather than British interests.[25] There were also unresolved questions over precedence between the ecclesiastical establishments of the court and the cathedral dating back to 1714.

The reasons for the cathedral's underemployment as a venue for state occasions between 1714 and 1760 did not lie entirely with unsympathetic Whig ministers and bishops; not until the latter stages of the Seven Years War (1756–63) did Britain have military successes that would justify the re-enactment of the thanksgivings that had marked the War of the Spanish Succession. Appropriately, the capture of the great French fortress of Louisburg guarding the mouth of the St Lawrence River in Canada prompted a St Paul's service on 6 September 1758 in which the captured flags were carried in procession to the cathedral and laid up. Popular interest in the event was greater than at any equivalent service since Marlborough's wars. One junior minister reported that 'the mob was immense on the occasion, and it has contributed very much to heighten popularity'.[26] This and other successes of the Pitt–Newcastle coalition recalled the first halcyon decade of the century, and completed the destruction of Jacobitism as a viable political cause that Cumberland's victory at Culloden had begun. In conjunction with the accession of a young, British-born monarch in George III in 1760 and the coming in from the cold of Tory politicians, the road seemed clear for a more intensive, celebratory use of St Paul's Cathedral uniting monarchy and nation via the mediation of the established church.

Yet still that trend was slow to emerge. The contested nature of the Peace of Paris (1763) that ended the Seven Years War and the imperial humiliation of losing the American War of Independence (1775–83) made holding a choreographed state event in the cathedral problematic. Then an unexpected opportunity occurred in 1789 that marked a variant in the pattern of services to date: thanksgiving not for battles won, but for the monarch's recovery from a fit of insanity. The symbolic link between the king's health and that of the British state was affirmed more forcibly than at any point in living memory. As Matthew Kilburn has put it, 'It was as if the king's subjects were to be restored to health alongside the king.'[27] More than any other state occasion observed since the rebuilt cathedral had opened, that of 23 April 1789 was marked not by triumphalism but spontaneous, widely felt rejoicing that the king was well again and could resume his reign as one who, as the bishop of London said in his sermon, 'in his person, [represents] every thing that is dear and valuable to us, as Men, as Britons, and as Christians'.[28] The service displayed the identification of the nation with the monarchy in a manner transcending confessional allegiance and which readied it for the long wars against revolutionary France:[29] less than a fortnight after George III met his people at St Paul's to cel-

ebrate the constitutional ties which bound them, Louis XVI of France met his at Versailles when the Estates-General convened to begin work on unstitching the traditional monarchical order.

The idea of a thanksgiving service for his recovery belonged to George III personally, articulated as early as the last week of February 1789, when he was still quite feeble. Ministers were apprehensive, the archbishop of Canterbury advised against it, but the king insisted on 'an affecting though highly proper act of devotion' in the public gaze.[30] He also stipulated the Psalm for the day, the Old Testament lesson (Isaiah 12) and the anthem. The arrangements were put together at short notice by the new dean, George Pretyman (Fig. 38), former private secretary to the prime minister, William Pitt the Younger, and concurrently bishop of Lincoln. Pretyman had been criticized in the press for greediness in securing two prime appointments at the age of thirty-seven only two years previously, but he brought to both his posts an undeniable energy and a relative youthfulness. His deanship from 1787–1820 coincided with the struggle for survival of the British state against France, and Pretyman's proximity to Pitt made St Paul's rather than Westminster Abbey central to the defiant and public celebration of church and state. Pretyman took his opportunities and gave St Paul's a place in national life unknown since Stuart times.

The 1789 St George's Day service brought a monarch to the cathedral for the first time since 1715. Less than three years after

308. Plan by Robert Mylne showing the fitting-up of the choir for the Thanksgiving Service for the recovery of George III, 23 April 1789. The east end is at the top of plan. (GL)

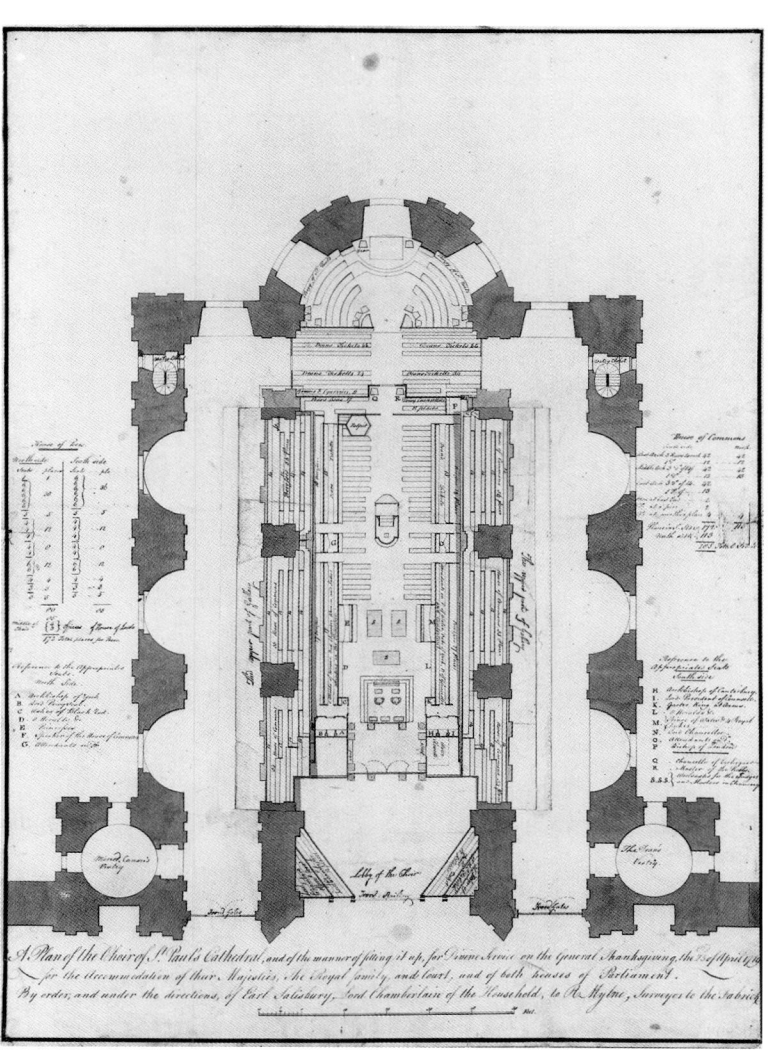

309. *The Grand Procession to St Paul's*, showing George III and Queen Charlotte *en route* to the cathedral, 23 April 1789, by Thomas Rowlandson. (GL)

the demented Quaker, Margaret Nicholson, had attempted to assassinate King George, security was a priority: three regiments of footguards lined the roads from St James's to Temple Bar, dragoons closed off every entrance into the processional route, and peace officers were on duty by 5 a.m.[31] Apprehensions evaporated when the popular mood proved benign: cheering crowds lined the streets, public buildings and houses were decked out with crowns, candles illuminated windows, and flags flew from all church steeples in Westminster and the city. For most members of the royal party, the journey east was nothing short of a triumphant progress, arriving at St Paul's just before noon, whereupon a rocket was fired from the statue of Queen Anne as a signal for the

guns at the Tower of London to be fired in salute. They were greeted at the west door of the cathedral by both archbishops (Moore of Canterbury and Markham of York) as well as Dean Pretyman and the bishop of London (Beilby Porteus); they then processed down to the choir where both houses of parliament were already seated. Some 167 MPs and most of the peers had convened at Westminster at 6 a.m. and then packed into carriages to convey themselves to St Paul's. It was reported that the cathedral arrangements were 'very judicious, and not marked by the least confusion, not withstanding the numerous assemblage of all the Lords and Commons now in town, without distinction of party'.[32] In a three-hour act of worship, the sermon of thanksgiv-

310. The choir looking west during the Thanksgiving Service of 23 April 1789, by Edward Dayes. (GL)

ing was preached by Porteus. After paying tribute to the king's personal trust in God, he reminded the congregation that they were present

> for the dedication of a WHOLE PEOPLE, with their SOVEREIGN at their head, to their Almighty Protector, their common benefactor and deliverer . . . Let this place be the grave of every unchristian sentiment and passion; let this day be the era of general harmony and concord. We have met here in joy; let us depart in peace.[33]

The day amounted to a triumphant début for Pretyman as master of ceremonies, taking (with the king's assistance) the Queen Anne state occasions as the model – there was even a search for the survivors of the 1713 service – but creatively and successfully adapting them to non-martial purposes. An act of private worship had been combined with popular celebration 'to create an act of royal theatre with St Paul's as a stage'.[34] As an exercise in popularizing the monarchy and the Church of England (currently under pressure from dissenters to repeal the Test and Corporation Acts), Pretyman had taken advantage of the national mood with acute timing, on 'an occasion where universal thanksgiving and general joy pervaded what may be truly called the people'.[35] In a masterstroke, dean and monarch had inspirationally selected St George's Day as the day for national thanksgiving, thereby linking up England's king with her patron saint so as to reinforce symbolically the interconnections of patriotism, piety, and praise. Loyalists eagerly anticipated the event: Hannah More expected 'one of the most awful scenes since the opening of Solomon's temple' (Figs 279, 299, 308–10).[36]

The crowds fêted Pretyman's former Cambridge pupil, Pitt, almost as much as King George, both for the premier's loyalty during the Regency crisis and for the rapid recovery of national prosperity after the loss of the American colonies, making the occasion 'in truth his triumph as much as the King's'.[37] The processional route had, as before, allowed Londoners to make their feelings towards the nation's leaders amply clear. Charles James Fox, the leading opposition politician and defender of the prince of Wales's claims to full powers as Regent, was recognized as his carriage passed Temple Bar 'and received an universal hiss which continued with very little intermission until he alighted at St Paul's', obliging him to sit back in his seat; in contrast, the crowd surrounded Pitt's carriage on the return journey, took off the horses and drew it back to Downing Street. George, prince of Wales – who, with his brother the duke of York, had munched biscuits during the service – had to endure catcalls on both the outward and return journey.[38] If the princes had at least made an effort and worn their father's favourite Windsor uniform, it was hard for them and their Whig friends to conceal their apartness on what was supposed to be a day of national unanimity when even their sisters, the royal princesses, proudly sported bandeaux of Indian gold muslin inscribed 'God Save the King' in letters of gold, a device imitated by most ladies in the congregation.

Eight years later, the cathedral reverted to thanking the Almighty for British successes in war. There had been few excuses for so doing since the outbreak of hostilities in 1793, though preachers did what they could to stir up patriotic sentiments as the nation – and the city of London in particular – hurriedly established volunteer companies to meet the invasion threat. Sermons on appropriate themes ('The duty of loving our country') could be heard regularly in the cathedral during the 1790s as volunteers assembled to worship in their regimentals. In 1798

Thomas Bowen thus warned the Temple Bar and St Paul's District Military Association that 'Our inveterate foe strikes at our government; he aims the blow at that happy constitution which is the source and security of all the blessings, civil or religious, that we enjoy!' Urging his congregation to meet the 'danger as men, as Britons, and as Christians', he warned them of the catastrophic results of defeat:

> Every distinction which originates in birth, property, or station, would be confounded; all that we now hold high, honourable, or sacred, would be levelled with the ground; and the vilest of our own countrymen would, in sarcastic malice, be selected by the victor to rule over us.[39]

The previous year had brought decisive victories first to Admiral Jervis over the Spanish at Cape St Vincent and then to Admiral Duncan over the Dutch at Camperdown, especially welcome so soon after the Spithead naval mutinies. The hard-pressed Pitt government was desperate to mark the moment with special services to commemorate 'the many signal and important victories, which His Divine Providence hath vouchsafed to HM's fleets, in the course of the present war' (to quote the specially produced collect). George III was personally enthusiastic. The Pitt–Pretyman partnership once more made St Paul's the natural centrepiece for national celebrations which, it has been argued, acted as a Christian counter-cultural riposte to the revolutionary state festivals seen recently in France, masterminded by Jacques-Louis David.[40] Indeed, as a cheap repository tract noted:[41]

> Remember that we meet to celebrate not our own praises, but the praises of that God who hath delivered us. In France, indeed, where they speak not of God in their public festivals, nor pretend to honour Him by them, it is natural to expect that a spirit of national pride only will be cultivated. They meet to do honour to the memory of a Hoche, or to celebrate a Moreau, or a Buonaparte; but we meet in order to give the praise to God, and not to deify either a Howe, a St Vincent, or a Duncan. We also have our heroes whom we would thank, but we will not make Gods of them.

The emphasis was on England depicted as the bulwark not just of Protestantism, but of Christianity itself. As Pretyman, preaching in the cathedral, observed:

> While our enemies have insulted the majesty of Heaven, we have humbled ourselves before God, and acknowledged our transgressions. While they have impiously denied his all-controlling power, we have prayed unto the Lord to give wisdom to our councils, success to our arms, and steadiness to our people.[42]

This sermon was the climax of the great service held in the cathedral on 19 December 1797, with the king (the Admiralty sword carried before him by Earl Spencer, the first lord) and the royal family taking their places in the choir (the king sat on a throne placed under the organ). French, Spanish and Dutch flags captured in a run of naval actions since March 1795 were carried aloft through streets bulging with a well-behaved crowd of over 200,000[43] and into the cathedral by detachments of 250 marines and ratings led by flag officers and captains to take up station in a semi-circle under the dome.[44] The decision to give ordinary seamen a place of honour in the service was innovative and controversial with some senior officers (one ship's commander, ordered by Admiral Lord Duncan to release fifty men for the

311.   Ticket for admission to the Thanksgiving Service for naval victories, 19 December 1797, engraved by Corbould and Hemsley. Above, portraits of George III and of Admirals Howe, St Vincent and Duncan; below, naval and military attributes, a crude image of St Paul's and the arms of the City of London. (GL)

service, feared they would just get drunk in town);[45] in Anne's state services, none of Marlborough's troops had been so honoured. The king, however, had personally insisted on the sailors' inclusion, setting a precedent for Nelson's funeral. As befitted the occasion, the congregation clapped as Lord Duncan and Countess Howe (representing her husband, Richard, earl Howe, victor of the 'Glorious First of June' 1794, who was too frail to attend) and her daughters came down the nave.

Pitt left nothing to chance: Pretyman preached from a text Pitt had selected himself (2 Sam. XXII: 1–2 and part of 3). Prime minister and dean reviewed the sermon in Downing Street beforehand, with Pitt advising that sentences about the army and the mutiny in the first draft were omitted. (Mrs Pretyman urged her husband not to make concessions to the premier, and begged the bishop to 'remember that Mr. Pitt is a better politician than a divine, a better judge of writing than of doctrine'.[46] In the finished version, praise for the navy abounded: 'The commanders of our fleets have displayed an unexampled degree of zeal, promptitude, and skill; and our seamen have fought with a spirit and intrepidity which we should in vain seek even in the annals of this country.'[47] But it was set once more within the wider frame of providential deliverance and prophetical fulfilment, and an expression of national relief at the diminished threat of invasion.[48] The service offered the country the chance to reflect on the nature of the strife in which it was engaged: thus the thanksgiving prayer spoke of the war as one 'for religion and for public liberty, for the independence of their country, for the rights of civil society, for the maintenance of every ordinance, divine and human, essential to the well-being of man'.[49]

Despite Pretyman's uplifting words, ceremonial colour and that prerequisite of any state occasion – good weather[50] – not all the London public thought that there was much to celebrate. Security concerns were high enough in wartime for a House of Commons committee to discuss what arrangements might be needed to preserve order. They were right to be cautious. Pitt's

reception indicated a very different mood to that of 1789: his carriage was hissed and pelted in St Paul's Churchyard and he returned home under military escort.[51] There was unease at the projection of state power within a sacred setting, well captured in the black humour of the squib *A Creed for All Good and Loyal Subjects, who go to St Paul's on the 19th of December 1797*, worth quoting in full:

> I believe in God as by Law established – in BILLY PITT Heaven born Chancellor of the Exchequer, promoter of all court intrigues, visible and invisible, Creator and Master of Lords and Commons, whose Politics are pure, and Morals untainted; and in Secretary HARRY DUNDAS, the only beloved of BILLY PITT, Beloved before all Women, Men of Men, Head of Heads, Minister of Ministers; beloved, not hated, being of one opinion with his patron, by whom all ministers are made; who for us Men, and our Taxation, came out of Scotland, and talked much in the House of Integrity, and was appointed East India Comptroller, under BILLY PITT, and went into Scotland, and was there burnt in Effigy; and the third Day he came back again, (according to the Newspapers) and ascended into Office, and sitteth at the right hand of his patron; there to judge both loyal and disloyal, whose folly shall have no end. And I believe that Murder, Rapine, Plunder and burning are the true and proper means of conciliating the Affection of the Inhabitants of Ireland, who I believe to be the Natural slaves of the British Cabinet. And I believe in the House of BOROUGHS; the legal representatives of the people, elected by one hundred and sixty-two persons, either peers, sinecure placemen, or immediate servants of the K—g who can do no wrong.
>
> And I believe in GE—GE the T—D, Lord and Giver of Places, who, together with BILLY PITT, is worshipped and glorified, who spake by a Proclamation: And I believe in Paper Money and National bankruptcy as outward and visible signs of the Nation's prosperity. and I look not for a remission of taxes, no, not till the Resurrection of the dead, and I look for a better Government in the World to come. Amen.

War-weariness, high prices, and higher taxation certainly led many of the king's otherwise loyal subjects to point the finger at Pitt personally. The trampling of a woman by a city volunteer's horse also detracted from the occasion, leading the oppositionist *Morning Post* to suggest that the service had come close to misfiring: 'The result of the procession to St. Paul's was that one man returned thanks to Almighty God and one woman was kicked to death.'[52]

Thanksgiving services were only an exceptional part of the life of St Paul's, but related developments also contributed to the cathedral's emerging place at the centre of Hanoverian public culture. First was the decision to bury some of the most talented Britons of their day in the vaults of the cathedral after solemn and extended services. The composer William Boyce was interred on 16 February 1779 with, appropriately, the choirs of St Paul's, Westminster Abbey and the Chapel Royal taking part in the service under the centre of the dome. Boyce's commital was quite eclipsed in magnificence by that of Sir Joshua Reynolds on 3 March 1793. Reynolds's coffin was followed by forty-two coaches for the mourners and forty-nine more for the nobility and gentry; the pall was carried by no fewer than ten noblemen, including three dukes. It was appropriate that Reynolds was laid to rest in St Paul's. As founding president of the Royal Academy (1768–92), he had dedicated himself to bringing the Academy into the mainstream of national life and he had hoped, in the early 1770s, that an ambitious decorative scheme for the cathedral nave would facilitate that progress. A residual fear of 'popery' on the part of the bishop of London doomed the proposal.[53] Reynolds had been a moving force in urging that St Paul's should be the last resting place of illustrious Britons, in which their sculptural (and sometimes sepulchral) monuments would fulfil a permanent if silent commemorative function. The heroes of the Seven Years War had gone to Westminster Abbey; a statue of Chatham had been erected at the Guildhall. St Paul's remained embarrassingly empty as late as the 1780s, despite Gwynn's idea for a temple of fame to British worthies and the enthusiasm of Dean Thomas Newton (1764–82), whose own monument ended up cluttering the interior of St Mary-le-Bow. With the backing of Bishop Porteus, Dean Pretyman at last overcame capitular reluctance to allow monuments into St Paul's, drafted 'wise and liberal regulations' and commissioned John Bacon to provide three life-size standing figures garbed in the Roman manner.[54] The first figure to be so honoured (in 1796) was John Howard (Fig. 214), the penal reformer and Quaker; the choice indicates how St Paul's was, by the 1790s, demonstrating that its character was at least as much national as it was Anglican, though the second statue, erected at Reynolds's prompting, was of the greatest Anglican layman of the eighteenth century – Samuel Johnson (Fig. 215). There were also the fallen of the Revolutionary War to immortalize, parliament in 1795 having voted money for the commemoration of selected naval and military heroes, using the battle of the 'Glorious First of June' the previous year as the occasion.[55] Though there was some confusion of categories, the implication was that in future, Westminster Abbey would be reserved for dead politicians and poets. Thus, just as revolutionary France was turning the church of Sainte-Généviève into a dechristianized and deconsecrated Pantheon, so St Paul's became the British alternative, a cultural as well as Christian shrine (pp. 272–9).

The deaths in action of several eminent officers after 1793 and their interment in the cathedral created a Valhalla rather than a Pantheon, a character which was gloriously confirmed on 9 January 1806 when St Paul's received the mortal remains of Horatio, Lord Nelson. The funeral service for the hero of Trafalgar spectacularly mixed the great state occasion with the entombment, a combination which St Paul's was at last ready to use after ample experience with each separately over the previous century. There were innovations: the processional route was not from a royal palace but by barge up-river from Greenwich to the Admiralty and only then on to St Paul's, and the official presence

of members of the royal family at a public funeral was previously unknown. Another feature of the event – the participation of forty-eight sailors from HMS *Victory* and forty-eight pensioners from the Greenwich naval hospital – followed the popular precedent of 1797 (pp. 369, 382; Figs 282, 315).

The patriotic outpouring and pride in British identity so remarkably on display at the Nelson funeral was the culmination of a century of state services that had shown the scope afforded by St Paul's for large-scale, sacred performance. Public satisfaction with what, from 1 January 1801, was the United Kingdom of Great Britain and Ireland and its Hanoverian heads of state had been slow to take form partly because it had been denied adequate expression until George III, Pretyman and Pitt saw the uses of the dormant tradition of national thanksgiving. Pride in British institutions had been fuelled meanwhile by those lesser corporate loyalties on display in smaller-scale services hosted by St Paul's throughout the eighteenth century, as for the mayor and corporation of the City of London, the livery companies, or for the militia and volunteer companies set up in the 1790s. These were no less occasions for patriotic and Protestant parade, lower-key than the great state services perhaps, but still imaginatively combining worship with display in a manner that was as lavish and colourful as anything else on offer in the Church of England.

By the beginning of the nineteenth century, St Paul's was a primary focus for elaborate and evolving ceremonial, a venue in which the rituals of church and state (national, military and civic) were enmeshed so as to provide an outlet for state rejoicing or mourning and thereby fostering and focusing a strengthened sense of national unity and purpose, as well as popularizing the monarchy.[56] Such splendid occasions also put on display the acceptable sides of establishment and played an underestimated part in prolonging Anglican confessional supremacy. There were still limitations in the use of the building, as in the failure to hold a service to mark the controversial incorporation of Ireland into the United Kingdom on 1 January 1801, but the pattern was clear: St Paul's had become much more than a church for the capital. The services may have been impeccably Anglican, but the breadth of public participation, both in the cathedral and *en route* to it, stressed the increasingly inclusive character of a formally confessional state and a composite, British monarchy. St Paul's was well on the way to becoming a national emblem in its own right, a temple to Britishness with a commemorative and monumental function extending well beyond Anglicanism, right at the heart of the imperial state's public culture.

33

ST PAUL'S AND ITS PARISHES,
1750–1870

Mark Smith

On 30 July 1840, Charles James Blomfield, bishop of London, rose in the House of Lords to speak in defence of the Ecclesiastical Duties and Revenues Bill. This was intended to divert the 'surplus' income of the great cathedral establishments in order to finance an expansion of parochial ministry in the growing towns and conurbations of early Victorian England. 'I traverse the streets of this crowded City,' explained the bishop,

> with deep and solemn thoughts of the spiritual condition of its inhabitants. I pass the magnificent Church which crowns the metropolis, and is consecrated to the noblest of objects, the glory of God, and I ask of myself, in what degree it answers that object. I see there a Dean, and three residentiaries, with incomes, amounting in the aggregate to between £10,000 and £12,000 a year...I proceed a mile or two to the E. and N.E. and find myself in the midst of an immense population in the most wretched state of destitution and neglect, artisans, mechanics, labourers, beggars, thieves, to the number of at least 300,000. I find, upon the average, about one church, and one clergyman, for every 8,000 or 10,000 souls: in some districts, a much smaller amount of spiritual provision...I naturally look back to the vast endowments of St Paul's, a part of them drawn from these very districts, and consider whether some portion of them may not be applied to remedy, or alleviate, these enormous evils. No, I am told, you may not touch St Paul's.[1]

Blomfield's speech played an influential role not only in the parliamentary debate, but also in shaping a historiography of the nineteenth-century Church of England in which the Ecclesiastical Commissioners emerge as champions of a moderate reform essential to the survival of the church, and the cathedral chapters as obscurantist defenders of their own sectional interests at the expense of the church as a whole.[2] From this perspective, the relationship between a cathedral chapter and its parishes can be conceived of as entirely exploitative: the chapter received benefits in terms both of revenues and the influence that came from patronage while returning little or nothing in support for the parochial ministry. This essay seeks to explore the actual nature of the relationship in the case of St Paul's, and also to assess its consequences for the life of the church in its parishes.

THE CATHEDRAL AND ITS PARISHES

In the period 1750–1870, the dean and chapter had a direct relationship with fifty-one parishes. In forty-five it exercised the patronage of the benefice either in sole right or jointly with another patron. Nineteen benefices fell within the peculiar jurisdiction of the cathedral, where the chapter was responsible for many of the functions usually performed by the diocesan bishop. In thirteen of those benefices, the dean and chapter exercised both the patronage and the jurisdiction (Table 7, p. 375).[3]

Patronage
The dean and chapter were thus influential patrons with more benefices in their gift than any private individual or even than the majority of bishops.[4] How was this patronage exercised, and what sorts of persons were in receipt of it? One salient point emerges from even the briefest perusal of the records: capitular patronage, just like capitular income, may have been the property of the chapter corporately, but it was enjoyed by the residentiaries individually. Already by the mid-eighteenth century, they were clearly taking it in turns to make appointments.[5] In 1833 this system was

elaborated in order to distinguish between 'personal options', in which a member of the chapter presented himself to a benefice, and 'friendly options', in which he presented someone else. Under the revised system, vacant benefices were offered to each of the canons in rotation as a 'personal option' and then, if refused by all, as a 'friendly option'. Since the value of the benefices concerned ranged from Kingsbury (£46 p.a.) to St Giles Cripplegate (£2,018 p.a.) it was possible in some cases that no canon would wish to present, lest by giving up his place at the head of the rota he lost an opportunity to present to a much more valuable living in the future. Consequently, there was provision for benefices which were refused by all canons both as 'personal' and as 'friendly options' to be filled by the chapter acting together.[6] In 1850, even this vestigial role for corporate action was removed by the establishment of a rota for refused options, which allowed individual canons to present without consequences for their position on either of the first two rotas.[7] Theoretically, nominations to vacancies merely constituted recommendations, subject to approval by the chapter as a whole. In practice, however, this stipulation remained a dead letter, and there is no evidence of a veto ever having been employed or even considered.

Only a few of the chapter's livings (like St Giles Cripplegate, selected by Frederick Blomberg in 1833[8]) were sufficiently valuable to attract a canon of St Paul's, and the exercise of personal options was correspondingly rare – only six instances between 1750 and 1850. Most patronage was therefore dispensed via 'friendly options' and, in exercising these, the members of the chapter seem to have regarded themselves as under some obligation to reward the less wealthy members of the cathedral establishment. In 1842, for example, the chapter minutes noted,

> The Dean and Chapter having received most satisfactory Testimonials to the character of the Revd Henry Goldsmith Vigne, son in law of Mr Hodgson, their chapter clerk, resolved to present him to the vacant vicarage of Sunbury. And they are desirous of recording this Act, as a proof of their sincere respect for Mr Hodgson, and of the sense they entertain of his long and valuable services.[9]

Minor canons also received such patronage and arrangements for this were formalized in 1835 when it was agreed that any benefice held by a minor canon that became vacant in the future should automatically be presented to another minor canon.[10] The most spectacular beneficiary of this sort of patronage was Weldon Champneys, who was preferred by the chapter to the benefices of Kensworth, Caddington, Langdon Hills and finally, in 1797, to St Pancras.[11] Even in the 1790s, St Pancras represented a considerable plum not usually conferred on a minor canon, who would more typically receive one of the cathedral's less valuable benefices outside London, such as Willesden, Kensworth or Tillingham. Occasionally, however, city parishes were made available – perhaps as a reward or inducement, as in the case of SS Anne and Agnes with St John Zachary given, in 1840, to John Povah on the basis that 'it will be highly conducive to the welfare of the cathedral and to the encouragement of proper conduct on the part of the minor canons'.[12] Indeed, from 1854, following an intervention by Blomfield, city parishes not wanted by members of the chapter were reserved in the first instance for the minor canons on grounds of convenience.[13] While minor canons in general seem to have been content with their portion of patronage,[14] this was by no means always the case. The bishop's intervention in 1853–4, for example, arose from a complaint by

312. Sydney Smith, canon of St Paul's 1831–45. Bust of 1835 by Richard Westmacott the younger in the cathedral library. (SPL)

two minor canons about inequities in the disposal of chapter livings. More spectacular still was the case of Henry Knapp, the subdean, who in 1847 laid claim to St Giles Cripplegate on the basis of a thirteenth-century ordinance that attached the benefice to his office. When the chapter dismissed his claim, Knapp appealed to the bishop as visitor, who considered the matter but concluded that the sub-dean had failed to establish his case.[15] Knapp responded by publishing a pamphlet in which he complained that the dean and chapter had 'very much disregarded and disproportionately repaid the services of some of the members of the cathedral', and concluded 'Is there not, then, a just cause of complaint at such a state of things; when, year after year, it is manifest that the patronage of the chapter is bestowed on sons, and nephews, and friends?'[16] (p. 86).

Whatever the validity of his claim to St Giles's, Knapp was certainly correct in supposing that, just like other individual patrons, the canons of St Paul's bestowed most of their patronage on their friends, relations and other connections. For example, John Naish, vicar of St Helen Bishopsgate, explained in 1790 that 'My particular friend who presented me to the living was Bishop Newton, then dean of St Paul's',[17] while Sydney Smith for some years deliberately kept himself at the head of the list for friendly options in the hope of presenting his son to a valuable living.[18] Smith was also at the centre of perhaps the most celebrated use of a friendly option in this period, a presentation to the vicarage of

313. Edmonton parish church, a St Paul's living, *c.* 1800. (GL)

Edmonton in 1843. The vacancy had arisen from the death of James Tate, a member of the chapter, who through financial mismanagement had left his dependants with very slender means and principally reliant on his son Thomas, his curate at Edmonton. Smith, whose turn it was, decided to rescue the family by presenting the benefice to Thomas, and clearly enjoyed himself hugely in the process. He went down to Edmonton to confirm the presentation in person and, having teased the family that he had given the living to a man called Tate who must be a relation, revealed the good news and then participated in an outburst of tearful rejoicing with the Tates, who had been expecting at any moment to be turned out by a new incumbent.[19] For the next few weeks Smith basked in congratulations on his generosity from, amongst others, the bishop of London[20] and the principal parishioners of Edmonton. In replying to the latter, he took the opportunity of describing the considerations that had actuated his exercise of patronage:

> I had to consult the character and dignity of the chapter, which would have been compromised by the nomination of a person merely because he was my friend and relation. I was to find a serious and diligent man in the prime of life, able and eager to fulfil the burdensome duties of so large a parish and I was to seek in him those characters of gentleness and peace which are of such infinite importance to the character of the church, and the happiness of those who live under the beautiful influence of those qualities. Lastly I had to show my strong respect for the memory of one of the kindest and best men that ever lived and to lift up, if I could, from poverty and despair, his widow and his children.[21]

It is perhaps understandable that in none of the correspondence subsequent to the presentation did Smith elect to reveal that Tate had not been his first choice. He had earlier attempted to present the living to John Grey, a man who, as rector of Stanhope in the diocese of Durham (worth almost £5,000 p.a. in 1835), was unlikely to have required lifting up from poverty. Grey did possess

the recommendation, however, of being a son of Earl and Lady Grey – among Smith's most important political connections – and when he turned down the offer, Smith wrote to Lady Grey commenting on the fact that her son had managed to avoid the 'very unpleasant task of getting dilapidations from Taite's [*sic*] ruined family'.[22]

PECULIAR JURISDICTION

For the nineteen parishes within its peculiar jurisdiction, the relationship with the cathedral had an additional dimension. From the point of view of the clergy and churchwardens, the most important additional feature was the chapter's assumption of the visitatorial role. For the parishioners, the most important feature was the chapter's provision of the court of first instance in matters of ecclesiastical law, including matrimonial cases and probate. The visitations followed a standard pattern: twice a year, at Michaelmas and Easter, the churchwardens of fourteen of the peculiar parishes were cited by the chapter's commissary to attend at St Paul's with their credentials and to pay the appropriate visitation fees. The wardens of the remaining five, all parishes in Essex, were cited to appear separately once a year at Heybridge.[23] The churchwardens were also required to make a presentment of the state of their parishes and, from the point at which the surviving records begin until 1835, these were made on a printed form to which the churchwardens were expected to add a report and their signatures. As in other jurisdictions at this period, the presentment usually consisted of an uninformative 'All Well'. However, judging by the handwriting, in the case of the St Paul's presentations the 'All Well' was inscribed in advance – almost certainly by the commissary's clerks – the wardens being simply asked to agree that this report should stand.[24] It is difficult to imagine a form of visitation less likely to yield useful information about the parishes. At the Michaelmas visitation of 1835, a new form was introduced, requiring answers to nine questions about

TABLE 7
St Paul's Benefices c.1832

County	Place	Jurisdiction	Patron	Value p.a.(£)
Beds	Caddington	Bishop of Lincoln	Dean & Chapter	319
Essex	Barling	Dean & Chapter	Dean & Chapter	308
Essex	Belchamp St Paul	Dean & Chapter	Dean & Chapter	240
Essex	High Easter with Good Easter	Bishop of London	Dean & Chapter	169
Essex	Heybridge	Dean & Chapter	Dean & Chapter	159
Essex	Horndon on the Hill	Bishop of London	Dean & Chapter	210
Essex	Hutton	Bishop of London	Dean & Chapter	313
Essex	Langdon Hills	Bishop of London	Dean & Chapter	245
Essex	Mucking	Bishop of London	Dean & Chapter	219
Essex	Navestock	Dean & Chapter	Trinity College Oxford	422
Essex	Tillingham	Dean & Chapter	Dean & Chapter	287
Essex	Wickham St Paul	Dean & Chapter	Dean & Chapter	200
Herts	Albury	Dean & Chapter	Treasurer of St Paul's	395
Herts	Ardeley	Bishop of Lincoln	Dean & Chapter	242
Herts	Hemel Hempstead	Bishop of Lincoln	Dean & Chapter	709
Herts	Kensworth	Bishop of Lincoln	Dean & Chapter	180
Herts	Brent Pelham with Furneaux Pelham	Dean & Chapter	Treasurer of St Paul's	320
Herts	Sandon	Bishop of Lincoln	Dean of St Paul's	227
Herts	Therfield	Bishop of Lincoln	Dean & Chapter	937
Herts	Walden St Paul	Bishop of Lincoln	Dean & Chapter	142
Kent	Charing	Bishop of London	Dean & Chapter	250
Kent	Egerton chapel	Archbishop of Canterbury	Dean & Chapter	111
London	St Alban Wood St with St Olave Silver St (Monkwell St)	Bishop of London	Dean & Chapter alternating with Crown	247
London	St Anne & St Agnes Aldersgate with St John Zachary	Bishop of London	Dean & Chapter alternating with Bishop of London	239
London	St Antholin with St John the Baptist (Walbrook)	Bishop of London	Dean & Chapter alternating with Crown	222
London	St Augustine at the Gate with St Faith	Dean & Chapter	Dean & Chapter	296
London	St Benet Gracechurch with St Leonard Eastcheap	Bishop of London	Dean & Chapter alternating with Dean & Chapter of Canterbury	300
London	St Clement Eastcheap with St Martin Orgar	Bishop of London	Dean & Chapter alternating with Bishop of London	290

County	Place	Jurisdiction	Patron	Value p.a.(£)★
London	St George Botolph Lane with St Botolph Billingsgate	Bishop of London	Dean & Chapter alternating with Crown	320
London	St Giles Cripplegate	Dean & Chapter	Dean & Chapter	2,018
London	St Gregory with St Mary Magdalen Old Fish St	Dean & Chapter	Dean & Chapter	245
London	St Helen Bishopsgate	Dean & Chapter	Private	209
London	St Lawrence Jewry with St Mary Magdalen Milk St	Bishop of London	Dean & Chapter alternating with Balliol College Oxford	300
London	St Mary Aldermanbury with St Thomas the Apostle	Bishop of London	Parishioners	255
London	St Michael Bassishaw	Bishop of London	Dean & Chapter	239
London	St Michael Queenhithe with Holy Trinity the Less	Bishop of London	Dean & Chapter alternating with Dean & Chapter of Canterbury	270
London	St Michael Le Querne with St Vedast	Bishop of London		
London	St Nicholas Cole Abbey with St Nicholas Olave	Bishop of London	Dean & Chapter alternating with Crown	287
London	St Peter Paul's Wharf with St Benet Paul's Wharf	Bishop of London	Dean & Chapter	251
London	St Peter le Poor	Bishop of London	Dean & Chapter	629
Middx	Chiswick	Dean & Chapter	Dean & Chapter	601
Middx	Edmonton	Bishop of London	Dean & Chapter	1,550
Middx	Friern Barnet	Dean & Chapter	Dean & Chapter	255
Middx	Kingsbury	Bishop of London	Dean & Chapter	46
Middx	St Luke	Dean & Chapter	Dean & Chapter	578
Middx	St Pancras	Dean & Chapter	Dean & Chapter	1,910
Middx	Stoke Newington	Dean & Chapter	Prebendary of Newington	438
Middx	Sunbury	Bishop of London	Dean & Chapter	336
Middx	Tottenham	Bishop of London	Dean & Chapter	978
Middx	West Drayton	Dean & Chapter	Private	530
Middx	Willesden	Dean & Chapter	Dean & Chapter	130
Surrey	Barnes	Archbishop of Canterbury	Dean & Chapter	375

Note The values are the mean net income over the three years ending 1831. Along with other information in the table, they are derived from: PP 1835 xxii (54), 'First Report of the Ecclesiastical Duties and Revenues Commission'; GL. MS CF box 115, AB 1831 (Dean and Chapter Visitation process); LPL, Fulham Papers Randolph, vols. 9–12 (bishop of London's visitation Returns).

the state of the church and associated property and the performance of duty by the minister and parish officers. This did at least demand a response from the churchwardens themselves, and initially it produced rather more detail. Within a few years, however, some churchwardens discovered that it was possible to get away with simply answering 'yes' or 'no' to the questions – thus rendering the new form little more useful than the old.[25]

What is generally missing from the peculiar jurisdiction of St Paul's is any real sense of actual visitation or of any form of superintendence being exercised over the parishes. This impression is confirmed by the case of Albury in Hertfordshire. In April 1831, its incumbent, William Cowling, wrote to the dean to call his attention to the neglected state of the church in general and the belfry in particular, which was in a 'ruinous as well as a dangerous state', and concerning which he had been unable to stimulate the churchwardens to take action. At the same time he noted that 'as the Living is a *Peculiar*, and within your Lordship's jurisdiction, the church has never been visited during the period of my incumbency "twenty years" and is consequently in a state that calls for immediate inspection'.[26] It seems that Cowling was eventually promised that the commissary would call in on his way to Cambridge. However, by 1838 (despite another strong plea in 1836) the visit had still not been made and Cowling protested that

the present fearful state of the part of the church before alluded to demands immediate interference on the part of the dean and chapter. And unless peremptory orders are issued to this effect, it will be neglected as heretofore, and the result may prove very calamitous.[27]

Throughout this period, the churchwardens' presentments had reported that repairs were under way or that there was nothing wanting more serious than a new pulpit cushion.[28] On one occasion the chapter did go beyond its usual practice when, in 1790, a set of queries was issued by the dean asking questions similar to those asked prior to contemporary episcopal visitations. The replies provided useful information on a range of issues, but there is no evidence that this information was acted on, or that the experiment was ever repeated.[29]

From the point of view of the laity, residence within a peculiar may have produced more ready access to ecclesiastical law than in some larger jurisdictions. Certainly, however supine the chapter's exercise of pastoral superintendence, its courts continued to be active throughout the period. In addition to a steady stream of probate and matrimonial cases and matters involving church property, the peculiar court was a resort for those seeking redress for slander.[30] These cases demonstrate continuing life in older forms of ecclesiastical sanction, including excommunication for defying the authority of the court and public penance (exacted as late as 1833 in the parish of St Pancras, for slander).[31] The small size of the jurisdiction may also have made it easier for parishioners to complain about their clergy, and there is some evidence that the chapter, at least by the second quarter of the nineteenth century, was sensitive to such concerns. In 1830, for example, having received a series of complaints from one Sarah Brooke about the minister and wardens of Heybridge, the dean wrote to the incumbent to demand a response and threatened an official inquiry if one was not forthcoming. He was, nevertheless, perhaps too readily satisfied by the incumbent's assurance that the complainant was 'an infamous woman who has often been troublesome to other authorities in this neighbourhood', and that (apparently worse) she dominated her husband.[32] More satisfactory from the point of view of the complainants was the reception of a deputation from a London parish in 1835, who, according to R. H. Barham, 'went away very much pleased with their reception, delighted with the courtesy shown them by the dean, and resolved to do all in their power to annoy their new incumbent'.[33] However pleased complainants might be by their reception, it is none the less difficult to find evidence of the chapter actually taking action in these cases – the main exception being an intervention by the dean in a dispute about the manner of performing divine service at Stoke Newington in 1845.[34]

THE PARISHES AND THE CATHEDRAL

The relationship between St Paul's and its parishes was clearly influenced by the fact that their primary connection was one of patronage – that, is a question of property. In particular, the chapter appears to have maintained a policy of attempting to secure and, within limits, to increase the value of its property. This had a direct bearing on proposals to change the shape of parishes. In general, a favourable attitude was taken to proposals for the amalgamation of livings. In 1771, for example, the chapter approved the consolidations of High Easter with Good Easter, and Brent Pelham with Furneaux Pelham. In giving its consent to the latter, the chapter noted that the

> emoluments of the said vicarages are so small that they now are and very probably will be insufficient to support and bear the necessary expenses of an incumbent in each of the said benefices with the decency and dignity suitable to the honour of his functions.[35]

Such amalgamations may have benefited the parishes by securing to them a resident minister. They certainly benefited the dean and chapter by increasing the attractiveness of its livings.

However, when proposals came forward for parochial subdivision, which potentially decreased the value of the patronage, the chapter was generally much less favourable. In the mid-1830s, for example, it sought to resist proposals from the bishop of London to subdivide the parish of Edmonton by carving out an income and a district for the chapel of ease at Winchmore Hill. The chapter's argument was based partly on a suggestion that the value of Edmonton might significantly decrease in future and partly on Sydney Smith's claim that it was better to maintain a few rich benefices to which clergymen might aspire than to spread the income more evenly, but also much more thinly, over the church as a whole.[36] This latter contention was repeated at length in Smith's first *Letter to Archdeacon Singleton* with specific reference to the Edmonton case.[37] It was also based on the assumption that the existing pastoral arrangements were perfectly adequate. 'I see no reason', wrote Smith to Bishop Blomfield, 'why the Parish may not go on quite as well with a Curate under the Rector as with a small autocratical clergyman in the midst of it.'[38] The rashness of this assumption became all too apparent when Thomas Tate succeeded to Edmonton and, much to Smith's own consternation, promptly dismissed the curate at Winchmore Hill, probably with a view to securing for himself its income of £200, finally conceded by the chapter in 1843.[39] The issue of the value of a living and thus its attractiveness as a piece of patronage often seems to have been a paramount consideration, and when Smith attempted to interest John Grey in Edmonton he took pains to assure him that the living might not be divided.[40]

Prior to 1833, there is no evidence of the chapter having intervened directly to increase the value of its livings by endowing them out of its own resources. Indeed, it may sometimes have allowed financial gain in the short term to erode the longer-term prospects of its livings. The incumbent of Ardeley, for example, complained that the rectorial tithe had been 'shamefully sold by the dean and chapter of St Paul's in 1808'.[41] In 1833, however, there was a brief flurry of activity when the chapter granted four small augmentations, worth £133 p.a. in total, under the authority of the Augmentations Act of 1831.[42] Thereafter, such augmentations seem largely to have dried up, and in 1846 an application from St Helen Bishopsgate was refused.[43] When other routes by which it might have contributed to parish life are examined, it is difficult to convict the chapter of much activity. In 1836 it declined to make any corporate contribution to the London Churches Building Fund, and it rarely acceded to requests for grants from its own parishes. Four grants totalling £200 were made between 1834 and 1839, but this seems to have exhausted the chapter's generosity, and Barnes was refused a grant towards rebuilding in 1850.[44] The chapter did live up to its responsibilities as rector for maintaining the chancels of churches (though frequently this expense was evaded because the rectorial tithes were leased out), but it was reluctant to contribute to new amenities in churches. Sunbury, for example, was refused a grant for an organ in 1842.[45] The chapter did, however, contribute to the building of schools, making ten grants worth a total of £145 5s. between 1835 and 1849.[46] St Paul's did not always have a good record of providing parsonages on its livings. In 1790 the incumbent of Friern Barnet reported that

I reside personally upon my cure, but not in the parsonage house. The dean and chapter of St Paul's, London, Patrons of my living, in the year 1776 sold the house that had been appropriated for the residence of the Rector, and in which my predecessors had always resided.[47]

The provision of decent accommodation, however, clearly increased the value of the chapter's patronage, and in the 1830s a few substantial grants were made for building or rebuilding parsonages. In 1837, Egerton was granted £100 and Wickham St Paul £50, though in making the latter gift it was resolved 'that it has not been the practice of the chapter to subscribe to the repair of the Parsonage Houses in their gift – nor is it their intention to set a precedent'. This resolution clearly had its effect, since only one other such grant – to Mucking in 1843 – is recorded before 1850, and the Kensal Green chapel in Willesden was refused a grant in 1848 on the ground that the chapter had 'no fund applicable to this case'.[48]

In 1857, however, an inquiry initiated by Canon Champneys into the chapter's support for parochial schools proposed an increase in annual grants, from an existing total of £10 5s. given to two schools to around £160 divided between fourteen schools. The next two years saw a significant increase in the number of annual grants awarded.[49] Less dramatic, but still noticeable, was a corresponding increase in the chapter's willingness to make grants towards the enlargement, restoration and rebuilding of churches and parsonage houses – especially from the mid-1860s. Wickham St Paul, for example, received a grant of £50 towards a new transept and re-pewing in 1866, and two years later Belchamp St Paul received £100 towards the cost of church restoration.[50]

Two reasons might be suggested for this sea-change in attitudes towards the use of chapter funds. One is a change in the character of the chapter itself, with the arrival of canons who had made their name as the pastors of large urban parishes and who possessed a passion for the improvement of the parochial ministry – especially the evangelicals Thomas Dale and William Weldon Champneys.[51] The second is the change in cathedral finances introduced by the Ecclesiastical Commission. By an order-in-council of 1845, the commissioners appropriated almost a third of the chapter's corporate income, leaving the remainder to be divided among the dean and canons in a ratio that was estimated to give an annual income of approximately £2,000 to the former and £1,000 to the latter. A subsequent order-in-council fixed the incomes at these sums for all canons appointed after 1853 and transferred the whole of the surplus to the commissioners.[52] The consequences of these changes were noted in the 1857 report on grants to schools:

as the revenues have increased as late, and will assuredly continue to supply more than the stated fixed incomes, the present may be considered a convenient time for adopting a new system in accordance with public opinion for the furtherance of education, especially as the Ecclesiastical Commissioners will bear a large portion of the sums proposed to be contributed.[53]

Cathedral reform had created a situation in which self-interest not only ceased to conflict with pastoral concern but positively reinforced it. The chapter could now transfer income to increase the value of its patronage not from the pockets of its own members but from the funds of the Ecclesiastical Commission.

Concern to increase the attractiveness and even extent of its

patronage remained a cornerstone of chapter policy in the reform era. Although the chapter did agree to the endowment of a new church out of the enormous income of St Giles Cripplegate in 1856, this was exceptional, and the maintenance of the value of its more important vicarages remained a key objective. Similar schemes were vetoed in Tottenham in 1851 and 1870 and in Edmonton in 1863.[54] The same policy can be detected in the chapter's attitude to the Union of Benefices Act (1860), which provided a mechanism for the union of contiguous benefices in the metropolis.[55] Once it had ensured, at the request of the minor canons, that the proposed unions would leave them with a sufficient number of benefices at a reasonable distance from St Paul's and with light enough parish work to enable the minor canons to pay due attention to their cathedral duties, the act was generally to the benefit of the chapter.[56] Its patronage might be reduced in quantity, but, like the parish unions promoted by the chapter itself in the eighteenth century, this was more than compensated for by a corresponding improvement in quality. The new benefices would usually enjoy an increased income and also a house of residence for the incumbent – a benefit of considerable value in a city parish. Accordingly, the chapter readily co-operated in the schemes promoted under the act by the bishop of London. Of fourteen proposed unions involving chapter benefices, only two had succeeded by 1870, but in no case was the failure due to

314. St Pancras New Church, built in 1819–22 at the start of a campaign to revitalize the Church of England in this fast-expanding parish, a St Paul's living. View in 1973

opposition from the chapter,[57] and in 1865 it received a letter of thanks from the bishop for its assistance in his attempt to unite St Clement Eastcheap with St Mary Abchurch.[58] In all the cases considered so far, the chapter had been responding to initiatives generated elsewhere, but in late 1869 it began to take an initiative itself to improve and extend its patronage. It first negotiated an exchange in which the patronage of Belchamp St Paul was transferred to the dean and chapter of Windsor in return for securing the sole right of patronage in the benefice of St Peter le Poor – a city parish with a small and declining population and a rapidly rising endowment.[59] Then it embarked on a scheme to alienate £1,000 p.a. of the endowment of St Peter, in favour first of poor livings in the chapter's patronage, and then (with the bulk of the fund) to raise the income of other poor city livings to £500 p.a. in return for the patronage being surrendered to the chapter.[60] Clearly, though the incomes of the deans and canons had been fixed by statute in 1853, their enjoyment of patronage remained a benefit capable of extension.

PARISH LIFE AND CHANGE

For the purpose of considering parochial life, St Paul's parishes can be divided into three groups. First were the seventeen city parishes. According to successive censuses, most of these were already small in population in 1801 and declined further over the nineteenth century. Although three had over 1,000 inhabitants in 1851, only one fell into this category twenty years later, and the majority had populations of less than 400. Second were the country parishes, mostly in Essex and Hertfordshire and again generally with small or medium-sized populations, mostly under 2,000 in 1851 and in five cases under 500, although they also included a substantial town parish – Hemel Hempstead – with a population of 7,073. Finally there were the large parishes of the metropolis and its immediate hinterland, including those that experienced substantial population growth in the first half of the nineteenth century, such as Edmonton, with 9,708 people. This last group also included four very large parishes with populations in excess of 10,000: Tottenham (13,076), St Giles Cripplegate (14,361), St Luke Old Street (54,055), and St Pancras, whose population of 166,956 in 1851 exceeded that of all the other fifty benefices put together.[61] Together, the St Paul's benefices represent a cross-section of parishes in the church as a whole, facing a range of challenges, from maintaining the parish system in small rural or declining city parishes to meeting the demands for change produced by urbanization and demographic growth.

Patterns of ministry

A good insight into key features of parochial activity can be gleaned from the returns to visitation queries issued by the dean and the bishops of London. These reveal distinctive patterns of ministry in each of the three groups. At first sight, the city parishes were characterized by comparatively low levels of clerical residence: according to the returns of 1790 and 1810, only five incumbents were legally resident and performing duty in their parishes. The main reason for this was the difficulty in finding accommodation in the city: as the incumbent of St Peter le Poor explained, 'In so very opulent a part of the town it would be scarcely possible to procure a proper house for the rector or curate from the profits of the living or curacy.'[62] Consequently, 'non-resident' city clergy frequently lived nearby and served their own cures or shared the duty with a curate. There were seven such 'virtual residents' in

1790–1810, and the remaining five city parishes were all served by resident or virtually resident curates. These parishes were also characterized by high levels of liturgical activity, with two services every Sunday supplemented by an elaborate pattern of weekday services. In a few churches, services were provided every day with the exception of Saturdays – often supported by teams of lecturers;[63] more usually, however, they were held two or three times a week and on holidays. Communion, too, was celebrated with a high level of frequency by eighteenth- and early nineteenth-century standards – the standard pattern being one celebration a month with additional celebrations at the three great festivals.[64] By contrast, other forms of pastoral activity stood at a relatively low level in the city parishes. Catechizing of the young, for example, where it took place at all, was already by 1763 largely confined to Lent and tended to move out of church to become a private or a school-based activity, or to be limited to children preparing for confirmation.[65]

Low levels of activity do not, however, necessarily indicate neglect on the part of the clergy. Some faced difficulties as a consequence of the existence of civic institutions that cut across the parish system. Education, for example, was organized on a ward rather than a parish basis and this tended to limit the clergy's involvement.[66] City clergy who attempted to exercise pastoral authority in their parishes also faced difficulties, as Francis Wollaston of St Michael le Querne complained in 1810: 'Those within the city can do very little towards regulating their parishes without giving umbrage to the corporation.'[67] However, judging by responses to the visitation of 1810, for example, the most significant influence on patterns of ministry in the city was the lifestyle of the population, of whom many resided during the week, but not at the weekend. The rector of St Clement Eastcheap and St Martin Orgar reported that, 'there are so many occupants of counting houses whose residence is only partial that I should be at a loss whether to consider them as parishioners'.[68] George Gaskin of St Benet Gracechurch Street was similarly exercised:

> in a parish circumstanced as mine is, where the parishioners are altogether involved in business and as soon as that is over, get to their country residences, a clergyman can have little intercourse or connexion with or knowledge of them...I meet very few even of the well disposed part of them at Divine Service and where Heads of families are dispersed, Servants are not likely to be regular in their attendance of a City parish church, but are more apt to wander abroad, either in secular dissipation, or to gratify itching ears by following strange and fanatical preachers.[69]

The tendency of the most influential members of their communities to be absent on Sundays explains the low number of communicants in city parishes – never more than forty at ordinary celebrations and sometimes in single figures – and may also go some way to accounting for the prevalence of weekday services. Moreover, it limited the extent to which these churches could provide a link between the cathedral and the city.

The pattern of ministry in the country parishes contrasted sharply with that in the city. Incumbents were more likely to be non-resident than resident, and even the curates might serve more than one cure.[70] As a consequence, in the eighteenth and early nineteenth centuries the majority of such parishes had only one service on a Sunday – often held alternately with a differently timed service in a neighbouring church. By 1851, however, two services, morning and afternoon, had become the universal pattern – probably a consequence of rising rates of clerical residence following the legislation of the 1830s. There is little evidence, however, of any complementary increase in the number of communion services, and the eighteenth-century pattern of four celebrations a year was still visible in 1842.[71] Other forms of pastoral activity were also at a relatively low level, with day and Sunday schools being thin on the ground and ministers having problems in attracting children for catechetical instruction.[72] By 1842, however, there is clear evidence of a quickening of pace in this area, as at Brent and Furneaux Pelham, where the incumbent had established day and Sunday schools, was contemplating opening an evening school and had an active Bible distribution programme.[73]

The large and growing parishes of Middlesex and the metropolitan fringe displayed a third pattern of ministry. Their incumbents were likely to be resident and, in the larger parishes, often supported by teams of curates. The parish churches typically had two services on a Sunday, and these were often supplemented by services in dependent chapels and occasionally by a third service or lecture in the church. They commonly had prayers on two weekdays and at major festivals, and celebrated communion at least monthly with respectable numbers of communicants ranging from forty to eighty in 1790.[74] These parishes also saw the early development of day and Sunday schools and other innovative pastoral practices like the introduction of catechetical lectures for the whole congregation. Such parishes were potentially extremely important to the cathedral – not merely because, in some cases, their sheer size gave it a measure of contact with and interest in the development of a new London, but also because, in places like Tottenham and Edmonton, the cathedral's nominees were rather more likely to find the leaders of the city in their Sunday congregations than were the incumbents of the city parishes.[75]

Clearly the nature of the clergy appointed to its benefices could have a significant effect, not only on parish life but also on the reputation of the chapter as patrons. A review of the 210 presentations and collations made by the dean and chapter between 1750 and 1850 makes it clear that their preference was for graduate clergy – 207 (98.6 per cent) were identified as possessing a degree. Parishes in south-east England were notable in this period for the high density of graduates among their clergy, but St Paul's parishes appear to have been a graduate preserve to a quite remarkable extent.[76] In other respects, however, St Paul's appointees seem fairly representative of the clergy as a whole. When, in the nineteenth century, party labels became prominent, men of all varieties of churchmanship could be found in their ranks. A list of influential London clergy prepared for the editor of *The Times* in 1844 included one future and four current St Paul's incumbents, whom it identified largely as moderates, two of whom inclined towards high churchmanship and one to evangelicalism.[77] Only Thomas Dale, future incumbent of St Pancras, was identified more firmly with a particular variety of churchmanship – in his case, evangelicalism. Surveying his county in 1847, however, the Hertfordshire Baptist William Upton found rather more definite views among five St Paul's clergy, including one evangelical, one high churchman and three whose views were categorized as 'Decidedly Puseyite', 'Direct Puseyism' and 'Rank Puseyism'.[78] It is possible that St Paul's livings, at least in the country, provided an early home for parish Tractarianism, though, as an evangelical dissenter, Upton may have been exceptionally sensitive on this point. St Paul's did make its share of unfortunate appointments, including one

whose living was sequestered for debt on no fewer than five separate accounts in 1813. In the opinion of Upton, the incumbent of Therfield was 'Indefinite' and 'Haughty', that of Walden St Paul was 'most uninteresting and erroneous', and that of Kensworth was 'irreligious and dissolute'.[79] Nevertheless, surviving complaints against the clergy are rare and the chapter clearly found excellent incumbents too, including the indefatigable Dale at St Pancras and Barham, who, on leaving St Gregory's, was given 'A substantial "testimonial of respect and friendship" in the shape of a silver salver…presented to himself and Mrs Barham, who as a clergyman's wife devoted herself to those duties which a woman alone can comprehend and discharge'.[80]

Change in the parishes

Few of the chapter's parishes would have escaped the pressure of change in the nineteenth century. Even small country livings like Ardeley felt the consequences of population growth in the late 1830s, which led to a re-pewing of the church and the construction of a chapel of ease.[81] Similarly, even in the city, the reviving forces of nonconformity were beginning to register in the consciousness of incumbents, as at St Michael Bassishaw which reported the presence of 'many dissenters' in 1810.[82] The Middlesex parishes, especially those on the northern fringe of the city, experienced these challenges to an even greater extent. St Luke's, Old Street in 1790 already contained 3,000 houses. 'We swarm with Methodists,' lamented its incumbent, and there were meeting houses of dissenters of all denominations.[83] Nowhere, however, was the challenge to the parochial system so acute as in St Pancras.

Originally comprising a series of small settlements served by a small parish church and a chapel of ease, St Pancras had experienced major population growth in the later eighteenth century but no corresponding extension of the parish system. The chapel of ease was enlarged in 1780–4 and several proprietary chapels were built. These were served by Anglican ministers licensed by the chapter and attracted large congregations, but they were established on a free-enterprise basis and not integrated into the parochial system. When T. F. Middleton was appointed to the living in 1811, he found a population of over 46,000 in a parish with church accommodation for only 5,500, of which 4,750 was in the proprietary chapels.[84] His response was the promotion of a scheme to build a large new parish church, but little progress had been achieved before James Moore brought a new impetus on succeeding Middleton in 1815.[85] In 1816 an Act of Parliament empowered trustees to borrow up to £40,000 to build a new church and a parochial chapel, and to levy a rate to pay off the loan.[86] It was eventually agreed that when the new church was finished the old parish church should become a chapel of ease and a second large chapel of ease should also be built. A contract for the new church was let in 1819 for just over £42,000, but before the extremely elaborate building was finished, the trustees ran out of money and in 1821 had to secure a further Act to borrow an additional £40,000 (also intended to cover the cost of sites for two further chapels to be built by the Church Building Commissioners). In total, the new parish church (Fig. 314) cost the ratepayers of St Pancras a massive £82,601.[87] It is difficult not to conclude that the project had been allowed to get out of hand. It certainly left an unfortunate legacy in relation both to the governance of the parish, uncomfortably divided between the trustees and the vestry, and to the support of the ratepayers, many of whom were dissenters determined never again to allow a church rate to be levied. This imposed severe restrictions on church extension, and Moore's efforts to accommodate his parishioners had thenceforward to be pursued using voluntary effort and grants from bodies like the Church Building Society. Four further churches were erected on this basis between 1837 and 1846, and in 1842 Moore inaugurated the St Pancras Church Extension Fund to support church-building and the housing and stipends of the clergy.[88]

When Thomas Dale succeeded Moore in 1846, he 'became at once painfully conscious of the inadequate provision which had been made for the spiritual charge of so vast a population'. Part of the problem was church accommodation, but perhaps more serious was a shortage of clergy: at the parish church, for example, two clergymen were responsible for a district containing 60,000 people.[89] Dale's response was a scheme to build ten more churches and to divide the parish into seventeen roughly equal districts, each with at least one clergyman. The proposal won the support of the trustees, but was rejected by the vestry, which refused to 'lend itself to any scheme that might now or hereafter jeopardize their present freedom from the payment of Church Rates, or TO INCREASE THE POWER AND PATRONAGE OF THE CHURCH OF ENGLAND AS BY LAW ESTABLISHED'.[90] It took a further five years of skirmishing and the careful navigation of numerous legal complexities before the scheme began to bear fruit. By 1852, however, Dale could already claim an increase in clergy from twenty-five to forty-one, in church accommodation from 21,313 to 27,713 seats, and in children attending church schools from 5,996 to 8,100.[91] After 1860, Dale's policy was continued by his successor, the energetic Canon Champneys, who had made his name as rector of the slum parish of Whitechapel. Several more churches were built, most paid for by local voluntary contributions, but including three financed by major private benefactions. For example, Christ Church Somers Town (1868) and its associated school for 600 children were financed at a cost of more than £14,000 by George Moore, an evangelical glove manufacturer, on condition that the patronage belong to the Simeon Trust.[92] The legal difficulties of the parish were not, however, resolved until 1868, when the St Pancras Ecclesiastical Regulation Act formally divided the old parish into twenty-two separate districts, each with its own vicar.[93]

In the exercise of their responsibilities to this most challenging of parishes, the dean and chapter seem (save for Dale and Champneys) to have been remarkably inert. At no point do they ever appear to have taken an initiative and while they generally approved church-extension schemes when put before them, they did not actively promote them. The limit of the chapter's involvement seems to have been its consideration of complaints arising out of the tension between the incumbent and the vestry.[94] When the subdivision of the parish was first mooted in 1846, the chapter predictably made its consent conditional on an income of £1,200 together with a house being secured to the vicar – a stipulation

reiterated in 1851.[95] Indeed, as late as 1862, Champneys and the incumbent of Camden chapel had to exhort the chapter to give 'not only no opposition but all the support that can be given short of pecuniary aid' to a scheme for regularizing the ecclesiastical district associated with the chapel.[96] The contrast with Blomfield's energetic activity on his assumption of jurisdiction when the peculiar was reformed in the 1840s is striking. He preached at the inauguration of a new appeal for the church-extension fund in 1847, and promoted amendments to legislation to clear legal obstructions. When Dale proposed that prebendal income from ground-rents in the parish which had been transferred to the Ecclesiastical Commissioners should be applied directly to St Pancras rather than being subsumed into a common fund, Blomfield 'unequivocally expressed his entire concurrence in the equity of the proposed appropriation, and his readiness to promote it, by all legitimate means'.[97]

The link between St Paul's and its parishes was clearly of benefit to the chapter in terms of both revenue and influence. But from the parochial point of view, was it beneficial or harmful? The chapter's exercise of its patronage was neither creative nor exceptionally corrupt, and there is no reason to think that its appointments were any more or less likely to be conscientious pastors than those made by other contemporary patrons. Its visitatorial responsibilities, however, were exercised so lightly as to be virtually intangible, leaving the parishes in the St Paul's peculiars as islands of poor practice in the otherwise well-run diocese of London. When the patterns of parish life and ministry are examined, it nevertheless becomes clear that local circumstances, rather than the nature of patronage or jurisdiction, were the primary influences at work. On all measures, including a comparison of evidence from visitation returns and from the religious census of 1851, both the range of activities and church attendance in St Paul's parishes were comparable to those observed in similar parishes under other patronage or jurisdiction.[98] The city parishes, by the end of the eighteenth century, were clearly losing any capacity to link the cathedral to leading citizens, and the percentage of the population attending Anglican services was lower in some of these parishes than in St Pancras.[99] However, the problems in the city were primarily demographic; the chapter's involvement had little or no effect. In the rapidly growing parishes of the metropolitan fringe, on the other hand, the chapter's conservatism and inactivity clearly delayed desirable pastoral developments, and even in the country parishes its lack of drive and initiative could leave problems to fester. The story of the chapter's relationship with its parishes, especially in the century between 1750 and 1850, is in the last analysis rather an inglorious one. The passing of its peculiar jurisdiction, at least, can have been regretted by few – apart, perhaps, from those clergymen who were in consequence subjected to the rather more bracing superintendence of Bishop Blomfield.[100]

34

NATIONAL OCCASIONS AT ST PAUL'S SINCE 1800

John Wolffe

No description in words could convey an adequate idea of the majestic beauty of a solemn national religious ceremony in St Paul's. It is hard to believe that there is any other building in the world that is so well adapted to be the setting of such symbolical acts of communal worship.[1]

Dean Matthews's reflections on George V's Silver Jubilee thanksgiving service in 1935 encapsulate a predominant reaction to national occasions in St Paul's during the two centuries between the funeral of Lord Nelson in January 1806 and the Golden Jubilee of Elizabeth II in June 2002. For such services the great scale and splendour of the building, which has its drawbacks in relation to regular daily and Sunday worship, at once becomes its greatest asset. Outside, the approach up Ludgate Hill, the open area around Queen Anne's statue and the steps up to the west door provide an outstanding location for public ceremonial, whether for the alighting of dignitaries passing on into the cathedral itself or for open-air services. The nave is an ideal setting for stately processions, while the space under the dome is a splendid stage both for grandiose celebration and for poignantly magnificent mourning. The seating capacity greatly exceeds that of any other London church, thus enabling attendance and participation to be maximized. When stands were erected in the nave and under the dome, a congregation of 10,000 or more could be accommodated.

The full ceremonial potential of St Paul's was, however, only realized on a relatively small number of full-scale state occasions: the funerals of Nelson (1806), Wellington (1852) and Churchill (1965); the jubilees of 1897, 1935, 1977 and 2002; the thanksgiving for the recovery of Albert Edward, prince of Wales from typhoid in 1872; and the marriage of Charles, prince of Wales in 1981. Whereas Westminster Abbey was the historic setting for coronations, and St George's, Windsor the scene of royal funerals from the reign of George III onwards, there was not any specific kind of occasion for which St Paul's was the automatic choice. Initially in 1852 there was talk of the duke of Wellington being buried at Westminster;[2] Queen Victoria's Golden Jubilee service in 1887 was held in the Abbey; and during this period St Paul's was not used for a royal wedding until 1981. There was, however, a broad tradition, maintained since the eighteenth century, of St Paul's as the setting for national thanksgiving services, and also of association with the armed forces. Hence it was the scene of the funerals of those pre-eminent secular saviours of the nation in moments of supreme military crisis, Nelson, Wellington and Churchill, and, from 1897 onwards, the recurrent choice for jubilee thanksgiving services. On these rare occasions, the cathedral became a central focus for something even bigger than itself, a ceremonial sequence also involving lengthy street processions and other events, and all organized by a bewildering variety of agencies, departments and institutions.

These nine major state occasions need, however, to be viewed in the context of two other main ways in which St Paul's exercised a national function. First, there were numerous other special services, which, whether by the inherent nature of the event or through the participation of the sovereign or other senior members of the royal family, had a clearly representative significance. These included funerals and memorial services for prominent individuals, generally military leaders, artists and musicians, thus complementing the political and literary associations of Westminster Abbey. Examples include the painter Edwin Landseer (1873), the soldier-engineer Baron Napier of Magdala

315. Admiral Nelson's funeral, 13 January 1806: the catafalque before St Paul's. Aquatint by Merigot and A. C. Pugin. (Museum of London)

(1890) and Lord Kitchener (1916). There were intercessions in time of war, as in 1899, 1914 and 1941, and thanksgivings for peace, for example in 1814, 1902, 1919 and 1945. Services also expressed national grief and solidarity at times of particular catastrophe, notably the sinking of the *Titanic* in April 1912 and the attack on the World Trade Center in September 2001. Celebrations in the life of the royal family, such as the silver weddings of George V and Queen Mary in 1918 and of George VI and Queen Elizabeth in 1948, and the hundredth birthday of Queen Elizabeth the Queen Mother in 2000, were also marked by worship in St Paul's.

Second, like other cathedrals and major churches, St Paul's was a focal point for diocesan and civic spiritual responses to national events, even when there were no royal visitors, or the central ceremonial took place elsewhere. Thus in October 1809 the Corporation of London attended a service to celebrate George III's jubilee,[3] and on the Sunday following Queen Victoria's death in January 1901 an estimated 30,000 people had to be turned away from an already packed morning service.[4] On VE Day in 1945, numerous successive services were held, and it is estimated that as many as 35,000 people attended.[5] The national prominence of St Paul's tended, however, to ensure that such spontaneous local London participation acquired wider significance in the eyes of the press and public.

The sheer extent, variety and richness of the role of St Paul's on national occasions therefore defies detailed description and analysis within the space of a single essay. All that can be done here is to indicate key trends and to give a brief account of some particularly significant events. The emphasis will be on the major state ceremonies, although account will also be taken of the wider context of other national services and of London's responses to national events. Important themes that run through the period include the sometimes contested nature of the cathedral's national role, and issues of ecumenical and, eventually, inter-faith inclusiveness in relation to liturgy and participation.

Lord Nelson's interment in the crypt on 9 January 1806 concluded an impressive pageant that had begun with a lying-in-state at Greenwich, followed by processions by river to Westminster and through the streets from the Admiralty (Fig. 315).[6] It was indeed the culmination of a late eighteenth-century revival in the use of St Paul's for major state occasions (pp. 367–71). The interior was arranged following the example of George III's most recent visit in 1797.[7] The scale and magnificence of the ceremonial, however, exceeded anything that had preceded it, and set important precedents. Inside the cathedral, large stands were erected along the nave and under the dome, thereby not only providing space for a congregation of about 9,000[8] but also creating a splendid amphitheatre of onlookers. The royal mourners were led by the prince of Wales, as at that period the attendance of the sovereign himself at the funeral of a subject, however illustrious, would have been considered a breach of protocol. The liturgy was a protracted one, with the coffin first taken into the choir for the singing of evensong and then moved to an octagonal platform under the dome, where a mechanism had been constructed to lower it slowly into the crypt. Dean Milman, who was present as a boy, recalled the poignant drama of this moment: 'I heard, or fancied that I heard, the low wail of the sailors who bore and encircled the remains of their admiral.'[9]

In the event, nearly half a century was to pass before the potential of St Paul's as a setting for state ceremonial was again to be so fully realized. The death of William Pitt a few weeks after Nelson's funeral brought to an end Dean Pretyman's close links with Downing Street, while the old age and mental incapacity of George III precluded his participation in any further services. On 7 July 1814, following initial victory over Napoleon, the Prince Regent, accompanied by the duke of Wellington, went in state to St Paul's to 'return thanks to the Almighty for the restoration of the blessings of peace to this country and to Europe'.[10] This was an occasion very much in the tradition of the state thanksgivings

316.   The duke of Wellington's funeral car arrives at St Paul's, 18 November 1852. (GL)

317. Wellington's funeral service in the crossing, 18 November 1852. (GL, St Paul's collection)

318. Wellington's funeral car in the cathedral crypt, where it could be admired by visitors until the 1960s. The most striking achievement of the German architect Gottfried Semper during his English exile, its flamboyance evoked mixed reactions. It was eventually moved to Wellington's country home at Stratfield Saye, Hampshire. (SPCL)

of 1789 and 1797 and the more remote ones of Anne's reign, but it was the last official service of this kind until 1872.

In November 1820, George IV's estranged wife Queen Caroline, supported by the Lord Mayor and Common Council, decided to go in procession to St Paul's to give thanks for the collapse of the parliamentary proceedings against her. This news was highly unwelcome both to the Tory government and to the chapter. Dean Van Mildert initially reacted with hysterical alarm, fearing 'gross irreverence and profanation' and possible violence.[11] The prime minister, Lord Liverpool, pointed out that 'it is quite impossible for the Government to prevent the Queen going to any Public Church to which she may think proper to resort during the regular time of Divine Service'. He counselled that steps should be taken to ensure there would be no breach of the peace or damage to the building, and that the service should be performed in the 'usual manner', without making any explicit acknowledgement of the queen's presence.[12] Van Mildert accordingly allowed a compromise, in which the queen was to be received with courtesy and the time of service changed to suit her convenience; to minimize the risk of disorder the proceedings were completed by nightfall. He did not, however, attend himself.[13] In the event, the visit passed off peacefully, with the queen's procession from Hammersmith on 29 November watched by large crowds of her supporters (Fig. 283).[14] It highlighted the power of St Paul's as a national symbol, which was normally consensual but could be contested, and also showed how the use of the cathedral for such purposes could not be fully controlled by the chapter. Royal indignation at Queen Caroline's visit helps to explain why neither George IV nor William IV ever attended St Paul's as king, and Victoria did not do so until she had

been on the throne for nearly thirty-five years. St Paul's accordingly suffered particularly badly from a general recession in state ceremonial in the three decades after 1821.

Not until the funeral of the duke of Wellington on 18 November 1852 did the cathedral again come into its own (Fig. 316–18). Again, the chapter's capacity to do more than execute the instructions of others was a limited one: a memorandum drawn up in the lord chamberlain's office made it clear that the dean's direct responsibility was only for the organization of the service itself. Layout and seating allocations were to be made in consultation with the lord chamberlain and the College of Arms.[15] Queen Victoria, Prince Albert and the prime minister, the earl of Derby, had decided on St Paul's for the interment, primarily out of conscious parallelism with Nelson, so that 'the greatest military [might rest] by the side of the greatest naval chief who ever reflected lustre on the annals of England'. A long interval was allowed between the death, on 14 September 1852, and the funeral, but systematic preparations did not begin until mid October. Accordingly the elaborate arrangements necessary were rushed, and in particular a plan to block out all natural light so that the funeral, like Nelson's, could take place under dramatic and partial artificial light was imperfectly executed. Seating was nevertheless provided for a congregation of at least 10,000. As with Nelson's funeral, the cathedral service was the final phase in an elaborate pageant, which had begun with a lying-in-state at Chelsea Hospital and continued with an impressive procession from Horse Guards watched by an a crowd estimated at over 1,000,000 people. Prince Albert represented the queen. The spectacle inside St Paul's itself impressed those attending, who were particularly moved by the dignity of the old soldiers gathered around the duke's remains and, as in 1805, by the slow disappearance of the coffin into the crypt.[16]

Wellington's interment consolidated the position of St Paul's as the natural place for the funerals of great military and naval heroes, with the patriotic associations of the building further enhanced by the resonances of Alfred Lord Tennyson's 'Ode on the Death of the Duke of Wellington':

> Under the cross of gold
> That shines over city and river,
> There he shall rest for ever
> Among the wise and the bold.[17]

Nevertheless, during the next twenty years, although services were held for occasions such as thanksgiving for the suppression of the Indian 'Mutiny' in May 1859,[18] the cathedral's role remained more a civic than a national one.

A significant new departure came with the thanksgiving on 27 February 1872 for the prince of Wales's recovery from typhoid (Fig. 319). For some days in December 1871 the prince had appeared to be dying, and his plight had captured public sympathy at a time when the royal family was being subjected to significant radical and republican criticism. Hence William Gladstone, the prime minister, saw the opportunity for a major public ceremony that would help to restore the popular image of the monarchy. He carefully studied earlier precedents, especially that of 1789. The queen herself was initially very reluctant to participate, partly because of her deep-seated dislike of any public appearances but also because she thought such ceremonial 'in point of religion, false and hollow'. Gladstone succeeded in overcoming her objections, but she insisted that the service should be kept short and simple.[19]

319.   Queen Victoria and the royal family cross Ludgate Circus on their way to the thanksgiving service for the recovery
of the Prince of Wales, 27 February 1872, painting by Nicholas Chevalier. (Royal Collection)

The prince of Wales and the government were preoccupied rather with securing as large and representative an attendance as possible. The prince complained when it was suggested that the seating capacity would be limited to 8,000, and pushed for greater numbers to be accommodated: 12,480 tickets were eventually distributed.[20] The lord chamberlain's office took considerable pains to secure representation of the working class and of nonconformist bodies, although some groups, including the Primitive Methodists and the Church of Scotland, still complained of inadequate ticket allocations.[21] Cardinal Henry Manning received an invitation, which he courteously declined, but the chief rabbi, Hermann Adler, accepted his.[22] Other faiths were further represented by the attendance of Maharajah Duleep Singh, the Nawab Nazim of Bengal and Prince Higashi of Japan.[23] It is noteworthy that religious inclusivity in a state service was already being sought and achieved in the later nineteenth century, albeit arising from the initiative of the government rather than the church, and without making non-Anglicans active participants in the proceedings.

The service followed a carriage procession from Buckingham Palace through cheering and largely orderly crowds.[24] Despite its brevity, the worship was impressive, consisting of a *Te Deum* sung by a choir of 200 voices, prayers, an anthem, a sermon from Archbishop Tait and a hymn.[25] The chapter, following the recent arrivals of Church, Gregory and Liddon, were willing collaborators in the spectacle. Indeed, Gregory believed that the whole idea had originated with Liddon, and saw the service as leading to significant public realization that 'Cathedrals might be made to fill an important position in the development of Church life'.[26] St Paul's sought immediately to capitalize on its renewed place in the nation's affections by launching an appeal to complete work on the building 'as a perpetual memorial of the thankfulness of the nation' for the prince's recovery.[27]

Both St Paul's and the royal family therefore benefited from the 1872 thanksgiving, and from that date an increasingly close association developed between them. This was despite the queen's private feelings: she thought the interior 'dull, cold, dreary and dingy', and short though the thanksgiving service was, she still found it 'cold and too long'.[28] She was not to be coaxed back for another quarter of a century, and even then she did not go inside. Nevertheless, the prince and princess of Wales attended a hospital service in June 1873, and in May 1876 there was a thanksgiving service for the prince's safe return from India. The princess of Wales was present at a memorial service for General Gordon in March 1885. In 1889 Archdeacon Sinclair noted in his chronicle based on Virger Green's diary that 'The royal visits became so numerous and regular that it is not necessary to quote them.'[29]

This trend reached an initial culmination in the Diamond Jubilee of June 1897. Numerous members of the royal family, led by the prince of Wales, attended a thanksgiving service on 20 June,[30] and then on 22 June Victoria herself drove to St Paul's through enormous and ecstatic crowds. The aged monarch's

320. Queen Victoria arrives at St Paul's for the Diamond Jubilee ceremony, 22 June 1897. Painting by Andrew Carrick Gow. As the queen was unable to walk up the steps, the brief service was held in the open. (Guildhall Art Gallery, Corporation of London)

321. Ticket for thanksgiving service for Edward VII's recovery of health, following the postponement of the coronation, 3 July 1902. (SPCL)

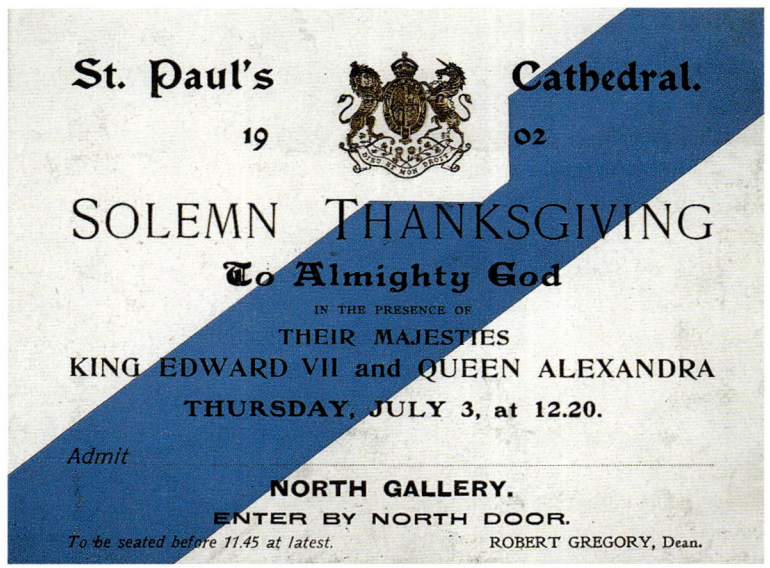

inability to climb the steps into the cathedral had initially seemed to present a major problem. A committee chaired by Archbishop Frederick Temple, however, proposed that the clergy and choir should stand on the steps outside the west front and lead a short service while Victoria remained in her carriage at the bottom. After some hesitation, this scheme was adopted and proved triumphantly successful.[31] Although space for onlookers was limited, the service still appeared a fully public part of the celebrations, on the boundaries of secular and ecclesiastical space, rather than being secluded in the interior of St Paul's. It lasted only twenty minutes and consisted of a *Te Deum*, performed by 650 voices and 200 instruments, prayers, benediction and the 'Old Hundredth', but the scene, favoured with glorious summer sunshine, was an unforgettable one of 'unparalleled splendour and enthusiasm'. A chorister recalled the ringing cheer that greeted Victoria's approach and wrote 'a more exciting moment I have or shall never live'.[32]

In the splendid sunset of her reign, Victoria thus in spite of herself confirmed a potent linkage in the public mind between St Paul's and the monarchy as symbols of national identity. It was, however, her death that opened the way to further strengthening of the tie, as her successors were prepared to visit the cathedral much more frequently. Edward VII, by attending services on 8 June 1902 to celebrate peace in South Africa and on 26 October 1902 to give thanks for his recovery from illness, equalled within two years of his accession his mother's record over than more than sixty years.[33] He returned on several other occasions during his short reign.[34] Moreover, in further contrast to Victoria, his general delight in ceremonial was evident in an ecclesiastical as well as secular context, and royal services could accordingly become more elaborate and lengthy. For example, the thanksgiving of

322. Bishop Winnington-Ingram preaches to troops on the steps of St Paul's, 1915. (SPCL)

October 1902 included psalms, the *Benedictus*, readings, prayers, sermon, the *Te Deum*, three hymns and the national anthem. It concluded with holy communion, albeit after the departure of the king and queen.[35]

George V was, if anything, an even more frequent visitor than his father. In 1911 the distribution of the royal maundy was held in St Paul's because Westminster Abbey was being prepared for the coronation. It was to St Paul's that the new king came again in June 1911 to give thanks for his coronation, and in February 1912 to mark his safe return from India. George V also departed from the previous protocol that the sovereign did not attend the funerals of subjects by attending the memorial service for Scott of the Antarctic and his comrades in 1913 and Lord Roberts's funeral in 1914.[36]

The impact of war, first in South Africa at the turn of the century, and then on a hitherto unimagined scale in Europe between 1914 and 1918, added further to the national role of St Paul's. Special services held during the South African War were memorable for a tone of penitence and quiet intercession rather than of patriotic self-assertion, and a similar tone was apparent in the cathedral's initial response to the First World War.[37] At the same time, there was also ample opportunity for Bishop Winnington-Ingram to indulge his more militaristic inclinations. An open-air service on the cathedral steps for a military parade in July 1915, a location that stirred recollections of the Diamond Jubilee, culminated with the bishop's address on 'The Soul of a Nation' and the singing of 'O God our help in ages past' (Fig. 322).[38] A packed memorial service in October 1915 for Nurse Edith Cavell, executed by the Germans, was attended by Queen Alexandra and numerous contingents of nurses. It was regarded as 'a great tribute paid by women to heroic womanhood' and was thus a noteworthy counterbalance to the otherwise predominantly male associations of St Paul's at this period.[39]

A memorial service on 13 June 1916 was the central event in national mourning for Lord Kitchener, who had drowned when his ship, HMS *Hampshire*, was sunk by a German mine off the Orkneys. Although attended by the king and queen, the service lacked state ceremonial, a reflection both of sober wartime conditions and of a concern not to detract from a future funeral were the body eventually to be recovered. Its sombre and restrained tone was hailed as an expression of national resolve, notably by *The Times* reporter, who wrote that 'All about us were black and khaki, the symbols of grief and of strenuous labour ... The music welded both together into a revealing union of woe and triumph, of striving and of proud assurance.'[40] The language of the concluding hymn, William Walsham How's 'For All the Saints who from their Labours Rest', elevated Kitchener from his assured status as national hero to still more glorious company. This was a theme very much developed in the striking All Souls' Chapel in the north-west tower, dedicated in 1925 in memory of Kitchener and of all others who had fallen in the war. The field marshal's cenotaph is flanked by the warrior saints, St Michael and St George, and faces a *pietà* conceived as the ultimate symbol of sacrifice.

In 1917 there was a solemn service to mark the entry of the United States into the war, notable for the first singing in St Paul's of 'The Star Spangled Banner' and the 'Battle Hymn of the Republic'.[41] On Armistice Day in November 1918, crowds of people came spontaneously to St Paul's and demanded a service, which was hastily arranged.[42] The official thanksgiving for peace in July 1919 was another service that echoed the Diamond Jubilee by being held partially in the open air, the royal family standing at the top of the steps as the multitudes in the churchyard and in Ludgate Hill joined in singing the 'Old Hundredth'.[43] During the war years, Canon Newbolt recalled, 'we sometimes seemed to sing

323. George V and Queen Mary arrive at St Paul's for the Silver Jubilee Thanksgiving Service, 6 May 1935. Painting by Frank O. Salisbury. (Guildhall Art Gallery, Corporation of London)

Te Deum when we ought to have sung dirges, and dirges when we ought to have sung *Te Deum*, yet it was always the same whatever happened, St. Paul's was expected to give expression to popular emotions.'[44]

The 1920s, however, saw another recession in the national role of St Paul's, attributable in part to the competing patriotic associations of Westminster following the building of the Cenotaph and the interment of the Unknown Warrior in 1920. The need for prolonged repairs to the fabric of the dome precluded elaborate ceremonial, while Dean Inge was not the man to encourage such events when they were not imposed upon him. Nevertheless, on 25 June 1930 a large and representative service, attended by George V and Queen Mary, celebrated the completion of the restoration of the cathedral and also reflected thanksgiving for the king's own recovery from recent serious illness.[45]

As in the 1870s, a sustained revival required both new leadership and a major state occasion. This opportunity came with the arrival of Dean Matthews in 1934 and the Silver Jubilee of 1935 (Fig. 323). A cabinet committee initiated plans for the celebration, with the thanksgiving service at St Paul's being the central religious focus of a royal procession through London on 6 May.[46] The chapter's role was an essentially subordinate one, but Matthews entered enthusiastically into the grandest service to be held inside St Paul's since the thanksgiving of 1872. Consideration was given to erecting stands, as for the three great nineteenth-century state services, but the idea was rejected, apparently largely on grounds of cost. Hence the seating capacity was much reduced, being calculated at 4,207.[47] As in 1897, the 'Old Hundredth' and *Te Deum* were prominent features of the worship, which also included Psalms, prayers, two other hymns and an address by Archbishop Lang. The jubilee service was noteworthy for the first actual participation – as opposed to mere attendance – of a non-Anglican church leader, Dr S. M. Berry, the moderator of the Federal Council of Evangelical Free Churches, who read the lesson.[48] A further significant new development was the broadcasting of the service on radio. Matthews wrote: 'Never before has any National Service been so really an act of worship of the whole Nation, for thousands, even millions of listeners will be taking part not only in spirit but by actual hearing.'[49]

Following the outbreak of the Second World War, less than five years later, St Paul's became, to a greater extent even than in the First World War, a symbol of civic and national purpose. Government, church and palace all perceived advantages in cultivating that image, and during the war years there were numerous services with a national dimension, many attended by George VI and Queen Elizabeth. Wartime constraints on travel and damage to the fabric of the building inevitably limited participation and ceremonial, but a consciousness of the role of such events in sustaining morale ensured great efforts were made to sustain an appearance of normality.[50] One notable example was a service on Sunday 26 September 1943 to mark the third anniversary of the Battle of Britain, attended by the king and queen and many members of the government, with the majority of the congregation consisting of contingents from the RAF and civil-defence units. Security considerations meant that the event could not be publicized in advance, and Matthews was very anxious not to turn away the normal Sunday matins congregation who would inevitably turn up unaware that a special ticket-only service was taking place. The solution adopted was to direct these worshippers into the crypt, to listen to a relay of the service on the main floor above. Herbert Morrison, the home secretary, thanked Matthews most warmly for the trouble that he had taken and added that 'we were all very pleased at the selection of popular and well-known hymns – and the ceremonial impressively performed'.[51] Such sensitivity under pressure to varied spiritual constituencies was the foundation for the effectiveness of St Paul's in the war years. It gives some substance to the claim, made on VE Day in 1945, that 'St Paul's belongs to the people and they know within themselves that somehow it binds them to God'.[52]

The legacy of the war remained a predominant theme for twenty years after 1945. Ties with the United States were particularly acknowledged, in a memorial service for Franklin Roosevelt in 1945, and then on Independence Day (4 July) 1951 in the presentation by General Eisenhower of a Roll of Honour of the 28,000 Americans who had died in Europe. The order of service made explicit the historic associations of St Paul's, now extended across the Atlantic:

St Paul's, which is the national cathedral, enshrines not a little of the history of British valour and sacrifice. Within its walls are commemorated a glorious muster of our fighting leaders, headed by the greatest of sea captains and the victor of Waterloo. The American comrades-at-arms of our people commemorated in St Paul's keep noble company.

As befitted the occasion, an enhanced ecclesiastical inclusiveness was apparent, in a reading from John Bunyan, the greatest of nonconformist writers, and in the use of a prayer of Abraham Lincoln's. The moderator of the General Assembly of the Church of Scotland, the presiding bishop of the Protestant Episcopal Church in the United States and several English nonconformist leaders all took part in the procession.[53] A similar service in November 1958 marked the dedication of the American Memorial Chapel.[54]

The immediate post-war era at St Paul's came to a splendidly elegiac conclusion with the state funeral of Sir Winston Churchill on 30 January 1965 (Fig. 324). This was a ceremony conceived 'on a scale unparalleled since the funeral of the Duke of Wellington' more than a century before, from which inspiration was drawn, and with which comparisons were naturally made.[55] Under the guise of the quaintly named 'Operation Hope

Not', secret plans had been in place since the late 1950s. The service in St Paul's was again a culminating religious moment in a lengthy pageant, including a lying-in-state at Westminster Hall, street and river processions, and eventual interment in the churchyard at Bladon in Oxfordshire.[56] Matthews was kept generally informed and was consulted on matters of specific ecclesiastical concern such as the position of the coffin during the service, but the earl marshal, the duke of Norfolk, firmly asserted his own control over the proceedings as a whole.[57] The service itself combined traditional elements, such as the Croft and Purcell sentences and the Handel *Dead March*, with rousing hymns (notably the 'Battle Hymn of the Republic', in celebration of Churchill's American links).[58] In obvious but significant contrast to Wellington's funeral, this was a ceremony in which there could be immediate world-wide engagement, represented in the presence of Commonwealth and world leaders brought rapidly by modern modes of transport, and in radio and television coverage. Paradoxically, this celebration of the life of the man who had come to embody defiant British patriotism was the most international occasion St Paul's had yet seen.

During the period since 1965, national services in St Paul's have been held in the context of a British national identity that has become increasingly diverse and contested. There has been a changed and diminished international role together with nationalist resurgence in Northern Ireland, Scotland and Wales, the settlement of substantial non-Christian minorities, and uncertainty over the future of the monarchy. Initially, however, it

324.   Funeral of Sir Winston Churchill under the dome, 30 January 1965

appeared that little had changed. Elizabeth II's Silver Jubilee thanksgiving service on 7 June 1977 had a similar structure to that of her grandfather more than forty years earlier. Indeed the service, with the addition of anthems and the reading of lessons by the archbishop of York and the archdeacon of London rather than by a Free Church representative, appeared if anything to have moved towards a more exclusive Anglicanism. In his sermon, Archbishop Coggan praised the royal family's 'stable and wonderfully happy' home life as an example to the nation.[59]

The next two major royal events in St Paul's, the Queen Mother's eightieth birthday thanksgiving in 1980 and the marriage of the prince of Wales in 1981 (Fig. 325), served initially to confirm that image. They did, however, show a markedly more ecumenical tone that both reflected the outlook of the new dean, Alan Webster, and showed a growing consciousness by church and palace alike of the multinational character of the United Kingdom. The moderator of the General Assembly of the Church of Scotland read the lesson in 1980 and said a prayer in 1981; the Roman Catholic archbishop of Westminster, Cardinal Basil Hume, led prayers on both occasions. At the prince of Wales's wedding the lesson was read by the Speaker of the House of Commons, George Thomas, a leading Welsh Free Churchman.[60] The very choice of St Paul's for the royal wedding was, moreover, itself a significant break with tradition. Nineteenth-century royal weddings had been private occasions, and the prince's grandparents, parents and sister had all been married at Westminster Abbey. This broadening of the royal associations of St Paul's confirmed a move away from the predominantly military character of national occasions in the cathedral in the period between 1939 and 1965.

That trend, however, did not go unchallenged. On 26 July 1982 a service was held to commemorate the recent military conflict between Britain and Argentina in the Falkland Islands. During the planning, it became apparent that two incompatible conceptions of the service were developing: would it be an ecumenical occasion in which pacifist perspectives were respected, or a nationalist and Christian militarist thanksgiving for victory? Webster, supported by Archbishop Robert Runcie and the leaders of other churches, adopted the former approach, whereas the prime minis-

ter, Margaret Thatcher, favoured the latter. Thatcher's outlook was consistent with the traditional character of services at St Paul's to mark military success, but, Webster later wrote, 'The traumas of modern war made a triumphalistic "Victory Service" a contradiction in terms.'[61] The eventual form of the service came much closer to the dean's vision than the prime minister's, although some compromises were made, notably the dropping of Webster's original idea for the saying of the Lord's Prayer in Spanish and the inclusion of readings by representatives of the armed forces. Nevertheless, the predominant note was one of reconciliation, as was apparent particularly in Runcie's denunciation of nationalism in his sermon as a 'most dangerous' 'God substitute', and in the prayers written by Dr Kenneth Greet, the secretary of the Methodist Conference, who had opposed British military action. The service was reputed to have angered the prime minister and was denounced by some right-wing Conservative MPs, notably Sir John Biggs-Davison, who said, 'It was revolting for cringing clergy to misuse St Paul's to throw doubt upon the sacrifices of our fighting men.'[62] Implicit in Biggs-Davison's complaint of 'misuse' of St Paul's was a view of the cathedral as a national symbol with a fixed meaning, whereas the controversy showed that in 1982, as with Queen Caroline's visit in 1820, services could sometimes be contested territory, highlighting divisions as well as reconciling them. Moreover, Webster saw the Falklands service as teaching lessons 'of great importance for the churches' in showing how ecumenical solidarity could make possible a stance independent of the government of the day.[63] This was a significant shift away from the exclusive Anglicanism and close ties with the state that had characterized national occasions in the mid twentieth century.

The problematic legacy of the Falklands service and of the 1981 royal wedding, once the difficulties in the marriage of the prince and princess of Wales became public knowledge, were probably factors in a further period of relative marginalization of St Paul's in the later 1980s and 1990s. At the dawn of the twenty-first century, however, a service on 11 July 2000 to mark the hundredth birthday of the Queen Mother,[64] and the thanksgiving service on 4 June 2002 for Elizabeth II's Golden Jubilee, both

326. Golden Jubilee service for Queen Elizabeth II, 4 June 2002

reasserted tradition and renewed innovation. The Golden Jubilee service was notable for an extended inclusiveness, not only with participation by non-Anglican church leaders that now began to appear routine, but also with the leading of prayers by women and black people, and the reading of Scripture passages by a Welsh and an Irish student. Leaders of non-Christian religious traditions in Britain were given prominent seats under the dome, facing the leaders of non-Anglican Christian churches. Liturgically, there were significant breaks with tradition, especially in the dropping of the *Te Deum*, which had been a prominent feature of the jubilee services of 1897, 1935 and 1977.[65]

The role of St Paul's as a religious focus for national conscious-ness has been subject to fluctuation and change just as the very

impulses and sentiments represented there have themselves shifted in intensity and character. During the century between 1872 and 1965, St Paul's was indeed in many respects the 'parish church of the British Empire'. It hosted many occasions of national consen-sus that marked the joys and sorrows of an imperial power, as reflected particularly in the sufferings and triumphs of the armed forces and in pivotal events in the lives of successive monarchs. During the earlier and later parts of the period, before 1872 and after 1965, the role of St Paul's in national life was, however, less continuous and sometimes contested. It remained very important, however, precisely because the uncertainties in its own role were a revealing mirror of wider changes in British national and reli-gious consciousness.

35

MUSIC, 1660–1800

Ian Spink

The choir took some time to get going again after the Restoration, but by July 1661 it was at full strength, including the boys.[1] The minor canons included Henry Smith as sub-dean, with Stephen Bing and Randall Jewett as senior and junior cardinals, the latter also being almoner.[2] Albertus Bryne, one of the vicars, was organist.[3] The organ itself had been 'broken all to peeces' in 1643,[4] but reinstatement was hindered by 'divers persons [who] to enrich themselves have sacrilegiously converted to their own private use and advantage, the Organs and Bells . . . and other materials heretofore prepared for the repair thereof'.[5] Nevertheless, we know from James Clifford's *Divine Services and Anthems* (1663; the imprimatur is dated 20 November 1662) that it was functioning both for playing voluntaries and accompanying the choir. It was usual for all harmonized music to be accompanied by the organ.

Clifford had become a minor canon in 1661.[6] His purpose in publishing the book was to provide the words of anthems so that puritan objections to the unintelligibility of choral singing might be mitigated. It begins with a section headed 'Brief Directions for the understanding of that part of *Divine Service* performed with the *Organ* in S. *Pauls* Cathedrall on Sundayes and Holy-dayes', and runs through the order of service for morning prayer and litany, the communion service, and evening prayer.[7] From this, it seems that two anthems were sung in the morning, the first after the third collect as now permitted by rubric in the 1662 prayer book (though anthems had been sung since Elizabethan times), the second after the sermon in the communion service. Similarly, in the evening, an anthem was sung after the third collect and another after the sermon. Organ voluntaries are specified after the psalms at morning and evening prayer, and after the blessing at the end of the litany (and presumably at the end of evening prayer). Most voluntaries at this time were probably improvised, but there is one surviving by Bryne.[8]

There follow the words of 172 anthems, among which thirty-three by Batten indicate a continued St Paul's representation. Anthems by local composers include several by Bryne and Jewett, and a few by minor canons Lawrence Fisher, Simon Ives and Richard Price. The much enlarged second edition (1664) includes a selection of what are called 'Common Tunes', that is, psalm tones based on traditional plainsong and sung without accompaniment. Some are also harmonized with the chant in the tenor, and as such are the forerunners of Anglican chants that were becoming widespread in the 1670s.[9] One of them, doubtless going back to pre-war years, is called 'Mr. *Adrian Battens* Tune'.

Services and anthems continued to be composed in both the full and verse styles. With the passage of time, the latter increased in popularity due to the greater scope it offered for solo singing and expressive treatment of the words, but the full service maintained its dominant position because the mainly chordal writing quickly disposed of lengthy texts such as the *Te Deum* without detriment to the intelligibility of the words.

In these early years everything points to a conservative repertoire such as would have been provided by Barnard's *Selected Church Musick*, which only came into general use after the Restoration. Services by William Child and Benjamin Rogers were probably also among those sung, as was Bryne's in G. A solitary countertenor partbook surviving from this time includes an anthem by Fisher, Bryne's service and four of his anthems.[10] With such a choir, it should have been possible to tackle quite demanding pieces, but it is sad to report Pepys's impression when he

327. John Blow, master of the choristers at St Paul's 1687–1703 engraving by Robert White published in 1700

328. Opening of John Blow's anthem *I Was Glad*, composed for the consecration of the chancel in 1697, from a copy in the hand of B. Isaack, *c.* 1700. (GL, Gresham Collection MS G Mus.452, p. 255)

dropped in to a service on 28 February 1664: 'before and after the sermon I was most impatiently troubled at the Quire, the worst I ever heard'.[11] The onset of the plague in the following year can hardly have improved matters and it is not surprising that choral services were broken off until March 1666,[12] only to be interrupted again by the Great Fire in September.

The extent to which musical worship continued during the months immediately following the Fire is difficult to determine. It was certainly intended that services should recommence as soon as makeshift arrangements could be made, but where they were held (if at all) is not known.[13] Various members of the choir went elsewhere – Bryne to Westminster, Jewett to Winchester, Bing to Lincoln – but nevertheless, it is possible that a rump struggled on, for abandoning the *Opus Dei* for even a few years (still less for thirty) can hardly have been contemplated. From 1674, a temporary wooden 'tabernacle' may have been used.[14] There were then probably five or six minor canons and three or four vicars still in post, though nothing is known about the boys. Hesitant steps began to be taken to fill some of the vacancies. The minor canons were boosted by the addition of the great bass John Gostling in 1682, and other appointments were made, including the music publisher John Playford as vicar choral.[15] In 1674 Playford published a collection of small-scale anthems entitled *Cantica Sacra*, including some by himself, which may well have furnished part of the repertoire at this time.

The best evidence we have for believing that services were still being sung is the fact that by 1677 Stephen Bing (who had returned in 1672) had copied out a set of partbooks, two of which are still in the cathedral library.[16] These contain services by Byrd, Gibbons, etc., and a number by Child and Restoration composers such as Pelham Humfrey and John Blow, whose services in A major and E minor are ascribed to 'Mr Blow'. Accounts show that in January 1677 Bing received £7 19s. 7d. in settlement 'of his bill for service bookes'.[17] Blow received his doctorate the following December.

By May 1687, the tabernacle had been taken over by the Office of Works, so services must have been held somewhere else.[18] About the same time, striking changes were occurring in the personnel of the choir. Michael Wise of Salisbury Cathedral and the Chapel Royal was appointed almoner in 1687 on the recommendation of the king, and six new minor canons and five new vicars were recruited.[19] Virtually all the statutory places in the choir were thus filled. Among the vicars were William Turner and Isaac Blackwell, the latter also being paid as organist from November 1687.[20] From then on, vacancies were filled as they occurred – most notably, Blow succeeding Wise as almoner in August 1687.[21] Everything was in place to usher in the great days of the St Paul's choir.

It therefore appears that it was 1687, not 1697 (cf. pp. 220, 223) that the choir – the singing choir if not the architectural one – was completed. The choir continued to take on the best singers, many of whom were also Gentlemen of the Chapel Royal or in the choir of Westminster Abbey, sometimes both. In January 1690, John Gostling was promoted sub-dean. John Howell became a vicar choral in 1697, Richard Elford in 1700, John Freeman in 1702 – virtuoso countertenors who, along with Gostling, were stars of the Chapel Royal.[22] Jeremiah Clarke took over from Blackwell as organist in 1698 and from Blow as almoner in 1703.[23] The repertoire of the choir at this time is represented by the contents of a second incomplete set of partbooks in the library.[24] These are in the hand of Gostling, who was paid £80 for eight books of anthems, two organ books to go with them and two more for services in the July–September quarter of 1699.[25] They must have been begun before 'Mr' Turner got his doctorate in 1696.

During Blackwell's tenure, the organ was presumably some kind of portable organ, but in 1694 a new one was ordered from Bernard ('Father') Smith 'bigger & lowder than the Temple Organ' which had made his reputation.[26] The contract was agreed

329. Detail of Robert Trevitt's engraving of the thanksgiving service on 31 December 1706, showing Bernard Smith's organ and musicians. See Fig. 154 (GL)

two anthems for this double occasion, though perhaps *Praise the Lord, O my soul* was written for the Chapel Royal and *I was glad* (the text of Henry Compton's sermon) for St Paul's. With regard to the latter, one wonders what the state of the echo was at this stage,[28] for Blow seems to have made the most of it – witness the opening tonic and dominant pedals and the pealing trumpets. Countertenors call to each other across the choir, long notes swell and erupt in dazzling cascades of sound, their vocal flourishes echoed by trumpets.

The years between the Peace of Ryswick and the Peace of Utrecht coincided with a period of unrivalled magnificence in the music of St Paul's. Marlborough's victories and other great occasions of state such as the Act of Union between England and Scotland in 1707 were celebrated with a panache and triumphalism that almost matched the building. Harris, Bernard Smith's rival, even proposed a grand ceremonial organ at the west end with six manuals and pedals 'for the Reception of the Queen on all publick Occasions of Thanksgiving', though nothing came of it.[29] Among the pieces specially written for these services were Clarke's *The Lord is my strength* for Ramillies (27 June 1706) and Croft's *Te Deum* and *Jubilate* in D with trumpets and oboes for Malplaquet (1709) '[p]erform'd twice before her most Gracious Majesty . . . at yᵉ Chapell Royall at Sᵗ James's on dayes of Thanksgiving, & thrice, at St Pauls, on yᵉ like Occasions'. Although it suffers from too many short sections, certain movements make a fine effect, notably 'The father of an infinite majesty' for the four countertenors – Elford, Freeman, Howell and Turner – suspensions piling on top of each other with hair-raising effect.

Somehow the music of Croft and Clarke, though inclined to be bland, suits the scale of St Paul's, whereas Purcell's, for all its richness, seems almost dwarfed. Indeed, the baroque grandeur of Wren's building never quite got the music it deserved, and even Handel's 'Utrecht' *Te Deum* (7 July 1713) failed to measure up. Nevertheless, the years between 1697 and 1713 represent an undoubted peak in the musical history of the cathedral.

THE CHOIR IN THE EIGHTEENTH CENTURY

The choir was maintained at the statutory level throughout the eighteenth century – except that about three-quarters of the way through, the choristers were reduced from ten to eight. But since many of the minor canons and virtually all the vicars were also members of the Chapel Royal and Westminster Abbey choirs, the question arises as to how far they can be regarded as distinct entities. Geographical separation, and to some extent clashing times of service, meant that they could not be in two (or three) places at once; thus, one might wonder how a full choir was ever possible at any of them.

The reason, indeed the need, for such pluralism was basically financial. Operatic styles and tastes were dominant, and though few wanted operatic church music or opera singers in church, to some extent it was unavoidable. Obviously there are superficial similarities between Handel's operas and the eighteenth-century verse anthem, for both were essentially made up of a string of 'numbers'. Not only were they typical products of their time, they operated in the same market. Professional singers of a high standard were required, and, with what were in effect three cathedral establishments in London, such men were in short supply. They therefore needed to be paid more than individual institutions could afford separately. Even so, Richard Bellamy, Robert

on 19 December 1694; the organ was to be placed on the choir screen, the case 22 feet high, 18 feet wide and 6 feet deep (in the end it was rather deeper) and finished by 25 March 1696. In fact, it was still not complete for the opening service more than twenty months later, progress having been set back by a fire in Smith's workshop. A last-minute change of plan to increase the compass of the instrument down to 16ft C (instead of F) was not put into effect until some time later, necessitating alterations to the case and perhaps calling forth Wren's exasperated 'confounded box of whistles' remark. In the end (*c.*1700), it probably had thirteen stops on the great including three mixtures and (by this date) the inevitable trumpet, eight on the chair and six on the echo. Until Renatus Harris's Salisbury organ of 1710, it was the largest in England. One in particular of Blow's thirty or so organ voluntaries – the one requiring a three-manual instrument – was probably written for it.[27] Blow, of course, was almoner, not organist, but the organ at Westminster Abbey where he officially presided was a two-manual affair.

The grand ceremonial opening of the new choir was held on Thursday, 2 December 1697 – the same day as the thanksgiving service for the Peace of Ryswick. Blow appears to have composed

Hudson, Francis Hughes, Francis Rowe, John Sale, William Savage, John Soaper, Robert Wass and Samuel Weely, all of whom served as vicars choral, were permitted to supplement their incomes with teaching and professional engagements.[30]

At St Paul's there appear to have been no official arrangements to deal with the problem of pluralism in the choir – at least, none that we are now aware of – although it must be presumed that a system of deputies was in operation.[31] From the records of the 'Cupola Fund', attendances seem to have been reasonable. This fund, set up in 1707 from the proceeds of admission charges to the dome and library, was used from 1711 to reward minor canons, vicars choral and virgers in proportion to their monthly attendances.[32] Individually, these were surprisingly respectable, but some members alternated monthly with others (no doubt by arrangement) so that the strength was normally between twelve and fifteen. To some extent, however, the music of the period could cope with depleted choirs, since verse anthems needed only a few soloists, and the increasingly popular solo anthem only one. Choruses, of course, needed one of each voice, at least.

Minor canons and vicars received not only individual stipends from the dean and chapter, but also income from property owned by them as independent corporations. Their stipends hardly changed over the years. In the middle of the eighteenth century, a minor canon received between £11 8s. 2d. and £19 13s. 2d. a year, depending on the endowment of his stall, plus a share of wedding fees and small extra payments for holding offices such as sacrist, gospeller, etc. Vicars were paid a flat rate of £9 14s. 2d., augmented by £12 or £16 to bring their wages up to a more realistic level. The almoner received £47 13s. 4d., with augmentation of £40; the organist's augmentation was £50.[33] As regards rental income, in 1748–9 each minor canon received £9 16s., and each vicar £17 0s. 2½d. Both these sums, however, were increased by fines negotiated when leases were renewed. Indeed, one property at Steeple Bumpstead in Essex, which the vicars owned, came up for renewal that year and produced £700 for a further twenty-one years' lease.[34] All in all, it was a bumper year for them, bearing in mind their earnings from the Chapel Royal and Westminster Abbey as well. Of course, some of the minor canons also had places there, or held other livings.

The minor canons may already have begun their decline to gentleman-amateurs, but they were still quite a formidable body, musically speaking. Originally they had obtained their places as singers – albeit ordained – and though singing the minister's part in the liturgy was their preserve, they were there to perform in anthems and services as well. The sub-dean chose the music, assigned the singers and had overall charge of the choir; the cardinals checked the attendance and catechized the boys. At the end of the century, it appears that several minor canons had been pupils of Philip Hayes, professor of music at Oxford,[35] and that 'ten out of twelve of the Minor Canons not only assisted in the general choral service but were principally looked up to, to sing the Anthems, perhaps even superior to the Vicars Choral of that time'.[36] Typical was the Revd William Hayes (younger brother of Philip), an ex-chorister of Magdalen College and a minor canon from 1764 to 1790. He was the author of 'Rules necessary to be observed by all Cathedral Singers in this Kingdom' published in the *Gentlemen's Magazine* (May 1765), though of little import.[37] It was he who sang the bass solo in Croft's 'O Lord, thou hast searched me out' by request of King George III at the thanksgiving service for the king's 'recovery' on St George's Day, 1789.[38] Another well-known singer among the minor canons was the

Revd Benjamin Mence, a countertenor, for whom Charles Wesley wrote the anthem 'My soul hath patiently tarried'.[39] Others, such as the Revd Anselm Bayly and the Revd Thomas [or Weldon] Champneys are also recorded as minor composers. Bayly, who became sub-dean of the Chapel Royal, published several thoughtful works touching on music and *A Collection of Anthems used in His Majesty's Chapel Royal and most Cathedral Churches* (1769), a book of anthem texts with an interesting preface on church music.[40]

Up to 1794, the choristers lodged with the almoner, from whom they received their maintenance and instruction in the theory of music, singing and reading at sight. Whatever its defects, the system produced some first-rate musicians, among them Maurice Greene and William Boyce.[41] The endowments, which included rents from fifteen houses in the city and two small estates in Acton, were intended to provide both a musical and general education for the boys.[42] There is no evidence, however, that the senior boys attended St Paul's School, as they had before the Fire (if Randall Jewett's indenture is to be believed).

Charles King, whose period as almoner covered most of the first half of the century, seems to have maintained a somewhat mild regime, judging by this piece of choristers' doggerel.

> Indulgence ne'ver was sought in vain,
> He never smote with stinging cane,
> He never stop't the penny fees,
> His boys were let do what they please.[43]

By contrast, his successor William Savage seems to have lived up to his name. According to one of his choristers, the glee composer R. J. S. Stevens, '[h]e was hasty and passionate when teaching the boys, but by constant attention to their elementary rules every morning before breakfast, he made them correct and ready performers. The four senior boys, could generally sing at sight. They were also instructed in playing the harpsichord.'[44] Rather surprisingly, it was said 'that Savage could not sing at sight himself' and even Stevens had to allow that '[p]erhaps, he was not so ready at first sight as could have been wished'.

Boys whose parents could afford an apprenticeship might be indentured to him or one of the other vicars with a view to becoming professional musicians. Indeed, Stevens has left a fascinating account of his apprenticeship under Savage.[45] After the afternoon service, choristers often performed at concerts in town. They provided trebles for the Academy of Vocal Musick at the Crown and Anchor in the Strand from 1726 under Greene, and for the break-away Apollo Society Concerts in 1731.[46] Along with boys from the Chapel Royal, they sang in Handel oratorios, and were in demand at meetings of the Madrigal Society in the 1740s.[47] At various times Savage and his successor Richard Bellamy were paid for supplying choristers for Drury Lane.[48]

It was probably during Savage's time that the number of choristers was reduced to eight.[49] Undoubtedly the financial situation was deteriorating and by the end of the century, with the growth of social conscience, the lack of provision for the choristers' education was becoming a scandal – hence Maria Hackett's assault on the dean and chapter (pp. 80, 85, 404). It seems that the endowments of the almonry had been rolled up into an allowance for the almoner which had now become inadequate. However this had come about – the rise in costs during the French wars was partly to blame, no doubt – Miss Hackett's case against the cathedral authorities was a damning indictment of their appalling complacency and neglect in maintaining the choristers.

330. Maurice Greene, organist at St Paul's 1718–55, with John Hoadley, author of the text for some of Greene's anthems. A painting by Francis Hayman, 1747. (NPG)

EIGHTEENTH–CENTURY ORGANISTS AND ALMONERS

Despite the difficulty of identifying particular musicians with particular institutions, it is fair to say that the almoners and organists of St Paul's were its truest representatives. In the first half of the eighteenth century, these were effectively two men, Charles King and Maurice Greene, whose years of service covered most of the period.[50] The two posts were normally separate, but Jeremiah Clarke held them jointly for a few years until his suicide in 1707 – the result of an unhappy love affair, it was said. His successor as organist, Richard Brind, was 'no very celebrated performer' according to Hawkins, but died in 1717, leaving the way clear for Greene (Fig. 330).[51]

King and Greene had both been choristers under Clarke. The former took the Bachelor of Music degree at Oxford in 1707 and was already a minor canon – though not ordained. (It was only in 1730 that the anomaly was rectified by his being made a vicar choral.)[52] His easy-going attitude as almoner has already been noted; it even carried over into his music, which seems designed to cause little trouble to performers and auditors alike. As a result, it circulated widely, especially the services. Indeed, Greene was fond of calling him 'a very serviceable man' on account of the number he wrote. There are eight in all – five printed in Arnold's *Cathedral Music* (1790) – scarcely distinguishable from each other to the listener.[53] At least seventeen anthems are known, for the most part avoiding the flamboyant style then fashionable. Hawkins, perhaps, hit the nail on the head when he observed that King's compositions 'leave the mind as they found it'.[54]

Greene's appointment as vicar choral and organist dates from 1718.[55] He was already organist of St Dunstan's in the West, and had recently been appointed organist of St Andrew's, Holborn in addition; but, against the trend, he relinquished both on becoming organist of St Paul's. The authorities seem to have been fully aware

of his worth, for they immediately doubled his augmentation to £50 over and above his vicar's income, and soon put in hand some improvements to the organ, including the addition of a set of 'pull-down' pedals and a swell mechanism. Thus in 1720, Christopher Shrider, Smith's son-in-law, was paid 'For Adding six large Trumpet pipes down to 16 foot Tone to be used with a pedal or without [£]36 / for the pedal & its Movements [£]20 / for adding the Loudening and Softening…and Its Movements… [£]12'.[56] The swell was said to produce 'the finest effect of any in the kingdom' – not that there were many contenders for the honour.[57] It was perhaps merely the echo organ fitted with some device to open and close the box. A new swell was added by John Crang in 1757. As for the pedals, it may be noted that none of Greene's organ voluntaries seems to make use of them.[58]

Whether the addition of pedals was the suggestion of Greene or Handel (who often played the St Paul's organ about this time) is not known. According to Hawkins, the latter would play following the afternoon service to an audience 'as great as ever filled the choir', after which 'it was his practice to adjourn with the principal persons of the choir to the Queen's Arms tavern in St Paul's church-yard, where was a great room, with a harpsichord in it; and oftentimes an evening was there spent in music and musical conversation'.[59] The reopening of the organ in 1720 was marked by a new anthem by Greene – probably *My soul truly waiteth still upon God* – performed on Sunday, 23 October 1720, Mist's *Weekly Journal* adding with the confidence of ignorance that 'it is now reckoned the best in Europe'.[60]

At this stage, Handel and Greene were still on good terms. Despite the coolness that later developed between them, they were hardly rivals – Handel's *métier* was, after all, opera, Greene's church music. In any case, Greene's career prospered and in 1727 he was made organist and composer to the Chapel Royal; in 1735 he became Master of the King's Musick. It seems reasonable to assume that most of the anthems written before his appointment to the Chapel Royal were intended specifically for St Paul's, among them *Lord, let me know mine end*, best known and (according to one copyist) '[t]he Finest Anthyme y[t] Ever was Made'.[61] Most critics agree that it is his masterpiece. An organ accompaniment book in the cathedral library contains sixteen anthems by 'Mr' Greene probably dating from this period – he received his Doctor of Music degree from Cambridge in 1730. The first few are probably in the hand of William Boyce, at that time a pupil of Greene, the rest in the hand of John Travers, another pupil, described as 'Sub-Organist of S[t] Paul's Cathedral' in the subscription list to Handel's *Admeto* (1727).[62]

Altogether Greene wrote almost eighty anthems, not counting twenty-four with orchestral accompaniment for the Chapel Royal and Festivals of the Sons of the Clergy. The verse anthems have been criticized for being too secular, florid and prone to cliché, but what militates most against their use today is their length. Nevertheless, their workmanship is admirable and without doubt they are the best of their kind, *pace* Dr Burney, who was somewhat severe with them. Full anthems such as *Lord, how long wilt thou be angry* and *O clap your hands together* have, on the other hand, been much admired, conforming as they do to what was then (and still is) regarded as an ideal for church music.

Apart from numerous orchestral *Te Deum*s written for non-liturgical occasions, he composed only one service. It is a marvellous piece in C major, comprising morning and evening canticles in up to eight parts.[63] Technically and aesthetically, it rises well above the perfunctoriness of so much eighteenth-century service music. Written in 1737, no special occasion that might have called for it is known, though its magnificent sonority makes it especially suitable for St Paul's.

In 1743 Greene published his *Forty Select Anthems*, followed in 1747 by *Six Solo Anthems*. In later years, he busied himself with compiling a historical collection of English church music, but left its completion to William Boyce, who saw it through to publication.[64] Boyce succeeded Greene as conductor of the Festival of the Sons of the Clergy on the latter's death in 1755, but not as cathedral organist – perhaps because of increasing deafness.[65] No doubt many of his anthems were written for the Chapel Royal, but again, because of his connections it seems likely that many early works were first heard at St Paul's; he is certainly well represented in the cathedral choir books. His funeral service was held in the cathedral and he is buried in the crypt under a stone now shared with Maurice Greene, whose body was moved from St Olave, Old Jewry in 1888.

Greene's successor was John Jones, a chorister under King and another pupil of Greene.[66] Appointed organist of the Temple Church (1749), the Charterhouse (1753) and St Paul's (1755), he held all these posts until his death. The allegation that he was unworthy to succeed Greene because 'he could not play from score',[67] and thus needed to write out his accompaniments, is, on the face of it, unjust, since he was like any other cathedral organist in this respect. Most anthems were not available in score unless already printed, like Greene's or Croft's. Burney, it is true, thought that 'his abilities as a performer or composer were not above mediocrity',[68] but judging by the set of harpsichord lessons he published in 1754, and two later volumes, this view must be questioned.

Jones's organ scores are still in the cathedral library.[69] They give a good idea of what was sung during his time, and include services by Tallis, Byrd (two), Gibbons, Batten, etc., from the Tudor and early Stuart periods; Child (five), Humfrey, Blow (three) and Purcell from the Restoration period; and Croft, King (five), Greene and Boyce (two) from the eighteenth century – to mention only well-known names. The anthems show a similar spread, from Gibbons (five), Batten (four), Farrant (three) and Byrd (three), through Blow (nine), Aldrich (seven), Purcell (six), Child (three) Wise (three), Clarke (three) and Weldon (three), to Greene (twenty-six), Croft (twenty), Nares (nineteen), Boyce (fifteen), King (thirteen), Kent (eight) and William Hayes, senior (three) – to mention only those with three or more to their names. Jones himself wrote two services, a Morning Service in G and an Evening Service in F, both still in the cathedral library.

He also published a collection of *Sixty Chants Single and Double* in 1785. It was one of these – no. 24 (in D) of the double chants – which Joseph Haydn heard at the charity children's service at St Paul's in either 1791 or 1792, and entered into his notebook (in E – the organ was probably a tone sharp).[70] Four thousand children singing together in unison clearly overwhelmed him:

> I stood there and wept like a child…the voices sounded like angels' voices…the fall in the first three bars to a low B brought both a fearsome quality that gripped the heart, as the notes died away in the delicate throats of the children and ended in a hovering breath of tone; then as it went on, the melody gradually grew in life and strength as it progressed upwards; thus the melody was full of light and shadow and its effect mighty.[71]

Another collection entitled *Sixty Chants, Single and Double*, 'Compos'd by the Choristers of St Paul's', was published in 1795.

While Jones was organist, the almoners were successively William Savage, Robert Hudson and Richard Bellamy.[72] According to Burney, Savage's voice was 'a powerful, and not unpleasant, bass', but added that '[h]e was a vain, pompous man, and felt and made others feel his importance'.[73] Stevens, however, found 'all this vanished when you were acquainted with him'. As for his voice, he thought it 'a pleasant bass voice of the compass of two octaves: he had a clear articulation, perfect intonation, great volubility of voice and chaste and good expression. In sacred music particularly, his pathos and feeling were excellent and very impressive.'[74] Close on forty anthems by Savage survive in manuscript, many carrying dates between 1765 and 1786.[75] *O Lord, rebuke me not* and *Hearken unto my voice, O Lord* Stevens thought 'not unworthy' of Purcell. There is also a service in C (1767) parts of which still survive in the cathedral library.

Robert Hudson, his successor, was often heard in the London pleasure gardens as a tenor soloist, and many of his songs were published.[76] He composed a service in E flat, several chants and hymn tunes. One of his choristers was Thomas Dibden, whose *Reminiscences* published in 1827 contain some appreciative references. Of Richard Bellamy it was reported that he 'bought his [vicar's] place of M[r] Savage' in 1777 with a life annuity.[77] He sang bass in the Handel commemoration of 1784 and at Drury Lane in 1786, where he was also paid for supplying choristers in 1794, 1797, 1798 and 1800.[78] He had taken the Bachelor of Music degree at Cambridge in 1775, and composed an orchestral *Te Deum* for the installation ceremony of the Knights of the Bath at Westminster Abbey in 1788. It was published together with a set of seven anthems, some of which are quite remarkable in their way. Naïve in some respects, they nevertheless display a spacious and dramatic approach to their texts, hinting at early romantic tendencies.

When it came to finding a successor for Jones as organist in 1796, several candidates were scouted. One of them, apparently, was Thomas Battishill, the outstanding church composer of the time and much admired as an organist, particularly as an improvisor.[79] As an ex-chorister and articled pupil of Savage, he had maintained links with the cathedral. One of his earliest anthems, 'I waited patiently', carries the date 1758 in the cathedral library; later, he published *Two Anthems as they are Sung at St Paul's Cathedral* (1767), containing *Call to remembrance*, a full anthem still much admired, and *How long wilt thou forget me, O Lord*, an equally fine verse anthem. His *O Lord, look down from heaven*, has been called 'one of the really great anthems of the English church'.[80] At its best, his church music combines modern harmonic feeling (diminished sevenths, etc.) with imaginative choral textures, rejecting alike 'baroque' and 'galant' idioms. Unfortunately his reputation as a drunkard went against him, and Stevens in his 'Recollections' recalls how even the archbishop of Canterbury quizzed him on this.[81]

In the end, Thomas Attwood was appointed organist, probably with royal backing.[82] As a chorister in the Chapel Royal he had attracted the attention of the prince of Wales, who sent him abroad to study, first in Naples (1783–5), then Vienna (1785–7), where he had lessons from Mozart. On his return, he became music teacher to the duchess of York, then to the princess of Wales, besides receiving other marks of recognition. Most of his church music belongs to the next century; only the Service in F (1796) and one or two anthems date from our period.

Doubtless the repertoire at the end of the century is reflected in the three volumes of John Page's *Harmonia Sacra* (1800), a sequel to Boyce and Arnold. Page himself was appointed vicar choral in 1800, and his collection includes, among others, anthems by Greene (seven), Clarke (four), King (four), Battishill (four), Attwood (one), and David Wood (described as 'Deputy Vicar Choral of St Paul's Cathedral').[83] Other publications include *The Anthems & Psalms as Performed at St Paul's Cathedral* (c.1795),

containing music for 'The Anniversary Meeting of the Charity Children' which Page himself conducted. It includes arrangements of *Zadok the priest* and the Hallelujah Chorus.

It is customary to regard the period around 1800 as marking the nadir of English church music. Certainly the modern view would be that things were better at St Paul's a hundred years earlier, or a hundred years later, and that at the turn of the century the cathedral authorities were scandalously self-satisfied. On the other hand, Maria Hackett's principal complaint, when it came, was against the inadequate provision for the general education of the choristers, their maintenance and moral welfare, not their musical training. More ominous for the future was the declining musical role of the minor canons who should have formed two-thirds of the choir, but whose increasing dilettantism made them ineffective. No doubt a largely clerical choir was an anachronism, but until that problem was solved – which meant more and better paid vicars – no great improvement could be expected. Nevertheless, the eighteenth-century achievement was solid and respectable. Above all, it kept alive a 250-year tradition of English church music stretching back to the Reformation, and brought it to the threshold of the nineteenth century as a still living force.

ALMONERS (MASTERS OF THE CHORISTERS) AND ORGANISTS
1660–1800

Almoners	Organists
Randall Jewett (1661–75)	Albertus Bryne (1660–68)
Michael Wise (1687)	
John Blow (1687–1703)	Isaac Blackwell (1687–99)
Jeremiah Clarke (1704–7)	Jeremiah Clarke (1699–1707)
Charles King (1707–48)	Richard Brind (1708–18)
William Savage (1748–73)	Maurice Greene (1718–55)
Robert Hudson (1773–93)	John Jones (1755–96)
Richard Bellamy (1793–1800)	Thomas Attwood (1796–1838)

36

ORCHESTRAS IN THE NEW CATHEDRAL

Donald Burrows

Thus wrote Thomas Tudway, professor of music at the University of Cambridge, in his preface (dated 1720) to the sixth and last volume of English church music that he had compiled and copied for Edward, Lord Harley.[2] It is uncertain whether the D major setting of the *Te Deum* and *Jubilate* composed by Henry Purcell (d. 1695) was indeed written in anticipation of performance at St Paul's Cathedral, but Tudway's statements reflect two subjects relevant to an exciting period in the cathedral's musical experience: the development of orchestrally accompanied church music in London during the 1690s, when the new cathedral was in a significant building phase, and the thanksgiving services of Queen Anne's reign, when the cathedral became the site for ceremonial state occasions attended by the monarch more frequently and more regularly than at any other time during its history.

The evolution of orchestrally accompanied church music in the 1690s is fairly easy to trace, but difficult to account for.[3] Although the principal developments took place at the 'city' end of London, the impetus may well have come principally from musicians associated with the court. One of the musical innovations of King Charles II's reign had been the 'Symphony Anthems' accompanied by stringed instruments which were performed at the Chapel Royal (then at Whitehall) when the king attended: when King James II withdrew to a separate Roman Catholic chapel, the practice continued, at least occasionally, when Princess Anne attended the Chapel Royal. However, King William III's Calvinist tastes were reflected in a command in 1689 that 'there shall be no musick [i.e. instruments] in the Chapell, but the Organ'.[4] The string players from the royal musicians and the singers from the Chapel Royal still regularly performed together in the odes which were given at court at New Year and on royal birthdays, but there was probably some regret at the attenuation of the 'symphony anthem'. The reintroduction of 'musick' came about through the 'Musical Society' which since 1683 had arranged annual celebrations of St Cecilia's Day with the performance of odes, much on the lines of the court odes but with texts referring to the beneficial power of music.[5] In 1693 the St Cecilia celebrations added a sermon, at St Bride's, Fleet Street, by Ralph Battel, the sub-dean of the Chapel Royal, subsequently published as *The Lawfullness and Expediency of Church-music*. Battel made a specific defence of the use of musical instruments in church, but as far as is known, no musical performance was undertaken to complement the sermon. The next year, however, the church component of the St Cecilia celebrations (again at St Bride's) included the first performance of the D major setting of the *Te Deum* and *Jubilate* by Purcell, probably given in the context of a service of morning prayer.

As Tudway noted, Purcell's canticle settings set a new style for English church music. Hitherto, the recent London traditions of instrumentally accompanied church music had comprised the symphony anthems in the Chapel Royal – essentially chamber-scale works involving a small string group – and the occasional grand anthem for which the presence of a relatively large (though in some ways disparate) group of musicians at royal coronations at

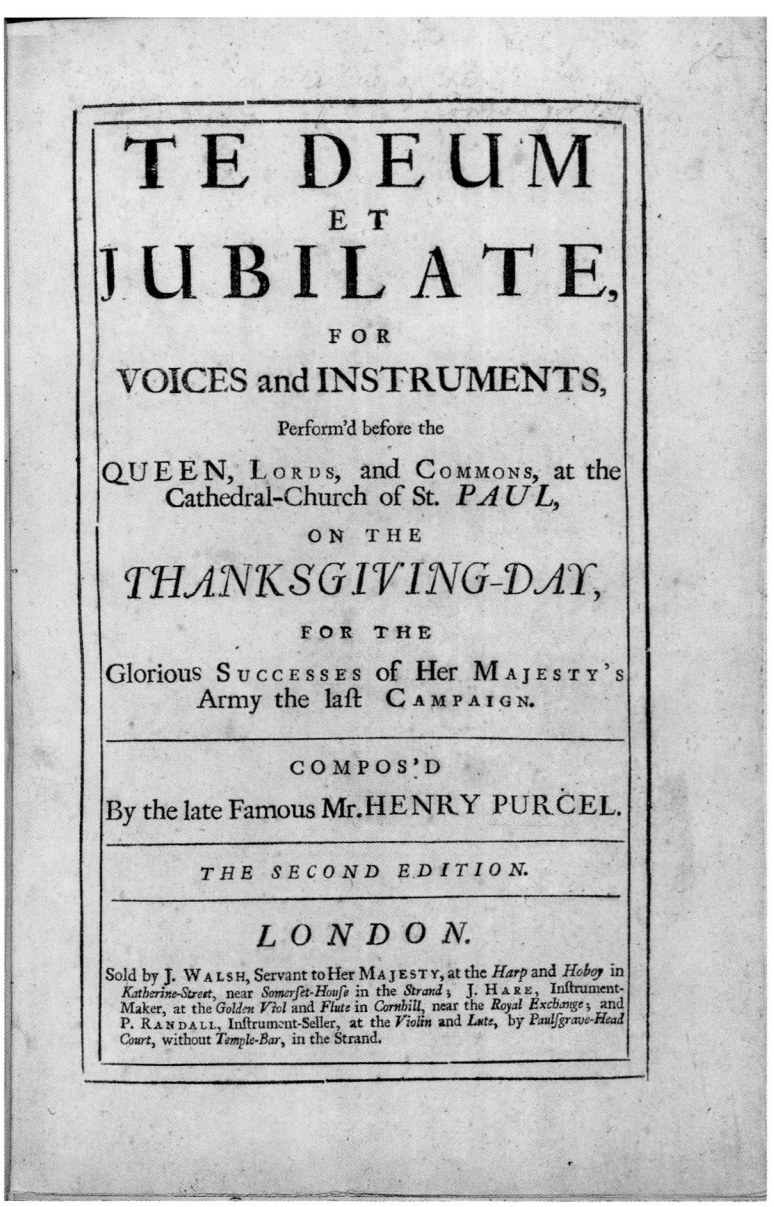

TE DEUM
ET
JUBILATE,
FOR
VOICES and INSTRUMENTS,
Perform'd before the
QUEEN, LORDS, and COMMONS, at the
Cathedral-Church of St. *PAUL*,
ON THE
THANKSGIVING-DAY,
FOR THE
Glorious SUCCESSES of Her MAJESTY'S
Army the laſt CAMPAIGN.

COMPOS'D
By the late Famous Mr. HENRY PURCEL.

THE SECOND EDITION.

LONDON.

Sold by J. WALSH, Servant to Her MAJESTY, at the *Harp* and *Hoboy* in *Katherine-Street*, near *Somerſet-Houſe* in the *Strand*; J. HARE, Instrument-Maker, at the *Golden Viol* and *Flute* in *Cornhill*, near the *Royal Exchange*; and P. RANDALL, Inſtrument-Seller, at the *Violin* and *Lute*, by *Paulſgrave-Head Court*, without *Temple-Bar*, in the *Strand*.

331. Title page of Henry Purcell's *Te Deum*, sung at the cathedral throughout Queen Anne's reign. (BL)

tions attended church services which followed the special published liturgies for the day and incorporated suitable sermons: the king usually attended morning prayer at the Chapel Royal, while the House of Lords went to Westminster Abbey and the House of Commons went to St Margaret's, Westminster. The Lord Mayor of London and the City Corporation now had the opportunity to attend their service at St Paul's, and it was rumoured that (no doubt on account of the significance of the re-opening) King William would make this a royal occasion:[6]

His majestie intends on the thanksgiving day to goe to St Paul's Cathedral, where the doctors of musick, singing men, etc., are to perform all the ceremonies.

In the event, the king went to the Chapel Royal instead, but nevertheless the service at St Paul's was celebrated with due ceremony and included a new anthem by John Blow, 'I was glad', written with the same orchestral scoring as Purcell's canticles.[7] On this occasion, it seems probable that there was a considerable concentration of London's talent in orchestral musicians and choral singers at St Paul's. It has to be borne in mind that, although there was some rivalry between London's major ecclesiastical establishments, the adult singers in the choirs were drawn from a common pool: London's professional church singers assembled their livelihood by combining simultaneous places at the Chapel Royal, Westminster Abbey and even St George's Chapel, Windsor, which they served in turn.

If there was some disappointment that the opening of the choir of St Paul's in 1697 was not marked as a royal event, there was considerable compensation during the following decade. Very soon after her accession in 1702, Queen Anne took up the opportunity to celebrate one of the national thanksgivings at St Paul's:[8]

(November 3) The queen hath given orders to the bishop of London to draw up a form of prayer to return God thanks next Sunday in St Paul's church for the great victory obtained over the French at Vigo, and that she intends to be present.

(November 5) The queen goes to St Paul's Cathedrall, (the like done in queen Elizabeth's reign) both houses of parliament will also be there.

The reference to 'queen Elizabeth's reign' is to that queen's attendance at St Paul's in November 1588 on the thanksgiving day after the defeat of the Spanish armada (p. 52): Anne was the first monarch to attend St Paul's for such a service since then, and in all she attended seven thanksgiving services at St Paul's between 1702 and 1708 (p. 365).[9] The thanksgivings were grand ceremonial occasions, combining the attendance of the various groups that had hitherto held separate services, with coach processions for the houses of parliament and the judges, and guards in attendance: the streets of the procession route were lined by spectators and by members of the city livery companies in their gowns. The description of the thanksgiving on 31 December 1706 describes what was probably the regular procedure:[10]

At Temple Bar her majestie was met by the lord mayor, aldermen, and sheriffs on horseback, who conducted her to St Paul's church, where a fine anthem was sung, and the bishop of Salisbury preacht the sermon.

After which she returned to St James's, and at night were discharged bonefires and illuminations, and the Tower guns were thrice discharged, viz. at her majesties first setting out, at the anthem, and at her return.

Westminster Abbey provided the opportunity in 1685 and 1689. Purcell's new canticles were, by contrast, orchestral in a more modern sense, scored for trumpets and strings and implying a larger group of string players than the symphony anthems: vocally, the pieces displayed the talents of London's best church soloists, in alternation and contrast with the full weight of the choral ensemble. Purcell's model was followed by similar settings of the *Te Deum* and *Jubilate* by John Blow and William Turner for the subsequent Cecilian celebrations in 1695 and 1696; his canticles also provided his successors with a more general stylistic model for orchestrally accompanied anthems.

It is against this musical background that the first stage in the opening of Wren's cathedral took place. By mid-1697 the choir of the cathedral was approaching completion, Father Smith's organ was in place and, some ten years after their refoundation, the musical institutions of St Paul's (choristers, minor canons and vicars choral) had the prospect of settling in their new home. An occasion for a celebratory reopening presented itself with the thanksgiving day for the Peace of Ryswick on 2 December 1697. On national thanksgiving days, London's major political institu-

Other reports of the services make it clear that the 'anthem' which was the signal for the second firing of the guns was the *Te Deum*. It is remarkable that Purcell's 1694 setting was the one that was regularly performed, rather than that by John Blow, who was still alive and was the principal Chapel Royal composer in the period following Purcell's death.

A report of the Blenheim thanksgiving service in 1704 mentions that the *Te Deum* was 'perform'd by her Majesty's Choir and Music', and there seems no doubt that these services assembled the best available talent from London's musicians, probably combining the forces of London's ecclesiastical choirs and adding extra instrumentalists to the regular group of string players from the Queen's Musicians. A remarkable picture of one of the thanksgivings by Robert Trevitt shows an array of musicians in the gallery, assembled for the performance of the *Te Deum* and *Jubilate*:[11] about twenty-five musicians are shown, in a view which does not encompass the whole gallery. Clearly the performing forces were more substantial then those for the old Chapel Royal symphony anthems: the ensemble depicted seems to show an interesting transitional stage between the rather heterogeneous large instrumental groups from the late seventeenth century and the recognizably modern orchestra that had developed by 1710 as a result of the establishment of an opera company at the King's Theatre, Haymarket. Although there may have been some artistic licence in the depiction of details, Trevitt's picture reflects the grandness of the musical contribution to the occasions (Figs 154, 329).[12]

In 1709–10 three further thanksgivings followed, but the queen withdrew to the Chapel Royal (now at St James's Palace), probably from a mixture of personal and political motives, and the various estates returned to services at separate venues, leaving the city to celebrate alone at St Paul's. There was one further combined thanksgiving at St Paul's, however, in July 1713, to celebrate the Peace of Utrecht (p. 365).[13] This was remarkable because new settings of the *Te Deum* and *Jubilate* were provided by the twenty-eight-year old George Frideric Handel. Just as Purcell's settings had set a new style for English church music in 1694, so Handel's did again in 1713. The new scale is apparent in a comparison of Purcell's and Handel's settings of the opening two verses. In one and a half minutes Purcell moves briskly from an instrumental introduction through a trio of soloists to the full chorus, but the same text takes more than four minutes in Handel's setting, with a more substantial orchestral sound (oboes with a full string section, and trumpets added) and more extended writing for the full body of singers: the second verse, treated imitatively by Purcell in just over half a minute, becomes a substantial fugal chorus movement with Handel.

The 'Utrecht' service probably precipitated Handel's formal dismissal from his post at the court of Hanover, but the severance was in one sense short-lived because the elector of Hanover succeeded to the British throne the next year as King George I. Early in his reign there was a further combined royal thanksgiving service at St Paul's, on 20 January 1715, celebrating (rather prematurely, as it turned out) 'bringing his Majesty to a Peaceable and Quiet possession of the Throne, and thereby Disappointing the Designs of the Pretender and all his adherents'. The *Te Deum* and *Jubilate* for this occasion were provided by William Croft, the leading Chapel Royal composer after Blow's death: this was actually a revival of music that Croft had composed previously, but adapted and strengthened on the model of Handel's settings.[14] However, the first two Hanoverian monarchs did not have much taste for the type of public display involved with the

thanksgivings,[15] and no grand royal service was seen again until King George III went to St Paul's to celebrate the recovery of his health and sanity in 1789. Circumstantial evidence from Handel's scores does, however, suggest that the composer anticipated that there might have been a couple of such services during the 1740s for the thanksgivings after the battle of Dettingen and the Peace of Aix-la-Chapelle, though in the end the king celebrated both in his own chapel. The service in January 1715 had apparently raised an issue as to whether the conduct of the service was the privilege of the Chapel Royal or the cathedral:[16] this probably did not affect the singers, many of whom held dual appointments in both.

The discontinuance of the royal thanksgiving services after 1708 seems to have left something of a vacuum: by then, St Paul's was associated with ceremonial public services in which orchestrally accompanied church music played a significant part. The vacuum was filled almost immediately by the regular incorporation of such music into the annual festival services for the Corporation of the Sons of the Clergy. These charity services, which had been held at St Michael's, Cornhill and Bow Church in the period following the Great Fire of 1666, moved back to St Paul's within a week of the opening of the choir in 1697: in 1698, when Blow was a steward for the festival, he contributed an anthem, 'Blessed is the Man that feareth the Lord' (with the Purcellian orchestral scoring for trumpet and strings) for the service, but thereafter a decade passed without any performances of a similar type. For the festival service in 1709, however, orchestrally accompanied music was reintroduced, almost certainly comprising Purcell's famous canticles. A rather confused memorandum written later in the eighteenth century suggests that the dean of St Paul's was initially opposed to the presence of the orchestra (which may have been enforced for the thanksgiving services by royal tastes), but was persuaded to permit the practice in order to increase the public attendance, and thus the financial contribution to the clergy charity.[17] By the 1720s, and possibly earlier, collections were made for the charity in the cathedral at the public rehearsals for the music, and these even came to exceed the collections at the service itself.

The musical programmes for the services are rather unclear for the years immediately after 1709, but from at least 1715 onwards orchestrally accompanied pieces were regularly performed, for the canticles and sometimes specially composed anthems as well.[18] The canticle settings by Purcell and Croft naturally featured in the early years. Maurice Greene was appointed organist at St Paul's in 1718, and seems to have taken over the management of musical aspects of the services, so it is not surprising that his own compositions were also introduced into the programmes, sometimes in alternation with Purcell's canticles. For some reason, Handel's music did not feature until 1731, when the 'Utrecht' *Te Deum* and *Jubilate* were introduced, and thereafter his music rather dominated the services. Additional pieces by Handel also crept in: by 1735 the overture to *Esther* was played before the service, and his anthem 'God save the King' (presumably from *Zadok the Priest*) was sung; both of these seem to have been adopted subsequently as regular features of the service. 1735 was a year that saw an important change in the physical arrangements for the musicians, as noted in a newspaper report of the public rehearsal:

> Dr Green play'd on the Organ, Mr Powel of Oxford sung, and Mr Carbonelli was the first Fiddle, and above 130 Instruments more, besides about 40 voices. Seats were built up at the Altar, for the Musick [i.e. performers] to face the Audience, which was never done before.

This allowed the participation of a much greater number of performers than had been possible in the organ gallery, and it also brought the musical element of the service into greater public prominence.

After Greene's death in 1755, William Boyce took over musical direction of the services: one of his first actions seems to have been to make a 'modernized' arrangement of Purcell's canticles. By then, the institutional arrangements for the participation of the orchestra had been secured on a permanent basis through an agreement with the Society of Musicians, a charity founded in 1738. As time went on, the musical programme became rather rigidly fixed, but nevertheless for the rest of the century the Sons of the Clergy Festival at St Paul's (and its preceding rehearsal) became one of the annual events at which some of the glories of English orchestrally accompanied church music could be heard.

37

MUSIC, 1800–2002

Timothy Storey

In 1800, and indeed for more than half of the nineteenth century, the two-and-a-half easternmost bays were the only part of St Paul's regularly used for worship, enclosed by an organ-screen placed some distance from the dome, rather east of the position occupied by the present-day organ and singers.[1] This restricted place could seat a surprisingly large number of people, for there were 'closets' (most of which still remain) within the panelling between the stone piers, and seats above these on top of the woodwork. On Sundays it might be necessary to bribe the virgers to secure a seat. The ten choristers provided for in the cathedral's statutes had dwindled to eight by the mid eighteenth century: these made up the choir, together with six vicars choral who were an independent corporation outside the chapter's control, protected by the security of a freehold. By long tradition, the organist took one of the freeholds, his place in the choir being taken by a deputy paid by the chapter.

The apse at St Paul's gives considerable assistance to the sound at the eastern end of the building: there is every reason to suppose that at its best such a small body of voices was adequate for the portion of the building then in use.[2] The organ's tone was gentle and mellow, ineffective under the dome but ideal for choral accompaniment. The organist, Thomas Attwood, had been in post four years: he was a genial man, a talented composer who had studied with Mozart and a fine player (Fig. 332). Like many a new organist, he was about to enjoy a rebuild and restoration of the organ, which was carried out in 1803.[3] Sadly, the choir was not always at its best, for the boys tended to be kept on long after their voices had begun to change,[4] and 'the efficiency of even this small body [of men] was marred by the fact that the vicars gradually grew into a corporation . . . holding estates and using the proceeds of their property. This independence made the vicars negligent of their ordinary duties, and careless of the reputation of their cathedral. They attended irregularly, and were disinclined to bend to any authority whatsoever.'[5]

In common with his successors until Sir George Martin (1888), Attwood had no official responsibilities beyond playing the organ. There were no practices for the full choir, and the boys were trained by the almoner, currently John Sale, who had just been appointed to this office. Conditions at this time were not good, as the former boarding-house in Carter Lane had been given up through lack of funds, and the boys now lived at home, being paid a pittance for singing. Morning and evening prayer (matins and evensong) were sung every day of the year. On Sundays the choir remained for the first part of the communion service, singing the Responses to the Commandments, the Nicene Creed and (if the composer had set it) the *Sanctus*, not in its proper place but as an introit. The musical repertoire was largely limited to the collected works of William Boyce, William Croft and Maurice Greene, supplemented by the anthologies edited by Boyce and Samuel Arnold. In the very year under review John Page, a vicar choral of St Paul's, published his *Harmonia Sacra*, whose three volumes usefully filled various gaps in the earlier collections. Page also published the music for Nelson's funeral in the cathedral on 9 January 1806, a strange mixture of the burial service and evening prayer, to which Attwood contributed a Dirge and his *Magnificat* and *Nunc Dimittis* in F.[6] The music for the daily services was chosen by the succentor, a minor canon. The greater offices of chancellor, precentor and treasurer were sinecures, and for much of the nineteenth century the precentor was the Revd C. A. Belli, who attended the cathedral so infrequently that he was once refused admission to his stall because no one recognized him.[7] There was

332.   Thomas Attwood, cathedral organist 1796–1838. (SPCL)

333.   Maria Hackett (1783–1874), persistent champion of reform of the choir and improved education for the boys. (SPCL)

no published weekly music scheme, and anthems might be changed at short notice to take account of absences from the choir. There was a preponderance of compositions for solo, duet or trio, the contribution of the full choir (such as it was) being confined to a brief final chorus.

Sale struggled on until 1812, failing to persuade the chapter to increase the funds available for the choristers.[8] His succcessor, William Hawes, met with rather more success, and was able to house the boys at Craven Street, Charing Cross, moving the establishment to Adelphi Terrace (off the Strand) in 1827 when he took on the Chapel Royal boys as well: from either address, the boys had a long walk to and from St Paul's twice a day. Miss Maria Hackett (p. 80; Fig. 333) complained of this, and much else, in a remarkable twenty-year series of letters to bishop, dean, almoner and many others. Her interest in the St Paul's choristers began in 1811 when she placed in the choir an orphan for whom she had responsibility, expecting that he would receive a good classical education. In 1814 she was successful in an application to the Master of the Rolls for the restoration of school property left in trust for the choristers,[9] and she subsequently extended her crusade to other cathedrals. Hawes ran his boarding-house as a kind of private enterprise, supplementing his income by hiring out the boys to sing at functions in the city of London, an arrangement he defended as broadening their musical education. He was a kindly if demanding master, but the arrangements did not survive his death in 1846, and the boys once more lived at home, travelling in daily and being left much to their own devices during the middle of the day. First a canon, then a minor canon was appointed almoner, and the boys were trained by a succession of vicars choral; but the arrangement could not be regarded as satisfactory, though it endured until the early 1870s.

Attwood died in 1838 and was succeeded by John Goss, a talented composer, distinguished tenor and competent organist.

Together with James Turle, organist of Westminster Abbey, he edited a three-volume anthology of church music, which was duly added to the choir library at St Paul's; and his anthem for the duke of Wellington's funeral on 18 November 1852, 'If we believe that Jesus died and rose again', is still widely sung. Goss has been quite unfairly pilloried for the chaotic state of the cathedral's services during his time, and the more colourful incidents of his declining years have been frequently recounted, such as the organist playing one chant while the choir sang another, the anthem having to be changed because of a lack of the necessary singers and (the most notorious of all) a performance of the 'Hallelujah Chorus' with only two of the men present;[10] but his responsibilities included neither the management of the choir nor the choice of the music it had to sing. He also had to contend with the whole series of alterations to the building from 1859 until his retirement in 1872. The screen was removed in 1860, the organ was re-erected under the second arch of the choir and a second-hand organ was set up in the south transept to accompany newly instituted Sunday evening services under the dome, for which a large voluntary choir of ladies and men was formed to lead the singing.

Now that the entire length of the building had been thrown open, the cathedral choir's inadequacy was all too obvious. Criticism in the press was widespread, and a report of a Sunday service in 1871 makes depressing reading: 'at no time did there appear to be more than an irregular confused hum of children's voices, trying to sing something of which the majority seemed incapable'.[11] The dome area was now the focus of the cathedral's worship, and the decision had been taken that the organ should be rebuilt and placed nearby, on either side of the entrance to the chancel.[12] There was a need for a larger and thus more powerful cathedral choir, and a wider vision for the cathedral's music in general. Goss departed in an unexpected blaze of glory, with a knighthood for his part in a special service held on 27 February

334.   Choirboys and vicars choral robing and preparing to enter the choir from the south chancel aisle. This view of *c.* 1852 by Jules Arnout was made shortly before the choirstalls were rearranged. (GL)

335.   Vicars choral with John Stainer (organist 1872–88) and George Martin (sub-organist 1876–88, organist 1888–1916, left and right in centre of front row, probably on the occasion of Stainer's retirement in 1888. (SPCL)

1872 in thanksgiving for the prince of Wales's recovery from typhoid, and was succeeded by John Stainer (Fig. 335).

The years following Stainer's appointment showed how much could be achieved by the fortunate coincidence of a number of like-minded individuals. Within the short space of the years 1868 to 1871, three high churchmen had been appointed to St Paul's, Dean Church and Canons Gregory and Liddon, and the chapter was united in its sympathies as seldom before or since. There was a desire to impart dignity and reverence to worship and to realize the full glories of Anglican worship as set out in the *Book of Common Prayer*, especially in emphasizing the primacy and importance of the holy communion.[13] When St Paul's needed a new

organist, Canon Liddon brought from Oxford his former colleague Stainer, who had been organist of Ouseley's fledgeling St Michael's College (set up to provide a model for cathedral services) and had then made the musical services of Magdalen College into exactly what seemed to be needed at St Paul's. He was a talented composer: his songs and cathedral music are far better than the work for which he is best known and which has been most reviled, *The Crucifixion*, a Passiontide cantata written in simple and direct style for a pupil's parish church choir. That he was a former chorister of St Paul's was a bonus.

Like his predecessors, Stainer was appointed organist – precisely that, with no other official responsibility. He would have to get

336. The old choir school in Carter Lane, built to designs by F. C. Penrose, 1874–5: view in 1989

337. George Martin at the console of the organ, after 1900. (SPCL)

along with the existing succentor and singing-master as best he could for the time being. The singers were too few for the building now that the whole length of the cathedral had been thrown open, and the boys, by now twelve in number, were bereft of proper schooling and of poor quality. Though supernumerary men had been appointed, making a total of ten, there was still no certainty that a balanced choir would be in attendance on weekdays, and the organ, much more brilliant in tone after its rebuild by Willis, swamped the choir's feeble singing. As a first step, twelve more boys were appointed in January 1873 and eight more men, making a total of eighteen of whom twelve in rotation were on duty on weekdays; and from this time, at Stainer's suggestion, a music-list was printed and put up every week. The twelve additional boys were boarded at No. 1, Amen Court, the former dozen choristers continuing as day-boys in a somewhat uneasy co-existence: the choristers did not reach their full complement of forty until 1875, after the opening of a new residential choir school in Carter Lane (Fig. 336).[14]

Stainer had no right or duty to rehearse the choir, and it says much for his 'charm and winning ways' that he managed to institute a weekly choir practice almost as soon as he arrived. Of course, the additional men appointed in 1873 were of his choosing, and by good fortune only two of the six freehold vicars choral were active in the choir,[15] heavily outnumbered by sixteen other men who were more biddable. Of these two freeholders, Thomas Francis was a thorough nuisance and pursued an extraordinary single-handed campaign in defence of his right to be absent without supplying a deputy and generally to do exactly as he pleased; but to everyone's relief he was persuaded to retire in 1876. Matters could easily have been very much worse.

If it would take some time for the cathedral choir to be

improved, there were other things possible of achievement meanwhile. Stainer's lecture to the Church Congress at Leeds in October 1872 was in effect a statement of intent for what he would do at St Paul's, the general thesis being that cathedrals should provide music in all styles, especially the expressive modern music of composers such as Mendelssohn. He was rather dismissive of the contrapuntal style, but perhaps as a chorister he had sung rather too much of it. There should, he urged, be good congregational singing; and to provide for this the special choir of volunteer men was refounded in January 1873, with the sopranos who had sung from its inception in 1861 replaced by the cathedral choristers. It sang at the congregational service on Sunday evenings, which was intended to be a model of good parish church worship with hymns and chanted canticles, in complete contrast to the statutory services at which the congregation remained dutifully dumb.

Stainer also advocated the occasional performance of oratorios with full orchestra, and thus on 25 January 1873, the feast of the Conversion of St Paul, selections from Mendelssohn's *St Paul* were given with full orchestra and augmented choir at evensong, the instrumentalists being clad in surplices to make it obvious that this was not to be regarded as a secular concert. Similar treatment was given to the traditional Festival of the Sons of the Clergy (whose orchestra had been given up in the 1840s). In the same year came the first performance of Bach's *St Matthew Passion* at St Paul's, so that every year until the Second World War there were the three great services with orchestra and augmented choir. After 1878, Spohr's *Last Judgement* was added to the annual cycle, sung on the second Tuesday in Advent but by the cathedral choir alone, without a conductor and with the orchestral accompaniment brilliantly realized upon the organ by Stainer. There had of course been occasional great events which filled the whole cathedral, such as Nelson's and Wellington's funerals and the annual service of the London charity schools,[16] but these new services were a regular part of the annual round of devotion. They were supplemented by annual festivals of such bodies as the London Church Choirs Association (1874 onwards), the London Gregorian Choral Association (from 1873) and Sion College Choral Union (1874).[17]

All of this was unofficial, voluntary and beyond his statutory duties, and it says much for the mutual trust between Stainer and the chapter that such innovations were allowed. Soon came his chance to apply a little influence to the cathedral choir, for there would be a need for a resident music master in the new choir school. The boys were being taught by Fred Walker, a vicar choral and a professor at the Royal Academy of Music, who was content to withdraw gracefully at the beginning of 1874 in favour of one George Clement Martin (Figs 335, 337), a former pupil of Stainer's at Oxford, who had been organist of the private chapel at Dalkeith Palace, where there was a daily choral service. Two years later came the death of the veteran suborganist, George Cooper, and with a sort of easy inevitability Martin took his place, becoming organist on Stainer's retirement in 1888 (but continuing to train the boys) and, by now Sir George Martin, dying in post in 1916. For the rest of Stainer's time, he did most of the work, playing for half the services and taking all the boys' practices, and he was an excellent voice-trainer, able to meet the demands of the building's unique acoustic:

> The tone emitted by these forty picked boys is tremendously shrill. But, with all its shrillness, there is none of the clatter of the forced 'chest' register so common with untrained boys. It is loud singing, but not shouting.[18]

This might well be a description of the current 'St Paul's sound'.

Thus Stainer's man was installed in one of the two positions vital to the choir's success: the other was soon to be filled by an ardent supporter, who almost out-Stainered him in his enthusiasm for all things modern. Having inherited the Revd W. C. Fynes Webber as succentor, Stainer tried to influence him by placing copies of Gounod and other similar composers in the library, but he was not to be moved. He retired on 25 March 1876, and, Easter falling late that year, the new succentor had five anthems by Gounod in the list in the ten days before Good Friday. William Sparrow Simpson was no outsider (pp. 424–5; Fig. 349), for he had been a minor canon since 1861 and had apparently been the first to suggest dividing the organ either side of the choir, the position it still occupies. Despite his long association with the cathedral – or because of it – he was full of ideas about the kind of music best suited to the grand, 'High Victorian' style of worship that was developing, and St Paul's became noted for colourful, expressive contemporary music, not without some complaint from those who preferred the old school of cathedral composers. He made sure that settings of the canticles and the communion service were restricted in number and used regularly according to a strict rota; but the repertory of anthems was extensive, those appropriate to a particular season being sung only once a year, so most of the choir's weekly full rehearsal would perforce be spent on these. He enjoyed excellent relations with the choir, in contrast to the rather harsh Canon Gregory, who famously promised that if a choirman fell down dead on the cathedral steps his widow would be fined for his non-attendance. Sparrow Simpson enjoyed putting his views into print, just like Stainer, and every two years he published a report with a complete catalogue of the music cur-

rently in use, which he would post free of charge to any interested party; and it is almost certain that other musical foundations were influenced thereby, for much Gounod, Spohr and Mendelssohn came into use elsewhere. Stainer was adamant that without Sparrow Simpson's influence the reforms desired by the chapter would have been difficult or impossible to achieve,[19] for friction between succentor and organist could have rendered the best plans worthless.

Stainer's honourable place in the history of St Paul's is secure. He was a truly inspired and inspiring musician, a devout churchman, famously good company and above all an excellent administrator. His and Sparrow Simpson's successors, supported by Canon Henry Scott Holland, who had been appointed the first-ever residentiary canon-precentor on Belli's death in 1886, consolidated and extended what had been set in place. From 1889, the communion service on St Paul's Day was enhanced by settings with orchestral accompaniment by native composers or adapted from continental settings of the mass, as was the Advent performance of *The Last Judgement*, which in due course was replaced by Brahms's *German Requiem* or (as today) Handel's *Messiah*. The daily repertory was kept up-to-date, with such classics as *Harwood in A flat*, *Noble in B minor* and *Stanford in C* introduced as soon as they were published; and Martin's adaptation of Palestrina's masses and his editing of other 'early music' were signs of a new trend. The boys were well taught in school, and enjoyed excellent relations with their choirmaster, famously photographed playing cricket with them on the school's roof-top playground (Fig. 339). Charles Macpherson (a former chorister appointed in 1895) was music master in the school and suborganist, and gradually took over the day-to-day choir training as Martin grew older.

Others were growing older too, for several of the men appointed in 1873 were still in the choir, becoming inefficient and cantankerous with age. The problem of freehold vicars choral had returned to haunt the chapter, Goss (died 1880) and Stainer (retired 1888) having been succeeded by singers active in the choir who could remain until death or terminal incapacity. Only in 1931 were cathedral freeholds abolished. What made the problem more obvious was that the boys now had holidays for a week after Christmas and Easter (from 1896), having been granted a complete month's summer holiday ten years earlier, so that the men were singing on their own much more often.

The arrival of the self-confessedly unmusical Dean Inge in 1911 had little immediate effect on the choir; nor did the outbreak of war in August 1914, as many of the men were too old to enlist. The daily round of services continued, as did most of the great festivals with orchestra, though the special music in Advent (and the Sunday evening services) had to be cancelled after the imposition of the blackout in 1915. But a sudden exodus of men in 1916 caused a drastic rearrangement, with the singing on Mondays and Saturdays left entirely to the boys so that the available men could be concentrated on Sundays and the other four weekdays. The full choir's repertory was much reduced, and though the boys rapidly learned suitable anthems, the canticles were nearly always sung to chants. It was while the boys were singing one Monday morning that there was a direct hit on the telegraph office 150 yards from the cathedral: they calmly carried on, which so impressed the dean that he 'went round to the choir house to thank the boys for their courage'.[20] Martin died in 1916 and Macpherson was immediately appointed to succeed him, with Stanley Marchant of St Peter's, Eaton Square becoming suborganist.

The choir was more or less complete again by February 1919, but recovery was slow. The choir school had to be closed several times owing to illness, including two outbreaks of diphtheria in 1921.[21] The men's salaries had not kept pace with wartime inflation, and several of the non-freeholders were kept on after retiring age, this presumably being easier than trying to replace them. The day-to-day music appeared both repetitive and perfunctory, the 'men-only' services being especially dreary, with canticles sung to Anglican chant and sometimes a couple of verses of a hymn doing duty as the anthem. More attention seemed to be lavished on the special services with orchestra: the *Requiems* of Brahms and Mozart had become the usual choice for the Advent service, and additionally on 23 December 1924 the first and second parts of Bach's *Christmas Oratorio* were given with orchestra, with 'Come, Jesu, come' thrown in for good measure. By the mid 1920s a new succentor, the Revd M. F. Foxell, was beginning to give the repertoire a more up-to-date look. While this chiefly involved his removal of virtually all the remaining Gounod and Stainer, and a great deal of Mendelssohn, Spohr and Sullivan, he also introduced early numbers of *Tudor Church Music*, newly published in octavo by Oxford University Press.

The cathedral had survived the Great War with its musical programme substantially intact and with the choir once more at full strength. The condition of the building was another matter, and an emergency in peacetime dealt the cathedral's music a blow which wartime had failed to inflict, for at the end of March 1925 all weekday morning services were suspended, except on Good Friday and Christmas Day, to allow work to proceed on underpinning the piers of the dome. Not even the patronal festival was exempt at first, the festival communion service with orchestra being cancelled altogether in 1926. Choirstalls were set up in the nave, and the grand organ was re-erected down there in the north aisle, the small 'Willis-on-wheels' which had been purchased in 1881 doing duty meanwhile (Fig. 342). Fortunately the grand organ sounded well in its new location, and Macpherson would have been glad to play it again and to see the restoration of the Choral Eucharist on St Paul's Day in 1927. Sadly, he died on 28 May of that year, Marchant being appointed at once in his place, with a former chorister, Douglas Hopkins, becoming suborganist. With the work on the dome completed much more quickly than anyone expected, organ and choir were back in their rightful places by July 1930,[22] the occasion being marked by a splendid series of festival communion services, sung to *Macpherson in E flat*, *Byrd (Mass for five voices)* and *Vaughan Williams in G minor*, the last two in English versions. The series was rounded off by a concert performance of Bach's *Mass in B minor*, a significant innovation, though concerts were to remain rare events for another forty years or so.

Somewhat surprisingly and perhaps as a consequence of the dean's lack of interest in anything that smacked of liturgical innovation, the daily morning choral services were restored in full in 1930, at a time when they were being whittled down in most other cathedrals; but not without some difficulty, as the men had meanwhile found other uses for their time, and the BBC was beginning to be a fruitful source of casual employment. There were soon to be changes, however, for Inge retired in September 1934. His successor, Dean Matthews, was aware of the cathedral's noble traditions, but though 'the worship was beautiful and dignified [and] the music...maintained the high standard which had been set by Stainer, Martin and Macpherson, many felt a lack of warmth and fellowship in the services'.[23] It fell to the new dean

to appoint a new headmaster to the choir school, and to break the long tradition of internal appointments in the selection of a new organist.

In the Revd Albert Jessop Price, appointed headmaster in 1937, the dean and chapter found a disciplinarian of awesome reputation, whose reform of the school extended to such details as the boys' uniform, where flannel suits replaced Etons on weekdays and ruffs replaced Eton collars. The new dean had already appointed a new organist. Marchant was becoming seriously affected by arthritis and resigned in 1936 to become principal of the Royal Academy of Music.[24] His recommendation that his assistant Douglas Hopkins be appointed his successor was not supported by the succentor and the retiring headmaster, and in any event there seemed to be a need for a fresh approach to the music. After three other candidates[25] had been interviewed and rejected, the appointment went to John Dykes Bower, only thirty-one years of age but already highly experienced.[26]

He made significant changes to the choir's repertoire, bringing in more Stanford and Wood and the products of contemporary organist-composers, but also reviving music of earlier generations, including anthems by Byrd, Hassler and Palestrina, some sung in the original Latin. Stainer was totally out of fashion. Two elderly vicars choral were persuaded to surrender their freeholds in 1937 and another died in 1938, but the sole remaining freeholder, the octogenarian alto Henry Dutton, proved impossible to dislodge and died in office on Easter Day 1948. With this one exception, the men's average age was lower than for some years and their standard higher. There were regular weekly broadcasts of evensong, and the choir sang at the Coronation in 1937 and at a concert in Westminster Abbey on 21 June 1938 during the National Festival of Modern Music. A London music festival in the spring of 1939 culminated in a concert in St Paul's in which the cathedral choir was joined by those of Westminster Abbey, the Chapel Royal and the Temple Church to give a programme entitled 'Four centuries of cathedral music', which included works by Weelkes, Purcell, Greene, Samuel Wesley and Wood, the omission of the late nineteenth century being typical of current taste.

The boys returned from their summer holiday on 27 August 1939, but on 3 September they made a hasty departure for Cornwall, in anticipation of the declaration of war against Germany: a proposal to disband the choir school in the event of war had already been rejected by the chapter. Their removal to Truro Cathedral School was part of HM Government's scheme to remove the population of large cities to places of safety. By the end of 1940 Dykes Bower was in the RAF, with Marchant recalled from retirement to play whenever the suborganist was at Truro with the boys. There were rumours that at least three cathedrals were 'contemplating closing their choir schools as a measure of economy',[27] and in such a climate the resolve of the dean and chapter to persevere with the arrangements at Truro seemed all the more praiseworthy. In contrast, Westminster Abbey's choristers were disbanded in the autumn of that year. The boys did not sing with the Truro choir, except on Sundays, when they sat in the canons' stalls behind the lay-clerks. During the week the two cathedrals' choristers sang on different days, and the St Paul's repertory was kept alive after a fashion by having the boys sing the men's parts of full-choir settings, transposed up an octave as necessary.

Meanwhile, at St Paul's the men faithfully continued to sing the services, morning and evening, seven days a week; but problems began to arise from the call-up of the younger men, and in the

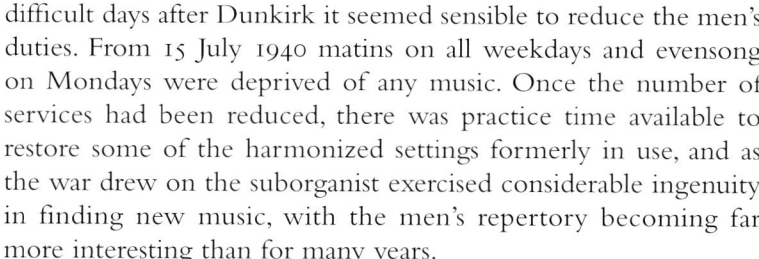

338. *A Hymn for Peace*, from George Martin's *Autograph Hymn Tunes*, showing 'the Lord Mayor's Own' volunteers entering the cathedral prior to departure for the Transvaal, 1900. (SPCL)

339. Choirboys playing cricket on the roof of the old choir school in Carter Lane, probably in the 1950s. (GL)

difficult days after Dunkirk it seemed sensible to reduce the men's duties. From 15 July 1940 matins on all weekdays and evensong on Mondays were deprived of any music. Once the number of services had been reduced, there was practice time available to restore some of the harmonized settings formerly in use, and as the war drew on the suborganist exercised considerable ingenuity in finding new music, with the men's repertory becoming far more interesting than for many years.

The first warning of an air-raid came on the very day that war was declared, to be followed by many more. After evensong had been abandoned on two consecutive days, 3 and 4 October 1940, it was transferred to the crypt. When this was damaged by a bomb on 10 October (which put the grand organ out of action[28] and wrecked Bodley's reredos), services had to be transferred to St Dunstan's Chapel for a while, but for most of the war services continued to be held in the crypt to the accompaniment of Dean Matthews's grand piano. Even the festival of the Sons of the Clergy was held there, the men singing to the accompaniment of a string orchestra in the suborganist's arrangements and orchestrations of anthems by Boyce or Croft and settings by Macpherson and E. W. Naylor, and thus the tradition of special music with orchestra was somewhat tenuously maintained.

The boys of St Mary's Choir School, Reigate sang on many occasions, from 1941 until the end of hostilities, and the cathedral's own choristers sometimes sang during school holidays if they lived near enough: after 1941 it became a regular arrangement for them to sing at Christmas and through Holy Week to Easter Sunday, and the *St Matthew Passion* was sung in 1944. The boys returned to London in May 1945, and on 8 May, the day of Germany's surrender, the full cathedral choir sang at no fewer than ten identical services of thanksgiving attended by some 35,000 people in all.

Though St Paul's had the basis of a full choir once again (unlike Westminster Abbey), there was much rebuilding to be done. The grand organ had to be restored; the number of choristers had dwindled to seventeen, who learned afresh some two hundred services and anthems in the first post-war year; and weekday morning services were not reintroduced until 1947, with the men

singing on their own on Monday and Thursday, and with matins on Wednesday and Friday replaced by short lunch-time services. The emphasis was on caution, safety and the restoration of pre-war standards, though sadly the orchestra never returned to the patronal festival, and the scale of the Sons of the Clergy festival was much reduced. *Sumsion in G* seemed a startling novelty when sung for the first time in 1946, and the *Collegium Regale* evening service of Howells took most of a term to learn, as did the *St Paul's Service* which he wrote for the cathedral choir.[29]

Membership of the choir had become quite an attractive proposition for aspiring young concert singers, for the attendance requirements had been considerably reduced during the war. The most famous recruit was the countertenor Alfred Deller, but there were many others of similar quality, the drawback being that all too frequently they did not appear in person, for it was the heyday of the BBC Third Programme and the Royal Festival Hall. Despite this problem, which had reached epidemic proportions by the 1960s, the choir was in great demand for broadcasts and recordings in the late 1940s and for some years afterwards: a tour of the United States and Canada in the autumn of 1953 found the St Paul's choir at the height of its fame and capabilities. The tour fell conveniently in Coronation year, though its true purpose was to commemorate the building of the American Memorial Chapel in St Paul's. The choir arrived in New York on 29 September, and began the tour with an opening service in the cathedral of St John the Divine, going on to give forty-one concerts and finally appearing at Carnegie Hall before returning to Britain. An important dual precedent had been set, of the regular choir's extended absence and the entrusting of its duties to visiting substitutes, now an accepted feature of the routine of most cathedral establishments.

Post-war plans included the widening of Carter Lane, with the attendant demolition of the choir school.[30] The new school at the east end of the cathedral included the tower of St Augustine's, Watling Street and was eventually opened in May 1967, its construction an act of faith in a decade when all sorts of traditions were being questioned (Fig. 340; p. 446). It still housed only the thirty-eight choristers when the trend elsewhere was for their

340. The east end in 1989 looking south from the churchyard, with the tower of Wren's St Augustine Watling Street and the new choir school designed by the Architects Co-Partnership, 1962–7

341. Portable organ ('Willis on wheels') being hauled across the cathedral, *c.* 1965. (SPCFA)

incorporation into larger schools. Nor was this the only respect in which the cathedral's music seemed old-fashioned, repertoire and performance practice having changed little from the pre-war years, with secular concerts in the cathedral completely unheard of. The organ had not really recovered from wartime upheavals and would soon need major attention once again. When both dean and organist retired at the end of the year, it was inevitable that their successors would wish to make significant changes.

Dykes Bower's successor was Christopher Dearnley, organist of Salisbury Cathedral, who took up his duties early in 1968. He was a noted proponent of both eighteenth-century and contemporary music, had made several acclaimed recordings with the Salisbury choir, and had revived the Southern Cathedrals Festival. He made an immediate impact on St Paul's, whose choir, the largest in the country, he regarded as a woefully under-used asset: its repertoire soon stretched from medieval to contemporary, with even the Victorians enjoying something of a revival. Concerts and recordings became a regular part of its routine. The chapter was strongly in favour, and in the summer of 1971 requested a report from the organist 'on the future development and use of the choir in respect of more frequent performances in the cathedral of major works, concerts outside and occasional tours abroad'.[31] The decisions taken then have provided a blueprint for the cathedral's music ever since.

The practice of performing large-scale works with orchestra and augmented choir in Advent (*Messiah*) and Holy Week[32] was confirmed, and on Sundays in July the cathedral choir would sing classical masses with orchestral accompaniment, thus reviving the former use of orchestral settings at the patronal festival but at a time more convenient to worshippers. There would be occasional tours abroad, the first of which duly took place in 1972, and regular concerts. An Advent carol service was instituted, and the historic festival of the Sons of the Clergy reinvigorated by the participation of choirs from other cathedrals. The strain was beginning to show, however, as there was still only the one weekly full rehearsal, Dearnley was increasingly occupied with planning the largest remodelling of the grand organ since 1872,[33] and the suborganist, Harry Gabb, was also organist of the Chapel Royal. When Gabb retired in 1974, Dearnley secured as his replacement Barry Rose, a choir trainer of unique quality who had created a first-rate choir at the new Guildford Cathedral: he gradually took over the boys' training, a situation formally recognized in 1978 by his being styled 'Master of the Choir'. These were golden years, with the organist exploring the riches of the rebuilt organ, heard nationwide at the Queen's Silver Jubilee Service in 1977, and a new polish and discipline being applied to the choir. John Scott, a brilliant young organist from St John's College, Cambridge, was appointed part-time assistant organist.

Sadly, it all turned very sour. The boys were doing so much outside work (not always with the chapter's prior agreement) that their education seemed to be suffering; the organization of tours and recordings was called into question;[34] and Rose, though popular with the choir, was proving a difficult colleague, whose relations with the organist had deteriorated. He seemed to be following an agenda entirely his own and was 'admonished' by the dean for a 'disgraceful' speech at a choir school prize-giving.[35] A severe financial crisis in 1981 caused further tensions. The number

342. The choir in front of the baldacchino

of vicars choral was reduced to twelve, augmented by six part-timers on Sundays, with matins on Saturday the only surviving weekday morning service and evensong on Thursday deprived of music altogether for a term, until the precentor (Canon Collins) raised enough money for it to be sung by six men in the north transept chapel. A lengthy wrangle (May 1983–March 1984) over the terms of a proposed recording by the Decca company and a complaint (not the first) of the making of an unauthorized recording resulted in the dean and chapter's unanimous decision to dismiss Rose. He left St Paul's in the summer of 1984 amid considerable public controversy.[36] Christopher Dearnley took charge of the choir once more, with John Scott appointed his full-time assistant.

Both men and boys resented the manner of Rose's departure, which placed Dearnley in an unenviable position. He seemed to have lost his self-confidence, and he was glad to let Scott take over most of the choir-training, with such conspicuous success that he was the natural choice to succeed him as 'Organist and Director of Music' in 1990. Dearnley retired to Australia, returning to St Paul's in the spring of 2000 for a memorable recital on the organ he had done so much to enhance. His death in December of that year was a shock, and his memorial service in St Paul's a moving tribute to a modest and deeply religious man, whose influence on the musical establishment had in its way been as significant as that of Stainer a century earlier.

John Scott has been tireless in encouraging composers to write for the cathedral choir, and the list includes Andrew Carter, Patrick Gowers, Jonathan Harvey, Philip Moore and John Tavener. He also has a deep affection for the established classics, as evinced by a series of seven recordings of English anthems: a notable project, completed in 2000, was the recording of the complete Psalter. The lack of an extended rehearsal for the full choir can cause problems, the men only arriving half an hour before each service, and often a difficult new composition is best tackled by scheduling it for a recording session. There has been a succession of talented soloists among the boys, including Anthony Way, who achieved national fame through his appearance in the televised version of Joanna Trollope's *The Choir*: the choir school has been expanded to include not only dayboys but also girls under the age of seven, though as yet there has been no move to establish a girls' choir.

The choir's singing is uniquely shaped by the need to produce a sound that will get out of the chancel into the dome and nave, but the recordings made during the last fifty years contain quite different versions of the 'St Paul's sound'. The constant factor has been the mature, professional quality of the men's singing, though it is much better blended and balanced nowadays. In contrast, there has been quite a change in the boys' tone, though they have always had to sing quite loudly. The boys 'just sang' under Dykes Bower, but Dearnley created a very thin and bright sound, presumably aiming at the maximum possible clarity. This was developed by Rose into a full-bodied tone which yet retained considerable brightness, and this sound has been retained and refined, more relaxed and mellow now than a few years ago, but no less powerful. The demands on the choir for special services are heavier than ever, with December's round of carol services for outside bodies especially exhausting, and St Paul's is still the favoured place for events of national mourning or rejoicing.[37] The cathedral's programme of music involves organ, choral and orchestral concerts, though sadly the gatherings of church choirs are no more, except for the Royal School of Church Music's London area festival in alternate years. At the heart of St Paul's is still the daily round of worship, and the music offered by the cathedral choir is perhaps as fine as it has ever been.

38

THE LIBRARY
AND ARCHIVES TO 1897

Nigel Ramsay

The recorded history of the cathedral's library begins in the twelfth century, with the mention of a chapter dignitary, the master of the schools, who was charged with the custody of books of secular and divine learning and had a wider responsibility for schools in the city (p. 27). Master Durand, a canon by 1086, is the first known holder of the office, which was granted in the 1110s or 1120s to his successor, Hugh.[1] Hugh and his successors were directed to list the books and place a copy of the list in the cathedral treasury; he was also entrusted with the keys to cupboards beside the altar, and so it can be presumed that at least some of the books were kept in these.

The nature of the cathedral's book collection at this time can only be guessed at. The earliest surviving book-lists are of 1245 (revised in 1255) and 1295, and these contain service books and certain other precious or ancient books that needed to be kept in the treasury.[2] A handful of them probably pre-dated the Norman Conquest: a psalter with interlinear English translation, and a psalter described as English and old, as well as the very old psalter of Saint Erkenwald. Others were gifts from more recent bishops of London. Of 'books of learning', little is known: such books were first listed in full in 1458 (Fig. 343), when the twelfth- and thirteenth-century collection had doubtless already suffered losses. In common with other English cathedrals in the late eleventh century, St Paul's would have acquired a collection of patristic texts. Probable survivors from the library of that time include three works by St Augustine: *De verbis domini* and his commentaries on Psalms 1–50 (written perhaps in a Canterbury hand) and Psalms 51–100. These all date from the early to mid twelfth century and were certainly in the library by 1458.[3] Some of the twelfth-century canons were doubtless benefactors of their library. The list of service books made in 1245 shows Master Alberic (canon *c.*1148–62) as donor of a missal, antiphonary and breviary, and a book of his (*le livre mestre albri*) at St Paul's was used in the later years of the century as the source for a translation into Anglo-Norman of a collection of miracles of the Virgin Mary.[4] Alberic was probably responsible for a recension of a well-known handbook of classical mythology (p. 153); if so, the cathedral's collection is likely to have included a copy.

Almost nothing is known about the ordering of the cathedral's muniments until late in the twelfth century. As soon as the cathedral's estates began to be distinguished from those of the bishop of London, in the mid tenth century (pp. 12–13), it is likely that the cathedral's canons would have started to treat some documents as pertaining to it rather than to the see of London – even if the two institutions' archives were still kept in one place (as was the case with some other English cathedrals in the early twelfth century). By 1127 the cathedral's muniments were housed in the treasury, and this was to continue to be their repository until the seventeenth century.[5] Many pre-Conquest documents were extant at the cathedral in the early twelfth century, but, as Kelly remarks, 'the known documents which seem to reflect genuine pre-Conquest title-deeds relate to estates which were controlled in 1086 by the bishop, as opposed to the canons', and 'one might speculate that the pre-Conquest title-deeds of the canons' lands were destroyed or otherwise lost'.[6] The matter is complicated by the cathedral having forged pre-Conquest title-deeds in the early twelfth century.[7] It is puzzling that at about this time the cathedral was nevertheless able to furnish ancient texts for transcription on to the flyleaves of one of its books – notably, a list of its estates and their obligations towards manning a ship, which unquestionably originated as a text no later than *c*.1000 (pp. 14–15). A few years later, in the mid twelfth century, the more significant step was taken of compiling a cartulary — a register based on the charters in the cathedral's possession. By good fortune, this survives as the first fifty-six leaves of *Liber L*.[8]

It was a peculiarity of St Paul's that some of the cathedral's dignitaries were late in gaining independent status, in part because of the power retained by the archdeacons. The office of precentor – responsible for the choir at St Paul's, and at other cathedrals often also serving as librarian – was not endowed until 1204 (p. 23). This must explain why at St Paul's responsibility for the books rested with the mastership of the schools, and passed to the chancellor when that office evolved into the chancellorship and was endowed *c*.1200. [9]

Within a few months of becoming dean in 1180, the very capable Ralph de Diceto,[10] accompanied by two canons, conducted a survey of the lands and churches belonging to the canons in common – the first such survey that is known. Diceto clearly believed in good record-keeping and while he was ready to resort to the old-fashioned method of entering copies of charters on blank leaves in a martyrology,[11] he also had two whole new registers made. The greater of these was in the fifteenth century designated *Liber B*, and the lesser *Liber C*. To judge from the bifolium that survives from *Liber B*, they were handsome and substantial volumes.[12] On one leaf there is a list of contents of the 1181 survey, a section of which is described as being 'about charters, placed in order or marked with such-and-such a mark'. Diceto ensured the charters were well arranged and the system of marks on them perhaps originated in his time, paralleling the system of symbols that he used in his historical compilations (p. 152). More certainly, he donated to the cathedral's collection of library and service books a psalter, homiliaries and martyrologies, his own chronicle and his postills (commentaries or lectures) on the books of Ecclesiasticus and Wisdom.[13]

Several canons in Diceto's time were also benefactors to the library – notably his co-adjutors in the survey, Henry of Northampton and Robert de Clifford. Significantly, his survey and registers are known because they entered the chapter archive: Diceto may have felt constrained to place them there, whereas later deans, more assured of their authority, retained such records for the deanery archive, which, though never mentioned, was undoubtedly substantial. The mid fifteenth-century account of books in the cathedral archive, which includes *Libri B* and *C* also features a *Liber F*, which was a register of Diceto and four successor deans, but it makes no mention of the eight registers known to have been made by deans.[14] Such registers must have formed part of the dean's archive, and were essential for the efficient administration of the cathedral and its estates.

Archivally, the principal task facing Diceto's successors was to keep up to date in the sorting-out and ordering of the documentation that resulted from developments in its ordinances and liturgy and from the proliferation of chantries with their own endowments. St Paul's conservatism and need for record-keeping must have been heightened by the prevalence of absentee prebendaries, who would not have entrusted the running of the cathedral to the residentiary canons, if their own interests risked being threatened. Many payments were made for so many years that they came to be seen as unalterable rights. The office of bookbinder (*ligator librorum*), for example, which may have dated back to the early thirteenth century and was unquestionably a sinecure

by the mid fourteenth century, yielded its holder a considerable annual income[15] and endured until at least 1556–7 (p. 418).

It is always tempting to link archival initiatives with the impact of individuals or events. *Liber L*, the cathedral's first cartulary, might thus be seen as part of the canons' response to the disastrous London fire of 1136. There is, however, no discernible trigger for the compilation in 1241–2 of the next cartulary, the *Liber Pilosus* or 'hairy book' (so called from the skin of its binding).[16] The dean at the time was either Geoffrey de Lucy or the obscure William de Ste Mère Eglise III. Yet the next dean, Henry of Cornhill (1243–54), probably had a major impact on the archives. His compilation of a coherent body of statutes for St Paul's reveals him as a thorough investigator of the cathedral's records,[17] and he was presumably also responsible for the detailed inventory of the non-archival contents of the treasury – the cathedral's vestments, plate, books and other valuables – made in 1245 and the earliest to survive from St Paul's.[18]

Subsequently, various attempts were made to search through the cathedral's records and reduce to order their mass of often-contradictory statements of practice. The aim was not so much to produce a new and consistent body of rules – that was not attempted until Dean Colet's day – as to record in a logical sequence the details that were discoverable. The 'able, ambitious and bookish'[19] Dean Ralph Baldock (1294–1304) made the most thoroughly researched set of statutes on these lines. He went back to pre-Conquest materials to get to the beginnings of things, and incorporated the ancient Rule of St Paul's, the fragment of a rule for canons of Carolingian origin.[20] Moreover, in April 1295 he carried out a 'visitation' of the treasury, listing its valuable contents.[21] The register in which one of the surviving copies of this record was written goes on to inventory the goods and endowments of a number of altars, chapels and chantry chapels, and continues with lists of *instrumenta* (charters and similar records) for a large number of the cathedral's estates. As successive manors were treated, this became less of a listing and more like a cartulary, more and more entire texts being included. Was Baldock himself the compiler? It certainly fits with what is known of his interests, and so it is he who has been declared to have misread an Old English charter and thus to have misattributed to a grant by King Cnut the cathedral's ownership of the church of Lambourn (Berks).[22] Extensive annotation to a psalter which he owned suggests a concern on his part to regularize his cathedral's liturgy (p. 120). Later, when he had become bishop of London (1304–13), Baldock is known to have presented to St Paul's a set of 'tables' (*tabulae*) with lists of bishops of London and deans of the cathedral.[23] He also showed his continuing attachment to it by the bequest of his enormous and miscellaneous collection of about 150 volumes:[24] a useful assortment of canon-law texts and commentaries, a little civil law, some scholastic theology with quite a few biblical commentaries, a little medicine and science, an illuminated Apocalypse, 'Bede in English', Henry of Huntingdon's chronicle, and, suggestively, a 'chronicle of Ralph Baldock'.[25] To judge from the library catalogue of 1458, the cathedral kept the theological books but rejected most of the legal works.

For the century after Baldock's time, it is harder to map out development in the library and the archives. No major accession to the cathedral's book collections is known, apart from the bequest by William de Tolleshunt (1329) and the gift by William Ravenstone (1358),[26] each to the almonry — benefactions which are puzzling because they do not directly square with what is known of the almoner's responsibilities for the choirboys and their schooling. Only part of Tolleshunt's legacy – books of grammar – was actually for the use of the boys, while books on logic, medicine and civil law were for lending to ex-pupils of the school.[27] Ravenstone's bequest was unequivocally for the almonry school, but many books in the collection were far over the heads of choirboys and cannot be explained away. Nothing is known of the later history of these books.

The archives must have increased enormously with annual accruals of manorial court rolls and account rolls, together with a growing number of chapter documents. Most of the latter have perished. Two may stand for a great many: a single surviving account of offerings received in May 1344,[28] and the contract for making some of the parts of the cathedral clock in 1344.[29] One residentiary canon, Roger of Waltham (pp. 164–6) worked through the 'books and memorials of the church' to compile a list of pittances.[30] Did he have anything to do with the making of a rather summary 'Inventory of the church's charters and muniments kept in cupboards'?[31]

FROM 1400 TO 1540

The corporate life of the St Paul's chapter sank to a low ebb in the early years of the fifteenth century. In October 1400 there was only one residentiary canon.[32] From 1406, the deanery was held by Thomas More, who cared deeply for his cathedral (pp. 35–6), but who retired from the personal exercise of his office in about 1417, leaving Reginald Kentwood, archdeacon of London, to deputize for him in chapter. No other dignitary was then in residence.[33] Yet this was not a period of inactivity for St Paul's library and muniments. The chapter clerk, a notary called William Godman, began a full record of chapter decisions, with copies of related documents, which ran from the time he took up office in 1411 until 1447.[34] It is thanks to this survival that the composition and activities of the chapter can be so closely gauged in these years, as for no other period in the Middle Ages. Dean More and his successors doubtless continued to keep registers of their own: More's register survived into the 1650s,[35] while a volume called *Liber AB* served as a register of the years 1400 onwards.[36] Kentwood may have had a care for the library, for he once gave a book to the English hospital in Rome, and he bequeathed a collection of books of civil and canon law to All Souls College, Oxford.[37] From some time around 1400 a paper register was compiled with summaries of dean and chapter charters that are so full that the book might almost be described as a cartulary.[38]

In the 1440s and 1450s the chapter's records and library were overhauled and added to on such a scale that they can fairly be described as transformed. These changes were principally the achievements of two men: Walter Sherrington, prebendary from 1440 until his death in 1449, and Thomas Lisieux, prebendary and residentiary canon from 1436, and dean from 1441 to 1456. The two men were friends, and part of a small circle of ecclesiastics centred on St Paul's: Sherrington's executors included Lisieux and the prebendaries (perhaps already residentiaries) Nicholas Sturgeon and William Brewster, as well as Roger Mersh, once keeper of the rolls and registers of the duchy of Lancaster.[39] Lisieux's testamentary supervisor was Thomas Kemp, bishop of London, while his executors included both Brewster and Mersh.[40] Neither Sherrington – a royal clerk who rose to be chancellor of the duchy of Lancaster (1431–49) and left over £4,000 in gold and money at his death[41] – nor Lisieux was himself an outstanding scholar, but each sought to encourage scholar-

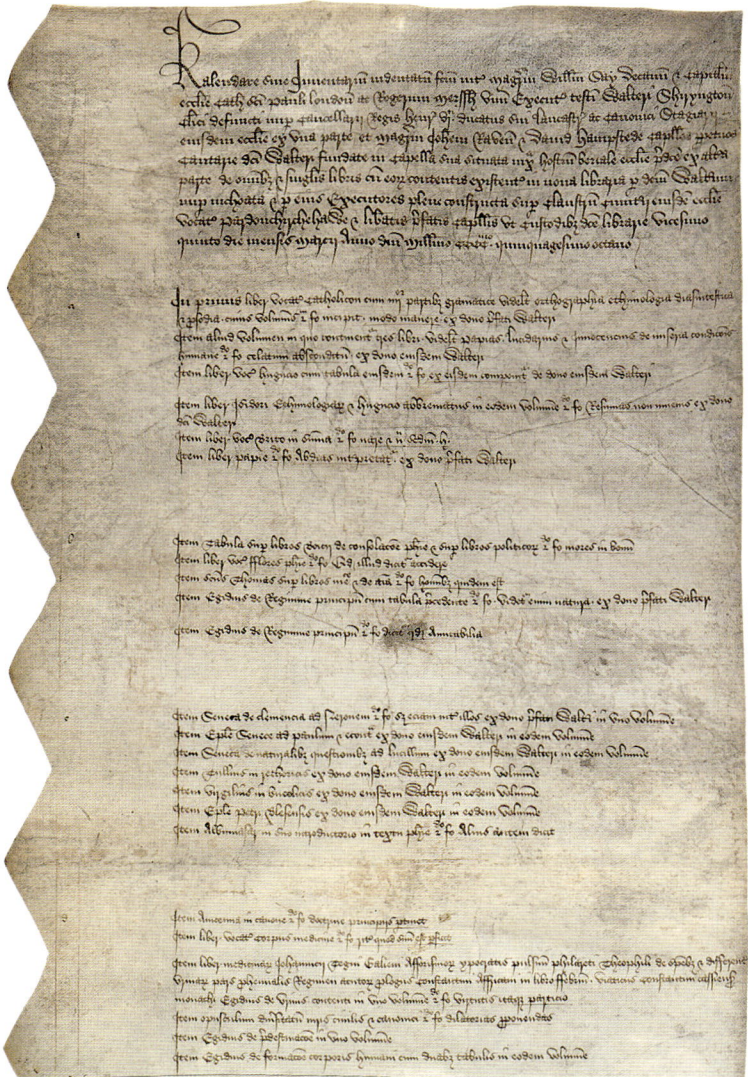

343. Catalogue of Sherrington's library, drawn up in indenture-form on Lady Day 1458 (BL, Cotton Charter xiii. 11)

ship. By the 1440s, new libraries were seen as valuable adjuncts to cathedrals, as Archbishop Chichele demonstrated by building a library room at Canterbury, and Sherrington decided to perform the same service at St Paul's. He was probably motivated by the wish to improve the learning of the London clergy generally, this being a particular concern of the bishops of London from about this time. He can hardly have expected the residentiary canons to be frequent readers, while the minor canons presumably had their own library.[42] John Stow later recorded an inscription which invoked prayers for Sherrington 'which in his life began this library, to the edificacion of clerkes and incresen of cristen faith'.[43] Even if the new library only served the cathedral's wider community, that was itself to be numbered in the hundreds, including the minor canons, vicars, chantry priests and incumbents of the St Paul's churches in the city (pp. 33–4). Even the chapter's rent collectors were sometimes chaplains.[44] Simply by being available to these people, the library would have been of use to a potential readership as large as that of the Guildhall Library, its nearby lay or public counterpart, set up in about 1425.

Sherrington made his new library into a permanent institution by linking it to an endowed chantry, for which he obtained the Crown's permission in 1446.[45] As elsewhere, the architectural link between the library and a chapel nearby was a feature of the scheme.[46] The chantry chapel was to be close to the north door

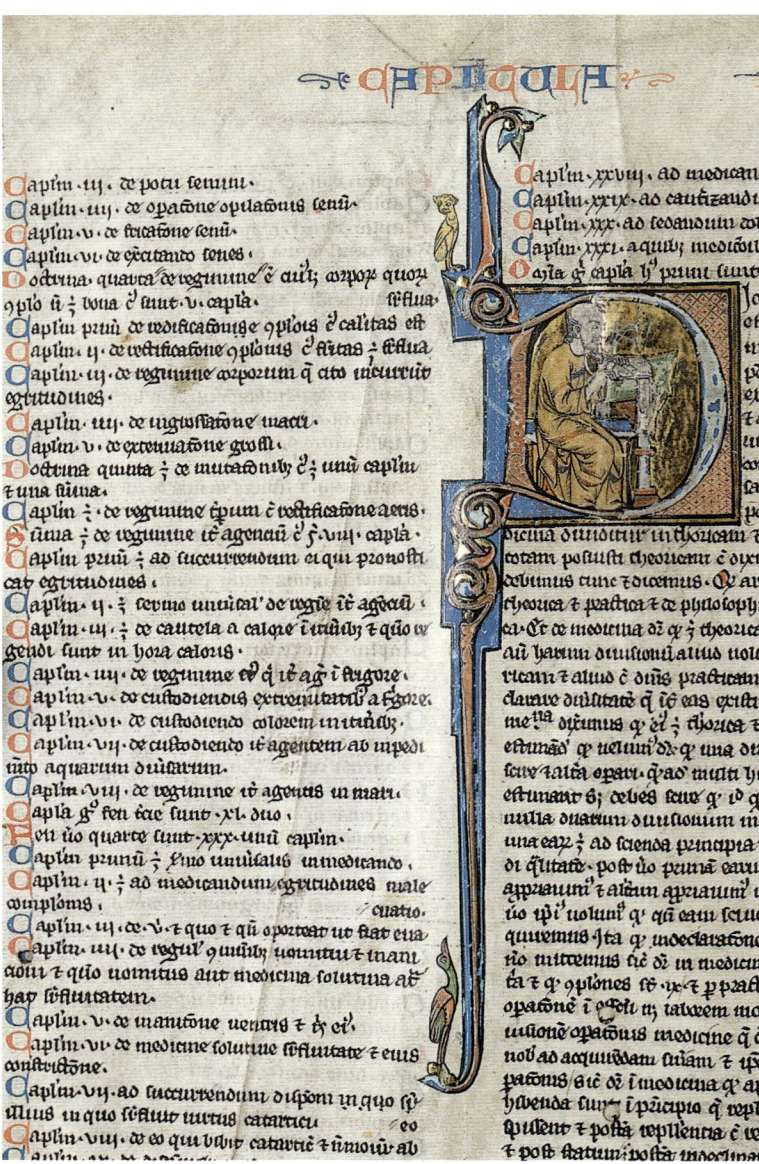

344. Avicenna at his desk, from a fourteenth-century manuscript of his *Canon of Medicine* given to the cathedral library in 1451 by Henry IV's physician, Dr John Somerset, who had purchased it from the rector of St Michael Wood Street. (SPCL, MS 3)

As early as 1452, Thomas Warde, doctor of canon law, a residentiary canon, bequeathed five books of canon law to the 'new library'.[49] However, it may not have commenced operations until March 1458, when an indented list of its contents was drawn up, as required in its ordinances.[50] That catalogue includes twenty-four books given by Sherrington – mostly biblical and psalter texts, the biblical commentaries of Nicholas of Lyre and guides for the priesthood such as John of Genoa's *Catholicon*, John de Burgo's *Pupilla oculi* and Ranulph Higden's *Speculum curatorum*. It lists 161 volumes (containing many more individual works), classed by subject matter under different letters of the alphabet: A for grammar (six volumes), B for philosophy (five volumes), C for classical literature (seven volumes), D for medicine (six volumes), F and G for history (eight volumes in all), H, I, K and L for biblical commentaries (forty volumes in all), followed by patristic and later commentators and theologians in presses M–S, and concluding with canon law in T (twelve volumes) and civil law in U (nine volumes). The omission of E was perhaps because it was hoped to obtain more books on medicine or history. The presses were perhaps along just one side of the room, and perhaps took the form of long sloping desks, fitted with a shelf below with space for up to at least seventeen volumes (the number in press O).[51]

345. Tripartite guide to the St Paul's chapter records, compiled in 1447 by Dean Thomas Lisieux. It is open at the start of a list of the records in location order. (GL, St Paul's collection, MS 25511)

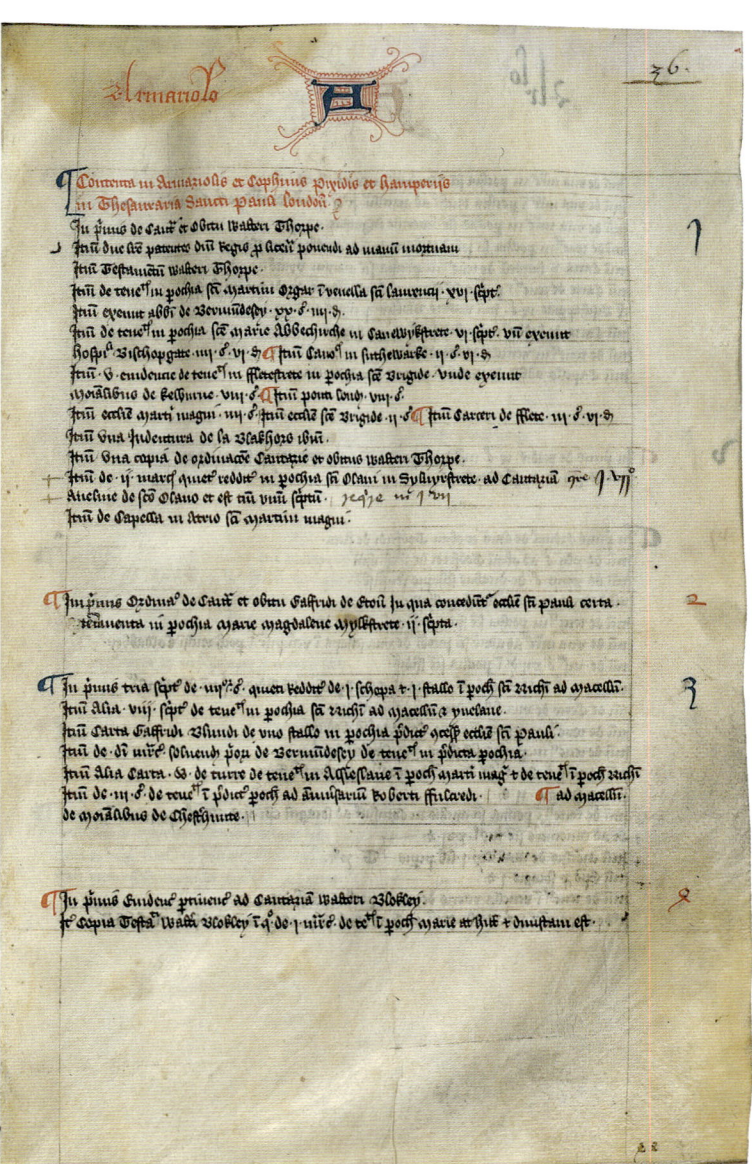

of the cathedral, and two chaplains were to serve both this and the library which was built above the east walk of the Pardon Churchyard cloister (pp. 33–4). Like the nearly contemporary libraries built in similar positions at Wells and Salisbury cathedrals, Sherrington's library was probably long and narrow. Since this side of the cloister was left intact by Protector Somerset in 1549,[47] the structure probably survived until the 1630s. An adjacent room, between the library and the chapel, seems to have been intended as the chaplains' permanent office. They were to be graduates of any faculty of the universities of Oxford or Cambridge. Sherrington's executors saw the work to completion and on 12 December 1457 sealed the ordinances.[48] The chaplains were to keep the library open for two periods every day (6 a.m. to the ninth hour after high mass, and from 1 p.m. to the end of compline, between 25 March and 8 September; and from sunrise to the ninth hour after high mass, and again from 1 p.m. to the end of compline or until sunset, between 8 September and 25 March). The books were doubtless to be kept chained; loans are stated to be possible, for a term of up to six months, but only if approved by the dean and chapter and upon the giving of sufficient surety.

The new library room was not large (and the chapter's most precious and ancient books remained in the treasury), but it contained a well-balanced collection with interesting rarities. On a visit in 1435 or 1436, Aeneas Silvius Piccolomini (the future Pope Pius II) believed that he was shown an ancient Latin version of Thucydides.[52] In 1451 Henry VI's physician, John Somerset, donated an early fourteenth-century copy of Avicenna's 'Canon of Medicine' (Fig. 324), and probably also a copy of the book of surgery of Guy de Chauliac which William Worcestre read at St Paul's in 1464.[53] The theologian and polymath Thomas Gascoigne (d. 1458) – a book lover who gave books to half a dozen libraries – donated at least three books to St Paul's (homilies of Gregory the Great, *De Vitiis et Virtutibus* of William Peraldus, and works by Hugh and Richard of St Victor, together with further homilies of Gregory the Great).[54] Only one of Gascoigne's donations appears in the 1458 catalogue. A few years later the precentor, Thomas Graunt (d. 1474), reinforced the new library's standing with a gift of at least seven books.[55] Three of these were in the treasury when its books were listed in 1486, and so the new library may have been running out of space for new accessions. There is no general catalogue after that of 1458, but comparison with two selective lists of 1535 × 40 and *c.*1622 suggests that the cathedral's total stock of books almost doubled between 1458 and *c.*1540, to 340 volumes.[56]

Sherrington's reorganization of the library had its counterpart in Lisieux's rationalization of the muniments. In 1447 Lisieux inventoried his cathedral's records with a thoroughness without match in medieval England (Fig. 345). He worked through the loose documents, cartularies and registers kept in the treasury, as well as the overflow stored below certain altars. Such of the documents as needed it were endorsed with their cupboard letter and *cophinus* or pyx number (Ai, etc.; with many variants as supplements), and such of the books as needed it were foliated, leaf by leaf. Then – and this is the most impressive part of the operation – he compiled a tripartite guide to the records, in which he first listed the documents in strict alphabetical order, with references to their location, then listed the same documents in location order, and finally set out the contents of each of seventeen registers, *Liber A* or *Pilosus* being described in particular detail. For good measure, Lisieux also produced a full list of the cathedral's chantries, with references to the books in which they are mentioned, and an alphabetical list of people commemorated on obit days, with references to the original instrument for each day's distribution. Lisieux's guide is an exceptionally thorough piece of work, still entirely usable and – in as much as it offers a guide to registers and documents that have since been lost – of enormous historical value.[57] He was a records manager to his fingertips, and may have been responsible for other pieces of administrative clarification, such as the list of accounts that had to be rendered at St Paul's annually, quarterly or at other times.[58]

Just as the new library attracted further gifts and readers, so the excellence of the archive's ordering caused searches to be made in it for materials that might otherwise have been sought elsewhere. St Paul's had, for instance, duplicates of documents relating to religious houses such as St Helen's, Bishopsgate, and Elsing Spital (within Cripplegate) that were under its supervision, as well as copies of many documents relating to the see of London. In a late fifteenth-century ecclesiastical lawyer's compilation, transcripts of some thirteenth-century charters are accompanied by the note: 'All these and many others, with seals, concerning the church of Ardeleye, can be found and seen in the archives of St Paul's,

London, in container (*scrinium*) U5'.[59] Late fifteenth-century St Paul's was well set up, so far as its library and archive were concerned.

The deanship of John Colet (1505–19; Fig. 19) may or may not have seemed to contemporaries to be a time of intellectual resurgence for St Paul's: it is very hard to assess his impact, such is the dearth of contemporary chapter records. His immediate predecessor, Robert Sherborn, was a capable administrator and a bibliophile who had been secretary or scribe of Oxford University, and in 1496, when in Rome, had been asked to take over and reform the English hospital there. At St Paul's, both he and Colet maintained the customary dean's register.[60] A year after Colet became dean, he carried out the usual visitation of the churches and manors of the common estate, and an account roll of this time is annotated in his hand.[61] In 1507 he provided a new parchment book into which the ordinances and deeds of the confraternity of Jesus in the crypt of St Paul's were to be copied.[62] For the better governance of the chantry priests, he read through the cathedral statutes and gathered the relevant portions into a small book which he placed in the choir.[63] Potentially of greater importance was the wholly new set of statutes for the cathedral that he drew up in 1518, but – no doubt because he died the next year – these were never put into force.[64] Of his significance for the cathedral's library, nothing can be discovered, save that in 1505–6 he lent manuscripts from it to his friend Erasmus.[65]

1540–1660

While during the religious upheaval of the 1530s, 1540s and 1550s, chantry chapels and elements of the choral staff were done away with, St Paul's, like other secular cathedrals, retained its staff intact and its statutes unaltered. The library needed supplementation, not replacement; and the process of adding printed books to its stock had begun long before the Reformation, perhaps even in the closing years of the fifteenth century. Certain books of canon law in the St Paul's library today are likely to have been at the cathedral for some five centuries, since they are early editions that cannot have been thought desirable acquisitions except when newly published.[66]

The archives were presumably disturbed as little as possible. Papal documents and perhaps some relating to the endowments of altars, lights and images may have been destroyed, yet St Paul's retains a greater number of medieval letters of indulgence than perhaps anywhere else in the British Isles,[67] and the documentation of its chantries is still extensive.[68] Archive maintenance seems to have been remarkably low down the list of priorities at all English cathedrals in the mid to late sixteenth century, and responsibility for the archive was allowed to pass to relatively junior staff. In such circumstances, title deeds and many other documents – especially if ancient and hard to understand – were likely to be left alone. At St Paul's, access to them seems to have passed to the sacrist and virgers, even though in principle the dean had charge of the muniments, then and for a further three centuries.[69] In September 1559 the former dean, Henry Cole, handed over to his successor, William May, certain 'Bookes and other writings appertayning to the Cathedral Church... and to the Deane onlye, and the Deane and Chapitor', but these were just thirteen volumes, at least half of them from the sixteenth century, comprising texts likely to be of immediate administrative value.[70]

Such neglect was not an option for the library. All English cathedrals were required to augment their libraries and, in 1549, to obtain within a year copies of the works of Saints Augustine, Basil, Gregory Nazianzen, Jerome, Ambrose, John Chrysostom, Cyprian and Theophylact, as well as Erasmus.[71] St Paul's already had many of these in manuscript. Printed editions were presumably intended, but records from this period are not sufficiently detailed for it to be possible to say whether these or any other books were acquired. The bookbinder continued to receive his annual fee of 13s. 4d. and 10d. a week commons until at least 1556–7. By 1570–1, he has disappeared and a new office makes its first appearance – that of library keeper (*custos bibliothecae*), with a salary of £4 13s. 4d. Its first two holders served also (and primarily) as the cathedral's sacrist.[72]

While the manuscript books were no longer relevant as contemporary reading matter, they began to be seen in a new light by scholars and collectors. 'The tyme hath bene, whan [London] hath had a great nombre of the noblest libraries in all Christendome', wrote the ex-Carmelite John Bale,[73] lamenting a process of disintegration to which he himself contributed by drawing attention to the rare texts that these libraries housed. In 1560, in a letter addressed to Archbishop Parker, he singled out at St Paul's the *Ymagines historiarum* of Ralph de Diceto (p. 152),[74] and within a few years this manuscript was being drawn on by William Harrison, a former schoolboy at St Paul's, for his 'Chronology'.[75] Before long it was removed to Lambeth Palace.[76] Parker (d. 1575) himself obtained from St Paul's at least one early and important manuscript of Anglo-Saxon laws.[77]

Two generations later, the cathedral's collections came under attack from a much more single-minded and unscrupulous collector of historical manuscripts, Sir Robert Cotton. He doubtless obtained access to both the library and the archives through his friendship with Patrick Young – royal librarian and prebendary of St Paul's (1621–52). Young himself was surely responsible for the fact that the largest number of survivors from the cathedral's medieval library are to be found at Aberdeen University Library,[78] to which they were bequeathed in 1624 by his friend Thomas Reid. The extent of Cotton's depredations cannot be ascertained, partly because (like Parker) he sought to cover his tracks by erasing ex-libris inscriptions and other signs of former ownership. It is not certain that any of the books among the Cotton collection is from St Paul's.[79] A dozen and more of the Cotton charters are demonstrably from St Paul's, but – as will be seen – most of these seem to have entered the Cotton library a generation after Sir Robert's death (1631). It is, however, certain that he obtained from the cathedral the thirteenth-century dish-base which had been cut down to serve as a tonsure plate; it is a unique survival of its kind (Fig. 12).[80]

In the early seventeenth century, awareness of the historical significance of the contents of English cathedral libraries and archives spread sufficiently that Crown action resulted and Patrick Young was commissioned to make lists. The poacher was now to act as gamekeeper.[81] A list for St Paul's is one of five that survive, all thought to date from 1622 or 1623.[82] It provides the fullest descriptions extant of the medieval manuscripts that remained in place: 195 books – still more than the 161 listed in 1458. John Stow had sadly reported that the cathedral library 'hath beene well furnished with faire written bookes in Vellem: but few. of them now do remaine there',[83] but Young's catalogue shows that he exaggerated. In 1626, when Thomas Roper was named library-keeper, he was specifically directed to keep an inventory of the volumes in his care.[84] He may even have been capable of reading the medieval manuscripts, for in 1634 he borrowed deeds from

the cathedral vestry.[85] Scholars continued to be given access to the older books and to the archives; but they now had to transcribe what interested them, and not seek to remove it. John Selden, in his *Historie of Tithes* (1618), cited an early copy in the St Paul's library of the collection of canons made by Ivo of Chartres,[86] and transcribed from the archives portions of a medieval roll with texts of pre-Conquest documents.[87] The roll has since been lost, but that may be no fault of Selden's, who did, however, obtain some archival items from St Paul's.[88] Episcopal concern for the safekeeping of the cathedral's archives, voiced in Richard Bancroft's visitation in 1598, was at last bearing fruit.[89]

The years of civil war and interregnum were far more devastating than the Reformation in their impact on both the library and the archives. The dissolution of the dean and chapter (1649, but realizing a policy intended since 1643: pp. 61–2) put the cathedral's goods at the mercy of its employees, as the canons and other prebendaries, with their monarchical and episcopal sympathies, felt it prudent to leave London. In 1648 many of the St Paul's books were removed to the library of Sion College, 'there to remayne for the publique use of the said College'.[90] A catalogue made on 13 March 1648 by the college's librarian lists 164 manuscripts and sixty-seven printed books from St Paul's.[91] Dean Barwick for a time read in the bishop of Durham's library, in London, and then went to stay with Sir Thomas Ersfield in Sussex, 'for in his house he had the use of a library well furnished with the writers of the Primitive Church, with which Mr Barwick most desired to converse'.[92]

The cathedral's archives were removed, in circumstances that remain obscure, into the charge of a legal official named John Reading. About 1655 the herald and antiquary William Dugdale (1605–86) chanced to meet Reading, and, in Dugdale's words,

> he freindly invited Mr Dugdale to his house at Scriveners' Hall, (neere Silver street) promising to show him divers old Manuscripts, originall Charters, and other antient writings: who coming thither accordingly, he brought forth five antient Manuscripts in folio, which were Cartularies of the Lordships and Lands first given to the Cathedrall of St Paul in London, freely lending them to him, into the Country, till Michaelmasse-term ensuing: promising him the use of many more upon his next returne to London.

When Dugdale came to return the books, he found that Reading was dead; but his executor was no less obliging and showed Dugdale 'many other Manuscript-bookes, originall Charters, old Rolls, and other very antient writings in Baggs and Hampers, all relating to that great Cathedrall: he freely lent them to him, to be carried to his own lodgings, which amounted to no lesse than ten porters burthens'.[93] Dugdale was nothing if not prolific, and he rapidly set about making the most of this windfall of source materials: his *History of St Paul's Cathedral* was published in 1658, a substantial folio volume, made marketable by its many etchings of the cathedral and monuments, and rendered of enduring scholarly value by the many texts printed in full.

Historians must rejoice that Dugdale chanced to meet Reading, for it is clear that many books and documents were lost from the cathedral's archive for ever before his visit to the Scriveners' Hall, whereas most of what Dugdale prints or cites in his *History* is still extant.[94] On the other hand, while Dugdale was 'bestowing paynes to sort them into order',[95] he apparently took the opportunity to remove a considerable number of documents that were of particular interest to him: most of these he seems to have passed on to his friend Sir Christopher Hatton (d. 1670), and then to have obtained for the Cotton Library in Westminster; as part of the Cotton collection, they are today in the British Library.[96] Some related to religious houses over which St Paul's had oversight,[97] but others were of immediate importance, like the St Paul's library catalogues of 1458 and 1486.[98]

1660–1897

The re-establishment of the Church of England in 1660 should have led to the restoration of each cathedral's archive and library to its historic location. In the case of St Paul's it is unclear how far this happened. Either the archive had been split into two main elements – one part in the possession successively of Reading and Dugdale, and another located with other dean and chapter records successively at Gurney House and (from 1654) at the Excise Office in Broad Street – or it was placed with sets of records from other cathedrals. Documents from several other cathedral archives became mixed in with those of St Paul's, and that can only have happened in the 1650s or 1660s.[99] Dugdale declared that what had been in his hands, he delivered to Dean Barwick soon after the Restoration.[100] It may in part have been self-interest, then, that in July 1661 led the dean and chapter to set aside

> the place or Chappell at the East End & North side of the Cathedrall Church [to] be for 6 moneths lent unto the persons who have the Custody of the Records bookes &c. belonging to the Bishops, Deanes & other … for the laying ordering and sorting of the said Records, bookes, deedes & writeings & for the better delivering of them out to their right & proper owners.[101]

Whether or not this sorting was effective, it was decided in 1662 to send the records of all cathedrals – presumably including those of St Paul's – to Lambeth Palace, where Dugdale volunteered to sort them. His expertise, applied perhaps over two years, must have been invaluable, and it is not a little shocking that, while the bishops each gave 10s., most of the chapters (including St Paul's) failed to provide any monetary reward.[102]

Only the more historic of the cathedral records can have been entrusted to Dugdale's care: the most pressing concern of each chapter was for the recovery of its estates and the income obtained by granting new leases. Estate management by the lease-hold system depended upon good record-keeping, but often these documents were held by the lessees themselves or by chapter officials residing away from the cathedral. When Sir Erasmus Fountaine sought, in 1661, to renew his lease of Belchamp St Paul's – a matter which was to take several months' negotiation – chapter had to direct the bringing in of all that estate's court rolls, surveys, surrenders and recoveries.[103] The library of St Paul's is ill-documented for this date. Dean Barwick was presumably quick to seek the recovery of the books from Sion College, and the presence today at St Paul's of fifteenth- and sixteenth-century folio volumes seems to be testimony to some success. On the other hand, a portion of the St Paul's library certainly remained at Sion College.[104]

The Great Fire of London destroyed tens of thousands of volumes at St Paul's. Most belonged to booksellers who had placed their stock in the crypt.[105] Chapter officials also had time to make arrangements for saving their movable goods, and their efforts

concentrated on the cathedral's muniments. John Tillison, Clerk of the Works and Dean Sancroft's right-hand man, later asserted that 'in the later Dreadfull fire Anno 1666, I secured all [the] Plate, Charters, Books, and Records, not without great labour, dilligence and charge, both in my own person, and in employing of others; of all which things, not the least particle had been saved, had I been either slack or negligent.'[106] Yet Tillison seems to have failed to save many contemporary and recent records: the Acquittance Books begin only in 1669,[107] and the main series of account-books of the chamberlain and receiver-general also begins only in 1666 (although there are a few earlier volumes),[108] and quite a few of the sets of the manor court books begin in 1668.[109] An overhaul of contemporary record-keeping or accountancy practice was instigated by Dean Sancroft, doubtless in response to these losses. The main chapter account-book for Michaelmas 1666 to Michaelmas 1667, immediately following the Great Fire, is written entirely in Sancroft's hand, and shows some rearrangement of the account's format.[110] Having been removed to Fulham at the time of the Fire, the records were now brought back to London, as two boatloads, together with a further quantity from Dr Barwick's house.[111] Sancroft kept them for a couple of years in his own lodgings, and then in 1669 three 'rooms' were erected for them in Convocation House Yard.[112]

Other manuscript materials were also saved from the Fire. Thomas Quartermain, a minor canon, arranged for the choir books to be taken to Oxfordshire.[113] The minor canons as a group put their plate and evidences into a chest, which was then taken to Islington.[114] The chapter's library of printed books seems to have been overlooked. Or was it remembered that some of it remained at Sion College? Still at St Paul's is a sheet of paper, on which are listed three Latin manuscripts (*Avicenna*, *Mariale B.V.* and *Remediarium Conversorum*) and twenty-four printed works, poignantly endorsed 'The Remains of yᵉ Library of Sᵗ Pauls preserv'd from yᵉ fire at Sion-Colleg' (Fig. 346). Virtually all of these works are today at St Paul's, some with extensive water-staining.

In the years preceding the Civil War, it had been part of the Laudian churchmen's justification of cathedrals to assert that they were centres of learning. On the eve of their destruction, in 1641, John Hacket, prebendary of St Paul's, had claimed in a speech to the House of Commons that the higher clergy of the cathedral and collegiate churches were 'studied and able men' and that their churches were 'usually supplied with large and copious libraries… [containing] the monuments of antiquity, councils, fathers, modern authors, schoolmen, casuists, and [that] many books must be turned over by him that will utter that which should endure the test and convince gainsayers.'[115] A few years later, blame for the wanton physical destruction wreaked upon cathedrals and their contents, including muniments and libraries, formed part of the royalist attack on the parliamentarians. Inevitably, then, the re-establishment of cathedral libraries was a general rule in the 1660s, and it was equally clear that a rebuilt St Paul's should include substantial accommodation for a library. That Dean Sancroft was one of the most enthusiastic bookmen among the higher clergy must have reinforced such a feeling.

In February 1673 Christopher Wren was said to be adding a library to his Great Model for St Paul's.[116] Subsequently, the present Library and Trophy Room (as they are now called) feature as unnamed spaces in Wren's 'Definitive Design'. Both rooms seem from the start to have been intended for books: like the Wren Library at Trinity College, Cambridge, and other libraries designed by Wren, they have windows placed high up, so as to

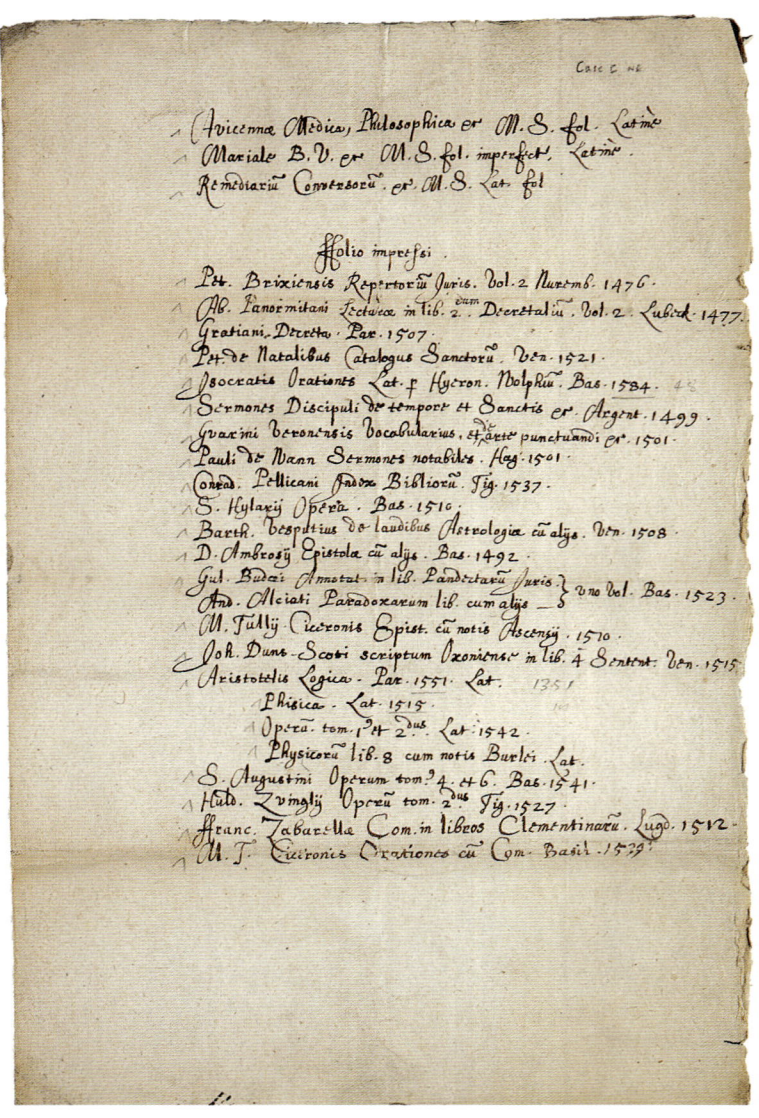

346.   *The Remains of yͤ Library of Sͭ Paul's preserv'd from yͤ fire at Sion-Colleg.* List of three manuscripts and twenty-four printed works which survived the Fire of London, 1666: the Avicenna manuscript and almost all of the printed books are still in St Paul's Library. (SPCL)

was paid to Mrs Gery.[120] The South Library, as it was called, began to fill respectably, and the carver Jonathan Maine was commissioned to provide trusses to support its gallery, for which he was paid in 1709.[121]

In September 1710 Humfrey Wanley, librarian to the earl of Oxford and himself England's pre-eminent palaeographer, offered to sell his collection of biblical editions to the commissioners for £60. The offer was instantly accepted, the commissioners 'being very desirous to lay hold on so good an opportunity for so curious an Addition to yͤ sᵈ. library',[122] but it is not clear why Wanley made it, for he had a continuing interest in biblical texts.[123] This celebrated collection is recorded in a catalogue in Wanley's own hand, arranged under such headings as 'Bibles in English', 'New Testaments', 'Concordances, Expositions and other Biblical Books', 'Popish Primers [Books of Hours] and other Prayer Books' and 'Dissenters Books' (Fig. 347).[124] It is a scholar's collection: the importance of the books for Wanley was their earliness of date, not their condition, and he was collecting in an area without any clear guides in print. He knew that he had parts of a Bible translated by Coverdale, printed in 1535; and he knew that his New Testament translated by Tyndale, 'printed in a German letter, 16ᵗᵒ, imperfect' [it lacks a title page, etc.], was 'one of the first editions'. But nobody at that date could have stated for certain that the latter was in fact one of the three surviving copies of the first printing of Tyndale's New Testament, now believed to have been

347.   Catalogue by Humfrey Wanley of his collection of biblical and liturgical books, acquired for St Paul's in 1710. It includes (line 2) a copy of the first printing of Tyndale's New Testament; Wanley only partly realised what a treasure he owned. (GL, St Paul's collection)

maximize space for shelving below. Accounts of 1701–9 for their completion, together with carved panels on the upper parts of the pilasters featuring books and other library equipment, confirm that both were destined for library use. In the event, only the southern room was occupied by the Library, while the northern one had no distinct initial use beyond that of housing Wren's Great Model.

Sancroft and his immediate successors may have set about acquiring a new stock of books for the cathedral, but the evidence for this is weak.[117] An alphabetically arranged catalogue of 1,459 printed books, almost all in Latin, may show book-purchasing by Sancroft and others.[118] The list was begun about 1692 and continued until about 1707, by when the total number of books had been doubled, but it is not certain to whose library it refers.

The dean and chapter in effect were sidelined in the matter of rebuilding their cathedral, and in similar fashion their book-buying activities – if any – were ignored by the Commissioners for Rebuilding St Paul's. Attention has focused on the commissioners' decision in 1707 to acquire the library of Robert Gery, late vicar of Islington, 'according to the Catalogue delivered', and that 'Sir Christopher Wren do fit up the Library of St Paul's fit for receiving Books with all expedition'.[119] The following year, £450 printed at Worms in 1526 for smuggling into England.[125] As the first complete edition of the New Testament in English, it has for over a century been regarded as the greatest treasure in the library of St Paul's.

The first ten years of the new library's existence were a high point in other ways, too. One of the clergymen on the Commission for Rebuilding – perhaps Archbishop Tenison – asked Wanley to set down in writing his suggestions for 'the Preservation & Enlargement of the New Library'. He did so at some length,[126] beginning with the comment – which was surely expected to be in accord with his patron's views – that

> I look upon this Library, not only as a Library belonging to the Dean & Chapter of a Cathedral Church, but as the Chiefest Public Library in the Metropolis (if I may say so) of Great Britain. As such I believe both Natives and Foreigners will take it; as Such I would have it Endow'd & Furnish'd; and as Such, I would have its Honor & Reputation Consider'd upon all Occasions.

His suggestions were wide-ranging, dealing with the necessary qualities of the library-keeper and his deputy, opening hours (8 a.m. to 12 noon, and 1 to 4 p.m. in winter, but 2 to 5 or 6 p.m. in summer), the need for the library-keeper to help both students (whose reading-matter should be entered in a register) and 'strangers' (who should be shown 'the Chief Curiosities of the Library'), admission charges (nil for clergy and students; 3*d.* for others, who should be met by a servant at the bottom of the library stairs), loans (never sanctioned), placing (by size; without chains) and so forth. It was at about this date, too, that someone of influence in Parliament – by tradition, the bishop of London, Henry Compton (Fig. 348) – had the library of St Paul's added to the copyright bill, but in the event Sion College was substituted for St Paul's as one of the libraries that would receive a free copy of each book protected by the Copyright Act.[127]

William Beveridge, bishop of St Asaph, had in 1708 bequeathed to St Paul's such of his books as were deemed 'fit for a Publick Library'.[128] Bishop Compton's relations with his cathedral chapter were often strained, but when he died, in 1713, it was found that he had bequeathed to St Paul's half of his library.[129] This was a transforming gift: the pick of a major, up-to-date, scholarly collection of biblical, patristic, liturgical and general theological works.[130] Most of the books are in Latin, including a fair number of sixteenth-century works by the continental reformers, but there are some catechetical books and works of controversial and other theology in English, and several dozen quartos and octavos in French. The authors represented by the greatest numbers of separately published works are Jean de Launoy (twenty-two works, including such rarities as his *Assertio inquisitionis in chartam immunitatis quam Beatus Germanus Parisiorum episcopus suburbano monasterio dedisse fertur* (Paris, 1658), which one can imagine Compton turning to as he struggled to enforce his visitation rights upon the chapter of his own cathedral), Jean Daillé the elder (fifteen works) and Edward Stillingfleet (fifteen works). Compton liked to keep up with French Protestant writings, and himself issued (anonymously) an English translation of part of André Lortie's *Traité de la Sainte Cène* (La Rochelle, 1674).[131] Many of the books have neatly written notes by Compton on their flyleaves and margins, showing how much he used them.

For want of documentation, it is impossible to say how much use the dean and chapter made of the richly stocked library that they now possessed. Certainly there were learned prebendaries,

348. Henry Compton, bishop of London 1675–1713, portrait of 1710 by J. Hargrave in the cathedral library

who could have used it profitably. For instance, Francis Hare, DD (prebendary 1707–40; dean 1726–40), editor of the Hebrew Psalms, might have drawn usefully on the library's resources. William Stanley, DD, residentiary 1692–1731 and bookish in the extreme,[132] would be another obvious candidate. In 1709 he showed his appreciation of the library by giving it what were regarded as two of its greatest treasures, Brian Walton's six-volume folio *Biblia Sacra Polyglotta* (London, [1653–]7) – the last of the great polyglot Bibles to be published – and Edmund Castell's *Lexicon Heptaglotton*, in two volumes (London, 1669), all on large paper and bound in turkey. In 1722 Dean Godolphin gave a copy of the second polyglot Bible (Antwerp, 1569–72). Perhaps of greater significance for the library, however, was his gift of a rent of £20 p.a. to endow the librarian's post. This income was annexed to the ninth minor canon's stall, which meant that henceforth whoever held that stall would be the librarian.[133] Unfortunately, at this date and until 1730, the ninth minor canon was Edward de Chair, a nonentity who fell short of what was needful.

Even before the cathedral had been completed, it is probable that the library, like Wren's Great Model,[134] was shown to visitors for a fee. Wanley had suggested that such fee-money could be used to purchase books. Within a few years, £5 a year was being paid to Mr Pigot 'for taking care of the library',[135] a sum suggesting that he was not allowed to keep the fees.

The German bibliophile Zacharias Conrad von Uffenbach is the earliest visitor to have recorded his impressions: he came in 1710 – before the library acquired the books and portrait of Bishop Compton.

The room is of moderate size but very high, so that many books can be housed there. For in the upper part there is one shelf above another, which are reached by a gallery… There are as yet scarcely a thousand volumes here, though these are mostly folios and some are very fine works, notably a copy of Castelli Lexicon. The keeper of the library is an Englishman, that is to say a person who concerns himself little about it. In answer to my enquiries he said that there were no manuscripts… If I had such a room, though perhaps somewhat larger, and such shelves for my books, I should be only too delighted to fill them. The place was somewhat dark for a library.[136]

Von Uffenbach was an unusually well-informed (and opinionated) tourist. Most subsequent notices of the library by visitors or in guidebooks merely refer to the oak floor, made up of 2,487 pieces laid without nail or peg to fasten them, the portrait of Compton that still hangs over the fireplace at the east end (Fig. 348), and perhaps some of the curios that found a resting-place here. The library was part of a tourist itinerary that made a feature of the geometrical staircase and also included the wooden model (kept in the Trophy Room, as the intended second library room came to be called) and the cupola (or Whispering Gallery). The earliest recorded figures for the actual numbers of visitors to the library date from the 1770s: one to three dozen then came daily (Monday to Saturday), paying 2*d*. each, the same sum as for seeing the bell or model.[137] Receipts between Christmas 1783 and Christmas 1790 indicate over a hundred visitors a week.[138] Until the 1780s, the dean and chapter may have spent little money on the library, beyond paying the man whose job it was to show it to the 'strangers, country people and little masters and misses', as one guidebook characterizes the visitors. In English cathedrals at this date, it was usual for library accessions to come principally as gifts from individual prebendaries, with supplementation from subscriptions and perhaps canonical installation fees. Such accessions will not feature in financial accounts, and it is only from chance notes that it is known that, for instance, Dean Secker gave £50 to the library in 1763.[139] It would also be a mistake to infer a lack of gifts from their absence in the Library Benefactors Book,[140] since that was not in use at this time. For at least part of the eighteenth century, there was a designated 'Library money' account, known today only from cancelled entries in the main chapter account for 1735–6 when payments were mistakenly recorded for subscriptions to a new edition of Robert Estienne's *Thesaurus Linguae Latinae* (1734–5) and to David Wilkins's *Concilia Magnae Britanniae et Hiberniae* (1737).[141]

The library certainly functioned adequately in this time. Since perhaps the 1710s, an interleaved copy of the Bodleian Library catalogue by Thomas Hyde (1674) had served well as a guide to its contents.[142] By mid century, each book had had its press number and shelf letter supplemented by its number on the shelf. From July 1744 until 1763, and again from December 1777 to the present day, a record of library borrowings was maintained.[143] This admittedly imperfect evidence suggests that St Paul's was the least heavily used of the eight cathedral libraries for which loan records survive from approximately this period: just 127 different works were taken out, by fifty-seven different borrowers, as a total of 726 separate loans.[144] Walton's *Biblia Polyglotta* was borrowed only once, apparently (as compared with fourteen times at Gloucester, thirteen at Canterbury and nine times each at Carlisle and Durham), and Dugdale's *History of St Paul's* (1658) not at all.[145]

The explanation lies partly in the method of recording loans, but also in the nature of the chapter's residence arrangements, combined with the existence of an alternative library for the clergy at Sion College. Only the canon in residence would find it convenient to borrow; the minor canons (whose library presumably had been destroyed in the Great Fire; it is never mentioned afterwards) borrowed less than the canons or even the prebendaries, despite being resident nearby for far more of the time, and they doubtless preferred to go to Sion College. To a degree that was perhaps unusual even by the standards of cathedral libraries, the library of St Paul's was a collection of patristic and later theology, biblical texts and commentaries and ecclesiastical history, very largely in Latin. It did not have sermons, or works of literature; nor was it strong in ecclesiastical law.

The ecclesiastical historian John Lewis visited the library in 1731, to look at the early translations of the Bible. In the long introduction to his edition of the Wycliffite New Testament, he made considerable use of the collection, and would thus have helped publicize it.[146] In 1782 the prebendary John Mangey died, and St Paul's took up the option of buying the combined libraries belonging to him and his father (Thomas Mangey, prebendary of Durham) for a fairly nominal £150.[147] 1,511 volumes were received, but a good many were promptly disposed of as duplicates. It was a fine collection, rich in works of learning, and at St Paul's it was thoroughly weeded of anything lightweight – English literature, modern history or the like. The *Letters of Lord Chesterfield*, the *Negotiations* of Matthew Prior and Edward Bysshe's *Art of English Poetry* were disposed of, for instance, while books retained included Origen's *Philocalia* (Paris, 1619) and quite a few works in French, including Lucian, in the French translation of Nicolas Perrot, sieur d'Ablancourt (Paris, 1660), *Les Provinciales* by Louis de Montalle (Cologne, 1657) [about the Jesuits], and Molière's *Œuvres* (Amsterdam, 1698). Many of the books still have the bookplate of Thomas Mangey, and notes thought to be in his hand, all in Latin, Greek or Hebrew, fill the pages of a Hebrew bible. Four years later, in 1787, chapter paid to have a bookplate engraved.[148]

The cathedral's archives in the eighteenth century were both less well looked after than the library and less accessible to those who might have wished to consult them. At the end of the seventeenth century, Dr Matthew Hutton was able to make extracts from the medieval *Libri B, F* and *G*,[149] but no subsequent scholar has seen them intact, with the possible exception of Richard Newcourt around 1700. No researcher is known to have obtained access to the archives in the eighteenth century, and so it is difficult to be sure when such books and other records disappeared. Five manuscripts in the collection of the London-based collector Richard Rawlinson (1690–1755)[150] were derived from the chapter archive. They include a bifolium from *Liber B* and a minute-book coming down to 1744, suggesting that these manuscripts left the cathedral in the 1740s or 1750s. There were later losses: a charter of Henry I which was still in the archive in the mid eighteenth century was recorded as missing in the 1840s and remains untraced.[151]

The cathedral's records, whether of purely historic significance or of immediate practical value, came under the immediate control of the register (or registrar, as the chapter clerk at St Paul's was then called). There is little sign of any eighteenth-century dean or prebendary taking an interest in the historic records, while successive bishops in their visitations were concerned only with whether rentals or terriers were being kept up for the various estates. Exceptionally, Bishop Gibson in 1724 asked whether the muniments were 'deposited in a convenient place and preserved from dust and wet and kept in good order and method',[152] but even he concentrated on the terriers and leases. This emphasis is understandable, since many such records were kept on the estates themselves and it was necessary to call in and copy them from time to time.[153]

The neglect of the historic records was not total. About 1700, some rearrangement of 186 bundles of (mainly) medieval documents took place, the documents being grouped by subject and, within that, in chronological order.[154] In the 1730s a professional transcriber was engaged for a total of fifty-three weeks to 'put the Records in order', a task that involved both the listing of title deeds (divided into two series, for London and country properties; initially numbered at random, as they 'came to hand promiscuously', but latterly sorted by property or parish) and the extensive use of parchment for strengthening or protecting them.[155] Each deed was endorsed with a number, corresponding to its entry in a calendar.[156]

The records were stored in the new chapter house (completed in 1714), in a series of drawers within presses. London deeds occupied seven drawers and the country deeds eight; royal grants occupied three further drawers.[157] Space must rapidly have come to be at a premium,[158] and in 1772–3 the title deeds and others of the older documents were moved to a secure new location: a muniment room that was created in the octagonal chamber directly above the dean's vestry in the cathedral.[159] In retrospect, the move can be seen as marking the first stage in the separation of control over the records from the office of register; physically, however, the records were now even less easy of access for any outsider. It may be that in the opening years of the nineteenth century the first outside scholar for a century to consult the medieval records was J. P. Malcolm, who asserted that he was the first person since Dugdale's time to have been 'indulged with the perusal of the Archives' – for which he thanked the prebendary Henry Meen.[160] Some members of chapter had looked into the older records from time to time. For instance, Dean Secker about 1753 arranged for the records of St Faith's church to be put in order, and 'examined all the Registers & Books in the Chapter House, & extracted out of them what seemed material, and left these Extracts in the hands of my Successor'.[161] It was perhaps to fulfil a commission from the chapter that the antiquary John Caley in 1791 looked at the thirteenth-century *Liber Pilosus* and compared its index with the 'general index' in Dean Lisieux's book.[162]

THE NINETEENTH CENTURY

From about 1800 onwards, parliament took a markedly greater interest in public records. In May of that year, the registrar reported on the chapter's records to the select committee on public records.[163] The Record Commission was set up in 1801, to publish documents concerning the nation's history, while the decision to publish a new edition of the *Statutes of the Realm* resulted in searches being carried out in many collections. Initially, such activities may have had little impact on St Paul's, and the library was perhaps the only direct beneficiary, as it was given a set of the commission's publications. However, the raising of the English historical consciousness made many areas of debate take a more historical turn. Nationally, the calls for church reform, especially in the 1830s, led to much research into the historical genesis of the church's organization. For St Paul's, this meant trouble from some of the minor canons, as they saw a new means to assert grievances in the face of an increasingly prosperous chapter.

Up to a point, the prebendaries and minor canons had a great many interests in common, not least the fact that a large part of their income came from London parish churches. The canons would have had nothing to lose and perhaps something to gain from giving access to their archives to the minor canon John Moore, rector of St Michael Bassishaw, as he sought to justify London parish clergy's claims to tithes; but his *Case respecting the Maintenance of the London-Clergy, briefly stated and supported by reference to Authentick Documents* (1802) had to be written without the benefit of resort to the chapter muniments.[164] A decade later, in 1812–13, the canons found themselves opposed by an extraordinarily persistent (and ultimately successful) campaigner for the quality of choral music, Maria Hackett, who suspected that they were in breach of ancient bequests to support the choristers' education.[165] She sought access to the chapter muniments, and, when she was refused this by the dean, instituted proceedings in Chancery. When legal action failed to achieve her ends, she continued the struggle and her researches elsewhere: in 1827, for instance, she printed extensive excerpts from the medieval Almoner's Register from a transcript in the British Museum.[166] A few years later, the minor canon who held the ninth stall (and was thus librarian), R. C. Packman, proved to be almost Miss Hackett's equal as an irritant, by his publication of a pamphlet on the *Spiritualities and Temporalities of St Paul's Cathedral* (London, [1839]), using historical materials to show how the minor canons had been unfairly treated, especially in the matter of benefices.[167]

It was, then, very much to the chapter's credit that at this time it embarked on major changes of policy affecting the archives and the library. The changes were advanced, however, not by the chapter corporately but by two individual canons. Sydney Smith, residentiary from 1831, became friends with R. H. Barham, a minor canon since 1821.[168] Smith was a Whig, while Barham was a Tory of a romantic, antiquarian cast of mind (as he was to show in his *Ingoldsby Legends*, published in 1840–7). In 1839 Smith offered his residentiary's house to Barham to live in.[169] Barham probably would not have cared to exercise the librarian's office, and certainly would not have been interested in updating its book-stock since he could read recent publications in the library of Sion College (of which he was elected president in 1842). But he did enjoy engaging in antiquarian researches in the St Paul's library, and in so far as he felt that things needed to be done there, he had a powerful and generous ally in Sydney Smith. Smith arranged for a stove to be installed, so that the library was properly heated for the first time,[170] and with chapter funds and from his own pocket paid for repairs to the books' bindings.[171] Barham realized what a treasure the cathedral had in its collection of early bibles, and he did his best to identify the various editions (being helped in this by the collector George Offor) and had them placed for safe keeping with the archives.[172] His care to have them rebound may now be regretted, however, as some books were cropped by the binder's plough while others – including the Tyndale first edition of the New Testament – had their integrity damaged by his well-intentioned changes to their pagination or structure.

The second canon who was a major instigator of changes was a tory of the old school, William Hale Hale (1795–1870), a lifelong friend and protégé of Charles James Blomfield.[173] Like Smith, a good man of business and a prolific author, he took a close interest in the cathedral library, especially in 1830. During the forty

W. Sparrow Simpson. Minor Canon 1861—1897. Mr W. ASH 119 NEWINGTON CAUSEWAY Librarian 1862.. Succentor 1876.

349. *Carte de visite* of W. Sparrow Simpson, minor canon and librarian, 1861–97. (SPCL)

way; characteristically, Hale was not keen on having new statutes, preferring if possible to apply a cy-pres interpretation to the existing ones.[176] Also in the early to mid 1840s, he had a set of catalogues made of the documents other than title deeds down to the mid eighteenth century – that is to say, of rent-collector's and other accounts, documents relating to the chantries, and the books of charters and statutes.[177] For most of these categories, Hale's was the first listing ever; for some, it is still the most detailed (even though it would be difficult to use today, because of subsequent rearrangements). In 1843 Hale procured access to *Liber A* for a solicitor and record agent named Thomas Edlyne Tomlins, who suggested to him that a complete transcript would be worth publishing.[178] Whether in response to this or not, Hale went on to edit the text of *Liber K* (GL, MS 25514) for the newly founded Camden Society.[179] It is a careful and reliable piece of work, with a lengthy and at times lively introduction, and has not been superseded: Hale enjoyed comparing the business of estate management in the thirteenth century with that in his own life-time. His next step in this area was to borrow a medieval register from Worcester Cathedral and set about editing that.

At some point in the early nineteenth century, a new general catalogue of the library's collections was drawn up.[180] But the years of Packman's tenure of the librarianship (1824–61) were effectively fallow ones, so far as the library's modern book-stock was concerned. For both the library and the archives, it was only in 1862 that a long-needed overhaul was commenced, with Dean Milman's transfer of William Sparrow Simpson from the tenth to the ninth minor canonry and his appointment as librarian (Fig. 349).

Sparrow Simpson (1828–97) was unquestionably the ideal man for the post. He had acted as librarian when an undergraduate at Queen's College, Cambridge; he was a devout churchman and a lover of cathedral music (p. 407), who delighted in being a minor canon and was happy to devote himself to the history of St Paul's; he was an antiquary to his core, and, in the words of his son, 'possessed an insatiable love of detail and of fact';[181] and he was ready to work for an almost interminable number of hours, for a nominal reward (£20 a year). He was a man of action and, where the library was concerned, of vision.

He immediately focused on the physical condition of the books. 'The librarian would grow eloquent and pathetic, as he described the emotions with which he first stood among the ruins of what had once been fine and costly bindings, reduced by decay to dust and dilapidation'.[182] When he delivered his first report as librarian in November 1862,[183] he could say that there were 7,617 books (5,965 on the ground floor, 1,433 in the gallery and 219 in locked cases) and that he had taken down every single one, cleaned it and replaced it; he had made a catalogue of the pamphlets and a complete shelf-list of the whole library, and he had assessed the immediate bookbinding needs (109 folios, 207 quartos and 515 octavos and smaller books had loose covers or no covers; Lewis, bookbinder to Sion College, estimated for these, at a total of £66 10s. 6d). He had rapidly made a favourable impression on the chapter, and in March 1862 it was agreed not only that he should get such books repaired as needed it, but also that it was 'desirable to appoint a proper person to arrange and keep in order all the muniments of the church' and that the dean would confer with Simpson about the best mode of proceeding.[184] Milman proceeded to entrust Simpson with this task, too.

Simpson's catalogue of the contents of the muniment room is characteristically clear-headed.[185] Neatly and summarily, he described the presses of this octagonal chamber and their con-

years that he was a prebendary, he borrowed far more books than anyone else, resorting to the library throughout the year. Presumably he or Smith proposed that the library-keeper's salary be raised from £8 a year to £20. His approach to the cathedral's management was partly founded on a sense of historic rights and obligations that led him to take an interest in its archives. For Hale, taking an interest meant taking action. 'His vigour and sense, his strong narrow opinions, his constant readiness to do battle for them, and the various dignities which he enjoyed, made his name well known, and those who came into contact personally with him always respected though they might often have occasion to oppose him', it was written immediately after his death.[174]

In 1840 Hale was made a residentiary canon, and was thus put in a position of power. The close interest that he took in the medieval archives resulted in a marked weakening in the control that the dean had customarily exercised over them. More immediately, Hale had more material removed physically from the custody of the chapter clerk: most notably, on 6 July 1841 he brought the eighteen medieval books of charters and statutes (*Liber A* or *Pilosus*, *Liber C*, etc.) from the first lower drawer in the chapter house to the muniment room.[175] That action may have been prompted by the perceived need to revise the cathedral's statutes, because of the Cathedrals Act and other legal changes then under tents. Chapter again was impressed, and agreed, tactfully, to offer £30 to Simpson 'rather as a compliment than compensation for his very valuable services in arranging the Records'.[186]

As librarian and *de facto* archivist, Sparrow Simpson went from strength to strength. In 1863 he compiled an index to the 3,620 wills proved before the dean and chapter between 1535 and 1672.[187] He won further gratitude from Milman by helping him with materials for his *Annals of S. Paul's Cathedral* (1868).[188] At Hale's suggestion, the archbishop of Canterbury made him an honorary librarian of Lambeth Palace Library in 1869, and for years to come he spent Fridays there, compiling a catalogue of its printed books.[189] He also set about developing his vision for the St Paul's collection of printed books: that it should be not so much a library of biblical and patristic and later theology as a series of special collections. Patiently but methodically, he built up collections relating specifically to St Paul's: views and plans of the cathedral; sermons preached in the cathedral or at St Paul's Cross; and the publications of members of the cathedral body. For the latter, with chapter permission, he circularized the prebendaries, minor canons and others in 1871, inviting donations. For purchases, he at first had to eke out the annual grant of £20; but from 1872 he received £100 a year, and was able to accelerate the filling of gaps and to embark on subscriptions to learned societies and journals.

In March 1872 the dean and chapter paid him the further compliment of commissioning him to edit the cathedral statutes;[190] characteristically, the work was completed and printed by Christmas.[191] It is a complete edition of all the statutes of St Paul's, medieval and later, and must be reckoned Sparrow Simpson's *magnum opus*. The pre-eminent medievalist William Stubbs, canon of St Paul's from 1879, carefully described it as 'about the best piece of work on such a subject as has been done'. Simpson gathered together transcripts of the various texts, and to some extent collated them; but his opaque way of indicating his sources and the fact that the volume was never published (but merely issued to prebendaries during their tenure of a stall) have reduced its standing, availability and utility.

Sparrow Simpson was happiest with printed materials. There is no reason to think that he sought out the task of editing the statutes. As G. F. Browne wrote, he 'was at his strongest as a compiler'.[192] For the Camden Society, he edited a volume of *Documents illustrating the History of St Paul's Cathedral* (1880) in which he printed Henry Wharton's extracts from the *Annales Paulini* (LPL, MS 590), collated with the manuscript (LPL, MS 1106) which was actually the original from which Wharton had made his transcript.[193]

Sparrow Simpson was probably also untroubled by the lack of readers. Casual visitors, supervised by a guide, continued to inspect the library from a sort of pen set up adjacent to its entrance (Fig. 330), but he did not need to concern himself with such people.[194] The pressure that English cathedrals had come under to improve access to their libraries probably affected St Paul's less than elsewhere because the library of Sion College was available to the London clergy. In 1879 Sparrow Simpson stated that it was open daily from 11 a.m. to 4 p.m., but only to diocesan clergy, and that it had no artificial light.[195] When a Mrs Matthew Hall was granted permission by chapter in 1871 to inspect certain books and papers from the muniment room, it was on condition that her references be found satisfactory and that 'the Librarian collate the books she may require before they are given to her and after they are returned'.[196]

William Stubbs may have been responsible for the next set of improvements in access to the archives. In his first winter as residentiary, 1879–80, he made investigations in the loft of the chapter house and found a considerable number of medieval documents. Then in 1881 the old muniment room was vacated and its contents moved to new presses in the gallery leading to the library, where there was room for expansion.[197] Stubbs's was no doubt the voice in chapter that led to the decision in 1881 to spend £50 on a medieval roll with copies of writs of Edward the Confessor, William I, William II and Henry I in favour of St Paul's.[198]

It was also in 1881, if not 1880, that Henry Maxwell Lyte was engaged by the Historical Manuscripts Commission to report on the capitular collections of medieval and later documents of historical interest – no doubt resulting from a chapter invitation to the commission. Lyte's report, published in 1883, is a detailed guide to a very large quantity of material;[199] it is selective and unmethodical, but shows a very sound understanding of what others were likely to think significant and is still of great utility, not superseded by the unprinted late twentieth-century catalogue of the same materials. The writer of Lyte's obituary in *The Times* described it as 'perhaps the best thing of the kind ever done';[200] certainly it was a remarkable achievement for a man in his mid thirties, and exceeds anything that Sparrow Simpson could have done.

Sparrow Simpson became succentor in 1876, and for the next few years was much engaged in creating a major music library for St Paul's.[201] In 1889 he was able to purchase a considerable quantity of papers which had belonged to Bishop Gibson, but many of them were subsequently claimed by descendants of Gibson and were surrendered to them by the decision of the dean and chapter.[202] In 1890 he explained to the dean how he had been spending the annual library grant of £100: on bookbinding and repairing, 'the annual cleaning of the books by an expert' and subscriptions to the Rolls Series, Surtees Society, Camden Society, Palaeographical Society, etc.; the rest had gone on books and other materials relating to St Paul's, Paul's Cross sermons, tracts on the Great Fire, Sir Christopher Wren, the Sacheverell controversy and other topics. His suggestion that he now publish a catalogue of these collections (at a cost to the dean and chapter of perhaps £50, which might be partly recouped from sales) was accepted, and it was issued two years later.[203]

He perhaps felt that his term as librarian was drawing to a close. In 1891 he presented six large albums of cuttings, service sheets and other ephemera relating to St Paul's – carefully indexed in a further volume. His wish to publish a catalogue of the special collections of older books, tracts and prints was surely an indication that he felt he had at least more or less completed what he wished in these areas. Overall, his achievement for the library and archive had been remarkable. His lists of the archival materials had always been kept up to date.[204] He had devised purchasing policies, carried through at very moderate cost. He had put the cathedral library on the map in areas beyond its established strengths, even coming up with a group of fine bindings for the *Exhibition of Bookbindings* in 1891.[205] And he had never neglected the maintenance and enlargement of the general collections of theological and other ecclesiastical works. From a total of 7,617 works in 1862, he had brought the library's holdings up to 21,176 in 1893; no doubt there were yet more by the time of his death, in March 1897.[206] Simpson lived in an age of capable cathedral librarians, but even by their standards he can be said to have been outstanding.

39

THE LIBRARY, 1897–2004

J. J. Wisdom

Sparrow Simpson cast a long shadow. It cannot have been easy for Lewis Gilbertson to succeed a librarian who had been in post for over thirty years and who had fostered assiduously all aspects of the library. Dean and chapter supported Simpson's work with slightly bemused approval: the activity of the library, however successful, remained on the periphery of their vision just as the library chamber itself was hidden from the mainstream life of the cathedral. While he was librarian Gilbertson published a guide to the cathedral which for thirty years was intermittently updated and republished.[1] In 1903 he became rector of St Martin Ludgate, and his successor as librarian was another minor canon, Walter Philip Besley.

In the century following Simpson's death the perils of the periphery were never more apparent than under Dean Inge (dean 1911–34).[2] In the middle of the First World War it was decided to 'suspend till further notice the allowance of £50 a year made for Library expenses';[3] an understandable economy, but appointments to a minor canonry and to the post of librarian were also deferred following the departure of Besley in 1920.[4] Drastic measures followed: 'The Dean [Inge] was appointed Librarian, and the Dean's Virger [Skinner] was asked to undertake the duties of Sub-Librarian. The stipend previously paid is to cease.'[5] The account book for this period closes with a balance returned to dean and chapter. For almost ten years the library is scarcely mentioned in subsequent chapter minutes, except as a place for the 'safe custody' of documents.[6]

By contrast, during the Second World War care was taken that the contents of the library should be evacuated to a place of safety. Gerald Henderson, who had been appointed sub-librarian in 1932,[7] anxiously oversaw the transfer by lorry of the rarer books to the National Library of Wales in Aberystwyth.[8] By the end of the war the library was thus an aspect of the cathedral's life long overdue a reappraisal, and in 1949 the newly appointed residentiary canon and chancellor John Collins instituted a brave attempt to put the library on a proper footing. Collins wanted to see the library accessible and a centre of scholarship. In 1948 he had discovered that the Fairhurst papers, a collection including many important ecclesiastical and secular documents of the sixteenth century, was for sale. He persuaded chapter to accept his offer to procure the papers for the library, without calling on the chapter's straitened financial resources, through an appeal for the £16,000 asking price.[9] Thus enhanced, the library would open to visitors from 2 May 1949.[10] A loan was secured to effect the purchase, while the Pilgrim Trust funded a cleaning programme in the library. The project came embarrassingly to grief, however, as aspects of the sale came into question and the appeal failed. The Fairhurst papers were ultimately resold by the underwriters.[11] A happier legacy of this renewed interest in the library was the agreement of the chapter to appoint a part-time librarian. W. M. Atkins, a minor canon with responsibilities in the choir school, took charge of manuscripts in March 1950[12] and was responsible independently of Henderson to Collins. Henderson was gently eased into an untenable position and resigned.[13] Atkins became librarian and carried on his duties while engaged in supporting Dean Matthews in the editing of the new history of the cathedral.[14] After his appointment as rector of St George Hanover Square in 1955, Atkins continued to work part time as librarian at

350. The cathedral library in about 1960

351. The Queen Mother visits the cathedral library, November 1950. On the left, with eye-patch, Gerald Henderson the sub-librarian; Dean Matthews is behind the Queen Mother. (SPCL)

the cathedral with the assistance of a new sub-librarian. This was Alexander R. B. Fuller, a retired public school master whose thesis had examined the minor canons of St Paul's, and who in 1960 himself became librarian.[15]

When cleaning of the exterior of the cathedral was undertaken in 1966 the books were temporarily removed from outer walls in case of water penetration.[16] Only the year before, Fuller had hotly defended retention of the books in the library chamber to the dean and chapter in response to an offer made to the latter by J. H. P. Pafford, Goldsmiths' Librarian of the University of London, to house them in the university library.[17] This development represented the first manifestation at St Paul's of a theme which in subsequent years would become a familiar and controversial subject of debate in the chapters of English cathedrals. In 1994 the Archbishop's Commission on Cathedrals headed by Elspeth Howe would note that 'the need to allocate financial resources to the maintenance of the library has to be weighed against other pressing needs. In some cathedrals the library occupies valuable space which members of the chapter believe could be better used in some other way.' On reading these sentences in his own copy of the report, Dean Eric Evans annotated the margin next to the last sentence 'S Pauls!'[18] The lack of a precinct to accommodate ancillary activities has certainly put additional pressure to justify their functions on the library and other non-liturgical spaces in St Paul's. The integrity of collections housed in the chamber for which they were built, and the value of the library as a resource for cathedral staff and researchers may, however precariously, be acknowledged, but they do not preclude the need for the library to seek new ways to serve the cathedral's mission.

Fuller's remonstrance to dean and chapter of 1965, written in haste and fury, nonetheless illustrates how the modern St Paul's library is more than the sum of its parts. The library and triforium have always been visited for sightseeing and educational purposes (pp. 421–5), and guide books indicate that in the first quarter of the twentieth century the library, whispering gallery and stone gallery were grouped as one extra charge of 6*d.* per visitor.[19] The librarian shares responsibility for guiding visits with

other staff, and in the early twentieth century a library attendant also assisted. In 1913, 'all these exhibits [library and triforium] are clearly and concisely explained by Mr Emerton, the courteous and well-informed attendant, especially to visitors whom he finds intelligently interested.'[20] From tonsure plate to 'Wren's waistcoat', the curiosities have been drawn to the attention of the paying visitor and the student.[21] Since 1998 'working friends' have led new triforium tours, but they expound the library and related treasures in a way that cannot have changed greatly from the early twentieth century. A vestige of the 'sheep pen' that was in use to corral visitors in the central space of the chamber (cf. p. 425 and Fig. 350) is still retained in the library as part of its working history.[22] Practical constraints on access at this level preclude visitor numbers comparable to those experienced on the cathedral floor and in the galleries, but recently the library has been included in plans to make previously 'hidden' areas of the cathedral available to as many visitors as possible, both physical and 'virtual'. To enable this to happen, while at the same time preserving and exploiting the library's historic collections, represents a considerable challenge.

Cataloguing was not mentioned by Fuller in his broadside to the dean and chapter, perhaps because the University of London might have served the collection rather better in this respect. The collections were trawled for the Short Title Catalogue and Wing (as in other cathedrals a large volume of correspondence crossed the Atlantic), and were fully included in the *Cathedral Libraries Catalogue*: these invaluably supplement the library's in-house cataloguing.[23] Simpson's legacy of cataloguing was a good one, and his 1893 volume is still useful for the highlights of the collections. A later card catalogue, compiled without code or authority files, is a hit-and-miss affair. Library databases are now the effective means of cataloguing, and building on a project commenced in the mid 1990s,[24] a database is currently under construction to help furnish the inventory required of the cathedral under The Care of Cathedrals Measure of 1990.

The special nature of the service given to visiting readers, and the range of enquiries that were answered in person and by correspondence, was one of the chief grounds cited by Fuller as requiring the continued separate existence of the cathedral library.[25] The library's resources have served scholarship well. In the 1930s, account and acquittance books and other archival material were borrowed by Arthur T. Bolton for transcription and publication in the monumental series of the Wren Society's publications, and Marion Gibbs was permitted to borrow the *Liber Pilosus* for six months in 1933 while she was working on the early charters of the cathedral. The loan book is largely a record of domestic loans to cathedral clergy and staff, especially the surveyor to the fabric, but the occasional carefully considered extramural loan shows how seriously the service of scholarship was taken.[26] Fuller characteristically notes 'Receipt in safe A. F.' against the loan of minute books to R. A. Beddard in 1971. The visitors' book shows that in the 1950s and 1960s the library and archives were used by scholars of considerable standing, and it is almost invidious to mention the names Christopher Brooke, Neil Ker, and Pierre Chaplais when so many others, including contributors to this *History*, would serve to illustrate the use to which the library was put.[27] Fruits range from theses to articles illuminating individual manuscripts and contributions to wide-ranging studies.[28] Domestically, guidebooks and numerous articles for *Dome* have emerged from the library. Genealogical enquiries are increasingly numerous, though not unwelcome as they rarely come from the 'dotty enquirers convinced they are descended from St Hereward the Wake', who bothered the archivist at Canterbury.[29]

Fuller suspected that an enquiry service of this quality could not be maintained if the library collections were transferred. Shortly after his death and before the appointment of Frank Atkinson in 1981 an analogous case was put to the test. Since the refurbishment undertaken with the support of the Pilgrim Trust had not achieved an adequate reading room for the archives,[30] the dean and chapter entered into negotiation with the Guildhall Library for the deposit of their archive. The connection between the archives and the cathedral library did not date back before the third quarter of the nineteenth century,[31] so the arguments for retention by the cathedral were not as strong as they were in the case of the library stock. The transfer was effected in September 1980, and the smaller archives of the minor canons and the cathedral school were deposited in 1994. Chapter minutes from 1832, later baptismal, marriage and burial registers, and some official papers of late twentieth-century greater persons, remain in the cathedral library, but the library does not seek to be an archival repository. That role is successfully fulfilled in the arrangement with Guildhall Library where the archive is in the care of professional archivists, sits alongside diocesan and other related material, and is publicly available to the growing number of readers who could never have been accommodated in the cathedral library. The cathedral library is thereby enabled to fulfil its two main functions. A collection of early printed books intimately connected to the chamber in which it is housed is preserved and exploited, and an adaptable and specialist information service supplies the needs both of the cathedral itself and of a far-reaching public.

40

ST PAUL'S PRECINCT AND THE BOOK TRADE TO *c.*1800

James Raven

From at least the early fourteenth to the early nineteenth centuries, the precinct of St Paul's was synonymous with the book trade. Long before the introduction of printing in the final third of the fifteenth century, the different yards and building ranges adjoining the cathedral – and at times even the cathedral cloisters and nave – had housed suppliers of vellum, paper, writing materials and books. As manuscript production and exchange tracked the varied evolution of cathedral and monastic centres across Britain, the streets around St Paul's became a particular focus for scriveners, limners and stationers, and with their book traditions well established, continued in the age of print as the premier site of book publishing in Britain. By 1800 St Paul's Churchyard – together with Paternoster Row to the immediate north – comprised one of the greatest publishing centres in Europe. From here, booksellers despatched books, magazines and other print to the country towns of England but also to the colonies in North America, the Caribbean, India, Africa, Australasia and the Far East. Fire and constant rebuilding transformed the physical appearance of the shops and stalls of the precinct, but the rituals of the book trade, many based on proud traditions and on memories of defiance and martyrdom, continued to be played out in the vicinity of the cathedral. No history of St Paul's is complete without an account of the publishing and bookselling cocoon that was the churchyard and row.

The ancient axis for the stationery, scribal, publishing and then printing trades of London ran from St Paul's to London Bridge, the sole road crossing of the Thames until 1755 and lined by shops and small crafts premises. The wealthy Bridge House, responsible for maintaining London Bridge, was also a dominant landlord in the fast-growing book-trading quarter of St Paul's and Paternoster Row. William de Southflete, a binder, is recorded at a shop in Paternoster Row in 1312, and several stationers and book artisans are known to have operated in the cathedral churchyard at the beginning of the fourteenth century. The first of the Bridge House shops in the row were erected in the early 1280s against the outside of the churchyard wall by the mayor Henry le Waleys to the north of the Pardon Churchyard and the Charnel House, between Paul's Alley (running right through Old St Paul's) and what was to become known as Pissing Alley. An early tenancy agreement by Waleys stipulated that noisy or tumultuous trades such as butchers, apothecaries, goldsmiths or cooks were not to occupy the shops.[1]

Bridge House rentals list sixty-six book artisans between 1395 and 1554, many of them prominent citizens. The majority contributed to a bustling commercial and civic community in St Paul's precinct that included lawyers operating in the cathedral nave from at least the fourteenth century. By about 1400 these lawyers had a particular devotion to the cult of St Erkenwald in the cathedral (pp. 40, 121). The legal dealings connected directly to commerce and finance in nearby parts of the city and it stimulated the trade of the scriveners. From the first, the premier book-trading sites adjoined the doors of the cathedral whose nave and transepts served as public thoroughfares. The bookmen worked in a centre long the focus of élite artistic production and consumption ranging from stonecarving, decorative carpentry and monumental brasses, to the making of stained glass and religious memorabilia and artefacts, including paternosters.[2]

The Bridge House shops were rebuilt in 1388, with further acquisitions stretching along the north of the dean's boundary wall to Paul's Gate at least 1358.[3] In all, some fifty-seven tenants occupied a line of thirty shops in Paternoster Row between

1404 and 1410, nineteen of whom were book traders and scriveners. Between 1460 and 1500 twenty-three different stationers, limners, scriveners, binders and textwriters tenanted thirty-six different Bridge House shops and solars in the row. John Pye, Warden of the Stationers in 1441, lived in Watling Street, just off the churchyard, east of St Paul's.[4] Another leading bookman, Peter Bylton (fl. 1404–54 and warden of the Stationers in 1426), rented three row premises, and later operated from his row house of *le Peter et Poule*, given to the Bridge House at his death.[5] Located on the northern side of the row on the corner of what was to become Queens Head Alley, the site continued to flourish as a cluster of bookshops for four more centuries until destroyed by the incendiary bombs of January 1941.[6]

The arrival of the printing press in London in the late fifteenth century transformed the book trades of St Paul's. Printers congregated in two broad areas of activity: one centred outside the city around Smithfield and the other reached from Paul's Wharf and the bridge in the south to Baynard's Castle and the cathedral in the north.[7] Julian Notary left to sell books first at Temple Bar and then in St Paul's Churchyard in the early six-

teenth century, with many early printers and sellers of printed books also setting up shops neighbouring the cathedral. The printer John Rastell operated from the Mermaid, first in the south churchyard 1512–15, and then at a Bridge House shop against Paul's Gate. His printed colophon is the first of any English stationer in the churchyard.[8]

The early sixteenth-century London book trade was dominated by aliens. A specific proviso excluded books from a 1484 Act prohibiting importations by foreign merchants, and before 1500 a French agent for a 1494 Paris printing of *Synonyma magistri Johanis de Garlandia* is the sole identified seller of printed books in the churchyard.[9] He was followed by various unnamed importers of French books, including those advertising at the sign of the Holy Trinity in the churchyard from 1505. English booksellers did continue to trade, however, even before the withdrawal of the proviso in 1534 brought a new generation of native printers to the city and to the cathedral precinct. By 1518 Henry Pepwell of the Cross Yard (including Paul's Cross) was publicly identified in his books, and five years later a tax list confirmed the Cross Yard as the focus of the Henrician trade with at least six identifiable

352. Book trades in St Paul's precinct and its neighbourhood during the eighteenth century.

premises associated with bookselling or printing in the eighteenth century

major or public buildings

other private houses

353. 'John Allen at the Rising Sunne, neare St Paul's', a signboard of 1656

stationers including Rastell (and a further three elsewhere in the churchyard). The apparent dominance of Pepwell was challenged by the establishment of Henry Tabbe as a publisher from at least 1542, while Thomas Dockwray became the first master of the Stationers' Company. Another eminent early trader was the alien Reyner Wolfe, who established the first printing shop in the Cross Yard by 1543 and flourished in the early years of Elizabeth's reign. By his death in 1573, his known accumulated properties, including the site of the charnel chapel, comprised 'a continuous stretch of more than 120 feet of the best bookselling frontage in England'.[10]

The book traders of St Paul's greatly increased in number and range in the second half of the sixteenth century. Importing stationers and wholesalers had long been more heavily capitalized and powerful than any other bookmen. By the 1580s, however, the leading printers (mostly outside the city walls) advanced a short-lived supremacy before they, too, were outranked by the publisher–booksellers who then consolidated their position by investment in copy during the seventeenth century. Among the most important of these early booksellers identified in Peter Blayney's full study of the churchyard shops of the period are Humphrey Toy (1562–74) and Thomas Chard (1578–85), who traded under the sign of the Helmet facing south on the churchyard. From the end of the sixteenth century, Robert Walley, Thomas Adams, John Drawater and then Joan Walley worked with others in shops near to the great north door of the cathedral.[11] Another, Francis Coldock, at the Green Dragon, became one of the largest book dealers (and later, master of the Stationers' Company in the 1590s). The celebrated printer and stationer Henry Bynneman opened at the Black Boy in the row in 1566 and was at the Three Wells at the north-west door of the cathedral by 1572, eleven years before his death in 1583.[12] It is perhaps

symptomatic of the changing trade that his first work seems to have been Crowley's *Apologie, or Defence of Predestination* printed in 1566, while one of his most important later productions was Holinshed's *Chronicles of England, Scotland and Ireland* (1577).

Equally prominent among the Tudor booksellers were the far from publicity-shy John Day, with his shop in Aldersgate, and his learned son, Richard. Day senior, who began work in 1546, established his reputation (and wealth) with the issue from 1563 of four folio editions of Foxe's Book of Martyrs (as the *History of the Acts and Monuments of the Church* was and is popularly known). Foxe probably served the Days as a corrector. Later patents for the metrical psalms, the ABC and the Little Catechism offered sure financial reward, and Day also published *Gorboduc* and Ascham's *Scholemaster*. He was the favoured printer of Archbishop Parker and Secretary Burghley, who sought to establish him in a new churchyard shop in the teeth of opposition from the mayor and aldermen.[13] Day finally moved to the churchyard in 1573, but the lease and shop proposed by Parker were never effected – although the plans for it give us a marvellous vignette both of the design of a two-storey bookshop with movable external counters and of the attempt by the archbishop to extend business premises right across Paul's Cross Churchyard.[14]

The commercial appearance of the bookshop itself accompanied the advertising stratagems of the title page and the issue of catalogues and fliers. Booksellers' signs suspended above the shop front provided a recognizable trade badge, many, of course, mentioned or even illustrated on the title-page or catalogue. Gordon Duff records thirty-seven different signs in the churchyard alone before 1558 and a further four in Paternoster Row, including the Row Greyhound of John Harrison and the Black Boy of Henry Sutton.[15] The sixteenth-century churchyard shops boasted a wonderfully whimsical range of names, most of them common throughout the city. Only the Bible and the Bishop's Head seemed to reflect the character of the neighbourhood (Fig. 353).

The establishment of the Stationers' Company further confirmed the importance of the book trade to this part of the City. From 1554 the hall and chambers of the company stood in the south-west corner of the precinct, modified from the buildings of St Peter's College, the foundation for the cathedral's chantry priests (Fig. 20). After 1606 the stationers moved headquarters to Abergavenny House, sited off Ave Maria Lane and dominating the westerly approach to Paternoster Row and the bookshops of the churchyard. The original Stationers' Hall became the Feathers Tavern, providing the company with rental income until its sale in 1671.[16] Incorporated in 1557, the Stationers' Company regulated apprenticeship, entry and the restrictive practices of the trade, and it oversaw the registration of books 'entered at Stationers' Hall'. Successive ordinances, injunctions and decrees granted company officers authority to search and seize unauthorized books. Just as significantly, the establishment of the joint-stock of the company created a financial corporation with arrangements for the successive distribution of dividends to members. The members of the company operated what was in effect a trading cartel, regulating not only the products and the manner of trade, but access to trading and the instruments of production.

As the book trade expanded, sections of the cathedral crypts were rented out as stock rooms for the financing and retailing publishers (almost always simply called 'booksellers') who, together with the greatest stationers, quickly began to surpass 'mechanick' printers in prestige and wealth-holding. So great was this concentration that by the time of the Civil War almost every premises fronting the Cross Yard was then or had in recent times been a bookshop.[17] At the same time, a few book and print shops began to appear in the south precinct and Carter Lane, the increased demand supporting shops more permanent than stall-board and shed lock-ups and developing from a new breadth of literature.[18]

In the century before the Civil War, most disputes about the stock of these precinct shops concerned religion – often at great personal cost. In 1546 John Day was sent 'for pryntyng of noythy bokes, to the Towre',[19] and a year later Richard Smith, Regius Professor of Divinity at Oxford, recanted his defence of traditional doctrine (his *Brief treatyse settynge divers truthes*) at Paul's Cross.[20] John Rogers, prebendary of St Paul's and publisher of the 1537 'Thomas Matthew' Bible, became the first person burned at the stake under Mary in 1555. An Act of the same year sanctioned the loss of a right hand for the circulation of any slander against the Crown – a penalty paid by John Stubbs and his bookseller William Page in 1581. Amongst many whose presses were seized were Abel Jeffes, sometime of St Paul's Churchyard, also imprisoned in 1595 for the printing of *Doctor Cipriano* 'and diverse other lewde ballades and thinges very offensive'. Another, Robert Waldegrave, printer in the Strand and later the churchyard, was imprisoned in 1584 and again in 1585 for printing Puritan literature. Toby Cooke at the Tiger's Head in the churchyard between 1577 and 1599 proved one of several conduits for new theological works, and several shops in the Cross Yard were certainly identified with 'advanced' belief and popular religious controversy.

The staple sales for most traders were bibles and prayer books, but the market for small publications advanced rapidly in the late sixteenth century, boosted from the 1590s by the association of English Ballad Partners collecting together relevant printing rights. The thousands of almanacs (the core of the Stationer's Company English stock), pamphlets and chapbooks peddled by chapmen and supplied by the shops of the churchyard generated a formidable commerce for secular bestsellers. A typical early bestseller was Barnaby Rich's *Roome for a Gentleman*, sold by Geoffrey Charlton at the North Door of St Paul's from 1609. Newsbooks, such as those by Richard Faques and Thomas Marsh, were the other major advancing publication, with the issue of 'corantos' and more ephemeral news books notably increasing in the years of the Civil War.

After the Restoration, greater toleration allowed more open diversity – if subject to the violent political reversals of the 1680s. Samuel Pepys notably sought his less respectable books from the east end of the churchyard. Here, under the shadow of the high altar, three bookshops were renowned suppliers of salacious and pornographic literature. In 1668 Pepys bought *L'Ecole des filles* (based on Aretine's *Postures*) from John Martin at the Bell in St Paul's Churchyard, 'a mighty lewd book, but not yet not amiss for a sober man once to read over, to inform himself in the villainy of the world'.[21] Nine years later, George Wells, also at the eastern end of the churchyard, had his Sun bookshop closed down for selling copies of the same book, just acquired from Amsterdam. Between these two shops stood the Crown, where another John Martin, surgeon of Hatton Garden, faced prosecution in 1709 for his *New System of all the Secret Infirmities and Diseases Natural Accidental and Venereal in Men and Women*. Numerous nearby publishers also invented spoof or vague imprints (such as 'near St Paul's Churchyard'[22]) to protect both themselves and their authors.

A form of self-governance also developed aside from the activities of the Stationers' Company and this was very much associated with leading booksellers in the streets around St Paul's. The fundamental division among the booksellers of the precinct (as indeed, across the whole city) was between those who invested and dealt in the ownership of the copyright to publication, and those who either printed, sold or distributed books for the copyholders or who traded entirely outside the bounds of copyright materials. Ever since the beginning of such divisions in the 1590s, the greatest profits in book publication in England resulted from the ownership of copyrights to successful works. Part-shares bought at the London trade auctions formed the staple investments and commerce was brisk.

Such expanding trade brought physical change and not a little grandeur to some of the booksellers' shops near the cathedral. The stalls and lock-ups against the cathedral walls (and the stationers' use of the crypts) did not survive the post-Fire rebuilding. With the relative decline of the peddling community in the area, fixed-site retailing became the norm. New ostentation was evident. At his death in 1670, James Allestree occupied a large shop on the churchyard with a separate counting house and an elaborate decorative shop division of 'double arch and two doors'. According to his post-mortem inventory, his dining-room boasted expensive printed hangings, gilt stars and pictures, a grand table, leather carpets and eight chairs.[23] Close by, at least eighteen new shops were built in the mid seventeenth century in the area then known as New Jewry, by London House Yard and Paul's Alley, between the Little North Door and the new west portico of the cathedral. Several of these shops were built to two storeys against the wall of the cathedral, together with a new block of twelve tenements, three storeys high, of which all but four can be documented as bookshops.[24] Although nine shops adjoining the cathedral were pulled down in 1665 and not rebuilt, this was an obvious premier site. The large shops in the triangular block bounded by Anchor Alley, New Jewry proper and Paul's Alley north were rebuilt before 1669, although eventually demolished by parliamentary Act before the end of 1702 because they were too close to the new cathedral.

After the Restoration, churchyard booksellers also hurriedly reprinted books and pamphlets suppressed or disowned during the Interregnum, and the Stationers' register reveals more and more of the important copyrights to have been concentrated in fewer hands. By the early eighteenth century, the Chapter Coffee House on the corner of Paul's Alley and Paternoster Row was recognized as the premier mart for the trade in copyrights. Access to these sales was strictly guarded, ensuring the *de facto* control of the book trade by a few established booksellers, almost all from the vicinity of the precinct. At the same time, the market in second-hand books proved increasingly active and well-organized, with the churchyard and row an obvious focus for the trade. This was especially so after the establishment of Christopher Bateman's shop in 1698 on the Ave Maria Lane–Paternoster Row corner. As Henry Plomer wrote, 'probably no bookseller's shop in London was better known in the days of Swift and his contemporaries'.[25] The German traveller, Conrad von Uffenbach, thought Bateman's shop 'the best in England... the floors piled up with books'.[26]

The higher gearing of all this literary activity brought many new booksellers and publishers into the churchyard and row. The bookshops hosted an increasing variety of news gathering and literary endeavours, with many penurious hacks lodging in the garrets high above the shops. The writer of a 1647 pamphlet observed: 'When I was lately in London, as I passed Pauls churchyard, I spyed a friend in a Stationer's Shop, who, after salutes passed, with some briefe discourse of the times, informed mee of some late newes out of Italy arrived at his hands in a Letter from a Friend.'[27] An early literary club, dating from 1695, met at the Castle Tavern, with entrances off Paternoster Row, and in 1749 Dr Johnson founded the Rambler Club in Ivy Lane at the King's Head. The Chapter Coffee House hosted many booksellers' and

literary societies, such as the Witanagemot and the Wet Paper Club, and its literati were featured in the first issue of the *Connoisseur* in 1754. From here Thomas Chatterton despatched his letters and Oliver Goldsmith presided over gatherings of admirers.[28] Joseph Johnson, radical publisher, founder of the *Analytical Review* and one of those prosecuted in the treason trials of the 1790s, extended more than most the literary

354. Harris's Juvenile Library in St Paul's Churchyard, from *Cries of London*, 1804. This shop continued the business of John Newbery

355. North side of St Paul's Churchyard looking east in 1822, drawing by Thomas Hornor. (GL)

NORTH SIDE OF ST PAUL'S CHURCH YARD, WITH THE END OF CHEAPSIDE.

sociability of booksellers' shops and living-rooms around the churchyard. From the early 1780s, Johnson presided over a kind of chic anti-establishment salon, attracting radical luminaries of the day to the rooms above his shop facing the cathedral on the north side.

After their close relationship with the cathedral in the four-teenth and fifteenth centuries, and the dynamic and often violent interaction of the Tudor and Stuart years, the eighteenth-century booksellers of the churchyard and the burgeoning Paternoster Row inhabited a more secular world. Certain key connections remained, most notably in the publication of cathedral music and sermons, but these supported rather than undermined the manu-facture of gentility. John Day had printed, under his patent, several church music books (including part books), but his 1562 *Whole Book of Psalmes* was the only one reissued. John Barnard, a minor canon of St Paul's, pioneered the printing of cathedral music with his 1641 *First Book of Selected Church Music*, but the market was demonstrably small. Most publication of music books remained with scribal copyists such as Stephen Bing (1610–81), minor canon of the cathedral,[29] while the greatest music publishers of the seventeenth century, John and Henry Playford, were based not in the churchyard but at Inner Temple, and they issued more sec-ular than religious music. Most cathedral music continued to be published more locally, and notably by Christopher Thompson and his family, whose music and music printing shop stood to the north of the west door of St Paul's. Many churchyard and row booksellers also combined to issue specially printed copies of fes-tival, fast day, thanksgiving and other notable sermons. Round-the-corner publishing enabled rapid dissemination, whether or not (as in the case of the Sacheverell sermon printed in some 50,000 copies: pp.343–4) officially sanctioned. The cathedral authorities and their preachers, however, accounted for a very small part of the overall clientele published by and buying from the precinct bookshops – St Paul's stood magnificently at the cen-tre of a literary engine room that now paid increasingly little attention to it.

The other outstanding feature of this activity was the despatch from around the churchyard of the books and pamphlets to the country. It was a commerce hugely expanded from the late seventeenth century and contributed greatly to the chaotic bustle of these streets. Some of the larger consignments were packed in barrels for coastal ships from the London wharves, but the fastest, most direct means of sending out stock was by common carrier. The churchyard's greatest coaching inn, The Goose and Gridiron, was grandly rebuilt after the Fire, as were the inns at Ludgate and the Poultry sited either side of the precinct. These inns acted rather like the great Victorian train stations that in many ways succeeded them. Each inn, like the Belle Sauvage, a bear-garden of a hostelry little more than a hundred yards from the Great West Door, served its own distinct route to the country.

The same traffic created particular images of the churchyard and its book trades, all carried far beyond the metropolis and conveyed all the more effectively by the books and prints them-selves. From at least the early seventeenth century, booksellers managed a high visibility through their own title-page addresses. These supplied what has been called 'imagéability' or the ways in which venues might be imagined by readers (many of whom were never to visit the St Paul's precinct at any time in their lives).[30] For coaching-inn or coffee-house readers in the coun-try towns, the world of books was constructed from these names: St Paul's Church Yard, the Great (or Little) North Door,

Pater-Noster Row, Amen Corner, Ave Maria Lane, Ivy Lane, Carter Lane, the Chapter Coffee House, and (much loved by the unlicensed) Pissing Alley. Many booksellers' trade cards and, later, circulating library and bookshop catalogues further included engravings of idealized interiors even if the reality proved more modest. Just as widely, the St Paul's printshops, bookshops and libraries came to be represented in literary tours and descriptions and, by the mid eighteenth century, in engrav-ings and illustrations in books, magazines and separately pub-lished prints (Figs 357–8).[31]

Those who did visit, or who worked or lived in Paternoster Row and St Paul's Churchyard were faced by extraordinary phys-ical confinement. Here, in the shadow of the cathedral, was an astonishing profusion and mixture of trades. Pungent smells met visitors at every corner, rising from printing troughs, stables, oil-shops, workshop fires and butchers' stalls in Newgate Market where carcasses were displayed on open stands and fifty-one cel-lars catered for the on-site slaughter of the hundreds of beasts driven there. The clusters of chimneys contributed to a murky atmosphere in a concentrated area. Crossing Blackfriars Bridge in 1785, the bookseller William West 'could only just perceive St. Paul's with its dome towering amid the smoke and fog that surrounded it'.[32]

After the Fire, the grander, more open churchyard, with a solitary elm tree in its north-eastern corner by the 1740s (Fig. 355),[33] had replaced the bookshop habitations of the Cross Yard and cathedral bays, but eighteenth-century book-seekers were now invited to a dark and crowded bookish world that lay beyond the northern churchyard façades. Even by 1720, John Strype noted that 'at the upper end [of Paternoster Row] some Stationers, and large Warehouses for Booksellers [are] well situated for learned and studious Mens access thither; being more retired and private'.[34] Leading booksellers' premises converged in the long strip of the row itself, and collaboration and sharing of ware-housing was well organized. Binders' houses were huddled together with small printers located in backhouses and yards. William West further recalled standing at the St Paul's entrance to London-house yard where 'my mind was pervaded with a kind of awe at the gloomy appearance of the stores of literature before me'.[35]

Both bookshops and printshops were distinguished by their narrowness and height. Buildings were four and sometimes five storeys, with split working levels contributing to what Sum-merson described as the 'insistent verticality' of the streetscape.[36] Despite the many Acts to regulate building, the restoration of the area around St Paul's included rapidly built houses in unpaved alleys which were once gardens or courts of adjoining large houses.[37] The most striking change to the streetscape was the removal of the hanging trade signs. Strype in 1720 had reported of the row that 'of all the Streets in the whole City, there is none to compare to it for handsome Signs, and uniformly hung'.[38] A gen-eration after, complaints about the hindrance to traffic and trade resulted in an Act of 1762 requiring the signs to be fixed flat against the walls. Action was also taken to bring some sort of order to the dozens of advertising rubric posts lining the precinct streets outside the bookshops and pasted with title pages and other printed sheets.[39]

What was clear by the time of Strype's report was the impor-tance of booksellers' concentration in one area, and here recent research using taxation records has allowed an appreciation of the physical layout of the bookshops impossible since the Second

356.   Paternoster Row, showing bookshops, from a trade card of *c.* 1800. (GL)

unavoidable. An overturned candle was certainly blamed for the notorious fire of January 1770 that burned down the booksellers Johnson and Payne, Upton, and Crowder and Dod's Bible warehouse off the row.

Surviving plans also show why relatively few printers (compared to the great number of booksellers) operated around the cathedral by the late eighteenth century. The shop of Francis Blyth, printer in an alley off the row, for example, could not have been larger than ten feet square on each level. Like many in the area, Blyth's press and several work rooms had to be on the upper floors.[41] Many properties of the Bridge House on the northern side of the precinct wall were just as shallow, and save for the Corporation's rental interests, they would have been demolished in the first of the post-Fire schemes to widen the row.[42] Obvious exceptions were large corner sites such as those occupied by John Beecroft and Henry Woodfall, or the tenement later numbered 16–18 in the row, once the Peter and Poule house, in multiple and distinguished occupancy through the eighteenth and nineteenth centuries. Tenants included Coote, Cooke, the Harrisons, Kendall and Hogg, all innovative booksellers and responsible for some of the greatest publishing successes of their age. The premises boasted a massive combined frontage of more than sixty feet, with a further frontage of thirty-three feet on Queens Head Alley and more back shops besides.[43]

Congested and colourful, the eighteenth-century churchyard and row attracted migrant young men (many untrained in publishing) to set up further bookshops, adding to the diversity of the literary trade in the precinct. In addition to Bateman's second-hand bookshop, most of the great booksellers of the eighteenth century lined Paternoster Row. They included the Longmans (partly on the site of the bishop's palace), the prolific and innovative Robinsons, and the equally successful Woodfalls. The first bookshop specializing in books for children and juveniles was managed by John Newbery in the churchyard from 1745. His shop almost adjoined the music shop of the Thompsons, but also the premises of the Bowles family, for long the greatest print and caricature shop in the country. Thomas Bowles traded at No. 69, next to the chapter house, from about 1712 to 1767. His nephew, Carington, son of his brother John who had also been in the trade since about 1720, continued the business until his own death in 1793 (Fig. 358). Thereafter, this most famous of print- and map-selling businesses was managed by the son of Carington Bowles, as 'Bowles and Carver', until 1832. The Bowles's materials were sometimes risqué, but more clandestine literature had also for long been available in the churchyard.[44] Also starting in the churchyard were William Bristow, 'next the Great Toy Shop' from about 1759 until 1766 when he moved to Fetter Lane, and John Wilkie, publishing topical tracts from the Bible, at no. 71, on the northern side near Ludgate Hill. Between his commencement in 1757 and his death in 1785, he issued about 760 publications, most of them in his own name only. He was succeeded by his sons, George and Thomas, who had also been publishing separately for at least four years. By 1800, total Wilkie publications surpassed 1,300 books and pamphlets.

Foremost among the new stationery and bookselling dynasties of St Paul's, however, were the Rivingtons, whose high-church Anglicanism clashed uncompromisingly with their noncon-formist neighbour and *Monthly Review* proprietor, Ralph Griffiths, who faced the Great North Door of the cathedral. Charles Rivington established the firm in 1711 at the Bible and Crown, no. 62, one door east of Canon Alley on the northern side

World War destruction of the street patterns and the loss, at the same time, of so many booksellers' business and personal papers.[40] From the mid eighteenth to the early nineteenth century, about sixty or so leading booksellers (and some two dozen at any one time) established the churchyard and the row as an international centre for the wholesaling of books and magazine and periodical publishing (Fig. 352). The row and churchyard clearly attracted booksellers wishing to join an area of noted trade specialism (agglomeration theory, in modern parlance). Commercial advantages included the sharing of warehousing and the proximity of allied trades including tallow chandlers, oilmen, leather-sellers and silversmiths (and other engravers). Crucial also were the sources of capital needed to set up and sustain publishing businesses, and shared operations became the most obvious form of risk limitation, especially where profitability was threatened by excess productive capacity.

It was the narrowness and height of individual dwellings that enabled such compactness in what was, after all, a total habitable area little larger than the floorspace of the cathedral itself. With a few prominent exceptions, most of the rented bookshops were small properties, crowded together with many upper storeys. Different tenants and subtenants might occupy parts of a single storey, with upstairs rooms opening up across neighbouring buildings. The confined light can also be linked to the fires that recur-rently plagued the cathedral precinct. If pressmen were to work fourteen hours a day throughout the year, candle and oil light was

357. *A view in St Paul's churchyard on a windy day.* Three quacks, Col. Dalmahoy, Dr Rock and Mr Ibbetson, interfere with a woman. Print published by Robert Sayer, 1740. (GL)

358. *A real scene in St Paul's churchyard on a windy day,* mezzotint by Robert Dighton, 1783. A later version on a similar theme, with the window of Bowles the printseller and the chapter house door behind. (GL)

of the churchyard (Fig. 352). Together with John Osborn, Rivington persuaded Samuel Richardson to write a series of moral letters 'in a common style, on such subjects as might be of use to those country readers who were unable to indite for themselves' – an undertaking which was to result in the publication of *Pamela* in 1740. On Charles's death in 1742, his son, John, succeeded to both his business and his mantle of saintliness. In John Nichols's words, John was 'universally esteemed' and enjoyed 'the especial patronage of the Clergy, particularly those of the higher order'.[45] In the next generation, Francis and Charles Rivington, trading jointly between 1792 and 1810, contributed to publishing standard editions of Milton, Shakespeare and Locke, and enhanced further the firm's reputation for theological and religious publications, including Cruden's *Concordance*.[46] The total number of eighteenth-century imprints bearing the name of Rivington is an astonishing 5,900 or more. Many were titles published by large associations of booksellers, but the family appears no less prolific in the early decades of the nineteenth century.

The Rivington piety was widely advertised. John Rivington was reportedly rarely absent from prayers in St Paul's at six or seven in the morning, even if this meant dressing in the cathedral.[47] His son Charles proudly recorded that the archbishop of Canterbury came in person to cast his vote for Rivington in the ballot for printer to the SPCK in 1781.[48] Finally, in 1791 the Rivingtons' *British Critic* was founded to promote Anglican loyalism in the face of revolution. The Rivingtons, indeed, could hardly expect to operate unchallenged and in a certain respect the late eighteenth-century churchyard publishers came to resemble their Elizabethan predecessors, with battle-lines drawn up over religious imprints and publishing emphases. In 1770 Fletcher's shop was taken over by Joseph Johnson, the most influential and notorious of the nonconformist booksellers trading in the precinct until 1815. The empire of reviewers created by Griffiths also stretched out to the bastions of old dissent (including the Norwich and Warrington academies) where distin-

guished scholars penned many of the articles that were sent back to the churchyard for monthly publication.[49] The Rivingtons made easy targets. According to the bookseller Dell, John Rivington was the great hypocrite, of 'a weak dishonest rotten heart',[50] and John Wolcot, as Peter Pindar, offered the following in 1806:

Ere long, the Huckster promises me more;
Lives of the Brother Rivingtons – great men!
Greater traders of the literary lore –
Encouragers of paper, ink, and pen.
In Paul's Church-yard, the Bible and the Key,
This wondrous pair is always to be seen –
Somewhat the worse for wear – a little gray,
One like a *Saint*, and one with Caesar's mien.[51]

Just as remarkable in this period were the confrontations between the various churchyard businesses of the Newbery and Carnan families. From their shops volleys of litigation and abuse were exchanged or hurled against the world. In 1743 John Newbery moved from Reading to continue his publishing business near Temple Bar. Within two years he set up as bookseller at the Bible and Sun, close to the chapter house at no. 65 on the north side of St. Paul's Churchyard, where he traded until his death in 1767. Newbery has claims to be the first specialist in children's books, or, as Dell put it, 'Renown'd for all, – He knowledge can supply, To lisping babes and babes of six foot high'. On his death he was succeeded by his son, Francis, in partnership with Francis's stepbrother, Thomas Carnan, a member of another Reading bookselling family. In 1779 shortly before the dissolution of the partnership, Francis opened new premises at no. 45 at the east end of the Churchyard. Here his lucrative business in patent medicines soon overshadowed his bookselling. Following a family quarrel, John Newbery's nephew (also named Francis) set up business at the opposite end of the Churchyard, on the corner of Ludgate Street, where he also traded in children's literature and was succeeded after his death in 1780 by his widow, Elizabeth. Thomas Carnan had traded with his stepfather from at least the late 1740s, publishing, among many titles Goldsmith's *Traveller*, *Deserted Village*, and *The Vicar of Wakefield*. A total of 1,352 eighteenth-century imprints are known to include the name Newbery, with 485 bearing the name Carnan. Between 1740 and 1799, at least 262 title pages included both names from several shops in the churchyard. The relationship between the Newberys and Carnans remained notoriously stormy, however, especially after Francis's move to no. 45 in 1779.

This was in the same year that Carnan overturned the Stationers' Company's monopoly in almanacs, and the cathedral precinct was now an arena for the battle over copyright. The other main protagonist, Alexander Donaldson, also traded in the churchyard between about 1773 and 1788, having arrived in London from Edinburgh in 1763. From mid century the exclusive booksellers' publishing associations, most meeting at the Chapter Coffee House and many operating from premises in the row and churchyard, successfully argued that the Copyright Act of 1710 sanctioned perpetual copyright under common law. Decisions of King's Bench and Chancery prohibiting Donaldson from continuing his cut-price reissues confirmed the ascendancy of the associations. In 1774, however, a ruling of the House of Lords ended the booksellers' invocation of common law to sanction perpetual copyright, and enabled those outside the charmed circle of leading booksellers to publish cheap reprint editions of classic works.[53] Carnan's confrontation with the Stationer's Company derived from his printing of almanacs. After the company's first chancery injuction against him in 1773 he was said always to keep a clean shirt in his pocket in readiness for court appearances. Finally, the company managed to secure a parliamentary Bill to legalize their monopoly, a ploy that backfired spectacularly when the Bill was thrown out by the House of Commons in May 1779. According to bookseller West, immediately after his almanac victory, Carnan 'drove repeatedly, in triumph, round St Paul's Churchyard and through Paternoster Row, in his lofty phaeton and pair'.[54]

Carnan's celebration acknowledged another important feature of publishing in the precinct. Religious, political and familial associations contributed to a sense of place explicable not only through the physical reality of the buildings but also by the remembered and the memorialized. The Stationers' Election Feast was held on the Sunday after St Peter's Day, 29 June, reflecting the original occupancy of St Peter's College. The feast marked the opening of the guild year and the incoming elections to office. The later barge-outings on the Thames by the stationers also represented a fine example of the invented tradition. Proud of the tradition of bookselling, influential booksellers and lovers of literary lore incorporated memories of trials and sufferings as well as triumphs, through printed anecdote, essay or even trade sign. The 'heads' in booksellers' signs in particular signalled deliberate and often contrasting allegiances. It was a self-referential world, and one in which puffing and commercial ingenuity was often indistinguishable from sincere reflection and commentary. Depictions and parodies of them all were to be found on sale in printshops such as those of Bowles in the churchyard (Fig. 358).

Victorian and early twentieth-century representations of the precinct and its wider bookworld have provided a nostalgic and selective account of the 'haunts of old booksellers', emphasizing individualism, eccentricity and a certain kind of élitism. For all the area's depiction as a quaint, higgledy-piggledy place, much regularity was in evidence by 1800, especially in the order necessary for efficient commercial production. From at least the early nineteenth century, when steam-driven presses transformed printing operations, there were in London many more, and not fewer, general locations for the book trade, but there was also a greater concentration of bookselling in the St Paul's district (and far fewer printshops). Impermanence was obvious, properties were reused by different trades, and buildings had to be adaptable. By the early nineteenth century many of the grander booksellers maintained properties well outside the city, or at least no longer lived over the shop. The Robinsons retreated to Streatham, the Longmans to Hampstead. The cosy world of the churchyard and row bookshops with booksellers in residence above was fractured. Visitors to the bookshops remembered the narrowness and height of the tenements, but also the historic associations with particular sites. And now physical remains have almost all been obliterated and all is a matter of written and drawn record.

41

THE PRECINCT AND SETTING OF ST PAUL'S FROM THE NINETEENTH CENTURY

Simon Bradley

The story of the setting of St Paul's Cathedral from the nineteenth century to the present can be read as a miniature of the City of London's own planning history: city-dwellers give way to commerce, trade in goods to finance and administration, small-scale architecture to ever bigger, bulkier or taller buildings. But St Paul's is also a unique story, shaped by recurrent concerns to protect or enhance views of Wren's masterpiece. For no other Anglican cathedral was so exposed, or had lost control over so much of its immediate surroundings. The dean, chapter and surveyor consequently feature much less in the story than developers, self-appointed experts, eager architects and well-meaning friends. As with the rest of the city, events were also violently interrupted by the Blitz, which suddenly offered architects and planners the possibility of a near-complete fresh start. The results were both disappointing and short-lived, however, and by the time this book appears a second rebuilding will be complete, on a scale almost as large as that of the 1950s and 1960s.

ST PAUL'S CHURCHYARD FROM 1837 TO THE SECOND WORLD WAR

The physical impact of the cathedral, powerful enough even today, must have been overwhelming in the tighter surroundings of centuries past. This domination is captured by J. H. Nixon's Turneresque painting of the south side *en fête* for Lord Mayor's Day, 9 November 1837, when the new queen went to dine at Guildhall for the first time (Fig. 361).[1] The streets around the churchyard proper then remained as they had been for more than a century, like twin currents of a stream parted by the smooth-worn shores of an islet. Major architectural incidents included the early eighteenth-century chapter house north of the nave, and St Paul's School on the east. Further east still were the baroque obelisk spires of St Vedast, Foster Lane, at the west end of Cheapside, and of St Augustine, Watling Street, at the east side of Old Change just beyond the churchyard. The idea of unity within this enclosure was reinforced by its numbering, anti-clockwise from no. 1 St Paul's Churchyard, at the junction with the present Ludgate Hill on the south side, to no. 80, its counterpart on the north.[2]

359.   Plan and elevations of St Paul's Churchyard in 1839 from John Tallis, *London Street Views* (1838–40)

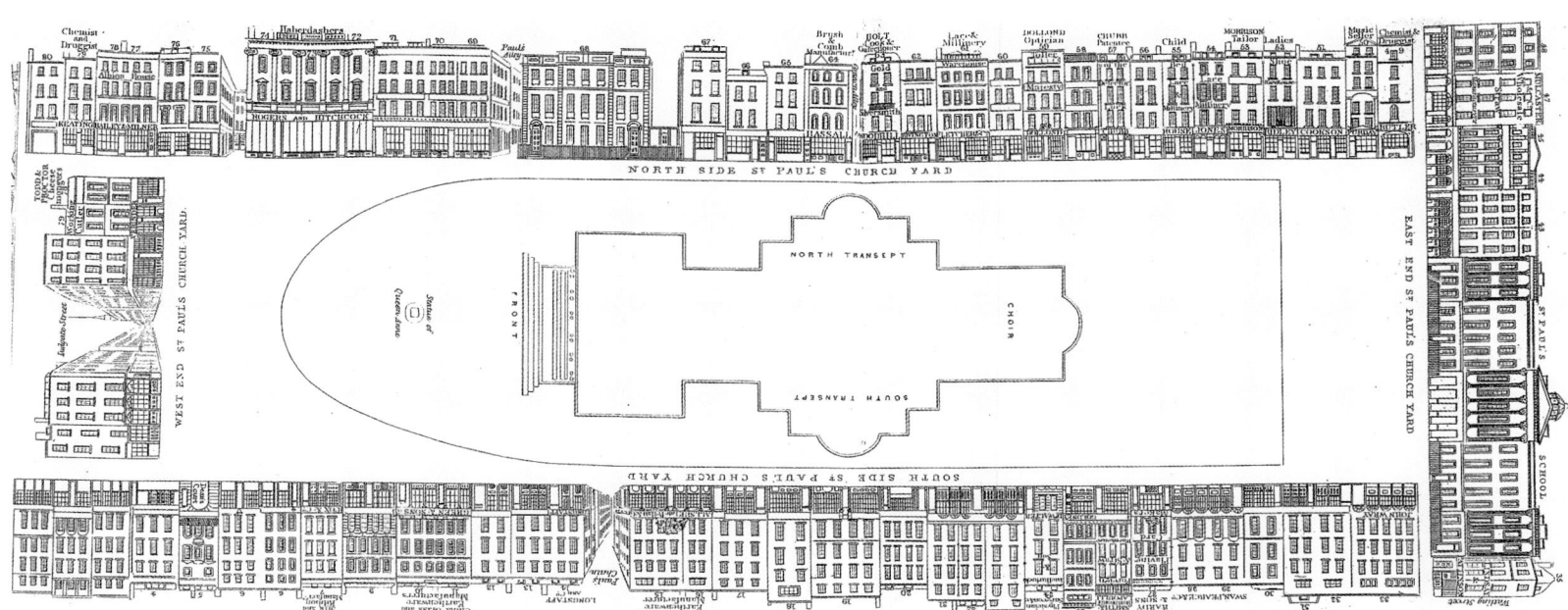

360.   St Paul's and the development of its precinct, 1676–2003. Modest changes up to the map of 1937 – chiefly the expansion of the open setting to the north, south-west and south-east, and the formation of Cannon Street West – contrast with the complete replanning of all but the extreme south-west area after the Second World War. Recent rebuilding on the north side echoes several features of the pre-war street plan.

A closer view can be had from one of John Tallis's *London Street Views*, first issued in 1838 (Fig. 359). The first really big newcomer to the churchyard fills most of the east side: George Smith's St Paul's School of 1823–4, a grandiose exercise in the classical manner associated with the so-called Metropolitan Improvements of *c*.1815–35. The rest is still lined mostly with unembellished upright house fronts of post-Great-Fire and Georgian type. Fancier elevations appear here and there, several of which represent rebuildings of more than one older property.

Passers-by would doubtless have noticed these embellishments less than they did the near-unbroken run of shopfronts below. These had long been a feature of the churchyard (Fig. 360). There would still have been much to attract behind the glass in Tallis's time, including the wares of several household names clustered on the north side, where sunlight fell most favourably and the absence of wheeled traffic encouraged a lingering inspection. The locksmiths Chubb & Son were at no. 57, where Jeremiah Chubb had moved from Portsmouth in 1820. At the start of the 1840s Chubb's entire output was still produced traditionally, without machines.[3] Two doors down at no. 59 was the distinguished optician George Dollond the elder, great-nephew of John Dollond, who had invented the achromatic lens in 1757.[4] For seekers after spiritual security and clear-sightedness, no. 62 housed the religious publishers J. G. F. & J. Rivington, which had kept up its earlier high-church reputation (see pp. 436–7) with such titles as the *Tracts for the Times* by John Henry Newman and his allies.[5] At no. 65 was the shop of the more evangelically inclined Religious Tract Society, whose genius for packaging improving literature in alluring forms would culminate with the long-running *Boy's Own Paper* in 1879.[6] But the dominant trades were increasingly tailoring and clothing – merchants of muslin, wool, lace, silk and millinery, all expanding from their traditional home around Cheapside – which already occupied twenty-eight of the eighty street addresses.

Victoria's reign saw a huge increase in the height and bulk of the buildings around St Paul's. A few six-storey fronts already appear in Tallis's views, as yet neither very wide nor very deep. A much higher density could be obtained by merging their sites with those of properties in streets beyond. The first great example was the warehouse of the wholesale drapers Messrs Cook at nos. 21–6, designed by James Knowles the elder and erected in 1853. This in its time represented an architecture of commercial modernity, recognized by contemporaries as a metropolitan version of the Italianate *palazzi* built for the booming cloth trade in Manchester; it took just ninety days to build, almost up to the level of the cathedral's top cornice.[7] Later premises of comparable mass remain to the west, including nos. 5–14 of 1896–7, built for the textile house of Pawson & Leaf, together making a continuous run from Godliman Street to the top of Ludgate Hill.[8] Before 1940 the warehouses and offices around the rest of the churchyard were generally similar, bending and swerving along the street lines in order to incorporate as much lucrative square footage as the site would allow.

While *laissez-faire* ruled, there could be no such thing as an architectural policy for St Paul's Churchyard, nor is it easy to tell whether its buildings had any inflections intended to complement the cathedral. There does seem to have been less Neo-Gothic than in some other City streets, though the use of round-arched medieval or mixed styles tends to blur the picture.[9] One instance of deliberate enhancement is recorded, after the newly vacated St Paul's School buildings were demolished in 1884: the site was taken for two separate warehouses meant for the Manchester wholesale trade, and the architects joined forces to produce a single coherent elevation.[10] But a petition to Common Council by Ewan Christian, President of the RIBA, that the site be used to open up a view of St Paul's was firmly rejected; design was one thing, sacrifice of precious building-land quite another.[11]

Christian's plea is a reminder that would-be improvers cared less about the style of buildings around St Paul's than about their effect on views of the cathedral itself. This much is apparent from the controversy that followed the creation of Cannon Street West by the Corporation in 1850–4.[12] The new road broke into the churchyard at the south-east, where a large area was cleared and

361. Queen Victoria's procession to Guildhall, 9 November 1837. Painting by J. H. Nixon, 1838, showing the south side of the cathedral. (Guildhall Art Gallery)

362.   The south side of the cathedral from the end of Cannon Street in 1905

363.   The west front glimpsed from the south-west during clearance in Dean's Court, 1895. (GL)

rebuilt (Fig. 362). It was much wider and straighter than the old eastward route down Watling Street, entering the churchyard a little to the north, which immediately became something of a backwater. Cannon Street West also created the first oblique, long-distance view of the cathedral's south flank. The effect is magical even today, and must have been doubly so in an age much less used to wholesale demolition. But the broad vista began to dwindle as offices and warehouses rose on the newly cleared plots along the route. By 1854 it was plain both that any building on the plot by the south-east corner of the churchyard would be particularly obstructive, and that its site value of £60,000 was beyond the resources of the City Improvement Fund to secure.[13] Hopes rose that Parliament might vote funds to buy it instead, and in December of that year a subcommittee of the RIBA, led by William Tite, attended on the Improvements Committee of the Corporation to plead against new construction.[14] The well-connected Tite also made representations to the prime minister, and questions were asked in the House of Commons.[15] In the end, a nice compromise was reached: the view was kept clear, but the Corporation created storage vaults for rent on the site, entered through a building in Old Change to the east. All that showed above ground was a round opening protected by a stone balustrade adorned with the city arms: a recurrent presence in maps and photographs into the 1950s.[16]

Another long-vanished Victorian practice was the inclusion in large buildings of a dormitory storey for employees, especially in the labour-intensive clothing trades. So many young warehouse

hands were accommodated in the new Cannon Street West that in 1855 a gallery was inserted for them in St Augustine's Church – possibly the last new gallery in a city church – balancing that for St Faith's parishioners in the north aisle.[17] Pawson & Leaf's warehouse went further, with fully three floors given over to residential uses, including dormitories, dining- and sitting-rooms.[18] These facilities may reflect the difficulty of attracting living-in staff by the 1890s, and it would be interesting to know when the last of these dormitories went out of use. They certainly stand as a correction to the commonsensical idea that depopulation always went hand in hand with the advance of commerce.

The enormous convulsions of the 1860s–70s for new streets and railways through the city bypassed St Paul's, and later changes were modest. Extra space for the southern roadway was secured by the easy option of taking an eight-foot-wide strip from the churchyard enclosure itself, in 1873–4.[19] A few small street widenings took place in addition when older premises were rebuilt. The most significant was the tidying-up of the south-west corner after 1895, when Dean's Court was also widened from a mere ten feet to a more acceptable twenty-two (Fig. 363).[20]

Meanwhile, a great plan for a new 'St Paul's Bridge' came and went. As first raised by Francis Bennoch in 1851 and endorsed by parliamentary committee three years later, it was to have crossed the Thames just south of the cathedral's east end, allowing an easy connection via a new road with the northward route up St Martin's-le-Grand and Aldersgate Street.[21] A Royal Commission on London Traffic of 1903–5 gave new impetus to the project (Fig. 365), and an Act for a bridge on the eastern alignment followed in 1911. Imperial self-aggrandizement was in the air, and the winning design in the competition that followed in 1914 (by the Scottish architect George Washington Browne) was suitably bombastic. But the First World War delayed progress and inflated costs, and a second Act in 1921 extending powers to build was never invoked. Parliament in 1929 then threw out the Corporation's Bill for a further extension – a relief to those who feared the effect of traffic vibration on the cathedral fabric.[22] Had it succeeded, the plan would have changed everyday experiences of St Paul's considerably, from a building usually passed length-ways and east–west to a dramatically looming presence encountered a few moments after crossing the river from the south. The extreme width of St Martin's-le-Grand, widened in connection with the bridge plan in 1926, gives a glimpse of what the great new highway might have been like.[23]

Whatever the intended route, the bridge and its approach were certainly meant as an enhancement to the setting of St Paul's. Those concerned with the look of London had also to guard against unwelcome intrusions, as new communications and building methods began to leave their mark on the city. As far back as the early 1850s objections were raised to the towering City Mills building in Upper Thames Street because it interfered with the view of St Paul's from Blackfriars Bridge.[24] A more enduring nuisance was the ornate cast-iron bridge put up across Ludgate Hill by the London, Chatham & Dover Railway in

1863–6, which lasted in de-Victorianized form until 1990.[25] This spoiled views of the west front first opened up when Ludgate was demolished in 1760–1. But it took the sudden obtrusion in 1932–3 of the Portland-faced slab of Faraday House, a nine-storey telephone exchange extension in Queen Victoria Street, to make the active protection of views a Corporation policy. New height guidelines were therefore imposed in 1938 between

365.   *St Paul's Bridge*: an ideal design on the axis of the south transept, by Beresford Pite, 1910. It precedes by four years the official but abortive competition for a bridge on an alignment further east

364.   North-east sector of the churchyard in the 1960s, showing the replacement Paul's Cross set up in 1910 'to recall and to renew the ancient memories' (Reginald Blomfield, architect; Bertram Mackennal, sculptor), against the background of the north transept and Holford's Juxon House

St Paul's and the river, drawn up in collaboration with Godfrey Allen, Surveyor to the Fabric (see p. 301), on the basis of a large-scale city survey presented two years previously. The newly limited heights were varied to suit the falling contour plane; the standard, hundred-foot limit of the London Building Acts took care of more distant views, from Hampstead, Highgate and Greenwich.[26]

Not long before, in 1931, the cloth trades were reinforced by the conversion of nos. 3–4 St Paul's Churchyard for the London Textile Exchange.[27] About the same time, the upper parts of nos. 74–8 on the opposite, north side were made into flats (ingratiatingly named Wren's View) – possibly the City's first 'warehouse conversion'.[28] Few of its new residents could have anticipated how little time remained for their ancient neighbourhood.

POST–WAR REPLANNING AND REBUILDING

The Blitz destroyed almost all the buildings east and south-east of the cathedral and most of those to the north and north-west.[29] The visual limits of its surroundings expanded gigantically as a result, to Bread Street and Cheapside, to Warwick Lane and Newgate Street, and south across Queen Victoria Street to Upper Thames Street. Post-war photographs show St Paul's looking strangely shrunken amidst horizontal wastes of streets lined with empty basements and dotted with burned husks of Wren churches.

Drapery and publishing firms survived in force to the west and south-west, however, and it took longer than is often realized for them all to slip away. Messrs Cook relaunched themselves under the brand name 'Cooks of St Paul's', along with textile fairs and fashion parades, but in 1960 their warehouse came down too.[30] The surviving buildings on the north side, the newly restored chapter house excepted, followed soon afterwards (by which time Paternoster Row looked like 'a narrow country lane bordered by weeds and bushes and wild flowers').[31] Oxford University Press held out at Amen House, Warwick Square until 1966, perhaps the last great publishing name within the orbit of St Paul's.[32] Plenty of shops were provided in the post-war buildings, but they filled up with general-purpose firms serving the hordes of new office workers, so that the churchyard was no longer a specialist retail enclave.

The new setting for St Paul's, the greatest emblem of London's wartime endurance, was from the outset a subject of the highest national interest. Three rival approaches rapidly emerged, all animated by a desire to show off the cathedral more effectively, but based on very different ideals of how London should renew itself. The first, proposed in 1942 by the Royal Academy Planning Committee under Sir Edwin Lutyens and developed up to 1944, was a rigid exercise in monumental classicism in which aesthetic effect overrode considerations of use and cost; even the preserved deanery and chapter house were duplicated, so as not to upset the symmetry.[33] The Corporation begged to demur. Its counter-proposal took the form of a series of recommendations conceived within a commercially minded rebuilding strategy, compiled under the City Engineer F. J. Forty and published as its Reconstruction Report in 1944. More open space was to be provided south, east and west of the cathedral, defined by very bulky new buildings of a uniform skyline and harmonious appearance 'so as to create a quiet formality, without forced symmetry'. Longer views were to be secured by widening Ludgate Hill and by making new vistas in line with the dome and transepts: a pedestrian approach from the north, and a broader corridor from the south, where steps would descend to a new embankment highway (Fig. 366). At the east end, a choice was presented between a new east–west thoroughfare formed by widening Watling Street or more limited clearance at the junction of Cannon Street and the churchyard.[34]

The Reconstruction Report seemed both greedy and unimaginative to most of those outside the city, however. Worse, its provision for a huge increase in the office-working population was at odds with the London County Council's objectives of decentralization and congestion control, as formulated in Forshaw and Abercrombie's *County of London Plan* of 1943. The new Ministry of Town and Country Planning therefore required the Corporation to come up with a replacement.[35] From a modernist point of view, the architectural provisions of the Forty plan were

366. Perspective by J. D. M. Harvey, showing opening-out of the cathedral vista from the river as proposed in *Reconstruction in the City of London*, 1944, by F. J. Forty, the Corporation's engineer. (GL)

367. The *Architectural Review* proposal for a new precinct around St Paul's. Axonometric view by Gordon Cullen, 1946

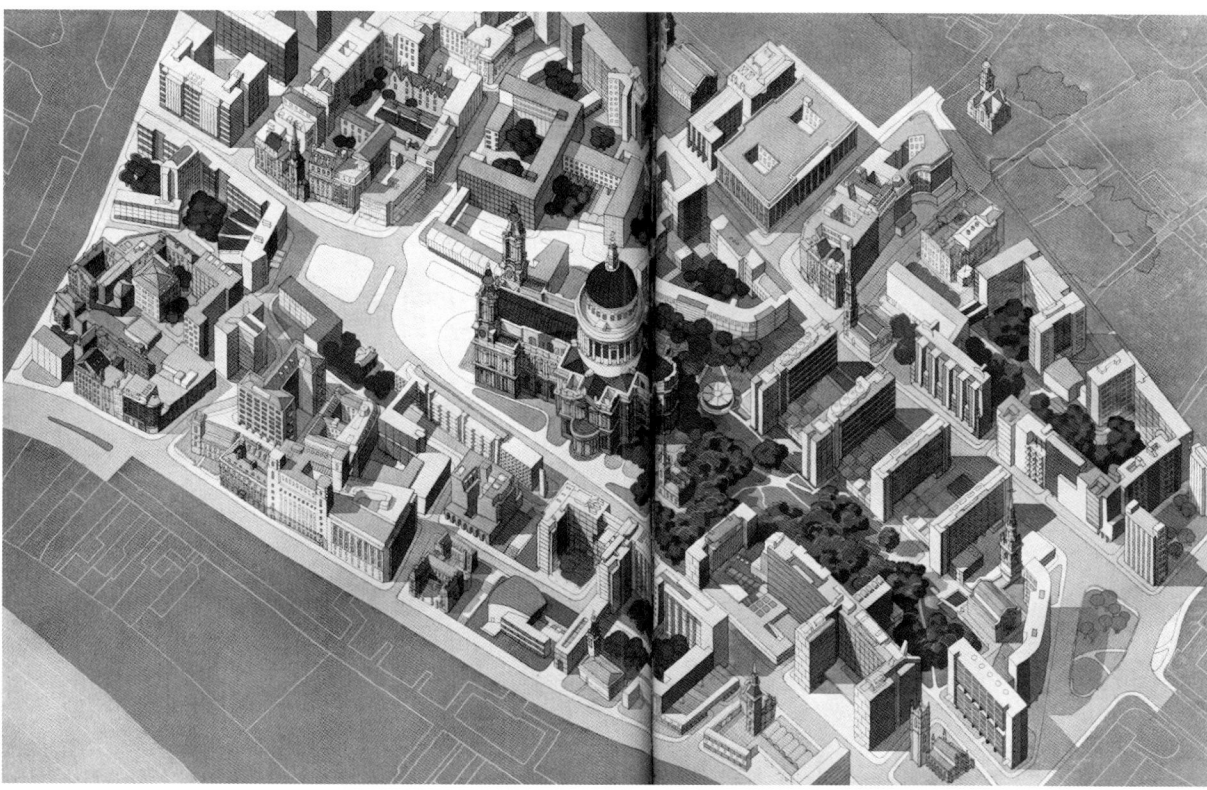

also painfully old-fashioned. The Royal Fine Art Commission said as much in its report of 1945.[36] The foremost mouthpiece of the progressives at that time was the *Architectural Review*, which was developing a new reconstruction aesthetic based on slabs and towers, deployed with a picturesque asymmetry meant to evoke a distinctively English tradition of place-making.[37] Mandatory height restrictions could be set aside in favour of plot-ratio controls (expressed by site area divided by floor area), allowing buildings to rise higher in return for leaving land clear for road widening, traffic-free precincts and public gardens. In 1946 the magazine published a project by 'Hugh Gordon-Peter' (the young architects Hugh Casson, Peter Shepheard and Gordon Stephenson), showing the intended effect of picturesque, freely composed blocks around St Paul's: the third and most radically new of the rival models for rebuilding (Fig. 367).[38]

Plot-ratio planning was duly adopted in the City's second reconstruction plan of 1946–7, drawn up by two architect members of the Royal Fine Art Commission, Charles Holden and W. G. Holford (of whom more later).[39] The final version was published in 1951 as *The City of London: a record of destruction and survival*, and adopted in essence in the County of London Development Plan of 1953. Where the setting of St Paul's was concerned, however, Holden and Holford advised caution. They recommended that the cathedral should remain the city's chief building, 'architecturally, as in other ways'; their suggestions took much from the 1944 plan, including the transept vistas and a (somewhat expanded) public open space to the south and east, where the Blitz had recreated the oblique view not seen since Cannon Street was extended a century before. A consistent, relatively low cornice line for new churchyard buildings was stipulated: 110 feet, with another eleven feet in a set-back storey. The facing was to be of brick with stone dressings.[40] While the recommendations were neutral on questions of style, their tendency was clearly much more conservative than the plot-ratio blocks outlined for other parts of the city, and it may be no coincidence that it was Holden, rather than the younger and generally

more progressive-minded Holford, who was chiefly responsible for this part of the plan.[41]

All of this was moreover perfectly in accord with city taste. The Corporation's own conservatism is shown by the classically detailed walls of Sir Albert Richardson's sunken garden southeast of the Cathedral, laid out on bombed sites as part of the Festival of Britain in 1951 and now looking rather bewildered in the wider open space; only the little circular Information Pavilion of the same date, since reconstructed further east, took up the lightweight, colourful modernism famously developed at the Festival site on the South Bank.[42] Nor were the early building designs implemented by city institutions any more adventurous: witness New Change Buildings, a giant Neo-Georgian office complex to the north-east, designed in 1953 by Victor Heal for the Bank of England and built in stages to 1960, which followed the cornice-line planning of the 1944–51 reports to the letter.[43] Older buildings to its west were demolished, saving the shell of St Augustine's church. To its south was Gateway House, the head office of the paper firm Wiggins Teape, completed in 1956 and also brick-faced, but detailed more in the Festival style and generously planned with a public garden within the southwest angle, where it allowed the best view from Cannon Street.[44]

Buildings of the type of Gateway House might have gone up north and west of the cathedral, too, were it not for two things: a shift from around 1954 towards modernist image-making and planning for new offices, and general misgivings that the new St Paul's Churchyard would be reactionary, incoherent, or both. Once more, the Government stepped in to procure what the Corporation seemed unable or unwilling to achieve alone. In 1955 the new Minister for Housing and Local Government, Duncan Sandys, required the Corporation to appoint a consultant who could draw up a comprehensive, three-dimensional plan. The recently knighted Holford was again appointed, subject to a committee on which the minister sat alongside the planning chairmen of the Corporation and of the LCC. The wrangling that followed

368. Proposed scheme for the south and east sides of the cathedral, by Burder, Cons, Moore & Pickering, published by the *Architects' Journal* in 1955. This student project shows the anti-contextual fundamentalism prevalent among younger architect-planners who addressed the surroundings of the cathedral in the 1950s.

would have confounded a less diplomatic architect than Holford: even after his informal outline design was published in 1956, Sandys continued vainly manœuvring in favour of his own pet option of a formal semicircular forecourt by the west front.[45] But the forces of modernism were enlisted in favour of informality – Nikolaus Pevsner even broadcast on the Home Service on its behalf – and Sandys eventually backed down.[46] It hardly mattered that the dean and chapter didn't like Holford's plan either; nor did the last-ditch symmetrical treatment drawn up for them by the Surveyor to the Fabric, Lord Mottistone, stand any chance at the public enquiry that followed in 1957.[47] Permission to rebuild north of the cathedral was duly granted in 1958.

Holford's design of 1956 is close in most respects to what was built north of the cathedral from 1961. It is also much closer in spirit to the *Architectural Review*'s suggestions of ten years before than to the proposals to which Holford had put his name in the plan of 1947.[48] Detailed design work was by the architects Trehearne and Norman, Preston and Partners, acting on behalf of the Church Commissioners, who formed a development consortium with the three building contractors. By 1967 work on the northern side was finished.[49] Planned on a single grid, the scheme had lower blocks of different heights placed with careful irregularity, a slim office tower at the north-west corner, where it would least disrupt views of the cathedral, and a pedestrian square raised over an access road and sunken car park on the north side. Differences from the Paternoster Square scheme of 1956 include the non-appearance of the Wren-era Temple Bar gateway from Fleet Street, exiled in 1878 to Hertfordshire, which Holford had wanted to re-erect as a feature just west of the chapter house, and the greater weight given to the elevated pedestrian deck, after the

Corporation adopted an all-embracing 'ped-way' network policy in 1959–60.[50]

In national terms, the result (Fig. 371) stands somewhere between the picturesquely arranged precincts of the 1950s, such as those of the New Towns, and the harsher norms of the 1960s, when higher traffic densities tended to force pedestrians up on to elevated decks and extreme contrasts of exposure and enclosure were thought tolerable. Only the western part showed a convincing and creative response to the cathedral, with its extension of Penrose's paved pedestrian area, screen of trees to the east, and broad flight of steps up to the new Paternoster Square on the podium. The offices themselves, many of which were taken by the Central Electricity Generating Board, were characteristic of upper-rank speculative projects in mid sixties London. Their frames were clad in Portland stone (not concrete, as hostile accounts sometimes have it) and varied with dark-grey slate panels and midnight blue and grey panelling and glazing: as deliberately subdued as a well-made business suit, and about as exciting.

Other criticisms concerned the failure to achieve attractive public spaces within the complex itself, the scanty pleasures of which seemed a poor return on the remarkably generous plot-ratio density of 2.6:1 (compare the pre-war figure of 3.1:1).[51] The new Paternoster Square was draughty and bleak (Fig. 370), the shopping courtyard to the east (called Cathedral Place) merely claustrophobic. Nor was the detailed relationship with St Paul's very satisfactory. Much offence was given by Juxon House, the block north-west of the cathedral, which appeared to jut forward due to the newly widened line of Ludgate Hill: an effect meant by Holford to achieve a gradual revelation of the west front, rather than the broader prospect outlined in the plans of 1944–51. But in other eyes the new block at once degraded and restricted the view, and in 1964 Dean Matthews even led a brief and futile protest campaign about it that must rank amongst the more unusual spats between the Church Commissioners and an Anglican dean.[52] Another undoubted failing was the view of St Paul's from Cathedral Place: a sudden erupting appearance of the dome, cut off below by a wing of new offices, through which a low-ceilinged pedestrian passage escaped on the axis of the north transept door: an effect like a textbook illustration of the symptoms of tunnel vision. Even if the complete plan had been realized, by rebuilding on similar lines to the south-east of the cathedral and by linking the north part with the elevated walkways of London Wall and the Barbican, it is hardly likely that the public would have liked Holford's plan much better, any more than that some other architectural practice could have realized it in a more appealing form.

The rather less ambitious reshaping of the east and south sides never attracted as much attention. To the east, part of the extended churchyard enclosure up to New Change was taken for a new choir school, designed in 1962 by the Architects' Co-Partnership as a counterpoint to St Paul's and completed in 1967 – a 'loving mother-and-child effect', according to the critic Ian Nairn.[53] Portland stone gives way to lead facing on the top storey, and the restored tower of St Augustine is incorporated (Fig. 340). The idea of a buffer of low buildings here can be traced back to the Corporation plan of 1944, the proposal of a resited choir school incorporating something of the church to Holden and Holford's report of 1951.[54] To the south, where height restrictions ruled out slabs or towers, some low office-blocks were built around a new, baldly paved square called Old Change Court,

369 (*above*).   The planner-architect in his element: Sir William Holford in Cannon Street, *c*.1956

370 (*above right*).   Holford's Paternoster Square looking south-east towards the dome

371 (*below*).   Aerial view of the cathedral and its surroundings from the north in 1968, showing Holford's Paternoster Square in the foreground

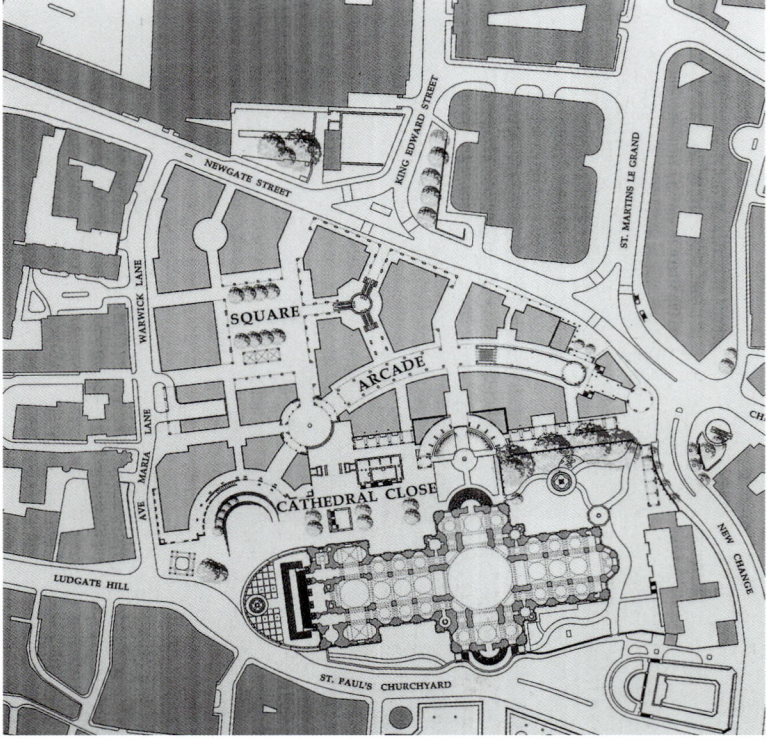

372. Plan for rebuilding the 1960s Paternoster Square by Arup Associates, 1988

373. Perspective of Paternoster Associates' proposals for the northern site, published in 1993, showing Paternoster Square recreated

which formed the top of a large car park entered from Queen Victoria Street; the particulars of the layout were not Holford's.[55] A more attractive public benefit was the broad stepped pedestrian street called Peter's Hill immediately to the west, aligned on the south transept, which in the 1980s was extended down to the river over the Thames Street underpass: another suggestion made in the 1944 plan. The area to its west was left alone, while schemes for a new road came and went; Holford's own second thoughts were worked up in 1964–8, and a version of the project lingered into the early 1970s, in connection with the unrealized Fleet Line extension for London Underground.[56] The following economic downturn, combined with a crescendo of concern for the loss of the historic streetscape, stopped these plans in their tracks.[57] So

the present-day approach to St Paul's from the south-west, along Carter Lane and up Dean's Court, is still that which the late Victorians knew.

SECOND THOUGHTS: ST PAUL'S CHURCHYARD SINCE THE 1980S

Financial deregulation in the mid 1980s created a sudden hunger for new office space, especially in relatively low buildings with large floor-plates; daylight and natural ventilation, the essential resources of 1950s planning and of Holford's scheme, could by that time be provided artificially. The Paternoster Square complex was an obvious case for treatment, and a partial change of ownership in 1986 was soon followed by a limited international competition for a new design, judged by a panel that included the architect William Whitfield as Surveyor to the Fabric. The winning design, by Arup Associates, abandoned slabs, towers and elevated decks in favour of broad, bulky 'groundscrapers', planned around a smallish square, with a broad covered route to its east following a segmental curve centred on the cathedral dome (Fig. 372). Externally, the scheme addressed the cathedral by twice setting back in segmental-ended public spaces, expressed in a kind of stripped postmodern classical architecture.[58]

Praise was less than universal, however, and from late 1987 an opposing plan by the architect John Simpson gathered momentum, publicized by the *Evening Standard* and enthusiastically supported by the prince of Wales. It took more than one change of ownership before this could progress, but from 1989 the site was all set for redevelopment by a new property consortium known as Paternoster Associates, to a modified version of the Simpson plan drawn up by the architects Terry Farrell & Co. in collaboration with the American Neoclassicist Thomas Beeby. This also featured a public square, this time sited east of old Paternoster Square, but was looser in its planning, with more effort made to recover the pre-war street network; an east–west street was included, close to the line of old Paternoster Row. It was also much more explicitly classical in its architectural language, with evocations by a number of practices of models ranging from Lutyens to American Beaux-Arts, deployed across nine major blocks which rose in height from south to north. The scheme was presented with seductive care, by contrast with the suicidally uncommunicative work-in-progress images put out by Arups: watercolours showed sunny spaces alive with workers, tourists and well-behaved children (Fig. 373), using perspectives that tended to play down the much greater bulk of office space that would have risen on the site.[59] In 1993 the plan was approved, after changes suggested by the Royal Fine Art Commission that tended to reduce its volume.

Further revisions continued into 1995, without addressing the flaw that its shared basement would have made the scheme one indivisible structure; a more subjective criticism, that its image was a hopelessly nostalgic one for the financial capital of modern Europe, also seems vindicated by the subsequent course of commercial architecture in London.[60] Once again, a different developer – the Mitsubishi Estate Co. – took over; once again, a new masterplan was drawn up. Its architect was Sir William Whitfield (Whitfield Partners), who took over the principle of separately replaceable blocks by different architects facing an irregular central piazza, fronted this time by open pedestrian arcades on its northern edges. (To protect it from any acquisitive rebuilding schemes in the future, this new Paternoster Square has been designated public space).

374. The rebuilt Paternoster Square in 2003

375. St Paul's seen from the south bank of the Thames in 2001, showing the new Millennium Bridge

The new precinct finally opened to the public in September 2003, five years after the first parts of Holford's group were demolished. The buildings include several by Whitfield Partners facing the cathedral, most of which are in versions of traditional styles. The historical, or historicist, mood is strengthened by the fountain in the square (Fig. 374), which is topped by a Corinthian column fashioned after the newly rediscovered dimensions of Inigo Jones's portico, and which doubles as a ventilation duct by means of perforations in its stepped stone base. It is placed deliberately off the main axis, to reinforce the effect of an irregular townscape.[61] New buildings by other architects include the extreme north-western block, finished in 2000 (and not part of the Whitfield masterplan), which briefly confronted the last Holfordian survivor at the south-east across the excavated car-park basement. This north-western block and its two neighbours to the east are all in a modern idiom, though faced largely in the traditional materials of stone, terracotta and brick. The central and largest building will house the relocated London Stock Exchange: a nice, if distorted echo of the medieval exchange for coins that gave its name to the lost street of Old Change, just east of the cathedral, and a notable instance of the march of high finance into St Paul's Churchyard.[62]

The final touch is scheduled for 2004, when the stones of old Temple Bar will be re-erected between the two new buildings at the south east: the culmination of decades of attempts to return the structure from its Victorian exile to Theobalds Park, Hertfordshire.

In the long run, however, it is the relationship to the cathedral that counts for most, and there will be few who do not respond to the vistas that have been created, or to the new freedom to move easily through traffic-free spaces, magnetized by intermittent glimpses of Wren's dome and towers. It will be interesting to see how far the atmosphere of calm contemplation will endure once the shop units are filled and the offices are busy with tenants.

Meanwhile, the 1960s precinct south of the cathedral has also been rebuilt, almost without wider comment. The architecture, by Rolfe Judd Planning, returns to the template of the 1944–51 plans in its brick facing and in the composition of low, straight-topped blocks (restricted, of course, by the St Paul's height limits), restoring the widened line of the churchyard enclosure.[63] The corresponding part of St Paul's Walk to its west was remodelled too, with a slanting ramp cutting across staggered steps, designed by Charles Funke Associates.

Beyond the bottom of the steps is, of course, the Millennium Footbridge opened in 2001, which spans across to the Tate Modern gallery in the old Bankside Power Station (Fig. 375).[64] Holden and Holford proposed that the steps should end instead at a formal terrace, where the public could watch the river traffic and where a royal barge might draw up for the king's visits to St Paul's. The river traffic has gone, and few would now suggest that London should be reshaped to enhance royal ceremonies; in these respects, at least, 1951 seems suddenly closer to the age of Wren than to our own.

42

THE REPUTATION OF
ST PAUL'S

Andrew Saint

On the most rising part of the town there stands a huge house, big enough to contain the whole nation of which I am king... I am apt to think, that this prodigious pile was fashioned into the shape it now bears by several tools and instruments, of which they have a wonderful variety in this country. It was probably at first an huge misshapen rock that grew upon the top of the hill, which the natives of the country (after having cut it into a kind of regular figure) bored and hollowed with incredible pains and industry, till they had wrought in it all those beautiful vaults and caverns into which it is divided at this day. As soon as this rock was thus curiously scooped out to their liking, a prodigious number of hands must have been employed in chipping the outside of it, which is now as smooth as the surface of a pebble; and is in several places hewn out into pillars, that stand like the trunks of so many trees bound about the top with garlands of leaves. It is probable that when this great work was begun, which must have been many hundred years ago, there was some religion among this people, for they give it the name of a temple, and have a tradition that it was designed for men to pay their devotion in. And, indeed, there are several reasons which make us think, that the natives of this country had formerly among them some sort of worship: for they set apart every seventh day as sacred...[1]

Such is the first considered critique of St Paul's Cathedral. Purportedly written by a native Indian prince visiting London, the words are those of Joseph Addison, worked up for *The*

376. St Paul's as a looming presence: looking across the Thames in the 1850s

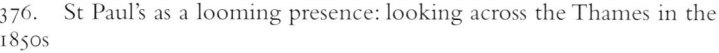

Spectator into a satirical fiction. The keynote in this passage of 1711 is bafflement: a sense that the new St Paul's Cathedral is alien – and too discrepant from religious ideals to be quite right. By putting his words into the mouth of an innocent, Addison also hints that he lacks the language for grappling with Wren's gargantuan creation.

There have been writers of every hue on St Paul's, but two sentiments pervade the literature. The first is one of certainty: that the cathedral symbolizes London, also perhaps England and the authority of its established church. From that standpoint, the very idea of St Paul's – the grandeur of its conception and the fact of its execution in a country and city uneasy with monumentality – is justification enough. In short, it is admirable because it is *there*. The other sentiment is summed up in Addison's backhanded appreciation. This tradition tells us that St Paul's is a puzzle. Seldom are buildings on its scale admired throughout; but seldom too has opinion been so torn between respect and contempt. Many writers have distinguished between an ebullient urban presence and an interior devoid of spirituality. As an essay in monumentality, the dome remains in the heart and head; so does the west front. But the interior of St Paul's has not been widely loved.

THE FIRST CRITICS

While St Paul's was being built, there were a few private expressions of difference about its architectural taste. Roger North sometimes went there when Wren was visiting the site for a 'snatch of discourse with him' and occasionally ventured criticisms: 'I observed to him the exility of his columnes, with Respect to the Grandure of his fabrick at Paulls'.[2] No sooner had the scaffolding been cleared from the choir in 1694 than John Evelyn came to comment. 'Some exceptions might yet perhaps be taken without [as] the placing Columns upon Pilasters, at the East Tribunal', he noted, adding quickly: 'As to the rest certainly a piece of Architecture without reproch'.[3] But these are rarities. Even in the controversy after Wren withdrew in 1710 from participation in St Paul's, the quality of his work went undiscussed. As yet, there was no public criticism of architecture in England, nor had it long begun in France. Hence the obliqueness of Addison's remarks, and an absence of immediate discourse about the completed cathedral.

The first full appraisal we have of the architecture of St Paul's comes indeed from a Frenchman, Georges Louis Le Sage, who visited England in 1713–14. Le Sage is well informed about the structure, but his tone anticipates the displeasure of later compatriots. He is struck by the triple dome, but finds it excessively high. Expert critics, he adds, judge that the church is too massive, bare and dark; the choir is on the small side, though he admires its woodwork; the columns on the western towers look like 'packets of candles'; and the stonework is failing in places because Wren's masons have not grasped the proper techniques for jointing masonry.[4]

Earliest of the native topographer-journalists to tackle the completed cathedral was John Macky. Though he feels that so 'robust' a building ought not to have been adorned with the Corinthian and Composite orders, whose effect is 'just as if one should put Embroidery on a Porter, or Carman's Coat', Macky's comments in *A Journey through England* (1714) are generally admiring.[5] But by the 1720s, homegrown criticism was clearly mounting. So much can be gleaned from the defensive tone detectable in a better-known topographical venture, Defoe's *Tour*

of the Whole Island of Great Britain. Purporting to rely in part on information vouchsafed by Wren himself, Defoe offers a lengthy reading of the cathedral's architecture, voicing a series of complaints only to rebut them. Here, for instance, is his defence of the plain interior:

> If all the square columns, the great pillasters, and the flat pannel work, as well within as without, which they now alledge are too heavy and look too gross, were filled with pictures, adorned with carved work and gilding, and crowded with adorable images of the saints and angels, the kneeling crowd would not complain of the grossness of the work; but 'tis the Protestant plainness, that divesting those columns, &c., of their ornaments, makes the work...be called gross and heavy; whereas, neither by the rule of order, or by the necessity of the building, to be proportioned and sufficient to the height and weight of the work, could they have been less so, or any otherwise than they are.[6]

By the time this was published in 1725, Defoe's positively baroque tastes were old-fashioned. In the next decade, another journalist and theatre critic, James Ralph, undertook an enlarged account of St Paul's in a series of weekly essays on London's architecture. Reissued in book form, they became the first full-length text of English architectural criticism.[7] Ralph spells out the complaints which Defoe had attempted to meet and which echo down the centuries. St Paul's suffers from 'a most notorious deficiency in point of view', requiring an open space all round it, a distant perspective from at least Temple Bar, and a vista towards the Thames. He dislikes the divided storeys of the exterior, which

> certainly indicates a like subdivision within: a circumstance abounding with absurdities, and defeating even the very end of erecting it at all. If, indeed, the architect had been embarrassed to reconcile the distance and height of his column, I am humbly of opinion, that a light and proper attick story had answered all ends, both of use and beauty, and left him room to have enlarged his imagination, and have given an air of majesty to the whole.

Inside, the scale of the dome detracts from the rest of the cathedral: 'after you have seen this you can look at no other part of it; whereas a judicious builder would husband his imagination, and still have something in reserve to delight the mind'. This prefaces an attack on the finishing of choir and altar, though Ralph excepts the stalls.

In Ralph's mind throughout, as in Defoe's, lies the comparison between St Paul's and St Peter's, Rome:

> Every body knows that the fund which raised it from its ruins to its present glory, was equal to any design of majesty or beauty; and as those who had it in trust went so far to this necessary end, it is a thousand pities they did not carry it on much farther, and make this pile not only the ornament of Britain, but the admiration and envy of all Europe. St Peter's, at Rome, was already built; a model which the most finished architect need not have been ashamed to imitate: and as all its particular beauties have been long publicly known and admired, I think it as incumbent on us to [have] equalled it at least; and if we had excelled it too, it would have been no more than might have been reasonably expected from such a nation as ours, and such a genius as Wren's.

377. Interior of St Peter's, Rome, in the 1730s, by G. P. Pannini. (Ca' Rezzonico, Venice)

For a century after its completion, the shadow of St Peter's looms over St Paul's (Fig. 378). The earliest guidebook to mention the building, Colsoni's *Le Guide de Londres* of 1693, alleges that St Paul's when finished will vie with St Peter's.[8] Almost all succeeding accounts allude to the parallel, often with comparative statistics for the rival cathedrals' dimensions. Early on, a few puffers claimed that St Paul's was bigger as well as better. According to Defoe, when this line was put to Wren, he answered with 'a merry hyperbole':

> I tell you, says Sir Christopher, you might set it in St Peter's, and look for it a good while, before you could find it.[9]

St Paul's champions therefore had to settle for phrases like 'deservedly esteemed the second in Europe' or 'the most magnificent protestant church in the world'.[10] Some found the west front of St Peter's secular-looking, or ill-related to the dome behind. Macky made the point that St Paul's was on an eminence and 'disengaged', while St Peter's was in a 'bottom' and encumbered by the Vatican and other buildings:

> And indeed all Cathedrals abroad have a Cloyster joyning to them, for the Conveniency of those that serve in the Church, which takes off very much from their Out-side Beauty.[11]

But such advantages could hardly stay an overwhelming verdict in favour of Rome.

PROTESTANTS AND CATHOLICS

The comparison with St Peter's was inevitable once the Great Model had been discarded in favour of a Latin cross with dome. To all appearances, Wren had built a Catholic cathedral without the trimmings, creating a compromise open to criticism from Catholics and Protestants alike.

Even Protestant visitors perceived the uselessness of the nave. Carl Philipp Moritz, visiting in 1782, had a proto-Romantic reaction:

> All around me I could see nothing but immense bare walls and pillars. Above me, at an astonishing height, was the vaulted

stone roof; and beneath me, a plain, flat, even floor, paved with marble... Did the great architects, who adopted this stile of building, mean by this to say that such a temple is most proper for the adoration of the Almighty? If this was their aim, I can only say, I admire the great temple of nature; the azure vaulted sky, and the green carpet with which the earth is spread. This is truly a large temple; but then there is in it no void, no spot unappropriated, or unfilled: but every where proofs in abundance of the presence of the Almighty.[12]

But it was from French Catholics that St Paul's got its severest mauling. The cathedral had not been without influence in France. It found its first foreign imitation in Servandoni's designs for the front of St Sulpice in Paris; and Wren's dome figured in the debates of the 1770s about how to complete Ste Geneviève.[13] The general view was less flattering. A broadside more lacerating than Le Sage's was fired by the Abbé Louis Maior in his *Temples anciens et modernes*, written in 1758–60 and republished in book form during the debate on Ste Geneviève.[14] The basis of his criticism was that only right religion could foster correct principles of taste; St Peter's, the centre of true Christianity, was therefore also the epigone of architecture. Protestantism, he argued, broke out in England and Germany just as architecture was improving, and blocked its progress in churches. In St Paul's, Maior found 'a blend of thinness and heaviness which has a tinge of Gothic discordance':

> Why are architrave and frieze suppressed above the nave and choir arcades, whereas everywhere else the entablature is complete? Why are the arcades too broad by almost a third in relation to their height, which makes the piers look extremely weak, thinner than they really are, and susceptible of being ornamented only by a single pilaster? Why do the tops of the arcades rise, as in the Temple of Peace, above the capitals of the pilasters, the whole height of the architrave and half that of the frieze? Why is there this giant cupola which feels as if it were crushing the church because of its height and external circumference, so out of proportion to the rest of the building? Why is the interior surface of the drum arranged like a

truncated cone, with the result that the pilasters that decorate it are out of alignment and lean towards the middle? To countless such questions it would be difficult to reply in such a way as to justify this utter English admiration, and to excuse the Chevalier Wren for frequently lacking taste.[15]

The trickle of Frenchmen who visited St Paul's turned into a flood between 1790 and 1815, when educated exiles rambled around London with time on their hands. Most of their comments were no kinder. 'What emptiness, what bareness!' exclaimed one:

> The only emotion summoned up by this dry architecture is astonishment. No chapels, no paintings, no seating; walls, pilasters and transepts are all white, cold and blank, leaving the soul undisturbed.[16]

A more enlightened reaction came from the duc de Lévis. This aristocrat saw in the 'poverty' and 'nakedness' of St Paul's interior the 'excessive simplicity' of the Protestant reformers and an echo of iconoclasm, '*dont les arts eurent tant à gémir*'. Protestants and Catholics alike, he reflected, aimed to excite piety. The answer was not to reject artistic embellishment, but to impose upon sculptors and painters 'the rules of the most austere reserve'. 'Ornaments of a particular kind', noted de Lévis, had lately found a place in the cathedral:

> Flags captured from Great Britain's enemies are suspended from the vaults, while a number of sepulchral monuments have been attached to the piers. I am aware that it is customary among almost all nations to install trophies in churches; yet I cannot approve a custom which consecrates, as it were, national hatreds that ought rather to be extinguished. The bloody tokens of victory were perhaps not out of place in the temple of the god Mars; but in our Christian religion, is not the admirable notion of a God of peace repulsive to them? In truth, these glorious rags may flatter national pride, but they shock the eye of the artist and sadden the friend of humanity.[17]

THE CULT OF WREN

Not just Catholics and foreigners felt that St Paul's was humilatingly bare. By the time the French exiles visited the cathedral, much ink had been spilled on the question.

Pertinent here is the way in which the campaign to embellish St Paul's ran alongside a growing tendency to view the building as bound up with the personality of Wren. As the cult of Wren took wing, the virtues of St Paul's seemed sometimes to emanate from him alone, while its deficiencies were credited to others' interference during the course of the design, or to their successors' inability to finish what he had conceived.

During construction, the idea had slowly developed that St Paul's was in a special sense Wren's – designed, built and all but completed in a single architect's lifetime. In James Wright's four dogged poems on the rebuilding of St Paul's, ranging in date from 1668 to 1709, one can see a shift taking place from a shared sense of glory to a focus on the unwearying surveyor. In 1677:

> And all who help this noble pile to rise,
> When from their happy labours here they rest,
>   Eternal fame shall mention their due praise...
>
> While every artist who is any way
>   Concern'd in this illustrious edifice,
> Like officers who their own pensions pay,
>   Builds his own monument in building this.

But in 1709:

> How will the much-admiring artists then
>   Applaud the builder? yielding all the fame
> Of former masters to the greater Wren,
>   That rais'd, and finsh'd this majestic frame.
> Kind Providence did happily permit
>   By his sole conduct the whole work to pass,
> Who built himself a monument with it,
>   Excelling pyramids, outlasting brass.[18]

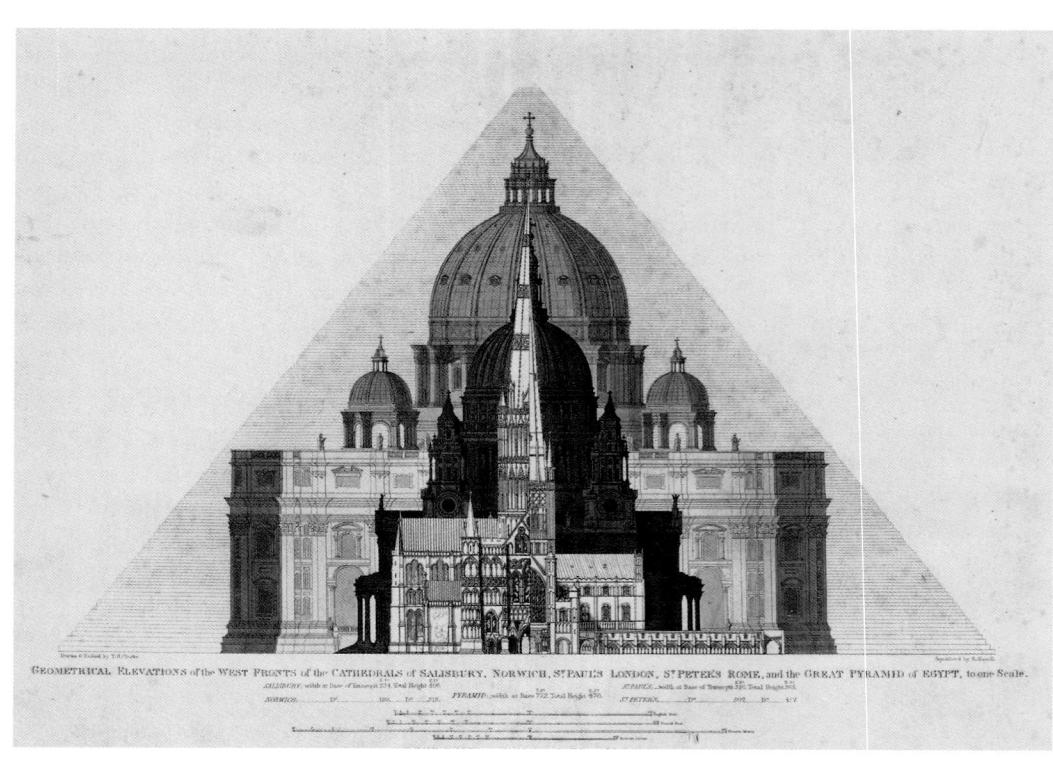

GEOMETRICAL ELEVATIONS of the WEST FRONTS of the CATHEDRALS of SALISBURY, NORWICH, ST PAUL'S LONDON, ST PETER'S ROME, and the GREAT PYRAMID of EGYPT, to one Scale.

378. Comparative elevations of the Great Pyramid of Giza with Salisbury and Norwich cathedrals, St Peter's, Rome and St Paul's. Drawing by T. H. Clarke, 1831. (GL)

Yet early guidebooks, historians and critics largely ignore Wren.[19] It is as if, following the shadow of his last years, his authorship of St Paul's had been censored. Two almost coincident events turned the tide. One was the publication in 1750 of *Parentalia*, which set out Wren's achievement as scientist and architect, told the story of his alienation from St Paul's, explained many of his decisions there and offered, with tantalizing brevity, his ideas for finishing the carcass.[20]

The other event was the beginnings of a campaign to embellish the interior (pp. 240–1), emanating from the circle of the St Martin's Lane academy. Hogarth, the central figure in this set, put up a spirited defence of St Paul's in *The Analysis of Beauty* (1753). But John Gwynn took things further. Gwynn invented a major element of the Wren myth, by alleging that Wren's plan for rebuilding London was considered and rejected by a mean-spirited City. This idea he first propagated in 1749, just before *Parentalia* appeared. Then in 1755–6 he published a section of St Paul's, purporting to show how Wren intended to finish it.[21]

When Gwynn returned to the charge in his *London and Westminster Improved* (1766), he argued that Protestantism was no obstacle to painted decoration. Wren, he claimed, would have

> never dreamed of the ridiculous objections that would be made to its being executed, as appears by the many compartments in that structure, which manifestly point out that great architect's intention.

For Gwynn, Wren was 'unquestionably the greatest geometrical and mathematical architect that ever existed', with 'more extent of invention than Inigo Jones, though, in point of elegance, he fell short of that master'. Yet his account of St Paul's was surprisingly critical. He reacted to the external double order like the ideal city-planner he was: if Wren adopted it because of the lack of space round the building, he should have trusted his first instinct and stuck to a giant order, as that might have forced the authorities to insist on an ampler setting. Inside, he preferred the compartmentalized nave of St Paul's to the barrel vault of St Peter's, but raised fresh objections to the chancel, always with a view to decoration:

> There is not perhaps a greater fault in the interior contrivance of this church, than that of perforating the east end of it. The prodigious glare of light produced by this means is useless and offensive, and totally destroys the grandeur and effect of the church in that part. Indeed this is a fault common in all our churches, but it never fails of rendering the altar obscure . . . In the present case, however, it not only produces this disgusting effect, but it has also prevented the making a proper use of this part, which undoubtedly should have been decorated with an altar of the utmost magnificence. The whole church, for want of such an object, is deplorably deficient in a part where decoration is undeniably necessary; the two middle windows therefore, ought to be stopped up, and the altar designed something like that proposed in a section of this church published by the Author in conjunction with Mr. Wale, in the year 1755.[22]

THE CONSTRUCTIVE INTERPRETATION

By 1800, tastes had shifted. According to the neoclassical canon for monumental buildings now prevalent, neither St Peter's nor St Paul's was a model for imitation; both lacked the chastity of Hellenic classicism and failed to reveal the logic of their structures.

The change was half-signalled when the architect–journalist James Elmes's first biography of Wren appeared in 1823. Elmes had pored over St Paul's during Robert Mylne's surveyorship, when he measured and drew what he was to call 'this fine machine of architecture'.[23] He argued that St Paul's was 'such a free imitation of St Peter's as the Aeneid is of the Iliad', and indeed 'rivalled and surpassed, in purity of taste, and scientific construction, the basilica of St Peter's, at Rome.'[24]

The key phrase here is 'scientific construction'. Wren's capacities as a constructor had always been recognized by a minority. Now the means of construction was becoming fashionable. When the German architect Schinkel visited Britain in 1826, he was everywhere more interested in engineering than architecture. This is borne out by his notes on St Paul's:

> The constructions are everywhere beautifully conceived and executed . . . The stone on the exposed surfaces has not any metal covering, because the climate is so mild, as frost is infrequent; even the gutters are of stone and not lined with metal . . . the walls behind the columns supporting the drum, which form the buttresses for the dome can hardly be seen from the outside.[25]

But there was a difficulty. According to French theory, widely accepted in England by the 1820s, construction should be so far as possible manifest. At St Paul's there were two major structural disguises or, as some came to see them, falsehoods. One was the triple dome, which involved not just inner and outer shells but the invisible brick cone inserted between the shells in order to carry the lantern. The other was the upward projection of the aisle walls into screens that hid the flying buttresses supporting the main vaults. The former might be forgiven or even admired. The latter, previously little noticed, now began to shock.

These issues of 'rational' construction surface in an absorbing essay of 1823 by Joseph Gwilt. Gwilt believes Wren heaped up problems of maintenance by building the outer dome of timber, and is uncomfortable with the voids over the corner piers at the base of the dome. But he goes on to argue that

> in estimating the merits of a building, and the constructive skill of its architect, that is superior in which the greatest effects are produced by use of the slenderest means. If we look at St. Paul's in this light, it claims our unqualified admiration.

Gwilt then compares 'the four largest modern churches of Europe' – Florence Cathedral, St Peter's, St Paul's and Ste Geneviève – for their efficiency in terms of plan, structure and usable space. While St Paul's gives a better result in proportion of clear area to support than the others except for Ste Geneviève (where the piers had proved inadequate and had to be strengthened), in terms of section and of internal to external area, it turns out unexpectedly wasteful. In conclusion, Gwilt notes that medieval Gothic cathedrals like Notre-Dame are more economical than classical ones: 'The builders of the middle ages seem to have found out the minimum of strength necessary to their purpose.'[26]

Gothic cathedrals: the cat was out of the bag, and who better to give it a run around than the younger Pugin? Ralph and Maior had carped at St Paul's for the hint of Gothic about it; now suddenly it was not Gothic enough. In his *True Principles* (1841), Pugin disposed of St Paul's with a pair of slashing sentences and sections (Fig. 379), showing the absolute deception of the screen wall in front of the buttresses – flying buttresses which

379. Comparative sections though aisles and buttresses of St Paul's and through a Gothic cathedral, from A. W. N. Pugin, *The True Principles of Pointed or Christian Architecture*, 1841

380. Looking along the roof of the north nave aisle, showing screen wall (left) and buttresses, *c.* 1930

in a Gothic cathedral would have been gloriously displayed, pinnacled and ornamented, but which the corruptions of Classicism and Protestantism had condemned to concealment. 'Miserable expedient!' thundered Pugin, 'worthy only of the debased style in which it has been resorted to'.[27]

Now followed the years when Gothic was the sole ideal for a cathedral, and commentators damned St Paul's for its very style. Yet the seductiveness of the Gothic Revival in the City of London was scant. St Paul's enjoyed a succession of sworn classicists as its Victorian surveyors. While neo-Gothic churches and public buildings proliferated across England, C. R. Cockerell and F. C. Penrose kept the Wren tradition going in-house; and the only plan of decoration antagonistic to the spirit of the building, by William Burges, came to grief (see pp. 250–1). Somers Clarke, Surveyor to the Fabric at the end of the century, remembered that his fellow assistants in Sir Gilbert Scott's office of the 1860s 'somewhat loftily, picked St Paul's to pieces'; yet 'even in the remote Gothic days I had a strong but lurking admiration'.[28]

In his *History of the Modern Styles of Architecture* (1862), James Fergusson followed the constructive interpretation, unperturbed by the Goths. For Fergusson, 'Wren was more of an engineer than an architect and, consequently, always preferred the display of his mechanical skill to the expression of his artistic feelings.' That was enough to excuse St Paul's lapses from the highest standards of classical taste.[29]

VOICES OF REFORM

Though the cathedral's bareness and want of sacred atmosphere were deplored, it is hard to catch a specifically religious criticism of the building before the church reforms of the 1830s. Then comes a change of tone, summed up in the well-known epigram from

Bishop Blomfield of London himself: 'I never pass St Paul's without thinking how little it has done for Christianity'.[30] If, in such terms, a cathedral ought to serve, the architecture and decoration of St Paul's mattered less than its management and purpose.

Henceforward, embellishments to the interior had to be harnessed to the gathering zeal for reforming the cathedral's liturgical life. The preparatory phase was attended by the violence of opinion inseparable from church restoration. Thus Gladstone, appealing for funds in 1870, denominated the cathedral's 'cold, dark columns and its almost repulsive general condition...a burning reproach to Englishmen...In its unfinished and unseemly condition it is so far from being the noblest church of modern times that it is almost the least noble.'[31]

Reactions of the resident clergy to the building now begin to be heard. Milman's *Annals of S. Paul's Cathedral* of the 1860s focuses on the area of the dome at a time when popular services are being instigated there, and regrets both the Thornhill paintings and their restoration. By contrast, the later memoirs of Dean Gregory and Canon Newbolt review with complacency the many managerial and decorative changes that have taken place since Milman.[32]

Notwithstanding these efforts to bring in the local faithful and adorn the fabric, jaundiced opinion persisted in identifying St Paul's with a too-easy accommodation between God and Mammon. As old-fashioned city trade gave way to *haute finance*, the bridging of that gap became fraught with peril. A gift of gold communion plate at the time of Victoria's Diamond Jubilee from the financial trickster Ernest Hooley was the kind of thing that armed the cynics (Fig. 381).[33] Wittiest among such critics of St Paul's was Edward Burne-Jones. He told his son:

I suppose you know the opening form of prayer used there – 'We, members of the stock exchange and of several banking companies (limited) gathered together in this handsome build-ing which the city of London erected at a vast outlay, humbly approach thy throne, O God, beseeching thee to turn thy all-seeing eye upon our present financial difficulties, which threaten to overturn the commercial pre-eminence of our city. It cannot be wholly unknown to thee, O God, that ever since the Argentine bankruptcy our affairs &c.' and so it goes on, rather a long form. Phil, dear, I assure you no other kind of prayer is possible in such a place, and so I was pleased to find that the Book of Common Prayer used there opens with this appeal.

Invited in 1891 to partake in the feast of mosaic work at 'the cen-tral edifice of metropolitan devotion', Burne-Jones after brief hes-itation 'couldn't face it':

and yet I love mosaics better than anything else in the world. It's nonsense to put mosaic there – nonsense I think to try to do anything with it but let it chill the soul of man and gently prepare him for the next glacial cataclysm. It wants carpets hung about and big, huge, dark oil pic-tures, and hangings of rich stuffs, and the windows let alone, no stained glass anywhere, no colour except black and silver, no chilling surplices, Bach always played, and me miles away. Me miles away, if possible, and I'll be content with it.[34]

IMPRESSIONISTS

For most random visitors, the cathedral was not an essay in struc-ture or style nor a mechanism for enhancing belief or the Church of England, but one of a number of metropolitan attractions. As the fashion grew for reacting to or revelling in London's terrible energy and size, verdicts on St Paul's became more impressionistic.

Blackness was one enduring impression. As early as 1710, the antiquarian von Uffenbach noted that St Paul's was 'already so black with coal-smoke that it has lost half its elegance'.[35] 'What a pity', echoed the Russian N. M. Karamzin in 1790,

that London's perpetual smoke has not spared this splendid temple, but has coated it with soot all the way up to the golden sphere which serves as its crown.[36]

For Théophile Gautier, St Paul's partook in the overall gloom and hideousness of an overcast city. The poet drew a Puginian moral:

The dome of St Paul's…suffers grievously from the influence of the London atmosphere. Despite the efforts they make to keep it white, it is always black, on one side at least. They can slop paint all over it, but the invisible coal dust sifted through the fog is faster still than the painter's brush. St Paul's is a fur-ther example proving that the cupola as a form belongs to the Orient and that the Northern sky requires to be pierced by the pinnacles and angular points of Gothic architecture.[37]

381.   Chalices and flagons designed by Edwin Lutyens and made by H. G. Murphy, 1933–4. The gold came from three sources, including plate given to St Paul's by the company promoter and fraudster Ernest Hooley, 1897, but later melted down. When his financial empire collapsed soon after the donation, Canon Scott Holland raised £1,500 which was paid to Hooley's defrauded creditors. (St Paul's Cathedral)

Occasionally people liked the soot. Louis Simond remarked in 1817:

> The colour struck me as strange, – very black and very white, in patches which envelope sometimes half a column; the base of one, the capital of another; – here, a whole row quite black – there, as white as chalk. It seems as if there had been a fall of snow, and it adhered unequally. The cause of this is evidently the smoke which covers London; but it is difficult to account for its unequal operation. This singularity has not the bad effect which might be expected from it.[38]

Nathaniel Hawthorne, visiting like Gautier in the 1850s, also felt that 'the edifice would not be nearly so grand without this drapery of black'.

Hawthorne was among the first of a more contemplative genre of tourists. He liked to stroll London's streets and savour St Paul's as a serene urban presence, an oasis. Returning to the cathedral often, sometimes encountering it almost by accident, he strikes the personal note:

> I love its remote distances and wide, clear spaces; its airy massiveness; its noble arches; its sky-like dome, which, I think, should be all over light with ground glass, instead of being dark, with diminutive windows...It is pleasant to stand in the centre of the Cathedral, and hear the noise of London, loudest all round that spot – how it is calmed into a sound as proper to be heard through the aisles, as the tones of its own organ.[39]

Writers and ramblers in Hawthorne's wake invert earlier criticism. In their reflections, the inside of St Paul's takes precedence over the outside, and its sounds coalesce with its sights. For William Dean Howells,

> a great congregation lost itself in the broken space of the London temple, dimmed rather than illumined by the electric blaze in the choir; a monotonous chanting filled the air as with a Rome of the worldliest period of the church, and the sense of something pagan that had arisen again in the Renaissance was, I perceive, the emotion that had long lain in wait for me.[40]

Making notes in 1909 for an unwritten book, Howells's friend and compatriot Henry James admires the

> spacious, vast *cheerful* effect of this crypt...with the great temple above it and the London sounds of only the ghostliest faintness...the Library most interesting and charming in high aloofness in the upper vastness of the church...with the London uproar rising more audibly, and yet fitful and *estompé*, than as it comes, or *doesn't* come, to the Crypt.[41]

Likewise Virginia Woolf:

> Directly we enter, we undergo that pause and expansion and release from hurry and effort which it is in the power of St. Paul's, more than any other building in the world, to bestow...Mind and body seem both to widen in this enclosure, to expand under this huge canopy where the light is neither daylight nor lamplight, but an ambiguous element something between the two...Very large, very square, hollow-sounding,

382. Visitors entering the great west door, by Joseph Pennell, 1893

383. *St Paul's. The King's Visit to Wren.* Painting by J. Seymour Lucas, exhibited at the Royal Academy, 1888. The event is fictional: no visit by Charles II to the cathedral is recorded

384. *Ludgate Hill – a block in the street*, by Gustave Doré, from Blanchard Jerrold, *London, A Pilgrimage* (1872)

385. 'Soul strivings from struggle into calm': symbolist frontispiece by A. H. Mackmurdo for his *Wren's City Churches* (1883)

echoing with a perpetual shuffling and booming, the Cathedral is august in the extreme; but not in the least mysterious.[42]

It is left to E. M. Forster in *Howards End* (1910) to give a final twist to the counterpoint of inside and out. In the compass of three sentences, Forster ties the exterior to Roger Fry's 'significant form', while turning the interior into a microcosm of the kaleidoscopic city in which the senses mingle:

She [Margaret Schlegel] went for a few moments into St Paul's, whose dome stands out of the welter so bravely, as if preaching the gospel of form. But within, St Paul's is as its surroundings – echoes and whispers, inaudible songs, invisible mosaics, wet footmarks crossing and recrossing the floor. *Si monumentum requiris, circumspice*: it points us back to London.[43]

WREN ASCENDANT

From the 1880s, Wren underwent reinterpretation. He began to be construed less as an aberrant classicist or wise constructor, more as a wholly English architect needing neither apology nor comparison. This could only happen after Britain had reached its apogee and St Paul's had become a symbol of empire – 'the central sanctuary in some sense of the English race', Liddon called it.[44]

The new mood of veneration is summed up by a history painting exhibited by J. Seymour Lucas in 1888, showing Wren receiving Charles II on an imaginary visit to St Paul's (Fig. 383). By then the long campaign for reform and refurbishment was

well forward. Lucy Phillimore's biography of Wren could salute a cathedral

set in green turf, and all around it is cared for instead of neglected, the once empty campanile is filled by twelve bells, whose music floats down over the roar of London, as if out of the sky itself, and the Dome is filled by vast congregations in the way Sir Christopher almost foresaw.[45]

That was in 1881. Two years later, the architect-craftsman A. H. Mackmurdo published his *Wren's City Churches* – a *mélange* of impressionism and Ruskinian history (Fig. 385). For Mackmurdo and many contemporaries, the craftsmanly City churches seemed more honest and English than the grandiose cathedral. St Paul's figures only obliquely in his text, as the grave mother around whose skirts the endangered daughter-churches play:

St Paul, bereft of its surrounding steeples, is to us as a parent bereft of her children – a Niobe in architecture. Likewise these churches, without their Metropolitan Cathedral, we regard as so many disconnected members, having neither head nor trunk to unite them.[46]

By 1900 even most of those older members of the Arts and Crafts Movement whose first love had been Gothic felt able to espouse Wren. Philip Webb, for instance, would take disciples to renew acquaintance with St Paul's:

When the shopping was done we had some food, then after a prowl to see any new thing, we wound up at St Paul's. It was inspiring to see his heart-felt enthusiasm for the work of a man

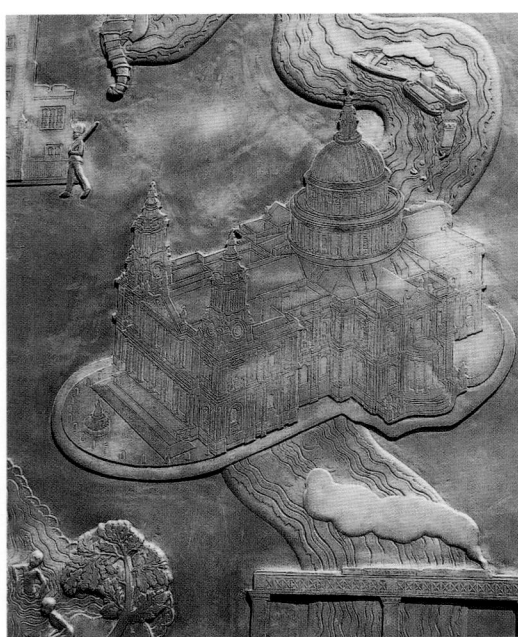

386. Belfast City Hall by A. Brumwell Thomas, architect, 1897–1906. One of many Edwardian buildings which liberally plunder the cathedral's architecture. Photograph of *c.*1960

387. Detail of bronze outer doors of the head-quarters of the Royal Institute of British Architects, London, made by James Woodford, 1934

whose form of expression was so opposed to his own. His criticisms were generous; he lost all thought of 'style', but he enjoyed the romantic abandon of Wren's compositions when compared to the pedantic stuff which goes by the same style name. For Wren's abrupt changes, his spontaneous introduction of inventions of his own and for all creative experiments Webb had the profoundest admiration and sympathy.[47]

For these generations, Wren was not a dogmatist. Even the mighty St Paul's could appear a liberal building, wherein the classical bonds were relaxed and multiple voices and hands found a place. The scholar-architect Walter Godfrey, for instance, believed that Wren's English common sense 'put off for half a century the academic and sterilised treatment of architecture'.[48] He relished the cathedral interior as a feast of craftsmanship in which Gibbons, Tijou and the rest became objects of enquiry and delight.

Wren-worship climaxed with the bicentenary of the architect's death in 1923. It prompted the founding of the Wren Society, whose twenty volumes of documentary publication were to transform scholarship on the architect's works, and an immediate memorial volume. A chapter of that book, 'The Crafts at St Paul's', looks upon the cathedral as 'a valuable object-lesson in the process of evolution which building methods have passed through between the completion of Westminster Abbey and that of the new County Hall': the mark of high tide, indeed, when the professional architect was in control but the craftsmen were 'still capable of delighting in and thus imparting life to the parts entrusted to them'.[49] In the epilogue, Canon Alexander sums up the mood of the moment: St Paul's is 'the symbol and expression of the best characteristics of the religious mind of the British people – its directness, its simplicity, truthfulness, its width of outlook'.[50]

St Paul's just then could look outwards as well, offering authority and parenthood. With swathes of the map red and the Modern Movement still infantile, the 'Wrenaissance' seemed pertinent to architecture throughout the Empire and beyond. Lutyens adapted the upper half of the west front into a façade for the British pavilion at the Rome exhibition of 1911 (subsequently the British School at Rome): one in the eye there for St Peter's.[51] The dome

had spawned countless imitations or adaptations – seldom without hints of control. Its outline stood vigil over the Protestant ascendancy from above the Four Courts at Dublin and the Belfast City Hall (Fig. 386); it received ironic tribute from half the state capitols of America; it even popped up sporadically in the Raj. On both the Albert Hall's frieze and the Royal Institute of British Architects' portals (Fig. 387), it was depicted as *the* icon for modern British architecture. And when Liverpool's Anglican cathedral was first mooted, the precentor there suggested that they execute the Great Model.[52] As it turned out, it was Liverpool's Catholic cathedral which in Lutyens's hands almost became the last great spin-off from the dome, synthesizing St Paul's and St Peter's. But by 1934, when Lutyens perfected his design and the second Great Model of British architecture was made, it was too late.[53]

A SHRINE IN PERIL

This moment of triumphalism refreshed an older interpretation of St Paul's as the imperial resting-place. That, though long promoted, seems to have been incompletely experienced before the First World War and the making of the chivalric chapels (pp. 259–61). It turns up among the inter-war Fleet Street school of populist historians like Arthur Mee and William Kent, adept at drawing a patriotic anecdote out of a St Paul's monument. But it is best presented from the periphery of the dominions, by Alan Mulgan's salute to the old country, *Home* (1927):

We New Zealanders may say without impropriety that, like the English, we are what the sea and the winds have made us, and here lie the greatest of these who bent the strength of the sea and the winds to the tremendous purpose of our race... In the Crypt there lies a man whose career for many years was bound up with New Zealand's history. I do not think it extravagant to say that Sir George Grey was the greatest man in the nineteenth century oversea development of the Empire... I would like to be sure that the average New Zealander who goes to St Paul's as an Imperial duty, could answer half a dozen simple questions about Grey's career.[54]

Should irony or aestheticism be preferred, James Pope-Hennessy's *London Fabric* supplies both. Pope-Hennessy squires an imaginary companion, the tiresome Perdita, around St Paul's. They make straight for the monuments, 'Perdita's heels clip-clipping on the black and white marble of the floor'. Sophisticates and modernists, they snigger at the hypocrisy and 'escape mechanisms' of the nineteenth century, 'the coy nudity of Burges, the lawn-sleeved Nazi salute of Bishop Middleton' (Figs 128, 217). But flippancy vanishes as the pair penetrate the crypt and confront the cherubim and dead babies upon the Martin tomb (Fig. 212). 'I used to find this crypt extraordinarily consoling when one was suffering from a bout of that black depression which I fancy attacks many people somewhere near nineteen,' admits the author.[55]

That was in 1939. In 1941 Pope-Hennessy is back, the smirk wiped off his face, to mourn the 'calcined Elizabethans' of his crypt and affirm the atavism intellectuals rediscover in war:

For many days colossal pieces of gilded masonry (some with fragments of mosaic stuck to them) lay strewn about the altar steps in the half light of the Cathedral. This grandiose litter had the majesty of a Piranesi; one thought of Gibbon and not of Wren... About the Abbey we feel far more intimately, far more deeply... But for the centuries since the Stuarts, for space and solemnity, for symmetry and style, you must turn to St Paul's.

To-day that unparalleled interior can give us something of momentous value: for by displaying the necessity (and simultaneously the grandeur) of true unity in architecture, does it not suggest the importance of this principle in other and more animated spheres?[56]

The metamorphosis of St Paul's into a symbol of togetherness, survival and suffering was best articulated in photographs, not words: above all in the snapshot taken by Herbert Mason on 29 December 1940 from the roof of the *Daily Mail*, showing the dome transfigured against white cloud, lit by invisible fires behind a screen of smoke (Fig. 388). A remarkable study by Brian Stater has shown how far this image was doctored: 'more of the picture has been changed than not'.[57] Yet so great was the hunger for it that it became instantly famous, within two months had been taken up even by a Berlin illustrated paper and still sells well in postcard form. Iconographically, it renews an old genre. The idea of the church transcending human destructiveness is fundamental to the marriage between Christianity and monumental architecture, while the experience of the dome illumined above cloud-bound streets had often been seen and even depicted. The photograph is powerful not just because of the historic moment it depicts. It also silences those who ask why we build monumentally at all.

388.   St Paul's from the roof of Northcliffe House, taken by Herbert Mason, 29 December 1940. Most memorable of all photographs of the cathedral

SKYLINE AND SCHOLARSHIP

St Paul's had now reached the limits of its capacity for meaning. Anti-climax ensued. The post-war cathedral had to adapt to loss of empire, weakening confidence in the national Church and forlorn surroundings. The hemming-in of former centuries was at least livelier than an isolation only enhanced by the banality of the new precinct. With the advent of easier images, people's verbal impressions seem shallower too. Fresh reactions to the cathedral are rare; foreign tourists lose interest, while English critics flounder.

One who tried was Ian Nairn. His response to St Paul's rambles, then slips into the fag-end of wartime chauvinism:

> Wren might have chosen grandeur, or drama or *terribilità* or excitement. Instead, there is overwhelming compassion, the common touch ennobled...All of St Paul's speaks individually and collectively at once: to all people and to this particular person...Because of its assiduous concern it floats, serene but not detached – the best kind of night-nurse – where St Peter's is still wound around with human passions. The dome is in an utter repose which transcends passion instead of ignoring it: the scale is huge and tiny at the same time. It is a stupendous, encompassing achievement of balanced feeling and maturity – and one that has come to the top again and again in this funny-shaped island just off Europe: Shakespeare's last plays, but also what England seems to have called out of people like Handel and T. S. Eliot. It is hard not to sound like a bad Churchillian parody, but in fact this is why we fought the war.[58]

Hollowness, too, can be detected in the role played by the cathedral in the battles of the late 1980s and early 90s between architectural modernists and recrudescent traditionalists, championed by the prince of Wales. Provision having been painstakingly made to guard the sacred silhouette from challenge in long-distance London views by means of the 'St Paul's heights' (see pp. 301, 444), one effect was to turn the cathedral in public perception into a cardboard cut-out 'framing' and defining the city. This two-dimensional image was espoused and exacerbated by the traditionalists. In Prince Charles's *A Vision of Britain* (1989), St Paul's graduates from being a prop in views by Canaletto from Westminster or by Turner from Greenwich into the centrepiece of Niels Lund's *Heart of Empire*, and finally an incident in a skyline desecrated by blunted office towers (Fig. 389).[59] At the heart of the picture lies only an ever fainter memory of national endurance.

These battles focused not upon St Paul's but upon its woebegone surroundings, which now assumed more importance than the cathedral itself. Occasionally Charles's architect-opponents, such as Richard Rogers or Maxwell Hutchinson, diverged into attacking features of the cathedral. But it was not St Paul's they cared about – only the freedom to build as they desired around and in its backdrop. Much of this debate was conducted on television, which rendered it wider but coarser.[60]

Not that the cathedral lacked respectful students in the post-war years. The burden of interpretation had passed to a new breed: historians of architecture, who claimed to bring fresh facts to the evaluation of buildings as works of art. Often the evaluation went forgotten in their relish for turning over the findings which the Wren Society's researches had unearthed.

For these scholars, St Paul's tended to mean Wren – but Wren with a difference. A first task was to sift out the anglocentric detritus and recall the cathedral's European lineage. That was undertaken by the Viennese Eduard Sekler in his *Wren and His Place in European Architecture* (1956), which paid a compliment back to Britain by setting out the influence of the dome and towers of St Paul's in Europe.[61] Another emigré, Nikolaus Pevsner, had already touched in his wartime *Outline of European Architecture* on the cathedral's continental pedigree. Pevsner's analysis of

St Paul's in *The Buildings of England* is precise rather than enthusiastic. He belonged to those who looked upon the Great Model as an affirmation of European culture, while the Warrant Design and its aftermath represented an English falling-off from that high ideal.[62]

For one native-born scholar, St Paul's was a quiet obsession: a building which he often revisited in search of fuller understanding. This was John Summerson, the student *par excellence* of English classical architecture. For the young Summerson, ideas came first. In a Hegelian spirit, he tried to demonstrate how Wren's work related 'to the social, political and philosophical thought of his time':

> St Paul's is a building into whose form the spiritual history of seventeenth-century England is as firmly built as it is into the writings of Locke and Dryden. There is the science of the Royal Society, the latinity of Restoration Oxford, the religious equivocation of the House of Stuart. That such a monument should rise, not among the new streets and squares of around Westminster but on the barren, unintellectual soil of the mercantile stronghold, is one of the freaks of history.[63]

Such was Wren's culture, argued Summerson, that his most ambitious buildings, St Paul's above all, were bound to reflect the gamut of influences which he absorbed. But in a paper of 1936, 'The Tyranny of Intellect', he also argued that Wren's approach to design was individual. According to that line of thought, his mathematical bent and his immersion in 'latinity' begat an architecture dominated by logic and science, and lacking French taste or Italian grace.[64]

Yet St Paul's is only spasmodically logical; it was for failings in consistency and clarity as much as of taste that it had long been criticized. 'Inconsistency' indeed is an idea running through Summerson's essay; only sometimes it seems to mean compromise forced on the architect by events or interests, sometimes a psycho-logical flaw in Wren. Like others, Summerson accepted that the Great Model represented Wren's own mind, and the Warrant Design the interference of tradition and the church. Faced, then, with the improvements of the final design, he drew back:

> In the finished structure it must be admitted that the strict intellectualism of his earlier maturity has to some extent dissolved, probably as a result of wider acquaintance with contemporary Italian work, but also under the influence of the changing viewpoint of the times. Nevertheless, Wren the empiricist emerges, on the whole, more consistently from the cathedral than Wren the Anglo-Baroque designer.[65]

By reminding his readers that not everything that Wren built should be adulated, Summerson had moved things on. He also relocated the achievement of St Paul's in a cerebral approach to design, not in some idealized collaboration between the classes. In his post-war *Architecture in Britain 1530–1830*, Summerson did include a section on the craftsmen of St Paul's. Instead of continuators of medieval tradition, they now became upholders of 'standards of workmanship which, once attained, remained the pride of English building for a century'. The craftsmen looked forward now, not back.[66]

Yet by juxtaposing Wren with Locke and Dryden more than Mansart, Perrault or Bernini, Summerson had again reinforced the Englishness of St Paul's – but an introspective Englishness now that interrogated its own history, not one that faced outward alongside the tub-thumping Canon Alexander. It was as if in a secular, contracting world, the 'national cathedral' could only be identified with the magnificent mind of one exceptional Englishman. And indeed that is how St Paul's has been mostly interpreted since Summerson. It is in Wren's name that scholars still sift the archive of St Paul's, few heeding the catalogue of enrichment and effort lavished upon the cathedral since Addison first pondered the enigmatic rock looming over London's river.

ABBREVIATIONS

AC	Alcuin Club
Arch	*Archaeologia*
ArchJ	Archaeological Journal
AUL	Aberdeen University Library
BAACT	British Archaeological Association Conference Transactions
BAR	British Archaeological Reports
BIHR	*Bulletin of the Historical Research*, subsequently *HR*
BL	British Library
BodL	Bodleian Library, Oxford
CBA	Council for British Archaeology
CCR	*Calendar of Close Rolls* + dates covered (HMSO, 1900–63)
CERC	Church of England Record Centre
CHJ	*Cambridge Historical Journal*
CJ	*Journals of the House of Commons, 1547–1761*, 28 vols. (n.p. [174262]).
CKS	Centre for Kentish Studies, Maidstone
CLRO	Corporation of London Records Office
CM	Chapter Minutes (in SPCL)
CPL	*Calendar of Entries in the Papal Registers relating to Great Britain and Ireland: Papal Letters* + dates covered (HMSO, 1894–1961)
CPR	*Calendar of Patent Rolls* + dates covered (HMSO, 1906–82)
CR	*Close Rolls* +date (HMSO, 1902–75)
CS	Camden Society
CSPDom	*Calendar of State Papers, Domestic Series* + dates covered (HMSO, 1856-97)
CSPFor	*Calendar of State Papers, Foreign Series* + dates covered (HMSO, 1861-1950)
CSPVen	*Calendar of State Papers and Manuscripts, Relating to English Affairs, Existing in the Archives and Collections of Venice* + dates coverered (HMSO, 1864–1947), plus date covered by the volume
CUL	Cambridge University Library
d.	died
DB	*Domesday Book*, see bibliography
DNB	*Dictionary of National Biography* (London)
EconHR	*Economic History Review*
EECM	Early English Church Music (British Academy, London, 1963–)
EHR	*English Historical Review*
ERO	Essex Record Office
ESTC	English Short Title Catalogue (British Library and elsewhere)
GD	Gallery Disbursments (Cupola Fund, 7 vols, 1732–1839, in SPCL)
GL	Guildhall Library, London
Grove	*Grove's Dictionary of Music and Musicians*, 5th ed., Supplementary Volume [ed. D. Stevens], London, 1961
HJ	*Historical Journal*
HMC 9	HMC, *Ninth Report* (1883), Part I, Appendix, 'Report on the manuscripts of the Dean and Chapter of St Paul's', 1–72 (by H. C. Maxwell Lyte)
HMC	Historical Manuscripts Commission (later Royal Commission on Historical Manuscripts); see bibliography
HMSO	Her Majesty's Stationary Office
HR	*Historical Research*, formerly *BIHR*
ILN	*Illustrated London News*
JBAA	*Journal of the British Archaeological Association*
JEcclH	*Journal of Ecclesiastical History*
L&P	*Calendar of Letters and Papers, Foreign and Domestic, Henry VIII* + vol. no. (HMSO, 1862 onwards)
LJ	*Journals of the House of Lords, 1510–1829*, 61 vols. (n.p. [1767–]).
LMA	London Metropolitan Archive
LonJ	*London Journal*
LPL	Lambeth Palace Library, London
LRS	London Record Society
LTR	*London Topographical Record*
LTS	London Topographical Society
MB	Musica Britannica (Royal Musical Association, London, 1951–)
MGH	Monumenta Germaniae Historica
MSE	*Miracula Sancti Erkenwaldi* in Whatley (1989)
n.s.	New Series
NCE	*New Catholic Encyclopaedia* 15 vols (New York, 1967)
NewDNB	*New Dictionary of National Biography* (Oxford, forthcoming)
NG	*The New Grove Dictionary of Music*, 2nd ed., ed. S. Sadie and J. Tyrell, 29 vols. (London, 2000)
PP	Parliamentary Papers
PR	Pipe Roll + regnal year (published by the Pipe Roll Society, London)
PRO	The National Archives (United Kingdom), Public Record Office
RC	Record Commission
RCHME	Royal Commission on Historical Monuments (England)
Rep.	Repertories of the court of Aldermen (in CLRO)
RIBA Journal	*Journal of the Royal Institute of British Architects* (continued, from 1965, as *RIBA Journal*)
RIBA	RIBA Library
RMARC	*Royal Musical Association Research Chronicle*
RS	Rolls Series
SAHGB	Society of Architectural Historians of Great Britain
SCH	Studies in Church History
ser.	series
SPC	St Paul's Cathedral
SPFA	St Paul's Cathedral, Fabric Archive (in the care of the Surveyor)
SPCL	St Paul's Cathedral Library
TLMAS	*Transactions of London and Middlesex Archaeological Society*
Trans RIBA	*Transactions. Royal Institute of British Architects Transactions*, continued from 1894 as *RIBA Journal*
TRHS	*Transactions of the Royal Historical Society*
VCH	*The Victoria History of the Counties of England*; identified by county names and volume numbers
VCR	Vicars Choral Records (6 boxes in SPCL).
VSE	*Vita Sancti Erkenwaldi* in Whatley (1989)
WAM	Westminster Abbey Muniments
WS	Bolton, A.T. and Henry, H.D., eds. (1924–43), *The Wren Society* (Oxford), 20 vols.

NOTES

2. *Before St Paul's*

1 The pattern of relief is well represented by the contours plotted on Museum of London (1981).
2 Keene (2001b).
3 Bentley (1987); Shepherd (1988); Schofield with Maloney (1998), 217, 287; Tyler (2000); Gaimster and Bradley (2002), 163.
4 Elsden (2002). A Palaeolithic axe in the Museum of London is said to have been found 'near St Paul's Cathedral', but lacks further documentation.
5 Coates (1998).
6 Perring and Roskams (1991) for the western Roman city. Excavations in the period 1907 to 1991 are summarized in Schofield with Maloney (1998). All excavations in and around the cathedral since the time of Wren are being brought together into a single monograph: Schofield (in prep).
7 Merrifield (1965), gazetteer sites 9, 10, 16, 17; Shepherd (1988); Perring and Roskams (1991).
8 RCHME (1928), 140 dates the recording of the main complex of kilns, by John Conyers (BL, MS Sloane 958, fo.105), to 1672; but Merrifield (1965), gazetteer site 22 gives the date of 1677. The accounts (WS XIII, 94) confirm that the later date is correct, and that the site was the north-east corner of the north transept. Merrifield, however, incorrectly places the site under the north-west tower.
9 Merrifield (1965), sites 18–21.
10 Grimes (1968), 149–50; Mattingley (1967).
11 Hill et al. (1980); Williams (1993).
12 Lobel (1989), 68; Gibbs (1939), nos. 79–80.
13 Wright (1991), 16–17.
14 Morey and Brooke (1965), 1511–3; Robertson and Sheppard (1875–85), vii. 10.
15 Camden mentions the supposed Temple of Diana and also relates the older and presumably rival tradition that there had been a Temple of Apollo on the site of Westminster Abbey: Camden (1772), ii. 334, 337. For the supposed Temple of Jupiter, see Kingsford (1971), i. 333. Wren gave little credit to the Diana story (Wren (1750), 266), which by his time appears to have been strengthened by reference to the ceremonial presentation to the Dean and Chapter each year of a buck (see p. 28 n. 57), and received a boost in the eighteenth century when a bronze statuette of Diana was found near St Paul's: Strype (1720), iii. 141, 165; RCHME (1928), 140; Clark (1996).
16 Lobel (1989), 20–2 (but the statements on the chronology of German settlement are not now accepted).
17 Mann (1961); Salway (1981), 340–1, 723–4; Sharpe (2002), 76–8.
18 Merrifield (1965), 61–5; Esmonde Cleary (1989), 35, 121–8, 162–4.
19 Maloney and Holroyd (2002), 8, site PNS01.
20 Schofield (in prep).
21 Kingsford (1971), i. 194; Taylor (1980); Wright (1988), 64–6; Wright (1991), 92–5; Colgrave and Mynors (1991), 24–5, 562–3; Kelly (2004).
22 Sankey (1998); cf. Sharpe (2002), 123.

3. *Foundation and Endowment: St Paul's and the English Kingdoms,* 604–1087

I am very grateful to all who have discussed this paper with me, especially Derek Keene, Susan Kelly, Julia Crick and Alan Thacker.

1 Colgrave and Mynors (1991), 134–41 (II.2); Thomas (1981), esp. 196–8; Sharpe (2002); Gameson (1999), esp. ch. 6; Sims-Williams (1990); Morris (1989).
2 Colgrave and Mynors (1991), 104–7 (I.29).
3 Colgrave and Mynors (1991), 142–3 (II.3).
4 Colgrave and Mynors (1991), 4–5 (Bede's preface).
5 Colgrave and Mynors (1991), 142–4 (II.3); I have amended the translation slightly.
6 Gibbs (1939), no. J.17, Sawyer (1968), no. 1786; Robertson (1956), 214–15; see below, 13, 18–20.
7 Blackmore (1997); Vince (1990), 13–18; Keene (2000a), 189–90; Coates (1999).
8 Taylor (2000), 219–20; Keene (2000a), 189.
9 See Dodwell (1982).
10 See Kelly (2004), whose forensic analysis of charters leads her to scepticism, not least about early and large-scale acquisition. I am grateful to Dr Kelly for discussion of the issues.
11 See comparable comments on the St Albans endowment by another sceptical charter analyst: Crick (2001), 83; Crick (forthcoming).
12 See below. Kelly (2004), no. 1, S 5; Chaplais (1969); Wormald (1984).
13 Gibbs (1939), xxiv and no. 11.
14 For the identification of Clerkenwell, see Taylor (1990); some labour services in Stepney were imposed on lands rather than tenants, suggestive of early obligations: Croot (1997), 6–7; Faith (1996), 207–10; Faith (1997).
15 At least part of Islington and, probably, Hornsey; see below.
16 Taylor (1980).
17 Dumville (1993), 20; Yorke (1990); Blair (1991a); Kirby (1991).
18 Dumville (1989); Davies and Vierck (1974); Dumville (1993), 11–13; Williamson (2000), 63–6.
19 Kirby (1966); see also Dumville (1993).
20 Gibbs (1939), no. J.9; Sawyer (1968), no 1784.
21 Colgrave and Mynors (1991), 152–3 (II.5).
22 Colgrave and Mynors (1991), 154–5 (II.6); I have altered the translation slightly.
23 Colgrave and Mynors (1991), 154–7 (II.6).
24 Colgrave and Mynors (1991), 280–5 (III.22); Mayr-Harting (1972), 100. The pamphlet histories in the still-surviving church of St Peter's Bradwell ignore the London connection.
25 Colgrave and Mynors (1991), 322–3 (III.30); I have altered the translation slightly; Yorke (1990); Dumville (1993), 28; Wood (1977), 18–20.
26 Colgrave and Mynors (1991), 234–5 (III.7); Whitelock (1975), 5, but see Kelly (2004).
27 See below, 114. The saint's *Life* (Whateley (1989) is a later hagiography; for what is known historically see especially *DNB*; Wormald, *New DNB*, to whom I am grateful for showing me a copy prior to publication; Wormald (1984). Kelly (2004) suggests that some of the credit may be owed to both Wine and Wealdhere.
28 Wormald, *New DNB*; Hart (1966), 117–45; Yorke (1985), 15–19.
29 Wormald (1984), esp. 9–11; Whitelock (1975), 5–10; Yorke (1990); Kirby (1991), ch. 6.
30 Dugdale (1818 ed), 3; the supposed privilege from Pope Agatho is a forgery.
31 Colgrave (1927), 86–7; Brooks (1984), 75–6.
32 Brooks (1984), 124; Cubitt (1995); Keynes (1994); Williamson (2000), 83–4.
33 *Nostrique pagi regnatores*: the rulers were probably Coenred of Mercia and the kings of the East Saxons. Kelly (2004), appendix 1. The

initial phrase is from Stenton (1971), 143. See also Chaplais (1978).
34 Hemel: Sawyer (1968), no. 1784; Gibbs (1939), no. J.9; Kelly (2004), no. 4. In 1066 Hemel was held as 10 hides by two men of Earl Leofric: *DB* i, fo. 136 (15.10). Twickenham: Sawyer (1968), no. 65; Gelling (1979), no. 191; Brooks (1984), 141–2.
35 Sawyer (1968), nos. 1783, 1785; Gibbs (1939), nos. J.6, J.7; Kelly (2004), nos. 2–3; Keynes (1993a), 307.
36 Sawyer (1968), no. 1787; Gibbs (1939), no. J.11; Hart (1957/1971), 30; Kelly (2004), no. 6.
37 See also below. Chich was transferred to the newly refounded St Osyth's Priory by bishop Richard de Belmeis (1107–27). On the Sokens, see Faith (1996).
38 John Blair, the model's originator, is more subtle. For a summary of the issues, see Cambridge and Rollason (1995) and Blair (1995).
39 For an attempt for Middlesex, see Bailey (1989); for Essex, where the evidence is stronger, Rodwell and Rodwell (1977); Rippon (1996).
40 Rodwell and Rodwell (1977), 56–8; 91–2; their puzzlement at the massive scale of the later parish churches at Clacton and Copford (102) overlooks the explanation that both were important episcopal estates. On St Osyth, see below, 116–17.
41 Bailey (1989), 117, suggests Fulham, but there is no supporting evidence: Taylor (1995b), 268–9.
42 Norden (1593), 38; Lee (1955).
43 I am grateful to Robert Whytehead of English Heritage for confirming the absence of archaeological finds, and to Alan Thacker and Chris Lewis for discussing St Pancras and his cult.
44 See below, 114; Thacker (2000), 257–60.
45 I am grateful to John Blair for information on the cross-type. Lee (1955) has useful detail but is unfootnoted and swings between balanced assessment and credulity. He has been followed uncritically by Ogden (1997), and on the cross, to her regret, by Cherry and Pevsner (1998), 348.
46 On St Albans, see Sharpe (2002), Crick (forthcoming), Crick (2001) and below; Westminster claimed patronage from Offa by at least the tenth century (Sawyer (1968), nos. 670, 1293), but this may have been Offa of Essex: see Harvey (1977), 20–1, Sullivan (1994), 79, 95.
47 On Waltham, Huggins and Bascombe (1992), 282–343; Huggins (1991) needs modification, see Taylor (1995b), 264–5.
48 Sawyer (1968), nos. 103a, 1787; Gibbs (1939), no. J.14; Kelly (1992); Kelly (2004), nos. 7, 8.
49 Keynes (1993d); Keynes (1994), 24–5. Brooks (1984).
50 Brooks (1984), 111–17.
51 Kirby (1991), 174–5, suggests that the new archdiocese may have been the expression of a new southern Anglian political community with Lichfield as its ecclesiastical centre and London and Ipswich its trading emporia, but London would surely then have been subject to Lichfield.
52 Keynes (1990); Keynes (1993c); Taylor (1995a); Taylor (1995b), 273; Crick (2001); Crick (forthcoming).
53 Blackburn (1986), especially Stewart (1986); Blunt (1961); Whitelock (1979), 420.
54 Whitelock (1979), 181.
55 Brooks (1984), 123–4; Lichfield reverted to a bishopric in 803.
56 Sawyer (1968), no. 1791. The description of Sigric the beneficiary makes it unlikely that he was Sigric, King of the East Saxons, who witnesses the transaction. Gibbs (1939), no. J.16; Kelly (2004), no. 9; *DB* i. fo. 137 (17.15).

57 Keynes (1993d); Keynes (1998), esp. 8; Keynes (1993b); Kelly, (2004), nos. 28–9.

58 Malcolm, Bowsher and Cowie (2003), 109–24, 128–34, 190; Keene (2003).

59 Blackburn and Dumville (1998), especially the chapters by Keynes and Blackburn; see below, pp. 20, 27.

60 Dumville (1992); Keynes (1998), 8.

61 Now Corpus Christi College, Cambridge MS 383, in a twelfth-century copy written under Bishop Maurice: Wormald, (1999), 235–6.

62 Dumville (1992); Williams (1996); Keynes (1998), 31–4.

63 Rodwell (1988), who disproves earlier beliefs that the Vikings reused an Iron Age or Roman earthwork.

64 Dumville (1992); Williams (1996); Gover, Mawer and Stenton (1938), xviii–xix, 26.

65 On the varieties of subjugation, see Campbell (1979/1986); Keynes (1993b).

66 Barrow (1994); Hadley (1996).

67 Whitelock (1974), 16; but see O'Donovan (1973), 92.

68 Nelson (1993), 155–7.

69 Rodwell (1976), but see Blair (2002), 518–19.

70 Bascombe (1987). The West Saxon royal house's involvement in post-Viking Barking, the only convent outside its heartlands so treated, still awaits explanation.

71 On the problem of the estates of defunct institutions, see Dumville (1992), 33.

72 Whitelock, (1974), 16, 30.

73 Dyson (1978); Dyson (1990); Keene (2003); Kelly (2004).

74 Dyson (1978); Dyson (1990); Keene (2003); Kelly (2004). Dr Kelly in a personal communication stresses that the surviving documentary copies are from a Canterbury-based memorandum and therefore incomplete. I nevertheless doubt if the memorandum would have excluded mention of key participants.

75 Keene (2003).

76 Dyson (1990), 106–7; Keene (2003).

77 Dyson (1990), 107; for Paul's Wharf, see below 20.

78 VI Æthelstan, translated in Whitelock (1979), 423–9. Liebermann (1903–16), i.172–83, iii.115–23; Liebermann (1908); Wormald (1999), 296–9, 303–6; Taylor (1995b), 277–8.

79 The *burh* of *Wigingamere* was more probably in Bucks than at Newport, Essex: Haslam (1997).

80 Taylor (1995b), 278–9; on London's uniqueness as a reason for its absence from the Burghal Hidage, Dumville (1992), 26.

81 Loyn (1974); Baring (1899); Round (1903), 406–7.

82 The phrase is Cam (1957), 55. The pattern is less widespread than is often thought. St Albans controlled Cashio Hundred, but Cam's allocation to St Paul's of Edwinstree (Herts) as a private half-hundred (1930, appendix 4) is mistaken: Taylor (1992), 302.

83 Whitelock (1975), 17–21; Bullough (1975), 33 and footnote; Dumville (1992), 159–62.

84 Hart (1957/1971), 34, followed by John (1964), 17, fn. 2, thought otherwise; for a detailed refutation, see Taylor (1992), 289–93, accepted by Kelly (2004).

85 *DB* ii. fo. 11 (3.14).

86 Kelly (2004) disagrees and sees all four estates as personal bequests.

87 Kelly (2004), who is sceptical about Stepney as early endowment, thinks the *Lundenebyri* estate probably intramural, but despite the name-form the text seems more naturally to refer to the activities of five comparably rural estates.

88 And therefore not separately named: *DB* i. fo. 30 (1.8).

89 *DB* i. fo. 34 (2.3).

90 Stafford (1989), 48.

91 Keynes (1995d), and above.

92 Whitelock (1975), 21.

93 For appraisals and summaries, see Farmer (1975), 10–19; Brooks and Cubitt (1996); on Westminster, Harvey (1977), 22–3.

94 Whitelock (1975), 23.

95 Whitelock (1975), 21–4; see also Dales (1988), 56.

96 Simpson (1873), 38–40; Brooke (1957), 11–15; Whitelock (1975), 27–9.

97 Whitelock (1975), 25–30; Wormald (1999).

98 Robertson (1956), 214–5, 465.

99 Sullivan (1994), esp. ch. 6.

100 Discarding the belief that Theodred's will provided a complete listing of the estates *c*.950 removed the need to posit a massive acquisition between then and the *c*.1000 list; cf. above.

101 Keynes (1993a), 303–16; Kelly (2004), no. 10.

102 *VCH Middx*, vi. 15, 17 (Friern), 55 (Finchley), 140 (Hornsey), 145 (Brownswood).

103 Stepney in Domesday Book had wood for 500 pigs and Fulham wood for 1,000; see also Taylor (1995b), 261–2.

104 Keynes (1993c); Taylor (1995b), 261.

105 On the 'Westminster Corridor', see Sullivan (1994).

106 Williamson (2000), 81–3, superceding Fenning (1915–22).

107 See Dumville (1992), 202.

108 For detail see Kelly (2004), and sources there cited.

109 Blake (1962), 105; Gibbs (1939), xxxix; Kelly (2004).

110 Whitelock (1930), no. 16.

111 Whitelock (1930), nos. 14–15; Gibbs (1939), no. J.1; Keynes (1993a), 306; Kelly (2004), no.17; Taylor (1992), 306.

112 See below, p. 21; Crosby (1994), 313–32, underplays the degree of early separation at St Paul's.

113 Gibbs (1939), supplemented by Keynes (1993a); BL, Lansdowne MS 364, fo.145v has what may be a related list, printed Gibbs (1939), viii; Kelly (2004), who stresses the unreliability of the charter relating to Navestock.

114 Sawyer (1968), no. 453; Gibbs (1939), x; Kelly (2004), no. 12; Rothe is Roe Green and Roe Wood within Sandon: Gover, Mawer and Stenton (1938), 165.

115 Corpus Christi College, Cambridge, MS 383, fo.107, in the same twelfth-century MS as the Alfred–Guthrum Treaty: Wormald (1999), 230–4; Liebermann (1900); Kelly (2004).

116 Whitelock (1975), 24.

117 *DB* ii. fo. 48 (24.63); see Taylor (2000), 12.

118 Wormald (1996); Taylor (1992), 300–1, and below.

119 Kelly (2004).

120 Taylor (1992), 310–11; Abels' guess (1988, 158–9, 276) that the ship list obligations were imposed on tenanted land is untenable.

121 See below, 115; Lawson (1993), 140–1; Hill (1994), 103–4.

122 Whitelock (1975), 33–4; see below, 115–16. The bishop's estate at Little Bentley was a post-Conquest acquisition. Spearhafoc was appointed in 1051, but expelled before consecration.

123 See below, 20; Keene (2003); Taylor (2002).

124 Wilson (1896); Brooks (1984), 275. The sacramentary had been written at either Winchester or Canterbury.

125 Gem (1981), 54.

126 Riley (1859), 26; Milman (1869), 17–18; Cownie (1998); on the chronicles, Bates (forthcoming).

127 As well as *DB*, see especially Round (1902); Round (1903); Taylor (1992), 303–11; Taylor (2002); Kelly (forthcoming).

128 See above and Taylor (1992), 310–11.

4. *From Conquest to capital: St Paul's c.1100–1300*

1 Whitelock, Douglas and Tucker (1961), 163.

2 Biddle (1976), 309–11; Gem (1983), 3–4; Gem (1990), 58.

3 Morey and Brooke (1965), 151–62; Brooke and Keir (1975), 120–1; see above, p. 4.

4 Whatley (1989), 65.

5 Brooke (1989), 81.

6 For an overview of London in this period, see Keene (2000a), (2000b).

7 Hollister (1986), 69, 133, 180, 197; Mortimer (1989).

8 Gibbs (1939), 28.

9 Page (1929), 129; but see Taylor (2002).

10 The palace will be the subject of a future essay by the author. For officials in this neighbourhood, see Gibbs (1939), no. 133; Chew and Weinbaum (1970), nos. 210, 279; Hodgett (1971), no. 824.

11 Davis (1972); Taylor (2002).

12 Colvin (1963), 17, 45, 491.

13 Fowler (1911), 756, 170.

14 Whatley (1989), 129–31.

15 Gibbs (1939), no. 198.

16 Hale (1858), xlviii–xlix; Greenway (1968), 27.

17 For this use of the quay, see GL, MS 25501, fo. 80b.

18 Gibbs (1939), no. 189.

19 Lobel (1989), 82.

20 Nightingale (1982).

21 Webster and Backhouse (1991), 285–6 (no. 265).

22 HMC 9, 26; Leach (1910); Gibbs (1939), no. 273; Neininger (1999), no. 24.

23 Stubbs (1882–3), i. 276–7; Riley (1859), 104, 119, 261, 270, 289; Riley (1860), 193; Fowler (1911), 91–3.

24 Lobel (1989), 82, 90, 93.

25 Gibbs (1939), no. 34; Clay (1944).

26 Lobel (1989), 80, 93.

27 Gibbs (1939), no. 13.

28 Gibbs (1939), no. 198; Blair (1991b).

29 Davis (1925). The wards named in this rental can be located by identifying properties with their corresponding entries in thirteenth-century rentals, where parishes are named: GL, MS 25504, fos. 107v–110v; MS 25512, fos. 1–7v.

30 GL, MS 25501, fo. 10.

31 Keene and Harding (1987), no. 104/0; Tatton-Brown (2002).

32 The complex story of the constitutional evolution of the cathedral establishment is more fully told in Brooke (1951), Brooke (1957) and Edwards (1967), to which this summary is heavily indebted and to which references on all points are not provided here. Those authors drew on Gibbs (1939), xvi–xxxix. Recently, the story has been modified in important ways: Crosby (1994), 313–32; Neininger (1999), xlii–lxiv. Greenway (1985) is very important for the development of this recent thinking, while Barrow (1986) puts the English prebendal system in context.

33 Harmer (1952), 237–9, 242–3;

34 Greenway (1985), 89 and n.

35 Gibbs (1939), nos. 8, 11, 13, 16, 27, 59; Harmer (1952), 237–9; Crosby (1994), 319–21; Bates (1998), 186; Neininger (1999), no. 8.

36 Neininger (1999), xlv.

37 Gibbs (1939), no. 63; Edwards (1967), 137–40.

38 Greenway (1968), 4, 8, 12, 14, 18; Brooke (1985).

39 Morey and Brooke (1965), 194–5.

40 Hale (1858), 109–17, 140–52; Simpson (1897a); Brooke and Keir (1975), 130 n. 3; Crosby (1994), 325–32.

41 Stapleton (1846), 41–2: the work was said to have begun before Easter in the shrieval year 1258–9.

42 Edwards (1967), 101–27, 147, 231–2.

43 Crosby (1994), 328–30; Neininger (1999), lvi, lvii, no. 69.

44 Brooke (1957), 71; Edwards (1967), 159–68.

45 Macleod (1990) is misleading on many aspects of this topic.

46 Stubbs (1876), ii. lxxii; GL, MS 25501, fo. 56a.

47 Gibbs (1939), nos. 103, 105.

48 Gibbs (1939), no. 277.

49 Gibbs (1939), nos. 198, 273; Neininger (1999), no. 24.

50 Edwards (1967), 339.

51 Gibbs (1939), nos. 132, 144–5; Edwards (1967), 340.

52 Simpson (1873), 9.

53 GL, MS 25501, fo. 66b.

54 I am grateful to Nicky Losseff for help with this account, based on Losseff (1994), 14–15, 27–35, 54, 161–3, 199–201. For the books, and a book of polyphony donated by a later almoner, see also Kerr (1969), 58, 63 and Baltzer (1987), 381–5. For the treasurer and prebendary, see Greenway (1968), 21, 36–7, 52.

55 Brooke (1957), 27–8; Greenway (1985), 92.

56 Stubbs (1876), ii. lxix–lxxiii; Brooke (1951); Edwards (1967), 36–8, 43, 51, 59–60, 75.

57 Stubbs (1882–3), i. 297. For the annual presentation

of a buck, instituted in 1274, see Kingsford (1971), i. 333–5.

58 HMC 9, 12; Gibbs (1939), nos. 79, 103, 200–2; Edwards (1967), 262–5, 276. Edwards's identification of the 'prebendary clerks' of 1162 as 'minor canons' is too categorical. Hennessy (1898), 320–1, n. r.140.

59 Gibbs (1939), no. 206; Edwards (1967), 253–4, 262–3.

60 For context, see Barrow (1989).

61 Edwards (1967), 260–2.

62 Simpson (1873), 63–5.

63 Gibbs (1939), nos. 170, 240, 295–6; GL, MS 25504, fos. 93–96v, MS 25512, fos 10–15v.

64 Gibbs (1939), nos. 221–2.

65 Illingworth and Caley (1812–18), i. 403; Stapleton (1846), 159; HMC 9, 12; Sharpe (1889–90), i. 36, 49–50; Williams (1963), 220, 236. Isabel Bukerel's will refers to a statute of 1279 and was proved in 1280.

66 Dugdale (1818), 330–5; see, p. 119 n. 98.

67 Edwards (1967), 39–40.

68 Astle, Ayscough and Caley (1802), 19–20; GL, MS 25504, fo. 90.

69 Edwards (1967), 43; GL, MS 25504, fo. 90.

70 The classic accounts covering the twelfth century, and to a lesser extent the thirteenth, are Brooke (1951) and (1957), elaborated in Morey and Brooke (1965), 202–16 and Brooke and Keir (1975), 338–59.

71 Brooke (1989), 83–9.

72 Stubbs (1876), i. 249; Whitelock, Brett and Brooke (1981), 751–4.

73 HMC 9, 26; *CPR 1281–92*, 174.

74 *DNB*, s.n. William of Cornhill.

75 Greenway (1968), 26, 44.

76 *DNB*, s.n. Henry and Ralph de Sandwich; Greenway (1968), 14, 61, 84.

77 Brooke (1957).

78 Greenway (1968), 68.

79 *DNB*.

80 Kealey (1972), 73–7, 235–7; Brooke and Keir (1975), 200, 203–4.

81 *DNB*.

82 Turner (1995); Brand (1992a).

83 Stubbs (1882–3), i. 28.

84 Brand 1992b; Dugdale (1818), 33, 68.

85 Stubbs (1882–3), i. 30, 54; Gibbs (1939), nos. 113–14; Brooke (1957), 46–7.

86 Edwards (1967), 188–9; Rathbone (1935), 176.

87 Hunt (1941–3), 208, 224–5.

88 Gibbs (1939), no. 275; Greenway (1968), 25; Neininger (1999), no. 41.

89 Rathbone (1935), 105, 132–3, 169.

90 Stubbs (1876), ii. lxix–lxxiii.

91 Rathbone (1935), 94–5; Kuttner and Rathbone (1949–51); Morey and Brooke (1967), 263–4.

92 Brooke (1927).

93 Edwards (1967), 189, 193.

94 Smalley (1935–6); Whatley (1989), 31–3.

95 Hunt (1936), 118.

96 Edwards (1967), 199–200; Greenway (1968), 53.

97 *DNB*; Greenway (1968), 54.

98 Simpson (1873), 187; Brooke (1957), 79; *DNB*.

99 Riley (1859), 279; Gibbs (1939), no. 177; Grierson (1972), 10–13, 17–19 Nightingale (1982), 41.

100 Simpson (1873), 78–9; Sharpe (1903), 38.

101 Round (1899); Haskins (1927), 333–5; Greenway (1968), 42, 59; Barrow (1993), xxxii–xxxiv; Barrow (2002), 1–2.

102 Haskins (1927), 120–6.

103 Riley (1860), 147–8, 343.

104 Davis (1925).

105 Illingworth and Caley (1812), 405, 417, 420, 429, 432; Stapleton (1846), 243–4; Riley (1860), 37–8; *PR 17 Henry II*, 147; *PR 2 John*, 150; Cam (1968–9), 212–13; Taylor (1976), 149–50; Taylor (1980).

106 Canterbury Cathedral Library, Register K, fo. 66.

107 Astle, Ayscough and Caley (1802), 8–13.

108 GL, MS 25504, fo. 90a, MS 25509, fos. 48v–53; Riley (1860), 233–4; Simpson (1897a).

109 HMC 9, 63.

110 Simpson (1897a); for the date, see Brooke and Keir (1975), 130.

111 Simpson (1873), 79–80; Riley (1859), 8–10; Powicke and Cheney (1964), i. 328–30; for the date 1302.

112 Illingworth and Caley (1812–18), i. 405; Weinbaum

113 Stubbs (1882–3), i. 91.

114 *CPR 1281–92*, 174.

115 GL, MS 25501, fo. 56.

116 Rule (1884), 210–11.

117 Bateson (1902), 487–8.

118 Luard (1872–83), iii. 414.

119 Stubbs (1876), ii. 31; Hewlett (1886–9), i. 131.

120 cf. Skinner (1999), 14–28.

121 Manley (1995), 223–5.

122 Stubbs (1876), ii. 114.

123 Luard (1864–9), ii. 329; Luard (1872–83), iv. 261; Stubbs (1882–3), i. 48.

124 Stubbs (1882–3), i. 84.

125 Luard (1872–83), iv. 641; Vincent (2001), 3, 7–19.

126 Stapleton (1846), 9.

127 Binski 1995.

128 Stubbs (1867), ii. 211; Appleby (1963), 48–9.

129 Stubbs (1876), ii. 143; Hewlett (1886–9), i. 244.

130 Hewlett (1886–9), ii. 83, 102–3; Richardson (1932), (1933); Michel (1840), 197.

131 Stubbs (1882), 46.

132 Stapleton (1846), 30–1.

133 Stapleton (1846), 44–5, 49, 63, 69, 73, 84, 92–3; Stubbs (1882), 54–5, 58.

134 Prestwich (1980), 126.

5. *St Paul's Cathedral: the city and the state, 1300–1540*

This chapter is an expanded and revised version of Barron (2003).

1 Brooke (1957), 85.

2 Brooke (1957), 69.

3 Rousseau (2003), 130.

4 *VCH London*, i, 426–7 (cf. HMC 9, 54–5); Kitching (1980), no. 113.

5 Saunders and Schofield (2001).

6 Simpson (1881a), 25–37.

7 Brooke (1957), 53, 60.

8 Simpson (1873), 238.

9 Simpson (1871); Simpson (1889), 3–31.

10 PRO, PROB 11/24, fos. 92v–93; PRO, PROB 111/27, fos. 234v–235v.

11 Kitching, (1980), nos. 108–11; Simpson (1894), ch. 5; *c*.1370 there were fifty-six chantry chaplains in the cathedral, GL, MS 25121/1954. See below, n. 74.

12 Leach (1910), 191–238; Rickert (1932), 257–74.

13 Macleod (1990), esp. 4–6.

14 Brooke (1957), 93.

15 Butler (1951), 254 and Appendix B 'Itinerary of Bishop Braybrook 1382–1401', 560–625. Even when Braybroke was not in his London palace, he was usually at Fulham or Stepney. Similarly, Bishops William Gray (1425–31), Robert fitz Hugh (1431–36) and Robert Gilbert (1436–48) appear rarely to have left the diocese and were frequently in London: Zadnik (1993), 228–56, Appendix 5, 270–82.

16 Riley (1868), 76.

17 Cam (1968), i. 32 and n. 4.

18 Riley (1860), 338–44.

19 Barron (1974), 21–2.

20 CLRO, Journal 4, fos. 60v, 69, 142; Journal 5, fos. 212, 214.

21 Calculated from Sharpe (1889–90).

22 Freeman (2001), 89–103, esp. 102.

23 Blayney (1990), 25–33, Fig. 10.

24 GL, MS 25271/79 (HMC 9, 48). For a contemporary reference to the 'little cemetery', see HMC 9, 46.

25 Watney (1892), 248–9; cf. Sharpe (1889–90), i. 29–30. For another legacy to the charnel chapel at that time, see HMC 9, 46. The executors of Aveline de Basing endowed a third chaplain in the chapel in 1281: GL, MSS 25271/79 and 25501, fos. 63, 68.

26 GL, MS, 25501, fo. 103; Cook (1955), 64–65.

27 GL, MS, 25121/1956; Dugdale (1818), 91–2.

28 PRO, C47/42/209a and b; Westlake (1919), 186–7.

29 cf. Sharpe (1889–90), ii. 302.

30 Sharpe (1909), 91, 194.

31 Dugdale (1818), 391–2; Sharpe (1911), 60, 115, 373; Sharpe (1912), 156, 271.

32 Price (1886), 123–5; Kingsford (1971), i. 330. In 1439 a chaplain was appointed to serve the chantry of Henry Barton and John Barry, but there is no other reference to Barton's celebration as a chantry: GL, MS 25513, fo. 177v.

33 Riley (1860), 343.

34 Schofield (in prep.).

35 Gibbs (1939), no. 306.

36 Sharpe (1889–90), i. 449, 652.

37 Wood (1994), 57; Harding (2002), 90–1.

38 CLRO, HR 195(44); Lee (1998).

39 Stratford (1994), 114, 117, 122, 128.

40 Sharpe (1889–90), ii. 467–8. For the chantry, see Kitching (1980), no. 111, and below, p. 36; its ordinances are LPL, MS 2018.

41 Emden (1957–9), ii. 1040; PRO, PROB 11/4, fo. 56v.

42 Kingsford (1971), i. 109, 327–8.

43 Binski (1996), 153–9; Harding (2002), 101–3.

44 Kingsford (1971), i. 109; Pearsall (1970), 177–9; Warren and White (1931); Simpson (2001), esp. 234–8; Brooke (1957), 65.

45 Brewer (1856), 131–44.

46 Imray (1968), 7, n. 1; see above, n. 31.

47 Petermann (2000), 26–41, 232, Abb. 1–2.

48 Riley (1859), 26; Kingsford (1971), ii. 346; cf. below p. 39.

49 Riley (1859), 28–9; Thomas, Sloane and Phillpotts, (1997), 127; Kitching (1980), no. 111; LPL, MS 2018.

50 Gilbert de Bruera (dean 1335–54), John Colet (dean 1505–19), Alan de Hotham (canon d. 1351–2), Hugh of St Edmund (canon d. 1264), James of Abbyngworth (canon d. 1275), Ralph Dunioun (canon d. 1286), Martin Elys (minor canon d.1393): Sharpe (1889–90), i. 9, 19, 77, 660, 682 and ii. 304–6, 640.

51 Sharpe (1889–90), ii. 305.

52 Sharpe (1889–90), ii. 640.

53 PRO, PROB 11/27, fos. 234v–235v.

54 Horn (1963), 26, 57; Thrupp (1962), 325, 366; Emden (1963), 519–20.

55 Horn (1963), 27; Butler (1951), 291–92; Sharpe (1889–90), ii. 385; Davis (2000).

56 Woolgar (1993), 695–6.

57 Butler (1951), 305–6, 407–12; Sharpe (1889–90), ii. 330–1.

58 Butler (1951), 130–41, 487, 525.

59 Butler (1951), 247.

60 Woolgar (1993), 721.

61 Butler (1951), 30–141.

62 Chew and Kellaway (1973), nos 69, 228, 250, 572, 579; Chew (1965), nos 184, 186, 191, 200, 250; Loengard (1989), nos 8, 24, 41, 123, 162, 177, 200, 222, 245, 254, 280, 373.

63 Sharpe (1911), 120.

64 Calculated from Hennessy (1898).

65 Fowler and Jenkins (1927), 148–82; Brooke (1957), 75–6; Rousseau (2003), 200.

66 Calculated from Kitching (1980).

67 Thomas (1929), 111; Thomas (1943), 144–5; Jones (1954), 82, 150; Simpson (1894), 81.

68 Harding (2002), 89; see pp. 27–8, 430–2.

69 Fowler (1911), 145–6; Riley (1868), 580.

70 Thomas (1926), 55.

71 Thomas (1932), 228–230; Barron (1971), 173–201, esp. 174–7; Rollenhagen (1993), 20–4.

72 The virgers' statutes were drawn up under Dean Baldock (1294–1304) and revised under Dean Lisieux (1441–56): Simpson (1889), 79–83.

73 Simpson (1873), 391–2; Thomas (1926), 36.

74 Simpson (1890); Simpson (1894), 95–124; Kitching (1980), nos 108–11; Gear (1996), 7–8, 84–7; Hill (1971), 242–55; Rousseau (2003), 57–60. The total does not include the chaplain serving Roger Beyuin's chantry and the canon serving Thomas Kempe's.

75 GL, MSS 25121/1754, 25271/35; Sharpe (1889–90), i. 609–11; Kitching (1980), no. 108. For city appointments of chaplains, see Sharpe (1907), 315, 338; Sharpe (1909), 45–6; Sharpe (1911) 58, 122–3, 191, 239; Sharpe (1912) 19, 71, 161, 191, 233, 260, 288. Pulteney's chantry was later amalgamated with those of two archdeacons of Colchester, with whose

76 Riley (1868), 224–5.
77 Sharpe (1889–90), i. 209; GL, MS 25505, fo. 65v.
78 Sharpe (1889–90), ii. 599.
79 GL, MS 25121/535.
80 Sharpe (1889–90), ii. 467–8, 504; GL, MS 25513, fo. 152v.
81 The parish or St Mary at Hill had, by the end of the fifteenth century, six or seven perpetual chantries: Burgess (1996), 247–9.
82 PRO, C47/41/187, 200; Strype (1720), iii. 145. The fraternity of the Virgin still existed in 1466, but only the light of the Virgin was mentioned in 1548: Corner (1858), 195; Kitching (1980), no. 222. For the other two see above, 35 and below, 39.
83 Sharpe (1889–90), ii. 157, 246, 303.
84 GL, MS 25121/513; we are grateful to Dave Rollenhagen for this reference and for providing us with a copy of his translation. See also Dugdale (1818), 76.
85 Sharpe (1889–90), ii. 203, but it is not certain that the fraternity mentioned in this will was at St Paul's.
86 Barron (1985), 25.
87 Brooke (1957), 96–7; New (1999), 38, 108–10; PRO, PROB 11/8, fos. 226v–228v (information supplied by Dr New).
88 Busson and Ledru (1891), 490–1; Racine (1980), 295–6; Williams (1993); Boucheron (2000).
89 Archer (1991), 10; Sharpe (1889–90), ii. 222–3.
90 GL, MS 25271/73; Archer (1991), 34; Kitching (1980), nos. 109, 220; Rousseau (2003), 122.
91 Sharpe (1889–90), ii. 272–3; Kitching (1980), no. 211; Davies and Saunders (2004), 23–8; Davies (2000), 80 and n. 97, 88 n. 121, 147 and n. 253. The tailors were intended as trustees for the chantry of Bishop fitz James (d. 1522), but this appears not to have been put into effect: Sharpe (1889–90), ii. 634–5; Kitching (1980), no. 108.
92 Maryfield (2000), 10. Armourers: *CPR 1452–1461*, 108; Cook (1955), 117. Dyers: GL, MS 9171/6, fo. 166; CLRO, Repertory 8, fo. 219v (we are grateful to John Oldland for these references).
93 Steer (1968), 10.
94 Sharpe (1889–90), ii. 637–8 and CLRO, HR 241/18; see Kitching (1980), no. 213.
95 Riley (1859), 24–6, 28.
96 Riley (1859), 27–8. Stow, at the end of the sixteenth century, noted that the mayor was attended by 'the fellowships' to St Paul's on the same seven days: Kingsford (1971), ii. 190.
97 Riley (1859), 29–30.
98 Riley (1859), 29; Riley (1868), 466.
99 HMC 9, 31 (GL, MS 25121/241); Simpson (1894), 62. For Barton's obit, see above, 35.
100 Sharpe (1889–90), ii. 649.
101 CLRO, Letter Book Q, fo. 94v (cited in Simpson (1894), 83).
102 Edwards (1967), 61–2; Brooke (1957), 86–7.
103 Dugdale (1818), 15–16, 339.
104 Johnson (1993), 11–13; Duffy (2003), 153.
105 Sharpe (1889–90), ii. 107–9, 139, 160; GL, MS 9171/1, fo. 234; Sharpe (1905), 107–8, 114; Dugdale (1818), 16.
106 Sharpe (1889–90), ii. 203 (where it is not stated that the fraternity was at St Paul's); GL, MS 9051/1, fo. 11r–v.
107 Gollancz (1922); Morse (1975); Johnson (1993), ch. 4; Duffy (2003), 154–9.
108 Baildon (1897–1902), i. 4; Dugdale (1680), 117.
109 Simpson (1880), 58.
110 Ellis (1812), 84, 90; Riddy (2001), 269–84, esp. 278.
111 [Nicolas] (1827), 174–87.
112 Davis (1971–6), i. 529; PRO, E36/248, fos. 45–6.
113 BL, Harley 565, printed in [Nicolas] (1827), 174–87.
114 Bodl, MSS Rawlinson B 355, fos. 67v–74, D 913.
115 Carpenter (1957), 106–16; Arnold (forthcoming).
116 For the text of the sermon, see Williams (1967), 652–60; Harper-Bill (1988), 191–210.
117 Simpson (1890); Simpson (1894), 95–124; Dugdale (1818), 360–7.
118 Barron (1996), esp. 226–7.
119 Nichols (1875), 1–34; Shahar (1994), 243–60.
120 See Colet's will drawn up in 1514, Sharpe (1889–90), ii. 640; Keene and Harding (1987), no. 105/18; Keene (1991), 13–15.
121 Courtenay (1987), 91–105, 142–6, 365–6. For the deputies: GL, MS 25121/1370.
122 Emden (1957–9), 398–9.
123 Emden (1963), 78–9.
124 Emden (1957–9), 1008–9; Warner and Gilson (1921), i. p. xli; a copy of Ive's *lectiones* is in BodL, MS Lat. theol. e. 25.
125 Lupton (1909), 139–40; Ashby (1950), 61.
126 Scott (1972), 6; Harrison (1980), 208 and n. 1.
127 Harrison (1980), 83; Rousseau (2003), 93.
128 Scott (1972), 7.
129 Harrison (1980), 83; Scott (1972), 8.
130 Bowers (1999), 211.
131 Mateer and New (2000), 513–14.
132 Rousseau (2003), 89–95.
133 BodL, MS 842; Harrison (1980), 113; Scott (1972), 7.
134 Scott (1972), 7–8.
135 Mateer and New (2000), 517; Rousseau (2003), 345.
136 Scott (1972), 10; Flynn (1995), 190.
137 Powicke and Cheney (1964), ii. no. 1265.
138 These public events are conveniently gathered together in Cook (1955), ch. 6.
139 Leland, cited by Anglo (1997), 49.
140 Anglo (1997), 56–94; Thomas and Thornley (1938), 308–9.
141 Scott (1972), 9–10; Anglo (1997), 128–30, 202.
142 Brooke (1957), 69.
143 Riley (1868), 415.
144 Copeland (2001), 2–3.
145 Simpson (1881a), 124–5; Kingsford (1971), i. 331. William Horne alias Littlesbery (d. 1496), left property to the Salters' Company, out of which 4*d*. was to be paid to each preacher at the cross, but this and other conditions were not performed: Kingsford (1971), i. 246; Salters' Hall, Deeds, H1/4/5A.
146 Sharpe (1909), 231; CLRO, Journal 6, fos. 123v, 49.
147 Simpson (1881), 168; Stow (1632), 454.
148 Thomas and Thornley (1938), 231–2; Emden (1963), 519–20.
149 Brigden (1989), 130, 151–3, 194, 271; Anglo (1997), 171–3.
150 In the six volumes of the Journals of the Court of Aldermen and Common Council covering 1416–62 (with a gap between 1429 and 1436) in CLRO there are only twelve references to St Paul's Cathedral and, of these, five refer to the dispute over the bars on Ludgate Hill (see above, n. 20).
151 Rymer (1739–45), vi (pt. 2). 194–5.
152 Brigden (1989), 291; Lehmberg (1988), 72–3.
153 Lehmberg (1988), 104, 116.
154 Lehmberg (1988), 120.
155 Simpson (1894), 138–44; Brigden (1989), 332; Kingsford (1971), ii. 328. By contrast, the parishioners of St Margaret's church at Westminster defended their church from Somerset's demolition squads: Rosser (1989), 275–6.

6. *Community, City and Nation*

I should like to thank the following for their assistance in the course of the research for this chapter: Trevor Cooper, Chris Faunch, Kenneth Fincham, Tom Freeman, Christopher Kitching, Elisabeth Leedham-Green, Nigel Ramsay, Janet Sidaway, Mark Smith, Jo Wheeler; my parents; and the staffs of Bristol Record Office, Cambridge University Library (particularly Ann Toseland), the University of Chicago Library, Gloucestershire Record Office, the Guildhall Library, Hull City Archives, the Huntington Library (particularly Dr Mary Robertson), the Isle of Wight County Record Office, the National Library of Wales, Wiltshire and Swindon Record Office, and York City Archives Department.

1 For recent overviews, see Boulton (2000), Spence (2000), O'Brien et al. (2001), Keene (2001a). On population, see de Vries (1984), Harding (1990).
2 Merritt (1998).
3 MacCulloch (1996), 129–35; Ayris (2000), 105–7; Douglas Hamilton (1875), 31; Brigden (1989), 236.
4 Douglas Hamilton (1875), 104; Elton (1972), 214–16; Brigden (1989), 233–5, 258; MacCulloch (1996), 139.
5 Douglas Hamilton (1875), 33–5, 47; Brigden (1989), 258–9; Corrie (1844), 33–57.
6 See standard accounts in Duffy (1992), Haigh (1993), MacCulloch (1996).
7 Nichols (1859), 286; Hopper (1859), 11–12; Douglas Hamilton (1875), 74–6; Brigden (1989), 289–90.
8 Hopper (1859), 13; Douglas Hamilton (1875), 84; Brigden (1989), 291.
9 Douglas Hamilton (1875), 59–60, 64–7, 71–2, 75–8, 90; Scarisbrick (1981), 355; Elton (1953).
10 Douglas Hamilton (1875), 89–90, 97–9; Duffy (1992), 410–12, 423; Haigh (1993), 136.
11 Douglas Hamilton (1875), 105–7; Brigden (1989), 308, 338; Hopper (1859), 16.
12 Janelle (1928–9), 13, 16–17, 167–72; Brigden (1989), 332–3, 339–40; Ryrie (1999), 62.
13 GL, MS 25648.
14 Nichols (1852), 49–50; Douglas Hamilton (1875), 147, 149, 161, 163–5.
15 Brodie (1905); Nichols (1852), 50–1; Douglas Hamilton (1875), 166–7, 170; Brigden (1989), 374, 376; Wabuda (1993).
16 Douglas Hamilton (1875), 161; MacCulloch (1996), 297–322, 328–32.
17 MacCulloch (1999), 4–5; Bernard (1998) and (1999).
18 Nichols (1852), 48, 52; Douglas Hamilton (1875), 152, 175.
19 GL, MS 25626/1, fos. 24r–v, 49r–v, 51r–v, 60v–61. On Ponet's association with Cranmer: MacCulloch (1996), *passim*.
20 Nichols (1852), 53; Stow and Howes (1615), 594; Loach (1999), 34.
21 Nichols (1852), 54–5; Douglas Hamilton (1877), 1; Stow and Howes (1615), 594–5; Brigden (1989), 433.
22 Kitching (1980), xxviii–xxx and nos. 108–13; GL, MS 25526.
23 Chambers (1966), 223, 234, 252, 283.
24 Nichols (1852), 55–6; Douglas Hamilton (1877), 2–3; Stow and Howes (1615), 595. William Lambard (1536–1601) remembered seeing the St Paul's Whitsuntide festivities as a child: Simpson (1881a), 79.
25 Nichols (1852), 56–7; Douglas Hamilton (1877), 2–3, 6.
26 See p. 432; Nichols (1852), 57; MacCulloch (1996), 66.
27 Bray (1994), 266–71; Douglas Hamilton (1877), 9; MacCulloch (1996), 410.
28 Nichols (1852), 58–61; Douglas Hamilton (1877), 10–14, 17–18, 20; Davis (1982); Brigden (1989), 371, 444, 447–52, 615; MacCulloch (1996), 423–5, 434–5.
29 Nichols (1852), 66–9; Dasent (1890–1907), iii. 138, 168–9; Douglas Hamilton (1877), 38, 41, 47; Brigden (1989), 468–9; MacCulloch (1996), 458.
30 Nichols (1852), 75–7; Douglas Hamilton (1877), 78–9, 83–4; Jordan (1970), 352; Walters (1939), 73–85.
31 Nichols (1852), 78; Douglas Hamilton (1877), 88; Ridley (1957), 303, n.; Boswell and Pauls (1989), 34; Brigden (1989), 524.
32 Nichols (1850), 11–12; Nichols (1852), 80, 82; Douglas Hamilton (1877), 88–9, 96; HMC (1913), 2–3; Loades (1989), 171–81, 188–9.
33 Nichols (1848), 41–2; Nichols (1850), 18; Nichols (1852), 83; Douglas Hamilton (1877), 97–100; Garnett (1892), 104–5; Dasent (1890–1907), iv. 317–18, 320–2; MacCulloch (1984), 272–3; Brigden (1989), 528–30.
34 Garnett (1892), 110; Nichols (1852), 84; Douglas Hamilton (1877), 101–2; Brigden (1989), 530–1.
35 Nichols (1848), 43, 45, 49, 61, 75; Nichols (1850), 27–30; Nichols (1852), 84–5, 88; Nichols (1859), 154–5, 288; Douglas Hamilton (1877), 104–5; Brigden (1989), 554–5.
36 Scarisbrick (1984), 37; Brigden (1989), 582–3; see above, p. 38, below, pp. 162–3.
37 Nichols (1848), 54; Nichols (1852), 87; Douglas Hamilton (1877), 110, 112; Brigden (1989), 533–45; Loades (1992), 1–137; Fletcher and MacCulloch (1997), 81–93.

38 Nichols (1850), 67; Douglas Hamilton (1877), 113.

39 Nichols (1852), 94; Dasent (1890–1907), iv. 321, 429; Brigden (1989), 484; Daniell (1994), 333–8.

40 Douglas Hamilton (1877), 113–14; Knowles (1959), 423–4, 427–31, 436–8, 442–3; Loach (1986), 108; PRO, SP46/124, fo. 242; Loades (1989), 246–7; Loades (1991), 268, 300.

41 Nichols (1848), 72, 77; Nichols (1850), 78–81; Nichols (1852), 90–1, 93; Douglas Hamilton (1877), 123–5; Schenk (1950), 129; Tyler (1954), 112, 122, 124.

42 CUL, Hengrave Hall Deposit, 88/1, item 43; Nichols (1848), 80–1; Nichols (1852), 94; Douglas Hamilton (1877), 126.

43 Brigden (1989), 530, 573–4, 608–9; Alexander (1987), 159, 164, 173–4; Loades (1991), 273; Freeman (2002); Douglas Hamilton (1877), 128–9, 132, 137.

44 Nichols (1848), 178; Boswell and Pauls (1989), 40; Jones (1982), 31, 36; McCullough (1998), 59.

45 Hudson (1980); Jones (1982), 83–168; Bernard (1984); Sutherland (1987); Williams (1995), 229–46; Bowers (2000).

46 Nichols (1848), 197, 200; Douglas Hamilton (1877), 145; *CSP For 1558–9*, 287–8; Birt (1907), 95–6, 210–14. Collinson (1979), 91; Boswell and Pauls (1989), 41.

47 Nichols (1848), 206, 212, 216; Douglas Hamilton (1877), 146.

48 GL, MS 25630/2, fos. 139v–140.

49 My fully referenced account of preferments to St Paul's will appear elsewhere.

50 Atherton, Bunny, Calfhill, Drant, James Grindal, Mullins, Palmer, Pilkington, Veron, Watts, Young.

51 Alley, Calfhill, Cole, Crowley, Gravett, Hutton, Mullins, Nowell, Padye, Veron, Young.

52 Alley, Bullingham, Calfhill, Hutton, Rogers, Westphaling, Young.

53 On Goodman, see Collinson (1979), 117.

54 Kingsford (1971), i. 331, ii. 347, 313; Collinson (1979), 153–61; Kitching (1986); Eiche (2001), 26.

55 Powell (1902), 129; 'Robert Parry's diary', 110; Donno (1976), 278; Rigg (1968), 145; BL, Add. MS 8937, fo. 4, Egerton MSS 806, fos. 5v–6, 2425, fo. 28v; CKS, CMB 1538–1812 (microfilm of Chelsfield St Martin parish register).

56 Simpson (1880), 123–4, 126–7; Pilkington (1563); Collinson (1979), 154–5; Walsham (1999); 117–24, 232–4, 297–8.

57 CLRO, Journal 17, fos. 316v, 317r–v, 328v; Nichols (1848), 260; Eiche (2001), 26.

58 BL, Add. MS 48023, fo. 356v; see also fo. 355r–v.

59 PRO, SP12/17/37, SP12/17/39, SP12/19/42; Bruce and Perowne (1853), 142–4, 152–3, 178–9; Nicholson (1843), 246–7; Corpus Christi College, Cambridge, Parker Library, MS 114B, p. 865; Hampshire Record Office, 21M65 A1/26, fo. 5v; BL, Lansdowne MS 6, fos. 133–4v; CUL, Ely Diocesan Records, G/1/8, fos. 51v–2; Norfolk Record Office, DN/SUN 3, fos. 100v–1v.

60 Chicago University Library, MS 4502; GL, MS 25589.

61 Nichols (1848), 271.

62 Kennedy (1908), 30, 42; Haugaard (1968), 54–6; Crankshaw (1998); MacCulloch (1999), 157–222; Inner Temple Library, Petyt MS 538/47, fos. 574–5v, 576r–7v, 581–4v, 588.

63 Primus (1960), 71–166; Collinson (1967), 74–5; Usher (2001), 444.

64 Frere and Douglas (1954), 32; Peel (1915), ii. 211.

65 Cross (1972); Marcombe (1991).

66 Collinson (1995), 154–7.

67 GL, MS 9537/3, fo. 3r–v.

68 Maclure (1958); Owen (1961); Boswell and Pauls (1989), 40–84.

69 Cargill Thompson (1969).

70 Owen (1957), 193–201; Owen (1961); BL, MS Harley 417, fo. 132.

71 Owen (1957), 627; Collinson (1964); Lake (1982), 16–24; McCullough (1998), 36–7, 48, 90–1. Stipends to Dering and other preachers and readers are recorded in GL, MS 25498.

72 On Mountain, see Brigden (1989), 440, 476–7, 527–8, 542, 587, 595, 617, 626.

73 E.g. Thomas Sampson, William Whitaker and George Withers.

74 PRO, SP12/48/36; Nichols (1848), 226, 251, 253, 259–60, 271–2, 276–80, 283–4, 293, 305; Boswell and Pauls (1989), 42–3, 45–8, 50, 62, 66; Gairdner (1880), 132; Bruce and Perowne (1853), 235, 254; McCullough (1998), 47–8, 64, 69, 70, 79, 84, 93.

75 O'Day and Berlatsky (1979), 136–7, 165; BL, Lansdowne MS 443, fos.123v, 125v, 224v, 225, 225v, 227, 230; Merchant Taylors' Company, London, Court Minute Book 2, fo. 30v; CLRO, Remembrancia I, fo. 89.

76 Milward (1977), 7, 8, 12; PRO, SP12/35, fos.12r–13v (stamped foliation); Owen (1957), 62–3.

77 BL, Lansdowne MS 443, fos. 123v, 128v, 140v, 144, 224v, 226, 227v, 230; Owen (1957), 20, 111–15.

78 Owen (1957), 607, 612, 618, 625–6, 629; Seaver (1970), 121–70.

79 Owen (1957), 245–7, 266, 281a, 632; Collinson (1967), 317, 336, 345, 348.

80 'Robert Parry's Diary', 112; Smith *et al.* (1979), 90; Milward (1977), 31.

81 GL, MS 7153, fo. 2v; PRO, SP12/218/38; CKS, U269/1 O185 and U350/Z7; Nichols (1823), ii. 537–9, 541–2; 'Robert Parry's diary', 117; Klarwill (1926), 184; *CSPFor Jan–Jul 1589*, 20; Boswell and Pauls (1989), 66.

82 GL, MSS 25175 (bills), 9537/9, fos. 42v–61v (transcripts); extracts in Simpson (1873), 272–80. The visitation continued in 1599 and 1600: GL, MS 25175, fols. 6–7v, 35–6v; Kennedy (1924), iii. 305–16.

83 Unless otherwise stated, this and the following seven paragraphs are based upon the original bills. My fully referenced account of this visitation will be published separately in due course.

84 Williams (1937), 176.

85 Cowie (1974), 41–2.

86 Pilkington (1563), sig.G5r.

87 Steane (1972), 92; Collinson (1979), 156; Hall (1602), 36; Frere and Douglas (1954); 31.

88 Earle (1966), 142–6.

89 GL, MS 25175, fos. 28–9v; Simpson (1873), 275–6.

90 Kitching (1986), 123; Barron, Coleman and Gobbi (1983), 142; PRO, SP12/35, fos. 12–13v (stamped foliation).

91 Fisher (1978); Collinson (1979), 144, 146–51; Dent (1983), 105–8, 110–25; Tyacke (1987), 58–60.

92 Grosart (1877), 184; BL, Harley MS 6994, fos. 179–80v; Porter (1958), 391–7; Tyacke (1987), *passim.*

93 Collinson (1979), 117; Tyacke (1987), 3, 16–17; Babbage (1962).

94 MacCulloch (1991), 8.

95 Sorlien (1976), 210; BL, Sloane MS 856, fo. 12.

96 Sorlien (1976), 67–8; Bülow (1892), 61.

97 Williams (1861), 162.

98 CKS, MS U951 Z16, fo.106r–v.

99 'The Puisnes Walks About London', in Baron (1997), i. 333.

100 Stow and Howes (1615), 886.

101 Dekker (1609), 21.

102 Dunn (1984), 342–3.

103 Caraman (1964), 430–40.

104 Loomie (1973), 82, 83 n. 7; Rye (1865), 127–8.

105 Cressy (1989), 143; Pearce (1929), 87.

106 Young (1890), 408.

107 Akrigg (1950–1), 80, 86. For winter use, see Boswell and Pauls (1989), 84–128, 95 (rain).

108 CLRO, Remembrancia VIII, nos. 110, 117, Rep. 47, fo. 210r–v; PRO, SP16/213, fo.37.

109 BL, Stowe MS 76, fo. 228v; Martin (1904), 986.

110 Pearce (1929), 91, also 90.

111 Boswell and Pauls (1989), on which the following observations are based.

112 Boswell and Pauls (1989), 86.

113 Boswell and Pauls (1989), 90, 104.

114 Boswell and Pauls (1989), 119.

115 BL, Stowe MS 76, fo. 228v; HMC *Fourth Report* (1874), 154.

116 Boswell and Pauls (1989), 90.

117 Boswell and Pauls (1989), 115.

118 Boas (1935), 43; Boswell and Pauls (1989), 121–2; Tyacke (1987), 103, 182, 261.

119 Tyacke (1987), 248–65.

120 Boswell and Pauls (1989), 84, 86, 89, 97, 100–1, 109, 116, 120.

121 See Walsham (1999), 285; Morrissey (2000), 43, 45.

122 Walsham (1999), 281–325.

123 Boswell and Pauls (1989), 110–11; Walsham (1999), 285, 298, 308. The foregoing discussion draws heavily on Morrissey (2000).

124 Boswell and Pauls (1989), 98; Salgado (1992), 30–3; Maclean (1860), 132.

125 Williams (1861), 90.

126 Farley (1616), 35.

127 *William Whiteway of Dorchester*, 28; BL, Stowe MS 76, fo. 226.

128 King (1620), 46–7.

129 BL, Stowe MS 76, fo. 228; PRO, PC2/41, p. 315; BL, India Office Records, MS H39, fo. 87; Heylyn (1668), 219; Seaver (1970), 58.

130 Heylyn (1668), 216.

131 Historians divide over whether Laud (Davies (1992), 79) or Charles (Carlton (1987), 94; Sharpe (1992), 322) should be seen as the author of the initiative.

132 LMA, ACC/1302/4/332, p. 17.

133 PRO, SP16/213, fos. 7v–8.

134 GL, MS 25478, p. 1.

135 CLRO, Remembrancia VIII, no. 85; Rep. 45, fos. 499r–500v.

136 PRO, PC 2/41, p. 234/fo. 117v; Merchant Taylors' Company, London, Court Minute Book 8, fo. 438; Young (1890), 129–30.

137 PRO, PC2/42, pp. 30, 57, 207, 251; Huntington Lib., California, Ellesmere MS 7406; GL, MS 25478, p. 52.

138 Hull City Archives, BRI 23 (formerly D831).

139 PRO, PC2/42, pp. 251–4.

140 PRO, PC2/41, p. 356/fo. 178v, p. 402/fo. 201v.

141 PRO, PC2/41, pp. 458–9/fos. 229v–230r; Simpson (1880), 131–3; PRO, SP16/229/116.

142 Gardiner (1886), 280–1; Trevor–Roper (1988), 123.

143 ERO, D/P 248/7/1, D/P 35/7/3.

144 ERO, D/DBa O1.

145 ERO, D/P 75/5/1, fo. 38r.

146 BL, Add. MSS 11044, fos. 247r–9r, 11051, fo. 192r; PRO, C115/72, nos. 6668–73. See Atherton (1999), 110–19.

147 Sharpe (1992), 323–6.

148 CKS, U570/01, 113–15.

149 Huntingdon Lib., Ellesmere MS 7422, analyzed Sharpe (1992), 324.

150 PRO, SP16/257/114; Davies (1992), 77; Scott and Bliss (1847–60), vi. 344–5.

151 PRO, SP16/266/58; GL, MS 25474/1, p. 8; Trevor–Roper (1988), 125.

152 Fleming (1634), 48. For a different perspective, see Lupton (1632), 9–14.

153 CUL, UA Grace Book Z, pp. 255–7.

154 PRO, PC2/42, pp. 373, 405; PC2/43, pp. 447–8/ fos. 228r–v.

155 PRO, SP 16/276/42; GL, MS 25475/1, fo. 124v; Sharpe (1992), 324.

156 Mason (1985), 80; BodL., MS Bankes 43/63.

157 See HMC *Fourth Report* (1874), 49.

158 PRO, PC2/42, pp. 578–9; SO1/2, fo. 177v; CLRO, Remembrancia VIII, no. 125.

159 Quoted Williams (1960), 32.

160 BL, Stowe MS 76, fos. 226, 228, trans. by Dr Elisabeth Leedham–Green; Dugdale (1818), 105, 108–9; Heylyn (1668), 221–3.

161 See e.g. Hill (1956), 265; Sharpe (1992), 324–5; Kishlansky (1996), 136.

162 GL, MSS 25475/1–2, 25478 (ledgers); 25474/1–6 (audit volumes). A detailed and fully referenced account of what follows will be published elsewhere.

163 Scott and Bliss (1847–60), iii. 442; £500 was eventually paid: CLRO, GLMS 272, fos. 7v, 13, 46v.

164 Bowle, Corbet, Dee, Juxon, Laud, Lindsell, Piers, Towers (100 per cent); Curle, Duppa, Skinner, Warner (>70 per cent), some contributing as deans prior to becoming bishops.

165 Wren, Montagu, Neile (terminated support); Howson, Bancroft, Mainwairing and White (non-givers).

166 Abbot, Potter, Thornborough (100 per cent records); Bridgeman, Owen, Davenant (>78 per cent); Hall, Morton, Wright, Coke, Williams (quitters).

167 Maltby (1998), 144.

168 GL, MSS 25478, pp. 18, 55; 25474/1, p. 4; 25474/2, p. 6; 25474/3, p. 7; 25475/1, fo. 98v; 25474/5, p. 6; 25474/6, p. 7.

169 GL, MS 25478, p. 53.

170 GL, MSS 25478, p. 65; 25474/1, p. 6; 25474/2, p. 8.

171 GL, MS 25478, p. 46.

172 GL, MS 25474/3, p. 8 (servants).

173 GL, MSS 25475/1, fos. 100v, 104; 25474/6, p. 16.

174 GL, MS 25478, p. 61.

175 Scott and Bliss (1847–60), iii. 240–1, 249 (Brooke).

176 Underperformers: Bishopsgate, Bridge Within, Cheap, Coleman Street, Cornhill, Farringdon Within, Farringdon Without, Queenhithe, Walbrook. Overperformers: Aldersgate, Aldgate, Basinghall, Broad Street, Cripplegate Within, Dowgate, Langborne, Tower. See Finlay (1981), 70–82.

177 Atherton (1999), 115.

178 Heylyn (1668), 222–3; Dugdale (1818), 108. For an indication of Pindar's importance to the appeal, see PRO, PC 2/42, p. 427A.

179 PRO, SP16/371/14.

180 PRO, SP16/378/73.

181 Davies (1992), 210–18; Sharpe (1992), 334–5.

182 Green (1856), 70.

183 'St. Gregories Complaint', in North (1659).

184 *The Jew's High Commendation*, quoted Sharpe (1992), 328.

185 Fincham (1998), 110–12, 114–15; HMC *Fourth Report* (1874), 154–6; BL, Add. MS 34268, fos. 18–19v.

186 PRO, SP16/213, fo. 40r–v.

187 Scott and Bliss (1847–60), iii. 229.

188 BL, Add. MS 11045, fo. 127v.

189 Scott and Bliss (1847–60), iii. 237; PRO, SP16/444/45, SP16/470/44; BL, Add. MS 11045, fos. 128v–9; *CSP Ven 1640–2*, 93; HMC *Twelfth Report* (1888), 262; Smith (1954), 110; Green (1856), 99; Quartermayne (1642).

190 BL, Add. MS 11045, fo. 130r–v; HMC, 12, 'Cowper MSS', 262; HMC (1966), 339; Smith (1954), 110.

191 HMC (1966), 339; Lindley (1997), 12.

192 Jansson *et al.* (2000), passim; Hamilton (1877), 5–6, 32; Notestein (1923), 223–4, 346, 386, 471; HMC *Fourth Report* (1874), 89; Scott and Bliss (1847–60), iii. 270; Heylyn (1668), 538; Cook (1955), 83 (full of errors); Seaver (1970), 362 n. 112.

193 For what follows, see Lindley (1997), 36–91.

194 For the former, see PRO, SP16/434A, fo. 29v; for the latter Smith (1954), 115.

195 BL, Sloane MS 3317, fo. 27; HMC (1971), 364; Lindley (1997), 44.

196 HMC *Twelfth Report* (1888), 291.

197 *The Brownists Synagogve*, 3.

198 *CSP Ven 1642–3*, 182; *To the Kings Most Excellent Majestie*, 5 (the second p. 5 in a confused pagination).

199 *A Perfect Diurnall*, 3; HMC *Fifth Report* (1876), 'Sutherland', 161.

200 HMC *Fifth Report* (1876), 'House of Lords', 56.

201 *Rump*, pt. 1, 145; Simpson (1881a), 268 (supplying a date, perhaps from a different edition).

202 Lindley (1997), 259 n. 20.

203 BL, Add. MS 55929, fos. 119, 110; Bruce (1845), 4–14; *CJ*, ii. 100, 110–14; Shaw (1900), i. 12, 37–56; Russell (1991), 255.

204 *CJ*, ii. 144–5, 151–2; BL, Harleian MS 163, fos. 165r–70r, Sloane MSS 3317, fo. 21, 1467, fo. 39v; Rushworth (1691), iv. 269–73; Bruce (1845), 75–7; Simpson (1881a), 256–7; Shaw (1900), i. 56–8; Fletcher (1981), 105; Russell (1991), 255.

205 *LJ*, iv. 296, 298, 308; Shaw (1900), i. 56, 65–9, 71–6, ii. 287–94; Gardiner (1906), 167–79.

206 Bruce (1845), 104–5; Shaw (1900), i. 77–88, 89–99; Coates (1942), 151; Fletcher (1977), 284–5; Fletcher (1981), 105; Russell (1991), 255.

207 Snow and Young (1992), 329; Scott and Bliss (1847–60), iii. 245; Simpson (1881a), 258; Shaw (1900), i. 119–20, 125–44.

208 Gardiner (1937), 17.

209 *CJ*, ii. 910.

210 *CJ*, iii. 110.

211 *CJ*, iii. 462, 468.

212 *CJ*, iii. 570; Firth and Rait (1911), i. 514–15; Shaw (1900), ii. 320.

213 Simpson (1880), 142–5.

214 See Seaver (1970), 273, 370 n. 24.

215 Lehmberg (1996), 106.

216 John Hansley is counted twice: he held the prebend of Oxgate 1639–40 and then that of Holbourn 1640–67.

217 PRO, SP16/489/73. For related petitions, revealing the king's ignorant interference, see HMC *Fifth Report* (1876), 'House of Lords', 19, 22–3.

218 Ogle and Bliss (1872), 227, 329, 332, 333, 356, 437–8; Matthews (1948), 10; Bosher (1951), 293.

219 Matthews (1948), 202.

220 *Articles Exhibited in Parliament*, 10 (as 'Laifield'); Matthews (1948), 53; Green (1978), 63, 121.

221 Matthews (1948), 44–5, 57.

222 *Articles Exhibited in Parliament*, 10; Coates (1942), 5; Matthews (1948), 50; Tyacke (1987), 263–5.

223 White (1643), 8, 13–14, 38–9; Matthews (1948), 201.

224 E.g. Samuel Baker, John Hacket, Benjamin Stone, Thomas Turner, Richard Bayley, Samuel Fell, Giles Bury, Thomas Wilson, Robert Adams and Richard Taylor.

225 Matthews (1948), 149; Bosher (1951), 50, 164, 287; Hicks (1977); Green (1978), 63–4.

226 Matthews (1948), 261–2.

227 Thomas Westfield, Samuel Hoard, Robert Kerch[i]er, Alexander Strange and Robert Thompson.

228 Matthews (1948), 81.

229 HMC *Sixth Report* (1877), 22; *CJ*, iii. 585; Matthews (1948), 11.

230 HMC *Fifth Report* (1876), 117; *An Ordinance of the Lords and Commons Assembled in Parliament*, 2.

231 *The Trve Informer*, 39 (second 39 in confused pagination).

232 BL, Stowe MS 76, fo. 228v; *Rump*, pt 1, 15.

233 Underdown (1963), 18; Russell (1971), 332; Christianson (1973), 227–8, 236–7, 239; Shaw (1900), I, II passim; Matthews (1934), 87–8; Kirby (1939); Wilson (1969), passim; Seaver (1970), 68–9, 258–9, 264–71, 294, 325–6, 369; Anderson (1986), 69–72; Laurence (1990), 106–7.

234 BL, Stowe MS 76, fo. 228v; *CJ*, iii. 421; *An Ordinance of the Lords and Commons Assembled in Parliament*, 1; Seaver (1970), 271.

235 PRO, SP16/310, fo. 2.

236 GL, MS 25471/4, p. 20; Peacham (1641).

237 *LJ*, v. 404; CLRO, Rep. 56, fo. 168v (uncancelled foliation); *CJ*, ii. 768, iii. 105.

238 CLRO, Rep. 56, fo.173v (uncancelled foliation).

239 *Mercurius, &c.*, 16; *CJ*, iii. 389.

240 Simpson (1881a), 266–7; Carpenter (1957), 168; Lehmberg (1996), 49.

241 Firth and Rait (1911), i. 522, 672–4; PRO, SP16/539, pt 3/311.

242 PRO, SP16/539 pt. 3/313 (1–3), 3/317–18, 3/350; Simpson (1880), 146–7.

243 Steig (1977), 37. For the Commons' interest, see *CJ*, iv. 538–9.

244 Simpson (1880), 147.

245 Firth and Rait (1911), i. 750; Mahony (1979), esp. 103–4; Lindley (1997), 276–7.

246 Shaw (1900), ii. 6, 109; Anderson (1986), 75.

247 Lindley (1997), 139.

248 Kishlansky (1979), 179–272; Kishlansky (1982); Gentles (1992), 140–97, 299; Ogle and Bliss (1872), 410; Young (1890), 406.

249 *The Kingdome's Weekly Intelligencer*, 1181; *Mercurius Elencticus* (1648), [532]; *Mercvrivs Pragmaticvs*, sig.[Ccc4r]; *The Perfect Weekly Account*, 309; *The Moderate Intelligencer*, [1778], [1787]. See also Bray (1850–2), iii. 33; Josten (1966), ii. 466.

250 *The Kingdome's Weekly Intelligencer*, 1184.

251 *Mercurius Elencticus* (1649), 564.

252 Simpson (1889), 283.

253 BL, Stowe MS 76, fo. 228r; *Mercurius Politicus*, [160]; de Beer (1955), ii. 555 (misleading dating).

254 Simpson (1880), 150.

255 Walcott (1872), 81; Tovey (1738), 259–60; Simpson (1881a), 269–70; Katz (1982), 179–80.

256 BL, Stowe MS 76, fo. 228v, translated by Dr Elisabeth Leedham-Green.

257 Heylyn (1668), 538–9. See also *Mercurius Melancholicus*, 1–3, *Rump*, pt 2, 122.

258 Shaw (1900), ii. 498, 590; Underdown (1963), 35; Matthews (1934), 13–14, 88; LPL, MS Comm. II/464.

259 Bachrach and Collmer (1982), 65, 79, 86.

260 Katz (1982), 116.

261 Simpson (1880), 151.

262 See *The Weekly Intelligencer* (1653a), 24; *The Perfect Account*, 1159; *Severall Proceedings of State Affaires*, [3355]; *The Weekly Intelligencer* (1653b), 26; *CSPVen 1653–4*, 142; Simpson (1880), 152; Woolrych (1982), 334–5. For the citadel, see Dick (1972), 280.

263 Simpson (1880), 153–5.

264 *CSPVen 1653–4*, 185; Lang (1956), 6; Macray and Coxe (1869), 311; Phillips (1973), 197.

265 Firth (1899), 129; Routledge (1932), 4.

266 Routledge (1932), 467, 478.

267 Firth (1901), 186–8; Routledge (1932), 484.

268 Spalding (1990), 568–9; Routledge (1932), 568; HMC (1899), 223–4; Gauden (1660).

269 Baxter (1660); Keeble (1974), 99.

270 Bosher (1951), 143.

271 Pierce (1660).

272 Hutton (1985), 143–6; Green (1978), 71.

273 GL, MS 25630/9, fos. 1–2; Green (1978), 67, 71–2.

274 Green (1978), 61–70.

275 William Braborn, Walter Jones, Richard Owen, Christopher Shute and John Wilton.

276 *Walker Revised*: see Matthews (1948).

277 John Barwick, John Dolben, Thomas Lant, Matthew Smallwood and George Stradling.

278 Beddard (1972), 161–4; Deputy Keeper of the Public Records (1886), 24, 89; Matthews (1948), 139, 378; Carpenter (1957), 211–12.

279 For Sancroft, see Carpenter (1957), 176–9, 212–15.

280 Carpenter (1957), 172; Hutton (1985), 150–2; Greaves (1986), 50–7.

281 Simpson (1889), 284; Hutton (1985), 170.

282 BL, Add. MS 10116, fos. 257v–8v; de Beer (1955), iii. 301 n. 4.

283 BL, Add. MS 10116, fo. 198.

284 Beddard (1972), 165; BL, Add. MS 10116, fo. 260; Bund (1915–20), i. 81.

285 Bund (1915–20), i. 80; BL, Add. MS 10116, fo. 257; Beddard (1972), 166–7.

286 Rutt (1828), iii. 539.

287 P., T. (1662), 1–2.

288 Carpenter (1957), 173–4; Bund (1915–20), i. 85; BL, Harley MS 4941, fos. 2–19v.

289 Beddard (1972), 168; CLRO, GLMS 272, fo. 1.

290 See Beddard (1972).

291 CLRO, GLMS 272, fos. 1–2v.

292 De Beer (1955), iii. 448–9.

293 This account draws on BL, Add. MS 10117, fos.175, 176v; de Beer (1955), iii. 450–64; Latham and Matthews (1995), vii. 267–82, 309–10, 367–8; Keeble (1974), 198–200; Harvey (1960); Elliott (1853), 10–14; Nicolson and Hutton (1992), 276–8; HMC (1930), 369–72; Barwick (1724), 352–4; Bell (1920), 124–40, 313–34; Hutton (1985), 247–9; Porter (2001).

294 Warwick (1701), 80.

295 Hawkins (1844), 83, 179; Bachrach and Collmer (1982), 131; de Beer (1955), ii. 513.

296 CLRO, GLMS 272, fos. 2v–10v; HMC (1901), 381.

297 Reddaway (1940), 84–5, 88–9 n. 4, 123 n. 3, 181–99, 237 n. 5, 242; Lang (1956), *passim*.

298 LPL, MS 2872, fos. 46–7v, 48–9v; HMC (1930), 328; BL, Stowe MS 208, fo. 38v.

299 Reddaway (1940), 313.

300 GL, MSS 25521, fos. [1r–2v], 25606.

301 GL, MS 25606; the archdeacons were Smith of Colchester and Bell of St Albans.

302 GL, MS 25567/13, fo. 27.

303 GL, MS 25606.

304 GL, MS CF box 54/2, and MSS 25570, 25566.

305 See GL, MS CF box 64, and MS 25747.

306 GL, MS 25566, letter of Dr Harcourt, Sept. 1678.

307 GL, MSS 25565/1–28.
308 GL, MS 25565/20, fo. 9A.
309 GL, MS 25565/1, fos. 25, 66.
310 CLRO, GLMS 272, fo. 170r–v.
311 CLRO, GLMS 272, fos. 12v–45v. A detailed analysis will be published elsewhere.
312 GL, MS 25489, fos. 10–11, 12–13.
313 Calculations based on BL, Harley MS 4941, fos. 244–5v.
314 BL, Add. MS 34268, fos. 20–7v; GL, MS 9537/26; Carpenter (1957), 202–3.
315 Simpson (1882), 121–3.
316 HMC (1930), 292.
317 De Beer (1955), v. 278–9.
318 Clay (1899), 5–39.
319 Jones and Holmes (1985), *passim*.
320 Carpenter (1957), 210; Kishlansky (1996), 314–15, 318, 331–2.
321 Morris (1982), 223–4.
322 Addleshaw and Etchells (1958), plate IX.
323 Dickinson (1967), 11.

7. *History, 1714–1830*

1 See, e.g., Jacob (1997); Knight (1995).
2 See Jones and Holmes (1985), 416; Paterson (1714).
3 Paterson (1714); Best (1746), 10.
4 Paterson (1714), *passim*.
5 Rose (1988), 113.
6 Squibb (1977).
7 GL, MS 25650/8; Prestige (1955), 55.
8 Prestige (1955), 5.
9 Prestige (1955), 29.
10 Prestige (1955), 175–6.
11 Prestige (1955), 43.
12 Edwards (1967), 253–63.
13 Prestige (1955), 56; Russell (1920), 29, 31.
14 For Hackett, see Garrett (1974b), quoting GL, MS 10189/5.
15 *Liber Ecclesiasticus*, 51.
16 Russell (1920), 29, 31.
17 Barrie-Curien (1993a).
18 Pruett (1976).
19 Tindal Hart (1949), 141.
20 GL, CF box 27, draft forms of proceeding on election of a bishop 1809 and 1828, and form of enthroning the bishop 1829.
21 Bell (1980), 161, 189.
22 Hackett (1832), 47.
23 Sykes (1934), 149; *Liber Ecclesiasticus*, 25.
24 BL, Add. MS 32719, fo. 180, quoted Sykes (1934), 149.
25 See Ralph (1985), 24; Fortescue (1926–8), i. 33, 35.
26 Taylor (1999), 183, 190.
27 Varley (1992), 223, n. 3; *Liber Ecclesiasticus*, 6.
28 GL, MS CF box 54/3.
29 BL, Egerton MS 2181.
30 See Simpson (1873), 304–11.
31 Information about chapter meetings is derived from the minute books, GL, MS 25738/3–6.
32 Bell (1980), 172.
33 Cowie (1956), 44.
34 Macaulay and Greaves (1988), 29–33.
35 See Twells (1816), i. 168–246.
36 See Thompson (1994), 224–5.
37 Varley (1992), 90, quoting BL, Add. MS 38286, fos. 120–2, Liverpool to Van Mildert 15 July 1820.
38 Hackett (1832), 3–78; Garrett (1974b), 153.
39 Varley (1992), 99–100. For further discussion, see p. 384, and for an illustration of the event, p. 328.
40 Varley (1992), 100–1, quoting BL, Add. MS 38294, fos. 230–4, Van Mildert to Liverpool 30 May 1823; Prestige (1955), 41.
41 GL, MS 25805.
42 GL, CF box 54/7.
43 GL, MS 25597, pt 1a.
44 BL, Egerton MS 2181.
45 BL, Egerton MS 2181.
46 BL, Egerton MS 2181.
47 *The Times*, 9 July 1824; Smith quoted in Prestige (1955), 3–4.

8. *St Paul's from 1830 to the present*

1 Thomas Randolph, prebendary of Cantlers, appointed in 1812.
2 Smith (1953), ii. 541 n. 1, Grey to Smith, 10 Sept. 1831; Prestige (1955), 14; for the adventures of Blomberg's violin, illuminating his sense of self-importance, Barham (1870), i. 55ff.
3 Smith (1953), letter 319.
4 Smith (1953), letter 643.
5 SPCL, CM, 24 Mar. 1835, 12 Mar. 1836; Prestige (1955), 20–1; Russell, 98. Beckwith is curiously and perhaps not unrelatedly omitted from the list of succentors in Simpson (1897b), 157.
6 SPCL, CM, 4 Dec. 1843.
7 Prestige (1955), 43–7.
8 See p. 73.
9 For the statute, see SPCL, CM, 10 July 1848.
10 SPCL, CM, 6 July 1841, 8 Dec. 1842.
11 For what follows, SPCL, CM, 27 May, 25 Nov. 1850, 9 May, 6 June 1853, bishop's judgement 9–10 Jan., 13 Apr. 1854; Prestige (1955), 64–7. For the 1830s, see Packman (1839).
12 BodL, MS Add. C. 290, fo. 17; Prestige (1955), 62.
13 PP 1835: XXII (no. 54), 10, 14, 20.
14 Blomfield (1864), 167.
15 SPCL, Smith to Blomfield, answered 10 Feb. 1837, reproduced Prestige (1955), 249–51.
16 Smith (1953), letter 751.
17 Smith (1869), 726.
18 Gladstone (1879), vii. 220.
19 SPCL, CM, 24 Mar. 1841; Case C, Hale MSS, Hale to Smith, 15, 23 Aug. 1842; Smith to Hale, 27 Aug. 1842.
20 See Prestige (1955), 174–83.
21 GL, MS 10189/II.i; Packman (1839), 15; Knapp (1848).
22 *ILN*, 15 Oct. 1853, 328, letter from Professor Donaldson.
23 PP 1841: VI (416).
24 Stanley (1870), 576.
25 *Plan* (1839), *passim*.
26 SPCL, CM, 24 Mar. 1859.
27 Russell (1920), 105.
28 See Burns (2003), introduction.
29 Church (1897), 242–3, 246.
30 Prestige (1955), 162; Church (1897), 262.
31 The number was further reduced to five in 1920, confirmed in the 1936 statutes.
32 Frost (n.d.), e.g. 37, 57.
33 Hutton (1912), 199.
34 Sinclair (1909), 322.
35 Chadwick (1966–97), ii. 381.
36 Paget (1921), 153.
37 Burns (1999), esp. ch. 6.
38 PP 1854: XXV [1822], 'Appendix to Report of Cathedral Commissioners', 42.
39 Newbolt [1921], 253.
40 Galloway (2000), ch. 14, esp. 289, 291, 319.
41 *Babylon* (n.d.), 12.
42 Paget (1921), 113.
43 Norman (1976), 180, 176.
44 Newbolt [1921], 171–4.
45 Sinclair (1909), 324.
46 Hutton (1912), 211–12.
47 Prestige (1955), 224–8; Newbolt [1921], 208.
48 Newbolt [1921], 229.
49 Prestige (1955), 206.
50 Hutton (1912), 259.
51 Ollard (1919), 216.
52 Inge (1949), 10.
53 Collins (1992), 72.
54 Fox (1960), 197, 209.
55 T. C. List, quoted in Fox (1960), 206.
56 Fox (1960), 202–3.
57 Dark (1928), 247.
58 Dark (1928), 225.
59 SPCL, Inge scrapbook.
60 Collins (1992), 72.
61 Fox (1960), 103.
62 Lockhart (1949), 265.
63 Inge (1949), 10–11; Fox (1960), 116.

64 Fox (1960), 115.
65 Fox (1960), 183; Inge (1949), 17, 11.
66 Alexander (1930b), 10.
67 SPCL, CM, 12 Jan. 1918; Atkins (1956), 290–1.
68 Alexander (1945), 3; Inge (1949), 19.
69 Inge (1949), 97; Alexander (1930a), 6.
70 SPCL, CM, 2 Nov. 1920.
71 Elliott (1951), 137, 140; Inge (1949), 139.
72 Collins (1966), 148, 149; Alexander (1930a), 29; LPL, Sheppard papers, MS 3746, fo. 194, Inge to Sheppard, 18 Sept. 1934.
73 LPL, Lang papers, 129, Johnson to Lang, 29 June 1933; Budge to Lang, 4 Nov. 1933; Inge to Lang, 13 Oct. 1933, 6 June 1934; Nevile Butler to Lang, 9 May 1934; memo fo. 431.
74 Collins (1992), 88.
75 Matthews (1969), 186.
76 Matthews (1938), 22.
77 LPL, MS 3744, fo. 39, memo 25 Feb. 1935.
78 Roberts (1942), 296.
79 LPL, MS 3744, fo. 31, Matthews to Sheppard, 18 Jan. 1935.
80 LPL, MS 3744, fos. 71 (draft 16 May 1935), 111–12 (Margaret Matthews, 1936).
81 Roberts (1942), 307.
82 Mozley (1938), 187.
83 Roberts (1942), 307.
84 Alexander (1930b), 8.
85 Roberts (1942), 254, 260.
86 Matthews (1946), 27.
87 SPCL, St Paul's Watch Night Shift Log 21 Sept. 1942–23 Mar. 1943, 20, 26 Oct. 1942.
88 BL, Add. MS 65254, fo. 238, Alexander to A. Mansbridge, 30 June 1941.
89 Imperial War Museum, LFB1, 'The Great Fire of London 29th Dec 1940'.
90 Chappell (1989–90), 45; Matthews (1946), 68.
91 Matthews (1946), 67.
92 Interview with Joyce Palmer, former employee of Hitchcock Williams, 30 July 2001.
93 Quoted Matthews (1957), 325.
94 Collins (1966), 92.
95 Collins (1966), 150; Matthews (1969), 325; Collins (1992), 169–70.
96 Collins (1992), 175.
97 Collins (1992), 166; Matthews (1969), 293, 325.
98 Collins (1966), 148.
99 Galloway (1996), for an exhaustive account; quotations at 119, 129.
100 Galloway (2000), 322.
101 Collins (1966), 155–6; Matthews (1969), 266–7.
102 Matthews (1957), 306.
103 Matthews (1969), 329–30; Webster (1978–9), 6.
104 Robbins (1995), 314; Cant (1977), 551; Hope, Lloyd and Erskine (1988), 85; Owen (1996), 631; Barrett (2000), 174.
105 Matthews (1969), 332–4; Shaw and Miller (2002), *passim*.
106 *Dome* 4 (1966–7), 1; *Dome* 1 (1963), 16; 2 (1964–5); Fitton (2002), 103–5.
107 *Dome* 2 (1964–5), 12–13; Wand (1965–6), 14.
108 *Dome* 6 (1968–9), 8.
109 Sullivan (1975), 184.
110 Webster (1994), 59–60, 86.
111 See the *Daily Telegraph* obituary in Beeson (2002), 42–4.
112 Conversation with Alan Webster 26 Oct. 2002.
113 Webster (1978–9), 2–4.
114 Webster (1978–9), 2–4; Potter (1979–80), 7–11.
115 Shears (1980–1), 15–16.
116 Webster (2002), 65.
117 'Cathedral finance: out of the red for 1981', 14; Shears (1983–4), 14.
118 *New York Times*, 10 July 1988; PP 1854: XXV [1822], 42.
119 Bawtree (2002), 94.
120 Conversation with A. Webster, 26 Oct. 2002; SPCL, CM, 28 Mar., 10 May 1990.
121 *Heritage and Renewal* (1994), 223.
122 *Annual Report* (2000), 16.

9. The Cult of Saints and the Liturgy in the Middle Ages

I am very grateful to all who have read and commented on all or part of this paper, especially Derek Keene, Pamela Taylor, Carol Davidson Cragoe, Diana Greenway and George Bernard. Special thanks are due to Nicholas Orchard for generously making available material from the calendar in GL, MS 25512 and an unpublished paper on the liturgy of St Paul's, and to Peter Kidd for his transcript of the calendar in Paris, Bibliothèque Nationale, lat. 10433, in advance of the publication of his study of the manuscript.

1 Sharpe (2002), 77, 122–3, arguing against Delehaye (1931), 301–5. Augulus and his companions are entered under 7 February in the martyrologies of Bede and Jerome.
2 Thacker (2000), 256–64; Thacker (2002a), 38–9.
3 Colgrave and Mynors (1991), 142–3 (II.3). We cannot be certain that this early church was on Ludgate Hill. The claims of St Peter Cornhill to be the first church in the city are, however, doubtful: p. 4.
4 Thacker (2002a), 14–20.
5 Rollason (1989), 196–214.
6 Brooke (1957), 8, 12–15; Simpson (1873), 38–43; see above, p. 1.
7 Wheeler (1934), 292–4; Tatton-Brown (1986), 22–3; Lobel (1989), 87–8.
8 Gibbs (1939), nos. 68–73. Note, however, that the dedication of the city church of St Pancras in Soper Lane, which belonged to Canterbury Cathedral Priory, probably reflects its Kentish affiliation: Keene and Harding (1987), no. 145/0.
9 Mellitus is expressly said to have been a leader of the party which brought necessaries of cult including relics of the apostles and martyrs from Rome in 601: Colgrave and Mynors (1991), 104–5 (I.29).
10 Colgrave and Mynors (1991), 320–1 (III.29). Since Pope Gregory was not a martyr, the relic may not be his; the choice, however, of an otherwise unknown but eponymous saint was presumably with reference to his English cult.
11 Colgrave and Mynors (1991), 156–9 (II.7).
12 For evidence that despite ecclesiastical protestations to the contrary secondary relics were never viewed as having the same status as the holy tomb, see Thacker (2002a), 18–19.
13 Colgrave and Mynors, 354–7 (IV.6); Whitelock (1975), 5–10; see above, pp. 8–9.
14 Sawyer (1968), no. 1247; Attenborough (1922), 36.
15 Levison (1913), 236–7 (cap. 43).
16 Wood (1994), pp. 176–7, 198–9; Fouracre and Geberding (1996), 97–114; Thacker (2002b), 58–9.
17 Colgrave and Mynors (1991), 354–69 (IV.6–11).
18 Colgrave and Mynors (1991), 354–5 (IV.6).
19 Tangl (1916), no. 36.
20 Blair (2002), 531; Blair (1989), 231–6; Rollason (1978), 64–5, 90.
21 Whatley (1989), 120–3 (Miracula Sancti Erkenwaldi, henceforth MSE, 4).
22 Whatley (1989), 120–1, 126–7 (MSE. 4); Thacker (2002b), 47, 62–4.
23 Whitelock, Douglas, and Tucker (1961), 75; see above, p. 13.
24 The miracle story in question tells of a violator of the saint's feast retrieving a bundle he had left contra sepulcrum sancti erkenwaldi extra monasterium and hurrying off into the churchyard, where he tripped over a protruding skull and fell to his death: Whatley (1989), 14–15 (MSE 2). The context suggests an open-air monument appropriate for the original grave site.
25 Biddle (1968), 275–8; Crook (2000), 163–4.
26 Blair (2002), p. 531.
27 Wormald (1934), 36.
28 The events recorded in Whatley (1989), 100–19 (MSE 1–3) appear to precede the fire of 1087.
29 Ker (1985), no. 107. I am grateful to Susan Kelly for this reference.
30 Yorke (1990), 55–6.
31 Colgrave and Mynors (1991), 364–9 (IV.11).
32 His cult is listed as late and dubious by Blair (2002), 564.
33 See e.g. Thacker (1985).

34 Whitelock (1930), 2–5; see pp. 12–13.
35 Simpson (1887), 496; Ker (1985), no. 2; Kelly (forthcoming).
36 Hamilton (1870), 144; Mellows (1949), 59; Whitelock (1975), 17–21.
37 Whitelock (1979), no. 106.
38 Arnold (1890–2), i. 43–6.
39 Rumble and Morris (1994).
40 Whitelock, Douglas and Tucker (1961), 99–100.
41 Lawson (1993), 141–2, 181–2.
42 Macray (1886), 158; Simpson (1997), 482.
43 Whitelock (1975), 33–4.
44 Macray (1886), pp. 157–8.
45 Arcoid makes much of this and of the inspection of the undamaged tomb in the smoking ruins by Bishop Maurice of London and Bishop Walkelin of Winchester: Whatley (1989), 120–9 (MSE 4).
46 Gem (1990), 57–9; Sharpe (1995); Gem (1983); Ridyard (1988), esp. 176–210.
47 Whatley (1989), 13–23, 86–7, 96–7 (Vita Sancti Erkenwaldi, henceforth VSE).
48 Whatley (1989), 90–7 (VSE).
49 Whatley (1989), 158–9 (MSE 5, 17). For its dedication, to St Faith, see pp. 29, 130.
50 Whatley (1989), 128–43, 158–61 (MSE 5–9, 16, 17).
51 Whatley (1989), 62, 142–5 (MSE 10).
52 Whatley (1989), 150–5 (MSE 14).
53 Whatley (1989), 63–4; Simpson (1880), 41.
54 Whatley (1989) VSE, 86–7, 124–5 (VSE; MSE 4, line 69); see p. 119.
55 Thacker (1999), 386; Henschenius and Papebrochius (1688), 429.
56 Whatley (1989), 120–1, 124–5, 154–5 (MSE 4, 14).
57 Wilson (1995), 456; see p. 132.
58 Mellows (1949), 59.
59 Colker (1965), 387, 398, 418.
60 Whatley (1989), 160–3 (MSE 18). Ethelburga's feast day, however, seems never to have been part of the Use of St Paul's: below.
61 e.g. Whatley (1989), 124–5 (MSE cap. 4), where he is referred to as 'Chedda, predecessor tuus'.
62 They were probably two different saints: Hohler (1966), pp. 61–72; Bethell (1980). Cf Blair (2002), 549.
63 Bethell (1970).
64 GL, MS 25122/1140; Bethell (1970), 307–8, 321.
65 Ward (1982), 36–42.
66 Whatley (1989), 158–9 (MSE 16).
67 Heslop (1995), 76.
68 The statutes are much concerned with the regulation of processions: Simpson (1873), 26, 79–80, 175, 184, 191, 240, 448. Cf. Cook (1955), 18.
69 Paris, BN lat. 10433; Kauffmann (1975), no. 89. I am most grateful to Peter Kidd for making available his transcript of this calendar and to him and Nicholas Orchard for discussion of it. It was first identified as a St Paul's calendar by Christopher Hohler: Avril and Stirnemann (1987), no. 74.
70 The calendar includes commemorations of the translation of 1148, but not of Thomas Becket (d. 1170).
71 This might suggest that the calendar copied into Paris lat. 10433 had been adapted for use in the church of St Gregory.
72 St Margaret's name was later erased.
73 The West Saxon king, Edward the Martyr, was also entered in red.
74 Lobel (1989), 86.
75 Lobel (19189), 88–91; below. St Leonard was also titular saint of the cathedral's parish of Shoreditch by the later twelfth century: Gibbs, nos 49, 57–8.
76 Ker (1985), no. 123.
77 Dugdale (1818), 18; Gibbs (1939), no. 186; GL, MS 25504, fo. 91v. (new fol. 93v.).
78 GL, MS 25502, new fo. 93; MS 25504, fo. 91; Gibbs (1939), no. 240.
79 Gibbs (1939), nos. 202, 237.
80 GL, MS 25512, fo. 13v.
81 Gibbs (1939), nos 248, 297. This was the location of the altar and chapel of St John the Evangelist by c.1300: Dugdale (1818), 334. The rood, however, was by then associated with altars in the north transept (p. 40).
82 Dugdale (1818), 337.

83 GL, MS 25512, fos. 10–15.
84 It was one of the unusual solemnities enforced by Roger Niger: below.
85 Gibbs (1939), no. 306.
86 Powicke and Cheney (1964), 329; Simpson (1873), 190–1.
87 Powicke and Cheney (1964), 653–6.
88 The bishop expressly attributes the high status of the feasts of Dunstan and Ethelbert in the city to reverence for the relics held there.
89 By c.1300 there was an altar to the Virgin in the south transept as well as in the nave: see pp. 132–3.
90 Gibbs (1939), nos. 98, 147–8, 202; GL, MS 25504, fo. 91 (new fol. 96).
91 GL, MS 25504, fo. 91 et sqq. (new fol. 93–6); Gibbs (1939), p. 279. The altar of St Chad was set up by Canon Alexander de Swereford (d. October 1246) who ordained a perpetual chantry for himself there: Dugdale (1818), 19; Greenway (1968), 43.
92 Simpson (1880), 2–3; Dugdale (1818), 10, 19.
93 Dugdale (1818), 15, 19; Simpson (1880), 179, 181; below p. 121.
94 CR 1242–7, 152, 199.
95 Ker (1985), nos. 51, 119; Dekkers (1995), no. 772.
96 Luard (1872–83), iv. 169–70, 378, v. 195; Madden (1866–9), ii. 493, iii. 93, 284, 318.
97 DNB, s.n. 'Roger Niger'.
98 Simpson (1887), 469–72; Dugdale (1818), 310–36, corrections in Simpson (1887), 460–3; GL, MS 25, 503.
99 Simpson (1887), 469–70; Dugdale (1818), 315.
100 Simpson (1887), 469–70.
101 Simpson (1887), 470–1.
102 Sharpe (1995), 7.
103 Dugdale (1818), 19; Simpson (1880), 2–3.
104 Simpson (1887), 461, 470–1; Dugdale (1818), 314, 337.
105 Simpson (1887), 471; Dugdale (1818), 314, 338.
106 Simpson (1887), 470; Dugdale (1818), 314.
107 For the location of this chapel see Simpson (1894), 295.
108 St Michael's altar was definitely in the New Work by 1321 when a chantry was established there; the fact that this chantry was later united with another chantry established at the altar of St Silvester perhaps suggests that it stood nearby: Dugdale (1818), 21.
109 Dugdale (1818), 330–6; Simpson (1880), 178–80; GL, MS 25502, fo. 100 (93). By the sixteenth century and probably long before there as an altar to St Mary Magdalen: Dugdale (1818), 29; above, p. 39.
110 For the location of the chapel of St John the Baptist, see Hollar's plan of the crypt: Dugdale (1818), 74–5.
111 Morris (1990), esp. at pp. 75–7.
112 Stubbs (1882–3), i. 311; Dugdale (1818), 15. The space housing the new shrine was later separated from the four bays to the east by a screen.
113 Stubbs (1882–3), i. 275; Simpson (1880), 44.
114 Stubbs (1882–3), i. 276.
115 Dugdale (1818), 20; Simpson (1880), 44; GL, MS 25137; Pfaff (1998).
116 Stubbs (1882–3), i. 311; Coldstream (1976), esp. 24–5.
117 Coldstream (1976), 24–5.
118 Stubbs (1882–3), i. 311.
119 Simpson (1880), 56; Stubbs (1882–3), i. 338, 368; Dugdale (1818), 20–1.
120 Luard (1890), iii. 213–14; Rymer (1816–69), ii. 525–6.
121 Simpson (1880), 10, 12–14.
122 See, for example, Simpson (1873), 52–5.
123 Dugdale (1818), 20, 22.
124 Simpson (1873), 393–4. Nicholas Orchard, in unpublished work, notes that the collect occurs in a late 13th- or early 14th-century service book from Ely: CUL, Ii. 4. 20, f. 227.
125 Dugdale (1818), 15.
126 Dugdale (1818), 14, 16–17.
127 Dugdale (1818), 15–16; Simpson (1873), 393–5; Simpson (1880), 15.
128 Dugdale (1818), 15–16, 339.
129 Simpson (1873), 398; Zadnik (1993), 248.
130 Dugdale (1818), 14.
131 Douet d'Arcq (1851), 265; Dugdale (1818), 14, 16–17, 21–2.

132 Dugdale (1818), 22.
133 Milman (1868), 516–18; GL, MS 25169.
134 Simpson (1894), 246, 252.
135 Legge (1907), 94–6.
136 Simpson (1891–3), 118–28. The exemptions also included SS David, Helen, Thomas of Hereford and the Venerable Bede. I am grateful to Nicholas Orchard for this reference and for analysis of its significance.
137 Simpson (1880), xxi–xxii, 35–9.
138 Eeles (1955–60).
139 King John of France's gift to the image of the Virgin 'beside the choir' was interpreted at St Paul's as a gift 'to the Annunciation': Dugdale (1818), 16–17.
140 Strype (1720), iii. 145, 148; Dugdale (1818), 76; Simpson (1880), 182.
141 Simpson (1887), 519; *CPR 1452–61*, 105.
142 *L&P*, vol. 13, pt. 2, no. 1393.
143 Douglas Hamilton (1875), 84.
144 Douglas Hamilton (1875), 98. See also a further passing reference to the shrine in September 1539: Douglas Hamilton (1875), 106.
145 *L&P*, vol. 15, no. 809 (p. 383).
146 Nichols (1852), 55. But Wriothesley alleges that only one person died and that certain others were injured 'by negligence of the labourers': Douglas Hamilton (1877), 1.
147 Nichols (1852), 57–8; Kingsford (1971), i. 328.
148 Nichols (1852), 59.
149 Nichols (1852), 67.
150 Nichols (1852), 73, 76.
151 Douglas Hamilton (1877), 114, 131, 143, 145–6.

10. *The archaeology of the cathedral*

1 Kingsford (1971), i. 333.
2 Archaeological discoveries in and around the cathedral since the time of Wren up to 2001 are now being brought together: Schofield (in prep.).
3 Wren (1760), 272.
4 Morgan (1885), 116, 118.
5 Burnby (1984), 77.
6 Tweddle et al. (1995), 228–9.
7 Penrose (1879), (1883).
8 Notably John Harvey (1978), who drew attention to the importance of the medieval chapter house and its cloister for the history of Perpendicular architecture.
9 Shepherd (1988), (1998); Schofield (1994), 94; Schofield with Maloney (1998).
10 To be reported by L. Blackmore in Schofield (in prep).
11 Harmer (1952), no. 55 and pp. 470–1.

11. *Fabric, Tombs and Precinct*

I am grateful to John Schofield, who kindly lent me the unpublished draft of his archaeological monograph on the cathedral, and to Nicola Coldstream, Matthew Cragoe, Eric Fernie, Richard Gem, Gordon Higgott, Derek Keene, Richard Lea, Richard Plant, Andrew Saint and Alan Thacker for their comments on aspects of this chapter.

1 Whately (1989), 128–9.
2 Hamilton (1870), 145–6.
3 Wren (1750), 272.
4 Schofield (in prep).
5 Whitelock, Douglas and Tucker (1961), 75; Biddle (1976), 306–9; Blockley, Sparks and Tatton-Brown (1997).
6 Whately (1989), 120–3; Hamilton (1870), 144; see pp. 114–15.
7 Whately 1989, 158–9. Claims that St Faith's was a separate church to the east of the cathedral until the late thirteenth century (Cook 1955, 34–5; Lobel (1989), 87) are incorrect.
8 Simpson (1880), 143–6; cf. below, p. 182.
9 *VCH London*, i. 432, pl. I; Birch (1887–1900), i. 299 and plate.
10 Roberts (2002), esp. ch. 4.
11 'The Miller's Tale', line 3318: Robinson (1966), 49.
12 Wren (1750), 272.
13 Lethaby (1930), 1091–2; Clapham (1934), 14 and Gem (1990), 55 favour the former. Fernie (2000), 247–53 discusses east ends in Anglo-Norman churches.
14 Dugdale (1818), 8.
15 Whateley (1989), 158–9.
16 Kingsford (1971), i. 329; Simpson (1880), xliii–iv.
17 Whateley (1989), 158–9.
18 Fernie (1998), Fig. 1.
19 These arches are just to the right of the crease in the lower part of the drawing. See below, p. 134 for a discussion of the treasury.
20 A stone structure against the north wall of the choir may be visible in an engraving for the title page of 'St Paul's church: the bill for parliament, 1621': Society of Antiquaries, London Views iv,. fo. 4.
21 Fernie, 2000, 122.
22 *tanta criptae laxitas*: Hamilton (1870), 145–6.
23 This view has been taken by most previous commentators.
24 Finch (1935), 730. Gem (1990), Fig. 2, shows compound piers in this position, but this does not fit the graphic evidence.
25 Fernie (1998); Crook (2000), 188–93; below, pp. 132–3 for discussion of the transepts.
26 Whately (1989), 122–3. I am grateful to Richard Plant for sharing these ideas with me.
27 *VCH Essex*, x. 151.
28 Wilson (1995), 456; see p. 116.
29 Norden (1593), 32; Holland (1614), 1; BL, Add. MS 71474, fo. 177r–v.
30 BL, Add. MS 71474, fos. 176v, 183v. These were omitted from Hollar's plan of the monuments.
31 Kingsford(1971), i. 337; see p. 163.
32 Gem (1990), but his argument (pp. 55–6) that the transepts were originally only three bays long is not supported by Wren's plan (Fig. 104), which shows a thick, presumably Romanesque, wall continuing unabated through the fourth bay and into the fifth.
33 Malcolm (1802–7), iii. 75.
34 WS XIII, 16, 20.
35 Dugdale (1818), 20. The 'chapter door' was in this location before the commencement of the new chapter house in 1332: HMC 9, 12.
36 Gibbs (1939), nos. 98, 148, 206.
37 Dugdale (1818), 28; Gibbs (1939), no. 202.
38 Dugdale (1818), 334.
39 Simpson (1880), xiv; Harvey (1987), 363.
40 HMC 9, 27 (Box A 24, 525); Malcolm (1802–7), iii. 75.
41 Sharpe (1889–90), i. 687, ii. 254; HMC 9, 55; Kingsford (1971), i. 328, 336; Dugdale (1818), 333.
42 HMC 9, 27 (Box A 24, 525).
43 Sharpe (1889–90), i. 609–10; Kingsford (1971), i. 335.
44 Dugdale (1818), 92; see pp. 415–16.
45 Fisher (1885), 104–5; below, p. 141 for discussion of the Pardon Churchyard.
46 Dugdale (1818), 315–27; Simpson (1887), 500–5.
47 Dugdale (1818), 33, 335. See pp. 164–6 for the chantry.
48 Pers. com. Gordon Higgott. See p. 177.
49 Whately (1989), 122–3; Chibnall (1978), 144.
50 See Gem (1990) for discussion of the dating of the nave.
51 GL, MS 11816A, fo. 320; Malcolm (1802–7), iii. 72; Simpson (1880), xliii–iv.
52 The transept west clerestory windows (Fig. 69) were shown with slightly arched heads, but as the south transept vault had collapsed, this may not be entirely accurate.
53 Cook (1955), 31; Fernie (2000), 130.
54 Whatley (1989), 60–1, 126–7.
55 Dugdale (1818), 14, 331.
56 Kingsford (1971), i. 332; Holland (1633), unpaginated; Dugdale (1818), 37.
57 Graham (1947–8); Morey and Brooke (1967), 306–8; trans. Gem (1990), 53.
58 Gibbs (1939), no. 257. For an earlier twelfth-century craftsman associated with the cathedral, see p. 20.
59 Gibbs (1939), nos. 117 (before 1218), 120 (late twelfth century), 177 (before 1200), 242 (late twelfth century), 285 (*c.*1193–8).
60 GL, MS 25504, fo. 93r–v.
61 Stow (1598), 302.
62 WS, XIII, 128–9; Wren (1750), 272.
63 Wren (1750), 279; WS XIII, 46.
64 London, Society of Antiquaries, London Plans and Views, vol. 4, 'Prospect of ye Citye of London'; Fig. 59; Schofield (1999), fig. 107.
65 Stow (1598), 302. Two woodcuts purporting to depict the interior of the southern tower appear in Foxe's *Book of Martyrs*, but their accuracy is uncertain. See McAleer (1990) for a different interpretation.
66 Simpson (180), 214–18.
67 McAleer (1988), 137–42.
68 Harvey (1987), 101.
69 Wren (1750), 275–6.
70 Luard (1864–9), iii. 66; Alexander and Binski (1987), 273.
71 GL, MS 25121/494; HMC 9, 26; Stubbs (1882–3), i. 338.
72 Stubbs (1882–3), i. 277.
73 WS XIII, 16.
74 Stubbs (1882–3), i. 276, 338.
75 Kingsford (1905), 156, 313; Kingsford (1971), i. 326.
76 Simpson (1880), 3–4, 175–7.
77 Lethaby (1930) and Morris (1990) argued that the choir was reworked in a single campaign begun in the 1250s, but both the graphic and documentary evidence suggest otherwise.
78 Stapleton (1846), 41–2.
79 HMC 9, 27 (Box A 24, 525); Kingsford (1971), i. 329.
80 Simpson (1873), 450, 457.
81 Dugdale (1818), 334. The latest commemoration in this inventory is John de Sta Maria (d. 1289); its date is confirmed by its omission of several early fourteenth-century chantries, including that of Reginald de Brandon (d. 1306–7), which was also said to be in the New Work (Dugdale (1818), 20).
82 Dugdale (1818), 331–2.
83 Bony (1979), 10–12; Morris (1990), 88 and passim; Wilson (1994), 135.
84 See Morris (1990) for a discussion of the architectural parallels of the New Work.
85 Bony (1979), 12; Morris (1990), 86.
86 Harvey (1978), 46.
87 Morris (1990), 90.
88 *VCH London*, i. 414; Simpson (1880), 175–7.
89 Kingsford (1971), i. 333.
90 Salzman (1967), 147, 419–20; BL, MS Lansdowne 874, fo. 115v.
91 Dugdale (1818), 11.
92 Fisher (1885), 16–7. Both he and Weever (1631, 358) give a date of 1532 for this tablet, but this was presumably a misreading of 1552.
93 Schofield (in prep.).
94 Dugdale (1818), 16.
95 Stubbs (1882–3), i. 338.
96 Stubbs (1882–3), i. 310.
97 Dugdale (1658), 172.
98 Morris (1990), 93, n.26.
99 Nicholas (1852), 69; Douglas Hamilton (1875), 47.
100 Harvey (1987), 242–3.
101 Wilson (1979), 197–219 discusses the significance of the chapter house.
102 Madge (1939), 26; Penrose (1883), 381–2.
103 HMC 9, 12.
104 Harvey (1978), 75.
105 For instance: London, Society of Antiquaries, London Plans and Views, vol. 4, 'Prospect of ye Citye of London'; Fig. 59.
106 Simpson (1880), 154; WS, XIII, plate facing p. 12.
107 Harvey (1978), Fig. 5; Penrose (1883), 381–2.
108 Wilson (1994), caption Fig. 139.
109 Hollar's view (Fig. 77) does not show this bridge, but it appears on his plan (Fig. 67).
110 BL, MS Add. 71474, fos. 164r–185v and Hollar's plates for Dugdale (1658), copied in Dugdale (1818).
111 Kingsford (1971), i. 328, 330; *VCH London*, i. 415–16. See also pp. 44, 48, 416.
112 Dugdale (1818), 45; Ramsay (1981), 9–10; Blair (1991), 54.
113 See, for instance, Harvey (1987), *passim*; Blair (1987); Blair (1991); Rogers (1991).
114 In 1228, only the bishops and Exeter and Salisbury had been commemorated with figural effigies. Wilson (1995), 458, n. 24; Rogers (1987), 40–1.

115 Binski (1987), 79; Coldstream (1994), 149.
116 Kingsford (1971), i. 333. Illustrated by Hollar.
117 Gee (1979) and Wilson (1979), 80–7 for a discussion of this group of tombs.
118 Wilson (1994) for a discussion of this phenomenon at Canterbury and elsewhere.
119 Kingsford (1971), i. 333.
120 Wilson (1995), 466.
121 Stubbs (1882–3), i. 311.
122 PRO, DL28/3/1, m.4.
123 Armitage-Smith (1911), ii. 212–3, no. 1394; Wilson (1979), 96.
124 BL, MS Lansdowne 874, fo. 115v.
125 Simpson (1889), 519–20.
126 Harvey (1987), 365.
127 Dugdale (1818), 24; Kingsford (1971), i. 337.
128 Kingsford (1971), i. 331, 337.
129 Gibbs (1939), nos. 28, 198. Lobel (1989), 92 is misleading in some respects; Dugdale (1818), 10 incorrectly states that the precinct was enlarged in the early thirteenth century: the market to which he refers was in Chelmsford.
130 HMC 9, 20, 26.
131 Gibbs (1939), no. 306; Chew and Weinbaum (1970), no. 363; GL, MS 25501, fo. 49a.
132 The most recent account of the precinct is Macleod (1990), which contains errors.
133 Dugdale (1818), 27.
134 cf. Blayney (1990), 3 and Fig. 1.
135 Gibbs (1939), no. 317.
136 Malcolm (1802–7), iii. 160–1.
137 Kingsford (1979), i. 328; Blayney (1990), 65.
138 Blayney (1990), 24–33, Fig. 10.
139 HMC 9, 26.
140 McAleer (2001).
141 Kingsford (1971), i. 330–1, 332; McAleer (2001), 59.
142 Kingsford (1971), i. 330–1; Blayney (1990), 5, 48, Fig. 1; New (1999), 289–91; Schofield (in prep.).
143 Malcolm (1802–7), iii. 24.
144 Cook (1963), 49, 144; Stow (1603), 337; see p. 39.
145 For instance, BL, MS Add. 71474, fo. 172r–v.

12. *Estates and Income, 1066–1540*

1 *DB Middlesex*, fo. 127d (3.14, 17); Gibbs (1939), xxii–xxiv.
2 *DB Middlesex*, fo. 127b (3.2), 127d (3.15,16).
3 *DB Essex*, fos. 12b–14a (5.1–12); *DB Herts.*, fo. 136b (13.1–5); *DB Beds.*, fo. 211a (12.1); for Middlesex, see Gibbs (1939), xxii–xxiv; Lambourn, Stepney and Acton: Gibbs (1939), xxxi; Taylor (1977).
4 *VCH Essex*, ii. 13, n. 1; for the dean and chapter's peculiar jurisdiction, see p. 21.
5 Faith (1996); Harvey (1977), 71.
6 Hale (1858), xxxviii–xliv, 122–39; 154–75.
7 GL, MSS 25404, 25523.
8 I am grateful to Dr Niall Brady for the following section, which is based on his thesis: Brady (1996).
9 GL, MSS 25122, 25112.
10 Hale (1858), cxxvii–cxxxvi (especially cxxix), 164★–75.
11 Gibbs (1939), xxi.
12 Hale (1858), 152; GL, MS 25404, fo. 90.
13 Hale (1858), 109–17.
14 Hale (1858), 112–13.
15 Hale (1858), 1–107.
16 GL, MSS 25122, 25516.
17 Faith (1994), 665–7.
18 Whatley (1989), 113.
19 GL, MS 25323.
20 HMC 9, 32–3; Faith (1994), 662–7.
21 Faith (1994), 670–4.
22 Sparvel-Bayley (1878), 205–19; Taylor (1976), 255.
23 GL, MS 25337.
24 GL, MS 25205; Hovland and Kleineke (2004), 23–5.
25 GL, MS 25337.
26 *VCH London*, i. 428; GL, MS 25205; Caley and Hunter (1810–34).

13. *Historical Writing at St Paul's, c.1100–1540*

1 Whatley (1989). For this and other cults at St Paul's, see pp. 113–22.
2 It is edited by Tyson (1987); see also Tyson (1990). For the identity of M. Ralph de Bohun as canon of St Paul's, see Greenway (1968), 88–9.
3 Stubbs (1876). For notes on his career, see Greenway (1968), 5–6, 15–16, 79, 90.
4 See Harrison (2002), 1–2, 25–8.
5 BodL, MS Rawlinson B. 372, fos. 3–4. Printed in Hale (1858), 109–17. For the use of symbols in the archives at St Paul's, see Gransden (1974), 234 n. 124.
6 Jones (1946), 116 (book I, c. 17. 2).
7 LPL, MS 8, and BL, Cotton MS Claudius E. iii. A third MS, BL, Royal MS 13 E. vi, was copied from Lambeth 8 before either it or Claudius E. iii were complete.
8 Stubbs (1876), i. 20. This explanation is itself a marginal addition in LPL, MS 8, fo. 5rb.
9 Adgar, the author of a cycle of *Miracles of the Blessed Virgin Mary*: see Legge (1963), 188–9.
10 Morey and Brooke (1965), 197–8; Greenway (1968), 86; Burnett (1981).
11 My recent re-examination of the style of the last portion suggests that it was not Ralph's own work. For an argument that Ralph died in November 1199 or November 1200, see Greenway (1966).
12 Corpus Christi College, Cambridge, MS 476; Liebermann (1888). For a description of the MS, see James (1912), 414–17.
13 Printed in Stubbs (1882–3), i. 3–251, with discussion of authorship at xxii–xxviii. The entry is at p. 49; cf. Liebermann (1888), 549.
14 Possibly the MS was the 'Chron. of Ralph of Baldock' which was no. cxxv in the list of books bequeathed by Baldock to St Paul's and no. xxiv in the list of his books at the bishop's manor of Stepney in 1313 (Emden (1957–9), iii. 2148); it was seen by Leland, but lost in the late seventeenth century. A copy of the *Flores* in Bodl., MS lat. hist. d. 4, was perhaps derived from Baldock's book, as it has an added note after the end of the account of the year 1308, fo. 205v, 'Explicit cronica Radulfi Baldok'.
15 Printed in Stubbs (1882–3), i. cxxvii–cxxix. Also printed from Henry Wharton's notes from LPL, MS 1106 (in LPL, MS 590) as 'A short chronicle of S. Paul's cathedral from 1140 to 1341', in Simpson (1880), 41–57.
16 Printed in Stubbs (1882–3), i. 255–370. It was shown by Richardson (1948) that the first section of these annals, covering 1307–8, actually originated at Westminster, and that the remainder, covering 1308–41, was written at St Paul's.
17 LPL, MS 1106, for which, see Luard (1890), i. xxvii–xxviii; Stubbs (1882–3), i. xlii–xlix.
18 Printed in Luard (1890), ii. 236; also Stubbs (1882–3), i. cxxvii.
19 Luard (1890), ii. 346; Stubbs (1882–3), i. cxxvii.
20 The commentary that follows owes much to Richardson (1948), and Gransden (1982), 25–30, 64, but differs from both in its assessment of the relationship between the *Annales* and Adam Murimuth's chronicle.
21 Thompson (1889).
22 He was born between Michaelmas 1274 and Michaelmas 1275, probably at the village of Fyfield, near Oxford. For his career, see Emden (1957–9), ii. 1329–30.
23 Stubbs (1882–3), i. lxv; Horn (1963), 35, 49.
24 Thompson (1889), xv.
25 Denholm-Young (1957). A new edition is in preparation by Dr Wendy Childs (Oxford Medieval Texts, forthcoming).
26 Hearne (1729). The medieval MS was lost in a fire in 1737, and Hearne's transcript, dated 1728, is the only surviving witness, Bodl., MS Rawlinson 180 fos. 162r–94v.
27 Denholm-Young (1956). He was prebendary of Weldland: Horn (1963), 66.
28 Childs (1997), expresses some doubt, but concedes the possibility, p. 178 n. 6.
29 'Chroniculi S. Pauli London', in BL, Add. MS 22142, fos. 7–10; entries concerning St Paul's printed in Simpson (1880), 58–60, 222–8.
30 For much of the following, I am indebted to the biography by Hay (1952), and to his edition of the final two books of Polydore's English history, Hay (1950).
31 Horn (1963), 54.
32 William Caxton's editions of the *Brut* (1480) and of Higden's *Polychronicon* (1482) were both in the English language, and offered a base text from a single manuscript, without apparatus criticus.
33 The standard edition is Mommsen (1898). This text, with an English translation, is reproduced with corrections by Winterbottom (1978).
34 Hay (1952), 170.
35 Horn (1963), 45, 49, 55.
36 It was printed as an addition to Hardyng's popular and influential *Chronicle*; see Gransden (1982), 440.

14. *The Lesser Clergy in the Later Middle Ages*

1 Barrow (1986), 564; Barrow (1989), 87–97; see above, pp. 21–3.
2 Edwards (1967), 33–51; Gibbs (1939), nos 224–5.
3 Fowler and Jenkins (1927–38), i. 86, 99.
4 Brooke (1957), 76.
5 Edwards (1967), 253–4, 259–63; see above, pp. 24, 33.
6 Simpson (1873), 84.
7 Brooke (1957), 74; HMC 9, 26.
8 *VCH London*, i. 426, citing Simpson (1873), 323 and Wilkins (1737), iii. 134–5.
9 On the physical setting of the vicars choral, see Schofield (forthcoming).
10 Simpson (1873), 322.
11 Simpson (1871).
12 *CPL 1396–1404*, 606–7.
13 *CPL 1471–84*, 463.
14 *CPL 1417–31*, 86.
15 Moorman (1945), 52–3.
16 McHardy (1989), 113.
17 McHardy (1977), nos. 1–38.
18 McHardy (1977), nos. 140–72.
19 Simpson, (1890).
20 Hennessy (1898), 62, n. e.170.
21 Hennessy (1898), 61, n. e.138.
22 Ordination lists for the diocese of London are recorded in most of the bishops' registers in London from 1361; see Davis (2000).
23 Hennessy (1898), 62–3; GL, MS 9531/3, fos. 16, 27, 37.
24 Hennessy (1898), 61, n. e.137.
25 Thompson (1947), 107–8.
26 Hennessy (1898), 60, n. e.125.
27 Sharpe, (1889–90), ii. 304–6; Hennessy (1898), 60, n. e.123.
28 Hill (1971).
29 Simpson (1873), 142–58.
30 Wilkins (1737), iii. 135–6.
31 Lines 507–11: Robinson (1966), 22.
32 Simpson (1873), 217–48; Simpson (1890).
33 Barron (2003), 136.
34 Figures derived from Hennessy (1898).
35 Emden (1957–9), 709; Hennessy (1898), 376.
36 Hennessy (1898), 320–1, n. r.140.
37 Hennessy (1898), 320–1, n. r.140.
38 Emden (1957–9), 379–80.
39 Hennessy (1898), 420–1, nn. 210–11.

15. *Fraternities in the cathedral: a case study of the Jesus Guild*

1 *CPR 1452–61*, 480. For a full account of the fraternity, see New (1999).
2 New (2000); see also p. 39.
3 BodL, MS Tanner 221. The author is preparing a calendar of this manuscript for publication by the London Record Society.
4 John 20:31; Acts 2:37, 4:30, 10:43; *NCE*, vii.76.

5 *NCE*, vii.76; Cabassut (1952) 47–8.

6 Duffy (1992), 235–6; Cabassut (1952), 54–5; *NCE*, vii. 76.

7 Cabassut (1952), 57; *NCE*, vii. 76.

8 BodL, Trinity College MS 8, fo. 286r. This missal belonged to Sir William Beauchamp.

9 New (1999), 29, 45–51, map 1.2

10 Lisieux's will is dated 29 November 1450, but he did not die until 1456, PRO, PROB 11/4, fos. 56v–58r. The 'great' crypt identifies this as the spacious Gothic undercroft.

11 PRO, PROB 11/4, fos. 44v–45v. I am grateful to Dr Anne Sutton for this reference. Brooke (1957), 96–8, suggests that the guild was founded either by Lisieux or his successor William Say.

12 Professor Caroline M. Barron has suggested that this concern for liturgical and musical improvement may have been one of Colet's main motives for his involvement with the guild. I am grateful to Professor Barron for her helpful comments on a draft of this essay.

13 *CPR 1555–7*, 274–6.

14 BodL, MS Tanner 221, fo. 6v.

15 BodL, MS Tanner 221, fo. 7v.

16 Dugdale (1818), 75–6.

17 Kingsford (1971), i. 339.

18 BodL, MS Tanner 221, fo. 113r.

19 BodL, MS Tanner 221: fos. 45v, 124r.

20 Harrison (1963), 9–14, 219; Pfaff, (1970), 79.

21 Mateer and New (2000).

22 New (1999), 394–402.

23 Dummelow (1973), 33; BodL, 221, fo. 13v.

24 BodL, MS Tanner 221, fo. 12r; PRO, PROB. 11/6, fo. 34v, PROB 11/6 fo. 159v, PROB. 11/18, fo. 69r and PROB 11/16, fo. 213r.

25 For example, Sir Stephen Jennyns was mayor of London in 1508–9, a year after serving as an Assistant of the fraternity. Beaven (1908), ii. 19.

26 Lang (1993) 107.

27 Barron (1985), 34.

28 Rosser, (1988), 30–2.

29 Brigden (1989), 39; Westlake (1919), 77.

30 de Worde (1522?), final page, an advertisement for the fraternity listing the benefits accrued by members, including an indulgence. I am grateful to Professor Mary Erler for drawing my attention to this almanac; Barron (1985), 26–7.

16. *The chantry chapel of Roger of Waltham*

This essay is a condensed version of Sandler (2003)

1 Cook (1963); Wood-Legh (1965); Colvin (2000).

2 Reduced by Bishop Braybrooke in 1391 to 31; Wood-Legh (1965), 194; see pp. 38, 160.

3 For thirteenth-century chantries at altars, see p. 24. For purpose-built structures, see: ordinance for a chantry for Canon John de Sancta Maria at a 'new' altar near the door of the chapter house, 1299 (GL, MS 25171/1677); ordinance for chantry of Canon William de Everdon at a newly constructed altar in the chapel of St Radegund in the crypt, 1349 (GL, MSS 25121/1940, 1969); ordinance for chantry of Adam de Bury in a newly built chapel near the north door, 1386 (GL, MS 25121/1737).

4 Leland (1709), 264–5.

5 Dugdale (1818), 32–3; HMC *Eighth Report* (1881), Part I, 'Queen Anne's Bounty', 632–5; HMC 9, 28, 40, 54 *et passim*. In addition, the following: GL, MSS 25161/1–10 (chaplains' accounts); 25121/9, 25121/14, 25121/19, 25121/179–180, 25121/208, 25121/582, 25121/1313, 25121/1316, 25121/1323, 25121/1329–1332, 25121/1630–1641, 25121/1643–1644, 25121/1647–1648 (leases and grants relating to properties given to establish chantries). See also GL, MS 25511 (Thomas Lyseux's Calendar of Deeds preserved in the Treasury of St Paul's, A.D. 1440), fos. 21v, 24, 25, 30, 33, 39v, 47v, 71v, 73v, 74v, 77, 93v.

6 GL, MS 25121/3037, attachment.

7 Fraser (1953), 122; cf. Horne (1963), 25.

8 For death date, see Hardy (1873–75), iii. 1339, 1340.

9 *CCR Edward II 1318–23*, 572, 576–9, 581, 602. Tout

(1920–33), ii. 267 n., 273, 275–6; iv. 91–3, 109 n.; vi. 26, 86–7, 123; also BL, Stowe MS 553, fo. 6v (account book) and Add. MS 36763 (roll of Wardrobe expenses).

10 Plummer (1885), 173–4.

11 Mynors (1963), 280–1.

12 Leland (1709), 264–5.

13 Six short pieces attributed to St Augustine, St Bernard and Hugh of St Victor; see BL, Roy. MS 8 G VI (English, fifteenth-century), fos. 142–6, 196, also Pembroke College, Cambridge, MS 254 (English, fifteenth-century), unfoliated, including four of the same items. One piece, *De cantu philomele*, also followed the main text of the copy of the *Compendium morale* seen by Leland at St Paul's and later recorded at Sion College; see London, LPL, MS Arc. L. 24.1/Si 7M, f. 2v.

14 Glasgow University Library, MS Hunter 231; see Young and Aitken (1908), 176–83 and Sandler (1993), 67–74.

15 Smalley (1960), xv–xvi and frontispiece.

16 GL, MSS 25241/13, 25241/23. For the property in Soper Lane: Keene and Harding (1987), nos. 145/5a–b and 25–6.

17 GL, MSS 25121/3036–3037.

18 GL, MSS 25241/22 (licence of alienation), 25241/3038 (indenture).

19 GL, MS 25121/1938, MS 25122/1341.

20 GL, MS 25121/3038. See p. 133.

21 GL, MSS 25121/1650, 25121/3039.

22 GL, MS 25121/1938 and MS 25122/1341.

23 GL, MS 25121/3040.

24 GL, MS 25121/1939; translated in Dugdale (1818), 21–2.

25 GL, MS 25121/1939.

26 Dugdale (1818), 313.

27 GL, MS 25121/3040.

28 GL, MS 25121/1939.

29 See Dawton (1983), 122–50.

30 Weever (1767), 170.

31 Thus described in 1684 by Payne Fisher (1885), 145.

32 Dugdale (1658), 68.

33 Illustrations in Cook (1963); cf. Binski (1996), 118.

34 GL, MS 25121/1939.

35 Morris (1990), 75–6.

36 GL, MS 25121/1939.

37 Cook (1955), 39.

38 GL, MS 25121/1953; see Wood-Legh (1965), 194. A chantry of three priests was founded in 1261 for Fulk Basset, bishop of London (1241–59); GL, MS 25504 (*Liber L*), fo. 146v. It was temporarily assigned to the altar of St John the Evangelist: GL, MS 25504 (*Liber L*), fo. 91. By 1295 this chantry, together with that of Philip Basset, had been transferred to the altar of the Virgin:; GL, MS 25520 (*Statuta minora*), fo. 70v.

39 Kreider (1979), 167–8, 186–9.

40 Nichols (1852), 54–5, 75.

17. *The Household and Daily Life of the Dean in the Fifteenth Century*

1 Sheppard (1960), 68–9; *VCH Middx*, x. 78.

2 This size is suggested by the will of Dean William Say which listed the members of his household according to their four grades: PRO, PROB11/5, fos. 199v–200v (PCC 26 Godyn).

3 PRO, PROB11/5, fos. 11v–200v (PCC 26 Godyn); GL, MS 25167/2.

4 Hovland and Kleineke (2004), *passim*; PRO, PROB11/6, fol. 34v (PCC 5 Wattys).

5 Woolgar (1999), 16–17; Dyer (1989), 51; Hovland and Kleineke (2004).

6 PRO, PROB11/4, fos. 56v–58 (PCC 8 Stokton); PROB11/5, fols. 199v–200v (PCC 26 Godyn); PROB11/6, fo. 34v (PCC 5 Wattys).

7 GL, MS 25125/94–99; New (1999), 431, 433.

8 Hovland and Kleineke (2004).

9 GL, MS 25166/7.

10 GL, MS 25166/3.

11 GL, MSS 25166/1, 7; 25167/2, mm. 4v, 5.

12 GL, MSS 25166/2–6A, 9; Woolgar (1999), 26–7;

Dyer (1989), 74; Rastall (1967); Southworth (1989); Southworth (1998), 35–47.

13 Lupton (1909), 148–9; Lupton (1883), 31, 40.

14 GL, MS 25166/4; Sutton and Visser-Fuchs (1998), 366–407.

15 Leach (1891), 40–3; GL, MS 25166/2.

16 GL, MS25166/3.

17 GL, MS 25166/2.

18 GL, MS 25166/1–9; Hovland and Kleineke (2004); Dyer (1989), 32.

19 GL, MS 25166/4.

20 Gairdner (1858), 69; Hay (1950), 72; Arthurson (1994), 84–6; GL, MS 25166/7.

21 GL, MS 25166/7; *CCR 1485–1500*, 795, 863, 910, 965; *CPR 1494–1509*, 23; Strachey (1767–7), vi. 489; C65/128, m. 17; C82/135/8 (We owe this reference to Dr David Grummitt).

22 Thomas and Thornley (1938), 257.

18. *The Fabric to 1670*

I am most grateful to Andrew Saint for his expert editorial guidance and in addition to those acknowledged in the text wish to thank Kerry Downes, Anthony Geraghty, John Newman and John Schofield for comments on the chapter in draft.

1 Dugdale (1818), 112; Cook (1955), 76. The rood was reinstated under Queen Mary for King Philip II of Spain's visit in October 1554, and was destroyed on Queen Elizabeth's orders in August 1559: Strype (1720), iii. 220.

2 Addleshaw and Etchells (1948), 26–8.

3 Stow (1592), 1029.

4 Kingsford (1971), i. 328; Dugdale (1658), 132.

5 AS II, 1, apparently an original drawing of *c.*1550–*c.*1630. The comment by James Elmes in his MS catalogue in 1807 (published in 1812): 'Mr Gutch tells me that Mr. Buckler copied it for Sir H. Englefield', is probably a reference to a copy made from this drawing and since lost; see WS I, 9.

6 Kingsford (1971), i. 331.

7 Kitching (1986), 131, n. 2; Dugdale (1818), 95–7.

8 WS XIII, 20–22; Soo (1998), 56–60.

9 Kitching (1986), 123–4.

10 Colvin (1975), 61–9.

11 Kingsford (1971), i. 332.

12 GL, MS 25618 (An account for the re-roofing July 1561–December 1564). A separate account that includes works by two Sergeant Plumbers is at PRO E164/66/8, 21–8; see Colvin (1975), 64–5.

13 Barron (1983), 142–3; Simpson (1881b), 132–3.

14 Colvin (1975), 65.

15 GL, MS 25618.

16 Kitching (1986), 128–9.

17 Kingsford (1971), i. 332.

18 Colvin (1975), 64.

19 Drawings (I), 22–3; Pierce (1963), 128–31. Kitching (1986), 128, corrects Pierce's reading, in PRO, E164/66/1, of 'one Col' to 'one Cob', and suggests the carpenter Richard Cobbe rather than Henry Cole as the author of the design. But neither man appears to have had the experience necessary to produce a drawing of this quality. I am grateful to Mark Girouard and Adam White for advice on this drawing.

20 Kingsford (1971), i. 327. Stow misinterpreted his source, see p. 135.

21 The drawing appears to scale at six feet to the inch. See Lethaby (1930) (July–Dec), 24–5 and 1088. Lethaby quotes a paper by Robert Hooke of 1664 addressed to Boyle and others, 'in the papers of Gresham College, or the Royal Society, at the British Museum', on the fall of bodies: 'We can try it here in the open air from the top of St. Paul's Church which is just 204 ft. high'.

22 GL, MS 25589 and PRO, E164/66/5. Income is set out in PRO, E164/66/7 and expenditure in PRO, SP12/22/69. The estimate is in PRO SP12/19/64. See Kitching (1986), 125–30.

23 Dugdale (1818), 101.

24 *Remembrancia* (1878), 322–7.

25 *Remembrancia* (1878), 325.

26 PRO, E164/66/1.

27 Dugdale (1658), 100.
28 PRO, SP14/35, no. 28; quoted in Dugdale (1818), 101–2.
29 GL, MS 25619; see also Dugdale (1818), 102.
30 Harris and Higgott (1989), 38; Summerson (1990), 53.
31 Somerville (1985); Saunders (2001), 21–4.
32 Dugdale (1658), 134–5.
33 Dugdale (1658), 136; on this issue in 1582–4, see *Remembrancia* (1878), 322–7.
34 PRO, SP14/131, no. 35.
35 Dugdale (1658), 137.
36 GL, MS 25490.
37 Dugdale (1658), 136.
38 Dugdale (1818), 103; Colvin (1975), 148.
39 Sharpe (1992), 275–402, especially 322–8; Colvin (1975), 147–52.
40 Trevor-Roper (1962), 121–6; Sharpe (1992), 132–45; Davies (1992), 46–86.
41 PRO, SP16/182/8.
42 Dugdale (1658), 158–9.
43 GL, MS 25474/2–5 (audited accounts for 1634–7 and 38–9); GL, MS 25475/1 and 2 (unaudited receipts from May 1631 to June 1644).
44 Stow (1633), 767; Dugdale (1658), 160; GL, MS 35471/9 (for Pindar's £2,618 contribution to the south transept).
45 On altar rails in this period, see Sharpe (1992), 333–45; Davies (1992), 205–50; and Newman (1993).
46 Colvin (1975), 149–50; Hart (1994a), 417–19.
47 GL, MS 25471/1, 3.
48 GL, MS 25471/13, p. 22; see also Colvin (1975), 150, n. 1; and Bold (1989), 168–70.
49 GL, MS 25490, fos. 14v–15v.
50 GL, MS 25471/1–15 (audited accounts up to September 1641, except account for west end, October 1639–September 1640, in LPL, MS F.P. 321); GL, MS 25473/1–9 (unaudited accounts up to September 1642).
51 GL, MS 25471/1, 2, 4, 7. Kinsman's first payment is in August 1636 (25471/5, 54). This appears to relate to a contract dated 31 January 1634 at BL Add. MS Ch.75846, in John Webb's hand. His second payment, for the next five bays, is in July 1637 (25471/7, 52).
52 GL, MS 25471/2 and 5 (p. 55, for first payments); and 25471/7, p. 51, for payment to Moore for work on five bays on the north side of the choir, including the 'Repaire of John a Gaunts Chappell and the vaulting within'.
53 GL, MS 25471/2, pp. 8–9. According to Cook (1956), 24–5 and 49, there was a chapel dedicated to the Virgin on the east side of the south transept, but in the second bay from the crossing, not at the 'South end', as indicated here.
54 GL, MS 25471/2, p. 26, and 25471/5, p. 15.
55 GL, MS 25471/5.
56 GL, MS 25471/5, p. 15.
57 GL, MS 25471/7, p. 7; 25471/11; For contemporary practice, see Bristow (1996), 6–21. I am very grateful to Dr Bristow for his advice on this topic.
58 Addleshaw and Etchells (1948), 133–47; Newman (1993), 172–5.
59 Dugdale (1818), 105–6, quoting Wilkins (1737), iv. 492.
60 GL, MS 25471/1. In January 1634, the king paid £500 for that year and two back payments of £500 for his second and third years' payments (1632 and 1633). His first £500 does not appear in the accounts, but may be the sum he gave as Prince of Wales in November 1620. Dugdale (1818) 'corrects' Wilkins (1737) by amending the king's words 'which for these years past we have duly paid' to 'for these *three* years'; but the king's vagueness appears to have been deliberate.
61 GL, MS 25471/4.
62 Now Saint-Paul-Saint-Louis (1627–41); Pérouse de Montclos (1989), 178–81.
63 Harris and Higgott (1989), 241–3; Hart (1995a), 202–9 (where the design is discussed as c.1620).
64 Hart (1995a), 209–11.
65 GL, MS 25471/13 (October 1639): 'Modells for two Statues', and 'Two Blocks for Statues Twelve Tonne'.
66 Tavernor and Schofield (1997), especially 285–96 on

67 Note of 'Feb. 12, 1672' (1673, New Style) in Gunther (1928), 196–8.
68 Summerson (1990), 56–60.
69 The frieze comes from a large engraving of the Baths of Diocletian by Hieronymus Cock, published in 1558, where it appears above a Corinthian order. See Harris and Higgott (1989), 240.
70 WS XIII, 46.
71 GL, MS 25471/15, p. 24.
72 GL, MS 25471/13, p. 73.
73 GL, MS 25475/2, fo. 15.
74 GL, MS 25471/9, p. 31. On Jones and St Gregory's see *DNB*; Gotch (1928), 155–60; Colvin (1975), 154–5.
75 Webb (1665), 27; WS XIV, xix–xx.
76 Tavernor and Schofield (1997), 241–7, 307–9; Chaney (1993), 42–53.
77 Tavernor and Schofield (1997), 248–51.
78 GL, MS 25471/9, p. 54; 25471/11, pp. 70–1; 25471/13, pp. 1–3, 11–12.
79 Higgott (1992), 71–2.
80 Summerson (2000), 99; Schofield (2002), i. 198–202. A replica of one of the columns, based on the archaeological evidence, was erected in 2001 in Paternoster Square, immediately north of the cathedral. The height of the order can only be deduced from the 1727 engraving (Fig. 97) and its source drawing by Henry Flitcroft (repr. in Higgott (1992), Fig. 15).
81 WS XIV, 30, 41, 45.
82 WS XIII, 21.
83 Webb (1665), 44, 226; Crayford (1997), 48–52. For the setting of the stones of the columns, see GL, MS 25471/8. Crayford gives the width and depth of the portico at main architrave level as 90 × 35 ft approximately, although this is not consistent with the plan in Fig. 101 when correctly scaled.
84 Dugdale (1658), 160.
85 GL, MS 25471, pp. 3–4, payments for 'plaine Ashler'.
86 GL, MS 25471/8, p. 15. Forty-three tons, supplied August 1637. In July 1637 Jones was procuring marble from Ireland, see Bold (1989), 168. A reference to 'about 2000' feet of Belgian Dinant black marble in the inventory of materials prepared for the City of London's 'Committee for Paules' on 25 February 1645 (see n. 98), indicates that the consignment of 'Black Marble Steps' delivered in November 1640 (GL, MS 25471/15, p. 8) was not used in the construction.
87 GL, MS 25473/8, 105; 25473/9, fo. 81.
88 GL, MS 25473/9, fos. 59v, 68, 68v.
89 Gunther (1928), 74.
90 GL, MS 25475/2, fo. 16.
91 Summerson (1990), 54 and n. 59.
92 GL, MS 25475/1 f. 20 and *passim*; 25475/2, *passim*.
93 Summary from audited accounts on sheet in GL, MS 25475/1.
94 See, for example, GL MS 25471/9, p. 54.
95 GL, MS 25475/2, totals to Michaelmas 1642.
96 GL, MS 25473/9, pp. 145, 163.
97 Dugdale (1658), 172; see p. 63.
98 Simpson (1880), 142.
99 GL, MS 25475/2; payment of 19 December 1644; Dugdale (1658), 172.
100 For Carter's career, see Colvin (1995), 226–7.
101 Dugdale (1658), 172–3.
102 *CSP Dom 1650*, 261.
103 Simpson (1880), xxiv; Whitelocke (1709), 580.
104 GL, MS 11770, incomplete minute on rear folio, from 1664–5 period.
105 Dugdale (1658), 174.
106 Simpson (1880), 153–5; WS XIII, 12 (with a plate of Webb's survey plan in the PRO).
107 Dugdale (1818), 115. Webb's valuation of the structures in the portico in 1663 is in GL, MS CF box 49.
108 Dugdale (1818), 116.
109 Wren (1750), 260; Downes (1982), 6–7.
110 Dugdale (1818), 116–23; WS XIII, 13.
111 GL, MS 11770.
112 On Cutler, see *DNB*; subscriptions to the repairs from 1663–6 are in Dugdale (1818), 143.
113 WS XIII, 13–14.

the Pantheon in Rome.

114 GL, MS CF box 49.
115 GL, MS 11770.
116 WS XIII, 14–15.
117 GL, MS 11770, p. 9.
118 GL, MS 25471/16, pp. 1–56.
119 Whinney (1971), 25–36; Downes (1982), 8–10.
120 WS XIII, 15–17; Soo (1998), 48–55. Wren's report may have accompanied his letter to Sancroft of 7 May 1666 (Tanner, 145/29, fos. 115–16; WS XIII, 44). Wren (1750), 274–7, prints an '*Ex Autographo*' version of the report which it states was 'laid before the King and Commissioners' on 1 May 1666, together with 'an accurate Survey' and 'the several respective drawings'.
121 WS XIII, 45; Whinney (1971), 28–36; Pérouse de Montclos (1989), 178–84.
122 WS XIII, 18.
123 WS XIII, 27; Dugdale (1818), 132–40.
124 WS XIII, 19. Evelyn may have replaced Denham, who became mentally ill in 1666.
125 WS XIII, 19.
126 Porter (1996), 52.
127 WS XIII, 20; de Beer (1955), iii. 448–9, 452.
128 WS XIII, 20–22; Soo (1998), 56–60.
129 GL, MS CF box 54/5 (5 March). See also Geraghty (2001), 474.
130 WS XIII, 46; Wren (1750), 278–9.
131 WS XIII, 47–8.
132 WS XIII, 49–50; Wren (1750), 279–80.
133 GL, MS 11770, fo. 17; and Dugdale (1818), 129, but with the word 'Works' missing.
134 GL, MS CF box 54/5, entry 'XVII'.
135 GL, MS 25471/16a, pp. 27, 29, 33 (payments to Clere, Wren and Woodroofe); Wren (1750), 281–2.
136 Wren (1750), 282; and a description by Pratt in 1673 in Gunther (1928), 213–14.
137 Wren (1750), 282.

19. *Wren and the new cathedral*

1 See n. 32.
2 WS XIII, 17.
3 Wren (1750), 283.
4 Downes (1988), 27–9; *Sir Christopher Wren and the Making of St Paul's* (1991), cat. 93.
5 Sir Henry Wotton's translation.
6 Oughtred, 1648, in Wren (1750), 184.
7 De Beer (1955), iii. 106.
8 Isaac Barrow, 1662, in Wren (1750), 346.
9 Sprat (1667), 311–19.
10 Summerson (1949); originally published in 1937 as 'The Tyranny of Intellect'.
11 Specifically e.g. Worsley (1995), xi.
12 Summerson (1953).
13 Gresham lecture, in Wren (1750), 200.
14 Wren (1750), 351.
15 *Ibid.*, 204.
16 WS XIII, 45.
17 WS XI, 74.
18 Wren (1750), 198.
19 Wren (1750), 261.
20 WS XIII, 17.
21 WS XIII, 47.
22 WS XIII, 15.
23 Wren (1750), 282.
24 WS XIII, 15–17, 44.
25 Authority was sought on 2 March 1676, and granted the next day, to begin the western piers. GL, MS 11770, fo.7; MS 25622/1, 19–20.
26 Summerson (1990), 71: one of 'divers designes' over a matter of years; Whinney (1971), 96: perhaps 1668, impossible to believe after the Great Model.
27 AS II.42, WS I, xxvia. Identified by G. Higgott, to whom I am much indebted.
28 Sancroft to Wren, WS XIII, 46.
29 Sancroft to Wren, WS XIII, 46–7.
30 Sancroft to Wren, WS XIII, 23.
31 Sancroft to Wren, WS XIII, 23.
32 Wren was made 'Surveyor Generall . . . of the Repairs' in succession to Sir John Denham on 30 July 1669 : GL, CF box 54/5, no.xvii.
33 Best seen in Summerson (1990), fig. 54.
34 WS XVI, 206; various diarists date the stone-laying

35 Hart (1995b), 20; expert advice from Ken Spencer, University of Hull.
36 Wren (1750), 286–7.
37 Wren is supposed to have wept when the future James II obliged him to add the two western chapels for Roman Catholic usage, or alternatively at the rejection of the Great Model. The first story, originating in eighteenth-century Parliamentary gossip, was recorded by Joseph Spence (1966), i. 326, and repeated by James Elmes (1823), 319–20, whose confusion between the model and the final building was elaborated by Francis Penrose (in the old *DNB*, s.v. Wren). The model was still accepted in the summer of 1674 when the east end was staked out; the dome centre had been set out, for the only time, the previous summer (WS XVI, 204, 201). Who ensured its rejection, and when, is unknown; the supposed meeting of 18 May 1674 described by Jane Lang and others never took place (Lang (1956), 68–71; Tinniswood (2001), 194–5; GL, MS 25622/1, 1–2).
38 *The Spectator*, 27 April 1711.
39 Ritual west, based on traditional orientation with the high altar to the east.
40 Wren (1750), 292.
41 Wren (1750), 352.
42 Palladio, bk ii.
43 WS XVI, 131.
44 Not quite: a rotated sector of 85°.
45 Clarke (1923), 73.
46 Wren (1750), 352. A comparable discrepancy between interior and exterior occurs in Wren's Trinity College Library at Cambridge.
47 WS XV, 145, 152.
48 This did not stop their being shown with glazing bars in successive editions of Banister Fletcher's *History of Architecture*.
49 WS XI, 21.
50 Uffenbach, 34.
51 The accounts do not specify the hue, but the normal specification for painting walls was 'stone colour', approximating to modern decorators' 'magnolia'.
52 An anonymous drawing (AS ii, 43) with comparative sections of Florence Cathedral and St Peter's (WS I, xxvii) is not evidence of Wren's knowledge of Florence; his knowledge of Pavia Cathedral is even more doubtful.
53 The rotation of a sector of 78°.
54 Downes (1982), fig. 4.
55 WS XIII, 16.
56 Wren (1750), 362–3.
57 Also known as the Basilica of Constantine or the Temple of Peace (begun AD 307, completed after 312 by Constantine). Neither Serlio, bk iii, nor Palladio, bk iv discusses the buttressing system.
58 Wren (1750), 289.
59 Wren (1750), 290.
60 Engraving *juxta priorem sententiam*.
61 Gribelin, Kip, Trevitt. William Emmett produced unauthorized and misleading prints.
62 The Dome of the Invalides is irrelevant to this design.
63 Downes (1988).
64 WS I, x–xiii. At a scale of about 30 feet to an inch, they leave many visual details, let alone structural ones, uncertain.
65 Wren (1750), 283.
66 Summerson (1990).
67 Downes (1988) and Downes (1994). A copy of a lost drawing (Jeffery (1992), Fig. 13) is also ambiguous.
68 Pointed out by Summerson in 1961 (Summerson (1990), 292, n. 2). The piers in front of the sanctuary would also be misplaced. The diagrams in Summerson (1953), 108–9, are simplified.
69 Summerson (1990), fig. 35.
70 Wren (1750), 357. The vaults in the pre-Fire design are not saucer-domes.
71 Not elliptical; the dual centres are pricked in some drawings.
72 Serlio, bk.iii.
73 Wren (1750), 353–4.
74 *Ibid.*, 281, explaining the absence of aisles in the First Model.

75 Dorn and Mark, (1981).
76 Clarke (1923), 80.
77 Wren (1750), 300–1.
78 Wren (1750), 362.
79 Wren (1750), 293.

20. *The Construction of the new cathedral*

1 In GL, reprinted in WS XIII–XVI.
2 Bodleian Library, Tanner 145, no. 129 quoted in WS XIII, 20–22; Soo (1998), 56–60.
3 GL, MS 25471/16, 7. We know Denham was 'Cathedral Surveyor' because Wren was appointed to 'replace him' in this position in 1669 (GL, MS CF box 54/5).
4 Colvin (1976), 15; Colvin (1995), 300.
5 GL, MS 25471/16, 12.
6 Geraghty (2001), 474.
7 GL, MS 25622/1, 2–3.
8 WS XIII, 13.
9 WS XIII, 19.
10 Gunther (1928), 11; Lang (1956), 26.
11 WS XIII, 20–2.
12 *Centre de Recherches sur les Monuments Historiques* (1985).
13 WS XIII, 45–6.
14 GL, MS 25471/16, 66.
15 WS XIII, 22–3.
16 GL, MS 25576.
17 WS XIII, 46.
18 GL, MS CF box 54/5.
19 GL, MS CF box 54/5.
20 GL MS 25471/16A, 19.
21 WS XVI, 190–213.
22 Eg. GL, MS 25471/16A, 49 (WS XVI, 197); GL, MS 25471/16A, 57 (WS XVI, 198); GL, MS 25471/16A 61 (WS XVI, 198); GL, MS 25471/16A 64 (WS XVI, 199) and GL, MS 25471/16A, 71 (WS XVI, 200).
23 Wren (1750), 284.
24 GL, MS 25471/16A, 57 (WS XVI, 198).
25 Lang (1956), 52–3.
26 GL, MS 25471/16, 47.
27 WS XIII, 12.
28 GL, MS 25471/16A, 36 (WS XVI, 195).
29 GL, MS 25471/16, 62.
30 GL, MS 25471/16, 68.
31 GL, MS 25471/16, 66.
32 GL, MS 25471/16, 65.
33 GL, MS 25554.
34 GL, MS 25471/16A, 47, 52.
35 GL, MS 25471/16A, 55.
36 GL, MS 25471/16A, 69.
37 GL, MS CF box 54/5; GL, MS 25471/16A, 73–80.
38 WS XIII, 33-x4.
39 Colvin (1995), 714–5.
40 GL, MS 25 471/27, 14 (WS XIV, 5).
41 WS XVI, 100.
42 WS XX, 1–33.
43 Downes (1988), 27–9.
44 Downes (1988), 29.
45 Colvin (1995), 641.
46 Colvin (1995), 935–6.
47 GL MS 25 471/19, 60–1 (WS XIII, 107).
48 Colvin (1995), 576.
49 WS XV, xiv.
50 WS XIV, frontispiece.
51 WS XV, xix.
52 GL, MS 25554.
53 Summerson (1961); Downes (1966), 28–30; Downes (1994), 50–4.
54 Whinney (1947), 9; Sekler (1956), 125–6; Downes (1959), 23–4; Geraghty (2000).
55 Soo (1998), 34–92.
56 Heyman (1995).
57 Jardine (2002), 412–14.
58 Wren (1750), 4.
59 Wren (1750), 286.
60 Wren (1750), 286.
61 Macartney (1913–14).
62 Wren (1750), 287.
63 Wren (1750), 286.
64 Soo (1998), 51–2; Wren (1750), 275.

65 WS XV, xiv.
66 Bettey (1971).
67 WS XV, xvi–xvii; Wren (1750), 320.
68 Downes (1988), 57, cat. no. 6.
69 Dorn and Mark (1981), 133.
70 WS XIII, 69–83.
71 WS XIII, 93, 113.
72 WS XIV, 45–63.
73 WS XV, pl. vii.
74 Yeomans (1986); Campbell (2002).
75 WS XV, xli–xlvi.
76 Wren (1750), 320.
77 Somers Clarke (1902).
78 WS XIII, 83.
79 Wren (1750), 283.
80 Heyman (1998).
81 Birch (1757), ii. 461, 464, 465.
82 Robinson and Adams (1935), 163.
83 Birch (1757), ii. 484.
84 SPFA 'survey drawing of section through the dome as built, probably made during Robert Mylne's surveyorship, c. 1785'.
85 Heyman (1998).
86 WS XV, 106–7, 136, 155, 157–8.
87 WS XV, 138.
88 Jardine (2002).
89 Birch (1757), i. 466.
90 Jardine (2002), 424.
91 Clutterbuck (1815–27), i. 168; Lang (1956), 241; Wren (1750), 293.
92 Colvin (1995), 1087.
93 Colvin (1995), 934–8.
94 For details see WS XV, part III, 141–81; Lang (1956), 231–44.

21. *Fittings and liturgy in post-Fire St Paul's*

Acknowledgements are due to Martin Stancliffe, Surveyor to the Fabric; Joseph Wisdom, Cathedral Librarian; Andrew Saint, for drawing attention to contemporary comments; and Dr Anthony Geraghty, for examining the drawing All Souls II. 30 with me and helping me to interpret it.

1 Hatton (1708), ii. 462.
2 Cobb (1980), 19.
3 Willis (1727, 1730).
4 Matthews and Atkins (1964), 108–9, 150.
5 Simpson (1880), 141.
6 Stow (1633), 767.
7 Matthews and Atkins (1964), 179, quoting BodL, Tanner MS 145, fos. 107, 114.
8 WS XIII, 16. Wren's reference to the Court of Arches is puzzling, as at no time before or since has it been accommodated in the cathedral.
9 BodL, MS Tanner 145, fo. 129v.
10 AS II. 42, reproduced in WS I, pl. xxvi.
11 AS II. 21, 23, reproduced in WS I, pls xvi and xviii.
12 Wren (1750), 282.
13 BodL, MS Tanner 45, f. 145v.
14 BodL, MSS Tanner 24, 32, 34, 123, 129, 141 *passim*.
15 Strype (1720), i. 649. Eleven printed sermons, delivered at thanksgiving services between 1639 and 1661, are listed in Simpson (1893), i. 99ff.
16 Minutes of Commissioners' meeting, 2 October 1693, printed in WS XVI, 75.
17 Building accounts, printed in WS XIV, 124, 130.
18 Minutes of Commissioners' meeting 1 May 1694, WS XVI, 16–17.
19 Simpson (1873), 281–5.
20 Simpson (1873), 285; Hatton (1708), ii. 463.
21 Matthews and Atkins, 148.
22 For the original seating plan see WS XIII, pl. xx.
23 WS XV, 41.
24 Matthews and Atkins, 179.
25 Simpson (1893), i. 99.
26 A model survives for the substructure of the stalls, and one for a reredos with paired twisted columns (discussed below). Both are preserved in the cathedral. The building accounts (WS XV, 10–11) record payments to Roger Davis and Hugh Webb for 'models and patterns for several parts of the joiners' work in the choir from Lady Day 1695 to Lady Day

'1696', and to Charles Hopson for models for 'the seats in the choir', for the altar (Communion table), for the organ case, for the organ bellows, for the dean's seat and for the chair organ case.

27   WS XIV, pl. v, and WS I, pl. xx (AS II. 30).

28   WS XV, 122.

29   The columns were reused in 1872 as part of inner porches at the north and south doors of the transepts. The north porch was destroyed by the bomb which fell on the north transept in 1941, but the south porch with the marble columns remains in place.

30   Recorded by F. C. Penrose in an elevational drawing reproduced in WS XVI, pl. xiv.

31   Building accounts under September 1696, WS XV, 16.

32   WS XVI, 77. For an important interpretation of the documentary evidence, disposing of myths, see Niland (1996), 90–101.

33   Dugdale (1658), pl. at 169.

34   GL, SP 183 and 184, reproduced in Downes (1988), Figs. 185–6. The drawings are both loaded with alternative designs for elaborate carved decoration in Grinling Gibbons's hand.

35   It was to these fifty-five people that Bishop Compton addressed his visitation instructions in 1696. They are named in the preamble to the manuscript text, GL, MS 9537/26.

36   The superseded scheme on AS II.30 had a less orthodox layout of the return stalls, curving round in a quadrant. For an elevation of this part of the scheme see GL, SP 83 published in WS II, pl xxvi–ii, and Downes (1988), Fig. 179.

37   WS XIV, 15: bishop's and lord mayor's thrones; 18: bishop's seat and bishop's throne, all among payments made in September 1696.

38   WS XIV, pls. xviii, xlvii.

39   The superseded scheme on AS II. 30 indicated gallery access in each bay by means of an enclosed spiral stair projecting into the aisle. A sketch elevation showing one of these stair projections is AS I. 99, published in WS I, pl. iii.

40   GL, SP 82, reproduced in WS II, pl. xxvii, and Downes (1988), fig. 170.

41   Building accounts printed in WS XV, 5, 17.

42   Evelyn (1955), v.192, under 5 October 1694, but almost certainly an addition made after the opening of the choir in December 1697.

43   Du Prey (2000), 141–2.

44   WS XV, 42, 44–5.

45   The engravings do not indicate that it was on wheels, but the building accounts include a payment in 1696 of £10 to a smith for '3 Engines for the Pulpit', WS XV, 26. Simpson (1880) prints a contemporary broadside which includes verses addressed 'To the Architect, upon his Happy Invention of a Pulpit on Wheels for the use of St Paul's Choir'.

46   WS XIV, pl. v.

47   Wren (1750), 292 n.

48   Wren (1750), 292 n.

49   A small model for a free-standing domed structure, presumably a baldacchino, survives in the cathedral library. This is of uncertain status, and is probably in part, and perhaps wholly, of the nineteenth century.

50   Contract with John Moore, gold beater, 23 March 1696/7, WS XVI, 35–6; Wren (1750), 292 note.

51   Hatton (1708), ii. 461.

52   Simpson (1873), 282, 285.

53   Building accounts, printed in WS XIV and XV, *passim*. The instructions to Wren given by the building commissioners on 23 March 1696/7, to estimate the cost of velvet for the altar, pulpit and cushions in the choir supports this interpretation, if the reference is to the velvet hangings in the apse described by Hatton.

54   WS XIII, pl. xxix.

55   Downes (1988), in colour pl. on 48. Some of the coloured marble slabs from the east end have been relaid to the west of the resited choir stalls.

56   The gates survive, within an enlarged composition by Bodley and Garner, created when they were moved to the easternmost of the main arcade arches in the choir. For payments to Tijou, WS XV, 42, es in the choir. For payments to Tijou, WS XV, 42,

150. Tijou's altar rail appears in Robert Trevitt's engraving of the thanksgiving service on 31 December 1706, probably newly erected for the occasion. A temporary wooden altar rail had been supplied by John Smallwell and paid for in 1698 (WS XV, 49). Tijou's rails are now at the west end of the choir, moved there by F. C. Penrose in 1872.

57   These may be the four-branch chandeliers now hanging one in the north nave aisle, the other in the south. A sketch for part of a much larger and more elaborate chandelier, dated 21 October 1697 and titled in French, records a design that seems not to have been proceeded with. (WS II, pl. xxxii and Downes (1988), no. 195).

58   WS XV, 60.

59   WS XVI, 174.

60   Dugdale (1658), 160.

61   Sherlock (1699).

62   Sherlock (1699), 12–14.

63   Stow (1633), 767.

64   Matthews and Atkins (1964), 199.

65   Luttrell (1857), iv. 313.

66   Reprinted in Dugdale (1818), which prints details of the services in 1702 and 1704 from College of Arms, MS M3. For the seating arrangements at the service on 31 December 1706, see the caption to Robert Trevitt's engraving.

67   Dugdale (1818), 438, and *LJ*, xvii. 164, 192.

68   See the representative collection of these printed sermons in the cathedral library.

69   The engraving is part of a supplement to Picart (1723).

70   For segregation of the sexes in parish churches during the eighteenth century see du Prey (2000), 40, and Yates (2000), 37.

71   WS XV, 116.

72   Macky (1714), 199–200.

73   Downes (1988), colour pl. on 48.

22.   *Embellishment and Decoration, 1696–1900*

Acknowledgements are due to Robert Crayford, former Architectural Archivist of St Paul's Cathedral; Dr Michael Hall; Canon John Halliburton; Dr Gordon Higgott; and Joseph Wisdom, St Paul's Cathedral Librarian, whose generous help with my research has been invaluable.

1   Wren (1750), 292.

2   Wren (1750), 261.

3   Wren (1750), 261.

4   Cardinal Richelieu stipulated that the cupola of the chapel of the Sorbonne should be painted to look like the mosaic in St Peter's, Rome. *Le Grand Siècle au Quartier Latin*, 170.

5   *Le Grand Siècle au Quartier Latin*, 170.

6   Mosaic was a very expensive form of decoration on account of the technical processes involved.

7   The only known drawing associated with Wren showing compartmentalized mosaic is a comparative study of the domes of St Peter's, Rome, and the Duomo, Florence, in the All Souls' Collection. WS I, pl. xxvii.

8   Chapel of Sorbonne, begun 1626, cupola decorated 1641–4; Val-de-Grâce, begun 1645, cupola decorated 1663; Saint-Paul-Saint-Louis, cupola and façade, 1629–41, decorated 1641–7.

9   Jestaz (1990), 36, 38.

10   Summerson (1990), 32–3.

11   Downes (1988), cat. no. 95. The drawing is there dated to 1675, but recent research ascribes it to the late 1680s or early 1690s: see Geraghty (2001), 478.

12   The writing on this drawing has been identified by Gordon Higgott as that of Hawksmoor.

13   The date for the le Pautre engraving illustrated here (Fig. 161) is found in Reuterswärd (1965), 89. Its attribution to Pierre le Pautre is argued for by Gordon Higgott in a forthcoming study on Les Invalides and Wren's Designs for St Paul's Cathedral. The engraving not illustrated here is a section by Jean Marot, published in Boulencourt (1683).

14   WS XV, 13.

15   WS XV, 35.

16   WS XV, 169.

17   WS XV, 188, 190.

18   WS XV, 190, 198.

19   WS XVI, 106.

20   Thornhill was commissioned to decorate the ceiling of the Great Hall of the Royal Hospital in 1707. Bold (2000), 132–4.

21   Croft-Murray (1962), 69–70.

22   Thornhill carried out at least ten decorative schemes for the architects of the Office of Works to Laguerre's five, one of which Laguerre gained because Thornhill was too expensive. Croft-Murray (1962), 250–4, 266–271.

23   Pozzo (1707).

24   There are five known sketches of 'architectural' schemes: three in the Witt Collection, Courtauld Institute, one in the Ashmolean Museum and one sold by Sotheby's in 1997.

25   WS XVI, 107.

26   WS X, 116–19.

27   The irregular form of the coffering in Thornhill's scheme for Blenheim is similar to that used by Wren in the dome at St Stephen, Walbrook.

28   WS XVI, 107.

29   WS XVI, 107.

30   WS XVI, 108.

31   WS XVI, 109.

32   WS XVI, 174.

33   Croft-Murray (1962), 72.

34   LPL, MS 2552, fo.63. The cathedral now has only two of the original set of eight paintings, while the Yale Center for British Art (Mellon Foundation) has one. The whereabouts of the other five paintings are not known.

35   Newton (1782), i. 105. In recent years, eight monochrome paintings belonging to the cathedral have been mistakenly referred to as the 'Presentation Set'. But these must have been painted after the death of Queen Anne, since they show the scheme actually painted on the dome some years later.

36   It has been suggested that Wren asked Laguerre to provide a decorative scheme for the dome in 1708 and authorized him to start work without first gaining the agreement of the Commissioners. Gibson-Wood (1993), 231. Not only would this have been uncharacteristic of Wren, but it cannot be reconciled with Vertue's account which says that Laguerre was unanimously chosen by the Commissioners, not Wren.

37   *Vertue Note Books*, II (Walpole Soc. 20, 1932), 125.

38   Lang (1956), 248–9.

39   WS XV, 219.

40   BL, Add. MS 21111, V18, B.M. 14b.

41   *The Gentleman's Magazine*, November 1790.

42   WS XVI, 116.

43   Ryder (1939), 306–8.

44   BL, Add. MS 34788. Thornhill records the artist as 'Adam an Italian'.

45   WS XV, 219.

46   *Vertue Note Books*, II (Walpole Soc. 18, 1930), 34.

47   Ryder (1939), 307.

48   WS XV, 222.

49   WS XVI, 132.

50   WS XVI, 135–6.

51   WS XVI, 136.

52   WS XVI, 136.

53   Ryder (1939), 308.

54   WS XV, 164.

55   For a figurative scheme to be easily seen so high above the ground, there need to be windows cut into the dome itself. A large number of windows in the peristyle merely produces a light barrier which makes it more difficult to see any paintings in the dome above.

56   The fact that Thornhill made alterations to the eye of the dome indicates that he was aware of the problem. WS XV, 218.

57   WS XV, 13.

58   WS XV, 35–6, 198. The wooden altar rail was replaced by a metal one prior to the Thanksgiving of 1706.

59   Parris pointed out that the figures in Thornhill's paintings had originally been much lighter in colour. *The Illustrated London News*, 9 August 1856.

60   Pears (1988), 154–6.

61   Hussey (1941), 24.

62 Gwynn (1749), (1761) and (1766).
63 Gwynn (1766), 40.
64 Gwynn (1766), 40.
65 Newton (1782), i. 105.
66 Newton (1782), i. 105.
67 Newton (1782), i. 105.
68 Newton (1782), i. 105.
69 Galt (1816), 53.
70 Henry Flitcroft, 'Account of Some Works now Necessary to be done'. LPL, MS 2027, fos. 44–5.
71 Thomas Secker, 'Observations relating to the Fabrick of the Church of St Pauls'. LPL, Herring Papers 2, fo. 154.
72 'Resolutions made by the Commissioners for the Church of St Pauls London', LPL, MS 2027, fos. 46–8 and Paymaster's Ledger Accounts, GL, MS 25621-2. Also bills and vouchers held in both LPL and GL.
73 GL, MS 25575/5.
74 LPL, MS 2552, fo. 158.
75 GL, MS 25621–2.
76 GL, MS 25621–2.
77 GL, MS 25621–2.
78 The pilasters at the east end of the choir had been painted to imitate Siena marble some time before Cockerell redecorated the cathedral in 1822. Watkin (1974), 116.
79 LPL, MS 2553, fos. 93–4.
80 Watkin (1974), 146.
81 'Fabrick of St Pauls Order Book', GL, MS CF box 41, fo. 1.
82 GL, MS CF box 41, fo. 3.
83 Watkin (1974), 116.
84 Watkin (1974), 116.
85 GL, Prints & Drawings Collection, C1.
86 'The Application of the Higher Branches of Painting especially in Fresco to Architecture', paper read by E. T. Parris at RIBA in 1842. RIBA, MS SP/4/9, fo. 2.
87 RIBA, MS SP/4/9, fo. 2.
88 GL, MS CF box 89, letter from Cockerell to the Dean.
89 RIBA MS SP/4/9, fo. 2.
90 Russell (1920), 57.
91 Russell (1920), 71.
92 Russell (1920), 76.
93 Russell (1920), 86.
94 Russell (1920), 69.
95 Milman (1868), 495.
96 Milman (1868), 495.
97 Milman (1868), 496.
98 'A few remarks on St Paul's and its appropriate Decorations', paper read by F. C. Penrose at RIBA, May 1852. RIBA, MS SP/11/5, fos. 1–33.
99 'On the decorations suitable to St Paul's', Discussion held at RIBA, July 1852. RIBA, MS SP/11/5 (Discussion), fos. 1–56.
100 RIBA, MS SP/11/5, fo.25.
101 RIBA, MS SP/11/5 (Discussion), fos. 1–2.
102 RIBA, MS SP/11/5 (Discussion), fos. 3–5.
103 RIBA, MS SP/11/5 (Discussion), fos. 32. This was John Woody Papworth, architect and antiquary.
104 RIBA, MS SP/11/5 (Discussion), fo. 46.
105 RIBA, MS SP/11/5 (Discussion), fos. 20, 23.
106 Prestige (1955), 82.
107 ILN, 9 August 1856.
108 GL, Prints and Drawings Collection, Box C3.
109 The first of these mosaics was installed in the cathedral in 1864 and the last in 1891–2. SPCL, CM, 1860–74, 1889–1906.
110 Physick (1970), 47.
111 A list of the members of this subcommittee appears at the top of a resolution it submitted to the dean and chapter in January 1860. SPCL, CM, 1860–74.
112 Annual Reports of F. C. Penrose, 1858–60. GL, MS CF box 89.
113 Penrose's Annual Report of 1859 refers to 'cleaning the drum'. SPCL, CM, 1852–60.
114 Annual Report of F. C. Penrose, March 1860. GL, MS CF box 89.
115 The limited extent of the decoration actually carried out can be seen in a photograph of c.1880. GL, Prints and Drawings Collection, A460/3.
116 Barrington (1906), i. 256.

117 Watts (1912), i. 209.
118 BodL, MS don e 69, fo. 107.
119 The Athenaeum, 21 Feb. 1863.
120 Milman (1868), 496.
121 Penrose Papers, RIBA, MS PeF/1/1/31.
122 The Builder, 30 July 1864, 567; The Art Journal, 1867, 135.
123 The Builder, 24 March 1855.
124 Royal Academy Exhibitors (1866), 801.
125 The Builder, 9 March 1867, 166.
126 RIBA, MS SP/11/5 (Discussion), fo.16.
127 Donated by Thomas Brown. The Art Journal, 1867, 94.
128 SPCL, Cathedral Scrapbook, fo. 262.
129 Description of decoration of apse included in review of 'Mr Longman's Book'. See The Edinburgh Review, October 1873.
130 Gregory (1912), 175.
131 The committees and their members are listed on a 1873 statement of the accounts of the St Paul's Cathedral Fund. SPCL, Decorations Box 1.
132 Longman (1873), 156.
133 Printed notice of the Public Meeting held on 17 July 1870. SPCL, Gregory scrapbook, 1.
134 Burges, 'Diary of St Paul's', 26 July 1870. RIBA, MS BuW/1, fo. 81.
135 The Architect, 3 September 1870.
136 Letter, George Cavendish Bentinck to the Cathedral Secretary, saying since Burges did not have a majority of votes his election was null and void. SPCL, Decorations Box 1.
137 Building News, 9 Aug. 1872.
138 Agreement as to the Completion of St Paul's Cathedral, 8 Aug. 1872, made between the dean and chapter and F. C. Penrose and W. Burges. StPL, Decorations Box 1.
139 Instructions on style and departure for Italy. Burges, 'Diary of St Paul's', RIBA, MS BuW/1, fo.121 and fo.148.
140 RIBA, MS BuW/1, fo. 204.
141 RIBA, MS BuW/1, fos. 246–8.
142 RIBA, MS BuW/1, fos. 310–4.
143 SPCL, CM, 1860–74, 7 May 1872.
144 Resolution of Decoration Subcommittee, 1877. SPCL, Decorations Box 3.
145 Gregory (1912), 207.
146 Report of the Decoration Subcommittee appointed June 1877. GL, MS 25809/2/1, fo. 71.
147 Letter from Leighton to the Cathedral Secretary, 28 Aug. 1877. GL, MS CF box 57.
148 GL, MS CF box 57.
149 GL, MS CF box 57.
150 'Mr Oldfield's Memoranda: Scheme of Subjects suggested for Dome', December 1877. GL, CF 57.
151 Poynter's report on replacement of supporting figures at base of ribs. GL, MS CF box 57.
152 SPCL, CM, 1884–9, 1889–1906.
153 Harding's Scrapbook. GL, MS 25809/2/1, fo. 30 verso.
154 Gregory (1912), 207.
155 Leeds Art Calendar, 76 (1975), 18–20. I am grateful to Michael Hall for drawing this to my attention.
156 Hall (1996), 41.
157 Hall (1996), 41.
158 Garner (1886), 168.
159 Garner (1886), 168.
160 GL, Prints & Drawings Collection, file marked 'For Bob'.
161 GL, MS 25809/1, fo. 26 verso.
162 Correspondence between W. Tapper, on behalf of Bodley and Garner, and Harding concerning erection of cartoons. GL, MS 25809/2/1, fos. 88–90.
163 SPCL, CM, 1889–1906, 29 July 1891; letter dated 23 July 1891 from Richmond to Harding, GL, MS 25809/2/1, fo. 98.
164 GL, MS 25809/1, fo. 31.
165 Powell (1894), 252–3.
166 SPCL, CM, 1889–1906; GL, MS 25809/1, fo. 31.
167 GL, MS 25809/1, fo. 32v.
168 GL, MS 25809/1, fo. 34.
169 Illustrated Carpenter and Builder, 9 March 1894, 195.
170 The Globe, 27 March 1899.
171 Minute of interview regarding the decoration of St Paul's Cathedral held at the Deanery on 15

April 1899. GL, MS CF box 41.
172 'Art Students and St Paul's Cathedral, May, 1899'. SPCL, Cathedral Scrapbook.
173 SPCL, Cathedral Scrapbook.
174 GL, MS 25809/1, fo. 40v.
175 GL, MS 25809/1, fo. 40v.
176 GL, MS 25809/1, fo. 41.

23. Decoration, furnishings and art since 1900

1 Clinch (1906), 155.
2 SPFA, Somers Clarke to Macartney, 7 March 1907.
3 WS XIV. Pl. xxvii, XIV. 106.
4 Physick (1970), 49, 101–4.
5 Galloway (2000), 289–93.
6 Galloway (2000), 295, Somers Clarke to Sir Robert Herbert, 28 Aug. 1902.
7 SPFA, Somers Clarke to dean and chapter, 29 Oct. 1903.
8 The Builder, 21 Oct. 1905, 412–13; see also Building News 15 June 1906, 840.
9 Galloway (2000), 295–8.
10 The Builder, 27 June 1908, p. 754; Nicholson and Spooner [1910], 118–22; SPFA, annual reports of surveyor, Nov. 1916; Galloway (2000), 298–306.
11 Galloway (2000), 305, 315.
12 Galloway (2000), 312–17; SPFA, annual reports of surveyor, 1922–37, passim. Somers Clarke's stalls were in part removed to Holy Innocents Church, Hammersmith, while his canopied chairs are said to have gone to 'the Hall of St Michael & St George in the palace at Valletta' (Galloway, 317).
13 Diaries of Venetia Benson, kindly communicated by Alan Crawford.
14 SPFA, report by S. E. Dykes Bower, Aug. 1946.
15 Wren (1750), 292.
16 It is now generally agreed that the model of such a baldacchino in St Paul's Library dates from Penrose's time rather than from the early eighteenth century, as has sometimes been believed.
17 Ward Perkins (1952), 21–33.
18 SPFA, annual report of surveyor, Jan. 1949.
19 The late Brian Thomas, in conversation with the author.
20 SPFA, report by S. E. Dykes Bower, Aug. 1946.

24. The post-Reformation monuments

1 The first and the last sections (pp. 269–72 and 282–92) were written by Roger Bowdler; the middle section (pp. 272–82) by Ann Saunders.
2 For monuments erected in Old St Paul's before the Reformation, see Fig. 67, p. 128.
3 Payne Fisher (1684).
4 Llewellyn (2000), 239.
5 One other monument did survive intact besides Donne's: the auricular cartouche to 'that worthy and learned Gent.' Sir Simon Baskerville (d. 1641), a doctor. It is now hidden from general view in the stock room of the cathedral shop.
6 The monument cost £120: Spiers (1919), 63–4 & 90; Gardner (1979); Hurtig (1983).
7 Harding Scrapbook, GL, MS 25809/1, fo. 1v.
8 See J. P. Malcolm's engraving in Gentleman's Magazine, Feb. 1820, opp. 113.
9 Mathew (1665), 351.
10 Walton (1675), 71–2.
11 Stone (1956), 74.
12 Wren (1750), 319.
13 Whinney (1988), 152.
14 The Mirror of Literature, Amusement and Instruction, 10 October 1825, 179.
15 Yarrington (1988), 85.
16 Newton (1782), i, 108–9.
17 Lewis and Wallace (1937), 280–2.
18 BL, Add. MS 26055 (minutes with correspondence, bills, etc.).
19 A copy of the haggard face and head of the sick man was Bacon's choice for his admission piece to the Royal Academy. For the best account of all this, see Whinney (1988), 304–7, 362.
20 BL, MS Add. 22549 (memoranda and letters); also

Saunders (1985), 632–6, giving a longer account of the story of the Johnson memorial and epitaph.

21 I am grateful to the late Professor Sir Ernst Gombrich for suggesting the relationship between the painting and the statue.

22 *Gentleman's Magazine*, March 1796, 180.

23 BL, Oriental Books: East India Company, Court of Directors, 12 April 1796, p. 1550.

24 I am most grateful to Dr Giles Tillotson for his help. The tablet shows the Churning of the Oceans, sitting on a pillar supported on a tortoise; Indra's elephant mount and Shiva's bull mount are also represented.

25 Cunningham (1829–33), iii. 238; Bailey (1927), 110.

26 Hudson (1958), 232.

27 *House of Commons' Journals* (1797), L, 428, 444, 490, 513, 578, 607; LIII, 33, 34.

28 I am grateful to Professor Judith Milhous for providing me with the libretto.

29 Cunningham (1829–33), iii. 115.

30 *The Times*, 7 Jan. 1806.

31 PRO, T27/53/400.

32 For further information on the Committee, see Garlick and Mcintyre (1978–98); also Herrmann (1972) and Guilding (2001).

33 *House of Commons Papers* 1841 (416), vi, 437.

34 Garlick and Macintyre (1978–98), 1 April 1802.

35 Garlick and Macintyre (1978–98), 24 August 1805.

36 Whinney and Gunnis (1967); Garlick and Macintyre (1978–98).

37 Models for the tablet are in the Flaxman Collection at University College London.

38 *Gentleman's Magazine* (1813), ii, 541–3.

39 Garlick and Macintyre (1978–98), 13 February 1804.

40 Garlick and Macintyre (1978–98), 16 and 24 March 1807.

41 Everyone wanted to commemorate Nelson. In the National Maritime Museum is a design with both the admiral's arms intact. I am grateful to Marianne Czisnik for telling me of it. See also Yarrington (1988). Even Canova published a colossal design to commemorate the heroic admiral.

42 Pope (1960–3), iii; Elwin (1950), 395.

43 Elwin (1950), 244.

44 See St Clair (1998); also, *Report of the Select Committee on National Monuments* (1841).

45 Garlick and Macintyre (1978–98), 13 June 1809.

46 Garlick and Macintyre (1978–98), 24 May 1802; 25 Aug. 1805; 29 March 1806; 2 March 1807; 21 April 1807.

47 Pope (1960–3), i, 261; cf. Elwin (1950), 173–4.

48 National Library of Scotland, MS 2732, Sederunt Book of the Committee of Subscribers. I am most grateful to Justin Howes for telling me of the manuscript, and for transcribing relevant passages.

49 Dalton (1890), p. 19.

50 Royal Academy, General Assembly Minutes, II, 113–22, 133–4, 136–42. A deputation called on the King at the Queen's Lodge at Windsor, with the proposal. George III, seriously ill at the time, talked about the arts solidly for two and a half hours. John Nash inserted a Valhalla into one of his designs for Regent's Park; it was never realized.

51 *House of Commons Papers* 1841 (416), VI, 437.

52 SPCL, Scrapbook No. 1, 204.

53 Hackett (1825), 8.

54 Montemont (c.1835), 92.

55 Kelly (1990), 138–9.

56 *ILN*, 6 Nov. 1847, 301.

57 Penny (1977), 76–8; see also Groseclose (1995), 95.

58 Lough and Merson (1987), 22, 62–3 and pl. 23; Groseclose (1995), 95.

59 Milman (1868), 491. The second viscount Melbourne is actually buried in the family vault at Hatfield.

60 *City Press*, 12 March 1870. Philip Ward-Jackson kindly passed on this reference.

61 *ILN*, 17 May 1856, 525.

62 Bowdler (2001), 220–1.

63 Letter signed 'DD': undated cutting in GL, Noble Collection, ref. A460/Crypt.

64 *ILN*, 4 November 1854, 431–2.

65 Prestige (1955), 77.

66 GL, Noble Collection, ref. A460/Wellington

(undated cutting from *London Journal*). Penrose had scoured Europe for a sufficiently massive monolith before a suitable stone was found on the Treffry estate at Luxullyan: unidentified cutting, SPCL, Scrapbook No. 1, 236.

67 Milman (1868), 494.

68 Picton fell at Waterloo, but his body was brought back to the burial ground of St George's, Hanover Square on the Bayswater Road.

69 Marochetti's monument in Exeter Cathedral to the 9th Lancers of 1860 repeats this approach.

70 *ILN*, 23 Aug. 1856, 199.

71 Blaxland (1977), 60–2.

72 Prestige (1955), 104.

73 GL, MS 25809/1, Harding scrapbook, fo. 17.

74 *A Guide to St Paul's Cathedral* (1874), 49.

75 *Illustrated London News*, 18 Oct. 1873, 373.

76 GL, MS 25809/1, fos. 63v ff.

77 Physick (1970).

78 Wolffe (2000), 44; SPCL, Scrapbook No. 1, 103, cutting.

79 Driskel (1993).

80 Longford (1971) 356.

81 Physick (1970), 129; Read (1982), 93–5, 276 etc.

82 GL, MS 25,809/1, fo. 63.

83 Wolffe (2000), 136–53.

84 Dimock (1900), 122.

85 Saunders (2001), 150–1.

86 Dugdale (1658), 94.

87 Read (1982), 330.

88 Atkinson (2000), 338; Cornford (1913), 63. The St Paul's bust is a cast by Rodin from his 1886 original, now in the National Portrait Gallery.

89 The monument has darkened considerably: its original appearance is illustrated in Macklin (1909), 116.

90 Burman (1987), 166. Creighton's monument was unveiled in 1905. Thornycroft returned to its mood in his now-damaged effigy of Bishop Yeatman Briggs (d. 1922) at Coventry Cathedral.

91 SPFA, draft letter (undated) from Somers Clarke.

92 *The Builder*, 28 Nov. 1913, 569.

93 Surridge (2001), 298–313; Royle (1985), 390.

94 A memorial tower was erected on Marwick Head, overooking the scene of the sinking one-and-a-half miles out to sea.

95 Butler (1950), 3, 45.

96 SPCL, CM (information from Joseph Wisdom); Elliott (1965), 30–2.

97 *Evening Standard*, 26 Jan. 1999. The memorial was paid for by an appeal launched by the paper.

98 *The Independent*, 6 Dec. 1999 (obituary of Skelton).

99 Approved in 1969, the tablet was unveiled in 1971 (SPCL, CM); Douglas Bader was among the onlookers, in tribute to Novello's genius as a morale-lifting song-writer: Webb (1999), 144.

25 · *The Conservation of the Fabric, 1720–2004*

1 WS XVI, 115, 116–8, 137, 141, 177–8; Colvin (1995), 536.

2 Clutterbuck (1815–27), i. 168.

3 *Frauds and Abuses*, 40–1.

4 LPL, MS box FP 448.

5 GL, MS CF box 89, 'The Humble Memorial of Henry Flitcroft . . . Architect and Surveyor'.

6 LPL, MS 2027, fos. 46–7.

7 Colvin (1995), 573; Woodley (1999).

8 SPFA, Mylne to the dean and chapter, 20 March 1781.

9 LPL, Cornwallis Papers, vol. 3, letter from the dean (Thomas Newton) to the bishop of London and the archbishop of Canterbury, 12 November 1778, fos. 80–1.

10 Colvin (1995), 573.

11 Colvin (1995), 262; *DNB*.

12 Watkin (1974), 20.

13 C. R. Cockerell to S. P. Cockerell, 18 August 1815, cited in Watkin (1974), 20.

14 WS XIV, 169. Cockerell worked in Smirke's office for a while.

15 In 1815 Cockerell had written to his father, then still

surveyor, urging the rejection of Canova's designs for Nelson's memorial, and praising Flaxman, who was in due course selected for this commission: Watkin (1974), 19.

16 *The Builder*, 19 Jan. 1856, 29; Watkin (1974), 109, 111, 121–2.

17 LPL, MS box FP 448.

18 Holland (1855), i. 249–53.

19 LPL, MS 2027, fo. 46.

20 Holland (1855), i. 249–53.

21 SPFA, Mylne, Annual Report to Chapter, 19 March 1852.

22 SPFA, Penrose, Annual Report to Chapter, June 1878.

23 J. T. Micklethwaite was also actively involved in aspects of the firm's work at St Paul's.

24 He paid for the provision and erection of the ironwork railings to the triforium out of his own pocket, continuing the payments long after his retirement.

25 *Architectural Review* 22 (1907), 111.

26 *Architectural Review* 22 (1907), 112.

27 Macartney (1907), 53–77.

28 Alexander (1927), 49.

29 SPFA, Macartney, Annual Report to Chapter, Nov.1914.

30 SPFA, Macartney, Annual Report to Chapter, Nov. 1915.

31 SPFA, Macartney, Annual Report to Chapter, Nov. 1921.

32 SPFA, Macartney, Annual Report to Chapter, Nov. 1922.

33 SPFA, Macartney, Annual Report to Chapter, Nov. 1923.

34 SPFA, Macartney, Annual Report to Chapter, Nov. 1924.

35 *The Builder*, 18 Jan. and 7 March 1924.

36 Fox (1924).

37 Barman (1925); Harvey (1925).

38 29 Dec. 1924 and 14 Feb. 1925: Alexander (1927), 54, 59.

39 13 March 1925: CLRO, Printed Reports, A/46N.

40 SPFA, Macartney, Annual Report to Chapter, Nov. 1925.

41 Godfrey Allen described Macartney's attitude to the project as being 'similar to that of Achilles in his tent': personal communication from Sir Bernard Feilden.

42 Poley (1927).

43 The drawing now belongs to the Victoria and Albert Museum, to which it is due to be returned. From this time also date the publication of the Building Accounts and other relevant material in the Wren Society volumes; a major photographic record by Royal Commission on Historical Monuments; and the meticulous measured drawings by Cecil Brown.

44 SPFA, Macartney, Annual Report to Chapter, Nov. 1930.

45 Obituary of Macartney, *RIBA Journal* 40 (Nov. 1932), 26.

46 SPFA, Macartney, Annual Report to Chapter, Nov. 1930.

47 *RIBA Journal* 43 (Sep. 1936). 1037–41.

48 SPFA, Allen, Annual Report to Chapter, Nov. 1932.

49 SPFA, Allen, Annual Report to Chapter, Dec. 1938.

50 Matthews and Atkins (1957), 314.

51 SPFA, Allen, notes for Annual Report to Chapter, Nov. 1944.

52 Matthews (1969), 326.

53 SPFA, Bernard Feilden, 'St Paul's Cathedral, notes 2.8.77', p. 10.

54 SPFA, Bernard Feilden, 'St Paul's Cathedral, notes 2.8.77', p. 24.

26 · *Estates and income, 1540–1714*

1 It is impossible to use the *Valor Ecclesiasticus* (even when supplemented by *Monasticon Anglicanum* [1817]) to make comparisons because the returns are incomplete, but whereas monastic lands were sold at market rates, profits could be made from exchanges. Habakkuk (1958), 376 and *passim*.

2 *L&P 1536*, 159 and *1540–46*, *passim*; *VCH Essex*. viii.

13. The chapter continued to receive other pensions payable from monasteries.
3 *L&P 1540*, 217; Saunders (1981), 21, 179.
4 *L&P 1543*, ii. 218, *1544*, i. 495; Dugdale (1818), 371–80, which also shows that Biggins was allocated to the dean in exchange for Acton.
5 *L&P 1544*, i. 496; ii. 72, 86, *Addenda*, i(ii), 548; *CPR 1550–53*, 135–6; *CPR 1560–63*, 388.
6 *L&P 1546*, 71, 324, 351, 409; *CPR 1547–48*, 147–8. Paget and the dean worked together on diplomatic missions.
7 Kitching (1980), 108–13.
8 Dugdale (1818), 29; *Valor Ecclesiasticus*, i. 367–9; *CSPD 1547–53*, 45; *CPR 1547–48*, 361–2, 394, *CPR 1548–49*, 35, 109. Kitching (1980), xxx calculates that the chapter made a profit of about £200 p.a.
9 *CSPD 1601–1603 with Addenda*, 520.
10 *CPR 1569–72*, 335–8. See also GL, MS 25787.
11 Simpson (1889), 257–9.
12 Topographical notes in this and the following paragraphs of this section are based on the Parliamentary surveys, GL, MSS 25631-2. See also Macleod (1990) and Blayney (1990). Peter College had been used by cathedral as well as chantry clergy.
13 *L&P 1545*, i. 304, *L&P 1546*, i. 217.
14 *CR 1547–8*, 395.
15 Kingsford (1971), ii. 19.
16 Somerville (1985), 163–7.
17 This resulted in St Faith's church becoming 'gloriously lighted'. Strype (1720), iii. 145b.
18 LPL, MS 909, fos. 313–18.
19 In 1474 Bishop Kemp appropriated the prebend of Pancratius to his chantry in St Paul's, which he had already endowed with Chigwell rectory. The prebendary retained the rectory after the suppression of the chantries. Morant (1768), 122.
20 *VCH Middx*, vii. 204, 213.
21 Johnson (1960), 29–35.
22 *CJ*, iii. 421; *LJ*, vi. 465–9.
23 CLRO, Rep. 57, fo. 8, Rep. 58, fo. 36 and *passim*.
24 HMC 6 (1877), 'Manuscripts of the House of Lords 1644–47', 103; Simpson (1880), 146–7.
25 Shaw (1900), *passim*.
26 Firth and Rait (1911), ii. 81–103. Impropriate tithes (though not manors and lands belonging to impropriate rectories) were not sold but (under the ordinance of 8 June 1649) were to be given on the expiration of any lease to the local incumbent to make up his salary to £100 p.a. The numerous ordinances regulating the sale of dean and chapter lands are listed in Firth and Rait, iii. 45–6.
27 GL, MSS 25631-2 (Parliamentary surveys), *passim*.
28 Ludlow (1894), 231.
29 This figure is derived from the deeds of bargain and sale in PRO Close Rolls (C/54); it includes the value of St Paul's land, calculated at minimum rates, sold in lots with land of other cathedrals.
30 GL, MS 25820; Power (1972), 240.
31 PRO, C54/3469/36, C54/3501/35.
32 PRO, C54/3582/1.
33 As argued in Hill (1940), 234, 239.
34 GL, MS 25633 (2 vols.).
35 See below under 'Receipts and Payments'.
36 When leasing Doctors Commons to the Fellows of Trinity Hall, Cambridge, the chapter made it a condition that the advocates residing there should provide free advice on ecclesiastical law if asked: GL, MS 25630/2, fo. 314.
37 *SR*, 13 Eliz. c.10, 14 Eliz. c.11. The one exception to the terms set in 1571–2 was for leases made to the queen herself. For example, in 1579 the chapter had to grant her a seventy-six-year lease of Barnes manor, commencing in 1600, which she rapidly assigned to Sir Francis Walsingham: GL, MS 25210, no. 10.
38 Wilkins (1737), 493; Hill (1956) 311–14.
39 GL, MSS 25630/1–16.
40 In 1697 the lease of Rickling parsonage was extended for fifteen years and 'to make up the same 21 years according to the usuall rule, the fine should be 3 yeares, 2 quarters, 1 month and 3 decimall points of a month': GL, MS 25738/3, p. 41.
41 Acroid's *Tables of Leases & Interest* (1628) and

[George Mabbutt], *Tables for the Renewing and Purchasing of the Leases of Cathedral Churches* (1686 et seq.) give a rate between 11 and 12 per cent. St Paul's used this traditional rate of interest in granting seven-year renewals of twenty-one-year country leases, but there is some evidence that they used the near current (and therefore more commercial) rate of 8 per cent in assessing fines on city leases. From 1651 to 1714 the legal maximum rate of interest was 6 per cent.
42 There are few references to estates being advertised, e.g. the great tithes of Aveley: GL, MS 25208, p. 3. Nepotism was common in prebendal leasing, unusual on capitular estates.
43 Chauncy (1700), i. 107; *VCH Middx*, vii. 193, 212, 217; PRO, C54/3583/29.
44 Even some lessees were allowed to pay their fines by instalments.
45 E.g. GL, MS 25208, p. 1.
46 Habakkuk (1978), 209–16.
47 GL, MS 25664/1, fo. 8v.
48 The chapter met approximately thirty times in both 1661 and 1662, less than ten thereafter.
49 Sancroft listed arrears of rent on city properties for the two years ending at Michaelmas 1668 amounting to £554,16s. 11d.: GL, MS 25643/2. This compares with arrears of £12 to £33 p.a. and receipts of about £410 p.a. for the period 1662–4: GL, MS 25640.
50 Jones (1966), introd. By *SR* 22 Car. II c.11 leases were not to be extended beyond sixty years.
51 CLRO, Fire Decrees B, fos. 231, 768; E, fo. 261; J fo. 159; GL, MS 25738/2, 44. The residentiaries set up a fund for the rebuilding of their houses to which they contributed from fines and other perquisites. GL, MSS 25643/1 (1669–70), 25643/2 (1666–7).
52 In April 1667 the chapter resolved to replace all rents in kind with a cash payment. GL, MS 25738/2, 17. It was calculated that the produce reserved to the chapter included seventy-seven capons at Easter and 184 at Christmas from the city and thirty-four from the country, five boars, twenty-four mallards, four quarters of oats, and thirty-six partridges: BL, Lansdowne MS 264, fo. 2.
53 GL, MS 25643/2.
54 GL, MSS 25636, 25638, 25642, 25643/1, 25677.
55 E.g. fines totalling £650 in 1667 and £2,108 in 1670. GL, MSS 25643/2, 41, 25650/1, fo. 24.
56 Sancroft was one of the few residentiaries who made substantial private donations. Dugdale (1818) 143 et seq.

27. *Music, 1540–1640*

1 HMC, *Fourth Report* (1874), 'Papers relating to Archbishop Laud's Visitations', 154. The choir of St Paul's is unique in having both minor canons and vicars choral. The former were the choir deputies of the canons and thus correspond to vicars choral in other cathedrals of the 'Old Foundation'. The latter were a supplementary body of professional singers, corresponding to lay clerks in cathedrals of the 'New Foundation'. At St Paul's both were corporate bodies owning rent-producing property. See pp. 24 Table 1), 158–9.
2 Minor canons are listed, not always reliably, in Hennessy (1898), 60–70.
3 Hofman and Morehen (1987); Daniel and le Huray (1972).
4 Bray (1994), 344–5.
5 Douglas Hamilton (1877), 2.
6 BodL, MS Mus. Sch. e. 420–2; see le Huray (1967), 172–81.
7 *NG*, xxvii. 352, s.n. Whytbroke.
8 Nichols (1852), 75.
9 Douglas Hamilton (1877), 89; Nichols (1852), 80.
10 Douglas Hamilton (1877), 124; Nichols (1852), 93.
11 BL, Add. MS 29996; Stevens (1969), no. 1. No choral music by ap Rhys is known, but there is a setting of *Dum transisset sabbatum* attributed to 'Roose' (Hofman and Morehen [1987], 53).
12 Caldwell (1966).
13 Plumley and Niland (2001), 18.

14 Hopkins and Rimbault (1855), 49; Ashbee and Lasocki (1998), 148–9.
15 BL, Add. MSS 17802-5; Mateer (1993), 19–43 and (1995), 21–50; Harrison (1958) 288–9.
16 *NG*, xvii. 390–1, s.n. Mundy.
17 Harrison (1963), no. 2.
18 There is an extensive literature; see especially Hillebrand (1926), 105–50, and Gair (1982).
19 Gair (1982), 5.
20 BL, Add. MS 15233. The play itself contains this couplet sung by one of the choristers (quoted in Flynn [1995], 191): 'Of all the creatures, less or moe / We lyttle poore boyes abyde much woe.'
21 Gair (1982), 80.
22 Gair (1982), 52–60.
23 *NG*, xxii. 54–6, s.n. Redford.
24 Grigson, (1984), 203.
25 *NG*, xxvii. 323, s.n. Westcote.
26 Brown (1952), 49.
27 Gair (1980b).
28 Hillebrand (1926), 327–8; Gair (1982), 21.
29 Arkwright (1913–14), especially 125–6 and 134–6; Shapiro (1968).
30 Brett (1967), no. 30.
31 Gair (1982), 89–90.
32 *NG*, xi. 477–8, s.n. Heywood. It may be mentioned (without speculating) that Redford's sister, Margaret Cox, had her will witnessed by a John Hayward, 'petycanon of poules' (Brown (1948), 509). Heywood and Hayward are probably of different generations, however.
33 *NG*, xvii. 382, s.n. Mulliner. The 'Mulliner Book' is BL Add. MS 30513; see Stevens (1951); Gifford (2002), 13–27.
34 *NG*, xix, 89–94, s.n. Philips.
35 Westcote left £5 to each minor canon in his will, £4 to each vicar choral and £5 to the choristers attending his funeral. He left a further £1 to each of seven ex-choristers (named), and £6 13s. 4d. to 'Peter Phillipp[es] likewise remayninge withe me' (Hillebrand (1926), 327–30).
36 Gair (1980b), 119.
37 Gair (1982), 9–12, 147–59.
38 Ravenscroft (1614), Sig. A2.
39 Jones (1993), 25.
40 BL, Add. MS 29289; Morehen (1969), 422–41.
41 Hillebrand (1926), 111.
42 Strype (1824), i. 298.
43 Le Huray (1965), 22–7.
44 Le Huray (1965), 28–32.
45 *NG*, xvii. 126–33, s.n. Morley; Shaw (1991), 172.
46 Hillebrand (1926), 111.
47 See fn. 49.
48 Anthems (including the Burial Service) in Morehen, (1991); services in Morehen, (1998).
49 Visitation Report in GL, MS 9537/9, abridged in Gair (1982) 176–81; see also Simpson (1873), 272–80.
50 Hentzner (1629), 178.
51 *NG*, ii. 739, s.n. Barnard.
52 Morehen (1969), 283–305.
53 London, Royal College of Music, MS 1045-51; Morehen (1969), 244–81.
54 Oxford, Bodleian Library, Tenbury MS 791; Morehen (1969), 215–43.
55 *NG*, ii. 910–11, s.n. Batten; Tomkins, NG, xxv, 575.
56 The maker may have been Thomas Hamlyn, '*demeurant en Trinite Leyn* [Lane]' – known to have carried out work on the organ at St James's Palace in 1613 – who had been approached by the ambassador of Archduke Albert to provide a similar instrument; Jeans (1986), 53, using the report of Baron de Hobocque dated '*v mars 1609*' (Vienna, Staatsarchiv, Belgien PC 45).
57 Furnivall (1908), 202.
58 Clark (1974), 71, also Clark (1968).
59 Daniel and le Huray (1972); *NG*, vi. 645–6, s.n. Cranford; *NG*, xxvii. 322, s.n. West; also Ashbee and Lasocki (1998), 1142.
60 *NG*, xix, 283–4, s.n. Peerson.
61 HMC *Fourth Report* (1874), 'Laud's visitation', 154.
62 Gee and Hardy (1910), 566; *CJ*, ii. 1803, 938.
63 Earliest and latest mentions.
64 According to Boyce (1760–73) ii. viii, Batten was

'Organist, and Vicar Choral', and the St Faith's burial register (GL, MS 8882, 15 Jan. 1651) describes Peerson as 'sometime Organist'. Both probably deputized for Tomkins while on duty at the Chapel Royal.

28. *Images of St Paul's*

1   Uffenbach (1934), 31–3.
2   No. 35 in Hind (1922); No. 1017 in Pennington (1982).
3   Pierce (1963), 128–32.
4   No. 1024 in Pennington (1982).
5   Several states described in Scouloudi (1953), 56–8.
6   No. 33 in Howgego (1978).
7   No. 15 in Adams (1983).
8   No. 17/11 in Adams (1983).
9   No. 18/1 in Adams (1983).
10 *Cal. of SP Dom 1698.*
11 No. 94 in Downes (1988).
12 No. 15 in O'Connell (1985), 27–42.
13 St Paul's Building Accounts, WS XIV, xi. payments in May 1702 and June 1703.
14 Downes (1994), 37–67.
15 *London Gazette*, 4–7 Jan. 1702/3.
16 The public was allowed to purchase them nevertheless, at his premises at the sign of the King's Arms, Coleman Street.
17 Society of Antiquaries, Harley Collection, 4.
18 *London Gazette*, 2 Jan. 1706/7, and key on print.
19 WS XIV, xii. The payment, for a view of the exterior (the 'Scenographia' plate) and the view of the choir, amounted to £300.
20 *London Gazette*, 4–8 Feb. 1702/3.
21 30 Aug.–2 Sept. 1703.
22 Copy in Pepys Collection: 163 in Aspital (1980).
23 WS XIV, xi.
24 Hodson (1984), 186–91. For successive deeds to the premises and plan of the shop see GL, MS 12660.
25 Tyacke (1978), 130–36; and Hodson (1989), pp. 186–9.
26 The only copy I have seen is item 101 in vol. 11 of the BM's Crowle Pennant.
27 *General Advertiser*, 28 Jan 1748.
28 Gwynn (1749); Gwynn (1766); Harris (1990), 214–17.
29 Colvin (1995), 440–1.
30 Conner (1984), 20.
31 Early proof of the dome section in GL, St Paul's Collection, 10/32; proof before letters in Sir John Soane's Museum.
32 The dedicatee on one copy in Sir John Soane's Museum has been changed to Hugh Richards.
33 Clayton (1997), 54–5. Thornhill was granted royal licence for sole printing of the engravings 1719.
34 Howgego (1978); and Webb (1975).
35 Clayton (1997), 140–1; Blake (2000); Stafford & Terpak (2001), 96–7.
36 135 in Adams (1983).
37 Lot 6 in Christies London sale, 26 Sept. 1999.
38 No. 432 in vol. 2 of Constable (1962).
39 BL Map Library, K.Top.23.36.f.
40 Advertised in *St James's Chronicle*, 12–14 Nov. 1789. Manuscript plans for the occasion in GL, St Paul's Collection, 11/10A. Also a pencil-drawn key in GL, Pr.460/PAU(2)int.
41 It persisted into the nineteenth century, nevertheless: John Buckler's, 'North West View of the Cathedral Church of St Paul's', for example, entirely ignores the cathedral's setting.
42 Advertisement in *The Times*, 18 Jan. 1801.
43 Advertisement in *The Times*, 18 Jan. 1801.
44 No. 219 in Adams (1983).
45 No. 220 in Adams (1983).
46 GL, St Paul's Collection 11/23.
47 Hyde (1982).
48 Hornor's annotated copy is in Yale Center for British Art.
49 Hyde (1987), 34–9.
50 Brooks (1998), 54–6.
51 Brooks (1998), 45–6.
52 Prestige (1955), 74.
53 'Funeral of the Duke of Wellington: Lying in State

at Chelsea Hospital'; 'Funeral of the Duke of Wellington: The Funeral Car Passing Apsley House'; and 'Funeral of the Duke of Wellington: The Ceremony in St Paul's Cathedral', after a painting by Louis Hague.
54 *ILN*, 24 June 1848.
55 *Punch*, 13 (1848), 84.
56 *ILN*, 9 Aug. 1856.
57 For contrasting opinion of Richmond's work see the caricature, 'The Dome of St Paul's. Shade of Sir Christopher (objecting to Sir W. Richmond's "improvements"…)' in SPCL, Newbolt Scrapbooks, 7, 4.
58 Hyde (2000).
59 A facsimile of it was published by Barracuda Books in 1984.
60 Currently hanging outside Trophy Room.
61 WS XIII, plates XXXIV–XXXVI. They are currently hanging in the north triforium aisle.
62 Matthews (1946); and *St Paul's in War and Peace,* (1960).
63 Flanders (1984), xiii.
64 In GL Print Room. Twenty-five drawings of St Paul's are listed in Flanders (1937–94). The view from Cannon Street belongs to dean and chapter and currently hangs in the chapter house.
65 Lingard (1993), 311–27.
66 Presented to GL by National Westminster Bank, and currently hanging in the members' dining-room.

29. *Estates and Income, 1714–2004*

1   See, e.g., the Durham statutes in Thompson (1929).
2   Order-in-council, 9 Aug. 1872.
3   GL, MSS 25697, fo. 221; 25730, fo. 40.
4   GL, MS 25697, esp. fo. 42.
5   Morrin (1997), 282 estimates that by 1840 the Durham chapter realized less than one quarter of the potential net annual value of their estate.
6   All fines were recorded by property from the 1730s in GL, MS 25730; examples cited here: fos. 5, 22, 25.
7   GL, MS CF box 102.
8   SPCL, CM, 31 Dec. 1855.
9   GL, MS CF box 31.
10 For example of annual valuation for fine, GL, MSS 20687/3, 25729. Fixed fines were charged on the manor of Kensworth alone in the communal estate in contrast to the prebendal estates where most of the fines on entry were fixed and small. CERC, S1, S2, and S4. Enfranchisement of copyhold continued until 1950 under the Ecclesiastical Commissioners. Morrin (1997), 45–72.
11 Turner and Beckett (1998), 102; GL, MS 14213/5.
12 PP 1837–8: IX (692), 1–91.
13 E.g. SPCL, CM, Aug. 1853; GL, MS 14212/17.
14 GL, MS 25697, fo. 5.
15 GL, MS CF box 41; SPCL, CM, 14 July 1833.
16 GL, MS 25729.
17 GL, MS 25730, fos. 2, 3, 7, 8, 20, 32.
18 SPCL, CM, 16 Mar. 1853; GL, MS 25647.
19 These figures were produced by chapter for the Ecclesiastical Commissioners based on surveys and reports of the rack rents paid by sublessees. This was the first occasion since the Interregnum land-sales on which the cathedral estate had been inventoried in this way. Chapter recorded the net annual value of properties based on surveys and evidence supplied by tenants. The dignitaries' and prebendal lands were not inventoried as they were outside the responsibility of the dean and chapter. SPCL, CM, 28 July 1853. Sellon's accounts for the chapter meeting show income from 1846 to 1852 varying from £11,000 to nearly £15,000 depending on fines. The income included rack rents on building leases, reserved rents, payments for redeemed land tax, profits of manors and woods, dividends on public securities, fines on leases for lives and years, and seal fees.
20 GL, MS 25729.
21 Figures from the papers prepared by the dean and chapter for the Ecclesiastical Commissioners showing the value of their communal estate in 1850: GL,

MS 25729.
22 GL, MS 25729.
23 CERC, S1. Most of the parish of Shadwell was let for ninety-nine years and the lessees had a perpetual right of renewal under the Act of Parliament 50 Geo III cap. 205 on payment of 20s., so the reversionary interest was not great.
24 All the valuations of dignitaries estates are from Ecclesiastical Commission records: CERC, S1.
25 PP 1837–8: IX (692), 436.
26 Smith (1838), 4; SPCL, CM, 24 Mar. 1859.
27 All valuations of prebendal lands from the Ecclesiastical Commission valuations: CERC, S1–2.
28 Still prebendary of Cantlers, Randolph declared his income from his prebend at £2,177 in 1857: SPCL, CM, 24 Feb. 1859; 53 Geo III cap. 49; CERC, S2, 401.
29 GL, MS 25697, fos. 20, 26.
30 SPCL, CM, 26 Jan. 1865; 24 Mar. 1859.
31 GL, MS 25697, fo. 18; SPCL, CM, 29 Nov. 1862.
32 CERC, S2.
33 GL, MS 25697; Cluttons could not find the land belonging to Weldland! CERC, S2.
34 GL, MS 25630/40, fo. 582.
35 Prestige (1955), 24–5.
36 SPCL, CM, 18 Jan. 1837; Charity Commission, High Court of Chancery, 18 Jan. 1837.
37 GL, MS CF box 41; BL, T 2328, fo. 131.
38 CERC, S4, p. 319; S1. Cluttons suggested tenants should be given notice to repair.
39 CERC, S1, S2.
40 SPCL, CM, 25 Mar. 1847; GL, MS 25647; CERC, S1, S2, S4.
41 Chadwick (1966–97), i. 26, 40.
42 Chadwick (1966–97), i. 105.
43 Chadwick (1966–97), i. 130–1; Prestige (1955), 32.
44 Chadwick (1966–97), i. 141.
45 Smith (1953), letter 814; Smith (1837), 3–7.
46 Gregory (1995), 245.
47 BL, T2328, fos. 115–17.
48 SPCL, CM, 24 Mar. 1859.
49 Barrett (1993), 219. Many cathedrals struggled with the costs of maintenance.
50 SPCL, CM, 24 Mar. 1859.
51 SPCL, CM, 9 May 1853. See pp. 88–9.
52 The surveys carried out on behalf of the Ecclesiastical Commissioners in the mid nineteenth century identified land ripe for development that should be retained for the Ecclesiastical Commission's estate. See CERC, S1–2.
53 Best (1964), 376–8.
54 PP 1851: XIII (589), 314–16.
55 SPCL, CM, 28 July 1853; Barrett (1993), 227–8; CERC, S1–2, 4. Valuations for prebendal lands and dignitaries' lands are taken from the surveys done (mainly by Cluttons) for the Ecclesiastical Commissioners in the mid nineteenth century. I have not found a valuation of the precentor's estate, and three of the very small prebends are not valued.
56 GL, MS 25630/46, fos. 18–19.
57 SPCL, CM, 31 Aug. 1853.
58 Barrett (1993), 220; Order-in-Council, 11 June 1858.
59 GL, MS CF box 13; SPCL, CM, 1868–71; Atkins (1957), 271; Barrett (1993), 229–30.
60 Order-in-council 9 Aug. 1872. Canterbury handed back its new estates between 1894 and 1902: Nockles (1995), 269–70.
61 Order-in-council 9 Aug. 1872; St Paul's Minor Canonries Act 1875. Dean Church supported this reform to bring the minor canons under dean and chapter control. The minor canons' grant remained at £2,000 a century later: SPCL, CM, 18 Dec. 1974; CERC, S2.
62 SPCL, CM, 15 July 1871.
63 SPCL, CM, 21 Nov. 1869, 15 Oct. 1869, 26 June 1872; Prestige (1955), 128–9. This inspector continued to operate until 1959: SPCL, CM, 3 Dec. 1959.
64 SPCL, CM, 31 Mar. 1871.
65 SPCL, CM, 21 Dec. 1878; Prestige (1955), 218. The fabric fund trustees continued to exist but seem to have played a lesser role after 1870.
66 GL, MS CF box 41. Public appeals for funds were becoming increasingly necessary: Canterbury

Cathedral launched a centenary appeal in 1895:
Nockles (1995), 282.

67 Atkins (1957), 290–3. See pp. 95–6.

68 GL, MS 25630/47, fos. 546–54; SPCL, CM, 13 Oct.
1876; GL, MS CF box 31.

69 Annual Report (2001).

70 Matthews (1957), 323; *Records of the Friends of St
Paul's* (1953), 10. See pp. 103–7.

71 Calculation from McCusker (2001).

72 *Annual Report* (2001).

73 Order-in-council 16 Oct. 1968, amending order-
in-council 9 Aug. 1872, under §§ 28 and 31 of the
Cathedrals Measure 1963. I am indebted to Philip
Gale of the CERC for this reference.

74 'The Cathedral's portfolio [of financial invest-
ments], entirely invested in the Central Board of
finance of the Church of England Investment and
Fixed Interest Securities Funds', lost nearly £1m in
value during 2001: *Annual Report* (2001). The investment properties of Tillingham and the Old
Deanery, however, gained nearly £0.5m in value
during 2001.

75 The City of London Endowment Trust contributed
£300,000 and legacies and donations £200,000 to
day-to-day running costs in 2001: *Annual Report*
(2001).

30. *Preaching Anglicanism at St Paul's,
1688–1800*

1   Bissett (1710), 1.

2   Sacheverell (1709), A2, 8–9, 23.

3   Holmes (1973), 91.

4   Ridpath (1710), 24.

5   *The Cherubim with a Flaming Sword*, 2, 3.

6   Burgess (1710), 1; *A True Answer to Dr Sacheverell's
Sermon*, 22.

7   Bennett (1975), 22.

8   Fleetwood (1708), 2–3, 15.

9   For some of these debates, and for their mapping on
to the political divisions of Tory and Whig, see
Speck (1970). For high-church clergy, see Every
(1956).

10 Altham (1706); Bisse (1710), 13; Bisse (1717), 42.

11 See Bennett (1975), 46–61, 65–73, 125–38; Sykes
(1959), 36–67.

12 Sykes (1934), 379.

13 See Downes (1982), 68–72, 77–82.

14 Ward (1716).

15 See *Ecclesia Restaurata*; Wright (1697); Wright (1709)

16 See Ralph (1734).

17 See Hart (1957), 190–2; above, pp. 68–9.

18 *An Historical Description of St Paul's*, 31.

19 *An Historical Description of St Paul's*, 30; Gregory
(1998), 85–110.

20 For a nineteenth-century detractor, see Wheaton
(1830), 134.

21 Curnock (1909–16), i. 472–3.

22 Curnock (1909–16), iii. 373.

23 Curnock (1909–16), ii. 127–9, 154, 281, 350–1, 354,
362–4, 374, 391, 393, 405, 419, 423, 425, 449.

24 Downes (1982), 60–2.

25 Wren (1750), 320.

26 See the comment in the 'Appendix' to Rennell
(1796), 12; Cox (1978), 64 observes that the
original sermon included some attacks on
the management of the Corporation and that the
printed version was much milder.

27 Bell (1713).

28 Maclure (1989); Walsham (1999), ch. 6; Morrisey
(2000), 43–58.

29 Holmes (1973), 75.

30 Majendie (1755).

31 See, e.g., Chambre (1710); Postlethwayt (1715);
Bellamy (1756). Brown (1763) recommended that
Protestant colleges be established to counteract the
influence of the Roman Catholic Church in India.

32 The phrase is Linda Colley's: Colley (1992), 19.

33 Sherlock (1712), 17.

34 Browne (1713), 12.

35 Scurlock (1733); for response, see *A Letter of Advice
to the Reverend Mr Scurlock*. Mischler (2001), 33–62.

36 Strype (1711), preface.

37 Venn (1740), 296, 299.

38 Crowe (1724), 2.

39 Crowe (1724), 11.

40 Sherlock (1712), 17.

41 Dane (1710), 2, 4, 10, 26.

42 Ibbot (1711), 17, 30.

43 Apthorp (1770), 22, 24.

44 For the SPCK, see Allen and McClure (1959). For
the Sons of the Clergy, see Cox (1978); on the charity-school festivals, see Jones (1938), esp. 56–61.

45 See Hart (1957), 227.

46 St John (1723), 14.

47 See the figures in Horsley (1793), 86.

48 Jones (1938), 61, ix, quoting Elliot, *Life and Letters*, i.
303–4.

49 Barton (1736), title page.

50 Holmes (1973), 263.

51 Sacheverell (1713), 3, 2, 28, 30, 34.

52 Sacheverell (1713), 34.

53 Sacheverell (1713), 37.

54 Lavington (1734), 19.

55 Marten (1738), 8.

56 Ridley (1757), 19, 6, 8, 11, 18. For a fuller discussion
of this issue, see Gregory (1987), 321–32, and for
related themes, see Bisse (1717), 13–17; Mangey
(1734), 9.

57 King (1751), 17.

58 Ibbetson (1758), 20.

59 Atterbury (1709), 8–16.

60 Salter (1755), 16.

61 Rhudde (1790), xiii.

62 Bisse (1710), 5; Ashton (1753), 2, 16; Dodwell (1760),
22; St John (1723), 38.

63 Mangey (1734), 18; Berriman (1737), 14.

64 Bisse (1710), 9; Bisse (1717), 13; Ibbetson (1758), 20.

65 Lewis (1717), 31.

66 Elon (1996), 17.

67 Cox shows that in the early eighteenth century the
Corporation had a potential income from its estates
of nearly £3,000, but that this was frequently in
arrears. Widows were paid £5 p.a. in the early eighteenth century, rising to £10 p.a. by the end of the
century: Cox (1978), 56, 75.

68 See 'Appendix' to Rennell (1796), 1–25. For
Handel's place in the cultural politics of the
eighteenth-century Church of England, see
Gregory (1991), 98–9.

69 Hodgson (1811), iii. 301, 305, 302.

70 Mason (1988), 250–1. The suggestion of satire comes
from the contrast with 'Holy Thursday' in *Songs of
Experience* (1793): ibid., 269. See Cowie (1977).

71 de Coetlogon (1790a–g).

72 Horsley (1793), 20, 27.

73 Bellinger (1982).

74 Porteus (1776), 7–11.

75 Layard (1795), xi–xiii.

76 Rennell (1796), xii. xvi, xviii, v.

31. *Liturgy, 1714–2004*

1   Martimort (1987), i. 94.

2   *Documents on the Liturgy*, §1.41, 13.

3   Legg (1914), vii–viii.

4   Eeles (1910), 1–2.

5   Staley (1904); Legg (1914).

6   Mather (1985); Nockles (1994), 4.

7   Paterson (1714), 217, 221.

8   Abbey and Overton (1887), 430; Frere and Kennedy
(1910), ii. 138. Bancroft's 1598 visitation articles for
St Paul's contain questions on the service: Kennedy
(1924), iii. 305.

9   Paterson (1714), *passim*.

10 Simpson (1873), 301; SPC, Liturgy Office, succentor's archives, worship bills. The last such service was
held on 28 June 1901.

11 Simpson (1873), 302.

12 As it was a century or more later: Hutton (1912),
158–9.

13 Simpson (1897), 312.

14 Milman (1869), 288–9.

15 Quoted Tindal Hart (1957), 239.

16 *London Gazette*, 20 Jan. 1715.

17 *London Gazette*, 2–25 Apr. 1789.

18 Milman (1869), 474.

19 Barham (1870), i. 288.

20 Barham (1870), i. 68; ii. 163.

21 Haweis (1801), 5.

22 Jebb (1843), 521–2.

23 Hutton (1912), 160.

24 *The Times*, 13 Oct. 1842; Barham (1870), ii. 149.

25 *The Times*, 18 Oct. 1842. The dean's letter was
accompanied by others from the warden of the
College of Minor Canons and from the virgers.

26 *The Times*, 6–9 Dec. 1842.

27 Russell (1920), 45–9.

28 *The Times*, 10, 15 Oct. 1842.

29 Jebb (1843), 495, 246, 371, 461.

30 Jebb (1843), 487; Walcott (1872), 116.

31 Russell (1920), title-page.

32 Pearson (1948), 270, 353.

33 Russell (1920), 72.

34 Russell (1920), 80.

35 Russell (1920), 93–4. The Nicene Creed was the
only part of the communion service sung in its
proper place at the time: *Parish Choir*, 2, 152.

36 Russell (1920), 96.

37 Russell (1920), 14, 104–5.

38 Prestige (1955), 61–2.

39 Russell (1920), 87.

40 SPCL, CM 1832–60, fo. 53.

41 SPCL, Diary of R. R. Green, dean's virger 1852–
1900, i. fo. 4; *ILN*, 7 Oct. 1854; Green Diary, i. fos,
3v, 12, 14v, 29.

42 Milman (1900), 282–3.

43 Wolffe (2000), ch. 2.

44 Hartford, Stevenson and Tyerer (1912), 377.

45 Milman (1900), 239.

46 Milman (1900), 240; SPCL, Diary of R. R. Green,
Dean's Virger 1852–1900, i. fo. 13. The first regular
Sunday evening nave service had been held in
Westminster Abbey on 2 Jan. 1858: Perkins (1952),
iii. 162.

47 Hutton (1912), 199–200.

48 Milman (1900), 242.

49 Milman (1900), 242. The Sunday evening services
were widely imitated in other cathedrals: Barrett
(1993), 119–20.

50 Hutton (1912), 158; Cadle (1999), 361–73.

51 Hutton (1912), 161.

52 SPCL, Diary of R. R. Green, dean's virger
1852–1900, i. fo. 33.

53 SPCL, CM, 9 Apr. 1870.

54 SPCL, CM, 7 Jan. 1871.

55 SPCL, CM, 31 Dec. 1870; Russell (1922), 16;
Simpson (1899), 49; SPCL, Diary of R. R. Green,
dean's virger 1852–1900, i. fo. 48.

56 Hutton (1912), 5.

57 Church (1894), 200. To further guarantee the high-
church tradition, Holland mischievously suggested
to Gladstone's daughter that the premier should
quit politics and himself take up a canonry, if not
the deanery: Ollard (1919), 48–9.

58 Church (1894), 218.

59 Church (1894), 246.

60 Chandler (2000), 86.

61 Chandler (2000), 88–9; Hutton (1912), 110; Bentley
(1978), 127.

62 Church (1894), 210–12.

63 Newbolt [1920], 192.

64 SPCL, Diary of R. R. Green, dean's virger
1852–1900, i. fos. 58–9, 65; Hutton (1912), 181;
Simpson (1899), 157–8.

65 Newbolt [1920], 195–6.

66 SPCL, CM, 29 June 1870.

67 Prestige (1955), 164.

68 SPCL, Liturgy Office, Service Bills.

69 WAM, Music/Service sheet Dec. 1873; Music Lists
1901; Stancliffe (1960), 333, 334.

70 SPCL, Diary of R. R. Green, dean's virger
1852–1900, i. fo. 51; Chandler (2000), 90; Prestige
(1955), 108; Church (1895), 242.

71 The Westminster Abbey copes had a rare outing
(save for coronations) at the Golden Jubilee service
in the abbey in 1887: Perkins (1938–52), iii. 81.

72 *Guardian*, 24 June 1897.

73 SPCL, CM 6 Apr. 1896, 28 Jan. 1897.

74 Simpson (1899), 123; Newbolt [1921], 199.

75 Hutton (1912), 212, 260.
76 PP 1906: XXXIV (Cd 3701), 274, §§.20941–2; Carpenter (1949), 197.
77 PP 1906: XXXIV (Cd 3701), 21, §§.99–102.
78 Inge (1949), 9.
79 Atkins (1957), 299.
80 Jasper (1989), 147–8.
81 Inge (1949), 144.
82 Elliott (1951), 141.
83 Roberts (1942), 251; Scott (1977), 206; Matthews (1969), 198.
84 Matthews (1969), 189–90.
85 Matthews (1969), 190–1.
86 Gray (1986), 4–6.
87 SPCL, CM, 2 Apr. 1955.
88 SPCL, CM, 26 Nov. 1955; 5, 26 May, 8 Sept., 3, 10 Nov. 1956; 18 May 1957; Jasper (1989), 173.
89 Collins (1966), 150; Collins (1992), 176.
90 Correspondence and conversations with past and present members of the St Paul's chapter.
91 SPC, Liturgy office, service sheets.
92 Gray (2002), 7–10.
93 *A Service of Remembrance with the American Community*, bidding prayer.

32. *St Paul's and the Public Culture of Eighteenth-Century Britain*

I am grateful to Robert Bucholz, Tony Claydon and Andrew Hanham for their comments on an earlier version of this essay.
1 Talbot (1707), 6.
2 *A Dialogue*, 35–6.
3 I owe this insight to Professor R.O. Bucholz.
4 Milman (1868), 427–8; Lang (1956), 188–9; Carpenter (1956), 181–2, 247.
5 Edmunds (2002).
6 Wright (1709).
7 Sherlock (1704), 17.
8 Cibber (1713), 12.
9 For details, see Dugdale (1818), 438–41; Milman (1868), 429–30; Lang (1956), 221–2, 229.
10 Quoted Gregg (1980), 277.
11 Jones and Holmes (1985), 406.
12 Hooper (1713), 1–2.
13 Wolfe (1968), 555.
14 Trelawny (1702), 33.
15 Stanhope (1706), 14.
16 Trelawny (1702), 38.
17 Willis (1705), 7, 9.
18 Harris (1991), 148.
19 Simpson (1894), 280–6, discusses the alleged 'plot', and dismisses it as 'an absurd *canard*, arising out of certain political exigencies' (286). See also Lord (1963–75), vii. 580, n. 46.
20 Willis (1715), 5, 6.
21 Trelawny (1702), 34.
22 An anonymous disgruntled Jacobite invoked Anne's statue to give vent to his horror at her successor. The *Pasquin to the Queen's Statue* includes such scurrilous lines as:

  'Behold he [George I] comes to make thy People groan,
  And with their curses to ascend thy Throne;
  A clod-pate, base, inhuman, jealous Fool,
  The Jest of EUROPE, and the Faction's Tool.
  Heav'n never heard of such a Right Divine,
  Nor earth e'er saw a Successor like thine:
  For if in Sense or Politicks you fail'd,
  T'was when his lousy long Succession you entail'd...

23 Smyth (2001), 128.
24 Lewis et al. (1937–68), xx. 46, to Sir Horace Mann.
25 See Colley (1992), 202–3, for the lower profile of state services during the reigns of the first two Georges.
26 Smith (1852–3), i. 25: Charles Jenkinson to George Grenville, 7 Sept. 1758. For first-hand accounts, see *Daily Advertiser*, 11 Sept. 1758, *London Chronicle*, iv. 231, 5–7 Sept. 1758.
27 Kilburn (1997), 228; for the thanksgiving service, see

227–37.
28 Porteus (1789), 19.
29 Cf. Rogers (1988), 184–8, who insists the nation-wide celebrations attending the king's recovery were essentially 'an orchestrated show' (186).
30 Aspinall (1962–70), i. 410, George III to Lord Sydney (home secretary), 20 Apr. 1789; Brooke (1972), 343.
31 BL, Add. MS 6307, fos. 45–6; *The History of All Royal Thanksgiving*, 11. Concerns were raised in the House of Commons about the safety of the scaffolding in the Strand.
32 Holland (1789), 24.
33 Porteus (1789), 17, 18, 22.
34 Kilburn (1989), 244.
35 Holland (1789), 23.
36 Roberts (1834), ii. 145: More to her sister, 9 Mar. 1789.
37 Ehrman (1969), 665. Hannah More interestingly noted: 'The mob was very joyful, but rather too temperate in their acclamations which is said to have proceeded from a fear of overpowering the king's feelings': Roberts (1834), ii. 153.
38 *The Times*, 24 Apr. 1789. See also *Public Advertiser*, 27 Apr. 1789; Hibbert (1972), 102–3.
39 Bowen (1798), 13, 14, 16.
40 Cf. Colley (1992), 215–16, citing the *Morning Chronicle*'s view that the occasion was a 'Frenchified farce'.
41 *Thanksgiving Day*, 5.
42 Pretyman (1798), 16. Pretyman's 1797 Christmas Day sermon also refers to French beliefs and the widely shared perception that these were the 'end days': Suffolk RO, Ipswich, Pretyman Papers, HA119/562/275.
43 *The Times*, 2 Dec. 1797, advertised rooms on the route and royal anchor ribbons for ladies to wear.
44 BL, Add. MS 6307, fos. 48–51 for more ceremonial details.
45 Garlick and Macintyre (1978–98), ii. 939, 10 Dec. 1797.
46 Ashbourne (1898), 345–8, Pretyman to Mrs Eliza Pretyman, n.d., 348–50.
47 Pretyman (1798), 17.
48 For the explicit identification of Britain with Old Testament Israel in other sermons of 1797, see Macleod (1998), 143–4. Macleod contends that laying-up the flags in the cathedral was in direct imitation of King David, who had laid the spoils of his victories before the Lord in the Temple at Jerusalem.
49 *Form of Prayer and Thanksgiving* (1797), 30.
50 It was 58° F 'and mild as April the air': Garlick and Macintyre (1978–98), ii. 950.
51 Garlick and Macintyre (1978–98), ii. 950; Duffy (2000), 156–7, 188; Stevenson (1992), 218.
52 *Thanksgiving Day*, 6.
53 See Aston (2001).
54 *European Magazine*, 19 (1791), 333–4, 341.
55 Whinney (1988), 362–3 for details. See also Yarrington, (1988), 61–7.
56 For the wider context, see Bayly, (1989), 109–15.

33. *St Paul's and its parishes, 1750–1870*

1 Blomfield (1840), 8.
2 Best (1964), 296–347.
3 The peculiars also included two precincts: Hoxton and Portpool.
4 PP 1835: XXII (67).
5 GL, MS 25738/5, 19 Apr. 1772.
6 SPCL, CM, 27 Mar. 1833, 12 Mar. 1836.
7 SPCL, CM, 29 Apr. 1850.
8 GL, MS 25664/7, 3 July 1833.
9 SPCL, CM, 16 Mar. 1842.
10 SPCL, CM, 21, 24 Jan. 1835.
11 Hennessy (1898), li.
12 Hennessy (1898), 61–70; SPCL, CM, 24 Feb. 1840.
13 SPCL, CM, 9 May 1853, 13 Apr. 1854.
14 E.g., Barham (1870), i. 265–7, ii. 138.
15 GL, MS 25664/7, 1 Apr.–10 May 1847.
16 Knapp (1848), 29–31.
17 GL, MS 25664/3, 4 Nov. 1752; GL, MS CF box 108,

Dean and Chapter Visitation Returns 1790.
18 Bell (1980), 167.
19 Smith (1953), ii. 803–5.
20 Smith (1953), ii. 805–6.
21 Holland and Austin (1855), 344–5.
22 Smith (1953), ii. 798–9. See also Bell (1980), 174–5.
23 Heybridge, Barling, Belchamp St Paul, Tillingham, Wickham St Paul.
24 Eg. GL, MS CF box 77, Annual Bundle 1827.
25 Eg. GL, MS CF box 114, Annual Bundle 1835, CF box 108, Annual Bundle 1839.
26 GL, MS CF box 115, Annual Bundle 1831.
27 GL, MS CF box 112, Annual Bundle 1838.
28 GL, MS CF box 115, Annual Bundle 1831, CF box 112, Annual Bundle 1838.
29 GL, MS CF box 108, Dean and Chapter Visitation Returns.
30 E.g., GL, MS 25664/3, 14 Mar. 1752; MS 25664/5, 20 June 1787; MS 25664/6, 4 June 1806; MS 25664/7, 29 July 1828; CF box 108, Annual Bundle 1808; CF box 83, Annual Bundle 1828.
31 GL, MS CF box 108, Annual Bundles 1807, 1808; CF box 34, Annual Bundle 1833.
32 GL, MS CF box 115, Annual Bundle 1831.
33 Barham (1870), i. 264–5.
34 SPCL, CM, 9 July 1845.
35 GL, MS 25664/4, 4 and 27 July 1771. High and Good Easter were, however, separated again and re-endowed by the dean and chapter in 1867. SPCL, CM, 6 Nov. 1867.
36 SPCL, CM, 23 Mar. 1836, Smith (1953), ii. 587–8.
37 Smith (1837), 28–30.
38 Smith (1953), ii. 585–6.
39 SPCL, CM, 10 Nov. 1843; Smith (1953), ii. 817.
40 Smith (1953), ii. 798–9.
41 Burg (1995), 125.
42 1&2 William IV, c.45; an augmentation of £50 was also granted to Cambourne, which was annexed to the deanery. SPCL, CM, 27 Mar., 31 June, 30 Nov. 1833.
43 One further augmentation was granted in 1850 subject to the consent of the commissioners: SPCL, CM, 10 Dec. 1846, 8 Nov. 1850; PP 1864: XLIV (282), 7.
44 SPCL, CM, 6 May 1836, 19 Mar. 1834, 4 Dec. 1843, 12 Apr. 1849, 27 May 1850.
45 SPCL, CM, 25 Mar. 1840, 11 Dec. 1847, 22 Mar. 1842.
46 SPCL, CM, 15 July 1835–24 Feb. 1849.
47 GL, MS CF box 108, Dean and Chapter Visitation Returns.
48 SPCL, CM, 15 Feb., 2 Mar. 1837, 4 Dec. 1843, 24 Jan. 1848.
49 SPCL, CM, 14 Dec. 1857, 1 Feb., 5 July 1858, 16 Feb., 7 Nov. 1859.
50 SPCL, CM, 22 Mar. 1866, 9 Dec. 1868.
51 Dale was canon 1843–70, Champneys 1851–68.
52 Prestige (1955), 56–70.
53 SPCL, CM, 14 Dec. 1857.
54 SPCL, CM, 17 Nov. 1851, 31 Dec. 1856, 11 Feb. 1863, 17 July 1870.
55 23&24 Vict., c. 142.
56 SPCL, CM, 21 Jan. 1861, copy letter to commissioners 9 Nov. 1861.
57 St Benet, Gracechurch with St Leonard, Eastcheap was united with All Hallows, Lombard Street in 1864; St Nicholas, Cole Abbey with St Nicholas, Olave was united with St Mary, Somerset with St Mary, Mounthaw in 1866. PP 1870: LIV (25).
58 SPCL, CM, 8 Aug. 1865.
59 SPCL, CM, 7 July, 22 Oct., 17 Dec. 1869.
60 SPCL, CM, 30 Dec. 1870.
61 PP 1852–3: LXXXV [1361], LXXXVI [1362]; PP 1872: LXVI, pt i [676].
62 LPL, Randolph MSS 10, no. 83.
63 LPL, Osbaldeston MSS 6, no. 123; LPL, Randolph MSS 9, nos. 169–76; PRO, HO129, 19/1–6.
64 E.g., GL, MS CF box 108; GL, Dean and Chapter Visitation Returns, St Augustine w. St Faith; LPL, Osbaldeston MSS 6, no. 91; LPL, Blomfield MSS 72, no. 5.
65 GL, MS CF box 108, Dean and Chapter Visitation Returns.
66 LPL, Blomfield MSS 72, no. 33.

67 LPL, Randolph MSS 11, no. 34.
68 LPL, Randolph MSS 9, nos. 930–7.
69 LPL, Randolph MSS 9, nos. 405–12.
70 LPL, Randolph MSS 10, no. 102, 11, no. 42.
71 GL, MS CF box 108, Dean and Chapter Visitation Returns; LPL, Blomfield MSS 72, no. 133.
72 E.g., LPL, Randolph MSS 10, no. 127.
73 LPL, Blomfield MSS 72, no. 133.
74 GL, MS CF box 108, Dean and Chapter Visitation Returns.
75 LPL, Randolph MSS 10, no. 21; 12, no. 80.
76 Gregory (2000), 73.
77 BodL., MS Add. C 290.
78 Burg (1995), 6, 36.
79 GL, MS 25664/6, 3 July–17 Dec. 1813; Burg (1995), 45, 74, 78.
80 Barham (1870), ii. 138–9.
81 PRO, HO129, 140/1/12/12.
82 LPL, Randolph MSS 11, no. 31.
83 GL, MS CF box 108, Dean and Chapter Visitation Returns.
84 Dale (1852), 3; Lee (1955), 31–5.
85 Middleton (1812).
86 56 Geo. III, c. 39.
87 Lee (1955), 37–40, PP 1852–3: LXXVIII (530).
88 Lee (1955), 44–55.
89 Dale (1852), 4.
90 Dale (1852), 5.
91 Dale (1852), 46.
92 Lee (1955), 64–5.
93 31 & 32 Vict., c.160.
94 SPCL, CM, 24–27 Jan. 1835.
95 SPCL, CM, 10 Mar. 1846; Dale (1852) 18.
96 SPCL, CM, 27 Mar. 1862.
97 Lee (1955), 56; Dale (1852), 14, 40.
98 PRO, HO129; Mather (1985), *passim*; Barrie-Curien (1993b).
99 PRO, HO129, 19/1/6, 19/2/16, 9/1–6.
100 LPL, Blomfield MSS 42, fo. 202; 43, fo. 122.

34. National Occasions at St Paul's since 1800

1 Matthews (1957), 311.
2 Wolffe (2000), 32–3.
3 *The Times*, 26 Oct. 1809.
4 Virger Green's diary, quoted by Sinclair (1909), 366.
5 Matthews (1946), 67.
6 There were numerous contemporary published accounts: see e.g. Duncan (1806); *Fairburn's Edition* (1806).
7 PRO, WORK 6/362/2, letter from Dean Pretyman, 11 Dec. 1805.
8 *An Official and Circumstantial Detail* (1806), 23.
9 Milman (1868), 485. For the wider context of the service, see Jenks (2000), where it is viewed as an assertion of Anglican religious hegemony in an environment of contested national identity.
10 *The Times*, 8 July 1814.
11 SPCL, Van Mildert to Lord Sidmouth, 19 Nov. 1820.
12 SPCL, Liverpool to Van Mildert, 21 Nov. 1820.
13 SPCL, Van Mildert to Manners Sutton, 26 Nov. 1821; *The Times*, 9 Dec. 1821.
14 *The Times*, 30 Nov. 1821.
15 Wolffe (2000), 291.
16 Wolffe (2000), 32–44.
17 Lines 47–50.
18 Sinclair (1909), 316.
19 Kuhn (1996), 38–42.
20 PRO, LC 2/91/4, Knollys to Ponsonby, 7 Feb. 1872; SPCL, Prince of Wales Thanksgiving Volume, printed list of seat distribution.
21 PRO, LC 2/91/4–8, *passim*, especially LC 2/91/5, list of nonconformist bodies; LC2/91/6, Dr Stevenson 20 Feb. 1872, Primitive Methodist Connexion, 24 Feb. 1872; LC 2/91/7, memorandum of conversation with Mr G. Potter, 16 Feb. 1872.
22 PRO, LC 2/91/5, Manning 11 Feb., Adler 13 Feb.
23 *Ceremonial: Thanksgiving at St Paul's Cathedral, 27 February 1872*, 11.
24 Kuhn (1996), 46–7.
25 Kuhn (1996), 45; SPCL, Prince of Wales Thanksgiving Volume, form of service.
26 Hutton (1912), 182.
27 SPCL, Prince of Wales Thanksgiving Volume, circulars of 27 Feb., 4 March 1872.
28 Buckle (1926), ii. 195.
29 Sinclair (1909), 327, 331, 341–2, 347.
30 Sinclair (1909), 359.
31 For the planning process, see PRO, LC 2/137, esp. notes of meetings chaired by the prince of Wales, 2, 27 Feb. 1897.
32 Sinclair (1909), 359–60; *A Form of Service to the Used at St Paul's Cathedral on the Occasion of the Royal Progress of Her Majesty the Queen, June 22 1897*; GL, FO Pam 8812, Extracts from the diary of F. S. Girdlestone, 22 June 1897. The bishop of London (Mandell Creighton) insisted, however, that the service was 'merely a beautiful and appropriate incident' in the queen's procession, and not 'a complete or adequate expression of religious feeling' (*The Times*, 21 April 1897).
33 Sinclair (1909), 368–9.
34 SPCL, Newbolt scrapbooks, iv. 104–5, v. 66, vi. 5–6.
35 *Order for Special Service to be Used at St Paul's Cathedral on Sunday, October 26th 1902, in Thanksgiving for the Recovery from Sickness of His Majesty King Edward VII.*
36 SPCL, Newbolt scrapbooks, vii. 26, 51, 93, viii. 38, 130.
37 *A Form of Prayer to be Used at a Memorial Service on Tuesday December 19 [1899] at 3 pm for those who have Fallen in the War; A Form of Prayer to be used at a Solemn Service of Humble Supplication to Almighty God that He would Vouchsafe to Prosper Our Arms in South Africa, on Friday December 29th [1899] at 10.30 am; Directions to those who take part in the Day and Night Watch of Intercession to be kept in St Paul's Cathedral from 8 am Dec 16th to 8 am Dec 17th 1914.*
38 Winnington-Ingram (1915).
39 SPCL, Newbolt scrapbooks, x. 45–8.
40 *The Times*, 14 June 1916.
41 Newbolt [1920], 277.
42 Newbolt [1920], 278.
43 SPCL, Newbolt scrapbooks, xi. 88–94.
44 Newbolt [1920], 277.
45 SPCL, Newbolt scrapbooks, xv. 87–106.
46 PRO, WORK 21/90; SPCL, George V silver-jubilee envelope.
47 PRO, WORK 21/90.
48 *Thanksgiving Service in Commemoration of the Twenty-Fifth Anniversary of the King's Accession to the Throne, on Monday, May 6th 1935 at 11.30 a.m.*
49 *Official Programme of the Jubilee Procession* (1935), 18.
50 Matthews (1946), 50–1.
51 PRO, HO 186/1223.
52 Quoted Matthews (1946), 67.
53 *In Honour of 28,000 American Dead: Service of Commemoration and of Dedication in St Paul's Cathedral July 4 1951*; Matthews (1957), 323. Illness prevented the king from attending, but the queen was present.
54 *Dedication of the American Memorial Chapel in the Presence of Her Majesty the Queen and the Vice President of the United States 26 November 1958*; PRO, WO32/17344.
55 SPCL, Churchill box, duke of Norfolk to Matthews, 19 May 1959; *The Times*, 30 Jan., 1 Feb. 1965.
56 Matthews had hoped Churchill would be buried in St Paul's in order that 'the three great war leaders of our modern history should be together' (SPCL, Churchill box, Matthews to H. Macmillan, 25 Mar. 1957).
57 SPCL, Churchill box, Sir George Bellew to Matthews, 24 Nov. 1958; Norfolk to Matthews, 29 Jan. 1959.
58 SPCL, Churchill box, order of service.
59 *The Times*, 8 June 1977; *A Form of Prayer and Thanksgiving to Almighty God Commemorating the Blessings Granted to the Queen's Most Excellent Majesty during the Twenty Five Years of Her Majesty's Reign, 7 June 1977 at 11.30.*
60 *The Times*, 26 July 1980, 29 July 1981.
61 Webster (2002), 91–101; SPCL, typescript account by Webster (in newspaper cuttings book).
62 *The Times*, 27 July 1982.
63 SPCL, typescript account by Webster (in newspaper cuttings book).
64 *The Times*, 12 July 2000.
65 *The Queen's Golden Jubilee: Ceremonial: A Thanksgiving Service at St. Paul's Cathedral at 11.30 am Tuesday 4th June 2002; A Service of Thanksgiving and Celebration on the Occasion of the Golden Jubilee of Her Majesty The Queen, St Paul's Cathedral Tuesday 4th June 2002.*

35. *Music, 1660–1800*

1 Boyer (1999), iii. 384, 394.
2 Boyer (1999), iii. 422–3, 399–400, 412–13; NG, iii. 594–5, s.n. Bing; NG, xiii. 23–4, s.n. Jewett.
3 Boyer (1999), iii. 401; NG, iv, 526–7, s.n. Bryne.
4 Furnivall (1908), 202.
5 Dugdale (1818), 119.
6 NG, vi. 57, s.n. Clifford.
7 The normal post-Restoration practice at morning prayer was to chant the *Venite* like a psalm. Musical settings of the holy communion usually contained only the responses to the Commandments (often called *Kyrie*) and the Creed; a *Sanctus* was frequently sung as an introit, the concluding *Gloria in excelsis deo* rarely sung at all. There was, of course, no place for hymns (in the modern sense) or metrical psalms in the official liturgy.
8 BL, Add MS 34695; Cox (1989), ii. 160–3.
9 Wilson (1996), 60–70.
10 Boyer (1991), 197–213; Boyer (1999), ii. 220–33.
11 Latham and Matthews (1997–83), v, 67.
12 Boyer (1999), i. 83.
13 WS XIII, 22–3, 46–9.
14 Robinson (1935), 109.
15 Boyer (1999), iii. 387–90; NG, x, 192, s.n. Gostling.
16 SPCL, 42B; Tenor (1/A1) and Countertenor (Alto 2/A1).
17 GL, MS 25707/1, 9; Spink (1995), 298.
18 WS XIV, 23, 25.
19 Boyer (1999), iii. 391; NG, xxvii. 447–8, s.n. Wise.
20 NG, xxv, 931–2, s.n. Turner; NG, iii. 6, 67, s.n., Blackwell.
21 NG, iii. 718–27, s.n. Blow.
22 NG, xi. 770, s.n. Howell; NG, viii. 114–15, s.n. Elford; NG, ix, 223, s.n. Freeman.
23 NG, v, 916–8, s.n. Clarke.
24 SPCL, 42B; Countertenor (Alto 2/A2), Tenor (2/A2), Bass (2/A2) and Bass (1/A2); see Ford (1984), 868–79, Boyer (1999), ii. 293–304, Spink (1995), 301.
25 WS XV. 55.
26 Niland (1996) 93; this paragraph is based on 91–8; also Plumley and Niland (2001), 20–37.
27 Cooper (1996), no. 29, see also p. 94.
28 The building was said to be 'the noblest for Eccho and Sound...in Europe' (Plumley and Niland [2001], 200), an observation probably made by Harris in the course of denigrating Smith's instrument.
29 Plumley and Niland (2001), Appendix C, 198–200.
30 See entries in Highfill, et al. (1973–83), also Thomas Baildon, David Cheriton, John Chelsum, Ralph Cowper [Cooper], Israel Gore, etc.
31 At Westminster Abbey in 1748 'Minor Canons take it by turns either themselves or by Deputies' (Pine (1953), 155); in 1796, individual members of the choir had their 'months of waiting' (Pine (1953), 171). There was a 'little door...by which they [choir members also in the Chapel Royal] could creep out unobserved' before the sermon (Bridge (1918), 73–4). This was in 1835, but probably a well-established practice. Gentlemen of the Chapel also had their 'months of waiting', and deputies were allowed with approval (Ashbee and Harley (2000), i. 305–7). It may just have been possible for members of the St Paul's choir to attend the 9.45 a.m. service in the cathedral and get to St James's Palace, almost two miles away, in time for the 11 a.m. service – much easier in the afternoon with 3.15 p.m. and 5 p.m. services, even with a longer anthem (Ashbee and

Harley (2000) ii. 54). About 1830, when times seem to have been more accomodating, E. J. Hopkins, a chorister at both institutions, apparently sang at the 9.45 am service at St Paul's, at noon in the Chapel Royal, then at 3.15 p.m. at St Paul's and 5.30 p.m. at the Chapel (Bumpus (1908), 421). Thomas Attwood, on the other hand, who was organist at both places, used to lunch at the Athenaeum after Sunday morning service at the chapel, and proceed to St Paul's for the afternoon service (Bumpus (1908), 419).

32 Accounts from September 1732 onwards are in SPCL. They show receipts for each month (daily except Sundays) and give attendances (down to half-days) with pro-rata dividends. It is interesting to note that in 1747–8 (for example) Greene, the organist, averaged thirteen and a half out of fourteen services a week, while the sub-dean and senior and junior cardinals averaged just over nine. Apart from Green and Savage (the almoner), vicars alternated monthly, two by two; Cheriton and Wass taking the even-numbered months, Rowe and Baildon the odd. Wass averaged more than twelve services a week, Rowe fewer than nine. Whether these figures were achieved using deputies cannot be said.

33 Quarterly payments for both groups are in GL, MS 25650/7 for the period 1735–65.

34 Details of rental income, etc., for minor canons in 1748–9, see GL, MS 25746, fos. 179v–184v, and for vicars in SPCL, VCR Box 3, 162–70.

35 Clarke-Whitfield [1805], 2 (preface).

36 R[ichard] C[lark], a vicar writing *c*.1832 but recalling twenty years earlier (SPCL, VCR Box 6/14). Attendance figures from the cupola accounts (SPCL, GD) confirm how reliant the choir was on minor canons, numerically at least.

37 *NG*, xi. 282–3, s.n. Hayes.

38 Bumpus (1891), 97.

39 Page (1800), ii. 168. For concert activities of minor canons (John Abbott, Thomas Baker, Thomas and/or Weldon Champneys, William Clarke, Hugh Cox, William Fitzherbert, Henry Fly, John Gibbons, William Hayes, John Horner, Edward Lloyd, Benjamin Mence, John Moore, etc.), see Highfill, et al. (1973–83). Several are listed among performers in the Handel commemoration of 1784 (Burney (1785), 17–21).

40 For the Champneys family, *NG*, v, 462–3; also Burrows (1981), Appendix 6, 166; *NG*, iii. 3, s.n. Bayly.

41 See section on the choristers in Dawe (1983), 5–7; also Garrett (1974a).

42 Simpson (1897b), 172; Bumpus (1891), 17, 100.

43 Bumpus (1891), 86.

44 This and the next two quotations are from Farmer (1936), 195.

45 Glasgow University Library, MS Euing R.d.23 (v–x); see Cudworth (1962), 754–6, 834–5.

46 Hawkins (1875), 884, also Grove, 2.

47 Hawkins (1875), 887, 889; Craufurd (1955–6), 37.

48 Highfill, et al. (1973–83), xiii. 218, ii. 20.

49 There were apparently eight boys boarding with the almoner from about 1760 onwards (Simpson (1897b), 172), though St Paul's provided ten boys for the Handel commemoration in 1784 (Burney (1785), 19).

50 *NG*, xiii. 605–6, s.n. King; *NG*, x, 361–5, s.n. Greene.

51 Hawkins (1875), 859; *NG*, iv, 355, s.n. Brind.

52 GL, MSS 25650/4 and 25650/6 under respective years.

53 There is also an orchestral *Te Deum* and *Jubilate*, another full setting of the *Te Deum* and a *Sanctus* 'Performed before the Bishops and the rest of the Clergy when they meet at St Paul's to choose a Prolocutor for the Convocation'.

54 This and the previous remark from Hawkins (1875), 798.

55 GL, MS 25650/6.

56 Plumley and Niland (2001), 37.

57 Burney (1785), ii. 346.

58 Johnstone (1966).

59 Hawkins (1875), 859.

60 Deutsch (1955), 115, emended in Johnstone (1967), 52–3.

61 CUL, MS Add. 3135 (hand of the Hon. Edward

Finch), also BodL, Tenbury MS 1027 with same comment.

62 SPCL, 42C; vol. 1 of a set of 4.

63 Johnstone (1966).

64 Johnstone (1975).

65 *NG*, iv, 152–62, s.n. Boyce.

66 *NG*, xiii. 194–5, s.n. Jones.

67 *The English Musical Gazette* (1 January 1819). In view of Burney's grudging remarks quoted below he may also have been responsible for this.

68 Rees (1819), xix, sig. ZZ4ᵛ.

69 SPCL 42B, Part 1 two vols, Part 2 one vol.

70 The year is uncertain; charity services were held on 9 June 1791 and 14 June 1792; see *A Sermon preached* …

71 Landon (1976), iii. 173.

72 For dates of vicars and almoners see SPCL, VCR Box 3 (front and rear fly leaves).

73 Rees (1819), xxxii, sig. 3Yᵛ.

74 Farmer (1936), 194, includes a list of anthems; see also *NG*, xxii. 337–8.

75 The main source is Glasgow University Library, MS Euing R.d.23, in the hand of R. J. S. Stevens.

76 *NG*, xi. 799, s.n. Hudson.

77 SPCL, R, Box 3; *NG*, iii. 186–7, s.n. Bellamy.

78 Highfill, et al. (1973–93), ii. 20–1.

79 *NG*, ii. 912–13, s.n. Battishill.

80 Long (1972), 310–11.

81 Trend (1932), 270.

82 *NG*, ii. 150–2, s.n. Attwood.

83 *NG*, xviii. 896, s.n. Page.

36. *Orchestras in the new cathedral*

1 BL, Harley MS 7342, fo. 12v.

2 Hogwood (1983).

3 Burrows (1981), ch. 2 and 4.

4 Quoted from the notebook of Marmaduke Alford, Yeoman of the Vestry to the Chapel Royal: Burrows (1981) i. 22; Ashbee and Harley (2000), ii. 287.

5 Husk (1857), ch. 2.

6 Luttrell (1857), vi. 307 (20 November 1697).

7 An annotation on a copy of the anthem in BL, Add. MS 31445 establishes its association of the anthem with the opening of St Paul's Cathedral, and a further anthem by Blow, without orchestral accompaniment, is attributed to the Peace of Ryswick in BL, Add. MS 31444: it seems that a single service combined both functions, and possibly both of Blow's anthems were performed then.

8 Luttrell (1857), v. 232.

9 For full details of the music performed at the thanksgivings, see Burrows (1981), i. 43–8.

10 Luttrell (1857), vi. 122–3.

11 Rather curiously, the anthems that were specially composed for the thanksgivings were accompanied only by the organ, without orchestra.

12 The engraving has the title 'A Prospect of the Choir of the Cathedral Church of St Paul on the General Thanksgiving the 31st of December 1706. Her Majesty and both Houses of Parliament present'. The copy in the collection of the Corporation of London at Guildhall Library has been coloured in. See also pp. 228, 321. Trevitt's picture may have been based on sketches taken at the previous royal thanksgiving service in June 1706: this would explain the inclusion of Prince George of Denmark in the picture. The picture is interesting because it shows singers and players in what appears to be a haphazard arrangement; instruments shown include a lute and a theorbo and apparently two oboes, in addition to the singers and expected string instruments.

13 Queen Anne almost certainly intended to attend this thanksgiving, but was prevented by doing so by the precarious state of her health. The other estates, however, went to St Paul's, and the queen was represented in the street procession by her coach.

14 Burrows (1981), i. 191–3.

15 See also Burrows (1981), i. 193, n. 16.

16 The sub-dean of the Chapel Royal claimed that St Paul's was the 'King's Chapell upon this Occasion', Ashbee and Harley (2000), i. 139.

---

17 Burrows (1981), i. 39 and n. 78.

18 Burrows (1981), ii. appendix four.

37. *Music, 1800–2002*

1 Plumley and Niland (2001), 64.

2 Bumpus (1891), 185.

3 Plumley and Niland (2001), 53.

4 Sydney Smith, quoted in Prestige (1955), 20.

5 Bevan and Stainer (1882), 76.

6 Bumpus (1891), 120 ff.

7 Prestige (1955), 9–10.

8 Bumpus (1891), 101.

9 Bumpus (1891), 104.

10 e.g. Prestige (1955), 148–9; Scott (1972), 25–6.

11 *The Musical Standard*, 14 Jan. 1871, 16–17.

12 SPCL, CM, 27 April 1871.

13 This was sung complete on Sundays from Easter 1873 and on all saints' days from 1876.

14 The building is now used by the Youth Hostels Association.

15 Goss occupied one place, Stainer another, and two were ill, represented by 'permanent deputies'.

16 A large choir of children was accommodated under the dome on temporary stands, whose erection and subsequent dismantling disrupted the cathedral for the whole of June each year. After 1873 chapter banned the temporary structures, and the service faded out altogether after 1877: Prestige (1955), 103–4.

17 The recorded attendance at some of these occasions defies belief; e.g. 10,000 at Nelson's funeral, 8,000 at the first performance of *St Paul*.

18 *The Guardian*, 2 April 1884.

19 Simpson (1899), 67 ff.

20 Inge (1949), 39.

21 SPCL, CM, 2 July and 24 September 1921.

22 Plumley and Niland (2001), 116 ff.

23 Matthews (1957), 302–3.

24 He was knighted in 1943 and died in 1949.

25 Hopkins, Thomas Armstrong and Harold Darke.

26 Organist of Truro Cathedral 1926–9; New College, Oxford 1929–33; Durham Cathedral 1933–6.

27 *English Church Music*, 10.4 (October 1940), 88 (editorial).

28 Plumley and Niland (2001), 150 ff.

29 Composed 1951, published (Novello) 1954, first sung on 19 October 1955.

30 This never happened.

31 SPCL, CM, 13 May 1971.

32 Usually the *St Matthew Passion*, though the *St John* replaced it from 1976 to 1993.

33 Plumley and Niland (2001), 163 ff.

34 SPCL, CM, 3 and 16 July, 3 and 24 September 1980: complaints regarding the organization and financial accounts of that year's tour of America and Canada.

35 SPCL, CM, 13 Jan. 1981.

36 Characteristically, he celebrated his departure by choosing different versions of 'There is no rose' to be sung every day of his last week.

37 In 2002, for example, there were televised broadcasts of a memorial service for the Queen Mother and the thanksgiving for the Golden Jubilee of HM the Queen.

38. *The library and archives to 1897*

This chapter has benefited greatly from the comments and corrections of Christopher Brooke, Derek Keene and Joseph Wisdom; help on specific points has been given by Helen Carron (Sancroft's Library), Susan Kelly (pre-Conquest material), Richard Palmer (Sion College), Julian Pooley (Pridden family) and Christopher Wilson (architecture)

1 Gibbs (1939), no. 273; Neininger (1999), no. 24.

2 Editions forthcoming in Ramsay and Willoughby (2004).

3 AUL, MSS 9, 4 and 5, respectively; dates etc. from the cards for Ker (1964, 1987) in BodL.

4 Southern (1958), 202–3.

5 Yeo (1986), 31; Gibbs (1939), no. 273; Neininger

(1999), no. 24. In the 1220s the bishop's copies of agreements in which he had acted as arbiter were to be kept in the treasury: Johnson (2003), xcvii.

6   Kelly (2004).

7   Gibbs (1939), x, 5 (no. J.10), 280; Kelly (2004), nos. 12, 16, 21, 26 and 29; see also pp. 7, 14.

8   GL, MS 25504 (formerly WD4).

9   Johnson (2003), no. 38.

10   Stubbs (1876), i. ix–c, and ii. vii–lx; Greenway (1966).

11   Mentioned in 1295; there was also a psalter prefixed by a list of ornaments given by Diceto: Ker (1985), 229, 232.

12   BodL, MS Rawl. B. 372, fos. 3–4; printed in Hale (1858), 109–17; the binding of *Liber C* survives as the cover of GL, MS 25502. Both registers were described in 1447 in GL, MS 25511.

13   Ramsay and Willoughby (2004). A catalogue of Diceto's books was on the last leaf of *Liber B* (now lost): BL, MS Harl. 6956, fos. 82v–85v.

14   Gilbert de Bruera, (dated) 1344 (onwards); John de Appleby, 1383; Thomas Stow and Thomas More, 1400 and 1405; Thomas Lisieux, 1447; Thomas Winterborne, 1475; Robert Sherborn and John Colet, undated; and John Colet, 1519. These were sent to Dr Edward Layfield, prebendary, in 1659: BL, MS Lansd. 364, fo. 136; two are also cited, *c.*1610–30(?), in GL, MS 25784, pp. 4 (Gilbert de Bruera), 18 (Sherborn and Colet). No later mention of any has been found, and they must be presumed lost. A volume of cathedral statutes, CUL, MS Ee.5.21, with annotation by Dean Sherborn, is a possible survivor from the deanery archive, as may be GL, MS 25511.

15   Simpson (1873), 13, 133; holders of the office included William Mulso, canon of Windsor and clerk of the works to Edward III (Evans (1948), 129).

16   GL, MS 25501, discussed in Gibbs (1939), xi–xiv, xl–xli.

17   Simpson (1873), 9–176 (Baldock's statutes, as augmented by Lisieux).

18   GL, MS 25509, fos. 5v–8v; the inventory is preceded by lists of rents and pensions, written apparently at the same time. Ker (1985), 211–13 argues that the inventory was not made *de novo* but was 'drawn up by several different persons or was in part based on an older and now lost inventory'.

19   Pfaff (1998), 19. His statutes are praised by Edwards (1967), 25.

20   Gibbs (1939), xviii–xix; Brooke (1950–2), 120; and Brooke and Keir (1975), 339–40.

21   GL, MSS 25503, fos. 1–13v, and 25516, fos. 9v–22r, and BodL, MS Ashmole 845, fos. 172–187v; Ramsay and Willoughby (2004).

22   GL, MSS 25514, fo. 36, and 25516, fo. 40v; for Baldock's misreading, see Gibbs (1939), xxx n. 1, and Kelly (2004). Late thirteenth-century endorsements on cathedral documents are noted by Yeo (1986), 37.

23   Printed by Leland (1770), i. 353–7; discussed by Brooke (1956), 235–6.

24   Summarily listed in Emden (1957–9), iii. 2147–9; Ramsay and Willoughby (2004).

25   The cathedral's copy of Baldock's chronicle was lost in the sixteenth or seventeenth century, but one from Bury St Edmunds abbey survives as BodL, MS Lat. hist. d. 4: Gransden (1974), 522–3.

26   McDonnell (1959), 16–24; Ramsay and Willoughby (2004).

27   Leach (1910), 198–9.

28   GL, MS 25169; Milman (1868), 152–3, 516–18.

29   BL, Cotton Charter xxi. 24; Madden and W[ay] (1855), 173–7.

30   GL, MSS 25520 (*Statuta Minora*), fos. 59–64v, and 25508 (*Liber Statutorum T*), fos. 20rv–23r.

31   In *Liber D* (now lost), fos. 191–c.202, according to GL, MS 25511, fo. 101.

32   Brooke (1957), 89–91.

33   Davies (1975–7), 7.

34   GL, MS 25513 (formerly WD13).

35   More's register is cited by Dugdale: (1818), 391.

36   Dean Lisieux indexed *Liber AB* in GL, MS 25511, fos. 135–6.

37   Emden (1957–9), ii. 1039–40; Ramsay and

Willoughby (2004).

38   BodL, MS Ashmole 801, fos. 50–73v: 24 leaves (only), once foliated lviij–lxxxj; cf. Davis (1958), no. 599.

39   LPL, Register of Archbishop Stafford, fos. 170–171v.

40   PRO, PROB 11/4, fos. 56v–57v.

41   Somerville (1953), 389–90, 460; GL, MS 25121/2073

42   Simpson (1871), 177, 196, and Simpson (1874), 249, for the minor canons' library regulations, as given in their statutes, revised *c.*1521.

43   Hearne (1722), xci.

44   Seventy-eight clergy signed the cathedral's acknowledgement of Henry VIII's supremacy in 1534: Wharton (1695), 286–92 cf. above, p.44. For the rent collectors: Kennedy (1987).

45   Crawford (1970–3), 588.

46   Catto and Evans (1992), 749–50.

47   Dugdale (1658), 132.

48   Hearne (1722), 169–204.

49   LPL, Register of Archbishops Stafford and Kempe, fos. 257v–258r, at 258r; none of these books appears in the catalogues of 1458 or later.

50   BL, Cotton ch. xiii.11; Ramsay and Willoughby (2004). It is dated 25 March '1458', and arguably should therefore be taken to be of 25 March 1459 in modern reckoning, but that would imply excessive delay in the start of the library's operation.

51   Clark (1899), 57–8. The catalogue has thirty-three volumes in P, but omits the headings Q and R, doubtless by mistake; counting E, Q and R, there would have been twenty presses.

52   This was simply one of a number of texts about Alexander the Great that were then current: Weiss (1967), 83 n. 1.

53   Worcestre's notes in BL, MS Sloane 4, fo. 56, transcribed *extra librum medicine magistri Johannis Somerset doctoris physice in quodam folio in principio libri Gydonis cirurgi remanente in librario Sancti Pauli.*

54   AUL, MSS 137 and 241; BodL, MS James 23, p. 32.

55   Graunt's gift can be reconstructed from the catalogue of 1486 (Ramsay and Willoughby [2004]) and from inscriptions in AUL, MSS 10, 219, 240 and 244. He also gave books to Canterbury College, Oxford, and, especially, to Syon Abbey: de Hamel (1991), 60–1.

56   Ramsay and Willoughby (2004).

57   Lisieux's inventory survives in two versions: GL, MSS 25511 and 25511A. The latter (paper) served as a draft for part of 25511 (parchment). 25511's treatment of obits is fuller and it alone has the account of the registers, but 25511A seems to have served as the working copy down to at least the 1530s (cf. fo. 48v). They remain unpublished, apart from the account of the registers: Hale (1858), xvi–xvii; Holtzmann (1930–52), i. 178–80.

58   GL, MS 25508 (*Liber Statutorum T*), fo. 38; another version in CUL, MS Ee. 5. 21, fo. 1v. Lisieux also had copies made of the cathedral statutes, prefixed by calendars: GL, MS 25501, CUL, MS Ee. 5. 21. The obits in the latter, 1319–1424 (supplementary to those in the *Statuta Minora*), were printed by Milman (1868), 515.

59   Oxford, Queen's College, MS 54, fo. 426v; cf. also fo. 444. 'Ardeleye' is Ardeley (Herts.).

60   See above, n. 14, and see Steer (1960).

61   GL, MS 25187. The identification of his hand is based upon comparison with Jayne (1963), 135–7 and plates I–V.

62   BodL, MS Tanner 221 (printed in Simpson (1873), 435–52); cf. Trapp (1990), §XI, 212.

63   Simpson (1890), 153, 161, citing the now-lost Jackson MS of Colet's compilation; see Trapp [1990], §XI, 212.

64   Simpson (1873), 237–48; cf. xlv–xlvii.

65   Allen (1914), 141.

66   The books are identifiable from the list of survivors from the Great Fire: see p. 419.

67   See Simpson (1880), 1–8, 175–7.

68   See GL catalogue, Kitching (1980), xxviii–xxx, and above, pp. 164–6.

69   Among the sacrist's duties, as specified in BL, MS Lansd. 364, fo. 149, were 'to look to & Conserve the Records & Evidences Reliques Jewells Vestments Plate & all ornaments what soever' of St Paul's, for

which purpose he had 'the Rome within the Chapter house & the other beneath with the Lavatory &c.'; undated, but early seventeenth-century.

70   GL, MS 25184; Dugdale (1818), 401. In 1561 Bishop Grindal directed that an inventory be made and that they be inspected annually: GL, MS 9537 (2), fo. 17r–v.

71   Frere and Kennedy (1910), i. 135, ii. 136.

72   GL, MS 25532, fos. 77v, 81v and 85v; MSS 25637/2 (1556–7), §Feoda & Vadia; 25498 (1570–84), fos. 35, 51, 108 etc.; 25638 (1592–4), §Feoda, in successive years. Seventeenth-century library keepers were paid £4 p.a.

73   Bale (1549), fo. G2 recto. Over two dozen works by medieval British authors were located at St Paul's by Bale and used for his *Index Britanniae Scriptorum*: Poole and Bateson (1902), 577.

74   Graham and Watson (1995), 25.

75   Now BL, Add. MS 70984; Parry (1989), 378.

76   LPL, MS 8.

77   Cambridge, Corpus Christi College, MS 383.

78   MSS 1–6, 8–10, 137, 205, 219, 240–1 and 244.

79   Possibilities are the chronicles of Ralph de Diceto in BL, Cotton MS Claudius E. iii. and the *Compendium morale* of Roger of Waltham in Vespasian B. xxi.

80   Formerly British Museum, Cotton Charter xvi. 73, it was transferred in 1916 to the Museum's Dept. of British & Medieval Antiquities (reg. no. 1916, 11–6, 1); discussed in Simpson (1882), 278–90. In the fifteenth century it was believed to have been used for the vicars of churches belonging to St Paul's – as was recorded on a parchment label damaged by fire in 1731, but earlier transcribed by Cotton's librarian: BodL, MS James 18 (*SC* 3855), fo. 100a.

81   Atkins and Ker (1944), 1–3.

82   GL, MS CF box 56; Ramsay and Willoughby (2004).

83   Kingsford (1908), i. 328.

84   Lehmberg (1996), 251, citing GL, MS 25630/7 (Chapter Acts, 1621–31), fo. 63.

85   Cf. BL, MS Lansdowne 364, fo. 2. Roper was succeeded as library-keeper by Robert Christmas, who received the keeper's salary of £4 p.a. from 1628–9 until 1641–2; in 1628–9 Roper was acting as auditor and rent collector: GL, MSS 25499, fos. 98 (1625–6), 137v (1628–9), 152v (1629–30), etc., *s.v.* §Feoda & Vadia; and 25677 (1641–2, etc.), §Feoda.

86   Selden (1618), 59.

87   Keynes (1993); printed in Kelly (2004).

88   LPL, MS 2018; Barratt (1950–1), 138, 257 (no. 15), 270 (no. 384) and 272 (no. 464).

89   GL, MS 9537(9), fo. 16v: direction that any writings or muniments which have been borrowed out of the treasury house be returned before 8 October next.

90   Pearce (1913), 245.

91   BodL, MS Rawl.D.888, fos. 2–5v, and LPL, Arc. L40.2/E5(2), last six folios.

92   Barwick, ed. (1903), 81. Barwick's love of books is apparent from his will (1664), printed by Thompson (1965) 245–9.

93   Hamper (1827), 26–7.

94   Lost items known to Dugdale include a collection of *exhibita* to Cardinal Wolsey, printed 'ex cartaceo Registro' in Dugdale (1818), 360–7, and reprinted with revisions in Simpson (1873), 217–48.

95   Hamper (1827), 27.

96   The presence of a St Paul's archival pressmark is the overlooked testimony of their medieval ownership.

97   E.g., BL, Cotton ch. v. 2 and 12 (Elsing Spital), v. 6 (St Helen's Bishopsgate) and xi. 6 and 8 (Markyate Priory).

98   BL, Cotton ch. xiii. 11 and 24.

99   Yeo (1986), 33; Owen (1967–8), 123–9.

100   Dugdale (1818), xxx.

101   GL, MS 25738 (1), p. 19.

102   Hamper (1827), 117–18.

103   GL, MS 25738 (1), p. 25.

104   Edwards (1859), ii. 85; some books may remain among the Sion College collection at LPL.

105   Bell (1923), 139.

106   BodL, MS Rawl. B. 372 (*S.C.* 11709), fo. 24.

107 GL, MS 25650.

108 GL, MS 25643; cf. GL, MSS 25677 and 25641–2.

109 For the loss of records in the Great Fire, see also Yeo (1986), 33–4.

110 GL, MS 25643/2; see fo. 28v for Sancroft's comparison of sums 'agreable to ye old Audit-Books, & modern Pay-Books too', and cf. fo. 31: 'These Dues to ye Officers of ye Church set down in ye 2 former Accounts under several Heads are All thus digested into ye Method of one Pay-Book; wherein every one may see presently, what his Dues are.'

111 GL, MS 25643/2, fo. 39.

112 Yeo (1986), 34.

113 Warner (1926), 82.

114 GL, MS 25746, fos. 37v, 38.

115 Plume (1675), preface, xix.

116 WS XIII, 5, citing Hooke's diary.

117 A letter congratulating Sancroft in 1669 on his purchase of Dr James Windet's library (Crossley and Christie (1847–86), ii. pt 2, 300) appears to refer to a purchase for his own library.

118 SPCL, in Case B.13; not listed in Read (1970), (1978).

119 GL, MS 25622/2, 10 and 13 Nov. 1707; printed, with some misreadings, in WS XVI, 104–5. The Gery catalogue is untraced, unless it is to be identified with one containing publications as late as 1705 that is bound up with that of *c*.1692 (see n. 119).

120 These and other details are provided in the Library Benefactors Book (SPCL, 37.B.10). Tenison's reimbursement of the balance actually set him back £256 17s.: see Le Neve (1720), pt. 1, 258 (Commissioners' receipt, 24 Dec. 1708).

121 Simpson (1896), from accounts in LPL, MS 670.

122 GL, MS 25622/2 (20 Sept. 1710); printed WS xvi. 110.

123 Doble et al. (1884–1918), i. 44. Wanley's notes on early printed Bibles: CUL, MS Mm.1.50; that he continued to collect biblical texts is apparent from his correspondence with Thomas Baker of Cambridge: Korsten (1985), 504. Baker transcribed into his own copy (now CUL, Adv.b.52.1) of Maunsell (1595), pt 2, 399–408, 'A Catalogue of some of the most valuable Old English Bibles, in My Lord Harley's Library, taken from the Catalogue drawn up by my Learned Friend Mr H. Wanley, with his Observations upon them.'

124 GL, in MS CF box 57.

125 Pollard and Redgrave (1986–91), no. 2824; most recently described in Arblaster et al. (2002), 148–9, but most fully in Simpson (1893), 18–19.

126 Heyworth (1989), 258–62, no. 119, dated 16 Sept. 1710.

127 Reading (1724), 38–9; Partridge (1938), 33–4.

128 GL, MS 25622/2, 27 July 1708; printed with some misreadings in WS XVI, 106. These books were ordered by the Commissioners for Rebuilding to be catalogued, that and the Gery catalogue to be compared, the better duplicates to be kept and have Beveridge's name added, and the less good duplicates disposed of and the proceeds applied to purchasing more books.

129 Cf. Carpenter (1956), 369. According to the Library Benefactors Book (SPCL, 37.B.10, where all the bequest is listed), St Paul's received its share on 11 July 1715. For Compton's book bequests (dated 31 Aug. 1708), see Wright (1963–4), 3–5; his collection included the Benedictional of St Ethelwold (now BL, Add. MS 49598).

130 According to W. S. Simpson's calculations (SPCL, Grangerized Dugdale (in case C), 527), there are 558 folios, 277 quartos, 452 volumes in quarto or octavo, and 605 in octavo or smaller, giving a total of 1,892 books.

131 *Treatise of Holy Communion* (London, 1677); cf. Macray (1873), 85, and Carpenter (1956), 327.

132 Some of his considerable book bills were paid by the chapter's steward out of the receipts held for him: GL, MS 25690/1, at e.g. 17 Mar. 1711 and 25 July 1716.

133 SPCL, 37.B.10, June 1722; quoted by Simpson (1889), 42.

134 BodL, MS Rawl. B.372, fos. 13–14.

135 GL, MS 25643 (31) (Residentiaries' accounts,

1708–22), 1718–19, § Expenses occasional.

136 Quarrell and Mare (1934), 34, slightly amended.

137 GL, MS CF box 92 (in contents of Minor Canons' Red Box). The charge was still 2*d*. in 1802, but 4*d*. by the 1840s and 6*d*. by 1854: *Picture* (1802), 38; GL, MS CF box 92 (in contents of Minor Canons' Red Box); Sims (1854), 391.

138 GL, MS 25689/3 (Steward's general account book, 1781–1871), fo. [i]: 'Mr Hyde's Profits for Showing the Library'.

139 BL, Add. MS 24692, fo. 12; Macauley and Greaves (1988), 46.

140 SPCL, 37.B.10.

141 GL, MS 25643/35 (1st Account Book), 1735–6, § Expenses occasional: payment made to [Samuel] Harding [bookseller].

142 SPCL, 37.A.10, 11 (being bound as two volumes); much thumbed and worn.

143 SPCL, 37.B.13 and unnumbered.

144 Kaufman (1963–4); abridged in Kaufman (1969).

145 Kaufman (1963–4), 661 and 48; note also Kaufman's caveat about St Paul's at 644.

146 Lewis (1731), 97–9 (Addenda), and cf. 29.

147 See SPCL, Case B.13, 'A Catalogue of the Library of the late REVD MR John Mangey': a list in shelf-order, presumably at Mangey's house. The purchase price is stated in GL, MS 25689/3 (Steward's general account book, 1781–1872), fo. 82; for the removal of the books from Dunmow to London, £11 15*s*. 6*d*. was paid to Mr [John] Pridden, bookseller, and he was paid a further ten guineas 'for his Attendance & Trouble'. Pridden was the father of John Pridden junior (1758–1825), a minor canon from Nov. 1782 and later a collector of details about the cathedral's history.

148 GL, MS 25689/3, § Fabrick Money, 17 July 1787: payment to Mr Delegal(?) of £6 3*s*. 2*d*. for 'Cleaning the Seal, Engraving a Book Plate &c.'

149 Cf. Hutton's notes in BL, Harl. MS 6956, fos. 82v–85v (*Liber B*), 86v–97v (*Liber F*) and 6r–v (*Liber G*).

150 Now BodL, MS Rawl. B.368–372.

151 Yeo (1986), 35.

152 GL, MS 9537 (30), fo. 17v.

153 GL, MS 25643/35 (1st Account Book), 1734–5 and 1735–6, § Expenses occasional.

154 GL, MS 25617 (once WA90).

155 GL, MS 25643/35, 1735–6 and 1736–7, § Expenses occasional; MS 25643/41 (Account book 2), § Expenses occasional; and Yeo (1986), 38–9.

156 Now GL, MSS 25616/1 and 2.

157 Yeo (1986), 39.

158 Cf. payment of £5 5*s*. in Feb. 1789 to Mr Goddard for writing a schedule of 'the Books and Papers in the Office': GL, MS 25689/3 (Steward's accounts, 1781–1871), fo. 3, 1789.

159 GL, MS 25643/43 (Account book 4), 1772–3, § Expenses occasional, entry of payment, 8*s*. 6*d*., for the removal of 'books &c. to the Muniment Room'.

160 Malcolm (1802–7), i. ii. and iii. 4.

161 Macauley and Greaves (1988), 34. Secker's extracts are not known to survive.

162 BL, MS Add. 24692, fos. 39–40v.

163 *Reports* (1800), 337–8. The return states that 'the ancient Records in general, are kept in a strong Room, in the Cathedral' and 'some of the more modern Books and Papers... in Oak Presses in the Chapter Room'.

164 Moore's sources included material at LPL and the Journals of the Common Council, at Guildhall.

165 Maria Hackett's campaign can be followed in her correspondence (GL, MS 10189/2, fos. 29–34v; see also Garrett (1974b) and above, pp. 80, 85, 404.

166 [Hackett] (1827). For leave in 1816 to transcribe and publish the transcript (MS Harl. 4080): GL, MS 10189/2, fo. 113. Unknown to her, the original was (and is) MS S.25, at St John's College, Cambridge.

167 Packman's pamphlet declares itself to have been published 'Under the Sanction of the Warden & Majority of the College of the Twelve Minor Canons'. Later in life, he fell out with most of his fellow minor canons over the question of appointments to minor canonries: an appeal by him and James Lupton to the bishop of London (as Visitor of

St Paul's) was disavowed by eight other minor canons in a letter to *The Times*, dated 20 Jan. 1854 (copy at back of GL, MS 22298; for the appeal, see *London Gazette*, 1855, vol. I (Jan.–Mar.), 538–41).

168 Barham (1870), i. 199–200.

169 Bell (1980), 161.

170 Bell (1980), 170.

171 Barham (1870), ii. 169, 171.

172 See Barham's note in the library catalogue (SPCL, 37.B.4 [= Read (1970), no. 275]), dated June 1836; many of the early bibles and testaments have bibliographic notes in Barham's hand. See also Bumpus (1913a), 269 and addenda. The St Paul's copy of Tyndale's New Testament had actually been discovered by the Revd Henry Cotton in 1821; see also Botfield (1849), 302–3.

173 The principal sources of information about Hale are Russell (1920), who drew on his now-lost diaries, and papers of his in GL, MS CF box 50.

174 'The Week', *The Guardian*, vol. 25 (1870), 1389.

175 Hale noted the event in his diary (see Russell (1920), 67) and further detail is given in GL, MS 25615/2, p. 28. Two more Books (19 and 21) were removed by him in 1847: GL, MS 25615/2, p. 41.

176 Letter to Sydney Smith, 1841, excerpted by W. S. Simpson in SPCL, Grangerized Dugdale (in case C), 169–284, at 33★.

177 GL, MS 25614 (comprising slips of paper bound into book form); that Hale was responsible for these lists being made is stated by W. S. Simpson in GL, MS 25613, fo. 66.

178 GL, MS CF box 50: letters from Tomlins, 17 April, 15 May and 1 Aug. 1843. Tomlins (1804–72) is best known as the first translator of Jocelin of Brakelond's chronicle.

179 Hale (1858).

180 Cf. Read (1970), no. 275.

181 Simpson (1899), 35; this work is a sketch of Simpson's life by his son, who followed him into the church.

182 Simpson (1899), 39.

183 Transcribed by him into SPCL, Grangerized Dugdale (in case C), 521–3; the chapter voted its 'warmest thanks' for this 'lucid and important Report' and for his labours in cataloguing the books, and agreed to allow £20 a year for the purposes set out in the report: SPCL, CM (1860–74), 32.

184 SPCL, CM (1860–74), 30.

185 GL, MS 25612: 'Index to the MSS. Books, Charters, Royal Grants, Indulgences, Deeds and Papers preserved amongst the Archives in the Cathedral Church of S. Paul, London. Compiled by me – W. Sparrow Simpson... 1863'.

186 SPCL, CM (1860–74), 47.

187 GL, MS 25627 (still the only index to these wills); the volumes are GL, MSS 25626/1–6.

188 Milman (1868), 161 n.

189 Simpson (1899), 48.

190 SPCL, CM, 10 Mar. 1872.

191 See further Simpson (1899), 60–3, and a packet of letters etc. in GL, MS CF box 89.

192 Simpson (1899), 163.

193 Simpson (1880), 41–57; Stubbs (1882–3), i. lviii.

194 In his Library Waste Book (SPCL, 37.B.15), Simpson carefully entered a verbatim transcript of the guide's inaccurate account of the library.

195 Reynolds (1879), App.

196 SPCL, CM (1860–74), p. 188.

197 See Yeo (1986), 42–3.

198 GL, MS 25272; formerly in Press A, no. 69; see Gibbs (1939), xliii. n.3, and Davis (1958), no. 598.

199 Lyte (1883); for earlier correspondence between the commission and chapter, see SPCL, CM, 5 April 1875.

200 Johnson (1940), 365. In what is presumably a sharp dig at Stubbs, Johnson observes that Lyte omits a roll of early charters 'then just discovered', which 'the Dean and Chapter reserved for publication by one of their own body'.

201 Simpson (1899), 67, 71 and 75.

202 GL, MS 25613/1, fo. 37v et seq., has Simpson's account of the whole affair, from 1889 to 1896; see further Sykes (1926), xxi and Burchnall (1993).

203 For copies of Simpson's letters on this topic, see SPCL, Grangerized Dugdale (in case C), 564–5, 590; the published catalogue is Simpson (1893).

204 GL, MSS 25613 and 25613A contain his 'Supplementary Index to Records', dealing with accessions down to 1897 (GL, MSS 25630–749).

205 [Prideaux] (1891), 52, 53, 66, 74 and 111.

206 Simpson (1893), v. The total had been swollen by the acquisition of 6,348 'tracts' (pamphlets) that had been Bishop Sumner's, 1,405 that had been Archdeacon Hale's and 402 that had been Prebendary Irons's.

39. *The Library, 1897–2004*

1 SPCL holds an issue dated 1935: Gilbertson (1935).

2 For background to the development of the library in the twentieth century, see Atkins (1954), Atkinson (1987–8), Atkinson (1990), Atkinson (1991–2), and Wisdom (1994–5).

3 SPCL, CM, 18 Mar. 1916.

4 SPCL, CM, 12 June 1920. Besley was appointed rector of St Lawrence Jewry.

5 SPCL, CM, 9 Oct. 1920.

6 SPCL, CM, 26 July 1924.

7 SPCL, CM, 16 Jan. 1932.

8 SPCL, CM, 29 July 1939; Matthews (1946), 25.

9 SPCL, CM, 18 Dec. 1948.

10 SPCL, CM, 23 Apr. 1949.

11 Bill (1966) 201–2; Collins (1992), 170.

12 SPCL, CM, 25 Feb 1950.

13 SPCL, CM, 15 Dec. 1951.

14 Matthews and Atkins (1957).

15 SPCL, CM, 8 June 1955, 6 Feb 1960; Fuller (1947).

16 'The £200,000 bath' (1966), 4.

17 Fuller (1965); SPCL, CM, 17 July 1965 mentions the initial approach of Lord Kenyon to dean and chapter.

18 *Heritage and renewal*, 47 (Dean Evans's copy, in possession of the author).

19 Gilbertson (1897), 32; Gilbertson (1914), 26; Gilbertson (1925), 21.

20 Bumpus (1913b), 211.

21 Gilbertson (1914), 48–9; Warner (1926), 114–25.

22 The triforium area and its presentation to visitors are now again under consideration as part of a larger review of visitor access.

23 McLeod (1984–98).

24 For the initial stages of this project see Norman (1996).

25 Fuller (1965), 2.

26 SPCL, Library files 6, Register of books borrowed from the library 1847–2003.

27 SPCL, Library files 6, Visitors' book, 1955–97.

28 A small sample includes Beddard (1972), Brooke (1951, 1956, 1957), Lowe (1953), Greenway (1968), Horn (1963, 1969), Ker (1969), Wilson (1996), Pfaff (1968).

29 Ramsay (1995), 406: W. Urry, copy of letter to C. R. Dodwell 29 July 1969.

30 Yeo (1986), 42, citing *The Times* 22 June 1949.

31 Yeo (1986), 42.

40. *St Paul's Precinct and the Book Trade to c.1800*

1 Christiansen (1989); see pp. 20, 31, 34.

2 See, for example, Blair (1991), esp. 43–4.

3 Detailed in Christiansen (1987, 1989 and 1990), but he confuses sites: the most westerly of his Bridge House blocks was actually part of the central block; nor are the thirty shop units of 1404 restricted to this.

4 Christiansen (1989); and esp. Christiansen (1987), 51 and Christiansen (1990), 31.

5 Christiansen (1987), 49–50; Pollard (1937), 16.

6 See Raven (2003).

7 Hetet (1987), 39.

8 Blayney (1990), 19; Christiansen (1990), 79.

9 ESTC 11608a.7; Blayney (1990), 19.

10 Blayney, (1990), 19.

11 Blayney (1990), 12–13, 15, 18–22, 48–9, 72–3.

12 Barnard and Bell (1991).

13 Cited in Mumby (1934), 74.

14 Blayney (2000), esp. 338–42, and Figs 16.5–16.10.

15 Duff (1905), appendix.

16 Blagden (1960), 208.

17 Blayney (1990), 5.

18 Harris (2003).

19 Duff (1905), 38.

20 King (1999), 166.

21 Pepys Diary, 8 Feb. 1668; Foxon (1964), 5–7.

22 Groom (2000), 101.

23 Mandelbrote (1995), 69.

24 Blayney (1990), 82–3.

25 Plomer (1968), 24.

26 Plomer (1968), 25.

27 Cited in Raymond (2001), 487.

28 West (1837), 92.

29 Chan (2002).

30 Lynch (1964), 9–13.

31 See Taubert (1966); Raven (1996); Raven (2001).

32 West (1837), 44.

33 Malcolm (1802–7), iii. 197.

34 Strype (1720), iii. 195b.

35 West (1837), 44.

36 Summerson (1962), 67.

37 Reddaway (1940), 80–2; Summerson (1962), chs 3–5.

38 Strype (1720), iii. 195b.

39 Malcolm (1810–11), ii. 3, 92

40 http://members.tripod.ox.ac/bookhistory, using rebuilding surveys, land tax assessments, property records of the dean and chapter of St Paul's, the Stationers' Company and other livery companies and the Corporation of London, and rental books of the Bridge House.

41 Raven (1997), 190–1.

42 Jones and Reddaway (1962–7); CLRO, Bridge House Rentals; GL, Taxation Records; and cf. Blayney (1990), fig. 2.

43 See Raven (2003).

44 Hetet (1987).

45 Nichols (1812–15), iii. 400.

46 See Rivington (1894), and Rivington (1919).

47 Rees and Britton (1896), 32.

48 Cited in Rivington (1919), 90.

49 See Raven (2000), 115–17.

50 Belanger (1977), 19.

51 [Wolcot] (1806), 103.

52 Belanger (1977), 19; Welsh (1885); Roscoe (1973).

53 Rose (1993), and Walters (1974).

54 West (1837), 21.

41. *The Precinct and Setting of St Paul's from the Nineteenth Century*

1 Guildhall Art Gallery, No. 10266. It was painted in 1838.

2 Expanded to No. 85 in 1892 (London County Council (1955), 671).

3 Briggs (1988), 1990 edition, 42–3; Howard and Newman (1951), 108.

4 *The House of Dollond* (1917), 4, 9. The firm moved here in the 1760s.

5 Rivington (1919), 113–42. The firm moved away in 1853.

6 Lovett (1890), 211–2; Turner (1975), Penguin edition, 1976, 96–103.

7 Metcalf (1980), 46–9.

8 For Nos. 5–13, see *Building News* 20 March 1896, 417, *The Architect* 57 (1897), 168, and Kynaston (1994–2001), i. 303–5. The warehouse was reconstructed behind the façade in 2002–3. Nos. 1–2 are a facsimile rebuilding: *Building Design*, 27 March 1987.

9 As at the Religious Tract Society's shop at No. 65, of 1876, for which see Lovett (1890), 212.

10 *The Builder*, 9 Oct. 1886, 518 and 5 March 1887, 348.

11 Welch (1896), 382.

12 The medieval Cannon Street (then Candlewick Street) is the east part of the present route of that name. Under Acts of 1847 and 1850 it was widened and extended westward into St Paul's Churchyard. The separate designation of Cannon Street West for

this end was dropped in 1866: Darby and Physick (1973), 140–1; *Post Office Directories*.

13 *The Building News*, first series (1854), 541.

14 *The Building News*, first series (1854), 514.

15 *Land and Building News* 1 (1855), 558–60.

16 *The Companion to the British Almanac*, 1861, 257.

17 *The Building News* 1 (1855), 751. The cost was borne by Burton's Charity. The gallery was removed in the early 1880s (*The Architect*, 4 Aug. 1883, 64).

18 *Building News*, 20 March 1896, 417–18.

19 Clunn (1951), 61.

20 *Building News*, 8 March 1895, 360.

21 Rival proposals, more aesthetically minded than practical, favoured an alignment on the axis of the dome and a new road debouching at midpoint into the churchyard: see Barker and Hyde (1982), 50–2.

22 *Guildhall* (1939), extracted and amended in Corporation of London, *Reconstruction* (1944), 20–1.

23 Clunn (1927), 41.

24 *The Builder* 23 July 1873, 475. Its bombed-out basement survives as the Mermaid Theatre.

25 Welch (1896), 236; Summerson (1973), 1. For a well-rehearsed lament, see Hare (1901), i. 106.

26 Bradley and Pevsner (1997), 343; Corporation of London (1944), 12–3, 15, and Plan II.

27 *Post Office Directories*.

28 *The Builder* 1 June 1934, 926; Clunn (1951), 60.

29 Corporation of London (1944), Plan Ia.

30 Howard and Newman (1951), 109–10.

31 Hudson (1961), 156.

32 Information from Martin Maw, Archivist, Oxford University Press.

33 Royal Academy (1942); Thorne (1991), 119–21.

34 Corporation of London (1944), 15–17.

35 Cherry and Penny (1986), 136.

36 Cited in Croft (1998), 9.

37 See Banham (1968).

38 *Architectural Review* 100 (1946), 142–9.

39 Cherry and Penny (1986), 136–41.

40 Holden and Holford (1951), 298.

41 Croft (1998), 11, 19.

42 Richardson went on in 1955 to design Bracken House, a new headquarters for the *Financial Times*, on the south side of Cannon Street at the junction with New Change, a late flowering of the stripped classical style of the 1920s: Bradley and Pevsner (1997), 444–6, 598.

43 Bradley and Pevsner (1997), 456.

44 Mais (1956), 19–27; Croft (1998), 41. The project architect was Harold Mortimer of Trehearne and Norman, Preston and Partners. Demolished in 1998, its replacement, completed in 2000, has a garden at the west end instead.

45 For a full account see Cherry and Penny (1986), 160–9, citing Holford (1956), *passim*; also Croft (1998), 41–4.

46 Pevsner (1956), 594–6; Games (2002), 240–8.

47 Croft (1998), 43.

48 To Holden's presumable chagrin: Karol (2001), 310.

49 Croft (1998), 43.

50 On the last, see Hebbert (1993), 433–51.

51 Thorne (1991), 136.

52 Kynaston (1994–2001), iv. 135.

53 Nairn (1966), 20.

54 Corporation of London (1944), 16; Holden and Holford (1951), 297.

55 Bradley and Pevsner (1997), 598.

56 Cherry and Penny (1986), 172; *Building* 5 Jan. 1973, 40.

57 For the conservationist case, see Freeman (1976), 21–32.

58 Murray (1991), 129–30.

59 Paternoster Associates (1991), e.g. 7–8.

60 *Building Design*, 15 Dec. 1995.

61 Information from Sir William Whitfield, September 2003.

62 Ekwall (1954), 197.

63 *Building Design*, 10 March 1995. For a previous scheme for the site by Edward Cullinan Architects, see *Architects' Journal*, 26 July 1989, 24–9.

64 Sudjic (2001).

42. *The Reputation of St Paul's*

1   *The Spectator*, 27 April 1711.
2   Colvin (1951), 257–60; Colvin and Newman (1981), xvii. 22.
3   De Beer (1955), v. 192.
4   Le Sage (1715), 182–7; Middleton (1968), 42 cites the author but does not identify him.
5   Macky (1714), 198–201.
6   Defoe (1725), 122–7; Defoe (1991), 142–4, an abridgement, omits two paragraphs.
7   Ralph (1734), 17–23; Harris (1990), 381–5.
8   Colsoni (1693/1951), 32–3.
9   Defoe (1725), 127; Defoe (1991), 144.
10   *London and its Environs Described* (1761), 114, 154.
11   Macky (1714), 198–9.
12   Moritz (1924), 90–1.
13   Middleton (1968), 46–55.
14   Middleton (1968), 50; Watkin (1996), 144, 151–2.
15   Maior (1774), 279–81.
16   Peignot (1836), 5.
17   De Lévis (1814), 95–105.
18   Lang (1956), 242–4.
19   E.g. Colsoni (1693); Miège (1707); Hatton (1708); Strype (1720); Smith (1726).
20   Wren (1750), 135–55; Harris (1990), 503–8.

21   Harris (1990), 214–17.
22   Gwynn (1766), 37–41.
23   Elmes (1852), 412.
24   Elmes (1823), 320–1.
25   Schinkel (1993), 203–4.
26   Gwilt (1825), 1–30.
27   Pugin (1841), 4.
28   Clarke (1923), 73–4.
29   Fergusson (1862), 266–74.
30   Cited in e.g. Phillimore (1881), 326.
31   Shone (1871), 33–6.
32   Milman (1868), 436–49, 495–7; Gregory (1912), 155–225; Newbolt [1921], 213–55.
33   Kynaston (1994–2001), ii. 161.
34   Burne-Jones (1909), ii. 218–20.
35   Uffenbach (1934), 35.
36   Karamzin (1957), 291.
37   Gautier (1852), 118.
38   Simond (1817), 23.
39   Hawthorne (1941), 204, 240–1.
40   Howells (1905), 90.
41   James (1987), 279–80.
42   Woolf (1975/1982), 31–2. From an essay originally published in *Good Housekeeping*, May 1932: see Squier (1985), 52, 64–5.
43   Forster (1910), ch. 34.

44   Shone (1871), 39.
45   Phillimore (1881), 334.
46   Mackmurdo (1883), 31.
47   Lethaby (1979), 227–8.
48   Godfrey (1911), 262.
49   Turner and Ward (1923), 83–4.
50   Alexander (1923), 267.
51   Crellin and Hopkins in Hopkins and Stamp (2002), 57–96.
52   Pite (1923), 58.
53   Summerson (1981), 45–52.
54   Mulgan (1927), 60.
55   Pope-Hennessy (1939), 7–20.
56   Beaton and Pope-Hennessy (1941), 78–82.
57   Stater (1996), 8–9.
58   Nairn (1966), 18–19.
59   Prince of Wales (1989), 55–9, 68–74.
60   Hutchinson (1989), 28–31; film, etc.
61   Sekler (1956), 183–94.
62   Pevsner (1957), 116–21; Pevsner (1963), 324–6; also Pevsner (1964), 87–8.
63   Summerson (1945), 45.
64   Summerson (1937), 373–90: see also revised version in Summerson (1937), 51–86.
65   Summerson (1937), 385–6.
66   Summerson (1970), 236–8.

BIBLIOGRAPHY

Sources

The close association between St Paul's and the capital city, and hence its long-established role in national life, mean that an exceptionally wide range of source material has a bearing on the history of the cathedral, as the notes in this History demonstrate. The national archives and those of the city of London and many other localities are all important for St Paul's. Just as valuable are numerous chronicles, histories, memoirs, sermons and tracts, of which a good many have been produced by St Paul's clergy or delivered at the cathedral itself (see chapters 6, 8, 13, 30, 42). The cathedral's own archive, touching on every aspect of its administration and interests, is immensely rich for the period from 1100 onwards; its development is outlined in chapter 38. Most of that archive has been deposited at Guildhall Library, where the card catalogue and the accessions register provide useful guides, although Maxwell-Lyte's descriptive list of 1883 (HMC 9) is still of great value. Much of the more recent St Paul's material at Guildhall Library has not been formally arranged and catalogued, but Dr Chris Faunch's typescript lists of the contents of the boxes in which this material is stored, compiled for the purposes of this history, are a valuable guide. These boxes include the semi-private papers of some cathedral servants. Current and recent records (including Chapter Minutes since 1832) are kept in various departments of the cathedral (see chapter 39).

Essential for identifying the bishops of London and the dignitaries and prebendaries of St Paul's up to 1857, along with their terms of office, are the relevant volumes of the *Fasti Ecclesiae Anglicanae*: Greenway (1968) and Horn (1963, 1969). Specific references to these works for individuals holding office at St Paul's have not normally been provided in this History. Hennessy (1898) provides lists (not always accurate) of the bishops, dignitaries and prebendaries (to 1897); the stagiaries (1670-1756); the four canons (*c.*1660 to 1897), and the minor canons (miscellaneous references, thirteenth to sixteenth centuries; lists *c.*1560 to 1897). *Crockford's Clerical Directory* provides an annual record from 1876. All bishops of London and deans of St Paul's, with their terms of office, are listed in the index to this History.

Major collections of sources in print include chronicles written at St Paul's (see chapter 31); early charters relating to the cathedral and diocese (Gibbs (1939), Kelly (2004)); acts and registers of the bishops of London (Neininger (1999), Johnson (2003); Fowler (1911), Fowler and Jenkins (1927-38)); the cathedral statutes (Simpson (1873); the extensive collections printed in Dugdale's *History* (Dugdale (1818)); documents and plans relating to the rebuilding of St Paul's after the Great Fire (WS).

Note: This bibliography serves primarily to identify the printed works referred to in the endnotes, and items appear in alphabetical order according to the form there cited. [ ] denotes interpolated information.

A Dialogue betwixt St Paul's Church and Salters Hall (London, 1698).

A Form of Prayer and Thanksgiving to Almighty God; to be Used on Tuesday 19 December 1797, being the Day Appointed by His Majesty's Royal Proclamation for a General Thanksgiving to Almighty God (London, 1797).

A Form of Prayer and Thanksgiving to Almighty God Commemorating the Blessings Granted to the Queen's Most Excellent Majesty during the Twenty-Five Years of Her Majesty's Reign, 7 June 1977 at 11.30 (n.d.).

A Form of Prayer to be Used at a Memorial Service on Tuesday December 19 at 3pm for Those who have Fallen in the War (n.d. [1899]).

A Form of Prayer to be Used at a Solemn Service of Humble Supplication to Almighty God that he would Vouchsafe to Prosper our Arms in South Africa, on Friday December 29th at 10.30 am (n.d. [1899]).

A Form of Service to be Used at St Paul's Cathedral on the Occasion of the Royal Progress of Her Majesty the Queen, June 22, 1897 (n.d.).

A Guide to St Paul's Cathedral (new edn. London, 1874).

A Letter of Advice to the Reverend Mr Scurlock: occasioned by his Extraordinary Sermon, preach'd at St Paul's Cathedral ... in vindication of the Excise Scheme (London, 1733).

A Perfect Account of the daily Intelligence from the Armies in England, Scotland, and Ireland, the Navy at Sea, and other transactions of, and in relation to this Common Wealth, No. 152: Wednesday 12 October to Wednesday 19 October 1653 (London) [BL, Thomason Tract E715/3].

A Perfect Diurnall of the Passages in Parliament. From the 24th of October, to the 31th of the same, 1642 (London, 1642) [BL, Thomason Tract E240/48].

A Sermon preached in the Cathedral Church of St Paul... June 14, 1792...by John [Warren], *Lord Bishop of Bangor* (London).

A Sermon preached in the Cathedral Church of St Paul... June 9, 1791...by Samuel Glasse (London).

A Service of Remembrance with the American Community in the United Kingdom, 14 September 2001.

A Service of Thanksgiving and Celebration on the Occasion of the Golden Jubilee of Her Majesty the Queen, St Paul's Cathedral Tuesday 4th June 2002 (n.d.).

A True Answer to Dr Sacheverell's Sermon, Before the Lord Mayor...In a Letter to one of the Aldermen (London, 1710).

Abbey, C. J. and Overton, J. H. (1887), *The English Church in the Eighteenth Century* (London).

Abels, R. P. (1988), *Lordship and Military Obligation in Anglo-Saxon England* (London).

Ackermann, R. (1808–9) *Microcosm of London*, 2 vols. (London).

Adams, B. (1983), *London Illustrated, 1604–1851* (London).

Addleshaw, G. W. O., and Etchells, F. (1948), *The Architectural Setting of Anglican Worship: an inquiry into the arrangements for Public Worship in the Church of England from the Reformation to the present day* (London).

Akrigg, G. P. V., ed. (1950–1), 'England in 1609', *Huntington Lib. Quart.* 14, 75–94.

Alcock, W. (1935), 'Sir John Stainer and church music,' *English Church Music* 5/4, 101.

Alexander, G. (1987), 'Bonner and the Marian persecutions', in Haigh, C., ed., *The English Reformation Revised* (Cambridge), 157–75.

Alexander, J. J. G. and Binski, P., eds. (1987), *The Age of Chivalry: Art in Plantagenet England, 1200–1400* (London).

Alexander, S. A. (1923), 'The Cross and the Dome (Epilogue)', in Dircks (1923).

Alexander, S. A. (1927; 2nd edn. 1930a), *The Safety of St Paul's* (London).

Alexander, S. A. (1930b), *The Cross and the Dome: Addresses on St Paul's Cathedral* (Oxford).

Alexander, S. A. (1945), *The Survival of St. Paul's: The Story of a Great Church in Perilous Times* (London).

Allen, P. S. (1914), *The Age of Erasmus* (Oxford).

Allen, W. O. B and McClure, E. (1898), *Two Hundred Years: The History of the SPCK, 1698–1898* (London).

Altham, R. (1706), *A Sermon Preach'd before the Sons of the Clergy at the Cathedral Church of St Paul, London on 26 November 1706* (London).

An Historical Description of St Paul's Cathedral (London, 1784).

An Official and Circumstantial Detail of the Grand National Obsequies at the Public Funeral of Britain's Darling Hero, the Immortal Nelson (London, 1806).

An Ordinance of the Lords and Commons Assembled in Parliament: Inabling the Lord Maior and Court of Aldermen to seize and sequester into their hands all the Houses, Rents and Revenues belonging to the Deane, Deane and Chapter and all other Officers belonging to the Cathedrall Church of Pauls London, And for the paying Doctor Burges 400. pounds per annum for a publike Lecture in the said Church. As also for the setling of Master Philip Goodwin in the Vicarage at Watford. (London, 1645).

Anderson, P. J. (1986), 'Sion College and the London provincial assembly, 1647–1660', *JEcclH* 37, 68–90.

Anglo, S (1997), *Spectacle, Pageantry and Early Tudor Policy* (2nd edn., Oxford).

Appleby, J. T., ed. (1963), *The Chronicle of Richard of Devizes* (London).

Apthorp, E. (1770), *A Sermon at St Paul's Cathedral 2 September MDCCLXX Being the Annual Commemoration of the Fire of London* (London).

Arblaster, P., Juhász, G., and Latré, G., eds. (2002), *Tyndale's Testament* (Turnhout).

Archer, I. (1991), *The History of the Haberdashers' Company* (Chichester).

Arkwright, G. E. P. (1913–14), 'Elizabethan choir-boy plays and their music', *Proc. of the [Royal] Musical Association* 40, 117–38.

Armitage-Smith, S., ed. (1911) *John of Gaunt's Register*, 2 vols. (CS, 3rd ser. 20–1).

Arnold, J. (forthcoming), 'John Colet, preaching and reform at St Paul's Cathedral, 1505–19', *HR*.

Arnold, S., ed. (1790), *Cathedral Music*, 4 vols. (London).

Arnold, T., ed. (1890–6), *Memorials of St Edmund's Abbey*, ed. T. Arnold, 3 vols. (RS 96).

Arthurson, I. (1994), *The Perkin Warbeck Conspiracy* (Stroud).

Articles Exhibited in Parliament against William Archbishop Of Canterbury, 1640 ([London, 1640]; repr. in facsimile, Amsterdam and New York, 1971).

Ashbee, A. and Harley, J. eds. (2000), *The Cheque Books of the Chapel Royal*, 2 vols. (Aldershot).

Ashbee, A. and Lasocki, D. (1998), *A Biographical Dictionary of English Court Musicians, 1485–1714*, 2 vols. (Aldershot).

Ashbourne, Lord (1898), *Pitt: Some Chapters of his Life and Times* (London).

Ashby, E. G. (1950), 'Aspects of parish life in the city of London, 1429–1529', MA thesis, University of London.

Ashton, T. (1753), *A Sermon Preached before the Sons of the Clergy. In the Cathedral Church of St Paul, Thursday 10 May 1753* (London).

Aspinall, A., ed. (1962–70), *The Later Correspondence of George III*, 5 vols. (Cambridge).

Aspital, A. W. (1980), *Catalogue of the Pepys Library at Magdalene College, Cambridge*, vol. III(i) (Woodbridge).

Astle, T., Ayscough, S. and Caley, J., eds. (1802), *Taxatio Ecclesiastica Angliae et Walliae, auctoritate Papae Nicholai IV circa A.D. 1291* (RC).

Aston, N. (2001), 'Popery, painting and the church of England: the failure of the St Paul's Cathedral decorative scheme in the 1770s' (unpublished paper to Georgian Group).

Atherton, I. (1999), *Ambition and Failure in Stuart England: The Career of John, First Viscount Scudamore* (Manchester).

Atkins, I., and Ker, N. R., eds. (1944), *Catalogus Librorum Manuscriptorum Bibliothecae Wigorniensis, made in 1622–1623 by Patrick Young* (Cambridge).

Atkins, W. M. (1954), 'St. Paul's cathedral: a short history of the library and archives', *A Record of the Friends of St. Paul's* (1954), 14–20.

Atkins, W. M. (1957), 'The age of reform: 1831–1934', in Matthews and Atkins (1957), 250–99.

Atkinson, D. (2000), *The Selected Letters of W. E Henley* (Aldershot).

Atkinson, F. (1987–8), 'The cathedral library', *Dome* 25, 49–51.

Atkinson, F. (1990), *St Paul's Cathedral, London: the Library of the Dean and Chapter* (London).

Atkinson, F. (1991–2), 'A final chapter', *Dome* 29, 29.

Attenborough, F. L., ed. (1922) *Laws of the Earliest English Kings* (Cambridge).

Atterbury, F. (1709), *A Sermon Preach'd before the Sons of the Clergy at their anniversary meeting in the Cathedral Church of St Paul, 6 December 1709* (London).

Avril, F. and Stirnemann, P. D. (1987), *Manuscrits enluminés d'origine insulaire, VIIe–XXe siècle* (Paris).

Ayris, P., ed. (2000), 'The Public Career of Thomas Cranmer', *Reformation and Renaissance Review* No. 4, 75–125.

Babbage, S. B. (1962), *Puritanism and Richard Bancroft* (London).

B[urne]-J[ones], G. (1909) *Memorials of Edward Burne-Jones*, 2 vols. (London).

Babylon in St. Paul's: or, the Eviction of Protestants from the Metropolitan Cathedral. A Letter of Protest and Rebuke to the Bishop of London. By a Retired Rector (London, n. d.).

Bachrach, A. G. H. and Collmer, R. G., eds. and trans., (1982), *Lodewijck Huygens: The English Journal 1651–1652* (Leiden, Publications Sir Thomas Browne Institute).

Backhouse, J., ed. (2003), *The English Medieval Cathedral: Papers in Honour of Pamela Tudor-Craig* (Donington, Harlaxton Medieval Studies 10).

Baecque, A. de (2001), *Glory and Terror: Seven Deaths under the French Revolution*, trans. Mandell, C. (London).

Baildon, W., ed. (1897–1902), *Records of the Honourable Society of Lincoln's Inn: The Black Books*, 5 vols. (London).

Bailey, K. (1989), 'The Middle Saxons', in Bassett (1989), 108–22.

Baily, A. (1769), *A Collection of Anthems used in His Majesty's Chapel Royal and Most Cathedrals in England* [London].

Baily, A. (1771), *A Practical Treatise on Singing and Playing with Just Expression and Real Elegance* [London].

Baily, A. (1789), *The Alliance of Musick, Poetry and Oratory* [London].

Bale, J. (1549), *The Laboryouse Journey & Serche of Johan Leylande, for Englandes Antiquitees …enlarged: by Iohan Bale* (London).

Baltzer, R. A. (1987), 'Notre Dame manuscripts and their owners: lost and found', *Journal of Musicology* 5, 380–99.

Banham, R. (1968), 'Revenge of the picturesque: English architectural polemics, 1945–1965', in Summerson, J., ed. (1968), *Concerning Architecture: Essays on Architectural Writers and Writing Presented to Nikolaus Pevsner*, 265–73.

Barham, R. H. D., ed. (1870), *The Life and Letters of the Rev. Richard Harris Barham,* 2 vols. (London).

Baring, F. (1899), 'The hidation of some southern counties', *EHR* 14, 290–9.

Barker, F. and Hyde, R. (1982), *London as it Might Have Been* (London).

Barman, C. (1925), *The Danger to St Paul's* (London).

Barnard, J. and Bell, M. (1991), 'The inventory of Henry Bynneman (1583): A Preliminary Survey', *Publishing History* 29 (1991), 5–46.

Baron, X., ed. (c.1997), *London 1066–1914: Literary Sources & Documents*, I, *Medieval, Tudor, Stuart and Georgian London 1066–1800* (Robertsbridge).

Barratt, D. M. (1950–1), 'The library of John Selden and its later history', *Bodleian Library Record* 3, 128–42, 208–13 and 256–74.

Barrett, P. L. S. (1993), *Barchester. English Cathedral Life in the Nineteenth Century* (London).

Barrett, P. L. S. (2000), 'From Victorian to modern times, 1832–1982', in Aylmer, G. and Tiller, J. eds. (2000), *Hereford Cathedral: A History* (London).

Barrie-Curien, V. (1993a), 'Clerical recruitment patterns in the Church of England during the eighteenth century', in Jacob, W. M. and Yates, N., eds. (1993), *Crown and Mitre: Religion and Society in Northern Europe since the Reformation* (Woodbridge), 93–104.

Barrie-Curien, V. (1993b), 'The clergy in the diocese of London in the eighteenth century', in Walsh J., Haydon C. and Taylor S., eds. (1993), *The Church of England c.1689–c.1833* (Cambridge), 86–109.

Barrington, Mrs R. (1906), *Life and Letters of Lord Leighton*, 2 vols. (London).

Barron, C. M. (1971), 'The quarrel of Richard II with London 1392–7', in Du Boulay and Barron, (1971) 173–201.

Barron, C. M. (1974), *The Medieval Guildhall of London* (London).

Barron, C. M. (1985), 'The parish fraternities of medieval London', in Barron, C. M., and Harper-Bill, C., eds., *The Church in Pre-Reformation Society: Essays in Honour of F. R. H. Du Boulay* (Woodbridge), (1985) 13–37.

Barron, C. M. (1996), 'The expansion of education in fifteenth-century London', in Blair, J. and Golding, B., eds., *The Cloister and the World: Essays in Medieval History in Honour of Barbara Harvey* (Oxford), (1996) 219–245.

Barron, C. M. (2003), 'London and St Paul's Cathedral in the later Middle Ages', in Backhouse (2003), 126–49.

Barron, C. M. and Sutton, A. F., eds. (1994), *Medieval London Widows 1300–1500* (London and Rio Grande).

Barron, C., Coleman, C. and Gobbi, C., eds. (1983), 'The London journal of Alessandro Magno 1562', *LonJ* 9, 136–152.

Barrow, J. (1986), 'Cathedrals, provosts and prebends: a comparison of twelfth-century German and English practice', *JEcclH* 37, 536–64.

Barrow, J. (1989), 'Vicars choral and chaplains in northern European cathedrals, 1100–1250', in Sheils and Wood (1989), 87–97.

Barrow, J. (1993), *English Episcopal Acta, VII, Hereford 1079–1234* (Oxford).

Barrow, J. (1994), 'English cathedral communities and reform in the late tenth and early eleventh centuries', in Rollason, D., ed. (1994), *Anglo-Norman Durham 1093–1193* (Woodbridge and Rochester NY).

Barrow, J. S. (2002), *John le Neve, Fasti Ecclesiae Anglicanae 1066–1300, VII, Hereford* (London).

Barton, P. (1736), *The Superior Excellency of Charity: A Sermon Preach'd before the Sons of the Clergy at their anniversary meeting in the Cathedral Church of St Paul on Thursday 19 February 1735* (London).

Barwick, G. F., ed. (1903), Peter Barwick, *The Life of Dr John Barwick, Dean of St Paul's, ...translated into English by Hilkiah Bedford* (London).

Barwick, P. (1724), *The Life Of The Reverend Dr. John Barwick, D.D. Sometime Fellow of St John's College in Cambridge ...* (London).

Bascombe, K. (1987), 'Two charters of Suabred of Essex', in Neale, K., ed. (1987), *An Essex Tribute* (London), 85–96.

Bassett, S., ed. (1989), *The Origins of Anglo-Saxon Kingdoms* (Leicester).

Bates, D. (forthcoming), *William the Conqueror* (New Haven and London).

Bates, D., ed. (1998), *Regesta Regum Anglo-Normannorum: the Acta of William I, 1066–1087* (Oxford).

Bateson, M. (1902), 'A London municipal collection of the reign of John', *EHR* 17, 480–511, 707–30.

Battishill, J. (1767), *Two Anthems as they are sung at St Paul's Cathedral* [London].

Bawtree, R. (2002), 'My five and a half years as secretary of the Friends of St Paul's', in Shaw and Miller (2002), 93–9.

Baxter, R. (1660), *Right Rejoycing: or The Nature and Order of Rational and Warrantable Ioy. Discovered in a Sermon preached at St Pauls before the Lord Maior and Aldermen, and the several Companies of the City of London, on May 10. 1660 appointed by both Houses of Parliament, to be a day of solemn Thanksgiving for Gods raising up and succeeding his Excellency, and other Instruments, in order to his Majesties restoration, and the settlement of these Nations* (London) [BL, Thomason Tract E1025/11].

Bayly, C. A. (1989), *Imperial Meridian: The British Empire and the World, 1780–1830* (Harlow).

Beaton, C. and Pope-Hennessy, J. (1941), *History under Fire* (London).

Beavan, I. (1998), '"The Best Library that ever the North Pairtes of Scotland Saw": Thomas Reid (Latin Secretary to James VI) and his books', in Isaac, P., and McKay, B., eds., *The Reach of Print: Making, Selling and Using Books* (Winchester and New Castle, DE), 205–20.

Beaven, A. B. (1908–13), *The Aldermen of the City of London, Temp. Henry III.–1912,* 2 vols. (London).

Beddard, R. A. (1972), 'Church and state in Old St. Paul's: Dean Barwick's assertion of the church's rights against the city', *Guildhall Miscellany* 4/3, 161–74.

Bede, see Colgrave and Mynors.

Beeson, T. (2002), *Priests and Prelates: The Daily Telegraph Clerical Obituaries* (London and New York).

Belanger, T. (1977), 'A directory of the London book trade, 1766', *Publishing History* 1, 7–48.

Bell, A. (1980), *Sydney Smith* (Oxford).

Bell, G. (1713), *St Paul's Behaviour in the Cause of the Gospel: A Sermon Preach'd before the Sons of the Clergy, at their Annual Feast in the Cathedral Church of St Paul, London, 4 December 1712* (London).

Bell, W. G. (1920; 3rd edn. 1923), *The Great Fire of London in 1666* (London).

Bellamy, D. (1756), *On Benevolence; with a Summary of the Life and Character of Dean Colet: A Sermon Preached in the Cathedral Church of St Paul, on Tuesday, 29 June 1756. Before the Gentlemen Educated at St Paul's School* (London).

Bellamy, R. (1788), *Te Deum for a Full Orchestra, Also a Set of Anthems* [London].

Bellinger, A. (1982), 'The émigré clergy and the English church, 1789–1815', *JEcclH* 34, 392–410.

Benham, H. (1977), *Latin Church Music in England, c.1460–1575* (London).

Bennett, G. V. (1975), *The Tory Crisis in Church and State, 1688–1730: The Career of Francis Atterbury, Bishop of Rochester* (Oxford).

Bentley, D. (1987), 'The western stream reconsidered: an enigma in the landscape', *London Archaeologist* 5, 328–34.

Bernard, G. W. (1984), review of N. L. Jones, *Faith by Statute: Parliament and the Settlement of Religion, 1559* (1982), *Heythrop Journal* 25, 228–32.

Bernard, G. W. (1998), 'The making of religious policy, 1533–1546: Henry VIII and the search for the middle way', *Historical Journal* 41, 321–49.

Bernard, G. W. (1999), 'The Piety of Henry VIII' in Amos, N. S., Pettegree, A. and van Nierop, H., eds. (1999), *The Education of a Christian Society: Humanism and the Reformation in Britain and the Netherlands* (Aldershot), 62–88.

Berriman, W. (1737), *The Tithing of the Third Year: A Sermon Preached before the Sons of the Clergy at the Cathedral Church of St Paul 21 April 1737* (London).

Best, G. F. A. (1964), *Temporal Pillars: Queen Anne's Bounty, the Ecclesiastical Commissioners and the Church of England* (Cambridge).

Best, W. (1746), *An Essay upon the Service of the Church of England, Considered as a Daily Service. With a View of Reviving a More General and Constant Attendance upon It* (London).

Bethell, D. (1970), 'Richard of Belmeis and the foundation of St Osyth's', *Trans. of Essex Archaeological Soc.,* 3rd ser. 2, 299–315.

Bethell, D. (1980), 'The lives of St Osyth of Essex and St Osyth of Aylesbury', *Analecta Bollandiana* 88, 75–127.

Bettey, J. H. (1971) 'The supply of stone for rebuilding St Paul's Cathedral', *ArchJ* 128, 176–85.

Bevan, G. and Stainer, J. (1882), *Handbook to the Cathedral of St Paul* (London).

Bevan, M., ed. (1958), *Adrian Batten: O clap your hands together* (London).

Bicknell, S. (1996), *The History of the English Organ* (Cambridge).

Biddle, M. (1968), 'Excavations at Winchester, 1967: sixth interim report', *Antiquaries Journal* 48, 250–84.

Biddle, M. (1986), 'Archaeology, architecture and the cult of Saints in Anglo-Saxon England', in Butler, L. A. S. and Morris, R. K. eds., (1986), *The Anglo-Saxon Church. Papers...in Honour of Dr. H. M. Taylor* (BAR 60), 1–31.

Biddle, M., ed. (1976), *Winchester in the Early Middle Ages: an Edition and Discussion of the Winton Domesday* (Oxford).

Bill, G (1966), 'Lambeth Palace library', *The Library,* 5th ser. 21, 192–206.

Binski, P. (1987) 'The stylistic sequence of London figure brasses', in Coales (1987), 69–132.

Binski, P. (1995), *Westminster Abbey and the Plantagenets: Kingship and the Representation of Power, 1200–1400* (New Haven and London).

Binski, P. (1996), *Medieval Death: Ritual and Representation* (London; Ithaca, NY).

Birch, T. (1757), *The History of the Royal Society of London* [page numbers from facsimile edn. printed in Paris, 1967].

Birch, W. de G. (1887–1900), *Catalogue of Seals in the Department of Manuscripts in the British Museum,* 6 vols. (London).

Birt, H. N. (1907), *The Elizabethan Religious Settlement: A Study of Contemporary Documents* (London).

Bisse, P. (1710), *A Sermon Preach'd at the Anniversary Meeting of the Sons of the Clergy in the Cathedral Church of St Paul on 2 December 1709* (London).

Bisse, T. (1717), *A Sermon Preach'd before the Sons of the Clergy at their Anniversary Meeting in the Cathedral-Church of St Paul on 6 December 1716* (London).

Bissett, W. (1710), *The Modern Fanatick: With a Large and True Account of the Life, Actions, Endeavours ... of the Famous Dr Sach—l* (London).

Blackburn, M. (1998), 'The London mint in the reign of Alfred', in Blackburn and Dumville (1998), 105–23.

Blackburn, M. A. S. and Dumville, D., eds. (1998), *Kings, Currency and Alliances. History and Coinage of Southern England in the Ninth Century* (Woodbridge).

Blackburn, M. A. S., ed. (1986), *Anglo-Saxon Monetary History. Essays in Memory of Michael Dolley* (Leicester).

Blackmore, L. (1997), 'From beach to burh: new clues to entity and identity in 7th- to 9th-century London', in de Boe, G. and Verhaeghe, F., eds. (1997), *Urbanism in Medieval Europe: papers of the 'Medieval Europe Brugge 1997' Conference,* vol. 1 (Zellik), 123–32.

Blagden, C. (1960), *The Stationers' Company: A History 1603–1959* (London).

Blagden, C. (1961), 'Thomas Carnan and the almanack monopoly', *Studies in Bibliography,* 14, 23–43.

Blair, J. (1987), 'English monumental brasses before 1350: patterns, types and workshops,' in Coales (1987), 133–75.

Blair, J. (1989), 'The Chertsey resting-place list and the enshrinement of Frithuwold', in Bassett (1989), 231–6, 287–8.

Blair, J. (1991a), *Early Medieval Surrey: Landholding, Church and Settlement* (Stroud).

Blair, J. (1991b), 'Purbeck Marble,' in Blair and Ramsay (1991), 41–56.

Blair, J. (1995), 'Debate: ecclesiastical organization and pastoral care in Anglo-Saxon England', *Early Medieval Europe,* 4, 193–212.

Blair, J. (2002), 'Handlist of Anglo-Saxon saints', in Thacker and Sharpe (2002), 495–565.

Blair, J., and Ramsay, N., eds. (1991), *English Medieval Industries: Craftsmen, Techniques, Products* (London, Rio Grande).

Blake, E. C. (2000), 'Zograscopes, perspective prints, and the mapping of polite space in mid-eighteenth century england', PhD thesis, Stanford University.

Blake, E. O., ed. (1962), *Liber Eliensis* (CS, 3rd ser. 92).

Blaxland, G. (1977), *The Middlesex Regiment* (London).

Blayney, P. W .M. (1990) *The Bookshops in Paul's Cross Churchyard* (Occasional Papers of the Bibliographical Soc. 5).

Blayney, P. W.M. (2000), 'John Day and the bookshop that never was', in Orlin, L.C., ed. (2000), *Material London ca. 1600* (Philadelphia), 322–43.

Blockley, K., Sparks, M. and Tatton-Brown, T. (1997), *Canterbury Cathedral Nave: Archaeology, History and Architecture* (Canterbury).

Blomfield, A. (1864), *A Memoir of Charles James Blomfield, D.D. Bishop of London, with Selections from his Correspondence* (London).

Blomfield, C. J. (1840), *Speech of the Lord Bishop of London in the House of Lords on Thursday July 30, 1840, on the Ecclesiastical Duties and Revenues Bill* (London).

Blunt, C. E. (1961), 'The coinage of Offa', in Dolley, R. H. M., ed. (1961), *Anglo-Saxon Coins* (London), 39–62.

Boas, F. S., ed. (1935), *The Diary of Thomas Crosfield M.A. B.D. Fellow of Queen's College, Oxford* (London).

Bold, J. (1989), *John Webb: Architectural Theory and Practice in the Seventeenth Century* (Oxford).

Bold, J. (2000), *Greenwich: An Architectural History of the Royal Hospital For Seamen and the Queen's House* (New Haven and London).

Bold, J. and Chaney, E., eds., *English Architecture Public and Private. Essays for Kerry Downes* (London and Rio Grande).

Bony, J. (1979) *The English Decorated Style: Gothic Architecture Transformed* (Oxford).

Bosher, R. S. (1951), *The Making of the Restoration Settlement: The Influence of the Laudians, 1649–1662* (London).

Boswell, J. C. and Pauls, P. (1989), *Register of Sermons Preached at Paul's Cross 1534–1642* (Centre for Reformation and Renaissance Studies, Victoria Univ. – Univ. of Toronto, Occasional Pub., 6 Ottawa).

Botfield, B. (1849), *Notes on the Cathedral Libraries of England* (London).

Boucheron, P. (2000), 'A qui appartient la cathédrale? La fabrique et la cité dans l'Italie médiévale', in Boucheron, P. and Chiffoleau, J., eds. (2000), *Religion et Société Urbaine au Moyen Âge: études offertes à Jean-Louis Biget par ses anciens élèves* (Paris), 95–117.

Boulencourt, L. de (1683), *Déscription Générale de L'Hostel royal des Invalides* (Paris).

Boulton, J. (2000), 'London 1540–1700', in Clark, P., ed. (2000), *The Cambridge Urban History of Britain, volume II, 1540–1840* (Cambridge), 315–46.

Bowdler, R. (2001), '*Ars longa, vita brevis*: Life, Death and John Everett Millais', in Mancoff, D. ed. (2001), *John Everett Millais. Beyond the Pre-Raphaelite Brotherhood* (London).

Bowen, T. (1798), *A Sermon Preached at the Cathedral Church of St Paul, on Sunday, July 22, 1798, before the Temple-Bar and St Paul's District Military Association* (London).

Bowers, R. (1999), 'The almonry schools of the English monasteries c.1265–1540', in Thompson, B. ed. (1999), *Monasteries and Society in Medieval Britain: Proceedings of the 1994 Harlaxton Symposium* (Stamford), 177–222.

Bowers, R. (2000), 'The Chapel Royal, the first Edwardian Prayer Book, and Elizabeth's settlement of religion, 1559', *Historical Journal* 43, 317–44.

Boyce, W., ed. (1760–73), *Cathedral Music*, 3 vols. (London).

Boyer, S. (1999), 'The cathedral, the city and the Crown: a study of the music and musicians of St Paul's Cathedral, 1660–1697', PhD thesis, University of Manchester, 3 vols.

Bradley, S. and Pevsner, N. (1997), *London 1: The City of London* (The Buildings of England Series, London).

Brady, N. (1996), 'The sacred barn: barn-building in southern England 1100–1550: a study of grain storage technology and its cultural context', PhD thesis, Cornell University.

Brand, P. (1992a), *The Origins of the English Legal Profession* (Oxford).

Brand, P. (1992b), 'Hengham Magna: a thirteenth-century English Common Law treatise', in his *The Making of the Common Law* (Oxford), 369–91.

Bray, G., ed. (1994), *Documents of the English Reformation* (Cambridge).

Bray, W., ed. (1850–52), *Diary and Correspondence of John Evelyn, F.R.S. Author of the 'Sylva' to which is subjoined the Private Correspondence between King Charles I. and Sir Edward Nicholas, and between Sir Edward Hyde, afterwards Earl of Clarendon, and Sir Richard Browne.*, 4 vols. (London).

[Brennan, J., Thistlethwaite, N. et al., eds.] (1996), *Fanfare for an Organ Builder. Essays presented to Noel Mander* (Oxford).

Brett, P., ed. (1967, 2nd edn. 1974), *Consort Songs* (MB 22, London).

Brewer, T. (1856), *Memoir of the Life and Times of John Carpenter* (London).

Brigden, S. (1989), *London and the Reformation* (Oxford).

Briggs, A. (1988), *Victorian Things* (London).

Bristow, I. C. (1996), *Architectural Colour in British Interiors 1615–1840* (New Haven and London).

Brodie, R. H., ed. (1905), 'The Case of Dr. Crome', *TRHS*, n.s. 19, 295–304.

Brooke, C. (1985), 'The archdeacon and the Norman Conquest', in Greenway, Holdsworth, and Sayers (1985), 1–19.

Brooke, C. N. L. (1951), 'The composition of the chapter of St Paul's, 1086–1163', *Cambridge Historical Journal* 10, 111–32.

Brooke, C. N. L. (1956), 'The deans of St Paul's, c.1090–1499', *BIHR* 29, 231–44.

Brooke, C. N. L. (1957), 'The earliest times to 1485', in Matthews and Atkins (1957), 1–99, 361–5.

Brooke, C. N. L. (1989), *The Medieval Idea of Marriage* (Oxford).

Brooke, C. N. L. and Keir, G. (1975), *London, 800–1216: The Shaping of a City* (London).

Brooke, J. (1972), *King George III* (London).

Brooke, Z. N. (1927), 'The register of Master David of London and the part he played in the Becket crisis', in Davis, H. W. C., ed. *Essays in History presented to Reginald Lane Poole* (Oxford), 227–45.

Brooks, D. (1998), *Thomas Allom* (London).

Brooks, N. (1984), *The Early History of the Church of Canterbury* (Leicester).

Brooks, N. and Cubitt, C., eds. (1996), *St Oswald of Worcester: Life and Influence* (Leicester).

Brown, A. (1948), 'Two notes on John Redford', *Modern Language Review* 43, 508–10.

Brown, A. (1952), 'Sebastian Westcote at York', *Modern Language Review* 47, 49–50.

Brown, J. (1763), *On Religious Liberty: A Sermon preached at St Paul's Cathedral 6 March 1763. On Occasion of the Brief for the Establishment of the Colleges of Philadelphia and New York* (London).

Browne, F. (1713), *A Sermon Preach'd before the Right Honourable the Lord Mayor, the Aldermen, and Citizens of London at the Cathedral Church of St Paul, Friday 30 January 1712–13* (London).

Browne, G. F. (1915), *Recollections of a Bishop* (London).

Bruce, J. and Perowne, T. T., eds. (1853), *Correspondence of Matthew Parker, D.D., Archbishop of Canterbury. Comprising Letters Written by and to him, from A.D. 1535, to his Death, A.D. 1575* (Cambridge, Parker Soc.).

Bruce, J., ed. (1845), *Verney Papers: Notes of Proceedings in the Long Parliament, Temp. Charles I, Printed from Original Pencil Memoranda taken in the House by Sir Ralph Verney, knight, Member for the Borough of Aylesbury ...* (CS 31).

Buckle, G. E., ed. (1926), *The Letters of Queen Victoria, Second Series. A Selection from Her Majesty's Correspondence and Journal between the Years 1862 and 1878*, 2 vols. (London).

Bullough, D. (1975), 'The continental background of the reform', in Parsons (1975), 20–36.

Bülow, G. von ed. (1892), 'Diary of the journey of Philip Julius, duke of Stettin-Pomerania, through England in the Year 1602', *TRHS* 6, 1–67.

Bumpus, J. S. (1891), *The Organists and Composers of S. Paul's Cathedral* [London].

Bumpus, J. S. (1908), *A History of English Cathedral Music, 1549–1889*, 2 vols. (London).

Bumpus, J. S. [1913a], *St Paul's Cathedral* (London).

Bumpus, J. S. [1913b], *Westminster Abbey by Jocelyn Perkins...and St.Paul's Cathedral by John S.Bumpus* (London).

Bund, J. W. W., ed. (1915–20), *Diary of Henry Townshend of Elmley Lovett, 1640–1663*, 4 pts in 2 vols. (Worcestershire Hist. Soc.).

Burchnall, R. A. (1993), 'Catalogue of the papers of Edmund Gibson (1669–1748), bishop of London, and his descendants', unpublished typescript in BodL.

Burg, J., ed. (1995), *Religion in Hertfordshire 1847–1851* (Hertfordshire Record Publications, 11).

Burgess, C. (1996), 'Shaping the parish: St Mary at Hill, London, in the fifteenth century', in Blair, J. and Golding, B., eds. (1996), *The Cloister and the World: Essays in Medieval History in Honour of Barbara Harvey* (Oxford), 245–86.

[Burgess, D.] (1710), *Dr Burgis's Answer to Dr Sacheverell's High Flown Sermon* (London).

Burman, P. (1987), *St Paul's Cathedral* (London).

Burnby, J. (1984), 'John Conyers, London's first archaeologist', *TLMAS* 35, 63–80.

Burnet, Gilbert (1707), *A Sermon preached before the Queen, and the two Houses of Parliament, at St Paul's, on the 31st of December, 1706. The Day of Thanksgiving for the Wonderful Successes of this Year. Psalm 72, v. 4* (London).

Burnett, C. S. F. (1981), 'A note on the origins of the Third Vatican Mythographer', *Journal of the Warburg and Courtauld Institutes* 44, 160–6.

Burney, C. (1785), *An Account of the Musical Performances in Westminster Abbey, and the Pantheon... in Commemoration of Handel* (London).

Burns, A. (1999), *The Diocesan Revival in the Church of England c.1800–1870* (Oxford).

Burrows, D. (1981), 'Handel and the English Chapel Royal during the reigns of Queen Anne and King George I', PhD thesis, Open University, 2 vols.

Burrows, D. (1993) 'Theology, politics and instruments in church: musicians and monarchs in London, 1660–1760' in Marx, H. J. ed. (1993), *Göttinger Händel-Beiträge,* Bd v (Kassel), 145–160.

Busson, G. and Ledru, A., eds. (1901), *Archives Historiques du Maine, II, Actus Pontificum Cenomannis in Urbe Degentium* (Le Mans).

Butler, A. S. G. (1950), *The Architecture of Sir Edwin Lutyens,* 3 vols. (London 1950).

Butler, L. H. (1951), 'Robert Braybrook, bishop of London (1381–1404) and his kinsmen', DPhil thesis, University of Oxford.

Cabassut, A. (1952), 'La dévotion au Nom de Jésus dans l'église d'occident', *La Vie Spirituelle* 86, 46–69.

Cadle, P. J. (1999), 'A new broom in the Augean stable: Robert Gregory and liturgical changes at St Paul's cathedral, London, 1868–1890', in Swanson, R. N., ed. (1999), *Continuity and Change in Christian Worship* (SCH 35), 361–73.

Caldwell, J., ed. (1966), *Early Tudor Keyboard Music: Music for the Office* (Early English Church Music 6, London).

Caley, J. and Hunter, J., eds. (1810–34), *Valor Ecclesiasticus, temp. Henrici VIII, auctoritate regia institutus,* 6 vols. (RC).

Cam, H. (1930), *The Hundred and the Hundred Rolls* (London).

Cam, H. (1957), 'The "private" hundred before the Norman Conquest', in Davies, J. C., ed., (1957), *Studies Presented to Sir Hilary Jenkinson* (London), 50–60.

Cam, H. M., ed. (1968–9), *The Eyre of London 14 Edward II, A.D. 1321,* 2 vols. (Selden Soc., 85–6).

Cambridge, E. and Rollason D. (1995), 'Debate: the pastoral organization of the Anglo-Saxon church: a review of the "minster hypothesis"', *Early Medieval Europe* 4, 87–104.

Camden, W. (1772), *Britannia,* trans. Edmund Gibson (4th edn., London).

Campbell, J. (1979/1986), *Bede's Reges and Principes* (Jarrow Lecture, 1979), reprinted in Campbell, J. (1986), *Essays in Anglo-Saxon History* (London), 85–98.

Campbell, J. W. P. (2002), 'Wren and the development of structural carpentry 1660–1710', *Architectural Research Quarterly* 6/1, 49–66.

Cant, R. (1977), 'From 1916 until 1975', in Aylmer, G. E., and Cant, R., eds. (1977), *A History of York Minster* (Oxford), 540–64.

Caraman, P. (1964), *Henry Garnet 1555–1606 and the Gunpowder Plot* (New York).

Cargill Thompson, W. D. J. (1969), 'A reconsideration of Richard Bancroft's Paul's Cross sermon of 9 February 1588/9', *JEcclH* 20, 253–66.

Carlton, C. (1987), *Archbishop William Laud* (London and New York).

Carpenter, E. (1956), *The Protestant Bishop: Being the Life of Henry Compton, 1632–1713 Bishop of London* (London).

Carpenter, E. F. (1957), 'The Reformation: 1485–1660', in Matthews and Atkins (1957), 100–71.

Carpenter, S. C. (1949), *Winnington-Ingram: The Biography of Arthur Foley Winnington-Ingram, Bishop of London 1901–1939* (London).

'Cathedral finance: out of the red for 1981', *Dome* 19 (1981–2), 14.

Catto, J. and Evans, R., eds. (1992), *The History of the University of Oxford, volume II, Late Medieval Oxford* (Oxford).

Centre de Recherches sur les Monuments Historiques (1985), *Charpentes d'assemblage du XVIe siècle au XIXe siècle* (Paris).

Ceremonial: Thanksgiving at St Paul's Cathedral, 27 February 1872 (n.d.).

Chadwick, W. O. (1966–97), *The Victorian Church, Pt 1* and *Pt 2,* 2 vols. (3 edns. of Pt 1; 2 edns. of Pt 2; (London).

Chambers, D. S., ed. (1966), *Faculty Office Registers 1534–1549: A Calendar of the First Two Registers of the Archbishop of Canterbury's Faculty Office* (Oxford).

Chambre, R. (1710), *The Duty of Being Public Spirited: A Sermon Preach'd at St Paul's Cathedral, 25 January 1709/10. Before the Gentlemen educated at St Paul's School* (London).

Chan, M. (2002) 'Music books', in Barnard, J. and McKenzie, D.F., eds. (2002), *The Cambridge History of the Book in Britain, Volume IV, 1557–1695* (Cambridge), 127–37.

Chandler, M. (2000), *The Life and Work of Henry Parry Liddon (1829–1890)* (Leominster).

Chaney, E. (1993), 'Inigo Jones in Naples', in Bold and Chaney (1993), 31–53.

Chaplais, P. (1969), 'Who introduced charters into England? The case for Augustine', *Journal of the Soc. of Archivists* 3, 526–42.

Chaplais, P. (1978), 'The letter from Bishop Wealdhere of London to Archbishop Brihtwold of Canterbury: the earliest original "Letter Close" extant in the west', in Parkes, M. B. and Watson, A. G., eds., (1978), *Manuscripts and Libraries: Essays Presented to N. R. Ker* (London); reprinted in Chaplais, P. (1981), *Essays in Medieval Diplomacy and Administration* (London), 3–23.

Chappell, C. (1989–90), 'St Paul's fire watch', *Dome* 27, 45–8.

Charlton, P. (1984), *John Stainer* (Newton Abbot).

Chauncy, H. (1700), *The Historical Antiquities of Hertfordshire* (London).

Cherry, B. and Pevsner N. (1998), *London 4: North* (The Buildings of England series, London)

Cherry, G. E. and Penny, L. (1986), *Holford: a study in architecture, planning and civic design* (London).

Chew, H. M. and Kellaway, W., eds. (1973), *London Assize of Nuisance 1301–1431* (LRS 10).

Chew, H. M. and Weinbaum, M., eds (1970), *The London Eyre of 1244* (LRS 6).

Chew, H. M., ed. (1965), *London Possessory Assizes: A Calendar* (LRS 1).

Chibnall, M., ed. (1978), *The Ecclesiastical History of Orderic Vitalis, VI* (Oxford).

Childs, W. (1997), 'Resistance and treason in the *Vita Edwardi Secundi*', in Prestwich, M., Britnell, R. H. and Frame, R. eds. (1997), *Thirteenth Century England 6* (Woodbridge), 177–91.

Christiansen, C. P. (1989), 'Evidence for the study of London's late medieval manuscript-book trade', in Griffiths, J. and Pearsall, D., eds. (1989), *Book Production and Publishing in Britain, 1375-1475* (Cambridge), 87-108.

Christianson, C. P. (1987), *Memorials of the Book Trade in Medieval London: The Artisans of Old London Bridge* (Cambridge).

Christianson, C. P. (1990), *A Directory of London Stationers and Book Artisans 1300–1500* (New York).

Christianson, P. (1973), 'From expectation to militance: reformers and Babylon in the first two years of the Long Parliament', *JEcclH* 24, 225–44.

Church, M. C., ed. (1894), *Life and Letters of Dean Church* (London).

Cibber, C. (1713), *The Triumph of Peace* (London).

Clark, J. (1996), 'The temple of Diana', in Bird, J., Hassall, M. and Sheldon, H. eds. (1996), *Interpreting Roman London: papers in memory of Hugh Chapman* (Oxford, Oxbow Monographs, 58), 1–10.

Clark, J. B. (1968), 'Adrian Batten and John Barnard: colleagues and collaborators', *Musica Disciplina* 22, 207–29.

Clark, J. B. (1974), *Transposition in Seventeenth-Century English Organ Accompaniments and the Transposing Organ* (Detroit).

Clark, J. W. (1899), 'On ancient libraries: … (3). S. Paul's Cathedral, London', *Proc. Cambridge Antiquarian Soc.* 9 (for 1894–8), 37–60.

Clarke, M., and Penny, N., eds. (1982), *The Arrogant Connoisseur, Richard Payne Knight, 1751–1824* (Manchester).

Clarke, S. (1902), 'Report on important works needed in St Paul's Cathedral, 13 Oct. 1902', unpublished report on the cathedral, from copy in the office of Alan Baxter Associates.

Clarke, S. (1923), 'St Paul's Cathedral: observations on Wren's system of buttresses for the dome piers and on some other things', in Dircks (1923).

Clarke, W. K. L. (1959), *A History of the SPCK* (London).

Clarke-Whitfield, J. [1805], *A Miscellaneous Volume of Morning and Evening Services in Score* [*Cathedral Music,* ii] (London).

Clay, C. T. (1944), 'The keepership of the old palace of Westminster', *EHR* 59, 1–21.

Clay, J. W., ed. (1899), *The Registers of St. Paul's Cathedral* (Harleian Soc. Registers, 26).

Clayton, T. (1997), *The English Print, 1688–1802* (New Haven and London).

Clifton, R. (1973), 'Fear of Popery', in Russell (1973).

Clinch, G. (1906), *St Paul's Cathedral, London* (London).

Clunn, H. P. (1927, 1951), *The Face of London* (London).

Clutterbuck, R. (1815–27), *The History and Antiquities of the County of Hertford,* 3 vols. (London).

Coales, J., ed. (1987), *The Earliest English Brasses: Patronage, Style and Workshop 1270–1350* (London).

Coates, R. (1998), 'A new explanation of the name London', *Trans. of the Philological Soc.* 92, 203–29.

Coates, R. (1999), 'New light from old wicks: the progeny of Latin *vicus*', *Nomina* 22, 75–116.

Coates, W. H., ed. (1942), *The Journal of Sir Simonds D'Ewes From the First Recess of the Long Parliament to the Withdrawal of King Charles from London* (New Haven, Conn.).

Cobb, G. (1980), *English Cathedrals, the Forgotten Centuries* (London).

Coldstream, N. (1976) 'English Decorated shrine bases', *JBAA* 129, 15–34.

Coldstream, N. (1994) *The Decorated Style: Architecture and Ornament 1240–1360* (London).

Coleridge, S. T. (1829), *On the Constitution of Church and State* (London).

Colgrave, B. and Mynors, R. A. B., eds., (1991), *Bede's Ecclesiastical History of the English People* (corr. reprint of the 1969 edn., Oxford). This provides both text and translation, but some of the translation is questionable. Bede's book and chapter numbers are indicated parenthetically in the form (I.3).

Colgrave, B., ed., (1927), *The Life of Bishop Wilfrid by Eddius Stephanus* (Cambridge).

Colker, M. L. (1965), 'Texts of Jocelyn of Canterbury which relate to the history of Barking abbey', *Studia Monastica* 7, 383–460.

Colley, L. (1992), *Britons: Forging the Nation, 1707–1837* (New Haven and London).

Collins, D. (1992), *Partners in Protest: Life with Canon Collins* (London).

Collins, L. J. (1966), *Faith under Fire* (London).

Collinson, P. (1964), *A Mirror of Elizabethan Puritanism: The Life and Letters of 'Godly Master Dering'*, (London, Friends of Dr Williams's Library, 17th Lecture, 1963).

Collinson, P. (1967), *The Elizabethan Puritan Movement* (London).

Collinson, P. (1979), *Archbishop Grindal 1519–1583: The Struggle for a Reformed Church* (London).

Collinson, P. (1995), 'The Protestant cathedral, 1541–1660', in Collinson, Ramsay and Sparks (1995), 154–203.

Collinson, P., Ramsay, N. and Sparks, M., eds. (1995), *A History of Canterbury Cathedral* (Oxford).

Colsoni, F. (1951), *Le Guide de Londres* (LTS reprint, Cambridge).

Colvin, H. (1951), 'Roger North and Sir Christopher Wren', *Architectural Review* 110, 257–60.

Colvin, H. (1995), *A Biographical Dictionary of British Architects, 1600–1840: Third Edition* (New Haven and London).

Colvin, H. (2000), 'The origin of chantries', *Journal of Medieval History* 26, 163–73.

Colvin, H. and Foister, S., eds. (1996), *The Panorama of London circa 1544 by Anthonis van den Wyngaerde* (LTS 151).

Colvin, H. and Newman, J. (1981), *Of Building: Roger North's Writings on Architecture* (Oxford).

Colvin, H. M., ed. (1963), *The History of the King's Works, Volume I, The Middle Ages* (London).

Colvin, H. M., ed. (1976), *History of the King's Works, Volume V, 1660–1782* (London).

Colvin, H. M., ed. (1975), *The History of the King's Works, Volume III, 1485–1660 (Part I)* (London).

Conner, P. (1984), *Michael Angelo Rooker* (London).

Constable, W. G. (1976), *Canaletto*, 2 vols. (Oxford).

Cook, G. H. (1955), *Old S. Paul's Cathedral: a Lost Glory of Mediaeval London* (London).

Cook, G. H. (1963), *Mediaeval Chantries and Chantry Chapels* (London, rev. edn.).

Cooper, B., ed. (1996), *John Blow: Complete Organ Music* (MB 69).

Copeland, R. (2001), *Pedagogy, Intellectuals and Dissent in the Later Middle Ages: Lollardy and Ideas of Learning* (Cambridge).

Corner, G. R. (1858), 'A collection of ancient wills, &c, relating to Southwark', *Surrey Archaeological Collections* 1, 190–202.

Cornford, L. C. (1913), *William Ernest Henley* (London).

Coronelli, V. (1697), *Viaggi*, pt. 2 (Venice).

Corporation of London Improvements and Town Planning Committee (1944), *Reconstruction in the City of London* (London).

Corrie, G. E., ed. (1844), *The Works of Hugh Latimer, Sometime Bishop of Worcester, Martyr, 1555*, I (Cambridge, Parker Soc.).

Courtenay, William J. (1987), *Schools and Scholars in Fourteenth-Century England* (Princeton).

Cowie, L. W. (1956), *Henry Newman: An American in London 1708–1743* (London).

Cowie, L. W. (1974), 'Paul's Walk', *History Today* 24, 41–47.

Cowie, L. W. (1977), 'Holy Thursday', *History Today* 27, 513–19.

Cownie, E. (1998), *Religious Patronage in Anglo-Norman England 1066–1135* (Woodbridge).

Cox, G. (1989), *Organ Music in Restoration England* (New York and London).

Cox, N. (1978), *Bridging the Gap: A History of the Corporation of the Sons of the Clergy over 300 years, 1655–1978* (Oxford).

Cox-Johnson, A. (1961), *John Bacon, R. A., 1740–1799* (London, St Marylebone Soc. Publications).

Crankshaw, D. J. (1998), 'Preparations for the Canterbury provincial convocation of 1562–63: a question of attribution', in Wabuda, S. and Litzenberger, C., eds. (1998), *Belief and Practice in Reformation England: A Tribute to Patrick Collinson from his Students* (Aldershot), 60–93.

Craufurd, J. G. (1955–6), 'The Madrigal Society', *Proc. of the Royal Musical Soc.* 82, 33–47.

Crawford, A. (1973), 'The charter of Shiryngton's chantry in the chapel of St Margaret, Uxbridge, 1459', *Journal of the Soc. of Archivists* 4, 588–92.

Crayford, R. (1997), 'Inigo Jones's portico on Old St Paul's', *Association for Studies in the Conservation of Historic Buildings, Trans.* 22, 44–55.

Crellin, D. (2002), '"When in Rome": Lutyens's architectural translations of Sanmicheli', in Hopkins, A. and Stamp, G. (2002).

Cressy, D. (1989), *Bonfires and Bells: National Memory and the Protestant Calendar in Elizabethan and Stuart England* (London).

Crick, J. (2001), 'Offa, Ælfric and the refoundation of St Albans', in Henig, M. and Lindley, P. eds., *Alban and St Albans. Roman and Medieval Architecture, Art and Archaeology* (BAACT, 24).

Crick, J. (forthcoming), *Charters of St Albans*, Anglo-Saxon Charters 11 (Oxford).

Croft, P. (1998), 'The rebuilding of the city of London 1945–1966', postgraduate diploma thesis, Architectural Association.

Croft-Murray, E. (1962–70), *Decorative Painting in England 1537–1837*, 2 vols. (London).

Crook, J. (2000), *The Architectural Setting of the Cult of the Saints in the Early Christian West c.300–1200* (Oxford).

Crook, J. M. (1981), *William Burges and the High Victorian Dream* (Southampton).

Croot, P. (1997), 'Settlement, tenure and land use in medieval Stepney: evidence of a field survey c.1400', *LonJ* 22, 1–15.

Crosby, E. U. (1994), *Bishop and Chapter in Twelfth-Century England: a Study of the 'Mensa Episcopalis'* (Cambridge).

Cross, C. (1972), '"Dens of Loitering Lubbers": Protestant protest against cathedral foundations, 1540–1640', in Baker, D., ed. (1972), *Schism, Heresy and Religious Protest* (SCH 9), 231–237.

Crossley, J. and Christie, R. C., eds. (1847–86), *Diary and Correspondence of Dr John Worthington*, 2 vols. in 3 parts (Chetham Soc. 13, 36, 114).

Crowe, W. (1724), *The Duty of Promoting the Public Peace. A Sermon Preached before the Right Honourable the Lord Major, the Aldermen, Sheriffs and Citizens of London, in the Cathedral Church of St Paul, 30 January 1724* (London).

Cubitt, C. R. E. (1995), *Anglo-Saxon Church Councils c.650–c.850* (London).

Cudworth, C. (1962), 'R. J. S. Stevens, 1757–1837', *Musical Times* 103, 754–6, 834–5.

Cudworth, C. (1967) 'An eighteenth-century musical apprenticeship', *Musical Times* 108, 602–4.

Cunningham, A. (1829–33), *Lives of the most Eminent British Painters, Sculptors and Architects*, 6 vols. (London).

Curnock, N. (1909–16), *The Journal of the Rev John Wesley: Enlarged from Original Mss. With Notes from Unpublished Diaries, Annotations, and Illustrations*, 8 vols. (London).

Dale, T. (1852), *Five Years of Church Extension in St Pancras* (London).

Dales, D. S. (1988), *Dunstan: Saint and Statesman* (Cambridge).

Dalton, C. (1890), *The Waterloo Roll Call* (London).

Dane, J. (1710), *The Reformation Protected by the Providence of God; or the Deliverance of the Protestant Church of Great Britain and Ireland from the Evil Design of Papists. A Sermon Preach'd in St Paul's Cathedral, London, Monday 23 October 1710. Before the Protestant Gentlemen of Ireland. It being their Anniversary-Day of Meeting in Commemoration of their Deliverance from the Barbarous Massacre Committed by the Papists in Ireland in the Year 1641* (London).

Daniel, R. T. and le Huray, P. (1972), *The Sources of English Church Music, 1549–1660* (EECM Supplementary Vol. 1).

Daniell, D. (1994), *William Tyndale: A Biography* (New Haven and London).

Darby, M. and Physick, J. (1973), 'Marble Halls': Drawings and Models for Victorian Secular Buildings (London, Victoria and Albert Museum).

Dark, S. (1928), *Five Deans* (London).

Dasent, J. R., ed. (1890–1907), *Acts of the Privy Council of England*, n.s., 32 vols. (London).

Davies, J. (1992), *The Caroline Captivity of the Church: Charles I and the Remoulding of Anglicanism 1625–1641* (Oxford).

Davies, M. and Saunders, A. (2004), *The History of the Merchant Taylors' Company* (Leeds).

Davies, M. P. (1994), 'The Tailors of London and Their Guild, c.1300–1500,' DPhil thesis, University of Oxford.

Davies, M., ed. (2000), *The Merchant Taylors' Company of London: Court Minutes 1486–1493* (Stamford).

Davies, R. G. (1975–7), 'Difficulties in the administration of the diocese of London, 1416–19', *Guildhall Studies in London History* 2, 1–10.

Davies, W. and Vierck, H. (1974), 'The contexts of the Tribal Hidage: social aggregates and settlement patterns', *Frümittelalterliche Studien* 8, 223–93.

Davis, G. R. C. (1958), *Medieval Cartularies of Great Britain: A Short Catalogue* (London).

Davis, H. W. C. (1925), 'London lands and liberties of St Paul's', in Little, A. G. and Powicke, F. M., eds. (1925), *Essays in Medieval History Presented to T. F. Tout* (Manchester), 45–59.

Davis, J. (1982), 'Joan of Kent, Lollardy and the English Reformation', *JEcclH* 33, 225–33.

Davis, N., ed. (1971–76), *Paston Letters and Papers of the Fifteenth Century*, 2 vols. (Oxford).

Davis, R. H. C. (1972), 'The college of St Martin-le-Grand and the Anarchy', *LTR* 23, 9–26.

Davis, V. (2000), *Clergy in London in the Late Middle Ages. A Register of Clergy Ordained in the Diocese of London based on Episcopal Ordination Lists 1361–1539* (London).

Dawe, D. (1983), *Organists of the City of London, 1666–1850* (Padstow, Cornwall).

Dawton, N. (1983), 'The Percy tomb at Beverley Minster: the style of the sculpture', in Thompson, F. H., ed. (1983), *Studies in Medieval Sculpture* (London), 122–50.

DB: Farley, A. and Ellis, H. eds. (1783–1816), *Liber Censualis vocatus Domesday-Book*, 4 vols. (RC). References are also provided to the numbered paragraphs in the Philimore edition, which appear in parenthesis after the folio number: *Domesday Book: Hertfordshire*, ed., Newman, M. and Wood, S. (Chichester, 1976); *Domesday Book: Middlesex*, ed. Wood, S. (Chichester, 1975); *Domesday Book: Bedfordshire*, ed. Sankaran, V. and Sherlock, D. (Chichester, 1977); *Domesday Book: Essex*, ed. Rumble, A. (Chichester, 1983).

de Beer, E. S., ed. (1955), *The Diary of John Evelyn*, 6 vols. (Oxford).

de Coetlogon, C. E. (1790a), *God and the King: A Sermon Delivered in the Cathedral-Church of St Paul, before the Lord Mayor, 25 October 1790* (London).

de Coetlogon, C. E. (1790b), *National Gratitude, for Providential Goodness, Recommended in a Sermon Preached before the Lord Mayor, Aldermen and Sheriffs, at St Paul's Cathedral on 29 May 1790, being the Anniversary of the Restoration of Charles II* (London).

de Coetlogon, C. E. (1790c), *Pious Memorials, a Public Good: A Sermon Delivered in the Cathedral Church of St Paul, before the Lord Mayor, 5 November 1790* (London).

de Coetlogon, C. E. (1790d), *Religion and Loyalty, the Grand Support of the British Empire. A Sermon on 30 January 1790, being the Anniversary of the Martyrdom of Charles I* (London).

de Coetlogon, C. E. (1790e), *The Essential Deity of the Messiah; and the Great Importance of that Article of the Christian Faith, to Every Conscientious Member of the Church of England, Considered in a Sermon Preached in the Cathedral Church of St Paul on 24 January 1790* (London).

de Coetlogon, C. E. (1790f) *The Harmony between Religion and Policy; or Divine and Human Legislation: A Sermon delivered before the Lord Mayor, in St Paul's, 25 April 1790* (London).

de Coetlogon, C. E. (1790g), *The Surprize of Death! A Commemorative Sermon on the Character, Sufferings, and Crucifixion of the Son of God: Deliver'd in St Paul's Cathedral, before the Right Honourable the Lord Mayor, Aldermen, and Sheriffs on 2 April 1790; Being Good Friday* (London).

de Hamel, C. F. R. (1991), *Syon Abbey: The Library of the Bridgettine Nuns and their Peregrinations after the Reformation* (Roxburghe Club).

De Lévis, P. M. G. (1814), *L'Angleterre au commencement du dix-neuvième siècle* (Paris).

de Vries, J. (1984), *European Urbanization, 1500–1800* (London).

de Worde, W. (1522?), *Almacke for. XV. yeres* (London) (BL shelfmark Huth 54).

Dearnley, C. (1969), 'The Need for a Reformed Approach to Church Music,' *English Church Music* 1969, 23.

Dedication of the American Memorial Chapel in the Presence of Her Majesty the Queen and the Vice President of the United States 26 November 1858 (n.d.).

Defoe, D. (1725), *A Tour of the Whole Island of Great Britain*, vol. 2 (London).

Defoe, D. (1991), *A Tour of the Whole Island of Great Britain*, ed. Furbank, P. N. and Owens, W. R. (New Haven and London).

Dekker, T. (1609), *The Gvls Horne-booke* (London).

Dekkers, E. (1995), *Clavis Patrum Latinorum*, (Steenbrugis, Corpus Christianorum Series Latina, 3rd edn.).

Delehaye, H. (1931), 'In Britannia dans le martyrologue hiéromynien', *Proc. of the British Academy* 17, 289–307.

Denholm-Young, N. (1956), 'The authorship of *Vita Edwardi Secundi*', *EHR* 71, 189–211.

Denholm-Young, N., ed. and trans. (1957), *Vita Edwardi Secundi* (Nelson's Medieval Texts, London and Edinburgh).

Dent, C. M. (1983), *Protestant Reformers in Elizabethan Oxford* (Oxford).

[Deputy Keeper of the Public Records] (1886), *The Forty-Sixth Annual Report of the Deputy Keeper of the Public Records*, Appendix I (London).

Deutsch, O. E. (1955), *Handel: a Documentary Biography* (London).

Dibden, T. J. (1827), *Reminiscences* (London).

Dick, O. L., ed. (1972), *Aubrey's Brief Lives* (Harmondsworth).

Dickinson, H. T., ed. (1967 for 1963), *The Correspondence of Sir James Clavering* (Surtees Soc., 178).

Dimock, A. (1900), *The Cathedral Church of St Paul* (London).

Dircks, R., ed. (1923), *Sir Christopher Wren A.D. 1623–1723: Bicentenary Memorial Volume published under the auspices of the Royal Institute of British Architects* (London).

Directions to those who take part in the Day and Night Watch of Intercession to be Kept in St Paul's Cathedral from 8 am Dec 16th to 8 am Dec 17th 1914 (n.d.).

Doble, C. E., et al., eds. (1884–1918), *Remarks and Collections of Thomas Hearne*, 11 vols. (Oxford Historical Soc., 2–72).

Documents on the Liturgy (1963–1979), Conciliar, Papal and Curial Texts (Collegevilla, MA, 1982).

Dodwell, R. (1982), *Anglo-Saxon Art: A New Perspective* (Manchester).

Dodwell, W. (1760), *A Sermon Preach'd before the Sons of the Clergy: in the Cathedral Church of St Paul, Thursday 8 May 1760* (London).

Donno, E. S., ed. (1976 for 1974), *An Elizabethan in 1582: The Diary of Richard Madox Fellow of All Souls* (Hakluyt Soc., 2nd ser. 147).

Dorn, H., and Mark, R. (1981), 'The architecture of Christopher Wren', *Scientific American* 245 (July 1981), 126–38.

Douët d'Arcq (1851), *Comptes d'argenterie des rois de France au XIV siècle* (Paris, Société de l'histoire de France).

Douglas Hamilton, W., ed. (1875), *A Chronicle of England During the Reigns of the Tudors, from A.D.1485 to 1559 by Charles Wriothesley, Windsor Herald*, i (CS, n.s. 11).

Douglas Hamilton, W., ed. (1877), *A Chronicle of England During the Reigns of the Tudors, from A.D.1485 to 1559 by Charles Wriothesley, Windsor Herald*, ii (CS, n.s. 20).

Downes, K. (1959), *Hawksmoor* (London).

Downes, K. (1966), *English Baroque Architecture* (London).

Downes, K. (1982), *The Architecture of Wren* (London).

Downes, K. (1988), *Sir Christopher Wren: the Design of St Paul's Cathedral* (London).

Downes, K. (1994), 'Sir Christopher Wren, Edward Woodroffe, J. H. Mansart, and architectural history', *Architectural History* 37, 37–67.

Downes, K. (2001), 'St Paul's Cathedral and its architecture', *LTR* 28, 1–22.

Draper, P. (1990), 'Seeing that it was done in all the noble churches in England', in Fernie, E. and Crossley, P. eds. (1990), *Medieval Architecture and its Intellectual Context. Studies in Honour of Peter Kidson* (London), 137–52.

Driskel, M. P. (1993), *As Befits a Legend. Building a Tomb for Napoleon* (Kent, Ohio).

Du Boulay, F. R. H. and Barron, C. M., eds. (1971), *The Reign of Richard II: Essays in Honour of May McKisack* (London).

du Prey, P. de la R. (2000), *Hawksmoor's London Churches. Architecture and Theology* (Chicago).

Duff, E. G. (1905), *A Century of the English Book Trade: Short Notices of all Printers, Stationers, Book-Binders, and Others connected with it from the Issue of the first dated Book in 1497 to the Incorporation of the Company of Stationers in 1557* (London).

Duffy, E. (1992), *The Stripping of the Altars: Traditional Religion in England c.1400–c.1580* (New Haven and London).

Duffy, E. (2003), 'St Erkenwald: London's cathedral saint and his legend', in Backhouse (2003), 150–67.

Duffy, M. (2000), *The Younger Pitt* (Harlow).

Dugdale, W. (1655–73), *Monasticon Anglicanum*, 3 vols. (1st edn., London).

Dugdale, W. (1658) *The History of St Paul's Cathedral in London: from its foundation untill these times: from its foundation untill these times / extracted out of originall charters. Records. Leiger books, and other manuscripts. Beautified with sundry prospects of the church, figures of tombes, and monuments* (London).

Dugdale, W. (1680), *Origines Judiciales* (London).

Dugdale, W. (1716), *The History of St Paul's Cathedral, from its Foundation…A continuation, setting forth what was done in the Structure of the New Church, to the year: 1685…The Second Edition corrected and enlarged by the Author's own Hand. To which is prefixed, his Life, written by himself. Published by Edward Maynard, D.D.* (London).

Dugdale, W. (1818), *The History of St Paul's Cathedral in London…with a continuation and additions by Henry Ellis* (London).

Dummelow, J. (1973), *The Wax Chandlers of London* (London and Chichester).

Dumville, D. (1993), 'Essex, Middle Anglia and the expansion of Mercia in the south-east Midlands', in Dumville (1993), 1–30; reprint of Dumville in Bassett (1989), 123-40, with footnotes added.

Dumville, D. N. (1989), 'The Tribal Hidage: an introduction to its texts and their history', in Bassett (1989), 225–30.

Dumville, D. N. (1992), 'The treaty of Alfred and Guthrum', in Dumville, D. N. (1992), *Wessex and England from Alfred to Edgar* (Woodbridge), 1–27.

Duncan, A. (1806), *A Correct Narrative of The Funeral of Horatio Lord Viscount Nelson* (London).

Dunn, R. D., ed. (1984), William Camden, *Remains Concerning Britain* (Toronto and Buffalo).

Dyer, C. (1989), *Standards of Living in the Later Middle Ages* (Cambridge).

Dyson, A. G. (1981), 'The terms "quay" and "wharf" and the early medieval waterfront of London', in Milne, G. and Hobley, B., eds. (1981), *Waterfront Archaeology in Britain and Northern Europe* (London, CBA Research Report 41), 37–8.

Dyson, T. (1978), 'Two Saxon land-grants for Queenhithe', in Bird, J., Chapman, H. and Clarke, J., eds. (1978), *Collectanea Londoniensia. Studies ... presented to R. Merrifield* (London), 200–15.

Eales, R., and Sharpe, R., eds (1995), *Canterbury and the Norman Conquest* (London).

Earle, J. (1966), *The Autograph Manuscript of Microcosmographie* (Leeds).

Ecclesia Restaurata: A Votive Poem to the Rebuilding of St Paul's Cathedral (London, 1677).

Edmunds, M. M. S. (2002), *Piety and Politics: Imagining Divine Kingship in Louis XIV's Chapel at Versailles* (Delaware).

Edwards, E. (1859), *Memoirs of Libraries: including a Handbook of Library Economy*, 2 vols. (London).

Edwards, K. (1967), *The English Secular Cathedrals in the Middle Ages: a constitutional study with special reference to the fourteenth century* (2nd edn., Manchester).

Eeles, F. C. (1910), *Traditional Ceremonial and Customs Connected with the Scottish Liturgy* (AC 17).

Eeles, F. C. (1955–60), 'Part of the kalendar of a XIIIth-century service book once in the church of Writtle', *Trans. of the Essex Archaeological Soc.* 25, n.s., 68–79.

Ehrman, J. (1969), *Pitt the Younger: The Years of Acclaim* (London).

Eiche, S. (May 2001), 'Read all about it', *BBC History Magazine*, 24–6.

Ekwall, E. (1954), *Street-Names of the City of London* (Oxford).

Elliott, C. R. (1965), 'Ambassador in armour', *Sussex Life* (Sept. 1965), 30–2.

Elliott, G. P., ed. (1853), 'Autobiography and anecdotes by William Taswell, D.D., sometime rector of Newington, Surrey, rector of Bermondsey, and previously student of Christ Church, Oxford. A.D. 1651–1682', *Camden Miscellany* 2 (CS 55), 1–40.

Elliott, W. H. (1951), *Undiscovered Ends: Autobiography* (London).

Ellis, H., ed. (1812), *The Chronicle of John Harding* (London).

Ellis Roberts, R. (1942), *H. R. L. Sheppard: Life and Letters* (London).

Elmes, J. (1823), *Memoirs of the Life and Works of Sir Christopher Wren* (London).

Elmes, J. (1852), *Sir Christopher Wren and his Times* (London).

Elon, A. (1996), *Founder: Meyer Amshel Rothschild and his Time* (London).

Elsden, N. (2002), *Excavations at 25 Cannon Street, City of London* (Museum of London Archaeology Service, Archaeology Studies 5).

Elton, G. R. (1953), 'An early Tudor Poor Law', *EconHR*, 2nd Ser. 6, 55–67.

Elton, G. R. (1972), *Policy and Police: The Enforcement of the Reformation in the Age of Thomas Cromwell* (Cambridge).

Elwin, M., ed. (1950), *The Autobiography and Journal of Benjamin Robert Haydon (1786–1846)* (London).

Emden, A. B. (1957–9), *A Biographical Register of the University of Oxford to A.D. 1500*, 3 vols. (Oxford).

Emden, A. B. (1963), *A Biographical Register of the University of Cambridge to 1500* (Cambridge).

English Baroque Sketches: the Painted Interior in the Age of Thornhill (Exhibition catalogue published by Greater London Council, 1974).

Erskine, A., Hope, V., and Lloyd, J. (1988), *Exeter Cathedral: A Short History and Description* (Exeter).

Esmonde Cleary, A. S. (1989), *The Ending of Roman Britain* (London).

Evans, A. K. B., *St George's Chapel, Windsor Castle, 1348–1416. A Study in Early Collegiate Administration* (Westminster, 1948).

Evans, D. (1968), *Four Anthems by Adrian Batten* (London).

Every, G. (1956), *The High Church Party, 1688–1718* (London).

Fairburn's Edition of the Funeral of Admiral Lord Nelson (London, 1806).

Faith R. (1994), 'Demesne resources and labour rent on the manors of St Paul's Cathedral, 1066–1222', *EconHR* 47, 657–78.

Faith, R. (1996), 'The topography and social structure of a small soke in the Middle Ages: The Sokens, Essex', *Essex Archaeology and History* 27, 202–13.

Faith, R. (1997), *The English Peasantry and the Growth of Lordship* (Leicester).

Farley, H. (1616), *The Complaint Of Pavles, To All Christian Sovles: Or an Humble Supplication, to our Good King and Nation, For Her Newe Reparation* [London].

Farmer, D. H. (1975), 'The progress of monastic reform', in Parsons (1975), 10–19.

Farmer, H. G. (1936), 'A forgotten composer of anthems: William Savage (1720–89)', *Music and Letters* 17, 188–99.

Félibien, J. F. (1706), *Description de la Nouvelle Eglise de l'Hostel Royal des Invalides* (Paris).

Fellowes, E. H. (1941), *English Cathedral Music* (London).

Fellowes, E. H. (1951), 'Sir John Stainer', *English Church Music* 21/1, 4.

Fenning, W. D. (1915–22), 'Elbow Lane', *East Herts Arch Soc. Trans.* 6, 68–71.

Fergusson, J. (1862), *History of the Modern Styles of Architecture* (London).

Fernie, E. (1998), 'The Romanesque church of Bury St Edmunds Abbey', in Gransden, A., ed. (1998), *Bury St Edmunds: Medieval Art, Architecture, Archaeology and Economy* (BAACT 20), 1–15.

Fernie, E. (2000), *The Architecture of Norman England* (Oxford).

Finch, R. H. C. (1935), 'Old St Paul's: a reconstruction', *The Builder* 148 (19 and 26 April 1935), 728–30, 772–3, 778–9.

Fincham, K., ed. (1998), *Visitation Articles and Injunctions of the Early Stuart Church*, ii (Church of England Record Soc., 5).

Finlay, R. (1981), *Population and Metropolis: the Demography of London, 1580–1650* (Cambridge).

Firth, C. H., ed. (1899), *The Clarke Papers: Selections From the Papers of William Clarke, Secretary to the Council of the Army, 1647–1649, and to General Monck and the Commanders of the Army in Scotland, 1651–1660*, iii (CS, n.s. 60).

Firth, C. H., ed. (1901), *The Clarke Papers: Selections From the Papers of William Clarke, Secretary to the Council of the Army, 1647–1649, and to General Monck and the Commanders of the Army in Scotland, 1651–1660*, iv (CS, n.s. 62).

Firth, C. H., and Rait, R. S., eds. (1911), *Acts and Ordinances of the Interregnum 1642–1660*, 3 vols. (London).

Fisher, P. (1885), *The tombs, monuments, &c., visible in S. Paul's Cathedral (and S. Faith's beneath it) previous to its destruction by fire A.D. 1666*, ed. G. Blacker Morgan (London).

Fisher, R. M. (1978), 'The origins of divinity lectureships at the Inns of Court, 1569–1585', *JEcclH* 29, 145–62.

Fitton, D. (2002), 'The first 50 years from a financial perspective', in Shaw and Miller (2002), 103–5.

Flanders, D. (1937–1994), 'Register of drawings, 1937–1994' (MS in GL Print Room).

Flanders, D. (1984), *Dennis Flanders' Britannia* (London).

Fleetwood, W. (1708), *A Sermon Preach'd before the Queen at St Paul's, 19 August 1708: the day of Thanksgiving for our Deliverance from the Late Invasion, and for the Victory Obtain'd near Audenard* (London).

Fleming, G. (1634), *Magnificence Exemplified: and, The Repaire of Saint Pauls exhorted unto* (London).

Fletcher, A. (1977), 'Concern for renewal in the Root and Branch debates of 1641', in Baker, D., ed. (1977), *Renaissance and Renewal in Christian History* (SCH 14), 279–86.

Fletcher, A. (1981), *The Outbreak of the English Civil War* (London).

Fletcher, A. and MacCulloch, D. (1997), *Tudor Rebellions* (4th edn., London).

Flynn, J. (1995), 'The education of choristers in England during the sixteenth century', in Morehen, J. ed., (1995), *English Choral Practice 1400–1650* (Cambridge), 180–99.

Forshaw, J. H. and Abercrombie, P. (1943), *County of London Plan* (London).

Forster, E. M. (1910), *Howards End* (London).

Fortescue, J., ed. (1927–8), *The Correspondence of King George the Third from 1760 to December 1783*, 6 vols. (London).

Foster, J. (1887–92), *Alumni Oxonienses: The Members of the University of Oxford, being the Matriculation Register of the University, Alphabetically Arranged, Revised and Annotated*, 8 vols. (Oxford).

Fouracre, P., and Geberding, R. (1996), *Late Merovingian France* (Manchester).

Fowler, R. C. and Jenkins, C. eds. (1927–38), *Registrum Simonis de Sudbiria, Diocesis Londoniensis, A.D. 1362–75*, 2 vols. (London, Canterbury and York Soc. 34, 38).

Fowler, R. C., ed. (1911), *Registrum Radulphi Baldock, Gilberti Segrave, Ricardi Newport, et Stephani Gravesend, Episcoporum Londoniensium AD MCCCIV–MDCCCXXXVIII* (London, Canterbury and York Soc. 7).

Fox, A. (1960), *Dean Inge* (London).

Fox, F. (1924), *Sixty-three years of Engineering, Scientific and Social Work* (London).

Fox, J. (1570), *The Ecclesiastical history contaynyng the Actes and Monumentes of … Martyrs …* (London, enlarged edn.).

Foxon, D. F. (1964), *Libertine Literature in England, 1660–1745* (London).

Fraser, C. M., ed. (1953), *Records of Antony Bek, Bishop and Patriarch* (Surtees Soc., 162).

Frauds and Abuses (15th April 1712) [pamphlet in SPCL].

Freeman, A. (1977), *Father Smith* (a revision of the 1926 edn. with new material by J. Rowntree, Oxford).

Freeman, J. (2001), 'Middlesex in the fifteenth century: community or communities?' in Hicks, M., ed. (2001), *Revolution and Consumption in late Medieval England* (Woodbridge), 89–103.

Freeman, T. (2002), 'Dissenters from a dissenting church: the challenge of the Freewillers, 1550–1558', in Marshall, P. and Ryrie, A., eds. (2002), *The Beginnings of English Protestantism* (Cambridge).

Frere, W. H. and Douglas, C. E., eds. (1954), *Puritan Manifestoes: A Study of the Origin of the Puritan Revolt* (London).

Frere, W. H., and Kennedy, W. M., eds. (1910), *Visitation Articles and Injunctions of the Period of the Reformation*, 3 vols. (AC 14–16).

Frost, W. A. [1925], *Early Recollections of St Paul's Cathedral: A Piece of Autobiography* (London).

Fuller, A. R. B. (1947), 'The minor corporations of the secular cathedrals of the province of Canterbury (excluding the Welsh sees) between the 13th century and 1536, with special reference to the minor canons of St Paul's cathedral from their origin in the 12th century to the visitation of Bishop Gibson in 1724,' MA thesis, University of London.

Fuller, A. R. B. (1965), 'The library', unpublished typescript, SPCL files, 5.

Fuller, A. R. B. (1967–8), 'A note on the cathedral library', *Dome* 5, 16–18.

Furnivall, F. J., ed. (1908), *Harrison's Description of England in Shakespeare's Youth… Part IV. The Supplement, 2* (London).

Gaimster, M. and Bradley, J., eds. (2002), 'Medieval Britain and Ireland, 2001', *Medieval Archaeology* 46, 146–264.

Gair, W. R. (1978), 'The presentation of plays at Second Paul's: the early phase, 1599–1602', *The Elizabethan Theatre, VI*, ed. G. Hibbard (Toronto), 21–47.

Gair, W. R. (1980a), '"Second Paul"; its theatre and personnel: its later repertoire and audience, 1602–6)', *The Elizabethan Theatre, VII*, ed. G. Hibbard (Port Credit) 21–46.

Gair, W. R. (1980b), 'The conditions of appointment for masters of choristers at Paul's (1553–1613),' *Notes and Queries* 225, 116–24.

Gair, W. R. (1982), *The Children of Paul's: the Story of a Theatre Company, 1553–1608* (Cambridge).

Gairdner, J., ed. (1858), *Memorials of King Henry VII* (RS 10).

Gairdner, J., ed. (1880), *Three Fifteenth-Century Chronicles, with Historical Memoranda by John Stowe, the Antiquary, and Contemporary Notes of Occurrences written by him in the Reign of Queen Elizabeth* (CS, n.s. 28).

Galloway, P. (1996), *The Order of the British Empire* [London?].

Galloway, P. (2000), *The Order of St Michael and St George* (Lingfield).

Galt, J. (1816), *Life and Works of Benjamin West Esq* (London).

Games, S., ed. (2002), *Nikolaus Pevsner: Pevsner on art and architecture, the radio talks* (London).

Gameson, R., ed. (1999), *St Augustine and the Conversion of England* (Stroud).

Gardiner, D., ed. (1937), *The Oxinden and Peyton Letters 1642–1670: Being the Correspondence of Henry Oxinden of Barham, Sir Thomas Peyton of Knowlton and their Circle* (London and New York).

Gardiner, S. R., ed. (1886), *Reports of Cases in the Courts of Star Chamber and High Commission* (CS, n.s. 39).

Gardiner, S. R., ed. (1906), *The Constitutional Documents of the Puritan Revolution 1625–1660* (3rd edn, Oxford).

Gardner, H. (1979), 'Dean Donne's monument in St Paul's', in Welleck, R. and Ribeiro, A., eds. (1979), *Evidence in Literary Scholarship* (Oxford), 29–44.

Garlick, K. and Macintyre, A., eds. (1978–98), *The Diary of Joseph Farington, July 1793–December 1821*, 17 vols. (New Haven and London).

Garner, T. (1886), 'The new altar screen in St Paul's cathedral', *Trans. of the St Paul's Ecclesiological Soc.* 2, 167–70.

Garnett, R., ed. (1892), *The Accession of Queen Mary: Being the Contemporary Narrative of Antonio De Guaras, a Spanish Merchant Resident in London* (London).

Garrett, K. I. (1974a), 'A list of some of St Paul's Cathedral choristers before 1873', *Guildhall Studies in London History* 1, 82–93.

Garrett, K. I. (1974b), 'Miss Hackett of Crosby Square', *Guildhall Studies in London History* 1, 150–62.

Gatens, W. (1986), *Victorian Cathedral Music in Theory and Practice* (Cambridge).

Gauden, J. (1660), Κάουργοι *sive Medicastri: Slight Healers of Publick Hurts set forth in a Sermon Preached In St. Pauls Church, London, before the Right Honorable the Lord Mayor, Lord General, Aldermen, Common-Council, and Companies of the honorable City of London. Febr. 28. 1659. Being a day of Solemn Thanksgiving unto God for restoring the Secluded Members of Parliament to the House of Commons …* (London) [BL, Thomason Tract E1019/4].

Gautier, T. (1852), *Caprices et Zigzags* (Paris).

Gear, N. (1996), 'The chantries in St Paul's Cathedral', MA thesis, University of London.

Gee, H. and Hardy, W. J., eds. (1910), *Documents illustrative of English Church History* (London).

Gee, L. L. (1979), '"Ciborium" tombs in England 1290–1330', *JBAA* 132, 29–41.

Gelling, M. (1979), *The Early Charters of the Thames Valley* (Leicester).

Gem, R. (1983), 'The Romanesque cathedral of Winchester: patron and design in the eleventh century', in Heslop and Sekules (1983), 1–12.

Gem, R. (1990), 'The Romanesque architecture of Old St Paul's cathedral and its late eleventh-century context', in Grant (1990), 47–63.

Gem, R. D. H. (1981), 'The Romanesque rebuilding of Westminster Abbey', *Anglo-Norman Studies* 3, 33–60.

Gentles, I. (1992), *The New Model Army in England, Ireland and Scotland, 1645–1653* (Oxford).

Geraghty, A. (2001), 'Edward Woodroffe: Sir Christopher Wren's first draughtsman', *Burlington Magazine* 143, 474–9.

Geraghty, A. (2000), 'Sir Christopher Wren and the dome of St Paul's', *Domes: papers read at the Annual Symposium of the Soc. of Architectural Historians of Great Britain 2000*, 75–81.

Gibb, A. and Freeman, R. (Nov. 1933), 'St Paul's Cathedral – investigation of foundations and subsoil – a report to the dean and chapter'.

Gibbs, M., ed. (1939), *Early Charters of the Cathedral Church of St Paul, London* (CS, 3rd ser. 58).

Gifford, G. (2002), 'The Mulliner book revisited: some musical perspectives and performance considerations', *The Consort* 58, 13–27.

Gilbertson, L. (1897), *Some notes chiefly on the fabric of the cathedral church of St. Paul in London* (London)

Gilbertson, L. (1914, 1925, 1935), *St. Paul's cathedral: the authorized guide* (London)

Gladstone, W. E. (1879), *Gleanings*, 7 vols. (London).

Godfrey, W. H. (1911), *A History of Architecture in London* (London).

Gollancz, I., ed. (1922), *Saint Erkenwald* (Oxford).

Gotch, J. A. (1928), *Inigo Jones* (London).

Gover, J. E. B., Mawer, A. and Stenton, F. M. (1938), *The Place-Names of Hertfordshire* (Cambridge, English Place-Name Soc. 15).

Graham, R. (1945–7), 'An appeal about 1175 for the building fund of St Paul's', *JBAA*, 3rd Series 10, 73–6.

Graham, T., and Watson, A. G. (1998), *The Recovery of the Past in Early Elizabethan England. Documents by John Bale and John Joscelyn from the Circle of Matthew Parker* (Cambridge Bibliographical Soc., Monograph no. 13).

Gransden, A. (1974), *Historical Writing in England*, I, c.550 to c.1307 (London).

Gransden, A. (1982), *Historical Writing in England*, II, c.1307 to the Early Sixteenth Century (London).

Grant, L., ed. (1990), *Medieval Art, Architecture, and Archaeology in London* (BAACT 10).

Gray, D. C. (1986), *Earth and Altar* (AC 68).

Gray, D. C. (2001), *Memorial Services* (AC Liturgy Guides, 1).

Greaves, R. L. (1986), *Deliver Us from Evil: The Radical Underground in Britain, 1660–1663* (New York and Oxford).

Green, I. M. (1978), *The Re-Establishment of the Church of England, 1660–1663* (Oxford).

Green, M. A. E., ed. (1856), *Diary of John Rous, Incumbent of Santon Downham, Suffolk, from 1625 to 1642* (CS 66).

Greenway, D. (1985), 'The false *Institutio* of St Osmund', in Greenway, Holdsworth and Sayers (1985), 77–102.

Greenway, D. E. (1966), 'The succession to Ralph de Diceto, dean of St Paul's', *BIHR* 39, 86–95.

Greenway, D. E. (1968), *John le Neve, Fasti Ecclesiae Anglicanae, 1066–1300*, 1, St Paul's, London (London).

Greenway, D., Holdsworth, C., and Sayers, J., eds. (1985), *Tradition and Change: Essays in Honour of Marjorie Chibnall* (Cambridge).

Gregg, E. (1980), *Queen Anne* (London).

Gregory, J. (1987), 'A just and sufficient maintenance: some defences of the clerical establishment in the eighteenth century', in Sheils, W. J., and Wood D., eds. (1987), *The Church and Wealth* (SCH 24), 321–32.

Gregory, J. (1991), 'Anglicanism and the arts: religion, culture and politics in the eighteenth century', in Black, J. and Gregory, J., eds. (1991), *Culture, Politics and Society in England, 1660–1800* (Manchester).

Gregory, J. (1998), '*Homo religious*: masculinity and religion in the long eighteenth century', in Hitchcock, T. and Cohen M., eds. (1998), *English Masculinities, 1660–1800* (London).

Gregory, J. (2000), *Restoration, Reformation and Reform, 1660–1828: Archbishops of Canterbury and their Diocese* (Oxford).

Gregory, R. (1912), *Robert Gregory 1819–1911, being the Autobiography of Robert Gregory, D.D., Dean of St. Paul's* (London).

Grierson, P. (1972), *English Linear Measures: an Essay in Origins* (Reading).

Grigson, G., ed. (1984), *Thomas Tusser: Five Hundred Points of Good Husbandry, 1557* (Oxford).

Grimes, W. F. (1968), *The Excavation of Roman and Mediaeval London* (London).

Groom, N. (2001), 'Forgery and plagiarism', in Womersley, D., ed. (2001), *A Companion to Literature from Milton to Blake* (Oxford), 94–113.

Grosart, A. B., ed. (1877), *The Spending of the Money of Robert Nowell of Reade Hall, Lancashire: Brother of Dean Alexander Nowell. 1568–1580 Edited from the Original MSS at Towneley Hall, Lancashire with Introduction, Notes and Illustrations* (n.p.).

Groseclose, B. (1995), *British Sculpture and the Company Raj* (Newark, N.J. 1995).

Guilding, R. (2001), *Marble Mania, Sculpture Galleries in England, 1640–1840* (London).

Gunther, R. T. (1928), *The Architecture of Sir Roger Pratt: Charles II's Commissioner for the rebuilding of London after the Great Fire* (Oxford).

Gwilt, J. (1825), 'St Paul's Cathedral', in Pugin, A. C. and Britton, J., *Illustrations of the Public Buildings of London* (London).

Gwynn, J. (1749), *Essay on Design Including Proposals for a Public Academy* (London).

Gwynn, J. (1766), *London and Westminster Improved* (London).

Gwynn, J. (1761), *Thoughts on the Coronation of George III* (London).

Habakkuk, H. J. (1958), 'The Market for Monastic Property 1539–1603', *EconHR* 10, 363–80.

Habakkuk, H. J. (1978), 'The land settlement and the restoration of Charles II', *TRHS* 28, 201–22.

Hackett, M. (1816), *Correspondence. Legal Proceedings and Evidence Respecting the Ancient School attached to Saint Paul's Cathedral* (London).

Hackett, M. (1825), *A Popular History of St Paul's Cathedral* (London).

Hackett, M. (1832), *Correspondence and Evidence respecting the Ancient Collegiate School attached to St Paul's Cathedral* (London).

[Hackett, M.], ed. (1827), *Registrum Eleemosynariae D. Pauli Londonensis* (London).

Haddan, A. W. and Stubbs, W., eds. (1869–78), *Councils and Ecclesiastical Documents*, 3 vols. (Oxford).

Hadley, D. (1996), 'Conquest, colonization and the church: ecclesiastical organization in the Danelaw', *HR* 69, 109–28.

Haigh, C. (1993), *English Reformations: Religion, Politics, and Society under the Tudors* (Oxford).

Hale, W. H., ed. (1858), *The Domesday of St. Paul's of the Year MCCXXII* (CS 69).

Hall, J. (1602), *Virgidemiarvm: Sixe Bookes. First three Bookes, of Tooth-lesse Satyrs 1. Poeticall 2. Academicall 3. Morall* (2nd edn., London).

Hall, M. (1996), 'Gothic and Renaissance: organ cases by Frederick Sutton and G. F. Bodley at Hoar Cross and Temple Newsam', *Journal of the British Institute of Organ Studies* 20, 21–43.

Hamilton, A. H. A., ed. (1877), *Note Book of Sir John Northcote Sometime M.P. for Ashburton, and afterwards for the County of Devon. Containing Memoranda of Proceedings in the House of Commons During the First Session of the Long Parliament, 1640* (London).

Hamilton, N. E. S. A. (1870), ed., *Willelmi Malmesbiriensis Monachi De Gestis Pontificum Anglorum* (RS 52).

Hamper, W., ed. (1827), *The Life, Diary, and Correspondence of Sir William Dugdale* (London).

Harding, V. (1990), 'The population of London, 1550–1700: a review of the published evidence', *LonJ* 15, 111–128.

Harding, V. (2002), *The Dead and the Living in Paris and London, 1500–1670* (Cambridge).

Hardwick, M. and M. (1980), *Alfred Deller, A Singularity of Voice* (London).

Hardy, T. D., ed. (1873–5), *Registrum palatinum Dunelmense*, 3 vols. (RS 62).

Hare, A. (1901), *Walks in London*, 2 vols. (7th edn., London).

Harper-Bill, C. (1988), 'Dean Colet's convocation sermon and the pre-Reformation church in England', *History* 73, 191–210.

Harris, E. (1990), *British Architectural Books and Writers, 1556–1785* (Cambridge).

Harris, F. (1991), *A Passion for Government: The Life of Sarah, Duchess of Marlborough* (Oxford).

Harris, J. and Higgott, G. (1989), *Inigo Jones, Complete Architectural Drawings* (London and New York).

Harris, M. (2003), 'Print in neighbourhood commerce: the case of Carter Lane' in Harris, M., Mandelbrote, G. and Myers, R. eds. (2003) *The London Book Trade: Topographies of Print in the Metropolis from the Sixteenth Century* (New Castle DE and London).

Harrison, F. Ll., (1958; 2nd edn. 1963, 4th edn., 1980), *Music in Medieval Britain* (London).

Harrison, F. Ll., ed. (1963), *William Mundy: Latin Antiphons and Psalms* (Early English Church Music 2, London).

Harrison, J. (2002), 'The English reception of Hugh of Saint-Victor's *Chronicle*', *Electronic British Library Journal*, 1–33.

Hart, A. T. (1957), 'The Age of Reason: 1660–1831', in Matthews and Atkins (1957), 172–249.

Hart, C. (1957; 2nd edn. 1971), *The Early Charters of Essex* (Leicester).

Hart, C. (1966), *The Early Charters of Eastern England* (Leicester).

Hart, V. (1994a), 'Inigo Jones's site organisation at St. Paul's Cathedral: "Ponderous Masses Beheld Hanging in the Air"', *Journal of the Soc. of Architectural Historians* 53/4, 414–27.

Hart, V. (1994b), *Art and Magic in the Court of the Stuarts* (London and New York).

Hart, V. (1995a), 'Imperial seat or ecumenical temple? On Inigo Jones's use of "Decorum" at St Paul's Cathedral', *Architettura* 30/2, 194–213.

Hart, V. (1995b), *St Paul's Cathedral: Sir Christopher Wren* (London).

Hartford, G., Stevenson, M. and Tyrer, E. W., eds. (1912), *The Prayer Book Dictionary* (London).

Harvey, B. (1977), *Westminster Abbey and its Estates in the Middle Ages* (Oxford).

Harvey, J. (1978), *The Perpendicular Style 1330–1485* (London).

Harvey, J. (1987), *English Medieval Architects: a Biographical Dictionary down to 1550.* (repr. of 1984 rev. edn.; Gloucester).

Harvey, P. D. A., ed. (1960), 'A foreign visitor's account of the Great Fire, 1666', *TLMAS* 20, 76–87.

Harvey, W. (1925), *The Preservation of St Paul's Cathedral and other famous buildings* (London).

Haskins, C. H. (1927), *Studies in the History of Medieval Science* (Cambridge, Mass.).

Haslam, J. (1997) 'The location of the *burh* of Wingingamere – a reappraisal', in Rumble, A. R. and Mills, A. D., eds., *Names Places and People. An Onomastic Miscellany in Memory of John McNeal Dodgson* (Stamford), 111–30.

[Hatton, E.] (1708), *A New View of London*, 2 vols. (London).

Haugaard, W. P. (1968), *Elizabeth and the English Reformation: The Struggle for A Stable Settlement of Religion* (Cambridge).

[Haweis, T.] (1801), *The Church of England Vindicated from Misrepresentation; Shewing her Genuine Doctrines as Contained in her Articles, Liturgy, and Homilies. With a Particular Reference to the Elements of Christian Theology, by the Bishop of Lincoln: By a Presbyter of the Church of England* (London).

Hawkins, E., ed. (1844), *Travels in Holland, The United Provinces, England, Scotland and Ireland, M.DC.XXXIV. – M.DC.XXXV* (Chetham Soc. 1).

Hawkins, J. (1875). *A General History of the Science and Practice of Music*, 1st edn., 5 vols. (1776), 3rd ed. 2 vols. (London, 1875).

Hawthorne, N. (1941), *The English Notebooks* (New York and London).

Hay, D. (1952), *Polydore Vergil. Renaissance Historian and Man of Letters* (Oxford).

Hay, D., ed. and trans. (1950), *The Anglica Historia of Polydore Vergil, 1485–1537* (CS, 3rd Ser. 74).

Hearne T., ed. (1722), *The History and Antiquities of Glastonbury to which are added the Endowment and Orders of Sherington's Chantry, founded in Saint Paul's Church, London* (Oxford), 161–223.

Hearne, T., ed. (1729), *Iohannis de Trokelowe annales Edu[ardi] II, Henrici de Blaneforde chronica, & Edu[ardi] II vita a monacho Malmesbur[iensi]* (Oxford).

Hebbert, M. (1993), 'The city of London walkway experiment', *Journal of the American Planning Association* 59, 433–51.

Hennessy, G. (1898), *Novum Repertorium Ecclesiasticum Parochiale Londinense; or, London Diocesan Clergy Succession from the earliest time to the year 1898. With copious notes* (London).

Henschenius, G. and Papebrochius, D., eds. (1688), *Acta Sanctorum: Mai VI* (Antwerp).

Hentzner, P. (1629), *Itinerarium Germaniae, Galliae, Angliae, Italiae* (Nuremberg).

Heritage and Renewal: the Report of the Archbishops' Commission on Cathedrals (London, 1994).

Herrmann, Frank (1972), *The English as Collectors: a Documentary Chrestomathy* (New York).

Heslop, T. and Sekules, V.A., eds. (1983), *Medieval Art and Architecture at Winchester Cathedral* (BAACT 6).

Heslop, T. A. (1995), 'The Canterbury calendars and the Norman Conquest', in Eales and Sharpe (1995), 53–85.

Hetet, J. S. T. (1987), 'A literary underground in Restoration England: printers and dissenters in the context of constraints 1660–1689', PhD thesis, University of Cambridge.

Hewlett, H. G., ed. (1886–9), *Rogeri de Wendover Liber qui dicitur Flores Historiarum*, 3 vols. (RS 84).

Heylyn, P. (1668), *Cyprianus Anglicus or the History of the Life and Death of...William [Laud]...Archbishop of Canterbury...Also the Ecclesiastical History of...England, Scotland and Ireland, from his First Rising till his Death* (London).

Heyman, J. (1995), *The Stone Skeleton: Structural Engineering of Masonry Architecture* (Cambridge).

Heyman, J. (1998), 'Hooke's cubico-parabolical conoid', *Notes and Records of the Royal Soc.* 52/1, 39–50.

Heyworth, P. L., ed. (1989), *Letters of Humfrey Wanley. Palaeographer, Anglo-Saxonist, Librarian, 1672–1726* (Oxford).

Hibbert, C. (1972), *George IV. Prince of Wales 1762–1811* (London).

Hicks, M. A. (1977), 'Draper v. Crowther: the prebend of Brownswood dispute 1664–92', *TLMAS* 28, 333–45.

Higgott, G. (1992), 'Varying with reason: Inigo Jones's theory of design', *Architectural History* 35, 51–77.

Highfill, P. H., Burnim, K. A. and Langhans, E. A. (1973–83), *A Biographical Dictionary of Actors, Actresses, Musicians... in London, 1660–1800*, 16 vols (Carbondale, Ill.).

Hill, C. (1940), 'The agrarian legislation of the Interregnum', *EHR* 55, 222–49.

Hill, C. (1956), *Economic Problems of the Church from Archbishop Whitgift to the Long Parliament* (Oxford).

Hill, C., Millett, M., and Blagg, T. (1980), *The Roman riverside wall and monumental arch in London: excavations at Baynard's Castle, Upper Thames Street, London, 1974–76* (London and Middlesex Archaeological Soc., Special Paper 3).

Hill, D. (1994), 'An urban policy for Cnut?', in Rumble (1994), 101–5.

Hill, R., (1971), 'A chaunterie for Souls: London chantries in the reign of Richard II', in Du Boulay and Barron (1971), 242–55.

Hillebrand, H. N. (1926), *The Child Actors: a Chapter in Elizabethan Stage History* (Urbana, Illinois).

Hind, A. M. (1922), *Wenceslaus Hollar and his Views of London and Windsor...* (London).

HMC (1899), *Report on the Manuscripts of F.W. Leyborne-Popham, Esq., of Littlecote, Co. Wilts* (London).

HMC (1901), *Report on Manuscripts in Various Collections*, I: *Berwick-upon-Tweed, Burford and Lostwithiel Corporations; The Counties of Wilts and Worcester; the Bishop of Chichester; and the Deans and Chapters of Chichester, Canterbury and Salisbury* (London).

HMC (1913), *Report on the Manuscripts of Allan George Finch Esq., of Burley-on-the-Hill, Rutland*, I (London).

HMC (1930), *Report on the Manuscripts of the late Reginald Rawdon Hastings, Esq., of the Manor House, Ashby-de-la-Zouche*, II (London).

HMC (1966), *Report on the Manuscripts of the Right Honourable Viscount De L'Isle, V.C., Preserved at Penshurst Place Kent*, VI, *Sidney Papers, 1626–1698* (London).

HMC (1971), *Calendar of the Manuscripts of the Most Honourable the Marquess of Salisbury, K.G., P.C., G.C.V.O., C.B., T.D., Preserved at Hatfield House, Hertfordshire*, XXII *(A.D. 1612–1668)* (London).

HMC *Fourth Report* (1874), Part I, *Report and Appendix*, 'Calendar of House of Lords Manuscripts', 'Papers Relating to Archbishop Laud's Visitations' (London).

HMC *Fifth Report* (1876), Part I, *Report and Appendix*, 'Calendar of House of Lords Manuscripts' and 'Manuscripts of His Grace the Duke of Sutherland, at Trentham, Co. Stafford' (London).

HMC *Sixth Report* (1877), Part I, *Report and Appendix*, 'Calendar of House of Lords Manuscripts' (London).

HMC *Eighth Report* (1881), Part I, *Report and Appendix*, 'Report of the governors of Queen Anne's Bounty'.

HMC 9: *Ninth Report*, part 1 (1883), Appendix, 1–72, 'Report on the manuscripts of the Dean and Chapter of St Paul's', by Maxwell-Lyte, H. C. (London).

HMC *Twelfth Report* (1888), Appendix II, 'The Manuscripts of the Earl Cowper, K.G., Preserved at Melbourne Hall, Derbyshire' (London).

Hodgett, G. A. J., ed. (1971), *The Cartulary of Holy Trinity Aldgate* (LRS 7).

Hodgson, R. ed. (1811), *The Works of Beilby Porteus*, 6 vols. (London).

Hodson, D. (1984), *County Atlases of the British Isles*, vol. 1 (Tewin).

Hodson, D. (1989), *County Atlases of the British Isles*, vol. 2 (Tewin).

Hoey, L. (2001), 'The Gothic reconstruction of the nave and presbytery of St Albans abbey', in Henig, M. and Lindley, P., eds. (2001), *Alban and St Albans Roman and Medieval Architecture, Art and Archaeology* (BAACT 24), 182–203.

Hofman, M. and Morehen, J. (1987), *Latin Music in British Sources, c.1485–c.1610* (EECM Supplementary Vol. 2).

Hogwood, C. (1983), 'Thomas Tudway's History of Music' in Hogwood, C. and Luckett, R., eds. (1983), *Music in Eighteenth-Century England* (Cambridge), 19–47.

Hohler, C. (1966), 'St Osyth and Aylesbury', *Records of Buckinghamshire* 18/1, 61–72.

Holden, C. H. and Holford, W. G. (1951), *The City of London: a record of destruction and survival* (London).

Holford, W. G. (1956), *Report to the Court of Common Council of the Corporation of the City of London on the Precincts of St Paul's* (London).

Hollaender A. E. J., and Kellaway W., eds. (1969), *Studies in London History Presented to P. E. Jones* (London).

Holland, H. (1614), *Monumenta Sepulchraria Sancti Pauli. The Monuments, Inscriptions, and Epitaphs of Kings, Nobles, Bishops, and Others Buried in the Cathedrall Church of St. Paul. London* (London).

Holland, H. (1633), *Ecclesia Sancti Pauli illustrata. The Monuments, inscriptions and epitaphs, of Kings, Nobles, Bishops, and others, buried in the Cathedrall Church of St. Paul. London* (2nd edn. of Holland (1614), London).

Holland, S. (1855), *A Memoir of the Rev. Sydney Smith by his daughter, Lady Holland. With a selection of his letters, edited by Mrs Austin* (London).

[Holland, William], *The Order of Procession of the King, Queen, & c. to St Paul's Church, (and the Whole of the Ceremony during Divine Service) on Thursday the 23rd of April 1789, etc.* (London, 1789).

Hollister, C. W. (1986), *Monarchy, Magnates and Institutions in the Anglo-Norman World* (London).

Holmes, G. (1973), *The Trial of Dr Sacheverell* (London).

Holtzmann, W. (1930–52), *Papsturkunden in England*, 3 vols. (Berlin and Göttingen).

Hooper, G. (1713), *A Sermon Preached before both Houses of Parliament, in the Cathedral Church of St Paul, on Tuesday, July 7, 1713. Being the Day Appointed by Her Majesty for a General Thanksgiving for the Peace* (London).

Hopkins, A. (2002), 'Lutyens's plans for the British School at Rome', in Hopkins and Stamp (2002).

Hopkins, A. and Stamp, G., eds. (2002), *Lutyens Abroad* (London).

Hopkins, E. J. and Rimbault, E. F. (1855), *The Organ; its History and Construction* (London).

Hopper, C., ed. (1859), 'London chronicle during the reigns of Henry the Seventh and Henry the Eighth', *Camden Miscellany* 4 (CS 73).

Horn, J. M. (1963), *John le Neve, Fasti Ecclesiae Anglicanae 1300–1541*, V, *St Paul's, London* (London).

Horn, J. M. (1969), *John le Neve, Fasti Ecclesiae Anglicanae 1541–1857*, I, *St Paul's, London* (London).

Hornor, T. (1823), *Prospectus: View of London and the Surrounding Country Taken with Mathematical Accuracy from an Observatory...*, (London).

Horsley, S. (1793), *A Sermon Preached in the Cathedral Church of St Paul, London, on 16 June 1793, Being the Time of the Yearly Meeting of the Children Educated in the Charity Schools in and about the Cities of London and Westminster* (London).

House of Commons Papers (1841), *Report from Select Committee on National Monuments, and Works of Art*.

Hovland, S., and Kleineke, H., eds. (2004), *The Household Accounts of William Worsley, Dean of St. Paul's, 1479–97* (Stamford).

Howard, A. and Newman, E., eds. (1951), *London Business Cavalcade* (London).

Howell, J. (1657), *Londinopolis: An Historicall Discourse or Perlustration of the City of London* (London).

Howells, W. D. (1905), *London Films* (London and New York).

Howgego, J. L. (1978), *Printed Maps of London, c.1553–1850* (Folkestone).

http//members.tripod.ox.ac/bookhistory.

Hudson, D. (1961), 'Publishing in the city', in Ian, N., ed. (1961), *The Book of the City* (London), 156–65.

Hudson, W. S. (1980), *The Cambridge Connection and the Elizabethan Settlement of 1559* (Durham, N. C.).

Huggins, P. (1991), 'First steps towards the minster parish of London', *London Archaeologist 6*, 292–300.

Huggins, P. J. and Bascombe, K. N., 'Excavations at Waltham Abbey, Essex, 1985–1991: Three pre-Conquest Churches and Norman Evidence', *ArchJ* 149, 282–343.

Hughes-Hughes, A. (1909), *Catalogue of Manuscript Music in the British Museum*, vol. 3 (London).

Hunt, R. W. (1936), 'English learning in the late twelfth century', *TRHS*, 4th ser. 19, 19–42, repr. in Southern, R. W., ed., *Essays in Medieval History* (London, 1968), 106–28.

Hunt, R. W. (1941–3), 'Studies in Priscian in the eleventh and twelfth centuries', *Medieval and Renaissance Studies* 1, 194–231.

Hunt, R. W. (1948), 'The disputation of Peter of Cornwall against Simon the Jew', in Hunt, R. W., Pantin, W. A. and Southern, R. W., eds., (1948) *Studies in Medieval History presented to Frederick Maurice Powicke* (Oxford), 143–56.

Hurtig, J. (1983), 'Seventeenth-century shroud tombs: classical revival and Anglican context', *Art Bulletin* 66, 603–15.

Husk, W.H. (1857), *An Account of the Musical Celebrations on St Cecilia's Day* (London)

Hussey, C. (1941), 'The art of Sir James Thornhill, 1675–1734', *Country Life* 90, 24–28.

Hutchinson, M. (1989), *The Prince of Wales: Right or Wrong?* (London).

Hutton, R. (1985), *The Restoration: A Political and Religious History of England and Wales 1658–1667* (Oxford).

Hutton, W. H., ed. (1912), *Robert Gregory 1819–1911: Being an Autobiography of Robert Gregory D.D. Dean of St Paul's* (London).

Hyde, R. (1982), *The Regent's Park Colosseum* (London).

Hyde, R. (1987), 'London as Seen through a Fish's Eye', *Map Collector* (Summer 1987), 34–39.

Hyde, R. (2000), 'William Monk's Calendar', *Print Quarterly* 17, 132–47.

Ibbetson, J. (1758), *A Sermon Preached before the Sons of the Clergy in the Cathedral Church of St Paul on the 20 April 1758* (London).

Ibbot, B. (1711), *The Dissolution of the World by Fire. A Sermon preach'd before the Right Hon Sir Gilbert Heathcote … 3 September 1711. The Day of Humiliation for the Dreadful Fire in 1666* (London).

Illingworth, W. and Caley, J., eds. (1812), *Rotuli Hundredorum*, vol. 1 (RC).

Imray, J. (1968), *The Charity of Richard Whittington* (London).

Imray, J. (1969), '"Les bonnes gentes de la Mercerye de Londres": a study of the membership of the medieval Mercers' Company', in Hollaender and Kellaway (1969), 155–80.

In Honour of 28,000 American Dead: Service of Commemoration and of Dedication in St Paul's Cathedral July 4 1951 (n.d.).

Inge, W. R. (1924), *Personal Religion and the Life of Devotion* (London).

Inge, W. R. (1926), *Lay Thoughts of a Dean* (London and New York).

Inge, W. R. (1949), *Diary of a Dean: St Paul's 1911–1934* (London).

Jackson, W. (1791), *Observations on the Present State of Music in London* (London).

Jacob, W. M. (1997), *Lay People and Religion in the Early-Eighteenth Century* (Cambridge)

James, H., ed. Edel, L. and Powers, L. H. (1987), *The Complete Notebooks of Henry James* (New York and London).

James, M. R. (1912), *Catalogue of the MSS of Corpus Christi College, Cambridge* (Cambridge).

Janelle, P., ed. (1928–9), 'An unpublished poem on bishop Stephen Gardiner', *BIHR* 6, 12–25, 89–96, 167–74.

Jansson, M., et al., eds. (2000), *Proceedings in the Opening Session of the Long Parliament: House of Commons*, I, *3 November–19 December 1640* (Rochester, NY, and Woodbridge).

Jardine, L. (2002), *On a Grander Scale: the Outstanding Career of Sir Christopher Wren* (London and New York).

Jasper, R. C. D. (1989), *The Development of the Anglican Liturgy* (London).

Jayne, S. R. (1963), *John Colet and Marsilio Ficino* (London).

Jeans, S. (1986), 'The English chaire organ from its origins to the Civil War', *The Organ*, 65, 49–55.

Jebb, J. (1843), *The Choral Services of the United Church of England and Ireland* (London).

Jeffery, P. (1992), 'Originals or apprentice copies? Some recently found drawings for St Paul's Cathedral, All Saints, Oxford and the City churches', *Architectural History* 35, 118–39.

Jenks, T. (2000), 'Contesting the nation: the funeral of Admiral Lord Nelson', *Journal of British Studies* 39, 422–53.

Jestaz, B. (1990), *L'Hôtel et l'Eglise des Invalides* (Paris).

John, E. (1964), *Land Tenure in Early England* (2nd edn., Leicester).

Johnson, C. (1940), 'Sir Henry Churchill Maxwell-Lyte, 1848–1940', *Proc. of the British Academy* 26, 363–79.

Johnson, D. J. (1960), 'The prebend of Ealdstreet', *A Record of the Friends of St Paul's*, 1960, 29–35.

Johnson, D. P., ed. (2003), *English Episcopal Acta, 26, London, 1189–1228* (Oxford).

Johnson, J. (1993), 'Medieval London and Saint Erkenwald', MA thesis, University of London.

Johnston, J. O. (1904), *Life and Letters of Henry Parry Liddon* (London).

Johnstone, H. D. (1967), 'The life and work of Maurice Greene (1696–1755)', PhD thesis, University of Oxford, 2 vols.

Johnstone, H. D. (1975), 'The genesis of Boyce's cathedral music', *Music and Letters* 56, 26–40.

Johnstone, H. D. ed. (1966), *Maurice Green: Magnificat and Nunc Dimittis from Service in C* (London).

Johnstone, H. D., ed. (1997), *Maurice Greene: Complete Organ Works* (Oxford).

Jones, C. and Holmes, G., eds. (1985), *The London Diaries of William Nicolson Bishop of Carlisle 1702–1718* (Oxford).

Jones, J. (1785), *Sixty Chants, Single and Double* [London].

Jones, Leslie W., trans. (1946), *An Introduction to Divine and Human Readings by Cassiodorus Senator* (New York).

Jones, M. G. (1938), *The Charity School Movement* (Cambridge).

Jones, N. L. (1982), *Faith by Statute: Parliament and the Settlement of Religion, 1559* (London).

Jones, N. L. (1993), *The Birth of the Elizabethan Age: England in the 1560s* (London).

Jones, P. E. and Reddaway, T. F., eds. (1962–7), *The Survey of Building Sites in the City of London after the Great Fire of 1666 by Peter Mills and Peter Oliver*, 5 vols. (LTS 97–9, 101, 103).

Jones, P. E., ed. (1954), *Calendar of Plea and Memoranda Rolls 1437–1457* (Cambridge).

Jones, P. E., ed. (1966), *The Fire Court*, I (London).

Jordan, W. K. (1970), *Edward VI: The Threshold of Power: The Dominance of the Duke of Northumberland* (London).

Josten, C. H., ed. (1966), *Elias Ashmole (1617–1692): His Autobiographical and Historical Notes, his Correspondence, and Other Contemporary Sources Relating to his Life and Work*, 5 vols. (Oxford).

Karamzin, N. M. (1957), *Letters of a Russian Traveller 1789–1790* (New York and London).

Karol, E. (2001), 'The life and architecture of Charles Holden', PhD thesis, University of Reading.

Katz, D. S. (1982), *Philo-Semitism and the Readmission of the Jews to England, 1603–1655* (Oxford).

Kauffmann, C. M. (1975), *Romanesque Manuscripts 1066–1190* (London).

Kaufman, P. (1963, 1964), 'Reading vogues at English cathedral libraries of the eighteenth century', *Bulletin of the New York Public Library* 67 (1963), 643–72; and 68 (1964), 48–64, 110–32, 191–202.

Kaufman, P. (1969), *Libraries and their Users. Collected Papers in Library History* (London).

Kealey, E. J. (1972), *Roger of Salisbury, Viceroy of England* (Berkeley and London).

Keeble, N. H. ed. (1974), *The Autobiography of Richard Baxter* (London).

Keene, D. (1991), 'Introduction', in Imray, J. (1991), *The Mercers' Hall* (LTS 143), 1–20.

Keene, D. (2000a), 'London from the post-Roman period to 1300', in Palliser, D. M., ed. (2000), *The Cambridge Urban History of Britain*, vol. 1, *600–1540* (Cambridge), 187–216.

Keene, D. (2000b), 'The South-East of England', in Palliser, D. M., ed. (2000), *The Cambridge Urban History of Britain*, vol. 1, *600–1540* (Cambridge), 545–82.

Keene, D. (2001a), 'Growth, modernisation and control: the transformation of London's landscape, *c.*1500–*c.*1760', in Clark, P. and Gillespie, R., eds. (2001), *Two Capitals: London and Dublin, 1500–1840* (Oxford, Proc. of the British Academy 107), 7–37.

Keene, D. (2001b), 'Issues of water in medieval London to *c.*1300', *Urban History* 28, 161–79.

Keene, D. (2003), 'Alfred and London', in Reuter, T., ed. (2003), *Alfred the Great: Papers from the Eleventh-Centenary Conferences* (Aldershot), 235–49.

Keene, D. and Harding, V. (1985), *A Survey of Documentary Sources for Property Holding in London before the Great Fire* (LRS 22).

Keene, D. and Harding, V. (1987), *Historical Gazetteer of London before the Great Fire, 1, Cheapside* (Cambridge).

Kelly, A. (1990), *Mrs Coade's Stone* (Upton-upon-Severn).

Kelly, S. (1992), 'Trading privileges from eighth-century England', *Early Medieval Europe* 1, 3–28.

Kelly, S. E., ed. (2004), *Charters of St Paul's, London, Anglo-Saxon Charters 10* (Oxford).

Kennedy, R. (1987), '"A Bird in Bishopswood": some newly-discovered lines of alliterative verse from the late fourteenth century', in Stokes, M., and Burton, T. L., eds. (1987), *Medieval Literature and Antiquities. Studies in Honour of Basil Cottle* (Cambridge), 71–87.

Kennedy, W. P. M., ed. (1908), *The 'Interpretations' of the Bishops & their Influence on Elizabethan Episcopal Policy (With an Appendix of the Original Documents)* (London, AC Tracts 7).

Kennedy, W. P. M., ed. (1924), *Elizabethan Episcopal Administration: An Essay in Sociology and Politics*, 3 vols. (AC 25–7).

Ker, N. R. (1964, 1987), *Medieval Libraries of Great Britain: a List of surviving Books*, 2nd edn, with supplement (London).

Ker, N. R. (1969, 1985), 'Books in St Paul's cathedral before 1313', in Hollaender and Kellaway (1969), 43–72, and in Watson (1985), 209–42.

Keynes, S. (1990), 'Changing faces: Offa, king of Mercia', *History Today* 40/11, 14–19.

Keynes, S. (1993a), 'A charter of King Edward the Elder for Islington', *HR* 66, 303–16.

Keynes, S. (1993b), 'The control of Kent in the ninth century', *Early Medieval Europe* 2, 111–31.

Keynes, S. (1993c), 'A lost cartulary of St Albans Abbey', *Anglo-Saxon England* 22, 253–79.

Keynes, S. (1993d), *An Atlas of Attestations in Anglo-Saxon Charters c.670–1066* (Cambridge).

Keynes, S. (1994), *The Councils of Clofesho* (Leicester).

Keynes, S. (1998), 'King Alfred and the Mercians', in Blackburn and Dumville (1998), 1–45.

Kilburn, M. C. (1997), 'Royalty and public in Britain: 1714–1789', DPhil thesis, University of Oxford.

King, A. (1751), *A Sermon Preached before the Sons of the Clergy in the Cathedral Church of St Paul 3 May 1751* (London).

King, D. (1656), *Cathedrall and Conventuall Churches of England and Wales Orthographically Delineated* (London).

King, J. (1620), *A Sermon at Paules Crosse, on behalfe of Paules Church, March 26. 1620* (London).

King, J. M. (1999), 'The book-trade under Edward VI and Mary I', in Hellinga, L. and Trapp, J.B., eds. (1999), *The Cambridge History of the Book in Britain: Vol. 5 1400–1557* (Cambridge), ch. 7.

Kingsford, C. L., ed. (1905), *Chronicles of London* (Oxford).

Kingsford, C. L., ed. (1908, 1971), *John Stow, A Survey of London, reprinted from the text of 1603*, 2 vols. (London, repr. 1971, with amendments from the 1st edn. of 1908).

Kirby, D. P. (1966), 'The Saxon bishops of Leicester, Lindsey (Syddenisis), and Dorchester', *Leicestershire Archaeological and Historical Soc. Trans.* 41, 1–7.

Kirby, D. P. (1991), *The Earliest English Kings* (London).

Kirby, E. W. (1939), 'Sermons before the Commons, 1640–42', *American Historical Review* 44, 528–48.

Kishlansky, M. (1982), 'Ideology and politics in the parliamentary armies, 1645–9', in Morrill, J. S., ed. (1982), *Reactions to the English Civil War*, 163–83.

Kishlansky, M. (1996), *A Monarchy Transformed: Britain 1603–1714* (Harmondsworth).

Kishlansky, M. A. (1979), *The Rise of the New Model Army* (Cambridge).

Kitching, C. (1986), 'Re-roofing Old St. Paul's Cathedral, 1561–66', *LonJ* 12, 123–33.

Kitching, C. J., ed. (1980), *London and Middlesex Chantry Certificate 1548* (LRS 16).

Klarwill, V. von, ed. (1926), *The Fugger News-Letters Second Series: Being a Further Selection from the Fugger Papers Specially Referring to Queen Elizabeth and Matters Relating to England During the Years 1568–1605* (London).

Knapp, H. J. (1848), *Particulars and the Result of an Appeal Made to the Lord Bishop of London, as Visitor of St Paul's Cathedral, by the Rev. H. J. Knapp, D.D., Sub Dean of the Said Cathedral* (London).

Knight, F. (1995), *The Nineteenth-Century Church and English Society* (Cambridge).

Knowles, D. (1959), *The Religious Orders in England*, III, *The Tudor Age* (Cambridge).

Korsten, F. (1985), 'Thomas Baker and his books', *Trans. Cambridge Bibliographical Soc.* 8, pt. 5, 491–513.

Kreider, A. (1979), *English Chantries: The Road to Dissolution* (Cambridge, MA).

Kuhn, W. M. (1996), *Democratic Royalism: The Transformation of the British Monarchy, 1861–1914* (Basingstoke).

Kuttner, S. and Rathbone, E. (1949–51), 'Anglo-Norman canonists of the twelfth century: an introductory study', *Traditio* 7, 279–358.

Kynaston, D. (1994–2001), *The City of London*, 4 vols. (London).

Lake, P. (1982), *Moderate Puritans and the Elizabethan Church* (Cambridge).

Landon, H. C. R. (1976), *Haydn: Chronology and Works*, (London) 5 vols.

Lang, J. (1956), *Rebuilding St Paul's after the Great Fire of London* (London).

Lang, R. G., ed. (1993), *Two Tudor Subsidy Assessment Rolls for the City of London: 1541 and 1582* (LRS 29).

Latham, R. C. and Matthews, W., eds. (1970–83), *The Diary of Samuel Pepys*, 11 vols. (London).

Latham, R., and Matthews, W., eds. (1995), *The Diary of Samuel Pepys, VII, 1666* (Berkeley and Los Angeles).

Laurence, A. (1990), *Parliamentary Army Chaplains 1642–1651* (Woodbridge).

Lavington, G. (1734), *A Sermon Preach'd before the Sons of the Clergy at their Anniversary Meeting in the Cathedral Church of St Paul, 13 February 1734* (London).

Lawson, M. K. (1993), *Cnut: the Danes in England in the Early Eleventh Century* (London).

Layard, C. P. (1795), *A Sermon Preached at the Anniversary Meeting of the Sons of the Clergy in St Paul's Cathedral on 7 May 1795* (London).

Le Grand Siècle au Quartier Latin: Exposition organisée par le Comité des fêtes de la mairie annexe du 5e arrondissement et par la Direction des Affaires culturelles de la Ville de Paris avec le concours du Musée Carnavalet (Paris, 1982).

Le Huray, P. (1967), *Music and the Reformation in England, 1549–1660* (London).

Le Huray, P., ed. (1965), *The Treasury of English Church Music, 1545–1650* (London).

Le Neve, J. (1720), *Lives and Characters ... of all the Protestant Bishops of the Church of England*, 1 vol. in 2 pts. (London).

Leach, A. F. (1910), 'St Paul's school before Colet', *Arch* 62, 191–238.

Leach, A. F., ed. (1891), *Visitations and Memorials of Southwell Minster* (CS, n.s. 48).

Lee, C. E. (1955), *St Pancras Church and Parish* (London).

Lee, V. (1998), 'The life and benefactions of John Hatherle, mayor and alderman of London', MA thesis, University of London.

Leff, D. (1868), *A Guide to St Paul's Cathedral including a copy of the inscription of every monument* (London).

Legg, J. W. (1914), *English Church Life from the Restoration to the Tractarian Movement Considered in Some of its Neglected or Forgotten Features* (London).

Legg, J. W. (1907), 'On a letter of to the archbishop of Canterbury from the pope, A.D. 1376, directing whether the Use of Salisbury should be followed at St Giles Cripplegate, instead of the Use of St Pauls', *Trans. of the St Paul's Ecclesiological Soc.* 6, 94–6.

Legge, M. D. (1963), *Anglo-Norman Literature and its Background* (Oxford).

Lehmberg, S. (1988), *The Reformation of Cathedrals: Cathedrals in English Society 1485–1603* (Princeton, New Jersey).

Lehmberg, S. E. (1996), *Cathedrals Under Siege: Cathedrals in English Society, 1600–1700* (Exeter).

Leland, J. (1709), *Commentarii de scriptoribus Britannicis* (London).

Leland, J. (1770), *De Rebus Britannicis Collectanea*, ed. T. Hearne, 6 vols. (London).

Lennam, T. (1970), 'The Children of Paul's, 1551–1582', *The Elizabethan Theatre, II*, ed. D. Galloway (Toronto), 20–36.

[Le Sage, G. L.] (1715), *Remarques sur l'état présent d'Angleterre, faites par un voyageur inconnu, dans les années 1713 & 1714* (Amsterdam).

Lethaby, W. R. (1930), 'Old St Paul's', *The Builder* 138 (Jan.–June), 671–3, 862–4, 1091–3; 139 (July–Dec.), 24–6, 193–5, 234–6, 393–5, 613–5, 791–3, 1005–7, 1088–90.

Lethaby, W. R. (1935), *Philip Webb and his Work* (Oxford).

Levison, W., ed. (1913), *Vita Sancti Wilfridi auctore Stephano*, (MGH, Scriptores Rerum Merovingicarum 6).

[Lewis, J.] (1717), *A Few English Notes on a Late Sermon Preached before the Sons of the Clergy by Dr Bisse, Intended to Vindicate the English Reformation from the Charge of Sacrilege and Fraud* (London).

Lewis, J. (1731), *The New Testament ... translated out of the Latin Vulgat by John Wiclif* (London).

Lewis, W. S., et al., eds. (1937–83), *Correspondence of Horace Walpole* (New Haven and London), 48 vols.

Liber Ecclesiasticus: An Authentic Statement of the Revenues of the Established Church compiled from the Report of the Commissioners appointed 'to Inquire into the Revenues and Patronage of the Established Church in England and Wales' (London, 1835).

Liebermann, F. (1900), 'Matrosenstellung aus Landguetern der Kirche London um 1000', *Archiv für das Studium der Neueren Sprachen und Literaturen* 104, 17–24.

Liebermann, F. (1908), 'Einleitung zum Statut der Londoner Friedensgilde unter Aethelstan', *Melanges Fitting*, ii. 77–103 (Montpellier).

Liebermann, F., ed. (1888), *Ex annalibus S. Pauli Londiniensis* in MGH, Scriptores 28 (Hannover), 548–51.

Liebermann, F., ed. (1903–16), *Die Gesetze der Angelsachsen*, 3 vols. (Halle).

Lightman, B. (1987), *The Origins of Agnosticism: Victorian Unbelief and the Limits of Knowledge* (Baltimore).

Lingard, J. B. (1993), 'Cyril A. Farey: a personal tribute to St Paul's cathedral and the city of London, 1940–44', in Bold and Chaney (1993).

Llewellyn, N. (2000), *Funeral Monuments in Post-Reformation England* (Cambridge).

Loach, J. (1986), *Parliament and the Crown in the Reign of Mary Tudor* (Oxford).

Loach, J. (1999), eds. Bernard, G. and Williams, P., *Edward VI* (New Haven, Conn., and London).

Loades, D. (1992), *Two Tudor Conspiracies* (2nd edn., Bangor).

Loades, D. M. (1989), *Mary Tudor: A Life* (Oxford).

Loades, D. M. (1991), *The Reign of Mary Tudor: Politics, Government and Religion in England, 1553–58* (2nd edn., London).

Lobel, M. D. ed. (1989), *The City of London from Prehistoric Times to c.1520* (Oxford, British Atlas of Historic Towns 3).

Lockhart, J. G. (1949), *Cosmo Gordon Lang* (London).

Lockyer, R. (1999), *The Early Stuarts* (Harlow).

Loengard, J. S., ed. (1989), *London Viewers and their Certificates 1508–1558* (LRS 26).

London and its Environs Described (1761) (London).

London County Council (1955), *Names of Streets and Places in the Administrative County of London* (4th edn., London).

Long, K. R. (1972), *The Music of the English Church* (London).

Longford, E. (1971), *Wellington. The Years of the Sword* (London).

Longman, W. (1873), *A History of Three Cathedrals dedicated to S. Paul's in London* (London).

Loomie, A. J., ed. (1973), *Spain and the Jacobean Catholics*, I, *1603–1612* (Catholic Record Soc. 64).

Lord, G. deF. *et al.* eds. (1963–75), *Poems on Affairs of State: Augustan Satirical Verse 1660–1714*, 7 vols. (New Haven and London).

Losseff, N. (1994), *The Best Concords: Polyphonic Music in Thirteenth-Century Britain* (New York and London).

Lough, J., and Merson, E. (1987), *John Graham Lough 1798–1876. A Northumbrian Sculptor* (Woodbridge).

Lovett, R. (1890), *London* (Religious Tract Soc., Pen and Pencil series, London).

Lowe, R. (1953), 'Herbert of Bosham's commentary on Jerome's Hebrew Psalter: a preliminary investigation into its sources', *Biblica* 34, 44–77, 159–92, 275–98.

Loyn, H. R. (1974), 'The Hundred in England in the tenth and early eleventh centuries', in Hearder, H. and Loyn, H. R., eds. (1974), *British Government and Administration. Studies Presented to S. B. Chrimes* (Cardiff), 1–15.

Luard, H. R., ed. (1864–9), *Annales Monastici*, 5 vols. (RS 36).

Luard, H. R., ed. (1872–83), *Matthaei Parisiensis, monachi sancti Albani, Chronica Majora*, 7 vols. (RS 57).

Luard, H. R., ed. (1890), *Flores Historiarum*, 3 vols. (RS 95).

Ludlow, E. (1894), *The Memoirs of Edmund Ludlow*, ed. Firth, C.H. (London).

Lupton, D. (1632), *London and the Covntrey Carbonadoed and Quartred into seuerall Characters* (London).

Lupton, J. H. (1909), *A Life of John Colet* (London).

Lupton, J. H., ed. (1883), *The Lives of Jehan Vitrier, warden of the Franciscan convent at St. Omer, and John Colet, dean of St. Paul's, London, by Erasmus of Rotterdam*.

Luttrell, N. (1857), *A Brief Historical Relation of State Affairs from September 1678 to April 1714*, 6 vols. (Oxford).

Lynch, K. (1964), *The Image of the City* (Cambridge, Mass).

McAleer, J. P. (1988), 'Particularly English? Screen façades of the type of Salisbury and Wells', *JBAA* 141, 124–58.

McAleer, J. P. (1990), 'The first façade of Old St Paul's Cathedral: did it have flanking towers?', in Grant ed. (1990), 64–73.

McAleer, J. P. (2001), 'Detached bell-towers at cathedral and monastic churches', *JBAA* 154, 54–83.

Macartney, M. (1913–14), 'Some investigations into the soil in and around St Paul's cathedral, and comparison with data in Parentalia', *Soc. of Antiquaries of London Proc.*, 2nd ser. 26, 218–28.

Macartney, M. E. (1907), 'The present condition of St Paul's cathedral', *RIBA Journal* 15, 1907, 53–77.

Macauley, J. S., and Greaves, R. W., eds. (1988), *The Autobiography of Thomas Secker, Archbishop of Canterbury* (Lawrence, Kansas).

McCormick, P. and Buxton, B., eds. (1938), *Dick Sheppard by his Friends* (London).

MacCulloch, D., ed. (1984), 'The *Vita Mariae Angliae Reginae* of Robert Wingfield of Brantham', *Camden Miscellany* 28 (CS, 4th ser. 29), 181–301.

MacCulloch, D. (1991), 'The myth of the English Reformation', *Journal of British Studies*, 30, 1–19.

MacCulloch, D. (1996), *Thomas Cranmer: A Life* (New Haven and London).

MacCulloch, D. (1999), *Tudor Church Militant: Edward VI and the Protestant Reformation* (London).

McCullough, P. E. (1998), *Sermons at Court: Politics and Religion in Elizabethan and Jacobean Preaching* (Cambridge).

McCusker, J. J. (2001), 'Comparing the purchasing power of money in Great Britain from 1264 to any other year including the present' (Economic History Services, URL: http://www.eh.net/hmit/ppowerbp/).

McDonnell, M. (1959), *The Annals of St Paul's School* (London).

McDonnell, M. (1977), *The Registers of St Paul's School, 1509–1748* (London).

McHardy, A. K. (1989), 'Careers and disappointments in the late-medieval church', in Sheils and Wood (1989), 111–30.

McHardy, A. K. (1995), 'The churchmen of Chaucer's London: seculars', *Medieval Prosopography* 16, 57–88.

McHardy, A. K., ed. (1977), *The Church in London 1375–92* (LRS 13).

McKenzie, D. F. (1966), *The Cambridge University Press 1696–1712* 2 vols. (Cambridge).

Macklin, A. E. (1909), 'Alfred Gilbert at Bruges', *The Studio* 48 (November 1909), 116 ff.

Mackmurdo, A. H. (1883), *Wren's City Churches* (Orpington).

[Macky, J.] (1714), *A Journey through England* [vol. 1] (London).

Maclean, J., ed. (1860), *Letters from George Lord Carew to Sir Thomas Roe, Ambassador to the Court of the Great Mogul, 1615–1617* (CS 76).

Macleod, E.V. (1998), *A War of Ideas: British Attitudes to the Wars Against Revolutionary France, 1792–1802* (Aldershot).

McLeod, M. S. G. et al. (1984–98), *The Cathedral Libraries Catalogue : books printed before 1701 in the libraries of the Anglican cathedrals of England and Wales*, 2 vols., ed. James, K. I., Shaw, D. J. et al. (London)

Macleod, R. (1990), 'The topography of St Paul's precinct, 1200–1500', *LTR* 26, 1–14.

MacLure, M. (1958, 1989), *The Paul's Cross Sermons, 1534–1642* (University of Toronto Department of English, Studies and Texts 6; rev. edn., Ottawa, 1989).

Macray, W. D. (1873), 'Bishop Henry Compton', *Notes and Queries*, 5th ser., 10 (Jul.–Dec.), 85.

Macray, W. D. and Coxe, H. O., eds. (1869), *Calendar of the Clarendon State Papers Preserved in the Bodleian Library*, II, *From the Death of Charles I, 1649, to the End of the Year 1654* (Oxford).

Macray, W.D., ed. (1886), *Chronicon Abbatiae Ramesiensis* (RS 83).

Madden, F., and W[ay], A. (1855), 'Agreement between the Dean and Chapter of St Paul's, London, and Walter the orgoner, of Southwark, relating to a clock in St Paul's Church', *ArchJ* 12, 173–7.

Madden, F., ed. (1866–9), *Matthaei Parisiensis, Historia Minor* 3 vols. (RS 44).

Madge, S. J. (1939), *The Mediaeval Records of Harringey alias Hornsey from 1216 to 1307* (Hornsey).

Mahony, M. (1979), 'Presbyterianism in the city of London, 1645–1647', *Historical Journal* 22, 93–114.

[Maior, Abbé]: 'M. L. M.' (1774), *Temples anciens et modernes, ou observations historiques et critiques sur les plus célèbres monumens d'architecture grecque et gothique* (London and Paris).

Mais, S. P. B. (1956), *Gateway House* (London).

Maitland, W. (1756), *The History and Survey of London from its Foundation to the Present Time*, 2 vols. (London).

Majendie, J. (1755), *The Double Deliverance: A Sermon Preached at the Cathedral of St Paul's, before the Right Honourable the Lord Mayor on 5 November 1755* (London).

Malcolm, G., Bowsher, D., and Cowie, R. (2003), *Middle Saxon London: Excavations at the Royal Opera House, 1989–99* (Museum of London Archaeology Service, Monograph 15).

Malcolm, J. P. (1802–7), *Londinium Redivivum; or, An Antient History and Modern Description of London*, 4 vols. (London).

Malcolm, J.P. (1810–11), *Anecdotes of the Manners and Customs of London during the Eighteenth Century*, 5 vols. (2nd edn., London).

Maloney, C., and Holroyd, I. (2002), 'London fieldwork and publication round–up 2001', *London Archaeologist* 10, supplement 1.

Maltby, J. (1998), *Prayer Book and People in Elizabethan and Early Stuart England* (Cambridge).

Malton, T. (1792–1801), *A Picturesque Tour through the Cities of London and Westminster* (London).

Mandelbrote, G., ed. (1995), 'From the warehouse to the counting-house: booksellers and bookshops in late 17th-century London', in

Myers, R., and Harris, M. (1995), *A Genius for Letters: Booksellers and Bookselling from the 16th to the 20th Century* (Winchester and New Castle DE), 49–84.

Mangey, T. (1734), *The Usefulness and Authority of the Christian Clergy's Instruction Set Forth in a Sermon Preach'd before the Sons of the Clergy, at their Anniversary Meeting in the Cathedral Church of St Paul, 21 February 1733* (London).

Manley, L. (1995), *Literature and Culture in Early Modern London* (Cambridge).

Mann, J.C. (1961), 'The administration of Roman Britain', *Antiquity* 35, 316–20.

Marcombe, D. (1991), 'Cathedrals and Protestantism: the search for a new identity, 1540–1660', in Marcombe, D. and Knighton, C. S., eds. (1991), *Close Encounters: English Cathedrals and Society since 1540* (Studies in Local and Regional History, 3, Nottingham), 43–61.

Marten, E. (1738), *The Usefulness of Assembling Ourselves to Promote Gods Works. A Sermon Preach'd before the Sons of the Clergy, at their Anniversary-Meeting in the Cathedral Church of St Paul 13 April 1738* (London).

Martimort, A. G. (1987), 'Structure and laws of the liturgical celebration', in Martimort, A. G., ed. and M. J. Connell, trans. (1987), *The Church at Prayer* (London), 4 vols., i. 85–225.

Martin, C.T., ed. (1904), *Minutes of Parliament of the Middle Temple, with an Inquiry into the Origin and Early History of the Inn by J. Hutchinson*, II, *1603–1649*, in Hopwood, C. H., ed., *Middle Temple Records* (London).

Maryfield, P. (2000), *'Love as Brethren': A Quincentennial History of the Coopers' Company* (London).

Mason, M., ed. (1988), *William Blake: The Oxford Authors* (Oxford).

Mason, T. A. (1985), *Serving God and Mammon: William Juxon, 1582–1663, Bishop of London, Lord High Treasurer of England, and Archbishop of Canterbury* (Newark, London and Toronto).

Mateer, D. (1993), 'The compilation of the Gyffard partbooks', *RMARC* 26, 19–43.

Mateer, D. (1995), 'The Giffard partbooks: composers, owners, date and provenance', *RMARC* 28, 21–50.

Mateer, D., and New, E. (2000), '"In Nomine Jesu": Robert Fayrfax and the guild of the Holy Name in St Paul's Cathedral', *Music and Letters* 81, 507–19.

Mather, F. C. (1985), 'Georgian churchmanship reconsidered: some variations in Anglican public worship, 1714–1830', *JEcclH* 36, 255–83.

Mathew, T. (1665), *A Collection of Letters made by Sir Tobie Mathew* (London).

Matthews, A. G. (1934), *Calamy Revised Being a Revision of Edmund Calamy's Account of the Ministers and Others Ejected and Silenced, 1660–2* (Oxford).

Matthews, A. G. (1948), *Walker Revised Being a Revision of John Walker's Sufferings of the Clergy During the Grand Rebellion 1642–60* (Oxford).

Matthews, W. R. (1938), 'The impatient parson', in McCormick and Buxton (1938).

Matthews, W. R. (1946), *St Paul's Cathedral in Wartime 1939–1945* (London).

Matthews, W. R. (1957), '1934 to the present day', in Matthews and Atkins (1957), 300–25.

Matthews, W. R. (1969), *Memories and Meanings* (London).

Matthews, W. R., and Atkins, W. M., eds. (1957; rev. edn. 1964), *A History of St Paul's Cathedral and the Men Associated with It* (London).

Mattingley, H. B. (1967), 'The Paternoster Row hoard of barbarous radiates', *Numismatic Chronicle*, 7th ser 7, 61–9.

Maunsell, A. (1595) *The Catalogue of English Printed Books* (London).

Mayr-Harting, H. (1972), *The Coming of Christianity to Anglo-Saxon England*, (London; rev. edns. 1977, 1991).

Mellows, W.T., ed. (1949), *Chronicle of Hugh Candidus* (Oxford).

Mercurius Elencticus, Communicating the unparalell'd Proceedings at Westminster, the Head-quarters, and other Places, discovering their Designes, reproving their Crimes, and advising the Kingdome, No. 55: Tuesday 5 December to Tuesday 12 December 1648 (n.p.) [BL, Thomason Tract E476/4].

Mercurius Elencticus, Communicating the unparalell'd Proceedings at Westminster, the Head-quarters, and other Places, discovering their Designes, reproving their Crimes, and advising the Kingdome, No. 59: Tuesday 2 January to Tuesday 9 January 1649 (n.p.) [BL, Thomason Tract E537/27].

Mercurius Melancholicus, Communicating the generall Affaires of the Kingdome Especially from Westminster and the Head-Quarters: Monday 25 December 1648 to Monday 1 January 1649 (n.p.) [BL, Thomason Tract E536/27].

Mercurius Politicus: Comprising the Summe of all Intelligence, with the Affairs, and Designs now on foot, in the three Nations of England, Ireland, and Scotland. In defence of the Common-wealth, and for Information of the People. No. 10: Thursday 8 August to Thursday 15 August 1650 (London) [BL, Thomason Tract E609/13].

Mercurius, &c. not –Veridicus, nor yet – Mutus; But –Cambro – (or if you please) – honest – Britannus: Communicating such Intelligence as is brought to him: which he verily believes to be plain truth; without favour or flattery, No. 2: Tuesday 31 [*sic*] January to Tuesday 6 February 1644 (n.p.) [BL, Thomason Tract E31/18].

Mercurius Pragmaticus: Communicating Intelligence from all Parts, touching all Affaires, Designes, Humors, and Conditions throughout the Kingdom. Especially from Westminster, and the Head-Quarters, Nos. 36, 37: Tuesday 5 December to Tuesday 12 December 1648 (n.p.) [BL, Thomason Tract E476/2].

Merrifield, R. (1965), *The Roman City of London* (London).

Merritt, J. F. (1998), 'Puritans, Laudians, and the phenomenon of church-building in Jacobean London', *Historical Journal* 41, 935–960.

Metcalf, P. (1980), *James Knowles: Victorian editor and architect* (Oxford).

Meyer, A. (1996), *Apostles in England: Sir James Thornhill and the Legacy of Raphael's Tapestry Cartoons* (New York).

Michel, F. (1840), *Histoire des ducs de Normandie et des rois d'Angleterre: publiée entier pour la première fois, d'après deux manuscrits de la Bibliothèque du roi* (Paris).

Middleton, R. D. (1968), 'French eighteenth-century opinion on Wren', in Summerson, J., ed. (1968), *Concerning Architecture: Essays on Architectural Writers and Writing presented to Nikolaus Pevsner* (Harmondsworth).

Middleton, T. F. (1812), *An Address to the Parishioners of St Pancras, Middlesex, on the Subject of the Intended Application to Parliament for a New Church* (London).

[Miège, G.] (1707), *The New State of England under Our Sovereign Queen Anne* (London).

Milman, A. (1900), *Henry Hart Milman, D.D. Dean of St. Paul's: A Biographical Sketch* (London).

Milman, H. H. (1868; 2nd edn. 1869), *Annals of S. Paul's Cathedral* (London).

Milward, P. (1977), *Religious Controversies of the Elizabethan Age: A Survey of Printed Sources* (Lincoln, Nebraska).

Mischler, G. (2001), 'English political sermons, 1714–1742: a case study in the theory of the "divine right of governors" and the ideology of order', *British Journal of Eighteenth-Century Studies* 24, 33–62.

Mommsen, T., ed. (1898), 'Gildae Sapientis de excidio et conquestu Britanniae', in MGH, Auctores Antiquissimi 13 (*Chronica Minora* iii) (Berlin), 25–85.

Montemont, A. [n.d., but c.1835], *Voyage à Londres* (Paris).

Moore, N. (1918), *The History of St Bartholomew's Hospital* (London).

Moorman, J. H. (1945), *Church Life in England in the Thirteenth Century* (Cambridge).

Morant, P. (1768), *The History and Antiquities of the County of Essex* (London).

Morden, R, and Lea, P. (c.1687–92), *Book of the Prospects of the Remarkable Places in and about the City of London* (London).

Morehen, J. (1969), 'The sources of English cathedral music, c.1617–c.1644', PhD thesis, University of Cambridge.

Morehen, J., ed. (1991), *Thomas Morley, I, Anthems* (EECM 38).

Morehen, J., ed. (1998), *Thomas Morley, II, Services* (EECM 41).

Morey, A. and Brooke, C. N. L. (1965), *Gilbert Foliot and his Letters* (Cambridge).

Morey, A. and Brooke, C. N. L., eds. (1967), *Letters and Charters of Gilbert Foliot* (Cambridge).

Morgan, G. B. ed. (1885), *The tombs, monuments etc visible in S Paul's Cathedral (and S Faiths beneath it) previous to its destruction by fire AD 1666*, by Payne Fisher (originally published 1684; corrected edn., London).

Moritz, C. P. (1924), *Travels of Carl Philipp Moritz in England in 1782* (London).

Morrin, E. J. (1997), 'Merrington: land, landlord and tenants 1541–1840: a study in the estate of the dean and chapter of Durham', PhD thesis, University of Durham.

Morris, C., ed. (1982), *The Illustrated Journeys of Celia Fiennes c.1682–c.1712* (London).

Morris, R. (1989), *Churches in the Landscape* (London).

Morris, R. K. (1990), 'The New Work at Old St Paul's Cathedral and its place in English thirteenth-century architecture', in Grant (1990), 74–100.

Morrissey, M. (2000), 'Elect nations and prophetic preaching: types and examples in the Paul's Cross jeremiad', in Ferrell, L. A. and McCullough, P., eds. (2000), *The English Sermon Revised: Religion, Literature and History, 1600–1750* (Manchester and New York), 43–58.

Morse, R., ed. (1975), *St Erkenwald* (Cambridge).

Mortimer, R. (1989), 'The Baynards of Baynard's Castle', in Harper-Bill, C., Holdsworth, C. J., and Nelson, J., eds. (1989), *Studies in Medieval History Presented to R. Allen Brown* (Woodbridge), 241–54.

Mozley, J. K. (1938), 'Dick Sheppard as a friend', in McCormick and Buxton (1938).

Mulgan, A. (1927), *Home* (London).

Mumby, F. A. (1934), *Publishing and Bookselling* (London).

Murphy, M. (1982), 'Humfrey Wanley on how to run a scholarly library', *The Library Quarterly* 52, 145–55.

Murray, P. (1991), 'Paternoster – post Holford', *LonJ* 16/2, 129–39.

Museum of London (1981), *Londinium: a descriptive map and guide to Roman London* (Southampton).

Mynors, R. (1963), *Catalogue of the Manuscripts of Balliol College, Oxford* (Oxford).

Nairn, I. (1966), *Nairn's London* (Harmondsworth).

Napier, A. S. and Stevenson, W. H., eds. (1895), *The Crawford Collection of Early Charters and Documents* (Oxford).

Nares, J. [1780] *A Treatise on Singing* [London].

Neininger, F., ed. (1999), *English Episcopal Acta, 15, London 1076–1187* (Oxford).

Nelson, J. (1993), 'The political ideas of Alfred of Wessex', in Duggan, A. ed., (1993), *Kings and Kingship in Medieval Europe* (London), 125–58.

New, E. A. (1999), 'The cult of the Holy Name of Jesus in late medieval England, with special reference to the fraternity in St Paul's Cathedral, London *c*.1450–1558', PhD thesis, University of London.

New, E. A. (2000), 'Fraternities in English cathedrals in the later medieval period', in Thornton, T., ed. (2000), *Social Attitudes and Political Structures in the Fifteenth Century* (Stroud), 41–58.

Newbolt, W. C. E. [1921], *Years that are Past: Being Some Recollections of a Long Life* (London).

Newman, J. (1993), 'Laudian literature and the interpretation of Caroline churches in London', in Howarth, D., ed. (1993), *Art and Patronage in the Caroline Courts* (Cambridge), 168–88.

Newton, T. (1782), *The works : of the Right Reverend Thomas Newton, ...With some account of his life, and anecdotes of several of his friends, written by himself*, 3 vols. (London).

Nichols, J. (1812–15), *Literary Anecdotes of the Eighteenth Century*, 9 vols. (London).

Nichols, J. G., ed. (1848), *The Diary of Henry Machyn, Citizen and Merchant-Taylor of London, from A.D.1550 to A.D.1563* (CS 42).

Nichols, J. G., ed. (1850), *The Chronicle of Queen Jane, and of Two Years of Queen Mary, and especially of the Rebellion of Sir Thomas Wyat. Written by a Resident in the Tower of London* (CS 48).

Nichols, J. G., ed. (1852), *Chronicle of the Grey Friars of London* (CS 53).

Nichols, J. G., ed. (1859), *Narratives of the Days of the Reformation, Chiefly from the Manuscripts of John Foxe the Martyrologist; with two Contemporary Biographies of Archbishop Cranmer* (CS 77).

Nichols, J. G., ed. (1875), 'Two sermons preached by the Boy Bishop,' in *Camden Miscellany* (CS, n.s.14), 1–34.

Nichols, J., ed. (1823), *The Progresses and Public Processions of Queen Elizabeth. Among which are Interspersed Other Solemnities, Public Expenditures, and Remarkable Events, During the Reign of that Illustrious Princess. Collected from Original Manuscripts, Scarce Pamphlets, Corporation Records, Parochial Registers, &c. &c. Illustrated with Historical Notes*, 3 vols. (London).

Nichols, J., ed. (1828), *The Progresses of King James I* (London).

Nicholson, C. and Spooner, C. [n..d, 1910?], *Recent English Ecclesiastical Architecture*

Nicholson, W., ed. (1843), *The Remains of Edmund Grindal, D.D., Successively Bishop of London, and Archbishop of York and Canterbury*, (Cambridge, Parker Soc.).

[Nicolas, N. H., ed.] (1827), *A Chronicle of London 1089–1483* (London).

Nicolson, M. H. and Hutton, S., eds. (1992), *The Conway Letters: The Correspondence of Anne, Viscountess Conway, Henry More, and their Friends 1642–1684* (2nd edn, Oxford).

Nightingale, P. (1982), 'Some London moneyers and reflections on the organisation of English mints in the eleventh and twelfth centuries', *Numismatic Chronicle* 142, 34–50.

Niland, A. (1996), 'Wren, Smith and the box of whistles story', in [Brennan, J., Thistlethwaite, N. et al., eds.] (1996).

Nilson, B. (1998), *The Cathedral Shrines of Medieval England* (Woodbridge).

Nockles, P. B. (1994), *The Oxford Movement in Context: Anglican High Churchmanship 1760–1857* (Cambridge).

Nockles, P. B. (1995), 'Aspects of cathedral life, 1828–1898', in Collinson, Ramsay and Sparks (1995), 256–96.

Noorthouck, J. (1773), *A New History of London* (London).

Norden, J. (1593), *Specvlvm Britanniae. The first parte: an historicall & chorographicall discription of Middlesex* (London).

Norman, E. (1996), 'St Paul's cathedral library lets in the sun', *Dome* 34, 34–6.

Norman, E. R. (1976), *Church and Society in England 1770–1970: A Historical Study* (Oxford).

[North, Dudley, 3rd Baron North] (1659), *A Forest Promiscuous of Several Seasons Productions* (London).

Notestein, W., ed. (1923), *The Journal of Sir Simonds D'Ewes from the Beginning of the Long Parliament to the Opening of the Trial of the Earl of Strafford* (Yale Historical Pubns: MSS and Edited Texts 7).

O'Brien, P., Keene, D., 't Hart, M., and van der Wee, H., eds. (2001), *Urban Achievement in Early Modern Europe: Golden Ages in Antwerp, Amsterdam and London* (Cambridge).

O'Connell, S. (1985), 'Simon Gribelin (1661–1733) printmaker and metal engraver', *Print Quarterly* 2, 27–42.

O'Day, R. and Berlatsky, J., eds. (1979), 'The letter-book of Thomas Bentham, bishop of Coventry and Lichfield', *Camden Miscellany* 27 (CS, 4th ser. 22).

O'Donovan, M. A. (1973), 'An interim revision of episcopal dates for the province of Canterbury, 850–950: Part II', *Anglo-Saxon England* 2, 91–114.

Ogden, M. (1997), 'Old St Pancras church and its fields', *Camden History Review* 21, 32–6.

Ogle, O., and Bliss, W. H., eds. (1872), *Calendar of the Clarendon State Papers Preserved in the Bodleian Library, I, To January, 1649* (Oxford).

Ollard, S. L. ed. (1919), *A Forty Years' Friendship: Letters from the late Henry Scott Holland to Mrs Drew* (London).

Order for Special Service to be Used at St Paul's Cathedral on Sunday, October 26th 1902, in Thanksgiving for the Recovery from Sickness of His Majesty King Edward VII (n.d.).

Orme, E. (1806), *Orme's Graphic History of the Life, Exploits, and Death of Horatio Nelson* (London).

Osman, W. R. (1950), 'A study of the work of Sir James Thornhill', PhD thesis, University of London.

Owen, D. (1996), 'The cathedral, 1840–1945', in Atherton, I., Fernie, E., Harper-Bill, C. and Smith, H., eds., *Norwich Cathedral: Church, City and Diocese 1096–1996* (London), 615–33.

Owen, D. M. (1967–8), 'Bringing home the records: the recovery of the Ely chapter muniments at the Restoration', *Archives* 8, 123–9.

Owen, H. G. (1957), 'The London parish clergy in the reign of Elizabeth I', PhD thesis, University of London.

Owen, H. G. (1961), 'Paul's Cross: the Broadcasting House of Elizabethan London', *History Today* 11, 836–842.

P., T. (1662), *A Poem On the Fall of the Southside of S. Paul's Cathedrall. To which is added, A Satyre Against the Fanatick Boutefeus of These Times. And a Memoriall Offer'd up at the Tomb of the Incomparable Mr John Cleaveland. Never before exactly Printed* (London).

Packman, R. C. (1839), *Spiritualities and Temporalities of St. Paul's Cathedral* (London).

Page, J. (1800), *Harmonia Sacra*, 3 vols. [London].

Page, J. [1780], *The Anthems & Psalms as Performed at St Paul's Cathedral. On the day of the Anniversary Meeting of the Charity Children* [London].

Page, J. [1798], *Divine Harmony* (London).

Page, W. (1929), *London: its Origin and Early Development* (London).

Paget, S. (1921), *Henry Scott Holland: Memoir and Letters* (London).

Palladio, A. (1676), *The First Book of Architecture*, (London).

Parry, G. (1981), *The Golden Age Restor'd. The Culture of the Stuart Court, 1603–42* (Manchester).

Parry, G. J. R. (1989), 'Inventing 'The Good Duke' of Somerset', *JEcclH* 40, 370–80.

Parsons, D., ed., (1975), *Tenth Century Studies* (Chichester).

Partridge, R. C. B. (1938), *The History of the Legal Deposit of Books throughout the British Empire* (London).

Pasquin to the Queen's Statue at St Paul's, during the Procession, Jan. 20 1714 [sic: 1715] (London, 1715?).

Paternoster Associates (1991), *Paternoster Square* (London).

Paterson, J. (1714), *Pietas Londinensis: or the Present Ecclesiastical State of London* (London).

[Peacham, H.] ('Pameach') (1641), *A Dialogue Between The Crosse in Cheap, and Charing Crosse. Comforting each other, as fearing their fall in these uncertaine times* (n.p.) [BL, Thomason Tract E238/9].

Pearce, A. (1929), *The History of the Butchers' Company* (London).

Pearce, E. H. (1913), *Sion College and Library* (Cambridge).

Pears, I. (1988), *The Discovery of Painting: The Growth of Interest in the Arts in England, 1680–1768* (New Haven and London).

Pearsall, D. (1970), *John Lydgate* (London).

Peel, A., ed. (1915), *The Seconde Parte of a Register Being a Calendar of Manuscripts under that Title Intended for Publication by the Puritans about 1593, and now in Dr. Williams's Library, London*, 2 vols. (Cambridge).

Peignot, G. (1836), *Souvenirs relatifs à St-Paul de Londres* (Paris and Dijon).

Pennington, R. (1982, *A Descriptive Catalogue of the Etched Work of Wenceslaus Hollar, 1607–1677* (Cambridge).

Penny, N. (1977), *Church Monuments in Romantic England* (New Haven and London).

Penrose, F. C. (1879), 'Notes on St Paul's Cathedral', *TransRIBA* 29, 93–104.

Penrose, F. C. (1883), 'On the recent discoveries of portions of Old St Paul's Cathedral', *Arch* 47, 381–92.

Perkins, J. (1938–52), *Westminster Abbey: Its Worship and Ornaments*, 3 vols. (AC 33–4, 38).

Pérouse de Montclos, J.-M. (1989), *Histoire de l'Architecture Française, de la Renaissance à la Révolution* (Paris).

Perring, D., and Roskams, S. (1991), *The development of Roman London west of the Walbrook* (London, CBA Research Report 70, The Archaeology of Roman London 2).

Petermann, K. (2000), *Bernt Notke: Arbeitsweise und Werkstattorganisationen im späten Mittelalter* (Berlin).

Pevsner, N. (1957), *The Buildings of England: London I, The Cities of London and Westminster* (Harmondsworth).

Pevsner, N. (1963), *An Outline of European Architecture* (Harmondsworth).

Pevsner, N. (1964), *The Englishness of English Art* (Harmondsworth).

Pfaff, R. (1970), *New Liturgical Feasts in Later Medieval England* (Oxford).

Pfaff, R. W. (1998), 'Bishop Baldock's book, St Paul's cathedral, and the Use of Sarum' in Pfaff, R. W. (1998), *Liturgical Calendars, Saints, and Services in Medieval England* (Aldershot), essay XI.

Phillimore, L. (1883), *Sir Christopher Wren, his Family and his Times* (London).

Phillips, J. (1973), *The Reformation of Images: Destruction of Art in England, 1535–1660* (Berkeley, Ca.).

Phoenix Paulina. A Poem on the New Fabrick of St Paul's Cathedral (London, 1709).

Physick, J. (1970), *The Wellington Monument* (London).

Picart, B. (1723), *Cérémonies et Coutumes Réligieuses de tous les Peuples du Monde*, 9 vols. (Paris).

Pierce, S. R. (1963), 'A drawing for a new spire for Old St Paul's, London', *Antiquaries Journal* 43, 128–31.

Pierce, T. (1660), *Englands Season For Reformation of Life: A Sermon Delivered in St Paul's Church, London. On the Sunday Next Following His Sacred Majesties Restauration* (London) [BL, Thomason Tract E1027/17].

Pilkington, J. (1563), *The burnynge of Paules church in London in the yeare of oure Lord 1561. and the iiii day of June by lyghtnynge, at three of the clocke, at after noone, which continued terrible and helplesse unto nyght* (London).

Pine, E. (1953), *The Westminster Abbey Singers* (London).

Pite, A. B. (1923), 'The design of St Paul's cathedral', in Dircks (1923).

Plan for a More Extensive Application to Divine Service, of the Hitherto Unoccupied Portions of the Cathedrals of England, but more especially of St Paul's Cathedral: … By a Clergyman (London, 1839).

Plomer, H. (1968), *A Dictionary of the Printers and Booksellers who were at Work in England, Scotland, and Ireland from 1668 to 1725* (London).

Plumley, N. and Niland, A. (2001), *A History of the Organs in St Paul's Cathedral* (Oxford).

Plummer, C., ed. (1885), *The Governance of England: otherwise called the difference between an absolute and a limited monarchy, by Sir John Fortescue* (Oxford).

Poley, F. E. (1927), *St Paul's Cathedral, London, Measured, Drawn and Described* (London).

Pollard, A. W., and Redgrave, G. R. (1976–91), *Short-Title Catalogue of Books Printed in England, Scotland & Ireland … 1475–1640*, rev. Jackson, W. A., Ferguson, F. S., and Pantzer, K. F., 3 vols. (2nd edn., London: The Bibliographical Soc.).

Pollard, G. (1937), 'The company of Stationers before 1557', *The Library*, 4th ser. 18, 1–38.

Poole, R. L., and Bateson, M., eds. (1902), *Index Britanniae Scriptorum*; reprinted with intro. by Brett, C. and Carley, J. P. (Cambridge, 1990).

Pope, W. B., ed. (1960–3), *The Diary of Benjamin Robert Haydon*, 5 vols. (Cambridge, Mass.)

Pope-Hennessy, J. (1939), *London Fabric* (London).

Porter, H. C. (1958), *Reformation and Reaction in Tudor Cambridge* (Cambridge).

Porter, S. (2001), *The Great Fire of London* (Stroud).

Porteus, B. (1776), *A Sermon Preached at the Anniversary Meeting of the Sons of the Clergy* (London).

Porteus, B. (1789), *A Sermon Preached at the Cathedral Church of St Paul, London, before his Majesty, and both Houses of Parliament, on Thursday, April 23, 1789* (London).

Postlethwayt, M. (1715), *The Necessity of Understanding the Grounds and Principles of Religion Briefly Represented. In a Sermon Preach'd in the Cathedral-Church of St Paul, on 25 January 1714/5. At the Anniversary Meeting of the Gentlemen Educated at St Paul's School* (London).

Potter, R. (1979–80), 'Work and plans', *Dome* 17, 7–11.

Powell, E., ed. (1902), 'The travels and life of Sir Thomas Hoby, Kt., of Bisham Abbey, written by himself, 1547–1564', *Camden Miscellany* 10 (CS, 3rd ser., 4).

Powell, J. C. (1894), 'Mosaic its materials and methods', *RIBA Journal*, 3rd Ser. 1/8, 248–254.

Power, M. J. (1972), 'East London housing in the seventeenth century', in Clark, P. and Slack, P., eds. (1972), *Crisis and Order in English Towns* (London), 237–62.

Powicke, F. M. and Cheney, C. R., eds. (1964), *Councils and Synods with other Documents relating to the English Church, II, A. D. 1205–1313*, 2 vols. (Oxford).

Pozzo, A. (1707), *Rules and Examples of Perspective for Painters and Architects*, ed. James, J. (London).

PP 1835: XXII, (67), 'Report of the Ecclesiastical Revenues Commission'.

PP 1837: XLI (242), 'Returns of fees for burials and monuments and cost of admission for the public at Westminster Abbey and St. Paul's', 475–80.

PP 1837–8: IX (692), 'Report from the Select Committee on mode of granting and renewing of leases of Ecclesiastical Bodies, 1838 and Minutes of Evidence, 1837–8', 1–91.

PP 1837–8: XXVI (119), 'Correspondence between Home Secretary and Others on Free Admittance to Public National Buildings'.

PP 1841 : VI (416), 'Report from the Select Committee on National Monuments and Works of Art with the Minutes of Evidence.'

PP 1851: XIII (589), 'Report from the Select Committee of the House of Lords appointed to consider the Bill entitled 'An Act for the Management and Regulation of Episcopal and Capitular Estates and Revenues in England and Wales'.

PP 1852–3: LXXVIII (530), 'Returns relating to the Church Trustees of the Parish of St Pancras'.

PP 1852–3: LXXXV (1361–2), 'Numbers of Inhabitants 1801–51', vols. I and II.

PP 1854: XXV [1822] Appendix to First Report of Cathedral Commissioners'.

PP 1906: XXXIV (Cd 3071), 'Royal Commission on Ecclesiastical Discipline', vol. 3 of evidence.

PP 1835: XXII (54), 'Report of the Ecclesiastical Duties and Revenues Commission'.

Prestige, G. L. (1955), *St Paul's in its Glory: A Candid History of the Cathedral 1831–1911* (London).

Prestwich, M., ed. (1980), *Documents illustrating the Crisis of 1297–8 in England* (CS, 4th ser. 24).

Pretyman, G. (1798), *A Sermon Preached at the Cathedral Church of St Paul, London, before His Majesty and both Houses of Parliament, on Tuesday, December 19th, 1797; being the Day Appointed for a General Thanksgiving* (2nd edn, London).

Price, J. E. (1886), *A Descriptive Account of the Guildhall of the City of London* (London).

[Prideaux, S. T.] (1891), *Exhibition of Bookbindings* (London: Burlington Fine Arts Club).

Primus, J. H. (1960), *The Vestments Controversy: An Historical Study of the Earliest Tensions within the Church of England in the Reigns of Edward VI and Elizabeth* (Kampen).

Prince of Wales, H. R. H. (1989), *A Vision of Britain* (London).

Prior, E. S. and Gardner, A. (1912), *An Account of Medieval Figure Sculpture in England* (Cambridge).

Pruett, J. H. (1976), 'Career patterns among the clergy of Lincoln Cathedral, 1660–1750', *Church History* 44, 204–16.

Pugin, A. W. N. (1841), *The True Principles of Pointed or Christian Architecture* (London).

Quatermayne, R. (1642), *Qvatermayns Conqvest Over Canterbvries Covrt. Or A Briefe Declaration of severall Passages between him and the Archbishop of Canterbury, with other Commissioners of the High Commission Court, at six severall appearances before them, and by them directed to Doctor Featly; with their severall Conferences; and the Doctors Reports to the Court …* (London).

Racine, P. (1980), *Plaisance du Xème à la fin du XIIIème siècle: essai d'histoire urbaine* (Lille, Reproduction des Thèses, Université de Lille III).

Ralph, E., ed. (1985), 'Bishop Secker's diocese book', in McGrath, P. (1985), *A Bristol Miscellany* (Bristol Record Soc. 37).

[Ralph, J.] (1734), *A Critical Review of the Publick Buildings, Statutes and Ornaments in, and about London and Westminster. To which is Prefix'd, The Dimensions of St Peter's Church at Rome, and St Paul's Cathedral at London* (London).

Ramsay, N. (1991), 'Alabaster', in Blair and Ramsay (1991), 29–40.

Ramsay, N. (1995), 'The cathedral archives and library', in Collinson, Ramsay and Sparks (1995), 341–407.

Ramsay, N. L., and Willoughby, J., eds. (2004), *Secular Cathedrals, Colleges and Hospitals*, (London, Corpus of British Medieval Library Catalogues).

Rastall, R. (1967), 'The minstrels of the English royal households', *RMARC* 4, 1–41.

Rathbone, E. (1935), 'The influence of bishops and members of cathedral bodies in the intellectual life of England, 1066–1216', PhD thesis, University of London.

Rathbone, E. (1941), 'Master Alberic of London, Mythographus Tertius Vaticanus', *Medieval and Renaissance Studies* 1, 35–8.

Raven, J. (1996), 'From promotion to proscription: arrangements for reading and eighteenth-century libraries' in Raven, J., Small, H. and Tadmor, N., eds. (1996), *The Practice and Representation of Reading in England* (Cambridge), 175–201.

Raven, J. (1997), 'Memorializing a London bookscape: the mapping and reading of Paternoster Row and St Paul's Churchyard, 1695–1814', in Alston, R., ed. (1997), *Order and Connexion: Studies in Bibliography and Book History* (Woodbridge, Suffolk), 177–200.

Raven, J. (2000), 'The novel comes of age', in Garside, P., Raven, J., and Schöwerling, R. eds. (2000), *The English Novel 1770–1829: A Bibliographical Survey of Prose Fiction Published in the British Isles*, 2 vols. (Oxford), I, 15–121.

Raven, J. (2001), 'Constructing bookscapes: experiments in mapping the sites and activities of the London book trades of the eighteenth century', in Murray, J., ed. (2001), *Mappa Mundi: Mapping Culture/Mapping the World* (Windsor, Ontario), 35–59.

Raven, J. (2003), 'A pursuit of permanence? The succession to key sites in the London book trades c.1600–1800', in Harris, M., Mandelbrote, G., and Myers, R., eds. (2003), *The London Book Trade: Topographies of Print in the Metropolis from the Sixteenth Century* (New Castle, DE, and London).

Ravenscroft, T. (1614), *A Briefe Discourse of the True (but Neglected) Use of Charact'ring the Degrees* (London).

Raymond, J. (2001), 'Pamphlets and news', in Womersley, D., ed. (2001), *A Companion to Literature from Milton to Blake* (Oxford), 483–96.

RCHME (1928), *An Inventory of the Historical Monuments in London, vol. III, Roman London* (London).

Read, B. (1982), *Victorian Sculpture* (London).

Read, E. A. (1970), *A Checklist of Books, Catalogues and Periodical Articles relating to the Cathedral Libraries of England* (Oxford Bibliographical Soc., Occasional Publication no. 6).

Read, E. A. (1978), 'Cathedral libraries: a supplementary checklist', *Library History* 4/5, 141–63.

Reading, W. (1724), *History of the Ancient and Present State of Sion-College…* (London).

Reddaway, T. F. (1940), *The Rebuilding of London after the Great Fire* (London).

Rees, A. (1819), *The Cyclopaedia, or Universal Dictionary of Arts, Sciences and Literature*, 39 vols. (London).

Rees, T., and Britton, J. (1896), *Reminiscences of Literary London from 1779 to 1853* (London).

Remembrancia (1878), *Analytical index to the series of records known as the Remembrancia, preserved in the Archives of the City of London, A.D.1579–1664* (London).

Rennell, T. (1796), *A Sermon Preached at the Anniversary Meeting of the Sons of the Clergy in the Cathedral Church of St Paul on Tuesday 10 May 1796* (London).

Report of the Select Committee of the House of Commons on the Earl of Elgin's Collection of Sculptured Marbles (1816).

Reports from the Select Committee appointed to inquire into the State of the Public Records of the Kingdom (ordered by the House of Commons to be printed, 1800).

Reuterswärd, P. (1965), *The two Churches of the Hôtel des Invalides* (Stockholm).

Reynolds, H. E. (1879), *Our Cathedral Libraries: Their History, Contents and Uses* (London).

Rhudde, D. (1790), *A Sermon Preached at the Anniversary Meeting of the Sons of the Clergy in the Cathedral Church of St Paul 20 May 1790* (London).

Richardson, H. G. (1932), 'William of Ely, the king's treasurer (?1195–1215)', *TRHS*, 4th ser. 15, 45–90.

Richardson, H. G. (1933), 'Letters of the legate Guala', *EHR* 48, 250–9.

Richardson, H. G. (1948), 'The *Annales Paulini*', *Speculum* 23, 630–40.

Rickert, E. (1932), 'Chaucer at school', *Modern Philology* 29, 257–74.

Riddy, F. (2001), 'Glastonbury, Joseph of Arimathea and the Grail in John Hardyng's Chronicle', in Carley, J., ed., *Glastonbury Abbey and the Arthurian Tradition* (Woodbridge), 269–84.

Ridley, G. (757), *A Sermon Preached before the Sons of the Clergy in the Cathedral Church of St Paul … 28 April 1757* (London).

Ridley, J. G. (1957), *Nicholas Ridley: A Biography* (London).

[Ridpath, G.] (1710), *The Peril of Being Zealously Affected: but Not Well; or Reflections on Dr Sacheverell's Sermon* (London).

Ridyard, S. J. (1988), *The Royal Saints of Anglo-Saxon England* (Cambridge).

Rigg, A. G., ed. (1968), *A Glastonbury Miscellany of the Fifteenth Century: A Descriptive Index of Trinity College, Cambridge, MS. O.9.38* (Oxford).

Riley, H. T., ed. (1859), *Liber Albus*, being vol. I of *Munimenta Gildhallae Londoniensis; Liber Albus, Liber Custumarum et Liber Horn* (RS 12); trans. as Riley (1861).

Riley, H. T., ed. (1860), *Liber Custumarum*, 2 parts, being vol. II of *Munimenta Gildhallae Londoniensis; Liber Albus, Liber Custumarum et Liber Horn* (RS 12).

Riley, H. T., ed. (1868), *Memorials of London and London Life in the XIIIth, XIVth and XVth Centuries* (London).

Riley, H. T., trans. (1861), *Liber Albus: the White Book of the City of London* (London); see Riley (1859).

Rippon, S. (1996), 'Essex c.700–1066', in Bedwin, O., ed. (1996), *The Archaeology of Essex* (Chelmsford), 117–28.

Rivington, S. (1894), *The Publishing House of Rivington* (London).

Rivington, S. (1919), *The Publishing Family of Rivington* (London).

Robbins, K. (1995), 'The twentieth century, 1898–1994', in Collinson, Ramsay and Sparks (1995), 297–340.

'Robert Parry's diary' (1915), *Archaeologia Cambrensis* 6th ser. 15, 109–139.

Roberts, M. (2002), *Dugdale and Hollar: History Illustrated* (Newark and London).

Roberts, M. (n.d. but c.1988), *The Emergence of Clarity: Images of English Cathedrals 1640–1840* (Charlottesville).

Roberts, R. E. (1942), *H. R. L. Sheppard: Life and Letters* (London).

Roberts, R. J., and Watson, A. G., eds. (1990), *John Dee's Library Catalogue* (London).

Roberts, W., ed. (1834), *Memoirs of the Life and Correspondence of Hannah More*, 4 vols. (London).

Robertson, A. J. (1956), *Anglo-Saxon Charters* (2nd edn., Cambridge).

Robertson, J. C. and Sheppard, J. B., eds. (1875–85), *Materials for the History of Thomas Becket, Archbishop of Canterbury*, 7 vols. (RS 67).

Robinson, F. N., ed. (1966), *The Works of Geoffrey Chaucer* (London).

Robinson, H. W. and Adams, W., eds. (1935), *The Diary of Robert Hooke, 1672–1680* (London).

Rodwell, W. (1976), 'The archaeological investigation of Hadstock church, Essex. An interim report', *Antiquaries Journal* 56, 55–71.

Rodwell, W. (1988), 'Fulham Palace, London, SW6. Archaeological appraisal and plan', for London Borough of Hammersmith and Fulham.

Rodwell, W. J. and Rodwell, K. (1977), *Historic Churches – A Wasting Asset* (London, CBA Research Report 19).

Rogers, N. (1988), *Crowds, Culture and Politics in Georgian Britain* (Oxford).

Rogers, N. J. (1987), 'English episcopal monuments, 1270–1350', in Coales, ed. (1987), 8–68.

Rollason, D. W. (1978), 'Lists of saints' resting-places in Anglo-Saxon England', *Anglo-Saxon England* 7, 61–93.

Rollason, D. W. (1989), *Saints and Relics* (Oxford).

Rollenhagen, D. D. (1993), 'Londoners at law: justice, public honour and private interest in the reign of Richard II', MPhil thesis, University of Cambridge.

Roscoe, S. (1973), *John Newbery and his Successors, 1740–1814: A Bibliography* (Wormley, Hertfordshire).

Rose, C. (1988), 'Politics, religion and charity, in Augustan London, c.1680–1720', PhD thesis, University of Cambridge.

Rose, M. (1993), *Authors and Owners: The Invention of Copyright* (Cambridge, Mass., and London).

Rosser, G. (1988), 'Communities of parish and guild in the later Middle Ages', in Wright, S. J., ed., *Parish, Church and People: Local Studies in Lay Religion 1350–1750* (London), 29–56.

Rosser, G. (1989), *Medieval Westminster 1200–1540* (Oxford).

Round, J. H. (1899), 'Ingelric the priest and Albert of Lotharingia', in his *The Commune of London and other Studies* (London), 28–38.

Round, J. H. (1902), 'Introduction to the Hertfordshire Domesday', *VCH Hertfordshire*, i. 263–99.

Round, J. H. (1903), 'Introduction to the Essex Domesday', *VCH Essex*, i. 334–426.

Round, J. H., (1909), *Feudal England : historical studies on the XIth and XIIth centuries* (London)

Rousseau, M.-H. (2003), 'Chantry foundations and chantry chaplains at St Paul's cathedral, London c.1200–1548', PhD thesis, University of London.

Routledge, F. J., ed. (1932), *Calendar of the Clarendon State Papers Preserved in the Bodleian Library, IV: 1657–1660* (Oxford).

Royal Academy of Arts (1942), *London Replanned: The Royal Academy Planning Committee Interim Report* (London).

Royle, T. (1985), *The Kitchener Enigma* (London).

Rule, M., ed. (1884), *Eadmeri Historia Novorum in Anglia* (RS 81).

Rumble, A. R., and Morris, R., eds and trans (1994), 'Translatio Sancti Ælfegi Cantuariensis archiespicopi et martyris (*BHL* 2519): Osbern's account of the translation of St Ælfeah's relics from London to Canterbury, 8–11 June 1023', in Rumble (1994), 283–315.

Rumble, A. R., ed. (1994), *The Reign of Cnut: King of England, Denmark and Norway* (Leicester).

Rump: or an Exact Collection Of the Choycest Poems and Songs Relating to the Late Times. By the most Eminent Wits, from Anno 1639 to Anno 1661. (London, 1662).

Rushworth, J. (1691), *Historical Collections …, IV* (London).

Russell, C. (1971), *The Crisis of Parliaments: English History 1509–1660* (Oxford).

Russell, C. (1990), *The Causes of the English Civil War* (Oxford).

Russell, C. (1991), *The Fall of the British Monarchies 1637–1642* (Oxford).

Russell, W. (1922), *St Paul's under Dean Church and his Associates* (London).

Russell, W,. ed. (1920), *St Paul's in the Early Nineteenth Century. Giving a Glimpse of What a Cathedral Establishment was Before and at the Beginning of the Great Church Revival. Based on Extracts from the Diary and Correspondence of the late William Hale Hale, Canon Residentiary and Archdeacon of London* (London).

Rutt, J. T., ed. (1828), *Diary of Thomas Burton, Esq. Member in the Parliaments of Oliver and Richard Cromwell, from 1656 to 1659: Now First Published from the Original Autograph Manuscript. With an Introduction, Containing an Account of the Parliament of 1654; From the Journal of Guibon Goddard, Esq. M.P. Also Now First Printed*, 4 vols. (London).

Ryder, D. (1939), *The Diary of Dudley Ryder, 1715–1716*, ed. Matthews, W. (London).

Rye, W. B., ed. (1865), *England As Seen By Foreigners in the Days of Elizabeth and James the First: Comprising Translations of the Journals of the Two Dukes of Wirtemberg in 1592 and 1610; both Illustrative of Shakespeare, with Extracts from the Travels of Foreign Princes and Others, Copious Notes, an Introduction, and Etchings* (London).

Rymer, T. (1739–45), *Foedera, conventiones, literae, et cujuscunque generis acta publica*, 10 vols, each in two separately paginated parts (The Hague).

Rymer, T., ed. (1816–69), *Foedera*, 4 vols. (RC edn.).

Ryrie, A. (1999), 'The unsteady beginnings of English Protestant martyrology', in Loades, D., ed. (1999), *John Foxe: An Historical Perspective* (Aldershot), 52–66.

Sabol, A. J. (1959), 'Ravenscroft's *Melismata* and the Children of Paul's', *Renaissance News* 12/1, 3–9.

Sacheverell, H. (1709), *The Perils of False Brethren, both in Church and State: Set Forth in a Sermon Preach'd before the Right Honourable the Lord-Mayor, Aldermen, and Citizens of London, at the Cathedral-Church of St Paul, on 5 November 1709* (London).

Sacheverell, H. (1713), *A Sermon Preach'd before the Sons of the Clergy* (London).

Salgado, G. (1992), *The Elizabethan Underworld* (Stroud).

Salter, S. (1755), *A Sermon Preached before the Sons of the Clergy in the Cathedral Church of St Paul* (London).

Salway, P. (1981), *Roman Britain* (Oxford).

Salzman, L. F. (1967) *Building in England* (corrected reprint of 1952 edn., Oxford).

Sandler (1993), 'The image of the book-owner in the fourteenth century: three cases of self-definition', in Rogers, N., ed. (1993), *England in the Fourteenth Century* (Harlaxton Medieval Studies 3), 58–80.

Sandler (2003), 'The chantry of Roger of Waltham in Old St Paul's', in Backhouse (2003), 168–90.

Sankey, D. (1998), 'Cathedrals, granaries, and urban vitality in late Roman London', in Watson, B. ed. (1998), *Roman London: recent archaeological work* (Journal of Roman Archaeology, Supplementary Ser. 24), 78–82.

Saunders, A. (1981), *Regent's Park from 1086 to the Present* (London).

Saunders, A. (1985), 'Samuel Johnson's funeral monument', *Journal of the Royal Soc. of Arts.*

Saunders, A. (2001), *St Paul's, the story of the Cathedral* (London).

Saunders, A. and Schofield, J., eds. (2001), *Tudor London: a Map and a View* (LTS 159).

Save the City: a conservation study of the City of London (1976) (London).

Sawyer, P.H. (1968), *Anglo-Saxon Charters: an Annotated List and Bibliography* (London).

Scarisbrick, J. J. (1981), *Henry VIII* (London).

Schenk, W. (1950), *Reginald Pole: Cardinal of England* (London).

Schinkel, K. F. (1993), *'The English Journey': Journal of a Visit to France and Britain in 1826*, eds. Bindman D. and Riemann, G. (New Haven and London).

Schofield, J. (1994), 'Saxon and medieval parish churches in the City of London: a review', *TLMAS* 45, 23–146.

Schofield, J. (forthcoming), 'The vicars choral at St Paul's and their context in the churchyard', in Hall, R. A. and Stocker, D. A., eds., *Cantate Domino: the English Colleges of Vicars Choral* (Oxford).

Schofield, J. (in prep), *Archaeology of St Paul's Cathedral, I: survey and excavation up to 2001*.

Schofield, J. with Maloney, C. eds. (1998), *Archaeology in the City of London 1907–91: a guide to the records of excavations by the Museum of London*, (Museum of London, Archaeological Gazetteer Ser. 1).

Scott, C. (1977), *Dick Sheppard: A Biography* (London).

Scott, D. (1972), *The Music of St Paul's Cathedral* (London).

Scott, W. and Bliss, J., eds. (1847–60), *The Works of the Most Reverend Father in God, William Laud, D.D.*, 7 vols. (Oxford).

Scouloudi, I. (1953), *Panoramic Views of London, 1660–1666* (London).

Scurlock, D. (1733), *A Caution Against Speaking Evil of our Governors and of one another. As it was Delivered in a Sermon Preached at St Paul's on Sunday the 7th of this Instant, October* (London).

Seaver, P. S. (1970), *The Puritan Lectureships: The Politics of Religious Dissent 1560–1662* (Stanford, Ca.).

Sekler, E. F. (1956), *Wren and his place in European architecture* (London).

Selden, J. (1618), *The Historie of Tithes* (London).

Severall Proceedings of State Affaires In England, Ireland and Scotland. With the Transactions of the Affaires in other Nations, No. 212: Thursday 13 October to Thursday 20 October 1653 (London) [BL, Thomason Tract E219/26].

Shahar, S. (1994), 'The boy bishop's feast: a case-study in church attitudes towards children in the high and late Middle Ages', in Wood, D., ed., *The Church and Childhood* (SCH 31), 243–60.

Shapiro, M. (1968), 'Music and song in plays acted by children's ompanies during the English Renaissance', *Current Musicology* 7, 97–110.

Sharpe, K. (1983), 'The personal rule of Charles I', in Tomlinson, H., ed. (1983), *Before the English Civil War* (London), 53–78.

Sharpe, K. (1987), 'The image of virtue: the court and household of Charles I, 1625–1642', in Starkey, D., ed. (1987), *The English Court: from the Wars of the Roses to the Civil War* (London and New York), 226–60.

Sharpe, K., (1992), *The Personal Rule of Charles I* (New Haven and London).

Sharpe, R. (1995), 'The setting of St Augustine's translation, 1091', in Eales and Sharpe (1995), 1–13.

Sharpe, R. (2002), 'Martyrs and local saints in late antique Britain', in Thacker and Sharpe (2002), 75–154.

Sharpe, R. R., ed. (1889–90), *Calendar of Wills Proved and Enrolled in the Court of Husting, London*, 2 vols. (London).

Sharpe, R. R., ed. (1903), *Calendar of Letter-Books…of the City of London, Letter-Book E.* (London).

Sharpe, R. R., ed. (1905), *Calendar of Letter-Books … of the City of London…Letter Book G.* (London).

Sharpe, R. R., ed. (1909), *Calendar of Letter-Books … of the City of London…Letter Book I.* (London).

Sharpe, R. R., ed. (1911), *Calendar of Letter-Books … of the City of London…Letter Book K.* (London).

Sharpe, R. R., ed. (1912), *Calendar of Letter-Books…of the City of London…Letter Book L.* (London).

Shaw, H. W. (1991), *The Succession of Organists of the Chapel Royal and the Cathedrals of England and Wales* (Oxford).

Shaw, S. and Miller, D., eds. (2002), *Who Would Have Thought…A Tribute to the Friends of St Paul's Cathedral 1952–2002* (London).

Shaw, W. A. (1900), *A History of the English Church During the Civil Wars and Under the Commonwealth, 1640–1660*, 2 vols. (London).

Shears, C. (1980–1), 'A difficult time for the cathedral', *Dome* 18, 15–16.

Shears, C. (1983–4), 'Cathedral finances', *Dome* 21, 14.

Sheils, W. J. and Wood, D., eds. (1989), *The Ministry: Clerical and Lay* (SCH 26).

Shepherd, J. (1988), 'The Roman occupation in the Paternoster Square area of the City of London', *TLMAS* 39, 1–30.

Shepherd, J. ed. (1998), *Post-War Archaeology in the City of London 1946–72: a guide to the records of excavations by Professor W F Grimes held by the Museum of London* (Museum of London, Archaeological Gazetteer Ser. 3).

Sheppard, F. H. W., ed. (1960), *Brooke House* (Survey of London 28/1).

Sherlock, D. (1978), 'The drawing of Old St Paul's in Ashwell church', *Hertfordshire Archaeology* 8, 96–100.

Sherlock, T. (1712), *A Sermon Preach'd before the Right Honourable Lord-Mayor, Aldermen, and Citizens of London, at the Cathedral-Church of St Paul, 5 November, 1712* (London).

Sherlock, W. (1699), *A Sermon Preach'd at St Paul's Cathedral November 22 1699 Being the Anniversary Meeting of the Lovers of Musick* (London).

Sherlock, W. (1704), *A Sermon preached before the Queen, at the Cathedral Church of St Paul, London, 7 September 1704, being the Thanksgiving Day for the Late Glorious Victory Obtained over the French and Bavarians at Blenheim near Hochfleet, on Wednesday 2 August, etc.* (London).

Simond, L. (1817), *Journal of a Tour and Residence in Great Britain during the years 1810 and 1811* (Edinburgh).

Simpson, J. (2001), 'Bulldozing the Middle Ages: the case of "John Lydgate"', in Scase, W., Capeland, R. and Lawton, D., eds. (2001), *New Medieval Literatures* (Oxford, 2001), vol. 4, 213–242.

Simpson, W. J. S. (1899), *Memoir of the Rev. W. Sparrow Simpson, D.D., Rector of St Vedast and Sub-Dean of St Paul's Cathedral* (London, etc.).

Simpson, W. S. (1871), 'The charters and statutes of the college of the Minor Canons in S. Paul's Cathedral, London', *Arch* 43, pt. 1, 165–200.

Simpson, W. S. (1874), 'Statutes of the college of the minor canons in S. Paul's Cathedral, London', *TLMAS* 4, 231–52.

Simpson, W. S. (1881a), *Chapters in the History of Old St Paul's* (London).

Simpson, W. S. (1881b), 'Some early drawings of Old St Paul's', *JBAA* 37, 123–34.

Simpson, W. S. (1882), 'The tonsure-plate in use in St Paul's cathedral during the thirteenth century', *JBAA* 38, 278–90.

Simpson, W. S. (1887), 'Two inventories of the cathedral church of St Paul, London, dated respectively 1245 and 1402', *Arch* 50, 439–524.

Simpson, W. S. (1889), *Gleanings from Old S. Paul's* (London).

Simpson, W. S. (1890), 'On a newly-discovered manuscript containing statutes compiled by Dean Colet for the government of the chantry priests and other clergy in St Paul's cathedral', *Arch* 52, pt. 1, 145–74; partially reprinted in Simpson (1894).

Simpson, W. S. (1891–3), 'A mandate of Bishop Clifford', *Proc. of the Soc. of Antiquaries of London*, 2nd ser. 14, 118–28.

Simpson, W. S. (1893), *S. Paul's Cathedral Library. A Catalogue…* (London).

Simpson, W. S. (1894), *St Paul's Cathedral and Old City Life: Illustrations of Civil and Cathedral Life from the Thirteenth to the Sixteenth Centuries* (London).

Simpson, W. S. (1896a), 'Edmund Gibson, bishop of London', *Notes and Queries*, 8th ser. 9 (Jan.–June), 81–3.

Simpson, W. S. (1896b), 'The Bateman manuscript in the Lambeth Library, and the rebuilding of St Paul's Cathedral', *Notes and Queries*, 8th ser., 9 (Jan.–June), 141–3.

Simpson, W. S. (1897a), 'Visitations of certain churches in the city of London in the patron-age of St Paul's cathedral, between the years 1138 and 1250', *Arch* 55, 283–300.

Simpson, W. S. (1905), 'The palaces or townhouses of the bishops of London', *TLMAS*, n.s. 1, 13–73.

Simpson, W. S., ed. (1873), *Registrum Statutorum et Consuetudinum Ecclesiae Cathedralis Sancti Pauli Londinensis* (London).

Simpson, W. S., ed. (1880), *Documents Illustrating the History of S. Paul's Cathedral* (CS, n.s. 26).

Simpson, W. S., ed. (1882), 'The misfortunes of St. Paul's Cathedral', *Notes and Queries*, 6th ser. 5, 121–3.

Simpson, W. S., ed. (1897b), *Registrum Statutorum et Consuetudinum Ecclesiae Cathedralis Sancti Pauli Londinensis: Supplement 1873–1897* (London).

Sims, R. (1854), *Handbook to the Library of the British Museum* (London).

Sims-Williams, P. (1990), *Religion and Learning in Western England, 600–800* (Cambridge).

Sinclair, W. M. (1909), *Memorials of St. Paul's Cathedral* (London).

Sir Christopher Wren A.D. 1623–1723: Bicentenary Memorial Volume published under the auspices of the Royal Institute of British Architects, ed. Dircks, R. (London, 1923).

Sir Christopher Wren and the Making of St Paul's (1991) [Exhibition catalogue, Royal Academy of Arts], (London).

Sixty Chants, Single & Double, also Twelve Sanctus's in Score, Compos'd by the Choristers of St Pauls Cathedral (1795).

Skinner, Q. (1999), 'Ambrogio Lorenzetti's Buon Governo frescoes: two old questions, two new answers', *Journal of the Warburg and Courtauld Institutes* 62, 1–28.

Smalley, B. (1935–6), 'Gilbertus Universalis, bishop of London (1128–34) and the problem of the "Glossa Ordinaria"', *Recherches de Théologie ancienne et médiévale* 7, 235–62, and 8, 24–60.

Smalley, B. (1960), *English Friars and Antiquity in the Early Fourteenth Century* (Oxford).

Smith, A. H., ed. (1905–7), *The Writings of Benjamin Franklin,* 10 vols. (New York).

Smith, A. H. et al., eds. (1979), *The Papers of Nathaniel Bacon of Stiffkey,* I, *1556–1577* (Norfolk Record Soc., 46).

Smith, B. A. (1958), *Dean Church: The Anglican Response to Newman* (London).

Smith, J. (1726), *A New Guide to London/Le Nouveau Guide de Londres* (London).

Smith, N. C., ed. (1953), *The Letters of Sydney Smith,* 2 vols. (Oxford).

Smith, S. (1837), *A Letter to Archdeacon Singleton on The Ecclesiastical Commission* (3rd edn., London).

Smith, S. (1869), *The Works of the Rev. Sydney Smith* (London).

Smith, W. J., ed. (1852–3), *The Grenville Papers,* 4 vols. (London).

Smith, W. J., ed. (1954), *Calendar of Salusbury Correspondence 1553–circa 1700. Principally from the Lleweni, Rûg and Bagot Collections in the National Library of Wales* (Cardiff).

Smyth, G. L. (1818), *The Monuments and Genii of St Paul's and Westminster Abbey,* 2 vols. (London).

Smyth, J. (2001), *The Making of the United Kingdom 1660–1800* (Harlow).

Snow, V. F. and Young, A. S., eds. (1992), *The Private Journals of the Long Parliament, 2 June to 17 September 1642* (New Haven and London).

Somerville, R. (1953), *History of the Duchy of Lancaster,* I, *1265–1603* (London).

Somerville, R. (1985), 'St Paul's cathedral repairs: the propaganda of Henry Farley', *LTR* 25, 163–75.

Soo, L. M. (1998), *Wren's "Tracts" on Architecture and Other Writings* (Cambridge).

Sorlien, R. P., ed. (1976), *The Diary of John Manningham of the Middle Temple, 1602–1603* (Hanover, New Hampshire).

Southern, R. W. (1958), 'The English origins of the "Miracles of the Virgin"', *Medieval and Renaissance Studies* 4, 176–216.

Southworth, J. (1989), *The English Medieval Minstrel* (Woodbridge).

Southworth, J. (1998), *Fools and Jesters at the English Court* (Stroud).

Spalding, R., ed. (1990), *The Diary of Bulstrode Whitelocke 1605–1675* (Oxford, Records of Social and Economic Hist., n.s. 13).

Sparvel-Bayley, J. A. (1878), 'Essex in insurrection, 1381', *Trans. of the Essex Archaeological Soc.* n.s. 1, 205–19.

Speck, W. A. (1970) *Tory and Whig. The Struggle in the Constituencies, 1701–1715* (London).

Spence, C. (2000), *London in the 1690s: a Social Atlas* (London).

Spence, J. (1966), *Observations, Anecdotes and Characters of Books and Men* (Oxford).

Spiers, W. L. (1919), 'The note-book and account book of Nicholas Stone', *WS* VII.

Spink, I. (1995), *Restoration Cathedral Music, 1660–1714* (Oxford).

Sprat, T. (1667), *The History of the Royal Society* (London).

Squibb, G. D. (1977), *Doctors' Commons: a history of the College of Advocates and Doctor of Law* (Oxford).

Squier, S. M. (1985), *Virginia Woolf and London* (Chapel Hill and London).

St Clair, W. (1998), *Lord Elgin and the Marbles* (3rd edn., London).

St John, P. (1723), *A Sermon Preach'd at the Anniversary-Meeting of the Sons of the Clergy at St Paul's Cathedral on the 13th December 1722* (London).

St Paul's in War and Peace (London, 1960).

Stafford, B. M. and Terpak, F. (2001), *Devices of Wonder: from the world in a box to images on a screen* (Los Angeles).

Stafford, P. (1989), *Unification and Conquest: A Political and Social History of England in the Tenth and Eleventh Centuries* (London).

Staley, V. ed., (1904), *Hierugia Anglicana: Documents and Extracts Illustrative of the Ceremonial of the Anglican Church after the Reformation,* 3 vols. (London).

Stancliffe, M. S. (1960), 'Victorian chapter: a new era', in Carpenter, E. ed. (1990), *A House of Kings* (London), 327–38.

Stanhope, G. (1706), *A Sermon Preached before the Queen at the Cathedral Church of St Paul, London, the 7th day of June 1706, Being the Day Appointed for a General Thanksgiving to Almighty God for the Success of Her Majesty's Arms in Flanders and Spain* (3rd edn., London).

Stanley, A. P. (1870), *Essays Chiefly on Questions of Church and State from 1850 to 1870* (London).

Stannus, H. (1891) *Alfred Stevens and his Work* (London).

Stapleton, T., ed. (1846), *De Antiquis Legibus Liber. Cronica Maiorum et Vicecomitum Londoniarum* (CS 34).

Stater, B. (1996), '"War's Greatest Picture": St Paul's Cathedral, the London Blitz and British national identity', MSc report, Bartlett School of Architecture, University College London.

Steane, J. B., ed. (1972), *Thomas Nashe, The Unfortunate Traveller and Other Works* (Harmondsworth).

Steer, F. W. (1960), *Robert Sherburne, Bishop of Chichester: some aspects of his life reconsidered* (Chichester Papers 16).

Steer, F. W., ed. (1968), *Scriveners' Company Common Paper 1357–1628* (LRS 4).

Steig, M. F., ed. (1977), *The Diary of John Harington, M.P. 1646–53* (Somerset Record Soc., 74).

Stenton, F. M. (1971), *Anglo-Saxon England*, 3rd ed. (Oxford).

Sternfeld, F. W. and Greer, D., eds. (1967), *English Madrigal Verse, 1588–1632* (Oxford).

Stevens, D., ed. (1951), *The Mulliner Book*, (MB 1).

Stevens, D., ed. (1969), *Early Tudor Organ Music: Music for the Mass* (EECM 10).

Stevens, R. J. S., ed. (1802), *Sacred Music*, 3 vols. (London).

Stevenson, J. (1992), *Popular Disturbances in England, 1700–1832* (2nd edn., London).

Stewart, D. A. (1988) 'George Frederick Watts: the social and religious themes', PhD thesis, Boston University.

Stewart, I. (1986), 'The London mint and the coinage of Offa', in Blackburn ed. (1986), 27–43.

Stone, L. (1956), 'The Verney tomb at Middle Claydon', *Records of Buckinghamshire* 16, 67–82.

Stone, L. (1972), *Sculpture in Britain: The Middle Ages* (2nd edn., Harmondsworth).

Storey, T. C. (1998), 'The music of St Paul's cathedral, 1872–1972', MMus thesis, University of Durham.

Stow, J. (1592), *The Annales of England, faithfully collected out of the most aut[h]enticated Authors, Records, and other Monuments of Antiquitie* (London).

Stow, J. (1632), *Annales, or, A generall chronicle of England Begun by John Stow; continued and augmented with matters forraigne and domestique, ancient and moderne, unto the end of this present yeere, 1631. by Edmund Howes* (London).

Stow, J. (1633), *The Survey of London … Afterwards inlarged by … A.M. [Anthony Munday] in the yeare 1618 And now completely finished by … A.M., H.D [Henry Dyson] and others, this present yeere 1633* (London).

Stow, J. and Howes, E. (1615), *The Annales, or Generall Chronicle of England, begun first by maister Iohn Stow, and after him continued and augmented with matters forreyne, and domestique, auncient and moderne, vnto the ende of this present yeere 1614. by Edmond Howes, gentleman* (London).

Strachey, J., ed. (1767–77), *Rotuli Parliamentorum*, 6 vols. (London).

Stratford, J. (1994), 'Joan Buckland (d.1462)', in Barron and Sutton (1994), 113–28.

Strype, J. (1711), *The Thankful Samaritan. A Sermon Preached at the Cathedral Church of St Paul before the lord Mayor and the Aldermen of the City of London on the 16 September 1711* (London).

Strype, J. (1720; 1754–5), *A Survey of the Cities of London and Westminster … written at first in the year MDXCVIII by John Stow*, 6 books separately paginated, bound as 2 vols.(London).

Strype, J. (1721), *Ecclesiastical Memorials: relating chiefly to religion and the reformation* (London).

Strype, J. (1824), *Annals of the Reformation*, 4 vols. (London).

Stubbs, W., ed. (1867), *The Chronicle of the Reigns of Henry II. and Richard I., A.D. 1169–1192, commonly known under the name of Benedict of Peterborough*, 2 vols. (RS 49).

Stubbs, W., ed. (1876), *Radulfi de Diceto Decani Lundoniensis Opera Historica*, 2 vols. (RS 68).

Stubbs, W., ed. (1882–3), *Chronicles of the Reigns of Edward I. and Edward II.*, 2 vols. (RS 76).

Sudjic, D. (2001), *Blade of Light: The Story of London's Millennium Bridge* (London).

Sullivan, D. (1994), *The Westminster Corridor* (London).

Sullivan, M. (1975), *Watch How You Go: An Autobiography* (London).

Summerson, J. (1937), 'The tyranny of intellect', *RIBA Journal*, 20 Feb. 1937.

Summerson, J. (1945, rev. edn. 1962), *Georgian London* (London).

Summerson, J. (1949), *Heavenly Mansions* (London).

Summerson, J. (1953), *Sir Christopher Wren* (London).

Summerson, J. (1961), 'The penultimate design for St Paul's', *Burlington Magazine* 103 (March 1961) reprinted in Summerson (1990a), 69–78.

Summerson, J. (1963), *Heavenly Mansions* (New York).

Summerson, J. (1970), *Architecture in Britain 1530–1830* (Harmondsworth).

Summerson, J. (1973), *The London Building World of the 1860s* (London).

Summerson, J. (1981), 'Arches of Triumph: the design for Liverpool Cathedral', in *Lutyens: The Work of the English Architect Sir Edwin Lutyens (1869–1944)* (Arts Council catalogue of exhibition at the Hayward Gallery, London).

Summerson, J. (1990a), *The Unromantic Castle and other essays* (London).

Summerson, J. (1990b), 'Inigo Jones: Covent Garden and the restoration of St Paul's cathedral', in Summerson (1990a), 41–62 (first published in the *Proc. of the British Academy*, 50 (1965), 169–92).

Summerson, J. (1990c), 'The penultimate design for St Paul's cathedral', in Summerson (1990a).

Summerson, J. (1990d), 'J. H. Mansart, Sir Christopher Wren and the dome of St Paul's', *Burlington Magazine*, 132, 32–6.

Summerson, J. (2000), *Inigo Jones*, ed. Colvin, H. (London and New Haven).

Sumner, W. (1931), *A History and Account of the Organs of St Paul's Cathedral* [London].

Surridge, K. (2001) 'More than a great poster: Lord Kitchener and the image of the military hero', *HR* 74, 298–313.

Sutherland, N. M. (1987), 'The Marian exiles and the establishment of the Elizabethan regime', *Archiv für Reformationsgeschichte* 78, 253–86.

Sutton, A. F., and Visser-Fuchs, L. (1998), 'The royal burials of the house of York at Windsor', *Ricardian* 11, 366–407.

Sykes, N. (1926), *Edmund Gibson, Bishop of London, 1669–1748* (London).

Sykes, N. (1934), *Church and State in England in the Eighteenth Century* (Cambridge).

Sykes, N. (1949), *Church and State in England in the XVIIth Century* (Cambridge).

Sykes, N. (1959), *From Sheldon to Secker. Aspects of English Church History, 1660–1768* (Cambridge).

Talbot, W. (1707), *A Sermon preached before the Queen at the Cathedral Church of St Paul on May the First 1707 being the day appointed by Her Majesty for a General Thanksgiving for the Happy Union of the Two Kingdoms of England and Scotland* (London).

Tallis, J. (1838–40), *London Street Views* (London; repub. as LTS 169 in 1969 and 2002).

Tangl, M., ed. (1916), *Die Briefe des heiligen Bonifatius und Lullus* (MGH, Epistolae Selectae in Usum Scholarum 1).

Tatham, G. B. (1913), *The Puritans in Power: A Study in the History of the English Church from 1640 to 1660* (Cambridge).

Tatton-Brown, T. (1986), 'The topography of Anglo-Saxon London', *Antiquity* 60, 21–8.

Tatton-Brown, T. (2002), 'The beginnings of Lambeth Palace', *Anglo-Norman Studies* 24, 203–14.

Taubert, S. (1966), *Bibliopola: Pictures and Texts about the Book Trade*, 2 vols. (Hamburg).

Tavernor, R. and Schofield, R. (1997), *Andrea Palladio: The Four Books of Architecture* (Cambridge, Mass., and London).

Taylor, P. (1976), 'The estates of the bishop of London, from the seventh century to the early sixteenth century', PhD thesis, University of London.

Taylor, P. (1977), 'A knight's fee at Acton, in the manor of Fulham', *TLMAS* 28, 316–22.

Taylor, P. (1980), 'The bishop of London's city soke', *BIHR* 53, 174–82.

Taylor, P. (1990), 'Clerkenwell and the religious foundations of Jordan de Bricett: a re-examination', *HR*, 63, 17–28.

Taylor, P. (1992), 'The endowment and military obligations of the see of London: a reassessment of three sources', *Anglo-Norman Studies* 14, 287–312.

Taylor, P. (1995a), 'The early St Albans endowment and its chroniclers', *HR* 68, 119–42.

Taylor, P. (1995b), 'Boundaries and margins: Barnet, Finchley and Totteridge', in Franklin, M. J. and Harper-Bill, C., eds., *Medieval Ecclesiastical Studies in Honour of Dorothy M. Owen* (Woodbridge).

Taylor, P. (2000), 'Introduction', *Little Domesday Book. Essex* (London, Alecto edn.).

Taylor, P. (2002), 'Ingelric, Count Eustace and the foundation of St Martin-le-Grand', *Anglo-Norman Studies* 24, 215–37.

Taylor, S. J. C. ed. (1999), 'Bishop Edmund Gibson's proposals for church reform', in Taylor, S. J. C., ed. (1999), *From Cranmer to Davidson: A Church of England Miscellany* (Church of England Record Soc. 7)

Thacker, A. (2000), 'In search of saints: the English church and the cult of Roman Apostles and Martyrs in the seventh and eighth centuries', in Smith, J. M. H., ed. (2000), *Early Medieval Rome and the Christian West: Essays in Honour of Donald Bullough* (Leiden, Boston).

Thacker, A. T. (1985), 'Kings, saints and monasteries in pre-Viking Mercia', *Midland History* 10, 1–26.

Thacker, A. T. (1999), 'In Gregory's shadow?', in Gameson (1999), 374–90.

Thacker, A. T. (2002a), '*Loca Sanctorum*: the significance of place in the study of the saints', in Thacker and Sharpe (2002), 1–43.

Thacker, A. T. (2002b), 'The making of a local saint', in Thacker and Sharpe (2002), 45–73.

Thacker, A. T. and Sharpe, R., eds. (2002), *Local Saints and Local Churches in the Early Medieval West* (Oxford).

Thanksgiving Day: An Address to All Persons, especially to our Brave Sailors, ...Showing what Great Reason we have for a NATIONAL THANKSGIVING, and how the Day Ought to be Kept by All Good Christians. To which is Added an Account of the Procession to St Paul's (London, 1797).

Thanksgiving Service in Commemoration of the Twenty-Fifth Anniversary of the King's Accession to the Throne, on Monday, May 6th 1935 at 11.30 am: Official Programme of the Jubilee Procession (1935).

'The £200,000 bath' (1966–7), *Dome* 4, 2–5.

The Brownists Synagogve or a late Discovery of their Conventicles, Assemblies, and places of meeting, Where they Preach, and the manner of their praying and preaching, With a Relation of the Names, places, and Doctrines of those which doe commonly Preach ... (1641) [BL, Thomason Tract E172/32].

The Cherubim with a Flaming Sword, that appear'd on the 5th of November last, in the Cathedral of St Paul, to the Lord Mayor, Aldermen, and Sheriffs, and many Hundreds of People etc. Being a Letter to my Lord Major, with Remarks upon Dr Sa – ll's Sermon (London. 1709).

The Guildhall of the City of London (7th edn., London, 1939).

The History of All Royal Thanksgiving Days and State Processions to St Paul's Cathedral (London, 1872).

The House of Dollond (London, 1917).

The Jew's High Commendation of the Metropolitan Cathedral Church of St Paul (1638).

The Kingdomes Weekly Intelligencer, Sent Abroad To prevent mis-information, no. 289: Tuesday 5 December to Tuesday 12 December 1648 (n.p.) [BL, Thomason Tract E476/9].

The Moderate Intelligencer: Impartially communicating Martiall Affairs to the Kingdom of England, No. 195: Thursday 7 December to Thursday 14 December 1648 (n.p.) [BL, Thomason Tract E476/24].

The Perfect Weekly Account Concerning Certain Speciall and Remarkable Passages from Both Houses of Parliament; from the Kings Majesty and the Commissioners, at Newport; from the Head-Quarters; and severall other parts of the Kingdome: Wednesday 6 December to Wednesday 13 December 1648 (n.p.) [BL, Thomason Tract E476/15].

The Picture of London, for 1802 ... (London, [1802]).

The Queen's Golden Jubilee: Ceremonial: A Thanksgiving Service at St. Paul's Cathedral at 11.30 am Tuesday 4th June 2002 (n.d.).

The Trve Informer, Who In the following Discovrs, or Colloquy, Discovereth unto the World the chiefe Causes of the sad Distempers in Great Brittany, and Ireland. Deduced from their Originals (Oxford, 1643) [BL, Thomason Tract E96/10].

The Weekly Intelligencer of the Common-Wealth. Faithfully communicating all Affairs both Martial and Civil, No. 139: Tuesday 11 October to Tuesday 18 October 1653 (London) [BL, Thomason Tract E715/1] (1653a).

The Weekly Intelligencer of the Common-Wealth. Faithfully communicating all Affairs both Martial and Civil, No. 140: Tuesday 18 October to Tuesday 25 October 1653 (London) [BL, Thomason Tract E715/8] (1653b).

Thomas, A. H., ed. (1926), *Calendar of Plea and Memoranda Rolls 1323–1364* (Cambridge).

Thomas, A. H., ed. (1929), *Calendar of Plea and Memoranda Rolls 1364–1381* (Cambridge).

Thomas, A. H., ed. (1932), *Calendar of Select Pleas and Memoranda of the City of London 1381–1412* (Cambridge).

Thomas, A. H., ed. (1943), *Calendar of Plea and Memoranda Rolls 1413–1437* (Cambridge).

Thomas, A. H. and Thornley I. D., eds. (1938), *The Great Chronicle of London* (London).

Thomas, C. (1981), *Christianity in Roman Britain to AD 500* (London).

Thomas, C., Sloane, B. and Phillpotts, C. (1997), *Excavations at the Priory and Hospital of St Mary Spital, London* (Museum of London Archaeology Service, Monograph 1).

Thompson, A. H. (1947), *The English Clergy and their Organisation in the Later Middle Ages* (Oxford).

Thompson, A. H., ed. (1929), *Statutes of the Cathedral Church of Durham* (Surtees Soc. 143).

Thompson, B. L. (1965), 'Dean Barwick and his will', *Trans. Cumberland and Westmorland Antiquarian and Archaeological Soc.*, n.s. 65, 240–83.

Thompson, D. M. (1994), 'Historical survey, 1750–1949', in Owen, D., ed. (1994), *Lincoln Minster* (Cambridge).

Thompson, E. M., ed. (1889), *Adae Murimuth Continuatio Chronicarum. Robertus de Avesbury de Gestis Mirabilibus regis Edwardi tertii* (RS 93).

Thorne, R. (1991), 'The setting of St Paul's cathedral in the twentieth century', *LonJ* 16/2, 117–28.

Thrupp, S. L. (1962), *The Merchant Class of Medieval London* (Ann Arbor).

Tindal Hart, A. (1949), *The Life and Times of John Sharp, Archbishop of York* (Church History Soc.).

Tinniswood, A. (2001), *His Invention So Fertile, A Life of Sir Christopher Wren* (London).

To the Kings most Excellent Majesty: the humble Petition of the City of London, presented to his Majestie, Octob. the 22. Wherein the particular grievances of the Tradesmen and common people of this City are declared, being occasioned by the Kings absenting himselfe, and maintaining a Civill Warre within this kingdome ... (London, 1642) [BL, Thomason Tract E124/25].

Tout, T. F. (1920–33), *Chapters in the Administrative History of Medieval England*, 6 vols. (Manchester).

Tovey, D'Blossiers (1738), *Anglia Judaica: or the History and Antiquities of the Jews in England, Collected from all our Historians, both Printed and Manuscript, as also from the Records in the Tower, and other Publick Repositories* (Oxford).

Trapp, J. B. [1990], *Essays on the Renaissance and the Classical Tradition* (Aldershot and Brookfield, Vermont).

Trelawny, J. (1702), *A Sermon Preached before the Queen and both Houses of Parliament: at the Cathedral Church of St Paul's Nov. 12, 1702 being the Day of Thanksgiving for the Signal Successes Vouchsafed to Her Majesty's Forces by Sea and Land [Low Countries, Vigo]...and likewise, for the Recovery of his Royal Highness the Prince of Denmark* (London).

Trend, J. B. (1932), 'Jonathan Battishill: from the unpublished recollections of R.J.S. Stevens', *Music and Letters* 13, 264–71.

Trevor-Roper, H. (1988), *Archbishop Laud, 1573–1645* (3rd edn, Basingstoke).

Turner, E. S. (1975), *Boys Will Be Boys* (3rd edn., London).

Turner, L. and Ward, W. H. (1923), 'The crafts at St Paul's', in Dircks (1923).

Turner, M. and Beckett, J. (1998), 'The lingering survival of ancient tenures in English agriculture in the 19th century', *Proc. of the 12th International Economic History Congress Madrid 1998*, section B2.

Turner, R. V. (1985), *The English Judiciary in the Age of Glanville and Bracton c.1176–1239* (Cambridge).

Tweddle, D., Biddle, M., and Kjølbye-Biddle, B. (1995), *Corpus of Ango-Saxon stone sculpture, IV: South-East England* (London).

Twells, L., *et al.* (1816), *The Lives of Dr Edward Pocock by Dr Twells, Dr Zachary Pearce, and of Dr Thomas Newton by themselves, and of the Revd Philip Skelton by Mr Purdy)*, 2 vols. (London).

Tyacke, N. (1987), *Anti-Calvinists: The Rise of English Arminianism c.1590–1640* (Oxford).

Tyacke, S. (1978), *London Mapsellers, 1660–1720* (Tring).

Tyler, K. (2000), 'The "Western Stream" reconsidered: excavations at the medieval Great Wardrobe, Wardrobe Place, City of London', *TLMAS* 51, 21–44.

Tyler, R., ed. (1954), *Calendar of Letters, Despatches and State Papers Relating to the Negotiations Between England and Spain Preserved in the Archives at Vienna, Simancas, Besançon, Brussels, Madrid and Lille*, XIII, *Philip and Mary, July 1554–November 1558* (London).

Tyson, D. B. (1990), 'Problem people in the *Petit Bruit* by Rauf de Boun', *Journal of Medieval History* 16, 351–61.

Tyson, D. B., ed. (1987), *Rauf de Boun, Le petit Bruit* (Anglo-Norman Text Soc., Plain Texts Ser. 4).

Uffenbach, Z. C. von (1934), *London in 1710, from the Travels of Zacharias Conrad von Uffenbach*, trans. and eds., Quarrell, W. H. and Mare, M. (London).

Underdown, D. (1963), 'A case concerning bishops' lands: Cornelius Burges and the Corporation of Wells', *EHR* 78, 18–48.

Usher, B. (2001), 'The Deanery of Bocking and the demise of the Vestiarian Controversy', *JEcclH* 52, 434–455.

Varley, E. A. (1992), *The Last of the Prince Bishops: William Van Mildert and the High Church Movement of the early nineteenth century* (Cambridge).

Venn, J. A. (1922–54), *Alumni Cantabrigienses: A Biographical List of all Known Students, Graduates and Holders of Office in the University of Cambridge, from the earliest Times to 1900*, 10 vols. (Cambridge).

[Venn, R.] (1740), *Tracts and Sermons of Several Occasions. By the Revd Richard Venn, A.M.* (London).

Vertue Note Books, 6 vols. plus index, Walpole Soc., 18, 20, 22, 24, 26, 29, 30 (Oxford, 1930–55).

Vince, A. (1990), *Saxon London: An Archaeological Investigation* (London).

Vincent, N. (2001), *The Holy Blood: King Henry III and the Westminster blood relic* (Cambridge).

Wabuda, S. (1993), 'Equivocation and recantation during the English Reformation: the "Subtle Shadows" of Dr Edward Crome', *JEcclH* 44, 224–242.

Walcott, M. E. C. (1872), *Traditions and Customs of Cathedrals* (2nd edn., London).

Walsham, A. (1999), *Providence in Early Modern England* (Oxford).

Walters, G. (1974), 'The booksellers in 1759 and 1774: the battle for literary property,' *Library* 5th ser. 29, 287–311.

Walters, H. B., ed. (1939), *London Churches at the Reformation with an Account of their Contents* (London).

Walton, I. (1665), *The Lives of Dr John Donne, Sir Henry Wotton, Mr Richard Hooker, Mr George Herbert* (4th edn., London).

Wand, W. C. (1965–6), 'Frederic Hood', *Dome* 3, 13–14.

Ward, B. (1982), *Miracles and the Medieval Mind* (London).

[Ward, E.] (1716), *St Paul's Church: or The Protestant ambulators. A burlesque poem* (London).

Ward Perkins, J. B. (1952), 'The shrine of St. Peter and its twelve spiral columns', *Journal of Roman Studies* 42, 21–33.

Warner, G. F., and Gilson, J. P. (1921), *British Museum. Catalogue of Western Manuscripts in the Old Royal and King's Collections*, 4 vols. (London).

Warner, S. A. (1926), *St. Paul's Cathedral* (London).

Warren, F. and White, B., eds. (1931), *The Dance of Death* (Oxford, Early English Text Soc. 181).

Warwick, Sir Philip (1701), *Memoires of the Reigne of King Charles I. with a Continuation to the Happy Restauration of King Charles II* (1st edn., London).

Watkin, D. (1974), *The Life and Work of C. R. Cockerell* (London).

Watkin, D. (1996), *Sir John Soane: Enlightenment Thought and the Royal Academy Lectures* (Cambridge).

Watney, J. (1892), *Some Account of the Hospital of St Thomas of Acon, in the Cheap, London, and of the Plate of the Mercers' Company* (London).

Watson, A., ed. (1985), N.R. Ker, *Books, Collectors and Libraries: Studies in the Medieval Heritage*, (London).

Watts, M. S. (1912), *The Annals of an Artist's Life*, 3 vols. (London).

Webb, D. (1975), 'Guide books to London before 1900', FLA thesis, Library Association.

Webb, J. (1665), *A Vindication of Stone-Heng Restored* … (London).

Webb, P. (1999), *Ivor Novello. A Portrait of a Star* (London).

Webster, A. (1978–9), 'Cathedrals are people,' *Dome* 16, 2–4.

Webster, A. (2002), *Reaching for Reality: Sketches from the Life of the Church* (London).

Webster, L. and Backhouse, J., eds. (1991), *The Making of England: Anglo-Saxon Art and Culture, A.D. 600–900* (London).

Webster, M. (1994), *A New Strength, a New Song: the Journey to Women's Priesthood* (London).

Weever, John (1631, 1767), *Ancient Funeral Monuments with the United Monarchie of Great Britaine, Ireland, and the Islands Adjacent…* (London).

Weinbaum, M., ed. (1976), *The London Eyre of 1276* (LRS 12).

Weiss, R. (1967), *Humanism in England during the Fifteenth Century* (3rd edn., Oxford).

Welch, C. (1896), *A Modern History of the City of London* (London).

Welsh, C. (1885), *A Bookseller of the Last Century, Being Some Account of the Life of John Newbery and of the Books he Published, and a Notice of the Later Newberys* (London and New York).

West, W. (1837), *Fifty Years' Recollections of an Old Bookseller* (London).

Westlake, H. F. (1919), *The Parish Gilds of Medieval England* (New York and London).

Wharton, H. (1695), *Historia de Episcopis & Decanis Londinensibus* (London).

Whatley, E. G., ed. (1989), *The Saint of London. The Life and Miracles of St. Erkenwald: Text and Translation* (Binghamton, NY, Medieval and Renaissance Texts and Studies 58).

[Wheaton, N. S.] (1830), *A Journal of a Residence … in London; including Excursions through Various Parts of England; … in the Years 1823 and 1824* (London).

Wheeler, R. M. (1934), 'The topography of Saxon London', *Antiquity* 8, 290–302.

Whinney, M. (1947), *St Paul's Cathedral* (London).

Whinney, M. (1971), *Wren* (London).

Whinney, M. (1988), *Sculpture in Britain, 1530–1830*, rev. Physick, J. (2nd edn., Harmondsworth).

Whinney, M., and Gunnis, R. (1967), *The Collection of Models by John Flaxman RA at University College* (London).

White, J. (1643), *The First Centvry of Scandalous, Malignant Priests, Made and admitted into Benefices by the Prelates, in whose hands the ordination of Ministers and government of the Church hath been … (London).*

Whitelock, D. (1975), *Some Anglo-Saxon Bishops of London* (Chambers Memorial Lecture, London); reprinted in her *History, Law and Literature in Tenth- to Eleventh-Century England* (London, 1981).

Whitelock, D., Brett, M. and Brooke, C. N. L., eds., *Councils and Synods with other Documents relating to the English Church, I, A. D. 871–1204*, 2 vols. (Oxford).

Whitelock, D., Douglas, D. C. and Tucker, S. I., ed. (1961), *The Anglo-Saxon Chronicle* (London).

Whitelock, D., ed. (1930), *Anglo-Saxon Wills* (Cambridge).

Whitelock, D., ed. (1979), *English Historical Documents*, vol. 1, c.500–1042, (2nd edn., London).

Whitelocke, B. (1709), *Memorials of the English Affairs* (London).

Wilkins, D., ed. (1737), *Concilia Magnae Britanniae et Hiberniae*, 4 vols. (London).

William Whiteway of Dorchester: His Diary 1618 to 1635 (Dorset Record Soc. 12, 1991).

Williams, A. (1996), 'The Vikings in Essex, 871–917', *Essex Archaeology and History* 27, 92–101.

Williams, C. H., ed. (1967), *English Historical Documents*, vol. 5, 1485–1588 (London).

Williams, C., ed. (1937), *Thomas Platter's Travels in England 1599* (London).

Williams, D. A. (1960), 'London Puritanism: the parish of St. Botolph without Aldgate', *Guildhall Miscellany* 2, 24–38.

Williams, G. A. (1963), *Medieval London: from Commune to Capital* (London).

Williams, J. W. (1993), *Bread , Wine & Money: the Windows of the Trades at Chartres Cathedral* (Chicago).

Williams, P. (1995), *The Later Tudors: England, 1547–1603* (Oxford).

Williams, S., ed. (1861), *Letters Written by John Chamberlain during the Reign of Queen Elizabeth* (CS 79).

Williams, T. (1993), *Public buildings in the south-west quarter of Roman London*, (CBA Research Report 88, The Archaeology of Roman London 3).

Williamson, T. (2000), *The Origins of Hertfordshire* (Manchester).

Willis, B. (1727–30), *A Survey of the Cathedrals…*, 2 vols. (London).

Willis, J. (1715), *The Bishop of Gloucester's Thanksgiving Sermon before the King at St Paul's, Jan. 20 [1715] 1714* (London).

Willis, R. (1705), *A Sermon preached before the Queen, at the Cathedral Church of St Paul, London, on the 23rd April 1705. Being the Day of Thanksgiving for the Late Glorious Success in Forcing the Enemies Lines in the Spanish Netherlands etc.* (London).

Wilson, C. (1979), 'The origins of the Perpendicular style and its development to *circa* 1360,' PhD thesis, University of London.

Wilson, C. (1980), 'The Neville screen,' in Coldstream, N. and Draper, P., eds. (1980), *Medieval Art and Architecture at Durham Cathedral* (BAACT 3), 90–104.

Wilson, C. (1994), *The Gothic Cathedral: The Architecture of the Great Church 1130–1530* (London).

Wilson, C. (1995), 'The medieval monuments', in Collinson, Ramsay and Sparks (1995), 451–510.

Wilson, H., ed. (1896), *The Missal of Robert of Jumièges* (Henry Bradshaw Soc. 11, repr. 1994, Woodbridge).

Wilson, J. F. (1969), *Pulpit in Parliament: Puritanism during the English Civil Wars, 1640–1648* (Princeton, N. J.).

Wilson, R. M. (1996), *Anglican Chant and Chanting in England, Scotland, and America, 1660 to 1820* (Oxford).

Winnington-Ingram, A. F. (1915), *The Soul of a Nation* (London).

Winterbottom, M., ed. and trans. (1978), *Gildas. The Ruin of Britain and other works* (London and Chichester).

Wisdom, J. J. (1994–5), 'St Paul's cathedral library', *Dome* 32, 10–11.

[Wolcot, J.] (1806), *Tristia; Or, The Sorrows of Peter … By P. Pindar, Esq* (London).

Wolfe, J. (1968), *Louis XIV* (London).

Wolffe, J. (2000), *Great Deaths. Grieving, Religion and Nationhood in Victorian and Edwardian Britain* (Oxford).

Wood, I. N. (1977), 'Kings, kingdoms and consent', in Sawyer, P. H. and Wood, I. N., eds. (1977), *Early Medieval Kingship* (Leeds).

Wood, I. N. (1994), *The Merovingian Kingdoms 450–751* (London).

Wood, R. A. (1994), 'Poor widows, *c.*1393–1415', in Barron and Sutton (1994), 55–69.

Wood-Legh, K. (1965), *Perpetual Chantries in Britain* (Cambridge).

Woolf, V. (1975/1982), *The London Scene: Five Essays* (New York and London).

Woolgar, C. M. (1999), *The Great Household in Late Medieval England* (New Haven and London).

Woolgar, C. M., ed. (1993), *Household Accounts from Medieval England*, Part ii, (Oxford).

Woolrych, A. (1982), *Commonwealth to Protectorate* (Oxford).

Wormald, F., ed. (1934), *English Kalendars before 1100* (Henry Bradshaw Soc. 72).

Wormald, P. (1984), *Bede and the Conversion of England: the Charter Evidence* (Jarrow Lecture; no publication details).

Wormald, P. (1996), 'Oswaldslow: an "Immunity"?', in Brooks, N. and Cubitt, C., eds., *St Oswald of Worcester: Life and Influence* (Leicester), 117–28.

Wormald, P. (1999), *The Making of English Law: King Alfred to the Twelfth Century*, vol. 1 (Oxford and Malden, Mass.)

Worsley, G. (1995), *Classical Architecture in Britain* (New Haven).

Wren, S. (1750), *Parentalia : or, Memoirs of the family of the Wrens; viz., of Mathew, bishop of Ely, Christopher, dean of Windsor, etc. but chiefly of Sir Christopher Wren ... in which is contained, besides his works, a great number of original papers and records ... compiled by his son Christopher. Now published by his grandson, Stephen Wren* (London; repr. Farnborough, 1965).

Wright, C. E. (1963–4), 'The Benedictional of St Ethelwold and Bishop Henry Compton', *British Museum Quarterly* 27, 3–5.

Wright, J. (1697), *Three Poems of St Paul's Cathedral* (London).

[Wright, J.] 'Pheonix Paulina' (1709), *A Poem on the New Fabrick of St Paul's Cathedral* (London).

Wright, N. ed. (1988), *The Historia Regum Britannie of Geoffrey of Monmouth*, II, *The first variant version: a critical edn.* (Cambridge).

Wright, N. ed. (1991), *The Historia Regum Britannie of Geoffrey of Monmouth*, V, *Gesta Regum Brittanie* (Cambridge).

Yarrington, A. (1988), *The Commemoration of the Hero 1801–1864: Monuments to the British Victors of the Napoleonic Wars* (New York and London).

Yates, W. N. (2000), *Buildings, Faith and Worship* (2nd edn., Oxford).

Yeo, G. (1986–7), 'Record-keeping at St Paul's Cathedral', *Journal of the Soc. of Archivists* 8, 30–44.

Yeomans, D. T. (1986), 'Inigo Jones's roof structures', *Construction History* 29, 85–101.

Yorke, B. (1985), 'The kingdom of the East Saxons', *Anglo-Saxon England* 14, 1–36.

Yorke, B. (1990), *Kings and Kingdoms of Early Anglo-Saxon England* (London).

Young, J. and Aitken, P. H. (1908), *A Catalogue of the Manuscripts in the Library of the Hunterian museum in the University of Glasgow* (Glasgow).

Young, S., ed. (1890), *The Annals of the Barber-Surgeons of London, Compiled from their Records and Other Sources* (London).

Zadnik, I. (1993), 'The administration of the diocese of London: bishops William Gray, Robert FitzHugh and Robert Gilbert (1426–1448)', PhD thesis, University of Cambridge.

INDEX

Numbers in *italics* indicate a page reference to a figure, caption or table. The former counties of places now within London, defined as the area under the Greater London Authority, are indicated by the form (Middx/London).

Substantial sections of the index are grouped under the headings LONDON and ST PAUL'S CATHEDRAL. The former covers all places and institutions in the historic city of London (the central district still under the jurisdiction of the Corporation of London), plus London-wide topics. Places outside the city are entered under their own names. A complete list of the bishops of London will be found under the LONDON heading, p. 522 and a complete list of the deans of St Paul's will be found under ST PAUL'S (subheading **3. Constitution**, p. 529). Lists of the dignitaries and the prebendaries of St Paul's up to 1857 are published in Horn (1963, 1969) and Greenway (1968). This index identifies all clergy and all the staff (both clerical and lay) of St Paul's Cathedral. Contemporary practice in identification is followed. Thus, prebendaries of St Paul's are normally described as canons up to the Reformation and as prebendaries thereafter. Residentiary canons cannot readily be identified before the later seventeenth century. They are identified in this index, when known, from c.1660 onwards, and a consolidated list of cross-references is provided. All minor canons, vicars choral and lay staff of the cathedral identified in the index are listed in a similar fashion, as are dignitaries in office from 1857 to the present.

Cardinals among the minor canons are identified as 'cardinal', while 'Cardinal' denotes a Roman cardinal.

The section headings are arranged as follows:

LONDON
1. **Miscellaneous**
2. **Bishop of London**
3. **City of London**
4. **Places and religious institutions in the city**
   a. *parishes and parish churches*
   b. *religious houses*
   c. *streets and places in the city of London*

ST PAUL'S CATHEDRAL
1. **Fabric and fittings**
   a. *before the 1087 fire*
   b. *1087 to c.1670 ('Old St Paul's' up to its demolition after the Great Fire)*
   c. *c.1670 to the present ('the Wren cathedral')*
2. **Precinct**
   a. *before the 1087 fire*
   b. *1087 to 1666*
   c. *1666 to the present*
3. **Constitution, clergy and staff**
   a. *before c.1100*
   b. *from c.1100 to the present*
4. **Liturgy and cult**
5. **Estates and income**
6. **Major public events at**
   a. *in the cathedral*
   b. *in the precinct*
7. **Other**

PHTOGRAPHIC ACKNOWLEDGEMENTS

The authors and publisher would like to thank the following individuals, libraries, galleries and photographic archives for permission to reproduce their material. Every care has been taken to trace copyright owners but if we have inadvertently infringed copyright we apologise and we will rectify it, if advised, in any future edition. The following numbers refer to the relevant page numbers:

Tracy Wellman: 3, 6, 18, 19, 26, 30, 42, 128, 129, 144, 180, 188, 208, 276, 306, 336, 431, 440

A.F. Kersting, London: 8, 170, 196 below, 199, 216 right, 234 left, 253, 257, 270 right, 287, 377, 426, 4443 left, 447 above right, 460 left

English Heritage, London: 10, 132, 133, 134, 136, 138, 139, 140 right, 177 below, 178 right, 180, 181.

Museum of London: 2 (Bridgeman Art Library), 11, 45 (by courtesy of Dessau Art Gallery), 55, 65 (Bridgeman Art Library), 137, 179 above, 382

British Library, London: 22 (Royal Ms.14.c.VII f.2r), 33 (Cotton Nero DII f.18), 34 (Royal 13.A.III f.14), 37 (Bridgeman Art Library), 44, 88, 140 left (Add. Ms. 71474 f.183r), 152 left (Ms. Cotton Claud. Eiii f.3v), 270 left (Add. Ms. 71474), 393 left (Bridgeman Art Library), 400 (Shelfmark G.99), 415 (Cotton Charter xiii 11)

The National Archives, Public Record Office: 24

British Museum, London: 25, 182, 197 left (Crase Collection XIX 163), 235 below (1881.6.11.203)

Dean and Chapter of St Paul's Cathedral, deposit at Guildhall Library (Bridgeman Art Library): 28, 116, 117, 148, 158, 193 above, 214 left, 225 above, 232, 235 left, 241, 244, 254 left, 296, 311, 322, 354, 364, 383 below, 416 below, 420 below

By courtesy of the Mercers' Company: 41

The Society of Antiquaries of London: 47, 49, 112, 173, 176, 177 above, 229 above

St Paul's Cathedral Library, Dean and Chapter of St Paul's: 56, 73, 85, 92 above and below, 93 right, 94, 95, 97, 98, 105, 124, 229 below, 230, 235 right, 245, 247 left, 250 above left and right, 260, 262 above, 264 right, 265 left and right, 271 below left, 272, 285 below, 300 right, 331 above and below, 342, 356 left, 373, 384, 386 below, 387, 404 left and right, 405 below, 406 right, 409 left, 416 above, 420 above, 421, 424, 428, 457.

Private Collection: 61 (Bridgeman Art Library), 69 left, 77 (Christie's Images), 93 left and right, 188, 192 (Bridgeman Art Library), 193 below, 209, 214 right, 236 below, 238 right and below, 275 above, 295 (Bridgeman Art Library), 432, 443 right, 456 left, 458 above, 459 right.

Private Collector, England: 87 (photograph courtesy of the Richard Green Gallery, London)

Guildhall Library, Corporation of London: 67, 69 right, 80, 81, 82, 99, 120 left and right, 130 (Bridgeman Art Library), 168, 197 right, 200 right, 202 above left and right, 225 below, 228 (Bridgeman Art Library), 231, 243, 249, 251, 267, 271 above left, 275 below left, 285 above, 288 below left, 297 below, 311, 315, 317, 318 above and below, 320 above, 321 left and right, 324 above (Bridgeman Art Library), 324 below, 326 above left and right, 327, 328 above and below left, 328 (Bridgeman Art Library), 330, 332 above and below, 333, 343, 345, 346, 359 below, 367, 368 above and below, 370, 374, 383 (Bridgeman Art Library), 393 right (Gresham Music Library G Mus. 452, by courtesy of the Joint Grand Gresham Committee), 394 (Bridgeman Art Library), 405 above, 409 right, 434 below, 436, 437 left and right, 439, 440, 442 right, 444, 454

Yale Center for British Art, Paul Mellon Collection: 68 (Bridgeman Art Library), 201, 238 left (Bridgeman Art Library)

The Provost and Fellows of Eton College, Windsor: 76

The National Portrait Gallery, London: 78, 365 right, 396

Lambeth Palace Library, London: 79, 152 right (Ms 8 f.57r), 154 (Ms. 1106 f.96v)

Hulton Archive, London: 100, 101,102, 104, 389, 390, 358 below

Philip Way: 106, 255, 259, 359 left, 361, 391, 411.

English Heritage (Derek Kendall): 109, 190, 205 below, 222, 226 left and right, 227 left, right and below, 246 below, 265 below, 266, 267 below, 271 above right, 449 above.

Sampson Lloyd: 125, 187, 218, 262 below, 278, 359 right, 449 below.

English Heritage, National Monuments Record: 128 above, 202 above and below right, 250 below, 252, 274 above (© Warburg Instiute), 281 left above and below, 358, 406 left, 410 above, 442 left, 451, 456 right.

Glasgow University: 165 (Ms Hunter 231 f.83)

The Warden and Fellows of All Souls College, Oxford: 172, 183, 184, 185, 186, 195, 204, 221 above and below, 224

Ashmolean Museum, Oxford: 174, 236 left

The Provost and Fellows of Worcester College, Oxford: 175

British Architectural Library, R.I.B.A., London: 178 left, 297 above.

The Bodleian Library, University of Oxford: 179 below (Gough Maps XX f.2v)

Kerry Downes: 196 above, 200 left, 203 left, 205 above

Yale University Arts Library, Visual Resources Collection, 201

Martin Charles: ii, 203 right

Imperial War Museum, London: 216 left

Bibliothèque Nationale, Paris: 234 right

Courtauld Institute of Art Gallery, London: 236 right, 237

Victoria & Albert Museum, London: 242 (Bridgeman Art Library), 248

Trustees of the Watts Gallery, Compton, Surrey: 246 above (Bridgeman Art Library)

St Paul's Cathedral Library, Dean and Chapter of St Paul's (Conway Library, Courtauld Institute of Art, London): 271 below right, 273 left and right, 274 below, 275 below, 275 right, 279, 280 left and right, 281 right, 283 left and right, 284 left, 286 left and right, 288 above and below right, 289, 290 left and right, 291, 292 left, 300 left.

Towneley Hall Art Gallery and Museum, Burnley, Lancashire: 276 (Bridgeman Art Library)

Evening Standard: 292 right

Tate Gallery, London: 294

St Paul's Cathedral Fabric Archive, Dean and Chapter of St Paul's: 206, 211, 247 right, above and below, 254 right, 264 left, 267 above, 298 above, 301 above and below, 302, 303, 410 below

Essex County Council: 308

The Pepys Library, Magdalene College Cambridge: 320 below

Lobkowicz Collection, Nelahozeves Castle, Czech Republic: 325 (Bridgeman Art Library)

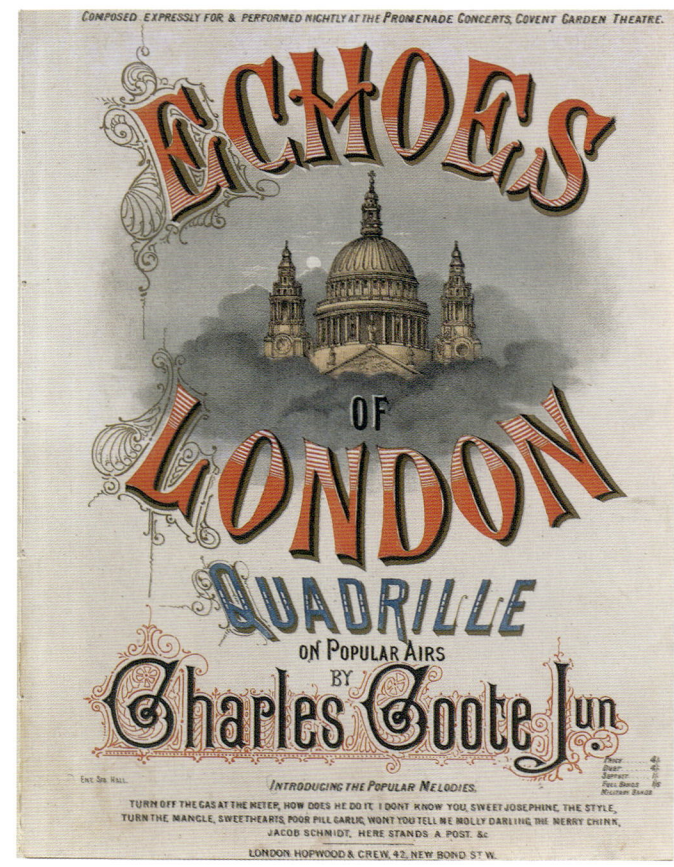